CIVIL PROCEDURE

ANDERSON'S
Law School Publications

ADMINISTRATIVE LAW ANTHOLOGY
by Thomas O. Sargentich

ADMINISTRATIVE LAW: CASES AND MATERIALS
by Daniel J. Gifford

ADMIRALTY LAW ANTHOLOGY
by Robert M. Jarvis

ANALYTIC JURISPRUDENCE ANTHOLOGY
by Anthony D'Amato

AN ANTITRUST ANTHOLOGY
by Andrew I. Gavil

APPELLATE ADVOCACY: PRINCIPLES AND PRACTICE (Second Edition)
Cases and Materials
by Ursula Bentele and Eve Cary

A CAPITAL PUNISHMENT ANTHOLOGY
by Victor L. Streib

CASES AND PROBLEMS IN CRIMINAL LAW (Third Edition)
by Myron Moskovitz

THE CITATION WORKBOOK
by Maria L. Ciampi, Rivka Widerman and Vicki Lutz

CIVIL PROCEDURE: CASES, MATERIALS AND PROBLEMS
by Richard D. Freer and Wendy C. Perdue

COMMERCIAL TRANSACTIONS: PROBLEMS AND MATERIALS
Vol. 1: Secured Transactions Under the UCC
Vol. 2: Sales Under the UCC and the CISG
Vol. 3: Negotiable Instruments Under the UCC and the CIBN
by Louis F. Del Duca, Egon Guttman and Alphonse M. Squillante

A CONSTITUTIONAL LAW ANTHOLOGY
by Michael J. Glennon

CONSTITUTIONAL LAW COURSEBOOK
by Phoebe A. Haddon, Donald E. Lively, Dorothy E. Roberts and Russell L. Weaver

CONSTITUTIONAL TORTS
by Sheldon H. Nahmod, Michael L. Wells, and Thomas A. Eaton

CONTRACTS
Contemporary Cases, Comments, and Problems
by Michael L. Closen, Richard M. Perlmutter and Jeffrey D. Wittenberg

A CONTRACTS ANTHOLOGY (Second Edition)
by Peter Linzer

CORPORATE AND WHITE COLLAR CRIME: AN ANTHOLOGY
by Leonard Orland

A CRIMINAL LAW ANTHOLOGY
by Arnold H. Loewy

CRIMINAL LAW: CASES AND MATERIALS
by Arnold H. Loewy

A CRIMINAL PROCEDURE ANTHOLOGY
by Silas Wasserstrom and Christie L. Snyder

CRIMINAL PROCEDURE: ARREST AND INVESTIGATION
by Arnold H. Loewy and Arthur B. LaFrance

CRIMINAL PROCEDURE: TRIAL AND SENTENCING
by Arthur B. LaFrance and Arnold H. Loewy

ECONOMIC REGULATION: CASES AND MATERIALS
by Richard J. Pierce, Jr.

ELEMENTS OF LAW
by Eva H. Hanks, Michael E. Herz and Steven S. Nemerson

ENDING IT: DISPUTE RESOLUTION IN AMERICA
Descriptions, Examples, Cases and Questions
by Susan M. Leeson and Bryan M. Johnston

AN EVIDENCE ANTHOLOGY
by Edward J. Imwinkelried and Glen Weissenberger

ENVIRONMENTAL LAW (Second Edition)
Vol. 1: Environmental Decisionmaking: NEPA and the Endangered Species Act
Vol. 2: Water Pollution; Vol. 3: Air Pollution; Vol. 4: Hazardous Wastes
by Jackson B. Battle, Mark Squillace, Maxine I. Lipeles and Robert L. Fischman

ENVIRONMENTAL PROTECTION AND JUSTICE
Readings and Commentary on Environmental Law and Practice
by Kenneth A. Manaster

FEDERAL EVIDENCE COURTROOM MANUAL
by Glen Weissenberger

FEDERAL INCOME TAXATION OF PARTNERSHIPS AND OTHER PASS-THRU ENTITIES
by Howard E. Abrams

FEDERAL RULES OF EVIDENCE (Second Edition)
Rules, Legislative History, Commentary and Authority
by Glen Weissenberger

FIRST AMENDMENT ANTHOLOGY
by Donald E. Lively, Dorothy E. Roberts and Russell L. Weaver

INTERNATIONAL ENVIRONMENTAL LAW ANTHOLOGY
by Anthony D'Amato and Kirsten Engel

INTERNATIONAL HUMAN RIGHTS: LAW, POLICY AND PROCESS
Problems and Materials
by Frank Newman and David Weissbrodt

INTERNATIONAL LAW ANTHOLOGY
by Anthony D'Amato

INTERNATIONAL LAW COURSEBOOK
by Anthony D'Amato

INTRODUCTION TO THE STUDY OF LAW: CASES AND MATERIALS
by John Makdisi

JUDICIAL EXTERNSHIPS: THE CLINIC INSIDE THE COURTHOUSE
by Rebecca A. Cochran

JUSTICE AND THE LEGAL SYSTEM
A Coursebook
by Anthony D'Amato and Arthur J. Jacobson

THE LAW OF DISABILITY DISCRIMINATION
by Ruth Colker

THE LAW OF MODERN PAYMENT SYSTEMS AND NOTES
by Fred H. Miller and Alvin C. Harrell

LAWYERS AND FUNDAMENTAL MORAL RESPONSIBILITY
by Daniel R. Coquillette

PATIENTS, PSYCHIATRISTS AND LAWYERS
Law and the Mental Health System
by Raymond L. Spring, Roy B. Lacoursiere, M.D., and Glen Weissenberger

PROBLEMS AND SIMULATIONS IN EVIDENCE (Second Edition)
by Thomas F. Guernsey

A PRODUCTS LIABILITY ANTHOLOGY
by Anita Bernstein

PROFESSIONAL RESPONSIBILITY ANTHOLOGY
by Thomas B. Metzloff

A PROPERTY ANTHOLOGY
by Richard H. Chused

Continued

THE REGULATION OF BANKING
Cases and Materials on Depository Institutions and Their Regulators
by Michael P. Malloy

A SECTION 1983 CIVIL RIGHTS ANTHOLOGY
by Sheldon H. Nahmod

SPORTS LAW: CASES AND MATERIALS (Second Edition)
by Raymond L. Yasser, James R. McCurdy and C. Peter Goplerud

A TORTS ANTHOLOGY
by Lawrence C. Levine, Julie A. Davies and Edward J. Kionka

TRIAL PRACTICE
Text by Lawrence A. Dubin and Thomas F. Guernsey
Problems and Case Files with *Video* Presentation
by Edward R. Stein and Lawrence A. Dubin

CIVIL PROCEDURE
CASES, MATERIALS, AND QUESTIONS

Richard D. Freer

Robert Howell Hall Professor of Law
Emory University School of Law
Atlanta, Georgia

Wendy Collins Perdue

Professor of Law
Georgetown University School of Law
Washington, D.C.

CINCINNATI
ANDERSON PUBLISHING CO.

FREER & PERDUE, CIVIL PROCEDURE: CASES, MATERIALS, AND QUESTIONS

©1996 by Anderson Publishing Co.
2035 Reading Road / Cincinnati, Ohio 45202
800 582-7295 / E-mail: andpubco@aol.com / FAX 513 562-8110

All rights reserved. No part of this book may be reproduced in any form or by any electronic or mechanical means including information storage and retrieval systems without permission in writing from the publisher.

Library of Congress Cataloging-in-Publication Data

Freer, Richard D., 1953-
    Civil procedure : cases, materials, and questions / Richard D. Freer, Wendy Collins Perdue.
       p.   cm.
    Includes index.
    ISBN 0-87084-267-6 (alk. paper)
    1. Civil procedure--United States--Cases. I. Perdue, Wendy Collins, 1953- . II. Title.
KF8839.F74 1995
347.73'5--dc20
[347.3075]
                                  95-44798
                                      CIP

Dedication

RDF: To Louise, Collin and Courtney
WCP: To David, Bill and Ben

Preface

Civil procedure is a challenging course both for students and teachers. Of all first the first year subjects, it is the most alien to students' pre-law school lives. As a result, the course sometimes seems to students to be unconnected to the "real world." Ironically, of all the first year courses, Civil Procedure is the most connected to the "real world" of what lawyers do. Graduates routinely report that Civil Procedure is central to their work.

Thus one challenge for professors (and casebook authors) is to bridge the gap in student experience. The book addresses this issue by including many problems and hypotheticals which are intended to make the material more concrete. We also include notes and questions that explore the strategic and ethical choices that real lawyers face.

A second challenge is that the course includes significant amounts of detail, but at the same time raises such fundamental questions as the role of justice, fairness and efficiency in the adjudication of rights. Students sometimes miss the richness of the course because they fail to see how its various aspects fit together — they may come away with a knowledge of individual trees but not an overall sense of the forest. This book seeks to avoid that result by stressing integration. The chapters are arranged in related blocks and each chapter begins with a section called "Introduction and Integration" which provides an overview and indicates how the section fits with other topics.

In some areas, we have arranged material differently from what seems to be the common approach. We do this to facilitate the integrative function. The first part of the book addresses where litigation can proceed and includes personal jurisdiction, subject matter jurisdiction, and venue. We have also included notice and service of process in this part because of its close relationship to personal jurisdiction. We end this block with *Erie*, which addresses some of the choice law implications of forum selection.

Next, the book moves to the phases of a law suit — pleading, discovery, and adjudication (with and without a jury). Joinder is covered later because we do not believe this topic is necessary to understanding the basic steps of litigation and by delaying it, we can cover it with the related issues of preclusion. Covering pleading and discovery back-to-back highlights that they are both methods of information exchange. The chapter on adjudication includes both summary judgment and judgment as a matter of law.

Following the chapter on adjudication are three chapters on preclusion and joinder. We view them as a unit on "packaging" of litigation. We begin with preclusion. That

Preface

chapter, which explores the goals of efficiency and finality, lays the foundation for the joinder chapters. Although we introduce supplemental jurisdiction briefly in the chapter on subject matter jurisdiction, we defer detailed analysis until the joinder chapters. This seems particularly necessary after the passage of § 1367 which students cannot understand without first studying the joinder rules. Following joinder, we address appeals.

This course stresses civil procedure as part of the litigation process — a publicly funded system of dispute resolution. We feel that students should be forced to consider whether the litigation system is a good way to resolve disputes. The last chapter of the book raises questions about alternative dispute resolution and comparative law. We feel that these issues are well treated at the end of the course, after the students have seen the litigation process fully.

This is a propitious time for a new book in civil procedure. In the past several years, Congress has been quite busy, changing rules on removal, diversity of citizenship, amount in controversy, venue, and codifying supplemental jurisdiction. The Rules Advisory Committee has been very (some would say too) busy of late, with mammoth changes in December 1993. The Supreme Court has decided several important cases in the past several years, and the lower courts have wrestled with thorny areas such as supplemental jurisdiction and Rule 11. The timing of this book enables us to take account of those changes and orient students for what might lie ahead.

Notes on Form

We indicate textual deletions from opinions and other materials by "* * *." We have not noted deletions of citations from opinions. Our footnotes are denoted by asterisks. We have retained the original number of footnotes appearing in opinions. We have adopted a short form of citing the several classic treatises to which we refer throughout the book. With apologies to the contributing authors on the two standard multi-volume treatises, we refer to them, respectively, as MOORE'S FEDERAL PRACTICE and WRIGHT & MILLER, FEDERAL PRACTICE AND PROCEDURE. CHARLES ALAN WRIGHT, FEDERAL COURTS (5th ed. 1994) is cited WRIGHT, FEDERAL COURTS; MARTIN REDISH, FEDERAL JURISDICTION: TENSIONS IN THE ALLOCATION OF JUDICIAL POWER (2d ed. 1990) is cited REDISH, FEDERAL JURISDICTION; JACK FRIEDENTHAL, MARY KAY KANE & ARTHUR MILLER, CIVIL PROCEDURE (2d. ed. 1993) is cited FRIEDENTHAL, KANE & MILLER, CIVIL PROCEDURE (4th ed. 1992) is cited JAMES, HAZARD & LEUBSDORF, CIVIL PROCEDURE, LARRY TEPLY & RALPH WHITTEN, CIVIL PROCEDURE (1994) is cited TEPLY & WHITTEN, CIVIL PROCEDURE.

Acknowledgments

Acknowledgments by Professor Freer

I have benefited greatly from the contributions of generous colleagues at Emory. Bill Ferguson has been a patient mentor from the first days of my career. The late Don Fyr was an avuncular mentor and close friend who convinced me to pursue scholarship in civil procedure. We discussed many aspects of this book and I regret that he is not here to see it. Tom Arthur is generous and insightful, and has contributed more to my work than the demands of friendship would justify. Professor Perdue and I are especially grateful to Tom for teaching from the manuscript version of this book and offering invaluable comments and criticisms.

I am also indebted to Dean Howard O. Hunter of Emory Law School for his unfailing support not only of this project but of all aspects of my career. I acknowledge with gratitude the generosity of Judge Robert Howell Hall, who endowed the professorship which I am honored to hold. Stephanie Shack provided excellent research and editorial assistance, for which I am very grateful. I also thank Glennis O'Neal and Radine Robinson for secretarial support.

I could not have completed work on this book — or anything else for that matter — without the encouragement and sacrifice of my family, Louise, Collin and Courtney.

Acknowledgments by Professor Perdue

I am grateful for the support I have received from the Georgetown University Law Center and all of my colleagues. I want to particularly thank the "civil procedure lunch brunch," a group of colleagues who share my passion for procedure and have offered invaluable ideas and encouragement. That group includes Sherman Cohn, Walter Kamiat, Florence Roisman, Kevin Quinn, and Phil Schrag. Cynthia Bright and David Hopper provided excellent research and editorial assistance.

My deepest thanks go to my family, David, Bill, and Ben. Although my sons occasionally questioned my choice of topic ("Why don't you do something useful — like write a book about basketball?), and my efficiency ("You're not done *yet*?"), their love and good humor were essential to keeping my sanity and perspective.

Acknowledgments

We acknowledge with gratitude the permission of the following copyright holders to quote material contained in the book:

American Bar Association Model Rules of Professional Conduct 3.1, 3.2, 3.3 & 3.4. Copyright ©1994 by the American Bar Association. Reprinted by permission. Copies of this publication are available from Service Center, American Bar Association, 750 Lake Shore Drive, Chicago, Illinois 60611.

Bone, Robert, *Rethinking the "Day in Court" Ideal and Nonparty Preclusion*, 67 N.Y.U.L. Rev. 193, 196 (1992). Copyright ©1992 by New York University Law Review. Reprinted by permission.

Branson, David and Andrea Johnson, *Aids Needed for Jury to Understand Instructions*, Legal Times, Mar. 5, 1984 at A-9. Copyright ©1984 by the Legal Times. Reprinted by permission.

Brilmayer, Lea, *How Contracts Count: Due Process Litigations on State Court Jurisdiction*, 1980 Sup. Ct. Rev. 77, 82-83, 95-96. Copyright © 1981 by the University of Chicago. Reprinted by permission.

Carrington, Paul, *The Seventh Amendment: Some Bicentennial Reflections*, 1990 U. Chi. Legal F. 33, 76. Copyright ©1990 by the University of Chicago. Reprinted by permission.

Clark, Charles, *Pleading Under the Federal Rules*, 12 Wyo. L. Rev. 177, 181 (1958). Copyright ©1958 by Land & Water Law Review. Reprinted by permission.

Council of Superior Court Judges of Georgia, Pattern Jury Instructions Committee, Suggested Pattern Jury Instructions, Vol. I: Civil Cases 231 (3d. ed. 1991). Copyright ©1991 by Carl Vinson Institute of Government. Reprinted by permission.

Coyle, Marcia, *High Court May Strike Sex-Based Challenges*, Nat'l L.J., Nov. 8, 1993. Copyright ©1993 by New York Law Publishing Co. Reprinted by permission.

Dobbs, Dan, *The Validation of Void Judgments: The Bootstrap Principle*, 53 Va. L. Rev. 1003, 1011-12 (1967). Copyright ©1967 by the Virginia Law Review Association. Reprinted by permission of the Virginia Law Review Association and Fred B. Rothman & Co.

Elliott, E. Donald, *Managerial Judging and the Evolution of Procedure*, 53 U. Chi. L. Rev. 306, 314, 335 (1986). Copyright ©1986 by University of Chicago. Reprinted by permission.

Ely, John Hart, *The Irrepressible Myth of Erie*, 87 Harvard L. Rev. 693, 713 (1974). Copyright © 1974 by Harvard Law Review Assoc. Reprinted by permission of publisher and author.

Fiss, Owen, *Against Settlement*, 93 Yale L.J. 1073, 1089-90 (1984), Copyright ©1984 by the Yale Law Journal Co. Reprinted by permission of the Yale Law Journal Co., Fred B. Rothman & Co., and the author.

Freer, Richard, *Avoiding Duplicative Litigation: Rethinking Plaintiff Autonomy and the Role of the Court in Defining the Litigative Unit*, 50 U. Pitt. L. Rev. 809, 824-25 (1989). Copyright ©1989 by the University of Pittsburgh Law Review. Reprinted by permission.

Friedenthal, Jack, *Cases on Summary Judgment: Has There Been a Material Change in Standards?* 63 Notre Dame L. Rev. 770, 783 (1988). Copyright © 1988 by Notre Dame Law Review, University of Notre Dame. Reprinted by permission.

Grillo, Trina, *The Mediation Alternative: Process Dangers for Women*, 100 Yale L.J. 1545, 1607-08 (1991). Copyright ©1991 by the Yale Law Journal Co. Reprinted by permission of the Yale Law Journal Co., Fred B. Rothman & Co., and the author.

Haley, John, *The Myth of the Reluctant Litigant*, 4 Journal of Japanese Studies 378-379 (1980). Copyright ©1980 by the Society of Japanese Studies, University of Washington. Reprinted by permission.

Hoffman, Morris, *Ten Trial Mistakes*, The Docket, Spring 1994 at 10. Copyright ©1994 by the National Institute for Trial Advocacy. Reprinted by permission.

Interim Report of the Committee on Civility of the Seventh Circuit, 143 F.R.D. 371, 389 (1991). Reprinted with permission of West Publishing Corporation.

James, Fleming, Hazard, Geoffrey, & Leubsdorf, John, Civil Procedure (4th ed. 1992). Copyright ©1992 by Geoffrey Hazard and John Leubsdorf. Reprinted by permission.

Kurland, Philip, *The Supreme Court, The Due Process Clause and the In Personam Jurisdiction of State Courts — From Pennoyer to Denckla: A Review*, 25 U. of Chi. L. Rev. 584-85 (1958). Copyright ©1958 by the University of Chicago. Reprinted by permission.

Langbein, John, *The German Advantage in Civil Procedure*, 52 U. Chi. L. Rev 823-866 (1985). Copyright ©1985 by the University of Chicago. Reprinted by permission.

Mayer, Jeffrey, *Prescribing Cooperation: The Mandatory Pretrial Disclosure Requirement of Proposed Rules 26 and 37 of the Federal Rules of Civil Procedure*, 12 Rev. Litig. 77, 113-14 (1992). Copyright ©1992 by the University of Texas at Austin School of Law Publications, Inc. Reprinted by permission.

Meador, Daniel John, and Jordana Simone Bernstein, Appellate Courts in the United States, 3-5 (1994). Copyright ©1994 by West Publishing Co. Reprinted by permission.

Mezibov, Marc, and Sirkin, H. Louis, *The Mapplethorpe Obscenity Trial*, Litig., Summer 1992, at 12, 13-15, 71. Copyright ©1992 by the American Bar Association. Reprinted by permission.

Acknowledgments

Miller, Arthur, *Problems of Giving Notice in Class Actions*, 58 F.R.D. 313, 322 (1972). Copyright ©1972 by West Publishing Co. Reprinted with permission of West Publishing Corporation.

Moore, J. Wm., & Freer, Richard, 3 Moore's Federal Practice ¶14.16 (2d ed. 1995). Copyright ©1995 Matthew Bender & Co. Reprinted by permission.

Moore, J. Wm., Lucas, Jo, 3A Moore's Federal Practice ¶22.02 [1] (2nd ed. 1995). Copyright ©1995 Matthew Bender & Co., Inc. Reprinted by permission.

Moore, J. Wm., Taggart, Walter, & Wicker, Jeremy, 6 Moore's Federal Practice ¶55.05 [2] (2nd ed. 1995). Copyright ©1995 Matthew Bender & Co., Inc. Reprinted by permission.

Restatement (Second) of Judgments §§ 24, 26(1), 27 Comment i, 28 & 41(1). Copyright ©1982 by the American Law Institute. Reprinted with the permission of the American Law Institute.

Riskin, Leonard, *Mediation and Lawyers*, 43 Ohio St. L.J. 29, 34 (1982). Copyright ©1982 by the Ohio State Universtiy. Reprinted by permission of the publisher and author.

Ritz, Wilfred, Rewriting the History of the Judiciary Act of 1789, at 148 (1990). Copyright ©1990 by the University of Oklahoma Press. Reprinted by permission.

Schwarzer, William, *Summary Judgment Under the Federal Rules: Defining Genuine Issues of Material Fact*, 99 F.R.D. 465 (1984). Copyright ©1984 by West Publishing Co. Reprinted by permission.

Sobol, Richard, Bending the Law 13 (1991). Copyright ©1991 by Richard Sobol. Reprinted by permission.

Stempel, Jeffrey, *Sanction, Symmetry, and Safe Harbors: Limiting Misapplications of Rule 11 by Harmonizing it with Pre-Verdict Dismissal Devices*, 60 Fordham L. Rev. 257, 261 (1991). Copyright ©1991 by Fordham Law Review. Reprinted by permission.

Sward, Ellen, *Appellate Review of Judicial Fact-Finding*, 40 Kan. L. Rev. 1, 4 (1991). Copyright ©1990 by the Kansas Law Review, Inc. Reprinted by permission.

Twitchell, Mary, *The Myth of General Jurisdiction*, 101 Harvard L. Rev. 610, 661-662 (1988). Copyright ©1988 by the Harvard Law Review Association. Reprinted by permission of publisher and author.

Underwood, James, A Guide to Federal Discovery Rules, at 40 (2d ed. 1985). Copyright ©1985 by the American Law Institute. Reprinted by permission.

Wagatsuma, Hiroshi, and Arthur Rosett, *The Implications of Apology: Law and Culture in Japan and the United States*, 20 Law and Society Review 461-495 (1986). Copyright ©1986 by the Law and Society Association. Reprinted by permission.

Weinstein, Jack, *Considering Jury "Nullification": When May and Should a Jury*

Reject the Law to Do Justice, 30 Am. Crim. L. Rev. 239, 244-245 (1993). Copyright ©1993 by Georgetown University Law Center. Reprinted by permission.

Wright, Charles Alan, Law of Federal Courts 100-02, 111, 474, 496, 732 & § 58 (5th ed. 1994). Copyright ©1994 by West Publishing Co. Reprinted with permission of West Publishing Corporation.

Wright, Charles Alan, and Arthur Miller, 4A Federal Practice and Procedure § 1096 (2d ed. 1987); 5A Federal Practice & Procedure 447-48 (2d ed. 1990); 9A Federal Practice and Procedure § 2529 (2d ed. 1995); 11 Federal Practice and Procedure § 2806 (2d ed. 1973). Copyright ©1987, 1990, 1995, & 1973 by West Publishing Co. Reprinted with permission of West Publishing Corporation.

Wright, Charles Alan, Arthur Miller, and Richard Marcus, 8 Federal Practice and Procedure § 2024 (2d ed. 1994). Copyright ©1994 by West Publishing Co. Reprinted by permission of West Publishing Corporation.

Table of Contents

Preface ix

Acknowledgments xi

Table of Contents xvii

Table of Cases xxxiii

CHAPTER 1 AN INTRODUCTION TO THE CIVIL ACTION AND PROCEDURE *1*

A. The Study of Procedure *1*

B. Federalism *3*

C. Overview of the Structure of a Court System *5*

    1. Trial Courts *5*

    2. Intermediate Appellate Courts *5*

    3. Supreme Courts *6*

    4. Appellate Practice and the Doctrine of Precedent *7*

D. The Adversary System *8*

E. Alternatives to Litigation *11*

F. A Brief History of Our English Judicial Roots *13*

G. General Topics of Civil Procedure *16*

    1. Selecting the Forum (Chapters 2-7) *17*

    2. Learning About the Opponent's Case (Chapters 8 & 9) *19*

    3. Adjudication With or Without a Jury (Chapter 10) *20*

    4. Preclusion, Joinder and Supplemental Jurisdiction (Chapters 11-13) *20*

    5. Appeal (Chapter 14) *20*

    6. Litigation Alternatives (Chapter 15) *21*

Contents

CHAPTER 2 PERSONAL JURISDICTION *23*

A. Introduction and Integration *23*

B. Constitutional Limits on Personal Jurisdiction *25*

   1. The Fountainhead — *Pennoyer v. Neff* *25*

      Notes and Questions *32*

   2. Interim Developments *35*

      Hess v. Pawloski *37*

      Notes and Questions *38*

   3. The Modern Era *40*

      International Shoe Co. v. Washington *40*

      Notes and Questions *45*

      Note on *McGee, Hanson* and *Gray* *46*

      World-Wide Volkswagen v. Woodson *49*

      Notes and Questions *58*

      Personal Jurisdiction in Federal Court *61*

      Note on *Keeton* and *Calder* *62*

      Why Litigants Care About Where Litigation Occurs *64*

      Burger King Corp. v. Rudzewicz *65*

      Notes and Questions *77*

      Asahi Metal Industry Co. v. Superior Court of California *78*

      Notes and Questions *84*

   4. General Jurisdiction *85*

      Helicopteros Nacionales de Colombia, S. A. v. Hall *85*

      Notes and Questions *91*

   5. Consent *94*

   6. In-Rem and Quasi-in-Rem Jurisdiction *95*

      Shaffer v. Heitner *96*

      Notes and Questions *107*

   7. Transient Presence *108*

      Burnham v. Superior Court of California *109*

      Notes and Questions *120*

C. A Different Perspective *122*

   1. The Purposes of Personal Jurisdiction *122*

   2. Personal Jurisdiction in Other Countries *123*

D. Statutory Limits on Personal Jurisdiction *125*

Flint v. Gust *127*

Gust v. Flint *130*

Notes and Questions *131*

CHAPTER 3 NOTICE AND OPPORTUNITY TO BE HEARD *133*

A. Introduction and Integration *133*

B. Notice *133*

    1. The Constitutional Requirement *133*

        Mullane v. Central Hanover Bank & Trust Co. *133*

        Notes and Questions *138*

    2. Statutory Requirements *141*

        National Dev. Co. v. Triad Holding Corp. *143*

        Notes and Questions *146*

    3. Immunity, Evasion and "Sewer Service" *148*

C. Opportunity to be Heard *149*

    Connecticut v. Doehr *150*

Notes and Questions *160*

CHAPTER 4 SUBJECT MATTER JURISDICTION *165*

A. Introduction and Integration *165*

B. State Courts and General Subject Matter Jurisdiction *165*

C. Federal Courts and Limited Subject Matter Jurisdiction *166*

    1. The Constitutional Grants and Role of Congress *166*

        Notes and Questions *167*

    2. Plaintiff's Burden to Establish Federal Subject Matter Jurisdiction *168*

    3. Diversity of Citizenship and Alienage Jurisdiction *169*

        a. Introductory Note *169*

        b. The Complete Diversity Rule *170*

            Strawbridge v. Curtiss *170*

            Notes and Questions *171*

        c. Determining Citizenship of Individuals *172*

            Mas v. Perry *172*

            Notes and Questions *175*

Contents

    d. Determining Citizenship of Entities *178*
     Randazzo v. Eagle-Picher Industries, Inc. *178*
     Notes and Questions *180*
     J. A. Olson Co. v. City of Winona *180*
     Notes and Questions *184*
    e. Representative Suits and Assignments of Claims *186*
    f. The Domestic Relations Exception *187*
    g. The Amount in Controversy Requirement *188*
     Notes and Questions *188*
  4. Federal Question Jurisdiction *192*
    a. Introductory Note *192*
    b. Narrow Interpretations of the Jurisdictional Grant *193*
     i. The Well-Pleaded Complaint Rule *193*
      Louisville & Nashville Railroad Co. v. Mottley *193*
      Notes and Questions *195*
     ii. Well-Pleaded Complaint Problems Raised by Declaratory Judgments *198*
     iii. Centrality of the Federal Issue to the Claim *200*
      Merrell Dow Pharmaceuticals, Inc. v. Thompson *202*
      Notes and Questions *211*
  5. Supplemental Jurisdiction *214*
  6. Removal Jurisdiction *214*
   Noble v. Bradford Marine, Inc. *215*
   Notes and Questions *217*

CHAPTER 5 VENUE *221*

A. Introduction and Integration *221*

B. Local and Transitory Actions *221*

C. State Venue Provisions *222*

 Notes and Questions *224*

D. Venue in Federal Court *225*

 1. The Basic Rules *225*

  Notes and Questions *227*
  Bates v. C & S Adjusters, Inc. *229*
  Notes and Questions *232*

E. Change of Venue *233*

 1. Transfer of Civil Cases in State Courts *233*

Contents

    2. Transfer of Civil Actions in Federal Court *233*

        a. Where Can Cases Be Transferred *234*

        b. *Goldlawr* Transfers *235*

        c. Forum Selection Clauses *235*

        d. Choice of Law *235*

        e. Standard for Transfer Under §§ 1404 and 1406 *237*

        f. Multidistrict Litigation *237*

F. Forum Non Conveniens *238*

    Piper Aircraft Co. v. Reyno *238*

    Notes and Questions *247*

CHAPTER 6 RAISING JURISDICTIONAL AND RELATED CHALLENGES *249*

A. Introduction and Integration *249*

B. The Traditional and Modern Approaches to Challenging Personal Jurisdiction *249*

    Notes and Questions *251*

    Jones v. Clinton *253*

    Notes and Questions *255*

C. Collateral and Direct Attacks on Personal Jurisdiction *256*

    Baldwin v. Iowa State Mens Traveling Association *257*

    Notes and Questions *259*

D. Challenging Federal Subject Matter Jurisdiction *259*

CHAPTER 7 WHAT LAW APPLIES IN FEDERAL COURT *263*

A. Introduction and Integration *263*

B. Determining What Law Applies *266*

    1. The *Erie* Doctrine *266*

        Erie Railroad Co. v. Tompkins *266*

        Notes and Questions *271*

        Note: Constitutional Bases of *Erie* *274*

    2. Distinguishing Substantive and Procedural Rules *276*

        Guaranty Trust Co. v. York *276*

        Notes and Questions *280*

        Byrd v. Blue Ridge Electrical Cooperative, Inc. *282*

Contents

    Notes and Questions *285*

  3. The Federal Rules of Civil Procedure *287*

    Hanna v. Plumer *287*

    Note on Understanding *Hanna* *294*

      a. What Happens When There Is a Federal Rule of Civil Procedure on Point--the Rules Enabling Act Prong *295*

        i. Determining Whether a Federal Rule of Civil Procedure Is Valid *296*

        Business Guides, Inc. v. Chromatic Communication Enterprises *297*

        Notes and Questions *299*

        Amendments to the Federal Rules of Civil Procedure *300*

        ii. Determining When a Federal Rule of Civil Procedure Is On Point *302*

      b. What Happens When There Is No Federal Rule of Civil Procedure on Point--the Rules of Decision Act Prong *304*

        Chambers v. Nasco, Inc. *305*

        Notes and Questions *311*

C. Determining the Content of State Law *312*

  DeWeerth v. Baldinger *313*

  Notes and Questions *316*

D. Federal Common Law *317*

E. Federal Law in State Court *318*

CHAPTER 8 PLEADINGS AND JUDGMENTS BASED ON PLEADINGS *319*

A. Introduction and Integration *319*

B. Historical Overview of the Evolution of Pleadings *320*

C. The Complaint *323*

  1. Requirements *323*

    a. Elements of the Complaint *323*

      i. A "short and plaint statement of the ground upon which the court's jurisdiction depends" *323*

      ii. A "short and plain statement of the claim showing that the pleader is entitled to relief" *324*

      iii. A "demand for judgment for the relief the pleader seeks" *324*

    b. Form of Pleadings *325*

    c. Legal Sufficiency *326*

      Notes and Questions *328*

    d. Factual (or "Formal") Sufficiency: The Debate Over Specificity *329*

      i. Code Pleading *329*

ii. **Federal Rules Pleading** *331*

Dioguardi v. Durning *331*

Notes and Questions *333*

iii. **The Commmon Counts** *336*

e. **Heightened Specificity Requirements in Certain Cases** *336*

Leatherman v. Tarrant County *337*

Notes and Questions *339*

f. **Pleading Inconsistent Facts and Alternative Theories** *342*

McCormick v. Kopmann *342*

Notes and Questions *345*

2. **Voluntary Dismissal** *346*

Notes and Questions *347*

3. **Involuntary Dismissal** *348*

Notes and Questions *349*

D. **Defendant's Options in Response** *350*

1. **Motions** *350*

Questions *351*

2. **The Answer** *352*

a. **Responses to the Plaintiff's Allegations** *352*

i. **Admissions** *352*

ii. **Denials** *352*

iii. **Denials for Lack of Knowledge or Information** *354*

b. **Affirmative Defenses** *354*

Notes and Questions *356*

3. **Claims by the Defendant** *357*

4. **Failure to Respond: Default and Default Judgment** *357*

Notes and Questions *357*

E. **Amended Pleadings** *360*

1. **Basic Principles Under Rule 15(a)** *360*

Notes and Questions *360*

2. **The Problem of Variance Under Rule 15(b)** *362*

Notes and Questions *362*

3. **Amendment and the Statute of Limitations Under Rule 15(c)** *364*

a. **Amendment to Claims or Defenses** *364*

Marsh v. Coleman Company *364*

Notes and Questions *367*

Contents

        b. Amendment Changing a Party *368*

F. Supplemental Pleadings *369*

G. Veracity in Pleading: Rule 11 and Other Devices *369*

    1. Rule 11 *369*

        Notes and Questions *373*

        Hadges v. Yonkers Racing Corp. *374*

        Notes and Questions *382*

    2. Other Sanctions *384*

CHAPTER 9 DISCOVERY *387*

A. Introduction and Integration *387*

B. Overview of the Discovery Devices *390*

    1. Depositions (Rules 30, 31) *390*

        Questions *391*

    2. Interrogatories (Rule 33) *391*

        Questions *392*

    3. Production of Documents and Things (Rule 34) *392*

        Questions *392*

    4. Medical Examination (Rule 35) *392*

        Questions *393*

    5. Requests for Admission (Rule 36) *393*

        Questions *394*

    6. Practice Problem *394*

C. Scope of Discovery *394*

    1. General Scope *394*

        Roesberg v. Johns-Manville Corp. *395*

        Notes and Questions *407*

    2. Privileged Material *408*

    3. Work Product *411*

        Hickman v. Taylor *411*

        Notes and Questions *419*

        Holmgren v. State Farm Mutual Insurance Co. *424*

        Notes and Questions *426*

    4. Experts *427*

Ager v. Jane C. Stormont Hospital & Training School for Nurses *428*

Notes and Questions *434*

5. Review Problem *436*

D. Timing, Scheduling and Mandatory Disclosure *437*

1. Timing *437*

2. Mandatory Initial Disclosures *438*

In re Lotus Development Securities Litigation *438*

Notes and Question *442*

3. Local Rules *446*

E. Sanctions *447*

Washington State Physicians Ins. Exchange & Ass'n v. Fisons Corp. *447*

Holmgren v. State Farm Mutual Automobile Insurance Co. *460*

Notes and Questions *462*

F. Scheduling and Pretrial Conferences and Orders *466*

CHAPTER 10 ADJUDICATION WITH AND WITHOUT A TRIAL OR A JURY *471*

A. Introduction and Integration *471*

B. The Right to a Jury *471*

1. Scope of the Constitutional Right *471*

a. "Actions at Common Law" and the Historical Test *473*

Chauffers Local, 391 v. Terry *473*

Notes and Questions *482*

b. The Complications of Merger and the Federal Rules *487*

c. Juries in non-Article III Courts *489*

Atlas Roofing Co. v. OSHRC *489*

Notes and Questions *493*

d. Juries in State Courts *495*

2. Selection and Size of the Jury *495*

a. The Venire and Voir Dire *495*

b. Peremptory Challenges *496*

J. E. B. v. Alabama *497*

Notes and Questions *513*

c. Two Views of Voir Dire and Peremptory Strikes *516*

The Mapplethorpe Obscenity Trial *516*

10 Trial Mistakes *520*

Contents

            d. Jury Size *520*
      3. Jury Nullification and Its Limits *521*

C. Summary Judgment — Adjudication Without Trial or Jury *522*

    Knapp v. Holiday Inns, Inc. *524*

    Notes and Questions *529*

    Anderson v. Liberty Lobby, Inc. *530*

    Notes and Questions *539*

    Celotex Corp. v. Catrett *544*

    Notes and Questions *551*

D. Controlling and Second-Guessing Juries *553*

    1. Judgment as a Matter of Law (Directed Verdict and JNOV) *553*

        Lavender v. Kurn *554*

        Notes and Questions *558*

    2. New Trials *561*

        Dadurian v. Underwriters at Lloyd's of London *562*

        Notes and Questions *567*

    3. Other Techniques for Controlling Juries *569*

            a. Jury Instructions *569*

            b. Forms of the Verdict *570*

            c. Judicial Comment *571*

            d. Juror Misconduct *572*

    4. Motions to Set Aside the Judgment *574*

CHAPTER 11 THE PRECLUSION DOCTRINES *577*

A. Introduction and Integration *577*

B. Claim Preclusion *579*

    1. Scope of a Claim *579*

        a. In General *579*

            Carter v. Hinkle *580*

            Notes and Questions *582*

        b. Contract Cases *586*

    2. Parties or Persons in Privity *587*

        a. Who Can Be Bound? *587*

            Notes and Questions *588*

b. Configuration of the Parties *589*
   Notes and Questions *590*
3. Valid, Final Judgment On the Merits *591*
   a. Validity *591*
   b. Finality *592*
   c. On the Merits *592*
   Notes and Questions *593*
4. Exceptions to the Operation of Claim Preclusion *595*
   Notes and Questions *596*

C. Issue Preclusion *598*
1. Same Issue Litigated and Determined *598*
   Cromwell v. County of Sac *599*
   Notes and Questions *601*
2. Issue Determined Was Essential to the Judgment *604*
   Rios v. Davis *605*
   Notes and Questions *606*
3. Against Whom Can Issue Preclusion be Asserted? *608*
   Hardy v. Johns-Manville Sales Corp. *608*
   Notes and Questions *610*
4. By Whom Can Issue Preclusion be Asserted? *613*
   a. Mutuality and Exceptions *613*
   b. Rejection of Mutuality for Defensive Use *615*
      Notes and Questions *617*
   c. Rejection of Mutuality for Offensive Use *619*
      Parklane Hosiery v. Shore *619*
      Notes and Questions *622*
5. Exceptions to the Operation of Issue Preclusion *624*
   Notes and Questions *625*

D. Problems of Federalism *626*
1. State-to-State *627*
2. State-to-Federal *627*
3. Federal-to-State *629*
4. Federal-to-Federal *629*

Contents

CHAPTER 12 SCOPE OF LITIGATION— JOINDER AND SUPPLEMENTAL JURISDICTION *631*

A. Introduction and Integration *631*

B. Real Party in Interest, Capacity, and Standing *632*

   Notes and Questions *634*

C. Claim Joinder by Plaintiffs *635*

   1. Procedural Aspects *635*

   2. Jurisdictional Aspects *636*

      United Mine Workers v. Gibbs *637*

      Notes and Questions *641*

D. Permissive Party Joinder by Plaintiff *644*

   1. Procedural Aspects *644*

      Schwartz v. Swan *644*

      Notes and Questions *648*

   2. Jurisdictional Aspects *652*

      Notes and Questions *654*

E. Claim Joinder by Defendants *655*

   1. Counterclaims *656*

      a. Compulsory Counterclaims *656*

         i. Procedural Aspects *656*

           Dindo v. Whitney *656*

           Carteret Savings & Loan Assn. v. Jackson *658*

           Notes and Questions *659*

         ii. Jurisdiction Aspects *662*

           Notes and Questions *663*

      b. Permissive Counterclaims *664*

         i. Procedural Aspects *664*

           Notes and Questions *665*

         ii. Jurisdictional Aspects *665*

   2. Cross-Claims *666*

      a. Procedural Aspects *666*

         Notes and Questions *666*

      b. Jurisdictional Aspects *668*

         Notes and Questions *668*

F. Overriding Plaintiff's Party Structure *669*

1. **Impleader (Third-Party Practice)** *669*
   - a. Procedural Aspects *669*
     - Markvicka v. Brodhead-Garrett Co. *670*
     - Notes and Questions *672*
   - b. Jurisdictional Aspects *674*
     - Owen Equipment & Erection Co. v. Kroger *675*
     - Notes and Questions *681*
2. **Compulsory Joinder (Necessary and Indispensable Parties)** *683*
   - a. Procedural Aspects *683*
     - Haas v. Jefferson National Bank *683*
     - Temple v. Synthes Corp. *687*
     - Notes and Questions *688*
   - b. Jurisdictional Aspects *691*
     - Notes and Questions *692*
3. **Intervention** *694*
   - a. Procedural Aspects *694*
     - Atlantis Development Corp. v. United States *695*
     - Notes and Questions *700*
   - b. Jurisdictional Aspects *702*
     - Notes and Questions *704*

CHAPTER 13 SPECIAL MULTIPARTY LITIGATION: INTERPLEADER AND THE CLASS ACTION *705*

A. Introduction and Integration *705*

B. Interpleader *705*

  1. Background *705*

  2. The Two Types of Interpleader in Federal Court *707*

  Pan American Fire & Casualty Co. v. Revere *707*

  Notes and Questions *711*

  3. The Limits of Interpleader to Avoid Duplicative Litigation *715*

  State Farm Fire & Casualty Co. v. Tashire *715*

  Notes and Questions *719*

C. The Class Action *720*

  1. Background *720*

  2. Policy and Ethical Issues *721*

  3. Constitutional Considerations *723*

Contents

    Hansberry v. Lee *725*

    Notes and Questions *728*

  4. **Practice Under Federal Rule 23** *730*

    a. Background *730*

    b. Filing and "Certification" of a Class Action *731*

    c. Requirements for "Certification" Under Rule 23 *732*

      i. Prerequisites of Rule 23(a) *732*

      Notes and Questions *733*

      ii. Types of class actions under Rule 23(b) *735*

      Notes and Questions *737*

    d. Notice to class members *738*

      Notes and Questions *739*

    e. Court's Role in Dismissal and Settlement *740*

  5. **Subject Matter Jurisdiction** *741*

    Free v. Abbott Laboratories *742*

    Notes and Questions *744*

  6. **Personal Jurisdiction** *745*

    Notes and Questions *747*

CHAPTER 14 APPEALS *749*

A. **Introduction and Integration** *749*

B. **Appellate Jurisdiction in the Federal Courts** *750*

  1. **Section 1291** *750*

  2. **Collateral Order Doctrine** *752*

    Coopers & Lybrand v. Livesay *753*

    Notes and Questions *757*

  3. **Section 1292** *760*

    Notes and Questions *760*

  4. **Rule 54(b)** *761*

    Notes and Questions *762*

  5. **Mandamus** *763*

  6. **Appealability of Discovery Orders** *764*

  7. **Mechanics of Filing an Appeal** *765*

  8. **Appellate Jurisdiction of the United States Supreme Court** *766*

C. **Appeals in State Courts** *766*

D. Scope of Review *767*

    Notes and Questions *769*

CHAPTER 15 ALTERNATIVE MODELS OF DISPUTE RESOLUTION *773*

A. **Introduction and Integration** *773*

B. **Models of Greater Judicial Control** *773*

    The German Advantage in Civil Procedure *773*

    Notes and Questions *783*

    Sempier v. Johnson & Higgins *784*

    Notes and Questions *789*

C. **Models of Non-Judicial Resolution** *791*

    The Implications of Apology: Law and Culture in Japan and in the United States *792*

    Notes and Questions *797*

Index 803

Table of Cases

Abuan v. General Electric Co., 85
Adam v. Saenger, 95
Adkins v. Allstate Ins. Co., 630
Aetna Cas. & Sur. Co. v. Spartan Mech. Corp., 654
Aetna Life Ins. Co. v. Alla Medical Serv., Inc., 252
Ager v. Jane C. Stormont Hospital & Training School for Nurses, 428, 764
Agrashell, Inc. v. Bernard Sirotta Co., 674
Aldinger v. Howard, 652
Alexander v. Fujitsu Bus. Commun. Sys., 360
Allen v. McCurry, 627
Allied Chemical Corp. v. Daiflon, Inc., 763
All West Pet Supply v. Hill's Pet Products, 428
Al-Site Corp. v. VSI Intern, Inc., 303
Alumax Mill Prods., Inc. v. Congress Fin. Corp., 654
American Airlines v. Ulen, 542
American Fire & Cas. Co. v. Finn, 260
American Hosp. Supply Corp. v. Hospital Products Ltd., 163
American National Red Cross v. S.G., 213
American Well Works Co. v. Layne & Bowler Co., 200, 212
Anderson v. Bessemer City, 768
Anderson v. Liberty Lobby, Inc., 530, 553
Andrews v. Christenson, 586
Ankenbrandt v. Richards, 187
Apex Oil Co. v. Belcher Co. of New York, Inc., 463
Arai v. Tachibana, 177
Arenson v. Southern University Law Center, 569
Arkansas Education Assn. v. Board of Education, 733
Armstrong v. Pomerance, 108
Asahi Metal Industry Co. v. Superior Court of California, 78, 251
Atlantis Development Corp. v. United States, 695
Atlas Roofing Co. v. OSHRC, 489
Averdick v. Republic Fin. Servs., Inc., 744
Baldwin v. Iowa State Mens Traveling Association, 257, 603
Baltimore & Carolina Line, Inc. v. Redman, 560
Banco Nacional de Cuba v. Sabbatino, 318
Bankhead Enterprises, Inc. v. Norfolk and W. Ry., 92
Barber v. Barber, 187
Bates v. C & S Adjusters, Inc., 229
Bates v. Union Oil Co., 630
Bauer v. Uniroyal Tire Co., 713
B. Braun Medical Inc. v. Abbott Laboratories, 409
Beacon Theatres v. Westover, 487, 488, 495, 764
Bearry v. Beech Aircraft Corp., 92
Beeck v. Aquaslide 'N' Dive Corp., 361
Bell v. Hood, 213, 642
Bendix Autolite Corp. v. Midwesco Enterprises, 121
Bennett v. Fieser, 409

Table of Cases

Bernhard v. Bank of America, 615
Berry v. Eagle-Picher, 303
Binks Manufacturing Co. v. National Presto Indus., Inc., 421
Black v. J. I. Case Co., 543
Blonder-Tongue Laboratories, Inc. v. University of Illinois Foundation, 616, 617
Boeing Co. v. Shipman, 559
Boerum v. Taylor, 584
Bogosian v. Gulf Oil Corp., 427
Boit v. Gar-Tec Products, Inc., 85
Boring v. Keller, 427
Bose Corp. v. Consumers Union of United States, Inc., 768
Boyle v. United Technologies Corp., 317
Braband v. Beech Aircraft Corp., 92
Brady v. Maryland, 445
Brady v. Southern Ry., 318
Branch v. Tunnell, 339
Brandon v. Holt, 363
Brokke v. Stauffer Chem. Co., 351
Brown v. Demco, Inc., 217
Brown v. Haley, 585
Brown v. Rahman, 588
Brown & Williamson Tobacco Corp. v. Jacobson, 341
Bryant v. Finnish Nat'l Airline, 92
Buchanan v. Dain Bosworth, Inc., 596
Buchanan v. Wilson, 148
Buck Creek Indus. v. Alcon Constr., Inc., 583
Budinich v. Becton Dickinson & Co., 765
Bumgarner v. Federal Dep. Ins. Corp., 250
Bunzl Pulp & Paper Sales, Inc. v. Golder, 435
Burger King Corp. v. Rudzewicz, 65, 233, 728
Burke v. Kleiman, 724
Burlington Northern Railroad Co. v. Woods, 302
Burnham v. Superior Court of California, 109, 228
Business Guides, Inc. v. Chromatic Communication Enterprises, 297, 311, 384
Byrd v. Blue Ridge Electrical Cooperative, Inc., 282, 304, 305, 312, 495
Cable Advertising Networks, Inc. v. DeWoody, 163
Calder v. Jones, 63, 64
Calero-Toledo v. Pearson Yacht Leasing Co., 161
Caliber Partners, Ltd. v. Affeld, 340
Cameco Industries Inc. v. Mayatrac, S.A., 107
Camelback Ski Corp. V. Behning, 94
Canuel v. Oskoian, 747
Capron v. Van Noorden, 260
Carden v. Arkoma Associates, 185
Carnival Cruise Lines v. Shute, 95
Carson v. Polley, 574
Carter v. Hinkle, 580
Carter v. Memphis, Tennessee, 465
Carteret Savings & Loan Assn. v. Jackson, 658
Casey v. Adams, 222
Catalano v. BRI, Inc., 252

Table of Cases

Catlin v. United States, 751
Catrett v. Johns-Manville Sales Corp., 551
Celotex Corp. v. Catrett, 544
Central Vermont Ry. v. White, 318
Chambers v. NASCO, Inc., 305, 385
Chauffers Local, 391 v. Terry, 473
Chevron, U.S.A. Inc. v. Natural Resources Defense Council, Inc., 771
Chicago, R.I. & P. Ry. Co. v. Martin, 217
Chicot County Drainage Distr. v. Baxter State Bank, 261, 598
China Basin Props. v. Allendale Mut. Ins., 185
China Resource Prod. v. FAYDA Int's, 427
Christianson v. Educational Service Unit No. 16, 336
Citizens Exchange Bank of Pearson v. Kirkland, 666
City of Los Angeles v. Superior Court, 596
Clearfield Trust Co. v. United States, 318
Clephas v. Fagelson, Shonberger, Payne & Arthur, 168
Coburn v. 4-R Corp., 738
Coca-Cola Bottling Co. v. Coca-Cola Co., 410
Coca-Cola Bottling Co. v. Coca-Cola Co. (*Coke VIII*), 410
Cohen v. Beneficial Industrial Loan Corp., 281, 752
Coleman v. Commissioner, 384
Colgrove v. Battin, 520
Colonial Penn Ins. Co. v. American Centennial Ins. Co., 704
Colosi v. Electri-Flex Co., 529
Commissioner of Internal Revenue v. Sunnen, 626
Companion Life Ins. Co. v. Schaffer, 715
Conley v. Gibson, 334, 335
Connecticut v. Doehr, 150
Consolidated Edison Co. v. Public Serv. Comm'n., 59
Coopers & Lybrand v. Livesay, 753
Cooter & Gell v. Hartmax Corp., 370, 384, 463, 769
Corsica Livestock Sales, Inc. v. Sumitomo Bank of Cal., 362
Cort v. Ash, 202
Cosmas v. Hassett, 340
Costello v. United States, 594
Cotton Bros. Baking Co. v. Industrial Risk Insurers, 341
Covey v. Town of Somers, 139
Covington Drawbridge Co. v. Shepherd, 184
Cromwell v. County of Sac, 599
Crouse-Hinds Co. v. Internorth, Inc., 662
Crowall v. Heritage Mutual Ins. Co., 625
Curtis v. Sears, Roebuck & Co., 703
Dadurian v. Underwriters at Lloyd's of London, 562
Daily v. Parker, 317
Dairy Queen v. Wood, 485, 488, 764
Dale Electronics, Inc. v. R.C.L. Electronics, Inc., 747
Dalrymple v. Dalrymple, 695
Danner v. Anskis, 668
Datskow v. Teledyne, Inc., 252
Davila Mendez v. Vatican Shrimp Co., 690
Davis & Cox v. Summa Corp., 666

xxxv

Table of Cases

Day & Zimmerman, Inc. v. Challoner, 274
Dehmlow v. Austin Fireworks, 85
Depex Reina 9 Partnership v. Texas International Petroleum Corp., 168
Deposit Guaranty National Bank v. Roper, 722
Des Moines Navigation & R.R. Co. v. Iowa Homestead Co., 261
DeTore v. Local No. 245, 359
DeWeerth v. Baldinger, 313, 574
D. Federico Co. v. New Bedford Redev. Auth., 362
D.H. Overmyer Co. v. Frick Co., 140
Dice v. Akron, Canton & Youngstown R. R., 318, 495
Dick Proctor Imports v. Sumitomo Corp., 313
Diefenthal v. Civil Aeronautics Board, 189
DiFrischia v. New York Cent. R.R. Co., 260
Digital Equipment Corp. v. Desktop Direct, Inc., 753, 758
Dimick v. Schredt, 568
Dindo v. Whitney, 656
Dioguardi v. Durning, 331
Dohany v. Rogers, 749
Dove v. Massachusetts Mut. Life Ins. Co., 713
Dugan v. EMS Helicopters, Inc., 346
Duncan v. Louisiana, 472
Dunn v. Pepsi-Cola Metropolitan Bottling Co., 219
Durfee v. Duke, 261
Dyer v. MacDougall, 523
Eisen v. Carlisle & Jacquelin, 739
Elder v. Holloway, 767
Elliott v. Perez, 336
Erie Railroad Co. v. Tompkins, 169, *266*, 311, 316, 317
Ernst & Ernst v. Hochfelder, 202
Estate of Portnoy v. Cessna Aircraft Co., 163
Executive Software of N. Am. v. United States Dist. Court, 643
Exxon Co. v. Banque de Paris et des Pays-bas, 317
Falkirk Mining Co. v. Japan Steel Works, Ltd., 85
Farmland Dairies v. Commissioner of the New York State Dept. of Agric. & Mkts., 702
Fauntleroy v. Lum, 24
Feathers v. McLucas, 126
Federated Dept. Stores, Inc. v. Moitie, 592, 597, 598
Fejta v. GAF Co., 363
Ferens v. John Deere Company, 236
Ferguson v. Mobil Oil Corp., 643
Fiandaca v. Cunningham, 702
Finkle v. Gulf & W. Mfg. Co., 682
Finley v. United States, 653
Fire Insurance Exchange v. Bell, 465
Firestone Tire & Rubber Co. v. Risjord, 757
First Nat. Bank & Trust Co. v. Ingerton, 146
First National Bank of Waukesha v. Warren, 764
Flanagan v. United States, 757
Fleming v. Kemp, 514
Flint v. Gust, 127
Flora, Flora & Montague, Inc. v. Saunders, 585

Table of Cases

Foman v. Davis, 360, 361
Ford v. Temple Hospital, 384
Fox v. Johnson & Wimsatt, Inc., 530
Franchise Tax Board v. Construction Laborers Vacation Trust, 199
Free v. Abbott Laboratories, *742*
Freedom National Bank v. Northern Illinois Corp., 354
Freeman v. Howe, 692
FTC v. Grolier Inc., 422
FTC v. Jim Walter Corp., 62
Fuentes v. Shevin, 163
Fullman v. Graddick, 336
Funding Systems Leasing Corp. v. Pugh, 357
Gallick v. Baltimore & Ohio R.R., 571
Gallion v. Woytassek, 331
Galloway v. United States, 560
Garza v. National American Ins. Co., 744
General Railway Signal Co. v. Corcoran, 713
General Tel. Co. of the Southwest v. Falcon, 733, 734
Gentile v. Missouri Department of Corrections & Human Resources, 789
Georgia v. McCollum, 513
Gerstein v. Pugh, 162
Gibbs v. Buck, 189
Gibson v. Bruce, 217
Gilmer v. Porterfield, 617
Goldlawr, Inc. v. Heiman, 235
Gonzalez v. Naviera Neptuno SA, 247
Goodwine v. Superior Court, 250
Goss v. Lopez, 149, 150
Granfinanciera, S.A. v. Norberg, 494
Grant v. Preferred Research, Inc., 357
Gray v. American Radiator & Standard Sanitary Corp., 48, 60, 126
Great Lakes Rubber Corp. v. Herbert Cooper Co., 662
Green v. Chicago, B. & Q. Ry., 36
Green v. Occidental Petroleum Corp., 764
Greene v. Lindsey, 140
Grover v. Eli Lilly Co., 346, 347
Guaranteed Systems, Inc. v. American National Can Co., 682
Guaranty Trust Co. v. York, *276*
Gulf Oil v. Gilbert, 248
Gust v. Flint, *130*
Gustin v. Sun Life Assurance Co., 312
Haas v. Jefferson National Bank, *683*
Hackney v. Newman Memorial Hosp., Inc., 186
Hadges v. Yonkers Racing Corp., *374*, 574
Hall v. E.I. DuPont De Nemours Co., 649
Hall v. Tower Land & Investment Co., 593
Hanna v. Plumer, *287*, 304, 311, 341, 672
Hansberry v. Lee, 588, *725*
Hanson v. Denckla, 46-48
Hardy v. Johns-Manville Sales Corp., *608*, 623
Harper v. Auto-Owner's Ins. Co., 422

xxxvii

Table of Cases

Harris v. Balk, 36, 95
Harrison Conference Services, Inc. v. Dolce Conference Services, Inc., 227
Hart v. American Airlines, Inc., 628
Hartley Pen Co. v. United States District Court, 410
Harvey's Wagon Wheel, Inc. v. Blitter, 303
Hatcher v. Emergency Medical Specialty Servs., Inc., 190
Hawkins v. South Plain Int'l Trucks, Inc., 422, 423
Helicopteros Nacionales de Columbia, S. A. v. Hall, 45, *85*
Henriksen v. Cameron, 596
Henry Doherty & Co. v. Goodman, 39
Hepburn & Dundas v. Ellzey, 177
Hernandez v. New York, 515
Hess v. Pawloski, 37, 58
H. F. Livermore Corp. v. Aktiengesellschaft Gebruder Loepfe, 359
Hickman v. Taylor, 411, 435, 764
Hinderlider v. LaPlata River and Cherry Creek Ditch Co., 317
Hodgson v. Bowerbank, 177
Hoffman v. Blaski, 234
Hoffman v. Owens-Illinois Glass Co., 423
Holmen v. Miller, 146
Holmes v. Bricker, 585
Holmgren v. State Farm Mutual Insurance Co., 424, 460
Honda Motor Co., Ltd. v. Oberg, 522
Hoover v. Gershman Investment Corp., 168
Hoppe v. G.D. Searle & Co., 351, 623
House v. Hanson, 660
Howard v. Senkowski, 515
Hubbard v. Brinton, 146
Huberman v. Duane Fellows, Inc., 654
Hulac v. Chicago & N.W. Ry. Co., 273
Hurn v. Oursler, 642
Illinois v. City of Milwaukee, 317
In re A.H. Robins Co., 189
In re Bank of New York, 141
In re Continental Bank & Trust Co., 141
In re Estate of Cochrane, 594
In re Japanese Electronic Prods. Antitrust Litigation, 483
In re Lotus Development Securities Litigation, 438
In re Mid-Atlantic Toyota Antitrust Litigation, 740
In re Northern District of California Dalkon Shield IUD Prods. Liability Litigation, 738
In re Rhone-Poulenc Rorer Inc., 764
In re Trans Ocean Tender Offer Securities Litigation, 628
In re Union Carbide Corporation Gas Plant Disaster at Bhopal, India, 248
Insurance Corp. v. Compagnie des Bauxites, 58, 95
International Harvester Co. v. Kentucky, 36
International Shoe Co. v. Washington, 40, 746
International Textbook Co. v. Prigg, 36
Ionian Shipping Co. v. British Law Ins. Co., 701
Irving v. Owns-Corning Fiberglas Corp., 85
James-Dickinson Farm Mortgage Co. v. Harry, 121
J. A. Olson Co. v. City of Winona, 180

Table of Cases

J.E.B. v. Alabama, *497*, 542
Jeub v. B/G Foods, Inc., 672
Johnson v. Fidelity & Cas. Co. of N.Y., 488
Johnson v. Manhattan Ry. Co., 651
Jones v. Clinton, *253*
Jones v. Maryland, 515
Jones Motor Co. v. Teledyne, Inc., 190
Julien v. Sarkes Tarzian, Inc., 770
Kahn v. Kahn, 188
Kalb v. Feurstein, 261
Kale v. Combined Ins. Co., 579
Kath v. Western Media Inc., 465
Keeton v. Hustler Magazine, Inc., 62-63, 92, 221
Kemner v. Monsanto Co., 484
Kenrose Mfg. Co. v. Fred Whitaker Co., 643
Kent County Bd. of Educ. v. Billbrough, 583
Kerney v. Fort Griffin Fandangel Assn., 745
Khalid Bin Talal v. E.F. Hutton & Co., 351
Kimberlin v. Quinlin, 339
King Fisher Marine Serv. v. 21st Phoenix Corp., 654
Kingston Square Tenants Association v. Tuskegee Gardens, Ltd., 303
Klaxon v. Stentor Elecric Manufacturing Co., 236, 273
Klee v. Pittsburgh & W. Va. Ry. Co., 260
Kliebert v. Upjohn Co., 219
Knapp v. Holiday Inns, Inc., *524*
Knight v. Knight, 721
Knowlton v. Allied Van Lines, 121
Konik v. Champlain Valley Physicians Hosp., 560
Kotteakos v. United States, 767
Kramer v. Caribbean Mills, Inc., 186
Kramer v. Kansas City Power & Light Co., 330
Kuisis v. Baldwin-Lima-Hamilton Corp., 579
Kulko v. Superior Court, 45, 60
Kyles v. Whitley, 445
Kyreacos v. Smith, 617
Lafayette Ins. Co. v. French, 36
Lake v. Jones, 596
Lambert Run Coal Co. v. Baltimore & Ohio R.R. Co., 250
Lavender v. Kurn, *554*
Leatherman v. Tarrant County, *337*
Leather's Best, Inc. v. S.S. Mormaclynx, 652
Leonen v. Johns-Manville, 422
Leroy v. Great Western United Corp., 226
Lesnick v. Hollingsworth & Vose Co., 85
Lewis v. Berry, 340
Lewis v. Rego Co., 217
Liberty Lobby, Inc. v. Anderson, 541
Lindsay v. Kvortek, 744
Link v. Wabash R. Co., 348
Livingston v. Jefferson, 222
Lopez Tijerina v. Henry, 732

Table of Cases

Los Angeles v. Salt Lake Railroad, 558
Louisville & Nashville Railroad Co. v. Mottley, 193, 197, 260
Magic Toyota, Inc. v. Southeast Toyota Distributors, Inc., 232
Malloy v. Trombley, 607
Manley v. Engram, 235
Marchand v. Mercy Medical Center, 463
Margeson v. Boston & M. R.R., 388
Marino v. Hyatt Corp., 93
Marks v. United States, 84
Markvicka v. Brodhead-Garrett Co., 670
Marrese v. American Academy of Orthopaedic Surgeons, 628, 629
Marsh v. Coleman Company, 364
Marshall v. Mulrenin, 295
Martin v. Hunter's Lessee, 167
Martin v. Wilks, 587, 691, 701
Mas v. Perry, 172
Mathews v. Eldridge, 160, 161
Matos v. Ashford Presbyterian Community Hospital, Inc., 341
Matsushita Elec. Indus. Co. v. Zenith Radio, 542
Mayo v. Key Fin. Servs., Inc., 744
Mayo v. Satan and His Staff, 142
McCarty v. Amoco Pipeline Co., 191
McCaughey v. Schuette, 330
McCormick v. Kopmann, 342, 355, 374
McDonald v. Mabee, 35
McDonnell Douglas Corp. v. United States District Court, 736
McDonough Power Equipment, Inc. v. Greenwood, 574
MCG Devel. Corp. v. Bick Realty Co., 361
McGee v. International Life Ins. Co., 46-48
McKennon v. Nashville Banner Publishing Co., 464, 465
McKibben v. Zamora, 596
Mebane Lumber Co. v. Avery & Bullock Builders, Inc., 331
Mells v. Billops, 596
Mendocino Environmental Ctr. v. Mendocino County, 339
Meredith v. Winter Haven, 317
Merrell Dow Pharmaceuticals, Inc. v. Thompson, 202, 221
Mid-American Title Co. v. Kirk, 339
Midland National Life Ins. Co. v. Emerson, 715
Midlantic National Bank v. Hansen, 185
Milliken v. Meyer, 36, 92
Mitchell v. Archibald & Kendall, Inc., 328
Mitchell v. Federal Intermediate Credit Bank, 591
Mitchell v. Forsyth, 758
Mitchell v. Neff, 33, 34
Miyano Machinery USA, Inc. v. Zonar, 664
Montana v. United States, 613
Moody v. Albemarle Paper Co., 736
Moor v. Madigan, 652
Moore v. Chesapeake & Ohio Ry., 201
Moore v. New York Cotton Exchange, 661
Morris v. Gilmer, 187

Table of Cases

Morris v. Jones, 592
Morris v. Union Oil Co., 583
Moses H. Cone Memorial Hospital v. Mercury Construction Corp., 757
Mower v. Boyer, 606
Mullane v. Central Hanover Bank & Trust Co., *133*, 728, 729, 745
Muniz v. Vidal, 359
Mucha v. King, 770
Murchu v. United States, 514
National Dev. Co. v. Triad Holding Corp., *143*
National Equip. Rental, Ltd. v. Szukhent, 94
National Mutual Insurance Co. v. Tidewater Transfer Co., 177
Neirbo Co. v. Bethlehem Shipbuilding Corp., 221
Nelson v. Zurich Insurance Co., 303
Newman-Green, Inc. v. Alfonzo-Lorraine, 176
New York Life Ins. Co. v. Dunlevy, 706
Nichols v. G. D. Searle & Co., 92
Nilsen v. City of Moss Point, 361
N.L.R.B. v. Jones & Laughlin Steel Corp., 273
Nobers v. Crucible, Inc., 219
Noble v. Bradford Marine, Inc., *215*
Nolan v. Transocean Air Lines, 273
North Central Illinois Laborers' Dist. Council v. S.J. Groves & Sons Co., 359
O'Connor v. G & R Packing Co., 598
Odum v. Penn Mutual Life Ins. Co., 706
Olan Mills, Inc. v. Hy-Vee Food Stores, Inc., 654
Olberding v. Illinois Central R. Co., 39
Oliveri v. Thompson, 384
Olympia Hotels Corp. v. Johnson Wax Dev. Corp., 346
Omni Capital Int'l v. Rudolf Wolff & Co., 62, 141
Orange County Calif. Airport Hotel Assoc. v. The Hongkong & Shanghai Banking Corp., 760
Osborn v. Bank of the United States, 200, 642
Owen Equipment & Erection Co. v. Kroger, 653, *675*
Oxford First Corp. v. PNC Liquidating Corp., 62
Pachinger v. MGM Grand Hotel-Las Vegas, Inc., 189
Palmer v. San Antonio, 336
Pan American Fire & Casualty Co. v. Revere, *707*, 719
Papin Builders, Inc. v. Litz, 331
Pappas v. Middle Earth Condominium Assoc., 170
Parker v. Moitzfield, 189
Parklane Hosiery Co. v. Shore, 488, *619*
Patton v. Yount, 496
Paul v. Virginia, 36
Pemberthy v. Beyer, 515
Pennoyer v. Neff, 3, *25*, 123
Penzoil Co. v. Texaco, Inc., 170, 765
People's Tobacco Co. v. American Tobacco Co., 36
Perkins v. Benguet Consolidated Mining Co., 92
Peterson v. United States, 420
Petrucelli v. Bohringer and Ratzinger GmBH Ausdereitungsanlagen, 147
Pfeiffer v. Ash, 250
Phillips Petroleum Co. v. Shutts, 745, 759

Table of Cases

Pierce v. Underwood, 769
Piper Aircraft Co. v. Reyno, 238
Polar Shipping Ltd. v. Oriental Shipping Co., 163
Portman v. American Home Products Corp., 568
Poster v. Central Gulf Steamship Corp., 649
Poulos v. Naas Foods, Inc., 218
Powell v. Allstate Ins. Co., 573
Prestenback v. Employers' Ins. Co., 690
Prinz v. Greate Bay Casino Corp., 363
Prosperity Realty Co. v. Haco-Canon, 635
Provident Tradesmens Bank & Trust Co. v. Patterson, 701
Puerto Rico Aqueduct & Sewer Authority v. Metcalf & Eddy, Inc., 758
Pullman-Standard v. Swint, 768
Quercia v. United States, 572
Ragan v. Merchants Transfer & Warehouse Co., 281
Railroad Co. v. Stout, 530
Rakus v. Erie-Lackawanna R.R., 422
Randazzo v. Eagle-Picher Industries, Inc., 178
Ranger Ins. Co. v. United Housing of New Mexico, Inc., 700
Reetz v. Michigan, 749
Reid v. San Pedro, 558
Reilly v. Sicilian Asphalt Paving Co., 585
Revere Copper & Brass, Inc. v. Aetna Cas. & Sur. Co., 674
Reynolds v. Clark, 321
Richardson v. Commissioner, 312
Richardson-Merrell, Inc. v. Koller, 757
Rios v. Davis, 605
Robinson v. Audi Aktiengesellschaft, 61
Robinson v. Brown, 488
Robinson v. Volkswagenwerk AG, 61
Roesberg v. Johns-Manville Corp., 395, 434, 443, 463
Rogers v. Bates, 770
Roller v. Holly, 149, 150
Romani v. Shearson Lehman Hutton, 340
Rose v. Giamatti, 215, 219
Ross v. Bernhard, 483, 484
Rubin v. Buckman, 260
Rush v. City of Maple Heights, 584, 586
Salve Regina College v. Russell, 316, 770
Sanders Co. Plumbing & Heating, Inc. v. B.B. Anderson Constr. Co., 185
Santa Clara County v. Southern Pacific R.R., 59
Scheetz v. Bridgestone/Firestone, Inc., 443
Scheuer v. Rhodes, 327
Schiavone v. Fortune, 368
Schlagenhauf v. Holder, 393, 764
Schroeder v. City of New York, 140
Schwartz v. Swan, 644
Scott v. Sandford, 175
Scott Paper Co. v. Ceilcote Co., 421
Scott Paper Co. v. National Cas. Co., 694
Sears, Roebuck & Co. v. Mackey, 762

Semegen v. Weidner, 340
Sempier v. Johnson & Higgins, 784
Shamrock Oil & Gas Corp. v. Sheets, 220
Shaffer v. Heitner, 96, 163
Shaumyan v. O'Neill, 160
Shelley v. Kraemer, 724
Sheridan v. Jackson, 330
Shields v. Barrow, 692
Shoshone Mining Co. v. Rutter, 212
Shute v. Carnival Cruise Lines, 93
Sibbach v. Wilson & Co., 296
Siemer v. Learjet Acquisition Corp., 121
Simblest v. Maynard, 542
Simer v. Rios, 735
Singh v. Daimler-Benz, AG, 177
6247 Atlas Corp. v. Marine Ins. Co., 714
Skelly Oil Co. v. Phillips Petroleum Co., 198
Slocum v. New York Life Insurance Co., 560
Smith v. Hutchins, 586
Smith v. Kansas City Title & Trust Co., 201
Smith v. Swormstead, 723
Soeder v. General Dynamics Corp., 422
Sopp v. Smith, 572
Southern R.R. v. Lanham, 423
Southwestern Stationery & Bank Supply, Inc. v. Harris Corp., 362
Stanford v. Tennessee Valley Authority, 651
State v. Spitter, 514
State ex rel Gooseneck Trailer Mfg. v. Barker, 313
State Farm Fire & Cas. Co. v. Century Home Components, Inc., 623
State Farm Fire & Cas. Co. v. Tashire, 172, 711, *715*
State of Utah v. American Pipe & Construction Co., 733
Stearn v. Malloy, 108
Stephan v. Yellow Cab Co., 585
Stewart Organization, Inc. v. Ricoh Corp., 235, 303, 305
Storer Cable Communications, Inc. v. City of Montgomery, 339
St. Paul Mercury Indem. Co. v. Red Cab Co., 189
Strawbridge v. Curtiss, 170, 711, 720, 741
Stringfellow v. Perry, 352
Stroud v. Doolittle, 225
Sun Ins. Office v. Clay, 317
Supreme Tribe of Ben-Hur v. Cauble, 724
Sure-Snap Corp. v. State Street Bank & Trust Co., 583
Sutphin v. Speik, 602
Sutton Place Dev. Co. v. Abacus Mortgage Inv. Co., 348
Swift v. Tyson, 265, 271
Swint v. Chambers County Commission, 761
Szantay v. Beech Aircraft Corp., 286
Tanner v. United States, 573
Taylor v. Louisiana, 495
Taylor v. Titan Midwest Construction Corp., 286
T.B. Harms Co. v. Eliscu, 212

Table of Cases

TBK Partners, Ltd. v. Western Union Corp., 741
Temple v. Synthes Corp., *687*
Thomson v. Gaskill, 190
Tobie v. Don Pepe Corp., 191
Torres v. Oakland Scavenger Co., 765
Touche Ross & Co. v. Redington, 202
Trans-Asiatic Oil, Ltd. v. Apex Oil Co., 163
Travelers Ins. Co. v. Riggs, 634
Trbovich v. United Mine Workers, 700
Troy Bank v. A. Whitehead & Co., 191
Tull v. United States, 486, 493
Turner v. Bank of North America, 167
Twin Disc, Inc. v. Big Bud Tractor, Inc., 369
Unique Concepts, Inc. v. Manuel, 665
United Mine Workers v. Gibbs, *637*
United States v. Angiulo, 514
United States v. Bagley, 445
United States v. Biaggi, 514
United States v. Chalan, 514
United States v. Cresta, 514
United States v. David, 514
United States v. Dennis, 514
United States v. Forbes, 515
United States v. Good, 161
United States v. Horsley, 515
United States v. Kimbell Foods, Inc., 318
United States v. Lopez, 275
United States v. Mensik, 146
United States v. Mendoza, 626
United States v. Nixon, 764
United States v. Odessa Union Warehouse Co-op, 162, 163
United States v. O'Neil, 650
United States v. Procter & Gamble Co., 388
United States v. Ringley, 603
United States v. Romero-Reyna, 513
United States v. Ruiz, 514
United States v. Weisman, 149
United States v. Wonson, 472
United States Fidelity & Guaranty Co. v. Algernon-Blair, Inc., 176
United States Fidelity & Guaranty Co. v. Mayberry, 227
Upjohn Co. v. United States, 409
Van Cauwenberghe v. Biard, 759
Van Dusen v. Barrack, 236
Vanier v. Ponsoldt, 495
Vasquez v. Superior Court, 734
Vaughan v. Southern Ry., 186
Velasquez v. Franz, 593
Virginia v. Johnson, 588
Visser v. Packer Engineering Assoc., 542
VT Investors v. R & D Funding Corp., 168
Wabash Western Rw. v. Friedman, 362

Wagner v. Taylor, 592
Walker v. Anderson Elec. Connectors, 468, 469
Walker v. Armco Steel Corp., 302
Wallace v. State, 515
Warwich Admin. Group v. Avon Prods., Inc., 339
Washington State Physicians Ins. Exchange & Ass'n v. Fisons Corp., 447
Watkins v. Resorts International Hotel & Casino, Inc., 594
Watts v. Smith, 652
West Coast Credit Corp. v. Pederson, 356
Western Maryland R. Co. v. Harbor Ins. Co., 688
Whitaker & Rambo Interior Designs, Inc. v. Prudential Property Cas. Ins. Co., 482
Whittenburg v. L.J. Holding Co., 341
Whyham v. Piper Aircraft Corp., 691
Will v. United States, 763
Williams v. Florida, 520
Williams v. North Carolina, 120
Willy v. Coastal Corp., 370
Wm. Passalacqua Bldrs. v. Resnick, Dev., 185
Wojan v. General Motors Corp., 260
Wolston v. Readers Digest Assoc. Inc., 530
Woods v. Interstate Realty Co., 281
World-Wide Volkswagen v. Woodson, 49
Wratchford v. S. J. Groves & Sons Co., 558
Yaffe v. Powers, 734
York v. Texas, 250
Zahn v. International Paper Co., 742
Zapata v. IBP, Inc., 409

CHAPTER 1

AN INTRODUCTION

TO THE CIVIL ACTION AND PROCEDURE

A. The Study of Procedure

The course in civil procedure focuses on the litigation process by which parties seek to resolve civil disputes in the courts. While it involves a significant amount of technical material, the course requires more than mastering discreet rules and doctrines. It should foster critical thinking about the principles underlying the rules and doctrines, and about the role of litigation as a method of resolving civil disputes. The stated goal of modern procedure is contained in Federal Rule 1: "to secure the just, speedy, and inexpensive determination of every action." Throughout this course, we should consider whether that goal is achieved.

The focus of this course is on the *litigation* process, through which parties seek to resolve their dispute by "going to court." Contrary to depiction in popular media, however, this process consists of far more than a trial. In addition, we should keep in mind that litigation is not the only method for resolving disputes. In Chapter 15, we will discuss alternatives to litigation. Indeed, most disputes in this country are not settled through litigation. And the vast bulk of those filed in court are resolved before the case can get to trial. See David Trubek, Austin Sarat, William Felstiner, Herbert Kritzer & Joel Grossman, *The Costs of Ordinary Litigation*, 31 UCLA L. REV. 72 (1983)(fewer than 12 percent of disputes are brought to a court system; approximately 10 percent of cases filed in a court system actually go to trial).

Although only a small percentage of all disputes will actually end in trial, use of alternatives, including voluntary settlement, are always made "in the shadow of the law." Any negotiated settlement will be influenced by the parties' assessment of what they could obtain through formal litigation. Thus, a full understanding of the litigation option is essential even for lawyers who ultimately pursue alternatives to it.

In this course, we are concerned with civil, as opposed to criminal, cases. The major goal of criminal law is to *punish* defendants for breaches of the general order rather than to *compensate* the victim of the crime. Civil cases, on the other hand, usually involve disputes between private parties,* in which the plaintiff seeks to recover a remedy from the defendant.

For example, suppose defendant drives her car while under the influence of alcohol, and runs into a car driven by plaintiff. Plaintiff is injured and her car is destroyed. Defendant's act constituted a violation of the criminal (or penal) law, for which the government may prosecute. If the prosecution is successful, the state can punish defendant, perhaps by imprisonment, or by payment of a fine, or by an order to perform community service. Generally, however, any fine goes to the government, and not to the injured person.

Defendant's act also constituted a *tort* for which the plaintiff can maintain a civil action against the defendant. The goal of that action will be to force defendant to compensate plaintiff for harm caused by her breach of a duty to plaintiff. The remedy may include reimbursement for the plaintiff's medical expenses and lost wages while recuperating, as well as compensation for pain and suffering and for the loss of her car. If the harm is permanent, the court may force defendant to pay for medical treatment over a long period.

Of course, not all civil cases involve criminal behavior. Breach of contract cases, for example, rarely involve misconduct that could constitute a crime. Similarly, the tort of negligence may be based on mere inadvertence which could not support a criminal prosecution. Civil cases play an important role in the administration of justice. They permit one party to sue another for breaching rules our society establishes governing relationships, even when those breaches fall short of criminal.

Throughout the law school curriculum, you will see procedural differences between criminal and civil cases. The prosecution must prove the criminal defendant guilty "beyond a reasonable doubt." The civil plaintiff generally must show that the defendant is liable "by a preponderance of the evidence." When charged, the criminal defendant is given warnings that the civil defendant is not. The court cannot compel the criminal defendant to testify at trial; the state must warn the criminal defendant that her statements may be used against her; the state must provide the criminal defendant with legal counsel if she cannot afford it. In short, more process is due the criminal defendant than the civil defendant.

The line between criminal and civil is not always bright. For example, in civil actions in which defendant has acted egregiously, our system may permit plaintiff to recover "punitive," or "exemplary," damages. Their purpose is expressly to punish — to "send a message" to defendant that her behavior is intolerable. To the extent that punitive

---

* The government can be a party to a civil action. For example, it might sue a contractor who breached an agreement to build some public work. In that instance, it is not enforcing a penal law, but is vindicating its private right. In addition, the government often enforces laws through civil actions, for example, by bringing an action to enjoin violations of antitrust laws.

damages serve a similar function to the criminal law, some observers have argued that the state should afford the defendant various heightened procedural protections given criminal defendants.

A civil litigant determines whether she has a claim and, if so, against whom, through the *substantive* law. In contrast, civil procedure provides the vehicle for attempting to vindicate rights created by substantive law. As we will see, however, the line between substance and procedure is sometimes ephemeral.

In many respects, procedure is the unique province of lawyers. Lawyers understand that *how* rights are vindicated can affect dramatically the scope of those rights. A claim or defense that one cannot prove is not worth much. Procedure is relatively invisible to most of the world, but seemingly technical procedural changes may effect significant alteration in the scope of substantive rights. Changes in the allocation of which party has the burden of proof on an issue, or how notice is given, or who is bound by a judgment can alter the underlying rights. Sir Henry Maine observed of English law that the substantive law was "secreted into the interstices of procedure." While this statement may overstate present reality, it certainly has a solid ring of truth. Throughout this course, we should consider whether seemingly neutral rules of procedure might have a distinctly substantive impact.

B. Federalism

Before there was a national government, the thirteen original states were separate sovereigns, governed by their individual constitutions and laws. Citizens concluded, however, that their interests might be better served by institution of a centralized government, at least for some purposes. After experimentation under the Articles of Confederation, the citizens undertook to create a national entity. Importantly, however, this national government did not replace or eliminate the separate state governments. The Constitution creates the United States government and cedes to it limited and enumerated powers.

In the first case in this book, Justice Stephen Field summarized these points succinctly:

> The several States of the Union are not, it is true, in every respect independent, many of the rights and powers which originally belonged to them being now vested in the government created by the Constitution. But, except as restrained and limited by that instrument, they possess and exercise the authority of independent States * * * .

Pennoyer v. Neff, 95 U.S. 714, 722 (1878).

CHAPTER 1 AN INTRODUCTION TO THE CIVIL ACTION AND PROCEDURE

While federal power is limited to those areas enumerated in the Constitution, the Supremacy Clause of that document provides that "This Constitution, and the Laws of the United States which shall be made in Pursuance thereof; and all Treaties made, or which shall be made, under the Authority of the United States, shall be the supreme Law of the Land. * * * " U.S. CONST, art. VI. Thus, where federal law exists and conflicts with state law, the federal law controls, so long as it concerns an issue properly within the purview of the federal government. Although most of the Constitution addresses the scope of federal power, it also imposes direct restrictions on the power of the states. For example, the Fourteenth Amendment provides that "No State shall * * * deprive any person of life, liberty, or property, without due process or law; * * * " Any state law violating this precept is unconstitutional and invalid.

The limited nature of the national government's power is reflected in the federal judiciary. Article III, section 2 of the Constitution sets the outer boundary of federal judicial power. Thus, as we will see in Chapter 4, litigants cannot file suit in a federal district court simply because they would like to be there. The case must be one as to which the Constitution and a congressional statute permit access. The two major types of cases which plaintiff can file in federal court are "diversity of citizenship" cases (in which the plaintiff and defendant are citizens of different states and in which the amount involved exceeds $50,000) and "federal question" cases (in which plaintiff's claim arises under a federal law).

What if the plaintiff has a dispute that cannot invoke one of these bases of federal subject matter jurisdiction? She can file in state court. Indeed, even the vast majority of those cases that can be filed in federal district court—all diversity of citizenship and most federal question cases—may also be filed in state court.* Thus, the existence of separate state and federal court systems will usually give the plaintiff a choice of fora. In fact, plaintiff may have a choice of filing in federal or in state court in several different states.

Although federal law can trump state law, it is important to note that the federal courts do not have general power to review actions of state courts. In most instances, a civil litigant in a state trial court can appeal an adverse judgment *only* to an appellate court of that state. Once the case is filed in one system—state or federal—it is subject to appellate review only in that system. There is one significant exception to this rule. The United States Supreme Court can review a decision of the highest court of a state. However, it can review that decision *only as to matters of federal law*.

Suppose, for example, that the supreme court of State A holds that unmarried people living together are not entitled to the same property law benefits as married people. The United States Supreme Court cannot review this holding, because it raises only a

---

* The only exception is with those federal question cases as to which federal district court jurisdiction is exclusive of the states. Such cases are rare. Examples include federal antitrust actions and some patent cases.

question of state law, as to which state courts are supreme. If, however, a party challenged this state law on the basis that it denied equal protection of the law as guaranteed by the Constitution, the Supreme Court would have the power to review the case. The reach of the Equal Protection Clause is a federal question, as to which the Supreme Court is the ultimate arbiter.

The American system of justice faces often thorny questions of federalism because American citizens are subject to regulation by both state and national governments. Few other countries have such dual governments. Interestingly, for example, England, from which we inherit so much of our law and legal tradition, is not a federal republic.

C. Overview of the Structure of a Court System

As we have noted, the federal government has a system of courts. Each state is free to establish its own judicial system as it sees fit. The federal courts and the courts of many (but not all) states are established in a tripartite model, consisting of (1) trial courts reviewed by (2) intermediate appellate courts reviewed by (3) a supreme court.

1. Trial Courts

These are the courts in which the plaintiff initiates civil litigation, usually by filing a complaint and having it and a court order (called a summons) delivered to defendant. Trial courts have *original* (as opposed to *appellate*) jurisdiction. Some states ascribe jurisdiction to different trial courts based upon subject matter. For example, they may have separate trial courts for probate matters, family law cases, and general civil disputes. Other states divide jurisdiction based upon the amount in dispute. For example, one court may take cases involving $15,000 or less while another takes cases of greater amount. States may use different names for their trial courts. Common names include superior, municipal, district and circuit courts. The trial court in the federal judicial system is the federal district court. This book focuses almost entirely on the jurisdiction and procedure in trial courts, where the bulk of the litigation is carried out.

2. Intermediate Appellate Courts

Despite a popular notion that a losing litigant can "fight to the highest court in the land," there is no constitutional right to appeal. Nonetheless, most American jurisdictions do provide one. In a tripartite model of court structure, states may permit an appeal of right to the intermediate appellate court.

In the federal judicial system, a litigant has a right to appeal an adverse district court judgment to the intermediate appellate court, which is known as the United States Court of Appeals. It consists of thirteen "circuits," eleven of which are grouped by geography into courts bearing a number. For example, the Fourth Circuit sits in Richmond, and hears appeals from federal district courts in Maryland, Virginia, West Virginia, North Carolina, and South Carolina. The twelfth is known as the Court of Appeals for the District of Columbia Circuit, which sits in Washington, D.C. and hears appeals from the federal district court in Washington.* The thirteenth United States Court of Appeals is for the "Federal Circuit," the jurisdiction of which is determined not by geography but by subject matter. It sits in Washington and considers appeals in specialized cases such as import transactions and patents.

Not all states have an intermediate court of appeals. In such states, a civil litigant who loses at the trial court may seek review at the state supreme court. Further, the existence of an intermediate appellate court does not guarantee a right of appeal in civil cases. In Virginia, for example, the intermediate appellate reviews criminal and administrative matters, not civil cases. Here, too, then, a civil litigant losing at the trial court may seek review by the supreme court.

3. Supreme Courts

Supreme courts are appellate courts.** Most states refer to their court of last resort as the supreme court. (In New York, however, it is called the Court of Appeals.) In the federal judicial system, the highest court is the United States Supreme Court. It consists of nine justices,*** and sits only at Washington, D.C. In most states, as in the federal system, the highest court is not required to hear all cases in which its review is sought. Indeed, in civil cases, supreme court review is almost always discretionary,**** In a typical year, for instance, the United States Supreme Court agrees to hear fewer than four percent of the cases (of any sort, criminal or civil) in which parties seek its review.

---

* Each of these courts of appeals reviews decisions by administrative agencies. Because it is in Washington, the District of Columbia Circuit hears more of these than any other Circuit.

** Interestingly, the United States Constitution gives the United States Supreme Court *original* (trial) jurisdiction over certain types of cases, including those in which a state is a party. U.S. Const., art. III, § 2.

*** The Constitution is silent on how many justices shall sit on the Supreme Court. The number is set by statute. See 28 U.S.C. § 1. The original Judiciary Act of 1789 provided the Court with only six justices.

**** In some states, a defendant in certain criminal cases, such as those involving capital punishment, has a right to review by the Supreme Court.

C. Overview of the Structure of a Court System

4. Appellate Practice and the Doctrine of Precedent

Appellate courts review dispositions of the case by the lower court(s). Appellate practice, however, is very different from trial practice. Appellate courts do not try cases, so they do not receive evidence or hear witnesses. Instead, they rely on the record below, briefs filed by counsel and, usually, oral argument on legal points. In intermediate courts of appeals, it is common to have a panel of three judges review each case. At the supreme court level, usually the entire panel of justices (commonly consisting of seven or nine) considers each case.

It is important to appreciate the role of appellate courts. The intermediate court (or the supreme court if it is reviewing the trial court directly) is not interested in whether it would have decided the case differently from the trial court; it does not retry the case. Rather, its role is to determine whether the trial court committed such error that the judgment should be reversed. Not every error is fatal. Indeed, the doctrine of "harmless error" allows an appellate court to affirm a judgment even when the lower court made a mistake, if the result would have been the same anyway.

When reading any opinion, note what court is deciding it. If it is an appellate court, note the issues as to which it is particularly deferential to the trial court. Note also the disposition of the appellate court. Does it affirm or reverse outright? Does it remand with instructions? How clear are the instructions?

Most supreme courts have a limited, though critical, role. Rather than simply correcting mistakes made by lower courts, most supreme courts act principally as final arbiter of the content of the jurisdiction's law. This role is reflected in the fact that most are not required to hear all cases in which parties seek their review. Thus, a supreme court may accept cases for review in particular substantive areas because it needs to clarify the law there.

Appellate pronouncements on questions of law are binding on all lower courts in the jurisdiction through the doctrine of *precedent*, or *stare decisis*. This doctrine lends consistency and stability to the law. In addition, under the same principle, an appellate decision on a point of law binds the same court in later cases. Thus, once a state supreme court has held that a plaintiff's contributory negligence bars her recovery, that court will apply the same rule in deciding subsequent cases. Stare decisis does not, however, freeze the law forever. Responding to relevant changes, the court that rendered an opinion (or a higher one) can overrule the precedent. Although overruling precedent is unusual, courts regularly elaborate on or modify rules announced in prior cases. This process of elaboration and gradual modification is at the heart of our common law system.

D. The Adversary System

One fundamental characteristic of American litigation is its adversarial nature. In our adversary system, each side to a dispute presents its case vigorously, in the best light possible. The parties take the initiative to bring suit, raise issues, present evidence, and persuade the factfinder. One obvious assumption of the system is that parties motivated by self-interest will only pursue worthwhile litigation and will invest the time and resources necessary to present their positions well. Another is that this clash of self-interested combatants hones the issues in such a way as to enhance the possibility of finding the truth and reaching a just result. Throughout the course, consider whether the adversary system relies too much on the notions that all lawyers are of equal ability and that all parties are of equal financial means.

The Constitution grants to federal courts jurisdiction only over "cases" or "controversies." Thus, courts may not render opinions on questions not presented in the context of an actual case. For example, assume that a legislature (federal or state) passes a statute that plainly violates the Constitution. No matter how egregious the violation, no federal court can declare the statute unconstitutional until the question is proffered in an actual case. The Founders expressly rejected a proposal that the Chief Justice sit with Congress to advise it on the constitutionality of its bills. Many (but not all) state court systems impose a similar limitation.

No plaintiff can sue unless she has "standing," which generally means that she must have suffered some injury before she can bring suit. Our system does not permit litigation simply because someone is upset over something or wants the courts to issue an advisory opinion; she has to be injured, to have a personal stake in the litigation, before the court is presented with the appropriate adversarial vehicle for resolution. Standing and similar doctrines governing "justiciability" of issues often present vexing questions; you will deal with them in detail in courses on constitutional law and federal courts.

Litigation is not unrestricted combat. Much like rules of a sporting contest, rules of procedure curb pure adversariness. For example, Federal Rule 11 imposes sanctions on litigants or counsel for various misdeeds, including documents filed "for any improper purpose, such as to harass or to cause unnecessary delay or needless increase in the cost of litigation." Rule 16 imposes sanctions for failure to cooperate in pretrial efforts to settle the case or to frame issues for trial. Rule 37 does the same for abuses in the area of discovery, through which litigants are permitted to find out contentions and evidence of opponents. In addition, rules of professional responsibility impose several important duties on counsel. Thus, a lawyer may not raise frivolous issues, conceal or destroy evidence, misrepresent facts, or offer false evidence. Counsel also must reveal controlling authority contrary to her position.

D. The Adversary System

Under the traditional adversary model, the judge is usually passive and reactive. The parties, not the court, are responsible for initiating and developing the case, framing the issues, discovering the evidence and presenting it at trial. Under this model, the judge rarely intervenes unless asked by the parties. For example, one might make a *motion*,* that is, a request for an order, on any of dozens of grounds, such as a motion to dismiss the case, or to transfer the case to another venue, or to strike a pleading. In addition, at trial, the judge monitors the admissibility of evidence. Here, although her need to rule is usually dictated by objections made by the parties, she can and will intervene to protect witnesses from harassment and to shield the jury from irrelevant or prejudicial evidence. Although the court is entitled to ask questions of witnesses at trial, historically courts have been reluctant to do so. In general, then, the decision makers (judge and jury) consider issues and evidence proffered by partisan advocates.

Not all judicial systems envision such a passive judge. In most of continental Europe, for example, the courts follow an "inquisitorial" model, in which the judge is expected to make an independent investigation into the merits of the case. She routinely questions witnesses and generally takes charge of the case in a way American lawyers would find intrusive.

Increasingly, American judges, particularly in federal courts, are borrowing some aspects of the inquisitorial system. In response to a perception that there is too much litigation (particularly too much expensive pretrial litigation), judges have assumed an activist role in managing cases, rather than simply reacting to the parties' requests. Recent amendments to the Federal Rules of Civil Procedure foster this new activism, which is changing (at least to a degree) the traditional view of the judge in the adversary system. Indeed, it is not uncommon now to hear some federal district judges complain that their job has become more "bureaucratic" or "managerial" than umpireal. The primary responsibility is often "keeping the parties' feet to the fire" and facilitating settlement.

Among many questions, the adversary system raises the issue of who should bear the cost of litigation. Litigation is expensive. Although the public provides the courthouse and the judges and juror, the adversary system puts the primary burden for expense on the parties. They pay the filing and other court fees, they pay to uncover evidence, they pay expert witnesses, and, most importantly, they pay attorney's fees. Attorneys are usually paid by the hour. Outside of small claims matters, cases do not get to trial without months, even years, of pretrial activity involving pleadings, motions, discovery, and settlement negotiations. Throughout these activities, the "meter is running."

---

* "Motion" is the noun. "Move" is the verb. Parties never "motion" the court. They "move" or "make a motion" for the desired order.

Under the "American Rule," each side pays her own attorney's fees.* The fact that it is called the American Rule implies that it is not followed in most other nations. Indeed, England now provides basically that the prevailing party recovers her costs *and* attorney's fees. In this country, there are exceptions to this rule (some created by courts, others by legislatures), and comentators and legislators increasingly advocate rejection of the American Rule. Still, it remains. Can you articulate policy support for the rule? Can you articulate policy reasons for rejecting the rule?

The expense of litigation — principally of attorney's fees — is an important factor in plaintiff's assessment of whether to attempt to enforce her substantive right. Suppose, for example, that D has swindled you out of $25,000; there is no question that D is liable to you for that sum. Suppose you retain a lawyer who charges $150 per hour. If she spends only 50 hours litigating the case through trial, her fee will be $7,500. Thus, even if you go to trial and win a judgment for $25,000, you will actually recover a net of $17,500. Moreover, you will have spent several months (perhaps years) in the litigation process.

Under these circumstances, you may instruct the lawyer to invest as little time as possible and to settle the case. Suppose the lawyer invests five hours and receives an offer from the other side to settle the case for $10,000. Will you agree to the settlement? It would give you $10,000, out of which you pay your lawyer (based on the hourly rate) $750. You end up with $9,250. On the other hand, you obviate the need to go to trial, and receive the money now rather than months or years from now.

Sometimes, plaintiff's lawyer bears the risk of attorney's fees by agreeing to take a case on a contingent fee arrangement. By this, the client agrees to pay the lawyer a percentage (typically one-third) of any recovery she gains. Some observers hail this arrangement, saying that it helps plaintiff bring some actions that would never be brought if plaintiff had to pay an hourly rate. Others criticize contingent fees for this very reason, saying the arrangement tends to foment litigation.

Other critics worry that the contingent fee arrangement gives the lawyer too great an incentive to settle a case quickly, rather than to go through trials. Suppose, for example, Lawyer could settle a case for $60,000 (and take a $20,000 contingent fee) after investing 30 hours. Suppose also that if the case goes to trial, plaintiff might win as much as $600,000; or, of course, plaintiff could win nothing. To go through trial will require several hundred attorney hours. It might be in the lawyer's economic interest to settle rather than litigate;

---

* It is important to distinguish between "costs" and attorney's fees. When lawyers speak of "costs" they mean "taxable" or "recoverable" costs. Generally, the prevailing party in litigation recovers her costs from the other side. These costs include such things as docket fees, court reporter fees, and clerk's costs, and usually amount to relatively little money. See 28 U.S.C. § 1920. They do not include attorney's fees, which will almost always be the most substantial cost of litigation.

critics are concerned that this economic incentive will color the advice the lawyer gives to her client.

Many lawyers, clients, judges, and commentators are addressing these and similar issues more seriously today than ever. Many are convinced that there is a "litigation crisis." Others disagree. But most observers seem to agree that litigation is too expensive and takes too long to resolve many disputes. Not surprisingly, people are looking to alternatives.

E. Alternatives to Litigation

This course focuses almost exclusively on litigation — the adversary system — to resolve disputes. That model has drawbacks. As noted, it is expensive. It relies in part on the fictive notions that all lawyers have equal ability and all litigants have equal financial resources. Litigation is a zero-sum game; someone wins, and someone loses. It is also retrospective, forcing litigants to look back to what happened in the past rather than focus on the future. All of this suggests that litigation may be better suited to some kinds of disputes than to others. We will address these issues in more detail in Chapter 15.

Alternative dispute resolution (ADR) has become an important topic for an upper division law school course. In our course, we hope to raise awareness of the possibility that litigation may not be the most appropriate method for resolution of your client's dispute. Our goal here is to survey the major methods of ADR. None is a panacea. None will ever totally supplant litigation. But throughout your law school career, consider whether the disputes you consider in your cases might have been handled better through ADR.

For example, consider a dispute between two persons who envision an ongoing relationship. This could be a dispute between family members over something personal, such as inheritance of a family heirloom. Or it could be the continuing relationship between a wholesale distributor and a retailer who, except for this disruption, have gotten along fine for years. Or perhaps it is an employer-employee relationship. In such situations, the best resolution may focus on the future, on continuing the relationship, on working out an arrangement to keep the relationship intact. Traditional, retrospective, zero-sum litigation may not be optimal. But what other choices are there?

Negotiation is the most widely used ADR tool. In fact, the vast majority of cases filed in court end up in a negotiated settlement. When negotiation works, and results in a settlement, it avoids the zero-sum-game aspects of litigation. The parties are free to structure the settlement in any way they see fit. This may take into account future relations and can be more creative than courts in fashioning remedies. An early settlement avoids the expense and trauma of trial and appeal, and can substantially lessen overall litigation costs.

Although parties can enter settlement negotiations at any time, often they do so only after the litigation dance has progressed for awhile, perhaps to the discovery stage. At that point, the lawyers begin to understand the facts of the dispute better, and may have a clearer idea of what the case is "worth."

At about that point as well, clients begin to realize not only the expense of protracted litigation, but that they are required to devote great time to the cause as well. For example, the other side will undoubtedly take the deposition of your client, in which she must respond under oath to questions by counsel for other parties. The experience is often traumatizing and sobering. On the other hand, it also gives the client a chance to speak directly to the other side and to "tell her story." This process is often cathartic. Indeed, there are some data showing that some litigants, especially those not routinely involved in litigation, consider the process a success (regardless of the outcome) if they get this opportunity.

Mediation is essentially negotiation through the auspices of a third party. This third party facilitates settlement of the dispute by helping the parties to find ground. It also avoids the zero-sum game nature of litigation. The mediator and the parties are usually free to structure the mediation sessions in any appropriate way. Usually, the mediator will allow each side to "tell its story" and to exchange information. She will sometimes suggest creative resolutions and can be especially helpful in disabusing one party of an unrealistic position.

Mediation is often voluntary, but an increasing number of courts require parties to submit to mediation sessions before continuing with litigation. Some litigants are offended by mandatory mediation; if they have a right to seek redress in the courts from a wrongdoer, why should they be made to sit down and try to negotiate a settlement?

Arbitration involves resolution of the dispute by a third party other than a court. Like litigation, then, someone wins and someone loses. The advantage is usually in time and expense. Arbitration can resolve the dispute more quickly than litigation. Because the discovery rules of civil litigation usually do not apply, the parties tend to spend less money in preparation for the hearing. The hearing is less formal than a civil trial, there is no jury, and the court rules governing admissibility of evidence do not apply. The arbitrator takes evidence and makes a decision. Sometimes, as in major league baseball arbitration, the parties require that the arbitrator choose between their respective offers. When this is not done, the arbitrator is free to fashion what she sees as an appropriate award, and may "split the difference" between the parties. At any rate, the dispute is resolved and the parties get on with their lives.

Arbitration is often consensual. Parties to a contract commonly agree that any dispute will be submitted to arbitration. They should spell out terms for selection and payment of the arbitrator(s), and for invocation of the process. Increasingly, commercial agreements include arbitration agreements for disputes. The terms of the agreements vary greatly. Under some, a party submitting to arbitration may waive significant rights, such as the right to jury trial and the right to seek some remedies, such as punitive damages, and the right to appeal. Most arbitration awards are reviewable only on very narrow grounds, which usually do *not* include the arbitrator's incorrect application of the law.

In some states, court-annexed arbitration requires parties to submit to arbitration before proceeding with litigation. For example, in several states, a plaintiff may not sue for medical malpractice until after she has gone through arbitration. Absent agreement of the parties, the arbitrator's decision is not binding. Either side can seek a trial de novo in court. Frequently, however, there are strong disincentives to this, such as provisions imposing various costs on that party unless she receives a better result at trial. As a result of collective bargaining agreements, many employees are required to submit to arbitration any grievances with their employers.

While arbitration offers advantages, it has its critics. Because the arbitrator is not a judge, and because her award is subject only to limited review, some have assailed arbitration as dispute resolution "without law." Moreover, there is a growing concern that the arbitration format favors "repeat players," particularly in the process of selecting the arbitrator.

Some disputes will involve traditional litigation and ADR. Indeed, much of ADR has found its way into the litigation process. As noted, it has long been true that parties negotiate a settlement to the vast majority of civil cases. Recent developments, particularly in federal courts, enhance that possibility. Several Federal Rules enhance the prospects of settlement by forcing litigating parties to work together at various stages of suit. In addition, creative lawyers have used ADR techniques such as arbitration to resolve specific issues in the course of litigation. Creative judges have also been able to bring ADR techniques and benefits into the litigation stream.

F. A Brief History of Our English Judicial Roots

We inherited much of our law and legal tradition from England. It is impossible to understand the American legal system fully without some background in English legal history.

Before the Norman Conquest of England in 1066, the administration of justice in what is now Great Britain was entrusted to a myriad of local courts, run by feudal lords, and enforcing rights in accord with local custom. William the Conqueror did not replace the local courts, but augmented them by establishing three royal courts: The King's Bench, the Exchequer, and the Court of Common Pleas. Litigants wishing to sue in one of the royal courts sought a writ (order) from the chancellor (a royal officer, akin to secretary to the King). Each court heard only certain types of cases, as defined by the writs each could entertain.

In early development, the royal courts heard a limited number of cases concerning possession of land, actions on contract (ex contractu), and actions in what today would be called tort (ex delicto). Over time, however, they expanded the number of writs which would invoke their jurisdiction. The feudal barons who controlled the local courts tried to stop this expansion of the royal courts' power. Ultimately, though, their efforts failed, and the royal courts developed a series of new writs in the thirteenth and fourteenth centuries.

While expanding their jurisdiction by recognizing new forms of action, the royal courts became increasingly inflexible in their administration of justice. Their rigidity denied justice to many suitors because of their failure to dot the "i" or cross the "t" on some arcane procedural point. The royal courts routinely dismissed cases despite proof at trial that the plaintiff was entitled to relief, simply because plaintiff had chosen the wrong writ at the outset of the case.

In addition, the royal courts became increasingly unwilling to give a successful plaintiff any remedy other than damages. To this day, of course, many plaintiffs seek exactly that; they want to be compensated in money for injuries inflicted in tort or to recover the benefit of their bargain in contract. Often, however, damages do not give the plaintiff true relief.

For example, suppose defendant steals a piece of plaintiff's jewelry. The jewelry has a market value of $500, but is a priceless sentimental treasure to the plaintiff. If money is the sole remedy available, however, the plaintiff cannot be made whole. What she wants is *specific* relief. She wants a court order commanding the defendant to return the jewelry. The royal courts largely refused to give this type of relief.

The hypertechnicality of royal court procedure, coupled with this limitation on remedies, led to pressure to reform the English practice. Suitors, used to petitioning the chancellor for a writ to sue in the royal courts, started to ask the King's Council (of which the chancellor was a minister) to intervene directly and to "do justice." In cases in which the remedy at law (through the royal courts) was inadequate, or in which a suitor alleged an enormous disparity of power between himself and his opponent, the chancellor started issuing orders on behalf of the Council to achieve equity. By the middle of the fourteenth century, Chancery (for the chancellor) was recognized as a separate court.

Over the next two centuries, this *equity* practice expanded. For example, the chancellor would enforce trusts (by which one could evade the common law rule that one could not devise land by will) and assignments of claims. The law courts would recognize neither. In addition — and most threatening to the royal courts — the chancellor could enjoin a party from enforcing a fraudulent judgment from a royal court. This seeming affront to the dignity of the common law judges led to a serious debate in the early seventeenth century. Francis Bacon, appointed by King James I as head of a commission addressing the matter, resolved the dispute in favor of equity practice. The commission upheld the chancellor's power to enjoin parties from enforcing royal court judgments procured by fraud. Because such orders were directed at a party, and not to the court that rendered the judgment, they did not constitute a direct infringement of the power of the royal courts.

After that, Chancery developed into a complete system of courts, procedures, and remedies. This system worked alongside the royal courts, which continued to administer the common law. Thus, England had a bifurcated system of civil justice—the royal (or "law") courts and Chancery (or "equity") courts. Law continued to award damages while equity developed a panoply of specific remedies, including the injunction, specific performance, rescission and reformation of contracts and other documents. A plaintiff could invoke equity's jurisdiction only by demonstrating that the remedy at law was inadequate. In addition, equity developed the "clean-up doctrine," by which it would award damages incidental to the issuance of equitable decree. For example, a plaintiff might win an injunction against further trespasses by the defendant, as well as an award of "clean-up" damages to compensate for past trespasses.

The two systems developed different procedures and terminology. Law courts used a jury to determine facts, while equity did not. Consequently, the law courts usually allowed live witness testimony. Equity came to permit more introduction of evidence through sworn statements. Law courts entered "judgments" while equity courts entered "decrees." Law courts had "judges," while equity courts had "chancellors."

Law and equity also differed dramatically in their methods of enforcing judicial decisions. Law enforced its judgments *in rem*, that is, against property. If plaintiff at law won a money judgment, and defendant refused to pay, the plaintiff could obtain a writ of execution, by which the sheriff would seize property owned by the defendant and sell it at public auction to satisfy the judgment. If defendant had no property to seize, plaintiff was out of luck. Equity, on the other hand, enforced its decrees *in personam*, that is, against the person. For example, if the chancellor ordered the defendant to return property to plaintiff, or to sign a deed conveying property, or to desist from some conduct, he could order defendant jailed until he agreed to do so. As the late Professor Fyr said, "Equity is into behavior modification."

Earlier in our history, most American states and the federal courts bifurcated law and equity practice. Some did so with separate courts, others with separate divisions of the same court. In 1938, Congress adopted the Federal Rules of Civil Procedure. Among many important advances, the Federal Rules abolished separate law and equity dockets in the federal courts and provided that there is a single form of action, known as the "civil action." Federal Rule 2. Although most states have done the same, this merger is not universal. In Virginia, for example, the circuit courts have separate equity and law "sides," in which rules of procedure are markedly different. In other states, such as Delaware, there are completely separate courts of law and equity.

Notwithstanding the widespread merger of law and equity, however, the distinction between the two continues to have practical importance in this country. For one, all jurisdictions differentiate between "legal" and "equitable" remedies. A plaintiff seeking equitable relief generally must demonstrate the inadequacy of a legal remedy. For another, the Seventh Amendment guarantees federal court litigants a jury trial in civil "[s]uits at common law."[*] Thus, consistent with historic practice, there is no constitutional right to a jury at equity. In Chapter 10, we will explore what this means after procedural merger of law and equity.

In other areas, equity practice came to dominate modern procedure. For instance, the joinder rules, which determine the scope of litigation by prescribing who may be parties and what claims may be asserted borrow liberally from equity practice. See Stephen Subrin, *How Equity Conquered Common Law: The Federal Rules of Civil Procedure in Historical Perspective*, 135 U. PA. L. REV. 909 (1987).

G. General Topics of Civil Procedure

Although fourteen chapters follow this one, it is helpful to view them as raising six groups of topics. Here we review these groups to provide a preview of the major procedural issues we will address in the course. We will do so using the facts from a case we will read in Chapter 2, World-Wide Volkswagen v. Woodson, 444 U.S. 286 (1980).

That case involved a tragic vehicular collision that seriously injured three members of a family in the process of moving from New York to Arizona. Harry and Kay Robinson had three children, Sam, Eva, and Sidney. Harry's doctors recommended that he leave his Massena, New York home and move to a drier climate. The family decided to move to Arizona. They set out in two vehicles — one a rented truck to carry furniture and the other their Audi 100 LS. They had bought the Audi from Seaway Volkswagen in Massena. The car was manufactured in Germany by Audi, imported to the United States by Volkswagen

---

[*] There are similar state constitutional provisions establishing a right to jury trial in state court in actions at law.

of America, and distributed to Seaway by World-Wide Volkswagen, which does business in New York and two neighboring states.

The trip went well until the family was driving on a freeway near Tulsa, Oklahoma. Harry and Sidney drove in the truck while Kay, Eva, and Sam followed in the Audi. Near Tulsa, a car driven by an inebriated Lloyd Hull, a citizen of Arkansas, collided with the rear of the Audi. The Audi caught fire. Kay and her two children were trapped inside the vehicle until a witness was able to smash the windows and rescue them. The three were burned horribly. Kay underwent more than thirty operations and spent 77 days in the intensive care unit of a Tulsa hospital. Each of the three was hospitalized for weeks.

The three Robinsons suffered enormous physical pain and incurred great financial loss. In inflicting this pain and loss, Lloyd Hull committed a crime. But, as we discussed above, the state's punishing him for driving while under the influence of alcohol would not compensate the Robinsons. Before commencing a civil case to seek compensation for the Robinsons, their lawyer had to review the substantive law to assess who might be liable and for what remedy. Obviously, as a matter of substantive law, the Robinsons could sue Lloyd Hull. Unfortunately, however, Hull had no appreciable assets from which to pay compensation. He also had no liability insurance. In short, Hull was "judgment proof"; any judgment against him would be uncollectible.

As a result, attorneys for the Robinsons had to consider whether the substantive law provided claims against any of the four corporations involved in manufacturing, importing, distributing and selling the Audi to the Robinsons. In your torts class, you will study the development of various products liability theories. The Robinsons were injured and brought suit in the 1970s, when such theories were emerging and when the law in Oklahoma was not completely clear. Still, the Robinsons' lawyers determined that they could assert claims against all four (the manufacturer (Audi), the importer (Volkswagen of America), the distributor (World-Wide) and the retailer (Seaway)). Put generally, the claims centered on the theory that the car was defective because the gas tank was mounted so as to make it susceptible to rupture in a rear-end collision. For a complete discussion of the facts of the case, see Charles Adams, World-Wide Volkswagen v. Woodson — *The Rest of the Story*, 72 NEB. L. REV. 1122 (1993).

1. Selecting the Forum (Chapters 2-7)

The first procedural issue is where to file the suit. The first group of chapters in this book addresses various constitutional and statutory limitations on plaintiff's choice of courts. It may not seem obvious at first blush, but the issue of where litigation takes place can be of enormous practical importance. Many plaintiffs, for instance, would like to sue "at home," without incurring the expense of travel and the inconvenience of hiring a lawyer in a distant forum. But not all plaintiffs can do this. The court must have *personal jurisdiction* over the defendants. Unless it does, the court cannot enter a valid judgment against the defendant. We will study the historical development of the constitutional and statutory limitations on a state's power to enter such binding judgments. Even in advance of that study, however, it makes some intuitive sense that the court of a state cannot enter binding orders over defendants who are not present there or who have no affiliation with the state.

Where does that leave the Robinsons? They no longer lived in New York; neither had they established a home in Arizona. Because of the lengthy hospitalization there, Oklahoma was about as convenient as anywhere else for them. Plus, the witnesses, police investigators, hospital records, and other important evidence was there. But would Oklahoma courts have personal jurisdiction over Audi, Volkswagen of America, World-Wide or Seaway? If not, would New York? If New York had personal jurisdiction, then the Robinsons would be forced to litigate far from most of the relevant witnesses and evidence.

Remember that civil litigation takes place under the auspices of a government. Thus, whatever state has personal jurisdiction over the defendants, its court must have a method for giving notice to them that they have been sued and telling them the time in which they must respond. The court gives this notice, and manifests the state's personal jurisdiction over the defendants, by prescribing rules for *service of process* on the defendants.

Even if the Robinsons' lawyer decides that Oklahoma would have personal jurisdiction over the four defendants and that there is a mechanism for serving process on them, she may then face another choice. Should she file the case in an Oklahoma state court or in the federal district court in Oklahoma? In other words, what court — state or federal — will have *subject matter jurisdiction* over the dispute? Recall from supra Section B that federal courts can hear (among others) cases arising under federal law and cases between citizens of different states.

The Robinsons' case does not involve federal law, but might qualify for diversity of citizenship jurisdiction. If so, their lawyer will have to choose whether to file in state or federal court. She will base this decision upon a variety of practical factors, including her experience with each court, how long it will take to get to trial, procedural mechanisms available, differences in choosing jury members, and many others. In *World-Wide Volkswagen*, the Robinsons' lawyer preferred state court because of the perception that juries in a particular county were extremely generous to plaintiffs. But should the plaintiffs' decision to eschew the federal court end the matter? As we will see, there may be a way for defendants to force the case into federal court.

The material on choosing a forum addresses other issues besides personal and subject matter jurisdiction and notice. One of them is the issue of whether federal or state law will provide the rule of decision for the case. Assessment of that question may affect one's choice of forum.

2. Learning About the Opponent's Case (Chapters 8 & 9)

The second major block of material addresses the rules governing how litigants learn about each other's contentions. The first tool is *pleadings*, documents in which each side alleges facts underlying their claims and defenses. Like all plaintiffs, the Robinsons initiated suit by filing what most jurisdictions call a complaint, in which they set forth factual allegations supporting their legal claims for relief. The defendants have several options in response. They might bring a motion to dismiss for any of myriad reasons, such as lack of personal jurisdiction. Or they may challenge the sufficiency of the complaint by arguing that it is unclear or incomplete.

Rather than bring a motion, the defendants may file a pleading which most jurisdictions call an *answer*, in which they respond to the allegations of the complaint and raise affirmative defenses. For example, if the defendants felt that Mrs. Robinson contributed to her own injuries by mishandling the car in some way, they could assert that in the answer. In some jurisdictions, the plaintiff responds to such affirmative defenses with a pleading called a *reply*.

After pleading, the parties embark on the *discovery* phase of the case, in which they have the right to require each other to produce relevant information through a variety of tools. They may request production of documents, send interrogatories that must be answered under oath, or take depositions of persons by asking questions under oath and "live," transcribed by a court reporter. Indeed, under recent amendments to the Federal Rules, parties must surrender specified information without a request by another party. Modern discovery provisions are extremely broad. This is consistent with modern theory that parties should not be required to plead facts in detail; factual detail is to be provided through discovery. What information would the Robinsons want to discover from the defendants? What sort of information would the defendants want to discover from the Robinsons?

Through the discovery process, the parties may find that they agree on certain facts, or that certain legal contentions are no longer tenable. Throughout this phase, the parties often start talking seriously about settlement. Recent developments foster such negotiations. The court can hold conferences to foster settlement and, if that fails, to narrow and clarify the issues remaining for adjudication.

3. Adjudication With or Without a Jury (Chapter 10)

After the discovery phase, counsel and the court start to focus on adjudication. Although the popular image of adjudication is plenary trial, in some instances other mechanisms can dispose of a case without the necessity of trial. If the case is tried, one important issue is whether the parties are entitled to have the case submitted to a jury. If so, counsel and the court must assess the division of labor at trial between the judge and the jury. Even after the jury has rendered its verdict, the court may have the power to change the result. Obviously, however, respect for the jury requires that this power be used narrowly.

4. Preclusion, Joinder and Supplemental Jurisdiction (Chapters 11-13)

By the end of Chapter 10, we will have taken a relatively simple dispute through adjudication. We then will address how a case can become more complicated. Two sets of rules foster the inclusive packaging of all related claims and parties into a single case. The first set consists of the *preclusion doctrines*, which prohibit parties from relitigating some issues already decided, and, in some instances, bar a plaintiff from raising things that she could have raised in an earlier case. These doctrines may counsel the Robinsons to raise all their claims in a single proceeding.

Against the background of the preclusion rules, litigants may make wiser use of the second set of rules promoting packaging — the joinder devices. These rules define the scope of litigation in terms of parties and claims. They delineate the plaintiffs' ability to join co-plaintiffs and multiple defendants in a single proceeding. In addition, they specify the circumstances under which the court, the defendants, and, in some instances, nonparties, can override the plaintiffs' structure of suit by adding new parties and claims. In *World-Wide Volkswagen*, these rules permitted the Robinsons to join together as co-plaintiffs and to sue the four defendants, all in a single case. In addition, the defendants may have been able to join claims against their insurance companies or, if the allegedly defective gas tank were manufactured by a subcontractor, to join the subcontractor to the pending litigation.

5. Appeal (Chapter 14)

All of the activities discussed to this point take place in a trial court. In Chapter 14, we will address appellate review. The most important restriction here is the final judgment rule, by which a party cannot appeal until the trial court has determined the entire dispute. In *World-Wide Volkswagen*, two defendants (World-Wide and Seaway) moved to dismiss on the ground that Oklahoma lacked personal jurisdiction over them. The trial judge dis-

G. General Topics of Civil Procedure

agreed. Unless they could invoke an exception to the final judgment rule, the defendants could not obtain appellate review of that order until after trial.

6. Litigation Alternatives (Chapter 15)

At the end of Chapter 14, we will have reviewed all major doctrines governing litigation. We will then be in a position to assess strengths and weaknesses of the litigation process by comparing it to alternatives. Such alternatives include not only mechanisms of ADR discussed in Section E, but dispute resolution mechanisms from other countries and cultures.

CHAPTER 2
PERSONAL JURISDICTION

A. Introduction and Integration

Before a plaintiff can initiate any law suit, she must decide where to sue. In deciding where to sue, the plaintiff must first determine which court has *jurisdiction*, that is, which court has the authority to decide this case.

When we speak of jurisdiction, we usually differentiate between two types—subject matter jurisdiction and personal jurisdiction. Subject matter jurisdiction deals with whether a court has authority to decide a particular type of case. For example, most state court systems have specialized courts such as probate courts, family law courts or small claims courts that can only hear certain types of cases. Similarly, the subject matter jurisdiction of the federal courts is limited to those areas specified in the Constitution and in federal statutes. Subject matter jurisdiction will be dealt with in a later chapter.

Personal jurisdiction is the topic of this chapter. It concerns the circumstances under which a court has authority to make decisions binding on these particular parties. By invoking the authority of the court, the plaintiff has consented to the power of that court to issue binding orders to her. But what about the defendant, who did not invoke or consent to the power of the court? What gives the court the power to enter binding orders against a particular defendant? At their root, concerns about personal jurisdiction are very similar to a question that has occupied political philosophers for centuries — what is it that makes the exercise of government authority legitimate? This chapter addresses this question not as an abstract philosophical one, but in the concrete context of litigation. Specifically, we will be analyzing whether particular judgments are valid or enforceable.

As a preliminary matter, you must know a little about the types of judgments available and how they are enforced. In some cases, the plaintiff gets a judgment in which the defendants are ordered by the court to do or refrain from doing something. This is called injunctive relief. For example, a school system might be ordered to desegregate, a town might be ordered to allow a group to hold a parade, a party to a contract to sell land might be ordered to transfer the land. In these cases, a defendant who defies the court order may be held in contempt of court and fined or imprisoned until she complies.

Awarding money damages, though, is far more common than injunctive relief. Indeed courts will usually issue an injunction only if money damages are an inadequate remedy. Where the plaintiff secures a money judgment, that award does not actually order the defendant to do anything. If the defendant refuses voluntarily to pay the judgment, she cannot be held in contempt of court or put in jail. Instead, the burden is on the person who secures the judgment to seek enforcement. To enforce or "execute" a judgment, the plaintiff typically "attaches" property owned by the defendant. With respect to physical property other than real estate, the property may literally be seized by the sheriff. Real estate is "attached" by posting notice on the property and making a notation in the property records. After attachment and notice to the owner, the property is auctioned and the proceeds are given to the judgment holder. If there are any proceeds in excess of the amount of the judgment plus expenses, that amount is returned to the judgment debtor.

In our nation of 50 independent and separate states, a serious problem could arise if states refused to enforce the judgments of other states. The drafters of the Constitution anticipated this problem and addressed it in the Full Faith and Credit Clause in Article IV of the Constitution, which provides that "Full faith and credit shall be given in each State to the public Acts, Records, and judicial Proceedings of every other State." Congress has by statute extended the requirement of full faith and credit to the federal courts. See 28 U.S.C. § 1738. The Full Faith and Credit Clause and Statute have been interpreted to require that every state must enforce the judgments of every other state. The Supreme Court has been extremely rigorous in upholding the requirements of the Full Faith and Credit Clause. For example, a state that makes gambling contracts illegal and unenforceable must nonetheless enforce a judgment entered by a sister state enforcing a gambling contract. See Fauntleroy v. Lum, 210 U.S. 230 (1908). One of the few exceptions to the strict requirement of full faith and credit is where the court that rendered the judgment lacked personal jurisdiction over the defendant.

This brings us back to the question with which we began: when does a court have personal jurisdiction? This chapter sets forth a largely chronological series of Supreme Court cases, in which the Court attempts to delineate the criteria for personal jurisdiction. As you will see, the criteria change over time — sometimes abruptly, sometimes gradually — and the area is still evolving.

B. Constitutional Limits on Personal Jurisdiction

1. The Fountainhead — *Pennoyer v. Neff*

Pennoyer v. Neff
95 U.S. 714, 24 L. Ed. 565, 5 Otto 714 (1877)

Justice Field delivered the opinion of the Court.

[In 1865, J.H. Mitchell sued Marcus Neff in Oregon state court. Mitchell claimed that Neff owed him $253.14 for legal services Mitchell performed. Mitchell submitted an affidavit asserting that Neff owned land in Oregon and further stating that Neff was living somewhere in California and could not be found. Notice of the suit was published for six weeks in the Pacific Christian Advocate, a weekly church newspaper. Neff did not answer or appear in the case, and the court entered a default judgment. Six months later, Mitchell secured a writ of execution against Oregon real estate owned by Neff. The land was sold at a sheriff's sale and purchased by Mitchell himself, presumably in exchange for the amount of the judgment plus costs. Three days later, Mitchell transferred title to Sylvester Pennoyer.

In September 1874, Neff sued Pennoyer in federal court seeking eviction. The trial court found for Neff holding that the judgment in *Mitchell v. Neff* was invalid. Specifically, the judge concluded that Mitchell's affidavit concerning Neff's whereabouts did not adequately describe the steps Mitchell had taken to locate Neff and that the affidavit by the newspaper attesting to the publication of the notice was also inadequate. Pennoyer appealed to the U.S. Supreme Court.]

* * *

The Code of Oregon provides for such service [by publication] when an action is brought against a nonresident and absent defendant, who has property within the State. It also provides, where the action is for the recovery of money or damages, for the attachment of the property of the nonresident. And it also declares that no natural person is subject to the jurisdiction of a court of the State, "unless he appear in the court, or be found within the State, or be a resident thereof, or have property therein; and, in the last case, only to the extent of such property at the time the jurisdiction attached." Construing this latter provision to mean, that, in an action for money or damages where a defendant does not appear in the court, and is not found within the State, and is not a resident thereof, but has property therein, the jurisdiction of the court extends only over such property, the declaration expresses a principle of general, if not universal, law. The authority of every tribunal is necessarily restricted by the territorial limits of the State in which it is established. Any attempt to exercise authority beyond those limits would be deemed in every other forum, as has been said by this court, an illegitimate assumption of power, and be resisted as mere abuse. In the case against the plaintiff, the property here in controversy sold under the judgment rendered was not attached, nor in any way brought under the jurisdiction of the court. Its first connection with the case was caused by a levy of the execution. It was not, therefore, disposed of pursuant to any adjudication, but only in enforcement of a personal judgment, having no relation to the property, rendered against a nonresident without service of process upon him in the action, or his appearance therein. The court below did not consider that an attachment of the property was essential to its jurisdiction or to the validity of the sale, but held that the judgment was invalid from defects in the affidavit upon which the order of publication was obtained, and in the affidavit by which the publication was proved.

[The Court held that the deficiencies in the affidavits upon which the lower court relied could only be a basis for appeal. They were not a basis for a collateral attack, that is, a separate law suit seeking to invalidate the prior judgment.]

* * *

If, therefore, we were confined to the rulings of the court below upon the defects in the affidavits mentioned, we should be unable to uphold its decision. But it was also contended in that court, and is insisted upon here, that the judgment in the State court against the plaintiff was void for want of personal service of process on him, or of his appearance in the action in which it was rendered, and that the premises in controversy could not be subjected to the payment of the demand of a resident creditor except by a proceeding in rem; that is, by a direct proceeding against the property for that purpose. If these positions are sound, the ruling of the Circuit Court as to the invalidity of that judgment must be sustained, notwithstanding our dissent from the reasons upon which it was made. And that they are sound would seem to follow from two well established principles of public law respecting the jurisdiction of an independent State over persons and property. The several States of the Union are not, it is true, in every respect independent, many of the rights and powers which originally belonged to them being now vested in the government created by the Constitution. But, except as restrained and limited by that instrument, they possess and exercise the authority of independent States, and the principles of public law to which we have referred are applicable to them. One of these principles is, that every State possesses exclusive jurisdiction and sovereignty over persons and property within its territory. As a consequence, every State has the power to determine for itself the civil status and capacities of its inhabitants; to prescribe the subjects upon which they may contract, the forms and solemnities with which their contracts shall be executed, the rights and obligations arising from them, and the mode in which their validity shall be determined and their obligations enforced; and also to regulate the manner and conditions upon which property situated within such territory, both personal and real, may be acquired, enjoyed, and transferred. The other principle of public law referred to follows from the one mentioned; that is, that no State can exercise direct jurisdiction and authority over persons or property without its territory. STORY, CONFL. LAWS, c. 2; WHEAT. INT. LAW, pt. 2, c. 2. The several States are of equal dignity and authority, and the independence of one implies the exclusion of power from all others. And so it is laid down by jurists, as an elementary principle, that the laws of one State have no operation outside of its territory, except so far as is allowed by comity; and that no tribunal established by it can extend its process beyond that territory so as to subject either persons or property to its decisions. "Any exertion of authority of this sort beyond this limit," says Story, "is a mere nullity, and incapable of binding such persons or property in any other tribunals." STORY, CONFL. LAWS, sect. 539.

But as contracts made in one State may be enforceable only in another State, and property may be held by nonresidents, the exercise of the jurisdiction which every State is admitted to possess over persons and property within its own territory will often affect persons and property without it. To any influence exerted in this way by a State affecting persons resident or property situated elsewhere, no objection can be justly taken; whilst any direct exertion of authority upon them, in an attempt to give ex-territorial operation to its laws, or to enforce an ex-territorial jurisdiction by its tribunals, would be deemed an encroachment upon the independence of the State in which the persons are domiciled or the property is situated, and be resisted as usurpation.

B. Constitutional Limits on Personal Jurisdiction

Thus the State, through its tribunals, may compel persons domiciled within its limits to execute, in pursuance of their contracts respecting property elsewhere situated, instruments in such form and with such solemnities as to transfer the title, so far as such formalities can be complied with; and the exercise of this jurisdiction in no manner interferes with the supreme control over the property by the State within which it is situated.

So the State through its tribunals, may subject property situated within its limits owned by nonresidents to the payment of the demand of its own citizens against them; and the exercise of this jurisdiction in no respect infringes upon the sovereignty of the State where the owners are domiciled. Every State owes protection to its own citizens; and, when nonresidents deal with them, it is a legitimate and just exercise of authority to hold and appropriate any property owned by such nonresidents to satisfy the claims of its citizens. It is in virtue of the State's jurisdiction over the property of the nonresident situated within its limits that its tribunals can inquire into that nonresident's obligations to its own citizens, and the inquiry can then be carried only to the extent necessary to control the disposition of the property. If the nonresident have no property in the State, there is nothing upon which the tribunals can adjudicate.

* * *

* * * If, without personal service, judgments in personam, obtained ex parte against nonresidents and absent parties, upon mere publication of process, which, in the great majority of cases, would never be seen by the parties interested, could be upheld and enforced, they would be the constant instruments of fraud and oppression. Judgments for all sorts of claims upon contracts and for torts, real or pretended, would be thus obtained, under which property would be seized, when the evidence of the transactions upon which they were founded, if they ever had any existence, had perished.

Substituted service by publication, or in any other authorized form, may be sufficient to inform parties of the object of proceedings taken where property is once brought under the control of the court by seizure or some equivalent act. The law assumes that property is always in the possession of its owner, in person or by agent; and it proceeds upon the theory that its seizure will inform him, not only that it is taken into the custody of the court, but that he must look to any proceedings authorized by law upon such seizure for its condemnation and sale. Such service may also be sufficient in cases where the object of the action is to reach and dispose of property in the State, or of some interest therein, by enforcing a contract or a lien respecting the same, or to partition it among different owners, or, when the public is a party, to condemn and appropriate it for a public purpose. In other words, such service may answer in all actions which are substantially proceedings in rem. But where the entire object of the action is to determine the personal rights and obligations of the defendants, that is, where the suit is merely in personam, constructive service in this form upon a nonresident is ineffectual for any purpose. Process from the tribunals of one State cannot run into another State, and summon parties there domiciled to leave its territory and respond to proceedings against them. Publication of process or notice within the State where the tribunal sits cannot create any greater obligation upon the nonresident to appear. Process sent to him out of the State, and process published within it, are equally unavailing in proceedings to establish his personal liability.

The want of authority of the tribunals of a State to adjudicate upon the obligations of nonresidents, where they have no property within its limits, is not denied by the court below: but the position is assumed, that, where they have property within the State, it is immaterial whether the property is in the first instance brought under the control of the court by attachment or some other equivalent act, and afterwards applied by its judgment to the satisfaction of demands against its owner; or such demands be first established in a personal action, and the property of the nonresident be afterwards seized and sold on execution. But the answer to this position has already been given in the statement, that the jurisdiction of the court to inquire into and determine his obligations at all is only incidental to its jurisdiction over the property. Its jurisdiction in that respect cannot be made to depend upon facts to be ascertained after it has tried the cause and rendered the judgment. If the judgment be previously void, it will not become valid by the subsequent discovery of property of the defendant, or by his subsequent acquisition of it. The judgment, if void when rendered, will always remain void: it cannot occupy the doubtful position of being valid if property be found, and void if there be none. Even if the position assumed were confined to cases where the nonresident defendant possessed property in the State at the commencement of the action, it would still make the validity of the proceedings and judgment depend upon the question whether, before the levy of the execution, the defendant had or had not disposed of the property. If before the levy the property should be sold, then, according to this position, the judgment would not be binding. This doctrine would introduce a new element of uncertainty in judicial proceedings. The contrary is the law: the validity of every judgment depends upon the jurisdiction of the court before it is rendered, not upon what may occur subsequently. * * *

The force and effect of judgments rendered against nonresidents without personal service of process upon them, or their voluntary appearance, have been the subject of frequent consideration in the courts of the United States and of the several States, as attempts have been made to enforce such judgments in States other than those in which they were rendered, under the provision of the Constitution requiring that "full faith and credit shall be given in each State to the public acts, records, and judicial proceedings of every other State;" and the act of Congress providing for the mode of authenticating such acts, records, and proceedings, and declaring that, when thus authenticated, "they shall have such faith and credit given to them in every court within the United States as they have by law or usage in the courts of the State from which they are or shall be taken." In the earlier cases, it was supposed that the act gave to all judgments the same effect in other States which they had by law in the State where rendered. But this view was afterwards qualified so as to make the act applicable only when the court rendering the judgment had jurisdiction of the parties and of the subject-matter, and not to preclude an inquiry into the jurisdiction of the court in which the judgment was rendered, or the right of the State itself to exercise authority over the person or the subject-matter. * * *

* * *

* * * In several of the cases, the decision has been accompanied with the observation that a personal judgment thus recovered has no binding force without the State in which it is rendered, implying that in such State it may be valid and binding. But if the court has no jurisdiction over the person of the defendant by reason of his nonresidence, and, consequently, no authority to pass upon his personal rights and obligations; if the whole proceeding, without service upon him or his appearance, is *coram non judice* and void; if to hold a defendant bound by such a judgment is contrary to the first principles of justice, — it is difficult to see how the judgment can legitimately have any force within the State. The language used can be justified only on the ground that there

B. Constitutional Limits on Personal Jurisdiction

was no mode of directly reviewing such judgment or impeaching its validity within the State where rendered; and that, therefore, it could be called in question only when its enforcement was elsewhere attempted. In later cases, this language is repeated with less frequency than formerly, it beginning to be considered, as it always ought to have been, that a judgment which can be treated in any State of this Union as contrary to the first principles of justice, and as an absolute nullity, because rendered without any jurisdiction of the tribunal over the party, is not entitled to any respect in the State where rendered.

Be that as it may, the courts of the United States are not required to give effect to judgments of this character when any right is claimed under them. Whilst they are not foreign tribunals in their relations to the State courts, they are tribunals of a different sovereignty, exercising a distinct and independent jurisdiction, and are bound to give to the judgments of the State courts only the same faith and credit which the courts of another State are bound to give to them.

Since the adoption of the Fourteenth Amendment to the Federal Constitution, the validity of such judgments may be directly questioned, and their enforcement in the State resisted, on the ground that proceedings in a court of justice to determine the personal rights and obligations of parties over whom that court has no jurisdiction do not constitute due process of law. Whatever difficulty may be experienced in giving to those terms a definition which will embrace every permissible exertion of power affecting private rights, and exclude such as is forbidden, there can be no doubt of their meaning when applied to judicial proceedings. They then mean a course of legal proceedings according to those rules and principles which have been established in our systems of jurisprudence for the protection and enforcement of private rights. To give such proceedings any validity, there must be a tribunal competent by its constitution — that is, by the law of its creation — to pass upon the subject-matter of the suit; and, if that involves merely a determination of the personal liability of the defendant, he must be brought within its jurisdiction by service of process within the State, or his voluntary appearance.

Except in cases affecting the personal status of the plaintiff, and cases in which that mode of service may be considered to have been assented to in advance, as hereinafter mentioned, the substituted service of process by publication, allowed by the law of Oregon and by similar laws in other States, where actions are brought against nonresidents, is effectual only where, in connection with process against the person for commencing the action, property in the State is brought under the control of the court, and subjected to its disposition by process adapted to that purpose, or where the judgment is sought as a means of reaching such property or affecting some interest therein; in other words, where the action is in the nature of a proceeding in rem. * * *

It is true that, in a strict sense, a proceeding in rem is one taken directly against property, and has for its object the disposition of the property, without reference to the title of individual claimants; but, in a larger and more general sense, the terms are applied to actions between parties, where the direct object is to reach and dispose of property owned by them, or of some interest therein. Such are cases commenced by attachment against the property of debtors, or instituted to partition real estate, foreclose a mortgage, or enforce a lien. So far as they affect property in the State, they are substantially proceedings in rem in the broader sense which we have mentioned.

It is hardly necessary to observe, that in all we have said we have had reference to proceedings in courts of first instance, and to their jurisdiction, and not to proceedings in an appellate tribunal to review the action of such courts. The latter may be taken upon such notice, personal or constructive, as the State creating the tribunal may provide. They are considered as rather a continuation of the original litigation than the commencement of a new action.

CHAPTER 2 PERSONAL JURISDICTION

HOLDING

It follows from the views expressed that the personal judgment recovered in the State court of Oregon against the plaintiff herein, then a nonresident of the State, was without any validity, and did not authorize a sale of the property in controversy.

To prevent any misapplication of the views expressed in this opinion, it is proper to observe that we do not mean to assert, by anything we have said, that a State may not authorize proceedings to determine the status of one of its citizens towards a nonresident, which would be binding within the State, though made without service of process or personal notice to the nonresident. The jurisdiction which every State possesses to determine the civil status and capacities of all its inhabitants involve authority to prescribe the conditions on which proceedings affecting them may be commenced and carried on within its territory. The State, for example, has absolute right to prescribe the conditions upon which the marriage relation between its own citizens shall be created, and the causes for which it may be dissolved. One of the parties guilty of acts for which, by the law of the State, a dissolution may be granted, may have removed to a State where no dissolution is permitted. The complaining party would, therefore, fail if a divorce were sought in the State of the defendant; and if application could not be made to the tribunals of the complainant's domicile in such case, and proceedings be there instituted without personal service of process or personal notice to the offending party, the injured citizen would be without redress.

Neither do we mean to assert that a State may not require a nonresident entering into a partnership or association within its limits, or making contracts enforceable there, to appoint an agent or representative in the State to receive service of process and notice in legal proceedings instituted with respect to such partnership, association, or contracts, or to designate a place where such service may be made and notice given, and provide, upon their failure, to make such appointment or to designate such place that service may be made upon a public officer designated for that purpose, or in some other prescribed way, and that judgments rendered upon such service may not be binding upon the nonresidents both within and without the State. * * * Nor do we doubt that a State, on creating corporations or other institutions for pecuniary or charitable purposes, may provide a mode in which their conduct may be investigated, their obligations enforced, or their charters revoked, which shall require other than personal service upon their officers or members. Parties becoming members of such corporations or institutions would hold their interest subject to the conditions prescribed by law.

In the present case, there is no feature of this kind, and, consequently, no consideration of what would be the effect of such legislation in enforcing the contract of a nonresident can arise. The question here respects only the validity of a money judgment rendered in one State, in an action upon a simple contract against the resident of another, without service of process upon him, or his appearance therein.

Judgment affirmed.

JUSTICE HUNT dissenting.

* * *

The judgment of the court below was placed upon the ground that the provisions of the statute were not complied with. This is of comparatively little importance, as it affects the present

B. Constitutional Limits on Personal Jurisdiction

case only. The judgment of this court is based upon the theory that the legislature had no power to pass the law in question; that the principle of the statute is vicious, and every proceeding under it void. It, therefore, affects all like cases, past and future, and in every State.

* * *

In my opinion, this decision is at variance with the long-established practice under the statutes of the States of this Union, is unsound in principle, and, I fear, may be disastrous in its effects. It tends to produce confusion in titles which have been obtained under similar statutes in existence for nearly a century; it invites litigation and strife, and over throws a well-settled rule of property.

The result of the authorities on the subject, and the sound conclusions to be drawn from the principles which should govern the decision, as I shall endeavor to show, are these: —

1. A sovereign State must necessarily have such control over the real and personal property actually being within its limits, as that it may subject the same to the payment of debts justly due to its citizens.

2. This result is not altered by the circumstance that the owner of the property is nonresident, and so absent from the State that legal process cannot be served upon him personally.

3. Personal notice of a proceeding by which title to property is passed is not indispensable; it is competent to the State to authorize substituted service by publication or otherwise, as the commencement of a suit against nonresidents, the judgment in which will authorize the sale of property in such State.

4. It belongs to the legislative power of the State to determine what shall be the modes and means proper to be adopted to give notice to an absent defendant of the commencement of a suit; and if they are such as are reasonably likely to communicate to him information of the proceeding against him, and are in good faith designed to give him such information, and an opportunity to defend is provided for him in the event of his appearance in the suit, it is not competent to the judiciary to declare that such proceeding is void as not being by due process of law.

5. Whether the property of such nonresident shall be seized upon attachment as the commencement of a suit which shall be carried into judgment and execution, upon which it shall then be sold, or whether it shall be sold upon an execution and judgment without such preliminary seizure, is a matter not of constitutional power, but of municipal regulation only.

To say that a sovereign State has the power to ordain that the property of nonresidents within its territory may be subjected to the payment of debts due to its citizens, if the property is levied upon at the commencement of a suit, but that it has not such power if the property is levied upon at the end of the suit, is a refinement and a depreciation of a great general principle that, in my judgment, cannot be sustained[.]

* * *

That a State can subject land within its limits belonging to nonresident owners to debts due to its own citizens as it can legislate upon all other local matters; that it can prescribe the mode and process by which it is to be reached — seems to me very plain.

I am not willing to declare that a sovereign State cannot subject the land within its limits to the payment of debts due to its citizens, or that the power to do so depends upon the fact whether its statute shall authorize the property to be levied upon at the commencement of the suit or at its termination. This is a matter of detail, and I am of opinion, that if reasonable notice be given, with an opportunity to defend when appearance is made, the question of power will be fully satisfied.

NOTES AND QUESTIONS

1. Like most judicial opinions, the Supreme Court's opinion in *Pennoyer* does not begin to tell the full story of the people involved in this famous case. Marcus Neff was an illiterate homesteader and one of the earliest settlers to claim land under the Oregon Donation Act. Mitchell and Pennoyer were somewhat better known. "J. H. Mitchell" was the Oregon alias of John Hipple, a Pennsylvania lawyer who abandoned his wife and headed west with his current paramour and four thousand dollars of client money. He wound up in Portland and quickly established himself as a successful lawyer specializing in land litigation. Scandal was a way of life for Mitchell. He was implicated, though never indicted, in a vote fraud scheme and an attempt to bribe the U.S. Attorney General. His private life was equally sordid. He married his second wife without bothering to divorce his first wife. Later, the *Oregonian* newspaper published a series of love letters Mitchell had written to his second wife's younger sister. None of this interfered with his political career. He was elected repeatedly to the U.S. Senate. In 1905, while serving in the Senate he was convicted of a massive land fraud scheme and sentenced to six months in jail. He died while his appeal was pending.

Sylvester Pennoyer went on to be governor of Oregon, but he remained bitter about his defeat in *Pennoyer v. Neff.* Ten years after the decision, he used his inaugural address as a forum to decry that decision as a usurpation of state power. His attacks on the Supreme Court were so frequent and vociferous that such attacks became known as *"Pennoyerism."* See Wendy Collins Perdue, *Sin, Scandal, and Substantive Due Process: Personal Jurisdiction and Pennoyer Reconsidered,* 62 WASH. L. REV. 479 (1987).

2. Justice Field distinguishes between in rem and in personam jurisdiction. "In rem" is Latin for "against the property" and "in personam" means "against the person." In an in personam case, because the court exercises jurisdiction over the person of the defendant, it can enter a judgment that creates a personal obligation to pay money or perform some act. A court can enforce an in personam judgment either by selling any of the defendant's property or, if the defendant defies an order, by jailing her.

In an in rem case, the court's jurisdiction is over the particular property attached. In rem cases fall into two broad categories. The first category involves cases in which the proceeding concerns the ownership of the attached property. Examples of this type are

B. **Constitutional Limits on Personal Jurisdiction**

condemnation or foreclosure proceedings. Suppose Penny and Dot each claim to own the same valuable painting. One might sue the other in personam and proceed to resolve the dispute. In the alternative, the one in possession could tender the painting to the court. The court, having jurisdiction over the property (the "res"), has the power to determine who owns it, even if other party is not served within the jurisdiction.

This first category of in rem cases is sometimes subdivided to differentiate true in rem cases from what are called quasi-in-rem "of the first type." True in rem cases are ones in which decide ownership as to the whole world. Government condemnation and certain admiralty cases fall into this category. After a condemnation proceeding, the government owns the land and no one else in the world does. Quasi-in-rem type 1 cases adjudicate ownership as between the litigants. For example, if I fail to pay my mortgage, a court may determine that as between the bank and me, the bank now owns the property. However, a third party could come along and prove that she has better title than the bank does.

What is important for our purpose is not the difference between true in rem and quasi-in rem type 1, but the similarity between the two. In both categories of cases, the court takes jurisdiction over the property so as to adjudicate ownership of in that property.

These cases should be distinguished from the second broad category of in rem jurisdiction in which the lawsuit has nothing to do with the property. Instead, the presence of the property is simply the basis upon which the court relies to assert jurisdiction in the case. This type of in rem proceeding is called quasi-in-rem "of the second type" (or just quasi-in-rem). In *Mitchell v. Neff*, Mitchell could have used quasi-in-rem jurisdiction by attaching Neff's land at the outset of the lawsuit. If he had done this, then even though Neff was not served in Oregon, the default judgment would have been valid. Following the default judgment, Mitchell would have been entitled to the proceeds from the auction of Neff's land, up to the amount of Mitchell's judgment.

3. Justice Field holds that in rem jurisdiction is available only if the property is attached at the beginning of the litigation. Because that did not occur in *Mitchell v. Neff*, he holds that there was no valid in rem jurisdiction. Why is it essential that attachment happen at the beginning of the suit?

4. Justice Field suggests that in an in rem proceeding, "substitute service by publication," plus attachment of the property, provides sufficient notice of the proceeding to the defendant. Do you think Neff would have in fact learned of the case against him if both these steps had in fact occurred? In the next chapter, we will explore in more detail the requirements of notice.

5. In addition to discussing the prerequisites for valid in rem jurisdiction, Justice Field also discusses in personam jurisdiction. In personam jurisdiction is jurisdiction "against the person." Unlike in rem judgments, an in personam judgment is not limited by the value of any property. Field's discussion of why there is no in personam jurisdiction lays important

CHAPTER 2 PERSONAL JURISDICTION

foundations for the future of personal jurisdiction. Interestingly, the discussion was unnecessary to deciding the particular case because both parties appear to have conceded that the judgment was not binding in personam.

6. Review Justice Field's explanation as to why there is no in personam jurisdiction over Neff. How do you think Justice Field would have responded to the following hypotheticals?

(a) Suit was brought in Oregon state court, with Neff served personally in California.

(b) Mitchell learned that Neff was vacationing in Arizona. Mitchell filed suit in Arizona state court, and Neff was served with process in Arizona. — *there is personal jurisdiction*

(c) At Mitchell's request, the Oregon sheriff goes to California where Neff is, knocks him unconscious, and takes him back to Oregon where he then serves Neff with process.

7. Field's analysis of personal jurisdiction seems to derive from what he describes as "well-established principles of public law," apparently relying on an international law analogy. Does it make sense to apply the rules of international jurisdiction to the states?

8. Field cites the Fourteenth Amendment as a basis for invalidating a state judgment. This citation apparently refers to the Due Process Clause of that Amendment, which provides: "No State shall * * * deprive any person of life, liberty or property, without due process of law." Why does Field conclude that service in the forum state is part of due process?

9. The Fourteenth Amendment was not ratified until 1868, several years after judgment in *Mitchell v. Neff* was entered and executed. Is the discussion of the Fourteenth Amendment dicta, or is Field suggesting that the clause should be applied retroactively? Either way, the Fourteenth Amendment has become the basis for challenges to state court jurisdiction. You should note that the standards under the Fourteenth Amendment and the Full Faith and Credit Clause are the same. Thus, if a state enters a judgment without jurisdiction, it violates due process and the judgment is not entitled to full faith and credit.

10. In early judicial proceedings, the court's authority, both civil and criminal, was thought to depend on the consent of the litigants. In criminal cases in Medieval England, the court developed an effective though brutal method of persuading defendants to "consent" — the piling of stones on the accused until he either consented or died. In civil cases, the defendant was summoned to appear, and if he refused, the court could levy fines that were enforceable against any of the defendant's property that could be found. Later, the English courts began to base its personal jurisdiction on the physical arrest of the defendant using a writ of *capias ad respondendum*. The defendant would be released only after posting sufficient bond to cover any adverse judgment. This form of civil arrest was not required in

all civil cases and was never widely practiced in the United States. See Albert Ehrenzweig, *The Transient Rule of Personal Jurisdiction: The "Power" Myth and Forum Conveniens*, 65 YALE L.J. 289, 296-98 (1956). Nonetheless, courts and commentators frequently point to this procedure as proof that "[h]istorically the jurisdiction of courts to render judgment in personam is grounded on their de facto power over the defendant's person." *International Shoe Co. v. Washington*. The classic statement of this view of jurisdiction is that of Justice Holmes:

> The foundation of jurisdiction is physical power, although in civilized times it is not necessary to maintain that power throughout proceedings properly begun * * *. We repeat also that the ground for giving subsequent effect to a judgment is that the court rendering it had acquired power to carry it out * * *.

McDonald v. Mabee, 243 U.S. 90, 91-92 (1917).

If the whole purpose of personal jurisdiction is to ensure that the rendering forum will have the physical power over the defendant or his property to enforce any judgment rendered, should that doctrine be applied to states, since states are bound by the Full Faith and Credit Clause? Put differently, isn't the whole purpose of the Full Faith and Credit Clause to ensure that judgments that are *not* physically enforceable in the rendering states are enforceable elsewhere?

2. Interim Developments

Field's approach to jurisdiction had the virtue of being easy to apply. Societal changes, however, including changes in the role of corporations, brought this approach under increasing pressure. In the 18th and early 19th centuries, the prevailing view was that corporations could be sued in personam only in the state of incorporation. A corporation was thought to "exist" only within the boundaries of the state that created it. This view of corporate existence arose from the economic reality at that time. Most corporate activities were confined to local activities such as operating bridges, toll roads, and intrastate railroads.

Industrialization brought with it significant multistate corporate activities and the need for states to be able to assert jurisdiction over out-of-state corporations conducting in-state activities. *Pennoyer* itself suggested one approach. Field asserts that states can require a corporation to appoint an agent for service of process as a condition for doing business in the state. Service could then be made on the in-state agent. This approach was premised, at least in part, on the understanding that states had the power to exclude foreign corporations and therefore had the power to condition entrance on consent to certain conditions. Under the Privileges and Immunities Clause of Article IV of the Constitution, one state could not exclude the citizens of another state. However, the Court held that corporations were not protected by the Privileges and Immunities Clause. See Paul v. Virginia, 75 U.S. 168, 177 (1869). As the Court explained in a pre-*Pennoyer* case, "A corporation created by Indiana can transact business in Ohio only with the consent, express or implied, of the latter state. This consent may be accompanied by such conditions as Ohio may think fit to impose * * *." Lafayette Ins. Co. v. French, 59 U.S. 404, 407 (1855).

By the early 20th century, the Court began to recognize that although the Privileges and Immunities Clause did not prohibit states from excluding out-of-state corporations, the Commerce Clause prohibited states from excluding corporations engaged solely in interstate commerce. See International Textbook Co. v. Prigg, 217 U.S. 91 (1910). Corporations were quick to exploit this limitation on state power. For example, in International Harvester v. Kentucky, 234 U.S. 579 (1914), the corporation had set up activities in Kentucky very carefully so that it would be in interstate commerce. The company contended that since Kentucky could not exclude it from the state, Kentucky also could not demand consent as a condition for entering the state. The Supreme Court responded by shifting its focus away from consent and upholding jurisdiction on the ground that regardless of consent, International Harvester was "present" in Kentucky. In a series of cases, the Supreme Court elaborated on what level of activity was necessary to make an out-of-state corporation "present." See, e.g., People's Tobacco Co. v. American Tobacco Co., 246 U.S. 79, 87 (1918); International Harvester Co. v. Kentucky, 234 U.S. 579 (1914); Green v. Chicago, B. & Q. Ry., 205 U.S. 530, 533-34 (1907).

The increased mobility of individuals put similar pressure on the jurisdictional doctrine. With increased travel, people were not always easy to locate for purposes of service of process. Moreover, the new mobility increased the ability of individuals to travel to distant locations and cause injuries which left victims who then had to travel to the defendant's state for any recourse.

One solution was to expand quasi-in-rem to include attachment of an intangible "res" such as a debt. As a result, a defendant was subject to quasi-in-rem type 2 jurisdiction wherever his debtors were found. See Harris v. Balk, 198 U.S. 215 (1905). This is discussed infra in Section B(6).

Another solution was to hold that an individual is subject to suit in his domicile, regardless of whether he is physically served there. The Supreme Court upheld this approach in Milliken v. Meyer, 311 U.S. 457, 462-64 (1940), explaining:

> Domicile in the state is alone sufficient to bring an absent defendant within the reach of the state's jurisdiction. * * * [As] in the case of the authority of the United States over its absent citizens, the authority of a state over one of its citizens is not terminated by the mere fact of his absence from the state. The state which accords him privileges and affords protection to him and his property by

B. Constitutional Limits on Personal Jurisdiction

virtue of his domicile may also exact reciprocal duties. * * * One such incident of domicile is amenability to suit within the state * * * where the state has provided and employed a reasonable method for apprising such an absent party of the proceedings against him.

This, however, was not a complete solution. States began to enact consent statutes for individuals that were similar to those used against corporations. The following case considers such a statute.

Hess v. Pawloski
274 U.S. 352, 47 S.Ct. 632, 71 L. Ed. 1091 (1927)

Justice Butler delivered the opinion of the Court.

This action was brought by defendant in error to recover damages for personal injuries. The declaration alleged that plaintiff in error negligently and wantonly drove a motor vehicle on a public highway in Massachusetts and that by reason thereof the vehicle struck and injured defendant in error. Plaintiff in error is a resident of Pennsylvania. No personal service was made on him and no property belonging to him was attached. The service of process was made in compliance with General Laws of Massachusetts, [statutory law] the material parts of which follow:

> "The acceptance by a nonresident of the rights and privileges conferred by section three or four, as evidenced by his operating a motor vehicle thereunder, or the operation by a nonresident of a motor vehicle on a public way in the commonwealth other than under said sections, shall be deemed equivalent to an appointment by such nonresident of the registrar or his successor in office, to be his true and lawful attorney upon whom may be served all lawful processes in any action or proceeding against him, growing out of any accident or collision in which said nonresident may be involved while operating a motor vehicle on such a way, and said acceptance or operation shall be a signification of his agreement that any such process against him which is so served shall be of the same legal force and validity as if served on him personally. * * *"

Plaintiff in error appeared specially for the purpose of contesting jurisdiction and filed an answer in abatement and moved to dismiss on the ground that the service of process, if sustained, would deprive him of his property without due process of law in violation of the Fourteenth Amendment. The court overruled the answer in abatement and denied the motion. * * * The jury returned a verdict for defendant in error. The exceptions were overruled by the Supreme Judicial Court. Thereupon the Superior Court entered judgment. * * *

The question is whether the Massachusetts enactment contravenes the due process clause of the Fourteenth Amendment.

The process of a court of one State cannot run into another and summon a party there domiciled to respond to proceedings against him. Notice sent outside the State to a nonresident is unavailing to give jurisdiction in an action against him personally for money recovery. *Pennoyer v.*

CHAPTER 2 PERSONAL JURISDICTION

Neff. There must be actual service within the State of notice upon him or upon some one authorized to accept service for him. A personal judgment rendered against a nonresident who has neither been served with process nor appeared in the suit is without validity. The mere transaction of business in a State by nonresident natural persons does not imply consent to be bound by the process of its courts. The power of a State to exclude foreign corporations, although not absolute but qualified, is the ground on which such an implication is supported as to them. But a State may not withhold from nonresident individuals the right of doing business therein. The privileges and immunities clause of the Constitution, § 2, Art. IV, safeguards to the citizens of one State the right "to pass through, or to reside in any other state for purposes of trade, agriculture, professional pursuits, or otherwise." And it prohibits state legislation discriminating against citizens of other States.

Motor vehicles are dangerous machines; and, even when skillfully and carefully operated, their use is attended by serious dangers to persons and property. In the public interest the State may make and enforce regulations reasonably calculated to promote care on the part of all, residents and nonresidents alike, who use its highways. The measure in question operates to require a nonresident to answer for his conduct in the State where arise causes of action alleged against him, as well as to provide for a claimant a convenient method by which he may sue to enforce his rights. Under the statute the implied consent is limited to proceedings growing out of accidents or collisions on a highway in which the nonresident may be involved. It is required that he shall actually receive a receipt for notice of the service and a copy of the process. And it contemplates such continuances as may be found necessary to give reasonable time and opportunity for defense. It makes no hostile discrimination against nonresidents but tends to put them on the same footing as residents. Literal and precise equality in respect of this matter is not attainable; it is not required. The State's power to regulate the use of its highways extends to their use by nonresidents as well as by residents. And, in advance of the operation of a motor vehicle on its highway by a nonresident, the State may require him to appoint one of its officials as his agent on whom process may be served in proceedings growing out of such use. Kane v. New Jersey, 242 U.S. 160, 167 [1916]. That case recognizes power of the State to exclude a nonresident until the formal appointment is made. And, having the power so to exclude, the State may declare that the use of the highway by the nonresident is the equivalent of the appointment of the registrar as agent on whom process may be served. The difference between the formal and implied appointment is not substantial so far as concerns the application of the due process clause of the Fourteenth Amendment.

Judgment affirmed.

NOTES AND QUESTIONS

1. The facts state that the defendant "appeared specially." A special appearance is a procedure that allows the defendant to come forward in a case and contest jurisdiction without thereby consenting to jurisdiction. All states permit defendants to contest personal jurisdiction without waiving the defense. Similarly, under the Federal Rules of Civil Procedure, a defendant may raise a jurisdictional objection without thereby consenting to jurisdiction. In Chapter 6 we will explore in greater detail the procedures for challenging jurisdiction.

B. Constitutional Limits on Personal Jurisdiction

2. Is the theory of the Massachusetts statute that by driving into the state, a driver "consented" to the appointment of the Secretary of State as her agent for service of process? Suppose that before heading to Massachusetts, Mr. Hess had sent a letter to the Secretary of State indicating in the strongest possible terms that he did *not* consent to the Secretary or anyone else being his agent. In such a case, could Hess still be sued in Massachusetts without personal service on him in state?

3. In a later case, a plaintiff argued that the defendant consented to venue in the state by driving into it. (Venue is a statutory limitation on where suits can be filed within a state. It will be addressed in detail in Chapter 5.) In rejecting this argument, Justice Frankfurter wrote:

> It is true that in order to ease the process by which new decisions are fitted into pre-existing modes of analysis there has been some fictive talk to the effect that the reason why a nonresident can be subjected to a state's jurisdiction is that the nonresident has "impliedly" consented to be sued there. In point of fact, however, jurisdiction in these cases does not rest on consent at all. The defendant may protest to high heaven his unwillingness to be sued and it avails him not. The liability rests on the inroad which the automobile has made on the decision of *Pennoyer v. Neff*, as it has on so many aspects of our social scene. The potentialities of damage by a motorist, in a population as mobile as ours, are such that those whom he injures must have opportunities of redress against him provided only that he is afforded an opportunity to defend himself. We have held that this is a fair rule of law as between a resident injured party (for whose protection these statutes are primarily intended) and a nonresident motorist, and that the requirements of due process are therefore met. *Hess v. Pawloski*. But to conclude from this holding that the motorist, who never consented to anything and whose consent is altogether immaterial, has actually agreed to be sued and has thus waived his federal venue rights is surely to move in the world of Alice in Wonderland.

Olberding v. Illinois Central R. Co., 346 U.S. 338, 340-41 (1953).

4. Although the Privileges and Immunities Clause clearly precludes a state from keeping out altogether citizens of other states, do *Hess* and *Kane* (discussed in *Hess*) allow them to exclude people who are in cars? What other state interest might justify implied consent theory? See Henry Doherty & Co. v. Goodman, 294 U.S. 623 (1935) (upholding jurisdiction over company whose agents were selling securities in forum; Court notes that selling of securities is highly regulated).

5. For a discussion of the impact of societal changes on personal jurisdiction doctrine, see Joseph Kalo, *Jurisdiction as an Evolutionary Process: The Development of Quasi in Rem and In Personam Principles*, 1978 DUKE L.J. 1147.

3. The Modern Era

In dealing with jurisdiction over corporations, the Court began moving away from the *Pennoyer*-based terms of "presence" and "consent" and focusing instead on whether the corporation was "doing business" in the state. Professor Kurland has explained:

> The law reports became cluttered with decisions as to what constituted "doing business." * * * The myriad of cases dealing with the question of "doing business" soon substituted that shibboleth for any theory. Without looking back of the words, the courts held that jurisdiction existed if the corporate defendant was "doing business" within the jurisdiction but no jurisdiction existed if the corporate defendant was not "doing business."

Philip Kurland, *The Supreme Court, the Due Process Clause and the In Personam Jurisdiction of State Courts — From* Pennoyer *to* Denckla: *A Review*, 25 U. CHI. L. REV. 569, 584-585 (1958). As you will see in the following case, the language of "doing business" ultimately gave way to another verbal formulation.

International Shoe Co. v. Washington
326 U.S. 310, 66 S.Ct. 154, 90 L. Ed. 95 (1945)

CHIEF JUSTICE STONE delivered the opinion of the Court.

The questions for decision are (1) whether, within the limitations of the due process clause of the Fourteenth Amendment, appellant, a Delaware corporation, has by its activities in the State of Washington rendered itself amenable to proceedings in the courts of that state to recover unpaid contributions to the state unemployment compensation fund exacted by state statutes, and (2) whether the state can exact those contributions consistently with the due process clause of the Fourteenth Amendment.

The statutes in question set up a comprehensive scheme of unemployment compensation, the costs of which are defrayed by contributions required to be made by employers to a state unemployment compensation fund. The contributions are a specified percentage of the wages payable annually by each employer for his employees' services in the state. The assessment and collection of the contributions and the fund are administered by appellees. Section 14(c) of the Act authorizes appellee Commissioner to issue an order and notice of assessment of delinquent contributions upon prescribed personal service of the notice upon the employer if found within the state, or, if not so found, by mailing the notice to the employer by registered mail at his last known address. * * *

In this case notice of assessment for the years in question was personally served upon a sales solicitor employed by appellant in the State of Washington, and a copy of the notice was mailed by registered mail to appellant at its address in St. Louis, Missouri. Appellant appeared specially before the office of unemployment and moved to set aside the order and notice of assessment on the ground that the service upon appellant's salesman was not proper service upon appellant; that appellant was not a corporation of the State of Washington and was not doing business within the state; that it had no agent within the state upon whom service could be made; and that appellant is not an employer and does not furnish employment within the meaning of the statute.

The motion was heard on evidence and a stipulation of facts by the appeal tribunal which denied the motion and ruled that appellee Commissioner was entitled to recover the unpaid contributions. That action was affirmed by the Commissioner; both the Superior Court and the Supreme Court affirmed. Appellant in each of these courts assailed the statute as applied, as a violation of the due process clause of the Fourteenth Amendment, and as imposing a constitutionally prohibited burden on interstate commerce. * * *

The facts as found by the appeal tribunal and accepted by the state Superior Court and Supreme Court, are not in dispute. Appellant is a Delaware corporation, having its principal place of business in St. Louis, Missouri, and is engaged in the manufacture and sale of shoes and other footwear. It maintains places of business in several states, other than Washington, at which its manufacturing is carried on and from which its merchandise is distributed interstate through several sales units or branches located outside the State of Washington.

Appellant has no office in Washington and makes no contracts either for sale or purchase of merchandise there. It maintains no stock of merchandise in that state and makes there no deliveries of goods in intrastate commerce. During the years from 1937 to 1940, now in question, appellant employed eleven to thirteen salesmen under direct supervision and control of sales managers located in St. Louis. These salesmen resided in Washington; their principal activities were confined to that state; and they were compensated by commissions based upon the amount of their sales. The commissions for each year totaled more than $31,000. Appellant supplies its salesmen with a line of samples, each consisting of one shoe of a pair, which they display to prospective purchasers. On occasion they rent permanent sample rooms, for exhibiting samples, in business buildings, or rent rooms in hotels or business buildings temporarily for that purpose. The cost of such rentals is reimbursed by appellant.

The authority of the salesmen is limited to exhibiting their samples and soliciting orders from prospective buyers, at prices and on terms fixed by appellant. The salesmen transmit the orders to appellant's office in St. Louis for acceptance or rejection, and when accepted the merchandise for filling the orders is shipped f. o. b. from points outside Washington to the purchasers within the state. All the merchandise shipped into Washington is invoiced at the place of shipment from which collections are made. No salesman has authority to enter into contracts or to make collections.

The Supreme Court of Washington was of opinion that the regular and systematic solicitation of orders in the state by appellant's salesmen, resulting in a continuous flow of appellant's product into the state, was sufficient to constitute doing business in the state so as to make appellant amenable to suit in its courts. But it was also of opinion that there were sufficient additional activities shown to bring the case within the rule frequently stated, that solicitation within a state by the agents of a foreign corporation plus some additional activities there are sufficient to render the corporation amenable to suit brought in the courts of the state to enforce an obligation arising out of its activities there. The court found such additional activities in the salesmen's display of samples sometimes in permanent display rooms, and the salesmen's residence within the state, continued over a period of years, all resulting in a substantial volume of merchandise regularly shipped by appellant to purchasers within the state. The court also held that the statute as applied did not invade the constitutional power of Congress to regulate interstate commerce and did not impose a prohibited burden on such commerce.

CHAPTER 2 PERSONAL JURISDICTION

Appellant's argument, renewed here, that the statute imposes an unconstitutional burden on interstate commerce need not detain us. [The Court rejects this argument, noting that Congress has by statute authorized states to establish such unemployment funds.] * * *

Appellant also insists that its activities within the state were not sufficient to manifest its "presence" there and that in its absence the state courts were without jurisdiction, that consequently it was a denial of due process for the state to subject appellant to suit. It refers to those cases in which it was said that the mere solicitation of orders for the purchase of goods within a state, to be accepted without the state and filled by shipment of the purchased goods interstate, does not render the corporation seller amenable to suit within the state. And appellant further argues that since it was not present within the state, it is a denial of due process to subject it to taxation or other money exaction. It thus denies the power of the state to lay the tax or to subject appellant to a suit for its collection.

Historically the jurisdiction of courts to render judgment in personam is grounded on their de facto power over the defendant's person. Hence his presence within the territorial jurisdiction of a court was prerequisite to its rendition of a judgment personally binding him. *Pennoyer v. Neff.* But now that the *capias ad respondendum* has given way to personal service of summons or other form of notice, due process requires only that in order to subject a defendant to a judgment in personam, if he be not present within the territory of the forum, he have certain minimum contacts with it such that the maintenance of the suit does not offend "traditional notions of fair play and substantial justice." Milliken v. Meyer, 311 U.S. 457, 463 (1940).

Since the corporate personality is a fiction, although a fiction intended to be acted upon as though it were a fact, it is clear that unlike an individual its "presence" without, as well as within, the state of its origin can be manifested only by activities carried on in its behalf by those who are authorized to act for it. To say that the corporation is so far "present" there as to satisfy due process requirements, for purposes of taxation or the maintenance of suits against it in the courts of the state, is to beg the question to be decided. For the terms "present" or "presence" are used merely to symbolize those activities of the corporation's agent within the state which courts will deem to be sufficient to satisfy the demands of due process. Those demands may be met by such contacts of the corporation with the state of the forum as make it reasonable, in the context of our federal system of government, to require the corporation to defend the particular suit which is brought there. An "estimate of the inconveniences" which would result to the corporation from a trial away from its "home" or principal place of business is relevant in this connection.

"Presence" in the state in this sense has never been doubted when the activities of the corporation there have not only been continuous and systematic, but also give rise to the liabilities sued on, even though no consent to be sued or authorization to an agent to accept service of process has been given. Conversely it has been generally recognized that the casual presence of the corporate agent or even his conduct of single or isolated items of activities in a state in the corporation's behalf are not enough to subject it to suit on causes of action unconnected with the activities there. To require the corporation in such circumstances to defend the suit away from its home or other jurisdiction where it carries on more substantial activities has been thought to lay too great and unreasonable a burden on the corporation to comport with due process.

While it has been held, in cases on which appellant relies, that continuous activity of some sorts within a state is not enough to support the demand that the corporation be amenable to suits unrelated to that activity, there have been instances in which the continuous corporate operations

B. Constitutional Limits on Personal Jurisdiction

within a state were thought so substantial and of such a nature as to justify suit against it on causes of action arising from dealings entirely distinct from those activities.

Finally, although the commission of some single or occasional acts of the corporate agent in a state sufficient to impose an obligation or liability on the corporation has not been thought to confer upon the state authority to enforce it, Rosenberg Bros. & Co. v. Curtis Brown Co., 260 U.S. 516 (1923), other such acts, because of their nature and quality and the circumstances of their commission, may be deemed sufficient to render the corporation liable to suit. Cf. *Hess v. Pawloski*. True, some of the decisions holding the corporation amenable to suit have been supported by resort to the legal fiction that it has given its consent to service and suit, consent being implied from its presence in the state through the acts of its authorized agents. But more realistically it may be said that those authorized acts were of such a nature as to justify the fiction.

It is evident that the criteria by which we mark the boundary line between those activities which justify the subjection of a corporation to suit, and those which do not, cannot be simply mechanical or quantitative. The test is not merely, as has sometimes been suggested, whether the activity, which the corporation has seen fit to procure through its agents in another state, is a little more or a little less. Whether due process is satisfied must depend rather upon the quality and nature of the activity in relation to the fair and orderly administration of the laws which it was the purpose of the due process clause to insure. That clause does not contemplate that a state may make binding a judgment in personam against an individual or corporate defendant with which the state has no contacts, ties, or relations. Cf. *Pennoyer v. Neff*.

But to the extent that a corporation exercises the privilege of conducting activities within a state, it enjoys the benefits and protection of the laws of that state. The exercise of that privilege may give rise to obligations, and, so far as those obligations arise out of or are connected with the activities within the state, a procedure which requires the corporation to respond to a suit brought to enforce them can, in most instances, hardly be said to be undue.

Applying these standards, the activities carried on in behalf of appellant in the State of Washington were neither irregular nor casual. They were systematic and continuous throughout the years in question. They resulted in a large volume of interstate business, in the course of which appellant received the benefits and protection of the laws of the state, including the right to resort to the courts for the enforcement of its rights. The obligation which is here sued upon arose out of those very activities. It is evident that these operations establish sufficient contacts or ties with the state of the forum to make it reasonable and just, according to our traditional conception of fair play and substantial justice, to permit the state to enforce the obligations which appellant has incurred there. Hence we cannot say that the maintenance of the present suit in the State of Washington involves an unreasonable or undue procedure.

We are likewise unable to conclude that the service of the process within the state upon an agent whose activities establish appellant's "presence" there was not sufficient notice of the suit, or that the suit was so unrelated to those activities as to make the agent an inappropriate vehicle for communicating the notice. It is enough that appellant has established such contacts with the state that the particular form of substituted service adopted there gives reasonable assurance that the notice will be actual. Nor can we say that the mailing of the notice of suit to appellant by registered mail at its home office was not reasonably calculated to apprise appellant of the suit.

* * *

Affirmed.

JUSTICE BLACK delivered the following opinion.

* * *

Certainly appellant cannot in the light of our past decisions meritoriously claim that notice by registered mail and by personal service on its sales solicitors in Washington did not meet the requirements of procedural due process. And the due process clause is not brought in issue any more by appellant's further conceptualistic contention that Washington could not levy a tax or bring suit against the corporation because it did not honor that State with its mystical "presence." For it is unthinkable that the vague due process clause was ever intended to prohibit a State from regulating or taxing a business carried on within its boundaries simply because this is done by agents of a corporation organized and having its headquarters elsewhere. To read this into the due process clause would in fact result in depriving a State's citizens of due process by taking from the State the power to protect them in their business dealings within its boundaries with representatives of a foreign corporation. Nothing could be more irrational or more designed to defeat the function of our federative system of government. Certainly a State, at the very least, has power to tax and sue those dealing with its citizens within its boundaries, as we have held before. Were the Court to follow this principle, it would provide a workable standard for cases where, as here, no other questions are involved. The Court has not chosen to do so, but instead has engaged in an unnecessary discussion in the course of which it has announced vague Constitutional criteria applied for the first time to the issue before us. It has thus introduced uncertain elements confusing the simple pattern and tending to curtail the exercise of State powers to an extent not justified by the Constitution.

* * *

It is true that this Court did use the terms "fair play" and "substantial justice" in explaining the philosophy underlying the holding that it could not be "due process of law" to render a personal judgment against a defendant without notice and an opportunity to be heard. * * * These cases, while giving additional reasons why notice under particular circumstances is inadequate, did not mean thereby that all legislative enactments which this Court might deem to be contrary to natural justice ought to be held invalid under the due process clause. None of the cases purport to support or could support a holding that a State can tax and sue corporations only if its action comports with this Court's notions of "natural justice." I should have thought the Tenth Amendment settled that.

I believe that the Federal Constitution leaves to each State, without any "ifs" or "buts," a power to tax and to open the doors of its courts for its citizens to sue corporations whose agents do business in those States. Believing that the Constitution gave the States that power, I think it a judicial deprivation to condition its exercise upon this Court's notion of "fair play," however appealing that term may be. Nor can I stretch the meaning of due process so far as to authorize this Court to deprive a State of the right to afford judicial protection to its citizens on the ground that it would be more "convenient" for the corporation to be sued somewhere else.

There is a strong emotional appeal in the words "fair play," "justice," and "reasonableness." But they were not chosen by those who wrote the original Constitution or the Fourteenth Amendment as a measuring rod for this Court to use in invalidating State or Federal laws passed by elected legislative representatives. No one, not even those who most feared a democratic govern-

B. Constitutional Limits on Personal Jurisdiction

ment, ever formally proposed that courts should be given power to invalidate legislation under any such elastic standards. * * *

True, the State's power is here upheld. But the rule announced means that tomorrow's judgment may strike down a State or Federal enactment on the ground that it does not conform to this Court's idea of natural justice. * * *

* * *

NOTES AND QUESTIONS

1. After *International Shoe*, it is no longer necessary to fit the defendant's activities into a model of consent or presence. The new test focuses on whether the defendant's activities constitute "minimum contacts such that jurisdiction is consistent with traditional notions of fair play and substantial justice." Justice Stone says of his new formulation that it is not new at all but simply reiterates what courts were doing all along under the old models of consent and presence. But hasn't the shift in paradigm from presence to fairness fundamentally altered jurisdiction doctrine?

2. Note that the Court requires that the defendant have minimum contacts with the forum "if he be not present." Does that mean that defendant's presence in the forum continues to be an independent basis for in personam jurisdiction, even in the absence of other contacts?

3. *International Shoe* involved a corporate defendant. Later cases made clear that the *International Shoe* test applies as well to individual defendants. See Kulko v. Superior Court, 436 U.S. 84, 92 (1978).

4. The Court differentiates between cases in which the cause of action is related to the contacts and those in which the case is unrelated. Later cases develop this distinction into two categories. See *Helicopteros Nacionales de Columbia, S. A. v. Hall*, infra at 85. Suits in which the contacts are related to the claim are referred to as *specific jurisdiction* cases. Those in which the contacts are unrelated are called *general jurisdiction*. Which type of case is *International Shoe*? The Court suggests that if the contacts are unrelated to the claim, then there will be jurisdiction only if the defendant's contacts are "continuous and systematic." At what point do a defendant's contacts move from being "casual" to "continuous and systematic?"

5. Consider the following hypotheticals. How should they come out under the *International Shoe* test?

    (a) An International Shoe delivery truck carrying shoes from Missouri to Washington drives through Colorado, where it hits a Colorado pedestrian. Can Pe-

CHAPTER 2 PERSONAL JURISDICTION

destrian sue International Shoe in Colorado? Would it matter if the truck driver had not planned to go through Colorado but got lost and ended up there?

(b) Could Pedestrian sue International Shoe in Washington?

(c) Could Pedestrian sue International Shoe in Missouri, where the defendant's headquarters were located?

(d) International Shoe's headquarters was located in St. Louis, Missouri, very close to Illinois. Suppose Pedestrian has a vacation home in Illinois and hence thinks it would be very convenient to litigate in Illinois. Can Pedestrian sue International Shoe in Illinois?

(e) Suppose International Shoe operates retail shoe outlets in Washington. A customer buys a pair of shoes there, but the shoes are defective. Can the customer sue International Shoe in Washington?

(f) International Shoe operates retail outlets in Washington but not in Oregon. An Oregon citizen visits the Washington store and buys a pair of defective shoes which she takes back to Oregon. Can she sue International Shoe in Oregon?

(g) Suppose that the Oregonian had seen the shoes at the Washington store but had returned home. She then contacted International Shoe directly and ordered a pair of shoes. The shoes were sent by International Shoe to the customer in Oregon. Could she sue International Shoe in Oregon?

(h) Suppose that instead of having the shoes shipped to Oregon, the customer picked them up in Missouri while she was vacationing in St. Louis. At the time she picks up the shoes, the customer makes it very clear she is going to take the shoes back to Oregon. Can she sue in Oregon?

(i) Suppose International Shoe makes shoe components such as heels and soles. International Shoe sells its heels to a Pennsylvania company. The Pennsylvania company incorporates the heels into its shoes which it then sells in Oregon. Can a person who buys the shoes in Oregon and is injured by a defective heel sue International Shoe in Oregon?

6. Reconsider *Pennoyer v. Neff.* Under the test of *International Shoe*, would there have been personal jurisdiction over Neff in the underlying suit of *Mitchell v. Neff*?

NOTE ON *MCGEE, HANSON* AND *GRAY*

During the 1950's, the Court decided a handful of personal jurisdiction cases. Two cases of note were McGee v. International Life Ins. Co., 355 U.S. 220 (1957), and Hanson v. Denckla, 357 U.S. 235 (1958).

B. Constitutional Limits on Personal Jurisdiction

In *McGee*, a California citizen purchased a life insurance policy from an Arizona insurance company. A Texas insurance company later took over the Arizona company. When it took over, the Texas company mailed a reinsurance certificate to the California insured. The insured in turn sent his premiums from California. The insured died in California, and a dispute arose concerning the policy. The beneficiaries sued the Texas insurance company in California state court. Although there was no evidence that the defendant had ever solicited or done any insurance business in California apart from this particular policy, the Supreme Court found that there was jurisdiction. The Court explained:

> Turning to this case we think it apparent that the Due Process Clause did not preclude the California court from entering a judgment binding on respondent. It is sufficient for purposes of due process that the suit was based on a contract which had substantial connection with that State. The contract was delivered in California, the premiums were mailed from there and the insured was a resident of that State when he died. It cannot be denied that California has a manifest interest in providing effective means of redress for its residents when their insurers refuse to pay claims. These residents would be at a severe disadvantage if they were forced to follow the insurance company to a distant State in order to hold it legally accountable. When the claims were small or moderate individual claimants frequently could not afford the cost of bringing an action in a foreign forum — thus in effect making the company judgment proof. Often the crucial witnesses — as here on the company's defense of suicide — will be found in the insured's locality. Of course there may be inconvenience to the insurer if it is held amenable to suit in California where it had this contract but certainly nothing which amounts to a denial of due process. There is no contention that respondent did not have adequate notice of the suit or sufficient time to prepare its defenses and appear.

355 U.S. at 223-24.

A year later, *Hanson* undercut the seemingly expansive approach of *McGee*. *Hanson* arose out of a family inheritance dispute. At issue was the validity of a trust. Dora Donner created the trust while she was domiciled in Pennsylvania. The trust instrument was executed in Delaware, naming a Delaware bank as trustee. Mrs. Donner reserved the trust income to herself and retained the power to designate who would receive the principle. Mrs. Donner later moved to Florida and designated the recipients of the trust. Following her death, a dispute developed between those family members who inherited money through Mrs. Donner's will and the trust beneficiaries.

Mrs. Donner's will was probated in Florida, and under Florida law, the Delaware bank was a necessary party to that litigation. The issue then arose as to whether Florida had personal jurisdiction over the Delaware bank. The Supreme Court held that Florida did not. In reaching this conclusion, the Court noted that when the trust was created, there was no connection with Florida. In addition, the Court found that Mrs. Donner's later move to Florida was not sufficient to create jurisdiction.

> The unilateral activity of those who claim some relationship with a nonresident defendant cannot satisfy the requirement of contact with the forum State. The application of that rule will vary with the quality and nature of the defendant's activity, but it is essential in each case that there be some act by which the defendant purposefully avails itself of the privilege of conducting activities within the forum State, thus invoking the benefits and protections of its laws.

357 U.S. at 253. The Court distinguished *McGee* explaining: "From Florida Mrs. Donner carried on several bits of trust administration that may be compared to the mailing of premiums in *McGee*. But the record discloses no instance in which the *trustee* performed any acts in Florida that bear the same relationship to the agreement as the solicitation in *McGee*." Id. at 252.

For 18 years following *Hanson*, the Supreme Court paid little attention to personal jurisdiction. During this period, state courts interpreted *McGee* expansively and largely ignored *Hanson*. A typical case is Gray v. American Radiator & Standard Sanitary Corp., 22 Ill.2d 432, 176 N.E.2d 761 (Ill. 1961). In *Gray*, the plaintiff sued the Titan Valve Co. alleging that it had negligently constructed a safety valve, and as a result of its negligence, a water heater had exploded. Plaintiff sued in Illinois, and Titan, an Ohio corporation, challenged personal jurisdiction. Titan had manufactured the valve in Ohio, then sold it to a Pennsylvania company which had incorporated it into the water heater. The water heater "in the course of commerce" was sold to the Illinois consumer. There was no evidence in the record that Titan had done any other business in Illinois either directly or indirectly. The Supreme Court of Illinois upheld jurisdiction stating:

> While the record does not disclose the volume of Titan's business or the territory in which appliances incorporating its valves are marketed, it is a reasonable inference that its commercial transactions, like those of other manufacturers, result in substantial use and consumption in this State. To the extent that its business may be directly affected by transactions occurring here it enjoys benefits from the laws of this State, and it has undoubtedly benefited, to a degree, from the protection which our law has given to the marketing of hot water heaters containing its valves. Where the alleged liability arises, as in this case, from the manufacture of products presumably sold in contemplation of use here, it should not matter that the purchase was made from an independent middleman or that someone other than the defendant shipped the product into this State.

176 N.E.2d at 766. Notice the court's willingness to presume that the defendant had substantial contacts with Illinois and that the products were sold "in contemplation of use" in Illinois.

In 1976, the Court began hearing personal jurisdiction cases again. In the fourteen years from 1976 to 1990, the Supreme Court decided twelve personal jurisdiction cases. The Court's major decisions during this period are considered below.

B. Constitutional Limits on Personal Jurisdiction

World-Wide Volkswagen v. Woodson
444 U.S. 286, 100 S.Ct. 559, 62 L. Ed. 2d 490 (1980)

JUSTICE WHITE delivered the opinion of the Court.

The issue before us is whether, consistently with the Due Process Clause of the Fourteenth Amendment, an Oklahoma court may exercise in personam jurisdiction over a nonresident automobile retailer and its wholesale distributor in a products-liability action, when the defendants' only connection with Oklahoma is the fact that an automobile sold in New York to New York residents became involved in an accident in Oklahoma.

I

Respondents Harry and Kay Robinson purchased a new Audi automobile from petitioner Seaway Volkswagen, Inc. (Seaway), in Massena, N. Y., in 1976. The following year the Robinson family, who resided in New York, left that State for a new home in Arizona. As they passed through the State of Oklahoma, another car struck their Audi in the rear, causing a fire which severely burned Kay Robinson and her two children.[1]

The Robinsons subsequently brought a products-liability action in the District Court for Creek County, Okla., claiming that their injuries resulted from defective design and placement of the Audi's gas tank and fuel system. They joined as defendants the automobile's manufacturer, Audi NSU Auto Union Aktiengesellschaft (Audi); its importer, Volkswagen of America, Inc. (Volkswagen); its regional distributor, petitioner *World-Wide Volkswagen Corp.* (World-Wide); and its retail dealer, petitioner Seaway. Seaway and World-Wide entered special appearances,[3] claiming that Oklahoma's exercise of jurisdiction over them would offend the limitations on the State's jurisdiction imposed by the Due Process Clause of the Fourteenth Amendment.

The facts presented to the District Court showed that World-Wide is incorporated and has its business office in New York. It distributes vehicles, parts, and accessories, under contract with Volkswagen, to retail dealers in New York, New Jersey, and Connecticut. Seaway, one of these retail dealers, is incorporated and has its place of business in New York. Insofar as the record reveals, Seaway and World-Wide are fully independent corporations whose relations with each other and with Volkswagen and Audi are contractual only. Respondents adduced no evidence that either World-Wide or Seaway does any business in Oklahoma, ships or sells any products to or in that State, has an agent to receive process there, or purchases advertisements in any media calculated to reach Oklahoma. In fact, as respondents' counsel conceded at oral argument there was no showing that any automobile sold by World-Wide or Seaway has ever entered Oklahoma with the single exception of the vehicle involved in the present case.

Despite the apparent paucity of contacts between petitioners and Oklahoma, the District Court rejected their constitutional claim and reaffirmed that ruling in denying petitioners' motion for reconsideration. Petitioners then sought a writ of prohibition in the Supreme Court of Oklahoma to

---

[1] The driver of the other automobile does not figure in the present litigation.

[3] Volkswagen also entered a special appearance in the District Court, but unlike World-Wide and Seaway did not seek review in the Supreme Court of Oklahoma and is not a petitioner here. Both Volkswagen and Audi remain as defendants in the litigation pending before the District Court in Oklahoma.

restrain the District Judge, respondent Charles S. Woodson, from exercising in personam jurisdiction over them. They renewed their contention that, because they had no "minimal contacts" with the State of Oklahoma, the actions of the District Judge were in violation of their rights under the Due Process Clause.

The Supreme Court of Oklahoma denied the writ holding that personal jurisdiction over petitioners was authorized by Oklahoma's "long-arm" statute, OKLA. STAT., Tit. 12, § 1701.03 (a)(4) (1971).[7] Although the court noted that the proper approach was to test jurisdiction against both statutory and constitutional standards, its analysis did not distinguish these questions, probably because § 1701.03 (a)(4) has been interpreted as conferring jurisdiction to the limits permitted by the United States Constitution. The court's rationale was contained in the following paragraph:

> "In the case before us, the product being sold and distributed by the petitioners is by its very design and purpose so mobile that petitioners can foresee its possible use in Oklahoma. This is especially true of the distributor, who has the exclusive right to distribute such automobile in New York, New Jersey and Connecticut. The evidence presented below demonstrated that goods sold and distributed by the petitioners were used in the State of Oklahoma, and under the facts we believe it reasonable to infer, given the retail value of the automobile, that the petitioners derive substantial income from automobiles which from time to time are used in the State of Oklahoma. This being the case, we hold that under the facts presented, the trial court was justified in concluding that the petitioners derive substantial revenue from goods used or consumed in this State."

We granted certiorari to consider an important constitutional question with respect to state-court jurisdiction and to resolve a conflict between the Supreme Court of Oklahoma and the highest courts of at least four other States. We reverse.

II

The Due Process Clause of the Fourteenth Amendment limits the power of a state court to render a valid personal judgment against a nonresident defendant. Kulko v. California Superior Court, 436 U.S. 84, 91 (1978). A judgment rendered in violation of due process is void in the rendering State and is not entitled to full faith and credit elsewhere. *Pennoyer v. Neff.* Due process requires that the defendant be given adequate notice of the suit, Mullane v. Central Hanover Trust Co., 339 U.S. 306, 313-314 (1950), and be subject to the personal jurisdiction of the court, *International Shoe Co. v. Washington.* In the present case, it is not contended that notice was inadequate; the only question is whether these particular petitioners were subject to the jurisdiction of the Oklahoma courts.

As has long been settled, and as we reaffirm today, a state court may exercise personal jurisdiction over a nonresident defendant only so long as there exist "minimum contacts" between

---

[7] This subsection provides:

"A court may exercise personal jurisdiction over a person, who acts directly or by an agent, as to a cause of action or claim for relief arising from the person's ... causing tortious injury in this state by an act or omission outside this state if he regularly does or solicits business or engages in any other persistent course of conduct, or derives substantial revenue from goods used or consumed or services rendered, in this state...." * * *

B. Constitutional Limits on Personal Jurisdiction

the defendant and the forum State. *International Shoe*. The concept of minimum contacts, in turn, can be seen to perform two related, but distinguishable, functions. It protects the defendant against the burdens of litigating in a distant or inconvenient forum. And it acts to ensure that the States, through their courts, do not reach out beyond the limits imposed on them by their status as coequal sovereigns in a federal system.

The protection against inconvenient litigation is typically described in terms of "reasonableness" or "fairness." We have said that the defendant's contacts with the forum State must be such that maintenance of the suit "does not offend 'traditional notions of fair play and substantial justice.'" *International Shoe*, quoting Milliken v. Meyer, 311 U.S. 457, 463 (1940). The relationship between the defendant and the forum must be such that it is "reasonable ... to require the corporation to defend the particular suit which is brought there." Implicit in this emphasis on reasonableness is the understanding that the burden on the defendant, while always a primary concern, will in an appropriate case be considered in light of other relevant factors, including the forum State's interest in adjudicating the dispute, see *McGee v. International Life Ins. Co.*; the plaintiff's interest in obtaining convenient and effective relief, see *Kulko v. California Superior Court*, at least when that interest is not adequately protected by the plaintiff's power to choose the forum, cf. Shaffer v. Heitner, 433 U.S. 186, 211, n.37 (1977); the interstate judicial system's interest in obtaining the most efficient resolution of controversies; and the shared interest of the several States in furthering fundamental substantive social policies. See *Kulko v. California Superior Court*.

The limits imposed on state jurisdiction by the Due Process Clause, in its role as a guarantor against inconvenient litigation, have been substantially relaxed over the years. As we noted in *McGee*, this trend is largely attributable to a fundamental transformation in the American economy:

> "Today many commercial transactions touch two or more States and may involve parties separated by the full continent. With this increasing nationalization of commerce has come a great increase in the amount of business conducted by mail across state lines. At the same time modern transportation and communication have made it much less burdensome for a party sued to defend himself in a State where he engages in economic activity."

The historical developments noted in *McGee*, of course, have only accelerated in the generation since that case was decided.

Nevertheless, we have never accepted the proposition that state lines are irrelevant for jurisdictional purposes, nor could we, and remain faithful to the principles of interstate federalism embodied in the Constitution. The economic interdependence of the States was foreseen and desired by the Framers. In the Commerce Clause, they provided that the Nation was to be a common market, a "free trade unit" in which the States are debarred from acting as separable economic entities. But the Framers also intended that the States retain many essential attributes of sovereignty, including, in particular, the sovereign power to try causes in their courts. The sovereignty of each State, in turn, implied a limitation on the sovereignty of all of its sister States — a limitation express or implicit in both the original scheme of the Constitution and the Fourteenth Amendment.

Hence, even while abandoning the shibboleth that "[t]he authority of every tribunal is necessarily restricted by the territorial limits of the State in which it is established," *Pennoyer v. Neff*, we emphasized that the reasonableness of asserting jurisdiction over the defendant must be assessed "in the context of our federal system of government," *International Shoe*, and stressed

CHAPTER 2 PERSONAL JURISDICTION

that the Due Process Clause ensures not only fairness, but also the "orderly administration of the laws." As we noted in *Hanson v. Denckla*:

> "As technological progress has increased the flow of commerce between the States, the need for jurisdiction over nonresidents has undergone a similar increase. At the same time, progress in communications and transportation has made the defense of a suit in a foreign tribunal less burdensome. In response to these changes, the requirements for personal jurisdiction over nonresidents have evolved from the rigid rule of *Pennoyer v. Neff*, to the flexible standard of *International Shoe*. But it is a mistake to assume that this trend heralds the eventual demise of all restrictions on the personal jurisdiction of state courts. Those restrictions are more than a guarantee of immunity from inconvenient or distant litigation. They are a consequence of territorial limitations on the power of the respective States."

Thus, the Due Process Clause "does not contemplate that a state may make binding a judgment in personam against an individual or corporate defendant with which the state has no contacts, ties, or relations." *International Shoe*. Even if the defendant would suffer minimal or no inconvenience from being forced to litigate before the tribunals of another State; even if the forum State has a strong interest in applying its law to the controversy; even if the forum State is the most convenient location for litigation, the Due Process Clause, acting as an instrument of interstate federalism, may sometimes act to divest the State of its power to render a valid judgment. *Hanson v. Denckla*.

III

Applying these principles to the case at hand, we find in the record before us a total absence of those affiliating circumstances that are a necessary predicate to any exercise of state-court jurisdiction. Petitioners carry on no activity whatsoever in Oklahoma. They close no sales and perform no services there. They avail themselves of none of the privileges and benefits of Oklahoma law. They solicit no business there either through salespersons or through advertising reasonably calculated to reach the State. Nor does the record show that they regularly sell cars at wholesale or retail to Oklahoma customers or residents or that they indirectly, through others, serve or seek to serve the Oklahoma market. In short, respondents seek to base jurisdiction on one, isolated occurrence and whatever inferences can be drawn therefrom: the fortuitous circumstance that a single Audi automobile, sold in New York to New York residents, happened to suffer an accident while passing through Oklahoma.

It is argued, however, that because an automobile is mobile by its very design and purpose it was "foreseeable" that the Robinsons' Audi would cause injury in Oklahoma. Yet "foreseeability" alone has never been a sufficient benchmark for personal jurisdiction under the Due Process Clause. In *Hanson v. Denckla*, it was no doubt foreseeable that the settlor of a Delaware trust would subsequently move to Florida and seek to exercise a power of appointment there; yet we held that Florida courts could not constitutionally exercise jurisdiction over a Delaware trustee that had no other contacts with the forum State. In *Kulko v. California Superior Court*, it was surely "foreseeable" that a divorced wife would move to California from New York, the domicile of the marriage, and that

B. Constitutional Limits on Personal Jurisdiction

a minor daughter would live with the mother. Yet we held that California could not exercise jurisdiction in a child-support action over the former husband who had remained in New York.

If foreseeability were the criterion, a local California tire retailer could be forced to defend in Pennsylvania when a blowout occurs there, see Erlanger Mills, Inc. v. Cohoes Fibre Mills, Inc., 239 F. 2d 502, 507 (4th Cir. 1956); a Wisconsin seller of a defective automobile jack could be haled before a distant court for damage caused in New Jersey, Reilly v. Phil Tolkan Pontiac, Inc., 372 F. Supp. 1205 (D.C.N.J. 1974); or a Florida soft-drink concessionaire could be summoned to Alaska to account for injuries happening there, see Uppgren v. Executive Aviation Services, Inc., 304 F. Supp. 165, 170-171 (Minn. 1969). Every seller of chattels would in effect appoint the chattel his agent for service of process. His amenability to suit would travel with the chattel.[11] * * *

This is not to say, of course, that foreseeability is wholly irrelevant. But the foreseeability that is critical to due process analysis is not the mere likelihood that a product will find its way into the forum State. Rather, it is that the defendant's conduct and connection with the forum State are such that he should reasonably anticipate being haled into court there. See *Kulko v. California Superior Court.* The Due Process Clause, by ensuring the "orderly administration of the laws," *International Shoe*, gives a degree of predictability to the legal system that allows potential defendants to structure their primary conduct with some minimum assurance as to where that conduct will and will not render them liable to suit.

When a corporation "purposefully avails itself of the privilege of conducting activities within the forum State," *Hanson v. Denckla*, it has clear notice that it is subject to suit there, and can act to alleviate the risk of burdensome litigation by procuring insurance, passing the expected costs on to customers, or, if the risks are too great, severing its connection with the State. Hence if the sale of a product of a manufacturer or distributor such as Audi or Volkswagen is not simply an isolated occurrence, but arises from the efforts of the manufacturer or distributor to serve, directly or indirectly, the market for its product in other States, it is not unreasonable to subject it to suit in one of those States if its allegedly defective merchandise has there been the source of injury to its owner or to others. The forum State does not exceed its powers under the Due Process Clause if it asserts personal jurisdiction over a corporation that delivers its products into the stream of commerce with the expectation that they will be purchased by consumers in the forum State. Cf.* Gray v. American Radiator & Standard Sanitary Corp., 176 N.E.2d 761 (Ill. 1961).

But there is no such or similar basis for Oklahoma jurisdiction over World-Wide or Seaway in this case. Seaway's sales are made in Massena, N.Y. World-Wide's market, although substantially larger, is limited to dealers in New York, New Jersey, and Connecticut. There is no evidence of

---

[11] Respondents' counsel, at oral argument, sought to limit the reach of the foreseeability standard by suggesting that there is something unique about automobiles. It is true that automobiles are uniquely mobile, that they did play a crucial role in the expansion of personal jurisdiction through the fiction of implied consent, e.g., *Hess v. Pawloski*, and that some of the cases have treated the automobile as a "dangerous instrumentality." But today, under the regime of *International Shoe*, we see no difference for jurisdictional purposes between an automobile and any other chattel. The "dangerous instrumentality" concept apparently was never used to support personal jurisdiction; and to the extent it has relevance today it bears not on jurisdiction but on the possible desirability of imposing substantive principles of tort law such as strict liability.

* [The Bluebook (15 ed. 1991) explains "cf." as follows: "Cited authority supports a proposition different from the main proposition but sufficiently lends analogous support.* * * The citation's relevance will usually be clear to the reader only if it is explained. Parenthetical explanations * * * are therefore strongly recommended." — EDS.]

CHAPTER 2 PERSONAL JURISDICTION

record that any automobiles distributed by World-Wide are sold to retail customers outside this tristate area. It is foreseeable that the purchasers of automobiles sold by World-Wide and Seaway may take them to Oklahoma. But the mere "unilateral activity of those who claim some relationship with a nonresident defendant cannot satisfy the requirement of contact with the forum State." *Hanson v. Denckla.*

In a variant on the previous argument, it is contended that jurisdiction can be supported by the fact that petitioners earn substantial revenue from goods used in Oklahoma. The Oklahoma Supreme Court so found drawing the inference that because one automobile sold by petitioners had been used in Oklahoma, others might have been used there also. While this inference seems less than compelling on the facts of the instant case, we need not question the court's factual findings in order to reject its reasoning.

This argument seems to make the point that the purchase of automobiles in New York, from which the petitioners earn substantial revenue, would not occur *but for* the fact that the automobiles are capable of use in distant States like Oklahoma. Respondents observe that the very purpose of an automobile is to travel, and that travel of automobiles sold by petitioners is facilitated by an extensive chain of Volkswagen service centers throughout the country, including some in Oklahoma.[12] However, financial benefits accruing to the defendant from a collateral relation to the forum State will not support jurisdiction if they do not stem from a constitutionally cognizable contact with that State. See *Kulko v. California Superior Court.* In our view, whatever marginal revenues petitioners may receive by virtue of the fact that their products are capable of use in Oklahoma is far too attenuated a contact to justify that State's exercise of in personam jurisdiction over them.

Because we find that petitioners have no "contacts, ties, or relations" with the State of Oklahoma, *International Shoe*, the judgment of the Supreme Court of Oklahoma is

Reversed.

JUSTICE BRENNAN, dissenting.

* * *

The Court's opinion[] focus[es] tightly on the existence of contacts between the forum and the defendant. In so doing, they accord too little weight to the strength of the forum State's interest in the case and fail to explore whether there would be any actual inconvenience to the defendant. * * *

Surely *International Shoe* contemplated that the significance of the contacts necessary to support jurisdiction would diminish if some other consideration helped establish that jurisdiction would be fair and reasonable. The interests of the State and other parties in proceeding with the case in a particular forum are such considerations. *McGee v. International Life Ins. Co.*, for instance, accorded great importance to a State's "manifest interest in providing effective means of redress" for its citizens.

---

[12] As we have noted, petitioners earn no direct revenues from these service centers.

B. **Constitutional Limits on Personal Jurisdiction**

* * *

In [this case], the interest of the forum State and its connection to the litigation is strong. The automobile accident underlying the litigation occurred in Oklahoma. The plaintiffs were hospitalized in Oklahoma when they brought suit. Essential witnesses and evidence were in Oklahoma. The State has a legitimate interest in enforcing its laws designed to keep its highway system safe, and the trial can proceed at least as efficiently in Oklahoma as anywhere else.

The petitioners are not unconnected with the forum. Although both sell automobiles within limited sales territories, each sold the automobile which in fact was driven to Oklahoma where it was involved in an accident.[8] It may be true, as the Court suggests, that each sincerely intended to limit its commercial impact to the limited territory, and that each intended to accept the benefits and protection of the laws only of those States within the territory. But obviously these were unrealistic hopes that cannot be treated as an automatic constitutional shield.[9]

An automobile simply is not a stationary item or one designed to be used in one place. An automobile is *intended* to be moved around. Someone in the business of selling large numbers of automobiles can hardly plead ignorance of their mobility or pretend that the automobiles stay put after they are sold. It is not merely that a dealer in automobiles foresees that they will move. The dealer actually intends that the purchasers will use the automobiles to travel to distant States where the dealer does not directly "do business." The sale of an automobile does *purposefully* inject the vehicle into the stream of interstate commerce so that it can travel to distant States.

This case is similar to Ohio v. Wyandotte Chemicals Corp., 401 U.S. 493 (1971). There we indicated, in the course of denying leave to file an original-jurisdiction case, that corporations having no direct contact with Ohio could constitutionally be brought to trial in Ohio because they dumped pollutants into streams outside Ohio's limits which ultimately, through the action of the water, reached Lake Erie and affected Ohio. No corporate acts, only their consequences, occurred in Ohio. The stream of commerce is just as natural a force as a stream of water, and it was equally predictable that the cars petitioners released would reach distant States.[10]

The Court accepts that a State may exercise jurisdiction over a distributor which "serves" that State "indirectly" by "deliver[ing] its products into the stream of commerce with the expectation that they will be purchased by consumers in the forum State." It is difficult to see why the Constitution should distinguish between a case involving goods which reach a distant State through a chain of distribution and a case involving goods which reach the same State because a consumer, using

---

[8] On the basis of this fact the state court inferred that the petitioners derived substantial revenue from goods used in Oklahoma. The inference is not without support. Certainly, were use of goods accepted as a relevant contact, a plaintiff would not need to have an exact count of the number of petitioners' cars that are used in Oklahoma.

[9] Moreover, imposing liability in this case would not so undermine certainty as to destroy an automobile dealer's ability to do business. According jurisdiction does not expand liability except in the marginal case where a plaintiff cannot afford to bring an action except in the plaintiff's own State. In addition, these petitioners are represented by insurance companies. They not only could, but did, purchase insurance to protect them should they stand trial and lose the case. The costs of the insurance no doubt are passed on to customers.

[10] One might argue that it was more predictable that the pollutants would reach Ohio than that one of petitioners' cars would reach Oklahoma. The Court's analysis, however, excludes jurisdiction in a contiguous State such as Pennsylvania as surely as in more distant States such as Oklahoma.

CHAPTER 2 PERSONAL JURISDICTION

them as the dealer knew the customer would, took them there.[11] In each case the seller purposefully injects the goods into the stream of commerce and those goods predictably are used in the forum State.[12]

Furthermore, an automobile seller derives substantial benefits from States other than its own. A large part of the value of automobiles is the extensive, nationwide network of highways. Significant portions of that network have been constructed by and are maintained by the individual States, including Oklahoma. The States, through their highway programs, contribute in a very direct and important way to the value of petitioners' businesses. Additionally, a network of other related dealerships with their service departments operates throughout the country under the protection of the laws of the various States, including Oklahoma, and enhances the value of petitioners' businesses by facilitating their customers' traveling.

Thus, the Court errs in its conclusion that "petitioners have no 'contacts, ties, or relations'" with Oklahoma. There obviously are contacts, and, given Oklahoma's connection to the litigation, the contacts are sufficiently significant to make it fair and reasonable for the petitioners to submit to Oklahoma's jurisdiction.

It may be that affirmance of the judgment * * * would approach the outer limits of *International Shoe*'s jurisdictional principle. But that principle, with its almost exclusive focus on the rights of defendants, may be outdated. * * *

* * *

As the Court acknowledges, both the nationalization of commerce and the ease of transportation and communication have accelerated in the generation since 1957. The model of society on which the *International Shoe* Court based its opinion is no longer accurate. Business people, no matter how local their businesses, cannot assume that goods remain in the business' locality. Customers and goods can be anywhere else in the country usually in a matter of hours and always in a matter of a very few days.

In answering the question whether or not it is fair and reasonable to allow a particular forum to hold a trial binding on a particular defendant, the interests of the forum State and other parties loom large in today's world and surely are entitled to as much weight as are the interests of the defendant. The "orderly administration of the laws" provides a firm basis for according some protection to the interests of plaintiffs and States as well as of defendants. Certainly, I cannot see how a defendant's right to due process is violated if the defendant suffers no inconvenience.

The conclusion I draw is that constitutional concepts of fairness no longer require the extreme concern for defendants that was once necessary. Rather, as I wrote in dissent from *Shaffer v. Heitner*, minimum contacts must exist "among the *parties*, the contested transaction, and the forum State." The contacts between any two of these should not be determinative. * * *

The Court's opinion * * * suggests that the defendant ought to be subject to a State's jurisdiction only if he has contacts with the State "such that he should reasonably anticipate being

---

[11] For example, I cannot understand the constitutional distinction between selling an item in New Jersey and selling an item in New York expecting it to be used in New Jersey.

[12] The manufacturer in the case cited by the Court, Gray v. American Radiator & Standard Sanitary Corp., 176 N. E. 2d 761 (Ill. 1961), had no more control over which States its goods would reach than did the petitioners in this case.

haled into court there."[18] There is nothing unreasonable or unfair, however, about recognizing commercial reality. Given the tremendous mobility of goods and people, and the inability of businessmen to control where goods are taken by customers (or retailers), I do not think that the defendant should be in complete control of the geographical stretch of his amenability to suit. Jurisdiction is no longer premised on the notion that nonresident defendants have somehow impliedly consented to suit. People should understand that they are held responsible for the consequences of their actions and that in our society most actions have consequences affecting many States. When an action in fact causes injury in another State, the actor should be prepared to answer for it there unless defending in that State would be unfair for some reason other than that a state boundary must be crossed.

In effect the Court is allowing defendants to assert the sovereign rights of their home States. The expressed fear is that otherwise all limits on personal jurisdiction would disappear. But the argument's premise is wrong. I would not abolish limits on jurisdiction or strip state boundaries of all significance; I would still require the plaintiff to demonstrate sufficient contacts among the parties, the forum, and the litigation to make the forum a reasonable State in which to hold the trial.

I would also, however, strip the defendant of an unjustified veto power over certain very appropriate fora — a power the defendant justifiably enjoyed long ago when communication and travel over long distances were slow and unpredictable and when notions of state sovereignty were impractical and exaggerated. But I repeat that that is not today's world. If a plaintiff can show that his chosen forum State has a sufficient interest in the litigation (or sufficient contacts with the defendant), then the defendant who cannot show some real injury to a constitutionally protected interest should have no constitutional excuse not to appear.

* * *

JUSTICE MARSHALL with whom Justice BLACKMUN joins, dissenting.

* * *

Petitioners are sellers of a product whose utility derives from its mobility. The unique importance of the automobile in today's society, * * * needs no further elaboration. Petitioners know that their customers buy cars not only to make short trips, but also to travel long distances. In fact, the nationwide service network with which they are affiliated was designed to facilitate and encourage such travel. Seaway would be unlikely to sell many cars if authorized service were available only in Massena, N.Y. Moreover, local dealers normally derive a substantial portion of their revenues from the service operations and thereby obtain a further economic benefit from the opportunity to service cars which were sold in other States. It is apparent that petitioners have not attempted to minimize the chance that their activities will have effects in other States; on the contrary, they have chosen to do business in a way that increases that chance, because it is to their economic advantage to do so.

---

[18] The Court suggests that this is the critical foreseeability rather than the likelihood that the product will go to the forum State. But the reasoning begs the question. A defendant cannot know if his action will subject him to jurisdiction in another State until we have declared what the law of jurisdiction is.

To be sure, petitioners could not know in advance that this particular automobile would be driven to Oklahoma. They must have anticipated, however, that a substantial portion of the cars they sold would travel out of New York. Seaway, a local dealer in the second most populous State, and World-Wide, one of only seven regional Audi distributors in the entire country, would scarcely have been surprised to learn that a car sold by them had been driven to Oklahoma on Interstate 44, a heavily traveled transcontinental highway. In the case of the distributor, in particular, the probability that some of the cars it sells will be driven in every one of the contiguous States must amount to a virtual certainty. This knowledge should alert a reasonable businessman to the likelihood that a defect in the product might manifest itself in the forum State — not because of some unpredictable, aberrant, unilateral action by a single buyer, but in the normal course of the operation of the vehicles for their intended purpose.

It is misleading for the majority to characterize the argument in favor of jurisdiction as one of "'foreseeability' alone." As economic entities petitioners reach out from New York, knowingly causing effects in other States and receiving economic advantage both from the ability to cause such effects themselves and from the activities of dealers and distributors in other States. While they did not receive revenue from making direct sales in Oklahoma, they intentionally became part of an interstate economic network, which included dealerships in Oklahoma, for pecuniary gain. In light of this purposeful conduct I do not believe it can be said that petitioners "had no reason to expect to be haled before a[n Oklahoma] court."

* * *

[The dissenting opinion of Justice Blackmun omitted.]

NOTES AND QUESTIONS

1. The Court asserts that the Due Process Clause of the Fourteenth Amendment is an "instrument of interstate federalism." Is this an historically accurate description of the purposes behind the Fourteenth Amendment?

2. Why would it upset the balance of interstate federalism to allow Oklahoma to hear this case? Doesn't Oklahoma have a significant territorial connection to this case? Compare this case with *Hess v. Pawloski*.

3. Three years after *World-Wide Volkswagen*, the Court backed away somewhat from its emphasis on federalism and explained: "The personal jurisdiction requirement recognizes and protects an individual liberty interest. It represents a restriction on judicial power not as a matter of sovereignty, but as a matter of individual liberty. * * * The restriction on state sovereign power described in *World-Wide Volkswagen Corp.*, however, must be seen as ultimately a function of the individual liberty interest preserved by the Due Process Clause." Insurance Corp. v. Compagnie des Bauxites, 456 U.S. 694, 702-03 & n.10 (1982). Thus, as the Court now describes personal jurisdiction, the defendant has a

B. Constitutional Limits on Personal Jurisdiction

constitutionally protected *liberty interest* in not being subject to the jurisdiction of a state with which that defendant has not purposefully connected herself. Do you agree that personal jurisdiction is one of the fundamental liberties protected by the Constitution?

4. Should corporations have a constitutionally protected right to "liberty?" Are corporations "persons" within the meaning of the Fourteenth Amendment? In Santa Clara County v. Southern Pacific R.R., 118 U.S. 394, 396 (1886), the Court held that they are. The Court offered no explanation for its holding and simply stated:

> The court does not wish to hear argument on the question whether the provision in the Fourteenth Amendment to the Constitution, which forbids a State to deny to any person within its jurisdiction the equal protection of the laws, applies to these corporations. We are of the opinion that it does.

More recently, the Court has held that corporations have freedom of speech rights protected by the First and Fourteenth Amendments. See Consolidated Edison Co. v. Public Serv. Comm'n, 447 U.S. 530, 533-35 (1980).

5. In *World-Wide Volkswagen*, the Court (quoting *Hanson*) stressed that the defendant must have "purposefully avail[ed] itself of the privilege of conducting activities within the forum state." The requirement of purposeful availment seems to reflect the Court's underlying belief that defendants should know in advance and be able to control where they will be subject to suit. Why should this be so? Defendants are sometimes held "strictly liable" for the injuries they cause without regard to whether they were negligent or took steps to prevent injuries. What would be wrong with "jurisdictional strict liability," under which manufacturers can be sued anywhere they or their products can cause injury? As one commentator has wryly observed, it is as if the Court thinks "an accused is more concerned with where he will be hanged than whether." Linda Silberman, Shaffer v. Heitner: *The End of an Era*, 53 N.Y.U. L. REV. 33, 88 (1978).

6. The Robinsons were badly burned in the accident. It may have been extremely difficult for them to travel to New York. Should the Court consider the burdens of distant litigation on the plaintiffs?

7. The Court states that in assessing a defendant's conduct, the foreseeability of a product's ending up in the forum is not the test. Instead, the relevant inquiry is whether in light of the defendant's conduct and connections with the state, he "should reasonably anticipate being haled into court there." Isn't this argument completely circular? Aren't reasonable expectations about where you can be haled into court a function of what the law provides? In other words, if the Supreme Court had decided in *World-Wide Volkswagen* that sellers can be sued wherever their products end up, then, from that time on, all sellers should reasonably expect to be haled into court wherever their products ended up.

CHAPTER 2   PERSONAL JURISDICTION

8. How can a company named *World-Wide* Volkswagen not expect to be sued in far away places?

9. Consider the following variations on *World-Wide Volkswagen*. Would the seller be subject to suit in Oklahoma?

   (a) When the Robinsons purchased their car, they explicitly and repeatedly told the salesman that they were planning to take the car to Oklahoma.

   (b) In addition to (a) above, at the Robinsons' request, the seller arranged to have the car titled and tagged in Oklahoma.

   (c) In addition to (a) and (b) above, the seller arranged to ship the car to Oklahoma for the Robinsons.

10. Review question 5(h) after *International Shoe*. Consider in particular the discussion in *World-Wide Volkswagen* about "corporation[s] that deliver [their] products into the stream of commerce." You will notice that the Court cites *Gray v. American Radiator & Standard Sanitary Corp*. That case is described supra at 48. Notice that the Court cited Gray with a "cf." Does this mean the Court agrees or disagrees with the result in *Gray*?

11. The Court also cites Kulko v. Superior Court, 436 U.S. 84 (1978). That case involved a suit for child support payments. Until their divorce, the Kulkos had been domiciled in New York. Following the divorce, the ex-wife moved to California, and the husband remained in New York with custody of their two children. Later the children requested that they be allowed to live with the mother. The father complied with that request and purchased a one-way plane ticket for one child (the mother sent a ticket for the other child). Upon their arrival in California, the mother filed suit in California seeking child support from the father. The Supreme Court held that California did not have jurisdiction over the father. The Court explained: "A father who agrees, in the interest of family harmony and his children's preferences, to allow them to spend more time in California than was required under a separation agreement can hardly be said to have 'purposefully availed himself' of the 'benefits and protections' of California's laws." Id. at 94. In its opinion, the Court seemed concerned that allowing jurisdiction would discourage parents from accommodating the "interests of family harmony." But doesn't this look at only half the transaction? After *Kulko*, custodial parents may be more willing to relinquish custody, but non-custodial parents may be less willing to accept custody knowing that they will not be able to get a support order without going to the other parent's home to litigate. Would the result in *Kulko* be different if Mr. Kulko had sent his ex-wife an exploding package rather than a teenager?

B. Constitutional Limits on Personal Jurisdiction

12. Following the Supreme Court's decision in *World-Wide*, the Robinsons' claim against Audi and Volkswagen was removed to federal court,* where it was tried. The Robinsons lost, but on appeal, the Court of Appeals for the Tenth Circuit ordered a retrial on their claim against Volkswagen. In the retrial, the Robinsons lost again, and this result was affirmed on appeal. The case did not end there. The Robinsons became acquainted with a University of Tulsa law professor who had previously owned a Volkswagen dealership and believed Audi and Volkswagen had concealed critical information about the corporate inter-relationship of those two companies. The Robinsons then filed a new lawsuit against both Volkswagen and their attorneys for fraudulently concealing information and against the Robinsons' prior lawyers for legal malpractice. This suit was filed in federal court in their new home state of Arizona. This suit generated its own personal jurisdiction battle and was transferred to the federal court in Oklahoma. In May 1995, the Robinsons lost their fraud claim. See Robinson v. Volkswagenwerk AG, 56 F.3d 1268 (10th Cir. 1995); Robinson v.Audi Aktiengesellschaft, 56 F.3d 1259 (10th Cir. 1995). See Charles Adams, World-Wide Volkswagen v. Woodson —*The Rest of the Story*, 72 Neb. L. Rev. 1122 (1993).

PERSONAL JURISDICTION IN FEDERAL COURT

At this point, students frequently suggest that it might be possible to avoid entirely the limits of personal jurisdiction by suing in federal court. Unfortunately, in most cases this will not work. Absent special congressional legislation, a federal court has personal jurisdiction only if the state in which it sits would have had personal jurisdiction. It is not obvious why this should be so. First of all, federal courts are organized by district, not by state.** Second, personal jurisdiction seems to focus on the relationship between the defendant and the sovereign government that is conducting the trial. When litigation is in federal court, the "sovereign" is the United States. One might conclude that so long as the defendant has connections with the United States, that should suffice for personal jurisdiction.

Notwithstanding the foregoing considerations, it is now clearly established that in most situations, a federal court has jurisdiction only if the state in which it sits would have jurisdiction. This understanding is embodied in Rule 4(k)(1)(A).

---

* Today the case could not have been removed because it became removable more than a year after the suit was filed. See § 1446 (b). Removal is discussed in detail in Chapter 4.

** Only one federal district includes more than one state, but many of the larger states include multiple federal districts. The District of Wyoming include those portions of Yellowstone National Park situated in Montana and Idaho. See 28 U.S.C. § 131.

The 1993 amendments to Rule 4 added one new exception to this general rule. Rule 4(k)(2) provides for personal jurisdiction in any federal court where: (1) the claim is based on federal law, (2) jurisdiction is constitutional, and (3) there is no state which would have personal jurisdiction. Can you describe a situation in which these three conditions would all be met? Rule 4(k)(2) overrides a prior Supreme Court case which interpreted the prior version of Rule 4 and had held that under the conditions described there was no personal jurisdiction. See Omni Capital Int'l v. Rudolf Wolff & Co., 484 U.S. 97 (1987).

In a few instances, Congress has passed special legislation providing for nationwide service of process. These statutes permit the defendant to be served anywhere in the United States and provide personal jurisdiction regardless of whether there would have been jurisdiction in any state court. Congress has authorized nationwide service of process in areas such as antitrust, securities, bankruptcy and interpleader.

Nationwide service of process presents its own potential due process problems, although the problem is governed by the Due Process Clause of the Fifth Amendment, rather than the Due Process Clause of the Fourteenth Amendment. With nationwide service of process, a defendant who lived his entire life in Florida and engaged in the alleged improper activities in Florida, might nonetheless be subject to suit in federal court in California. Would this be constitutional? If we focus only on the relationship between the defendant and the sovereign, the defendant clearly has connections with the United States. In addition to the contacts requirement, does the Fifth Amendment impose any fairness or convenience limitations? Compare FTC v. Jim Walter Corp., 651 F. 2d 251 (5th Cir. 1981) (rejecting 5th Amendment limitation on federal court jurisdiction) with Oxford First Corp. v. PNC Liquidating Corp., 372 F. Supp. 191 (E.D. Pa. 1974) (nationwide jurisdiction limited by fundamental notions of fairness).

NOTE ON *KEETON* AND *CALDER*

In 1984, the Supreme Court addressed personal jurisdiction issues in two libel cases. The first case, Keeton v. Hustler Magazine, Inc., 465 U.S. 770 (1984), concerned a libel suit brought against Hustler magazine in New Hampshire. The suit alleged defamation in one issue of Hustler magazine that was distributed in New Hampshire and nationwide. Keeton was a citizen of New York, with little connection to New Hampshire. She sued there because it was the only state in which her action would not have been barred by the statute of limitations. In her suit, Keeton sought damages for the injury to her reputation suffered in New Hampshire, as well as the injury which she suffered nationwide.

B. Constitutional Limits on Personal Jurisdiction

The Supreme Court upheld personal jurisdiction not only as to her injury suffered in New Hampshire from the copies of the magazine that were distributed in New Hampshire, but also for her injury suffered in all other states as a result of the copies that were distributed there. The Supreme Court explained that New Hampshire has a "substantial interest in cooperating with other States * * * to provide a forum for efficiently litigating all issues and damages claims arising out of a libel in a unitary proceeding." Id. at 777. The Court upheld jurisdiction despite the plaintiff's minimal connection with New Hampshire. "[W]e have not to date required a plaintiff to have 'minimum contacts' with the forum State before permitting that State to assert personal jurisdiction over a nonresident defendant. On the contrary, we have upheld the assertion of jurisdiction where such contacts were entirely lacking." Id. at 779.

Although the Supreme Court upheld suit in New Hampshire for all injuries suffered as a result of the distribution of the article, the Court did not hold that Hustler was subject to suit in New Hampshire on all possible causes of action. The Court held, "In the instant case, respondent's activities in the forum may not be so substantial as to support jurisdiction over a cause of action unrelated to those activities. But respondent is carrying on a 'part of its general business' in New Hampshire, and that is sufficient to support jurisdiction when the cause of action arises out of the very activity being conducted, in part, in New Hampshire." Id. at 779-80.

In the companion case of Calder v. Jones, 465 U.S. 783 (1984), the Court upheld jurisdiction in California against the editor and writer of an allegedly defamatory article about a California citizen. Both the writer and the editor were citizens of Florida. Neither traveled to California in connection with researching this article. The article was written and edited in Florida. The National Enquirer which is widely distributed in California, published the article. In upholding jurisdiction against the writer and editor (jurisdiction over the National Enquirer was not disputed), the Court explained:

> The allegedly libelous story concerned the California activities of a California resident. It impugned the professionalism of an entertainer whose television career was centered in California. The article was drawn from California sources, and the brunt of the harm, in terms both of respondent's emotional distress and the injury to her professional reputation was suffered in California. In sum, California is the focal point both of the story and of the harm suffered. Jurisdiction over petitioners is therefore proper in California based on the 'effects' of their Florida conduct in California.

* * *

* * *[P]etitioners are not charged with mere untargeted negligence. Rather, their intentional, and allegedly tortious, actions were expressly aimed at California.

> Petitioners South wrote and petitioner Calder edited an article that they knew would have a potentially devastating impact upon respondent. And they knew that the brunt of that injury would be felt by respondent in the State in which she lives and works and in which the National Enquirer has its largest circulation. Under these circumstances, petitioners must "reasonably anticipate being haled into court there" to answer for the truth of the statements made in their article.

Id. at 788-89, 789-90.

WHY LITIGANTS CARE ABOUT WHERE LITIGATION OCCURS

As you read the personal jurisdiction cases, one issue that may occur to you is why litigants seem to care so much about the location of the litigation. One reason might be that they want to avoid an inconvenient forum. Distant litigation could burden a party in several ways. First, it may make it more difficult to subpoena witnesses. Second, it may be more expensive to ship and store documents or other evidence. Third, the lawyer "back home," who may have counseled the party on the underlying transaction will probably not be a member of the bar in another state. Thus, the party will have to hire a new lawyer. Yet in an age of instant telecommunications and easy transportation, concern about inconvenience sometimes seems an unlikely explanation. Remember, a dismissal for lack of personal jurisdiction does not protect a defendant from litigation; it simply means that the litigation will occur in a different place. Therefore, the only expenses that a defendant would save are the incremental *additional* costs associated with litigating in one place rather than another.

Another possible reason litigants might care about the location of litigation is that they might believe that judges and juries in a particular location are more likely to be biased for or against them. As you will see in Chapter 4, the Constitution explicitly provides one solution to the problem of bias — it grants federal courts jurisdiction over cases between citizens of different states.

Probably the most common reason that litigants care about the location of jurisdiction has nothing to do with inconvenience or bias — it has to do with what law will be applied. We are a nation of 50 states, and the laws of those states vary. In *Keeton*, for example, New Hampshire was the only state with a six year statute of limitations for libel. The statute of limitations on this claim had expired in all the other states.

In any litigation, a fundamental question that the forum must decide is what law applies. A forum does not always apply its own laws. For example, suppose that there is an automobile accident in Virginia, but the lawsuit concerning the accident occurs in Connecticut. Connecticut will certainly refer to Virginia's traffic and speed laws in determining the negligence of either driver. While in the foregoing example it seems clear that the court should apply Virginia law, it is not always so clear which state's law should govern a dispute. Suppose that a husband and wife from Connecticut have an auto accident in Virginia. Under the law of Connecticut, one spouse can sue the other, but under the law of Virginia there is inter-spousal immunity which would bar the suit. Which state's rules concerning inter-spousal lawsuits should apply? States disagree about whose law to apply in this case. Some states apply the law of the place of the accident. Other states conclude that rules about inter-spousal immunity are really the concern of the state where the married couple resides.

Who decides what law will be applied? The forum does. Therefore, where different states would apply different laws, it may matter a great deal where the litigation occurs. Personal jurisdiction imposes significant limitations on the plaintiff's choice of forum and therefore limits the plaintiff's ability to choose a forum that will apply the most advantageous law.

Despite the practical and strategic implications of the plaintiff's choice of forum, the Supreme Court has never focused on these practical implications of personal jurisdiction in delineating the scope of the doctrine. Instead, the Court has focused on personal jurisdiction as a relatively abstract liberty interest. Would it be more appropriate for the Court to delineate the contours of personal jurisdiction by reference to the pragmatic concerns that motivate actual litigants?

Burger King Corp. v. Rudzewicz
471 U.S. 462, 105 S.Ct. 2174, 85 L. Ed. 2d 528 (1985)

JUSTICE BRENNAN delivered the opinion of the Court.

The State of Florida's long-arm statute extends jurisdiction to "[a]ny person, whether or not a citizen or resident of this state," who, inter alia, "[b]reach[es] a contract in this state by failing to perform acts required by the contract to be performed in this state," so long as the cause of action arises from the alleged contractual breach. Fla. Stat. § 48.193 (1)(g) (Supp. 1984). The United States District Court for the Southern District of Florida, sitting in diversity, relied on this provision in exercising personal jurisdiction over a Michigan resident who allegedly had breached a franchise agreement with a Florida corporation by failing to make required payments in Florida. The question presented is whether this exercise of long-arm jurisdiction offended "traditional conception[s] of fair play and substantial justice" embodied in the Due Process Clause of the Fourteenth Amendment.

CHAPTER 2 PERSONAL JURISDICTION

I

A

Burger King Corporation is a Florida corporation whose principal offices are in Miami. It is one of the world's largest restaurant organizations, with over 3,000 outlets in the 50 States, the Commonwealth of Puerto Rico, and 8 foreign nations. Burger King conducts approximately 80% of its business through a franchise operation that the company styles the "Burger King System" — "a comprehensive restaurant format and operating system for the sale of uniform and quality food products." Burger King licenses its franchisees to use its trademarks and service marks for a period of 20 years and leases standardized restaurant facilities to them for the same term. In addition, franchisees acquire a variety of proprietary information concerning the "standards, specifications, 11procedures and methods for operating a Burger King Restaurant." They also receive market research and advertising assistance; ongoing training in restaurant management;[3] and accounting, cost-control, and inventory-control guidance. By permitting franchisees to tap into Burger King's established national reputation and to benefit from proven procedures for dispensing standardized fare, this system enables them to go into the restaurant business with significantly lowered barriers to entry.

In exchange for these benefits, franchisees pay Burger King an initial $ 40,000 franchise fee and commit themselves to payment of monthly royalties, advertising and sales promotion fees, and rent computed in part from monthly gross sales. Franchisees also agree to submit to the national organization's exacting regulation of virtually every conceivable aspect of their operations. Burger King imposes these standards and undertakes its rigid regulation out of conviction that "[u]niformity of service, appearance, and quality of product is essential to the preservation of the Burger King image and the benefits accruing therefrom to both Franchisee and Franchisor."

Burger King oversees its franchise system through a two-tiered administrative structure. The governing contracts provide that the franchise relationship is established in Miami and governed by Florida law, and call for payment of all required fees and forwarding of all relevant notices to the Miami headquarters. The Miami headquarters sets policy and works directly with its franchisees in attempting to resolve major problems. Day-to-day monitoring of franchisees, however, is conducted through a network of 10 district offices which in turn report to the Miami headquarters.

The instant litigation grows out of Burger King's termination of one of its franchisees, and is aptly described by the franchisee as "a divorce proceeding among commercial partners." The appellee John Rudzewicz, a Michigan citizen and resident, is the senior partner in a Detroit accounting firm. In 1978, he was approached by Brian MacShara, the son of a business acquaintance, who suggested that they jointly apply to Burger King for a franchise in the Detroit area. MacShara proposed to serve as the manager of the restaurant if Rudzewicz would put up the investment capital; in exchange, the two would evenly share the profits. Believing that MacShara's idea offered attractive investment and tax-deferral opportunities, Rudzewicz agreed to the venture.

Rudzewicz and MacShara jointly applied for a franchise to Burger King's Birmingham, Michigan, district office in the autumn of 1978. Their application was forwarded to Burger King's

---

[3] Mandatory training seminars are conducted at Burger King University in Miami and at Whopper College Regional Training Centers around the country.

B. Constitutional Limits on Personal Jurisdiction

Miami headquarters, which entered into a preliminary agreement with them in February 1979. During the ensuing four months it was agreed that Rudzewicz and MacShara would assume operation of an existing facility in Drayton Plains, Michigan. MacShara attended the prescribed management courses in Miami during this period, and the franchisees purchased $165,000 worth of restaurant equipment from Burger King's Davmor Industries division in Miami. Even before the final agreements were signed, however, the parties began to disagree over site-development fees, building design, computation of monthly rent, and whether the franchisees would be able to assign their liabilities to a corporation they had formed. During these disputes Rudzewicz and MacShara negotiated both with the Birmingham district office and with the Miami headquarters.[7] With some misgivings, Rudzewicz and MacShara finally obtained limited concessions from the Miami headquarters, signed the final agreements, and commenced operations in June 1979. By signing the final agreements, Rudzewicz obligated himself personally to payments exceeding $1 million over the 20-year franchise relationship.

The Drayton Plains facility apparently enjoyed steady business during the summer of 1979, but patronage declined after a recession began later that year. Rudzewicz and MacShara soon fell far behind in their monthly payments to Miami. Headquarters sent notices of default, and an extended period of negotiations began among the franchisees, the Birmingham district office, and the Miami headquarters. After several Burger King officials in Miami had engaged in prolonged but ultimately unsuccessful negotiations with the franchisees by mail and by telephone, headquarters terminated the franchise and ordered Rudzewicz and MacShara to vacate the premises. They refused and continued to occupy and operate the facility as a Burger King restaurant.

B

Burger King commenced the instant action in the United States District Court for the Southern District of Florida in May 1981, invoking that court's diversity jurisdiction pursuant to 28 U. S. C. § 1332(a) and its original jurisdiction over federal trademark disputes pursuant to § 1338(a). Burger King alleged that Rudzewicz and MacShara had breached their franchise obligations "within [the jurisdiction of] this district court" by failing to make the required payments "at plaintiff's place of business in Miami, Dade County, Florida," and also charged that they were tortiously infringing its trademarks and service marks through their continued, unauthorized operation as a Burger King restaurant. Burger King sought damages, injunctive relief, and costs and attorney's fees. Rudzewicz and MacShara entered special appearances and argued, inter alia, that because they were Michigan residents and because Burger King's claim did not "arise" within the Southern District of Florida, the District Court lacked personal jurisdiction over them. The District Court denied their motions after a hearing, holding that, pursuant to Florida's long-arm statute, "a nonresident Burger King franchisee is subject to the personal jurisdiction of this Court in actions arising out of its franchise agreements." Rudzewicz and MacShara then filed an answer and a counterclaim seeking damages for alleged violations by Burger King of Michigan's Franchise Investment Law, Mich. Comp. Laws § 445.1501 et seq. (1979).

---

[7] Although Rudzewicz and MacShara dealt with the Birmingham district office on a regular basis, they communicated directly with the Miami headquarters in forming the contracts; moreover, they learned that the district office had "very little" decision making authority and accordingly turned directly to headquarters in seeking to resolve their disputes.

After a 3-day bench trial, the court again concluded that it had "jurisdiction over the subject matter and the parties to this cause." Finding that Rudzewicz and MacShara had breached their franchise agreements with Burger King and had infringed Burger King's trademarks and service marks, the court entered judgment against them, jointly and severally, for $ 228,875 in contract damages. The court also ordered them "to immediately close Burger King Restaurant Number 775 from continued operation or to immediately give the keys and possession of said restaurant to Burger King Corporation," found that they had failed to prove any of the required elements of their counterclaim, and awarded costs and attorney's fees to Burger King.

Rudzewicz appealed to the Court of Appeals for the Eleventh Circuit.[11] A divided panel of that Circuit reversed the judgment, concluding that the District Court could not properly exercise personal jurisdiction over Rudzewicz pursuant to Fla. Stat. § 48.193(1)(g) (Supp. 1984) because "the circumstances of the Drayton Plains franchise and the negotiations which led to it left Rudzewicz bereft of reasonable notice and financially unprepared for the prospect of franchise litigation in Florida." Accordingly, the panel majority concluded that" [j]urisdiction under these circumstances would offend the fundamental fairness which is the touchstone of due process."

* * *

II

A

The Due Process Clause protects an individual's liberty interest in not being subject to the binding judgments of a forum with which he has established no meaningful "contacts, ties, or relations." *International Shoe*.[13] By requiring that individuals have "fair warning that a particular activity may subject [them] to the jurisdiction of a foreign sovereign," *Shaffer v. Heitner* (Stevens, J., concurring in judgment), the Due Process Clause "gives a degree of predictability to the legal system that allows potential defendants to structure their primary conduct with some minimum assurance as to where that conduct will and will not render them liable to suit," *World-Wide Volkswagen Corp.*

Where a forum seeks to assert specific jurisdiction over an out-of-state defendant who has not consented to suit there, this "fair warning" requirement is satisfied if the defendant has "purposefully directed" his activities at residents of the forum, *Keeton v. Hustler Magazine, Inc.*, and the litigation results from alleged injuries that "arise out of or relate to" those activities, Helicopteros

---

[11] MacShara did not appeal his judgment. In addition, Rudzewicz entered into a compromise with Burger King and waived his right to appeal the District Court's finding of trademark infringement and its entry of injunctive relief. Accordingly, we need not address the extent to which the tortious act provisions of Florida's long-arm statute, may constitutionally extend to out-of-state trademark infringement. Cf. *Calder v. Jones* (tortious out-of-state conduct); *Keeton v. Hustler Magazine, Inc.* (same).

[13] Although this protection operates to restrict state power, it "must be seen as ultimately a function of the individual liberty interest preserved by the Due Process Clause" rather than as a function "of federalism concerns." *Insurance Corp. of Ireland v. Compagnie des Bauxites de Guinee*, 456 U.S. 694, 702-703, n.10 (1982).

B. Constitutional Limits on Personal Jurisdiction

Nacionales de Colombia, S.A. v. Hall, 466 U.S. 408, 414 (1984).[15] Thus "[t]he forum State does not exceed its powers under the Due Process Clause if it asserts personal jurisdiction over a corporation that delivers its products into the stream of commerce with the expectation that they will be purchased by consumers in the forum State" and those products subsequently injure forum consumers. *World-Wide Volkswagen.* Similarly, a publisher who distributes magazines in a distant State may fairly be held accountable in that forum for damages resulting there from an allegedly defamatory story. *Keeton v. Hustler Magazine, Inc.*, see also *Calder v. Jones*, (suit against author and editor). And with respect to interstate contractual obligations, we have emphasized that parties who "reach out beyond one state and create continuing relationships and obligations with citizens of another state" are subject to regulation and sanctions in the other State for the consequences of their activities. See also *McGee v. International Life Insurance Co.*

We have noted several reasons why a forum legitimately may exercise personal jurisdiction over a nonresident who "purposefully directs" his activities toward forum residents. A State generally has a "manifest interest" in providing its residents with a convenient forum for redressing injuries inflicted by out-of-state actors. See also *Keeton v. Hustler Magazine, Inc.* Moreover, where individuals "purposefully derive benefit" from their interstate activities, it may well be unfair to allow them to escape having to account in other States for consequences that arise proximately from such activities; the Due Process Clause may not readily be wielded as a territorial shield to avoid interstate obligations that have been voluntarily assumed. And because "modern transportation and communications have made it much less burdensome for a party sued to defend himself in a State where he engages in economic activity," it usually will not be unfair to subject him to the burdens of litigating in another forum for disputes relating to such activity. *McGee v. International Life Insurance Co.*

Notwithstanding these considerations, the constitutional touchstone remains whether the defendant purposefully established "minimum contacts" in the forum State. *International Shoe.* Although it has been argued that foreseeability of causing injury in another State should be sufficient to establish such contacts there when policy considerations so require, the Court has consistently held that this kind of foreseeability is not a "sufficient benchmark" for exercising personal jurisdiction. *World-Wide Volkswagen.* Instead, "the foreseeability that is critical to due process analysis ... is that the defendant's conduct and connection with the forum State are such that he should reasonably anticipate being haled into court there." In defining when it is that a potential defendant should "reasonably anticipate" out-of-state litigation, the Court frequently has drawn from the reasoning of *Hanson v. Denckla*:

> "The unilateral activity of those who claim some relationship with a nonresident defendant cannot satisfy the requirement of contact with the forum State. The application of that rule will vary with the quality and nature of the defendant's activity, but it is essential in each case that there be some act by which the defendant purposefully avails itself of the privilege of conducting activities within the forum State, thus invoking the benefits and protections of its laws."

---

[15] "Specific" jurisdiction contrasts with "general" jurisdiction, pursuant to which "a State exercises personal jurisdiction over a defendant in a suit not arising out of or related to the defendant's contacts with the forum." Helicopteros Nacionales de Colombia, S.A. v. Hall, 466 U.S., at 414, n. 9; see also Perkins v. Benguet Consolidated Mining Co., 342 U.S. 437 (1952).

This "purposeful availment" requirement ensures that a defendant will not be haled into a jurisdiction solely as a result of "random," "fortuitous," or "attenuated" contacts, or of the "unilateral activity of another party or a third person." Jurisdiction is proper, however, where the contacts proximately result from actions by the defendant *himself* that create a "substantial connection" with the forum State. Thus where the defendant "deliberately" has engaged in significant activities within a State, or has created "continuing obligations" between himself and residents of the forum, he manifestly has availed himself of the privilege of conducting business there, and because his activities are shielded by "the benefits and protections" of the forum's laws it is presumptively not unreasonable to require him to submit to the burdens of litigation in that forum as well.

Jurisdiction in these circumstances may not be avoided merely because the defendant did not *physically* enter the forum State. Although territorial presence frequently will enhance a potential defendant's affiliation with a State and reinforce the reasonable foreseeability of suit there, it is an inescapable fact of modern commercial life that a substantial amount of business is transacted solely by mail and wire communications across state lines, thus obviating the need for physical presence within a State in which business is conducted. So long as a commercial actor's efforts are "purposefully directed" toward residents of another State, we have consistently rejected the notion that an absence of physical contacts can defeat personal jurisdiction there. *Keeton v. Hustler Magazine, Inc.*; see also *Calder v. Jones*; *McGee v. International Life Insurance Co.*

Once it has been decided that a defendant purposefully established minimum contacts within the forum State, these contacts may be considered in light of other factors to determine whether the assertion of personal jurisdiction would comport with "fair play and substantial justice." *International Shoe*. Thus courts in "appropriate case[s]" may evaluate "the burden on the defendant," "the forum State's interest in adjudicating the dispute," "the plaintiff's interest in obtaining convenient and effective relief," "the interstate judicial system's interest in obtaining the most efficient resolution of controversies," and the "shared interest of the several States in furthering fundamental substantive social policies." *World-Wide Volkswagen*. These considerations sometimes serve to establish the reasonableness of jurisdiction upon a lesser showing of minimum contacts than would otherwise be required. See, e.g., *Keeton v. Hustler Magazine, Inc.*; *Calder v. Jones*; *McGee v. International Life Insurance Co.* On the other hand, where a defendant who purposefully has directed his activities at forum residents seeks to defeat jurisdiction, he must present a compelling case that the presence of some other considerations would render jurisdiction unreasonable. Most such considerations usually may be accommodated through means short of finding jurisdiction unconstitutional. For example, the potential clash of the forum's law with the "fundamental substantive social policies" of another State may be accommodated through application of the forum's choice-of-law rules. Similarly, a defendant claiming substantial inconvenience may seek a change of venue. Nevertheless, minimum requirements inherent in the concept of "fair play and substantial justice" may defeat the reasonableness of jurisdiction even if the defendant has purposefully engaged in forum activities. *World-Wide Volkswagen*; see also RESTATEMENT (SECOND) OF CONFLICT OF LAWS §§ 36-37 (1971). As we previously have noted, jurisdictional rules may not be employed in such away as to make litigation "so gravely difficult and inconvenient" that a party unfairly is at a "severe disadvantage" in comparison to his opponent. The Bremen v. Zapata Off-Shore Co., 407 U.S. 1, 18 (1972) (re forum-selection provisions); *McGee v. International Life Insurance Co.*

B. Constitutional Limits on Personal Jurisdiction

B

(1)

Applying these principles to the case at hand, we believe there is substantial record evidence supporting the District Court's conclusion that the assertion of personal jurisdiction over Rudzewicz in Florida for the alleged breach of his franchise agreement did not offend due process. At the outset, we note a continued division among lower courts respecting whether and to what extent a contract can constitute a "contact" for purposes of due process analysis. If the question is whether an individual's contract with an out-of-state party alone can automatically establish sufficient minimum contacts in the other party's home forum, we believe the answer clearly is that it cannot. The Court long ago rejected the notion that personal jurisdiction might turn on "mechanical" tests, or on "conceptualistic ... theories of the place of contracting or of performance." Instead, we have emphasized the need for a "highly realistic" approach that recognizes that a "contract" is "ordinarily but an intermediate step serving to tie up prior business negotiations with future consequences which themselves are the real object of the business transaction." It is these factors — prior negotiations and contemplated future consequences, along with the terms of the contract and the parties' actual course of dealing — that must be evaluated in determining whether the defendant purposefully established minimum contacts within the forum.

In this case, no physical ties to Florida can be attributed to Rudzewicz other than MacShara's brief training course in Miami.[22] Rudzewicz did not maintain offices in Florida and, for all that appears from the record, has never even visited there. Yet this franchise dispute grew directly out of "a contract which had a *substantial* connection with that State." *McGee v. International Life Insurance Co.* (emphasis added). Eschewing the option of operating an independent local enterprise, Rudzewicz deliberately "reach[ed] out beyond" Michigan and negotiated with a Florida corporation for the purchase of a long-term franchise and the manifold benefits that would derive from affiliation with a nationwide organization. Upon approval, he entered into a carefully structured 20-year relationship that envisioned continuing and wide-reaching contacts with Burger King in Florida. In light of Rudzewicz' voluntary acceptance of the long-term and exacting regulation of his business from Burger King's Miami headquarters, the "quality and nature" of his relationship to the company in Florida can in no sense be viewed as "random," "fortuitous," or "attenuated." *Hanson v. Denckla; Keeton v. Hustler Magazine, Inc.; World-Wide Volkswagen.* Rudzewicz' refusal to make the contractually required payments in Miami, and his continued use of Burger King's trademarks and confiden-

---

[22] The Eleventh Circuit held that MacShara's presence in Florida was irrelevant to the question of Rudzewicz' minimum contacts with that forum, reasoning that "Rudzewicz and MacShara never formed a partnership" and "signed the agreements in their individual capacities." The two did jointly form a corporation through which they were seeking to conduct the franchise, however. They were required to decide which one of them would travel to Florida to satisfy the training requirements so that they could commence business, and Rudzewicz participated in the decision that MacShara would go there. We have previously noted that when commercial activities are "carried on in behalf of" an out-of-state party those activities may sometimes be ascribed to the party, *International Shoe*, at least where he is a "primary participan[t]" in the enterprise and has acted purposefully in directing those activities, *Calder v. Jones*. Because MacShara's matriculation at Burger King University is not pivotal to the disposition of this case, we need not resolve the permissible bounds of such attribution.

CHAPTER 2   PERSONAL JURISDICTION

tial business information after his termination, caused foreseeable injuries to the corporation in Florida. For these reasons it was, at the very least, presumptively reasonable for Rudzewicz to be called to account there for such injuries.

The Court of Appeals concluded, however, that in light of the supervision emanating from Burger King's district office in Birmingham, Rudzewicz reasonably believed that "the Michigan office was for all intents and purposes the embodiment of Burger King" and that he therefore had no "reason to anticipate a Burger King suit outside of Michigan." This reasoning overlooks substantial record evidence indicating that Rudzewicz most certainly knew that he was affiliating himself with an enterprise based primarily in Florida. The contract documents themselves emphasize that Burger King's operations are conducted and supervised from the Miami headquarters, that all relevant notices and payments must be sent there, and that the agreements were made in and enforced from Miami. Moreover, the parties' actual course of dealing repeatedly confirmed that decisionmaking authority was vested in the Miami headquarters and that the district office served largely as an intermediate link between the headquarters and the franchisees. When problems arose over building design, site-development fees, rent computation, and the defaulted payments, Rudzewicz and MacShara learned that the Michigan office was powerless to resolve their disputes and could only channel their communications to Miami. Throughout these disputes, the Miami headquarters and the Michigan franchisees carried on a continuous course of direct communications by mail and by telephone, and it was the Miami headquarters that made the key negotiating decisions out of which the instant litigation arose.

Moreover, we believe the Court of Appeals gave insufficient weight to provisions in the various franchise documents providing that all disputes would be governed by Florida law. The franchise agreement, for example, stated:

> "This Agreement shall become valid when executed and accepted by BKC at Miami, Florida; it shall be deemed made and entered into in the State of Florida and shall be governed and construed under and in accordance with the laws of the State of Florida. The choice of law designation does not require that all suits concerning this Agreement be filed in Florida."

The Court of Appeals reasoned that choice-of-law provisions are irrelevant to the question of personal jurisdiction, relying on *Hanson v. Denckla* for the proposition that "the center of gravity for choice-of-law purposes does not necessarily confer the sovereign prerogative to assert jurisdiction." This reasoning misperceives the import of the quoted proposition. The Court in *Hanson* and subsequent cases has emphasized that choice-of-law *analysis*— which focuses on all elements of a transaction, and not simply on the defendant's conduct — is distinct from minimum-contacts jurisdictional analysis — which focuses at the threshold solely on the defendant's purposeful connection to the forum. Nothing in our cases, however, suggests that a choice-of-law *provision* should be ignored in considering whether a defendant has "purposefully invoked the benefits and protections of a State's laws" for jurisdictional purposes. Although such a provision standing alone would be insufficient to confer jurisdiction, we believe that, when combined with the 20-year interdependent relationship Rudzewicz established with Burger King's Miami headquarters, it reinforced his deliberate affiliation with the forum State and the reasonable foreseeability of possible litigation there. As Judge Johnson argued in his dissent below, Rudzewicz "purposefully availed himself of the benefits and protections of Florida's laws" by entering into contracts expressly providing that those laws would govern franchise disputes.[24]

(2)

Nor has Rudzewicz pointed to other factors that can be said persuasively to outweigh the considerations discussed above and to establish the *unconstitutionality* of Florida's assertion of jurisdiction. We cannot conclude that Florida had no "legitimate interest in holding [Rudzewicz] answerable on a claim related to" the contacts he had established in that State. *Keeton v. Hustler Magazine, Inc.*; see also *McGee v. International Life Insurance Co.* (noting that State frequently will have a "manifest interest in providing effective means of redress for its residents").[25] Moreover, although Rudzewicz has argued at some length that Michigan's Franchise Investment Law governs many aspects of this franchise relationship, he has not demonstrated how Michigan's acknowledged interest might possibly render jurisdiction in Florida *unconstitutional*.[26] Finally, the Court of Appeals' assertion that the Florida litigation "severely impaired [Rudzewicz'] ability to call Michigan witnesses who might be essential to his defense and counterclaim," is wholly without support in the record. And even to the extent that it is inconvenient for a party who has minimum contacts with a forum to litigate there, such considerations most frequently can be accommodated through a change of venue. Although the Court has suggested that inconvenience may at some point become so substantial as to achieve *constitutional* magnitude, this is not such a case.

The Court of Appeals also concluded, however, that the parties' dealings involved "a characteristic disparity of bargaining power" and "elements of surprise," and that Rudzewicz "lacked fair notice" of the potential for litigation in Florida because the contractual provisions suggesting to

---

[24] In addition, the franchise agreement's disclaimer that the "choice of law designation does not *require* that all suits concerning this Agreement be filed in Florida," reasonably should have suggested to Rudzewicz that by negative implication such suits *could* be filed there.

The lease also provided for binding arbitration in Miami of certain condemnation disputes, and Rudzewicz conceded the validity of this provision at oral argument. Although it does not govern the instant dispute, this provision also should have made it apparent to the franchisees that they were dealing directly with the Miami headquarters and that the Birmingham district office was not "for all intents and purposes the embodiment of Burger King."

[25] Complaining that "when Burger King is the plaintiff, you won't 'have it your way' because it sues all franchisees in Miami," Rudzewicz contends that Florida's interest in providing a convenient forum is negligible given the company's size and ability to conduct litigation anywhere in the country. We disagree. Absent compelling considerations, cf. *McGee v. International Life Insurance Co.*, a defendant who has purposefully derived commercial benefit from his affiliations in a forum may not defeat jurisdiction there simply because of his adversary's greater net wealth.

[26] Rudzewicz has failed to show how the District Court's exercise of jurisdiction in this case might have been at all inconsistent with Michigan's interests. To the contrary, the court found that Burger King had fully complied with Michigan law, and there is nothing in Michigan's franchise Act suggesting that Michigan would attempt to assert exclusive jurisdiction to resolve franchise disputes affecting its residents. In any event, minimum-contacts analysis presupposes that two or more States may be interested in the outcome of a dispute, and the process of resolving potentially conflicting "fundamental substantive social policies," *World-Wide Volkswagen*, can usually be accommodated through choice-of-law rules rather than through outright preclusion of jurisdiction in one forum.

the contrary were merely "boilerplate declarations in a lengthy printed contract." Rudzewicz presented many of these arguments to the District Court, contending that Burger King was guilty of misrepresentation, fraud, and duress; that it gave insufficient notice in its dealings with him; and that the contract was one of adhesion. After a 3-day bench trial, the District Court found that Burger King had made no misrepresentations, that Rudzewicz and MacShara "were and are experienced and sophisticated businessmen," and that "at no time" did they "ac[t] under economic duress or disadvantage imposed by" Burger King. Federal Rule of Civil Procedure 52(a) requires that "[f]indings of fact shall not be set aside unless clearly erroneous," and neither Rudzewicz nor the Court of Appeals has pointed to record evidence that would support a "definite and firm conviction" that the District Court's findings are mistaken. To the contrary, Rudzewicz was represented by counsel throughout these complex transactions and, as Judge Johnson observed in dissent below, was himself an experienced accountant "who for five months conducted negotiations with Burger King over the terms of the franchise and lease agreements, and who obligated himself personally to contracts requiring over time payments that exceeded $ 1 million." Rudzewicz was able to secure a modest reduction in rent and other concessions from Miami headquarters; moreover, to the extent that Burger King's terms were inflexible, Rudzewicz presumably decided that the advantages of affiliating with a national organization provided sufficient commercial benefits to offset the detriments.

III

Notwithstanding these considerations, the Court of Appeals apparently believed that it was necessary to reject jurisdiction in this case as a prophylactic measure, reasoning that an affirmance of the District Court's judgment would result in the exercise of jurisdiction over "out-of-state consumers to collect payments due on modest personal purchases" and would "sow the seeds of default judgments against franchisees owing smaller debts." We share the Court of Appeals' broader concerns and therefore reject any talismanic jurisdictional formulas; "the facts of each case must [always] be weighed" in determining whether personal jurisdiction would comport with "fair play and substantial justice."[29] The "quality and nature" of an interstate transaction may sometimes be so "random," "fortuitous," or "attenuated" that it cannot fairly be said that the potential defendant "should reasonably anticipate being haled into court" in another jurisdiction. We also have emphasized that jurisdiction may not be grounded on a contract whose terms have been obtained through "fraud, undue influence, or overweening bargaining power" and whose application would render litigation "so gravely difficult and inconvenient that [a party] will for all practical purposes be deprived of his day in court." The Bremen v. Zapata Off-Shore Co., 407 U.S., at 12, 18. Cf. Fuentes v. Shevin, 407 U.S. 67, 94-96 (1972); National Equipment Rental, Ltd. v. Szukhent, 375 U.S. 311, 329 (1964)(Black, J., dissenting) (jurisdictional rules may not be employed against small consumers so as to "crippl[e] their defense"). Just as the Due Process Clause allows flexibility in ensuring that commercial actors are not effectively "judgment proof" for the consequences of obligations they voluntarily assume in other States, so too does it prevent rules that would unfairly enable them to obtain default judgments against unwitting customers.

---

[29] This approach does, of course, preclude clear-cut jurisdictional rules. But any inquiry into "fair play and substantial justice" necessarily requires determinations "in which few answers will be written 'in black and white. The grays are dominant and even among them the shades are innumerable.'" *Kulko.*

B. Constitutional Limits on Personal Jurisdiction

For the reasons set forth above, however, these dangers are not present in the instant case. Because Rudzewicz established a substantial and continuing relationship with Burger King's Miami headquarters, received fair notice from the contract documents and the course of dealing that he might be subject to suit in Florida, and has failed to demonstrate how jurisdiction in that forum would otherwise be fundamentally unfair, we conclude that the District Court's exercise of jurisdiction pursuant to FLA. STAT. § 48.193(1)(g) (Supp. 1984) did not offend due process. The judgment of the Court of Appeals is accordingly reversed, and the case is remanded for further proceedings consistent with this opinion.

It is so ordered.

JUSTICE STEVENS, with whom JUSTICE WHITE joins, dissenting.

* * *

In my opinion there is a significant element of unfairness in requiring a franchisee to defend a case of this kind in the forum chosen by the franchisor. It is undisputed that appellee maintained no place of business in Florida, that he had no employees in that State, and that he was not licensed to do business there. Appellee did not prepare his French fries, shakes, and hamburgers in Michigan, and then deliver them into the stream of commerce "with the expectation that they [would] be purchased by consumers in" Florida. To the contrary, appellee did business only in Michigan, his business, property, and payroll taxes were payable in that State, and he sold all of his products there.

Throughout the business relationship, appellee's principal contacts with appellant were with its Michigan office. Notwithstanding its disclaimer, the Court seems ultimately to rely on nothing more than standard boilerplate language contained in various documents, to establish that appellee "'purposefully availed himself of the benefits and protections of Florida's laws.'" Such superficial analysis creates a potential for unfairness not only in negotiations between franchisors and their franchisees but, more significantly, in the resolution of the disputes that inevitably arise from time to time in such relationships.

Judge Vance's opinion for the Court of Appeals for the Eleventh Circuit adequately explains why I would affirm the judgment of that court. I particularly find the following more persuasive than what this Court has written today:

> "Nothing in the course of negotiations gave Rudzewicz reason to anticipate a Burger King suit outside of Michigan. The only face-to-face or even oral contact Rudzewicz had with Burger King throughout months of protracted negotiations was with representatives of the Michigan office. Burger King had the Michigan office interview Rudzewicz and MacShara, appraise their application, discuss price terms, recommend the site which the defendants finally agreed to, and attend the final closing ceremony. There is no evidence that Rudzewicz ever negotiated with anyone in Miami or even sent mail there during negotiations. He maintained no staff in the state of Florida, and as far as the record reveals, he has never even visited the state.

> "The contracts contemplated the startup of a local Michigan restaurant whose profits would derive solely from food sales made to customers in Drayton Plains.

The sale, which involved the use of an intangible trademark in Michigan and occupancy of a Burger King facility there, required no performance in the state of Florida. Under the contract, the local Michigan district office was responsible for providing all of the services due Rudzewicz, including advertising and management consultation. Supervision, moreover, emanated from that office alone. To Rudzewicz, the Michigan office was for all intents and purposes the embodiment of Burger King. He had reason to believe that his working relationship with Burger King began and ended in Michigan, not at the distant and anonymous Florida headquarters....

"Given that the office in Rudzewicz' home state conducted all of the negotiations and wholly supervised the contract, we believe that he had reason to assume that the state of the supervisory office would be the same state in which Burger King would file suit. Rudzewicz lacked fair notice that the distant corporate headquarters which insulated itself from direct dealings with him would later seek to assert jurisdiction over him in the courts of its own home state....

"Just as Rudzewicz lacked notice of the possibility of suit in Florida, he was financially unprepared to meet its added costs. The franchise relationship in particular is fraught with potential for financial surprise. The device of the franchise gives local retailers the access to national trademark recognition which enables them to compete with better-financed, more efficient chain stores. This national affiliation, however, does not alter the fact that the typical franchise store is a local concern serving at best a neighborhood or community. Neither the revenues of a local business nor the geographical range of its market prepares the average franchise owner for the cost of distant litigation....

"The particular distribution of bargaining power in the franchise relationship further impairs the franchisee's financial preparedness. In a franchise contract, 'the franchisor normally occupies [the] dominant role'....

"We discern a characteristic disparity of bargaining power in the facts of this case. There is no indication that Rudzewicz had any latitude to negotiate a reduced rent or franchise fee in exchange for the added risk of suit in Florida. He signed a standard form contract whose terms were non-negotiable and which appeared in some respects to vary from the more favorable terms agreed to in earlier discussions. In fact, the final contract required a minimum monthly rent computed on a base far in excess of that discussed in oral negotiations. Burger King resisted price concessions, only to sue Rudzewicz far from home. In doing so, it severely impaired his ability to call Michigan witnesses who might be essential to his defense and counterclaim.

"In sum, we hold that the circumstances of the Drayton Plains franchise and the negotiations which led to it left Rudzewicz bereft of reasonable notice and financially unprepared for the prospect of franchise litigation in Florida. Jurisdiction under these circumstances would offend the fundamental fairness which is the touchstone of due process."

Accordingly, I respectfully dissent.

B. Constitutional Limits on Personal Jurisdiction

NOTES AND QUESTIONS

1. *Burger King*, like *World-Wide Volkswagen*, addresses both the need for purposeful contacts and the requirement that the forum be reasonable. Review Justice Brennan's discussion of reasonableness. Is he suggesting, contrary to *World-Wide Volkswagen*, that if a forum is very reasonable and convenient, there might be jurisdiction, even if the defendant has no "contacts" with the forum. Can you imagine a fact pattern in which jurisdiction would be convenient and reasonable in a forum with which the defendant lacked sufficient contacts?

2. The *Burger King* Court notes that states have an interest in providing their citizens with a courtroom. However, *World-Wide Volkswagen* certainly made clear that a state interest is not a substitute for purposeful contacts. While *Burger King* reaffirms that, the Court seems to reintroduce state interest as a factor in the reasonableness analysis. What does state interest mean in this context? Aren't states the best judges of their own interests and, therefore, if a state wants to assert jurisdiction doesn't that necessarily mean that it has an interest? Should the fact that the state wants to assert jurisdiction be a factor that weighs in favor of jurisdiction?

3. Suppose a West Virginia construction company orders an expensive piece of equipment from a manufacturer in Wisconsin. The contract calls for the equipment to be delivered "F.O.B. at the seller's plant in Wisconsin," meaning the buyer takes title to and assumes the risk for the equipment at the sellers plant. When a dispute arises over payment, the Wisconsin seller sues the West Virginia buyer in Wisconsin. Is there jurisdiction? Would West Virginia have jurisdiction over the seller if the buyer brought suit there? Would your answer to either question change if the seller had arranged for the transportation of the equipment to West Virginia? Would your answer change if the item in question was a $300 tool purchased by a consumer from a catalogue?

4. In *Burger King*, the Court treats the choice of law clause in the contract as significant. In many respects, a choice of law clause is simply an alternative mechanism for the parties to specify in detail the meanings of terms in the contract. Rather than doing this directly, however, the parties select a body of law, thereby giving some additional certainty to the meanings of the terms. The parties might choose the law of a state that has nothing to do with the contract or the parties, simply because that state's law is clear and well defined on the matters that are of concern to the parties. See Restatement (Second) of the Law of Conflict of Laws § 187 (1971). If the parties had specified that this contract was to be interpreted under the laws of California, would that have subjected the defendant to jurisdiction in California?

5. In addition to choice of law clauses, parties sometimes include a forum selection clause in contracts. Such a clause specifies where any litigation is to occur. These clauses are usually used to reinforce a choice of law clause because the best way to insure that the "real" Florida law is applied is to litigate in Florida. See Richard Freer, Erie's *Mid-Life Crisis*, 63 TULANE L. REV. 1087, 1134-39 (1989). Why would the parties include a choice of law clause but not include a choice of forum clause? Professor Weintraub has suggested that one reason may have been that the Michigan Franchise Investment Act, as interpreted at that time, prohibited contract provisions requiring franchisees to litigate in other states. RUSSELL WEINTRAUB, COMMENTARY ON THE CONFLICT OF LAWS 139 (3d ed. 1986). Does Justice Brennan's reliance on the choice of law clause allow franchisors to achieve indirectly the prohibited effect of a choice of forum clause?

Asahi Metal Industry Co. v. Superior Court of California
480 U.S. 102, 107 S.Ct. 1026, 94 L. Ed. 2d 92 (1987)

JUSTICE O'CONNOR announced the judgment of the Court and delivered the unanimous opinion of the Court with respect to Part I, the opinion of the Court with respect to Part II-B, in which THE CHIEF JUSTICE, JUSTICE BRENNAN, JUSTICE WHITE, JUSTICE MARSHALL, JUSTICE BLACKMUN, JUSTICE POWELL, and JUSTICE STEVENS join, and an opinion with respect to Parts II-A and III, in which THE CHIEF JUSTICE, JUSTICE POWELL, and JUSTICE SCALIA join.

This case presents the question whether the mere awareness on the part of a foreign defendant that the components it manufactured, sold, and delivered outside the United States would reach the forum State in the stream of commerce constitutes "minimum contacts" between the defendant and the forum State such that the exercise of jurisdiction "does not offend 'traditional notions of fair play and substantial justice.'"

I

[In 1978, Gary Zurcher was seriously injured when he lost control of his Honda motorcycle. Zurcher alleged that the accident was caused by a defective rear tire which suddenly lost air. Zurcher sued several defendants, including Cheng Shin, the Taiwanese manufacturer of the tire tube. Cheng Shin in turn filed a third party claim for indemnification (see Fed. R. Civ. P. 14, for the federal court equivalent) against Asahi, the Japanese manufacturer of the tube's valve assembly. Zurcher ultimately settled with Cheng Shin and the other defendants, leaving only Cheng Shin's indemnification claim against Asahi. Asahi moved to dismiss this claim for lack of personal jurisdiction.]

* * *

In relation to the motion, the following information was submitted by Asahi and Cheng Shin. Asahi is a Japanese corporation. It manufactures tire valve assemblies in Japan and sells the assemblies to Cheng Shin, and to several other tire manufacturers, for use as components in finished

B. Constitutional Limits on Personal Jurisdiction

tire tubes. Asahi's sales to Cheng Shin took place in Taiwan. The shipments from Asahi to Cheng Shin were sent from Japan to Taiwan. Cheng Shin bought and incorporated into its tire tubes 150,000 Asahi valve assemblies in 1978; 500,000 in 1979; 500,000 in 1980; 100,000 in 1981; and 100,000 in 1982. Sales to Cheng Shin accounted for 1.24 percent of Asahi's income in 1981 and 0.44 percent in 1982. Cheng Shin alleged that approximately 20 percent of its sales in the United States are in California. Cheng Shin purchases valve assemblies from other suppliers as well, and sells finished tubes throughout the world.

In 1983 an attorney for Cheng Shin conducted an informal examination of the valve stems of the tire tubes sold in one cycle store in Solano County. The attorney declared that of the approximately 115 tire tubes in the store, 97 were purportedly manufactured in Japan or Taiwan, and of those 97, 21 valve stems were marked with the circled letter "A," apparently Asahi's trademark. Of the 21 Asahi valve stems, 12 were incorporated into Cheng Shin tire tubes. The store contained 41 other Cheng Shin tubes that incorporated the valve assemblies of other manufacturers. An affidavit of a manager of Cheng Shin whose duties included the purchasing of component parts stated: "'In discussions with Asahi regarding the purchase of valve stem assemblies the fact that my Company sells tubes throughout the world and specifically the United States has been discussed. I am informed and believe that Asahi was fully aware that valve stem assemblies sold to my Company and to others would end up throughout the United States and in California.'" An affidavit of the president of Asahi, on the other hand, declared that Asahi "'has never contemplated that its limited sales of tire valves to Cheng Shin in Taiwan would subject it to lawsuits in California.'" The record does not include any contract between Cheng Shin and Asahi.

* * *

[The California Supreme Court held that California had jurisdiction over Asahi.]

II

A

The Due Process Clause of the Fourteenth Amendment limits the power of a state court to exert personal jurisdiction over a nonresident defendant. "[T]he constitutional touchstone" of the determination whether an exercise of personal jurisdiction comports with due process "remains whether the defendant purposefully established 'minimum contacts' in the forum State." *Burger King Corp. v. Rudzewicz*, most recently we have reaffirmed the oft-quoted reasoning of *Hanson v. Denckla*, that minimum contacts must have a basis in "some act by which the defendant purposefully avails itself of the privilege of conducting activities within the forum State, thus invoking the benefits and protections of its laws." *Burger King*. "Jurisdiction is proper ... where the contacts proximately result from actions by the defendant *himself* that create a 'substantial connection' with the forum State."

Applying the principle that minimum contacts must be based on an act of the defendant, the Court in *World-Wide Volkswagen Corp.*, rejected the assertion that a *consumer's* unilateral act of bringing the defendant's product into the forum State was a sufficient constitutional basis for personal jurisdiction over the defendant. * * *

CHAPTER 2   PERSONAL JURISDICTION

* * *

* * * Since *World-Wide Volkswagen*, lower courts have been confronted with cases in which the defendant acted by placing a product in the stream of commerce, and the stream eventually swept defendant's product into the forum State, but the defendant did nothing else to purposefully avail itself of the market in the forum State. Some courts have understood the Due Process Clause, as interpreted in *World-Wide Volkswagen*, to allow an exercise of personal jurisdiction to be based on no more than the defendant's act of placing the product in the stream of commerce. Other courts have understood the Due Process Clause and the above-quoted language in *World-Wide Volkswagen* to require the action of the defendant to be more purposefully directed at the forum State than the mere act of placing a product in the stream of commerce.

* * *

We now find this latter position to be consonant with the requirements of due process. The "substantial connection" between the defendant and the forum State necessary for a finding of minimum contacts must come about by *an action of the defendant purposefully directed toward the forum State*. The placement of a product into the stream of commerce, without more, is not an act of the defendant purposefully directed toward the forum State. Additional conduct of the defendant may indicate an intent or purpose to serve the market in the forum State, for example, designing the product for the market in the forum State, advertising in the forum State, establishing channels for providing regular advice to customers in the forum State, or marketing the product through a distributor who has agreed to serve as the sales agent in the forum State. But a defendant's awareness that the stream of commerce may or will sweep the product into the forum State does not convert the mere act of placing the product into the stream into an act purposefully directed toward the forum State.

Assuming, arguendo, that respondents have established Asahi's awareness that some of the valves sold to Cheng Shin would be incorporated into tire tubes sold in California, respondents have not demonstrated any action by Asahi to purposefully avail itself of the California market. Asahi does not do business in California. It has no office, agents, employees, or property in California. It does not advertise or otherwise solicit business in California. It did not create, control, or employ the distribution system that brought its valves to California. There is no evidence that Asahi designed its product in anticipation of sales in California. On the basis of these facts, the exertion of personal jurisdiction over Asahi by the Superior Court of California exceeds the limits of due process.

B

The strictures of the Due Process Clause forbid a state court from exercising personal jurisdiction over Asahi under circumstances that would offend "'traditional notions of fair play and substantial justice.'"

B. Constitutional Limits on Personal Jurisdiction

We have previously explained that the determination of the reasonableness of the exercise of jurisdiction in each case will depend on an evaluation of several factors. A court must consider the burden on the defendant, the interests of the forum State, and the plaintiff's interest in obtaining relief. It must also weigh in its determination "the interstate judicial system's interest in obtaining the most efficient resolution of controversies; and the shared interest of the several States in furthering fundamental substantive social policies." *World-Wide Volkswagen*.

A consideration of these factors in the present case clearly reveals the unreasonableness of the assertion of jurisdiction over Asahi, even apart from the question of the placement of goods in the stream of commerce.

Certainly the burden on the defendant in this case is severe. Asahi has been commanded by the Supreme Court of California not only to traverse the distance between Asahi's headquarters in Japan and the Superior Court of California in and for the County of Solano, but also to submit its dispute with Cheng Shin to a foreign nation's judicial system. The unique burdens placed upon one who must defend oneself in a foreign legal system should have significant weight in assessing the reasonableness of stretching the long arm of personal jurisdiction over national borders.

When minimum contacts have been established, often the interests of the plaintiff and the forum in the exercise of jurisdiction will justify even the serious burdens placed on the alien defendant. In the present case, however, the interests of the plaintiff and the forum in California's assertion of jurisdiction over Asahi are slight. All that remains is a claim for indemnification asserted by Cheng Shin, a Taiwanese corporation, against Asahi. The transaction on which the indemnification claim is based took place in Taiwan; Asahi's components were shipped from Japan to Taiwan. Cheng Shin has not demonstrated that it is more convenient for it to litigate its indemnification claim against Asahi in California rather than in Taiwan or Japan.

Because the plaintiff is not a California resident, California's legitimate interests in the dispute have considerably diminished. The Supreme Court of California argued that the State had an interest in "protecting its consumers by ensuring that foreign manufacturers comply with the state's safety standards." The State Supreme Court's definition of California's interest, however, was overly broad. The dispute between Cheng Shin and Asahi is primarily about indemnification rather than safety standards. Moreover, it is not at all clear at this point that California law should govern the question whether a Japanese corporation should indemnify a Taiwanese corporation on the basis of a sale made in Taiwan and a shipment of goods from Japan to Taiwan. The possibility of being haled into a California court as a result of an accident involving Asahi's components undoubtedly creates an additional deterrent to the manufacture of unsafe components; however, similar pressures will be placed on Asahi by the purchasers of its components as long as those who use Asahi components in their final products, and sell those products in California, are subject to the application of California tort law.

World-Wide Volkswagen also admonished courts to take into consideration the interests of the "several States," in addition to the forum State, in the efficient judicial resolution of the dispute and the advancement of substantive policies. In the present case, this advice calls for a court to consider the procedural and substantive policies of other nations whose interests are affected by the assertion of jurisdiction by the California court. The procedural and substantive interests of other nations in a state court's assertion of jurisdiction over an alien defendant will differ from case to case. In every case, however, those interests, as well as the Federal Government's interest in its foreign relations policies, will be best served by a careful inquiry into the reasonableness of the assertion of jurisdiction in the particular case, and an unwillingness to find the serious burdens on an alien defendant outweighed by minimal interests on the part of the plaintiff or the forum State. "Great care and reserve should be exercised when extending our notions of personal jurisdiction into the international field." United States v. First National City Bank, 379 U.S. 378, 404 (1965) (Harlan, J., dissenting).

Considering the international context, the heavy burden on the alien defendant, and the slight interests of the plaintiff and the forum State, the exercise of personal jurisdiction by a California court over Asahi in this instance would be unreasonable and unfair.

III

Because the facts of this case do not establish minimum contacts such that the exercise of personal jurisdiction is consistent with fair play and substantial justice, the judgment of the Supreme Court of California is reversed, and the case is remanded for further proceedings not inconsistent with this opinion.

It is so ordered.

JUSTICE BRENNAN, with whom JUSTICE WHITE, JUSTICE MARSHALL, and JUSTICE BLACKMUN join, concurring in part and concurring in the judgment.

I do not agree with the interpretation in Part II-A of the stream-of-commerce theory, nor with the conclusion that Asahi did not "purposely avail itself of the California market." I do agree, however, with the Court's conclusion in Part II-B that the exercise of personal jurisdiction over Asahi in this case would not comport with "fair play and substantial justice," This is one of those rare cases in which "minimum requirements inherent in the concept of 'fair play and substantial justice' ... defeat the reasonableness of jurisdiction even [though] the defendant has purposefully engaged in forum activities." *Burger King Corp. v. Rudzewicz*. I therefore join Parts I and II-B of the Court's opinion, and write separately to explain my disagreement with Part II-A.

* * * The stream of commerce refers not to unpredictable currents or eddies, but to the regular and anticipated flow of products from manufacture to distribution to retail sale. As long as a participant in this process is aware that the final product is being marketed in the forum State, the possibility of a lawsuit there cannot come as a surprise. Nor will the litigation present a burden for which there is no corresponding benefit. A defendant who has placed goods in the stream of commerce benefits economically from the retail sale of the final product in the forum State, and indirectly benefits from the State's laws that regulate and facilitate commercial activity. These benefits accrue regardless of whether that participant directly conducts business in the forum State, or engages in additional conduct directed toward that State. Accordingly, most courts and commentators have found that jurisdiction premised on the placement of a product into the stream of commerce is consistent with the Due Process Clause, and have not required a showing of additional conduct.

The endorsement in Part II-A of what appears to be the minority view among Federal Courts of Appeals represents a marked retreat from the analysis in *World-Wide Volkswagen*. * * *

B. Constitutional Limits on Personal Jurisdiction

* * *

The Court [in that case] concluded its illustration by referring to *Gray v. American Radiator & Standard Sanitary Corp.* a well-known stream-of-commerce case in which the Illinois Supreme Court applied the theory to assert jurisdiction over a component-parts manufacturer that sold no components directly in Illinois, but did sell them to a manufacturer who incorporated them into a final product that was sold in Illinois.

The Court in *World-Wide Volkswagen* thus took great care to distinguish "between a case involving goods which reach a distant State through a chain of distribution and a case involving goods which reach the same State because a consumer ... took them there." The California Supreme Court took note of this distinction, and correctly concluded that our holding in *World-Wide Volkswagen* preserved the stream-of-commerce theory.

In this case, the facts found by the California Supreme Court support its finding of minimum contacts. The court found that "[a]lthough Asahi did not design or control the system of distribution that carried its valve assemblies into California, Asahi was aware of the distribution system's operation, and it knew that it would benefit economically from the sale in California of products incorporating its components." Accordingly, I cannot join the determination in Part II-A that Asahi's regular and extensive sales of component parts to a manufacturer it knew was making regular sales of the final product in California is insufficient to establish minimum contacts with California.

JUSTICE STEVENS, with whom JUSTICE WHITE and JUSTICE BLACKMUN join, concurring in part and concurring in the judgment.

The judgment of the Supreme Court of California should be reversed for the reasons stated in Part II-B of the Court's opinion. While I join Parts I and II-B, I do not join Part II-A for two reasons. First, it is not necessary to the Court's decision. * * * [T]his case fits within the rule that "minimum requirements inherent in the concept of 'fair play and substantial justice' may defeat the reasonableness of jurisdiction even if the defendant has purposefully engaged in forum activities." *Burger King*. Accordingly, I see no reason in this case for the plurality to articulate "purposeful direction" or any other test as the nexus between an act of a defendant and the forum State that is necessary to establish minimum contacts.

Second, even assuming that the test ought to be formulated here, Part II-A misapplies it to the facts of this case. The plurality seems to assume that an unwavering line can be drawn between "mere awareness" that a component will find its way into the forum State and "purposeful availment" of the forum's market. Over the course of its dealings with Cheng Shin, Asahi has arguably engaged in a higher quantum of conduct than "[t]he placement of a product into the stream of commerce, without more...." Whether or not this conduct rises to the level of purposeful availment requires a constitutional determination that is affected by the volume, the value, and the hazardous character of the components. In most circumstances I would be inclined to conclude that a regular course of dealing that results in deliveries of over 100,000 units annually over a period of several years would constitute "purposeful availment" even though the item delivered to the forum State was a standard product marketed throughout the world.

NOTES AND QUESTIONS

1. *World-Wide Volkswagen* specified the two separate concerns of contacts and reasonableness. While *World-Wide Volkswagen* treated these as entirely separate inquiries, *Burger King* seemed to be bringing these two prongs back together. Has *Asahi* split them entirely apart again?

2. Seven other Justices concurred in Justice O'Connor's Part 2B, which found that California was an unreasonable forum. Do you think the result would have been different if:

(a) Zurcher's claim against Cheng Shin had not settled.
(b) Zurcher had sued Asahi.
(c) Asahi were a New York corporation instead of a Japanese Corporation.

3. The Court expresses concern about "extending our notions of personal jurisdiction into the international field." Should the Court have considered whether other countries would exercise jurisdiction under similar circumstances? See Russell Weintraub, *Asahi Sends Personal Jurisdiction Down the Tubes*, 23 TEX. INT'L L.J. 55, 64-66 (1988).

4. Part II, concluding that Asahi does not have sufficient purposeful contacts with California, did not command a majority of the Court. Only four justices accepted that portion of the opinion. Similarly, Justice Brennan's analysis of Asahi's purposeful contacts garnered a total of four votes. Justice Stevens' analysis on this point garnered three votes. What are other courts to do when the Supreme Court issues only plurality opinions? In Marks v. United States, 430 U.S. 188, 193 (1977), the Supreme Court said of this situation: "When a fragmented Court decides a case and no single rationale explaining the result enjoys the assent of five Justices, 'the holding of the Court may be viewed as that position taken by those Members who concurred in the judgments on the narrowest grounds.'" Does this help in *Asahi*?

5. Consider Justice O'Connor's "contacts" analysis. Does she seem to believe that conduct directed at the forum is always required? Or is such conduct sufficient, but not necessary, evidence of "an intent or purpose to serve the market?"

6. Now consider Justice Brennan's position. Is he saying that a manufacturer's knowledge of where its component might end up is always sufficient? Does he believe that knowledge is necessary? Can a manufacturer avoid jurisdiction by not asking a distributor where the product is resold?

7. How different is Justice Stevens' position from that of Justice Brennan?

8. What advice would you give a component manufacturer that sought to limit where it was subject to personal jurisdiction?

9. After *Asahi*, lower courts have split on the question of how to evaluate stream of commerce cases. Some courts have applied the dicta of *World-Wide Volkswagen* as they did prior to *Asahi* and used an approach that resembles Justice Brennan's *Asahi* opinion. See Dehmlow v. Austin Fireworks, 963 F.2d 941, 947 (7th Cir. 1992); Irving v. Owens-Corning Fiberglas Corp., 864 F.2d 383, 386 (5th Cir.), *cert. denied*, 493 U.S. 823 (1989). Other courts have also looked to pre-*Asahi* law, but adopted an approach more closely resembling Justice O'Connor's *Asahi* opinion. See Lesnick v. Hollingsworth & Vose Co., 35 F.3d 939, 945-946 (4th Cir. 1994), *cert. denied*, 115 S. Ct. 1103 (1995); Boit v. Gar-Tec Products, Inc., 967 F.2d 671, 682-683 (1st Cir. 1992); Falkirk Mining Co. v. Japan Steel Works, Ltd., 906 F.2d 369, 375-376 (8th Cir. 1990). Finally, at least one court has explicitly adopted the approach articulated by Justice Stevens in *Asahi*. See Abuan v. General Electric Co., 735 F. Supp. 1479, 1485-86 (D. Guam 1990), *aff'd on other grounds*, 3 F.3d 329 (9th Cir.), *cert. denied*, 114 S. Ct. 1064 (1994).

10. While the *Asahi* case was pending in California, Cheng Shin sued Asahi in Japan. Following the Supreme Court's decidion and the dismissal of the suit in California, Asahi settled the Japanese suit for $20,000, a sum Asahi's lawyer considered minimal in light of litigation costs. See Christopher Cameron & Kevin Johnson, *Death of a Salesman? Forum Shopping and Outcome Determination Under* International Shoe, 28 U. C. DAVIS L. REV. 769, 860 (1995). Apparently the reason the settlement was so small was that by the time of the settlement, Asahi had acquired strong evidence that the valve in question was not manufactured by Asahi!

4. General Jurisdiction

Helicopteros Nacionales de Colombia, S. A. v. Hall
466 U.S. 408, 104 S.Ct. 1868, 80 L. Ed. 2d 404 (1984)

JUSTICE BLACKMUN delivered the opinion of the Court.

We granted certiorari in this case, to decide whether the Supreme Court of Texas correctly ruled that the contacts of a foreign corporation with the State of Texas were sufficient to allow a Texas state court to assert jurisdiction over the corporation in a cause of action not arising out of or related to the corporation's activities within the State.

I

Petitioner Helicopters Nacionales de Colombia, S. A. (Helicol), is a Colombian corporation with its principal place of business in the city of Bogota in that country. It is engaged in the business of providing helicopter transportation for oil and construction companies in South America. On January 26, 1976, a helicopter owned by Helicol crashed in Peru. Four United States citizens were

CHAPTER 2 PERSONAL JURISDICTION

among those who lost their lives in the accident. Respondents are the survivors and representatives of the four decedents.

At the time of the crash, respondents' decedents were employed by Consorcio, a Peruvian consortium, and were working on a pipeline in Peru. Consorcio is the alter ego of a joint venture named Williams-Sedco-Horn (WSH). The venture had its headquarters in Houston, Tex. Consorcio had been formed to enable the venturers to enter into a contract with Petro Peru, the Peruvian state-owned oil company. Consorcio was to construct a pipeline for Petro Peru running from the interior of Peru westward to the Pacific Ocean. Peruvian law forbade construction of the pipeline by any non-Peruvian entity.

Consorcio/WSH needed helicopters to move personnel, materials, and equipment into and out of the construction area. In 1974, upon request of Consorcio/WSH, the chief executive officer of Helicol, Francisco Restrepo, flew to the United States and conferred in Houston with representatives of the three joint venturers. At that meeting, there was a discussion of prices, availability, working conditions, fuel, supplies, and housing. Restrepo represented that Helicol could have the first helicopter on the job in 15 days. The Consorcio/WSH representatives decided to accept the contract proposed by Restrepo. Helicol began performing before the agreement was formally signed in Peru on November 11, 1974. The contract was written in Spanish on official government stationery and provided that the residence of all the parties would be Lima, Peru. It further stated that controversies arising out of the contract would be submitted to the jurisdiction of Peruvian courts. In addition, it provided that Consorcio/WSH would make payments to Helicol's account with the Bank of America in New York City.

Aside from the negotiation session in Houston between Restrepo and the representatives of Consorcio/WSH, Helicol had other contacts with Texas. During the years 1970-1977, it purchased helicopters (approximately 80% of its fleet), spare parts, and accessories for more than $4 million from Bell Helicopter Company in Fort Worth. In that period, Helicol sent prospective pilots to Fort Worth for training and to ferry the aircraft to South America. It also sent management and maintenance personnel to visit Bell Helicopter in Fort Worth during the same period in order to receive "plant familiarization" and for technical consultation. Helicol received into its New York City and Panama City, Fla., bank accounts over $5 million in payments from Consorcio/WSH drawn upon First City National Bank of Houston.

Beyond the foregoing, there have been no other business contacts between Helicol and the State of Texas. Helicol never has been authorized to do business in Texas and never has had an agent for the service of process within the State. It never has performed helicopter operations in Texas or sold any product that reached Texas, never solicited business in Texas, never signed any contract in Texas, never had any employee based there, and never recruited an employee in Texas. In addition, Helicol never has owned real or personal property in Texas and never has maintained an office or establishment there. Helicol has maintained no records in Texas and has no shareholders in that State. None of the respondents or their decedents were domiciled in Texas,[5] but all of the decedents were hired in Houston by Consorcio/WSH to work on the Petro Peru pipeline project.

---

[5] Respondents' lack of residential or other contacts with Texas of itself does not defeat otherwise proper jurisdiction. *Keeton v. Hustler Magazine, Inc.*; *Calder v. Jones*. We mention respondents' lack of contacts merely to show that nothing in the nature of the relationship between respondents and Helicol could possibly enhance Helicol's contacts with Texas. The harm suffered by respondents did not occur in Texas. Nor is it alleged that any negligence on the part of Helicol took place in Texas.

B. Constitutional Limits on Personal Jurisdiction

Respondents instituted wrongful-death actions in the District Court of Harris County, Tex., against Consorcio/WSH, Bell Helicopter Company, and Helicol. Helicol filed special appearances and moved to dismiss the actions for lack of in personam jurisdiction over it. The motion was denied. After a consolidated jury trial, judgment was entered against Helicol on a jury verdict of $ 1,141,200 in favor of respondents.

* * * In ruling that the Texas courts had in personam jurisdiction, the Texas Supreme Court first held that the State's long-arm statute reaches as far as the Due Process Clause of the Fourteenth Amendment permits. Thus, the only question remaining for the court to decide was whether it was consistent with the Due Process Clause for Texas courts to assert in personam jurisdiction over Helicol.

II

The Due Process Clause of the Fourteenth Amendment operates to limit the power of a State to assert in personam jurisdiction over a nonresident defendant. *Pennoyer v. Neff.* Due process requirements are satisfied when in personam jurisdiction is asserted over a nonresident corporate defendant that has" certain minimum contacts with [the forum] such that the maintenance of the suit does not offend 'traditional notions of fair play and substantial justice.'" *International Shoe Co. v. Washington.* When a controversy is related to or "arises out of" a defendant's contacts with the forum, the Court has said that a "relationship among the defendant, the forum, and the litigation" is the essential foundation of in personam jurisdiction. *Shaffer v. Heitner.*[8]

Even when the cause of action does not arise out of or relate to the foreign corporation's activities in the forum State,[9] due process is not offended by a State's subjecting the corporation to its in personam jurisdiction when there are sufficient contacts between the State and the foreign corporation. Perkins v. Benguet Consolidated Mining Co., 342 U.S. 437 (1952); see *Keeton v. Hustler Magazine, Inc.* In *Perkins*, the Court addressed a situation in which state courts had asserted general jurisdiction over a defendant foreign corporation. During the Japanese occupation of the Philippine Islands, the president and general manager of a Philippine mining corporation maintained an office in Ohio from which he conducted activities on behalf of the company. He kept company files and held directors' meetings in the office, carried on correspondence relating to the business, distributed salary checks drawn on two active Ohio bank accounts, engaged an Ohio bank to act as transfer agent, and supervised policies dealing with the rehabilitation of the corporation's properties in the Philippines. In short, the foreign corporation, through its president, "ha[d] been carrying on in Ohio a continuous and systematic, but limited, part of its general business," and the exercise of general jurisdiction over the Philippine corporation by an Ohio court was "reasonable and just."

---

[8] It has been said that when a State exercises personal jurisdiction over a defendant in a suit arising out of or related to the defendant's contacts with the forum, the State is exercising "specific jurisdiction" over the defendant. See Von Mehren & Trautman, *Jurisdiction to Adjudicate: A Suggested Analysis*, 79 HARV. L. REV. 1121, 1144-1164 (1966).

[9] When a State exercises personal jurisdiction over a defendant in a suit not arising out of or related to the defendant's contacts with the forum, the State has been said to be exercising "general jurisdiction" over the defendant. See Brilmayer, *How Contacts Count: Due Process Limitations on State Court Jurisdiction*, 1980 S. CT. REV. 77, 80-81; Von Mehren & Trautman, 79 HARV. L. REV. at 1136-1144; *Calder v. Jones.*

All parties to the present case concede that respondents' claims against Helicol did not "arise out of," and are not related to, Helicol's activities within Texas.[10] We thus must explore the nature of Helicol's contacts with the State of Texas to determine whether they constitute the kind of continuous and systematic general business contacts the Court found to exist in *Perkins*. We hold that they do not.

It is undisputed that Helicol does not have a place of business in Texas and never has been licensed to do business in the State. Basically, Helicol's contacts with Texas consisted of sending its chief executive officer to Houston for a contract-negotiation session; accepting into its New York bank account checks drawn on a Houston bank; purchasing helicopters, equipment, and training services from Bell Helicopter for substantial sums; and sending personnel to Bell's facilities in Fort Worth for training.

The one trip to Houston by Helicol's chief executive officer for the purpose of negotiating the transportation-services contract with Consorcio/WSH cannot be described or regarded as a contact of a "continuous and systematic" nature, as *Perkins* described it, and thus cannot support an assertion of in personam jurisdiction over Helicol by a Texas court. Similarly, Helicol's acceptance from Consorcio/WSH of checks drawn on a Texas bank is of negligible significance for purposes of determining whether Helicol had sufficient contacts in Texas. There is no indication that Helicol ever requested that the checks be drawn on a Texas bank or that there was any negotiation between Helicol and Consorcio/WSH with respect to the location or identity of the bank on which checks would be drawn. Common sense and everyday experience suggest that, absent unusual circumstances, the bank on which a check is drawn is generally of little consequence to the payee and is a matter left to the discretion of the drawer. Such unilateral activity of another party or a third person is not an appropriate consideration when determining whether a defendant has sufficient contacts with a forum State to justify an assertion of jurisdiction.

The Texas Supreme Court focused on the purchases and the related training trips in finding contacts sufficient to support an assertion of jurisdiction. We do not agree with that assessment, for the Court's opinion in Rosenberg Bros. & Co. v. Curtis Brown Co., 260 U.S. 516 (1923) (Brandeis, J., for a unanimous tribunal), makes clear that purchases and related trips, standing alone, are not a sufficient basis for a State's assertion of jurisdiction.

---

[10] Because the parties have not argued any relationship between the cause of action and Helicol's contacts with the State of Texas, we, contrary to the dissent's implication, assert no "view" with respect to that issue.

The dissent suggests that we have erred in drawing no distinction between controversies that "relate to" a defendant's contacts with a forum and those that "arise out of" such contacts. This criticism is somewhat puzzling, for the dissent goes on to urge that, for purposes of determining the constitutional validity of an assertion of specific jurisdiction, there really should be no distinction between the two.

We do not address the validity or consequences of such a distinction because the issue has not been presented in this case. Respondents have made no argument that their cause of action either arose out of or is related to Helicol's contacts with the State of Texas. Absent any briefing on the issue, we decline to reach the questions (1) whether the terms "arising out of" and "related to" describe different connections between a cause of action and a defendant's contacts with a forum, and (2) what sort of tie between a cause of action and a defendant's contacts with a forum is necessary to a determination that either connection exists. Nor do we reach the question whether, if the two types of relationship differ, a forum's exercise of personal jurisdiction in a situation where the cause of action "relates to," but does not "arise out of," the defendant's contacts with the forum should be analyzed as an assertion of specific jurisdiction.

B. Constitutional Limits on Personal Jurisdiction

The defendant in *Rosenberg* was a small retailer in Tulsa, Okla., who dealt in men's clothing and furnishings. It never had applied for a license to do business in New York, nor had it at any time authorized suit to be brought against it there. It never had an established place of business in New York and never regularly carried on business in that State. Its only connection with New York was that it purchased from New York wholesalers a large portion of the merchandise sold in its Tulsa store. The purchases sometimes were made by correspondence and sometimes through visits to New York by an officer of the defendant. The Court concluded: "Visits on such business, even if occurring at regular intervals, would not warrant the inference that the corporation was present within the jurisdiction of [New York]."

This Court in *International Shoe* acknowledged and did not repudiate its holding in *Rosenberg*. In accordance with *Rosenberg*, we hold that mere purchases, even if occurring at regular intervals, are not enough to warrant a State's assertion of in personam jurisdiction over a nonresident corporation in a cause of action not related to those purchase transactions.[12] Nor can we conclude that the fact that Helicol sent personnel into Texas for training in connection with the purchase of helicopters and equipment in that State in any way enhanced the nature of Helicol's contacts with Texas. The training was a part of the package of goods and services purchased by Helicol from Bell Helicopter. The brief presence of Helicol employees in Texas for the purpose of attending the training sessions is no more a significant contact than were the trips to New York made by the buyer for the retail store in *Rosenberg*.

III

We hold that Helicol's contacts with the State of Texas were insufficient to satisfy the requirements of the Due Process Clause of the Fourteenth Amendment.[13] Accordingly, we reverse the judgment of the Supreme Court of Texas.

It is so ordered.

JUSTICE BRENNAN, dissenting.

---

[12] This Court in *International Shoe* cited *Rosenberg* for the proposition that "the commission of some single or occasional acts of the corporate agent in a state sufficient to impose an obligation or liability on the corporation has not been thought to confer upon the state authority to enforce it." Arguably, therefore, Rosenberg also stands for the proposition that mere purchases are not a sufficient basis for either general or specific jurisdiction. Because the case before us is one in which there has been an assertion of general jurisdiction over a foreign defendant, we need not decide the continuing validity of *Rosenberg* with respect to an assertion of specific jurisdiction, i.e., where the cause of action arises out of or relates to the purchases by the defendant in the forum State.

[13] As an alternative to traditional minimum-contacts analysis, respondents suggest that the Court hold that the State of Texas had personal jurisdiction over Helicol under a doctrine of "jurisdiction by necessity." See *Shaffer v. Heitner*. We conclude, however, that respondents failed to carry their burden of showing that all three defendants could not be sued together in a single forum. It is not clear from the record, for example, whether suit could have been brought against all three defendants in either Colombia or Peru. We decline to consider adoption of a doctrine of jurisdiction by necessity — a potentially far-reaching modification of existing law — in the absence of a more complete record.

[Justice Brennan first disagrees with the majority's conclusion that there are insufficient contacts for general jurisdiction.]

* * *

II

The Court also fails to distinguish the legal principles that controlled our prior decisions in *Perkins* and *Rosenberg*. In particular, the contacts between petitioner Helicol and the State of Texas, unlike the contacts between the defendant and the forum in each of those cases, are significantly related to the cause of action alleged in the original suit filed by the respondents. Accordingly, in my view, it is both fair and reasonable for the Texas courts to assert specific jurisdiction over Helicol in this case.

By asserting that the present case does not implicate the specific jurisdiction of the Texas courts, the Court necessarily removes its decision from the reality of the actual facts presented for our consideration.[3] Moreover, the Court refuses to consider any distinction between contacts that are "related to" the underlying cause of action and contacts that "give rise" to the underlying cause of action. In my view, however, there is a substantial difference between these two standards for asserting specific jurisdiction. Thus, although I agree that the respondents' cause of action did not formally "arise out of" specific activities initiated by Helicol in the State of Texas, I believe that the wrongful-death claim filed by the respondents is significantly related to the undisputed contacts between Helicol and the forum. On that basis, I would conclude that the Due Process Clause allows the Texas courts to assert specific jurisdiction over this particular action.

The wrongful-death actions filed by the respondents were premised on a fatal helicopter crash that occurred in Peru. Helicol was joined as a defendant in the lawsuits because it provided transportation services, including the particular helicopter and pilot involved in the crash, to the joint venture that employed the decedents. Specifically, the respondent Hall claimed in her original complaint that "Helicol is ... legally responsible for its own negligence through its pilot employee." Viewed in light of these allegations, the contacts between Helicol and the State of Texas are directly and significantly related to the underlying claim filed by the respondents. The negotiations that took place in Texas led to the contract in which Helicol agreed to provide the precise transportation services that were being used at the time of the crash. Moreover, the helicopter involved in the crash

---

[3] Nor do I agree with the Court that the respondents have conceded that their claims are not related to Helicol's activities within the State of Texas. Although parts of their written and oral arguments before the Court proceed on the assumption that no such relationship exists, other portions suggest just the opposite:

"If it is the concern of the Solicitor General [appearing for the United States as amicus curiae] that a holding for Respondents here will cause foreign companies to refrain from purchasing in the United States for fear of exposure to general jurisdiction on unrelated causes of action, such concern is not well founded.

"Respondents' cause is not dependent on a ruling that mere purchases in a state, together with incidental training for operating and maintaining the merchandise purchased can constitute the ties, contacts and relations necessary to justify jurisdiction over an unrelated cause of action. However, regular purchases and training coupled with other contacts, ties and relations may form the basis for jurisdiction." Thus, while the respondents' position before this Court is admittedly less than clear, I believe it is preferable to address the specific jurisdiction of the Texas courts because Helicol's contacts with Texas are in fact related to the underlying cause of action."

was purchased by Helicol in Texas, and the pilot whose negligence was alleged to have caused the crash was actually trained in Texas. This is simply not a case, therefore, in which a state court has asserted jurisdiction over a nonresident defendant on the basis of wholly unrelated contacts with the forum. Rather, the contacts between Helicol and the forum are directly related to the negligence that was alleged in the respondent Hall's original complaint.[4] Because Helicol should have expected to be amenable to suit in the Texas courts for claims directly related to these contacts, it is fair and reasonable to allow the assertion of jurisdiction in this case.

Despite this substantial relationship between the contacts and the cause of action, the Court declines to consider whether the courts of Texas may assert specific jurisdiction over this suit. Apparently, this simply reflects a narrow interpretation of the question presented for review. It is nonetheless possible that the Court's opinion may be read to imply that the specific jurisdiction of the Texas courts is inapplicable because the cause of action did not formally "arise out of" the contacts between Helicol and the forum. In my view, however, such a rule would place unjustifiable limits on the bases under which Texas may assert its jurisdictional power.

Limiting the specific jurisdiction of a forum to cases in which the cause of action formally arose out of the defendant's contacts with the State would subject constitutional standards under the Due Process Clause to the vagaries of the substantive law or pleading requirements of each State. For example, the complaint filed against Helicol in this case alleged negligence based on pilot error. Even though the pilot was trained in Texas, the Court assumes that the Texas courts may not assert jurisdiction over the suit because the cause of action "did not 'arise out of,' and [is] not related to," that training. If, however, the applicable substantive law required that negligent training of the pilot was a necessary element of a cause of action for pilot error, or if the respondents had simply added an allegation of negligence in the training provided for the Helicol pilot, then presumably the Court would concede that the specific jurisdiction of the Texas courts was applicable.

Our interpretation of the Due Process Clause has never been so dependent upon the applicable substantive law or the State's formal pleading requirements. At least since *International Shoe Co. v. Washington*, the principal focus when determining whether a forum may constitutionally assert jurisdiction over a nonresident defendant has been on fairness and reasonableness to the defendant. To this extent, a court's specific jurisdiction should be applicable whenever the cause of action arises out of or relates to the contacts between the defendant and the forum. It is eminently fair and reasonable, in my view, to subject a defendant to suit in a forum with which it has significant contacts directly related to the underlying cause of action. Because Helicol's contacts with the State of Texas meet this standard, I would affirm the judgment of the Supreme Court of Texas.

NOTES AND QUESTIONS

1. The Court defines "general jurisdiction" as that applicable when a claim does not arise from or relate to the defendant's activity in the jurisdiction. The paradigm case of

---

[4] The jury specifically found that "the pilot failed to keep the helicopter under proper control," that "the helicopter was flown into a treetop fog condition, whereby the vision of the pilot was impaired," that "such flying was negligence," and that "such negligence ... was a proximate cause of the crash." On the basis of these findings, Helicol was ordered to pay over $ 1 million in damages to the respondents.

CHAPTER 2 PERSONAL JURISDICTION

general jurisdiction is Perkins v. Benguet Consolidated Mining Co., 342 U.S. 437 (1952). There, the defendant was a Philippine corporation which had fled the Philippine Islands during the Japanese occupation. The limited activities that the corporation conducted were all run from an office in Ohio. The Supreme Court upheld jurisdiction over the defendant in Ohio on a cause of action that had nothing to do with its Ohio activities. *Perkins* is a relatively easy case because there the Court upheld jurisdiction at the defendant's corporate headquarters. Prior to *Perkins*, it was well established that corporations could be sued in their place of incorporation on any claim. You will recall that an analogous rule for individuals permits them to be sued in their domicile. See Milliken v. Meyer, 311 U.S. 457 (1940), supra at 36.

2. Suppose this were a suit by Bell Helicopters against Helicol, alleging Helicol failed to pay for the parts it purchased from Bell. Could such a suit be brought in Texas? Does *Rosenberg*, relied on by the Court in *Helicopteros*, prohibit jurisdiction under these circumstances?

3. Suppose the defendant had four million dollars in *sales* in the forum. Would that be sufficient for general jurisdiction? See Nichols v. G. D. Searle & Co., 991 F.2d 1195 (4th Cir. 1993) (defendant had 17 to 21 employees in the forum and annual sales there of $9 to $13 million; no general jurisdiction); Bearry v. Beech Aircraft Corp., 818 F.2d 370 (5th Cir. 1987) (manufacturer's sales in products worth $250 million over 5 years to independent Texas dealers not sufficient for general jurisdiction in Texas). Cf. *Keeton v. Hustler Magazine, Inc.*, supra at 62 (noting that sales in New Hampshire of 10,000 to 15,000 copies per month of a magazine "may not be so substantial as to support jurisdiction over a cause of action unrelated to those activities"). Compare with Braband v. Beech Aircraft Corp., 382 N.E.2d 252 (Ill. 1978) (manufacturer sold products in Illinois through independent dealer and sponsored sales promotions in Illinois; dealer was required to perform warranty work on all of manufacturer's products and to make records and facilities available to manufacturer for inspection; the court held manufacturer subject to general jurisdiction in Illinois).

Suppose Helicol had a small office and employees located in Texas. Would that be enough? See, e.g., Bankhead Enterprises, Inc. v. Norfolk and W. Ry., 642 F.2d 802 (5th Cir. 1981) (finding general jurisdiction where defendant leased an office and employed sales agents and clerical staff); Bryant v. Finnish Nat'l Airline, 208 N.E.2d 439 (N.Y. 1965)(finding general jurisdiction over foreign airline which maintained a one and a half room office and employed several people). Unfortunately, the Court has never explained what to look for in establishing general jurisdiction. Will anything short of the headquarters suffice? Is the Court looking for a major component of the corporation, or will any physical office be sufficient?

B. Constitutional Limits on Personal Jurisdiction

4. Why have general jurisdiction at all? Isn't specific jurisdiction adequate to provide appropriate fora for litigation? On the other hand, maybe it is useful to have at least one "home base" for each defendant, that is, one place where everyone knows the defendant would be subject to suit on anything. However, if this is the function served by general jurisdiction, shouldn't it be limited to the corporate headquarters? See B. Glenn George, *In Search of General Jurisdiction*, 64 TULANE L. REV. 1097 (1990) (discussing waning importance of general jurisdiction in wake of expansion of specific jurisdiction).

5. Does general jurisdiction apply to individuals as well as corporations? See Burnham v. Superior Court, 495 U.S. 604, 610 n.1 (1990) (Scalia, J.), infra at 110.

6. You will notice that the Court assumes in *Helicopteros* that the cause of action is completely unrelated to the defendant's contacts with Texas. The Court makes this assumption because, according to it, the parties did not argue otherwise. Are the defendants' contacts with Texas really completely unrelated to the cause of action?

Justice Brennan thought that Helicol's contacts with Texas were sufficiently related to the cause of action to subject it to specific jurisdiction. The majority did not address this point because it assumed the parties had conceded that the contacts were completely and absolutely unrelated. How closely must the contacts be related to the cause of action for a case to be deemed a specific jurisdiction case? Is it sufficient that the contacts "relate to" the cause of action, or must the cause of action "arise out of" the contacts?

Suppose, for example, that a Hawaii hotel advertises in Massachusetts. A Massachusetts citizen sees the advertising and goes to the Hawaii hotel, where she slips and falls in her Hawaii hotel room. Can she sue the hotel in Massachusetts? Some courts have held no, reasoning that the advertising was not the proximate cause of the fall. See Marino v. Hyatt Corp., 793 F.2d 427 (1st Cir. 1986). Other courts have reached a contrary conclusion, reasoning that "but for" the advertising, the plaintiff would never have stayed in the defendant's facilities. See Shute v. Carnival Cruise Lines, 897 F.2d 377 (9th Cir. 1990), *rev'd on other grounds*, 498 U.S. 807 (1991).

If "but for" causation is a sufficient condition for specific jurisdiction, is it also a necessary condition? Consider the situation of Audi in *World-Wide Volkswagen*. Audi presumably sold cars to Oklahoma but not the car that blew up. Is this enough of a connection for specific jurisdiction? Professor Twitchell has argued that this should be enough for specific jurisdiction:

> [T]he fact that this accident occurred within the forum, coupled with similarity between the manufacturer's conduct in the forum and the conduct underlying the plaintiff's cause of action * * * makes exercising jurisdiction over this claim particularly reasonable. Having sold and serviced identical cars in the state, the manufacturer will have foreseen such suits and insured against them. Furthermore, the forum has a very strong interest in regulating the manufacturer's con-

duct in this suit, not just because this particular automobile malfunctioned there, but because state residents are buying many similar cars and operating them on the forum's highways. The fact that the car was not actually sold within the state is, in this context, fortuitous. A court need not decide whether it is fair to hold the manufacturer subject to jurisdiction on all causes of action in the forum in order to decide that it is fair in this particular case. Specific jurisdiction, in which the nature of the cause of action is taken into account when considering fairness, not general jurisdiction, is the key to proper jurisdictional analysis under these circumstances.

Mary Twitchell, *The Myth of General Jurisdiction*, 101 HARV. L. REV. 610, 661-62 (1988). Professor Brilmayer, in contrast, has argued for a narrower approach, explaining:

> A contact is related to the controversy if it is the geographical qualification of a fact relevant to the merits. A forum occurrence which would ordinarily be alleged as part of the comparable domestic complaint is a related contact. In contrast, an occurrence in the forum State of no relevance to a totally domestic cause of action is an unrelated contact, a purely jurisdictional allegation with no substantive purpose. If a fact is irrelevant in a purely domestic dispute, it does not suddenly become related to the controversy simply because there are multistate elements.

Lea Brilmayer, *How Contacts Count: Due Process Limitations on State Court Jurisdiction*, 1980 SUP. CT. REV. 77, 82-83. With whom would you agree in this debate? See also George, supra, 64 TULANE L. REV. 1097.

   7.   Some have suggested that the categories of general and specific jurisdiction are not really two separate categories, but are simply two ends of a continuum. See Camelback Ski Corp. v Behning, 539 A.2d 1107, 1111 (Md. 1988); William Richman, *Review Essay: Part I—Casad's Jurisdiction in Civil Actions; Part II—A Sliding Scale to Supplement the Distinction Between General and Specific Jurisdiction*, 72 CAL. L. REV. 1328 (1984). Where the cause of action is closely related to the contacts, as little as a single contact may be sufficient. At the other extreme — where the cause of action is completely unrelated to the contacts — a very high level of contacts will be required. As to the cases in between, the more closely the contacts are related to the cause of action, the fewer contacts are required. Conversely, the more attenuated the connection between the contacts and the cause of action, the greater the level of contacts required.

5. Consent

   Personal jurisdiction is a personal right that can be waived at anytime by the defendant. It is well established that a person may consent to jurisdiction even long in advance of litigation. Consent to jurisdiction is sometimes manifested by appointing an agent for service of process within the state. The Court has upheld this type of consent. See National Equip. Rental, Ltd. v. Szukhent, 375 U.S. 311 (1964).

B. Constitutional Limits on Personal Jurisdiction

Sometimes parties to a contract agree to litigate only in a designated forum. Such provisions have been upheld even where the designated forum is relatively burdensome for one litigant. See Carnival Cruise Lines v. Shute, 498 U.S. 807 (1991).

Parties may also consent to jurisdiction by virtue of their conduct in the litigation. In Adam v. Saenger, 303 U.S. 59 (1938), the Supreme Court held that by filing a complaint, the plaintiff consented to any counterclaim filed against the plaintiff by the defendant. Similarly, as you will see in Chapter 6, a failure to raise a timely objection to jurisdiction constitutes a waiver of the objection.

Insurance Corp. of Ireland v. Compagnie des Bauxites de Guinee, 456 U.S. 694 (1982), illustrates another type of consent. There, in response to a defendant's motion to dismiss for lack of personal jurisdiction, the plaintiff sought discovery of documents that might show that defendant had sufficient contacts with the forum. After a protracted discovery dispute, the district court ordered the defendant to produce the documents. When the defendant refused to comply with that order, the district court sanctioned the defendant under Rule 37(b)(2)(A). The sanction imposed was a finding that the court had personal jurisdiction over the defendant. The defendant appealed, arguing that it had no obligation to obey the orders of the court unless the court had personal jurisdiction. Therefore, the defendant continued, a finding of personal jurisdiction could not be imposed as a sanction, because such a finding was a pre-requisite to the court's authority to impose any sanction. The Supreme Court rejected this argument explaining: "By submitting to the jurisdiction of the court for the limited purpose of challenging jurisdiction, the defendant agrees to abide by that court's determination on the issue of jurisdiction." Id. at 706.

6. In-Rem and Quasi-in-Rem Jurisdiction

Quasi-in-rem jurisdiction allows a plaintiff to acquire jurisdiction over the defendant wherever the defendant has property in the forum simply by attaching it. Quasi-in-rem jurisdiction was recognized even before *Pennoyer v. Neff*, and subsequent cases specifically upheld its constitutionality. One extreme example is the case of Harris v. Balk, 198 U.S. 215 (1905). In that case, Harris owed Balk money, and Balk owed Epstein money. Epstein wished to sue Balk for the debt, but Epstein resided in Maryland, Balk lived North Carolina, and Epstein did not wish to travel to North Carolina. If Balk had property in Maryland, Epstein could have attached it and thereby litigated in Maryland. Balk did not have any property there, however, until Harris, his debtor, visited Maryland. When Epstein learned of Harris's presence in Maryland, he commenced a lawsuit in Maryland and "attached" Harris, contending that since Harris owed Balk money, his debt to Balk was "property" located in Maryland. The Supreme Court upheld jurisdiction finding that the debt was property attachable for purposes of quasi-in-rem jurisdiction, and that the debt was located wherever the debtor was.

Shaffer v. Heitner
433 U.S. 186, 97 S.Ct. 2569, 53 L. Ed. 2d 683 (1977)

Justice Marshall delivered the opinion of the Court.

The controversy in this case concerns the constitutionality of a Delaware statute that allows a court of that State to take jurisdiction of a lawsuit by sequestering any property of the defendant that happens to be located in Delaware. Appellants contend that the sequestration statute as applied in this case violates the Due Process Clause of the Fourteenth Amendment both because it permits the state courts to exercise jurisdiction despite the absence of sufficient contacts among the defendants, the litigation, and the State of Delaware and because it authorizes the deprivation of defendants' property without providing adequate procedural safeguards. We find it necessary to consider only the first of these contentions.

I

Appellee Heitner, a nonresident of Delaware, is the owner of one share of stock in the Greyhound Corp., a business incorporated under the laws of Delaware with its principal place of business in Phoenix, Ariz. On May 22, 1974, he filed a shareholder's derivative suit[*] in the Court of Chancery for New Castle County, Del., in which he named as defendants Greyhound, its wholly owned subsidiary Greyhound Lines, Inc., and 28 present or former officers or directors of one or both of the corporations. In essence, Heitner alleged that the individual defendants had violated their duties to Greyhound by causing it and its subsidiary to engage in actions that resulted in the corporations being held liable for substantial damages in a private antitrust suit and a large fine in a criminal contempt action. The activities which led to these penalties took place in Oregon.

Simultaneously with his complaint, Heitner filed a motion for an order of sequestration of the Delaware property of the individual defendants pursuant to Del. Code Ann., Tit. 10, § 366 (1975). This motion was accompanied by a supporting affidavit of counsel which stated that the individual defendants were nonresidents of Delaware. The affidavit identified the property to be sequestered as

> "common stock, Second Cumulative Preferred Stock and stock unit credits of the Defendant Greyhound Corporation, a Delaware corporation, as well as all

---

[*] [A shareholder's derivative suit is a suit brought by one or more corporate shareholders to enforce the corporation's rights. Often, such suits are brought against officers and directors of the corporation, alleging that their malfeasance harmed the corporation by causing it to lose money. Indeed, in this case, officers and directors were accused of breaching duties to the corporation by having the company engage in illegal activities which cost it millions of dollars. See Fed. R. Civ. P. 23.1. — EDS.]

options and all warrants to purchase said stock issued to said individual Defendants and all contractual [sic] obligations, all rights, debts or credits due or accrued to or for the benefit of any of the said Defendants under any type of written agreement, contract or other legal instrument of any kind whatever between any of the individual Defendants and said corporation."

The requested sequestration order was signed the day the motion was filed. Pursuant to that order, the sequestrator "seized" approximately 82,000 shares of Greyhound common stock belonging to 19 of the defendants, and options belonging to another 2 defendants. These seizures were accomplished by placing "stop transfer" orders or their equivalents on the books of the Greyhound Corp. So far as the record shows, none of the certificates representing the seized property was physically present in Delaware. The stock was considered to be in Delaware, and so subject to seizure, by virtue of Del. Code Ann., Tit. 8, § 169 (1975), which makes Delaware the situs of ownership of all stock in Delaware corporations.

All 28 defendants were notified of the initiation of the suit by certified mail directed to their last known addresses and by publication in a New Castle County newspaper. The 21 defendants whose property was seized (hereafter referred to as appellants) responded by entering a special appearance for the purpose of moving to quash service of process and to vacate the sequestration order. They contended that the ex parte sequestration procedure did not accord them due process of law and that the property seized was not capable of attachment in Delaware. In addition, appellants asserted that under the rule of *International Shoe Co. v. Washington*, they did not have sufficient contacts with Delaware to sustain the jurisdiction of that State's courts.

The Court of Chancery rejected these arguments in a letter opinion which emphasized the purpose of the Delaware sequestration procedure:

> "The primary purpose of 'sequestration' as authorized by 10 Del. C. § 366 is not to secure possession of property pending a trial between resident debtors and creditors on the issue of who has the right to retain it. On the contrary, as here employed, 'sequestration' is a process used to compel the personal appearance of a nonresident defendant to answer and defend a suit brought against him in a court of equity. It is accomplished by the appointment of a sequestrator by this Court to seize and hold property of the nonresident located in this State subject to further Court order. If the defendant enters a general appearance, the sequestered property is routinely released, unless the plaintiff makes special application to continue its seizure, in which event the plaintiff has the burden of proof and persuasion."

This limitation on the purpose and length of time for which sequestered property is held, the court concluded, rendered inapplicable the due process requirements enunciated in Sniadach v. Family Finance Corp., 395 U.S. 337 (1969); Fuentes v. Shevin, 407 U.S. 67 (1972); and Mitchell v. W. T. Grant Co., 416 U.S. 600 (1974). The court also found no state-law or federal constitutional barrier to the sequestrator's reliance on Del. Code Ann., Tit. 8, § 169 (1975). Finally, the court held that the statutory Delaware situs of the stock provided a sufficient basis for the exercise of quasi in rem jurisdiction by a Delaware court.

On appeal, the Delaware Supreme Court affirmed the judgment of the Court of Chancery. * * *

II

The Delaware courts rejected appellants' jurisdictional challenge by noting that this suit was brought as a quasi in rem proceeding. Since quasi in rem jurisdiction is traditionally based on attachment or seizure of property present in the jurisdiction, not on contacts between the defendant and the State, the courts considered appellants' claimed lack of contacts with Delaware to be unimportant. This categorical analysis assumes the continued soundness of the conceptual structure founded on the century-old case of *Pennoyer v. Neff.*

[The Court reviewed the cases from *Pennoyer* to *International Shoe*. The Court concluded that "the relationship among the defendant, the forum, and the litigation, rather than the mutually exclusive sovereignty of the States on which the rules of *Pennoyer* rest, became the central concern of the inquiry in to personal jurisdiction."] * * *

No equally dramatic change has occurred in the law governing jurisdiction in rem. There have, however, been intimations that the collapse of the in personam wing of *Pennoyer* has not left that decision unweakened as a foundation for in rem jurisdiction. Well-reasoned lower court opinions have questioned the proposition that the presence of property in a State gives that State jurisdiction to adjudicate rights to the property regardless of the relationship of the underlying dispute and the property owner to the forum. The overwhelming majority of commentators have also rejected *Pennoyer*'s premise that a proceeding "against" property is not a proceeding against the owners of that property. Accordingly, they urge that the "traditional notions of fair play and substantial justice" that govern a State's power to adjudicate in personam should also govern its power to adjudicate personal rights to property located in the State.

Although this Court has not addressed this argument directly, we have held that property cannot be subjected to a court's judgment unless reasonable and appropriate efforts have been made to give the property owners actual notice of the action. Walker v. City of Hutchinson, 352 U.S. 112 (1956); Mullane v. Central Hanover Bank & Trust Co., 339 U.S. 306 (1950). This conclusion recognizes, contrary to *Pennoyer*, that an adverse judgment in rem directly affects the property owner by divesting him of his rights in the property before the court. Moreover, in *Mullane* we held that Fourteenth Amendment rights cannot depend on the classification of an action as in rem or in personam, since that is

> "a classification for which the standards are so elusive and confused generally and which, being primarily for state courts to define, may and do vary from state to state."

It is clear, therefore, that the law of state-court jurisdiction no longer stands securely on the foundation established in *Pennoyer*. We think that the time is ripe to consider whether the standard of fairness and substantial justice set forth in *International Shoe* should be held to govern actions in rem as well as in personam.

B. Constitutional Limits on Personal Jurisdiction

III

The case for applying to jurisdiction in rem the same test of "fair play and substantial justice" as governs assertions of jurisdiction in personam is simple and straightforward. It is premised on recognition that "[t]he phrase, 'judicial jurisdiction over a thing,' is a customary elliptical way of referring to jurisdiction over the interests of persons in a thing." Restatement (Second) of Conflict of Laws § 56, Introductory Note (1971) (hereafter Restatement). This recognition leads to the conclusion that in order to justify an exercise of jurisdiction in rem, the basis for jurisdiction must be sufficient to justify exercising "jurisdiction over the interests of persons in a thing."[23] The standard for determining whether an exercise of jurisdiction over the interests of persons is consistent with the Due Process Clause is the minimum-contacts standard elucidated in *International Shoe*.

This argument, of course, does not ignore the fact that the presence of property in a State may bear on the existence of jurisdiction by providing contacts among the forum State, the defendant, and the litigation. For example, when claims to the property itself are the source of the underlying controversy between the plaintiff and the defendant,[24] it would be unusual for the State where the property is located not to have jurisdiction. In such cases, the defendant's claim to property located in the State would normally indicate that he expected to benefit from the State's protection of his interest. The State's strong interests in assuring the marketability of property within its borders and in providing a procedure for peaceful resolution of disputes about the possession of that property would also support jurisdiction, as would the likelihood that important records and witnesses will be found in the State,[28] The presence of property may also favor jurisdiction in cases, such as suits for injury suffered on the land of an absentee owner, where the defendant's ownership of the property is conceded but the cause of action is otherwise related to rights and duties growing out of that ownership.

It appears, therefore, that jurisdiction over many types of actions which now are or might be brought in rem would not be affected by a holding that any assertion of state-court jurisdiction must satisfy the *International Shoe* standard.[30] For the type of quasi in rem action typified by *Harris v. Balk* and the present case, however, accepting the proposed analysis would result in significant change. These are cases where the property which now serves as the basis for state-court jurisdiction is completely unrelated to the plaintiff's cause of action. Thus, although the presence of the

---

[23] It is true that the potential liability of a defendant in an in rem action is limited by the value of the property, but that limitation does not affect the argument. The fairness of subjecting a defendant to state-court jurisdiction does not depend on the size of the claim being litigated. Cf. *Fuentes v. Shevin*.

[24] This category includes true in rem actions and the first type of quasi in rem proceedings. [The Court then cites its prior note 17, which states:

"'A judgment in rem affects the interests of all persons in designated property. A judgment quasi in rem affects the interests of particular persons in designated property. The latter is of two types. In one the plaintiff is seeking to secure a pre-existing claim in the subject property and to extinguish or establish the nonexistence of similar interests of particular persons. In the other the plaintiff seeks to apply what he concedes to be the property of the defendant to the satisfaction of a claim against him. *Hanson v. Denckla*. As did the Court in *Hanson*, we will for convenience generally use the term in rem in place of 'in rem and quasi in rem.'"]

[28] We do not suggest that these illustrations include all the factors that may affect the decision, nor that the factors we mentioned are necessarily decisive.

CHAPTER 2 PERSONAL JURISDICTION

defendant's property in a State might suggest the existence of other ties among the defendant, the State, and the litigation, the presence of the property alone would not support the State's jurisdiction. If those other ties did not exist, cases over which the State is now thought to have jurisdiction could not be brought in that forum.

Since acceptance of the *International Shoe* test would most affect this class of cases, we examine the arguments against adopting that standard as they relate to this category of litigation. Before doing so, however, we note that this type of case also presents the clearest illustration of the argument in favor of assessing assertions of jurisdiction by a single standard. For in cases such as *Harris* and this one, the only role played by the property is to provide the basis for bringing the defendant into court. Indeed, the express purpose of the Delaware sequestration procedure is to compel the defendant to enter a personal appearance. In such cases, if a direct assertion of personal jurisdiction over the defendant would violate the Constitution, it would seem that an indirect assertion of that jurisdiction should be equally impermissible.

The primary rationale for treating the presence of property as a sufficient basis for jurisdiction to adjudicate claims over which the State would not have jurisdiction if *International Shoe* applied is that a wrongdoer "should not be able to avoid payment of his obligations by the expedient of removing his assets to a place where he is not subject to an in personam suit." RESTATEMENT § 66, Comment a. This justification, however, does not explain why jurisdiction should be recognized without regard to whether the property is present in the State because of an effort to avoid the owner's obligations. Nor does it support jurisdiction to adjudicate the underlying claim. At most, it suggests that a State in which property is located should have jurisdiction to attach that property, by use of proper procedures, as security for a judgment being sought in a forum where the litigation can be maintained consistently with *International Shoe*. Moreover, we know of nothing to justify the assumption that a debtor can avoid paying his obligations by removing his property to a State in which his creditor cannot obtain personal jurisdiction over him. The Full Faith and Credit Clause, after all, makes the valid in personam judgment of one State enforceable in all other States.[36]

It might also be suggested that allowing in rem jurisdiction avoids the uncertainty inherent in the *International Shoe* standard and assures a plaintiff of a forum.[37] We believe, however, that the fairness standard of *International Shoe* can be easily applied in the vast majority of cases. Moreover, when the existence of jurisdiction in a particular forum under *International Shoe* is unclear, the cost of simplifying the litigation by avoiding the jurisdictional question may be the sacrifice of "fair play and substantial justice." That cost is too high.

We are left, then, to consider the significance of the long history of jurisdiction based solely on the presence of property in a State. Although the theory that territorial power is both essential to and sufficient for jurisdiction has been undermined, we have never held that the presence of property in a State does not automatically confer jurisdiction over the owner's interest in that property.

---

[30] We do not suggest that jurisdictional doctrines other than those discussed in text, such as the particularized rules governing adjudications of status, are inconsistent with the standard of fairness.

[36] Once it has been determined by a court of competent jurisdiction that the defendant is a debtor of the plaintiff, there would seem to be no unfairness in allowing an action to realize on that debt in a State where the defendant has property, whether or not that State would have jurisdiction to determine the existence of the debt as an original matter.

[37] This case does not raise, and we therefore do not consider, the question whether the presence of a defendant's property in a State is a sufficient basis for jurisdiction when no other forum is available to the plaintiff.

B. Constitutional Limits on Personal Jurisdiction

This history must be considered as supporting the proposition that jurisdiction based solely on the presence of property satisfies the demands of due process, but it is not decisive. "[T]raditional notions of fair play and substantial justice" can be as readily offended by the perpetuation of ancient forms that are no longer justified as by the adoption of new procedures that are inconsistent with the basic values of our constitutional heritage. The fiction that an assertion of jurisdiction over property is anything but an assertion of jurisdiction over the owner of the property supports an ancient form without substantial modern justification. Its continued acceptance would serve only to allow state-court jurisdiction that is fundamentally unfair to the defendant.

We therefore conclude that all assertions of state-court jurisdiction must be evaluated according to the standards set forth in *International Shoe* and its progeny.[39]

IV

The Delaware courts based their assertion of jurisdiction in this case solely on the statutory presence of appellants' property in Delaware. Yet that property is not the subject matter of this litigation, nor is the underlying cause of action related to the property. Appellants' holdings in Greyhound do not, therefore, provide contacts with Delaware sufficient to support the jurisdiction of that State's courts over appellants. If it exists, that jurisdiction must have some other foundation.

Appellee Heitner did not allege and does not now claim that appellants have ever set foot in Delaware. Nor does he identify any act related to his cause of action as having taken place in Delaware. Nevertheless, he contends that appellants' positions as directors and officers of a corporation chartered in Delaware provide sufficient "contacts, ties, or relations," *International Shoe Co. v. Washington*, with that State to give its courts jurisdiction over appellants in this stockholder's derivative action. This argument is based primarily on what Heitner asserts to be the strong interest of Delaware in supervising the management of a Delaware corporation. That interest is said to derive from the role of Delaware law in establishing the corporation and defining the obligations owed to it by its officers and directors. In order to protect this interest, appellee concludes, Delaware's courts must have jurisdiction over corporate fiduciaries such as appellants.

This argument is undercut by the failure of the Delaware Legislature to assert the state interest appellee finds so compelling. Delaware law bases jurisdiction, not on appellants' status as corporate fiduciaries, but rather on the presence of their property in the State. Although the sequestration procedure used here may be most frequently used in derivative suits against officers and directors, the authorizing statute evinces no specific concern with such actions. Sequestration can be used in any suit against a nonresident, and reaches corporate fiduciaries only if they happen to own interests in a Delaware corporation, or other property in the State. But as Heitner's failure to secure jurisdiction over seven of the defendants named in his complaint demonstrates, there is no necessary relationship between holding a position as a corporate fiduciary and owning stock or other interests in the corporation.[43] If Delaware perceived its interest in securing jurisdiction over corporate fiduciaries to be as great as Heitner suggests, we would expect it to have enacted a statute more clearly designed to protect that interest.

---

[39] It would not be fruitful for us to re-examine the facts of cases decided on the rationales of *Pennoyer* and *Harris* to determine whether jurisdiction might have been sustained under the standard we adopt today. To the extent that prior decisions are inconsistent with this standard, they are overruled.

[43] Delaware does not require directors to own stock.

Moreover, even if Heitner's assessment of the importance of Delaware's interest is accepted, his argument fails to demonstrate that Delaware is a fair forum for this litigation. The interest appellee has identified may support the application of Delaware law to resolve any controversy over appellants' actions in their capacities as officers and directors.[44] But we have rejected the argument that if a State's law can properly be applied to a dispute, its courts necessarily have jurisdiction over the parties to that dispute.

> "[The State] does not acquire ... jurisdiction by being the 'center of gravity' of the controversy, or the most convenient location for litigation. The issue is personal jurisdiction, not choice of law. It is resolved in this case by considering the acts of the [appellants]." *Hanson v. Denckla.*

Appellee suggests that by accepting positions as officers or directors of a Delaware corporation, appellants performed the acts required by *Hanson v. Denckla*. He notes that Delaware law provides substantial benefits to corporate officers and directors, and that these benefits were at least in part the incentive for appellants to assume their positions. It is, he says, "only fair and just" to require appellants, in return for these benefits, to respond in the State of Delaware when they are accused of misusing their power.

But like Heitner's first argument, this line of reasoning establishes only that it is appropriate for Delaware law to govern the obligations of appellants to Greyhound and its stockholders. It does not demonstrate that appellants have "purposefully avail[ed themselves] of the privilege of conducting activities within the forum State," *Hanson v. Denckla*, in a way that would justify bringing them before a Delaware tribunal. Appellants have simply had nothing to do with the State of Delaware. Moreover, appellants had no reason to expect to be haled before a Delaware court. Delaware, unlike some States, has not enacted a statute that treats acceptance of a directorship as consent to jurisdiction in the State. And "[i]t strains reason ... to suggest that anyone buying securities in a corporation formed in Delaware 'impliedly consents' to subject himself to Delaware's ... jurisdiction on any cause of action." Appellants, who were not required to acquire interests in Greyhound in order to hold their positions, did not by acquiring those interests surrender their right to be brought to judgment only in States with which they had had "minimum contacts."

The Due Process Clause "does not contemplate that a state may make binding a judgment ... against an individual or corporate defendant with which the state has no contacts, ties, or relations." *International Shoe Co. v. Washington*. Delaware's assertion of jurisdiction over appellants in this case is inconsistent with that constitutional limitation on state power. The judgment of the Delaware Supreme Court must, therefore, be reversed.

It is so ordered.

JUSTICE POWELL, concurring.

---

[44] In general, the law of the State of incorporation is held to govern the liabilities of officers or directors to the corporation and its stockholders. The rationale for the general rule appears to be based more on the need for a uniform and certain standard to govern the internal affairs of a corporation than on the perceived interest of the State of incorporation.

B. Constitutional Limits on Personal Jurisdiction

I agree that the principles of *International Shoe Co. v. Washington*, should be extended to govern assertions of in rem as well as in personam jurisdiction in a state court. I also agree that neither the statutory presence of appellants' stock in Delaware nor their positions as directors and officers of a Delaware corporation can provide sufficient contacts to support the Delaware courts' assertion of jurisdiction in this case.

I would explicitly reserve judgment, however, on whether the ownership of some forms of property whose situs is indisputably and permanently located within a State may, without more, provide the contacts necessary to subject a defendant to jurisdiction within the State to the extent of the value of the property. In the case of real property, in particular, preservation of the common-law concept of quasi in rem jurisdiction arguably would avoid the uncertainty of the general *International Shoe* standard without significant cost to "'traditional notions of fair play and substantial justice.'"

Subject to the foregoing reservation, I join the opinion of the Court.

[handwritten: *But the prop might be enough.*]

JUSTICE STEVENS, concurring in the judgment.

The Due Process Clause affords protection against "judgments without notice." *International Shoe Co. v. Washington* (opinion of Black, J.). Throughout our history the acceptable exercise of in rem and quasi in rem jurisdiction has included a procedure giving reasonable assurance that actual notice of the particular claim will be conveyed to the defendant. Thus, publication, notice by registered mail, or extraterritorial personal service has been an essential ingredient of any procedure that serves as a substitute for personal service within the jurisdiction.

The requirement of fair notice also, I believe, includes fair warning that a particular activity may subject a person to the jurisdiction of a foreign sovereign. If I visit another State, or acquire real estate or open a bank account in it, I knowingly assume some risk that the State will exercise its power over my property or my person while there. My contact with the State, though minimal, gives rise to predictable risks.

Perhaps the same consequences should flow from the purchase of stock of a corporation organized under the laws of a foreign nation, because to some limited extent one's property and affairs then become subject to the laws of the nation of domicile of the corporation. As a matter of international law, that suggestion might be acceptable because a foreign investment is sufficiently unusual to make it appropriate to require the investor to study the ramifications of his decision. But a purchase of securities in the domestic market is an entirely different matter.

One who purchases shares of stock on the open market can hardly be expected to know that he has thereby become subject to suit in a forum remote from his residence and unrelated to the transaction. * * *

How the Court's opinion may be applied in other contexts is not entirely clear to me. I agree with Justice Powell that it should not be read to invalidate quasi in rem jurisdiction where real estate is involved. I would also not read it as invalidating other long-accepted methods of acquiring jurisdiction over persons with adequate notice of both the particular controversy and the fact that their local activities might subject them to suit. My uncertainty as to the reach of the opinion, and my fear that it purports to decide a great deal more than is necessary to dispose of this case, persuade me merely to concur in the judgment.

JUSTICE BRENNAN, concurring in part and dissenting in part.

I join Parts I-III of the Court's opinion. I fully agree that the minimum-contacts analysis developed in *International Shoe Co. v. Washington*, represents a far more sensible construct for the exercise of state-court jurisdiction than the patchwork of legal and factual fictions that has been generated from the decision in *Pennoyer v. Neff*. It is precisely because the inquiry into minimum contacts is now of such overriding importance, however, that I must respectfully dissent from Part IV of the Court's opinion.

I

[Justice Brennan argued that it was inappropriate for the Court to consider whether Delaware's assertion of jurisdiction met the "minimum contacts" test. He said of the Court's discussion of this point that "a purer example of an advisory opinion is not to be found."]

* * *

My concern with the inappropriateness of the Court's action is highlighted by two other considerations. First, an inquiry into minimum contacts inevitably is highly dependent on creating a proper factual foundation detailing the contacts between the forum State and the controversy in question. Because neither the plaintiff-appellee nor the state courts viewed such an inquiry as germane in this instance, the Court today is unable to draw upon a proper factual record in reaching its conclusion; moreover, its disposition denies appellee the normal opportunity to seek discovery on the contacts issue. Second, it must be remembered that the Court's ruling is a constitutional one and necessarily will affect the reach of the jurisdictional laws of all 50 States. Ordinarily this would counsel restraint in constitutional pronouncements. Certainly it should have cautioned the Court against reaching out to decide a question that, as here, has yet to emerge from the state courts ripened for review on the federal issue.

II

Nonetheless, because the Court rules on the minimum-contacts question, I feel impelled to express my view. While evidence derived through discovery might satisfy me that minimum contacts are lacking in a given case, I am convinced that as a general rule a state forum has jurisdiction to adjudicate a shareholder derivative action centering on the conduct and policies of the directors and officers of a corporation chartered by that State. Unlike the Court, I therefore would not foreclose Delaware from asserting jurisdiction over appellants were it persuaded to do so on the basis of minimum contacts.

It is well settled that a derivative lawsuit as presented here does not inure primarily to the benefit of the named plaintiff. Rather, the primary beneficiaries are the corporation and its owners, the shareholders. "The cause of action which such a plaintiff brings before the court is not his own

B. Constitutional Limits on Personal Jurisdiction

but the corporation's.... Such a plaintiff often may represent an important public and stockholder interest in bringing faithless managers to book."

Viewed in this light, the chartering State has an unusually powerful interest in insuring the availability of a convenient forum for litigating claims involving a possible multiplicity of defendant fiduciaries and for vindicating the State's substantive policies regarding the management of its domestic corporations. I believe that our cases fairly establish that the State's valid substantive interests are important considerations in assessing whether it constitutionally may claim jurisdiction over a given cause of action.

In this instance, Delaware can point to at least three interrelated public policies that are furthered by its assertion of jurisdiction. First, the State has a substantial interest in providing restitution for its local corporations that allegedly have been victimized by fiduciary misconduct, even if the managerial decisions occurred outside the State. The importance of this general state interest in assuring restitution for its own residents previously found expression in cases that went outside the then-prevailing due process framework to authorize state-court jurisdiction over non-resident motorists who injure others within the State. *Hess v. Pawloski*. More recently, it has led States to seek and to acquire jurisdiction over nonresident tort-feasor whose purely out-of-state activities produce domestic consequences. E.g., *Gray v. American Radiator & Standard Sanitary Corp.* Second, state courts have legitimately read their jurisdiction expansively when a cause of action centers in an area in which the forum State possesses a manifest regulatory interest. E.g., *McGee v. International Life Ins. Co.* (insurance regulation); Travelers Health Assn. v. Virginia, 339 U.S. 643 (1950) (blue sky laws). * * * Finally, a State like Delaware has a recognized interest in affording a convenient forum for supervising and overseeing the affairs of an entity that is purely the creation of that State's law. For example, even following our decision in *International Shoe*, New York courts were permitted to exercise complete judicial authority over nonresident beneficiaries of a trust created under state law, even though, unlike appellants here, the beneficiaries personally entered into no association whatsoever with New York. Mullane v. Central Hanover Bank & Trust Co., 339 U.S. 306, 313 (1950). I, of course, am not suggesting that Delaware's varied interests would justify its acceptance of jurisdiction over any transaction upon the affairs of its domestic corporations. But a derivative action which raises allegations of abuses of the basic management of an institution whose existence is created by the State and whose powers and duties are defined by state law fundamentally implicates the public policies of that forum.

To be sure, the Court is not blind to these considerations. It notes that the State's interests "may support the application of Delaware law to resolve any controversy over appellants' actions in their capacities as officers and directors." But this, the Court argues, pertains to choice of law, not jurisdiction. I recognize that the jurisdictional and choice-of-law inquiries are not identical. *Hanson v. Denckla*. But I would not compartmentalize thinking in this area quite so rigidly as it seems to me the Court does today, for both inquiries "are often closely related and to a substantial degree depend upon similar considerations." Id. (Black, J., dissenting). In either case an important linchpin is the extent of contacts between the controversy, the parties, and the forum State. While constitutional limitations on the choice of law are by no means settled, important considerations certainly include the expectancies of the parties and the fairness of governing the defendants' acts and behavior by rules of conduct created by a given jurisdiction. These same factors bear upon the propriety of a State's exercising jurisdiction over a legal dispute. At the minimum, the decision that it is fair to bind a defendant by a State's laws and rules should prove to be highly relevant to the fairness of permitting that same State to accept jurisdiction for adjudicating the controversy.

Furthermore, I believe that practical considerations argue in favor of seeking to bridge the distance between the choice-of-law and jurisdictional inquiries. Even when a court would apply the law of a different forum, as a general rule it will feel less knowledgeable and comfortable in interpretation, and less interested in fostering the policies of that foreign jurisdiction, than would the courts established by the State that provides the applicable law. See, e.g., Gulf Oil Co. v. Gilbert, 330 U.S. 501 (1947). Obviously, such choice-of-law problems cannot entirely be avoided in a diverse legal system such as our own. Nonetheless, when a suitor seeks to lodge a suit in a State with a substantial interest in seeing its own law applied to the transaction in question, we could wisely act to minimize conflicts, confusion, and uncertainty by adopting a liberal view of jurisdiction, unless considerations of fairness or efficiency strongly point in the opposite direction.

This case is not one where, in my judgment, this preference for jurisdiction is adequately answered. Certainly nothing said by the Court persuades me that it would be unfair to subject appellants to suit in Delaware. The fact that the record does not reveal whether they "set foot" or committed "act[s] related to [the] cause of action" in Delaware, is not decisive, for jurisdiction can be based strictly on out-of-state acts having foreseeable effects in the forum State. E.g., *McGee v. International Life Ins. Co.; Gray v. American Radiator & Standard Sanitary Corp.* I have little difficulty in applying this principle to nonresident fiduciaries whose alleged breaches of trust are said to have substantial damaging effect on the financial posture of a resident corporation. Further, I cannot understand how the existence of minimum contacts in a constitutional sense is at all affected by Delaware's failure statutorily to express an interest in controlling corporate fiduciaries. To me this simply demonstrates that Delaware did not elect to assert jurisdiction to the extent the Constitution would allow.[5] Nor would I view as controlling or even especially meaningful Delaware's failure to exact from appellants their consent to be sued. Once we have rejected the jurisdictional framework created in *Pennoyer v. Neff*, I see no reason to rest jurisdiction on a fictional outgrowth of that system such as the existence of a consent statute, expressed or implied.

I, therefore, would approach the minimum-contacts analysis differently than does the Court. Crucial to me is the fact that appellants voluntarily associated themselves with the State of Delaware, "invoking the benefits and protections of its laws," by entering into a long-term and fragile relationship with one of its domestic corporations. They thereby elected to assume powers and to undertake responsibilities wholly derived from that State's rules and regulations, and to become eligible for those benefits that Delaware law makes available to its corporations' officials. E.g., DEL. CODE ANN., Tit. 8, § 143 (1975) (interest-free loans); § 145 (1975 ed. and Supp. 1976) (indemnification). While it is possible that countervailing issues of judicial efficiency and the like might clearly favor a different forum, they do not appear on the meager record before us; and, of course, we are concerned solely with "minimum" contacts, not the "best" contacts. I thus do not believe that it is unfair to insist that appellants make themselves available to suit in a competent forum that Delaware might create for vindication of its important public policies directly pertaining to appellants' fiduciary associations with the State.

---

[5] In fact, it is quite plausible that the Delaware Legislature never felt the need to assert direct jurisdiction over corporate managers precisely because the sequestration statute heretofore has served as a somewhat awkward but effective basis for achieving such personal jurisdiction. E.g., Hughes Tool Co. v. Fawcett Publications, Inc., 290 A. 2d 693, 695 (Del. Ch. 1972): "Sequestration is most frequently resorted to in suits by stockholders against corporate directors in which recoveries are sought for the benefit of the corporation on the ground of claimed breaches of fiduciary duty on the part of directors."

B. Constitutional Limits on Personal Jurisdiction

NOTES AND QUESTIONS

1. *International Shoe* focused on whether jurisdiction offends "traditional notions of fair play and substantial justice." American courts have recognized quasi-in-rem jurisdiction for over a century. How could a traditionally accepted mechanism of jurisdiction violate traditional notions of fair play and substantial justice? What tradition was the Court looking to?

2. Consider how the following hypotheticals would be analyzed after *Shaffer*:

(a) Fred, a California citizen, owns real estate in Delaware. Fred doesn't make his mortgage payments. The bank which holds the mortgage wants to foreclose on the property. Is there personal jurisdiction for the bank to foreclose in Delaware?

(b) Fred owns property in Delaware. Someone trips and falls on his property. The injured person sues Fred in Delaware. Is there personal jurisdiction?

(c) Sally (a citizen of California) has a contract with Fred (also a citizen of California). The deal goes bad, and Sally sues Fred in California and wins. Fred refuses to pay the judgment. Sally goes to Delaware and enforces the judgment by attaching Fred's Delaware real estate. Is this permitted after *Shaffer*?

(d) In *Shaffer*, the property attached was stock. Suppose the directors had owned real estate in Delaware and Heitner had attached that instead of the stock. Would that have changed the result? Would it have changed the result for Justices Powell or Stevens?

3. Does the Court hold that a defendant can be subject to jurisdiction by attachment only if she would be subject to in personam jurisdiction? Some commentators have interpreted *Shaffer* this way. See GENE SHREVE & PETER RAVEN-HANSEN, UNDERSTANDING CIVIL PROCEDURE 63 (2d ed. 1994). In contrast, Professor Weintraub has argued that although all assertions of jurisdiction must be evaluated under the *International Shoe* standard, that "is not the same as saying that those standards must provide the same answer no matter what the form of jurisdiction asserted. In cases that would fall close to the due process line if full personal jurisdiction were asserted, the less drastic remedy of allowing the plaintiff to reach the defendant's assets in the state may be reasonable." RUSSELL WEINTRAUB, COMMENTARY ON THE CONFLICT OF LAWS 206 (3d ed. 1986). Which interpretation of *Shaffer* do you think is correct?

In Cameco Industries Inc. v. Mayatrac, S.A., 789 F. Supp. 200 (D. Md. 1992), the court upheld jurisdiction based solely on the attachment of a bank account in the forum. The court noted that the defendant lacked sufficient contacts to be subject to in personam jurisdiction, but held that quasi-in-rem jurisdiction was constitutional because the defendant voluntarily and purposefully maintained the bank account in the forum for fourteen years. Is Cameco consistent with the majority opinion in *Shaffer*?

4. Consider Part IV of the opinion. Why isn't becoming the director of a Delaware corporation a sufficient contact for those directors to be sued in personam in Delaware for breaches of their obligations as directors? Justice Marshall stresses that the directors "never set foot in Delaware" and that no act relating to the cause of action took place "in Delaware." Is physical presence in the state a prerequisite for jurisdiction? Is Part IV of *Shaffer* consistent with *Burger King*?

5. If personal jurisdiction is not proper in Delaware, where is it proper? Would there be personal jurisdiction over the officers and directors in Arizona (Greyhound's headquarters)? Does it matter whether the officers and directors have physically visited the headquarters? The alleged misconduct occurred in Oregon. Suppose several directors were not present in Oregon when the misconduct occurred, but learned about it at a later board meeting in Aspen. Colorado, and did nothing to correct the misconduct. Would those directors be subject to jurisdiction in Oregon? in Colorado?

6. Shortly after *Shaffer*, Delaware passed a statute providing that every nonresident director of a Delaware corporation appointed after September 1, 1977, shall "be deemed" to have consented to the appointment of the corporation's registered agent to be his agent for service of process in any suit in Delaware alleging that the director breached his duties as a director. 10 DEL. CODE § 3114. The Delaware Supreme Court upheld this statute in Armstrong v. Pomerance, 423 A.2d 174 (Del. 1980). See also Stearn v. Malloy, 89 F.R.D. 421 (E.D.Wis. 1981) (upholding a similar Wisconsin statute).

7. Transient Presence

Pennoyer established that service within the state is both necessary and sufficient to establish personal jurisdiction. Modern developments have changed the first part of that rule — in-state service is no longer necessary. But is it still sufficient? *Shaffer* held that the mere presence of property is not sufficient to establish jurisdiction. Similarly, one might argue that mere presence of the person should not be enough. Indeed, after *Shaffer*, many commentators predicted the demise of so called "transient" or "tag" jurisdiction. As you can see from the next case, rumors of its death were greatly exaggerated.

B. Constitutional Limits on Personal Jurisdiction

Burnham v. Superior Court of California
495 U.S. 604, 110 S.Ct. 2105, 109 L. Ed. 2d 631 (1990)

JUSTICE SCALIA announced the judgment of the Court and delivered an opinion in which THE CHIEF JUSTICE and JUSTICE KENNEDY join, and in which JUSTICE WHITE joins with respect to Parts I, II-A, II-B, and II-C.

The question presented is whether the Due Process Clause of the Fourteenth Amendment denies California courts jurisdiction over a nonresident, who was personally served with process while temporarily in that State, in a suit unrelated to his activities in the State.

I

Petitioner Dennis Burnham married Francie Burnham in 1976 in West Virginia. In 1977 the couple moved to New Jersey, where their two children were born. In July 1987 the Burnhams decided to separate. They agreed that Mrs. Burnham, who intended to move to California, would take custody of the children. Shortly before Mrs. Burnham departed for California that same month, she and petitioner agreed that she would file for divorce on grounds of "irreconcilable differences."

In October 1987, petitioner filed for divorce in New Jersey state court on grounds of "desertion." * * * Mrs. Burnham, after unsuccessfully demanding that petitioner adhere to their prior agreement to submit to an "irreconcilable differences" divorce, brought suit for divorce in California state court in early January 1988.

In late January, petitioner visited southern California on business, after which he went north to visit his children in the San Francisco Bay area, where his wife resided. He took the older child to San Francisco for the weekend. Upon returning the child to Mrs. Burnham's home on January 24, 1988, petitioner was served with a California court summons and a copy of Mrs. Burnham's divorce petition. He then returned to New Jersey.

Later that year, petitioner made a special appearance in the California Superior Court, moving to quash the service of process on the ground that the court lacked personal jurisdiction over him because his only contacts with California were a few short visits to the State for the purposes of conducting business and visiting his children. * * * [The California courts upheld personal jurisdiction on the ground that the defendant was served with process in the state.]

II

A

* * *

To determine whether the assertion of personal jurisdiction is consistent with due process, we have long relied on the principles traditionally followed by American courts in marking out the territorial limits of each State's authority. That criterion was first announced in *Pennoyer v.*

Neff. * * * In what has become the classic expression of the criterion, we said in *International Shoe Co. v. Washington*, that a state court's assertion of personal jurisdiction satisfies the Due Process Clause if it does not violate "'traditional notions of fair play and substantial justice.'" Since *International Shoe*, we have only been called upon to decide whether these "traditional notions" permit States to exercise jurisdiction over absent defendants in a manner that deviates from the rules of jurisdiction applied in the 19th century. We have held such deviations permissible, but only with respect to suits arising out of the absent defendant's contacts with the State.[1] See, e.g., *Helicopteros Nacionales de Colombia v. Hall*. The question we must decide today is whether due process requires a similar connection between the litigation and the defendant's contacts with the State in cases where the defendant is physically present in the State at the time process is served upon him.

B

Among the most firmly established principles of personal jurisdiction in American tradition is that the courts of a State have jurisdiction over nonresidents who are physically present in the State. The view developed early that each State had the power to hale before its courts any individual who could be found within its borders, and that once having acquired jurisdiction over such a person by properly serving him with process, the State could retain jurisdiction to enter judgment against him, no matter how fleeting his visit. That view had antecedents in English common-law practice, which sometimes allowed "transitory" actions, arising out of events outside the country, to be maintained against seemingly nonresident defendants who were present in England. Justice Story believed the principle, which he traced to Roman origins, to be firmly grounded in English tradition: "[B]y the common law[,] personal actions, being transitory, may be brought in any place, where the party defendant may be found," for "every nation may ... rightfully exercise jurisdiction over all persons within its domains." J. STORY, COMMENTARIES ON THE CONFLICT OF LAWS §§ 554, 543 (1846).

Recent scholarship has suggested that English tradition was not as clear as Story thought, see Hazard, *A General Theory of State-Court Jurisdiction*, 1965 S. Ct. Rev. 241, 253-260; Ehrenzweig, *The Transient Rule of Personal Jurisdiction: The "Power" Myth and Forum Conveniens*, 65 Yale L.J. 289 (1956). Accurate or not, however, judging by the evidence of contemporaneous or near-contemporaneous decisions, one must conclude that Story's understanding was shared by American courts at the crucial time for present purposes: 1868, when the Fourteenth Amendment was adopted. * * *

---

[1] We have said that "[e]ven when the cause of action does not arise out of or relate to the foreign corporation's activities in the forum State, due process is not offended by a State's subjecting the corporation to its in personam jurisdiction when there are sufficient contacts between the State and the foreign corporation." *Helicopters Nacionales de Colombia v. Hall*. Our only holding supporting that statement, however, involved "regular service of summons upon [the corporation's] president while he was in [the forum State] acting in that capacity." See *Perkins v. Benguet Consolidated Mining Co.* It may be that whatever special rule exists permitting "continuous and systematic" contacts to support jurisdiction with respect to matters unrelated to activity in the forum applies only to corporations, which have never fitted comfortably in a jurisdictional regime based primarily upon "de facto power over the defendant's person." *International Shoe Co. v. Washington*. We express no views on these matters — and, for simplicity's sake, omit reference to this aspect of "contacts"-based jurisdiction in our discussion.

B. Constitutional Limits on Personal Jurisdiction

* * *

Decisions in the courts of many States in the 19th and early 20th centuries held that personal service upon a physically present defendant sufficed to confer jurisdiction, without regard to whether the defendant was only briefly in the State or whether the cause of action was related to his activities there. [Citations to 13 state cases omitted.] Although research has not revealed a case deciding the issue in every State's courts, that appears to be because the issue was so well settled that it went unlitigated. Opinions from the courts of other States announced the rule in dictum. [Citations to eight state cases omitted.] Most States, moreover, had statutes or common-law rules that exempted from service of process individuals who were brought into the forum by force or fraud, or who were there as a party or witness in unrelated judicial proceedings. These exceptions obviously rested upon the premise that service of process conferred jurisdiction. Particularly striking is the fact that, as far as we have been able to determine, *not one* American case from the period (or, for that matter, not one American case until 1978) held, or even suggested, that in-state personal service on an individual was insufficient to confer personal jurisdiction.[3] Commentators were also seemingly unanimous on the rule.

This American jurisdictional practice is, moreover, not merely old; it is continuing. It remains the practice of, not only a substantial number of the States, but as far as we are aware all the States and the Federal Government — if one disregards (as one must for this purpose) the few opinions since 1978 that have erroneously said, on grounds similar to those that petitioner presses here, that this Court's due process decisions render the practice unconstitutional. See Nehemiah v. Athletics Congress of U.S.A., 765 F.2d 42, 46-47 (3d Cir. 1985); Schreiber v. Allis-Chalmers Corp., 448 F. Supp. 1079, 1088-91 (D.C. Kan. 1978), *rev'd on other grounds*, 611 F.2d 790 (10th Cir. 1979); Harold M. Pittman Co. v. Typecraft Software Ltd., 626 F. Supp. 305, 310-14 (N.D. Ill. 1986). We do not know of a single state or federal statute, or a single judicial decision resting upon state law, that has abandoned in-state service as a basis of jurisdiction. Many recent cases reaffirm it. [Citations to fourteen cases omitted.]

C

Despite this formidable body of precedent, petitioner contends, in reliance on our decisions applying the *International Shoe* standard, that in the absence of "continuous and systematic" contacts with the forum, a nonresident defendant can be subjected to judgment only as to matters

---

[3] Given this striking fact, and the unanimity of both cases and commentators in supporting the in-state service rule, one can only marvel at Justice Brennan's assertion that the rule "was rather weakly implanted in American jurisprudence," and "did not receive wide currency until well after our decision in *Pennoyer v. Neff*," I have cited pre-*Pennoyer* cases clearly supporting the rule from no less than nine States, ranging from Mississippi to Colorado to New Hampshire, and two highly respected pre-*Pennoyer* commentators. (It is, moreover, impossible to believe that the many other cases decided shortly after *Pennoyer* represented some sort of instant mutation — or, for that matter, that *Pennoyer* itself was not drawing upon clear contemporary understanding.) Justice Brennan cites neither cases nor commentators from the relevant period to support his thesis * * *, and instead relies upon modern secondary sources that do not mention, and were perhaps unaware of, many of the materials I have discussed. * * *

CHAPTER 2 PERSONAL JURISDICTION

that arise out of or relate to his contacts with the forum. This argument rests on a thorough misunderstanding of our cases.

The view of most courts in the 19th century was that a court simply could not exercise in personam jurisdiction over a nonresident who had not been personally served with process in the forum. *Pennoyer v. Neff*, [held] *** that when proceedings "involv[e] merely a determination of the personal liability of the defendant, he must be brought within [the court's] jurisdiction by service of process within the State, or his voluntary appearance." We invoked that rule in a series of subsequent cases, as either a matter of due process or a "fundamental principl[e] of jurisprudence."

Later years, however, saw the weakening of the *Pennoyer* rule. In the late 19th and early 20th centuries, changes in the technology of transportation and communication, and the tremendous growth of interstate business activity, led to an "inevitable relaxation of the strict limits on state jurisdiction" over nonresident individuals and corporations. *** We initially upheld these laws under the Due Process Clause on grounds that they complied with *Pennoyer's* rigid requirement of either "consent." As many observed, however, the consent and presence were purely fictional. Our opinion in *International Shoe* cast those fictions aside and made explicit the underlying basis of these decisions: Due process does not necessarily *require* the States to adhere to the unbending territorial limits on jurisdiction set forth in *Pennoyer*. The validity of assertion of jurisdiction over a nonconsenting defendant who is not present in the forum depends upon whether "the quality and nature of [his] activity" in relation to the forum, renders such jurisdiction consistent with "'traditional notions of fair play and substantial justice.'" Subsequent cases have derived from the *International Shoe* standard the general rule that a State may dispense with in-forum personal service on nonresident defendants in suits arising out of their activities in the State. ***

Nothing in *International Shoe* or the cases that have followed it, however, offers support for the very different proposition petitioner seeks to establish today: that a defendant's presence in the forum is not only unnecessary to validate novel, nontraditional assertions of jurisdiction, but is itself no longer sufficient to establish jurisdiction. That proposition is unfaithful to both elementary logic and the foundations of our due process jurisprudence. The distinction between what is needed to support novel procedures and what is needed to sustain traditional ones is fundamental, as we observed over a century ago:

> "[A] process of law, which is not otherwise forbidden, must be taken to be due process of law, if it can show the sanction of settled usage both in England and in this country; but it by no means follows that nothing else can be due process of law.... [That which], in substance, has been immemorially the actual law of the land ... therefor[e] is due process of law. But to hold that such a characteristic is essential to due process of law, would be to deny every quality of the law but its age, and to render it incapable of progress or improvement. It would be to stamp upon our jurisprudence the unchangeableness attributed to the laws of the Medes and Persians."

Hurtado v. California, 110 U.S. 516, 528-529 (1884).

The short of the matter is that jurisdiction based on physical presence alone constitutes due process because it is one of the continuing traditions of our legal system that define the due process standard of "traditional notions of fair play and substantial justice." That standard was

B. Constitutional Limits on Personal Jurisdiction

developed by *analogy* to "physical presence," and it would be perverse to say it could now be turned against that touchstone of jurisdiction.

D

Petitioner's strongest argument, though we ultimately reject it, relies upon our decision in *Shaffer v. Heitner*. * * *

It goes too far to say, as petitioner contends, that *Shaffer* compels the conclusion that a State lacks jurisdiction over an individual unless the litigation arises out of his activities in the State. *Shaffer*, like *International Shoe*, involved jurisdiction over an *absent defendant*, and it stands for nothing more than the proposition that when the "minimum contact" that is a substitute for physical presence consists of property ownership it must, like other minimum contacts, be related to the litigation. Petitioner wrenches out of its context our statement in *Shaffer* that "all assertions of state-court jurisdiction must be evaluated according to the standards set forth in *International Shoe* and its progeny." When read together with the two sentences that preceded it, the meaning of this statement becomes clear:

> "The fiction that an assertion of jurisdiction over property is anything but an assertion of jurisdiction over the owner of the property supports an ancient form without substantial modern justification. Its continued acceptance would serve only to allow state-court jurisdiction that is fundamentally unfair to the defendant.
>
> "We *therefore conclude* that all assertions of state-court jurisdiction must be evaluated according to the standards set forth in *International Shoe* and its progeny."

Shaffer was saying, in other words, not that all bases for the assertion of in personam jurisdiction (including, presumably, in-state service) must be treated alike and subjected to the "minimum contacts" analysis of *International Shoe*; but rather that quasi in rem jurisdiction, that fictional "ancient form," and in personam jurisdiction, are really one and the same and must be treated alike — leading to the conclusion that quasi in rem jurisdiction, i.e., that form of in personam jurisdiction based upon a "property ownership" contact and by definition unaccompanied by personal, in-state service, must satisfy the litigation-relatedness requirement of *International Shoe*. The logic of *Shaffer*'s holding — which places all suits against absent nonresidents on the same constitutional footing, regardless of whether a separate Latin label is attached to one particular basis of contact — does not compel the conclusion that physically present defendants must be treated identically to absent ones. As we have demonstrated at length, our tradition has treated the two classes of defendants quite differently, and it is unreasonable to read *Shaffer* as casually obliterating that distinction. *International Shoe* confined its "minimum contacts" requirement to situations in which the defendant "be not present within the territory of the forum," and nothing in *Shaffer* expands that requirement beyond that.

It is fair to say, however, that while our holding today does not contradict *Shaffer*, our basic approach to the due process question is different. We have conducted no independent inquiry into the desirability or fairness of the prevailing in-state service rule, leaving that judgment to the legislatures that are free to amend it; for our purposes, its validation is its pedigree, as the phrase

113

"*traditional notions* of fair play and substantial justice" makes clear. *Shaffer* did conduct such an independent inquiry, asserting that "'traditional notions of fair play and substantial justice' can be as readily offended by the perpetuation of ancient forms that are no longer justified as by the adoption of new procedures that are inconsistent with the basic values of our constitutional heritage." Perhaps that assertion can be sustained when the "perpetuation of ancient forms" is engaged in by only a very small minority of the States.[4] Where, however, as in the present case, a jurisdictional principle is both firmly approved by tradition and still favored, it is impossible to imagine what standard we could appeal to for the judgment that it is "no longer justified." While in no way receding from or casting doubt upon the holding of *Shaffer* or any other case, we reaffirm today our time-honored approach. For new procedures, hitherto unknown, the Due Process clause requires analysis to determine whether "traditional notions of fair play and substantial justice" have been offended. But a doctrine of personal jurisdiction that dates back to the adoption of the Fourteenth Amendment and is still generally observed unquestionably meets that standard.

III

A few words in response to Justice Brennan's opinion concurring in the judgment: It insists that we apply "contemporary notions of due process" to determine the constitutionality of California's assertion of jurisdiction. But our analysis today comports with that prescription, at least if we give it the only sense allowed by our precedents. The "contemporary notions of due process" applicable to personal jurisdiction are the enduring "*traditional* notions of fair play and substantial justice" established as the test by *International Shoe*. By its very language, that test is satisfied if a state court adheres to jurisdictional rules that are generally applied and have always been applied in the United States.

But the concurrence's proposed standard of "contemporary notions of due process" requires more: It measures state-court jurisdiction not only against traditional doctrines in this country, including current state-court practice, but also against each Justice's subjective assessment of what is fair and just. Authority for that seductive standard is not to be found in any of our personal jurisdiction cases. It is, indeed, an outright break with the test of "traditional notions of fair play and substantial justice," which would have to be reformulated "*our* notions of fair play and substantial justice."

The subjectivity, and hence inadequacy, of this approach becomes apparent when the concurrence tries to explain *why* the assertion of jurisdiction in the present case meets its standard of continuing-American-tradition-*plus*-innate-fairness. Justice Brennan lists the "benefits" Mr. Burnham derived from the State of California — the fact that, during the few days he was there, "[h]is health and safety [were] guaranteed by the State's police, fire, and emergency medical services; he [was] free to travel on the State's roads and waterways; he likely enjoy[ed] the fruits of the State's economy." Three days' worth of these benefits strike us as powerfully inadequate to establish, as an abstract matter, that it is "fair" for California to decree the ownership of all Mr. Burnham's worldly goods acquired during the 10 years of his marriage, and the custody over his children. We daresay

---

[4] *Shaffer* may have involved a unique state procedure in one respect: Justice Stevens noted that Delaware was the only State that treated the place of incorporation as the situs of corporate stock when both owner and custodian were elsewhere.

B. Constitutional Limits on Personal Jurisdiction

a contractual exchange swapping those benefits for that power would not survive the "unconscionability" provision of the Uniform Commercial Code. Even less persuasive are the other "fairness" factors alluded to by Justice Brennan. It would create "an asymmetry," we are told, if Burnham were *permitted* (as he is) to appear in California courts as a plaintiff, but were not *compelled* to appear in California courts as defendant; and travel being as easy as it is nowadays, and modern procedural devices being so convenient, it is no great hardship to appear in California courts. The problem with these assertions is that they justify the exercise of jurisdiction over *everyone, whether or not* he ever comes to California. The only "fairness" elements setting Mr. Burnham apart from the rest of the world are the three days' "benefits" referred to above — and even those, do not set him apart from many other people who have enjoyed three days in the Golden State (savoring the fruits of its economy, the availability of its roads and police services) but who were fortunate enough not to be served with process while they were there and thus are not (simply by reason of that savoring) subject to the general jurisdiction of California's courts. In other words, even if one agreed with Justice Brennan's conception of an equitable bargain, the "benefits" we have been discussing would explain why it is "fair" to assert general jurisdiction over Burnham-returned-to-New-Jersey-after-service only at the expense of proving that it is also "fair" to assert general jurisdiction over Burnham-returned-to-New-Jersey-*without*-service — which we *know* does not conform with "contemporary notions of due process."

There is, we must acknowledge, one factor mentioned by Justice Brennan that *both* relates distinctively to the assertion of jurisdiction on the basis of personal in-state service *and* is fully persuasive — namely, the fact that a defendant voluntarily present in a particular State has a "reasonable expectatio[n]" that he is subject to suit there. By formulating it as a "reasonable expectation" Justice Brennan makes that seem like a "fairness" factor; but in reality, of course, it is just tradition masquerading as "fairness." The only reason for charging Mr. Burnham with the reasonable expectation of being subject to suit is that the States of the Union assert adjudicatory jurisdiction over the person, and have always asserted adjudicatory jurisdiction over the person, by serving him with process during his temporary physical presence in their territory. That continuing tradition, which anyone entering California should have known about, renders it "fair" for Mr. Burnham, who voluntarily entered California, to be sued there for divorce — at least "fair" in the limited sense that he has no one but himself to blame. Justice Brennan's long journey is a circular one, leaving him, at the end of the day, in complete reliance upon the very factor he sought to avoid: The existence of a continuing tradition is not enough, fairness also must be considered; fairness exists here because there is a continuing tradition.

While Justice Brennan's concurrence is unwilling to confess that the Justices of this Court can possibly be bound by a continuing American tradition that a particular procedure is fair, neither is it willing to embrace the logical consequences of that refusal — or even to be clear about what consequences (logical or otherwise) it does embrace. Justice Brennan says that "[f]or these reasons [i.e., because of the reasonableness factors enumerated above], as a rule the exercise of personal jurisdiction over a defendant based on his voluntary presence in the forum will satisfy the requirements of due process." The use of the word "rule" conveys the reassuring feeling that he is establishing a principle of law one can rely upon — but of course he is not. Since Justice Brennan's only criterion of constitutionality is "fairness," the phrase "as a rule" represents nothing more than his estimation that, *usually*, all the elements of "fairness" he discusses in the present case will exist. But what if they do not? Suppose, for example, that a defendant in Mr. Burnham's situation enjoys not three days' worth of California's "benefits," but 15 minutes' worth. Or suppose we remove one of those "benefits" — "enjoy[ment of] the fruits of the State's economy" — by positing that Mr. Burnham had not come to California on business, but only to visit his children. Or suppose that Mr. Burnham were demonstrably so impecunious as to be unable to take advantage of the modern means of transportation and communication that Justice Brennan finds so relevant. Or suppose, finally, that the California courts lacked the "variety of procedural devices," that Justice Brennan says can reduce the burden upon out-of-state litigants. One may also make additional suppositions, relating not to the absence of the factors that Justice Brennan discusses, but to the presence of additional factors bearing upon the ultimate criterion of "fairness." What if, for example, Mr. Burnham were visiting a sick child? Or a dying child? Since, so far as one can tell, Justice Brennan's approval of applying the in-state service rule in the present case rests on the presence of all the factors he lists, and on the absence of any others, every different case will present a different litigable issue. Thus, despite the fact that he manages to work the word "rule" into his formulation, Justice Brennan's approach does not establish a rule of law at all, but only a "totality of the circumstances" test, guaranteeing what traditional territorial rules of jurisdiction were designed precisely to avoid: uncertainty and litigation over the preliminary issue of the forum's competence. It may be that those evils, necessarily accompanying a freestanding "reasonableness" inquiry, must be accepted at the margins, when we evaluate *non*traditional forms of jurisdiction newly adopted by the States, see, e.g., *Asahi Metal Industry Co. v. Superior Court of California*. But that is no reason for injecting them into the core of our American practice, exposing to such a "reasonableness" inquiry the ground of jurisdiction that has hitherto been considered the very *baseline* of reasonableness, physical presence.

The difference between us and Justice Brennan has nothing to do with whether "further progress [is] to be made" in the "evolution of our legal system." It has to do with whether changes are to be adopted as progressive by the American people or decreed as progressive by the Justices of this Court. Nothing we say today prevents individual States from limiting or entirely abandoning the in-state-service basis of jurisdiction. And nothing prevents an overwhelming majority of them from doing so, with the consequence that the "traditional notions of fairness" that this Court applies may change. But the States have overwhelmingly declined to adopt such limitation or abandonment, evidently not considering it to be progress.[5] The question is whether, armed with no authority other than individual Justices' perceptions of fairness that conflict with both past and current practice, this Court can compel the States to make such a change on the ground that "due process" requires it. We hold that it cannot.

* * *

Because the Due Process Clause does not prohibit the California courts from exercising jurisdiction over petitioner based on the fact of in-state service of process, the judgment is

Affirmed.

JUSTICE WHITE, concurring in part and concurring in the judgment.

---

[5] I find quite unacceptable as a basis for this Court's decisions Justice Brennan's view that "the *raison d'être* of various constitutional doctrines designed to protect out-of-staters, such as the Art. IV Privileges and Immunities

B. Constitutional Limits on Personal Jurisdiction

I join Parts, I, II-A, II-B, and II-C of Justice Scalia's opinion and concur in the judgment of affirmance. The rule allowing jurisdiction to be obtained over a nonresident by personal service in the forum State, without more, has been and is so widely accepted throughout this country that I could not possibly strike it down, either on its face or as applied in this case, on the ground that it denies due process of law guaranteed by the Fourteenth Amendment. Although the Court has the authority under the Amendment to examine even traditionally accepted procedures and declare them invalid, e.g., *Shaffer v. Heitner*, there has been no showing here or elsewhere that as a general proposition the rule is so arbitrary and lacking in common sense in so many instances that it should be held violative of due process in every case. Furthermore, until such a showing is made, which would be difficult indeed, claims in individual cases that the rule would operate unfairly as applied to the particular nonresident involved need not be entertained. At least this would be the case where presence in the forum State is intentional, which would almost always be the fact. Otherwise, there would be endless, fact-specific litigation in the trial and appellate courts, including this one. Here, personal service in California, without more, is enough, and I agree that the judgment should be affirmed.

JUSTICE BRENNAN, with whom JUSTICE MARSHALL, JUSTICE BLACKMUN, and JUSTICE O'CONNOR join, concurring in the judgment.

I agree with Justice Scalia that the Due Process Clause of the Fourteenth Amendment generally permits a state court to exercise jurisdiction over a defendant if he is served with process while voluntarily present in the forum State. I do not perceive the need, however, to decide that a jurisdictional rule that "'has been immemorially the actual law of the land,'" automatically comports with due process simply by virtue of its "pedigree." Although I agree that history is an important factor in establishing whether a jurisdictional rule satisfies due process requirements, I cannot agree that it is the *only* factor such that all traditional rules of jurisdiction are, ipso facto, forever constitutional. Unlike Justice Scalia, I would undertake an "independent inquiry into the ... fairness of the prevailing in-state service rule." I therefore concur only in the judgment.

I

I believe that the approach adopted by Justice Scalia's opinion today — reliance solely on historical pedigree — is foreclosed by our decisions in *International Shoe Co. v. Washington*, and *Shaffer v. Heitner*. In *International Shoe*, we held that a state court's assertion of personal jurisdic-

---

Clause and the Commerce Clause," entitles this Court to brand as "unfair," and hence unconstitutional, the refusal of all 50 States "to limit or abandon bases of jurisdiction that have become obsolete," "Due process" (which is the constitutional text at issue here) does not mean that process which shifting majorities of this Court feel to be "due"; but that process which American society — self-interested American society, which expresses its judgments in the laws of self-interested States — has traditionally considered "due." The notion that the Constitution, through some penumbra emanating from the Privileges and Immunities Clause and the Commerce Clause, establishes this Court as a Platonic check upon the society's greedy adherence to its traditions can only be described as imperious.

tion does not violate the Due Process Clause if it is consistent with "'traditional notions of fair play and substantial justice.'" In *Shaffer*, we stated that "*all* assertions of state-court jurisdiction must be evaluated according to the standards set forth in *International Shoe* and its progeny." The critical insight of *Shaffer* is that all rules of jurisdiction, even ancient ones, must satisfy contemporary notions of due process. * * *

While our *holding* in *Shaffer* may have been limited to quasi in rem jurisdiction, our mode of analysis was not. Indeed, that we were willing in *Shaffer* to examine anew the appropriateness of the quasi in rem rule — until that time dutifully accepted by American courts for at least a century — demonstrates that we did not believe that the "pedigree" of a jurisdictional practice was dispositive in deciding whether it was consistent with due process. We later characterized *Shaffer* as "abandon[ing] the outworn rule of *Harris v. Balk*, that the interest of a creditor in a debt could be extinguished or otherwise affected by any State having transitory jurisdiction over the debtor." *World-Wide Volkswagen Corp. v. Woodson.* If we could discard an "ancient form without substantial modern justification" in *Shaffer*, we can do so again. Lower courts, commentators, and the American Law Institute all have interpreted *International Shoe* and *Shaffer* to mean that *every* assertion of state-court jurisdiction, even one pursuant to a "traditional" rule such as transient jurisdiction, must comport with contemporary notions of due process. Notwithstanding the nimble gymnastics of Justice Scalia's opinion today, it is not faithful to our decision in *Shaffer*.

II

Tradition, though alone not dispositive, is of course *relevant* to the question whether the rule of transient jurisdiction is consistent with due process.[7] Tradition is salient not in the sense that practices of the past are automatically reasonable today; indeed, under such a standard, the legitimacy of transient jurisdiction would be called into question because the rule's historical "pedigree" is a matter of intense debate. The rule was a stranger to the common law[8] and was rather weakly implanted in American jurisprudence "at the crucial time for present purposes: 1868, when the Fourteenth Amendment was adopted." For much of the 19th century, American courts did not uniformly recognize the concept of transient jurisdiction, and it appears that the transient rule did not receive wide currency until well after our decision in *Pennoyer v. Neff*.[10]

---

[7] I do not propose that the "contemporary notions of due process" to be applied are no more than "each Justice's subjective assessment of what is fair and just." Rather, the inquiry is guided by our decisions beginning with *International Shoe Co. v. Washington*, and the specific factors that we have developed to ascertain whether a jurisdictional rule comports with "traditional notions of fair play and substantial justice." See, e.g., *Asahi Metal Industry Co. v. Superior Court of California* (noting "several factors," including "the burden on the defendant, the interests of the forum State, and the plaintiff's interest in obtaining relief"). This analysis may not be "mechanical or quantitative," but neither is it "freestanding," or dependent on personal whim. Our experience with this approach demonstrates that it is well within our competence to employ.

[8] As Justice Scalia's opinion acknowledges, American courts in the 19th century erected the theory of transient jurisdiction largely upon Justice Story's historical interpretation of Roman and continental sources. Justice Scalia's opinion conceded that the rule's tradition "was not as clear as Story thought," in fact, it now appears that as a historical matter Story was almost surely wrong. * * *

[10] One distinguished legal historian has observed that "notwithstanding dogmatic generalizations later sanctioned by the Restatement [of Conflict of Laws], appellate courts hardly ever in fact held transient service sufficient as such" and that "although the transient rule has often been mouthed by the courts, it has but rarely been applied." * * *

Rather, I find the historical background relevant because, however murky the jurisprudential origins of transient jurisdiction, the fact that American courts have announced the rule for perhaps a century (first in dicta, more recently in holdings) provides a defendant voluntarily present in a particular State *today* "clear notice that [he] is subject to suit" in the forum. Regardless of whether Justice Story's account of the rule's genesis is mythical, our common understanding *now,* fortified by a century of judicial practice, is that jurisdiction is often a function of geography. The transient rule is consistent with reasonable expectations and is entitled to a strong presumption that it comports with due process. "If I visit another State, ... I knowingly assume some risk that the State will exercise its power over my property or my person while there. My contact with the State, though minimal, gives rise to predictable risks." *Shaffer v. Heitner* (Stevens, J., concurring in judgment). Thus, proposed revisions to the RESTATEMENT (SECOND) OF CONFLICT OF LAWS § 28, p. 39 (1986), provide that "[a] state has power to exercise judicial jurisdiction over an individual who is present within its territory unless the individual's relationship to the state is so attenuated as to make the exercise of such jurisdiction unreasonable."[11]

By visiting the forum State, a transient defendant actually "avail[s]" himself of significant benefits provided by the State. His health and safety are guaranteed by the State's police, fire, and emergency medical services; he is free to travel on the State's roads and waterways; he likely enjoys the fruits of the State's economy as well. Moreover, the Privileges and Immunities Clause of Article IV prevents a state government from discriminating against a transient defendant by denying him the protections of its law or the right of access to its courts. Subject only to the doctrine of forum non conveniens, an out-of-state plaintiff may use state courts in all circumstances in which those courts would be available to state citizens. Without transient jurisdiction, an asymmetry would arise: A transient would have the full benefit of the power of the forum State's courts as a plaintiff while retaining immunity from their authority as a defendant.

The potential burdens on a transient defendant are slight. "'[M]odern transportation and communications have made it much less burdensome for a party sued to defend himself'" in a State outside his place of residence. *Burger King.* That the defendant has already journeyed at least once before to the forum — as evidenced by the fact that he was served with process there — is an indication that suit in the forum likely would not be prohibitively inconvenient. Finally, any burdens that do arise can be ameliorated by a variety of procedural devices.[13] For these reasons, as a rule the exercise of personal jurisdiction over a defendant based on his voluntary presence in the forum will satisfy the requirements of due process.

In this case, it is undisputed that petitioner was served with process while voluntarily and knowingly in the State of California. I therefore concur in the judgment.

---

[11] As the Restatement suggests, there may be cases in which a defendant's involuntary or unknowing presence in a State does not support the exercise of personal jurisdiction over him. The facts of the instant case do not require us to determine the outer limits of the transient jurisdiction rule.

[13] For example, in the federal system, a transient defendant can avoid protracted litigation of a spurious suit through a motion to dismiss for failure to state a claim or through a motion for summary judgment. Fed. Rules Civ. Proc. 12(b)(6) and 56. He can use relatively inexpensive methods of discovery, such as oral deposition by telephone (Rule 30(b)(7)), deposition upon written questions (Rule 31), interrogatories (Rule 33), and requests for admission (Rule 36), while enjoying protection from harassment (Rule 26(c)), and possibly obtaining costs and attorney's fees for some of the work involved (Rules 37(a)(4), (b)-(d)). Moreover, a change of venue may be possible. 28 U.S.C. § 1404. In state court, many of the same procedural protections are available, as is the doctrine of forum non conveniens, under which the suit may be dismissed.

JUSTICE STEVENS, concurring in the judgment.

As I explained in my separate writing, I did not join the Court's opinion in *Shaffer v. Heitner*, because I was concerned by its unnecessarily broad reach. The same concern prevents me from joining either Justice Scalia's or Justice Brennan's opinion in this case. For me, it is sufficient to note that the historical evidence and consensus identified by Justice Scalia, the considerations of fairness identified by Justice Brennan, and the common sense displayed by Justice White, all combine to demonstrate that this is, indeed, a very easy case.* Accordingly, I agree that the judgment should be affirmed.

NOTES AND QUESTIONS

1. Mr. Burnham contested California's jurisdiction to enter a monetary judgment against him in connection with a divorce. He did not contest the court's jurisdiction to grant the divorce itself. The reason for this is that in personam jurisdiction is not necessary for a court to enter a valid divorce. This rule predates *Pennoyer* and Justice Field specifically reaffirmed the rule. See supra at 30. The only jurisdictional prerequisite to a valid divorce is that at least one of the spouses be domiciled in the state which grants the divorce. See Williams v. North Carolina, 317 U.S. 287 (1942). While in personam jurisdiction is not required for the divorce, it is required for a money judgment of alimony or child support.

2. If you had represented the defendant, what arguments would you have made as to why transient jurisdiction is unconstitutional?

3. In *Shaffer*, the Court invalidated a type of jurisdiction that had long been allowed. How does Justice Scalia reconcile the result of *Shaffer* with his historical approach? Some have argued that Scalia's opinion suggests a very narrow reading of *Shaffer* which prohibits quasi-in-rem jurisdiction only in cases involving "intangible property that has no reasonable nexus with the forum." Russell Weintraub, A*n Objective Basis for Rejecting Transient Jurisdiction*, 22 RUTGERS L.J. 611, 623 (1991). Do you agree with this interpretation of Scalia's opinion? Is this a plausible reading of Scalia's opinion? Of *Shaffer*?

4. According to Justice Brennan, why is jurisdiction fair in this case? Do you agree that the benefits the defendant received from California were sufficient to warrant being subjected to personal jurisdiction? Would the benefits have been any different if the defendant had been served outside California? Would there have been jurisdiction in such a case?

---

* [Footnote in original.] Perhaps the adage about hard cases making bad law should be revised to cover easy cases.

5. Suppose the defendant were served with process while flying over California. Which Justices if any, would uphold jurisdiction?

6. Suppose the defendant had been involuntarily extradited to California or had been tricked or fraudulently induced into entering the state. Which Justices, if any, would uphold jurisdiction?

7. Does in-state service on a corporate agent subject the corporation to general jurisdiction? In James-Dickinson Farm Mortgage Co. v. Harry, 273 U.S. 119 (1927), the Supreme Court held: "Jurisdiction over a corporation of one State cannot be acquired in another State or district in which it has no place of business and is not found, merely by serving process upon an executive officer temporarily therein, even if he is there on business of the company." Id. at 122. Does it make sense to treat transient corporate agents differently from transient individuals?

8. What about in-state service on corporate agents who are not transient? States require out-of-state corporations seeking to do business within the state to register and to appoint an in-state agent for service of process. Would in-state service on a registered agent be constitutionally sufficient? Some courts have held that the appointment of such an agent operates as "consent" to general jurisdiction. See, e.g., Knowlton v. Allied Van Lines, 900 F.2d 1196 (8th Cir. 1990). Other courts have held that as a matter of state law, appointing an agent does not constitute consent to general jurisdiction. See, e.g., Siemer v. Learjet Acquisition Corp., 966 F.2d 179 (5th Cir. 1992), *cert. denied*, 113 S.Ct. 1047 (1993). Justice Scalia cites with apparent disapproval three lower federal court cases that held service on a corporate agent was a constitutionally insufficient basis for jurisdiction. See supra at 111. *Nehemiah* and *Harold M. Pittman Co.* involved service on corporate agents who happened to be passing through the state. *Schreiber* involved service on a registered agent. All three cases relied primarily on *International Shoe* and *Shaffer* and none cited *James-Dickinson Farm Mortgage Co.*.

9. In Bendix Autolite Corp. v. Midwesco Enterprises, 486 U.S. 888 (1988), the Supreme Court struck down an Ohio statute under which the Ohio statute of limitations was tolled indefinitely for any foreign corporation that had not appointed an agent for service of process in Ohio. The Court assumed, without analysis, that appointment of an in-state agent would subject the corporation to general jurisdiction in Ohio. However, the Court concluded that being subject to general jurisdiction was "a significant burden" and the Court struck down the statute, holding that "the burden imposed on interstate commerce by the tolling statute exceeds any local interest that the State might advance." Id. at 891. Could Mr. Burnham make a similar argument? Wasn't he subjected to a significant burden that may discourage interstate travel?

C. A Different Perspective

1. The Purposes of Personal Jurisdiction

The constitutional doctrine of personal jurisdiction imposes a federal restriction on state adjudicative authority. But why should there be any such limits? What is the problem for which personal jurisdiction is the solution? One might argue that personal jurisdiction is simply a guaranty of immunity from the inconvenience of distant litigation. The doctrine that has developed, however, does not focus primarily on convenience. Indeed, the Court in *World Wide Volkswagen* stated that even the most convenient forum may not have jurisdiction. Limitations on personal jurisdiction could be intended to protect a defendant from the bias of states with which she is not affiliated. Again, however, the developed doctrine is not aimed at protecting against bias. For example, there is no reason to believe that California will be less biased toward the defendants in *Calder* than Oklahoma would be toward the defendants in *World-Wide Volkswagen*.

Maybe personal jurisdiction is a concrete manifestation of a somewhat more philosophical problem. When one asks whether a court has personal jurisdiction, one in essence asks whether a sovereign has a legitimate right to exercise authority over a particular individual. If one conceives of states as wholly separate sovereigns, and one believes that legitimate authority stems only from the consent of the governed, then it may make sense to require that a defendant consent or otherwise purposefully connect herself with the sovereign. See Margaret Stewart, *A New Litany of Personal Jurisdiction*, 60 U. COLO. L. REV. 5 (1989).

This explanation is not without its difficulties. Even if one accepts a consent theory of political legitimacy, why isn't it the case that by becoming (or remaining) a citizen of the United States, one consents to the adjudicative authority of all the states? By participating in our interdependent nation with its free interstate flow of goods and services, all citizens get many benefits. One of the costs of interstate commerce is that harms can be inflicted far from the participants to a transaction. Having accepted the benefits of our free flowing economy, why isn't it fair to impose the burden of possible distant litigation in any of the states?

Professor Brilmayer has offered a related but somewhat different explanation for the purposefulness component of personal jurisdiction. She explains:

> The reason for limiting jurisdiction to cases where the defendant had some control over the eventual location of the product is to prevent the forum from always shifting the costs to persons to whom its sovereignty does not extend, namely, the out-of-state consumers who have no contact with the forum. If the defendant deliberately sent a product into the State, he has a choice to stop marketing there if the costs of doing business exceed the value to him of that

> market. And the State is unlikely to impose upon him jurisdictional burdens exceeding the actual cost of his activities there, because the State does not want to discourage his activities in the State unless the benefits of the activities are less than the burdens. But if jurisdiction can be asserted even where the defendant had no control, these checks cannot be assumed to be adequate. Since the defendant cannot structure his conduct in a way that makes him immune to suit there, the State is not adequately restrained by the possibility that the defendant will withdraw from its markets. And it cannot be inferred that taking advantage of activity in the forum was sufficiently profitable, even given the added jurisdictional costs, that the defendant may fairly be presumed to have agreed to take his chances.

Brilmayer, supra, 1980 S. Ct. Rev. at 95-96. Why can't states distribute the losses on out-of-staters? In the context of personal jurisdiction, someone, either plaintiff or defendant, will have to travel to an undesired (and undesirable?) forum. Is economic efficiency enhanced by making plaintiffs travel to defendants' states rather than the other way around?

Other commentators have suggested that personal jurisdiction should be viewed less as a protection of individual liberty and more as a device for regulating interstate federalism. Thus, Professor Stein has argued that the central issue in personal jurisdiction should be "whether the forum has any business regulating the controversy." Allan Stein, *Styles of Argument and Interstate Federalism in the Law of Personal Jurisdiction*, 65 Tex. L. Rev. 689, 751 (1987). Similarly, Professor Weinstein has argued that the rules of personal jurisdiction developed in this country as the "quid pro quo" for a strict application of the Full Faith and Credit Clause, under which all sister-state judgments (rendered with jurisdiction) must be enforced. James Weinstein, *The Early American Origins of Territoriality in Judicial Jurisdiction*, 37 St. Louis U. L.J. 1, 27 (1992). Finally, it has been argued that because plaintiffs frequently seek a forum that will apply the most advantageous law, personal jurisdiction, which limits plaintiffs' choices among fora, is an indirect way to limit plaintiffs' ability to choose the law. See Wendy Collins Perdue, *Personal Jurisdiction and the Beetle in the Box*, 32 B.C. L. Rev. 529, 570-73 (1991).

Which, if any, of these explanations make sense? Do any of them provide adequate justifications for the federal judiciary to override state attempts to exercise jurisdiction?

2. Personal Jurisdiction in Other Countries

In *Pennoyer*, Justice Field suggested that the principles of jurisdiction which he propounds are universally accepted. They are not. For example, the German Civil Procedure Code permits in personam jurisdiction over nonresident defendants who own property in Germany. There is no requirement that the claim be related to the property, there is no need for prior attachment and jurisdiction is not limited to the value of the German assets. France goes even further. Its Civil Code permits French citizens to sue anyone in French courts without regard to the defendant's connection to France. The Code further provides that French citizens can be sued only in France. Of course, the fact that Germany and France choose to exercise jurisdiction in these circumstances does not mean that other countries will enforce these judgments. Nonetheless, many countries permit jurisdiction in circumstances that we would consider exorbitant. See generally Friedrich Juenger, *Judicial Jurisdiction in the United States and in the European Communities: A Comparison*, 82 MICH. L. REV. 1195 (1984).

These international analogies may not seem entirely apt to the problem of interstate jurisdiction. After all, one of the purposes of the U.S. Constitution was to constrain the destructive chauvinistic instincts of the states. One of the most interesting international analogies to the problems we confront as a nation of states is the European Union (EU). In connection with the creation of the EU, the participating countries addressed the problems of jurisdiction by adopting the Lugano Convention on Jurisdiction and the Enforcement of Judgments in Civil and Commercial Matters, Sept. 16, 1988, 1988 O.J. (L 319). That Convention provides for general jurisdiction in the defendant's domicile or, in the case of a business, in its principal place of business. In addition, it includes a number of specific rules, some of which are set forth below. The Convention prohibits the use of certain types of jurisdiction, including transient jurisdiction. All of the limitations imposed by the Convention apply only to jurisdiction asserted over domiciliaries and nationals of signatory countries. The Convention does not limit assertions of jurisdiction over other foreigners.

TITLE II, SECTION 2

Article 5

A person domiciled in [an EU Country] may, in another [EU Country] be sued:

1. in matters relating to a contract, in the courts of the place of performance of the obligation in question; * * *
2. in matters relating to maintenance [e.g., child support and alimony], in the courts for the place where the maintenance creditor is domiciled or habitually resident * * *;
3. in matters relating to tort, delict or quasi-delict in the courts for the place where the harmful event occurred;

D. Statutory Limits on Personal Jurisdiction

* * *

Article 6

A person domiciled in [an EU Country] may also be sued:

1. where he is one of a number of defendants, in the courts for the place where any one of them is domiciled;
2. as a third party in an action on a warranty or guarantee or in any other third party proceedings, in the court seised of the original proceedings, unless these were instituted solely with the object of removing him from the jurisdiction of the court which would be competent in his case;
3. on a counter-claim arising from the same contract or facts on which the original claim was based, in the court in which the original claim is pending.

* * *

Consider *World-Wide Volkswagen*, *Kulko*, *Burger King*, *Asahi* and *Burnham*. Would the results in those cases be different under the EU treaty?

You will notice that the Convention does not appear to impose a requirement of "purposeful availment." Indeed, with respect to torts, the European Court of Justice has held that a tort suit can be filed either in the place of the damage or in the place of the events giving rise to the damage. See Bier v. Mines de Potasse D'Alsace S.A. [1976-8] E.C.R. 1736, 1743 (European Court of Justice). Does the Convention fail to recognize and protect the sovereignty of the signatory countries? Do you think the Convention is unfair to the citizens of those countries? See generally Patrick Borchers, *Comparing Personal Jurisdiction in the United States and the European Community: Lessons for American Reform*, 40 AM. J. COMP. L. 121 (1992).

D. Statutory Limits on Personal Jurisdiction

Up to this point, we have been dealing with limits imposed by the Constitution on states' ability to assert personal jurisdiction. States may also impose their own limits. Obviously, states cannot assert jurisdiction beyond that which the Constitution allows, but they may choose to exercise less than the full authority granted by the Constitution. Where states choose to impose restriction beyond those from the Constitution, their courts have jurisdiction only if (1) the case falls within the limits imposed by state statute, and (2) jurisdiction is constitutional. Thus, if the statute is not met, no constitutional analysis is needed. This is consistent with the general desire of courts to avoid constitutional questions when possible. If the state has elected not to assert jurisdiction over the case at hand, the fact that it could constitutionally have done so is irrelevant.

All states have so-called "long arm statutes" that specify the scope of that state's personal jurisdiction authority. These statutes were passed in reaction to *International Shoe* and vary state to state. Most consist of laundry lists of acts which would subject a nonresident to specific jurisdiction. A few are more open-ended. For example, California law provides "A court of this state may exercise jurisdiction on any basis not inconsistent with the Constitution of this state or of the United States." CAL. CODE OF CIV. PROC. § 410.10. Each state is free to interpret its long arm statute however it chooses, and sometimes identical language is interpreted differently in different states.

Consider the following situation. Suppose Valve Co. manufactures valves in State A. It sells the valves to Heater Co., a heater manufacturer in State B. Heater Co. incorporates the valves into its heaters, which it sells throughout a region of several states. One of the Valve Co. valves explodes in State X, injuring the plaintiff. Plaintiff wants to sue Valve Co. in State X. Its long arm statute grants jurisdiction over one who "commits a tortious act or omission in State X." Does it apply to Valve Co?

Courts in different states have interpreted this language differently. In Gray v. American Radiator & Std. Sanitary Corp., 176 N.E.2d 761 (Ill. 1961), supra at 48, the Illinois Supreme Court upheld jurisdiction under these facts. It reasoned that an act or omission cannot become "tortious" until someone is injured. Because plaintiff was injured in Illinois, defendant committed a tortious act or omission there.

The New York Court of Appeals interpreted an identical New York statue under similar circumstance and reached a different conclusion. It emphasized the statutory words "act or omission," and concluded that the statute could be met only if the defendant actually did (or omitted to do) something in New York. Where the negligent manufacture of the product took place in a different state, there was no tortious act or omission (and therefore no jurisdiction) in New York. Feathers v. McLucas, 209 N.E.2d 68, (N.Y. 1965).

Following *Feathers*, the New York legislature amended the New York statue to permit jurisdiction over nonresidents who committed tortious acts or omissions out of state that caused injury in state. Jurisdiction was proper, however, only if the defendant had other contacts with the state or could reasonably expect to derive substantial revenue there.

Review the Georgia statue, reproduced below. Notice that in subparts (2) and (3) the statue deal separately with cases in which the defendant acted in Georgia and those in which it acted out of state, causing injury in state. Notice also, that (3) imposes an additional

D. Statutory Limits on Personal Jurisdiction

requirement similar to that in the New York statue. Let's see what the Georgia courts did with this scheme.

9 Official Code of Georgia Annotated § 9-10-91 (1992)

9-10-91. Grounds for exercise of personal jurisdiction over nonresident.

A court of this state may exercise personal jurisdiction over any nonresident or his executor or administrator, as to a cause of action arising from any of the acts, omissions, ownership, use, or possession enumerated in this Code section, in the same manner as if he were a resident of the state, if in person or through an agent, he:

(1) Transacts any business within this state;
(2) Commits a tortious act or omission within this state, except as to a cause of action for defamation of character arising from the act;
(3) Commits a tortious injury in this state caused by an act or omission outside this state if the tort-feasor regularly does or solicits business, or engages in any other persistent course of conduct, or derives substantial revenue from goods used or consumed or services rendered in this state;
(4) Owns, uses, or possesses any real property situated within this state; or
(5) With respect to proceedings for alimony, child support, or division of property in connection with an action for divorce or with respect to an independent action for support of dependents, maintains a matrimonial domicile in this state at the time of the commencement of this action or, if the defendant resided in this state preceding the commencement of the action, whether cohabiting during that time or not. This paragraph shall not change the residency requirement for filing an action for divorce.

Flint v. Gust
180 Ga. App. 904, 351 S.E.2d 95 (1986)

BANKE, CHIEF JUDGE.

The appellant sued the appellees, a Wisconsin corporation and its president, to recover damages for fraud and conversion based on their alleged conduct of a "bait-and-switch" operation involving the sale of customized vans and trucks. Jurisdiction over the appellees, neither of whom are Georgia residents, was predicated on subsection (3) of our Long Arm Statute, OCGA § 9-10-91, which is applicable by its terms to tort actions arising from acts and omissions occurring outside the state which lead to injury inside the state. The appellant later amended his complaint to add a claim for breach of contract, predicating jurisdiction over the appellees with respect to that claim on subsection (1) of OCGA § 9-10-91, which applies if the nonresident defendant "[t]ransacts any business in this state." This appeal is from the grant of the appellees' motion to dismiss both counts of the complaint for lack of personal jurisdiction.

The appellant alleged that, acting in response to an ad appearing in a trade magazine distributed in this state, he had transmitted an order to the appellees in Wisconsin for a customized

Ford truck and trailer, following which, in response to the appellees' requirements, he had remitted a cashier's check to them for $6,000 as a deposit on the vehicle. He further alleged that, after receiving this check, the appellees had attempted to substitute a different type of vehicle from the one he had ordered and had subsequently refused numerous demands by him for the return of his deposit.

In support of their motion to dismiss the complaint for lack of personal jurisdiction, the appellees submitted affidavits in which they denied that they regularly conducted or solicited business in Georgia, or engaged in any other persistent course of conduct within this state, or derived substantial revenue from goods used or services rendered in this state. Indeed, they denied that they had ever done any business at all in Georgia with the exception of the transaction at issue in this suit. *Held*:

1. The trial court was correct in concluding that it had no jurisdiction over the appellees with respect to the breach of contract claim. In a breach of contract action not involving real property located in this state (see OCGA § 9-10-91(4)), jurisdiction over a nonresident defendant may be exercised by the courts of this state only upon a showing that the nonresident defendant "[t]ransacts any business in this state...." OCGA § 9-10-91(1). Jurisdiction over a nonresident exists on the basis of transacting business in this state only "if the nonresident has purposefully done some act or consummated some transaction in this state, if the cause of action arises from or is connected with such act or transaction, and if the exercise of jurisdiction by the courts of this state does not offend traditional fairness and substantial justice." Davis Metals v. Allen, 230 Ga. 623, 625, 198 S.E.2d 285 (1973). It is well settled that an out-of-state defendant will not be deemed to have engaged in purposeful business activity in this state merely because he has advertised products for sale in national trade magazines circulating in this state and has accepted orders for such products which have been transmitted to him from this state by mail, telephone, or other instrumentality of interstate commerce in response to such advertisements.

2. The issue of whether the trial court had jurisdiction over the appellees with respect to the tort action is somewhat more problematical. The appellees established without dispute by their affidavits that they had neither engaged in any regular or persistent business activity in this state nor obtained substantial revenue from goods used or services rendered in this state. Therefore, jurisdiction over them clearly could not be predicated on OCGA § 9-10-91(3), which authorizes the exercise of long-arm jurisdiction over a nonresident defendant who "[c]ommits a tortious injury in this state caused by an act or omission outside this state *if the tortfeasor regularly does or solicits business, or engages in any other persistent course of conduct, or derives substantial revenue from goods used or consumed or services rendered in this state....*" (Emphasis supplied.) It follows that any jurisdiction which may exist over the appellees with respect to this litigation must exist pursuant to OCGA § 9-10-91(2). By its terms, that subsection is applicable, without further restriction, to any nonresident defendant who "[c]ommit a tortious act or omission within this state, except as to a cause of action for defamation of character arising from the act...."

The predecessor to OCGA § 9-10-91(3) was enacted by the Legislature in response to prior decisions of this court adopting the "New York rule" in interpreting the predecessor to OCGA § 9-10-91(2). Under the "New York rule," a tort is deemed to have been committed within the state only if the tortious act or omission itself, and not merely the injury resulting therefrom, occurred therein. However, after the predecessor to OCGA § 9-10-91(3) was enacted, our Supreme Court, in *Coe & Payne Co. v. Wood-Mosaic Corp.*, 230 Ga. 58, 195 S.E.2d 399 (1973), rejected the "New York rule" in favor of the "Illinois rule," pursuant to which a tort resulting in damage inside the state is deemed to have occurred inside the state regardless of where the tortious act or omission took place.

At first blush, the holding in *Coe & Payne Co. v. Wood-Mosaic Corp.* would appear to have made the transaction-of-business requirements set forth in OCGA § 9-10-91(3) entirely superfluous. However, in Clarkson Power Flow v. Thompson, 244 Ga. 300, 301, 260 S.E.2d 9 (1979), the Supreme Court held that "limitations similar to those present in subsection [(3)] are constitutionally mandated under subsection [(2)]." The Court elaborated as follows: "A nonresident defendant is subject to the jurisdiction of the Georgia courts only if he has established 'minimum contacts' in this state so that the exercise of jurisdiction is consistent with 'traditional notions of fair play and substantial justice.' *International Shoe Co. v. Washington ... We thus conclude that there is no essential difference between subsections [(2)] and [(3)].*" (Emphasis supplied.)

Interpreted literally, the effect of this holding would appear to be to engraft onto subsection (2) of OCGA § 9-10-91 the transaction-of-business requirements set forth in subsection (3), making the establishment of long-arm jurisdiction over any nonresident tort feasor conditional upon a showing that the tort feasor regularly conducted or solicited business in this state, or engaged in some other persistent course of conduct in this state, or derived substantial revenue from goods used or services rendered in this state. However, it is quite clear that such restrictions are not constitutionally mandated in all cases, particularly where the cause of action is based on tort. See *McGee v. Intl. Life Ins. Co.* It is similarly apparent that the Georgia Supreme Court has never expressed any intention to renounce the principle, previously adopted in *Coe & Payne Co. v. Wood-Mosaic Corp.*, as a corollary of the "Illinois rule," that this state's Long Arm Statute is to be interpreted so as to permit the exercise of jurisdiction over nonresident parties "to the maximum extent permitted by procedural due process." Accordingly, we must conclude that what the Supreme Court really meant in *Clarkson Power Flow v. Thompson*, was simply that the exercise of long-arm jurisdiction is always conditional on the existence of constitutionally sufficient "minimum contacts" between the nonresident defendant and this state, regardless of which subsection of the statute is invoked as the basis for such jurisdiction. Having so interpreted the holding in *Clarkson Power Flow*, we [conclude] * * * that, while the exercise of jurisdiction over a nonresident tort feasor pursuant to OCGA § 9-10-91(2) "requires some activity by [the] nonresident defendant in or with Georgia, ... there is no engrafting on this 'tort' section the requirement that this activity amount to a 'transaction of business' within this state."

The appellees in the present case were alleged to have intentionally and fraudulently induced the appellant to send them a $6,000 deposit on a vehicle they did not intend to deliver to him. Such conduct goes well beyond the mere acceptance of an order for an item advertised in a national publication; and we have no hesitancy in holding that, being both intentional and specifically directed towards a Georgia resident, it would establish, if proved, a sufficient connection with this state to satisfy the "minimum contacts" requirement imposed by the due-process clause of the United States Constitution. Therefore, we hold that the trial court erred in granting the appellees' motion to dismiss the complaint with respect to the fraud and conversion claims.

Judgment affirmed in part and reversed in part.

CHAPTER 2 PERSONAL JURISDICTION

Gust v. Flint
257 Ga. 129, 356 S.E.2d 513 (1987)

WELTNER, JUSTICE.

George Flint, a resident of Georgia, responded to an advertisement printed in a trade paper published in Nebraska and mailed to Flint in Georgia. Roger Gust and Twin Grove Trailers & Pate Tractor, Inc., of Madison, Wisconsin, had inserted the advertisement for a customized truck and trailer which attracted Flint's interest, and by long distance telephone the parties struck a bargain, pursuant to which Flint sent a $6,000 deposit toward the purchase price of the truck and trailer. After the deposit was received the sellers informed Flint that they could not deliver the truck and trailer he had ordered and attempted to persuade Flint to accept a substitute. When Flint refused to do so, the sellers refused to return his deposit.

Flint filed suit against the sellers in Georgia, predicating personal jurisdiction over the Wisconsin parties on OCGA Section 9-10-91, this state's long-arm statute. The out-of-state defendants, who were served personally in Wisconsin, moved to dismiss Flint's complaint, contending that under Georgia's long-arm statute they were not subject to personal jurisdiction in this state. The affidavits filed in support of the motion to dismiss, which were not traversed, showed that the defendants: (1) did not regularly do business or solicit business within the State of Georgia, (2) did not engage in any persistent course of conduct within the State of Georgia, (3) did not derive substantial revenue from services rendered within the State of Georgia, (4) the only business done by them in the State of Georgia is the transaction which is the subject of the instant action, (5) the only communications or connection they have had with the State of Georgia had been via telephone communication, (6) that neither they nor any of their employees have ever been located within the State of Georgia, (7) the corporate defendant is not domesticated in or authorized to do business in the State of Georgia and does not manufacture goods or produce any services in the State of Georgia. Thus, they demonstrated that they had done none of the acts which OCGA Section 9-10-91 requires as a basis for personal jurisdiction. * * *

The trial court sustained the motion to dismiss. The Court of Appeals reversed, holding that the trial court had personal jurisdiction of the tort claim but not the claim for breach of contract. We granted certiorari to determine whether the issue in this case is controlled by *Coe & Payne Co., v. Wood-Mosaic Corp.*, and *Clarkson Power Flow, Inc. v. Thompson*, that is to say, by a literal construction of Georgia's long-arm statute.

The unrebutted affidavits filed in support of the out-of-state defendants' motion to dismiss clearly establish that the defendants have done none of the acts set forth in OCGA § 9-10-91 which must be done in order to subject them to personal jurisdiction of a Georgia court. We need not discuss the relative merits of a "New York rule" or an "Illinois rule." The rule that controls is our statute, which requires that an out-of-state defendant must do certain acts within the State of Georgia before he can be subjected to personal jurisdiction. Where, as here, it is shown that no such acts were committed, there is no jurisdiction.

Judgment reversed.

GREGORY, JUSTICE, concurring.

D. Statutory Limits on Personal Jurisdiction

I agree with the judgment of the majority opinion and its analysis. However, I suggest there may be a valid reason to pursue the relative merits of the "New York rule" versus the "Illinois rule." To do so might tend to focus public attention on the contrary philosophies underlying each. For my part, I fail to see why Georgia would not want its courts to have the maximum jurisdiction permissible within constitutional due process. A legislative act simply extending the jurisdiction of the Georgia courts to the maximum limit permitted within the restraints of due process of law would accomplish this result.

* * *

SMITH, JUSTICE, dissenting.

Under our Long-Arm Statute, OCGA § 9-10-91, as interpreted by the majority today, a civil defendant from another state who has committed the intentional tort of fraud against a citizen of this state is better off than a defendant from another state who sends a negligently manufactured product to Georgia. Unfortunately, it may appear that we punish carelessness but only wink at outright deception. We should not send the wrong message to those who would launch deceptive business practices into Georgia from afar.

As Justice Gregory states in his concurrence, Georgia should have a Long-Arm Statute that fits the contours of the limits of constitutional due process. * * *

* * *

NOTES AND QUESTIONS

1. Would it have been unconstitutional for Georgia to assert personal jurisdiction in this case?

2. Do you agree with the Georgia Supreme Court that the literal language of that statute was not met? The plaintiff alleged that defendants failed to return his deposit or the goods ordered. Where did that omission occur?

3. Oklahoma has a long arm statute similar to Georgia's. The Oklahoma Supreme Court has held that this statute extends jurisdiction to the full extent allowed by the Constitution. See *World-Wide Volkswagen*, supra, at 50 n.7. Do you think this is a plausible interpretation of the statute?

4. Why would choose not to reach to the full constitutional limit? Professor Leflar has said of a California-type statute:

> [S]uch enactments permit the exercise of jurisdiction which reaches to the very edge of fair play and substantial justice, almost to unfair play and actual injustice. The due process clause does not require ideal or even very good procedures. It

only prohibits procedures that are very bad. * * * "To say that a law does not violate the due process clause is to say the least possible good about it."

ROBERT LEFLAR, LUTHER MCDOUGAL & ROBERT FELIX, AMERICAN CONFLICTS LAW 102 (4th ed. 1986), quoting *Cheatham, Conflict of Laws: Some Developments and Some Questions,* 25 ARK. L. REV. 9, 25 (1975). If you were advising your state legislature, how far would you recommend that it extend its long arm statute? Are there any categories of cases for which jurisdiction is constitutional, but you believe the state should not assert jurisdiction?

CHAPTER 3
NOTICE AND OPPORTUNITY TO BE HEARD

A. Introduction and Integration

In the personal jurisdiction chapter, we explored one aspect of due process. While personal jurisdiction is a necessary condition on the exercise of authority, the Due Process Clauses of the Fifth and Fourteenth Amendments impose additional requirements. Two of these additional elements are reasonable notice and the opportunity to be heard. As you will recall, some personal jurisdiction cases, such as *Pennoyer*, addressed notice, but notice is not a central concern of personal jurisdiction. If notice were the issue, it would never matter where process was served. This chapter explores the additional due process requirements of notice and opportunity to be heard.

B. Notice

1. The Constitutional Requirement

Mullane v. Central Hanover Bank & Trust Co.
339 U.S. 306, 70 S.Ct. 652, 94 L. Ed. 865 (1950)

JUSTICE JACKSON delivered the opinion of the Court.

This controversy questions the constitutional sufficiency of notice to beneficiaries on judicial settlement of accounts by the trustee of a common trust fund established under the New York Banking Law. The New York Court of Appeals considered and overruled objections that the statutory notice contravenes requirements of the Fourteenth Amendment and that by allowance of the account beneficiaries were deprived of property without due process of law. * * *

Common trust fund legislation is addressed to a problem appropriate for state action. Mounting overheads have made administration of small trusts undesirable to corporate trustees. In order that donors and testators of moderately sized trusts may not be denied the service of corporate fiduciaries, the District of Columbia and some thirty states other than New York have permitted pooling small trust estates into one fund for investment administration. The income, capital gains, losses and expenses of the collective trust are shared by the constituent trusts in proportion to their contribution. By this plan, diversification of risk and economy of management can be extended to those whose capital standing alone would not obtain such advantage.

* * * [New York law authorizes the pooling of small trusts into a common fund. Under New York law, each] participating trust shares ratably in the common fund, but exclusive management and control is in the trust company as trustee, and neither a fiduciary nor any beneficiary of a participating trust is deemed to have ownership in any particular asset or investment of this common fund. The trust company must keep fund assets separate from its own, and in its fiduciary capacity may not deal with itself or any affiliate. Provisions are made for accountings twelve to fifteen months after the establishment of a fund and triennially thereafter. The decree in each such judicial settlement of accounts is made binding and conclusive as to any matter set forth in the account upon everyone having any interest in the common fund or in any participating estate, trust or fund.

In January, 1946, Central Hanover Bank and Trust Company established a common trust fund in accordance with these provisions, and in March, 1947, it petitioned the Surrogate's Court for settlement of its first account as common trustee. During the accounting period a total of 113 trusts, approximately half inter vivos and half testamentary, participated in the common trust fund, the gross capital of which was nearly three million dollars. The record does not show the number or residence of the beneficiaries, but they were many and it is clear that some of them were not residents of the State of New York.

The only notice given beneficiaries of this specific application was by publication in a local newspaper in strict compliance with the minimum requirements of N.Y. Banking Laws * * *. Thus the only notice required, and the only one given, was by newspaper publication setting forth merely the name and address of the trust company, the name and the date of establishment of the common trust fund, and a list of all participating estates, trusts or funds.

At the time the first investment in the common fund was made on behalf of each participating estate, however, the trust company, pursuant to the requirements of [N.Y. banking law], had notified by mail each person of full age and sound mind whose name and address were then known to it and who was "entitled to share in the income therefrom ... [or] ... who would be entitled to share in the principal if the event upon which such estate, trust or fund will become distributable should have occurred at the time of sending such notice." Included in the notice was a copy of those provisions of the Act relating to the sending of the notice itself and to the judicial settlement of common trust fund accounts.

Upon the filing of the petition for the settlement of accounts, appellant was, by order of the court pursuant to [the banking law], appointed special guardian and attorney for all persons known or unknown not otherwise appearing who had or might thereafter have any interest in the income of the common trust fund; and appellee Vaughan was appointed to represent those similarly interested in the principal. There were no other appearances on behalf of any one interested in either interest or principal.

Appellant appeared specially, objecting that notice and the statutory provisions for notice to beneficiaries were inadequate to afford due process under the Fourteenth Amendment, and therefore that the court was without jurisdiction to render a final and binding decree. Appellant's objections were entertained and overruled, the Surrogate holding that the notice required and given was sufficient. A final decree accepting the accounts has been entered, affirmed by the Appellate Division of the Supreme Court, and by the Court of Appeals of the State of New York.

B. Notice

The effect of this decree, as held below, is to settle "all questions respecting the management of the common fund." We understand that every right which beneficiaries would otherwise have against the trust company, either as trustee of the common fund or as trustee of any individual trust, for improper management of the common trust fund during the period covered by the accounting is sealed and wholly terminated by the decree.

We are met at the outset with a challenge to the power of the State — the right of its courts to adjudicate at all as against those beneficiaries who reside without the State of New York. * * * [T]he Surrogate is without jurisdiction as to nonresidents upon whom personal service of process was not made.

* * *

* * * [The Court upheld jurisdiction, explaining:] It is sufficient to observe that, whatever the technical definition of its chosen procedure, the interest of each state in providing means to close trusts that exist by the grace of its laws and are administered under the supervision of its courts is so insistent and rooted in custom as to establish beyond doubt the right of its courts to determine the interests of all claimants, resident or nonresident, provided its procedure accords full opportunity to appear and be heard.

Quite different from the question of a state's power to discharge trustees is that of the opportunity it must give beneficiaries to contest. Many controversies have raged about the cryptic and abstract words of the Due Process Clause but there can be no doubt that at a minimum they require that deprivation of life, liberty or property by adjudication be preceded by notice and opportunity for hearing appropriate to the nature of the case.

In two ways this proceeding does or may deprive beneficiaries of property. It may cut off their rights to have the trustee answer for negligent or illegal impairments of their interests. Also, their interests are presumably subject to diminution in the proceeding by allowance of fees and expenses to one who, in their names but without their knowledge, may conduct a fruitless or uncompensatory contest. Certainly the proceeding is one in which they may be deprived of property rights and hence notice and hearing must measure up to the standards of due process.

Personal service of written notice within the jurisdiction is the classic form of notice always adequate in any type of proceeding. But the vital interest of the State in bringing any issues as to its fiduciaries to a final settlement can be served only if interests or claims of individuals who are outside of the State can somehow be determined. A construction of the Due Process Clause which would place impossible or impractical obstacles in the way could not be justified.

Against this interest of the State we must balance the individual interest sought to be protected by the Fourteenth Amendment. This is defined by our holding that "The fundamental requisite of due process of law is the opportunity to be heard." This right to be heard has little reality or worth unless one is informed that the matter is pending and can choose for himself whether to appear or default, acquiesce or contest.

The Court has not committed itself to any formula achieving a balance between these interests in a particular proceeding or determining when constructive notice may be utilized or what test it must meet. Personal service has not in all circumstances been regarded as indispensable to the process due to residents, and it has more often been held unnecessary as to nonresidents. We disturb none of the established rules on these subjects. No decision constitutes a controlling or even a very illuminating precedent for the case before us. But a few general principles stand out in the books.

An elementary and fundamental requirement of due process in any proceeding which is to be accorded finality is notice reasonably calculated, under all the circumstances, to apprise interested parties of the pendency of the action and afford them an opportunity to present their objections. The notice must be of such nature as reasonably to convey the required information, and it must afford a reasonable time for those interested to make their appearance. But if with due regard for the practicalities and peculiarities of the case these conditions are reasonably met, the constitutional requirements are satisfied. "The criterion is not the possibility of conceivable injury but the just and reasonable character of the requirements, having reference to the subject with which the statute deals."

But when notice is a person's due, process which is a mere gesture is not due process. The means employed must be such as one desirous of actually informing the absentee might reasonably adopt to accomplish it. The reasonableness and hence the constitutional validity of any chosen method may be defended on the ground that it is in itself reasonably certain to inform those affected, or, where conditions do not reasonably permit such notice, that the form chosen is not substantially less likely to bring home notice than other of the feasible and customary substitutes.

It would be idle to pretend that publication alone, as prescribed here, is a reliable means of acquainting interested parties of the fact that their rights are before the courts. It is not an accident that the greater number of cases reaching this Court on the question of adequacy of notice have been concerned with actions founded on process constructively served through local newspapers. Chance alone brings to the attention of even a local resident an advertisement in small type inserted in the back pages of a newspaper, and if he makes his home outside the area of the newspaper's normal circulation the odds that the information will never reach him are large indeed. The chance of actual notice is further reduced when, as here, the notice required does not even name those whose attention it is supposed to attract, and does not inform acquaintances who might call it to attention. In weighing its sufficiency on the basis of equivalence with actual notice, we are unable to regard this as more than a feint.

Nor is publication here reinforced by steps likely to attract the parties' attention to the proceeding. It is true that publication traditionally has been acceptable as notification supplemental to other action which in itself may reasonably be expected to convey a warning. The ways of an owner with tangible property are such that he usually arranges means to learn of any direct attack upon his possessory or proprietary rights. Hence, libel of a ship, attachment of a chattel or entry upon real estate in the name of law may reasonably be expected to come promptly to the owner's attention. When the state within which the owner has located such property seizes it for some reason, publication or posting affords an additional measure of notification. A state may indulge the assumption that one who has left tangible property in the state either has abandoned it, in which case proceedings against it deprive him of nothing, or that he has left some caretaker under a duty to let him know that it is being jeopardized. As phrased long ago by Chief Justice Marshall in The Mary, 9 Cranch 126, 144[1815], "It is the part of common prudence for all those who have any interest in [a thing], to guard that interest by persons who are in a situation to protect it."

In the case before us there is, of course, no abandonment. On the other hand these beneficiaries do have a resident fiduciary as caretaker of their interest in this property. But it is their caretaker who in the accounting becomes their adversary. Their trustee is released from giving notice of jeopardy, and no one else is expected to do so. Not even the special guardian is required or apparently expected to communicate with his ward and client, and, of course, if such a duty were merely transferred from the trustee to the guardian, economy would not be served and more likely the cost would be increased.

This Court has not hesitated to approve of resort to publication as a customary substitute in another class of cases where it is not reasonably possible or practicable to give more adequate warning. Thus it has been recognized that, in the case of persons missing or unknown, employment of an indirect and even a probably futile means of notification is all that the situation permits and creates no constitutional bar to a final decree foreclosing their rights.

Those beneficiaries represented by appellant whose interests or whereabouts could not with due diligence be ascertained come clearly within this category. As to them the statutory notice is sufficient. However great the odds that publication will never reach the eyes of such unknown parties, it is not in the typical case much more likely to fail than any of the choices open to legislators endeavoring to prescribe the best notice practicable.

Nor do we consider it unreasonable for the State to dispense with more certain notice to those beneficiaries whose interests are either conjectural or future or, although they could be discovered upon investigation, do not in due course of business come to knowledge of the common trustee. Whatever searches might be required in another situation under ordinary standards of diligence, in view of the character of the proceedings and the nature of the interests here involved we think them unnecessary. We recognize the practical difficulties and costs that would be attendant on frequent investigations into the status of great numbers of beneficiaries, many of whose interests in the common fund are so remote as to be ephemeral; and we have no doubt that such impracticable and extended searches are not required in the name of due process. The expense of keeping informed from day to day of substitutions among even current income beneficiaries and presumptive remaindermen, to say nothing of the far greater number of contingent beneficiaries, would impose a severe burden on the plan, and would likely dissipate its advantages. These are practical matters in which we should be reluctant to disturb the judgment of the state authorities.

Accordingly we overrule appellant's constitutional objections to published notice insofar as they are urged on behalf of any beneficiaries whose interests or addresses are unknown to the trustee.

As to known present beneficiaries of known place of residence, however, notice by publication stands on a different footing. Exceptions in the name of necessity do not sweep away the rule that within the limits of practicability notice must be such as is reasonably calculated to reach interested parties. Where the names and post-office addresses of those affected by a proceeding are at hand, the reasons disappear for resort to means less likely than the mails to apprise them of its pendency.

The trustee has on its books the names and addresses of the income beneficiaries represented by appellant, and we find no tenable ground for dispensing with a serious effort to inform them personally of the accounting, at least by ordinary mail to the record addresses. Certainly sending them a copy of the statute months and perhaps years in advance does not answer this purpose. The trustee periodically remits their income to them, and we think that they might reasonably expect that with or apart from their remittances word might come to them personally that steps were being taken affecting their interests.

We need not weigh contentions that a requirement of personal service of citation on even the large number of known resident or nonresident beneficiaries would, by reasons of delay if not of

CHAPTER 3 NOTICE AND OPPORTUNITY TO BE HEARD

expense, seriously interfere with the proper administration of the fund. Of course personal service even without the jurisdiction of the issuing authority serves the end of actual and personal notice, whatever power of compulsion it might lack. However, no such service is required under the circumstances. This type of trust presupposes a large number of small interests. The individual interest does not stand alone but is identical with that of a class. The rights of each in the integrity of the fund and the fidelity of the trustee are shared by many other beneficiaries. Therefore notice reasonably certain to reach most of those interested in objecting is likely to safeguard the interests of all, since any objection sustained would inure to the benefit of all. We think that under such circumstances reasonable risks that notice might not actually reach every beneficiary are justifiable. "Now and then an extraordinary case may turn up, but constitutional law like other mortal contrivances has to take some chances, and in the great majority of instances no doubt justice will be done." Blinn v. Nelson, [222 U.S. 1,] 7 [1911].

The statutory notice to known beneficiaries is inadequate, not because in fact it fails to reach everyone, but because under the circumstances it is not reasonably calculated to reach those who could easily be informed by other means at hand. However it may have been in former times, the mails today are recognized as an efficient and inexpensive means of communication. Moreover, the fact that the trust company has been able to give mailed notice to known beneficiaries at the time the common trust fund was established is persuasive that postal notification at the time of accounting would not seriously burden the plan.

In some situations the law requires greater precautions in its proceedings than the business world accepts for its own purposes. In few, if any, will it be satisfied with less. Certainly it is instructive, in determining the reasonableness of the impersonal broadcast notification here used, to ask whether it would satisfy a prudent man of business, counting his pennies but finding it in his interest to convey information to many persons whose names and addresses are in his files. We are not satisfied that it would. Publication may theoretically be available for all the world to see, but it is too much in our day to suppose that each or any individual beneficiary does or could examine all that is published to see if something may be tucked away in it that affects his property interests. We have before indicated in reference to notice by publication that, "Great caution should be used not to let fiction deny the fair play that can be secured only by a pretty close adhesion to fact." McDonald v. Mabee, 243 U.S. 90, 91 [1917].

We hold that the notice of judicial settlement of accounts required by the New York Banking Law is incompatible with the requirements of the Fourteenth Amendment as a basis for adjudication depriving known persons whose whereabouts are also known of substantial property rights. Accordingly the judgment is reversed and the cause remanded for further proceedings not inconsistent with this opinion.

Reversed.

NOTES AND QUESTIONS

1. As to what group(s) of beneficiaries did the Court *reverse* the judgment of the New York Court of Appeals? Why was the notice directed toward them deficient? As to

what group(s) of beneficiaries did the Court *affirm* the New York judgment? Why was the notice directed toward them sufficient?

2. The Due Process Clause only applies to takings of "life, liberty or property." What property was taken from the beneficiaries as to whom notice was held deficient in *Mullane*?

3. In-person service would be more reliable than service by mail. If the right to notice is a fundamental constitutional right, why doesn't the Court require the most reliable form of notice?

4. Does the Court require that notice actually be received? Could a valid judgment be entered against a defendant who had no actual knowledge of the suit? What justification can there be for permitting a valid judgment under such circumstances?

5. In *Mullane* the Court does not require the bank to attempt to notify individually everyone whose rights might be affected. How does the Court justify allowing a judgment that affects the property of individuals whom no one even tried to notify?

6. What is the purpose of notice? One possible purpose is that notice, at least when it is combined with the opportunity to be heard, may increase the likelihood of an accurate result in the ensuing litigation. The court will hear both sides and have the benefit of an adversarial presentation. If accuracy through an adversarial presentation is the goal, is notice always necessary to achieve this goal? In *Mullane* itself the court had appointed a lawyer to represent the interests of the absent beneficiaries. Why isn't that step alone sufficient? How likely is it that the small and scattered beneficiaries will get involved in the litigation? Moreover, how would individual involvement of the beneficiaries in this type of case enhance the presentation of issues? With such a homogeneous group, wouldn't the court be likely to conclude that "once you've heard one, you've heard them all?"

Does notice serve some interest besides the utilitarian concern for accuracy? Professor Jerry Mashaw argues that "a lack of personal participation [in decisions affecting oneself] cause[s] alienation and a loss of that dignity and self-respect that society properly deems independently valuable." Jerry Mashaw, *The Supreme Court's Due Process Calculus for Administrative Adjudication in* Mathews v. Eldridge: *Three Factors in Search of a Theory of Value*, 44 U. CHI. L. REV. 28, 50 (1976). Should the Due Process Clause be interpreted to require procedures that enhance individual dignity? How might such a requirement affect the law with respect to notice?

7. In *Mullane*, the Court held that mailed notice was sufficient even as to those beneficiaries whose names and addresses were known, (and, therefore, as to whom personal service would have been possible). But what if the person to whom notice is sent cannot understand the notice for some reason? For example, in Covey v. Town of Somers, 351 U.S. 141 (1956), the Court refused to uphold notice mailed to a person known to be mentally incompetent.

(a) If the recipient's mental deficiencies were not known to the sender, would due process require that the sender make an inquiry into her mental capacity? Suppose the incapacity were a matter of public record because a conservator had been appointed to handle her affairs, what notice would due process require?

(b) Along similar lines, what if the defendant does not speak English? Does due process require that notice be given in a language the defendant understands?

8. *Mullane* suggested that posting of notice on physical property would be adequate notice. In Schroeder v. City of New York, 371 U.S. 208 (1962), the Court held that publication in a newspaper and posting of notices near the property was insufficient if the defendant's name and address were easily ascertainable from public records. In Greene v. Lindsey, 456 U.S. 444 (1982), the Court held that under the facts of the case, posting notice of eviction on an apartment door was not sufficient notice. Nonetheless, the Court reaffirmed the general adequacy of notice by posting:

> It is * * * reasonable to assume that a property owner will maintain superintendence of his property, and to presume that actions physically disturbing his holdings will come to his attention. * * * Upon this understanding, a State may in turn conclude that in most cases, the secure posting of a notice on the property of a person is likely to offer that property owner sufficient warning of the pendency of proceedings possibly affecting his interests.

Id. at 451-52.

Do you agree that it is reasonable to assume an owner will "maintain superintendence" over her property? Recall Justice Field's statement in *Pennoyer*, that "[t]he law assumes that property is always in the possession of its owner * * * and it proceeds upon the theory that its seizure will inform him, not only that it is taken into the custody of the court, but that he must look to any proceedings authorized by law * * * for its condemnation and sale."

Would it be reasonable to post notice on the door of a cabin in the woods? Suppose the owner only uses it occasionally. See generally Arthur Greenbaum, *The Postman Never Rings Twice: The Constitutionality of Service of Process by Posting after* Greene v. Lindsey, 33 AM. U.L. REV. 601 (1984).

In *Greene* the Court ultimately held that posting was inadequate because the process servers knew that "notices posted on apartment doors in the area where these tenants lived were 'not infrequently' removed by children or other tenants before they could have their intended effect." 456 U.S. at 453. The Court required service by mail.

9. The right to notice and a hearing are waivable personal rights. In D.H. Overmyer Co. v. Frick Co., 405 U.S. 174 (1974), the Court considered an extreme form of waiver known as a cognovit note, in which the debtor consents in advance to a creditor's obtaining a judgment without notice to the debtor or a hearing! The Court held that a cognovit note is

not per se unconstitutional, although it stressed that under some circumstances, such as where the cognovit was part of a contract of adhesion, it might be unconstitutional.

10. Kenneth Mullane, the special guardian appointed to represent income beneficiaries of the trust, argued for greater notice. James Vaughan, the special guardian appointed to represent principal beneficiaries, argued that the statutorily described notice was adequate. Why did the two guardians take opposite positions? Consider the following: Under New York law, the ordinary expenses associated with the accounting procedure could be billed to the common fund trust and were payable out of the principal. See In re Bank of New York, 67 N.Y.S. 2d 444, 448 (1946); In re Continental Bank & Trust Co., 67 N.Y.S.2d 806, 807 (1946). Therefore, the costs of more expensive notice were paid by those Vaughan represented. Of course, a reduction of the principal also has some effect on income beneficiaries because there would be less principal upon which to earn interest.

Do you think Mullane acted in the best interest of the income beneficiaries he represented by (1) insisting on more expensive notice, and (2) litigating the issue of notice all the way to the United States Supreme Court and thereby increasing the expenses for guardians chargeable against the trust?

2. Statutory Requirements

The Due Process Clause, as interpreted in *Mullane* and other cases, sets the constitutional minimum standards for notice. In addition to the constitutional minimum, all courts have rules or statutes that spell out in detail the mechanics and form for giving notice. These rules for service of process are frequently more demanding than the Constitution. For example, some courts may require actual in-hand personal service when the constitutional minimum would be met by mailing notice. Service of process must comply with both the constitutional minimum and any additional statutory or rule requirements.

Service of process is not a mere technicality. The Supreme Court has explained that service is integral to a court's acquiring jurisdiction:

> [B]efore a court may exercise personal jurisdiction over a defendant, there must be more than notice to the defendant and a constitutionally sufficient relationship between the defendant and the forum. There also must be a basis for the defendant's amenability to service of summons. Absent consent, this means there must be authorization for service of summons on the defendant.

Omni Capital International v. Rudolf Wolff & Co., 484 U.S. 97, 104 (1987).

In federal court, service of process is governed by Rule 4. Rule 4(c)(1) provides, "A summons shall be served together with a copy of the complaint."* Obviously, the latter

---

* The word "shall" is mandatory. It requires something be done. Contrast it with the use of "may" in many of the Rules.

CHAPTER 3 NOTICE AND OPPORTUNITY TO BE HEARD

document gives the defendant notice of the allegations made against her. What, then, does the summons do? What must the summons contain? See Rule 4(a).

The Federal Rules are accompanied by a set of Forms which, under Rule 84, are deemed sufficient to satisfy the requirements of the Rules. See Forms 1 and 1-A to see what a summons looks like.

Form summonses are available at the clerk's office of any federal district court. Counsel generally has a stack of them at the office for use when needed. She simply has the names of the parties typed in and takes the summons, with the original complaint and copies thereof, to the clerk's office for filing. At that point, the clerk signs the summons (see Rule 4(b)), the case is assigned a docket number, and the plaintiff arranges to have service effected.

Why couldn't the function of the summons be performed by a letter from plaintiff's counsel to the defendant? Although notice is technically a separate requirement from personal jurisdiction, the two concepts are related. Service of process is the ceremonial method in which the sovereign's right to exercise personal jurisdiction is validated. As Justice Stone said in *International Shoe*, "the capias ad respondendum has given way to service of process." The capias, an order of the court, commanded that the defendant be arrested. This is still done in criminal cases. In civil cases today, we feel less strongly about the need of the sovereign to make such an overbearing demonstration of its power over the defendant. Nonetheless, we have retained a ceremonial demonstration that the government is asserting power over the defendant.

We require the ceremonial show of force only once in a lawsuit. After the summons has been served, subsequent pleadings, motions and other papers can be served by mailing a copy to the other party or her attorney. See Rule 5(b).

In earlier times, service was routinely effected by the marshal's office, thereby emphasizing the fact that the summons represented the power of the sovereign. Today, any non-party at least 18 years old can serve process, although the court can order service by a marshal. See Rule 4(c)(2). When the marshal's office is to effect service, the plaintiff may be required to instruct the marshal on how to do so. In Mayo v. Satan and His Staff, 54 F.R.D. 282 (W.D. Pa. 1971), the court dismissed the case because the plaintiff failed to render such aid when asking the marshal to serve the devil himself.

Following service, the person effecting service is required to file with the court proof that she did so. See Rule 4(l). If a civilian serves process, this proof must be made by affidavit, which is a statement made under penalty of perjury. The Rule explicitly provides, however, that "[f]ailure to make proof of service does not affect the validity of the service."

National Dev. Co. v. Triad Holding Corp.
930 F.2d 253 (2d Cir. 1991)

McLaughlin, Circuit Judge.

For more than a half-century, the Federal Rules of Civil Procedure have permitted service upon an individual by leaving a summons and complaint "at the individual's dwelling house or usual place of abode." For a half-century before that, Equity Rule 13 had the same provision. With approximately 1.16 billion passengers annually engaging in international airline travel, and an estimated five million people with second homes in the United States, determining a person's "dwelling house or usual place of abode" is no longer as easy as in those early days of yesteryear.

We ponder this problem upon review of an order of the United States District Court for the Southern District of New York * * * refusing, under Fed.R.Civ.P. 60(b)(4), to vacate a default judgment entered against defendant-appellant Adnan Khashoggi ("Khashoggi"). In essence, Khashoggi argues that, although he has numerous residences world-wide, his "dwelling house or usual place of abode" is in Saudi Arabia and, absent personal delivery, service of process pursuant to Rule 4(d)(1) is proper only at his compound there. [Under the current Rule 4, this provision appears at 4(e)(2) — Eds.] Therefore, he concludes that a purported service at his apartment at the Olympic Tower in New York was void and conferred no jurisdiction. We disagree and affirm the order of the district court.

Background

* * *

It is the service of the summons and complaint on Khashoggi on December 22, 1986 that forms the basis of this appeal. On that day, NDC handed a copy of the summons and complaint to Aurora DaSilva, a housekeeper at Khashoggi's Olympic Tower condominium apartment on Fifth Avenue. * * *

* * *

The district court held an evidentiary hearing on the service of process issue, at which Khashoggi and his housekeeper, Ms. DaSilva, testified. Ms. DaSilva confirmed that Khashoggi was in New York and staying at his Olympic Tower apartment from December 15 through December 23, 1986. The parties stipulated that Ms. DaSilva accepted delivery of a copy of the summons and complaint on December 22, 1986. Ms. DaSilva testified that during 1986, Khashoggi stayed at his Olympic Tower apartment for a total of 34 days.

To call it an apartment is perhaps to denigrate it. Valued at approximately $20-25 million, containing more than 23,000 square feet on at least two floors, the Olympic Tower apartment contains a swimming pool, a sauna, an office and four separate furnished "apartments" to accommodate guests and Khashoggi's brother. The complex requires the attention of two full-time and three part-time staff persons.

Khashoggi testified that he is a citizen of Saudi Arabia and resides in a ten-acre, six-villa compound in its capital city, Riyadh. In 1986, Khashoggi stayed in the Riyadh compound for only three months. During the remaining nine months, Khashoggi traveled throughout the world, staying another two months at a "home" in Marabella, Spain. Khashoggi testified that he purchased the Olympic Tower apartment in 1974. Shortly thereafter, Khashoggi transferred ownership to Akorp, N.V., a company that is wholly owned by A.K. Holdings, Ltd., which, in turn, is wholly owned by Khashoggi. Before Khashoggi transferred ownership of the Olympic Tower apartment to Akorp, he personally hired contractors to complete a remodeling project costing over $1 million. The results of the remodeling project were prominently featured in the June 1984 issue of *House and Garden*.

* * *

* * * [T]he district court found that the Olympic Tower apartment was not a "dwelling house or usual place of abode" for purposes of either Fed.R.Civ.P. 4(d)(1) or N.Y.C.P.L.R. § 308(2), but that service was nevertheless proper because Khashoggi had actual notice. We reject the notion that "actual notice" suffices to cure a void service, but we affirm the district court because we conclude that the Olympic Tower apartment is properly characterized under Rule 4(d)(1) as Khashoggi's "dwelling house or usual place of abode," and service at that location was therefore valid.

Discussion

Rule 4(d)(1) permits service

[u]pon an individual other than an infant or an incompetent person, by delivering a copy of the summons and of the complaint to the individual personally or by leaving copies thereof at the individual's dwelling house or usual place of abode with some person of suitable age and discretion then residing therein ...

There is no dispute that Ms. DaSilva, with whom the papers were left, is a "person of suitable age and discretion then residing" at the Olympic Tower apartment. We are called upon only to determine whether the Olympic Tower apartment was Khashoggi's "dwelling house or usual place of abode," terms that thus far have eluded "any hard and fast definition." Indeed, these quaint terms are now archaic and survive only in religious hymns, romantic sonnets and, unhappily, in jurisdictional statutes.

The phrase "dwelling house or usual place of abode" to describe where service can be made has its origin in Equity Rule 13. Yet, "[d]espite the length of time the language ... has been a part of federal practice, the decisions do not make clear precisely what it means." We do not here intend to reconcile decades of conflicting authority. Instead, we decide this case on the facts presented with a recognition of the realities of life in this the winter of the twentieth century.

As leading commentators observe, "[i]n a highly mobile and affluent society, it is unrealistic to interpret Rule 4(d)(1) so that the person to be served has only one dwelling house or usual place of abode at which process may be left." This case presents a perfect example of how ineffectual so wooden a rule would be.

B. Notice

Khashoggi is a wealthy man and a frequent intercontinental traveler. Although he is a citizen of Saudi Arabia and considers the Riyadh compound his domicile, he spent only three months there in 1986. Khashoggi testified that the Olympic Tower apartment was only one of twelve locations around the world where he spends his time, including a "home" which he owns in Marabella, Spain, and "houses" in Rome, Paris and Monte Carlo. The conclusion that only *one* of these locations is Khashoggi's "usual place of abode," since he does not "usually" stay at any one of them, commends itself to neither common sense nor sound policy.

There is nothing startling in the conclusion that a person can have two or more "dwelling houses or usual places of abode," provided each contains sufficient indicia of permanence. State courts construing state statutes containing similar language have arrived at this result where the defendant maintained one residence for certain days of the week or certain months of the year and another residence for the balance of his time. Some courts have expressly required that the defendant sought to be served be actually living at the residence at the time service is effected. [S]ee also J. MOORE, MOORE'S FEDERAL PRACTICE ¶. 4.11[2], at 132 ("Where a party has several residences which he permanently maintains, occupying one at one period of the year and another at another period, service is valid when made at the dwelling house in which the party is then living.") (footnote omitted).

Although federal practice under Rule 4(d)(1) has not produced consistent results, compare Capitol Life Ins. Co. v. Rosen, 69 F.R.D. 83 (E.D. Pa. 1975) (service at defendant's brother's house sufficient where defendant frequently journeyed but kept a room and personal belongings at brother's house and paid rent therefor) and Blackhawk Heating & Plumbing Co. v. Turner, 50 F.R.D. 144 (D. Ariz. 1970) (service at house in Arizona deemed proper where evidence suggested that defendant was living at the time in California but received actual notice) with First Nat'l Bank & Trust Co. v. Ingerton, 207 F.2d 793 (10th Cir. 1953) (usual place of abode was hotel in New Mexico notwithstanding defendant's temporary stay in Denver) and Shore v. Cornell-Dubilier Elec. Corp., 33 F.R.D. 5 (D. Mass. 1963) (service on defendant who divided his time between residences in New York and New Jersey improper where made at a house he owned in Massachusetts that was used by him only when conducting business there), we believe that application of the rule to uphold service is appropriate under these facts.

It cannot seriously be disputed that the Olympic Tower apartment has sufficient indicia of permanence. Khashoggi owned and furnished the apartment and spent a considerable amount of money remodeling it to fit his lifestyle. Indeed, in July 1989, Khashoggi listed the Olympic Tower apartment as one of his residences in a bail application submitted in connection with the criminal proceedings. Since Khashoggi was actually living in the Olympic Tower apartment on December 22, 1986, service there on that day was, if not the most likely method of ensuring that he received the summons and complaint, reasonably calculated to provide actual notice of the action. See *Mullane v. Central Hanover Bank & Trust Co.* Surely, with so itinerant a defendant as Khashoggi, plaintiff should not be expected to do more.

We conclude, therefore, that service of process on Khashoggi should be sustained under Rule 4(d)(1) because the Olympic Tower apartment was a "dwelling house or usual place of abode" in which he was actually living at the time service was effected. We express no opinion upon the validity of service had Khashoggi not been actually living at the Olympic Tower apartment when service was effected.

Conclusion

Since service was properly effected on Khashoggi, his motion pursuant to Rule 60(b)(4) to vacate the default judgment entered on the original complaint for want of personal jurisdiction was properly denied. Accordingly, we affirm.

NOTES AND QUESTIONS

1. The district court found that because Khashoggi received actual notice, compliance with Rule 4 was not required. The court of appeals rejected this argument. Why? Shouldn't actual notice always be sufficient?

2. Would the result have been different if Khashoggi had not been in New York at the time of service?

3. Should this case have come out differently if it involved Joe Smith, not Adnan Khashoggi, and service had been at Joe's summer cabin (which has never been featured in *House and Garden*)?

4. What constitutes "the individual's dwelling house or usual place of abode?" Does this phrase include a hotel room? See First Nat. Bank & Trust Co. v. Ingerton, 207 F.2d 793 (10th Cir. 1953) (yes); the parental home of a college student while the student was away at school? See Hubbard v. Brinton, 26 F.R.D. 564 (E.D. Pa. 1961) (yes); the penitentiary from which a prisoner had escaped? See United States v. Mensik, 57 F.R.D. 125 (M.D. Pa. 1972) (no). One treatise observes: "Despite the extensive factual analyses and attempts at careful statutory construction that often are undertaken by the courts, an examination of the cases reveals that the actual receipt of the summons and complaint at the particular place where it is served may be the real key to the disposition of many cases." 4A WRIGHT & MILLER, FEDERAL PRACTICE & PROCEDURE § 1096, at 77-78.

5. According to the court, there was no dispute that Ms. DaSilva was of "suitable age and discretion." How old must the person be to meet this requirement? Is a 13 year old of "suitable age and discretion?" See Holmen v. Miller, 296 Minn. 99, 206 N.W.2d 916 (1973) (no). Consider also the requirement that the recipient "reside therein." Would this language apply to a house guest visiting for two weeks?

6. Review Rule 4(h). Who constitutes "a managing or general agent?" Would service on the manager of one small store owned by a large corporation meet the rule? Should the focus be on the job title or instead on whether the position is "of sufficient responsibility so that it is reasonable to assume that the person will transmit notice of the commencement of the action to organizational superiors?" 4A WRIGHT & MILLER, FEDERAL PRACTICE & PROCEDURE § 1103, at 113.

7. Read Rule 4(m). Under what circumstances must or may the court extend the 120 day limit? See Petrucelli v. Bohringer and Ratzinger GmBH Ausdereitungsanlagen, 46 F. 3d 1298 (3rd Cir. 1995).

8. *National Development Co.* was decided before the 1993 revisions to Rule 4. Under the current versions of Rule 4:
   (a) Could service properly be made on Khashoggi by mailing it or delivering it to his office in New York? By mailing it to his home in Saudi Arabia?
   (b) Suppose the plaintiff had learned that Khashoggi would be visiting in Florida and wanted to serve him there. By what methods could he have Khashoggi served in Florida?

9. Service of process, like an objection to personal jurisdiction, is waivable. Read Rule 4(d). Suppose the plaintiff in *National Development Co.* wanted to use this provision:
   (a) What must the plaintiff do to request waiver of service by Khashoggi? Could a request for waiver of service have been faxed to him at his New York apartment? His New York office? His home in Saudi Arabia?
   (b) What advantage, if any, would Khashoggi get from waiving formal service? Does waiver prejudice any defenses he may have as to personal jurisdiction or venue?
   (c) How would Khashoggi manifest his intention to waive formal service?
   (d) If Khashoggi does not waive service, what should the plaintiff do next? Notice the sanction available if the defendant refuses to waive formal service. How big an incentive do you think this is?

10. In serving process (as opposed to seeking a waiver), the plaintiff may follow either the procedures of the state in which the district court sits, or the procedures of the state in which service is effected, or the procedures set forth in Rule 4. Many states permit service of process by certified or registered mail. You should not confuse actual service by mail with waiver of service under Rule 4(d). The distinction between the two can be particularly significant for purposes of statutes of limitation.

In many situations, federal courts apply state statutes of limitation. In some states, the limitations period is tolled by filing a complaint, while in other states, the period runs until service on the defendant. Where the statute of limitations is of the latter type, it may be that neither the receipt of a request for waiver of service nor completion of a waiver form by the defendant will toll the statute.

11. Read Rule 4(k)(1). Suppose suit is brought in the Federal District Court in El Paso, Texas. Defendant is a citizen of New Mexico, residing in Santa Inez, New Mexico,

CHAPTER 3 NOTICE AND OPPORTUNITY TO BE HEARD

which is 87 miles from the federal court house in El Paso. Would the federal court have personal jurisdiction over the defendant? How can service be effected?

12. Review Rule 4(k)(2). We discussed this section in connection with personal jurisdiction. See supra at 62.

13. Are there methods of notice that are constitutionally permissible that are not permitted by Rule 4? Why would the drafters exclude any constitutionally permissible method of service?

14. Although service was ultimately upheld in *National Development Co.*, the focus of the court of appeals was on the language of Rule 4, not on the constitutional requirement of notice. Would it have been better to provide a more open-end standard rather than specific rules for service? For example, Rule 4 might simply provide that "service shall be effectuated using any method reasonably calculated to notify the other party." Would this be an improvement?

15. Service of process in a foreign country can present some complications. Rule 4(f) specifies several possible mechanisms for service of process abroad: compliance with the Hague Convention on Service Abroad of Judicial and Extrajudicial Documents; use of a "letter rogatory" requesting the assistance of a foreign court; compliance with the local rules for service of the foreign country; or, if permitted by the foreign country, personal service or mail service. The last method is frequently not available because in many countries, particularly civil law countries, service of process is regarded as a "sovereign act" that can be performed in their territory "only by the state's own officials and in accordance with its own law." RESTATEMENT (THIRD) FOREIGN RELATIONS LAW OF THE UNITED STATES § 471, cmt. b (1987).

3. Immunity, Evasion and "Sewer Service"

Both state and federal courts recognize common law and statutory immunity from service under certain circumstances. See 4 WRIGHT & MILLER, FEDERAL PRACTICE & PROCEDURE § 1076. For example, witnesses, litigants or lawyers who come into the state to participate in one suit may be immune from process concerning other suits. Immunity is also sometimes granted to persons who are induced to enter the state through fraud or deceit. See, e.g., Buchanan v. Wilson, 254 F.2d 849 (6th Cir. 1958). In addition, some state statutes prohibit service on Sunday. See, e.g., FLA. STAT. § 48.20; N. Y. GEN. BUS. LAW § 11. Adam Clayton Powell, a Congressman from New York, evaded service of a civil contempt citation for several years by returning to his district only on Sundays.

Some defendants without the protection of immunity will seek to evade service and thereby delay or avoid suit completely. In response to this problem, creative process servers specialize in serving the hard-to-find defendant. Such a process server may masquerade as florist's delivery-person and tuck a summons in among the roses or serve process on a groom in a wedding receiving line. One enterprising process server bought a ticket to dance on a Donny Osmond TV special, waltzed past Donny, and served him with process on live television. Martin Grayson & Bart Schwartz, *Adventures in Serving Process*, 11 LITIGATION 11, 12 (1985).

The flip side of evasive defendants is the problem of "sewer service," that is, dishonest process servers who certify that process was served when in fact it was not. This practice was shockingly common in New York during the 1960s and early 1970s and resulted in several publicized criminal prosecutions. See United States v. Wiseman, 445 F.2d 792 (2d Cir.), *cert. denied*, 404 U.S. 967 (1971); Frank Tuerkheimer, *Service of Process in New York City: A Proposed End to Unregulated Criminality*, 72 COLUM. L. REV. 847 (1972). The practice was apparently exacerbated by New York's rigid requirement of personal service on the defendant. Because process could not ordinarily be left with someone other than the defendant, process servers falsified affidavits and threw the summons away rather than track down the defendant.

New York responded by authorizing service on a person of suitable age and discretion at the defendant's actual place of business or abode, with a second copy mailed to the defendant's last known address. N.Y. CIV. PRAC. L.& R. § 308(2)(1990). Notwithstanding this change, problems persist. A 1986 report by the New York City Departments of Consumer Affairs and Investigation found that at least one-third of all default judgments were based on perjured affidavits. See Margaret Taylor, *A Court Fails, an Old Woman Dies, and the Police Stand Trial*, NEW YORK TIMES, March 19, 1987, at A26.

C. Opportunity to be Heard

In addition to notice, the Due Process Clauses of the Fifth and Fourteenth Amendments require an opportunity to be heard. This opportunity does not necessarily require a full blown trial. In some circumstances less formal procedures will suffice. Thus, for example, in Goss v. Lopez, 419 U.S. 565 (1975), the Court held that prior to suspension from a public school, a student is entitled to notice of the charges and an opportunity to offer an explanation of her version of events. In this regard, however, the school need not hold a formal hearing with confrontation of witness and cross-examination. An informal discussion between the student and the school official was sufficient.

Regardless of the formality of the hearing, the defendant must ordinarily receive sufficient advance warning to allow time to prepare an adequate defense. For example, in Roller v. Holly, 176 U.S. 398 (1900), the defendant was served with process in Virginia requiring him to defend the action in Texas five days later. The Court held that in light of the distance to be traveled, "five days was not reasonable notice, or due process of law." Id. at 413. However, the amount of advance warning required depends on the nature of the proceeding. Thus, in the context of school discipline, it is sufficient for the school official to discuss with the student the alleged misconduct immediately following the incident. See *Goss v. Lopez*, supra.

The requirement of due process raises particularly difficult questions when the plaintiff seeks so-called "provisional" relief. Suppose, for example, you live near a nuclear power plant and you have just learned that the plant is about to vent radioactive steam into the air. You might wish to get a temporary restraining order (TRO), prohibiting the release of steam until a full hearing can be conducted on the lawfulness of the power plant's conduct. The power company's position may be that the steam poses no health risk and is completely lawful. Further, it may argue that if it is not allowed to vent the steam, it will have to shut down the plant, thereby incurring economic losses and interrupting services to the community. In this situation the court does not have the luxury of time to figure out who is correct. If it grants the TRO, it risks great harm to the defendant for what may prove to be groundless allegations. If it does not stop the venting, the plaintiff may suffer irreparable harm. What does due process require under these circumstances? Notice how Federal Rule 65(b) deals with this situation. Consider the following case involving the less dramatic but very common situation of pre-judgment attachment.

Connecticut v. Doehr
501 U.S. 1, 111 S.Ct. 2105, 115 L.Ed.2d 1 (1991)

JUSTICE WHITE delivered an opinion, Parts I, II, and III of which are the opinion of the Court.[*]

This case requires us to determine whether a state statute that authorizes prejudgment attachment of real estate without prior notice or hearing, without a showing of extraordinary circumstances, and without a requirement that the person seeking the attachment post a bond, satisfies the Due Process Clause of the Fourteenth Amendment. We hold that, as applied to this case, it does not.

I

On March 15, 1988, Petitioner John F. DiGiovanni submitted an application to the Connecticut Superior Court for an attachment in the amount of $75,000 on respondent Brian K. Doehr's home

---

[*] The CHIEF JUSTICE, JUSTICE BLACKMUN, JUSTICE KENNEDY, JUSTICE SOUTER join Parts I, II, and III of this opinion, and JUSTICE SCALIA joins Parts I and III.

in Meridan, Connecticut. DiGiovanni took this step in conjunction with a civil action for assault and battery that he was seeking to institute against Doehr in the same court. The suit did not involve Doehr's real estate nor did DiGiovanni have any pre-existing interest either in Doehr's home or any of his other property.

Connecticut law authorizes prejudgment attachment of real estate without affording prior notice or the opportunity for a prior hearing to the individual whose property is subject to the attachment. The State's prejudgment remedy statute provides, in relevant part:

> "The court or a judge of the court may allow the prejudgment remedy to be issued by an attorney without hearing as provided in sections 52-278c and 52-278d upon verification by oath of the plaintiff or of some competent affiant, that there is probable cause to sustain the validity of the plaintiff's claims and (1) that the prejudgment remedy requested is for an attachment of real property ...." CONN. GEN. STAT. § 52-278e (1991).

The statute does not require the plaintiff to post a bond to insure the payment of damages that the defendant may suffer should the attachment prove wrongfully issued or the claim prove unsuccessful.

As required, DiGiovanni submitted an affidavit in support of his application. In five one-sentence paragraphs, DiGiovanni stated that the facts set forth in his previously submitted complaint were true; that "I was willfully, wantonly and maliciously assaulted by the defendant, Brian K. Doehr"; that "[s]aid assault and battery broke my left wrist and further caused an ecchymosis to my right eye, as well as other injuries"; and that "I have further expended sums of money for medical care and treatment." The affidavit concluded with the statement, "In my opinion, the foregoing facts are sufficient to show that there is probable cause that judgment will be rendered for the plaintiff."

On the strength of these submissions the Superior Court judge, by an order dated March 17, found "probable cause to sustain the validity of the plaintiff's claim" and ordered the attachment on Doehr's home "to the value of $75,000." The sheriff attached the property four days later, on March 21. Only after this did Doehr receive notice of the attachment. He also had yet to be served with the complaint, which is ordinarily necessary for an action to commence in Connecticut. As the statute further required, the attachment notice informed Doehr that he had the right to a hearing: (1) to claim that no probable cause existed to sustain the claim; (2) to request that the attachment be vacated, modified, or that a bond be substituted; or (3) to claim that some portion of the property was exempt from execution.

Rather than pursue these options, Doehr filed suit against DiGiovanni in Federal District Court, claiming that § 52-278e (a)(1) was unconstitutional under the Due Process Clause of the Fourteenth Amendment. The District Court upheld the statute and granted summary judgment in favor of DiGiovanni. On appeal, a divided panel of the United States Court of Appeals for the Second Circuit reversed. * * *

CHAPTER 3 NOTICE AND OPPORTUNITY TO BE HEARD

* * *

II

With this case we return to the question of what process must be afforded by a state statute enabling an individual to enlist the aid of the State to deprive another of his or her property by means of the prejudgment attachment or similar procedure. Our cases reflect the numerous variations this type of remedy can entail. In Sniadach v. Family Finance Corp. of Bay View, 395 U.S. 337 (1969), the Court struck down a Wisconsin statute that permitted a creditor to effect prejudgment garnishment of wages without notice and prior hearing to the wage earner. In Fuentes v. Shevin, 407 U.S. 67 (1972), the Court likewise found a due process violation in state replevin provisions that permitted vendors to have goods seized through an ex parte application to a court clerk and the posting of a bond. Conversely, the Court upheld a Louisiana ex parte procedure allowing a lien holder to have disputed goods sequestered in Mitchell v. W.T. Grant Co., 416 U.S. 600 (1974). *Mitchell*, however, carefully noted that *Fuentes* was decided against "a factual and legal background sufficiently different ... that it does not require the invalidation of the Louisiana sequestration statute." Those differences included Louisiana's provision of an immediate post-deprivation hearing along with the option of damages; the requirement that a judge rather than a clerk determine that there is a clear showing of entitlement to the writ; the necessity for a detailed affidavit; and an emphasis on the lienholder's interest in preventing waste or alienation of the encumbered property. In North Georgia Finishing, Inc. v. Di-Chem, Inc. 419 U.S. 601 (1975), the Court again invalidated an ex parte garnishment statute that not only failed to provide for notice and prior hearing but that also failed to require a bond, a detailed affidavit setting out the claim, the determination of a neutral magistrate, or a prompt post-deprivation hearing.

These cases "underscore the truism that '[d]ue process, unlike some legal rules, is not a technical conception with a fixed content unrelated to time, place and circumstances.'" Mathews v. Eldridge, [424 U.S. 319, 334 (1976)] (quoting Cafeteria Workers v. McElroy, 367 U.S. 886, 895 (1961)). In *Mathews*, we drew upon our prejudgment remedy decisions to determine what process is due when the government itself seeks to effect a deprivation on its own initiative. That analysis resulted in the now familiar threefold inquiry requiring consideration of "the private interest that will be affected by the official action"; "the risk of an erroneous deprivation of such interest through the procedures used, and the probable value, if any, of additional or substitute safeguards"; and lastly "the Government's interest, including the function involved and the fiscal and administrative burdens that the additional or substitute procedural requirement would entail."

Here the inquiry is similar but the focus is different. Prejudgment remedy statutes ordinarily apply to disputes between private parties rather than between an individual and the government. Such enactments are designed to enable one of the parties to "make use of state procedures with the overt, significant assistance of state officials," and they undoubtedly involve state action "substantial enough to implicate the Due Process Clause." Nonetheless, any burden that increasing procedural safeguards entails primarily affects not the government, but the party seeking control of the other's property. For this type of case, therefore, the relevant inquiry requires, as in *Mathews*, first, consideration of the private interest that will be affected by the prejudgment measure; second, an examination of the risk of erroneous deprivation through the procedures under attack and the prob-

C. Opportunity to be Heard

able value of additional or alternative safeguards; and third, in contrast to *Mathews*, principal attention to the interest of the party seeking the prejudgment remedy, with, nonetheless, due regard for any ancillary interest the government may have in providing the procedure or forgoing the added burden of providing greater protections.

We now consider the *Mathews* factors in determining the adequacy of the procedures before us, first with regard to the safeguards of notice and a prior hearing, and then in relation to the protection of a bond.

III

We agree with the Court of Appeals that the property interests that attachment affects are significant. For a property owner like Doehr, attachment ordinarily clouds title; impairs the ability to sell or otherwise alienate the property; taints any credit rating; reduces the chance of obtaining a home equity loan or additional mortgage; and can even place an existing mortgage in technical default where there is an insecurity clause. Nor does Connecticut deny that any of these consequences occurs.

Instead, the State correctly points out that these effects do not amount to a complete, physical, or permanent deprivation of real property; their impact is less than the perhaps temporary total deprivation of household goods or wages. But the Court has never held that only such extreme deprivations trigger due process concern. To the contrary, our cases show that even the temporary or partial impairments to property rights that attachments, liens, and similar encumbrances entail are sufficient to merit due process protection. Without doubt, state procedures for creating and enforcing attachments, as with liens, "are subject to the strictures of due process."

We also agree with the Court of Appeals that the risk of erroneous deprivation that the State permits here is substantial. By definition, attachment statutes premise a deprivation of property on one ultimate factual contingency — the award of damages to the plaintiff which the defendant may not be able to satisfy. For attachments before judgment, Connecticut mandates that this determination be made by means of a procedural inquiry that asks whether "there is probable cause to sustain the validity of the plaintiff's claim." The statute elsewhere defines the validity of the claim in terms of the likelihood "that judgment will be rendered in the matter in favor of the plaintiff." What probable cause means in this context, however, remains obscure. The State initially took the position, as did the dissent below, that the statute requires a plaintiff to show the objective likelihood of the suit's success. DiGiovanni, citing ambiguous state cases, reads the provision as requiring no more than that a plaintiff demonstrate a subjective good faith belief that the suit will succeed. At oral argument, the State shifted its position to argue that the statute requires something akin to the plaintiff stating a claim with sufficient facts to survive a motion to dismiss.

We need not resolve this confusion since the statute presents too great a risk of erroneous deprivation under any of these interpretations. If the statute demands inquiry into the sufficiency of the complaint, or, still less, the plaintiff's good-faith belief that the complaint is sufficient, requirement of a complaint and a factual affidavit would permit a court to make these minimal determinations. But neither inquiry adequately reduces the risk of erroneous deprivation. Permitting a court to authorize attachment merely because the plaintiff believes the defendant is liable, or because the plaintiff can make out a facially valid complaint, would permit the deprivation of the defendant's property when the claim would fail to convince a jury, when it rested on factual allegations that were sufficient to state a cause of action but which the defendant would dispute, or in the case of a mere good-faith standard, even when the complaint failed to state a claim upon which relief could be granted. The potential for unwarranted attachment in these situations is self-evident and too great to satisfy the requirements of due process absent any countervailing consideration.

Even if the provision requires the plaintiff to demonstrate, and the judge to find, probable cause to believe that judgment will be rendered in favor of the plaintiff, the risk of error was substantial in this case. As the record shows, and as the State concedes, only a skeletal affidavit need be and was filed. The State urges that the reviewing judge normally reviews the complaint as well, but concedes that the complaint may also be conclusory. It is self-evident that the judge could make no realistic assessment concerning the likelihood of an action's success based upon these one-sided, self-serving, and conclusory submissions. And as the Court of Appeals said, in a case like this involving an alleged assault, even a detailed affidavit would give only the plaintiff's version of the confrontation. Unlike determining the existence of a debt or delinquent payments, the issue does not concern "ordinarily uncomplicated matters that lend themselves to documentary proof." *Mitchell*. The likelihood of error that results illustrates that "fairness can rarely be obtained by secret, one-sided determination of facts decisive of rights .... [And n]o better instrument has been devised for arriving at truth than to give a person in jeopardy of serious loss notice of the case against him and an opportunity to meet it." Joint Anti-Fascist Refugee Committee v. McGrath, 341 U.S. 123, 170-172 (1951) (Frankfurter, J., concurring).

What safeguards the State does afford do not adequately reduce this risk. Connecticut points out that the statute also provides an "expeditiou[s]" post-attachment adversary hearing; notice for such a hearing; judicial review of an adverse decision; and a double damages action if the original suit is commenced without probable cause. Similar considerations were present in *Mitchell* where we upheld Louisiana's sequestration statute despite the lack of pre-deprivation notice and hearing. But in *Mitchell*, the plaintiff had a vendor's lien to protect, the risk of error was minimal because the likelihood of recovery involved uncomplicated matters that lent themselves to documentary proof, and plaintiff was required to put up a bond. None of these factors diminishing the need for a pre-deprivation hearing is present in this case. It is true that a later hearing might negate the presence of probable cause, but this would not cure the temporary deprivation that an earlier hearing might have prevented. "The Fourteenth Amendment draws no bright lines around three-day, 10-day or 50-day deprivations of property. Any significant taking of property by the State is within the purview of the Due Process Clause." *Fuentes*.

Finally, we conclude that the interests in favor of an ex parte attachment, particularly the interests of the plaintiff, are too minimal to supply such a consideration here. Plaintiff had no existing interest in Doehr's real estate when he sought the attachment. His only interest in attaching the property was to ensure the availability of assets to satisfy his judgment if he prevailed on the merits of his action. Yet there was no allegation that Doehr was about to transfer or encumber his real estate or take any other action during the pendency of the action that would render his real estate unavailable to satisfy a judgment. Our cases have recognized such a properly supported claim would be an exigent circumstance permitting postponing any notice or hearing until after the attachment is effected. Absent such allegations, however, the plaintiff's interest in attaching the property does not justify the burdening of Doehr's ownership rights without a hearing to determine the likelihood of recovery.

No interest the government may have affects the analysis. The State's substantive interest in protecting any rights of the plaintiff cannot be any more weighty than those rights themselves.

C. Opportunity to be Heard

Here the plaintiff's interest is de minimis. Moreover, the State cannot seriously plead additional financial or administrative burdens involving pre-deprivation hearings when it already claims to provide an immediate post deprivation hearing.

Historical and contemporary practices support our analysis. Prejudgment attachment is a remedy unknown at common law. Instead, "it traces its origin to the Custom of London, under which a creditor might attach money or goods of the defendant either in the plaintiff's own hands or in the custody of a third person, by proceedings in the mayor's court or in the sheriff's court." Generally speaking, attachment measures in both England and this country had several limitations that reduced the risk of erroneous deprivation which Connecticut permits. Although attachments ordinarily did not require prior notice or a hearing, they were usually authorized only where the defendant had taken or threatened to take some action that would place the satisfaction of the plaintiff's potential award in jeopardy. Attachments, moreover, were generally confined to claims by creditors. As we and the Court of Appeals have noted, disputes between debtors and creditors more readily lend themselves to accurate ex parte assessments of the merits. Tort actions, like the assault and battery claim at issue here, do not. Finally, as we will discuss below, attachment statutes historically required that the plaintiff post a bond.

Connecticut's statute appears even more suspect in light of current practice. A survey of state attachment provisions reveals that nearly every State requires either a pre-attachment hearing, a showing of some exigent circumstance, or both, before permitting an attachment to take place. Twenty-seven States, as well as the District of Columbia, permit attachments only when some extraordinary circumstance is present. In such cases, pre-attachment hearings are not required but post-attachment hearings are provided. Ten States permit attachment without the presence of such factors but require pre-writ hearings unless one of those factors is shown. Six States limit attachments to extraordinary circumstance cases but the writ will not issue prior to a hearing unless there is a showing of some even more compelling condition. Three States always require a pre-attachment hearing. Only Washington, Connecticut, and Rhode Island authorize attachments without a prior hearing in situations that do not involve any purportedly heightened threat to the plaintiff's interests. Even those States permit ex parte deprivations only in certain types of cases: Rhode Island does so only when the claim is equitable; Connecticut and Washington do so only when real estate is to be attached, and even Washington requires a bond. Conversely, the States for the most part no longer confine attachments to creditor claims. This development, however, only increases the importance of the other limitations.

We do not mean to imply that any given exigency requirement protects an attachment from constitutional attack. Nor do we suggest that the statutory measures we have surveyed are necessarily free of due process problems or other constitutional infirmities in general. We do believe, however, that the procedures of almost all the States confirm our view that the Connecticut provision before us, by failing to provide a pre-attachment hearing without at least requiring a showing of some exigent circumstance, clearly falls short of the demands of due process.

IV

A

Although a majority of the Court does not reach the issue, Justices Marshall, Stevens, O'Connor, and I deem it appropriate to consider whether due process also requires the plaintiff to post a bond or other security in addition to requiring a hearing or showing of some exigency.[7]

As noted, the impairments to property rights that attachments affect merit due process protection. Several consequences can be severe, such as the default of a homeowner's mortgage. In the present context, it need only be added that we have repeatedly recognized the utility of a bond in protecting property rights affected by the mistaken award of prejudgment remedies.

Without a bond, at the time of attachment, the danger that these property rights may be wrongfully deprived remains unacceptably high even with such safeguards as a hearing or exigency requirement. The need for a bond is especially apparent where extraordinary circumstances justify an attachment with no more than the plaintiff's ex parte assertion of a claim. We have already discussed how due process tolerates, and the States generally permit, the otherwise impermissible chance of erroneously depriving the defendant in such situations in light of the heightened interest of the plaintiff. Until a post-attachment hearing, however, a defendant has no protection against damages sustained where no extraordinary circumstance in fact existed or the plaintiff's likelihood of recovery was nil. Such protection is what a bond can supply. Both the Court and its individual members have repeatedly found the requirement of a bond to play an essential role in reducing what would have been too great a degree of risk in precisely this type of circumstance.

But the need for a bond does not end here. A defendant's property rights remain at undue risk even when there has been an adversarial hearing to determine the plaintiff's likelihood of recovery. At best, a court's initial assessment of each party's case cannot produce more than an educated prediction as to who will win. This is especially true when, as here, the nature of the claim makes any accurate prediction elusive. In consequence, even a full hearing under a proper probable-cause standard would not prevent many defendants from having title to their homes impaired during the pendency of suits that never result in the contingency that ultimately justifies such impairment, namely, an award to the plaintiff. Attachment measures currently on the books reflect this concern. All but a handful of States require a plaintiff's bond despite also affording a hearing either before, or (for the vast majority, only under extraordinary circumstances) soon after, an attachment takes place. Bonds have been a similarly common feature of other prejudgment remedy procedures that we have considered, whether or not these procedures also included a hearing.

---

[7] Ordinarily we will not address a contention advanced by a respondent that would enlarge his or her rights under a judgment, without the respondent filing a cross-petition for certiorari. Here the Court of Appeals rejected Doehr's argument that § 52-278e(a)(1) violates due process in failing to mandate pre-attachment bond. Nonetheless, this case involves considerations that in the past have prompted us to "consider question highlighted by respondent." First, as our cases have shown, the notice and hear question and the bond question are intertwined and can fairly be considered facets of the same general issue. Thus "[w]ithout undue strain, the position taken by the respondent before this Court...might be characterized as an argument in support of the judgement below" insofar as a discussion of notice and a hearing cannot be divorced from consideration of a bond. Second, this aspect of prejudgment attachment "plainly warrants our attention, and with regard to which the lower courts are in need of guidance." Third, "and perhaps most importantly, both parties have briefed and argued the question."

C. Opportunity to be Heard

The State stresses its double damages remedy for suits that are commenced without probable cause. CONN. GEN. STAT. § 52-568(a)(1). This remedy, however, fails to make up for the lack of a bond. As an initial matter, the meaning of "probable cause" in this provision is no more clear here than it was in the attachment provision itself. Should the term mean the plaintiff's good faith or the facial adequacy of the complaint, the remedy is clearly insufficient. A defendant who was deprived where there was little or no likelihood that the plaintiff would obtain a judgment could nonetheless recover only by proving some type of fraud or malice or by showing that the plaintiff had failed to state a claim. Problems persist even if the plaintiff's ultimate failure permits recovery. At best a defendant must await a decision on the merits of the plaintiff's complaint, even assuming that a § 52-568(a)(1) action may be brought as a counterclaim. Settlement, under Connecticut law, precludes seeking the damages remedy, a fact that encourages the use of attachments as a tactical device to pressure an opponent to capitulate. An attorney's advice that there is probable cause to commence an action constitutes a complete defense, even if the advice was unsound or erroneous. Finally, there is no guarantee that the original plaintiff will have adequate assets to satisfy an award that the defendant may win.

Nor is there any appreciable interest against a bond requirement. Section 52-278e(a)(1) does not require a plaintiff to show exigent circumstances nor any pre-existing interest in the property facing attachment. A party must show more than the mere existence of a claim before subjecting an opponent to prejudgment proceedings that carry a significant risk of erroneous deprivation.

B

Our foregoing discussion compels the four of us to consider whether a bond excuses the need for a hearing or other safeguards altogether. If a bond is needed to augment the protections afforded by pre-attachment and post-attachment hearings, it arguably follows that a bond renders these safeguards unnecessary. That conclusion is unconvincing, however, for it ignores certain harms that bonds could not undo but that hearings would prevent. The law concerning attachments has rarely, if ever, required defendants to suffer an encumbered title until the case is concluded without any prior opportunity to show that the attachment was unwarranted. Our cases have repeatedly emphasized the importance of providing a prompt post-deprivation hearing at the very least. Every State but one, moreover, expressly requires a pre-attachment or post-attachment hearing to determine the propriety of an attachment.

The necessity for at least a prompt post-attachment hearing is self-evident because the right to be compensated at the end of the case, if the plaintiff loses, for all provable injuries caused by the attachment is inadequate to redress the harm inflicted, harm that could have been avoided had an early hearing been held. An individual with an immediate need or opportunity to sell a property can neither do so, nor otherwise satisfy that need or recreate the opportunity. The same applies to a parent in need of a home equity loan for a child's education, an entrepreneur seeking to start a business on the strength of an otherwise strong credit rating, or simply a homeowner who might face the disruption of having a mortgage placed in technical default. The extent of these harms, moreover, grows with the length of the suit. Here, oral argument indicated that civil suits in Connecticut commonly take up to four to seven years for completion. Many state attachment statutes require that the amount of a bond be anywhere from the equivalent to twice the amount the plaintiff seeks. These amounts bear no relation to the harm the defendant might suffer even assuming that money damages can make up for the foregoing disruptions. It should be clear, however, that such an assumption is fundamentally flawed. Reliance on a bond does not sufficiently account for the harms that flow from an erroneous attachment to excuse a State from reducing that risk by means of a timely hearing.

If a bond cannot serve to dispense with a hearing immediately after attachment, neither is it sufficient basis for not providing a pre-attachment hearing in the absence of exigent circumstances even if in any event a hearing would be provided a few days later. The reasons are the same: a wrongful attachment can inflict injury that will not fully be redressed by recovery on the bond after a prompt post-attachment hearing determines that the attachment was invalid.

Once more, history and contemporary practice support our conclusion. Historically, attachments would not issue without a showing of extraordinary circumstances even though a plaintiff bond was almost invariably required in addition. Likewise, all but eight States currently require the posting of a bond. Out of this 42 State majority, all but one requires a pre-attachment hearing, a showing of some exigency, or both, and all but one expressly require a post-attachment hearing when an attachment has been issued ex parte. This testimony underscores the point that neither a hearing nor an extraordinary circumstance limitation eliminates the need for a bond, no more than a bond allows waiver of these other protections. To reconcile the interests of the defendant and the plaintiff accurately, due process generally requires all of the above.

V

Because Connecticut's prejudgment remedy provision, CONN. GEN. STAT. § 52-278e(a)(1), violates the requirements of due process by authorizing prejudgment attachment without prior notice or a hearing, the judgment of the Court of Appeals is affirmed, and the case is remanded to that court for further proceedings consistent with this opinion.

It is so ordered.

CHIEF JUSTICE REHNQUIST with whom JUSTICE BLACKMUN joins, concurring in part and concurring in judgment.

I agree with the Court that the Connecticut attachment statute, "as applied in this case," fails to satisfy the Due Process Clause of the Fourteenth Amendment. I therefore join Parts I, II and III of its opinion. Unfortunately, the remainder of the Court's opinion does not confine itself to the facts of this case, but enters upon a lengthy disquisition as to what combination of safeguards are required to satisfy Due Process in hypothetical cases not before the Court. I therefore do not join Part IV.

As the Court's opinion points out, the Connecticut statute allows attachment not merely for a creditor's claim, but for a tort claim of assault and battery; it affords no opportunity for a pre-deprivation hearing; it contains no requirement that there be "exigent circumstances," such as an effort on the part of the defendant to conceal assets; no bond is required from the plaintiff; and the property attached is one in which the plaintiff has no pre-existing interest. The Court's opinion is, in my view, ultimately correct when it bases its holding of unconstitutionality of the Connecticut statute as applied here on our cases of *Sniadach, Fuentes, Mitchell,* and *Di-Chem*. But I do not believe that the result follows so inexorably as the Court's opinion suggests. All of the cited cases dealt with personalty — bank deposits or chattels — and each involved the physical seizure of the property itself, so that the defendant was deprived of its use. These cases, which represented something of a revolution in the jurisprudence of procedural due process, placed substantial limits on the methods by which creditors could obtain a lien on the assets of a debtor prior to judgment. But in all of them the debtor was deprived of the use and possession of the property. In the present case, on the other hand, Connecticut's pre-judgment attachment on real property statute, which secures an incipient lien for the plaintiff, does not deprive the defendant of the use or possession of the property.

The Court's opinion therefore breaks new ground, and I would point out, more emphatically than the Court does, the limits of today's holding. In Spielman-Fond, Inc. v. Hanson's, Inc., 379 F. Supp. 997, 999 (D. Ariz. 1973), the District Court held that the filing of a mechanics' lien did not cause the deprivation of a significant property interest of the owner. We summarily affirmed that decision. 417 U.S. 901 (1974). Other courts have read this summary affirmance to mean that the mere imposition of a lien on real property, which does not disturb the owner's use or enjoyment of the property, is not a deprivation of property calling for procedural due process safeguards. I agree with the Court, however, that upon analysis the deprivation here is a significant one, even though the owner remains in undisturbed possession. "For a property owner like Doehr, attachment ordinarily clouds title; impairs the ability to sell or otherwise alienate the property; taints any credit rating; reduces the chance of obtaining a home equity loan or additional mortgage; and can even place an existing mortgage in technical default when there is an insecurity clause." Given the elaborate system of title records relating to real property which prevails in all of our states, a lienor need not obtain possession or use of real property belonging to a debtor in order to significantly impair its value to him.

But in *Spielman-Fond, Inc.*, supra, there was, * * *, an alternate basis available to this Court for affirmance of that decision. Arizona recognized a pre-existing lien in favor of unpaid mechanics and materialmen who had contributed labor or supplies which were incorporated in improvements to real property. The existence of such a lien upon the very property ultimately posted or noticed distinguishes those cases from the present one, where the plaintiff had no pre-existing interest in the real property which he sought to attach. Materialman's and mechanic's lien statutes award an interest in real property to workers who have contributed their labor, and to suppliers who have furnished material, for the improvement of the real property. Since neither the labor nor the material can be reclaimed once it has become a part of the realty, this is the only method by which workmen or small businessmen who have contributed to the improvement of the property may be given a remedy against a property owner who has defaulted on his promise to pay for the labor and the materials. To require any sort of a contested court hearing or bond before the notice of lien takes effect would largely defeat the purpose of these statutes.

* * *

Justice Scalia, concurring in part and concurring in the judgment.

Since the manner of attachment here was not a recognized procedure at common law, I agree that its validity under the Due Process Clause should be determined by applying the test we set forth in *Mathews v. Eldridge*; and I agree that it fails that test. I join Parts I and III of the Court's opinion, and concur in the judgment of the Court.

NOTES AND QUESTIONS

1. How significant was the deprivation in *Doehr*? Mr. Doehr still had physical possession of his home and there is no indication that he was trying to sell or refinance the property. Under these circumstances, why wasn't the post-deprivation hearing sufficient?

2. In *Mathews v. Eldridge*, discussed in *Doehr*, the issue was whether a recipient of social security disability benefits was entitled to a hearing before the government terminated his payments. The Court held that a pre-termination hearing was not required. It noted, however, that the recipient was entitled to a post-deprivation hearing — a process that took over a year. The Court also suggested that being deprived of disability benefits was not particularly onerous because not all recipients were impoverished. This was so even though Mr. Eldridge lost his home and most of his possessions as a result of losing his income for a year. Is the result in *Doehr* consistent with the result in *Mathews*?

3. The Court held that the Connecticut statute was unconstitutional "as applied to this case." Are there other situations in which the procedures set forth in that statute would be constitutionally adequate? In Shaumyan v. O'Neill, 987 F.2d 122 (2d Cir. 1993), the Second Circuit upheld the statute. Mr. Shaumyan had contracted for repairs, including window replacements to his home. After the work was completed, Mr. Shaumyan was dissatisfied with the work and refused to make the final payment. The contractor sued for breach of contract in Connecticut state court and attached the Shaumyan home without a hearing or bond. Shaumyan then brought suit in federal court challenging the attachment. The Second Circuit distinguished *Doehr* and upheld the attachment. The court found that the contractor, unlike the plaintiff in *Doehr*, had an interest in the property and could have filed a mechanic's lien. The court also found that there was much less risk of a wrongful deprivation because the case concerned a contract that was for a sum certain and was easily documented. How persuasive do you find these reasons? The dispute between the homeowner and the contractor concerned the adequacy of performance. Is that something that is easily documented?

4. In 1993, Connecticut amended its prejudgment attachment statute. The new statute provides:

> (a) The court or judge of the court may allow the prejudgment remedy to be issued by an attorney without hearing * * * upon the filing of an affidavit sworn to by the plaintiff or any competent affiant setting forth a statement of facts sufficient to show that there is probable cause that a judgment in the amount of the prejudgment remedy ought, or in an amount greater than the amount of the prejudgment remedy sought, taking into account any known defenses, counterclaims or set-offs, will be rendered in the matter in favor of the plaintiff and that there is reasonable likelihood that the defendant (1) has hidden himself so that

process cannot be served on him or (2) is about to remove himself or his property from the state or (3) is about to fraudulently dispose of or has fraudulently disposed of any of his property with intent to hinder, delay or defraud his creditors or (4) has fraudulently hidden or withheld money, property or effects which should be liable to the satisfaction of his debts.

CONN. GEN. STAT. § 52–278e. The defendant may move to modify or dissolve the prejudgment remedy and the court must hold a hearing within 7 days of the filing of such a motion. Id. at subsection (e). At the hearing or upon motion, the defendant may request that the court order the plaintiff to post bond. Id. at § 52–278d(d). If the court grants this request and the defendant prevails at trial or the prejudgment attachment is later dissolved, the plaintiff must pay the defendant for any damages caused by the prejudgment attachment. Is this revised statute constitutional?

5. Federal law permits the forfeiture of property used to commit or facilitate the commission of a federal drug offense. 21 U.S.C. § 881. In United States v. Good, 114 S.Ct. 492 (1993), several years after Good was convicted of drug offenses, the United States brought an ex parte procedure to seize Good's property. The property was seized without prior notice or a hearing. The Court held that there was not a sufficient government justification to support seizure without notice or a hearing. The Court noted that although it has permitted seizure without prior notice of movable forfeitable property such as a yacht, see Calero-Toledo v. Pearson Yacht Leasing Co., 416 U.S. 663 (1974), no exigent circumstances justified a similar approach regarding the seizure of real property.

6. The three part test of *Mathews v. Eldridge* can be read to suggest that in deciding how much process the Constitution requires, courts should do a kind of cost-benefit analysis and weigh the value of the right against the cost of the additional process. The *Mathews* Court itself invoked such terms, noting that "[a]t some point the benefit of an additional safeguard to the individual affected by the [government] action and to society in terms of increased assurance that the action is just, may be outweighed by the cost." 424 U.S. at 828. Some have applauded this approach, because it seeks to ensure an "efficient" amount of procedure. As Judge Richard Posner has explained, "in general we would not want to increase the direct costs of the legal process by one dollar in order to reduce the error costs by 50 (or 99) cents." Richard Posner, *An Economic Approach to Legal Procedure and Judicial Administration,* 2 J. LEGAL STUDIES 399, 401 (1973). Do you agree that the purpose of the Due Process Clause is to ensure an efficient level of procedure? If so, how should a court go about estimating the costs and benefits of a procedure? What should a court do when it lacks solid data about costs and benefits?

7. Consider the following situation: The City of Parksburg is planning a program of "booting" cars that have accumulated parking tickets totaling more than $300. (A "boot"

CHAPTER 3 NOTICE AND OPPORTUNITY TO BE HEARD

is a device that is attached to the wheel of a car and makes it impossible to drive.) The City also plans to tow and dispose of abandoned cars. The City Attorney has asked you to describe what, if any, procedures must be in place in order for these programs to be constitutional.

8. The Court in *Doehr* asserts that "fairness can rarely be obtained by secret, one-sided determination of facts decisive of rights" (quoting Justice Frankfurter's concurrence in *Joint Anti-Fascist Refugee Committee v. McGrath*). In the criminal arena, arrest warrants and search warrants are routinely issued by the court on an ex parte basis. Indeed, the affidavit that DiGiovanni submitted likely would have provided sufficient probable cause for a court to issue a warrant for Doehr's arrest. On the basis of an arrest warrant, Doehr could have been jailed (subject to a later hearing on bail). Thus, the procedures which were an inadequate basis for depriving Doehr of his property would have been sufficient for depriving him of his liberty. The Court has explained this anomaly as follows:

> The historical basis of the probable cause requirement is quite different from the relatively recent application of variable procedural due process in debtor-creditor disputes and termination of government-created benefits. The Fourth Amendment was tailored explicitly for the criminal justice system, and its balance between individual and public interests always has been thought to define the "process that is due" for seizures of person or property in criminal cases, including the detention of suspects pending trial.

Gerstein v. Pugh, 420 U.S. 103, 125 n.27 (1975).

9. Even if the defendant is entitled to a hearing prior to the grant of any preliminary relief, what standards should be applied at that hearing? Should a plaintiff be entitled to preliminary relief based on a showing that the plaintiff may prevail or is likely to prevail? Why shouldn't the plaintiff have actually to prevail before getting any relief? In some contexts, such as the nuclear power plant example at the beginning of the section, the plaintiff faces an immediate and irreparable injury. The plaintiff will not be able to prevail without a complete trial. If nothing is done in the interim, however, any final remedy may be inadequate. In deciding whether to grant preliminary relief in such cases, courts typically consider a list of factors including: the plaintiff's probability of success on the merits, risk of irreparable injury to the plaintiff, the balance of hardships between the parties, and the public interest. Some courts treat this list of factors as "a sliding scale in which the required degree of irreparable harm increases as the probability of success decreases." United States v. Odessa Union Warehouse Co-op, 833 F.2d 172, 174 (9th Cir. 1987). Indeed, Judge Posner has distilled this into an algebraic formula:

C. Opportunity to be Heard

$$P \times HP > (1 - P) \times HD$$

P is the probability that the plaintiff will prevail. (1 - P is the probability that the defendant will prevail.) HP is the irreparable harm the plaintiff will suffer if the preliminary relief is denied, and HD is the irreparable harm the defendant will suffer if the preliminary relief is granted. American Hosp. Supply Corp. v. Hospital Products Ltd., 780 F.2d 589, 593 (7th Cir. 1986). Thus, if the likely harm to the plaintiff of denying relief is greater than the likely harm to the defendant of granting relief, the injunction should be granted.

10. Suppose a plaintiff attaches property to secure quasi-in-rem jurisdiction. What pre-attachment process is required? In Fuentes v. Shevin, 407 U.S. 67 (1972), the Supreme Court in enumerating several circumstances under which attachment without a prior hearing has been permitted, stated: "Another case involved attachment necessary to secure jurisdiction in state court — clearly a most basic and important public interest. Ownbey v. Morgan." Relying on this statement, the Delaware Supreme Court upheld the ex parte sequestration procedure at issue in *Shaffer v. Heitner*, Chapter 2, despite the lack of pre-attachment procedures. Because the Supreme Court reversed for lack of jurisdiction, it did not reach the issue of pre-attachment procedures. However, in a footnote the Court commented on the Delaware Supreme Court's treatment of this issue and observed:

> The [Delaware] court relied on our decision in *Ownbey v. Morgan* and references to that decision in [*Di-Chem, Mitchell, Fuentes* and several other cases]. The only question before the Court in *Ownbey* was the constitutionality of a requirement that a defendant whose property has been attached file a bond before entering an appearance. We do not read the recent references to *Ownbey* as necessarily suggesting that *Ownbey* is consistent with more recent decisions interpreting the Due Process Clause.

433 U.S. at 194 n.10.

Admiralty courts have upheld quasi-in-rem attachment without a prior hearing. See, e.g., Trans-Asiatic Oil, Ltd. v Apex Oil Co., 743 F.2d 956 (1st Cir. 1984); Polar Shipping Ltd. v. Oriental Shipping Co., 680 F.2d 627 (9th Cir. 1982). Outside the admiralty context, the issue appears to have arisen infrequently and the cases are divided. Compare Cable Advertising Networks, Inc. v. DeWoody, 632 A.2d 1383 (Del. Chanc. 1993) (pre-attachment safeguards required in quasi-in-rem attachment) with Estate of Portnoy v. Cessna Aircraft Co., 603 F. Supp. 285, 294-96 (S.D. Miss. 1985) (pre-attachment safeguards not required in quasi-in-rem attachment).

CHAPTER 4
SUBJECT MATTER JURISDICTION

A. Introduction and Integration

"Jurisdiction" is a chameleon word; it means different things in different contexts. We have spent considerable time determining whether the forum has personal jurisdiction over the defendant, and now turn to a separate requirement: the plaintiff must file suit in a court permitted by relevant law to entertain the type of claim asserted. In other words, the court must have subject matter jurisdiction. Subject matter jurisdiction is independent of personal jurisdiction. Throughout this chapter, we assume that the plaintiff has established personal jurisdiction over the defendant in a particular state. Now the question is what court does plaintiff go to in that state?

The principal choice will be between a state court and a federal court. In each state, there are various state trial courts, which bear a variety of names, and there is at least one federal trial court, which is always called the federal district court. The federal district court (like all federal courts) has *limited subject matter jurisdiction*; it can hear only certain kinds of cases, as prescribed by the United States Constitution and federal statutes. In contrast, the trial courts of each state collectively have *general subject matter jurisdiction*; they can, with rare exceptions, hear any cognizable claim. Many cases will satisfy subject matter jurisdiction of both the state and federal court. Such situations are examples of the two court systems' having *concurrent subject matter jurisdiction*. In cases of concurrent jurisdiction, the plaintiff decides in which court to file, usually guided by a variety of pragmatic and strategic considerations.

B. State Courts and General Subject Matter Jurisdiction

The states are free to divide subject matter jurisdiction among whatever courts they decide to establish. In some states, the matter is treated in the constitution, while in others, it is addressed in statutes. There is considerable variation as to the names given the trial courts (popular names include County, District, Municipal, Circuit, and Superior Courts), and as to how to divide subject matter among them.

CHAPTER 4 SUBJECT MATTER JURISDICTION

Many states establish specialized tribunals to handle specific cases, such as Probate Courts, Juvenile Courts, Traffic Courts, and the like. In some, subject matter is divided along monetary lines. For example, civil cases involving less than a particular monetary amount might go to one court while those involving a greater sum go to another. Many states employ a combination of these approaches, with specialized courts hearing specific substantive cases and other courts dividing the remaining general civil cases along monetary lines.

No matter how a state chooses to allocate its trial jurisdiction, however, the key point is that within each state a plaintiff virtually always will be able to find some tribunal of that state in which to assert her claim. Thus, while not all courts in a state can hear all cases, the courts of a particular state, in the aggregate, have general subject matter jurisdiction. There is one narrow exception to the general subject matter jurisdiction of state courts. It involves those areas in which Congress has vested the federal district courts with exclusive subject matter jurisdiction. These include some admiralty proceedings (28 U.S.C. § 1333), bankruptcy matters (28 U.S.C. § 1334), patent and copyright infringement claims (28 U.S.C. § 1338(a)), and certain cases arising under federal antitrust and securities laws (15 U.S.C. §§ 15126, 78aa).

Most grants of federal jurisdiction, including other specific grants, are not exclusive. For example, 28 U.S.C. § 1343 allows federal courts to hear cases involving violations of federally protected civil rights, but such cases may also be brought in state court. The same is true with the general federal question statute, 28 U.S.C. § 1331, which we will address in detail in Section C(4) below. It is a catchall provision, allowing assertion of claims that arise under federal laws but that do not have their own specialized jurisdictional grant. It does not carry exclusive federal jurisdiction.

Why would Congress establish exclusive jurisdiction in the federal courts as to *any* matters? Why wouldn't Congress establish exclusive jurisdiction over *all* matters cognizable by the federal courts?

C. Federal Courts and Limited Subject Matter Jurisdiction

1. The Constitutional Grants and Role of Congress

As discussed in Chapter 1, Section B, the Constitution creates the federal government and grants it only specified powers. Article III of the Constitution specifies the powers of the federal courts. Read Sections 1 and 2 of Article III in your rules supplement and consider the following notes and questions.

C. Federal Courts and Limited Subject Matter Jurisdiction

NOTES AND QUESTIONS

1. Note the extraordinary protections accorded federal judges. They cannot be forced to retire. They never face an electorate. Their pay cannot be reduced. They can be removed from office only through impeachment, which has occurred fewer than a dozen times in the history of the nation. In contrast, the judges of most state courts must face an electorate at some point. Keep these protections of the federal judiciary in mind as we study the various types of cases heard by federal courts, always asking why the Founders felt it necessary to insulate federal judges from ongoing review by an electorate.

2. Compare the provisions of the first sentence of Art. III, Section 1 with the second paragraph of Section 2. What federal court(s) must exist? Could Congress abolish federal district courts and federal courts of appeals? If Congress did abolish the lower federal courts, where would cases that are now filed there go?

3. The nine separate categories, or "heads," of jurisdiction provided in the first paragraph of Section 2 of Article III delineate the outer limits of jurisdiction of the federal courts. Congress cannot exceed these limits in conferring jurisdiction upon the federal courts. But *must* Congress vest the federal courts with the power to decide all of the types of disputes contained in Article III, Section 2? Although Justice Story asserted that Article III imposed that obligation on Congress, see Martin v. Hunter's Lessee, 14 U.S. 304, 327-37 (1816), Congress has never felt obliged to follow that theory. For example, Congress did not grant the lower federal courts jurisdiction over cases "arising under * * * the laws of United States" until 1875.

4. Even within a particular category of jurisdiction, Article III does not require that Congress grant jurisdiction to the full constitutional limit. For example, Congress has always imposed an amount in controversy requirement in diversity of citizenship cases, although no such limit exists in the Constitution. 28 U.S.C. § 1332(a)(1).

5. Would it be wise for Congress to vest the federal courts with judicial power over particular types of cases to the full extent of Article III? Consider Justice Chase's remarks nearly two centuries ago in Turner v. Bank of North America, 4 U.S. 8, 10 (1799): "[I]t would, perhaps, be inexpedient, to enlarge the jurisdiction of the federal courts, to every subject, in every form, which the constitution might warrant." Why would it be "inexpedient?" Should that view hold sway today?

It is extremely rare for Congress to overreach the power given by Article III. Instead, Congress generally follows Justice Chase's advice and refuses to grant the courts jurisdiction to the full extent that the Constitution would allow. Thus, most problems regarding the proper invocation of federal jurisdiction involve interpretation of the jurisdictional *statutes* passed by Congress, and not the provisions of Article III.

2. Plaintiff's Burden to Establish Federal Subject Matter Jurisdiction

Several important consequences flow from the fact that federal court jurisdiction is limited to those areas granted by the Constitution and statutes. First, the parties to litigation cannot confer subject matter jurisdiction on a federal court by "consent".

Second, a federal court's lack of subject matter jurisdiction is a defense that is never waived. See Rule 12(h)(3). Any party or the court can raise the issue at any time in the case, even after the court has entered judgment. Indeed, even the plaintiff, who originally invoked the jurisdiction of the federal court, can seek dismissal for lack of subject matter jurisdiction. There are a surprising number of cases in which disputes bounce through different levels of the federal judiciary for years before someone notices that the case must be dismissed for want of subject matter jurisdiction. See, e.g., Depex Reina 9 Partnership v. Texas International Petroleum Corp., 897 F.2d 461 (10th Cir. 1990) (ordering dismissal after case had been through full trial, appeal, remand by the appellate court and subsequent treatment by the district court). Ordinarily, the plaintiff will then have to start the case over in state court. The plaintiff may be without remedy, however, if the federal jurisdictional problem is not discovered until after the statute of limitations has run for a state court action. See Clephas v. Fagelson, Shonberger, Payne & Arthur, 719 F.2d 92 (4th Cir. 1983). We will discuss the timing and methods of jurisdictional challenges in Chapter 6.

Third, there is a presumption *against* federal jurisdiction. Thus, the plaintiff must properly plead that federal jurisdiction exists. Indeed, Rule 8(a)(1), to be discussed further in Chapter 8, requires "a short and plain statement of the grounds upon which the court's jurisdiction depends." If the defendant challenges the allegation, the plaintiff assumes the burden of proving that jurisdiction exists. See Hoover v. Gershman Investment Corp., 774 F. Supp. 60 (D. Mass. 1991) (case dismissed after plaintiff failed to show facts establishing federal jurisdiction).

It is critical, therefore, that counsel understand not only the burden of invoking jurisdiction, but the elements required to establish it. Detailed understanding of these elements "is not a hypertechnicality." VT Investors v. R & D Funding Corp., 733 F. Supp. 823, 826 (D. N.J. 1990). Instead, it is fundamental to the competent practice of law and critical to assure that the federal courts not decide cases beyond their power.

Although Article III listed nine separate categories of federal jurisdiction, we will focus on three: diversity of citizenship, alienage, and federal question jurisdiction.

3. Diversity of Citizenship and Alienage Jurisdiction

a. Introductory Note

Compare the constitutional grants of diversity of citizenship and alienage jurisdiction in Article III to the statutory grants in 28 U.S.C. § 1332(a)(1) and § 1332(a)(2). The term "original jurisdiction," in contrast to "appellate jurisdiction," refers to jurisdiction of a trial court.

The Founders provided for alienage jurisdiction for two related reasons. First, it gave aliens involved in litigation with American citizens a forum free from local political influence. Second, it thereby demonstrated to foreign countries that the United States treats litigation involving their citizens or subjects as a matter of such importance as to justify a place on the dockets of the national, as opposed to the local, courts. Alienage jurisdiction accounts for a small percentage of the federal court caseload. In part because of this, and because the underlying principles for alienage remain vital, no one seriously contends that alienage jurisdiction ought to be restricted or abolished.

The same is not true of diversity of citizenship jurisdiction, which accounts for approximately one-quarter of the filings in the federal courts, and which has always had opponents. The orthodox view is that diversity jurisdiction provided a neutral forum — free from local bias or influence — for resolution of cases between citizens of different states. It provided a federal forum for an out-of-state litigant who feared that she might be the victim of local bias, or be "hometowned," if forced to litigate before the locally selected state court judge. It seems clear that the Founders were most interested in relieving anxiety of commercial interests. The availability of an impartial federal forum may have made it easier for enterprises to invest in other states, and thus may have fostered economic expansion. Indeed, President and Chief Justice Taft concluded that diversity jurisdiction "was the single most important element in securing capital for the development of the southern and western United States." William Howard Taft, *Possible and Needed Reforms in Administration of Justice in Federal Courts*, 8 A.B.A.J. 601, 604 (1922). See EDWARD PURCELL, LITIGATION AND INEQUALITY: FEDERAL DIVERSITY JURISDICTION IN INDUSTRIAL AMERICA, 1870-1958 (1992).

Many critics feel that diversity jurisdiction has outlived its usefulness. They assert that local bias and the fear of local bias have largely evaporated in the modern era of mass communication and travel. Moreover, diversity jurisdiction only changes the judge who presides — it does not change the law that applies, and thus cannot protect litigants from biased laws. On the contrary, since the landmark case of Erie Railroad v. Tompkins, 304 U.S. 64 (1938), infra Chapter 7, a federal court sitting in a diversity case must apply the same law that the state in which it sits would have applied — biases and all. Thus, argue

CHAPTER 4 SUBJECT MATTER JURISDICTION

critics, diversity jurisdiction no longer provides much benefit and, given our limited resources, federal judges should be freed up to work on cases involving federal substantive law. See, e.g., REPORT OF FEDERAL COURTS STUDY COMMITTEE 38-43 (1990); Larry Kramer, *Diversity Jurisdiction*, 1990 B.Y.U. L. REV. 97; Thomas Rowe, *Abolishing Diversity Jurisdiction: Positive Side Effects and Potential for Further Reforms*, 92 HARV. L. REV. 963 (1979).

Others disagree, contending that the historic justification remains vital today. They point to cases such as Pennzoil Co. v. Texaco, Inc., 481 U.S. 1 (1987) — in which a Texas state court entered a judgment of $11 billion in favor of a Texas company against a New York entity — as evidence of local bias, or, at least, as evidence of why the fear of local bias is not irrational. See, e.g., Pappas v. Middle Earth Condominium Assoc., 963 F.2d 634 (2d Cir. 1992) (involving lawyers' appeal to regional bias); 1 MOORE'S FEDERAL PRACTICE ¶ 0.71 [3.-2]; Charles Brieant, *Diversity Jurisdiction: Why Does the Bar Talk One Way But Vote the Other Way With Its Feet?*, 1989 N.Y. ST. B.J. 20; John Frank, *The Case for Diversity Jurisdiction*, 16 HARV. J. LEGIS. 403 (1979).

Consider, for example, the comments of Justice Neely of the West Virginia Supreme Court: "As long as I am allowed to redistribute wealth from out-of-state companies to injured in-state plaintiffs, I shall continue to do so. Not only is my sleep enhanced when I give someone else's money away, but so is my job security, because the in-state plaintiffs, their families and their friends will re-elect me." RICHARD NEELY, THE PRODUCT LIABILITY MESS: HOW BUSINESS CAN BE RESCUED FROM THE POLITICS OF STATE COURTS 4 (1988). Advocates of diversity of citizenship jurisdiction also note that federal courts generally draw their juries from wider geographic areas than state courts, which may lessen the impact of local bias.

The debate over the need for diversity of citizenship jurisdiction will continue, as it has for two centuries. As a general rule, diversity has proved quite popular with members of the bar, in part because it affords them an option of fora. Because the bar is such a powerful lobbying force, it seems unlikely that Congress will abolish diversity of citizenship jurisdiction wholesale.

b. The Complete Diversity Rule

Strawbridge v. Curtiss
7 U.S. 267, 2 L. Ed. 435 (1806)

This was an appeal from a decree * * * which dismissed the complainants' bill for want of jurisdiction.

Some of the complainants were alleged to be citizens of the State of Massachusetts. The defendants were also stated to be citizens of the same State, excepting Curtiss, who was averred to be a citizen of the State of Vermont, and upon whom the subpoena was served in that State.

MARSHALL, CHIEF JUSTICE, delivered the opinion of the Court.

The court has considered this case, and is of opinion that the jurisdiction cannot be supported.

The words of the act of congress are, "* * * the suit is between a citizen of a State where the suit is brought, and a citizen of another State."

The court understands these expressions to mean, that each distinct interest should be represented by persons, all of whom are entitled to sue, or may be sued, in the federal courts. That is, that where the interest is joint, each of the persons concerned in that interest must be competent to sue, or liable to be sued in those courts. * * *

NOTES AND QUESTIONS

1. After *Strawbridge*, diversity jurisdiction exists only if all plaintiffs are of diverse citizenship from all defendants. Professor David Currie has observed, "[t]he assumption apparently underlying *Strawbridge* is that the presence of Massachusetts people on both sides of a case will neutralize any possibility of bias affecting litigants from other states," meaning that no federal forum was necessary. David Currie, *The Federal Courts and the American Law Institute*, 36 U. CHI. L. REV. 1, 18 (1968). What do you think of this rationale? Does Chief Justice Marshall suggest this or any other rationale for the Court's holding?

2. Compare the wording of the statutory grant of diversity jurisdiction quoted by Chief Justice Marshall in *Strawbridge* with the current wording of that grant at 28 U.S.C. § 1332 (a)(1). Which version is more consistent with the historic justification for diversity of citizenship jurisdiction?

3. In 1917, Congress passed the Federal Interpleader Act, 28 U.S.C. §§ 1335, 1397, & 2361. It applies only to a very specialized type of litigation concerning ownership of property, as we will see in Chapter 13. For present purposes, it is enough to note that the statute grants federal subject matter jurisdiction based upon "minimal diversity," that is, based upon having one adverse claimant of diverse citizenship from another. In other words, if an interpleader proceeding involved adverse claims by citizens of Vermont and Maryland against a citizen of Maryland, the statute would permit jurisdiction.

The Supreme Court upheld the constitutionality of the Federal Interpleader Act in

State Farm Fire & Cas. Co. v. Tashire, 386 U.S. 523, 530-31 (1967). The Court explained:

> In *Strawbridge v. Curtiss,* * * * this Court held that the diversity of citizenship statute required "complete diversity": where co-citizens appeared on both sides of a dispute, jurisdiction was lost. But Chief Justice Marshall there purported to construe only "The words of the act of Congress," not the Constitution itself. And in a variety of contexts this Court and the lower courts have concluded that Article III poses no obstacle to the legislative extension of federal jurisdiction, founded on diversity, so long as any two adverse parties are not co-citizens. Accordingly, we conclude that the present case is properly in the federal courts.

4. *Strawbridge* governs cases brought under § 1332(a)(1) today. As made clear in *Tashire, Strawbridge* interprets merely the statutory, not the constitutional, grant of diversity of citizenship jurisdiction. But how can identical language in the Constitution ("between citizens of different states") and in the statute ("between citizens of different states") mean different things? Especially since some of the same persons who drafted Article III also drafted the original statutory grant of diversity jurisdiction interpreted by Chief Justice Marshall, how likely is it that they intended to make the two mean different things?

5. It is important to remember that both the Constitution and the statute grant jurisdiction over cases involving diversity of *citizenship*. As we will see, citizenship is not necessarily the same as *residence*, and the terms should not be used interchangeably. Competent counsel will be careful to use only the term *citizenship* when speaking of diversity jurisdiction.

c. Determining Citizenship of Individuals

Mas v. Perry
489 F.2d 1396 (5th Cir.), *cert. denied,* 419 U.S. 842 (1974)

AINSWORTH, CIRCUIT JUDGE.

This case presents questions pertaining to federal diversity jurisdiction under 28 U.S.C. § 1332, which, pursuant to article III, section II of the Constitution, provides for original jurisdiction in federal district courts of all civil actions that are between, *inter alia*, citizens of different States or citizens of a State and citizens of foreign states and in which the amount in controversy is more than $10,000. [Note: The statute now requires an amount in excess of $50,000 - EDS.]

Appellees Jean Paul Mas, a citizen of France, and Judy Mas were married at her home in Jackson, Mississippi. Prior to their marriage, Mr. and Mrs. Mas were graduate assistants, pursuing coursework as well as performing teaching duties, for approximately nine months and one year, respectively, at Louisiana State University in Baton Rouge, Louisiana. Shortly after their marriage, they returned to Baton Rouge to resume their duties as graduate assistants at LSU. They remained in Baton Rouge for approximately two more years, after which they moved to Park Ridge, Illinois. At the time of the trial in this case, it was their intention to return to Baton Rouge while Mr. Mas finished his studies for the degree of Doctor of Philosophy. Mr. and Mrs. Mas were undecided as to where they would reside after that.

Upon their return to Baton Rouge after their marriage, appellees rented an apartment from appellant Oliver H. Perry, a citizen of Louisiana. This appeal arises from a final judgment entered on a jury verdict awarding $5,000 to Mr. Mas and $15,000 to Mrs. Mas for damages incurred by them as a result of the discovery that their bedroom and bathroom contained "two-way" mirrors and that they had been watched through them by the appellant during three of the first four months of their marriage.

At the close of the appellees' case at trial, appellant made an oral motion to dismiss for lack of jurisdiction. The motion was denied by the district court. Before this Court, appellant challenges the final judgment below solely on jurisdictional grounds, contending that appellees failed to prove diversity of citizenship among the parties and that the requisite jurisdictional amount is lacking with respect to Mr. Mas. Finding no merit to these contentions, we affirm. Under section 1332(a)(2), the federal judicial power extends to the claim of Mr. Mas, a citizen of France, against the appellant, a citizen of Louisiana. Since we conclude that Mrs. Mas is a citizen of Mississippi for diversity purposes, the district court also properly had jurisdiction under section 1332(a)(1) of her claim.

It has long been the general rule that complete diversity of parties is required in order that diversity jurisdiction obtain; that is, no party on one side may be a citizen of the same State as any party on the other side. *Strawbridge v. Curtiss*. This determination of one's State citizenship for diversity purposes is controlled by federal law, not by the law of any State. As is the case in other areas of federal jurisdiction, the diverse citizenship among adverse parties must be present at the time the complaint is filed. Jurisdiction is unaffected by subsequent changes in the citizenship of the parties. The burden of pleading the diverse citizenship is upon the party invoking federal jurisdiction, and if the diversity jurisdiction is properly challenged, that party also bears the burden of proof.

To be a citizen of a State within the meaning of section 1332, a natural person must be both a citizen of the United States, see Sun Printing & Publishing Association v. Edwards, 194 U.S. 377, 383 (1904); U.S. Const. Amend. XIV, § 1, and a domiciliary of that State. For diversity purposes, citizenship means domicile; mere residence in the State is not sufficient.

A person's domicile is the place of "his true, fixed, and permanent home and principal establishment, and to which he has the intention of returning whenever he is absent therefrom...." A change of domicile may be effected only by a combination of two elements: (a) taking up residence in a different domicile with (b) the intention to remain there.

It is clear that at the time of her marriage, Mrs. Mas was a domiciliary of the State of Mississippi. While it is generally the case that the domicile of the wife - and, consequently, her State citizenship for purposes of diversity jurisdiction - is deemed to be that of her husband, we find no precedent for extending this concept to the situation here, in which the husband is a citizen of a foreign state but resides in the United States. Indeed, such a fiction would work absurd results on the facts before us. If Mr. Mas were considered a domiciliary of France — as he would be since he had lived in Louisiana as a student-teaching assistant prior to filing this suit, — then Mrs. Mas would also be deemed a domiciliary, and thus, fictionally at least, a citizen of France. She would not be a citizen of any State and could not sue in a federal court on that basis; nor could she invoke the alienage jurisdiction to bring her claim in federal court, since she is not an alien. On the other hand, if Mrs. Mas's domicile were Louisiana, she would become a Louisiana citizen for diversity purposes and could not bring suit with her husband against appellant, also a Louisiana citizen, on the basis of diversity jurisdiction. These are curious results under a rule arising from the theoretical identity of person and interest of the married couple.

An American woman is not deemed to have lost her United States citizenship solely by reason of her marriage to an alien. 8 U.S.C. § 1489. Similarly, we conclude that for diversity purposes a woman does not have her domicile or State citizenship changed solely by reason of her marriage to an alien.

Mrs. Mas's Mississippi domicile was disturbed neither by her year in Louisiana prior to her marriage nor as a result of the time she and her husband spent at LSU after their marriage, since for both periods she was a graduate assistant at LSU. Though she testified that after her marriage she had no intention of returning to her parents' home in Mississippi, Mrs. Mas did not effect a change of domicile since she and Mr. Mas were in Louisiana only as students and lacked the requisite intention to remain there. Until she acquires a new domicile, she remains a domiciliary, and thus a citizen, of Mississippi.[2]

Appellant also contends that Mr. Mas's claim should have been dismissed for failure to establish the requisite jurisdictional amount for diversity cases of more than $10,000. In their complaint Mr. and Mrs. Mas alleged that they had each been damaged in the amount of $100,000. As we have noted, Mr. Mas ultimately recovered $5,000.

It is well settled that the amount in controversy is determined by the amount claimed by the plaintiff in good faith. Federal jurisdiction is not lost because a judgment of less than the jurisdictional amount is awarded. That Mr. Mas recovered only $5,000 is, therefore, not compelling. As the Supreme Court stated in St. Paul Mercury Indemnity Co. v. Red Cab Co., 303 U.S. 283, 288-290:

> [T]he sum claimed by the plaintiff controls if the claim is apparently made in good faith.
> It must appear to a legal certainty that the claim is really for less than the jurisdictional amount to justify dismissal. The inability of the plaintiff to recover an amount adequate to give the court jurisdiction does not show his bad faith or oust the jurisdiction....
> ... His good faith in choosing the federal forum is open to challenge not only by resort to the face of his complaint, but by the facts disclosed at trial, and if from either source it is clear that his claim never could have amounted to the sum necessary to give jurisdiction there is no injustice in dismissing the suit.

Having heard the evidence presented at the trial, the district court concluded that the appellees properly met the requirements of section 1332 with respect to jurisdictional amount. Upon examination of the record in this case, we are also satisfied that the requisite amount was in controversy.

---

[2] The original complaint in this case was filed within several days of Mr. and Mrs. Mas's realization that they had been watched through the mirrors, quite some time before they moved to Park Ridge, Illinois. Because the district court's jurisdiction is not affected by actions of the parties subsequent to the commencement of the suit, the testimony concerning Mr. and Mrs. Mas's moves after that time is not determinative of the issue of diverse citizenship, though it is of interest insofar as it supports their lack of intent to remain permanently in Louisiana.

C. Federal Courts and Limited Subject Matter Jurisdiction

Thus the power of the federal district court to entertain the claims of appellees in this case stands on two separate legs of diversity jurisdiction: a claim by an alien against a State citizen; and an action between citizens of different States. We also note, however, the propriety of having the federal district court entertain a spouse's action against a defendant, where the district court already has jurisdiction over a claim, arising from the same transaction, by the other spouse against the same defendant. In the case before us, such a result is particularly desirable. The claims of Mr. and Mrs. Mas arise from the same operative facts, and there was almost complete interdependence between their claims with respect to the proof required and the issues raised at trial. Thus, since the district court had jurisdiction of Mr. Mas's action, sound judicial administration militates strongly in favor of federal jurisdiction of Mrs. Mas's claim.

Affirmed.

NOTES AND QUESTIONS

1. The notion that a married woman takes the domicile of her husband has eroded today. See 1 MOORE'S FEDERAL PRACTICE ¶ 0.74[6.-1]. Regarding the court's treatment of why the monetary amount of Mr. Mas's judgment did not affect jurisdiction, see 28 U.S.C. § 1332(b).

2. In the notorious *Dred Scott* decision, the Supreme Court held that to be a "citizen of a state" within the meaning of the Constitution, a person must be a "citizen" of the United States. The Court further held that "a negro, whose ancestors were imported into this country" was not a "citizen" of the United States and therefore could not be a citizen of a state for diversity purposes. Scott v. Sandford, 60 U.S. 393, 403 (1856). As a result, when a slave, who claimed to have been freed, sued for assault, the Court dismissed for lack of diversity of citizenship jurisdiction.

3. It is clear from *Mas* that a person can have only one domicile at a time, and thus can be a citizen of only one state at a time. Everyone is ascribed a domicile at birth, usually based upon the domicile of her parents. She retains that domicile until she affirmatively changes it. *Mas* sets forth a standard statement of how one changes her domicile: by taking up residence in another state with the intent to make that her "true, fixed, and permanent home and principal establishment." Note, then, that there are two requirements for changing domicile: the physical requirement of moving to the new state and the mental requirement of intending to make the new state one's fixed home. While Mrs. Mas resided in Louisiana and Illinois, she never intended to make either state her domicile. Thus, she remained a domiciliary, and therefore a citizen, of Mississippi.

Obviously, the question of whether one forms the intent to establish a new domicile raises potentially difficult problems of proof. Sometimes, people move to a different state

175

CHAPTER 4 SUBJECT MATTER JURISDICTION

without the intent to stay. At some point, however, they may form the subjective intent to make that state their domicile. Identifying that point can be difficult, and courts look to a variety of factors in assessing this intent, including voter registration, purchase of a house, and payment of taxes and of instate college tuition. See 1 MOORE'S FEDERAL PRACTICE 787-89.

4. Suppose the court in *Mas* found that Mrs. Mas was a citizen of Louisiana. Would the court have had to dismiss the entire case, or could it simply have dismissed Mrs. Mas from the action? Federal Rule 21 gives district courts the authority to dismiss non-diverse parties from the suit (so long as they are not "indispensable"). The Supreme Court has held that the courts of appeals also have this authority. Newman-Green, Inc. v. Alfonzo-Lorraine, 490 U.S. 826 (1989). Thus, on such facts, the Fifth Circuit could have dismissed Mrs. Mas's claim, but allowed Mr. Mas's judgment to stand.

5. The plaintiff is responsible for alleging the facts establishing diversity of citizenship jurisdiction. The court retains power to "realign" the parties according to its assessment of their true interests. If the realignment destroys diversity, the court will dismiss. See, e.g., United States Fidelity & Guaranty Co. v. Algernon-Blair, Inc., 705 F.Supp. 1507 (M.D. Ala. 1987).

6. Reconsider the final paragraph of the opinion in *Mas*. The court is suggesting the use of something now called "supplemental jurisdiction," which we will note in Section 5 below and in Chapter 12. Based upon the court's discussion in *Mas*, how can such jurisdiction be reconciled with the complete diversity rule of *Strawbridge v. Curtiss?*

7. Pat, a citizen of New York, forms the intent to change her domicile to California, and sets out to drive there to establish her home. On the way, in Nevada, she is involved in an auto wreck with Dan, a citizen of California, suffering damages of more than $50,000. Can she invoke diversity of citizenship jurisdiction against Dan? Why or why not?

8. Paul, a citizen of Texas, properly institutes a diversity of citizenship action against Donna, a citizen of Oklahoma. After filing, but before the case proceeds to trial, Paul becomes a citizen of Oklahoma. Donna then moves to dismiss the case for lack of subject matter jurisdiction. Based upon the discussion in *Mas*, what result? If you represented Paul, and knew that he planned to change his domicile from Texas to Oklahoma, would it be proper for you to recommend that he delay doing so until after filing the case?

9. Pam, a citizen of the United States domiciled in New York, sues Doris, a citizen of the United States domiciled in New Zealand, asserting a state law claim for $75,000. Do you see why there is neither diversity nor alienage jurisdiction? Explain why an American citizen domiciled abroad cannot sue or be sued under diversity or alienage jurisdiction. Unless there is some other basis of federal jurisdiction, such as federal question, cases involving such persons must be filed in a state court.

C. Federal Courts and Limited Subject Matter Jurisdiction

10. Patty, a citizen of the United States domiciled in the District of Columbia, sues Don, a citizen of the United States domiciled in California, asserting a state law claim for $75,000. Review 28 U.S.C. § 1332(d). The District of Columbia is not a state. Neither are American territories and possessions such as Puerto Rico and Guam. So how can Patty be considered a citizen of a state, as required in both § 1332(a)(1) and Article III, Section 2 of the Constitution? The notion that she can seems especially troublesome in view of a Supreme Court case, decided before enactment of § 1332(d), holding that a citizen of the District of Columbia is not a citizen of a state for diversity purposes. Hepburn & Dundas v. Ellzey, 6 U.S. 445, 453 (1804).

Nonetheless, the Supreme Court upheld the predecessor of § 1332(d) in National Mutual Insurance Co. v. Tidewater Transfer Co., 337 U.S. 582 (1949). This decision is especially odd because there is no rationale for it. Although five justices concluded that the statute was constitutional, they did so in two separate opinions, neither of which commanded a majority. Thus, we know that section 1332(d) is constitutional, but we have no reason for the holding!

11. Congress occasionally oversteps its constitutional authority and confers jurisdiction beyond that authorized by Article III. For example, Congress originally authorized federal jurisdiction over cases in which "an alien is a party." In Hodgson v. Bowerbank, 9 U.S. 303 (1809), the Supreme Court held this statute unconstitutional as applied to a case in which alienage was the sole basis for jurisdiction and in which the plaintiff was an alien and there was no allegation concerning the citizenship of the defendants. Do you see why such a case exceeds the scope of Article III? Shortly after the decision in *Hodgson*, Congress changed the statute providing for "alienage" jurisdiction. Notice how the statutory provision reads today. See 28 U.S.C. § 1332(a)(2).

12. In 1990, Congress amended § 1332(a)(2) to provide that an alien admitted to the United States for permanent residence shall be deemed for diversity purposes to be a citizen of the state in which she is domiciled. Suppose an alien admitted for permanent residence brings suit in federal court against another alien. Would this exceed the scope of Article III? Some commentators have suggested that it would. See 1 MOORE'S FEDERAL PRACTICE ¶¶ 0.71[4.-7], 0.75[1.-2]. One court has avoided the constitutional problem by holding that the permanent resident provision of § 1332(a)(2) applies only to *defeat* diversity jurisdiction and cannot be used to create jurisdiction between two aliens. See Arai v. Tachibana, 778 F. Supp. 1535 (D. Haw. 1991).

In Singh v. Daimler-Benz, AG, 9 F.3d 303 (3d Cir. 1993), a citizen of India admitted to the United States for permanent residence and domiciled in Virginia sued a German corporation and its American distributor (which was a citizen of states other than Virginia). The Third Circuit upheld jurisdiction and avoided the constitutional issue. In its view, Congress provided for jurisdiction in such a case based upon minimal diversity between the parties. A different result might follow had the American distributor not been joined. Do you agree with the court's holding?

d. Determining Citizenship of Entities

Many cases involve claims by or against entities which are formed in compliance with laws that vary from state to state. These non-human litigants fall into two general categories: corporate and non-corporate. 28 U.S.C. § 1332(c)(i) addresses the citizenship of corporations for diversity of citizenship purposes, while the citizenship of non-corporate entities (such as labor unions, insurance associations, joint ventures, and partnerships (including law firms)), is not addressed statutorily.

Randazzo v. Eagle-Picher Industries, Inc.
117 F.R.D. 557 (E.D. Pa. 1987)

LORD, SENIOR DISTRICT JUDGE.

This is an asbestos case. The complaint incorporates by reference the master long form complaint filed in re Asbestos Litigation, No. 86-0457. In a written order dismissing the complaint I pointed out that the complaint failed to allege either the state of incorporation or the principal place of business of defendant Bevco Industries or the principal place of business of defendant C.E. Refractories. The complaint therefore failed to show complete diversity and was jurisdictionally deficient. Plaintiff was granted ten days to file an amended complaint.

Plaintiff's counsel, apparently laboring under the impression that I am not dealing with a full deck and that my knowledge of diversity requirements is about equal to that of a low-grade moron, chose to disregard the directional signals posted in my memorandum. Counsel brazenly, discourteously, defiantly, arrogantly, insultingly and under the circumstances rather obtusely threw back into my face the very allegations I had held insufficient by reiterating and incorporating those same crippled paragraphs. The so-called "amended complaint" itself cheekily informs me that these paragraphs allege the states of incorporation *or* (emphasis added) principal places of business of the defendant corporations. Of course, any law school student knows that both the state of incorporation and principal place of business must be diverse, but I suppose I can hardly expect any more from counsel whose familiarity with Title 28 U.S.C. § 1332 could be no more than a friendly wave from a distance visible only through a powerful telescope.

In view of counsel's demonstrated ignorance of diversity requirements, I think it may be profitable to set forth the rules of the game. Every plaintiff bears the burden of alleging in his pleading "a short and plain statement of the grounds upon which the court's jurisdiction depends." Fed. R. Civ. Pro. 8(a)(1). It is well established that "a plaintiff suing in a federal court must show in his pleading, affirmatively and distinctly, the existence of whatever is essential to federal jurisdiction; and if he does not do so, the court, on having the defect called to its attention or on discovering the same, *must* dismiss the case, unless the defect be corrected by amendment." For purposes of the diversity statute, "a corporation shall be deemed a citizen of any state by which it has been incorporated and of the State where it has its principal place of business." 28 U.S.C. § 1332(c) [Now § 1332(c)(1)-EDS]. Courts have consistently interpreted § 1332(c) to mean exactly what it says: a party must allege a corporation's state of incorporation and principal place of business. The requirements of § 1332 and Rule 8 "are straightforward and the law demands strict adherence to them."

The master complaint alleges that defendant C.E. Refractories "is a corporation organized and existing under the laws of the State of Delaware with a registered office situate [sic] at 123 S. Broad Street, Philadelphia, Pennsylvania...." The allegation that defendant has a "registered office" in Pennsylvania is not equivalent to an allegation that defendant's principal place of business is in Pennsylvania. Because the complaint fails to properly allege the principal place of business, I have no jurisdiction over this defendant and the complaint will be dismissed as to it.

Similarly, the master complaint alleges that defendant Bevco Industries "is a corporation duly organized to do business within the Commonwealth of Pennsylvania ... and is domiciled in the Commonwealth of Pennsylvania." The reference to domicile may mean that defendant is incorporated in Pennsylvania but I have no way of knowing that. Again, plaintiff has simply failed to allege the principal place of business of defendant or its state of incorporation. Section 1332 makes clear that corporations have dual citizenship, and plaintiff "does not have a choice of alleging only one of the corporation's citizenships." Therefore, the complaint will be dismissed as to this defendant.

It is important to state why I take the apparently harsh step of dismissal with prejudice. Adequately pleading the jurisdictional requirements is not an exercise in mindless formalism. "Subsection (c) of § 1332 was adopted in 1958 by Congress as part of legislation designed to reduce the caseload of the Federal courts." It is axiomatic that "Federal courts are not courts of general jurisdiction; they have only the power that is authorized by Article III of the Constitution and the statutes enacted by Congress pursuant thereto." * * * To rebut the presumption that a Federal court lacks jurisdiction over a particular case the facts that establish jurisdiction must be affirmatively alleged. These jurisdictional principles are fundamental. That is why I have an obligation to notice want of jurisdiction *mea sponte*. See Fed. R. Civ. Pro. 12(h)(3). In the context of our federal system, to consider a case not properly within the jurisdiction of the Federal courts is not "simply wrong but indeed an unconstitutional invasion of the powers reserved to the states."

Plaintiff's counsel was given ample opportunity to amend the complaint. The language of § 1332 could not be more clear. It would have taken counsel only moments to set forth the allegations that the diversity statute so plainly requires. I fail to understand why, after having the deficiencies of the complaint explicitly identified in a written order, counsel insisted on resubmitting the exact same complaint. I understand that the asbestos bar has a heavy caseload, and applaud steps, such as the master complaint, taken to ease the administrative burden asbestos cases place upon both bench and bar. However, a heavy caseload can neither excuse faulty pleadings nor justify the retention of jurisdiction beyond that permitted by statute.

An appropriate order follows.

CHAPTER 4 SUBJECT MATTER JURISDICTION

NOTES AND QUESTIONS

1. Why were allegations of a corporation's "registered office" and "domicile" inappropriate?

2. The court first dismissed the complaint in *Randazzo* "with leave to amend." Courts sometimes refer to this as dismissal "without prejudice," meaning that the plaintiff can refile the action. In *Randazzo,* the court apparently also instructed counsel about the defects of his jurisdictional allegations. When counsel reasserted the improper allegations, the court dismissed "with prejudice," meaning that the plaintiff could not refile the case.

3. Do we know that the plaintiff could not establish diversity jurisdiction in *Randazzo*? If not, is it fair to let the errors of counsel rob the plaintiff of a federal forum? On the other hand, how many chances should counsel need to make jurisdictional allegations correctly?

4. Judges can get angry.

J. A. Olson Co. v. City of Winona
818 F.2d 401 (5th Cir. 1987)

JOLLY, CIRCUIT JUDGE.

In this case we address the question whether the principal place of business of a corporation that has its executive offices in Chicago and its sole manufacturing plant in Mississippi is an Illinois or Mississippi entity for purposes of diversity jurisdiction.

J.A. Olson Company (Olson), is an Illinois corporation with its sole manufacturing plant in Winona, Mississippi. It brought suit in federal court against the City of Winona (Winona), an incorporated municipality of Mississippi, basing jurisdiction on diversity of citizenship. After appropriate discovery, Winona moved to dismiss for lack of jurisdiction on the ground that diversity of citizenship was lacking because Olson's principal place of business was in Mississippi. The district court agreed * * *. Accordingly, the district court granted Winona's motion and dismissed Olson's complaint. This appeal followed.

Olson, a wholly owned subsidiary of Stamatakis [Industries, Inc.], is engaged in the manufacture of wooden picture and mirror frames, molding in lengths, and cornices. Its only manufacturing plant and storage facility is located in Winona, Mississippi. The plant also houses the administrative offices that provide accounting, bookkeeping, payroll and data processing services and a photography studio used to prepare Olson's sales catalogues. Olson also has a retail showroom in Winona that accounts for approximately three percent of the company's sales. Proceeds from these sales are remitted directly to Olson at Winona. At the time of the hearing the plant employed 113 people, with an annual payroll in 1984 of over $1.7 million.

Bea Sullivan, as the general manager of the plant, generally oversees the functions of the facility. She is authorized to hire and fire employees, supervise employee training, and process employee grievances and workers' compensation claims. She also has input into decisions regarding the scheduling of production.

Olson maintains three bank accounts in Winona, two payroll accounts and one general account. Checks on these accounts, which are funded as needed by Olson's Chicago office based on information provided by Winona personnel, are processed in the Winona data processing office. Mr. Stamatakis is the authorized signatory on all the Winona accounts but his name is signed mechanically in Winona. Accounts receivable and payable are also handled by personnel at Winona.

In 1985, the plant purchased approximately $200,000 in supplies locally and over $500,000 in supplies in Mississippi. Olson belongs to the Mississippi Economic Council, the Mississippi Manufacturers Association, and the Mississippi Glass Association; Olson is not a member of any such organization in any other state. In sum, Olson has its base of operations in the State of Mississippi.

Much of its operation, however, is directed from outside the State of Mississippi. Olson's corporate office, as well as that of Stamatakis, is located in Chicago, Illinois. The Chicago office maintains Olson's corporate records, prepares and files Olson's corporate tax returns, compiles Olson's financial reports, and negotiates insurance coverage for Olson. Ninety-seven percent of the proceeds of Olson's sales are remitted to the Chicago office and deposited in a bank there. After consultation with the manager of Olson's Winona plant, Olson's corporate treasurer, Donald Kes, transfers the necessary funds from Chicago to Olson's bank accounts in Winona. According to Roger Miller, an executive vice president of Olson, most if not all of the major corporate and financial decisions are made in the Chicago office.

Miller, whose office is located in Dallas, Texas, visits Winona about once a month, but his address as shown on his business card and stationery is that of Olson's Winona plant. He coordinates Olson's marketing efforts, including the hiring of independent sales representatives, the extension of credit to customers, and determination of pricing. He consults with Bea Sullivan, the Winona plant manager, regarding hiring decisions at the plant, and he is also responsible for decisions regarding the equipment and the number of employees needed at the plant.

Olson's other business functions are conducted in scattered locations. Olson's thirty-five to thirty-seven salespeople, termed by Sullivan as independent contractors, live in their different sales areas throughout the country. The majority of sales, however, are made through leased showrooms in Dallas and Atlanta where Olson employs only part-time secretaries. Donald Lull, Olson's controller, lives and works in St. Paul and Olson's independent auditor lives in Phoenix. * * *

Our court has stated that we apply the "total activity" test to determine principal place of business. We have, however, failed to give form to that term except to say that it incorporates two tests that we have also neglected to explicate: the "nerve center" test and the "place of activity" test. In this case we attempt to give meaning to the "total activity" test as a means of determining a corporation's principal place of business. * * *

Although many factors have been considered and emphasized [by courts trying to define "principal place of business"], two major focal points have evolved: the nerve center of the corporation and the place of activity of the corporation. These focal points have often been referred to as separate tests as though the application of one precluded the application of the second, but as we shall see, the ultimate question is not which test to apply, but rather which consideration, on the basis of the totality of the facts, predominates. Stated differently, we have observed that the "total activity" test applied in this circuit combines considerations of both the nerve center and the place of activity of the corporation in question. * * *

The "nerve center" test was coined in Scot Typewriter Co. v. Underwood Corp., 170 F. Supp. 862 (S.D.N.Y. 1959). In that case, [Scot Typewriter Co. (Scot) sued Underwood Corp. (Underwood). Scot was a citizen of New York. The issue was whether Underwood's principal place of business was New York or Connecticut.]

Underwood manufactured typewriters and business machines in Connecticut, office and related supplies in New Jersey, and missile and radar components in California. All of these products were distributed and serviced in branch offices across the United States. Underwood's executive offices were located in New York. Underwood conceded that its "New York City offices function[ed] on the executive level in the determination of policy and the coordination of all of its various policies." * * * [Nonetheless,] its major corporate function, the development and manufacture of typewriters and business machines, was located in Connecticut. * * * In Connecticut, Underwood had its largest number of employees, largest payroll and most tangible property. Additionally, most of its shipments were made from there as well as the majority of its purchases. * * *

The court observed that manufacturing is but one component of a corporation's business, and that other elements are equally significant. Additionally, the court relied on data showing that the volume of typewriters and business machine sales ranked third behind sales of products it manufactured in California and New Jersey, to conclude that the Connecticut operations did not constitute Underwood's major corporate function. In holding New York to be Underwood's principal place of business, the court reasoned:

> Where a corporation is engaged in far-flung and varied activities which are carried on in different states, its principal place of business is the nerve center from which it radiates out to its constituent parts and from which its officers direct, control and coordinate all activities without regard to locale, in the furtherance of the corporate objective. The test applied by our Court of Appeals, is that place where the corporation has an "office from which its business was directed and controlled" — the place where "all of its business was under the supreme direction and control of its officers."

Scot Typewriter. * * *

The "place of activity" test was first enunciated in Kelly v. United States Steel Corp., 284 F.2d 850 (3d Cir. 1960). In that case the plaintiffs, Pennsylvania citizens, brought suit against and obtained judgment against U.S. Steel. On appeal, U.S. Steel asserted that the district court did not have jurisdiction because its principal place of business was in Pennsylvania. * * * The court rejected identifying the state in which shareholders and the Board of Directors hold their meetings as the principal place of business for the reason that state law and corporate charters generally allow these meetings to be held in places totally unrelated to the business of the corporation. The court also declined to adopt the "nerve center" test in this case because the organization of U.S. Steel provided for "a good many collections of nerve cells serving the common function of making the corporate enterprise go."

The court then turned to the method of operation of U.S. Steel. It noted that activities which took place in New York included the filing of tax returns, meetings of the board of directors (although the board could and sometimes did meet elsewhere), the executive committee, the finance committee, the corporation's major banking and the management of its government securities and pension plan. Additionally, the chairman of the board, the president, the secretary, the treasurer and general counsel of U.S. Steel were in New York. The court concluded that "[if] the test of 'principal place of

C. Federal Courts and Limited Subject Matter Jurisdiction

business' is where ... final decisions are made on corporate policy, then New York was U.S. Steel's principal place of business."

The board of directors, however, had delegated to its operation policy committee the authority to conduct the corporation's business. That committee was in Pennsylvania, and its duties included appointment of division presidents and corporation officers. Additionally, all of the executive vice presidents and most of the other vice presidents and their staffs were in Pennsylvania. The court also noted that Pennsylvania had far more U.S. Steel employees and tangible property than had New York or any other state.

Balancing the facts relating to the business operations in Pennsylvania and New York, the Third Circuit held: "All this points us to the conclusion that business by way of activities is centered in Pennsylvania and we think it is the activities rather than the occasional meeting of policy-making Directors which indicate the principal place of business." * * *

It is clear * * * that the place of activity and the nerve center are two of the components of the "total activity" test. It is further apparent that our determination of the principal place of business begins with the general rules of these component tests: (1) when considering a corporation whose operations are far flung, the sole nerve center of that corporation is more significant in determining principal place of business, (2) when a corporation has its sole operation in one state and executive offices in another, the place of activity is regarded as more significant, but (3) when the activity of a corporation is passive and the "brain" of the corporation is in another state, the situs of the corporation's "brain" is given greater significance. These general rules, however, are only a starting point. In each case we must fully examine the corporation's operations and its nerve center in the context of the organization of that business. * * *

With this fuller understanding of the "total activity" test, we turn to the facts before us today. * * *

The district court found that Winona is the situs of by far the most significant number of Olson's employees as well as all of Olson's manufacturing and storage facilities. Additionally, the Winona office, through the supervision of its general manager, processes Olson's orders, maintains bookkeeping records, and sales showrooms, and coordinates employee training and grievance procedures. The district court further found that Olson's Chicago office handles the company's significant financial activities and insurance transactions and maintains Olson's corporate records. The district court weighed these facts and concluded that Winona was Olson's principal place of business.

* * * Olson's sole manufacturing activity is in Winona, Mississippi, and its executive offices are located in Chicago. In such a situation, the place of activity is regarded as significant. * * *

Olson's sole activities are the operation of a single plant in Winona, and sale of the products manufactured there. Its plant is a labor-intensive activity and brings it into contact with the local community as employer and consumer and as a member of local and state trade associations. Olson's sales activities are conducted in various places, including Winona, particularly through part-time showrooms in Dallas and Atlanta.[16]

Olson's nerve center is located primarily in Chicago for it is there that primary financial and other management decisions are made; additionally, Olson's corporate records and major bank accounts are maintained in Chicago. Significant management decisions, however, are also made in

---

[16] Neither party contends that Atlanta or Dallas is Olson's principal place of business, and rightly so, as neither city contains substantial activity or corporate decision-making authority

Winona; these decisions involve scheduling production, hiring and firing of employees, employee grievances and workers compensation matters. Accounts receivable and payable are handled in Winona where some other corporate records and bank accounts are kept. Additionally, we note that the decisions made in Chicago are based on information initially compiled by the Winona facility.

Winona is therefore not only the locale of Olson's only substantial activity but also the place in which some significant business decisions are made. And, as we have noted, Winona is where the vast majority of Olson's employees are located, is where Olson is most visible, is where its products are manufactured, is where it has its most substantial investment, and indeed is where, more than any other place, its corporate purpose is fulfilled. Although decisions made in Chicago are clearly important, they cannot outweigh the greater significance of the activities conducted in Winona. Thus, when we consider the total activity of Olson, the balance of the relevant factors demonstrates with force that Winona is the corporation's principal place of business. For these reasons, we hold that the district court did not err. * * *

NOTES AND QUESTIONS

1. Before 1958, courts treated corporations as citizens of the state(s) in which they were incorporated. They reached this conclusion by treating an action by or against the corporation as an action by or against the shareholders, and by manufacturing an irrebuttable presumption that all shareholders were citizens of the state in which the corporation was chartered. Covington Drawbridge Co. v. Shepherd, 61 U.S. 227, 233 (1858).

In 1958, Congress passed what is now codified at § 1332(c)(1). It was the first legislative effort to define a corporation's citizenship for jurisdictional purposes. Congress felt that adding the corporation's "principal place of business" to the definition of citizenship would reduce "abuse" of diversity jurisdiction. Under the prior practice, for example, a corporation with all operations in Baltimore, but incorporated in Delaware, could invoke diversity of citizenship jurisdiction against a Maryland citizen even though its business presence in Baltimore would seem to ensure that it would not suffer local bias in an action with a Maryland citizen. Commentators hailed this addition as likely to reduce the backlog of diversity cases as well. See, e.g., 1 MOORE'S FEDERAL PRACTICE ¶ 0.77[1].

2. Note, however, that under § 1332(c)(1), every corporation has only *one* principal place of business. Obviously, many large corporations may have facilities that, while quite substantial, nonetheless are not the one principal place of business. If the purpose of diversity of citizenship jurisdiction is to redress out-of-state bias, why shouldn't corporations be deemed citizens of *every* state in which they do significant business? What would be the effect of such a change?

In passing § 1332(c)(1), Congress gave no indication of what factors would determine a corporation's principal place of business. Judge Jolly's opinion in *J. A. Olson* summarizes the different approaches to the issue, and provides a sensible guide to their application. Why does the "nerve center" test make most sense when a corporation is "engaged in far-flung and varied activities which are carried on in different states?" To what sorts of businesses does the "place of activities" test (sometimes called a "muscle center" test) seem to apply best?

Most importantly, *J. A. Olson* demonstrates a court's careful *analysis* of the relevant issues, rather than unthinking adherence to a label. Most courts recognize that determining a corporation's principal place of business requires consideration of all the factors discussed in *J. A. Olson*. Thus, no matter what label they use, most courts appear to approach the issue by viewing the "total activities." See 1 MOORE'S FEDERAL PRACTICE ¶ 0.77 [3-4].

3. Note that the language of § 1332(c)(l) also deems a corporation to be a citizen of "the states" in which it is incorporated, implying that corporations can be chartered in more than one state. Although multiple incorporation was once common, it is now very rare. Today, almost all corporations incorporate in just one state.

4. What is the citizenship of a corporation that is not actively engaged in business? For example, a corporation may dissolve but remain in existence until its assets are liquidated. Or a corporation may be inactive because of government order, such as when regulators order a bank to cease operations. All courts consider such corporations to be citizens of the state(s) of incorporation. But does an inactive corporation have a principal place of business?

Some courts conclude that they do not, and thus look only to the state of incorporation to determine corporate citizenship. See, e.g., Midlantic National Bank v. Hansen, 48 F. 3d 693 (3d Cir. 1995); Sanders Co. Plumbing & Heating, Inc. v. B.B. Anderson Constr. Co., 660 F. Supp. 752 (D.Kan.1987)(alternative holding). Other courts conclude that an inactive corporation can have a principal place of business, but disagree as to what constitutes such a place. The Second Circuit, for example, looks to where the corporation last transacted business. Wm. Passalacqua Bldrs. v. Resnick, Dev., 933 F.2d 131 (2d Cir. 1991). Other courts look to various factors, including how long the company has been inactive. See, e.g., China Basin Props. v. Allendale Mut. Ins., 818 F. Supp 1301 (N.D. Cal. 1992). In light of the policies underlying diversity of citizenship jurisdiction, which approach makes most sense?

5. Partnerships and other unincorporated associations, unlike corporations, do not have an entity citizenship separate from the citizenship of the partners or members. Hence a partnership or other unincorporated association is considered a citizen of every state in which one or more partners is a citizen. In Carden v. Arkoma Associates, 494 U.S. 185 (1990), the Supreme Court held that this rule applies to limited partnerships and that courts must consider the citizenship of *all* partners — both general and limited partners. If a non-corporate association had members who were citizens of every American jurisdiction, it could not sue or be sued under diversity of citizenship jurisdiction.

6. Plaintiff is incorporated in Delaware and does business there and in Maryland, Virginia, Pennsylvania, and the District of Columbia. It sues an unincorporated insurance association that has members who are citizens of Maryland and the District of Columbia. Assuming the requisite amount in controversy, might there be diversity of citizenship? What facts would you need to know to decide?

e. Representative Suits and Assignments of Claims

A plaintiff who is not of diverse citizenship from the defendant but who wants to sue in federal court might try to manufacture diversity by assigning her claim to someone who could invoke diversity of citizenship jurisdiction. Unfortunately for such a plaintiff, 28 U.S.C. § 1359 provides that the district court has no jurisdiction over cases "in which any party, by assignment or otherwise, has been improperly or collusively made or joined to invoke the jurisdiction of such court." The Supreme Court has applied the statute to an assignment in which the assignee is a mere collection agent for the assignor invokes the statute. Kramer v. Caribbean Mills, Inc., 394 U.S. 823 (1969). The result is that the court ignores the citizenship of the assignee and uses that of the assignor. This means, of course, that there is no diversity of citizenship. On the other hand, an assignment for adequate consideration, in which the assignee is not a mere collection agent for the assignor, does not run afoul of § 1359.

Another technique sometimes used to create diversity of citizenship jurisdiction involved cases brought by or against a decedent's estate. For example, assume Decedent was a citizen of Michigan, and that he died under circumstances that made his family want to bring a malpractice action against Hospital, which is also a citizen of Michigan. If the family members wanted to bring the case in federal court, they might agree to have Uncle Fred, who is a citizen of Montana, appointed as executor. Uncle Fred would then sue, and argue that his citizenship — not Decedent's — was relevant for jurisdiction. Hospital would then argue that the appointment of Uncle Fred violated § 1359, and should be ignored for purposes of determining diversity of citizenship.

Such situations resulted in a remarkable body of inconsistent opinions. Some courts upheld jurisdiction, even if the representative was appointed for the purpose of creating diversity. See, e.g., Hackney v. Newman Memorial Hosp., Inc., 621 F.2d 1069 (10th Cir.), cert. denied, 449 U.S. 982 (1980). Others ignored the appointment, even when it was not made with the intent to create diversity of citizenship. See, e.g., Vaughan v. Southern Ry., 542 F.2d 641 (4th Cir. 1976). Happily, § 1332(c)(2), which became effective in 1989, resolves the issue, as well as the closely related question of citizenship when a legal representative sues or is sued on behalf of a minor or incompetent. Thus § 1359 remains vital today generally only in the area of assignment of claims.

C. Federal Courts and Limited Subject Matter Jurisdiction

Because § 1359 is aimed at *collusive* creation of jurisdiction, it is not applied to a single litigant's changing her domicile to create diversity. So long as the change of domicile comports with the rules discussed in *Mas v. Perry*, and occurs before filing, such a change can create diversity, even if motivated solely by a desire to gain access to federal court. See Morris v. Gilmer, 129 U.S. 315 (1889).

f. The Domestic Relations Exception

Even if the requirements for diversity of citizenship jurisdiction are met, the federal courts refuse to hear "domestic relations" cases. This exception dates back to Barber v. Barber, 62 U.S. 582 (1859). Although the majority opinion in that case offered little explanation for its conclusion, the dissenters discussed a rationale. They noted that the original Judiciary Act of 1791 gave jurisdiction over suits "at common law or in equity." This, according to the argument, did not include domestic relations cases because in England, such disputes were heard neither by law nor equity courts, but by ecclesiastical courts.

In Ankenbrandt v. Richards, 504 U.S. 689 (1992), the Supreme Court reaffirmed the domestic relations exception, explaining the exception on both statutory and policy grounds. The Court noted that Congress had amended the diversity statute in 1948 to replace the law/equity distinction with the phrase "all civil actions." The Court then "presume[d that] Congress did so with full cognizance of the Court's nearly century-long interpretation of the prior statutes, which had construed the statutory diversity jurisdiction to contain an exception for certain domestic relations matters." Id. at 700. The Court offered a policy explanation for the exception:

> As a matter of judicial economy, state courts are more eminently suited to work of this type than are federal courts, which lack the close association with the state and local government organizations dedicated to handling issues that arise out of conflict over divorce, alimony, and child custody decrees. Moreover, as a matter of judicial expertise, it makes far more sense to retain the rule that federal courts lack power to issue these types of decrees because of the special proficiency developed by state tribunals over the past century and a half in handling issues that arise in the granting of such decrees.

Id. at 704. What do you think of these policy justifications? Could they be used to justify a court's refusal to hear any diversity of citizenship cases?

Although the *Ankenbrandt* Court endorsed the domestic relations exception, it emphasized that the exception is quite narrow and applies only in cases "involving the issuance of a divorce, alimony, or child custody decree." Thus, it does not preclude jurisdiction over cases simply because they involve conflict between family members. In *Ankenbrandt* itself, for instance, a mother, suing on behalf of her minor children, sought tort damages from her ex-husband (the children's father) and his companion. She alleged that the defendants had abused the children when they were visiting their father. The lower courts invoked the domestic relations exception and refused to hear the case. The Supreme Court reversed, since the case did not involve divorce, alimony, or a child custody decree. See generally 1 MOORE'S FEDERAL PRACTICE ¶ 0.71[5.-5].

In Kahn v. Kahn, 21 F.3d 859 (8th Cir. 1994), the court refused to hear tort claims for conversion and fraud by a woman against her ex-husband. It held that the claims were "so inextricably intertwined with the property settlement incident to the divorce proceeding that subject matter jurisdiction does not lie." Id. at 861. Does this holding extend *Ankenbrandt*?

g. The Amount in Controversy Requirement

Article III contains no amount in controversy limitations. Such limitations are established in jurisdictional statutes and traditionally have served two functions. First, they reflect the notion that a federal tribunal should not be a small claims court. Second, and related, they are a method of docket control. Historically, diversity of citizenship, alienage, and general federal question cases contained such requirements. Today, they remain in diversity of citizenship and alienage jurisdiction.

In 1989, Congress increased the amount in controversy limitation in § 1332 to one in excess of $50,000. Congress had not increased this amount since 1959, when it raised the figure from an amount in excess of $3,000 to one in excess of $10,000. The most recent increase was intended to cut down on the number of diversity of citizenship cases filed, without capitulating to those who sought total abolition of diversity jurisdiction. Does the existence of a substantial amount in controversy requirement demonstrate that alienage and diversity of citizenship cases are "less important" than federal question cases? Or is it consistent with the traditional justification of alienage and diversity jurisdiction because fear of local bias will be stronger in more substantial cases?

NOTES AND QUESTIONS

For each of the hypotheticals in Notes 1 through 3, assume that the complete diversity rule is satisfied.

1. Plaintiff sues for exactly $50,000. Is there jurisdiction?
2. Suppose plaintiff sues for $100,000. After trial, the jury finds that plaintiff is entitled to damages of $18,000. Defendant then moves to dismiss, asserting that the amount

C. Federal Courts and Limited Subject Matter Jurisdiction

in controversy, it turns out, was only $18,000. The motion will be denied. Why? Remember that *Mas v. Perry*, supra, addressed this issue. See also 28 U.S.C. § 1332(b). Why is it important to determine whether plaintiff satisfies the amount in controversy early in the case, rather than to await the outcome of the litigation? [handwritten: "good faith" / because they may get way less than what they are asking for]

3. Ordinarily, the prevailing party is entitled to have her costs paid by the other party. See Rule 54(d). Under § 1332(b), however, a prevailing plaintiff who recovers less than $50,000 may be ordered to pay the defendant's costs. "Costs" is a term of art which includes most expenses of litigation *except* attorney's fees. Included in "costs" are such things as filing and other fees assessed by the court clerk's office, some costs of discovery, witness fees, and disbursements and copying costs of certain papers. Under the "American Rule," however, each party bears its own attorney's fees. In almost every case, attorney's fees are the "big ticket" item, and will far exceed costs. Note that § 1332(b) does not *require* the court to order a plaintiff recovering less than the jurisdictional amount to pay defendant's costs. When might the court not order such a recovery?

4. Courts dismiss very few cases for failure to satisfy the amount in controversy requirement because the standard for satisfying the requirement is so low. In *St. Paul Mercury*, discussed in *Mas*, the Supreme Court held that the plaintiff's good faith allegation that the jurisdictional amount is satisfied will invoke jurisdiction unless it appears "to a legal certainty that the claim is really for less than the jurisdictional amount * * *." St. Paul Mercury Indem. Co. v. Red Cab Co., 303 U.S. 283, 289 (1938). Courts rarely undertake an investigation into the matter unless it is clearly raised by the defendant or by the pleadings or evidence. In re A.H. Robins Co., 880 F.2d 709, 724 (4th Cir. 1989) (no affirmative obligation on the court absent some "apparent reason" to inquire). When the issue is raised, plaintiff assumes the burden of showing that it is not clear "to a legal certainty" that the jurisdictional amount is *not* met. Gibbs v. Buck, 307 U.S. 66 (1939).

Obviously, some plaintiffs fail to meet even this low burden. A clear example is when one seeks recovery of damages not allowed by law. Suppose, for instance, that plaintiff sues for $35,000 damages for breach of contract and for $100,000 punitive damages for the breach. Under the traditional rule, punitive damages are not recoverable for breach of contract. Thus, it would be clear "to a legal certainty" that plaintiff's case involved only $35,000, and the case would be dismissed. See Pachinger v. MGM Grand Hotel-Las Vegas, Inc., 802 F.2d 362 (9th Cir. 1986) (as matter of law, innkeeper's liability limited to less than jurisdictional amount); Parker v. Moitzfield, 733 F. Supp. 1023 (E.D. Va. 1990) (applicable law did not recognize damages for anticipatory breach).

Occasionally, a court will rule as a matter of law that the plaintiff could not recover the requisite amount even in the absence of a legal limitation on damages. For example, in Diefenthal v. Civil Aeronautics Board, 681 F.2d 1039 (5th Cir. 1982), the court dismissed as trivial the plaintiffs' claims that they were humiliated and embarrassed by a flight attendant's "brusque" refusal to re-seat them in an airliner's smoking section.

   5. One difficult area concerns *aggregation* of claims — when may a plaintiff add together separate claims to satisfy the amount in controversy requirement? The statute does not address the issue; although the courts have established clear rules, the rules are not always logical or consistent with policy.

   (a) *One plaintiff v. one defendant.* The plaintiff in such a case may aggregate all of her claims to meet the jurisdictional requirement, even if the claims are unrelated legally or transactionally. For instance, a plaintiff with a $25,000 contract claim and an unrelated $30,000 tort claim against the same defendant may aggregate them to meet the amount in controversy requirement. The record appears to be set in Jones Motor Co. v. Teledyne, Inc., 690 F.Supp. 310 (D. Del. 1988), in which the plaintiff aggregated 54 separate, relatively insignificant claims against the defendant to satisfy the amount in controversy requirement.

   Clearly, this rule is inconsistent with the premise that Congress imposes the amount in controversy requirement to prevent the federal courts from becoming tribunals for small claims. If aggregation is to be permitted, would it make more sense to allow aggregation only of transactionally related claims?

   (b) *Multiple parties on either side.* If there is more than one plaintiff or more than one defendant, aggregation is not allowed. Thus, if (1) two or more plaintiffs have claims of $35,000 and $20,000 against one defendant or (2) if one plaintiff has such claims against two or more defendants, or (3) if two or more plaintiffs have such claims against two or more defendants, the claims cannot be aggregated, and the amount in controversy requirement is not be met. This is true even if the claims are transactionally related. See, e.g., Thomson v. Gaskill, 315 U.S. 442, 447 (1942)(aggregation "cannot be made merely because the claims are derived from a single instrument...or because the plaintiffs have a community of interest")(citations omitted). The courts have not articulated a logical explanation for this rule. 1 MOORE'S FEDERAL PRACTICE ¶ 0.97[2]-[4].

   It is important to remember that aggregation concerns the adding together of two or more separate claims. There is no rule that requires an amount in controversy of over $50,000 for each defendant. For example, if a plaintiff asserted a single claim of $50,000.01 against two joint tort feasors, or against defendants in the alternative, the jurisdictional amount would be satisfied. There would be no aggregation issue because there would be nothing to aggregate. There is a single claim, and it exceeds $50,000. Aggregation only becomes a concern when *two or more* claims must be added together to satisfy the amount requirement.

   For example, in Hatcher v. Emergency Medical Specialty Servs., Inc., 643 F. Supp. 1124 (D. N.J. 1986), plaintiff could not aggregate separate claims against a doctor, on the one hand, and a hospital, on the other, concerning the alleged wrongful death of her child. See generally 1 MOORE'S FEDERAL PRACTICE ¶ 0.97[2].

(c) *Common, Undivided, or Joint Claims.* Courts allow aggregation — even if multiple parties are present as plaintiffs or defendants — if the claims are "common, undivided, or joint." It is not allowed if the claims are "several, separate, or distinct." Unfortunately, these terms are not self-defining and are encumbered with arcane historical distinctions. Professor Redish criticizes the use of such amorphous terms as "attempting to drive a Model T on a superhighway." Martin Redish, *Reassessing the Allocation of Judicial Business Between State and Federal, Courts: Federal Jurisdiction and "The Martian Chronicles,"* 78 Va. L.Rev. 1769, 1808 (1992).

Despite this ambiguity, courts appear to be fairly consistent in most cases. For example, personal injuries suffered by different people are separate and distinct, even if suffered in a single accident. Tobie v. Don Pepe Corp., 646 F. Supp. 620 (D. P.R. 1986). In contrast, a suit brought by joint owners to foreclose on a mortgage or to quiet title to property is common and undivided. Troy Bank v. A. Whitehead & Co., 222 U.S. 39 (1911). Thus, if two joint plaintiffs sue to quiet title to property worth $60,000, the amount in controversy would be met, even though we might be tempted to see their claims as separate assertions of $30,000 each. It is important to note, however, that very few claims are common, undivided, or joint for these purposes. Indeed, outside the property area noted, it is difficult to find any claims satisfying this test. See generally 1 MOORE'S FEDERAL PRACTICE ¶ 0.97[1]-[4].

6. Another difficult area concerns cases seeking equitable relief. For example, suppose the plaintiff seeks to enjoin the defendant from polluting a stream running through plaintiff's land. How does one put a dollar value on a claim for an injunction? Courts have taken different approaches. The traditional view is to ask whether the defendant's alleged acts *harm the plaintiff* by more than $50,000. Some courts, however, look at whether complying with the injunction would *cost the defendant* more than $50,000.

The difference in approach may make quite a difference. Suppose, for example, that defendant built her house so that it encroached on plaintiff's property by six inches. While the damage to plaintiff may be minimal, it would cost defendant a considerable sum to remedy the encroachment. Today, most courts will uphold jurisdiction if the amount is met from *either* the plaintiff's or the defendant's viewpoint. See McCarty v. Amoco Pipeline Co., 595 F.2d 389 (7th Cir. 1979).

7. The class action device allows a representative to sue on behalf of a group. If the class seeks to invoke diversity of citizenship, courts look only to the citizenship of the class representative (not to that of all class members). Oddly, however, with regard to the amount in controversy, courts traditionally have required that the claim of each class member satisfy the jurisdictional amount. We will discuss this issue in Chapter 13.

4. Federal Question Jurisdiction

a. Introductory Note

Compare the constitutional grant of federal question jurisdiction in Article III to the statutory grant in 28 U.S.C. §1331.

Section 1331 is known as the "general" federal question statute, an omnibus provision allowing a claim arising under any federal law to be brought in federal court. While we will address only §1331 in detail, note that there are many specialized federal question statutes allowing jurisdiction over claims arising under specific federal laws. For example, §1337 grants jurisdiction over federal antitrust cases; §1338 creates jurisdiction over patent and trademark cases; §1343 relates to civil rights claims.

The historic justifications for giving federal courts jurisdiction over cases arising under federal law are obvious. Federal judges could be expected to be more sympathetic to policies underlying federal legislation and would develop expertise in the interpretation of federal law. State court judges, on the other hand, might be less likely to do the former or have the time to do the latter. Still, it is interesting that the Founders clearly envisioned that state courts would decide cases arising under federal law. Although such specialized federal question statutes are as old as the federal judiciary itself, Congress did not pass a general federal question statute until 1875.[*] Thus, for 84 years, claims arising under federal law and not addressed by a specialized grant of jurisdiction could be heard only in the state courts. You will recall from Chapter 1 that the state courts' interpretation of federal law is ultimately subject to review by the Supreme Court, thereby ensuring, at least in theory,[**] that the federal judiciary remained the ultimate interpreter of federal law.

Note that §1331 does not impose an amount in controversy requirement. It did carry the same requirement as that imposed in diversity of citizenship cases from 1875 until 1980, when Congress abolished it. In part, Congress was motivated by the fact that most of the specialized grants of federal question jurisdiction had no amount in controversy requirement. As is clear from the face of §1331, its grant of jurisdiction is not exclusive to the federal courts. Thus, cases brought under it can be filed either in state or federal court. Indeed, this is also true under the specialized grants of federal question jurisdiction, *except*

---

[*] There was a brief grant of general federal question jurisdiction in the famous Midnight Judges Act of 1801. It was repealed the following year, however, and was of no particular importance.

[**] We say "in theory" because the Supreme Court can review only a very limited number of cases in a given year. If federal question cases were filed only in the federal courts, however, they would be assured of review by a federal district court and, if a party chose to appeal, by a federal court of appeals. The fact that general federal question jurisdiction is not exclusive to the federal courts suggests that Congress is not terribly bothered (as the Founders were not bothered) by the fact that state courts are often the final arbiters of the meaning of federal law. Justice Marshall made this point in dissent in the *Merrell Dow* case, infra at 202.

in those fairly rare situations in which the federal grant is exclusive, which we noted in Section B above.

b. Narrow Interpretations of the Jurisdictional Grant

Courts have long struggled to interpret the seemingly simple language of § 1331 and its complementary constitutional grant. In particular, the term "arising under" has caused problems in two areas. First is a requirement that the federal law be set forth as a claim, not as a defense. This raises the problem of the curiously named "well-pleaded complaint" rule. Second, and more difficult to fathom, is an assessment of whether federal law is sufficiently central to the claim asserted in a well-pleaded complaint. With each of these restrictions, the federal courts have read the statutory language "arising under" more narrowly than the constitutional language. This should not surprise us. Remember that "citizens of different states" in the diversity of citizenship statute is read more narrowly than the same language in the Constitution.

i. The Well-Pleaded Complaint Rule

Louisville & Nashville Railroad Co. v. Mottley
211 U.S. 149, 29 S. Ct. 42, 53 L. Ed. 126 (1908)

JUSTICE MOODY delivered the opinion of the court.

Two questions of law were raised by the demurrer to the bill, were brought here by appeal, and have been argued before us. They are, first, whether that part of the act of Congress of June 29, 1906 (34 Stat. 584), which forbids the giving of free passes or the collection of any different compensation for transportation of passengers than that specified in the tariff filed, makes it unlawful to perform a contract for transportation of persons, who in good faith, before the passage of the act, had accepted such contract in satisfaction of a valid cause of action against the railroad; and, second, whether the statute, if it should be construed to render such a contract unlawful, is in violation of the Fifth Amendment of the Constitution of the United States. We do not deem it necessary, however, to consider either of these questions, because, in our opinion, the court below was without jurisdiction of the cause. Neither party has questioned that jurisdiction, but it is the duty of this court to see to it that the jurisdiction of the Circuit Court, which is defined and limited by statute, is not exceeded. This duty we have frequently performed of our own motion.

There was no diversity of citizenship and it is not and cannot be suggested that there was any ground of jurisdiction, except that the case was a "suit ... arising under the Constitution and laws of the United States." It is the settled interpretation of these words, as used in this statute, conferring jurisdiction, that a suit arises under the Constitution and laws of the United States only when the plaintiff's statement of his own cause of action shows that it is based upon those laws or that

Constitution. It is not enough that the plaintiff alleges some anticipated defense to his cause of action and asserts that the defense is invalidated by some provision of the Constitution of the United States. Although such allegations show that very likely, in the course of the litigation, a question under the Constitution would arise, they do not show that the suit, that is, the plaintiff's original cause of action, arises under the Constitution. In Tennessee v. Union & Planters' Bank, 152 U.S. 454 [1894], the plaintiff, the State of Tennessee, brought suit in the Circuit Court of the United States to recover from the defendant certain taxes alleged to be due under the laws of the State. The plaintiff alleged that the defendant claimed an immunity from the taxation by virtue of its charter, and that therefore the tax was void, because in violation of the provision of the Constitution of the United States, which forbids any State from passing a law impairing the obligation of contracts. The cause was held to be beyond the jurisdiction of the Circuit Court, the court saying, by Mr. Justice Gray, "a suggestion of one party, that the other will or may set up a claim under the Constitution or laws of the United States, does not make the suit one arising under that Constitution or those laws." Again, in Boston & Montana Consolidated Copper & Silver Mining Company v. Montana Ore Purchasing Company, 188 U.S. 632 [1903], the plaintiff brought suit in the Circuit Court of the United States for the conversion of copper ore and for an injunction against its continuance. The plaintiff then alleged, for the purpose of showing jurisdiction, in substance, that the defendant would set up in defense certain laws of the United States. The cause was held to be beyond the jurisdiction of the Circuit Court, the court saying, by Mr. Justice Peckham.

"It would be wholly unnecessary and improper in order to prove complainant's cause of action to go into any matters of defence which the defendants might possibly set up and then attempt to reply to such defence, and thus, if possible, to show that a Federal question might or probably would arise in the course of the trial of the case. To allege such defence and then make an answer to it before the defendant has the opportunity to itself plead or prove its own defence is inconsistent with any known rule of pleading so far as we are aware, and is improper.

"The rule is a reasonable and just one that the complainant in the first instance shall be confined to a statement of its cause of action, leaving to the defendant to set up in his answer what his defence is and, if anything more than a denial of complainant's cause of action, imposing upon the defendant the burden of proving such defence.

"Conforming itself to that rule the complainant would not, in the assertion or proof of its cause of action, bring up a single Federal question. The presentation of its cause of action would not show that it was one arising under the Constitution or laws of the United States.

"The only way in which it might be claimed that a Federal question was presented would be in the complainant's statement of what the defence of defendants would be and complainant's answer to such defence. Under these circumstances the case is brought within the rule laid down in *Tennessee v. Union & Planters' Bank*. That case has been cited and approved many times since, ..."

The interpretation of the act which we have stated was first announced in Metcalf v. Watertown, 128 U.S. 586 [1888], and has since been repeated and applied in [many cases]. The application of this rule to the case at bar is decisive against the jurisdiction of the Circuit Court.

C. Federal Courts and Limited Subject Matter Jurisdiction

It is ordered that the judgment be reversed and the case remitted to the Circuit Court with instructions to dismiss the suit for want of jurisdiction.

NOTES AND QUESTIONS

1. Do not become so carried away with the requirements of one form of jurisdiction that you overlook another possible basis for taking a case to federal court. Obviously, if Mr. and Mrs. Mottley had met the citizenship and amount in controversy requirements, they could have invoked diversity of citizenship jurisdiction. (In fact, as the opinion noted, the Mottleys could not have done so.)

2. *Mottley* establishes the "well-pleaded complaint" rule, which is one of the most inaccurately named doctrines in the law. Despite the clear implication of the name, the doctrine has nothing to do with writing ability, grammar, spelling, sentence structure, or syntax. A well-pleaded complaint, for purposes of this rule, is one that sets forth *only* a claim, unadorned by anticipated defenses or other extraneous material. If the court determines that a complaint contains matter beyond the claim itself, it does not give the plaintiff a bad grade in English Composition or ask her to redraft it. Instead, it ignores the surplus language, and looks only to what would have been included had the complaint been well-pleaded; that is, it looks to the essential elements of the claim itself. Why was the Mottleys' complaint not well-pleaded in this sense?

In *Mottley*, the claim was for breach of contract. To plead such a claim properly, the plaintiff must allege that there was a contract, that the defendant breached the contract, and, in some jurisdictions, that the plaintiff satisfied all conditions required by the contract. These are the only elements to be considered in a well-pleaded complaint. The Mottleys' lawyer, like most good lawyers, considered not only the elements of their claim, but the railroad's likely defense as well. The lawyer accurately predicted that the railroad would assert that the federal statute precluded it from honoring the passes given to the Mottleys and thus that federal law required it to breach the contract. The railroad's assertion is called an "affirmative defense." With it, the defendant says, in essence, "I may have done the bad things you say, but I still win because of this statute."

There are numerous other potential affirmative defenses. For example, a defendant might assert that the statute of limitations bars plaintiff's claim, or that plaintiff is barred by contributory negligence. For a lengthy (albeit partial) list of affirmative defenses, see Rule 8(c), which we will address in Chapter 8. Whether an allegation is considered part of plaintiff's claim or an affirmative defense reflects a policy decision about which side should bear the burden of raising the issue.

CHAPTER 4 SUBJECT MATTER JURISDICTION

There is nothing wrong with a lawyer's anticipating a defense. The well-pleaded complaint rule simply provides that for purposes of determining federal jurisdiction, the court will consider only those aspects of the complaint that are essential to the claim.

3. The well-pleaded complaint rule has the effect of funneling many questions of federal law *out* of the federal courts and into state courts. In *Mottley*, the only issues to be litigated were federal: whether the federal statute required the railroad to refuse to honor the Mottleys' pass, and, if so, whether it violated the Constitution. Yet, under the holding in *Mottley*, a state trial court had to decide these federal issues.

Indeed, the well-pleaded complaint rule results in state court determinations even as to issues supposedly in the exclusive jurisdiction of the federal courts. Note that 28 U.S.C. § 1338 gives exclusive jurisdiction to the federal courts for "any civil action arising under any Act of Congress relating to patents." Courts generally have concluded that exclusive jurisdiction under the statute applies only for actions alleging the *infringement* of a patent. See 1 MOORE'S FEDERAL PRACTICE ¶ 0.62[5].

Suppose Pam holds a patent for the X-83 Widget. She enters a contract with Dave under which Dave is permitted to manufacture and sell the X-83, and is to pay Pam a royalty of $5.00 per widget sold. After ten months, Pam discovers that Dave has sold 12,000 widgets on which he has paid no royalty. She sues to recover damages of $60,000 under the contract. Dave argues that he is not required to pay the royalty, since Pam's patent is invalid. Pam contends that her patent is valid. Notice that because of the well-pleaded complaint rule, this case would not arise under federal law, even though the only issue to be litigated is the validity of the patent under federal law. Interestingly, because of this, the validity of most federal patents may actually be decided by state courts! See Donald Chisum, *The Allocation of Jurisdiction Between State and Federal Courts in Patent Litigation*, 46 WASH. L. REV. 633, 657-64 (1971).

4. Proponents of the well-pleaded complaint rule argue that it serves the valuable function of allowing the court to decide at the outset whether a case arises under federal law. Specifically, if defendant's pleading could invoke federal question jurisdiction, a court would be in limbo as to whether it had jurisdiction, at least until the defendant filed her answer or otherwise raised a federal defense. See FRIEDENTHAL, KANE & MILLER, CIVIL PROCEDURE 22 (rule "fulfills a useful and necessary function"). Opponents of the rule (and there are many) note what we have already seen — that the rule does not funnel litigation centering on federal issues to federal court. They also argue that the question of what elements are considered part of the claim and what matters are considered defenses raises a policy issue that has no particular relation to federal jurisdiction. Further, the critics note that the rule is particularly difficult to apply in the context of a suit for declaratory judgment, as we will explore below. See generally Donald Doernberg, *There's No Reason For It; It's*

C. Federal Courts and Limited Subject Matter Jurisdiction

Just Our Policy: Why the Well-Pleaded Complaint Rule Sabotages the Purposes of Federal Question Jurisdiction, 38 HAST. L.J. 597 (1987).

   5. The Supreme Court held that Mr. and Mrs. Mottley's claim did not "arise under" federal law and thus could not invoke the jurisdiction of a federal trial court. After the Court issued the opinion we just read, the Mottleys took their claim against the railroad to state court, where they lost on the merits. After they appealed the case through the entire state court system, the United States Supreme Court heard it, ruling on the issues of whether the federal statute precluded the railroad from giving the pass to the Mottleys and whether the statute was unconstitutional. Louisville & Nashville Railroad v. Mottley, 219 U.S. 467 (1911). (By the way, the Railroad won.) Thus, just three years after the opinion you read, the Supreme Court addressed the very question it said could not fall within the trial court's jurisdiction!

   The explanation for this anomaly lies in the mechanisms by which the two *Mottley* cases reached the Supreme Court. The first *Mottley* case originated in federal trial court. As a result, when the case was appealed to the Supreme Court, the Court had to determine whether the trial court had properly asserted jurisdiction under the precursor to § 1331. The second *Mottley* case originated in state court. Following the state court determination, an appeal was properly taken to the Supreme Court pursuant to 28 U.S.C. § 1257, which gives the Court appellate jurisdiction over final state court judgments in which a federal statute or constitutional provision is "drawn in question."

   The fact that the Supreme Court ultimately heard the *Mottley* case highlights that the well pleaded complaint rule is solely an interpretation of § 1331 and is not a constitutional limitation on the federal judicial power. Otherwise, then there would have been no constitutional authority for the Supreme Court to review the second *Mottley* case.

   6. You will recall that most of the personal jurisdiction cases we read in Chapter 2 originated in state court. Although these cases raised important federal constitutional questions concerning the scope of the due process clause, this constitutional defense is not a sufficient basis to create original jurisdiction in the federal district court. If one reason for creating federal question jurisdiction is the fear that state judges may be less receptive to federal claims, shouldn't we also fear that they will be less receptive to federal defenses? In *World-Wide Volkswagen*, the Oklahoma state judge responded to the motion to dismiss by telling a defense lawyer that the Fourteenth Amendment did not "carry much water in Creek County." Of course, *World-Wide Volkswagen* was ultimately appealed to the United States Supreme Court, but that Court hears fewer than 200 cases a year.

ii. Well-Pleaded Complaint Problems Raised by Declaratory Judgments

In most cases, plaintiffs seek coercive relief — a remedy that will force the defendant to do something. For example, the plaintiff seeking damages wants the defendant to pay her money; the plaintiff seeking an injunction wants the defendant to do (or desist from doing) something. In such cases, the well-pleaded complaint rule is relatively easy to apply; if the plaintiff's claim for such relief is based upon federal law, it satisfies the well-pleaded complaint rule.

Sometimes, however, plaintiff will seek the noncoercive remedy of a declaratory judgment, in which she requests that the court declare the relative rights between the parties. For instance, an insurance company might seek a declaration that it is not required to pay under a policy because the insured breached a condition. A patent holder might seek a declaration that its patent is valid and has been infringed.

The declaratory judgment raises potentially serious questions about justiciability. Article III, Section 2 of the Constitution provides that the federal courts may be given jurisdiction only over "cases" and "controversies." Among other things, this requires that issues come to the federal bench only through contested litigation, and not through simple requests for the court's opinion on a matter. The federal courts cannot give advisory opinions. Thus, in providing for the remedy in the Federal Declaratory Judgment Act, 28 U.S.C. §§ 2201, 2202, Congress was careful to require that the request be made only "in cases of actual controversy."

In addition, the availability of declaratory relief can alter the alignment of parties one would expect in a case involving a coercive remedy. For example, just as the holder of a patent might sue for a declaration of validity, so an infringer might sue for a declaration of invalidity. And just as an insurer might seek a declaration that its policy is inoperative, so the insured might ask the court to declare that the policy is in force. In other words, the person bringing the declaratory judgment action would have been the defendant in a coercive suit.

How does this fact affect the well-pleaded complaint rule? One is tempted to say that the existence of the Federal Declaratory Judgment Act ensures that *any* declaratory judgment action will meet the well-pleaded complaint test. After all, any request for a declaratory judgment under the Act will set forth elements specified in a federal statute. But the Supreme Court rejected such a broad invocation of federal jurisdiction in Skelly Oil Co. v. Phillips Petroleum Co., 339 U.S. 667 (1950), in which it held that the Act merely creates a remedy, and does not provide a jurisdictional basis. Thus, declaratory judgment actions are proper under the Act only if supported by an independent basis of jurisdiction, such as diversity of citizenship or federal question jurisdiction.

Of course, this fact merely begs the question of how to apply the well-pleaded complaint rule to a claim for declaratory relief. Professor Charles Alan Wright has synthesized the relevant case law in a helpful way. He concludes that "the declaratory action may be entertained in federal court only if the coercive action that would have been necessary, absent declaratory judgment procedure, might have been so brought." WRIGHT, FEDERAL COURTS 111. For example, the patent holder who seeks a declaration that its patent is valid and is being infringed invokes federal jurisdiction because it could just as easily have sought coercive relief in the form of damages or an injunction for the same behavior.

Moreover, as Professor Wright demonstrates, it does not matter who would bring the coercive action, as long as one could be brought by one of the parties. For example, consider the flip side of the patent infringement case. Suppose the alleged infringer seeks a declaration that the manufacturer's patent is invalid or, alternatively, that its actions do not constitute infringement. It would have no right, of course, to bring a coercive action on these issues; they would be raised as defenses in a suit by the patent holder. Nonetheless, because the patent holder could have brought a coercive suit raising the same federal issues, jurisdiction is upheld. Id. at 100-02.

The Supreme Court reaffirmed this approach in Franchise Tax Board v. Construction Laborers Vacation Trust, 463 U.S. 1 (1983), the facts of which led Professor Wright to dub it "the Exam Question from Hell masquerading as a federal lawsuit." WRIGHT, FEDERAL COURTS 108-09, n. 3 (quoting Professor John Oakley in a different context). In that case, a labor union pooled money as a vacation trust for its members. The Franchise Tax Board, a California agency responsible for collecting state income tax, was unable to collect taxes from three union members. It sued the union vacation trust in state court, seeking tax money from the three employees' vacation fund. Among other things, the Franchise Tax Board sought a declaration that federal employee pension law did not prevent it from recovering the money from the trust.

The Supreme Court held that this claim did not create federal question jurisdiction and, thus, that the defendant could not "remove" the case to federal court. (We will discuss removal below; it permits a defendant to have a case transferred from state to federal court, but only if the case invoked federal subject matter jurisdiction.) The Franchise Tax Board's claim was based upon state law. The question of whether federal law preempted the claim was raised by defense. Unless a coercive suit would arise under federal law, a declaratory judgment case cannot invoke federal question jurisdiction.

What, then, about *Mottley*? Could the Mottleys have invoked federal question jurisdiction for a declaration that federal law did not preclude the railroad from giving them their passes? Clearly not, since, as we saw, the Mottleys could not have brought a coercive action for the same claim. What about the railroad? Could it have invoked federal question jurisdiction by seeking a declaration that it was precluded from giving the passes to the Mottleys? Clearly not. Why?

iii. Centrality of the Federal Issue to the Claim

In addition to the requirement that the federal issue be injected in a well-pleaded complaint, the federal courts have imposed another statutory limitation on the words "arising under" in § 1331. Although this limitation is more difficult to describe, it basically concerns whether the federal issues set forth in the well-pleaded complaint are central enough to the dispute. In other words, to invoke federal question jurisdiction, the federal issue must be part of a well-pleaded complaint *and* must also be a sufficient or central enough part of the dispute.

Does every aspect of the case have to be addressed by federal law, or can there be some state law elements? Suppose, for example, a federal statute creates a right to sue but directs the courts to determine liability by reference to state law. Does such a claim arise under federal law? These are the sorts of questions that can arise in this area. There is no question that the constitutional grant of federal question jurisdiction requires only that federal law be "an ingredient" of the case. Osborn v. Bank of the United States, 22 U.S. 738 (1824). Thus any case involving title to land in any part of the United States where the title is ultimately traced to a federal grant could constitutionally be heard in federal courts. But the statutory grant of federal question jurisdiction is narrower, and it is our focus here. We set the stage with a summary of three important Supreme Court opinions before reading the Court's most recent effort in the area.

The plaintiff in American Well Works Co. v. Layne & Bowler Co., 241 U.S. 257 (1916), manufactured a pump. It sued under state trade libel law, alleging that the defendant had wrongfully accused the plaintiff of infringing the defendant's patent on the pump. The complaint also alleged that the defendant had driven away customers by improperly threatening to sue anyone who bought the plaintiff's pump. Clearly, the litigation would focus solely on the federal issue of whether the plaintiff's pump actually did infringe defendant's patent. Nonetheless, the Supreme Court, in an opinion by Justice Oliver Wendell Holmes, held that the case did *not* arise under federal law. Holmes adopted a mechanical approach, concluding simply that "[a] suit arises under the law that creates the cause of action." Id. at 260. Because the claim for trade libel was based upon state law, there was no federal question jurisdiction.[*]

---

[*] Although the case addressed the predecessor to § 1338, concerning patent cases, and not the predecessor to § 1331, the interpretation of "arising under" applies to both.

Five years later, the Court took a different tack. In Smith v. Kansas City Title & Trust Co., 255 U.S. 180 (1921), the plaintiff sued a corporation in which he held stock, seeking to enjoin the company from using corporate funds to invest in bonds issued under the Federal Farm Loan Act. He asserted that such an investment was illegal according to Missouri banking law because the Farm Loan Act was unconstitutional. Missouri law created the cause of action; thus, the case would not arise under federal law according to the *American Well Works* test. Nonetheless, the Court upheld jurisdiction, saying (over Justice Holmes's strong dissent) that "where it appears from the bill or statement of the plaintiff that the right to relief depends upon the construction or application of the Constitution or laws of the United States, and that such federal claim . . . rests upon a reasonable foundation, the District Court has jurisdiction." Id. at 199. Because *Smith* directly involved the construction of a federal act and the federal Constitution, jurisdiction existed.

The Court did not clarify matters when it decided Moore v. Chesapeake & Ohio Ry., 291 U.S. 205 (1934). There, the plaintiff sued under a state employers' liability act. Under that state law, contributory negligence could not bar an employee's recovery if the employer had violated a statute "enacted for the safety of employees." One such statute, incorporated into the state statute, was the Federal Safety Appliance Act. Thus, the question was whether the railroad employer had violated that federal law. The *American Well Works* case would counsel that the case did not arise under federal law because state law created the cause of action. *Smith*, however, would seem to require a finding of jurisdiction, since the case turned on the "construction or application" of federal law. The *Moore* Court found no jurisdiction, creating considerable confusion.

Thus, in *Smith* and *Moore*, plaintiffs brought state causes of action, but their cases raised significant questions of federal law. Yet, one case arose under federal law for purposes of § 1331, and the other did not. The following case, *Merrell Dow*, is the Supreme Court's most recent decision in this thorny area. In it, the majority opinion, by Justice Stevens, purports to reconcile *Smith* and *Moore*. The dissenting opinion, by Justice Brennan, concludes that *Smith* and *Moore* are irreconcilable. As you read them, analyze which you find more persuasive.

Two pieces of background information will assist in your understanding of *Merrell Dow*. First, as we will address in detail in Section 6 of this chapter, the process of "removal" allows a defendant sued in state court to remove (transfer) the case to the federal trial court in the same locality. The defendant may do so, however, only if the case is one over which the federal court would have subject matter jurisdiction. In *Merrell Dow*, the defendant attempted to remove the case to federal court on the basis of federal question jurisdiction. Thus, the question is the same as it would have been if the plaintiff had tried to invoke federal question jurisdiction, i.e., did plaintiff's claim "arise under" federal law for purposes of § 1331?* The defendant especially wanted to litigate in federal court, since that particular district judge had previously dismissed a similar case on grounds of forum non conveniens.

Second, it is important to understand that Congress does not always create a private right to sue to enforce the laws it passes. For example, many criminal and regulatory statutes proscribe specific inappropriate behavior but do not provide that someone hurt by such behavior can sue to recover damages. Rather, they allow administrative enforcement or criminal prosecution. Sometimes, the federal courts find that Congress intended to give a private right of action even though the legislation does not provide expressly for one. For example, the Supreme Court has recognized that a federal criminal provision regarding misrepresentation in the purchase or sale of securities impliedly created a right to sue for buyers or sellers injured by the misrepresentation. See, e.g., Ernst & Ernst v. Hochfelder, 425 U.S. 185 (1976).

Such "implied rights of action" are controversial. After all, it is Congress's — not the courts' — job to write the laws. If Congress wanted to give a private right of action, it could have said so. Sensitive to this concern, the Supreme Court has been less willing to find implied rights of action in recent times. The test for when such implication remains appropriate, however, is not clear. Compare, e.g., Cort v. Ash, 422 U.S. 66 (1975), with Touche Ross & Co. v. Redington, 442 U.S. 560 (1979). In *Merrell Dow*, as we will see, the parties agreed that the regulatory law involved did not create a private right of action for its enforcement. As you read the case, focus on the importance of that fact to the majority opinion.

Merrell Dow Pharmaceuticals, Inc. v. Thompson
478 U.S. 804, 106 S. Ct. 3229, 92 L. Ed. 2d 650 (1986)

JUSTICE STEVENS delivered the opinion of the Court.

The question presented is whether the incorporation of a federal standard in a state-law private action, when Congress has intended that there not be a federal private action for violations of that federal standard, makes the action one "arising under the Constitution, laws, or treaties of the United States," 28 U.S.C. § 1331.

---

* The defendant could not remove the case to federal court based upon alienage jurisdiction because of the limitation of 28 U.S.C. § 1441(b), which precludes removal of alienage and diversity cases if any defendant is a citizen of the forum. We will discuss this point in Section 6 of this chapter. Thus, federal question was the only possible jurisdictional basis.

C. Federal Courts and Limited Subject Matter Jurisdiction

I

The Thompson respondents are residents of Canada and the MacTavishes reside in Scotland. They filed virtually identical complaints against petitioner, a corporation, that manufactures and distributes the drug Bendectin. The complaints were filed in the Court of Common Pleas in Hamilton County, Ohio. Each complaint alleged that a child was born with multiple deformities as a result of the mother's ingestion of Bendectin during pregnancy. In five of the six counts, the recovery of substantial damages was requested on common-law theories of negligence, breach of warranty, strict liability, fraud, and gross negligence. In Count IV, respondents alleged that the drug Bendectin was "misbranded" in violation of the Federal Food, Drug, and Cosmetic Act (FDCA), because its labeling did not provide adequate warning that its use was potentially dangerous. Paragraph 26 alleged that the violation of the FDCA "in the promotion" of Bendectin "constitutes a rebuttable presumption of negligence." Paragraph 27 alleged that the "violation of said federal statutes directly and proximately caused the injuries suffered" by the two infants.

Petitioner filed a timely petition for removal from the state court to the Federal District Court alleging that the action was "founded, in part, on an alleged claim arising under the laws of the United States." After removal, the two cases were consolidated. Respondents filed a motion to remand to the state forum on the ground that the federal court lacked subject-matter jurisdiction. Relying on our decision in Smith v. Kansas City Title & Trust Co., 255 U.S. 180 (1921), the District Court held that Count IV of the complaint alleged a cause of action arising under federal law and denied the motion to remand. It then granted petitioner's motion to dismiss on forum non conveniens grounds.

The Court of Appeals for the Sixth Circuit reversed. After quoting one sentence from the concluding paragraph in our recent opinion in Franchise Tax Board v. Construction Laborers Vacation Trust, 463 U.S. 1 (1983),[2] and noting "that the FDCA does not create or imply a private right of action for individuals injured as a result of violations of the Act," it explained:

> Federal question jurisdiction would, thus, exist only if plaintiffs' right to relief *depended necessarily* on a substantial question of federal law. Plaintiffs' causes of action referred to the FDCA merely as one available criterion for determining whether Merrell Dow was negligent. Because the jury could find negligence on the part of Merrell Dow without finding a violation of the FDCA, the plaintiffs' causes of action did not depend necessarily upon a question of federal law. Consequently, the causes of action did not arise under federal law and, therefore, were improperly removed to federal court.

We granted certiorari, and we now affirm.

---

[2] "'Under our interpretations, Congress has given the lower courts jurisdiction to hear, originally or by removal from a state court, only those cases in which a well-pleaded complaint establishes either that federal law creates the cause of action or that the plaintiff's right to relief necessarily depends on resolution of a substantial question of federal law.'" (quoting *Franchise Tax Board*, 463 U.S. at 28).

II

Article III of the Constitution gives the federal courts power to hear cases "arising under" federal statutes. That grant of power, however, is not self-executing, and it was not until the Judiciary Act of 1875 that Congress gave the federal courts general federal-question jurisdiction. Although the constitutional meaning of "arising under" may extend to all cases in which a federal question is "an ingredient" of the action, Osborn v. Bank of the United States, 9 Wheat. 738, 823 (1824), we have long construed the statutory grant of federal-question jurisdiction as conferring a more limited power.

Under our longstanding interpretation of the current statutory scheme, the question whether a claim "arises under" federal law must be determined by reference to the "well-pleaded complaint." A defense that raises a federal question is inadequate to confer federal jurisdiction. Louisville & Nashville R. Co. v. Mottley, 211 U.S. 149 (1908). Since a defendant may remove a case only if the claim could have been brought in federal court, 28 U.S.C. § 1441(b), moreover, the question for removal jurisdiction must also be determined by reference to the "well-pleaded complaint."

As was true in *Franchise Tax Board*, the propriety of the removal in this case thus turns on whether the case falls within the original "federal question" jurisdiction of the federal courts. There is no "single, precise definition" of that concept; rather, "the phrase 'arising under' masks a welter of issues regarding the interrelation of federal and state authority and the proper management of the federal judicial system." Id. at 8.

This much, however, is clear. The "vast majority" of cases that come within this grant of jurisdiction are covered by Justice Holmes' statement that a "'suit arises under the law that creates the cause of action.'" Id., at 8-9, quoting American Well Works Co. v. Layne & Bowler Co., 241 U.S. 257, 260 (1916). Thus, the vast majority of cases brought under the general federal-question jurisdiction of the federal courts are those in which federal law creates the cause of action.

We have, however, also noted that a case may arise under federal law "where the vindication of a right under state law necessarily turned on some construction of federal law." Franchise Tax Board.[5] Our actual holding in *Franchise Tax Board* demonstrates that this statement must be read with caution; the central issue presented in that case turned on the meaning of the Employee Retirement Income Security Act of 1974, but we nevertheless concluded that federal jurisdiction was lacking.

---

[5] The case most frequently cited for that proposition is Smith v. Kansas City Title & Trust Co., 255 U.S. 180 (1921). In that case the Court upheld federal jurisdiction of a shareholder's bill to enjoin the corporation from purchasing bonds issued by the federal land banks under the authority of the Federal Farm Loan Act on the ground that the federal statute that authorized the issuance of the bonds was unconstitutional. The Court stated:

> The general rule is that where it appears from the bill statement of the plaintiff that the right to relief depends upon the construction or application of the Constitution or laws of the United States, and that such federal claim is not merely colorable, and rests upon a reasonable foundation, the District Court has jurisdiction under this provision. Id. at 199.

The effect of this view, expressed over Justice Holmes' vigorous dissent, on his *American Well Works* formulation has been often noted. See, e.g., Franchise Tax Board, 463 U.S. at 9 ("[I]t is well settled that Justice Holmes' test is more useful for describing the vast majority of cases that come within the district courts' original jurisdiction than it is for describing which cases are beyond district court jurisdiction"); T.B. Harms Co. v. Eliscu, 339 F.2d 823, 827 (2d Cir. 1964) (Friendly, J.) ("It has come to be realized that Mr. Justice Holmes' formula is more useful for inclusion than for the exclusion for which it was intended").

C. Federal Courts and Limited Subject Matter Jurisdiction

This case does not pose a federal question of the first kind; respondents do not allege that federal law creates any of the causes of action that they have asserted.[6] This case thus poses what Justice Frankfurter called the "litigation-provoking problem," Textile Workers v. Lincoln Mills, 353 U.S. 448, 470 (1957) (dissenting opinion) — the presence of a federal issue in a state-created cause of action.

In undertaking this inquiry into whether jurisdiction may lie for the presence of a federal issue in a nonfederal cause of action, it is, of course, appropriate to begin by referring to our understanding of the statute conferring federal-question jurisdiction. We have consistently emphasized that, in exploring the outer reaches of § 1331, determinations about federal jurisdiction require sensitive judgments about congressional intent, judicial power, and the federal system. "If the history of the interpretation of judiciary legislation teaches us anything, it teaches the duty to reject treating such statutes as a wooden set of self-sufficient words.... The Act of 1875 is broadly phrased, but it has been continuously construed and limited in the light of the history that produced it, the demands of reason and coherence, and the dictates of sound judicial policy which have emerged from the Act's function as a provision in the mosaic of federal judiciary legislation." Romero v. International Terminal Operating Co., 358 U.S. at 379. * * *

In this case, both parties agree with the Court of Appeals' conclusion that there is no federal cause of action for FDCA violations. For purposes of our decision, we assume that this is a correct interpretation of the FDCA. Thus, as the case comes to us, it is appropriate to assume that, under the settled framework for evaluating whether a federal cause of action lies, some combination of the following factors is present: (1) the plaintiffs are not part of the class for whose special benefit the statute was passed; (2) the indicia of legislative intent reveal no congressional purpose to provide a private cause of action; (3) a federal cause of action would not further the underlying purposes of the legislative scheme; and (4) the respondents' cause of action is a subject traditionally relegated to state law. [These are factors set out in Cort v. Ash, 422 U.S. 66, 78 (1975), regarding the propriety of finding an implied right of action — EDS.] In short, Congress did not intend a private federal remedy for violations of the statute that it enacted.

* * *

The significance of the necessary assumption that there is no federal private cause of action thus cannot be overstated. For the ultimate import of such a conclusion, as we have repeatedly emphasized, is that it would flout congressional intent to provide a private federal remedy for the violation of the federal statute. We think it would similarly flout, or at least undermine, congressional intent to conclude that the federal courts might nevertheless exercise federal-question jurisdiction and provide remedies for violations of that federal statute solely because the violation of the federal statute is said to be a "rebuttable presumption" or a "proximate cause" under state law, rather than a federal action under federal law.[10]

---

[6] Jurisdiction may not be sustained on a theory that the plaintiff has not advanced. See Healy v. Sea Gull Specialty Co., 237 U.S. 479, 480 (1915) ("[T]he plaintiff is absolute master of what jurisdiction he will appeal to"); The Fair v. Kohler Die & Specialty Co., 228 U.S. 22, 25 (1913) ("[T]he party who brings a suit is master to decide what law he will rely upon").

[10] When we conclude that Congress has decided not to provide a particular federal remedy, we are not free to "supplement" that decision in a way that makes it "meaningless." * * *

CHAPTER 4 SUBJECT MATTER JURISDICTION

III

Petitioner advances three arguments to support its position that, even in the face of this congressional preclusion of a federal cause of action for a violation of the federal statute, federal-question jurisdiction may lie for the violation of the federal statute as an element of a state cause of action.

First, petitioner contends that the case represents a straightforward application of the statement in *Franchise Tax Board* that federal-question jurisdiction is appropriate when "it appears that some substantial, disputed question of federal law is a necessary element of one of the well-pleaded state claims." 463 U.S. at 13. *Franchise Tax Board*, however, did not purport to disturb the long-settled understanding that the mere presence of a federal issue in a state cause of action does not automatically confer federal-question jurisdiction. Indeed, in determining that federal-question jurisdiction was not appropriate in the case before us, we stressed Justice Cardozo's emphasis on principled, pragmatic distinctions: "'What is needed is something of that common-sense accommodation of judgment to kaleidoscopic situations which characterizes the law in its treatment of causation ... a selective process which picks the substantial causes out of the web and lays the other ones aside.'" Id. at 20-21 (quoting Gully v. First National Bank, 299 U.S. 109, 117-118 (1936)).

Far from creating some kind of automatic test, *Franchise Tax Board* thus candidly recognized the need for careful judgments about the exercise of federal judicial power in an area of uncertain jurisdiction. Given the significance of the assumed congressional determination to preclude federal private remedies, the presence of the federal issue as an element of the state tort is not the kind of adjudication for which jurisdiction would serve congressional purposes and the federal system. This conclusion is fully consistent with the very sentence relied on so heavily by petitioner. We simply conclude that the congressional determination that there should be no federal remedy for the violation of this federal statute is tantamount to a congressional conclusion that the presence of a claimed violation of the statute as an element of a state cause of action is insufficiently "substantial" to confer federal-question jurisdiction.[12]

---

[12] Several commentators have suggested that our § 1331 decisions can best be understood as an evaluation of the nature of the federal interest at stake. See, e.g., Shapiro, *Jurisdiction and Discretion*, 60 N.Y.U. L. Rev. 543 568 (1985); C. WRIGHT, FEDERAL COURTS 96 (4th ed. 1983); Cohen, *The Broken Compass: The Requirement That a Case Arise "Directly" Under Federal Law*, 115 U. PA. L. REV. 890, 916 (1967). Cf. Kravitz v. Homeowners Warranty Corp., 542 F.Supp. 317, 320 (ED Pa. 1982) (Pollak, J.) ("I cannot identify any compelling reasons of federal judicial policy for embracing a case of this kind as a federal question case. The essential Pennsylvania elements of plaintiffs' suit for rescission would be more appropriately dealt with by a Court of Common Pleas than by this court; and, with respect to the lesser-included issue of federal law, Pennsylvania's courts are fully competent to interpret the Magnuson-Moss Warranty Act and the relevant F.T.C. regulations, subject to review by the United States Supreme Court").

Focusing on the nature of the federal interest, moreover, suggests that the widely perceived "irreconcilable" conflict between the finding of federal jurisdiction in Smith v. Kansas City Title & Trust Co., 255 U.S. 180 (1921), and the finding of no jurisdiction in Moore v. Chesapeake & Ohio R. Co., 291 U.S. 205 (1934), see, e.g., M. REDISH, FEDERAL JURISDICTION: TENSIONS IN THE ALLOCATION OF JUDICIAL POWER 67 (1980), is far from clear. For the difference in results can be seen as manifestations of the differences in the nature of the federal issues at stake. In *Smith*, as the Court emphasized, the issue was the constitutionality of an important federal statute. See 255 U.S. at 201 ("It is ... which is directly drawn in question. The decision depends upon the determination of this issue"). In *Moore*, in contrast, the Court emphasized that the violation of the federal standard as an element of state tort

C. Federal Courts and Limited Subject Matter Jurisdiction

Second, petitioner contends that there is a powerful federal interest in seeing that the federal statute is given uniform interpretations, and that federal review is the best way of insuring such uniformity. In addition to the significance of the congressional decision to preclude a federal remedy, we do not agree with petitioner's characterization of the federal interest and its implications for federal-question jurisdiction. To the extent that petitioner is arguing that state use and interpretation of the FDCA pose a threat to the order and stability of the FDCA regime, petitioner should be arguing, not that federal courts should be able to review and enforce state FDCA-based causes of action as an aspect of federal-question jurisdiction, but that the FDCA pre-empts state-court jurisdiction over the issue in dispute. Petitioner's concern about the uniformity of interpretation, moreover, is considerably mitigated by the fact that, even if there is no original district court jurisdiction for these kinds of action, this Court retains power to review the decision of a federal issue in a state cause of action.

Finally, petitioner argues that, whatever the general rule, there are special circumstances that justify federal-question jurisdiction in this case. Petitioner emphasizes that it is unclear whether the FDCA applies to sales in Canada and Scotland; there is, therefore, a special reason for having a federal court answer the novel federal question relating to the extraterritorial meaning of the Act. We reject this argument. We do not believe the question whether a particular claim arises under federal law depends on the novelty of the federal issue. Although it is true that federal jurisdiction cannot be based on a frivolous or insubstantial federal question, "the interrelation of federal and state authority and the proper management of the federal judicial system," Franchise Tax Board, 463 U.S. at 8, would be ill served by a rule that made the existence of federal-question jurisdiction depend on the district court's case-by-case appraisal of the novelty of the federal question asserted as an element of the state tort. The novelty of an FDCA issue is not sufficient to give it status as a federal cause of action; nor should it be sufficient to give a state-based FDCA claim status as a jurisdiction-triggering federal question.

---

recovery did not fundamentally change the state tort nature of the action. See 291 U.S. at 216-217 ("The action fell within the familiar category of cases involving the duty of a master to his servant. This duty is defined by the common law, except as it may be modified by legislation. The federal statute, in the present case, touched the duty of the master at a single point and, save as provided in the statute, the right of the plaintiff to recover was left to be determined by the law of the State'") (quoting Minneapolis, St. P. & S.S.M. R. v. Popplar, 237 U.S. 369, 372 (1915)).

The importance of the nature of the federal issue in federal-question jurisdiction is highlighted by the fact that, despite the usual reliability of the Holmes test as an inclusionary principle, this Court has sometimes found that formally federal causes of action were not properly brought under federal-question jurisdiction because of the overwhelming predominance of state-law issues. See Shulthis v. McDougal, 225 U.S. 561, 569-570 (1912) ("A suit to enforce a right which takes its origin in the laws of the United States is not necessarily, or for that reason alone, one arising under those laws, for a suit does not so arise unless it really and substantially involves a dispute or controversy respecting the validity, construction or effect of such a law, upon the determination of which the result depends. This is especially so of a suit involving rights to land acquired under a law of the United States. If it were not, every suit to establish title to land in the central and western States would so arise, as all titles in those States are traceable back to those laws"); Shoshone Mining Co. v. Rutter, 177 U.S. 505, 507 (1900) ("We pointed out in the former opinion that it was well settled that a suit to enforce a right which takes its origin in the laws of the United States is not necessarily one arising under the Constitution or laws of the United States, within the meaning of the jurisdiction clauses, for if it did every action to establish title to real estate (at least in the newer States) would be such a one, as all titles in those States come from the United States or by virtue of its laws").

IV

We conclude that a complaint alleging a violation of a federal statute as an element of a state cause of action, when Congress has determined that there should be no private, federal cause of action for the violation, does not state a claim "arising under the Constitution, laws, or treaties of the United States." 28 U.S.C. § 1331.

The judgment of the Court of Appeals is affirmed.

It is so ordered.

JUSTICE BRENNAN, with whom JUSTICE WHITE, JUSTICE MARSHALL and JUSTICE BLACKMUN join, dissenting.

* * *

I

While the majority of cases covered by § 1331 may well be described by Justice Holmes' adage that "[a] suit arises under the law that creates the cause of action," American Well Works Co. v. Layne & Bowler Co., 241 U.S. 257, 260 (1916), it is firmly settled that there may be federal-question jurisdiction even though both the right asserted and the remedy sought by the plaintiff are state created. The rule as to such cases was stated in what Judge Friendly described as "[t]he path-breaking opinion" in Smith v. Kansas City Title & Trust Co., 255 U.S. 180 (1921). T.B. Harms Co. v. Eliscu, 339 F.2d 823, 827 (2d Cir. 1964). * * *

The continuing vitality of *Smith* is beyond challenge. We have cited it approvingly on numerous occasions, and reaffirmed its holding several times — most recently just three Terms ago by a unanimous Court in Franchise Tax Board v. Construction Laborers Vacation Trust. * * *[1]

---

[1] Some commentators have argued that the result in *Smith* conflicts with our decision in Moore v. Chesapeake & Ohio R. Co., 291 U.S. 205 (1934). * * *

The Court suggests that *Smith* and *Moore* may be reconciled if one views the question whether there is jurisdiction under § 1331 as turning upon "an evaluation of the *nature* of the federal interest at stake." Thus, the Court explains, while in *Smith* the issue was the constitutionality of "an important federal statute," in *Moore* the federal interest was less significant in that "the violation of the federal standard as an element of state tort recovery did not fundamentally change the state tort nature of the action."

In one sense, the Court is correct in asserting that we can reconcile *Smith* and *Moore* on the ground that the "nature" of the federal interest was more significant in *Smith* than in *Moore*. Indeed, as the Court appears to believe, ante, n.12, we could reconcile many of the seemingly inconsistent results that have been reached under § 1331 with such a test. But this is so only because a test based upon an ad hoc evaluation of the importance of the federal issue is infinitely malleable: at what point does a federal interest become strong enough to create jurisdiction? What principles guide the determination whether a statute is "important" or not? Why, for instance, was the statute in *Smith* so "important" that direct review of a state-court decision (under our mandatory appellate jurisdiction) would have been inadequate? Would the result in *Moore* have been different if the federal issue had been a more important element of the tort claim? The point is that if one makes the test sufficiently vague and general, virtually any set of results can be "reconciled." However, the inevitable — and undesirable — result of a

C. Federal Courts and Limited Subject Matter Jurisdiction

* * *

There is, to my mind, no question that there is federal jurisdiction over the respondents' fourth cause of action under the rule set forth in *Smith* and reaffirmed in *Franchise Tax Board*. Respondents pleaded that petitioner's labeling of the drug Bendectin constituted "misbranding" in violation of §§ 201 and 502(f)(2) and (j) of the Federal Food, Drug, and Cosmetic Act (FDCA), and that this violation "directly and proximately caused" their injuries. Respondents asserted in the complaint that this violation established petitioner's negligence *per se* and entitled them to recover damages without more. No other basis for finding petitioner negligent was asserted in connection with this claim. As pleaded, then, respondents' "right to relief [d]epended upon the construction or application of the Constitution or laws of the United States." *Smith*, 255 U.S. at 199. Furthermore, although petitioner disputes its liability under the FDCA, it concedes that respondents' claim that petitioner violated the FDCA is "colorable, and rests upon a reasonable foundation." *Smith*, supra, at 199.[3] Of course, since petitioner must make this concession to prevail in this Court, it need not be accepted at face value. However, independent examination of respondents' claim substantiates the conclusion that it is neither frivolous nor meritless. As stated in the complaint, a drug is "misbranded" under the FDCA if "the labeling or advertising fails to reveal facts material ... with respect to consequences which may result from the use of the article to which the labeling or advertising relates ...." 21 U.S.C. § 321(n). Obviously, the possibility that a mother's ingestion of Bendectin during pregnancy could produce malformed children is material. Petitioner's principal defense is that the Act does not govern the branding of drugs that are sold in foreign countries. It is certainly not immediately obvious whether this argument is correct. Thus, the statutory question is one which "discloses a need for determining the meaning or application of [the FDCA]," and the claim raised by the fourth cause of action is one "arising under" federal law within the meaning of § 1331.

---

test such as that suggested in the Court's footnote 12 is that federal jurisdiction turns in every case on an appraisal of the federal issue, its importance and its relation to state law issues. Yet it is precisely because the Court believes that federal jurisdiction would be "ill served" by such a case-by-case appraisal that it rejects petitioner's claim that the difficulty and importance of the statutory issue presented by its claim suffices to confer jurisdiction under § 1331. The Court cannot have it both ways.

My own view is in accord with those commentators who view the results in *Smith* and *Moore* as irreconcilable. See, e.g., REDISH [FEDERAL JURISDICTION: TENSIONS IN THE ALLOCATION OF JUDICIAL POWER] 67; D. CURRIE, FEDERAL JURISDICTION IN A NUTSHELL 109 (2d ed. 1981). That fact does not trouble me greatly, however, for I view *Moore* as having been a "sport" at the time it was decided and having long been in a state of innocuous desuetude. Unlike the jurisdictional holding in *Smith*, the jurisdictional holding in *Moore* has never been relied upon or even cited by this Court. *Moore* has similarly borne little fruit in the lower courts, leading Professor Redish to conclude after comparing the vitality of *Smith* and *Moore* that "the principle enunciated in *Smith* is the one widely followed by modern lower federal courts." REDISH 67. Finally, as noted in text, the commentators have also preferred *Smith*. *Moore* simply has not survived the test of time; it is presently moribund, and, to the extent that it is inconsistent with the well-established rule of the *Smith* case, it ought to be overruled.

[3] *Franchise Tax Board* states that the plaintiff's right to relief must necessarily depend upon resolution of a "substantial" federal question. In context, however, it is clear that this was simply another way of stating that the federal question must be colorable and have a reasonable foundation. This understanding is consistent with the manner in which the *Smith* text has always been applied, as well as with the way we have used the concept of a "substantial" federal question in other cases concerning federal jurisdiction. See, e.g., Hagans v. Lavine, 415 U.S. 528, 536-537 (1974); Bell v. Hood, 327 U.S. 678, 682 (1946).

The Court apparently does not disagree with any of this — except, of course, for the conclusion. According to the Court, if we assume that Congress did not intend that there be a private federal cause of action under a particular federal law (and, presumably, *a fortiori* if Congress' decision not to create a private remedy is express), we must also assume that Congress did not intend that there be federal jurisdiction over a state cause of action that is determined by that federal law. Therefore, assuming — only because the parties have made a similar assumption — that there is no private cause of action under the FDCA, the Court holds that there is no federal jurisdiction over the plaintiffs' claim. * * *

The Court nowhere explains the basis for [its] conclusion. Yet it is hardly self-evident. Why should the fact that Congress chose not to create a private federal *remedy* mean that Congress would not want there to be federal *jurisdiction* to adjudicate a state claim that imposes liability for violating the federal law? Clearly, the decision not to provide a private federal remedy should not affect federal jurisdiction unless the reasons Congress withholds a federal remedy are also reasons for withholding federal jurisdiction. Thus, it is necessary to examine the reasons for Congress' decisions to grant or withhold both federal jurisdiction and private remedies, something the Court has not done.

A

In the early days of our Republic, Congress was content to leave the task of interpreting and applying federal laws in the first instance to the state courts; with one short-lived exception, Congress did not grant the inferior federal courts original jurisdiction over cases arising under federal law until 1875. The reasons Congress found it necessary to add this jurisdiction to the district courts are well known. First, Congress recognized "the importance, and even necessity of uniformity of decisions throughout the whole United States, upon all subjects within the purview of the constitution." Martin v. Hunter's Lessee, 1 Wheat. at 347-348 (Story, J.) (emphasis in original). Concededly, because federal jurisdiction is not always exclusive and because federal courts may disagree with one another, absolute uniformity has not been obtained even under § 1331. However, while perfect uniformity may not have been achieved, experience indicates that the availability of a federal forum in federal-question cases has done much to advance that goal. This, in fact, was the conclusion of the American Law Institute's Study of the Division of Jurisdiction Between State and Federal Courts.

In addition, § 1331 has provided for adjudication in a forum that specializes in federal law and that is therefore more likely to apply that law correctly. Because federal-question cases constitute the basic grist for federal tribunals, "[t]he federal courts have acquired a considerable expertness in the interpretation and application of federal law." Id. at 164-165. By contrast, "it is apparent that federal question cases must form a very small part of the business of [state] courts." Id. at 165. As a result, the federal courts are comparatively more skilled at interpreting and applying federal law, and are much more likely correctly to divine Congress' intent in enacting legislation.[6]

---

[6] Another reason Congress conferred original federal-question jurisdiction on the district courts was its belief that state courts are hostile to assertions of federal rights. See Hornstein, *Federalism, Judicial Power and the "Arising Under" Jurisdiction of the Federal Courts: A Hierarchical Analysis*, 56 IND. L.J. 563, 564-565 (1981). Although this concern may be less compelling today than it once was, the American Law Institute reported as recently as 1969 that "it is difficult to avoid concluding that federal courts are more likely to apply federal law

C. Federal Courts and Limited Subject Matter Jurisdiction

These reasons for having original federal-question jurisdiction explain why cases like this one and *Smith* — i.e., cases where the cause of action is a creature of state law, but an essential element of the claim is federal — "arise under" federal law within the meaning of § 1331. Congress passes laws in order to shape behavior; a federal law expresses Congress' determination that there is a federal interest in having individuals or entities conform their actions to a particular norm established by that law. Because all laws are imprecise to some degree, disputes inevitably arise over what specifically Congress intended to require or permit. It is the duty of courts to interpret these laws and apply them in such a way that the congressional purpose is realized. As noted above, Congress granted the district courts power to hear cases "arising under" federal law in order to enhance the likelihood that federal laws would be interpreted more correctly and applied more uniformly. In other words, Congress determined that the availability of a federal forum to adjudicate cases involving federal questions would make it more likely that federal laws would shape behavior in the way that Congress intended.

By making federal law an essential element of a state-law claim, the State places the federal law into a context where it will operate to shape behavior: the threat of liability will force individuals to conform their conduct to interpretations of the federal law made by courts adjudicating the state-law claim. It will not matter to an individual found liable whether the officer who arrives at his door to execute judgment is wearing a state or a federal uniform; all he cares about is the fact that a sanction is being imposed — and may be imposed again in the future — because he failed to comply with the federal law. Consequently, the possibility that the federal law will be incorrectly interpreted in the context of adjudicating the state-law claim implicates the concerns that led Congress to grant the district courts power to adjudicate cases involving federal questions in precisely the same way as if it was federal law that "created" the cause of action. It therefore follows that there is federal jurisdiction under § 1331.

* * *

NOTES AND QUESTIONS

1. *Merrell Dow* is unusual in that both the plaintiffs and the defendant argued that there was no private cause of action. Usually, of course, the plaintiff argues in favor of a private cause of action. Why did the plaintiffs not do so in *Merrell Dow*? Why wouldn't

---

sympathetically and understandingly than are state courts." ALI 166. In any event, this rationale is, like the rationale based on the expertise of the federal courts, simply an expression of Congress' belief that federal courts are more likely to interpret federal law correctly.

One might argue that this Court's appellate jurisdiction over state-court judgments in cases arising under federal law can be depended upon to correct erroneous state-court decisions and to insure that federal law is interpreted and applied uniformly. However, as any experienced observer of this Court can attest, "Supreme Court review of state courts, limited by docket pressures, narrow review of the facts, the debilitating possibilities of delay, and the necessity of deferring to adequate state grounds of decision, cannot do the whole job." CURRIE 160. Indeed, having served on this Court for 30 years, it is clear to me that, realistically, it cannot even come close to "doing the whole job" and that § 1331 is essential if federal rights are to be adequately protected.

the defendant argue in favor of a private cause as a way of strengthening its argument for federal jurisdiction?

2. Is anything left of *Smith*? If so, what? Does the majority in *Merrell Dow* hold that there is no federal jurisdiction if federal law does not create a right to sue?

(a) If this is the holding, hasn't the majority simply adopted Justice Holmes's test from *American Well Works?*

(b) If this is not the holding, under what circumstances might there be federal question jurisdiction without a federal cause of action?

3. Professor Redish criticizes the majority opinion in *Merrell Dow* for failing to give "a coherent, generalizable jurisdictional doctrine." Instead, he says, the majority's test "resembles more the free-standing, subjective, and individualized determination of Judge Wapner." Martin Redish, *Reassessing the Allocation of Judicial Business Between State and Federal Courts: Federal Jurisdiction and "The Martian Chronicles,"* 78 VA. L. REV. 1769, 1794 (1992). Do you agree? Why? For detailed criticism of *Merrell Dow*, see Patti Alleva, *Prerogative Lost: The Trouble With Statutory Federal Question Doctrine After* Merrell Dow, 52 OHIO ST. L.J. 1477 (1991).

4. *Merrell Dow* highlights the importance of footnotes. The debate over whether *Smith* and *Moore* can be reconciled is waged entirely in footnotes. In your opinion, which side won? See REDISH, FEDERAL JURISDICTION 99-105.

5. What does Justice Stevens seem to think is the primary reason for federal question jurisdiction? What does Justice Brennan seem to think?

6. Judge Henry Friendly concluded that "Justice Holmes' formula [from *American Well Works*] is more useful for inclusion than for the exclusion for which it was intended." T.B. Harms Co. v. Eliscu, 339 F.2d 823, 827 (2d Cir. 1964). Do you agree? If the FDCA had created a private right of action, would Justice Holmes's formula have dictated that there be federal question jurisdiction?

Interestingly, Justice Holmes's opinion in *American Well Works* did not overrule Shoshone Mining Co. v Rutter, 177 U.S. 505 (1912), in which a federal law empowered federal courts to hear disputes. involving mining claims on federal lands. The statute provided that local customs would decide such disputes. Although federal law clearly created the cause of action, the Supreme Court held that there was no federal question jurisdiction, since the case would involve merely the interpretation and application of local law. The Court has never overruled *Shoshone*, but "there are no recent decisions in which the Court has denied the existence of a federal question when a federal law created a cause of action." ERWIN CHEMERINSKY, FEDERAL JURISDICTION 269 (2d ed. 1994). For an older but helpful discussion of this area, see William Cohen, *The Broken Compass: The Requirement that a Case Arise "Directly" Under Federal Law*, 115 U. PA. L. REV. 890 (1967).

C. Federal Courts and Limited Subject Matter Jurisdiction

7. Suppose a State enacted this statute:

> Any person who suffers injury as a result of a violation of federal drug labelling requirements shall be entitled to sue therefor, and, if successful, to recover three times his or her actual damages, plus attorney's fees.

Would a claim brought solely on the basis of this statute invoke federal question jurisdiction? Should such a case come out differently from *Merrell Dow*?

8. How would finding jurisdiction in *Merrell Dow* have served the policies Justice Brennan sees at underlying federal question jurisdiction? Would they be served by allowing invocation of federal question jurisdiction based upon federal defenses (as opposed to claims)? How is Justice Brennan's desire for a broader invocation of federal question jurisdiction served by his rather extraordinary admission in footnote 6, that the Supreme Court "cannot even come close to 'doing the whole job?'"

9. The majority notes that federal question jurisdiction does not require that the federal law involved be novel. Neither does it need to be an outright, clear winner. Remember, the assessment here is simply whether a federal court has jurisdiction to hear the case. The court will not know whether plaintiff's legal and factual contentions prevail until it addresses the merits of the case. As long as federal law is part of a well-pleaded complaint and is not "plainly insubstantial," Bell v. Hood, 327 U.S. 678 (1946), the federal court can hear the case.

10. Section 1331 is known as the "general" federal question statute, an omnibus provision allowing a claim arising under any federal law to be brought in federal court. While we will address only §1331 in detail, note that there are many specialized federal question statutes allowing jurisdiction over claims arising under specific federal laws. For example, §1337 grants jurisdiction over federal antitrust cases; §1338 creates jurisdiction over patent and trademark cases; §1343 relates to civil rights claims. In American National Red Cross v. S.G., 505 U.S. 247 (1992), plaintiffs sued the Red Cross, alleging that they contracted AIDS from tainted blood provided by that organization. The Red Cross is a corporation chartered by the federal government. The statute creating it authorizes it "to sue and be sued in courts of law and equity, State and Federal, within the jurisdiction of the United States." 36 U.S.C. § 2. The Supreme Court concluded that this provision not only gives the Red Cross the capacity to litigate, but constitutes a grant of federal subject matter jurisdiction for all cases involving it. Thus, any state law claim by or against the Red Cross invokes federal jurisdiction. Such cases are brought directly under 36 U.S.C. § 2, and not the general federal question statute (28 U.S.C. §1331) we have addressed.

5. Supplemental Jurisdiction

A case that invokes federal subject matter jurisdiction — diversity of citizenship, alienage, or federal question — might include individual claims or issues that do not. For example, a plaintiff might have a federal question claim and a state law claim against a single defendant. If she cannot invoke diversity of citizenship, there is no independent basis of jurisdiction for the state law claim. Similarly, a defendant might have a state law cross-claim for indemnity against her co-defendant. Again, if she is not of diverse citizenship from her co-defendant (or if her claim does not exceed $50,000), there is no independent basis of jurisdiction for the cross-claim.

The federal courts have long recognized their power to hear such claims, as long as they are so closely related to the underlying dispute as to constitute part of the same "case or controversy" under Article III. Jurisdiction over such claims has been called "pendent" or "ancillary" jurisdiction, and has a rich, controversial history. In 1990, Congress codified the area, employing the generic rubric of "supplemental" jurisdiction.

Problems involving supplemental jurisdiction are common and often difficult. Because they arise when someone joins a claim that does not have an independent basis of subject matter jurisdiction such as diversity of citizenship, alienage, or federal question, They are best addressed in the context of the joinder rules. Thus, we will investigate this area in depth in Chapter 12.

6. Removal Jurisdiction

We encountered the concept of removal briefly with the *Merrell Dow* case. The removal statutes give the *defendant* some say in whether a case will proceed in federal or state court. They permit the defendant to have a case originally filed in state court removed to federal court. The case must be one over which the federal courts have subject matter jurisdiction. This procedure simply effects a transfer of the case from the state trial court to the federal trial court. It is not an appeal; you will recall from Chapter 1 that the federal courts have no general power to sit in judgment of what the state courts do. We deal only with the general removal provisions of the Judicial Code. We do not address specialized provisions for specific cases. See, e.g., 28 U.S.C. §§1442 (suit or prosecution against federal officer); 2679(d)(tort by federal employee).

Read 28 U.S.C. §§1441, 1446, and 1447. The defendant does not ask the federal court's permission to remove; she simply removes the case. See §1446(d). If removal is improper, the federal court *remands* the case to state court. It might do so because the defendant failed to follow the procedures for removal or because the federal court lacks subject matter jurisdiction.

Note that the defendant can remove only to the federal district court "for the district * * * embracing the place where such action is pending." For example, a case pending in the proper state court in St. Louis can be removed only to the Eastern District of Missouri, which encompasses St. Louis.* It could not be removed to the district court in Kansas City, which is in the Western District of Missouri.

A defendant might choose to remove a case to federal court for any of several reasons. Commonly, the defendant will remove a case upon the basis of diversity of citizenship for the same reasons many plaintiffs invoke that jurisdiction — to avoid possible bias of a local state court with its locally elected judge. When baseball great Pete Rose challenged his banishment from the game by suing the Commissioner of Baseball and others in state court in Cincinnati (Rose's hometown), the defendants thought it wise to remove the case to federal court. Rose v. Giamatti, 721 F. Supp. 906 (S.D. Ohio 1989). For an interesting discussion, see Note, *Maintaining the Home Field Advantage: Rose v. Federal Court*, 10 LOY. ENT. L.J. 695 (1990).

What about timing?

Noble v. Bradford Marine, Inc.
789 F. Supp. 395 (S.D. Fla. 1992)

JAMES C. PAINE, DISTRICT JUDGE.

This matter comes before the court *sua sponte*. After an extreme close-up review of the record and excellent authorities, the court enters the following order.

Hurling Chunks

On October 11, 1988, while berthed at the facilities of BRADFORD MARINE, INC. ("BRADFORD"), a fire spewed from the M/V Prime Time, a boat owned by PRIME TIME CHARTERS, INC. ("PRIME TIME"). The blaze hurled chunks of flaming debris to other vessels, destroying those owned by LYN C. NOBLE ("NOBLE") and ROBERT C. MUIR ("MUIR"). Thereafter, NOBEL and MUIR commenced, on June 7, 1989, and July 15, 1989, respectively, separate actions in the Circuit Court for the Seventeenth Judicial Circuit, in and for Broward County, Florida.

After NOBLE amended her Complaint so as to add PRIME TIME as a new party, that Defendant, on May 9, 1990, removed the proceeding to federal court, claiming original jurisdiction insofar as the Plaintiff's causes of action [invoked admiralty jurisdiction under 28 U.S.C. § 1333(1)]. PRIME TIME asserted that removal was timely because it came within thirty days of service of the Amended Complaint. Similarly, the MUIR action was also removed after that Plaintiff amended his Complaint so as to add PRIME TIME as a Defendant. * * *

---

* Thus, the venue provisions of 28 U.S.C. § 1391, which apply to cases filed by plaintiff in federal court, and which we will address in Chapter 5, do not apply to removed cases.

Upon BRADFORD's objection, this court, by Order dated June 28, 1990, remanded the NOBLE action to the state court for the failure of all Defendants to join in the removal. * * * Thereafter, PRIME TIME filed a Supplemental Notice of Removal, bearing both the NOBLE and MUIR captions, attempting to effect a phoenix-like ascent to federal court through the MUIR proceeding.

Like a Winged Monkey Flying Out of the Ashes...
A district court may, and always should, determine sua sponte whether its subject matter jurisdiction has been properly invoked. In addition, the removal statutes should be strictly construed, and "if at anytime before final judgment it appears that the district court lacks subject matter jurisdiction, the case shall be remanded." 28 U.S.C. § 1447(c).

The Notice of Removal of a civil action must be filed "within thirty days after the receipt by the defendant, through service or otherwise, of a copy of the initial pleading setting forth the claim for relief upon which such action or proceeding is based. . . ." 28 U.S.C. § 1446(b). If the case, as stated by the initial pleading, is not removable, removal may be effected within thirty days after receipt or otherwise, of a copy of an amended pleading from which it may be ascertained that the case is removable. Id. As time limitations in removal statutes are mandatory and strictly construed in accordance with Rule 6 of the Federal Rules of Civil Procedure, the failure to comply with time requirement of Section 1446(b) is a defect causing "improvident" removal.

Not!
The addition of a new Defendant in an Amended Complaint, however, does not start the time for removal anew when the original Complaint itself was removable. Unless the amendment sets forth a new basis of federal jurisdiction, subsequent events do not make a removable case "more removable" or "again removable." Thus, the failure of initial Defendants to remove during the original thirty day time period is deemed a waiver of the right of removal which is binding on subsequently added Defendants.

A Schwing and a Miss
Because of the court's admiralty jurisdiction, MUIR'S original Complaint, like his Amended Complaint, provided BRADFORD with a basis for removal. BRADFORD'S failure or waiver of the removal right, therefore, is binding on PRIME TIME, the subsequently added Defendant, since the Plaintiff's amendment did not change the nature of the "action as to constitute 'substantially a new suit begun that day.'"

As a result, PRIME TIME's removal, almost ten months after MUIR commenced suit, is untimely and is a defect deemed "way" improvident. For similar reasons, the court finds that removal of the NOBLE case, which had been remanded, was also untimely. In short, PRIME TIME's most bogus attempt at removal is "not worthy" and the Defendants must "party on" in state court.

In view of all the foregoing, it is hereby ORDERED and ADJUDGED that the above styled action is REMANDED to the Seventeenth Judicial Circuit in and for Broward County, Florida from which it was improvidently removed. * * *

C. Federal Courts and Limited Subject Matter Jurisdiction

NOTES AND QUESTIONS

1. Who was the original defendant in both cases? Why should its failure to remove either case foreclose Prime Time from doing so? Although § 1446(a) does not expressly address the question, it is clear that all defendants must agree to remove. If one refuses, the others simply cannot remove the case, Chicago, R.I. & P. Ry. Co. v. Martin, 178 U.S. 245 (1900), except that defendants not yet served with process in the state case need not join in the removal. Lewis v. Rego Co., 757 F.2d 66 (3d Cir. 1985). As *Noble* shows, this rule bars subsequently added defendants from removing a case if the original defendant failed to do so. See also Brown v. Demco, Inc., 792 F.2d 478 (5th Cir. 1986). Can you articulate a policy supporting this rule?

Note, however, 28 U.S.C. § 1441(c), which seems to allow an exception to this rule. Under that provision, a single defendant may remove an entire case, so long as there is a "separate and independent" federal question claim against her. The federal court can then either adjudicate the non-federal issues in the case or remand them to state court. The provision raises interesting possibilities and has captivated academics. It has not captivated litigants or judges, however, and is almost never successfully invoked, because of the difficulty in defining "separate and independent." See generally 1A MOORE'S FEDERAL PRACTICE ¶ 0.163 [4.-5].

2. Perry, a citizen of Missouri, sues Dale, a citizen of California, for $100,000 tort damages in an appropriate state court in St. Louis. Can Dale remove the case to federal court? When may Dale do so? What steps does Dale take to do so? What happens if, after removal, Perry seeks to add David as a defendant, and David is a citizen of Missouri?

3. Same facts as in Question 2, except the case is originally filed in the appropriate state court in Los Angeles. Why can Dale *not* remove this case to federal court? Does this rule make sense in light of the underlying theory of diversity of citizenship jurisdiction? Articulate how and why removal jurisdiction is narrower than original jurisdiction in this case.

4. Pat, a citizen of North Carolina, sues Defendant-1, a citizen of Oklahoma, and Defendant-2, a citizen of Wyoming, in an appropriate state court in Wyoming. Pat asserts breach of contract and seeks $500,000 damages. Obviously, the case is not removable, as we explored in Question 3. But suppose the claim against Defendant-2 is dismissed from the case two months after it was filed in state court. May Defendant-1 remove the case? Historically, courts concluded that diversity of citizenship must exist *both* when the defendant removes the case *and* when the plaintiff files it. Gibson v. Bruce, 108 U.S. 561 (1883). This rule would "prevent the defendant from acquiring a new domicile after commencement of the suit and then removing on the basis of diversity." WRIGHT, FEDERAL COURTS 231. But the reason for this limitation does not apply if the claim against the nondiverse

defendant is dropped, "since this is action over which defendant has no control." Id. Courts thus distinguished between (1) cases in which the plaintiff voluntarily dismissed the claim against the nondiverse defendant and (2) cases in which the court dismissed the claim against the nondiverse defendant. In the former, courts permitted the remaining diverse defendant to remove the case. In the latter, they did not, because the dismissal might be reversed on appeal.

In 1949, however, Congress amended § 1446(b) to add the provision permitting removal upon "receipt by the defendant * * * of an amended pleading, motion, order or other paper from which it may first be ascertained that the case is one which is or has become removable." Although this language appears to make no distinction as to why the claim against the nondiverse defendant is dismissed, most courts continue to make the historic distinction. See Poulos v. Naas Foods, Inc., 959 F.2d 69 (7th Cir. 1992). Thus, most courts will allow D-1 to remove the case only if Pat voluntarily dismissed the claim against D-2.

5. Why would your answer to Question 4 be different if the claim against Defendant-2 is dismissed from the case thirteen months after the case was filed in state court? Does this rule make any sense in light of the underlying theory of diversity of citizenship jurisdiction? After Defendant-2 is dismissed from the case, isn't Defendant-1 in exactly the situation for which diversity of citizenship jurisdiction was granted?

6. You will recall the case of *World-Wide Volkswagen* from the materials on personal jurisdiction. There, the Robinsons, citizens of New York, sued the manufacturer of their car, as well as the regional distributor and dealership from which they bought it, seeking damages for personal injuries. The Robinsons were injured when their car burst into flames after being struck by another vehicle. The Robinsons claimed that their injuries were the result of defective design and manufacture of the gas tank, as well as the manufacturer's failure to provide sufficient fire protection between the gas tank and the passenger compartment. Why, then, would they join the distributor and retailer?

The answer lies in their desire to litigate in state court. The accident occurred in Creek County, Oklahoma. Juries in that county had a reputation for being unusually generous to plaintiffs. If a case filed there were removed to federal court, the jury would be drawn from the entire federal district, a far wider geographic area, which could dilute the largesse of the Creek County residents. The case would be removable on alienage grounds if the Robinsons sued only the manufacturer. They joined the distributor and retailer (also New York citizens) to destroy diversity of citizenship jurisdiction and thus to ensure that the case could not be removed to federal court.

The defendants knew what was at stake. The distributor and retailer were unlikely to be held liable, and therefore were unwilling to spend much money contesting jurisdiction. The manufacturer bankrolled the litigation to the Supreme Court, where the focus was on the due process rights of the distributor and retailer. See Adams, supra, 72 NEB. L. REV. 1122.

It is clear, however, that a plaintiff cannot defeat removal by joining a nondiverse defendant against whom she has no bona fide claim. Such joinder is said to be "fraudulent," although that word is a term of art and does not impugn the interigity of plaintiff or her attorney. Nobers v. Crucible, Inc., 602 F. Supp. 703, 706 (W.D. Pa. 1985). When Pete Rose sued the Commissioner of Baseball in a Cincinnati state court, he added the Cincinnati Reds and Major League Baseball as defendants. Because they shared Ohio citizenship with Rose, it appeared that the defendants could not remove the case. The district court upheld removal, however, finding that joinder of the team and Major League Baseball was "fraudulent." They were merely nominal defendants. Rose's real dispute was with the Commissioner, who was of diverse citizenship. Rose v. Giamatti, 721 F. Supp. 906 (S.D. Ohio 1989).

7. Plaintiff, a citizen of Alaska, sues Defendant, a citizen of Maine, in an appropriate state court in Alaska, seeking breach of contract damages of *exactly* $50,000. Why can this case *not* be removed? Can the plaintiff effectively thwart removal by clever pleading of the amount in controversy? In most jurisdictions, the plaintiff's prayer for damages does not limit the amount she can recover if the case goes to trial. If a plaintiff thwarts removal by seeking exactly $50,000, should she have to waive any possibility of recovery over $50,000 in state court? See Kliebert v. Upjohn Co., 915 F.2d 142 (5th Cir. 1990) (remanding such a case to state court unless defendant could show to a legal certainty that plaintiff could recover more than the amount requested in the complaint). But see Dunn v. Pepsi-Cola Metropolitan Bottling Co., 850 F.Supp. 853 (N.D. Cal. 1994) (denying remand to state court; although plaintiff sought $49,900, allegations in the complaint showed that he could recover twice that amount).

8. If Plaintiff feels that a case should not have been removed because Defendant failed to satisfy the procedure for removal, what should Plaintiff do? When must Plaintiff do so? If the federal court agrees with Plaintiff, what will it do?

9. How would your answer to Question 8 be different if the federal court lacked subject matter jurisdiction over the case?

10. Plaintiff, a citizen of Florida, sues Defendant, a citizen of Arizona, in an appropriate state court in Arizona, seeking $25,000 damages for Defendant's alleged violation of Plaintiff's rights under the federal civil rights laws. Defendant can remove this case. Why? (Remember, do not become so focused on one form of jurisdiction that you overlook another.)

11. The Mottleys, citizens of Kentucky, sue Railroad, also a citizen of Kentucky, in an appropriate state court, seeking breach of contract damages. The Mottleys' complaint

CHAPTER 4 SUBJECT MATTER JURISDICTION

alleges that the Railroad's reliance on a federal statute as an excuse for not giving them their lifetime passes is ill-founded. Why can this case not be removed?

12. Plaintiff sues Defendant in an appropriate state court on a claim that could not be removed. Defendant files a counterclaim against Plaintiff, setting forth a claim that does invoke federal jurisdiction. Can Plaintiff remove the case? The courts say no, interpreting the grant of removal power to "defendants" to be limited to those persons sued by the plaintiff; thus, the plaintiff, even though a defendant on the counterclaim, is not a defendant for purposes of the removal statutes. Shamrock Oil & Gas Corp. v. Sheets, 313 U.S. 100 (1941).

13. Suppose Plaintiff sues Defendant in state court for violating federal securities laws. Such cases are in the exclusive jurisdiction of federal courts. Can Defendant remove the case even though the state court obviously lacked subject matter jurisdiction? Historically, courts viewed removal jurisdiction as "derivative." Thus, if the state court had no subject matter jurisdiction, as in federal securities cases, the defendant could not remove! Congress changed this result in 1986 by adding 28 U.S.C. § 1441(e).

14. Plaintiff, a citizen of Iowa, sues Defendant, a citizen of Minnesota, for violation of a federal statute, seeking damages of $100,000. This is a so-called "hybrid" case, meaning that it would invoke *either* diversity of citizenship or federal question jurisdiction. Thus, we are tempted to say that it is removable on either basis.

Let's complicate it a bit, though. Suppose the case is brought in Minnesota state court. Does the limitation on removal of diversity of citizenship cases (addressed above in Question 2) apply? Take a close look at 28 U.S.C. § 1441(b). Congress could have done a better job here, by making it clear whether one treats the hybrid case as a diversity case or as a federal question case.* Based on the policies underlying each type of jurisdiction, how should the hybrid case be treated?

---

* In Chapter 5, on venue, we will see that Congress did foresee the hybrid case, making one provision for cases in which jurisdiction is based "solely" on diversity of citizenship and another for "all other cases."

CHAPTER 5

VENUE

A. Introduction and Integration

As you will recall from Chapters 2 and 4, a court cannot properly hear a case unless it has both personal and subject matter jurisdiction. In this chapter we address a third requirement — venue.

Subject matter jurisdiction determines what categories of cases a court *system* (e.g., the federal courts) has authority to decide. Likewise, personal jurisdiction, at least as applied to states, determines whether a court *system* has power over a defendant. Venue determines where *within* a court system a case can be brought. It is primarily a matter of convenience.

Venue is largely defined by statute. All states have venue statutes or rules which determine where within the state cases are to be filed. Similarly, there are federal venue statutes that control the location of cases within the federal court system. There is no federal constitutional right to venue in a particular place. Neirbo Co. v. Bethlehem Shipbuilding Corp., 308 U.S. 165 (1939).

If subject matter jurisdiction, personal jurisdiction, and venue are all proper in a court, then that court has authority to hear the case. However, even where all three of these requirements are met, a case may have little connection with the forum. (Remember *Keeton v. Hustler Magazine, Inc.*, Chapter 2), and *Merrell Dow Pharmaceuticals v. Thompson,* Chapter 4) In such a case, the court may invoke the doctrine of forum non conveniens and decline as a matter of discretion to hear the case. Forum non conveniens is addressed at the end of the chapter.

B. Local and Transitory Actions

One abiding distinction in venue rules is that between "local" and "transitory" actions. Basically, local actions involve land and historically include three major categories of disputes:

(1) in rem or quasi-in-rem cases, in which real property is the basis of jurisdiction;
(2) cases in which the plaintiff seeks a remedy in or to realty, such as a claim for quiet title, ejectment, foreclosure of a mortgage, enforcement of removal of a lien; and
(3) claims for damages for injury to land, such as trespass.

Most state venue statutes provide that in cases such as these, venue must be laid where the land is located. Even absent a statute, most courts invoke a common law local action rule, concluding that the distinction is so well rooted in history that "no one has ever supposed laws which prescribed generally where one should be sued, included such suits as were local in their character." Casey v. Adams, 102 U.S. 66, 67-68 (1880). See generally 1A MOORE'S FEDERAL PRACTICE ¶ 0.342[2].

The general federal venue statute does not include an explicit local action rule. Nonetheless, the courts have implied such a limitation. The most celebrated venue case of all time involved a claim against Thomas Jefferson, in which the plaintiff sought damages against the former President for trespass to the plaintiff's land in Louisiana. Plaintiff sued Jefferson in Virginia because in that pre-*International Shoe* era, he could not get personal jurisdiction in Louisiana. Chief Justice Marshall, sitting at Circuit Court, dismissed the case, and held that it was a local action in which venue must be laid in Louisiana. Livingston v. Jefferson, 15 Fed. Cas. 660 (C.C.D. Va. 1811). Marshall noted that it would be sensible to limit the local action rule to in rem cases. Nonetheless, he reluctantly (Marshall was no friend of Jefferson's) concluded that precedent established that in personam actions for damages to realty were local actions. For a fascinating account of the case and its famous participants, see Ronan Degnan, Livingston v. Jefferson — *A Freestanding Footnote*, 75 CAL. L. REV. 115 (1987).

Any case that is not a local action is a transitory action and the vast majority of cases are transitory. As to these, the venue statutes of the state and for federal court prescribe appropriate places for trial. Before turning to the federal venue provisions, we will consider a state venue statute.

C. State Venue Provisions

Personal jurisdiction determines whether the state as a whole has power over the defendant. Venue restrictions identify where within the state — in which county, parish or other subdivision — cases are to be adjudicated. Most states provide a general rule for civil actions and also set out special venue rules for particular types of cases (usually including local actions). The following Maryland venue statute is typical.

C. State Venue Provisions

ANNOTATED CODE OF MARYLAND
Court and Judicial Proceedings (1989)
Subtitle 2. Venue

§ 6-201. General rule

(a) *Civil actions.* — Subject to the provisions of §§ 6-202 and 6-203 and unless otherwise provided by law, a civil action shall be brought in a county where the defendant resides, carries on a regular business, is employed, or habitually engages in a vocation. In addition, a corporation also may be sued where it maintains its principal offices in the State.

(b) *Multiple defendants.* — If there is more than one defendant, and there is no single venue applicable to all defendants, under subsection (a), all may be sued in a county in which any one of them could be sued, or in the county where the cause of action arose.

§ 6-202. Additional Venue Permitted

In addition to the venue provided in § 6-201 or § 6-203, the following actions may be brought in the indicated county:

(1) Divorce — Where the plaintiff resides;

(2) Annulment — Where the plaintiff resides or where the marriage ceremony was performed;

(3) Action against a corporation which has no principal place of business in the State — Where the plaintiff resides;

(4) Replevin or detinue — Where the property sought to be recovered is located;

(5) Action relating to custody, guardianship, maintenance, or support of a child — Where the father, alleged father, or mother of the child resides, or where the child resides;

(6) Suit on a bond against a corporate surety — Where the bond is filed, or where the contract is to be performed;

(7) Action for possession of real property — Where a portion of the land upon which the action is based is located;

(8) Tort action based on negligence — Where the cause of action arose;

(9) Attachment on original process — Where the property is located or where the garnishee resides;

(10) Nondelivery or injury of goods against master or captain of a vessel — Where the goods are received on board the vessel or where delivery is to be made under the contract;

(11) Action for damages against a nonresident individual — Any county in the State;

(12) Action against a person who absconds from a county or leaves the State before the statute of limitations has run — Where the defendant is found;

(13) In a local action in which the defendant cannot be found in the county where the subject matter of the action is located — In any county in which the venue is proper under § 6-201.

§ 6-203. Exceptions to General Rule

(a) *In general.* — The general rule of § 6-201 does not apply to actions enumerated in this section.

(b) *Interest in land.* — The venue of the following actions is in the county where all or any portion of the subject matter of the action is located:

(1) Partition of real estate;
(2) Enforcement of a charge or lien on land;
(3) Eminent domain;
(4) Trespass to land;
(5) Waste.

(c) *Property in more than one county.* — If the property lies in more than one county, the court in which proceedings are first brought has jurisdiction over the entire property.

(d) *Injury to livestock by railroad.* — The venue of an action to recover damages against a railroad company for injury to livestock is the county where the injury occurred.

(e) *Adoption.* — The venue for a proceeding for adoption of a person who is physically within the State or subject to the jurisdiction of an equity court is in a county in which:

(1) The petitioner is domiciled;
(2) The petitioner has resided for at least 90 days next preceding the filing of the petition;
(3) A licensed child placement agency having legal or physical custody of the person to be adopted is located;
(4) The person to be adopted is domiciled, if he is related to the petitioner by blood or marriage or is an adult; or
(5) An equity court has continuing jurisdiction over the custody of the person to be adopted.

NOTES AND QUESTIONS

1. Note the cases in which Maryland allows venue to be laid where the *plaintiff* resides. Why might such a provision be appropriate in those types of cases?

2. Which provision embodies Maryland's local action rule? Note that it, like most statutory provisions for local actions, allows venue to be laid in the political subdivision in which "any portion" of the land lies.

3. Section 6-201(b) is a typical provision regarding multiple defendants. Suppose plaintiff sues D-1, who resides in County A and D-2, who resides in County B. She lay venue in County A. Suppose the claim against D-1 is dismissed before trial. Should the court in County A proceed with the case, adjudicating the claim against D-2? In many jurisdictions, the case would proceed. In some, the court would transfer to County B upon motion by D-2.

The most bizarre result is that dictated in Georgia. There, joint tortfeasors residing in different counties may be sued in the county in which either defendant resides. However, to maintain such a suit against the non-resident of the forum county, the suit against the resident defendant must be alleged and *proved*. Thus, in the above hypothetical, if D-1 wins at trial and D-2 loses, the judgment against D-2 is of no effect. Instead, the case must be transferred to D-2's home county and the entire case retried. See Stroud v. Doolittle, 213 Ga. 32, 96 S.E.2d 876, 880 (Ga. 1957). Thus, after the taxpayers and the parties have paid for full litigation in County A, the case must be started afresh against D-2 in County B!

D. Venue in Federal Court

1. The Basic Rules

In the federal system, it is somewhat harder to conceptualize the relationships between venue and personal jurisdiction. You will recall that absent a federal statute or rule extending service of process, a federal court has personal jurisdiction over an out-of-state defendant only if the state in which that federal court sits would have personal jurisdiction. Thus, state personal jurisdiction doctrine limits the places in which a defendant can be sued within the federal system. In addition, Congress has enacted venue statutes which specify where within the federal system particular types of cases must be filed. The reason for this overlap is primarily historical. Venue and personal jurisdiction doctrines developed largely independently and without much reference to each other. The result is that both personal jurisdiction and venue restrictions exist side by side in the federal courts, and both must be met.

The general venue statute governing federal civil practice is 28 U.S.C. §1391. Note that Congress qualified the provisions of §1391(a) and (b) with the phrase "except as otherwise provided by law." Just as the Maryland statute above had exceptions to its general provisions, federal law provides particular venue provisions for specialized actions. For example, 12 U.S.C. § 94 governs venue for cases against national banks; 28 U.S.C. §1396 provides the venue choices for cases involving collection of federal taxes; and 28 U.S.C. §1397 addresses venue under the federal interpleader act. Although there are other special venue provisions, see generally 1A MOORE'S FEDERAL PRACTICE ¶ 0.344, venue in most cases in federal court is governed by the general provisions of §1391.

That statute has a long history dating back to the first Judiciary Act of 1789. It provided that a suit could be brought in the district where the defendant "is an inhabitant, or in which he shall be found." In 1887, as part of a general narrowing of access to the federal courts, Congress eliminated the "or could be found" clause. At the same time an inexplicable anomaly was introduced. The statute differentiated between diversity of citizenship

CHAPTER 5 VENUE

cases and all other cases (such as federal question cases) and provided broader venue choices in diversity cases. In diversity cases, venue was proper where all plaintiffs or all defendants resided, whereas in other cases it was proper only where all defendants resided. The anomaly persisted for over 100 years, though a 1990 revision of the statue sought to eliminate it.

After 1887, the statute remained largely unchanged until 1966. Before 1966, there was no provision allowing plaintiffs to sue multiple defendants in the district in which any defendant resided. A 1966 amendment attempted to fill this "gap" in the statute by making venue proper in the district "where the claim arose." This change created its own problems. The Court interpreted "where the claim arose" to mean there was one and only one place where each claim arose. In more complex cases there was frequently uncertainty and litigation over where that one place was. See Leroy v. Great Western United Corp., 443 U.S. 173 (1979). The 1990 revision eliminated the need for the sometimes metaphysical debate (similar to those we saw with regard to long-arm statutes) about where a tort occurs or whether a contract is breached at the place it was made or where it was to have been performed. The plaintiff need not identify the district in which the claim arose; where a part of the claim arose suffices.

Read §1391 with care. Although the statute includes a detailed definition of residence for a corporate defendant, see §1391(c), it contains no such definition for individual defendants. One could argue that since venue primarily concerns convenience, venue should be proper wherever a defendant has a significant actual residence, regardless of domicile. Nonetheless, courts have generally assumed that "resides" as applies to individuals is synonymous with domicile. See 15 WRIGHT & MILLER, FEDERAL PRACTICE & PROCEDURE at 33-37. Notice also the special treatment of alien defendants. See §1391(d). This section has been applied to both alien individuals and alien corporations.

Finally, you will observe that the statute continues to deal separately with cases in which subject matter jurisdiction is based solely on diversity and all other cases, but the only actual difference in treatment for these two categories occurs in subparts (3). Compare (a)(3) with (b)(3). The difference between the two subparts used to be even greater. The 1990 version of (a)(3) did not include the phrase "if there is no district in which the action may otherwise be brought." As a result, (a)(3) appeared to make (a)(1) and (a)(2) superfluous because so long as there was personal jurisdiction, venue would be proper under (a)(3) without the need to meet the more limited provisions of (a)(1) and (a)(2). To make sense of the statute, commentators suggested that (a)(3) was available only where there were multiple defendants. See 15 WRIGHT & MILLER, FEDERAL PRACTICE & PROCEDURE § 3802.1; John Oakley, *Recent Statutory Changes in the Law of Federal Jurisdiction and Venue: The Judicial Improvements Acts of 1988 and 1990*, 24 U.C. DAVIS L. REV.

D. Venue in Federal Court

735, 780-81 (1991). Several courts adopted this interpretation. See United States Fidelity & Guaranty Co. v. Mayberry, 789 F.Supp. 901, 904 (E.D. Tenn. 1992); Harrison Conference Services, Inc. v. Dolce Conference Services, Inc., 768 F.Supp. 405, 407-08 (E.D. N.Y. 1991). In 1992, Congress again amended §1391, this time adding the language at the end of (a)(3) which makes that provisio0n a fall-back provision. The House and Senate Reports on this change do not discuss whether (a)(3) should continue to be interpreted to apply only in cases involving multiple defendants. See H.R. Rep. No. 102-1006 (1992); Sen. Rep. No. 102-342 (1992).

While state statutes and rules place venue in various political subdivisions of the state, federal venue keys into federal districts. Congress has divided the country into 91 federal districts, plus ones for Puerto Rico, and other possessions such as Guam and the Virgin Islands. With one inconsequential exception (the district of Wyoming includes parts of Yellowstone National Park that are in Idaho and Montana), no federal district crosses state lines. Not all states have the same number of federal districts. California, New York, and Texas each have four districts. Other states have three or two districts and many states comprise a single federal district each.

Sometimes Congress divides a district into separate "divisions." For example, Minnesota consists of a single federal district. It is divided, however, into six divisions, with a statute spelling out which counties are in each division and where the court shall be held. 28 U.S.C. §103. (There is such a statute for each state.)

Read §1391 before addressing the following.

NOTES AND QUESTIONS

1. Paula is in an auto accident with Doug. Paula is a Massachusetts citizen. Doug is a New York citizen, with his home in the Eastern District of New York. The accident occurred in Maine. Assume that Paula's claim exceeds $50,000.
   (a) Paula wants to sue Doug in federal court. Where would venue be proper?
   (b) Paula sues Doug in federal court in Vermont, where Doug resides while attending college in Vermont. Is venue proper in Vermont? (There is only one federal district in Vermont.)
   (c) Assume that Doug is a citizen of France. Where would venue be proper? Would it matter if he were admitted for permanent residence? See §1332(a).
   (d) Paula sues Doug in federal court in Massachusetts, serving him while he is in Massachusetts doing business. Is venue proper in Massachusetts? (There is only one federal district in Massachusetts.)

2. Suppose Paula decides to sue Car Inc., the manufacturer of her car, alleging defective design and manufacture of the vehicle. Car Inc. is incorporated in Delaware with its headquarters and a factory in the Western District of Michigan. It also has factories in the Western District of Tennessee and the Northern District of Georgia. Assume Paula's claim exceeds $50,000.

   (a) In Paula v. Car Inc., where is venue proper?
   (b) Assume that Car Inc. did not acquire the factory in Tennessee until after the accident between Paula and Doug. In Paula v. Car Inc. would venue be proper in the Western District of Tennessee?
   (c) In addition to the facts described above, Car Inc. is licensed to do business in New York and has an agent for service of process there. The agent is located in the Western District of New York. Currently, Car Inc. has no operations in New York. In Paula v. Car Inc. would venue be proper in the Western District of New York? The Eastern District of New York?
   (d) Assume the facts are as described in 2(c). Paula sues Doug and Car Inc. Would venue be proper in the Western District of Michigan? The Eastern District of New York? The Western District of New York? The Western District of Tennessee?

3. Assume in Notes 1 and 2 above that there was federal question jurisdiction. Would this change any of your answers?

4. Compare §1391(a)(1) and §1392. Does §1392 add anything?

5. Section 1392(b) is the only federal venue provision referring to local actions. Note that this provision only addresses local actions in which the property is located in two districts of the same state.

6. Under the current version of §1391, what is the significance of the different phrasing of (a)(3) and (b)(3)? Under (a)(3) would venue be proper in a place where the sole basis for jurisdiction is in-state service (as in *Burnham*)? In cases of transient jurisdiction, is a defendant "subject to personal jurisdiction *at the time the action is commenced*?"

7. Under (b)(3) does "found" include the situation in which the defendant is not physically present in the place but is subject to long-arm personal jurisdiction? There is similar language in other specialized venue statutes and the cases interpreting those statutes are not entirely consistent. See, e.g., 15 WRIGHT & MILLER, FEDERAL PRACTICE & PROCEDURE §3819 n.11.

8. Can you describe a situation in which (a)(3) would be the basis for venue?

9. In what circumstances will there be personal jurisdiction but no venue? Why not simply make venue proper wherever there is personal jurisdiction? Isn't that what § 1391 now in essence provides if the defendant is a corporation?

D. Venue in Federal Court

10. Remember that cases removed from state to federal court have their own venue provision. Such cases can only be removed to the federal court "embracing the place where such action is pending." 28 U.S.C. §1441(a). Thus, the provisions of §1391 are irrelevant to removed cases.

11. Recall from subject matter jurisdiction that some cases can be supported by more than one basis of federal jurisdiction. For example, a New York citizen may assert a federal question claim against a Texas citizen, seeking more than $50,000. Such a case could invoke either diversity of citizenship or federal question jurisdiction, and is known as a "hybrid case." Congress foresaw this possibility and provided for it. Read §1391(a). How does it make clear that hybrid cases are to be treated as federal question (not diversity) cases?

Bates v. C & S Adjusters, Inc.
980 F.2d 865 (2d Cir. 1992)

NEWMAN, CIRCUIT JUDGE.

This appeal concerns venue in an action brought under the Fair Debt Collection Practices Act, 15 U.S.C. §§1692-1692o (1988). Specifically, the issue is whether venue exists in a district in which the debtor resides and to which a bill collector's demand for payment was forwarded. The issue arises on an appeal by Phillip E. Bates from the May 21, 1992, judgment of the District Court for the Western District of New York (William M. Skretny, Judge), dismissing his complaint because of improper venue. We conclude that venue was proper under 28 U.S.C.A. § 1391(b)(2) (West Supp. 1992) and therefore reverse and remand.

BACKGROUND

Bates commenced this action in the Western District of New York upon receipt of a collection notice from C & S Adjusters, Inc. ("C & S"). Bates alleged violations of the Fair Debt Collection Practices Act, and demanded statutory damages, costs, and attorney's fees. The facts relevant to venue are not in dispute. Bates incurred the debt in question while he was a resident of the Western District of Pennsylvania. The creditor, a corporation with its principal place of business in that District, referred the account to C & S, a local collection agency which transacts no regular business in New York. Bates had meanwhile moved to the Western District of New York. When C & S mailed a collection notice to Bates at his Pennsylvania address, the Postal Service forwarded the notice to Bates' new address in New York.

In its answer, C & S asserted two affirmative defenses and also counterclaimed for costs, alleging that the action was instituted in bad faith and for purposes of harassment. C & S subsequently filed a motion to dismiss for improper venue, which the District Court granted.

229

DISCUSSION

1. Venue and the 1990 amendments to 28 U.S.C. § 1391(b)

Bates concedes that the only plausible venue provision for this action is 28 U.S.C.A. § 1391(b)(2), which allows an action to be brought in "a judicial district in which a substantial part of the events or omissions giving rise to the claim occurred." Prior to 1990, section 1391 allowed for venue in "the judicial district ... in which the claim arose." 28 U.S.C. § 1391(b) (1988). This case represents our first opportunity to consider the significance of the 1990 amendments.

Prior to 1966, venue was proper in federal question cases, absent a special venue statue, only in the defendant's state of citizenship. If a plaintiff sought to sue multiple defendants who were citizens of different states, there might be no district where the entire action could be brought. Congress closed this "venue gap" by adding a provision allowing suit in the district "in which the claim arose." This phrase gave rise to variety of conflicting interpretations. Some courts thought it meant that there could be only one district; others believed there could be several. Different tests developed, with courts looking for "substantial contacts," the "weight of contacts," the place of injury or performance, or even to the boundaries of personal jurisdiction under state law. District courts within the second Circuit used at least three of these approaches.

The Supreme Court gave detailed attention to section 1391(b) in Leroy v. Great Western United Corp., 443 U.S. 173 (1979). The specific holding of *Leroy* was that Great Western, a Texas corporation, which had attempted to take over an Idaho corporation, could not bring suit in Texas against Idaho officials who sought to enforce a state anti-takeover law. Although the effect of the Idaho officials' action might be felt in Texas, the Court rejected this factor as a basis for venue, since it would allow the Idaho officials to be sued anywhere a shareholder of the target corporation could allege that he wanted to accept Great Western's tender offer. The Court made several further observations: (1) the purpose of the 1966 statute was to close venue gaps and should not be read more broadly than necessary to close those gaps, (2) the general purpose of the venue statute was to protect defendants against an unfair or inconvenient trial location, (3) location of evidence and witnesses was a relevant factor, (4) familiarity of the Idaho federal judges with the Idaho anti-takeover statute was a relevant factor, (5) plaintiff's convenience was not a relevant factor, and (6) in only rare cases should there be more than one district in which a claim can be said to arise.

Subsequent to *Leroy* and prior to the 1990 amendment to section 1391(b), most courts have applied at least a form of the "weight of contacts" test. Courts continued to have difficulty in determining whether more than one district could be proper.

Against this background, we understand Congress' 1990 amendment to be at most a marginal expansion of the venue provision. The House Report indicates that the new language was first proposed by the American Law Institute in a 1969 Study, and observes:

> The great advantage of referring to the place where things happened ... is that it avoids the litigation breeding phrase "in which the claim arose." It also avoids the problem created by the frequent cases in which substantial parts of the underlying events have occurred in several districts.

H.R. Rep. No. 734, 101st Cong., 2d Sess. 23. Thus it seems clear that *Leroy*'s strong admonition against recognizing multiple venues has been disapproved. Many of the factors in *Leroy* — for instance, the convenience of defendants and the location of evidence and witnesses — are most useful in distinguishing between two or more plausible venues. Since the new statute does not, as a general matter, require the District Court to determine the best venue, these factors will be of less significance. Apart from this point, however, *Leroy* and other precedents remain important sources of guidance.

2. Fair Debt Collection Practices Act

Under the version of the venue statute in force from 1966 to 1990, at least three District Courts held that venue was proper under the Fair Debt Collection Practices Act in the plaintiff's home district if a collection agency had mailed a collection notice to an address in that district or placed a phone call to a number in that district. None of these cases involved the unusual fact, present in this case, that the defendant did not deliberately direct a communication to the plaintiff's district.

We conclude, however, that this difference is inconsequential, at least under the current venue statute. The statutory standard for venue focuses not on whether a defendant has made a deliberate contact — a factor relevant in the analysis of personal jurisdiction[1] — but on the location where events occurred. Under the new version of section 1391(b)(2), we must determine only whether a "substantial part of the events ... giving rise to the claim" occurred in the Western District of New York.

In adopting this statute, Congress was concerned about the harmful effect of abusive debt practices on consumers. See 15 U.S.C. § 1692(a) ("Abusive debt collection practices contribute to the number of personal bankruptcies, to marital instability, to the loss of jobs, and to invasions of individual privacy."). This harm does not occur until receipt of the collection notice. Indeed, if the notice were lost in the mail, it is unlikely that a violation of the Act would have occurred. Moreover, a debt collection agency sends its dunning letters so that they will be received. Forwarding such letters to the district to which a debtor has moved is an important step in the collection process. If the bill collector prefers not to be challenged for its collection practices outside the district of a debtor's original residence, the envelope can be marked "do not forward." We conclude that receipt of a collection notice is a substantial part of the events giving rise to a claim under the Fair Debt Collection Practices Act.

The relevant factors identified in *Leroy* add support to our conclusion. Although "bona fide error" can be a defense to liability under the Act, 15 U.S.C. § 1692k(c), the alleged violations of the Act turn largely not on the collection agency's intent, but on the content of the collection notice. The most relevant evidence — the collection notice — is located in the Western District of New York. Because the collection agency appears not to have marked the notice with instructions not to forward, and has not objected to the assertion of personal jurisdiction, trial in the Western District of New York would not be unfair.

---

[1] C&S has waived whatever claim it might have had that the District Court lacked personal jurisdiction over it. Waiver resulted from C&S's failure to allege lack of personal jurisdiction in its answer or motion to dismiss. See Fed. R. Civ. P. 12(b)(2), (h).

Conclusion

The judgment of the District Court is reversed, and the matter is remanded for further proceedings consistent with this decision.

NOTES AND QUESTIONS

1. The Fair Debt Collection Practices Act, 15 U.S.C. §1692 et seq., regulates communications between debt collectors and consumers, prohibiting harassment, abuse and false representations made by debt collectors. The statute permits suits for damages against debt collectors who violate the Act.

2. Suppose Mr. Bates, in a hurry to leave on a trip, had taken his unopened mail with him. He later opened the offending letter in California. Would venue be proper in California?

3. In the *Leroy* case (discussed in *Bates*), the Supreme Court rejected an economic effects test under which venue would be proper where the plaintiff's business was economically injured. In rejecting this test, the Court held that "such a reading of §1391(b) is inconsistent with the underlying purpose of the provision, for it would leave the venue decision entirely in the hands of plaintiffs, rather than making it primarily a matter of convenience of litigants and witnesses." 443 U.S. at 186-87. Does *Bates* revive the approach rejected in *Leroy*?

4. Notice that in *Bates*, the defendant waived its objection to personal jurisdiction. Does this make venue proper in New York under §1391(b)(1) and (c)?

5. Compare *Bates* with Magic Toyota, Inc. v. Southeast Toyota Distributors, Inc., 784 F. Supp. 306 (D.S.C. 1992). In *Magic Toyota*, the plaintiff purchased a South Carolina Toyota dealership from defendant. According to plaintiff, defendant had promised plaintiff that he would be permitted to relocate the dealership to another city in South Carolina, but defendant breached that promise. Plaintiff further alleged that when he refused to participate in various illegal activities, defendant set out to destroy plaintiff's business. Plaintiff brought suit in federal court in South Carolina, alleging violations of the Racketeering Influenced and Corrupt Organization Act (RICO), as well as state claims for breach of contract, fraud and violation of the Automobile Dealers Day in Court Act. The district court dismissed for improper venue, finding that §1391(b)(2) was not met because the alleged fraudulent inducement to purchase the South Carolina dealership happened during negotiations that occurred in Florida and that the other activities in support of defendants' supposed illegal scheme also occurred outside South Carolina.

Why isn't it sufficient for §1391(b)(2) that both the alleged fraudulent inducement and the attempt to destroy plaintiff's business were directed at the South Carolina dealership? The court noted that §1391(b)(2) focuses not on "contacts" but "events." Id. at 317. Does this wording in the statute justify the holding in the case?

E. Change of Venue

1. Transfer of Civil Cases in State Courts

All states have provisions permitting the transfer of civil cases from one county (or relevant political subdivision) to another. The reasons for ordering transfer differ and may depend on whether venue in the original court is proper. Most states permit a defendant to seek transfer if she is unlikely to get a fair trial where the case is filed. Florida has an unusual provision allowing a defendant to seek transfer on grounds that she "is so odious to the inhabitants of the county" that she could not receive a fair trial. FLA. STAT. § 47.101(1)(b). In some states, transfer can be ordered only on motion; in others, it can be ordered sua sponte.

It is important to note that such transfers are *within* the state. Because the individual states are separate political sovereigns, no state can unilaterally transfer a case from one of its courts to a court in a different state. Recently, the American Law Institute and the Commissioners on Uniform State Laws recommended legislation that would permit transfer among states, but such legislation has not yet been enacted. See AMERICAN LAW INSTITUTE, COMPLEX LITIGATION: STATUTORY RECOMMENDATIONS AND ANALYSIS WITH REPORTER'S STUDY: A MODEL SYSTEM FOR STATE-TO-STATE TRANSFER AND CONSOLIDATION (1994).

A state court that concludes the action before it ought to be litigated in another state cannot transfer the case, but it has the option to dismiss the case under the doctrine of "forum non conveniens." After the dismissal, the plaintiff can file a new action in the other state. Forum non conveniens is addressed in Section F, below.

2. Transfer of Civil Actions in Federal Court

The federal government is not restricted by state lines. 28 U.S.C. §§1404(a) and 1406(a) permit transfer of civil actions from one federal district court to another. The fact that the latter court sits in another state is irrelevant; this is not a transfer from one sovereign to another, but from one federal court to another federal court. Recall Justice Brennan's statement in *Burger King*, supra at 70, that the inconvenience of the Florida forum for the

Michigan defendants might be ameliorated by a change of venue. Such a transfer was conceivable in that case only because it was brought in federal court. Had the case been in state court in Florida, no transfer to Michigan would have been possible. In such situations, it is not uncommon for a state court defendant to remove the case to federal court (assuming there is subject matter jurisdiction) and then seek transfer to federal court in another state.

a. Where Can Cases Be Transferred?

Section 1404(a) permits transfer to any district where the suit "might have been brought." Section 1406(a) contains similar language. In Hoffman v. Blaski, 363 U.S. 335 (1960), the Supreme Court interpreted this language to mean that cases can be transferred only to a district in which venue and personal jurisdiction would be proper. Consider the following situation: a defendant requests transfer to a district in which, absent the defendant's consent, venue or personal jurisdiction would not be proper. The defendant, however, consents to venue and personal jurisdiction in that location. Couldn't one argue that since the defendant has consented to litigation in a particular location that it is now a place where the case "might have been brought?"

In *Hoffman*, the Supreme Court rejected this argument, explaining:

> We do not think the § 1404(a) phrase "where it might have been brought" can be interpreted to mean, as petitioners' theory would require, "where it may now be rebrought, with defendants' consent." * * *
>
> * * *
>
> The thesis urged by petitioners would not only do violence to the plain words of § 1404(a), but would also inject gross discrimination. That thesis, if adopted, would empower a District Court, upon a finding of convenience, to transfer an action to any district desired by the *defendants* and in which they were willing to waive their statutory defenses as to venue and jurisdiction over their persons, regardless of the fact that such transferee district was not one in which the action "might have been brought" by the plaintiff. Conversely, that thesis would not permit the court, upon motion of the *plaintiffs* and a like showing of convenience, to transfer the action to the same district, without the consent and waiver of venue and personal jurisdiction defenses by the defendants. Nothing in § 1404(a), or in its legislative history, suggests such a unilateral objective and we should not, under the guise of interpretation, ascribe to Congress any such discriminatory purpose.

Id. at 342-44 (emphasis original). Although *Hoffman* involved a transfer under §1404, note that the language in §1404 concerning the transferee court is similar to that in §1406. There is no question that the reasoning of *Hoffman* applies to transfers under §1406. Manley v. Engram, 755 F.2d 1463 (11th Cir. 1985).

b. *Goldlawr* Transfers

Section 1406(a) permits transfer of cases filed in an improper venue. Suppose, however, that the case is filed in a district in which not only venue is improper, but which also lacks personal jurisdiction. Can this case be transferred? Some argued that if the court lacked jurisdiction, it also lacked the authority to transfer. In Goldlawr, Inc. v. Heiman, 369 U.S. 463 (1962), the Supreme Court held otherwise. It concluded that allowing the transfer of such cases was consistent with the objective of the statute of "removing whatever obstacles may impede an expeditious and orderly adjudication of cases and controversies on their merits." Id. at 466-67.

c. Forum Selection Clauses

Some contracts include a "forum selection clause" specifying where litigation concerning the contract is to occur. Where such a clause exists, are federal courts required to honor the clause in making a transfer determination? In Stewart Organization, Inc. v. Ricoh Corp., 487 U.S. 22 (1988), the Supreme Court held that although such an agreement will be "a significant factor that figures centrally in the district court's calculus," it is not entitled to dispositive weight in deciding whether to transfer a case. Id. at 29.

Several commentators have criticized *Stewart*. Among other things, some argue that the existence of a forum selection clause is irrelevant to §1404 and that the Court's use of it as a factor in transfer federalizes the issue of whether forum selection clauses are enforceable. That issue, they assert, should be governed by state law. See, e.g., Richard Freer, Erie's *Mid-Life Crisis*, 63 TULANE L. REV. 1087 (1989); Linda Mullenix, *Another Choice of Forum, Another Choice of Law: Consensual Adjudicatory Procedure in Federal Court*, 57 FORDHAM L. REV. 291 (1988). See Chapter 7 at 303.

d. Choice of Law

In connection with personal jurisdiction, we noted that in many situations a court might apply any one of several states' laws to a single transaction or occurrence. Suppose two citizens of one state travel to another state and enter into an oral contract. Suppose further that the law of their home state would enforce this contract, but the law of the place of making would require the contract to be in writing. Which State's law should govern the validity of the contract? Each state has its own choice of law doctrine or rules to decide which state's law to apply. The choice of law doctrines vary among the states and, therefore, different courts may apply different law when confronted with the same situation.

Given that choice of law rules vary, the logical next question is whose choice of law rules apply? The answer is easy when litigation occurs in state court, the forum applies its choice of law rules. When litigation occurs in federal court, the matter becomes more complex. What law applies in federal court is a difficult question to which we devote an entire Chapter. See Chapter 7. Briefly stated, on matters of substantive law (as opposed to matters of procedure), where there is no federal statute on point, a federal court ordinarily applies state law. Therefore, in a contract case in federal court, the question of whether a contract has to be in writing is a matter as to which federal courts would apply state law. But suppose that some states would require that the contract be in writing, but others would not. Which state's law should the federal court apply? In Klaxon v. Stentor Elec. Mfr. Co., 313 U.S. 487 (1941), the Court held that a federal court should apply the choice of law rules of the state in which it sits. Therefore, in our contract hypothetical, a federal court would apply whichever state's law the state in which it sits would have applied.

Because choice of law rules vary from state to state, one next must determine which state's rules govern once a federal case is transferred. Should the federal court apply the law of the transferee district or the law of the state of the transferor district? In Van Dusen v. Barrack, 376 U.S. 612 (1964), the Supreme Court held that when a defendant seeks a §1404(a) transfer, that transfer is simply a change of courtroom and should not change the law that is applied. The Court was concerned that if a change of venue brought with it a change of law, then §1404(a) would be used "by defendants to defeat the advantages accruing to plaintiffs who have chosen a forum which, although it was inconvenient, was a proper venue." Id. at 634. Therefore, the Court held that the district court to which the case is transferred should apply whatever law the transferring court would have applied.

In Ferens v. John Deere Company, 494 U.S. 516 (1990), the Supreme Court went even further and held that even where the *plaintiff* requests the §1404 transfer, the transferee court (the receiving court) should apply the law that the transferor court (the original court) would have applied. The facts of *Ferens* are quite striking. The plaintiff lost his right hand when it was caught in his John Deere harvester. The accident occurred in Pennsylvania, which has a two-year statute of limitations in such cases. After that period expired, the plaintiff brought suit against John Deere in federal court in Mississippi. John Deere apparently had an agent for service of process in Mississippi or did sufficient business there to be subject to general personal jurisdiction.

The Mississippi statute of limitations was six years. If the case had been in Mississippi state court, Mississippi would have applied its statute of limitations to this case. Therefore, it was undisputed that if the case were litigated in federal court in Mississippi, the federal court would apply the six year time limit.

The case did not, however, stay in Mississippi. Shortly after filing his complaint, the plaintiff moved for a change of venue to Pennsylvania. The motion was granted, and the Supreme Court held that the federal court in Pennsylvania should apply the law that the federal court in Mississippi would have applied, i.e., the Mississippi statute of limitations. Thus, the plaintiff got to take advantage of Mississippi law without having to litigate there.

Van Dusen and *Ferens* involved transfers under §1404. Can you articulate why their holdings ought not to apply to §1406 transfers?

e. Standard for Transfer Under §§ 1404 and 1406

Section 1404 expressly provides that in deciding whether to transfer, the court shall consider the convenience of the parties, convenience of the witnesses, and "the interest of justice." On the other hand, §1406 prescribes no such factors, providing that if the case is filed in an improper venue, the court "shall dismiss, or if it be in the interest of justice, transfer." If there is a federal court to which the case can be transferred, won't transfer rather than dismissal always be in the interest of justice? As some commentators have noted, "In the main * * * dismissal will not usually be necessary, nor generally proper." 1A MOORE'S FEDERAL PRACTICE 4405.

f. Multidistrict Litigation

In mass torts such as airplane crashes or toxic torts, there may be a number of cases pending in different districts, all of which raise one or more common question (e.g., why did the plane crash?). Section 1407 permits all of these cases to be transferred to one district and consolidated for pretrial proceedings. These transfers need not meet other venue requirements. The decision whether to permit such transfers is made by "the judicial panel on multidistrict litigation," a seven member panel composed of district and circuit judges appointed by the Chief Justice. Although §1407 requires that following completion of pretrial proceedings, the cases "shall be remanded," it is not uncommon for cases consolidated under §1407 to be tried together, usually by consent of the parties.

F. Forum Non Conveniens

Piper Aircraft Co. v. Reyno
454 U.S. 235, 102 S.Ct. 252, 70 L. Ed. 2d 419 (1981)

JUSTICE MARSHALL delivered the opinion of the Court.

These cases arise out of an air crash that took place in Scotland. Respondent, acting as representative of the estates of several Scottish citizens killed in the accident, brought wrongful-death actions against petitioners that were ultimately transferred to the United States District Court for the Middle District of Pennsylvania. Petitioners moved to dismiss on the ground of *forum non conveniens*. After noting that an alternative forum existed in Scotland, the District Court granted their motions. The United States Court of Appeals for the Third Circuit reversed. The Court of Appeals based its decision, at least in part, on the ground that dismissal is automatically barred where the law of the alternative forum is less favorable to the plaintiff than the law of the forum chosen by the plaintiff. Because we conclude that the possibility of an unfavorable change in law should not, by itself, bar dismissal, and because we conclude that the District Court did not otherwise abuse its discretion, we reverse.

I

A

In July 1976, a small commercial aircraft crashed in the Scottish highlands during the course of a charter flight from Blackpool to Perth. The pilot and five passengers were killed instantly. The decedents were all Scottish subjects and residents, as are their heirs and next of kin. There were no eyewitnesses to the accident. At the time of the crash the plane was subject to Scottish air traffic control.

The aircraft, a twin-engine Piper Aztec, was manufactured in Pennsylvania by petitioner Piper Aircraft Co. (Piper). The propellers were manufactured in Ohio by petitioner Hartzell Propeller, Inc. (Hartzell). At the time of the crash the aircraft was registered in Great Britain and was owned and maintained by Air Navigation and Trading Co., Ltd. (Air Navigation). It was operated by McDonald Aviation, Ltd. (McDonald), a Scottish air taxi service. Both Air Navigation and McDonald were organized in the United Kingdom. The wreckage of the plane is now in a hangar in Farnsborough, England.

* * *

In July 1977, a California probate court appointed respondent Gaynell Reyno administratrix of the estates of the five passengers. Reyno is not related to and does not know any of the decedents or their survivors; she was a legal secretary to the attorney who filed this lawsuit. Several days after her appointment, Reyno commenced separate wrongful-death actions against Piper and

Hartzell in the Superior Court of California, claiming negligence and strict liability. Air Navigation, McDonald, and the estate of the pilot are not parties to this litigation. The survivors of the five passengers whose estates are represented by Reyno filed a separate action in the United Kingdom against Air Navigation, McDonald, and the pilot's estate. Reyno candidly admits that the action against Piper and Hartzell was filed in the United States because its laws regarding liability, capacity to sue, and damages are more favorable to her position than are those of Scotland. Scottish law does not recognize strict liability in tort. Moreover, it permits wrongful-death actions only when brought by a decedent's relatives. The relatives may sue only for "loss of support and society."

On petitioners' motion, the suit was removed to the United States District Court for the Central District of California. Piper then moved for transfer to the United States District Court for the Middle District of Pennsylvania, pursuant to 28 U.S.C. § 1404(a). Hartzell moved to dismiss for lack of personal jurisdiction, or in the alternative, to transfer.[5] In December 1977, the District Court quashed service on Hartzell and transferred the case to the Middle District of Pennsylvania. Respondent then properly served process on Hartzell.

B

In May 1978, after the suit had been transferred, both Hartzell and Piper moved to dismiss the action on the ground of forum non conveniens. The District Court granted these motions in October 1979. It relied on the balancing test set forth by this Court in Gulf Oil Corp. v. Gilbert, 330 U.S. 501 (1947), and its companion case, Koster v. Lumbermens Mut. Cas. Co., 330 U.S. 518 (1947). In those decisions, the Court stated that a plaintiff's choice of forum should rarely be disturbed. However, when an alternative forum has jurisdiction to hear the case, and when trial in the chosen forum would "establish ... oppressiveness and vexation to a defendant ... out of all proportion to plaintiff's convenience," or when the "chosen forum [is] inappropriate because of considerations affecting the court's own administrative and legal problems," the court may, in the exercise of its sound discretion, dismiss the case. To guide trial court discretion, the Court provided a list of "private interest factors" affecting the convenience of the litigants, and a list of "public interest factors" affecting the convenience of the forum.[6]

After describing our decisions in *Gilbert* and *Koster*, the District Court analyzed the facts of these cases. It began by observing that an alternative forum existed in Scotland; Piper and Hartzell had agreed to submit to the jurisdiction of the Scottish courts and to waive any statute of limitations defense that might be available. It then stated that plaintiff's choice of forum was entitled to little

---

[5] The District Court concluded that it could not assert personal jurisdiction over Hartzell consistent with due process. However, it decided not to dismiss Hartzell because the corporation would be amenable to process in Pennsylvania.

[6] The factors pertaining to the private interests of the litigants included the "relative ease of access to sources of proof; availability of compulsory process for attendance of unwilling, and the cost of obtaining attendance of willing, witnesses; possibility of new premises, if view would be appropriate to the action: and all other practical problems that make trial of a case easy, expeditious and inexpensive." *Gilbert*. The public factors bearing on the question included the administrative difficulties flowing from court congestion; the "local interest having localized controversies decided at home"; the interest in having the trial of a diversity case in a forum that is at home with the law that must govern the action; the avoidance of unnecessary problems in conflict of laws, or in the application of foreign law; and the unfairness of burdening citizens in an unrelated forum with jury duty.

weight. The court recognized that a plaintiff's choice ordinarily deserves substantial deference. It noted, however, that Reyno "is a representative of foreign citizens and residents seeking a forum in the United States because of the more liberal rules concerning products liability law," and that "the courts have been less solicitous when the plaintiff is not an American citizen or resident, and particularly when the foreign citizens seek to benefit from the more liberal tort rules provided for the protection of citizens and residents of the United States."

The District Court next examined several factors relating to the private interests of the litigants, and determined that these factors strongly pointed towards Scotland as the appropriate forum. Although evidence concerning the design, manufacture, and testing of the plane and propeller is located in the United States, the connections with Scotland are otherwise "overwhelming." The real parties in interest are citizens of Scotland, as were all the decedents. Witnesses who could testify regarding the maintenance of the aircraft, the training of the pilot, and the investigation of the accident — all essential to the defense — are in Great Britain. Moreover, all witnesses to damages are located in Scotland. Trial would be aided by familiarity with Scottish topography, and by easy access to the wreckage.

The District Court reasoned that because crucial witnesses and evidence were beyond the reach of compulsory process, and because the defendants would not be able to implead potential Scottish third-party defendants, it would be "unfair to make Piper and Hartzell proceed to trial in this forum." The survivors had brought separate actions in Scotland against the pilot, McDonald, and Air Navigation. "[I]t would be fairer to all parties and less costly if the entire case was presented to one jury with available testimony from all relevant witnesses." Although the court recognized that if trial were held in the United States, Piper and Hartzell could file indemnity or contribution actions against the Scottish defendants, it believed that there was a significant risk of inconsistent verdicts.[7]

The District Court concluded that the relevant public interests also pointed strongly towards dismissal. The court determined that Pennsylvania law would apply to Piper and Scottish law to Hartzell if the case were tried in the Middle District of Pennsylvania.[8] As a result, "trial in this forum would be hopelessly complex and confusing for a jury." In addition, the court noted that it was unfamiliar with Scottish law and thus would have to rely upon experts from that country. The court also found that the trial would be enormously costly and time-consuming; that it would be unfair to burden citizens with jury duty when the Middle District of Pennsylvania has little connection with the controversy; and that Scotland has a substantial interest in the outcome of the litigation.

In opposing the motions to dismiss, respondent contended that dismissal would be unfair because Scottish law was less favorable. The District Court explicitly rejected this claim. It reasoned

---

[7] The District Court explained that inconsistent verdicts might result if petitioners were held liable on the basis of strict liability here, and then required to prove negligence in an indemnity action in Scotland. Moreover, even if the same standard of liability applied, there was a danger that different juries would find different facts and produce inconsistent results.

[8] Under Klaxon v. Stentor Electric Mfg. Co., 313 U.S. 487 (1941), a court ordinarily must apply the choice-of-law rules of the State in which it sits. However, where a case is transferred pursuant to 28 U.S.C. § 1404(a), it must apply the choice-of-law rules of the State from which the Case was transferred. Van Dusen v. Barrack, 376 U.S. 612 (1946). Relying on these two cases, the District Court concluded that California choice-of-law rules would apply to Piper, and Pennsylvania choice-of-law rules would apply to Hartzell. It further concluded that California applied a "governmental interests" analysis in resolving choice-of-law problems, and that Pennsylvania employed a "significant contacts" analysis. The court used the "governmental interests" analysis to determine the Pennsylvania liability rules would apply to Piper, and the "significant contacts" analysis to determine that Scottish liability would apply to Hartzell.

that the possibility that dismissal might lead to an unfavorable change in the law did not deserve significant weight; any deficiency in the foreign law was a "matter to be dealt with in the foreign forum."

C

On appeal, the United States Court of Appeals for the Third Circuit reversed and remanded for trial. The decision to reverse appears to be based on two alternative grounds. First, the Court held that the District Court abused its discretion in conducting the *Gilbert* analysis. Second, the Court held that dismissal is never appropriate where the law of the alternative forum is less favorable to the plaintiff.

* * *

II

The Court of Appeals erred in holding that plaintiffs may defeat a motion to dismiss on the ground of forum non conveniens merely by showing that the substantive law that would be applied in the alternative forum is less favorable to the plaintiffs than that of the present forum. The possibility of a change in substantive law should ordinarily not be given conclusive or even substantial weight in the forum non conveniens inquiry.

We expressly rejected the position adopted by the Court of Appeals in our decision in Canada Malting Co. v. Paterson Steamships, Ltd., 285 U.S. 413 (1932). That case arose out of a collision between two vessels in American waters. The Canadian owners of cargo lost in the accident sued the Canadian owners of one of the vessels in Federal District Court. The cargo owners chose an American court in large part because the relevant American liability rules were more favorable than the Canadian rules. The District Court dismissed on grounds of forum non conveniens. The plaintiffs argued that dismissal was inappropriate because Canadian laws were less favorable to them. This Court nonetheless affirmed:

> "We have no occasion to enquire by what law the rights of the parties are governed, as we are of the opinion that, under any view of that question, it lay within the discretion of the District Court to decline to assume jurisdiction over the controversy.... '[T]he court will not take cognizance of the case if justice would be as well done by remitting the parties to their home forum.'"

The Court further stated that "[t]here was no basis for the contention that the District Court abused its discretion."

It is true that *Canada Malting* was decided before *Gilbert*, and that the doctrine of forum non conveniens was not fully crystallized until our decision in that case.[13] However, *Gilbert* in no

---

[13] * * * In previous forum non conveniens decisions, the Court has left unresolved the question whether under Erie R. Co. v. Tompkins, 304 U.S. 64 (1938), state or federal law of forum non conveniens applies in a diversity case. The Court did not decide this issue because the same result would have been reached in each case under federal or state law. The lower courts in these cases reached the same conclusion: Pennsylvania and California law on forum non conveniens dismissals are virtually identical to federal law. Thus, here also, we need not resolve the *Erie* question.

way affects the validity of *Canada Malting*. Indeed, by holding that the central focus of the forum non conveniens inquiry is convenience, *Gilbert* implicitly recognized that dismissal may not be barred solely because of the possibility of an unfavorable change in law. Under *Gilbert*, dismissal will ordinarily be appropriate where trial in the plaintiff's chosen forum imposes a heavy burden on the defendant or the court, and where the plaintiff is unable to offer any specific reasons of convenience supporting his choice.[15] If substantial weight were given to the possibility of an unfavorable change in law, however, dismissal might be barred even where trial in the chosen forum was plainly inconvenient.

The Court of Appeals' decision is inconsistent with this Court's earlier forum non conveniens decisions in another respect. Those decisions have repeatedly emphasized the need to retain flexibility. In *Gilbert*, the Court refused to identify specific circumstances "which will justify or require either grant or denial of remedy." Similarly, in *Koster*, the Court rejected the contention that where a trial would involve inquiry into the internal affairs of a foreign corporation, dismissal was always appropriate. "That is one, but only one, factor which may show convenience." And in Williams v. Green Bay & Western R. Co., 326 U.S. 549, 557 (1946), we stated that we would not lay down a rigid rule to govern discretion, and that "[e]ach case turns on its facts." If central emphasis were placed on any one factor, the forum non conveniens doctrine would lose much of the very flexibility that makes it so valuable.

In fact, if conclusive or substantial weight were given to the possibility of a change in law, the forum non conveniens doctrine would become virtually useless. Jurisdiction and venue requirements are often easily satisfied. As a result, many plaintiffs are able to choose from among several forums. Ordinarily, these plaintiffs will select that forum whose choice-of-law rules are most advantageous. Thus, if the possibility of an unfavorable change in substantive law is given substantial weight in the forum non conveniens inquiry, dismissal would rarely be proper.

* * *

The Court of Appeals' approach is not only inconsistent with the purpose of the forum non conveniens doctrine, but also poses substantial practical problems. If the possibility of a change in law were given substantial weight, deciding motions to dismiss on the ground of forum non conveniens would become quite difficult. Choice-of-law analysis would become extremely important, and the courts would frequently be required to interpret the law of foreign jurisdictions. First, the trial court would have to determine what law would apply if the case were tried in the chosen forum, and what law would apply if the case were tried in the alternative forum. It would then have to compare the rights, remedies, and procedures available under the law that would be applied in each forum. Dismissal would be appropriate only if the court concluded that the law applied by the alternative forum is as favorable to the plaintiff as that of the chosen forum. The doctrine of forum non conveniens, however, is designed in part to help courts avoid conducting complex exercises in comparative law. As we stated in *Gilbert*, the public interest factors point towards dismissal where the court would be required to "untangle problems in conflict of laws, and in law foreign to itself."

---

[15] In other words, *Gilbert* held that dismissal may be warranted where a plaintiff chooses a particular forum, not because it is convenient, but solely in order to harass the defendant or take advantage of favorable law. This is precisely the situation in which the Court of Appeals' rule would bar dismissal.

Upholding the decision of the Court of Appeals would result in other practical problems. At least where the foreign plaintiff named an American manufacturer as defendant,[17] a court could not dismiss the case on grounds of forum non conveniens where dismissal might lead to an unfavorable change in law. The American courts, which are already extremely attractive to foreign plaintiffs,[18] would become even more attractive. The flow of litigation into the United States would increase and further congest already crowded courts.[19]

The Court of Appeals based its decision, at least in part, on an analogy between dismissals on grounds of forum non conveniens and transfers between federal courts pursuant to § 1404(a). In Van Dusen v. Barrack, 376 U.S. 612 (1964), this Court ruled that a § 1404(a) transfer should not result in a change in the applicable law. Relying on dictum in an earlier Third Circuit opinion interpreting *Van Dusen*, the court below held that that principle is also applicable to a dismissal on forum non conveniens grounds. However, § 1404(a) transfers are different than dismissals on the ground of forum non conveniens.

Congress enacted § 1404(a) to permit change of venue between federal courts. Although the statute was drafted in accordance with the doctrine of forum non conveniens, it was intended to be a revision rather than a codification of the common law. District courts were given more discretion to transfer under § 1404(a) than they had to dismiss on grounds of forum non conveniens.

The reasoning employed in *Van Dusen v. Barrack* is simply inapplicable to dismissals on grounds of forum non conveniens. That case did not discuss the common-law doctrine. Rather, it focused on "the construction and application" of § 1404(a). Emphasizing the remedial purpose of the statute, *Barrack* concluded that Congress could not have intended a transfer to be accompanied by a change in law. The statute was designed as a "federal housekeeping measure," allowing easy change of venue within a unified federal system. The Court feared that if a change in venue were

---

[17] In fact, the defendant might not even have to be American. A foreign plaintiff seeking damages for an accident that occurred abroad might be able to obtain service of process on a foreign defendant who does business in the United States. Under the Court of Appeals' holding, dismissal would be barred if the law in the alternative forum were less favorable to the plaintiff -- even though none of the parties are American, and even though there is absolutely no nexus between the subject matter of the litigation and the United States.

[18] First, all but 6 of the 50 American States -- Delaware, Massachusetts, Michigan, North Carolina, Virginia, and Wyoming -- offer strict liability. Rules roughly equivalent to American Strict liability are effective in France, Belgium, and Luxembourg. West Germany and Japan have a strict liability statute for pharmaceuticals. However, strict liability remains primarily an American innovation. Second, the tort plaintiff may choose, at least potentially, from among 50 jurisdictions if he decides to file suit in the choice-of-laws rules. Third, jury trials are almost always available in the United States, while they are never provided in civil law jurisdictions. Even in the United Kingdom, most civil actions are not tried before a jury. Fourth, unlike most foreign jurisdictions, American courts allow contingent attorney's fees, and do not tax losing parties with their opponents' attorney's fees. Fifth, discovery is more extensive in American than in foreign courts.

[19] In holding that the possibility of a change in law favorable to the plaintiff should not be given substantial weight, we also necessarily hold that the possibility of a change in law favorable to the defendant should not be considered. Respondent suggests that Piper and Hartzell filed the motion to dismiss, not simply because trial in the United States would be inconvenient, but also because they believe the laws of Scotland are more favorable. She argues that this should be taken into account in and analysis of private interests. We recognize, of course, that Piper and Hartzell may be engaged in reverse forum-shopping. However, this possibility ordinarily should not enter into a trial court's analysis of private interests. If the defendant is able to overcome the presumption in favor of plaintiff by showing that trial in the chosen forum would be unnecessarily burdensome, dismissal is appropriate -- regardless of the fact that defendant may also be motivated by a desire to obtain a more favorable forum.

accompanied by a change in law, forum-shopping parties would take unfair advantage of the relaxed standards for transfer. The rule was necessary to ensure the just and efficient operation of the statute.

We do not hold that the possibility of an unfavorable change in law should *never* be a relevant consideration in a forum non conveniens inquiry. Of course, if the remedy provided by the alternative forum is so clearly inadequate or unsatisfactory that it is no remedy at all, the unfavorable change in law may be given substantial weight; the district court may conclude that dismissal would not be in the interests of justice.[22] In these cases, however, the remedies that would be provided by the Scottish courts do not fall within this category. Although the relatives of the decedents may not be able to rely on a strict liability theory, and although their potential damages award may be smaller, there is no danger that they will be deprived of any remedy or treated unfairly.

III

The Court of Appeals also erred in rejecting the District Court's *Gilbert* analysis. The Court of Appeals stated that more weight should have been given to the plaintiff's choice of forum, and criticized the District Court's analysis of the private and public interests. However, the District Court's decision regarding the deference due plaintiff's choice of forum was appropriate. Furthermore, we do not believe that the District Court abused its discretion in weighing the private and public interests.

A

The District Court acknowledged that there is ordinarily a strong presumption in favor of the plaintiff's choice of forum, which may be overcome only when the private and public interest factors clearly point towards trial in the alternative forum. It held, however, that the presumption applies with less force when the plaintiff or real parties in interest are foreign.

The District Court's distinction between resident or citizen plaintiffs and foreign plaintiffs is fully justified. In *Koster*, the Court indicated that a plaintiff's choice of forum is entitled to greater deference when the plaintiff has chosen the home forum.[23] When the home forum has been chosen, it is reasonable to assume that this choice is convenient. When the plaintiff is foreign, however, this

---

[22] At the outset of any forum non conveniens inquiry, the court must determine whether there exists an alternative forum. Ordinarily this requirement will be satisfied when the defendant is "amenable to process" in the other jurisdiction. In rare circumstances, however, where the remedy offered by another forum is clearly unsatisfactory, the other forum may not be an adequate alternative, and the initial requirement may not be satisfied. Thus, for example, dismissal would not be appropriate where the alternative forum does not permit litigation of the subject matter of the dispute. Cf. Phoenix Canada Oil Co. Ltd. v. Texaco, Inc., 78 F.R.D. 445 (Del. 1978) (court refuses to dismiss, where alternative forum is Ecuador, it is unclear whether Ecuadorian tribunal will hear the case, and there is no generally codified Ecuadorian legal remedy for the unjust enrichment and tort claims asserted).

[23] In *Koster*, we stated that "[i]n any balancing of conveniences, a real showing of convenience by a plaintiff who has sued in his home forum will normally outweigh the inconvenience the defendant may have shown."

As the District Court correctly noted in its opinion, the lower federal courts have routinely given less weight to a foreign plaintiff's choice of forum.

assumption is much less reasonable. Because the central purpose of any forum non conveniens inquiry is to ensure that the trial is convenient, a foreign plaintiff's choice deserves less deference.[24]

B

The forum non conveniens determination is committed to the sound discretion of the trial court. It may be reversed only when there has been a clear abuse of discretion; where the court has considered all relevant public and private interest factors, and where its balancing of these factors is reasonable, its decision deserves substantial deference. * * *

(1)

In analyzing the private interest factors, the District Court stated that the connections with Scotland are "overwhelming." This characterization may be somewhat exaggerated. Particularly with respect to the question of relative ease of access to sources of proof, the private interests point in both directions. As respondent emphasizes, records concerning the design, manufacture, and testing of the propeller and plane are located in the United States. She would have greater access to sources of proof relevant to her strict liability and negligence theories if trial were held here.[25] However, the District Court did not act unreasonably in concluding that fewer evidentiary problems would be posed if the trial were held in Scotland. A large proportion of the relevant evidence is located in Great Britain.

The Court of Appeals found that the problems of proof could not be given any weight because Piper and Hartzell failed to describe with specificity the evidence they would not be able to obtain if trial were held in the United States. It suggested that defendants seeking forum non conveniens dismissal must submit affidavits identifying the witnesses they would call and the testimony these witnesses would provide if the trial were held in the alternative forum. Such detail is not necessary. Piper and Hartzell have moved for dismissal precisely because many crucial witnesses are located beyond the reach of compulsory process, and thus are difficult to identify or interview. Requiring extensive investigation would defeat the purpose of their motion. Of course, defendants must provide enough information to enable the District Court to balance the parties' interests. Our examination of the record convinces us that sufficient information was provided here.

A citizen's forum choice should not be given dispositive weight, however. Citizens or residents deserve somewhat more deference than foreign plaintiffs, but dismissal should not be automatically barred when a plaintiff has filed suit in his home forum. As always, if the balance of conveniences suggests that trial in the chosen forum would be unnecessarily burdensome for the defendant or the court, dismissal is proper.

[24] Respondent argues that since plaintiffs will ordinarily file suit in the jurisdiction that offers the most favorable law, establishing a strong presumption in favor of both home and foreign plaintiffs will ensure that defendants will always be held to the highest possible standard of accountability for their purported wrongdoing. However, the deference accorded to a plaintiff's choice of forum has never been intended to guarantee that the plaintiff will be able to select the law that will govern the case.

[25] In the future, where similar problems are presented, district courts might dismiss subject to the condition that defendant corporations agree to provide the records relevant to the plaintiff's claims.

Both Piper and Hartzell submitted affidavits describing the evidentiary problems they would face if the trial were held in the United States.[27]

The District Court correctly concluded that the problems posed by the inability to implead potential third-party defendants clearly supported holding the trial in Scotland. Joinder of the pilot's estate, Air Navigation, and McDonald is crucial to the presentation of petitioners' defense. If Piper and Hartzell can show that the accident was caused not by a design defect, but rather by the negligence of the pilot, the plane's owners, or the charter company, they will be relieved of all liability. It is true, of course, that if Hartzell and Piper were found liable after a trial in the United States, they could institute an action for indemnity or contribution against these parties in Scotland. It would be far more convenient, however, to resolve all claims in one trial. The Court of Appeals rejected this argument. Forcing petitioners to rely on actions for indemnity or contributions would be "burdensome" but not "unfair." Finding that trial in the plaintiff's chosen forum would be burdensome, however, is sufficient to support dismissal on grounds of forum non conveniens.

(2)

The District Court's review of the factors relating to the public interest was also reasonable. On the basis of its choice-of-law analysis, it concluded that if the case were tried in the Middle District of Pennsylvania, Pennsylvania law would apply to Piper and Scottish law to Hartzell. It stated that a trial involving two sets of laws would be confusing to the jury. It also noted its own lack of familiarity with Scottish law. Consideration of these problems was clearly appropriate under *Gilbert*; in that case we explicitly held that the need to apply foreign law pointed towards dismissal. The Court of Appeals found that the District Court's choice-of-law analysis was incorrect, and that American law would apply to both Hartzell and Piper. Thus, lack of familiarity with foreign law would not be a problem. Even if the Court of Appeals' conclusion is correct, however, all other public interest factors favored trial in Scotland.

Scotland has a very strong interest in this litigation. The accident occurred in its airspace. All of the decedents were Scottish. Apart from Piper and Hartzell, all potential plaintiffs and defendants are either Scottish or English. As we stated in *Gilbert*, there is "a local interest in having localized controversies decided at home." 330 U.S. at 509. Respondent argues that American citizens have an interest in ensuring that American manufacturers are deterred from producing defective products, and that additional deterrence might be obtained if Piper and Hartzell were tried in the United States, where they could be sued on the basis of both negligence and strict liability. However, the incremental deterrence that would be gained if this trial were held in an American court is likely to be insignificant. The American interest in this accident is simply not sufficient to justify the enormous commitment of judicial time and resources that would inevitably be required if the case were to be tried here.

---

[27] The affidavit provided to the District Court by Piper states that it would call the following witnesses: The relatives of the descendents; the owners and employees of McDonald; the persons responsible for the training and licensing of the pilot; the persons responsible for servicing and maintaining the aircraft; and two or three of its own employees involved in the design and manufacture of the aircraft.

IV

The Court of Appeals erred in holding that the possibility of an unfavorable change in law bars dismissal on the ground of forum non conveniens. It also erred in rejecting the District Court's *Gilbert* analysis. The District Court properly decided that the presumption in favor of the respondent's forum choice applied with less than maximum force because the real parties in interest are foreign. It did not act unreasonably in deciding that the private interests pointed towards trial in Scotland. Nor did it act unreasonably in deciding that the public interests favored trial in Scotland.

Thus, the judgment of the Court of Appeals is reversed.

NOTES AND QUESTIONS

1. *Piper* involves several interesting procedural wrinkles. First, the case was removed from California Superior Court in Los Angeles to the federal district court for the Central District of California. Without knowing anything about the residence of the parties or where the claim arose, why was venue proper in the Central District? Second, the case was transferred to the Middle District of Pennsylvania. Because venue was proper in the transferor court, the transfer was under §1404. Finally, the case was dismissed under forum non conveniens.

2. What law applied after the case was transferred? See *Piper*, supra at n.8. Why would the district court have applied California choice of law rules to Piper but not as to Hartzell?

3. Would the result in *Piper* have been different if one of the decedents had been a U.S. citizen? What if all decedents were Scottish, but the beneficiary of one of their estates was a U.S. citizen? See William Reynolds, *The Proper Forum for a Suit: Transnational Forum Non Conveniens and Counter-Suit Injunctions in the Federal Courts*, 70 TEX. L. REV. 1663 (1992).

4. Notice that the Supreme Court grants the district judge broad discretion in ruling on forum non conveniens motions and that such rulings will not be reversed on appeal absent abuse of discretion. As you will see in Chapter 14, abuse of discretion is the most deferential of the various standards of review. For a rare case in which a district court's denial of a forum non conveniens dismissal was reversed on appeal following a trial on the merits, see Gonzalez v. Naviera Neptuno SA, 832 F.2d 876, 881 (5th Cir. 1987).

5. The federal transfer provisions were first enacted in 1948. Before that, dismissal on grounds of forum non conveniens was the only option available. Now that transfer is available, forum non conveniens is used in federal court only where the alternative forum is in a foreign country.

6. The Court in *Piper* adopts and applies principles established in *Gulf Oil v. Gilbert*. In that case, a Virginia plaintiff sued a Pennsylvania defendant in federal court in New York. The accident underlying the suit occurred in Virginia. Virtually all relevant trial witnesses and evidence were in Virginia, and it is clear that Virginia law would govern. The Court reinstated the district court's order of dismissal for forum non conveniens. Congress passed §1404 expressly in reaction to *Gilbert*.

7. States are free to develop their own common law doctrines of forum non conveniens. In most states these are quite similar to he federal doctrine. A few states, such as Florida, Georgia, Louisiana, and Texas, have significantly limited the availability of such dismissals. See Russell Weintraub, *International Litigation and Forum Non Conveniens*, 29 TEX. INT'L L.J. 321, 334 n. 101 & 343-51 (1994).

8. A forum non conveniens dismissal may be conditioned on the defendants waiving in the other forum defenses such as the statute of limitations or personal jurisdiction, see, e.g., CAL. CODE CIV. PRO. 410.30; OHIO RULES CIV. PRO., Rule 3D, or agreeing to discovery that may not be available in the other forum. See In re Union Carbide Corporation Gas Plant Disaster at Bhopal, India, 809 F.2d 195 (2d Cir.), *cert. denied*, 484 U.S. 871 (1987); Weintraub, supra, 29 TEX. INT'L L.J. at 330-32.

9. In *Piper*, the federal court had both subject matter jurisdiction and personal jurisdiction. Nonetheless, the federal court refused to adjudicate the case. Where do federal courts get the authority to do this? When Congress grants subject matter jurisdiction over a category of cases to the federal courts, is that simply a request to the courts that they adjudicate the described cases (if the court feels like it), or are such grants mandates? There is another category of discretionary refusal to assert jurisdiction, known as "abstention." Under various abstention doctrines, federal courts will sometimes decline to decide a case where it involves a particularly sensitive or unsettled issue of state law, or where another case dealing with the same issue is pending in state court. See WRIGHT, FEDERAL COURTS 322-39. Like forum non conveniens, the abstention doctrines are entirely court-made and is not addressed by statute. Professor Redish argues that these court-made doctrines constitute a judicial abdication of congressionally conferred jurisdiction and, thus violates the principle of separation of powers. See Martin Redish, *Abstention, Separation of Powers, and the Limits of the Judicial Function*, 94 YALE L.J. 71 (1984).

10. "As a moth is drawn to the light, so is a litigant drawn to the United States. If he can only get his case into their courts, he stands to win a fortune." Weintraub, supra, 29 TEX. INT'L L.J. at 322 (quoting Lord Denning). The attractions of U.S. courts include extensive pretrial discovery, generous tort laws and choice of law rules that make it more likely U.S. laws will be applied, and trial by jury. See id. at 323-24. Should the United States continue to play this role?

CHAPTER 6
RAISING JURISDICTIONAL
AND RELATED CHALLENGES

A. Introduction and Integration

To this point, we have explored doctrines governing the plaintiff's selection of a court: personal jurisdiction, subject matter jurisdiction, and venue. In this chapter, we consider how and when a defendant may object to the plaintiff's selection.

The nature of the defense affects the time in which it may be asserted. As we have seen, the rules governing personal jurisdiction and venue give the defendant personal rights, which she may waive. In addition, it is efficient to resolve questions of personal jurisdiction and venue early in the lawsuit. Consequently, courts impose strict rules as to how and when these defenses must be raised.

Subject matter jurisdiction, however, stands on a different footing. It involves not a personal waivable right of the defendant, but governmental structure. Federal courts have limited subject matter jurisdiction, reflecting the constitutional allocation of judicial power between the national and state governments.* Thus, although it would be efficient to resolve this issue at the outset of litigation, parties are not free to waive subject matter jurisdiction. By the well established rule, this defense can be raised anytime, by any party or by the court itself (sua sponte). Although some have questioned the wisdom of this rule, it remains.

B. The Traditional and Modern Approaches to Challenging Personal Jurisdiction

There are two general approaches for raising a direct objection to in personam jurisdiction. The traditional method is the "special appearance," some form of which is still

---

* Recall also that states are free to allocate their judicial power between various courts, prescribing the subject matter jurisdiction of each.

used in a considerable number of states. The second, more modern, approach is embodied in Federal Rule 12. Of course, Rule 12 governs practice only in federal court, but many states have adopted a version of it. Both approaches address the dilemma faced by a defendant wishing to challenge in personam jurisdiction: by going to the forum and arguing that it lacks jurisdiction, does the defendant risk submitting herself to jurisdiction there through "appearance" or "consent?"

Appreciating this difficulty, courts developed the notion of the special appearance, allowing a defendant to "appear" in a forum for the *sole* purpose of contesting in personam jurisdiction. While the requirements for making the special appearance vary among the states, the important point is that the defendant generally may raise *only* the in personam jurisdiction issue. If the defendant does more, for example, if she asserts an additional defense, or, in some states, if she merely makes a motion for continuance of proceedings, she is deemed to have made a "general appearance," which subjects her to in personam jurisdiction. See, e.g., Bumgarner v. Federal Dep. Ins. Corp., 764 P.2d 1367 (Okla. App. 1988)(continuance); Pfeiffer v. Ash, 206 P.2d 438 (Cal. App. 1949)(same).

Over a century ago, the Supreme Court held that due process does not require states to provide for a special appearance or like manner of objecting to personal jurisdiction. York v. Texas, 137 U.S. 15 (1890). Nonetheless, every state now allows defendants to raise the jurisdictional issue without submitting to general jurisdiction, either through a form of the special appearance or of Federal Rule 12. Despite the rigor with which some state courts apply the special appearance doctrine, raising an objection to personal jurisdiction along with a petition to remove the case to federal court does not constitute a general appearance. Lambert Run Coal Co. v. Baltimore & Ohio R.R. Co., 258 U.S. 377 (1922). Moreover, some states allow a defendant to challenge in personam and subject matter jurisdiction simultaneously. See, e.g., Goodwine v. Superior Court, 407 P.2d 1 (Cal. 1965).

A defendant wishing to contest in rem or quasi in rem jurisdiction faces the problem of limiting her potential liability to the value of the property attached. States have taken different approaches to this problem. In some, any appearance, even simply to contest jurisdiction, may convert the action into one in personam. In others, defending on the merits of the underlying claim opens the defendant to in personam jurisdiction. Many states permit the defendant to make a "limited appearance," which permits her to appear and defend without facing liability beyond the value of the property attached. See FRIEDENTHAL, KANE & MILLER, CIVIL PROCEDURE 186-89.

Although Federal Rule 4(n) authorizes quasi in rem jurisdiction, the Rules do not address the availability of the limited appearance in federal court. The federal courts addressing the question have reached differing conclusions. Id. at 187. In view of the increasing availability of in personam jurisdiction and the concomitant decline in importance

B. The Traditional and Modern Approaches to Challenging Personal Jurisdiction

of in rem and quasi in rem jurisdiction, the availability of the limited appearance may be less important than previously.

Federal Rule 12 abolishes the distinction between general and special appearances by allowing the defendant to raise several defenses simultaneously with an objection to personal jurisdiction. See the third sentence of Rule 12(b). It is a mistake to assume, however, that Rule 12 is so liberal that defendants cannot get into trouble. The lawyer who does not read Rule 12 very carefully can easily commit malpractice.

Read Rules 12(a), 12(b), 12(g), and 12(h). Note that Rule 12(b) permits the defendant to raise seven specific defenses either in a "responsive pleading" or "by motion." What's the difference? *Pleadings* are documents setting forth factual and legal contentions of the parties. Read Rule 7(a). *Motions* are requests that the court order something. Read Rule 7(b)(1). Motions can be made for a nearly infinite variety of reasons. For example, a party might move* for a continuance of a trial date, for an extension of time in which to answer, for an order that certain evidence not be admitted at trial, for an order that certain witnesses be excluded from the courtroom while not testifying, for a transfer of venue, and, of course, for dismissal. A party raising Rule 12(b) defenses in a motion usually will be moving to dismiss the case for one of the specified reasons.

NOTES AND QUESTIONS

1. Under what circumstances might a defendant prefer to raise a Rule 12(b) defense by motion rather than in a pleading? Under what circumstances might a defendant prefer to raise a Rule 12(b) defense in a pleading rather than by motion?

2. Defendant moves to dismiss for insufficiency of service of process. After the motion is denied, Defendant moves to dismiss for lack of personal jurisdiction. Why is the personal jurisdiction defense waived? Under what subsection(s) of Rule 12?

3. Defendant moves to dismiss for insufficiency of service of process. After the motion is denied, Defendant files an answer, asserting the defense of lack of personal jurisdiction. Why is the personal jurisdiction defense waived? Under what subsection(s) of Rule 12? Consider the situation in *Asahi*, supra Chapter 2. Under California procedure, objections to personal jurisdiction must be raised by special appearance. A defendant who enters a general appearance waives all personal jurisdiction objections, see CALIFORNIA CIVIL CODE § 410.50, and raising defenses other than jurisdiction, filing other motions, or

---

* As noted before, a party may "move" for or can "make a motion" for something. But "motion" is never used as a verb here. Thus, a party does not "motion" the court for anything.

CHAPTER 6 RAISING JURISDICTIONAL AND RELATED CHALLENGES

contesting the merits constitute a general appearance. In *Asahi,* Asahi's lawyer made the understandable decision to focus initially on jurisdiction. However, after the jurisdictional challenge was well under way, a Japanese engineer came to California inspected the valve in question, and concluded that the valve had not been manufactured by Asahi. Nonetheless, although Asahi had a strong defense on the merits, under California procedure it could not waive that defense without waiving jurisdiction. If the case had been in federal court, what would the defendant's options have been?

4. Which four of the Rule 12(b) defenses must be raised either in a preanswer Rule 12 motion or (if no such motion is made) in Defendant's answer? These four are commonly called the "waivable defenses" because they will be waived if not asserted early. This label is a bit confusing because two of the remaining three Rule 12(b) defenses are also readily waivable, but under different circumstances. See Rule 12(h)(2). Why do you think the rule requires early assertion of the four "waivable defenses?"

5. Defendant moves to dismiss for lack of personal jurisdiction and improper venue. After the motion is denied, Defendant files an answer, asserting the defense of failure to state a claim under Rule 12(b)(6). Is that defense timely? The case proceeds to trial, during which Defendant moves to dismiss for failure to join an indispensable party. Is that defense timely?

6. Suppose Defendant raises a Rule 12(b)(6) or 12(b)(7) defense for the first time on appeal. Why would that not be timely? But Defendant could raise the Rule 12(b)(1) defense for the first time on appeal. What part of Rule 12 makes this clear?

7. Defendant moves for an extension of time in which to respond to the complaint. The motion is granted, after which Defendant files a motion to dismiss for lack of personal jurisdiction. Is the personal jurisdiction defense waived? Is the motion for extension of time a defense "motion under this rule?" Rule 12(g). Would you reach the same conclusion if the initial motion were for a stay of proceedings? How about an initial motion for transfer under 28 U.S.C. § 1404(a)? See Aetna Life Ins. Co. v. Alla Medical Serv., Inc., 855 F.2d 1470 (9th Cir. 1988)(stay; no waiver); Catalano v. BRI, Inc., 724 F. Supp. 1580 (E.D. Mich. 1989)(transfer; no waiver).

8. According to some courts, a party may waive a defense even though she originally raised it in a timely manner. In Datskow v. Teledyne, Inc., 899 F.2d 1298 (2d Cir. 1990), the defendant filed a timely answer in which it asserted insufficient service of process. The defendant failed to raise the issue in a subsequent conference between litigants and the court. Later, after the statute of limitations had expired, the defendant moved to dismiss on the service of process grounds. The court denied the motion, holding that the defendant, despite timely filing of the answer, had waited too long to revisit the question. As we will see in Chapter 9, a pretrial conference order of the court basically supersedes the pleadings; issues not included in such an order generally are waived.

Jones v. Clinton
858 F. Supp. 902 (E.D. Ark. 1994)

SUSAN WEBBER WRIGHT, JUDGE.

* * *

I

This complaint, which was filed on May 6, 1994, arises out of an alleged incident that is said to have occurred on May 8, 1991, when President Clinton was Governor of the State of Arkansas. The plaintiff was a state employee at the time, and she claims that the President sexually harassed and assaulted her during a conference being held at a hotel in Little Rock, Arkansas.

* * *

The President informs the Court that he will file a motion to dismiss the complaint without prejudice to its reinstatement after he leaves office, on grounds that sitting presidents are constitutionally immune from having to litigate private suits for civil damages. He states that the immunity motion will raise serious issues which go to the constitutionality of compelling a sitting President to litigate private civil damages claims, as well as to this Court's authority to proceed in this case in the first instance. The President argues that the Court should allow him initially to assert the immunity issue alone, thereby permitting that question to be resolved prior to filing any other pleadings in the case.

II

The President states that his immunity motion will be based substantially on the Supreme Court's decision in Nixon v. Fitzgerald, 457 U.S. 731 (1982), a case decided on a narrow 5-4 margin. The plaintiff in that case, a former employee of the Department of the Air Force, had alleged that then-President Nixon abolished his position in retaliation for his testimony before a Congressional Committee. * * * The Supreme Court * * * held that "in view of the special nature of the President's constitutional office and functions, we think it appropriate to recognize absolute Presidential immunity from damages liability for acts within the 'outer perimeter' of his official responsibility." In so holding, the Court identified immunity as "a functionally mandate incident of the President's unique office, rooted in the constitutional tradition of the separation of powers and supported by our history."

Fitzgerald involved official actions by a sitting President while the allegations here relate to conduct that purportedly occurred prior to President Clinton's assumption of office. The President acknowledges this distinction and states that his motion will not assert absolute immunity such as was afforded in *Fitzgerald*, but will recognize the plaintiff's right to reinstate the lawsuit after he leaves office. In asserting such a claim of immunity, the President will seek entitlement to a fundamental protection from suit previously unrecognized in any court. This claim may or may not succeed. Nevertheless, because of the "singular importance of the President's duties," and because suits for civil damages "frequently could distract a President from his public duties, to the detriment of not only the President and his office but also the nation that the Presidency was designed to serve," the Court concludes that the issue of presidential immunity deserves threshold consideration, prior to the filing of any other motions or pleadings.

In allowing the President to first assert the issue of immunity, the Court is permitting a procedure that is entirely consistent with the principles underlying absolute immunity. The "essence of absolute immunity is its possessor's entitlement not to have to answer for his [alleged] conduct in a civil damages action." Mitchell v. Forsyth, 472 U.S. 511, 525 (1985). * * * Because the entitlement is an immunity from suit, the Supreme Court has stressed that immunity questions should be resolved at the earliest possible stage in litigation.

* * *

Nevertheless, plaintiff argues that the Federal Rules of Civil Procedure require every defendant, including the President of the United States, to either answer a complaint or file a single dispositive motion raising all available grounds for dismissal, including absolute immunity. Certainly, that is one way to handle a case, but it is not the only way it can be done. Plaintiff asserts, however, that the briefing schedule sought by the President is "nothing less than a categorical suspension of the Federal Rules of Civil Procedure." To the contrary, Rule 12 specifically allows for successive motions to dismiss for failure to state a claim. "Although defenses of lack of jurisdiction over the person, improper venue and insufficiency of process are waived if not raised in a party's first responsive pleading, '[a] defense of failure to state a claim upon which relief can be granted . . . may be made in any pleading permitted or ordered under Rule 7(a), or by motion for judgment on the pleadings, or at the trial on the merits.'" (citing Fed. R. Civ. P. 12(h)). See also 2A Moore's Federal Practice ¶ 12.07[3] at 12-102 (2d ed. 1994)(affirmative defenses not enumerated in Rule 12(b) may be made by motion under Rule 12(b)(6)); 5A Charles A. Wright & Arthur R. Miller, Federal Practice and Procedure § 1361 at 447-43 [sic] (1990)(Rule 12(b)(6) motions are exempted by Rule 12(g) from the consolidation requirement). The briefing schedule sought by the President is in conformity with the Federal Rules of Civil Procedure and does not afford him privileges unavailable to other defendants.

To be sure, the plaintiff's interest in seeking prompt relief for the alleged violation of her rights is certainly legitimate and not to be minimized. The Court, however, finds that plaintiff's concern that the briefing schedule proposed by the President will entail undue delay is unfounded. Should the Court deny the President's claim of immunity, such order would be immediately appealable. This would be so regardless of the Court's ruling on any other Rule 12(b) motions.

B. The Traditional and Modern Approaches to Challenging Personal Jurisdiction

* * *

III

For the foregoing reasons, the Court will allow the President to file a motion to dismiss on the grounds of presidential immunity on or before August 10, 1994, and to defer and preserve the filing of any other motions or pleadings that may or must be filed under the Federal Rules of Civil Procedure until such time as the issue of presidential immunity has been resolved by this Court.

NOTES AND QUESTIONS

1. As the court suggests, the President's motion to dismiss because of immunity may be considered under Rule 12(b)(6). Couldn't one also argue that immunity is not a "motion under this rule," as required in Rule 12(g)? Professor Moore concluded that any defense not already specified in Rule 12(b), but which could be raised as an affirmative defense, can be asserted in a motion to dismiss under Rule 12(b)(6). 2A MOORE'S FEDERAL PRACTICE ¶ 12-102. Could immunity also be raised under Rule 12(b)(1)? What difference would it make?

2. Does Rule 12(h)(2) authorize the filing of a preanswer motion raising failure to state a claim?

3. Suppose defendant files a Rule 12(b)(6) motion and the court denies it. Then defendant files another Rule 12(b)(6) motion based upon a different theory. According to the court in *Jones*, is this permitted? It appears that the President wants to file a Rule 12(b)(6) motion based upon immunity now and, if unsuccessful, file another Rule 12(b)(6) motion without having to file an answer. Does Rule 12 permit this?

4. As Rule 12(h)(2) makes clear, the Rule 12(b)(6) defense need not be raised in the defendant's first Rule 12 response. But the court in *Jones* goes farther, concluding that the defendant's Rule 12(b)(6) motion will not preclude him from raising other defenses later. Although it is unlikely that the President would be able to assert the defenses under Rule 12(b)(2), (3), (4), or (5) in *Jones*, doesn't Rule 12(g) clearly provide that he has waived those defenses by failing to join them in this motion? For its conclusion that Rule 12(b)(6) is "exempted from the consolidation requirement," the court cites 5A WRIGHT & MILLER, FEDERAL PRACTICE AND PROCEDURE 443-47. Consider this statement from that book:

> According to Rule 12(g), once a party has chosen to make a Rule 12(b) motion, any available Rule 12(b) defenses must be joined in that motion or those that are omitted will be waived. Again, this does not apply to defenses under Rules

12(b)(1), 12(b)(6), and 12(b)(7), which are exempted by Rule 12(g) from the consolidation requirement and are protected against waiver by Rules 12(h)(2) and 12(h)(3).

Id. at 447-48.

Does this language support a conclusion that a defendant bringing a Rule 12(b)(6) motion does not waive defenses included in Rule 12(b)(2) through (b)(5) by not joining them in that motion?

5. Under Rule 12(a), if a motion is denied, the defendant must answer within ten days "unless a different time is fixed by the court." Does this provision give the court authority to do what it did in *Jones*?

6. In a subsequent order in the *Jones* case, Judge Wright held that the President was not immune from suit, that trial would be delayed until after the President left office, but that discovery could proceed. 869 F. Supp. 690 (E.D. Ark. 1994). Later she stayed the discovery order pending appeal. 879 F. Supp. 86 (E.D. Ark. 1995).

C. Collateral and Direct Attacks on Personal Jurisdiction

You practice law in Virginia. Client has been served properly with summons and complaint in Richmond in a case filed in a Hawaii state court. After investigating, you conclude that it is not clear whether Hawaii has personal jurisdiction over Client. Of course, Client could make an appearance in the Hawaii case (as permitted by Hawaii law) and object to personal jurisdiction. This would be a *direct attack* on Hawaii's jurisdiction. But Client has another option.

Client could ignore the process and allow the Hawaii court to enter a default judgment against her. Then, when the plaintiff attempts to enforce the default judgment in Virginia, Client could make a *collateral attack*. In this attack, she would argue that the Hawaii judgment is not entitled to full faith and credit because Hawaii did not have personal jurisdiction. Strategically, this course has the advantage of allowing Client to litigate at home (and would also save travel expense). But it could be a risky course.

First, the plaintiff may enforce the judgment anywhere Client has property. If Client has property in Hawaii or, say, Montana, she will have to raise the collateral attack in a distant forum.

Second, even if the plaintiff does seek to enforce the Hawaii judgment in Virginia, the collateral attack permits Client to raise *only* the issue of whether the Hawaii court had jurisdiction; she cannot contest the merits of the plaintiff's claim. Thus, if Virginia (or any other state in which the plaintiff seeks to enforce the judgment) determines that Hawaii did have jurisdiction, the default judgment against Client is enforced, without litigation concerning the merits of underlying dispute. Obviously, if the court in the collateral attack determines that Hawaii did not have jurisdiction over Client, it will refuse to enforce the judgment. At that point, the plaintiff may decide to sue in Virginia. In this litigation, the defendant will be permitted to litigate the merits of the underlying dispute.

There are also problems, however, with making a direct attack. For one, if you are not also licensed to practice law in Hawaii, Client will have to find an attorney to appear on her behalf there. That counsel will have to learn enough about the case and the jurisdictional challenge to proceed appropriately. This process is expensive for Client and must be completed quickly because of time limits imposed for making defensive responses. The expense and tension will be forgotten, however, if Client prevails in the direct attack; in that event, of course, the Hawaii court will dismiss the case.

But what if the Hawaii court rejects Client's direct attack? The traditional rule, followed in most jurisdictions as we will see in Chapter 14, allows appellate review of right only after the trial court has entered a final judgment, which is one determining the merits of the entire underlying dispute between the parties. Some jurisdictions have an exception for personal jurisdiction, allowing review by appeal or, more commonly, by extraordinary writ, before trial on the merits. For example, the defendants in *World-Wide Volkswagen, Asahi,* and *Burnham,* which we read in Chapter 2, obtained appellate review of the jurisdictional issue in this way.

Absent such an exception to the general rules of appealability, however, Client cannot appeal the jurisdictional ruling until after she litigates the entire case on the merits. Should she lose at trial, she can appeal both on jurisdiction and the merits. Thus, any defendant making a direct attack should understand that rejection of the challenge may necessitate her staying for trial. Also, as a practical matter, which court—Hawaii or Virginia—is more likely to hold that Hawaii lacks jurisdiction?

Competent counsel must be mindful of the advantages and disadvantages of the direct and collateral attacks. Most importantly, however, counsel must try not to mix the approaches.

Baldwin v. Iowa State Mens Traveling Association
283 U.S. 522, 51 S. Ct. 517, 75 L. Ed. 2d. 1224 (1931)

MR. JUSTICE ROBERTS delivered the opinion of the Court.

A writ of certiorari was granted herein to review the affirmance by the Circuit Court of Appeals of a judgment for respondent rendered by the District Court for Southern Iowa. The action was upon the record of a judgment rendered in favor of the petitioner against the respondent in the United States District Court for Western Missouri.

CHAPTER 6 RAISING JURISDICTIONAL AND RELATED CHALLENGES

The defense was lack of jurisdiction of the person of the respondent in the court which entered the judgment. After hearing, in which a jury was waived, this defense was sustained and the action dismissed. The first suit was begun in a Missouri state court and removed to the District Court. Respondent appeared specially and moved to quash and dismiss for want of service. The court quashed the service, but refused to dismiss. An alias summons was issued and returned served, whereupon it again appeared specially, moved to set aside the service, quash the return, and dismiss the case for want of jurisdiction of its person. After a hearing on affidavits and briefs, the motion was overruled, with leave to plead within thirty days. No plea having been filed within that period, the cause proceeded and judgment was entered for the amount claimed. Respondent did not move to set aside the judgment nor sue out a writ of error.

The ground of the motion made in the first suit is the same as that relied on as a defense to this one, namely, that the respondent is an Iowa corporation, that it never was present in Missouri, and that the person served with process in the latter State was not such an agent that service on him constituted a service on the corporation. The petitioner objected to proof of these matters, asserting that the defense constituted a collateral attack and a retrial of an issue settled in the first suit. The overruling of this objection and the resulting judgment for respondent are assigned as error.

* * * The respondent * * * insists that to deprive it of the defense which it made in the court below, of lack of jurisdiction over it by the Missouri District Court, would be to deny the due process guaranteed by the Fourteenth Amendment; but there is involved in that doctrine no right to litigate the same question twice.

The substantial matter for determination is whether the judgment amounts to res judicata on the question of the jurisdiction of the court which rendered it over the person of the respondent. * * * The special appearance gives point to the fact that the respondent entered the Missouri court for the very purpose of litigating the question of the jurisdiction over its person. It had the election not to appear at all. If, in the absence of appearance, the court had proceeded to judgment and the present suit had been brought thereon, respondent could have raised and tried out the issue in the present action, because it would never have had its day in court with respect to jurisdiction. It had also the right to appeal from the decision of the Missouri District Court, as is shown by Harkness v. Hyde, 98 U.S. 476 (1878) * * * . It elected to follow neither of those courses, but, after having been defeated upon full hearing in its contention as to jurisdiction, it took no further steps, and the judgment in question resulted.

Public policy dictates that there be an end of litigation; that those who have contested an issue shall be bound by the result of the contest, and that matters once tried shall be considered forever settled as between the parties. We see no reason why this doctrine should not apply in every case where one voluntarily appears, presents his case and is fully heard, and why he should not, in the absence of fraud, be thereafter concluded by the judgment of the tribunal to which he has submitted his cause.

While this court has never been called upon to determine the specific question here raised, several federal courts have held the judgment res judicata in like circumstance. And we are in accord with this view. * * *

The judgment is reversed and the cause remanded for further proceedings in conformity with this opinion.

Reversed.

D. Challenging Federal Subject Matter Jurisdiction

NOTES AND QUESTIONS

1. Do we know that the Missouri court properly concluded that it had jurisdiction over the defendant? After all, the Iowa federal court found that Missouri lacked personal jurisdiction. Will we ever know which court was correct?

2. The Supreme Court says that its holding in *Baldwin* is based upon the doctrine of res judicata, which is also called claim preclusion. We will study this and related doctrines in Chapter 11. For present purposes, it is enough to understand that our system generally provides a litigant "one bite at the apple," and does not allow relitigation of an issue already decided. Thus, a defendant is permitted to challenge personal jurisdiction once — either in a direct attack or a collateral attack.

There was nothing wrong with the defendant's choice of a direct attack in *Baldwin*. The mistake was in not following through with that attack in Missouri. Having lost on the jurisdictional issue before the trial court in Missouri, the defendant (as part of its direct attack) could have appealed an adverse judgment to the appropriate court of appeals (and, if accepted, to the United States Supreme Court). As noted above, though, the issue probably could not have been raised on appeal until after resolution of the underlying litigation.

3. Assume again that you practice law in Virginia and that Client has been served with process for a suit in Hawaii. The issue of whether Hawaii has jurisdiction over Client is a close one.

   (a) If Client has a weak case on the merits (i.e., it is fairly clear that she will be held liable), why might you recommend a collateral, rather than a direct, attack?

   (b) If Client has a strong case on the merits (e.g., has overwhelming proof that she is not liable), why (despite the expense) might you recommend a direct, rather than a collateral, attack? For example, assume the plaintiff asserted that Client owed her on a note. Client has the canceled check showing that she paid the note on time. Suppose Client allows Hawaii to enter a default judgment and makes a collateral attack when the plaintiff seeks to enforce the judgment in Virginia. What is the only issue the Virginia court will address? If it finds that Hawaii had jurisdiction over Client, what good is the canceled check?

D. Challenging Federal Subject Matter Jurisdiction

In the usual case, the defendant will challenge subject matter jurisdiction by moving to dismiss under Rule 12(b)(1). A plaintiff may challenge subject matter jurisdiction of a removed case by moving to remand the case to state court under 28 U.S.C. §1447(c). What happens, though, when the objecting party does not raise the issue early in the proceedings at the trial court? What does Rule 12(h) provide regarding timing of the defense?

In *Louisville & Nashville R.R. v. Mottley*, which we read in Chapter 4, the Supreme Court raised lack of subject matter jurisdiction *sua sponte*. The case had to be dismissed, even though the jurisdictional problem was not discovered until after decision at the trial court and appeal and even though all parties wanted an answer. Remember also that after dismissal, plaintiffs sued in state court and, after review by the highest state tribunal, successfully invoked Supreme Court appellate jurisdiction to address the merits.

The notion that lack of subject matter jurisdiction is not a waivable defense is so strong that even the party purporting to invoke federal jurisdiction can raise it after losing on the merits. In Capron v. Van Noorden, 6 U.S. 126 (1804), the plaintiff sued in federal court, apparently under diversity of citizenship jurisdiction. After losing at trial, he appealed on the grounds that the court lacked subject matter jurisdiction, since there was no diversity after all! The Supreme Court held that the case must be dismissed. In American Fire & Cas. Co. v. Finn, 341 U.S. 6 (1951), a defendant who removed a case to federal court and then lost on the merits did the same thing. Again, the case was dismissed.

The nonwaivability of the subject matter jurisdiction defense can result in waste of judicial and private resources. It can also countenance outrageous gamesmanship. In some cases, plaintiffs have concealed the lack of jurisdiction until after losing on the merits. While their concealment may be punishable under various rules, such as Federal Rule 11, the judgment must be set aside. See, e.g., Rubin v. Buckman, 727 F.2d 71 (3d Cir. 1984). Similarly, defendants have successfully concealed a lack of jurisdiction until after the state court statute of limitations has run. Again, the federal case must be dismissed, perhaps leaving the plaintiff without remedy. See, e.g., Wojan v. General Motors Corp., 851 F.2d 969 (7th Cir. 1988).

Such abuse led some commentators to argue that litigants be estopped from raising lack of subject matter jurisdiction in instances of bad faith. See, e.g., 1 MOORE'S FEDERAL PRACTICE ¶ 0.60[4]; Dan Dobbs, *Beyond Bootstrap: Foreclosing the Issue of Subject Matter Jurisdiction Before Final Judgment*, 51 MINN. L. REV. 491 (1967); Comment, *Second Bites at the Jurisdictional Apple: A Proposal for Preventing False Assertions of Diversity of Citizenship*, 41 HAST. L.J. 1417 (1990). Two cases seemed to indicate a move in that direction, DiFrischia v. New York Cent. R.R. Co, 279 F.2d 141 (3d Cir. 1960) and Klee v. Pittsburgh & W. Va. Ry. Co., 22 F.R.D. 252 (W.D. Pa. 1958), but they have had no serious impact on the traditional rule. Indeed, the Third Circuit later repudiated *DiFrischia* in light of Supreme Court decisions reasserting the traditional rule. Rubin v. Buckman, 727 F.2d 71 (3d Cir. 1984).

All of these cases involved direct attacks on the court's jurisdiction — that is, challenges made in the proceedings against the defendant either at the trial court or on appeal from judgment of the trial court. Does the same rule apply in collateral attacks? Remember, a litigant only gets "one bite at the apple." Thus, consistent with what we have seen with personal jurisdiction, a defendant who litigates the issue of subject matter jurisdiction and loses cannot challenge it again in a separate action. Durfee v. Duke, 375 U.S. 106 (1963). This rule is subject to narrow exceptions. For example, the Supreme Court found an exception in the policy underlying federal bankruptcy legislation. Kalb v. Feuerstein, 308 U.S. 433 (1940). See generally Karen Moore, *Collateral Attack on Subject Matter Jurisdiction: A Critique of the Restatement (Second) of Judgments*, 66 CORNELL L. REV. 534 (1981).

What if the parties litigate the merits of the case without raising the issue of subject matter jurisdiction? We know that a party can assert the lack of subject matter jurisdiction on appeal, but can she raise it in a collateral suit? The answer appears to be no. Chicot County Drainage Distr. v. Baxter State Bank, 308 U.S. 371 (1940).

Chicot County involved a collateral attack of a judgment in which federal jurisdiction had been based upon a statute later held unconstitutional. Although the parties would have had no reason to suspect the lack of jurisdiction during the pendency of the prior suit and did not raise or litigate the issue, the Supreme Court refused to allow a collateral attack. According to the Court, the validity of the statute should have been raised during the first proceeding, and not after the court approved the final decree. As we will see in Chapter 11, claim preclusion can bar further litigation not only of issues actually litigated but of issues that could have been raised. 308 U.S. 378. See also Des Moines Navigation & R.R. Co. v. Iowa Homestead Co., 123 U.S. 552 (1887).

The usual explanation for this rule is that courts have jurisdiction to decide their own jurisdiction—a concept that Professor Dobbs calls the "bootstrap principle." Dan Dobbs, *The Validation of Void Judgments: The Bootstrap Principle*, 53 VA. L. REV. 1003, 1241 (pts. 1 & 2)(1967). Subject matter derives from the legislative body or constitution that creates the court. Professor Dobbs argues that we should assume in most cases that the body creating the court intended for it to have jurisdiction to determine its own jurisdiction. He explains:

> [U]nder settled rules, if a court has jurisdiction to dismiss for want of jurisdiction, it has jurisdiction to retain the case. It may be error to dismiss or retain the case, but in either event it has jurisdiction to decide the issue. Of course, the legislature might change this rule by fiat. It might say that courts have jurisdiction to decide correctly and not other jurisdiction. But unless a legislature says this specifically, there is no reason to assume that it intended such a rule, because such a rule would not be consonant with a court's power to dismiss for want of jurisdiction.

53 VA. L. REV. at 1011-12.

And what about a collateral attack on a default judgment? There, the defendant has litigated nothing, but has suffered an adverse judgment. May she attack the default judgment for lack of subject matter jurisdiction in a collateral action? While *Chicot County* seems to indicate that she may not, remember that a defendant in a similar situation would be able to make a collateral attack based upon personal jurisdiction.* Should the concept of jurisdiction to decide jurisdiction be applied to default judgments? Does a court in fact decide whether it has jurisdiction before entering a default judgment?

The Restatement (Second) of Judgments does not permit defendant to make a collateral attack on a default judgment based upon lack of subject matter jurisdiction. The drafters were quick to point out, however, that few modern decisions have sustained a collateral attack on a default judgment where the sole issue is lack of subject matter jurisdiction. RESTATEMENT (SECOND) OF JUDGMENTS § 12, cmt. f (1982). Often, there will be some other problems, such as lack of proper notice, which support collateral attack. Id. Professor (now Judge) Karen Moore provides a very helpful analysis of this area. Moore, supra, 66 CORNELL L. REV. at 551-53.

---

* The claimants in *Chicot County* did not appear in the original proceeding. 103 F. 2d 847 (8th Cir. 1939). Because many other parties were involved and did appear, the underlying case itself was litigated. The Supreme Court did not address the claimants' absence, and made no mention of a default judgment. Some commentators, however, regard *Chicot County* as a default case. *See, e.g.*, Moore, supra, 66 CORNELL L. REV. at 553.

CHAPTER 7

WHAT LAW APPLIES IN FEDERAL COURT

A. Introduction and Integration

As mentioned in earlier chapters, when an issue is controlled by state law, a court frequently faces the question of which state's law applies. Each state has its own choice of law rules to answer this question. You may study the various choice of law rules in a different course, usually entitled "Choice of Law" or "Conflict of Laws." The problem of which of several states' laws apply is sometimes referred to as a "horizontal" choice of law problem. For purposes of this course you need to understand that there are choice of law rules, that these rules vary among the states, and that, as a result, different courts may apply different state laws to the same incident or transaction.

This chapter focuses on a "vertical" choice of law problem, that is, whether federal or state law governs a decision. Students sometimes assume that federal courts only apply federal law, but that is not the case. As we already saw in personal jurisdiction, absent a federal provision, a federal court has personal jurisdiction only if the state court in which it sits has personal jurisdiction. As you will see in this chapter, federal courts apply state law on other matters as well.

Our starting point for analyzing when federal courts apply state law is the Rules of Decision Act, the original version of which was contained in Section 34 of the Judiciary Act of 1789. The current version, codified at 28 U.S.C. § 1652, provides:

> The laws of the several states, except where the Constitution or treaties of the United States or Acts of Congress otherwise require or provide, shall be regarded as rules of decision in civil actions in the courts of the United States, in cases where they apply.

Notice that the statute requires the use of state law only if there is no federal statute, treaty, or constitutional provision on point. The Supremacy Clause of the Constitution makes federal law "the supreme law of the land." Because of the Supremacy Clause, Congress may, if it wishes, completely preempt state law in a particular area so long as Congress has authority to legislate in that area. For example, Congress could pass a statute requiring that all railroads provide at least a two foot right of way on either side of the track.

CHAPTER 7 WHAT LAW APPLIES IN FEDERAL COURT

Such a statute would preempt or override a conflicting state statute requiring only a one foot right of way.

Whether a federal statute preempts state law depends entirely on the meaning of that federal statute. Thus, in the right of way example, suppose the federal statute requires a two foot right of way but one state requires three feet. Whether the federal statute preempts the state law turns on whether Congress intended the federal statute merely to provide a minimum standard or instead to provide a nationwide uniform standard. A court ascertains the intent of Congress from the statutory language and, when appropriate, from the legislative history. If the court determines that the federal statute is preemptive and on point, then that federal statute applies, not only in federal court, but also in state court.

If no preemptive federal law is on point then the Rules of Decision Act provides that "the laws of the several states * * * shall be regarded as rules of decision." Close examination of the statute raises several questions.

First, does this language mean that if there is no preemptive federal law, that state law controls as to every issue? If a state passes a statute that requires that no trial can start before 10 a.m. and there is no federal statute addressing this issue, would federal courts be required to abide by the state law? Notice that the Rules of Decision Act provides that state law shall be the "rules of decision." This phrase might mean that state law is required only as to those issues that concern the decision on the merits. In other words, it might refer only to laws relating to the substance of the claims and not to matters of procedure.

History provides some support for this view. Shortly after the First Congress passed the Judiciary Act, it passed another statute, the Process Act (later revised and called the Conformity Act), which required that federal courts apply state law concerning "the forms of writs and execution, except their style, and modes of process and rates of fees." Although this statute is no longer in effect, the fact that the First Congress thought it necessary might suggest that Congress believed that at least some matters of procedure were not covered by section 34 of the Judiciary Act. There is, however, little legislative history available on the Rules of Decision Act, so this argument is largely speculative.

It is now accepted that the Rules of Decision Act does not require the use of state law on all matters. As a rough generalization, one can say that where there is no preemptive federal law, state law applies on all substantive matters, but not on procedural matters. As we will see, however, the line between these two categories is uncertain and the labels of "substance" and "procedure" often are not helpful as analytical tools.

Second, the Rules of Decision Act refers to the "laws of the several states." It does not specify which state law a federal court should apply. It is now established that a federal court is to apply the law that the state in which it sits would apply, but this result is not obvious from the language of the Rules of Decision Act.

264

A. Introduction and Integration

Third, what is included within the phrase "laws of the several states" — does "laws" include common law doctrine as well as statutes? In Swift v. Tyson, 41 U.S. 1 (1842), the Supreme Court held that the "laws of the several states" included only statutory laws, plus court-made doctrine on matters of "local" law. However, according to the Court, that phrase did not include court-made doctrine on matters of "general" law. The Court explained:

> In the ordinary use of language, it will hardly be contended, that the decisions of courts constitute laws. They are, at most, only evidence of what the laws are; and are not, of themselves, laws. They are often re-examined, reversed, and qualified by the courts themselves, whenever they are found to be either defective, or ill-founded, or otherwise incorrect. The laws of a state are more usually understood to mean the rules and enactments promulgated by the legislative authority thereof, as long-established customs having the force of laws. * * * It never has been supposed by us, that the section [§ 34] did apply, or was designed to apply, to questions of a more general nature * * * as, for example, * * * questions of general commercial law * * * .

41 U.S. at 18-19.

The distinction between matters of general and local law proved elusive and produced great uncertainty. The legal realists of the twentieth century ridiculed the idea that judges' decisions are only "evidence of the law" and not law themselves. Judges make law every bit as much as legislatures do, the legal realists declared. It was against this backdrop that the Supreme Court decided Erie Railroad Co. v. Tompkins, 304 U.S. 64 (1938), a case later described by Justice Black as "one of the most important cases at law in American history." Hugo Black, *Address*, 13 Mo. B.J. 173, 174 (1942).

B. Determining What Law Applies

1. The *Erie* Doctrine

Erie Railroad Co. v. Tompkins
304 U.S. 64, 58 S. Ct. 817, 82 L. Ed. 1188 (1938)

JUSTICE BRANDEIS delivered the opinion of the Court.

The question for decision is whether the oft-challenged doctrine of *Swift v. Tyson* shall now be disapproved.

Tompkins, a citizen of Pennsylvania, was injured on a dark night by a passing freight train of the Erie Railroad Company while walking along its right of way at Hughestown in that State. He claimed that the accident occurred through negligence in the operation, or maintenance, of the train; that he was rightfully on the premises as licensee because on a commonly used beaten footpath which ran for a short distance alongside the tracks; and that he was struck by something which looked like a door projecting from one of the moving cars. To enforce that claim he brought an action in the federal court for southern New York, which had jurisdiction because the company is a corporation of that State. It denied liability; and the case was tried by a jury.

The Erie insisted that its duty to Tompkins was no greater than that owed to a trespasser. It contended, among other things, that its duty to Tompkins, and hence its liability, should be determined in accordance with the Pennsylvania law; that under the law of Pennsylvania, as declared by its highest court, persons who use pathways along the railroad right of way — that is a longitudinal pathway as distinguished from a crossing — are to be deemed trespassers; and that the railroad is not liable for injuries to undiscovered trespassers resulting from its negligence, unless it be wanton or wilful. Tompkins denied that any such rule had been established by the decisions of the Pennsylvania courts; and contended that, since there was no statute of the State on the subject, the railroad's duty and liability is to be determined in federal courts as a matter of general law.

The trial judge refused to rule that the applicable law precluded recovery. The jury brought in a verdict of $30,000; and the judgment entered thereon was affirmed by the Circuit Court of Appeals, which held that it was unnecessary to consider whether the law of Pennsylvania was as contended, because the question was one not of local, but of general, law and that "upon questions of general law the federal courts are free, in the absence of a local statute, to exercise their independent judgment as to what the law is; and it is well settled that the question of the responsibility of a railroad for injuries caused by its servants is one of general law.... Where the public has made open and notorious use of a railroad right of way for a long period of time and without objection, the company owes to persons on such permissive pathway a duty of care in the operation of its trains.... It is likewise generally recognized law that a jury may find that negligence exists toward a pedestrian using a permissive path on the railroad right of way if he is hit by some object projecting from the side of the train."

The Erie had contended that application of the Pennsylvania rule was required, among other things, by § 34 of the Federal Judiciary Act of September 24, 1789, [28 U.S.C. § 1652] which provides:

"The laws of the several States, except where the Constitution, treaties, or statutes of the United States otherwise require or provide, shall be regarded as rules of decision in trials at common law, in the courts of the United States, in cases where they apply."

Because of the importance of the question whether the federal court was free to disregard the alleged rule of the Pennsylvania common law, we granted certiorari.

First. Swift v. Tyson held that federal courts exercising jurisdiction on the ground of diversity of citizenship need not, in matters of general jurisprudence, apply the unwritten law of the State as declared by its highest court; that they are free to exercise an independent judgment as to what the common law of the State is — or should be; and that, as there stated by Justice Story:

"the true interpretation of the thirty-fourth section limited its application to state laws strictly local, that is to say, to the positive statutes of the state, and the construction thereof adopted by the local tribunals, and to rights and titles to things having a permanent locality, such as the rights and titles to real estate, and other matters immovable and intraterritorial in their nature and character. It never has been supposed by us, that the section did apply, or was intended to apply, to questions of a more general nature, not at all dependent upon local statutes or local usages of a fixed and permanent operation, as, for example, to the construction of ordinary contracts or other written instruments, and especially to questions of general commercial law, where the state tribunals are called upon to perform the like functions as ourselves, that is, to ascertain upon general reasoning and legal analogies, what is the true exposition of the contract or instrument, or what is the just rule furnished by the principles of commercial law to govern the case."

The Court in applying the rule of § 34 to equity cases * * * said: "The statute, however, is merely declarative of the rule which would exist in the absence of the statute." The federal courts assumed, in the broad field of "general law," the power to declare rules of decision which Congress was confessedly without power to enact as statutes. Doubt was repeatedly expressed as to the correctness of the construction given § 34, and as to the soundness of the rule which it introduced. But it was the more recent research of a competent scholar, who examined the original document, which established that the construction given to it by the Court was erroneous; and that the purpose of the section was merely to make certain that, in all matters except those in which some federal law is controlling, the federal courts exercising jurisdiction in diversity of citizenship cases would apply as their rules of decision the law of the State, unwritten as well as written.[1]

Criticism of the doctrine became widespread after the decision of Black & White Taxicab Co. v. Brown & Yellow Taxicab Co., 276 U.S. 518 (1928). There, Brown and Yellow, a Kentucky corporation owned by Kentuckians, and the Louisville and Nashville Railroad, also a Kentucky corporation, wished that the former should have the exclusive privilege of soliciting passenger and baggage transportation at the Bowling Green, Kentucky, railroad station; and that the Black and White, a competing Kentucky corporation, should be prevented from interfering with that privilege. Knowing

---

[1] Charles Warren, *New Light on the History of the Federal Judiciary Act of 1789* (1923) 37 HARV. L. REV. 49. 51-52, 81-88, 108.

that such a contract would be void under the common law of Kentucky, it was arranged that the Brown and Yellow reincorporate under the law of Tennessee, and that the contract with the railroad should be executed there. The suit was then brought by the Tennessee corporation in the federal court for western Kentucky to enjoin competition by the Black and White; an injunction issued by the District Court was sustained by the Court of Appeals; and this Court, citing many decisions in which the doctrine of *Swift v. Tyson* had been applied, affirmed the decree.

Second. Experience in applying the doctrine of *Swift v. Tyson*, had revealed its defects, political and social; and the benefits expected to flow from the rule did not accrue. Persistence of state courts in their own opinions on questions of common law prevented uniformity; and the impossibility of discovering a satisfactory line of demarcation between the province of general law and that of local law developed a new well of uncertainties.[8]

On the other hand, the mischievous results of the doctrine had become apparent. Diversity of citizenship jurisdiction was conferred in order to prevent apprehended discrimination in state courts against those not citizens of the State. *Swift v. Tyson* introduced grave discrimination by non-citizens against citizens. It made rights enjoyed under the unwritten "general law" vary according to whether enforcement was sought in the state or in the federal court; and the privilege of selecting the court in which the right should be determined was conferred upon the non-citizen. Thus, the doctrine rendered impossible equal protection of the law. In attempting to promote uniformity of law throughout the United States, the doctrine had prevented uniformity in the administration of the law of the State.

The discrimination resulting became in practice far-reaching. This resulted in part from the broad province accorded to the so-called "general law" as to which federal courts exercised an independent judgment. In addition to questions of purely commercial law, "general law" was held to include the obligations under contracts entered into and to be performed within the State, the extent to which a carrier operating within a State may stipulate for exemption from liability for his own negligence or that of his employee; the liability for torts committed within the State upon persons resident or property located there, even where the question of liability depended upon the scope of a property right conferred by the State; and the right to exemplary or punitive damages. Furthermore, state decisions construing local deeds, mineral conveyances, and even devises of real estate were disregarded.

In part the discrimination resulted from the wide range of persons held entitled to avail themselves of the federal rule by resort to the diversity of citizenship jurisdiction. Through this jurisdiction individual citizens willing to remove from their own State and become citizens of another might avail themselves of the federal rule. And, without even change of residence, a corporate citizen of the State could avail itself of the federal rule by re-incorporating under the laws of another State, as was done in the *Taxicab* case.

The injustice and confusion incident to the doctrine of *Swift v. Tyson* have been repeatedly urged as reasons for abolishing or limiting diversity of citizenship jurisdiction. Other legislative relief has been proposed. If only a question of statutory construction were involved, we should not

---

[8] Compare 2 WARREN, THE SUPREME COURT IN UNITED STATES HISTORY (rev. ed. 1935) 89: "Probably no decision of the Court has ever given rise to more uncertainty as to legal rights; and though doubtless intended to promote uniformity in the operation of business transactions, its chief effect has been to render it difficult for businessmen to know in advance to what particular topic the Court would apply the doctrine..." The Federal Digest, through the 1937 volume, lists nearly 1000 decisions involving the distinction between questions of general and of local law.

be prepared to abandon a doctrine so widely applied throughout nearly a century. But the unconstitutionality of the course pursued has now been made clear and compels us to do so.

Third. Except in matters governed by the Federal Constitution or by Acts of Congress, the law to be applied in any case is the law of the State. And whether the law of the State shall be declared by its Legislature in a statute or by its highest court in a decision is not a matter of federal concern. There is no federal general common law. Congress has no power to declare substantive rules of common law applicable in a State whether they be local in their nature or "general," be they commercial law or a part of the law of torts. And no clause in the Constitution purports to confer such a power upon the federal courts. As stated by Justice Field when protesting in Baltimore & Ohio R. Co. v. Baugh, 149 U.S. 368, 401 (1893), against ignoring the Ohio common law of fellow servant liability:

> "I am aware that what has been termed the general law of the country — which is often little less than what the judge advancing the doctrine thinks at the time should be the general law on a particular subject — has been often advanced in judicial opinions of this court to control a conflicting law of a State. I admit that learned judges have fallen into the habit of repeating this doctrine as a convenient mode of brushing aside the law of a State in conflict with their views. And I confess that, moved and governed by the authority of the great names of those judges, I have, myself, in many instances, unhesitatingly and confidently, but I think now erroneously, repeated the same doctrine. But, notwithstanding the great names which may be cited in favor of the doctrine, and notwithstanding the frequency with which the doctrine has been reiterated, there stands, as a perpetual protest against its repetition, the Constitution of the United States, which recognizes and preserves the autonomy and independence of the States — independence in their legislative and independence in their judicial departments. Supervision over either the legislative or the judicial action of the States is in no case permissible except as to matters by the Constitution specifically authorized or delegated to the United States. Any interference with either, except as thus permitted, is an invasion of the authority of the State and, to that extent, a denial of its independence."

The fallacy underlying the rule declared in *Swift v. Tyson* is made clear by Justice Holmes. The doctrine rests upon the assumption that there is "a transcendental body of law outside of any particular State but obligatory within it unless and until changed by statute," that federal courts have the power to use their judgment as to what the rules of common law are; and that in the federal courts "the parties are entitled to an independent judgment on matters of general law":

> "but law in the sense in which courts speak of it today does not exist without some definite authority behind it. The common law so far as it is enforced in a State, whether called common law or not, is not the common law generally but the law of that State existing by the authority of that State without regard to what it may have been in England or anywhere else....

> "the authority and only authority is the State, and if that be so, the voice adopted by the State as its own [whether it be of its Legislature or of its Supreme Court] should utter the last word."

CHAPTER 7 WHAT LAW APPLIES IN FEDERAL COURT

Thus the doctrine of *Swift v. Tyson* is, as Justice Holmes said, "an unconstitutional assumption of powers by courts of the United States which no lapse of time or respectable array of opinion should make us hesitate to correct." In disapproving that doctrine we do not hold unconstitutional § 34 of the Federal Judiciary Act of 1789 or any other Act of Congress. We merely declare that in applying the doctrine this Court and the lower courts have invaded rights which in our opinion are reserved by the Constitution to the several States.

Fourth. The defendant contended that by the common law of Pennsylvania as declared by its highest court * * * the only duty owed to the plaintiff was to refrain from wilful or wanton injury. The plaintiff denied that such is the Pennsylvania law. In support of their respective contentions the parties discussed and cited many decisions of the Supreme Court of the State. The Circuit Court of Appeals ruled that the question of liability is one of general law; and on that ground declined to decide the issue of state law. As we hold this was error, the judgment is reversed and the case remanded to it for further proceedings in conformity with our opinion.

Reversed.

JUSTICE CARDOZO took no part in the consideration or decision of this case.

JUSTICE REED.

I concur in the conclusion reached in this case, in the disapproval of the doctrine of *Swift v. Tyson*, and in the reasoning of the majority opinion except in so far as it relies upon the unconstitutionality of the "course pursued" by the federal courts.

* * *

To decide the case now before us and to "disapprove" the doctrine of *Swift v. Tyson* requires only that we say that the words "the laws" include in their meaning the decisions of the local tribunals. As the majority opinion shows, by its reference to Mr. Warren's researches and the first quotation from Justice Holmes, that this Court is now of the view that "laws" includes "decisions," it is unnecessary to go further and declare that the "course pursued" was "unconstitutional," instead of merely erroneous.

The "unconstitutional" course referred to in the majority opinion is apparently the ruling in *Swift v. Tyson* that the supposed omission of Congress to legislate as to the effect of decisions leaves federal courts free to interpret general law for themselves. I am not at all sure whether, in the absence of federal statutory direction, federal courts would be compelled to follow state decisions. There was sufficient doubt about the matter in 1789 to induce the first Congress to legislate. No former opinions of this Court have passed upon it. * * * If the opinion commits this Court to the position that the Congress is without power to declare what rules of substantive law shall govern the federal courts, that conclusion also seems questionable. The line between procedural and substantive law is hazy but no one doubts federal power over procedure. The Judiciary Article and the "necessary and proper" clause of Article One may fully authorize legislation, such as this section of the Judiciary Act.

In this Court, stare decisis, in statutory construction, is a useful rule, not an inexorable command. It seems preferable to overturn an established construction of an Act of Congress, rather than, in the circumstances of this case, to interpret the Constitution.

There is no occasion to discuss further the range or soundness of these few phrases of the opinion. It is sufficient now to call attention to them and express my own non-acquiescence.

NOTES AND QUESTIONS

1. In the Supreme Court, as in the lower courts, the parties in *Erie* framed their arguments in terms of *Swift v. Tyson*, with Tompkins arguing that the issue (the standard of care owed by the railroad to trespassers) was an issue of "general law" as to which federal courts could apply federal law. The railroad argued that the issue was of "local law" and therefore was controlled by state law. Neither party argued that *Swift v. Tyson* should be overruled. Imagine their surprise when they read the opening sentence of Justice Brandeis' opinion. If you had represented Tompkins and the railroad had argued for overruling *Swift*, what arguments could you have made in support of *Swift*?

2. In his opinion in *Swift*, Justice Story supported his call for a general common law with Cicero's statement that the law cannot be one thing in Rome and another in Athens. 41 U.S. at 19. How would Justice Brandeis respond to this argument?

3. Consider Justice Brandeis' arguments for overruling *Swift*. Which arguments do you find most persuasive?

4. Suppose a federal statute provided that railroads are not liable to trespassers injured on a railroad right of way. An injured trespasser files suit in federal court in a state in which property owners are liable for negligence toward trespassers. After *Erie*, must the federal court apply state law on the federal statute?

5. Justice Brandeis uses *Black & White Taxicab* as an illustration of the mischief caused by *Swift*. At the time of *Erie*, corporations were considered citizens only of their state of incorporation for diversity purposes. Thus, as in *Black & White Taxicab*, a corporation could change its citizenship relatively easily by reincorporating in a different state. In 1958, Congress amended § 1332 to add subpart (c) which makes corporations also citizens of their principal place of business. See supra at 184. Is *Erie* an overreaction to a problem with a simple statutory solution?

6. The Court refers to a draft of Section 34 of the Judiciary Act discovered by Professor Charles Warren. That draft provided: "the Statute law of the several States in force for the time being and their unwritten or common law now in use, whether by adoption from the common law of England, the ancient statutes of the same or otherwise * * * " shall be the rules of decision in federal court. The final version of the statute substituted the phrase "laws of the several states" in place of the longer draft version. Professor Warren concluded that the final version was intended to mean the same thing as the earlier version, and the change was simply stylistic. Charles Warren, *New Light on the History of the Federal Judiciary Act of 1789*, 37 HARV. L. REV. 49, 86 (1923). Is this the only possible explanation for the change?

Another historian, Wilfred Ritz, draws a different conclusion from this earlier draft. While he agrees that the change in language was probably stylistic, he argues that the draft demonstrates that "the laws of the several states" meant American law as opposed to English law. He concludes that Section 34 of the Judiciary Act of 1789

> is a direction to the national courts to apply American law, as distinguished from English law. American law is to be found in the "laws of the several states" viewed as a group of eleven states in 1789, and not viewed separately and individually. It is not a direction to apply the law of a particular state, for if it had been so intended, the section would have referred to the "laws of the respective states."

WILFRED J. RITZ, REWRITING THE HISTORY OF THE JUDICIARY ACT OF 1789, 148 (1990). See Patrick Borchers, *The Origins of Diversity Jurisdiction, The Rise of Legal Positivism, and a Brave New World for Erie and Klaxon*, 72 TEX. L. REV. 79 (1993).

7. *Erie* has come to be understood as a cornerstone of our federalism. But the opinion was issued without much fanfare or immediate recognition of the opinion's significance. Then Professor Frankfurter wrote to President Roosevelt: "I certainly didn't expect to live to see the day when the Court would announce, as they did on Monday, that it itself has usurped power for nearly a hundred years. And think of not a single New York paper — at least none that I saw — having a nose for the significance of such a decision. How fluid it all makes the Constitution." ROOSEVELT AND FRANKFURTER: THEIR CORRESPONDENCE 1928-1945, at 456 (Max Freedman ed., 1967).

8. The year 1938 marked dramatic change in federal court practice. With *Erie*, the federal courts began looking to state law on matters of substantive law that had previously been governed by federal common law. However, the year brought another dramatic change. In 1934, Congress had enacted the Rules of Enabling Act authorizing the Supreme Court to promulgate a uniform set of procedural rules to be applied in the federal courts. An advisory committee worked for several years on these rules and in 1938 these rules went into effect. Thus, prior to 1938, federal courts, pursuant to the Conformity Act, applied state procedural rules but federal common law on matters of general law; whereas after 1938, federal courts applied federal procedural rules but state substantive law on matters covered by *Erie*. See Mary Kay Kane, *The Golden Wedding Year:* Erie Railroad Company v. Tompkins *and the Federal Rules*, 63 NOTRE DAME L. REV. 671 (1988). See also Jack Weinstein, *The Ghost of Process: The Fiftieth Anniversary of the Federal Rules of Civil Procedure and* Erie, 54 BROOKLYN L. REV. 1 (1988).

The year 1938 was also at the beginning of the New Deal revolution in which the Court legitimized a massive expansion of federal power at the expense of the states. See, e.g., N.L.R.B. v. Jones & Laughlin Steel Corp., 301 U.S. 1 (1937). *Erie*, with its concern about overstepping limits on federal power, seems out of place with this trend. Professors Fink and Tushnet have suggested that the explanation may lie in the then prevailing view that diversity jurisdiction had become an oppressive tool of big corporations. See HOWARD FINK & MARK TUSHNET, FEDERAL JURISDICTION: POLICY AND PRACTICE 190 (2d ed. 1987). Federal courts were perceived to be pro-business and individual plaintiffs generally preferred state court. As one federal judge noted in 1912,

> It is a well-recognized fact in judicial history that plaintiffs, in actions brought by employees against railway companies for damages resulting from personal injuries, have quite generally and for many years sought to bring and retain their actions in the state courts * * *. The expense of trials and of appeals in the federal courts have been deterrents, and the variance in the rules of law in such cases has * * * also been well understood.

Hulac v. Chicago & N.W. Ry. Co., 194 F. 747, 748-749 (D.Neb. 1912). See generally EDWARD PURCELL, JR., LITIGATION AND INEQUALITY: FEDERAL DIVERSITY JURISDICTION IN INDUSTRIAL AMERICA, 1870-1958 (1992). Thus, *Erie* may be seen as an anti-corporate decision. Of course, it is doubtful that Mr. Tompkins viewed the decision as anti-corporate.

9. Notice that although the Court decides that the state "laws" referred to in § 34 of the Judiciary Act includes all common law as well as statutory laws, the majority does not discuss whether reference to these state laws is required on absolutely every issue. Indeed, Justice Reed states in concurrence, that "no one doubts federal power over procedure." It is Justice Reed's concurrence that may have given birth to the jurisprudence of labels about "substance" and "procedure." See Gregory Gelfand & Howard Abrams, *Putting* Erie *on the Right Track*, 49 U. PITT. L. REV. 937, 958-64 (1988).

10. The accident in *Erie* occurred in Pennsylvania but Tompkins filed suit in federal court in New York. Although the Court decided that the issue of standard of care was to be governed by state law, it did not discuss *which* state law controlled, though it assumed that the relevant law was that of Pennsylvania. A few years later, in Klaxon Co. v. Stentor Electric Manufacturing Co., 313 U.S. 487 (1941), the Supreme Court held that in a diversity case, federal courts must follow the choice of law rules of the state in which it sits. Thus, in *Erie*, the federal court in New York should apply whatever state's law a New York state court would apply. Because New York would have almost certainly applied Pennsylvania law, the Court's assumption in *Erie* that Pennsylvania law applied is not inconsistent with *Klaxon*. The *Klaxon* rule led Judge Friendly to observe in a diversity case, "Our principle task * * * is to determine what New York Courts would think California Courts would think on an issue about which neither has thought." Nolan v. Transocean Air Lines, 276 F.2d.

280, 281 (2d. Cir. 1960). Although some commentators have criticized *Klaxon*, see, e.g., William Baxter, *Choice of Law and the Federal System*, 16 STAN. L. REV. 1, 41-42 (1963), the Supreme Court reaffirmed its holding in Day & Zimmerman, Inc. v. Challoner, 423 U.S. 3, 4 (1975).

11. At trial, Tompkins won a verdict of $30,000. Shortly thereafter, the Railroad offered to settle with Tompkins for $7,500. To Tompkins, who was unemployed and had a wife and child to support, the sum was substantial and accepting it would have avoided the delay and uncertainty associated with appeals. Although Tompkins was inclined to accept, the lawyer advised him strongly against it. Reportedly, his lawyer was so concerned that Tompkins might settle precipitously that he invited Tompkins to visit him at his home in New York where Tompkins stayed for two weeks until the appeal was well underway and the settlement offer withdrawn. On remand the court held that under Pennsylvania law, the railroad was liable to Tompkins only if it acted with "wanton negligence." Because Tompkins had neither pleaded nor proved that degree of culpability, the court entered judgment for the railroad. See Irving Younger, *What Happened in* Erie, 56 TEX. L. REV. 1011, 1021-22 (1978).

NOTE: CONSTITUTIONAL BASES OF *ERIE*

Although the Court in *Erie* referred to the "unconstitutionality of the course pursued" under the regime of *Swift v. Tyson,* it held that the Rules of Decision Act itself is not unconstitutional. The Court cites no provision of the Constitution that was violated. As Professor Wright observes that "it is unusual to have a constitutional decision that avoids making specific reference to the constitutional provision involved." WRIGHT, FEDERAL COURTS 382. It is especially perplexing because Brandeis was known for avoiding constitutional issues if possible. In a letter, Justice Stone called the language "unfortunate dicta." Id. Others also criticized the idea of a constitutional underpinning. See Charles Clark, *State Law in the Federal Courts: The Brooding Omnipresence of* Erie v. Tompkins, 55 YALE L.J. 267, 273, 278 (1946). Judge Friendly's rejoinder is the best: if the Court says it's making a constitutional ruling, we should take it at its word until it says otherwise. Henry Friendly, *In Praise of* Erie — *And of the New Federal Common Law*, 39 N.Y.U. L. REV. 383, 386 n.15 (1964). Of course, this still begs the question of what provision was violated.

Under *Swift*, federal courts were required to apply state law only where there was an applicable state statute or the issue was one of "local law." Where there was no statute and the issue was one of "general law," the Rules of Decision Act was thought to be silent. This created a gap, and the federal courts assumed that they had the authority to fill the gap by creating general federal common law. It was this judicially assumed power to create general federal common law that *Erie* held to be unconstitutional.

While it is relatively clear what the Court held unconstitutional, it is less clear *why* it did so. The generally accepted argument about why the federal courts were acting unconstitutionally under *Swift* focuses on the fact that the federal government is limited to those powers enumerated in the Constitution. As Dean John Hart Ely has explained, "[t]he Constitution is * * * a sort of checklist, enumerating in a general way those things the central government may do and by implication denying it power to do anything else." John Ely, *The Irrepressible Myth of* Erie, 87 HARV. L. REV. 693, 701 (1974) (quoting M'Culloch v. Maryland, 17 U.S. 316, 404 (1819)). Under the Tenth Amendment, those powers not granted to the federal government "are reserved to the States, respectively, or to the people." Thus, the constitutional problem is that "nothing in the Constitution provided the central government with a general lawmaking authority of the sort the Court had been exercising under Swift." Ely, supra, at 703. As Professor Wright explains, *Erie* "returns to the states a power that had for nearly a century been exercised by the federal government." WRIGHT, FEDERAL COURTS 377.

One difficulty with this arguement is that the enumerated powers of Congress, particularly its power under the Commerce Clause, have been broadly construed. Although the Commerce Clause has some limits, see United States v. Lopez, 115 S. Ct. 1624 (1995), there is no doubt that it extends to the regulation of interstate railroads, as was at issue in *Erie*. If Congress could have legislated in this area, why can't the courts act in the area to create common law?

The answer may be that while *Congress* has *legislative* authority, the federal courts' judicial authority is not as broad. The more limited authority of the courts reflects separation of power concerns about the appropriate role for courts. It may also reflect federalism concerns because, although the interests of states are represented in Congress through Senators and Representatives, those interests are less likely to be represented in the federal judiciary. See Thomas Merrill, *The Common Law Powers of Federal Courts*, 52 U. CHI. L. REV. 1, 13-24 (1985).

The argument that federal courts exceeded their constitutional authority in creating general federal common law assumes that nothing in the Constitution confers such authority on the courts. However, one might argue that the grant of diversity jurisdiction in Art. III, sec. 2 of the Constitution carried with it authority to make general federal common law to be applied in diversity cases. After all, the whole purpose of diversity jurisdiction was to prevent bias against citizens of another state, and the laws themselves might be biased. Indeed, the Supreme Court has long held that the grant of jurisdiction over cases in admiralty carried with it just such a common law authority. Why couldn't the same be true of diversity jurisdiction?

Consider, for example, the reported remarks of John Wilson, arguing in favor of ratification of the Constitution before the Pennsylvania convention. He praised diversity jurisdiction, explaining:

> [I]s it not necessary, if we mean to restore either public or private credit, that foreigners, as well as ourselves, have a just and impartial tribunal to which they may resort? I would ask how a merchant must feel to have his property be at the mercy of the laws of Rhode Island. * * * [S]ecurity [for contracts] cannot be obtained, unless we give the power of deciding upon those contracts to the general government.

2 THE DEBATES IN THE SEVERAL STATE CONVENTIONS ON THE ADOPTION OF THE FEDERAL CONSTITUTION 491-492 (J. Elliot ed., 2d ed. 1836). Does Wilson's concern about "the laws of Rhode Island" suggest that he assumed federal diversity courts would not be bound by the law of that state?

Concerning the argument that diversity jurisdiction carries with it a grant of law making authority, Dean Ely has responded:

> It would not be irrational to fight bias against out-of-staters by giving them access to a body of law, developed by persons beholden to no particular state, unavailable in suits between co-citizens. Not irrational, but the founders of our Republic — by not including any such power in the Constitution, and even more clearly by enacting the Rules of Decision Act — refused to do it. Bias against out-of-staters was to be resisted, but only by providing an unbiased tribunal. To provide more, or so it was felt, would create an unfairness in the other direction.

Ely, supra, 87 Harv. L. Rev. at 713.

Regardless of whether you are persuaded by this argument, *Erie* unequivocally rejected the notion that federal courts have authority to make general common law.

2. Distinguishing Substantive and Procedural Rules

Guaranty Trust Co. v. York
326 U.S. 99, 65 S. Ct. 1464, 89 L. Ed. 2079 (1945)

JUSTICE FRANKFURTER delivered the opinion of the Court.

* * *

The suit, instituted * * * in a federal court solely because of diversity of citizenship, is based on an alleged breach of trust by Guaranty in that it failed to protect the interests of the noteholders * * *. On appeal, the Circuit Court of Appeals, one Judge dissenting, * * * held that in a suit brought on the equity side of a federal district court that court is not required to apply the State statute of limitations that would govern like suits in the courts of a State where the federal court is sitting even though the exclusive basis of federal jurisdiction is diversity of citizenship. * * *

* * *

Our starting point must be the policy of federal jurisdiction which *Erie R. Co. v. Tompkins* embodies. In overruling *Swift v. Tyson, Erie R. Co. v. Tompkins* did not merely overrule a venerable case. It overruled a particular way of looking at law which dominated the judicial process long after its inadequacies had been laid bare. Law was conceived as a "brooding omnipresence" of Reason, of which decisions were merely evidence and not themselves the controlling formulations. Accordingly, federal courts deemed themselves free to ascertain what Reason, and therefore Law, required wholly independent of authoritatively declared State law, even in cases where a legal right as the basis for relief was created by State authority and could not be created by federal authority and the case got into a federal court merely because it was "between Citizens of different States" under Art. III, § 2 of the Constitution of the United States.

* * *

In relation to the problem now here, the real significance of *Swift v. Tyson* lies in the fact that it did not enunciate novel doctrine. Nor was it restricted to its particular situation. It summed up prior attitudes and expressions in cases that had come before this Court and lower federal courts for at least thirty years, at law as well as in equity. The short of it is that the doctrine was congenial to the jurisprudential climate of the time. Once established, judicial momentum kept it going. Since it was conceived that there was "a transcendental body of law outside of any particular State but obligatory within it unless and until changed by statute," State court decisions were not "the law" but merely someone's opinion — to be sure an opinion to be respected — concerning the content of this all-pervading law. Not unnaturally, the federal courts assumed power to find for themselves the content of such a body of law. The notion was stimulated by the attractive vision of a uniform body of federal law. To such sentiments for uniformity of decision and freedom from diversity in State law the federal courts gave currency, particularly in cases where equitable remedies were sought, because equitable doctrines are so often cast in terms of universal applicability when close analysis of the source of legal enforceability is not demanded.

In exercising their jurisdiction on the ground of diversity of citizenship, the federal courts, in the long course of their history, have not differentiated in their regard for State law between actions at law and suits in equity. Although § 34 of the Judiciary Act of 1789, directed that the "laws of the several states ... shall be regarded as rules of decision in trials at common law ...," this was deemed, consistently for over a hundred years, to be merely declaratory of what would in any event have governed the federal courts and therefore was equally applicable to equity suits. Indeed, it may fairly be said that the federal courts gave greater respect to State-created "substantive rights," in equity than they gave them on the law side, because rights at law were usually declared by State courts and as such increasingly flouted by extension of the doctrine of *Swift v. Tyson,* while rights in

CHAPTER 7 WHAT LAW APPLIES IN FEDERAL COURT

equity were frequently defined by legislative enactment and as such known and respected by the federal courts.

Partly because the States in the early days varied greatly in the manner in which equitable relief was afforded and in the extent to which it was available, Congress provided that "the forms and modes of proceeding in suits ... of equity" would conform to the settled uses of courts of equity. 28 U.S.C. § 723. But this enactment gave the federal courts no power that they would not have had in any event when courts were given "cognizance," by the first Judiciary Act, of suits "in equity." From the beginning there has been a good deal of talk in the cases that federal equity is a separate legal system. And so it is, properly understood. The suits in equity of which the federal courts have had "cognizance" ever since 1789 constituted the body of law which had been transplanted to this country from the English Court of Chancery. But this system of equity "derived its doctrines, as well as its powers, from its mode of giving relief." In giving federal courts "cognizance" of equity suits in cases of diversity jurisdiction, Congress never gave, nor did the federal courts ever claim, the power to deny substantive rights created by State law or to create substantive rights denied by State law.

This does not mean that whatever equitable remedy is available in a State court must be available in a diversity suit in a federal court, or conversely, that a federal court may not afford an equitable remedy not available in a State court. * * * State law cannot define the remedies which a federal court must give simply because a federal court in diversity jurisdiction is available as an alternative tribunal to the State's courts. Contrariwise, a federal court may afford an equitable remedy for a substantive right recognized by a State even though a State court cannot give it. Whatever contradiction or confusion may be produced by a medley of judicial phrases severed from their environment, the body of adjudications concerning equitable relief in diversity cases leaves no doubt that the federal courts enforced State-created substantive rights if the mode of proceeding and remedy were consonant with the traditional body of equitable remedies, practice and procedure, and in so doing they were enforcing rights created by the States and not arising under any inherent or statutory federal law.

Inevitably, therefore, the principle of *Erie R. Co. v. Tompkins*, an action at law, was promptly applied to a suit in equity.

And so this case reduces itself to the narrow question whether, when no recovery could be had in a State court because the action is barred by the statute of limitations, a federal court in equity can take cognizance of the suit because there is diversity of citizenship between the parties. Is the outlawry, according to State law, of a claim created by the States a matter of "substantive rights" to be respected by a federal court of equity when that court's jurisdiction is dependent on the fact that there is a State-created right, or is such statute of "a mere remedial character," which a federal court may disregard?

Matters of "substance" and matters of "procedure" are much talked about in the books as though they defined a great divide cutting across the whole domain of law. But, of course, "substance" and "procedure" are the same keywords to very different problems. Neither "substance" nor "procedure" represents the same invariants. Each implies different variables depending upon the particular problem for which it is used. And the different problems are only distantly related at best, for the terms are in common use in connection with situations turning on such different considerations as those that are relevant to questions pertaining to ex post facto legislation, the impairment of the obligations of contract, the enforcement of federal rights in the State courts and the multitudinous phases of the conflict of laws.

Here we are dealing with a right to recover derived not from the United States but from one of the States. When, because the plaintiff happens to be a non-resident, such a right is enforceable in a federal as well as in a State court, the forms and mode of enforcing the right may at times, naturally enough, vary because the two judicial systems are not identic. But since a federal court adjudicating a State-created right solely because of the diversity of citizenship of the parties is for that purpose, in effect, only another court of the State, it cannot afford recovery if the right to recover is made unavailable by the State nor can it substantially affect the enforcement of the right as given by the State.

And so the question is not whether a statute of limitations is deemed a matter of "procedure" in some sense. The question is whether such a statute concerns merely the manner and the means by which a right to recover, as recognized by the State, is enforced, or whether such statutory limitation is a matter of substance in the aspect that alone is relevant to our problem, namely, does it significantly affect the result of a litigation for a federal court to disregard a law of a State that would be controlling in an action upon the same claim by the same parties in a State court?

It is therefore immaterial whether statutes of limitation are characterized either as "substantive" or "procedural" in State court opinions in any use of those terms unrelated to the specific issue before us. *Erie R. Co. v. Tompkins* was not an endeavor to formulate scientific legal terminology. It expressed a policy that touches vitally the proper distribution of judicial power between State and federal courts. In essence, the intent of that decision was to insure that, in all cases where a federal court is exercising jurisdiction solely because of the diversity of citizenship of the parties, the outcome of the litigation in the federal court should be substantially the same, so far as legal rules determine the outcome of a litigation, as it would be if tried in a State court. The nub of the policy that underlies *Erie R. Co. v. Tompkins* is that for the same transaction the accident of a suit by a non-resident litigant in a federal court instead of in a State court a block away should not lead to a substantially different result. And so, putting to one side abstractions regarding "substance" and "procedure," we have held that in diversity cases the federal courts must follow the law of the State as to burden of proof, as to conflict of laws, Klaxon Co. v. Stentor Co., 313 U.S. 487 (1941), as to contributory negligence. *Erie R. Co. v. Tompkins* has been applied with an eye alert to essentials in avoiding disregard of State law in diversity cases in the federal courts. A policy so important to our federalism must be kept free from entanglements with analytical or terminological niceties.

Plainly enough, a statute that would completely bar recovery in a suit if brought in a State court bears on a State-created right vitally and not merely formally or negligibly. As to consequences that so intimately affect recovery or non-recovery a federal court in a diversity case should follow State law. * * *

* * *

To make an exception to *Erie R. Co. v. Tompkins* on the equity side of a federal court is to reject the considerations of policy which, after long travail, led to that decision. Judge Augustus N. Hand thus summarized below the fatal objection to such inroad upon *Erie R. Co. v. Tompkins*: "In my opinion it would be a mischievous practice to disregard state statutes of limitation whenever federal courts think that the result of adopting them may be inequitable. Such procedure would promote the choice of United States rather than of state courts in order to gain the advantage of different laws. The main foundation for the criticism of *Swift v. Tyson* was that a litigant in cases where federal jurisdiction is based only on diverse citizenship may obtain a more favorable decision by suing in the United States courts."

Diversity jurisdiction is founded on assurance to nonresident litigants of courts free from susceptibility to potential local bias. The Framers of the Constitution, according to Marshall, entertained "apprehensions" lest distant suitors be subjected to local bias in State courts, or, at least, viewed with "indulgence the possible fears and apprehensions" of such suitors. And so Congress afforded out-of-State litigants another tribunal, not another body of law. The operation of a double system of conflicting laws in the same State is plainly hostile to the reign of law. Certainly, the fortuitous circumstance of residence out of a State of one of the parties to a litigation ought not to give rise to a discrimination against others equally concerned but locally resident. The source of substantive rights enforced by a federal court under diversity jurisdiction, it cannot be said too often, is the law of the States. Whenever that law is authoritatively declared by a State, whether its voice be the legislature or its highest court, such law ought to govern in litigation founded on that law, whether the forum of application is a State or a federal court and whether the remedies be sought at law or may be had in equity.

* * *

The judgment is reversed and the case is remanded for proceedings not inconsistent with this opinion.

So ordered.

NOTES AND QUESTIONS

1. The Court in *York* says that the policy underlying *Erie* was to ensure that litigants would get the same result in federal court as in state court. Was that really the focus of *Erie*? Wasn't the *Erie* Court's focus on the unconstitutionality of federal courts' making general federal common law?

2. Isn't it true that any procedural rule which includes a potential sanction of dismissal can affect outcome? Suppose that on the last day before the expiration of the statute of limitations, the federal clerk refuses to accept your filing because it is on the wrong size paper. If the state court would have accepted the filing and the federal court would not, does a rule about paper size significantly affect the outcome? Yet, does that mean a federal court has no power to prescribe something so obviously procedural as paper size?

3. *York* was an equity suit and at the time of that decision, § 34 of the Judiciary Act did not explicitly apply to equity actions. Justice Frankfurter finessed this potential problem by explaining that § 34 was "merely declaratory of what would in any event have governed the federal courts and therefore was applicable to equity suits." The expansion of the Rules of Decision Act to include equity actions produced an analytical complication for Frankfurter. The remedies available in federal equity were generally considered an issue of federal, not state, law. Frankfurter explicitly reaffirms this principle. It is difficult to square this principle, however, with the outcome test Frankfurter announces. If different remedies are available in state and federal court, wouldn't that significantly affect the results of litigation? See David Crump, *The Twilight Zone of the* Erie *Doctrine: Is There Really a Different Choice of Equitable Remedies in the "Court a Block Away?,"* 1991 WIS. L. REV. 1233.

    4. The approach of *York* was applied a few years later in a trilogy of cases all handed down the same day.

    (a) Ragan v. Merchants Transfer & Warehouse Co., 337 U.S. 530 (1949). Rule 3 of the Federal Rules provides that "an action is commenced by filing a complaint." Nonetheless, relying on *York*, the Court held that state law controls when an action is "commenced" for purposes of the statute of limitations.

    (b) Woods v. Interstate Realty Co., 337 U.S. 535 (1949). A Mississippi "door closing statute" provided that out-of-state corporations that had failed to properly register in Mississippi were barred from suing in state court. The Supreme Court held that a Mississippi federal court should apply the state statute and bar such corporations from suing in federal court.

    (c) Cohen v. Beneficial Industrial Loan Corp., 337 U.S. 541 (1949). To discourage so-called strike suits, state law required plaintiffs in shareholder derivative actions to post a substantial bond. Although Rule 23.1 enumerates the criteria for shareholder derivative actions and does not require a bond, the Court held that the state bond requirement applied in a shareholder derivative action in federal court.

    5. The development of vertical choice of law has gone in waves, with various periods suggesting state or federal hegemony. In the 20 years after *Erie*, the pendulum swung quite far toward application of state law. *Ragan, Woods,* and *Cohen* led to concern that federal law would never be found to prevail and that the Federal Rules were in trouble. Judge Clark said that few of the rules "[could] be considered safe from attack" after *Ragan*. Charles Clark, Book Review, 36 CORNELL L.Q. 181, 183 (1950). Some commentators urged repeal of the Federal Rules in diversity cases. See Bernard Gavit, *States' Rights and Federal Procedure*, 25 IND. L.J. 1, 26 (1949); Edward Merrigan, Erie *to* York *to* Ragan — A TRIPLE PLAY ON THE FEDERAL RULES, 3 VAND. L. REV. 711 (1950). As we will see, concern about the validity of the Federal Rules of Civil Procedure proved unfounded.

CHAPTER 7 WHAT LAW APPLIES IN FEDERAL COURT

Byrd v. Blue Ridge Electrical Cooperative, Inc.
356 U.S. 525, 78 S. Ct. 893, 2 L. Ed. 2d 953 (1958)

JUSTICE BRENNAN delivered the opinion of the Court.

This case was brought in the District Court for the Western District of South Carolina. Jurisdiction was based on diversity of citizenship. The petitioner, a resident of North Carolina, sued respondent, a South Carolina corporation, for damages for injuries allegedly caused by the respondent's negligence. He had judgment on a jury verdict. The Court of Appeals for the Fourth Circuit reversed and directed the entry of judgment for the respondent. We granted certiorari, and subsequently ordered reargument.

The respondent is in the business of selling electric power to subscribers in rural sections of South Carolina. The petitioner was employed as a lineman in the construction crew of a construction contractor. * * *

One of respondent's affirmative defenses was that, under the South Carolina Workmen's Compensation Act, the petitioner — because the work contracted to be done by his employer was work of the kind also done by the respondent's own construction and maintenance crews — had the status of a statutory employee of the respondent and was therefore barred from suing the respondent at law because obliged to accept statutory compensation benefits as the exclusive remedy for his injuries. Two questions concerning this defense are before us: (1) whether the Court of Appeals erred in directing judgment for respondent without a remand to give petitioner an opportunity to introduce further evidence; and (2) whether petitioner, state practice notwithstanding, is entitled to a jury determination of the factual issues raised by this defense.

I

[As to the first issue, the Court held that the court of appeals erred in directing judgment for respondent. The Court ordered the case remanded to permit petitioner an opportunity to present evidence on the question of whether respondent was a statutory employee within the meaning of the South Carolina Workers Compensation statute.]

II

A question is also presented as to whether on remand the factual issue is to be decided by the judge or by the jury. The respondent argues on the basis of the decision of the Supreme Court of South Carolina in Adams v. Davison-Paxon Co., 230 S.C. 532, 96 S.E. 2d 566 (1957), that the issue of immunity should be decided by the judge and not by the jury. * * *

The respondent argues that this state-court decision governs the present diversity case and "divests the jury of its normal function" to decide the disputed fact question of the respondent's immunity under § 72-111. This is to contend that the federal court is bound under *Erie R. Co. v. Tompkins* to follow the state court's holding to secure uniform enforcement of the immunity created by the State.

First. It was decided in *Erie R. Co. v. Tompkins* that the federal courts in diversity cases must respect the definition of state-created rights and obligations by the state courts. We must, therefore, first examine the rule in *Adams v. Davison-Paxon Co.* to determine whether it is bound up with these rights and obligations in such a way that its application in the federal court is required.

The Workmen's Compensation Act is administered in South Carolina by its Industrial Commission. The South Carolina courts hold that, on judicial review of actions of the Commission under § 72-111, the question whether the claim of an injured workman is within the Commission's jurisdiction is a matter of law for decision by the court, which makes its own findings of fact relating to that jurisdiction. The South Carolina Supreme Court states no reasons in *Adams v. Davison-Paxon Co.* why, although the jury decides all other factual issues raised by the cause of action and defenses, the jury is displaced as to the factual issue raised by the affirmative defense under § 72-111. * * * A State may, of course, distribute the functions of its judicial machinery as it sees fit. The decisions relied upon, however, furnish no reason for selecting the judge rather than the jury to decide this single affirmative defense in the negligence action. They simply reflect a policy, that administrative determination of "jurisdictional facts" should not be final but subject to judicial review. The conclusion is inescapable that the *Adams* holding is grounded in the practical consideration that the question had theretofore come before the South Carolina courts from the Industrial Commission and the courts had become accustomed to deciding the factual issue of immunity without the aid of juries. We find nothing to suggest that this rule was announced as an integral part of the special relationship created by the statute. Thus the requirement appears to be merely a form and mode of enforcing the immunity, *Guaranty Trust Co. v. York*, and not a rule intended to be bound up with the definition of the rights and obligations of the parties. The situation is therefore not analogous to that in Dice v. Akron, C. & Y. R. Co., 342 U.S. 359 (1952), where this Court held that the right to trial by jury is so substantial a part of the cause of action created by the Federal Employers' Liability Act that the Ohio courts could not apply, in an action under that statute, the Ohio rule that the question of fraudulent release was for determination by a judge rather than by a jury.

Second. But cases following *Erie* have evinced a broader policy to the effect that the federal courts should conform as near as may be — in the absence of other considerations — to state rules even of form and mode where the state rules may bear substantially on the question whether the litigation would come out one way in the federal court and another way in the state court if the federal court failed to apply a particular local rule. E.g., *Guaranty Trust Co. v. York*. Concededly the nature of the tribunal which tries issues may be important in the enforcement of the parcel of rights making up a cause of action or defense, and bear significantly upon achievement of uniform enforcement of the right. It may well be that in the instant personal-injury case the outcome would be substantially affected by whether the issue of immunity is decided by a judge or a jury. Therefore, were "outcome" the only consideration, a strong case might appear for saying that the federal court should follow the state practice.

But there are affirmative countervailing considerations at work here. The federal system is an independent system for administering justice to litigants who properly invoke its jurisdiction. An essential characteristic of that system is the manner in which, in civil common-law actions, it distributes trial functions between judge and jury and, under the influence — if not the command[10] — of the Seventh Amendment, assigns the decisions of disputed questions of fact to the jury. The policy of uniform enforcement of state-created rights and obligations, see, e.g., *Guaranty Trust Co. v. York*,

---

[10] Our conclusion makes unnecessary the consideration of — and we intimate no view upon — the constitutional question whether the right of jury trial protected in federal courts by the Seventh Amendment embraces the factual issue of statutory immunity when asserted, as here, as an affirmative defense in a common-law negligence action.

cannot in every case exact compliance with a state rule — not bound up with rights and obligations — which disrupts the federal system of allocating functions between judge and jury. Herron v. Southern Pacific Co., 283 U.S. 91 (1931). Thus the inquiry here is whether the federal policy favoring jury decisions of disputed fact questions should yield to the state rule in the interest of furthering the objective that the litigation should not come out one way in the federal court and another way in the state court.

We think that in the circumstances of this case the federal court should not follow the state rule. It cannot be gainsaid that there is a strong federal policy against allowing state rules to disrupt the judge-jury relationship in the federal courts. In *Herron v. Southern Pacific Co.*, the trial judge in a personal-injury negligence action brought in the District Court for Arizona on diversity grounds directed a verdict for the defendant when it appeared as a matter of law that the plaintiff was guilty of contributory negligence. The federal judge refused to be bound by a provision of the Arizona Constitution which made the jury the sole arbiter of the question of contributory negligence. This Court sustained the action of the trial judge, holding that "state laws cannot alter the essential character or function of a federal court" because that function "is not in any sense a local matter, and state statutes which would interfere with the appropriate performance of that function are not binding upon the federal court under either the Conformity Act or the 'rules of decision' Act." Perhaps even more clearly in light of the influence of the Seventh Amendment, the function assigned to the jury "is an essential factor in the process for which the Federal Constitution provides." Concededly the *Herron* case was decided before *Erie R. Co. v. Tompkins*, but even when *Swift v. Tyson* was governing law and allowed federal courts sitting in diversity cases to disregard state decisional law, it was never thought that state statutes or constitutions were similarly to be disregarded. Yet *Herron* held that state statutes and constitutional provisions could not disrupt or alter the essential character or function of a federal court.

Third. We have discussed the problem upon the assumption that the outcome of the litigation may be substantially affected by whether the issue of immunity is decided by a judge or a jury. But clearly there is not present here the certainty that a different result would follow, cf. *Guaranty Trust Co. v. York*, or even the strong possibility that this would be the case, cf. Bernhardt v. Polygraphic Co., [350 U.S. 198 (1956)]. There are factors present here which might reduce that possibility. The trial judge in the federal system has powers denied the judges of many States to comment on the weight of evidence and credibility of witnesses, and discretion to grant a new trial if the verdict appears to him to be against the weight of the evidence. We do not think the likelihood of a different result is so strong as to require the federal practice of jury determination of disputed factual issues to yield to the state rule in the interest of uniformity of outcome.

The Court of Appeals did not consider other grounds of appeal raised by the respondent because the ground taken disposed of the case. We accordingly remand the case to the Court of Appeals for the decision of the other questions, with instructions that, if not made unnecessary by the decision of such questions, the Court of Appeals shall remand the case to the District Court for a new trial of such issues as the Court of Appeals may direct.

Reversed and remanded.

NOTES AND QUESTIONS

1. Suppose the South Carolina Workers' Compensation statute had explicitly required that determinations about who is an employee be made by judges not juries. Suppose further that it is clear from the statute and its legislative history that the reason for this requirement was the perception that juries tended to be moved by sympathy for the injured worker and to find workers were or were not employees depending on what would ensure the largest recovery. Would this have changed the result in *Byrd*?

2. *Byrd* requires that federal courts analyze the state and federal interests in having their respective rules applied. However, the Court does not elaborate on how those interests are to be assessed. Professor Redish and Mr. Phillips have offered a framework for analyzing these interests. See Martin Redish & Carter Phillips, Erie *and the Rules of Decision Act: In Search of the Appropriate Dilemma,* 91 HARV. L. REV. 356 (1977). As to the state interest, they have argued that the state rules which need to be respected are those that affect "primary conduct," that is, what people do outside of litigation. Obviously, basic rules of liability or standard of care meet this criteria. They note that in addition to these obviously "substantive" state rules, there are some state rules that regulate procedure but which nonetheless affect primary conduct, and should therefore be regulated. Two categories of these substantive procedural rules are (1) rules designed to provide behavioral guides such as evidentiary privilege, and (2) rules for conducting trials that tend to benefit one party more than the other such as burdens of proof.

As to the federal interest, Redish and Phillips have argued that as an "independent system for administering justice," the federal court system has an interest in conducting its business in "what it deems the fairest and most efficient manner." They caution that courts should not put too much weight on the federal interest in using what the federal courts deem the fairest procedure. Id. at 391. They explain that "[i]n the face of a relatively significant countervailing state interest, the 'doing justice' factor should be outbalanced. But where the competing state interest is of relatively slight significance, the interest of a federal court in determining for itself what procedures are 'just' should prevail." Id. Redish and Phillips argue that the one federal interest that should always prevail over state interests is the federal interest in avoiding costs or inconvenience to the federal court.

3. Professor Stein has argued for a somewhat different approach in assessing the state and federal interests. See Allan Stein, Erie *and Court Access,* 100 YALE L.J. 1935 (1991). Stein argues that the first step in a *Byrd* analysis is to determine whether the policy underlying the state rule would be hampered by application of a different rule in federal court. One asks, in essence, whether the state would care if the federal court applied a different rule. Thus, for example, where a state rule is designed simply to cut the costs of operating the state judicial system, the rule can be disregarded in federal court. Of course, in some situations the state policy may be undermined by the application of a different rule in federal court, creating a "true conflict" between the state and federal interests. Where a true conflict exists, Stein argues that the federal practice must be justified by a "paramount federal interest." Id. at 2000. Stein disagrees with Redish and Phillips' willingness to allow federal courts to ignore state rules that impose costs on federal courts. "Most state laws enforced in federal courts implicate the expenditure of federal resources," he argues. Id. at 2001. Stein would allow federal courts to apply federal rules where the purposes underlying federal jurisdiction are implicated, as for example, where a state rule discriminates against out-of-staters.

4. What law should apply when the court concludes that the state and federal interests are equal? For example, in Taylor v. Titan Midwest Construction Corp., 474 F. Supp. 145, 147 (N.D. Tex. 1979), the court found the relative state and federal interests "equally strong," and applied federal law. Is the presence of an equally strong interest sufficient to justify the vertical non-uniformity that results from application of federal law?

5. The Court in *Byrd* refers to "the influence — if not the command" of the Seventh Amendment. What does this mean? If the Seventh Amendment commands a jury trial could the Rules of Decision Act or state law ever override that command? If the Seventh Amendment does not require a jury trial, how can that Amendment have "influence?"

6. Under South Carolina law, the South Carolina state courts have no jurisdiction over cases brought by an out-of-state plaintiff against an out-of-state corporation for a cause of action that arises out-of-state. Under *Byrd*, would a federal court in South Carolina be required to apply this state door-closing statute? See Szantay v. Beech Aircraft Corp., 349 F.2d 60 (4th Cir. 1965).

7. Professor Ely has described the *Byrd* opinion as one that "exhibits a confusion that exceeds even that normally surrounding a balancing test." Ely, supra, 87 HARV. L. REV. at 709. In a similar vein, Professor Wright described *Byrd* as "the most Delphic of the Supreme Court's major *Erie*-doctrine decisions." WRIGHT, FEDERAL COURTS 403.

8. Despite its weaknesses, several commentators praised Byrd for restoring some equilibrium to vertical choice of law, see Friendly, supra, 39 N.Y.U. L. REV. at 403 n.95; Allen Smith, *Blue Ridge and Beyond: A Byrd's Eye View of Federalism in Diversity Litigation,* 36 TULANE L. REV. 443 (1962), and for breathing life back into the Federal Rules. Although *Byrd* did not involved a Federal Rule of Civil Procedure, some saw it as a providing "a formula by which the rules might co-exist with the *Erie* doctrine." WRIGHT, FEDERAL COURTS 403.

B. Determining What Law Applies

3. The Federal Rules of Civil Procedure

Hanna v. Plumer
380 U.S. 460, 85 S. Ct. 1136, 14 L. Ed. 2d 8. (1965)

CHIEF JUSTICE WARREN delivered the opinion of the Court.

The question to be decided is whether, in a civil action where the jurisdiction of the United States district court is based upon diversity of citizenship between the parties, service of process shall be made in the manner prescribed by state law or that set forth in Rule 4 (d)(1) of the Federal Rules of Civil Procedure.

On February 6, 1963, petitioner, a citizen of Ohio, filed her complaint in the District Court for the District of Massachusetts, claiming damages in excess of $10,000 for personal injuries resulting from an automobile accident in South Carolina, allegedly caused by the negligence of one Louise Plumer Osgood, a Massachusetts citizen deceased at the time of the filing of the complaint. Respondent, Mrs. Osgood's executor and also a Massachusetts citizen, was named as defendant. On February 8, service was made by leaving copies of the summons and the complaint with respondent's wife at his residence, concededly in compliance with Rule 4 (d)(1), which provides:

"The summons and complaint shall be served together. The plaintiff shall furnish the person making service with such copies as are necessary. Service shall be made as follows:

"(1) Upon an individual other than an infant or an incompetent person, by delivering a copy of the summons and of the complaint to him personally or by leaving copies thereof at his dwelling house or usual place of abode with some person of suitable age and discretion then residing therein ...."

Respondent filed his answer on February 26, alleging, inter alia, that the action could not be maintained because it had been brought "contrary to and in violation of the provisions of Massachusetts General Laws Chapter 197, Section 9." That section provides:

"Except as provided in this chapter, an executor or administrator shall not be held to answer to an action by a creditor of the deceased which is not commenced within one year from the time of his giving bond for the performance of his trust, or to such an action which is commenced within said year unless before the expiration thereof the writ in such action has been served by delivery in hand upon such executor or administrator or service thereof accepted by him or a notice stating the name of the estate, the name and address of the creditor, the amount of the claim and the court in which the action has been brought has been filed in the proper registry of probate...."

On October 17, 1963, the District Court granted respondent's motion for summary judgment, citing *Ragan v. Merchants Transfer Co.* and *Guaranty Trust Co. v. York* in support of its conclusion that the adequacy of the service was to be measured by § 9, with which, the court held, petitioner had not complied. On appeal, petitioner admitted noncompliance with § 9, but argued that Rule 4 (d)(1) defines the method by which service of process is to be effected in diversity actions. The Court of Appeals for the First Circuit, finding that "[r]elatively recent amendments [to § 9] evince a clear legislative purpose to require personal notification within the year,"[1] concluded that the conflict of state and federal rules was over "a substantive rather than a procedural matter," and unanimously affirmed. Because of the threat to the goal of uniformity of federal procedure posed by the decision below, we granted certiorari.

We conclude that the adoption of Rule 4 (d)(1), designed to control service of process in diversity actions, neither exceeded the congressional mandate embodied in the Rules Enabling Act nor transgressed constitutional bounds, and that the Rule is therefore the standard against which the District Court should have measured the adequacy of the service. Accordingly, we reverse the decision of the Court of Appeals.

The Rules Enabling Act, 28 U.S.C. § 2072, provides, in pertinent part:

> "The Supreme Court shall have the power to prescribe, by general rules, the forms of process, writs, pleadings, and motions, and the practice and procedure of the district courts of the United States in civil actions.
>
> "Such rules shall not abridge, enlarge or modify any substantive right and shall preserve the right of trial by jury ...."

Under the cases construing the scope of the Enabling Act, Rule 4 (d)(1) clearly passes muster. Prescribing the manner in which a defendant is to be notified that a suit has been instituted against him, it relates to the "practice and procedure of the district courts."

> "The test must be whether a rule really regulates procedure, — the judicial process for enforcing rights and duties recognized by substantive law and for justly administering remedy and redress for disregard or infraction of them." Sibbach v. Wilson & Co., 312 U.S. 1, 14 (1941).

In Mississippi Pub. Corp. v. Murphree, 326 U.S. 438 (1946), this Court upheld Rule 4 (f), which permits service of a summons anywhere within the State (and not merely the district) in which a district court sits:

> "We think that Rule 4 (f) is in harmony with the Enabling Act .... Undoubtedly most alterations of the rules of practice and procedure may and often do affect the

---

[1] Section 9 is in part a statute of limitations, providing that an executor need not "answer to an action...which is not commenced within one year from the time of his giving bond..." This part of the statute, the purpose of which is to speed the settlement of estates, is not involved in this since the action clearly was timely commenced. * * *

Section 9 also provides for the manner of service. Generally, service of process must be made by "delivery by hand," although there are two alternatives: acceptance of service by the executor, or filing of a notice of claim, the components of which are set out in the statute, which *is* involved here, is, as the court below noted, to insure that executors will receive actual notice of claims. Actual notice is of course also the goal of Rule 4 (d) (1); however, the Federal Rule reflects a determination that this goal can be achieved by a method less cumbersome than that prescribed in § 9. In this case the goal seems to have been achieved; although the affidavit filed by respondent in the District Court asserts that he had not been served in hand nor had he accepted service, it does not allege lack of actual notice.

rights of litigants. Congress' prohibition of any alteration of substantive rights of litigants was obviously not addressed to such incidental effects as necessarily attend the adoption of the prescribed new rules of procedure upon the rights of litigants who, agreeably to rules of practice and procedure, have been brought before a court authorized to determine their rights. *Sibbach v. Wilson & Co.* The fact that the application of Rule 4 (f) will operate to subject petitioner's rights to adjudication by the district court for northern Mississippi will undoubtedly affect those rights. But it does not operate to abridge, enlarge or modify the rules of decision by which that court will adjudicate its rights."

Thus were there no conflicting state procedure, Rule 4 (d)(1) would clearly control. However, respondent, focusing on the contrary Massachusetts rule, calls to the Court's attention another line of cases, a line which — like the Federal Rules — had its birth in 1938. *Erie R. Co. v. Tompkins,* overruling *Swift v. Tyson,* held that federal courts sitting in diversity cases, when deciding questions of "substantive" law, are bound by state court decisions as well as state statutes. The broad command of *Erie* was therefore identical to that of the Enabling Act: federal courts are to apply state substantive law and federal procedural law. However, as subsequent cases sharpened the distinction between substance and procedure, the line of cases following Erie diverged markedly from the line construing the Enabling Act. *Guaranty Trust Co. v. York* made it clear that *Erie*-type problems were not to be solved by reference to any traditional or common-sense substance-procedure distinction:

> "And so the question is not whether a statute of limitations is deemed a matter of 'procedure' in some sense. The question is ... does it significantly affect the result of a litigation for a federal court to disregard a law of a State that would be controlling in an action upon the same claim by the same parties in a State court?"

Respondent, by placing primary reliance on *York* and *Ragan,* suggests that the *Erie* doctrine acts as a check on the Federal Rules of Civil Procedure, that despite the clear command of Rule 4 (d)(1), *Erie* and its progeny demand the application of the Massachusetts rule. Reduced to essentials, the argument is: (1) *Erie,* as refined in *York,* demands that federal courts apply state law whenever application of federal law in its stead will alter the outcome of the case. (2) In this case, a determination that the Massachusetts service requirements obtain will result in immediate victory for respondent. If, on the other hand, it should be held that Rule 4 (d)(1) is applicable, the litigation will continue, with possible victory for petitioner. (3) Therefore, *Erie* demands application of the Massachusetts rule. The syllogism possesses an appealing simplicity, but is for several reasons invalid.

In the first place, it is doubtful that, even if there were no Federal Rule making it clear that in-hand service is not required in diversity actions, the *Erie* rule would have obligated the District Court to follow the Massachusetts procedure. "Outcome-determination" analysis was never intended to serve as a talisman. *Byrd v. Blue Ridge Cooperative.* Indeed, the message of *York* itself is that choices between state and federal law are to be made not by application of any automatic, "litmus paper" criterion, but rather by reference to the policies underlying the *Erie* rule. *Guaranty Trust Co. v. York.*

The *Erie* rule is rooted in part in a realization that it would be unfair for the character or result of a litigation materially to differ because the suit had been brought in a federal court.

CHAPTER 7 WHAT LAW APPLIES IN FEDERAL COURT

* * *

The decision was also in part a reaction to the practice of "forum-shopping" which had grown up in response to the rule of *Swift v. Tyson*. That the *York* test was an attempt to effectuate these policies is demonstrated by the fact that the opinion framed the inquiry in terms of "substantial" variations between state and federal litigation. Not only are nonsubstantial, or trivial, variations not likely to raise the sort of equal protection problems which troubled the Court in *Erie*; they are also unlikely to influence the choice of a forum. The "outcome-determination" test therefore cannot be read without reference to the twin aims of the *Erie* rule: discouragement of forum-shopping and avoidance of inequitable administration of the laws.[9]

The difference between the conclusion that the Massachusetts rule is applicable, and the conclusion that it is not, is of course at this point "outcome-determinative" in the sense that if we hold the state rule to apply, respondent prevails, whereas if we hold that Rule 4 (d)(1) governs, the litigation will continue. But in this sense *every* procedural variation is "outcome-determinative." For example, having brought suit in a federal court, a plaintiff cannot then insist on the right to file subsequent pleadings in accord with the time limits applicable in the state courts, even though enforcement of the federal timetable will, if he continues to insist that he must meet only the state time limit, result in determination of the controversy against him. So it is here. Though choice of the federal or state rule will at this point have a marked effect upon the outcome of the litigation, the difference between the two rules would be of scant, if any, relevance to the choice of a forum. Petitioner, in choosing her forum, was not presented with a situation where application of the state rule would wholly bar recovery; rather, adherence to the state rule would have resulted only in altering the way in which process was served.[11] Moreover, it is difficult to argue that permitting service of defendant's wife to take the place of in-hand service of defendant himself alters the mode of enforcement of state-created rights in a fashion sufficiently "substantial" to raise the sort of equal protection problems to which the *Erie* opinion alluded.

There is, however, a more fundamental flaw in respondent's syllogism: the incorrect assumption that the rule of *Erie R. Co. v. Tompkins* constitutes the appropriate test of the validity and

---

[9] The Court of Appeals seemed to frame the inquiry in terms of how "important" § 9 is to the State. In support of its suggestion that § serves some interest the State regards as vital to its citizens, the court noted that something like § 9 has been on the books in Massachusetts a long time, that § 9 has been amended a number of times, and that § 9 is designed to make sure that executors receive actual notice. See note 1, supra. The apparent lack of relation among these three observations is not surprising, because it is not clear to what sort of question the Court of Appeals is addressing itself. One cannot meaningfully ask how important something is without first asking "important for what purpose?" *Erie* and its progeny make clear that when a federal court sitting in a diversity case is faced with a question of whether or not to apply state law, the importance of a state rule is indeed relevant, but only in the context of asking whether application of the rule would make so important a difference to the character or result of the litigation that failure to enforce it would unfairly discriminate against citizens of the forum state, or whether application of the rule would have so important an effect upon the fortunes of one or both of the litigants that failure to enforce it would be likely to cause a plaintiff to choose the federal court.

[11] We cannot seriously entertain the thought that one suing estate would be led to choose the federal court because of a belief that adherence to Rule 4(d)(1) is less likely to give the executor actual notice than § 9, and therefore more likely to produce a default judgment. Rule 4(d)(1) is well designed to give actual notice, as it did in this case. See note 1, supra.

B. Determining What Law Applies

therefore the applicability of a Federal Rule of Civil Procedure. The *Erie* rule has never been invoked to void a Federal Rule. It is true that there have been cases where this Court has held applicable a state rule in the face of an argument that the situation was governed by one of the Federal Rules. But the holding of each such case was not that *Erie* commanded displacement of a Federal Rule by an inconsistent state rule, but rather that the scope of the Federal Rule was not as broad as the losing party urged, and therefore, there being no Federal Rule which covered the point in dispute, *Erie* commanded the enforcement of state law.

> "Respondent contends, in the first place, that the charge was correct because of the fact that Rule 8 (c) of the Rules of Civil Procedure makes contributory negligence an affirmative defense. We do not agree. Rule 8 (c) covers only the manner of pleading. The question of the burden of establishing contributory negligence is a question of local law which federal courts in diversity of citizenship cases must apply." Palmer v. Hoffman, 318 U.S. 109, 117 (1943).

(Here, of course, the clash is unavoidable; Rule 4 (d)(1) says — implicitly, but with unmistakable clarity — that in-hand service is not required in federal courts.) At the same time, in cases adjudicating the validity of Federal Rules, we have not applied the *York* rule or other refinements of *Erie*, but have to this day continued to decide questions concerning the scope of the Enabling Act and the constitutionality of specific Federal Rules in light of the distinction set forth in *Sibbach*.

Nor has the development of two separate lines of cases been inadvertent. The line between "substance" and "procedure" shifts as the legal context changes. "Each implies different variables depending upon the particular problem for which it is used." *Guarantee Trust Co. v. York*; Cook, The Logical and Legal Bases of the Conflicts of Laws 154-83 (1942). It is true that both the Enabling Act and the Erie rule say, roughly, that federal courts are to apply state "substantive" law and federal "procedural" law, but from that it need not follow that the tests are identical. For they were designed to control very different sorts of decisions. When a situation is covered by one of the Federal Rules, the question facing the court is a far cry from the typical, relatively unguided *Erie* choice: the court has been instructed to apply the Federal Rule, and can refuse to do so only if the Advisory Committee, this Court, and Congress erred in their prima facie judgment that the Rule in question transgresses neither the terms of the Enabling Act nor constitutional restrictions.

We are reminded by the *Erie* opinion that neither Congress nor the federal courts can, under the guise of formulating rules of decision for federal courts, fashion rules which are not supported by a grant of federal authority contained in Article I or some other section of the Constitution; in such areas state law must govern because there can be no other law. But the opinion in *Erie*, which involved no Federal Rule and dealt with a question which was "substantive" in every traditional sense (whether the railroad owed a duty of care to Tompkins as a trespasser or a licensee), surely neither said nor implied that measures like Rule 4 (d)(1) are unconstitutional. For the constitutional provision for a federal court system (augmented by the Necessary and Proper Clause) carries with it congressional power to make rules governing the practice and pleading in those courts, which in turn includes a power to regulate matters which, though falling within the uncertain area between substance and procedure, are rationally capable of classification as either. Neither *York* nor the cases following it ever suggested that the rule there laid down for coping with situations where no Federal Rule applies is coextensive with the limitation on Congress to which *Erie* had adverted. Although this Court has never before been confronted with a case where the applicable Federal Rule is in direct collision with the law of the relevant State, courts of appeals faced with such clashes have rightly discerned the implications of our decisions.

"One of the shaping purposes of the Federal Rules is to bring about uniformity in the federal courts by getting away from local rules. This is especially true of matters which relate to the administration of legal proceedings, an area in which federal courts have traditionally exerted strong inherent power, completely aside from the powers Congress expressly conferred in the Rules. The purpose of the *Erie* doctrine even as extended in *York* and *Ragan*, was never to bottle up federal courts with 'outcome-determinative' and 'integral-relations' stoppers — when there are 'affirmative countervailing [federal] considerations' and when there is a Congressional mandate (the Rules) supported by constitutional authority."

Erie and its offspring cast no doubt on the long-recognized power of Congress to prescribe housekeeping rules for federal courts even though some of those rules will inevitably differ from comparable state rules. "When, because the plaintiff happens to be a non-resident, such a right is enforceable in a federal as well as in a State court, the forms and mode of enforcing the right may at times, naturally enough, vary because the two judicial systems are not identic." *Guaranty Trust Co. v. York*; *Cohen v. Beneficial Loan Corp.* Thus, though a court, in measuring a Federal Rule against the standards contained in the Enabling Act and the Constitution, need not wholly blind itself to the degree to which the Rule makes the character and result of the federal litigation stray from the course it would follow in state courts, it cannot be forgotten that the *Erie* rule, and the guidelines suggested in *York*, were created to serve another purpose altogether. To hold that a Federal Rule of Civil Procedure must cease to function whenever it alters the mode of enforcing state-created rights would be to disembowel either the Constitution's grant of power over federal procedure or Congress' attempt to exercise that power in the Enabling Act. Rule 4 (d)(1) is valid and controls the instant case.

Reversed.

JUSTICE HARLAN, concurring.

It is unquestionably true that up to now *Erie* and the cases following it have not succeeded in articulating a workable doctrine governing choice of law in diversity actions. I respect the Court's effort to clarify the situation in today's opinion. However, in doing so I think it has misconceived the constitutional premises of *Erie* and has failed to deal adequately with those past decisions upon which the courts below relied.

Erie was something more than an opinion which worried about "forum-shopping and avoidance of inequitable administration of the laws," although to be sure these were important elements of the decision. I have always regarded that decision as one of the modern cornerstones of our federalism, expressing policies that profoundly touch the allocation of judicial power between the state and federal systems. *Erie* recognized that there should not be two conflicting systems of law controlling the primary activity of citizens, for such alternative governing authority must necessarily give rise to a debilitating uncertainty in the planning of everyday affairs. And it recognized that the scheme of our Constitution envisions an allocation of law-making functions between state and federal legislative processes which is undercut if the federal judiciary can make substantive law affecting state affairs beyond the bounds of congressional legislative powers in this regard. Thus, in diversity cases *Erie* commands that it be the state law governing primary private activity which prevails.

The shorthand formulations which have appeared in some past decisions are prone to carry untoward results that frequently arise from oversimplification. The Court is quite right in stating that the "outcome-determinative" test of *Guaranty Trust Co. v. York*, if taken literally, proves too much, for any rule, no matter how clearly "procedural," can affect the outcome of litigation if it is not obeyed. In turning from the "outcome" test of *York* back to the unadorned forum-shopping rationale of *Erie*, however, the Court falls prey to like oversimplification, for a simple forum-shopping rule also proves too much; litigants often choose a federal forum merely to obtain what they consider the advantages of the Federal Rules of Civil Procedure or to try their cases before a supposedly more favorable judge. To my mind the proper line of approach in determining whether to apply a state or a federal rule, whether "substantive" or "procedural," is to stay close to basic principles by inquiring if the choice of rule would substantially affect those primary decisions respecting human conduct which our constitutional system leaves to state regulation.[2] If so, *Erie* and the Constitution require that the state rule prevail, even in the face of a conflicting federal rule.

The Court weakens, if indeed it does not submerge, this basic principle by finding, in effect, a grant of substantive legislative power in the constitutional provision for a federal court system and through it, setting up the Federal Rules as a body of law inviolate. * * * So long as a reasonable man could characterize any duly adopted federal rule as "procedural," the Court, unless I misapprehend what is said, would have it apply no matter how seriously it frustrated a State's substantive regulation of the primary conduct and affairs of its citizens. Since the members of the Advisory Committee, the Judicial Conference, and this Court who formulated the Federal Rules are presumably reasonable men, it follows that the integrity of the Federal Rules is absolute. Whereas the unadulterated outcome and forum-shopping tests may err too far toward honoring state rules, I submit that the Court's "arguably procedural, ergo constitutional" test moves too fast and far in the other direction.

The courts below relied upon this Court's decisions in *Ragan v. Merchants Transfer Co.* and *Cohen v. Beneficial Loan Corp.* Those cases deserve more attention than this Court has given them, particularly *Ragan* which, if still good law, would in my opinion call for affirmance of the result reached by the Court of Appeals. Further, a discussion of these two cases will serve to illuminate the "diversity" thesis I am advocating.

In *Ragan* a Kansas statute of limitations provided that an action was deemed commenced when service was made on the defendant. Despite Federal Rule 3 which provides that an action commences with the filing of the complaint, the Court held that for purposes of the Kansas statute of limitations a diversity tort action commenced only when service was made upon the defendant. The effect of this holding was that although the plaintiff had filed his federal complaint within the state period of limitations, his action was barred because the federal marshal did not serve a summons on the defendant until after the limitations period had run. I think that the decision was wrong. At most, application of the Federal Rule would have meant that potential Kansas tort defendants would have to defer for a few days the satisfaction of knowing that they had not been sued within the limitations

---

[2] *Byrd v. Blue Ridge Coop., Inc.* indicated that state procedures would apply if the State had manifested a particularly strong interest in their employment. However, this approach may not be of constitutional proportions.

period. The choice of the Federal Rule would have had no effect on the primary stages of private activity from which torts arise, and only the most minimal effect on behavior following the commission of the tort. In such circumstances the interest of the federal system in proceeding under its own rules should have prevailed.

Cohen v. Beneficial Loan Corp. held that a federal diversity court must apply a state statute requiring a small stockholder in a stockholder derivative suit to post a bond securing payment of defense costs as a condition to prosecuting an action. Such a statute is not "outcome determinative"; the plaintiff can win with or without it. The Court now rationalizes the case on the ground that the statute might affect the plaintiff's choice of forum, but as has been pointed out, a simple forum-shopping test proves too much. The proper view of *Cohen* is, in my opinion, that the statute was meant to inhibit small stockholders from instituting "strike suits," and thus it was designed and could be expected to have a substantial impact on private primary activity. Anyone who was at the trial bar during the period when *Cohen* arose can appreciate the strong state policy reflected in the statute. I think it wholly legitimate to view Federal Rule 23 [now Fed. R. Civ. P. 23.1] as not purporting to deal with the problem. But even had the Federal Rules purported to do so, and in so doing provided a substantially less effective deterrent to strike suits, I think the state rule should still have prevailed. That is where I believe the Court's view differs from mine; for the Court attributes such overriding force to the Federal Rules that it is hard to think of a case where a conflicting state rule would be allowed to operate, even though the state rule reflected policy considerations which, under *Erie*, would lie within the realm of state legislative authority.

It remains to apply what has been said to the present case. The Massachusetts rule provides that an executor need not answer suits unless in-hand service was made upon him or notice of the action was filed in the proper registry of probate within one year of his giving bond. The evident intent of this statute is to permit an executor to distribute the estate which he is administering without fear that further liabilities may be outstanding for which he could be held personally liable. If the Federal District Court in Massachusetts applies Rule 4 (d)(1) of the Federal Rules of Civil Procedure instead of the Massachusetts service rule, what effect would that have on the speed and assurance with which estates are distributed? As I see it, the effect would not be substantial. It would mean simply that an executor would have to check at his own house or the federal courthouse as well as the registry of probate before he could distribute the estate with impunity. As this does not seem enough to give rise to any real impingement on the vitality of the state policy which the Massachusetts rule is intended to serve, I concur in the judgment of the Court.

NOTE ON UNDERSTANDING *HANNA*

Notice that *Hanna* identified two distinct prongs of analysis for *Erie* cases. Where there is a Federal Rule on point, the proper analysis is the Rules Enabling Act prong (described in the second half of the opinion). In contrast, the Rules of Decision Act prong (discussed in the first part of the opinion) applies only if there is no Federal Rule on point. The Court stressed that it is a "fundamental flaw" to apply Rules of Decision Act analysis to a Federal Rule. Notwithstanding the Court's explicit bifurcation of the analysis, courts as well as still sometimes loosely refer to "the *Erie* doctrine" as if it were a unitary principle.

For an excellent analysis of the two separate prongs of analysis, see Ely, supra, 87 HARV. L. REV. 693. Dean Ely was a law clerk to Chief Justice Warren the term *Hanna* was decided. In the sections below, we analyze the two prongs separately.

a. What Happens When There Is a Federal Rule of Civil Procedure on Point — the Rules Enabling Act Prong

The Federal Rules were made possible by the Rules Enabling Act, which directed the Supreme Court to promulgate a set of rules of procedure for the federal courts. The Rules Enabling Act is preemptive federal legislation that requires that the Federal Rules of Civil Procedure apply in federal court. Indeed, the Rules Enabling Act explicitly provides that "[a]ll laws in conflict with such rules shall be of no further force or effect after such rules have taken effect." 28 U.S.C. § 2072(b). Where a Federal Rule is involved, if the rule is valid and on point, then the Supremacy Clause dictates that the rule governs.

This holding of *Hanna* has been described as "hard-hearted and heavy-handed," Richard Freer, *Erie's Mid-Life Crisis*, 63 TULANE L. REV. 1087, 1120 (1989), and a few courts have resisted applying it. For example, in Marshall v. Mulrenin, 508 F.2d 39 (1st Cir. 1974), the plaintiff was injured while on business premises and sued the defendant whom she believed owned the property. The suit was filed in federal court in Massachusetts. While the suit was pending but after the statute of limitations had expired, the plaintiff learned that the defendant she sued had owned the property but had sold it before the accident occurred. The plaintiff then attempted to amend her complaint to name the current owner. Massachusetts law permitted any amendments that would "sustain the action for the cause for which it was intended to be brought." On the other hand, Rule 15(c) of the Federal Rules is more restrictive. The First Circuit refused to apply Rule 15(c), explaining:

> We do not accept the "singularly hard-hearted" view that *Hanna* commands that the Federal Rules be woodenly applied irrespective of a discoverable substantive, as distinguished from a merely procedural, state purpose. * * * Such a constriction does not, of course, render Federal Rules inoperative in their procedural aspects. It merely means that a rule is not to be applied to the extent, if any, that it would defeat rights arising from state substantive law as distinguished from state procedure.

Id. at 44.

Notwithstanding *Marshall*, the Rules Enabling Act prong of *Hanna* is clear — if there's a valid Federal Rule of Civil Procedure on point, it must be applied. *Hanna*'s holding is surely correct under the Supremacy Clause. The escape from its "hard–hearted" effects is to find, where appropriate, that a Rule does not cover the particular point at issue. See Section ii, infra.

CHAPTER 7 WHAT LAW APPLIES IN FEDERAL COURT

i. Determining Whether a Federal Rule of Civil Procedure Is Valid

As with any statute, a Federal Rule is valid only if it is constitutional, and a statute beyond the scope of Congress' authority would, of course, be unconstitutional. In *Hanna*, the Court delineated the scope of Congress' authority with respect to rules of procedure for the federal courts. The Court explained that Congress' authority to create a federal court system carries with it authority to mandate the procedural rules for those courts. The Court concluded that although the line between substance and procedure is fuzzy, Congress' constitutional power over federal procedure extends to anything "rationally capable of classification" as procedure. Thus, so long as any Federal Rule is arguably procedural, it is constitutional.

Finding that a Federal Rule is constitutional is only the first step in determining the Rule's validity. Congress did not itself enact the Rules, but instead delegated authority to the Supreme Court to promulgate them. Therefore, for a Rule to be valid, it must be within the delegated authority. It is the Rules Enabling Act, 28 U.S.C. § 2072, that delegates this authority to the Supreme Court. That statute provides:

> (a) The Supreme Court shall have the power to prescribe general rules of practice and procedure and rules of evidence for cases in the United States district courts (including proceedings before magistrates thereof) and courts of appeals.
>
> (b) Such rules shall not abridge, enlarge or modify any substantive right. All law in conflict with such rules shall be of no further force or effect after such rules have taken effect.

Although subpart (a) appears to delegate broad authority, subpart (b) appears to restrict that authority. In essence the statute says that the Supreme Court may promulgate procedural rules, but not procedural rules that alter or amend substantive rights.

The first challenge to the Rules came three years after their promulgation, in Sibbach v. Wilson & Co., 312 U.S. 1 (1941). There, pursuant to Rule 35, the court ordered the plaintiff to submit to physical examination. State law did not permit a court to order such examinations, and the plaintiff argued that Rule 35 was invalid because it abridged a substantive right to be free from the indignity and intrusion of court-ordered physical exams. The Supreme Court rejected this argument, concluding that subsection (b) of the statute simply restated, but did not modify, subsection (a). According to the Court, the categories of substance and procedure are mutually exclusive. The test for the validity of a federal rule, the Court explained, is whether that Rule "really regulates procedure." If the Rule does concern procedure, then, by definition, it cannot be one that alters or amends substantive rights.

Notwithstanding *Sibbach*, subsection (b) appears to have some constraining effect on what Rules are promulgated. On at least one occasion the Court declined to promulgate a proposed Rule because of concern that it might violate subsection (b) of the Rules Enabling Act. See Rule 11(b)(1) (Proposed 1991), 137 F.R.D. 75-76 (Draft Committee Notes).

Business Guides, Inc. v. Chromatic Communication Enterprises
498 U.S. 533, 111 S. Ct. 922, 112 L. Ed. 2d 1140 (1991)

JUSTICE O'CONNOR delivered the opinion of the Court.

In this case we decide whether Rule 11 of the Federal Rules of Civil Procedure imposes an objective standard of reasonable inquiry on represented parties who sign pleadings, motions, or other papers. [Rule 11 was substantially amended in 1993, but those amendments do not effect the points made here -- EDS.]

[The Court held that Rule 11 applies to represented parties who sign papers and that the standard is an objective one of reasonableness under the circumstances.] * * *

III

One issue remains: Business Guides asserts that imposing sanctions against a represented party that did not act in bad faith violates the Rules Enabling Act, 28 U.S.C. § 2072. The Act authorizes the Court "to prescribe general rules of practice and procedure," but provides that such rules "shall not abridge, enlarge, or modify any substantive right." Business Guides argues that Rule 11, to the extent that it imposes on represented parties an objective standard of reasonableness, exceeds the limits of the Court's power in two ways: (1) It authorizes fee shifting in a manner not approved by Congress; and (2) it effectively creates a federal tort of malicious prosecution, thereby encroaching upon various state law causes of action.

We begin by noting that any Rules Enabling Act challenge to Rule 11 has a large hurdle to get over. The Federal Rules of Civil Procedure are not enacted by Congress, but "Congress participates in the rulemaking process." Additionally, the Rules do not go into effect until Congress has had at least seven months to look them over. See 28 U.S.C. § 2074. A challenge to Rule 11 can therefore succeed "only if the Advisory Committee, this Court, and Congress erred in their prima facie judgment that the Rule ... transgresses neither the terms of the Enabling Act nor constitutional restrictions." *Hanna v. Plumer*.

This Court's decision in Burlington Northern R. Co. v. Woods, 480 U.S. 1 (1987), presents another hurdle. There, the Court considered the Act's proscription against interference with substantive rights and held, in a unanimous decision, that "Rules which *incidentally* affect litigants' substantive rights do not violate this provision if reasonably necessary to maintain the integrity of that system of rules." There is little doubt that Rule 11 is reasonably necessary to maintain the integrity of the system of federal practice and procedure, and that any effect on substantive rights is incidental. We held as much only last Term in *Cooter & Gell*: "It is now clear that the central purpose of Rule 11 is to deter baseless filings in district court and thus, consistent with the Rule Enabling Act's grant of authority, streamline the administration and procedure of the federal courts."

Petitioner's challenges do not clear these substantial hurdles. In arguing that the monetary sanctions in this case constitute impermissible fee shifting, Business Guides relies on the Court's statement in Alyeska Pipeline Service Co. v. Wilderness Society, 421 U.S. 240, 247 (1975), that, in the absence of legislative guidance, courts do not have the power "to reallocate the burdens of litigation" by awarding costs to the losing party in a civil rights suit; they have only the power to sanction a party for bad faith. The initial difficulty with this argument is that *Alyeska* dealt with the courts' inherent powers, not the Rules Enabling Act. Rule 11 sanctions do not constitute the kind of fee shifting at issue in *Alyeska*. Rule 11 sanctions are not tied to the outcome of litigation; the relevant inquiry is whether a specific filing was, if not successful, at least well founded. Nor do sanctions shift the entire cost of litigation; they shift only the cost of a discrete event. Finally, the Rule calls only for "an appropriate sanction" — attorney's fees are not mandated. As we explained in *Cooter & Gell*: "Rule 11 is not a fee-shifting statute.... 'A movant under Rule 11 has no entitlement to fees or any other sanction.'"

Also without merit is Business Guides' argument that Rule 11 creates a federal common law of malicious prosecution. We rejected a similar claim in *Cooter & Gell*. The main objective of the Rule is not to reward parties who are victimized by litigation; it is to deter baseless filings and curb abuses. Imposing monetary sanctions on parties that violate the Rule may confer a benefit on other litigants, but the Rules Enabling Act is not violated by such incidental effects on substantive rights. Additionally, we are confident that district courts will resist the temptation to use sanctions as substitutes for tort damages. This case is a good example. Chromatic asked that the sanctions award include consequential damages, but the District Court refused. "[W]hile sympathetic to [Chromatic's] plight," the court was "not persuaded that such compensation is within the purview of Rule 11." In the event that a district court misapplies the Rule in a particular case, the error can be corrected on appeal. "But misapplications do not themselves provide a basis for concluding that Rule 11 was the result of ... distinct errors in prima facie judgment during the development and promulgation of the rule."

* * *

Affirmed.

JUSTICE KENNEDY, with whom JUSTICE MARSHALL and JUSTICE STEVENS join, and with whom JUSTICE SCALIA joins as to Parts I, III, and IV, dissenting.

* * *

Our potential incursion into matters reserved to the States also counsels against adoption of the majority's rule. Just as the various statutory fee-shifting mechanisms reflect policy choices by Congress regarding the extent to which certain types of litigation should be encouraged or discouraged, state tort law reflects comparable state policies. As interpreted by the majority, Rule 11 places on those represented parties who sign papers subject to the Rule duties far exceeding those imposed by state tort law. In general, States permitting recovery for malicious prosecution or abuse of process require the plaintiff to prove malice or improper purpose as a necessary element. As interpreted by the majority, Rule 11 creates a new tort of "negligent prosecution" or "accidental abuse of process," applicable to any represented party ignorant enough to sign a pleading or other Rule 11 paper.

In this case, the District Court imposed sanctions on a corporation for the actions of its agents taken in reliance on business records developed to safeguard the company's property rights in its own research. The decision to impose sanctions required the court, sitting without a jury, to make judgments about the skill and care that companies of this kind must use in their business practices. We tolerate judgments about the care an attorney must use because we deem judges to know the standards appropriate for the practice of law. We do not have similar expertise in the workings of private enterprise or the conduct and supervision of investigations made by a company to protect and defend its rights. And though the majority would seem to suggest it, I should not have thought that before a person or entity seeks the aid of the federal courts, it ought to know the contents of the Federal Rules of Civil Procedure, rules that, at least until now, were the domain of lawyers and not the community as a whole.

A rule sanctioning misconduct during the litigation process will often satisfy the Rules Enabling Act because it "affects only the process of enforcing litigants' rights and not the rights themselves." *Burlington Northern R. Co. v. Woods.* As applied to attorneys, and perhaps those who act as their own attorneys, the same can be said of Rule 11's sanctions for failure to conduct a reasonable prefiling inquiry. That much we established in *Cooter & Gell v. Hartmarx Corp.* But the presumption that a Federal Rule is valid carries less weight in a case such as this, where "the intended scope of [the] Rule is uncertain," and the construction of Rule 11 adopted today extends our role far beyond its traditional and accepted boundaries. Whether or not Rule 11 as construed by the majority exceeds our rulemaking authority, these concerns weigh in favor of a reasonable, alternative interpretation, one which, as I said at the outset, is more consistent with the text of the Rule. See *Cooter & Gell*, ("We ... interpret Rule 11 according to its plain meaning, ... in light of the scope of the congressional authorization [in the Rules Enabling Act]"); 19 WRIGHT, MILLER, & COOPER, at 148 ("If a federal court concludes it is uncertain whether a Civil Rule truly governs a given question of practice, and if a relevant state rule of law differs, the extent to which application of the Civil Rule would interfere with substantive rights is certainly one of the factors that should be considered in deciding whether the Civil Rule applies. In effect, the 'substantive rights' limitation, and the concern it reflects for the integrity of state substantive policies, is relevant to determining the scope of the Civil Rules").

* * *

NOTES AND QUESTIONS

1. Would the following Rules be within the scope of the Rules Enabling Act?
(a) a Rule providing that where a judgment is rendered, the loser shall pay the costs, including attorney's fees, of the winner;

(b) a Rule providing for a three year statute of limitations in all cases in federal court;

(c) a Rule providing for nationwide service of process in all cases in federal court.

2. The process by which the Federal Rules are promulgated is described below in a statement Justice White issued in connection with the 1993 amendments to the Rules. Given the limited involvement of the Supreme Court in the actual drafting of the Rules, one might expect the Court to do more probing analysis of Rules whose validity is challenged. Nonetheless, as *Business Guides* suggests, the Court appears to treat the Rules as having a heavy presumption of validity.

Amendments to the Federal Rules of Civil Procedure
113 S. Ct. 575 (1993)

Statement of JUSTICE WHITE.

28 U.S.C. § 2072 empowers the Supreme Court to prescribe general rules of practice and procedure and rules of evidence for cases in the federal courts, including proceedings before magistrates and courts of appeals. But the Court does not itself draft and initially propose these rules. Section 2073 directs the Judicial Conference to prescribe the procedures for proposing the rules mentioned in § 2072. The Conference is authorized to appoint committees to propose such rules. These rules advisory committees are to be made up of members of the professional bar and trial and appellate judges. The Conference is also to appoint a standing committee on rules of practice and evidence to review the recommendations of the advisory committees and to recommend to the Conference such rules and amendments to those rules "as may be necessary to maintain consistency and otherwise promote the interest of justice." § 2073 (b). Any rules approved by the Conference are transmitted to the Supreme Court, which in turn transmits any rules "prescribed" pursuant to § 2072 to the Congress. Except as provided in § 2074 (b), such rules become effective at a specified time unless Congress otherwise provides.

* * *

During my 31 years on the Court, the number of advisory committees has grown as necessitated by statutory changes. During that time, by my count at least, on some 64 occasions we have "prescribed" and transmitted to Congress a new set of rules or amendments to certain rules. Some of the transmissions have been minor, but many of them have been extensive. Over this time, Justices Black and Douglas, either together or separately, dissented 13 times on the ground that it was inappropriate for the Court to pass on the merits of the rules before it. Aside from those two Justices, Justices Powell, Stewart and then-Justice Rehnquist dissented on one occasion and Justice O'Connor on another as to the substance of proposed rules. Only once in my memory did the Court refuse to transmit some of the rule changes proposed by the Judicial Conference.

B. Determining What Law Applies

That the Justices have hardly ever refused to transmit the rules submitted by the Judicial Conference and the fact that, aside from Justices Black and Douglas, it has been quite rare for any Justice to dissent from transmitting any such rule, suggest that a sizable majority of the 21 Justices who sat during this period concluded that Congress intended them to have a rather limited role in the rulemaking process. The vast majority (including myself) obviously have not explicitly subscribed to the Black-Douglas view that many of the rules proposed dealt with substantive matters that the Constitution reserved to Congress and that in any event were prohibited by § 2072's injunction against abridging, enlarging or modifying substantive rights.

Some of us, however, have silently shared Justice Black's and Justice Douglas' suggestion that the enabling statutes be amended

> "to place the responsibility upon the Judicial Conference rather than upon this Court. * * * The Judicial Conference can participate more actively in fashioning the rules and affirmatively contribute to their content and design better than we can. Transfer of the function to the Judicial Conference would relieve us of the embarrassment of having to sit in judgment on the constitutionality of rules which we have approved and which as applied in given situations might have to be declared invalid."

Despite the repeated protestations of both or one of those Justices, Congress did not eliminate our participation in the rulemaking process. Indeed, our statutory role was continued as the coverage of § 2072 was extended to the rules of evidence and to proceedings before magistrates. Congress clearly continued to direct us to "prescribe" specified rules. But most of us concluded that for at least two reasons Congress could not have intended us to provide another layer of review equivalent to that of the standing committee and the Judicial Conference. First, to perform such a function would take an inordinate amount of time, the expenditure of which would be inconsistent with the demands of a growing caseload. Second, some of us, and I remain of this view, were quite sure that the Judicial Conference and its committees, "being in large part judges of the lower courts and attorneys who are using the Rules day in and day out, are in a far better position to make a practical judgment upon their utility or inutility than we."

I did my share of litigating when in practice and once served on the Advisory Committee for the Civil Rules, but the trial practice is a dynamic profession, and the longer one is away from it the less likely it is that he or she should presume to second-guess the careful work of the active professionals manning the rulemaking committees, work that the Judicial Conference has approved. At the very least, we should not perform a de novo review and should defer to the Judicial Conference and its committees as long as they have some rational basis for their proposed amendments.

Hence, as I have seen the Court's role over the years, it is to transmit the Judicial Conference's recommendations without change and without careful study, as long as there is no suggestion that the committee system has not operated with integrity. If it has not, such a fact, or even such a claim, about a body so open to public inspection would inevitably surface. This has been my practice, even though on several occasions, based perhaps on out-of-date conceptions, I had serious questions about the wisdom of particular proposals to amend certain rules.

* * *

In conclusion, I suggest that it would be a mistake for the bench, the bar, or the Congress to assume that we are duplicating the function performed by the standing committee or the Judicial Conference with respect to changes in the various rules which come to us for transmittal. As I have said, over the years our role has been a much more limited one.

ii. Determining When a Federal Rule of Civil Procedure Is On Point

Although the Court has never struck down a Federal Rule of Civil Procedure, it has on some occasions concluded that a Rule which might appear to control is not in fact applicable.

In Walker v. Armco Steel Corp., 446 U.S. 740 (1980), state law provided that an action has not "commenced" for purposes of the statute of limitations until the defendant is actually served. In contrast, Rule 3 of the Federal Rules provides that "an action is commenced by filing a complaint." Despite Rule 3, the Supreme Court reaffirmed its ruling in *Ragan*, and held that state law controlled. The Court explained that Rule 3 was not intended to toll a state statute of limitations.

A similar explanation can be offered for *Cohen*. There, the Court held that federal courts must apply a state law requirement that plaintiffs in shareholder derivative actions post bond. Rule 23.1 of the Federal Rules specifically addresses shareholder derivative actions and specifies the requirements for such actions. The Rule includes nothing about a bond requirement. One can reconcile Rule 23.1 and *Cohen* by concluding that the Rule simply does not address the question of bond — it does not require bond, but it also does not prohibit it.

Should Federal Rules generally be read narrowly to avoiding infringing on the rights of states? Justice Kennedy argues for such an approach in his dissent in *Business Guides*. However, the Court does not always give the narrowest possible interpretation to a Federal Rule. In Burlington Northern Railroad Co. v. Woods, 480 U.S. 1 (1987), the Court dealt with Rule 38 of the Federal Rules of Appellate Procedure. That Rule provides: "If a court of appeals shall determine that an appeal is frivolous, it may award just damages and single or double costs to the appellee." A state law imposed a mandatory fixed penalty of ten percent of the judgment on appellants who obtain stays of judgment and then lose their appeals. The Court held that Rule 38 controls, and the state rule does not. It concluded that Rule 38, by permitting, but not requiring, sanctions, prohibits mandatory sanctions and that the only sanctions available were those that fell within Rule 38.

Consider the following situations:

(1) Rule 41(b) of the Federal Rules permits dismissal for failure to prosecute a claim. The Nevada rules of procedure mandate dismissal for failure to prosecute after five

B. Determining What Law Applies

[handwritten: 1. The Nevada Rule b/c it set the time limit.]

years. Should a federal court in Nevada apply the Nevada rule? See Harvey's Wagon Wheel, Inc. v. Van Blitter, 959 F.2d 153 (9th Cir. 1992).

(2) Illinois law provides that in tort cases "no complaint shall be filed containing a prayer for relief for punitive damages. However, a plaintiff may, pursuant to pretrial motion and after a hearing before the Court, amend the complaint to include a prayer for relief seeking punitive damages." Federal Rule 8 provides that the complaint "shall contain * * * a demand for judgment for the relief the pleader seeks." Rule 9 sets forth special pleading rules for certain specified situations but says nothing about punitive damages. Should a federal court in Illinois apply the Illinois rule? Compare Berry v. Eagle-Picher, 1989 U.S.Dist. LEXIS 7671 (N.D. Ill. 1989) (refusing to apply state law); Kingston Square Tenants Ass'n v. Tuskegee Gardens, Ltd., 792 F. Supp. 1566, 1579 (S.D. Fla. 1992) (same) with Al-Site Corp. v. VSI Intern, Inc., 842 F. Supp. 507, 511-514 (S.D. Fla. 1993) (applying state law); Nelson v. Zurich Insurance Co., 1992 U.S.Dist. LEXIS 12955 (N.D.D. 1992) (same).

(3) Forum selection clauses are contractual terms providing that where litigation arising from the contract must be filed. The modern view, adopted by the federal courts in cases in which state law does not govern, upholds such clauses as long as they are not the product of overreaching. Although most states adopt this modern approach, about a dozen do not. To them, such clauses violate a public policy by "ousting" a court of jurisdiction. Suppose P, a citizen of Alabama, and D, a citizen of New York, enter a contract which contains a clause mandating that any dispute arising from the contract be filed in New York.

A dispute arises and P sues in state court in Alabama. D moves to dismiss, based on the forum selection clause. Because Alabama law does not allow enforcement of such provisions, the court will deny the motion. Suppose, however, that D removes the case to federal court based upon diversity of citizenship. Should the federal court follow Alabama law?

The Supreme Court held that the transfer of venue statute, 28 U.S.C. section 1404(a) applied to this situation, noting that "when the federal law sought to be applied is a congressional statute, the first and chief question * * * is whether the statute is 'sufficiently broad to control the issue before the court.'" Stewart Organization Inc. v. Ricoh Corp., 487 U.S. 22 (1988). In the Court's view, Congress intended courts to consider the existence of a forum selection clause as one of the factors in determining whether to transfer under section 1404(a). It is not apparent that Congress ever considered the issue when it passed § 1404(a), and several commentators criticize the Court's interpretation of § 1404(a). See, e.g., Freer, supra, 63 TUL. L. REV. 1089; Linda Mullenix, *Another Choice of Forum, Another Choice of Law: Consensual Adjudicatory Procedure in Federal Court*, 57 FORDHAM L. REV. 291 (1988).

After *Stewart*, what is the law regarding enforceability of forum selection clauses in Alabama (or in the other states that refuse to enforce them)? Does the answer depend upon whether the litigation is in federal or state court? How is this situation different from *Swift v. Tyson*? Some people may think it "unfair" that P breached the forum selection clause by suing in Alabama. But shouldn't a party seeking to include such a clause in a contract be responsible for checking whether the law of the other party's state permits enforcement of such clauses?

b. What Happens When There Is No Federal Rule of Civil Procedure on Point — the Rules of Decision Act Prong

Although *Hanna* found that there was a valid Federal Rule of Civil Procedure on point in that case, the Court nonetheless explained how to analyze cases where there is no such Rule. A few commentators have pointed out that this portion of the opinion is dicta. (Do you see why?) See REDISH, FEDERAL JURISDICTION POWER 220 n.71. According to the Court, this analysis should focus on the "twin aims of *Erie*" — discouraging forum shopping and avoiding inequitable administration of the laws.

1. Are the "twin aims of *Erie*" really only one aim? Several commentators have argued that "the 'twin aims' collapse into a single concern for equality: forum shopping results from and contributes to different treatment of litigants on the basis of their citizenship." Stein, supra, 100 YALE L.J. at 1947. See REDISH, FEDERAL JURISDICTION at 225. In a similar vein, the test articulated by the Court in *Hanna* has been called a "modified outcome test." As Professor Freer has explained, "Instead of assessing outcome determination at the point at which it is raised in litigation — when it will always make a difference in outcome — it should be assessed ex ante, as of the outset of litigation." Freer, supra, 63 TUL. L REV. at 1106. See Ely, supra, 87 HARV. L. REV. at 717-718.

2. What's so bad about "forum shopping?" Isn't the whole point of diversity jurisdiction to provide out-of-state litigants with an alternative forum?

3. Reconsider Note 6 after *Byrd*. Would this situation be analyzed differently under the *Hanna* test?

4. The *Hanna* Court suggests that the difference between the state and federal service rules was not sufficient to affect a litigant's choice of forum. But is this really true? In Hanna, the plaintiff filed suit a little more than three weeks before the statute of limitations expired. Isn't it possible that a litigant who had only three weeks within which to effectuate service might chose federal court because federal court does not require in-hand personal service?

5. How is *Hanna* different from *York*? What is left of *York* after *Hanna*?

6. Does *Hanna* overrule *Byrd*? Professor Laura Little concludes that *Byrd* "did not survive * * * *Hanna*." *Out of Woods and Into the Rules: The Relationship Between*

State Foreign Corporation Door-Closing Statutes and Federal Rule of Civil Procedure 17(b), 72 VA. L. REV. 767, 788 (1986). Do you agree?

7. Notwithstanding the apparent rejection of *Byrd* by *Hanna*, a number of lower courts have continued to rely on *Byrd*. Some courts ignore *Hanna* entirely, other courts acknowledge *Hanna* but conclude that *Byrd* is the proper test in at least some situations, and still others attempt to use both *Byrd* and *Hanna*. See REDISH, FEDERAL JURISDICTION at 221-25. Professor Freer has concluded that of the scores of cases analyzing forum selection clauses, "Justice Scalia, dissenting in *Stewart* is the only federal judge to undertake any meaningful assessment of the * * * issue under the twin aims test in a published opinion." Freer, supra, 63 TUL. L. REV. at 1112 n. 122. What explanations might there be for this phenomenon? Professor Redish has argued:

> The lower federal courts' widespread refusal to apply *Hanna* as the exclusive Rules of Decision test * * * may well represent more than failure to grasp the subtleties of the *Hanna* Court's analysis. Instead, it may reflect the view that *Hanna*'s modified outcome determination test inadequately accommodates all of the significant social interests to be served by both *Erie* and the Rules of Decision Act.

REDISH, FEDERAL JURISDICTION at 225. Do you agree? Do you think *Byrd* or *Hanna* better captures the underlying purposes of *Erie* and the Rules of Decision Act?

8. Consider the following case which is the Supreme Court's latest word in this area.

Chambers v. NASCO, Inc.
501 U.S. 32, 111 S. Ct. 2123, 115 L. Ed. 2d 27 (1991)

JUSTICE WHITE delivered the opinion of the Court.

This case requires us to explore the scope of the inherent power of a federal court to sanction a litigant for bad-faith conduct. Specifically, we are asked to determine whether the District Court, sitting in diversity, properly invoked its inherent power in assessing as a sanction for a party's bad-faith conduct attorney's fees and related expenses paid by the party's opponent to its attorneys. We hold that the District Court acted within its discretion, and we therefore affirm the judgment of the Court of Appeals.

[This case began as a suit for specific performance. Chambers had contracted to sell his television station to NASCO. When Chambers tried to back out of the deal, NASCO sued in federal court for specific performance. Throughout the litigation, Chambers and his attorneys engaged in an ongoing pattern of delay and abuse of the judicial process. Chambers was personally held in contempt of court once and came very close on two other occasions. Even after he lost on the merits, Chambers attempted to circumvent the court's orders.

Following Chambers' unsuccessful appeal, NASCO moved for sanctions. The district court held that sanctions were appropriate "for the manner in which this proceeding was conducted from ... the time that the plaintiff gave notice of its intention to file suit to this date." The court imposed sanctions against Chambers in the form of attorneys fees and expenses totaling $996,644.65, which was the entire amount of NASCO's litigation costs paid to its attorneys. In imposing these costs, the court relied not on Rule 11 or § 1927. It relied instead on its "inherent power."

The Supreme Court upheld this exercise of inherent power, rejecting the argument that the court's power to sanction was limited to the sanctions available under Rule 11 or § 1927.]

* * *

III

Chambers asserts that even if federal courts can use their inherent power to assess attorney's fees as a sanction in some cases, they are not free to do so when they sit in diversity, unless the applicable state law recognizes the "bad-faith" exception to the general rule against fee shifting. He relies on footnote 31 in *Alyeska*, in which we stated with regard to the exceptions to the American Rule that "[a] very different situation is presented when a federal court sits in a diversity case. '[I]n an ordinary diversity case where the state law does not run counter to a valid federal statute or rule of court, and usually it will not, state law denying the right to attorney's fees or giving a right thereto, which reflects a substantial policy of the state, should be followed.'"

We agree with NASCO that Chambers has misinterpreted footnote 31. The limitation on a court's inherent power described there applies only to fee-shifting rules that embody a substantive policy, such as a statute which permits a prevailing party in certain classes of litigation to recover fees. * * *

Only when there is a conflict between state and federal substantive law are the concerns of *Erie R. Co. v. Tompkins* at issue. As we explained in *Hanna v. Plumer*, the "outcome determinative" test of *Erie* and *Guaranty Trust Co. v. York*, "cannot be read without reference to the twin aims of the *Erie* rule: discouragement of forum-shopping and avoidance of inequitable administration of the laws." Despite Chambers' protestations to the contrary, neither of these twin aims is implicated by the assessment of attorney's fees as a sanction for bad-faith conduct before the court which involved disobedience of the court's orders and the attempt to defraud the court itself. In our recent decision in *Business Guides, Inc. v. Chromatic Communications Enterprises, Inc.*, we stated, "Rule 11 sanctions do not constitute the kind of fee shifting at issue in *Alyeska* [because they] are not tied to the outcome of litigation; the relevant inquiry is whether a specific filing was, if not successful, at least well founded." Likewise, the imposition of sanctions under the bad-faith exception depends not on which party wins the lawsuit, but on how the parties conduct themselves during the litigation. Consequently, there is no risk that the exception will lead to forum-shopping. Nor is it inequitable to apply the exception to citizens and noncitizens alike, when the party, by controlling his or her conduct inlitigation, has the power to determine whether sanctions will be assessed. As the Court of Appeals expressed it, "*Erie* guarantees a litigant that if he takes his state law cause of action to federal court, and abides by the rules of that court, the result in his case will be the same as if he had brought it in state court. It does not allow him to waste the court's time and resources with cantankerous conduct, even in the unlikely event a state court would allow him to do so."

***

Chambers argues that because the primary purpose of the sanction is punitive, assessing attorney's fees violates the State's prohibition on punitive damages. Under Louisiana law, there can be no punitive damages for breach of contract, even when a party has acted in bad faith in breaching the agreement. Indeed, "as a general rule attorney's fees are not allowed a successful litigant in Louisiana except where authorized by statute or by contract." It is clear, though, that this general rule focuses on the award of attorney's fees because of a party's success on the underlying claim. Thus, in Frank L. Beier Radio, Inc. v. Black Gold Marine, Inc., 449 So. 2d 1014 (La. 1984), the state court considered the scope of a statute which permitted an award of attorney's fees in a suit seeking to collect on an open account. This substantive state policy is not implicated here, where sanctions were imposed for conduct during the litigation.

Here the District Court did not attempt to sanction petitioner for breach of contract, but rather imposed sanctions for the fraud he perpetrated on the court and the bad faith he displayed toward both his adversary and the court throughout the course of the litigation. We agree with the Court of Appeals that "[w]e do not see how the district court's inherent power to tax fees for that conduct can be made subservient to any state policy without transgressing the boundaries set out in *Erie, Guaranty Trust Co.*, and *Hanna*," for "[f]ee-shifting here is not a matter of substantive remedy, but of vindicating judicial authority."

IV

[The Court upheld the sanctions imposed.]

Affirmed.

Justice Kennedy, with whom The Chief Justice and Justice Souter join, dissenting.

Today's decision effects a vast expansion of the power of federal courts, unauthorized by rule or statute. I have no doubt petitioner engaged in sanctionable conduct that warrants severe corrective measures. But our outrage at his conduct should not obscure the boundaries of settled legal categories.

With all respect, I submit the Court commits two fundamental errors. First, it permits the exercise of inherent sanctioning powers without prior recourse to controlling rules and statutes, thereby arrogating to federal courts Congress' power to regulate fees and costs. Second, the Court upholds the wholesale shift of respondent's attorney's fees to petitioner, even though the District Court opinion reveals that petitioner was sanctioned at least in part for his so-called bad faith breach of contract. The extension of inherent authority to sanction a party's prelitigation conduct subverts the American Rule and turns the *Erie* doctrine upside down by punishing petitioner's primary conduct contrary to Louisiana law. Because I believe the proper exercise of inherent powers requires exhaustion of express sanctioning provisions and much greater caution in their application to redress prelitigation conduct, I dissent.

I

The Court's first error lies in its failure to require reliance, when possible, on the panoply of express sanctioning provisions provided by Congress.

A

The American Rule prohibits federal courts from awarding attorney's fees in the absence of a statute or contract providing for a fee award. Alyeska Pipeline Service Co. v. Wilderness Society, 421 U.S. 240, 258-259 (1975). The Rule recognizes that Congress defines the procedural and remedial powers of federal courts, *Sibbach v. Wilson & Co.*; and controls the costs, sanctions, and fines available there, Kaiser Aluminum & Chemical Corp. v. Bonjorno, 494 U.S. 827, 835 (1990) ("[T]he allocation of the costs accruing from litigation is a matter for the legislature, not the courts"); *Alyeska Pipeline Co.* ("[T]he circumstances under which attorney's fees are to be awarded and the range of discretion of the courts in making those awards are matters for Congress to determine").

* * *

In addition to dismissing some of our precedents and misreading others, the Court ignores the commands of the Federal Rules of Civil Procedure, which support the conclusion that a court should rely on rules, and not inherent powers, whenever possible. Like the Federal Rules of Criminal Procedure, the Federal Rules of Civil Procedure are "as binding as any statute duly enacted by Congress, and federal courts have no more discretion to disregard the Rule[s'] mandate than they do to disregard constitutional or statutory provisions." See also Fed. Rule Civ. Proc. 1 (Federal Rules "*govern* the procedure in the United States district courts in all suits of a civil nature") (emphasis added). Two of the most prominent sanctioning provisions, Rules 11 and 26(g), mandate the imposition of sanctions when litigants violate the Rules' certification standards. See Fed. Rule Civ. Proc. 11 (court "shall impose ... an appropriate sanction" for violation of certification standard); Fed. Rule Civ. Proc. 26(g) (same); see also *Business Guides, Inc. v. Chromatic Communications Enterprises, Inc.* (Rule 11 "requires that sanctions be imposed where a signature is present but fails to satisfy the certification standard").

The Rules themselves thus reject the contention that they may be discarded in a court's discretion. Disregard of applicable rules also circumvents the rulemaking procedures in 28 U.S.C. § 2071 et seq., which Congress designed to assure that procedural innovations like those announced today "shall be introduced only after mature consideration of informed opinion from all relevant quarters, with all the opportunities for comprehensive and integrated treatment which such consideration affords."

B

Upon a finding of bad faith, courts may now ignore any and all textual limitations on sanctioning power. By inviting district courts to rely on inherent authority as a substitute for attention to the careful distinctions contained in the rules and statutes, today's decision will render these sources of authority superfluous in many instances. A number of pernicious practical effects will follow.

* * *

Nothing in the foregoing discussion suggests that the fee-shifting and sanctioning provisions in the Federal Rules and Title 28 eliminate the inherent power to impose sanctions for certain conduct. Limitations on a power do not constitute its abrogation. Cases can arise in which a federal court must act to preserve its authority in a manner not provided for by the Federal Rules or Title 28. But as the number and scope of rules and statutes governing litigation misconduct increase, the necessity to resort to inherent authority — a predicate to its proper application — lessens. Indeed, it is difficult to imagine a case in which a court can, as the District Court did here, rely on inherent authority as the exclusive basis for sanctions.

* * *

II

When a District Court imposes sanctions so immense as here under a power so amorphous as inherent authority, it must ensure that its order is confined to conduct under its own authority and jurisdiction to regulate. The District Court failed to discharge this obligation, for it allowed sanctions to be awarded for petitioner's prelitigation breach of contract. The majority, perhaps wary of the District Court's authority to extend its inherent power to sanction prelitigation conduct, insists that "the District Court did not attempt to sanction petitioner for breach of contract, but rather imposed sanctions for the fraud he perpetrated on the court and the bad faith he displayed toward both his adversary and the Court throughout the course of the litigation." Based on this premise, the Court appears to disclaim that its holding reaches prelitigation conduct. This does not make the opinion on this point correct, of course, for the District Court's opinion, in my view, sanctioned petitioner's prelitigation conduct in express terms. Because I disagree with the Court's characterization of the District Court opinion, and because I believe the Court's casual analysis of inherent authority portends a dangerous extension of that authority to prelitigation conduct, I explain why inherent authority should not be so extended and why the District Court's order should be reversed.

The District Court's own candid and extensive opinion reveals that the bad faith for which petitioner was sanctioned extended beyond the litigation tactics and comprised as well what the District Court considered to be bad faith in refusing to perform the underlying contract three weeks before the lawsuit began. The Court made explicit reference, for instance, to "this massive and absolutely unnecessary lawsuit forced on NASCO by Chambers' arbitrary and arrogant refusal to honor and perform this perfectly legal and enforceable contract." 124 F.R.D. at 136. See also id., at 143 ("Chambers arbitrarily and without legal cause refused to perform, forcing NASCO to bring its suit for specific performance"); ibid. ("Chambers, knowing that NASCO had a good and valid contract, hired Gray to find a defense and arbitrarily refused to perform, thereby forcing NASCO to bring its suit for specific performance and injunctive relief"); id., at 125 (petitioner's "unjustified and arbitrary refusal to file" the FCC application "was in absolute bad faith"). The District Court makes the open and express concession that it is sanctioning petitioner for his breach of contract:

"[T]he balance of ... fees and expenses included in the sanctions, would not have been incurred by NASCO if Chambers had not defaulted and forced NASCO to bring this suit. There is absolutely no reason why Chambers should not reimburse in full all attorney's fees and expenses that NASCO, by Chambers' action, was forced to pay."

Id. at 143. The trial court also explained that "the attorney's fees and expenses charged to NASCO by its attorneys ... *flowed from and were a direct result of this suit.* We shall include them in the attorney's fees sanctions." Id. at 142 (emphasis added).

Despite the Court's equivocation on the subject, it is impermissible to allow a District Court acting pursuant to its inherent authority to sanction such prelitigation primary conduct. A Court's inherent authority extends only to remedy abuses of the judicial process. By contrast, awarding damages for a violation of a legal norm, here the binding obligation of a legal contract, is a matter of substantive law, see Marek v. Chesny, 473 U.S. 1, 35 (1985) ("right to attorney's fees is 'substantive' under any reasonable definition of that term"); see also *Alyeska*, which must be defined either by Congress (in cases involving federal law) or by the States (in diversity cases).

The American Rule recognizes these principles. It bars a federal court from shifting fees as a matter of substantive policy, but its bad faith exception permits fee shifting as a sanction to the extent necessary to protect the judicial process. The Rule protects each person's right to go to federal court to define and to vindicate substantive rights. "[S]ince litigation is at best uncertain one should not be penalized for merely defending or prosecuting a lawsuit." When a federal court, through invocation of its inherent powers, sanctions a party for bad-faith prelitigation conduct, it goes well beyond the exception to the American Rule and violates the Rule's careful balance between open access to the federal court system and penalties for the willful abuse of it.

By exercising inherent power to sanction prelitigation conduct, the District Court exercised authority where Congress gave it none. The circumstance that this exercise of power occurred in a diversity case compounds the error. When a federal court sits in diversity jurisdiction, it lacks constitutional authority to fashion rules of decision governing primary contractual relations. See E*rie R. Co. v. Tompkins*; *Hanna v. Plumer*. See generally Ely, *The Irrepressible Myth of* Erie, 87 HARV. L. REV. 693, 702-706 (1974). The *Erie* principle recognizes that "[e]xcept in matters governed by the Federal Constitution or by Acts of Congress, the law to be applied in any [diversity] case is the law of the State." The inherent power exercised here violates the fundamental tenet of federalism announced in Erie by regulating primary behavior that the Constitution leaves to the exclusive province of States.

The full effect of the District Court's encroachment on State prerogatives can be appreciated by recalling that the rationale for the bad-faith exception is punishment. To the extent that the District Court imposed sanctions by reason of the so-called bad-faith breach of contract, its decree is an award of punitive damages for the breach. Louisiana prohibits punitive damages "unless expressly authorized by statute," and no Louisiana statute authorizes attorney's fees for breach of contract as a part of damages in an ordinary case. One rationale for Louisiana's policy is its determination that "an award of compensatory damages will serve the same deterrent purpose as an award of punitive damages." Ricard v. State, 390 So. 2d 882, 886 (La. 1980). If respondent had brought this suit in state court he would not have recovered extra damages for breach of contract by reason of the so-called willful character of the breach. Respondent's decision to bring this suit in federal rather than state court resulted in a significant expansion of the substantive scope of his remedy. This is the result prohibited by *Erie* and the principles that flow from it.

As the Court notes, there are some passages in the District Court opinion suggesting its sanctions were confined to litigation conduct. See ante, n.17. ("[T]he sanctions imposed 'appl[ied] only to sanctionable acts which occurred in connection with the proceedings in the trial Court'"). But these passages in no way contradict the other statements by the trial court which make express reference to prelitigation conduct. At most, these passages render the court's order ambiguous, for the District Court appears to have adopted an expansive definition of "acts which occurred in connection with" the litigation. There is no question but that some sanctionable acts did occur in court. The problem is that the District Court opinion avoids any clear delineation of the acts being sanctioned and the power invoked to do so. This confusion in the premises of the District Court's order highlights the mischief caused by reliance on undefined inherent powers rather than on Rules and statutes that proscribe particular behavior. The ambiguity of the scope of the sanctionable conduct cannot be resolved against petitioner alone, who, despite the conceded bad-faith conduct of his attorneys, has been slapped with all of respondent's not inconsiderable attorney's fees. At the very least, adherence to the rule of law requires the case to be remanded to the District Court for clarification on the scope of the sanctioned conduct.

III

My discussion should not be construed as approval of the behavior of petitioner and his attorneys in this case. Quite the opposite. Our Rules permit sanctions because much of the conduct of the sort encountered here degrades the profession and deserves justice. District courts must not permit this abuse and must not hesitate to give redress through the Rules and statutes prescribed. It may be that the District Court could have imposed the full million dollar sanction against petitioner through reliance on federal Rules and statutes, as well as on a proper exercise of its inherent authority. But we should remand here because a federal court must decide cases based on legitimate sources of power. I would reverse the Court of Appeals with instructions to remand to the District Court for a reassessment of sanctions consistent with the principles here set forth. For these reasons, I dissent.

NOTES AND QUESTIONS

1. Justice White appears to be relying on *Business Guides* to show that assessing attorney's fees would not affect a plaintiff's choice of forum. Is *Business Guides* a Rules of Decision Act on a Rules Enabling Act case? What about *Chambers*?

2. Do you agree that the availability in federal court of the sanctions upheld in *Chambers* is unlikely to affect a plaintiff's choice of forum?

3. Look at Justice White's discussion of whether applying the federal practice will result in an equitable administration of the laws. Is he saying that there will be no such inequity because the federal rule is fair? Is that the kind of inequity *Erie* and *Hanna* are talking about?

4. Is *Byrd* dead? If so, why does Justice White bother to argue that a "substantive state policy is not implicated here?" What does he mean when he says that he does "not see how the district court's inherent power to tax fees for conduct can be made subservient to any state policy." Is he saying that the federal interest always is so great that it would outweigh even a substantive state policy?

C. Determining the Content of State Law

Once the federal court has determined that it should apply state law (and, under *Klaxon*, has determined which state's law applies), it next must ascertain the content of that state law. This can, at times, be a difficult task. In *Erie*, Justice Brandeis stated that federal courts had to follow the state law as decided by the "highest court" of the state. 304 U.S. at 78. But what if there were no supreme court decisions? Courts went through a fairly comical period in which they focused on whatever authority there was — no matter how low. In Gustin v. Sun Life Assurance Co., 154 F.2d 961 (6th Cir. 1946), the court felt absolutely bound by an unpublished Ohio intermediate court of appeals opinion even though state law provided that it was of no precedential value. This sort of thing led Judge Jerome Frank to utter his wonderful line: federal judges were now "to play the role of the ventriloquist's dummy to the courts of some particular state." Richardson v. Commissioner, 126 F.2d 562, 567 (2d Cir. 1942).

Later, federal courts came to accept that in addressing issues of state law, a federal court should do what it believed the state supreme court would have done. As Professor Wright has explained:

> Thus, the federal judge need no longer be a ventriloquist's dummy. Instead he or she is free, just as state judges are, to consider all the data the highest court of the state would use in an effort to determine how the highest court of the state would decide. This is as it should be. Unless this much freedom is allowed the federal judge, the *Erie* doctrine would simply have substituted one kind of forum-shopping for another. The lawyer whose case was dependent on an old or shaky state court decision that might no longer be followed within the state would have a strong incentive to maneuver the case into federal court, where, on the mechanical jurisprudence that the *Erie* doctrine was once thought to require, the state decision could not have been impeached.

WRIGHT, FEDERAL COURTS 395. See also Geri Yonover, *Ascertaining State Law: The Continuing* Erie *Dilemma*, 38 DEPAUL L. REV. 1 (1989).

Thus, the federal court is to look to all available data to make its best guess as to the content of state law. Particularly where the law is in flux or the relevant state precedents are old, the federal courts may have difficulty accurately predicting state law. It is hard to generalize whether a federal court will be more or less conservative than its state counterparts in declaring state law to have changed. For example, a federal court may be reluctant to predict that the state supreme court will overrule itself. On the other hand, the federal court can get ahead of state law, predicting change before the state court is willing to make it. Compare Dick Proctor Imports v. Sumitomo Corp., 486 F. Supp. 815 (E.D. Mo 1980) with State ex rel Gooseneck Trailer Mfg. v. Barker, 619 S.W. 2d 928, 930 (Mo. App. 1981).

What happens when a federal judgment is based on an incorrect interpretation of state law? Consider the following case:

DeWeerth v. Baldinger
38 F.3d 1266 (2d Cir.), *cert. denied*, 115 S. Ct. 512 (1994)

WALKER, CIRCUIT JUDGE.

This appeal is the latest episode in a decade-long dispute over the ownership of an oil painting entitled "Champs de Blé à Vétheuil" by Claude Monet. The work by the celebrated French Impressionist was previously owned by plaintiff Gerda Dorothea DeWeerth, a German citizen. It was discovered missing from DeWeerth's family castle after World War II, and was subsequently purchased by defendant Edith Marks Baldinger, a New York resident, from * * * Wildenstein & Co., a New York art gallery. * * *

* * *

In 1982, DeWeerth discovered that Baldinger was in possession of the Monet and demanded its return. When Baldinger refused, DeWeerth promptly commenced a diversity action to recover it. * * *

[Although the district court found for DeWeerth, the court of appeals] reversed the district court's judgment on the ground that New York limitations law required a showing of reasonable diligence in locating stolen property and that DeWeerth had failed to make such a showing. * * *

[Several years later, in an entirely separate action,] the New York Court of Appeals that held that the New York statute of limitations applicable to this action did not require a showing of reasonable diligence in locating stolen property. * * *

[DeWeerth then returned to the district court and asked that her case be reopened under Rule 60 and judgment entered in her favor.]

* * *

Based on the New York Court of Appeals' opinion, the district court determined that DeWeerth would have prevailed in this case had she originally brought her suit in the New York state courts. It then held that *Erie Railroad Co. v. Tompkins*, and its progeny entitled plaintiff to a modification of the final judgment in this case to avoid this inconsistency. It determined that the countervailing interest of both the parties and the courts in the finality of litigation was outweighed by the need "to prevent the working of an extreme and undue hardship upon plaintiff, to accomplish substantial justice and to act with appropriate regard for the principles of federalism which underlie our dual judicial system."

* * * In our view, *Erie* simply does not stand for the proposition that a plaintiff is entitled to reopen a federal court case that has been closed for several years in order to gain the benefit of a newly-announced decision of a state court, a forum in which she specifically declined to litigate her claim. The limited holding of *Erie* is that federal courts sitting in diversity are bound to follow state law on any matter of substantive law not "governed by the Federal Constitution or by Acts of Congress." 304 U.S. at 78. However, the fact that federal courts must follow state law when deciding a diversity case does not mean that a subsequent change in the law of the state will provide grounds for relief under Rule 60(b)(6). See Brown v. Clark Equip. Co., 96 F.R.D. 166, 173 (D. Me. 1982) ("mere change in decisional law does not constitute an 'extraordinary circumstance'" under Rule 60(b)(6), especially where "[p]laintiffs elected to proceed in the federal forum, thereby voluntarily depriving themselves of the opportunity to attempt to persuade the [state court]"); Atwell v. Equifax, Inc., 86 F.R.D. 686, 688 (D. Md. 1980) (change in the state decisional law upon which appellate court based decision held "insufficient to warrant reopening a final judgment"). This principle also applies in federal cases where the Supreme Court has changed the applicable rule of law.

* * *

When confronted with an unsettled issue of state law, a federal court sitting in diversity must make its best effort to predict how the state courts would decide the issue. The comprehensive opinion by now Chief Judge Jon O. Newman in *DeWeerth* accordingly surveyed New York case law and determined that a New York court called upon to decide the issue would be likely to impose a requirement of due diligence. The decision was based in part on the fact that plaintiff's argument would create an incongruity in the treatment of bona fide purchasers and thieves. In New York, the three-year statute of limitations starts running against thieves once the owner discovers that the art object has been stolen, while under plaintiff's theory, it would not start running against a good faith purchaser until he refused the owner's request to return the art object. The court determined in *DeWeerth* that this rule conflicted with a policy inherent in certain New York cases of protecting bona fide purchasers of stolen objects from stale claims by alleged owners. Based on this incongruity, New York's policy of discouraging stale claims in other settings, and the fact that in most other states the limitations period begins to run when a good faith purchaser acquires stolen property thereby prompting due diligence on the part of the previous owner, we determined that New York courts would adopt a due diligence requirement for owners attempting to locate stolen property.

It turned out that the *DeWeerth* panel's prediction was wrong. However, by filing her state law claim in a federal forum, DeWeerth assumed the risk that her adversaries would argue for a change in the applicable rules of law and that any open question of state law would be decided by a federal as opposed to a New York state court. * * *

C. Determining the Content of State Law

* * *

We conclude that the prior *DeWeerth* panel conscientiously satisfied its duty to predict how New York courts would decide the due diligence question, and that *Erie* and its progeny require no more than this. The fact that the New York Court of Appeals subsequently reached a contrary conclusion * * * does not constitute an "extraordinary circumstance" that would justify reopening this case in order to achieve a similar result. There is nothing in *Erie* that suggests that consistency must be achieved at the expense of finality, or that federal cases finally disposed of must be revisited anytime an unrelated state case clarifies the applicable rules of law. Attempting to obtain such a result through Rule 60(b)(6) is simply an improvident course that would encourage countless attacks on federal judgments long since closed. While our conclusion relies in part on our belief that the prior *DeWeerth* decision fully comported with *Erie* and did not, as plaintiffs suggest, mistakenly apply settled state law and reach a clearly wrong result, we note that even if those were the circumstances, the doctrine of finality would still pose a considerable hurdle to reopening the final judgment in this case. Whether, in such circumstances, the result would be different if the issue were raised within one year pursuant to Rule 60(b)(1) is an issue we need not decide.

* * *

For the foregoing reasons, we reverse the judgment of the district court.

OWEN, DISTRICT JUDGE.

I respectfully dissent.

* * *

The clear applicability of Rule 60(b)(6) to this case was well-stated by Judge Broderick below, 804. F. Supp. at 547:

> The range of fundamental policy and constitutional considerations which have informed the *Erie* doctrine are fully evident in the present case. Failure to act on the present Rule 60 motion would deny Mrs. DeWeerth the right to recover her property solely because she initially brought this action in federal rather than state court. Had Mrs. DeWeerth brought suit in state court, her claim would have been deemed timely commenced under the applicable statute of limitations.
>
> Such inconsistency is exactly the type of result that *Erie* was enacted to avoid. As Justice Frankfurter noted, "[t]he nub of the policy that underlies *Erie R. Co. v. Tompkins* is that for the same transaction the accident of a suit by a non-resident litigant in a federal court instead of in a State Court a block away should not lead to a substantially different result." *Guaranty Trust Company of New York v. York.*

I am, of course, unhesitatingly one with the majority as to the "integrity of the [prior] *DeWeerth* decision [and] . . . the fairness of the process that was accorded *DeWeerth*." However, given the majority's acknowledgment "that the [prior] *DeWeerth* panel's prediction was wrong[,] I cannot accept the result here * * *. Should not the impact of [the New York Court of Appeals decision] * * * be shouldered by us, notwithstanding the integrity of our error? While the doctrine of finality of judgments does address an important interest, it should not deter us from using Rule 60 today to do justice because we may have to deal hereafter with the Rule's invocation in unworthy cases.

* * *

Accordingly, contrary to the majority, I * * * would affirm on the scholarly and thorough opinion of Judge Broderick below.

NOTES AND QUESTIONS

1. In this case, it was the plaintiff who was disadvantaged by the incorrect interpretation of state law by the federal court. The majority concludes that by choosing the federal forum, the plaintiff "assumed the risk" that this might happen. Suppose it was the defendant who lost because of an incorrect interpretation. Does a defendant (who does not choose the forum) "assume" the same risk?

2. Do you think the majority put too much weight on concerns of finality and gave too little weight to the underlying concerns of *Erie*?

3. In ruling on the motion to reopen, should the federal court have considered whether a New York state court would have allowed a New York judgment to be reopened under similar circumstances?

4. A federal district judge is likely to be a member of the bar of the state in which she sits, and to have practiced law in the courts of the state. A federal appeals court panel of three judges may be drawn from judges covering the various states in the circuit. Thus, it is possible that the appellate panel will have no judge who is a member of the bar of the state whose law applies. To them, it might seem reasonable to defer to the judgment of the local district judge on a question of state law. Indeed, some appellate courts announced that they would defer to such judgments unless they appeared clearly erroneous. The Supreme Court rejected this practice in Salve Regina College v. Russell, 499 U.S. 225 (1991), in which it held that the courts must review determinations of state law just as they would any question of law. Thus, they are to review the questions de novo, and without deference to the local judge. See Dan Coenen, *To Defer or Not to Defer: A Study of Federal Circuit Court Deference to District Court Rulings on State Law*, 73 MINN. L. REV. 899 (1989).

5. If there is absolutely no state law on point, can the federal court refuse to hear the case? No. The court's "duty is tolerably clear. It is to decide, not avoid, the question."

Daily v. Parker, 152 F.2d 174, 177 (7th Cir. 1945). See also Meredith v. Winter Haven, 320 U.S. 228 (1943) (federal court may not abstain because of difficulty in determining state law).

6. One mechanism for eliminating uncertainty about the content of state law is certification. Under this procedure, when a federal court is confronted with an uncertainty in state law, it can certify the state law issue to that state's highest court and request the opinion of that court on the issue. Certification is not always a solution because it is not available in every state, some states will not decide certified questions that depend on issues of fact, see Exxon Co. v. Banque de Paris et des Pays-bas, 889 F.2d 674 (5th Cir. 1989), *cert. denied*, 496 U.S. 943 (1990), and sometimes the federal court simply doesn't understand the answer it receives, see Sun Ins. Office v. Clay, 319 F.2d. 505, 509-10 (5th Cir. 1963), *rev'd*, 377 U.S. 179 (1964). See generally Ira P. Robbins, *Interstate Certification of Questions of Law: A Valuable Process in Need of Reform*, 76 JUDICATURE 125 (1992).

D. Federal Common Law

Although *Erie* held that there is no *general* federal common law, in a few limited areas of unique federal interest there is federal common law that survives *Erie*. Indeed, on the very day the Court decided *Erie*, it also held that issues of interstate water allocation are governed by federal common law. See Hinderlider v. LaPlata River and Cherry Creek Ditch Co., 304 U.S. 92 (1938). Federal common law is limited to those areas in which there is an overwhelming need to have one federal rule, and where Congress could but has not provided that rule. As the Supreme Court has explained, "we have held that a few areas, invoking 'uniquely federal interests' are so committed by the Constitution and laws of the United States to federal control that state law is pre-empted and replaced, where necessary, by federal law of a content prescribed (absent explicit statutory directive) by the courts — so-called 'federal common law.'" Boyle v. United Technologies Corp., 487 U.S. 500, 504 (1988).

This judicially created federal common law is in many respects treated as if it were statutory law. It can be changed by Congress through legislation (a constitutional amendment is not required). It is preemptive of state law and binding on state courts. It has even been held that "laws" as used in §1331, includes federal common law. See Illinois v. City of Milwaukee, 406 U.S. 91, 98-101 (1972).

Where do the federal courts get the authority to make law? Sometimes the authority can be said to derive from some broad federal statute that appears to contemplate a single federal rule, but does not specify what the rule is. In other cases one might be able to argue that the Constitution itself grants this authority. In many respects, a court's creation of federal common law is like its intervention in the "dormant commerce clause" area. In both situations, the court is operating in an area in which Congress could legislate, but has not done so. Rather than simply leaving it to Congress to recognize the need for federal legislation, the federal courts act on their own.

You should remember that these areas of true federal common law are quite narrow. Federal common law is largely confined to the areas of admiralty, interstate border disputes, certain issues affected by international relations, and issues affecting the proprietary interests of the U.S. government. See United States v. Kimbell Foods, Inc., 440 U.S. 715, 726-29 (1979); Banco Nacional de Cuba v. Sabbatino, 376 U.S. 398, 426-27 (1964); Clearfield Trust Co. v. United States, 318 U.S. 363 (1943). See generally WRIGHT, FEDERAL COURTS 411-421.

E. Federal Law in State Court

As discussed in Chapter 4, states have concurrent jurisdiction over most federal causes of action. The only exception is where Congress has granted the federal courts exclusive jurisdiction. Thus, for example, a railroad employee injured on the job can bring suit against her employer based on the Federal Employees' Liability Act (FELA) and can file that suit in either state or federal court. Under the Supremacy Clause, a state court adjudicating that claim is required to apply federal law. But how far does this obligation extend? Must the state court apply all the same procedures that would be applied in federal court?

State courts must follow federal procedures "essential to effectuate" the purposes behind the federal law. Dice v. Akron, Canton & Youngstown R. R., 342 U.S. 359, 361 (1952). Thus, in *Dice*, an FELA case, the Court held that the right to a jury is "part and parcel of the remedy afforded" by that statute and therefore, federal law governs the availability of juries in FELA cases in state court. Id. at 363. Compare this holding with *Byrd*. In other FELA cases, Court has held that states must also follow federal law concerning burden of proof on contributory negligence, Central Vermont Ry v. White, 238 U.S. 507 (1915), and sufficiency of evidence to sustain a verdict, see Brady v. Southern Ry., 320 U.S. 476 (1943). See generally Daniel Meltzer, *State Court Forfeitures of Federal Rights*, 99 HARV. L. REV. 1130 (1986), Martin Redish & John Muench, *Adjudication of Federal Causes of Action in State Court*, 75 MICH. L. REV. 311 (1976).

CHAPTER 8
PLEADINGS AND JUDGMENTS BASED ON PLEADINGS

A. Introduction and Integration

Television and motion picture depictions of trials often have dramatic surprise witnesses and stunning new revelations from the witness stand. Although such things make for good theater, they are not terribly accurate, at least not in civil cases. American civil procedure does not countenance "trial by ambush." Instead, it embraces the notion that litigants should be aware of all the contentions and all the evidence of their opponents before trial. Through this broad disclosure, the system seeks to find the truth, and not simply reward parties for the quick reactions of their lawyers to surprise evidence.

In this chapter and the next, we address pleadings and discovery, which are the two major tools through which litigants gain information about each other's claims and defenses. It is helpful to think of the two tools as establishing an education process for the parties, one that routinely consumes many months and sometimes years. The starting point in that process — the first opportunity to learn about the opponent's contentions — is the pleading stage. Under modern practice, this is a relatively short part of the overall education of the litigants. It gives way to the discovery process, during which parties can determine what factual support exists for their contentions and for those of other litigants. As we will see in the next chapter, discovery may serve as a "reality check" to foster stipulations about the scope of the dispute or to spur settlement.

Pleadings are documents filed by litigants, setting forth their claims and defenses. The plaintiff initiates suit by filing what most jurisdictions call a *complaint*. You will recall from Chapter 3 that the plaintiff must arrange to give notice to the defendant through service of process, which consists of the court summons and a copy of the plaintiff's pleading. The defendant has a choice of how to respond to the complaint. One option is to file her own pleading, which most jurisdictions call an *answer*, in which she responds to the allegations in the complaint and may raise new matter called affirmative defenses. In some jurisdictions, the plaintiff may then respond to any such new matter in another pleading, the *reply*.

CHAPTER 8 PLEADINGS AND JUDGMENTS BASED ON PLEADINGS

Rules governing pleading have a long and rich history, a glimpse of which we will see below. The history is important because it reflects the debate over the role pleadings should play in an overall system of civil procedure. The earliest system expected pleadings to perform at least four functions: (1) putting parties on notice of claims and defenses of their opponents; (2) stating facts each party believed it could prove; (3) narrowing the number and scope of issues needing trial; and (4) providing a quick method for resolving meritless claims and defenses. WRIGHT, FEDERAL COURTS 468. Modern systems expect less from pleadings and tend to limit their function to giving notice. Modern practice has provided other mechanisms — such as broadranging discovery and the motion for summary judgment (which we will see in Chapter 10) — to perform the other functions.

It is helpful to think of pleading requirements as a gatekeeper to judicial machinery. Earlier systems used difficult and arcane pleading rules to erect a high barrier to entry. Most jurisdictions today, on the other hand, recognize that because pleadings are filed early in the dispute, it is inappropriate to expect the parties to be fully familiar with the underlying facts. They therefore lower the barrier to entry by requiring less rigor and detail in pleading; they permit ready amendment of pleadings and place the burden for factual development on the discovery process. This choice is not without cost. Discovery can be very expensive. Some ctitics feel that by erecting a low barrier to entry and placing more emphasis on the expensive discovery process, modern theory makes litigation more time consuming, more difficult to settle, and more expensive.

Before looking in more detail at the evolution of rules governing pleading, it is important to emphasize two things. First, pleading rules in modern systems are not unimportant. Pleadings are still gatekeepers to the judicial system. The fact that they erect a lower barrier to entry than in earlier times does not mean that they raise no barrier at all. Many cases are won or lost because of the pleadings. Second, although we may speak generally of modern theories of pleading, jurisdictions disagree somewhat about the amount of detail to be required in pleading. Although every American jurisdiction has rejected the strictures of the earliest systems, there is some debate over how high a barrier pleadings ought to impose for entry to the judicial system.

B. Historical Overview of the Evolution of Pleadings

Three great theories have dominated the history of pleading: common law, "code," and the Federal Rules. Thus, we can speak of common law pleading, code pleading, and Federal Rules pleading (sometimes called "notice pleading"). Although the common law theory dominated English practice for centuries and American procedure for generations, it

B. Historical Overview of the Evolution of Pleadings

is now abandoned. Nonetheless, we need to know something about common law pleading for two reasons. First, some vestiges of it remain in modern theory. Second, and more importantly, the other two theories evolved in reaction to the common law system. It is impossible to understand the advances made by the codes and Federal Rules, then, without some grounding in the common law. You may wish to reread the overview of English legal history in Chapter 1, Section F.

The codes and the Federal Rules may be considered generically as modern. Most of the American states adopt the Federal Rules approach to pleading. A significant minority of states, however, including such populous states as California and New York, adhere to code pleading rules.

Common law pleading on both sides of the Atlantic was dominated by the "writ system." The plaintiff stated her substantive cause of action by invoking the writ for her claim. Choice of the writ determined not only the pleading rules for the case, but other aspects of procedure as well. The plaintiff asked the court to issue the particular writ for her type of case, and had to plead the "form of action" appropriate to that type of case, such as trespass, trover, assumpsit, etc. The common law system included no plenary right to discovery. Thus, pleadings constituted the primary method not only for putting litigants on notice but for factual development and narrowing issues for trial as well. The parties went through round after round of pleadings, with the goal of framing a single disputed factual issue to be tried.

But the plaintiff had a serious problem if that single disputed issue did not fit the writ she had chosen at the outset of the case. In that instance, the court dismissed the entire suit, and the plaintiff had to start again by choosing another writ. This happened quite frequently, not only because the writs were extremely narrow but because the parties had no way to determine the underlying facts until trial.

One example should suffice. The writ of "trespass" covered what today would be considered intentional torts. The writ of "trespass on the case," on the other hand, covered what we would consider negligence. Suppose the plaintiff was injured when her carriage hit a large rock in the roadway and that she sued the defendant in trespass, contending that the defendant had put the rock there intentionally. At trial, the evidence shows that the defendant had negligently dislodged the rock, causing it to come to rest in the roadway. Even though the plaintiff had showed a right to relief, the court would dismiss her suit. She had pleaded trespass but proved trespass on the case. The variance was fatal. See TEPLY & WHITTEN, CIVIL PROCEDURE 29-30 (1994). Cf. Reynolds v. Clarke, 93 Eng. Rep. 747 (K.B. 1726).

Common law pleading was a nightmarish exercise. It was part of a system not well calculated to reach a decision on the merits. Indeed, pleadings were an end in themselves, and seemed more important than any factfinding function of the court.* The situation led to calls for reform both here and in England in the mid-nineteenth century. In the United States, the effort was spearheaded by the remarkable David Dudley Field,** a lawyer from Albany, New York, whose devotion to codification of reforms (including abolishing common law pleading) led to adoption of the "Field Code" in that state in 1848.

Field's effort ushered in the second great theory of pleading. "Code pleading" abolished the writ system and the forms of action. It also abolished distinctions between procedure at law and equity. More importantly for our purposes, it stated a role for pleadings. They were to be simplified and focused on giving notice to the parties and the court; they were to facilitate a decision on the merits. The role of developing the facts would be shifted to discovery, which the codes liberalized considerably. Accordingly, the codes limited the number of pleadings. No longer would the parties plead back and forth to frame a single disputed issue. Instead, generally, the plaintiff would file a complaint, the defendant would file an answer and the plaintiff may file a reply to the answer.

Over time, the code approach came to dominate, largely (but not completely) supplanting common law rules throughout the United States by the 1930s. The centerpiece of code pleading is its emphasis on pleading *facts*. Specifically, the code complaint should contain "a statement of the facts constituting the cause of action, in ordinary and concise language, without repetition, and in such a manner as to enable a person of common understanding to know what is intended." This seemingly straightforward and pragmatic undertaking replaced the near-mystical exercise of selecting the correct writ under common law practice.

Unfortunately, however, some courts were incapable of interpreting the code provision in the liberalizing spirit that was intended. As we will see, some judges seized on the requirement that plaintiff plead "facts" to impose stiflingly subtle distinctions. Pleading again became an end in itself, rather than a means to the end of decisionmaking based upon the merits.

The failure of code pleading to realize its potential led to the drive for further reform in the Federal Rules, which embody the third great theory of pleading. It is not a revolutionary break from the theory of code pleading. Indeed, the Federal Rules reaffirm David Dudley Fields's central goals. Pleadings are designed to give notice and provide a mecha-

---

* Meanwhile, equity developed different pleading rules. Because no jury was available in equity, the pleadings were often used as a surrogate for evidentiary presentations at trial. Accordingly, equity pleading was prolix and often argumentative.

** David Dudley's youngest brother was Stephen Field, whom we remember as the author of the Supreme Court opinion in *Pennoyer v. Neff*, Chapter 2. Before serving on the Supreme Court, Stephen Field was a political leader and Chief Justice of the then-new state of California, and may have influenced its legislature to adopt his brother's code from New York. Another brother, Cyrus Field, played an important role in establishing the trans-Atlantic telegraph cable.

nism for ready testing of the legal sufficiency of a claim. To avoid the major problems invented by courts in code states, the Federal Rules eschew the term "facts." Instead of pleading facts, the plaintiff makes a short and plain statement of her claim, showing that she is entitled to relief. The limited role of pleadings was buttressed by startlingly liberal discovery provisions, sanctions for abusive pleading, and retooled provisions for summary judgment.

Of course, the Federal Rules govern pleading in federal court. As noted, most states have adopted the Federal Rules approach as well. Remember, however, that code pleading is alive and well today in a good many states. The difference between its approach and the Federal Rules essentially is one of detail. Code pleading requires more detailed allegations than the Federal Rules.

C. The Complaint

Both the codes and the Federal Rules limit the number of pleadings, generally to a complaint, answer, and a reply. See Rule 7(a). Nearly all states refer to the plaintiff's initial pleading as the complaint, though some states use other terms, such as "petition" or "declaration." Regardless of the label, most of the code and Federal Rules provisions governing complaints are substantially similar.

1. Requirements

a. Elements of the Complaint

Read Rule 8(a). Like many state counterparts, Rule 8(a) requires every complaint[*] to contain three things. A complaint lacking any of the three must be dismissed, although the plaintiff will be permitted to amend to correct a formal deficiency.

i. A "short and plain statement of the grounds upon which the court's jurisdiction depends"

Because federal courts have limited subject matter jurisdiction, it is essential that the plaintiff allege that the case is properly within the court's jurisdiction. (The exception in

---

[*] Actually, Rule 8 applies to all pleadings setting forth a "claim for relief," specifically listing several. While the complaint is the major pleading setting forth a claim for relief (as an original claim), it is not the only one. For example, the defendant may file a counterclaim against the plaintiff or a cross-claim against her co-defendant. All must satisfy Rule 8(a). For our present purposes, though, we need only address the complaint.

Rule 8(a)(1) for cases in which the court's subject matter jurisdiction is already established will not apply to the original complaint, since it is the document that institutes the proceeding.) Many state rules require such an allegation as well, so the plaintiff must aver that she has selected the proper trial court for her dispute. In addition, some state provisions require the plaintiff to allege facts supporting personal jurisdiction if the defendant is a nonresident, and a statement of facts supporting venue.

You should be familiar with the Appendix of Forms printed behind the Federal Rules in your Rules pamphlet. Rule 84 provides that these forms "are sufficient under the rules and are intended to indicate the simplicity and brevity of statement which the rules contemplate." Counsel are not required to use the Forms, but may find them instructive. Form 2, setting forth acceptable allegations of subject matter jurisdiction, is particularly helpful.

ii. A "short and plain statement of the claim showing that the pleader is entitled to relief"

This is the liberal Federal Rules approach to plaintiff's statement of her claim. As noted above, code states commonly require the plaintiff to allege a "statement of the facts constituting a cause of action, in ordinary and concise language, without repetition." In Section C(1)(d) below, we will explore this difference between code and Federal Rules pleading.

iii. A "demand for judgment for the relief the pleader seeks"

In the demand — often called the "prayer" — the plaintiff must tell the court what she wants to recover. Interestingly, under Federal Rule 54(c) and many state provisions, the demand does not limit plaintiff's recovery. She is entitled to recover whatever relief she proves at trial, even if that is more money than she asked for, and even if it is of a different type than she requested (e.g., equitable versus legal). This is not true in default judgment cases, as we will see in Section D(4) below.

In federal and state practice, the prayer is a simple statement, universally preceded by the word "Wherefore." In Form 3, the entire demand consists of: "Wherefore plaintiff demands judgment against defendant for the sum of ____ dollars, interest, and costs." Damages generally can be pleaded as a lump sum. We will see below that parties must plead certain kinds of damages — "special damages" — with particularity.

The requirement of a demand does not mandate that the plaintiff set forth a dollar figure on damages. Instead, plaintiff can "demand damages in an amount to be shown at trial." The statement of damages in the demand differs from the allegation that the case

C. The Complaint

satisfies the amount in controversy requirement for diversity of citizenship or alienage jurisdiction in federal court. The amount in controversy allegation is part of the statement of subject matter jurisdiction, as shown in Form 2. There is nothing improper about alleging that the matter in controversy exceeds $50,000.00 for jurisdictional purposes and making a demand in an amount to be shown at trial.

Of course, as we noted in Chapter 1, damages are not the only relief available. Plaintiff might seek equitable relief, such as an injunction, specific performance, or declaratory judgment. See the demands for such relief in Forms 12, 16, and 18. The demand may be especially important in determining whether the case will be tried to a jury. As we will see in Chapter 10, the Seventh Amendment guarantees a jury trial for legal claims but not for equitable claims. A claim for damages is the quintessential legal claim.

b. Form of Pleadings

Federal Rule 10 governs the form of all pleadings in federal court. Under Rule 10(a), the caption of any pleading must state the name of the court, title of the case (by parties' names) and the identity of the document itself. It also lists the file number (sometimes called the "case number" or "docket number"), which the clerk assigns to each case when it is filed. In most districts, civil case numbers are preceded by the designation "CV." The first number following that denomination in the file number indicates the year in which the case was filed. This is followed by a number assigned sequentially to each case. Thus, the first case filed in a particular district in 1996 would have the file number "96-00001." In most districts, these numbers are followed by the initials of the judge assigned to the case. Here is a caption for a mythical case assigned to Judge Schwartz. Every pleading by each party in the case will bear the same case number.

CHAPTER 8 PLEADINGS AND JUDGMENTS BASED ON PLEADINGS

United States District Court
Southern District of California

Sally Johnson,	)	
	)	
Plaintiff,	)	
	)	CV-97-0506-S
vs.	)	
	)	COMPLAINT
Terri Benson,	)	
	)	
Defendant	)	

The body of the pleading sets forth claims or defenses in numbered paragraphs, as required by Rule 10(b). Note that the rule requires the plaintiff to state separate counts only when claims are founded on separate transactions. In practice, however, courts are usually stricter, and it is common for plaintiffs to set forth separate counts for different claims, even if transactionally related. Thus, a plaintiff injured in a car wreck generally will allege two counts, one for personal injuries and one for property damage to the car.

Rule 10(c) allows parties to adopt by reference allegations found elsewhere in the document. For example, suppose plaintiff alleges two counts against the defendant — one for personal injuries and the other for property damage sustained in an automobile wreck. In the first count, the plaintiff will allege facts common to both counts, such as the circumstances of the accident, and the defendant's breach of duty to her. Rather than reiterate this common material in the second count, the plaintiff can merely adopt those allegations by reference. In addition, Rule 10(c) allows parties to attach to their pleading a copy of a written instrument, which then becomes a part of the pleading "for all purposes." In contract cases, for example, lawyers routinely attach to a complaint a copy of the contract, which can streamline their pleadings.

c. Legal Sufficiency

Plaintiff's complaint must be legally sufficient. If on the face of the complaint the allegations could not support a judgment for the plaintiff, the case can be dismissed at the outset, without the wasted effort of a trial. At common law and today under code pleading, the defendant tested the legal sufficiency of a complaint by filing a *general demurrer* to the complaint. (It is also proper to say that the defendant demurred to the complaint. Neither demurrer nor demur is pronounced with a long "u" sound as in "demure." Instead, the "u" sound is like that in "fur.") In federal court, technically there is no such thing as a demurrer. See Rule 7(c). The same function is served, however, by the motion to dismiss for failure to state a claim under Rule 12(b)(6).

In ruling on a general demurrer or a Rule 12(b)(6) motion, the court looks only to the face of the complaint; it does not consider evidence that may support the allegations or sharpen the dispute between the parties. "The issue is not whether a plaintiff will ultimately prevail but whether [she] is entitled to offer evidence to support the claims." Scheuer v. Rhodes, 416 U.S. 232, 236 (1974). The court asks itself one question: if the plaintiff proved everything she alleged in her complaint, would the law provide a remedy for her? If not, the court sustains the general demurrer or grants the Rule 12(b)(6) motion and dismisses the case. It will usually do so "with leave to amend," which means that the plaintiff has another opportunity to allege a draft a legally sufficient complaint.

For example, suppose relevant precedent established that a spouse of a person injured by defendant's negligence may sue to recover her loss of "consortium," which it defines as "conjugal fellowship and sexual relations between wife and husband." Assume now that the plaintiff sues to recover for loss of "consortium" because of injuries inflicted upon someone she names in the complaint, but whose relationship she does not allege. Because the plaintiff has not alleged that the injured person is her spouse, the law will not afford a remedy. The court will sustain defendant's general demurrer or grant defendant's Rule 12(b)(6) motion and dismiss the case. It will give the plaintiff leave to amend, however, because it is possible that she can allege that she and the injures person are married.

Let's say the plaintiff files an amended complaint seeking damages for loss of "consortium" and alleging that she and the injured person are live-in lovers. Because the relevant precedent does not permit a recovery by non-married persons, the court would sustain defendant's demurrer or grant defendant's Rule 12(b)(6) motion, and dismiss the case. This time, it will probably do so without leave to amend, and will enter final judgment for the defendant. Plaintiff may now appeal and attempt to convince the appellate court to establish a right of consortium between non-married persons.

Defendants often will want to raise substantive challenges to the sufficiency of the complaint as their initial response in the suit. If successful, the defendant is spared the expense of preparing an answer and otherwise litigating. Note, however, that the defendant does not lose the substantive challenge by failing to assert it at the outset. See Rule 12(h)(2). She may not become aware of the deficiency until later in the proceedings, and can raise it then. This rule recognizes that "[i]t would make no sense whatsoever to allow evidence to come in on a claim * * * that, if proved, would have no substantive effect in the case." FRIEDENTHAL, KANE & MILLER, CIVIL PROCEDURE 298.

Defendant need not attack the entire complaint through a general demurrer or Rule 12(b)(6) motion. She can, for example, address one of several claims made by the plaintiff.

NOTES AND QUESTIONS

1. Plaintiff is a truck driver hauling goods from New Jersey to the Defendant's warehouse in Chicago. When he arrived at the warehouse, Defendant's loading dock was already in use. Defendant's employees directed Plaintiff to park his rig on the public street, adjacent to the driveway leading to the warehouse, and to wait for the loading dock to clear. Plaintiff parked the truck and waited in his rig as directed. Two unidentified men then attempted to rob Plaintiff. One of the men shot Plaintiff, inflicting serious personal injuries. In each of the following variations, assume that Plaintiff sued Defendant alleging these facts and that he was an "invitee" to whom Defendant owed a duty to guard from criminal acts of third parties.

Assume there is no question that Plaintiff was an "invitee" under the applicable law. But case law clearly establishes a duty to guard an invitee from criminal acts of third parties only *while the invitee is on the defendant's "premises."* (This fact pattern is adapted from Mitchell v. Archibald & Kendall, Inc., 573 F.2d 429 (7th Cir. 1978).)

   (a) Plaintiff alleges that he was sitting in his rig, parked on a public street when he was shot. Defendant files a general demurrer or Rule 12(b)(6) motion. What result?

   (b) Plaintiff alleges that he was sitting in his rig, parked where directed by Defendant's employees when he was shot. Defendant files a general demurrer or Rule 12(b)(6) motion. What result?

   (c) Plaintiff alleges that he was sitting in his rig, parked on Defendant's "premises" when he was shot. Defendant contends that Plaintiff was parked on a public street instead. Defendant cannot raise this issue through a general demurrer or Rule 12(b)(6) motion, since those devices do not address actual evidence or allow the court to determine disputed facts. Again, they assess only the sufficiency of the allegations of the complaint. In this situation, Defendant would file an answer denying Plaintiff's allegation that he was parked on Defendant's "premises." At that point, the pleadings would have framed a disputed factual issue requiring resolution.

   (d) If Defendant or Plaintiff felt that evidence (perhaps from witnesses or from the parties themselves) would show no dispute as to this factual issue of where the rig was parked, it or he could move for summary judgment. See Rule 56.

C. The Complaint

Summary judgment permits the court to go beyond the allegations of the pleadings and to assess evidence. The court makes a determination as to whether, on the evidence proffered (as opposed to in the pleadings), there is a disputed issue requiring resolution. Suppose the uncontradicted evidence showed that Plaintiff was parked on the public street. Would Defendant be entitled to summary judgment?

2. Is there anything ethically improper about Plaintiff's alleging that he was on Defendant's "premises" when shot (paragraph (c) in Note 1)?

3. As noted, a court can consider evidence in ruling on a motion for summary judgment, but not in ruling on a general demurrer or Rule 12(b)(6) motion. Under modern practice, however, if a court looks to evidentiary materials in ruling on demurrer or a motion to dismiss, it simply converts the motion into one for summary judgment. See the last sentence of Rule 12(b)(6).

d. Factual (or "Formal") Sufficiency: The Debate Over Specificity

In the previous section, we were concerned with barriers erected by the substantive law. In this section, we will assume that the law affords a claim for the plaintiff. Now, the question is whether the plaintiff has pleaded that claim in sufficient detail to proceed in the litigation. Here, the code system and the Federal Rules diverge more than with any other issue relating to pleading. Stated simply, the code system requires plaintiff to plead with greater specificity than the Federal Rules. Although most code states have liberalized their practice, the distinction between the two pleading systems persists, and reflects a continuing debate over the independent importance of the pleading exercise. In code states, a defendant challenges the factual sufficiency of the plaintiff's pleading with a *special demurrer*. In federal practice, she does so with a Rule 12(b)(6) motion.

i. Code Pleading

As we have seen, code states generally require that the plaintiff make "a statement of facts constituting a cause of action, in ordinary and concise language, without repetition." Unfortunately, courts in most code states refined the word "facts" in ways that have created traps for the unwary. They came to require the plaintiff to state not just "facts" but the "ultimate facts" constituting her claim. The problem, of course, is that "ultimate facts" is not a self-defining term.

A plaintiff who alleges facts too specifically could be guilty of "pleading the evidence," for which the court would sustain defendant's special demurrer. On the other hand,

CHAPTER 8 PLEADINGS AND JUDGMENTS BASED ON PLEADINGS

a plaintiff who alleges facts too generally could be guilty of "pleading conclusions of law," for which the court would also sustain defendant's special demurrer. Thus, counsel in code states can find themselves stuck between the Scylla of pleading evidence (too much detail) and the Charybdis of pleading conclusions of law (too little detail). What was intended as a liberal reform of common law pleading can become an exercise in formalism, every bit as arcane and frustrating as the writ system.

Let's consider an example. A plaintiff suing in ejectment (to oust a defendant from possession of property) must plead and prove several issues, one of which is that her title to the disputed property is superior to that of the defendant. Suppose the plaintiff had purchased the property from defendant and could prove due execution of the contract, payment, and even that defendant had given her a deed to the property. Which, if any, of the following is a pleading of the "ultimate fact" of her superior title?

a. Plaintiff alleges that she "has superior title to the property."
b. Plaintiff alleges that she is "entitled to possession of the property."
c. Plaintiff alleges that she "had paid for the property pursuant to contract and that the defendants had given her a deed to the property."

Today, it is probable that courts in code states would accept any of these allegations. There is old authority, however, that the plaintiff in situations (a) and (b) alleged improper conclusions of law. See, e.g., Sheridan v. Jackson, 72 N.Y. 170 (1878). In (c), the California Supreme Court held that plaintiff had pleaded too specifically, and thus was setting forth evidentiary facts instead of ultimate facts. McCaughey v. Shuette, 117 Cal. 223 (1896). The result in *McCaughey* was especially absurd because it reversed a judgment for the plaintiff after full trial. The court remanded the case to the trial court, where it permitted the plaintiff to amend his complaint to state the "ultimate facts" of his superior title. Then the case was to be retried! How would you formulate an allegation of "ultimate facts" that the plaintiff had superior title to property?

In Kramer v. Kansas City Power & Light Co., 279 S.W. 43 (Mo. 1925), the plaintiff was a lineman who fell thirty feet because a spike in the pole he was climbing broke. The spikes were put into the pole by the defendant. They were nine inches long, and the defendant generally drove them halfway into the pole, meaning that four and one-half inches protruded, on which linemen could step. The plaintiff alleged that the defendant "negligently caused said step to be driven and placed in said pole not far enough to make it reasonably safe." Id. at 47. Although the plaintiff won at trial, the Missouri Supreme Court reversed, holding that the trial court should have sustained defendant's demurrer. How would you formulate an allegation of "ultimate facts" that the defendant placed the spike into the pole negligently?

Many of the cases concerning pleading "ultimate facts" simply cannot be reconciled. Is an allegation that "defendant drove his car negligently" a statement of ultimate fact? How about "defendant became indebted to the plaintiff in the amount of $500?" As some observers put it, "the difficulty of determining what is a properly pleaded 'ultimate fact' appears to place an attorney in a 'no win' situation; precedents are available to attack the pleadings no matter how the allegations are phrased." FRIEDENTHAL, KANE & MILLER, CIVIL PROCEDURE 250.

We don't want to overstate the horribles. It is clear that the practice has relaxed considerably in code states. Id. at 251-52. By the same token, we don't want to give the impression that code pleading practice is as liberal as the Federal Rules. It is not. See, e.g., Papin Builders, Inc. v. Litz, 734 S.W.2d 853 (Mo. App. 1987). Courts in code states still appear especially tough on pleaders who allege conclusions of law rather than ultimate facts. Some modern opinions remind counsel that allegations of conclusions of law are disregarded in determining whether the plaintiff has stated a cause of action. See, e.g., Gallion v. Woytassek, 504 N.W.2d 76, 79 (Neb. 1993)(on demurrer, court considers "the pleaded facts, as distinguished from legal conclusions"); Mebane Lumber Co. v. Avery & Bullock Builders, Inc., 154 S.E.2d 665 (N.C. 1967)(allegation that contract was entire and indivisible improper is improper conclusion of law).

In addition to the special demurrer, code states generally permit the defendant to seek amplification of the plaintiff's pleading through a motion for more definite statement or bill of particulars. They also permit the defendant to move to strike redundant or scandalous matter from a pleading.

ii. Federal Rules Pleading

Rule 8(a)(2) avoids terms such as "ultimate facts," "conclusions of law," and "evidentiary facts." Indeed, it avoids "facts" altogether.

Dioguardi v. Durning
139 F.2d 774 (2d Cir. 1944)

CLARK, CIRCUIT JUDGE

In his complaint, obviously home drawn, the plaintiff attempts to assert a series of grievances against the Collector of Customs at the Port of New York growing out of his endeavors to import merchandise from Italy "of great value," consisting of bottles of "tonics." We may pass certain of his claims as either inadequate or inadequately stated and consider only these two: (1) that on the auction day, October 9, 1940, when defendant sold the merchandise at "public custom," "he sold my merchandise to another bidder with my price of $110, and not of his price of $120," and (2) "that three weeks before the sale, two cases, of 19 bottles each case, disappeared." The plaintiff does not make wholly clear how these goods came into the collector's hands, since he alleges compliance with the revenue laws; but he does say he made a claim for "refund of merchandise which was two-third paid in Milano, Italy," and that the collector denied the claim. These and other circumstances alleged indicate (what, indeed, the plaintiff's brief asserts) that his original dispute was with his consignor as to whether anything more was due upon the merchandise, and that the collector, having held it for a year (presumably as unclaimed merchandise under 19 U.S.C.A. 1491), then sold it, or such part of it as was left, at public auction. For his asserted injuries the plaintiff claimed $5,000 damages, together with interest and costs, against the defendant individually and as collector. This complaint was dismissed by the District Court, with leave, however, to the plaintiff to amend, on motion of the United States Attorney, appearing for the defendant, on the ground that it "fails to state facts sufficient to constitute a cause of action."

Thereupon the plaintiff filed an amended complaint, wherein, with an obviously heightened conviction that he was being unjustly treated, he vigorously reiterates his claims, including those quoted above and now stated as that his "medicinal extracts" were given to the Springdale Distilling Company "with my betting (bidding?) price of $110: and not their price of $120," and "It isn't so easy to do away with two cases of 37 bottles of one quart. Being protected, they can take this chance." An earlier paragraph suggests that defendant had explained the loss of the two cases by "saying that they had leaked, which could never be true in the manner they were bottled." On defendant's motion for dismissal on the same ground as before, the court made a final judgment dismissing the complaint, and the plaintiff now comes to us with increased volubility, if not clarity.

It would seem, however, that he has stated enough to withstand a mere formal motion, directed only to the face of the complaint, and that here is another instance of judicial haste which in the long run makes waste. Under the new rules of civil procedure, there is no pleading requirement of stating "facts sufficient to constitute a cause of action," but only that there be "a short and plain statement of the claim showing that the pleader is entitled to relief," Federal Rules of Civil Procedure, rule 8(a), and the motion for dismissal under Rule 12(b) is for failure to state "a claim upon which relief can be granted." The District Court does not state why it concluded that the complaints showed no claim upon which relief could be granted; and the United States Attorney's brief before us does not help us, for it is limited to the prognostication— unfortunately ill founded so far as we are concerned— that "the most cursory examination" of them will show the correctness of the District Court's action.

We think that, however inartistically they may be stated, the plaintiff has disclosed his claims that the collector has converted or otherwise done away with two of his cases of medicinal tonics and has sold the rest in a manner incompatible with the public auction he had announced— and, indeed, required by 19 U.S.C.A. 1491, above cited, and the Treasury Regulations promulgated under it. As to this latter claim, it may be that the collector's only error is a failure to collect an additional ten dollars from the Springdale Distilling Company; but giving the plaintiff the benefit of reasonable intendments in his allegations (as we must on this motion), the claim appears to be in effect that he was actually the first bidder at the price for which they were sold, and hence was entitled to the merchandise. Of course, defendant did not need to move on the complaint alone; he could have disclosed the facts from his point of view, in advance of a trial if he chose, by asking for a pre-trial hearing or by moving for a summary judgment with supporting affidavits. But, as it stands, we do not see how the plaintiff may properly be deprived of his day in court to show what he obviously so firmly believes and what for present purposes defendant must be taken as admitting. It appears to be well settled that the collector may be held personally for a default or for negligence in the performance of his duties.

On remand, the District Court may find substance in other claims asserted by the plaintiff, which include a failure properly to catalogue the items [as the relevant Regulations provide], or to allow the plaintiff to buy at a discount from the catalogue price just before the auction sale (a claim whose basis is not apparent), and a violation of an agreement to deliver the merchandise to the plaintiff as soon as he paid for it, by stopping the payments. In view of the plaintiff's limited ability to write and speak English, it will be difficult for the District Court to arrive at justice unless he consents to receive legal assistance in the presentation of his case. The record indicates that he refused further help from a lawyer suggested by the court, and hisbrief (which was a recital of facts, rather than an argument of law) shows distrust of a lawyer of standing at this bar. It is the plaintiff's privilege to decline all legal help; but we fear that he will be indeed ill advised to attempt to meet a motion for summary judgment or other similar presentation of the merits without competent advice and assistance.

Judgment is reversed and the action is remanded for further proceedings not inconsistent with this opinion.

NOTES AND QUESTIONS

1. You may be interested to read the actual allegations of Mr. Dioguardi's amended complaint:

Plaintiff, as and for his bill of amended complaint the defendant, respectfully alleges:

FIRST: I want justice done on the basis of my medicinal extracts which have disappeared saying that they had leaked, which could never be true in the manner they were bottled,

SECOND: Mr. E.G. Collord Clerk in Charge, promised to give me my merchandise as soon as I paid for it. Then all of a sudden payments were stopped.

THIRD: Then, he didn't want to sell me my merchandise at catalogue price with the 5% off, which was very important to me, after I had already paid $5,000 for them, beside a few other expenses.

FOURTH: Why was the medicinal given to the Springdale Distilling Co. with my betting price of $110; and not their price of $120.

FIFTH: It isn't so easy to do away with two cases with 37 bottles of one quart. Being protected, they can take this chance.

SIXTH: No one can stop my rights upon my merchandise, because of both the duly and the entry.

WHEREFORE: Plaintiff demands judgment against the defendant, individually and as Collector of Customs at the Port of New York, in the sum of Five

Thousand Dollars ($5,000) together with interest from the respective dates of payment as set forth herein, together with the costs and disbursements of this action.

JOHN COUND, JACK FRIEDENTHAL, ARTHUR MILLER & JOHN SEXTON, CIVIL PROCEDURE CASES AND MATERIALS 513-14 (6th ed. 1993). In a code pleading jurisdiction, would a court sustain a special demurrer to Mr. Dioguardi's complaint? Why?

 2. Consider the views of Professor Wright on *Dioguardi*:

> It is difficult to see what the Second Circuit could have done other than reverse in the Dioguardi case. Had it affirmed the judgment below, Dioguardi would have been out of court without ever having any hearing on the merits of his claims. These claims had merit if the facts were as Dioguardi believed them to be. The critics have made much of the fact that, after the decision the case went to trial, Dioguardi failed to prove his claims, and a judgment was entered against him and affirmed by the Second Circuit. [151 F.2d 501 (1945)] The fact, however, that a litigant ultimately loses on the merits hardly shows that he should be thrown out of court without any opportunity to prove the merits of his case.
>
> Those who criticize the result in the *Dioguardi* case necessarily must believe that "good pleading" is a sufficiently important goal that even possibly meritorious claims should be dismissed if they are not properly pleaded. [Such a position] is contrary to the fundamental notion of all modern procedural reform, that the object of procedure should be to secure a determination on the merits rather than to penalize litigants because of procedural blunders.

WRIGHT, FEDERAL COURTS 474.

 3. As the court points out, a litigant may eschew the services of an attorney, as Mr. Dioguardi did. Such a party is said to litigate "pro se" or "in propria persona." Not surprisingly, courts are more lenient with such parties than with parties represented by counsel. Should *Dioguardi* be read narrowly because the plaintiff acted pro se?

 Apparently not. The Supreme Court embraced *Dioguardi* avidly in Conley v. Gibson, 355 U.S. 41 (1957), in which all parties were represented by counsel. There, the Court cited *Dioguardi* as authority for what it called the "accepted rule that a complaint should not be dismissed for failure to state a claim unless it appears beyond doubt that that plaintiff can prove no set of facts in support of his claim which would entitle him to relief." Id. at 45. Obviously, however, the rules require something more than "defendant is liable to me." The Court spoke to this need later in the opinion when it discussed the function of the complaint as "giv[ing] the defendant fair notice of what the plaintiff's claim is and the grounds upon which it rests." Id. at 47. See TEPLY & WHITTEN, CIVIL PROCEDURE 500-03.

 4. Seizing upon the "fair notice" language in *Conley*, many lawyers and judges speak of the Federal Rules as having established "notice pleading." Thus, pleadings are sufficient if they put the other litigants "on notice" of what is claimed. Some observers dislike the term because it is abstract. See, e.g., WRIGHT, FEDERAL COURTS 472. Judge Clark, who wrote the opinion in *Dioguardi*, is the same Charles E. Clark who, as Dean of the Yale Law School, was the principal architect of the Federal Rules of Civil Procedure. He also eschewed the term "notice pleading" because "it isn't anything that we can use with any precision." Charles Clark, *Pleading Under the Federal Rules*, 12 WYO. L. REV. 177, 181 (1958). Judge Clark continued:

> [Federal pleading] is a beautiful nebulous thing. * * * What we require is a general statement of the case, and our best precedents are those that have been honored over the years, which show that we haven't done anything really violent. We do not require detail. We require a general statement. How much? Well, the answer is made in what I think is probably the most important part of the rules so far as this particular topic is concerned, namely, the Forms. These are important because when you can't define you can at least draw pictures to show your meaning.

Id. Forms 3 through 18 are intended to show how little detail is needed in federal court.

    5.   The defendants in *Dioguardi* and *Conley* challenged the pleadings by filing Rule 12(b)(6) motions to dismiss for failure to state a claim on which relief can be granted. Such motions are usually brought in lieu of filing an answer. The Rule 12(c) motion for judgment on the pleadings does the same thing as a Rule 12(b)(6) motion, but is raised "[a]fter the pleadings are closed." At what point are pleadings closed in federal court? See Rule 7(a).

    In addition, parties can challenge pleading through the Rule 12(e) motion for more definite statement and Rule 12(f) motion to strike. When would these latter two be appropriate instead of a Rule 12(b)(6) motion?

    6.   Liberal pleading rules are not without costs. By making it easier to meet the formal requirement of factual sufficiency, the Federal Rules also make it easier to proceed to more expensive phases of litigation, notably discovery. This may provide effective leverage to settle the case to avoid such expense.

    It is important to remember that pleading rules do not alter the substantive law. Thus, regardless of the detail of the pleadings, the plaintiff must prove all elements of her claim when the case goes to trial. Counsel must be careful not to let relaxed pleading rules lull her into failing to consider all the elements of a cause of action at an early stage of litigation. Otherwise, she could find herself at trial without proof on a crucial issue.

    Consider the assessment of one court in a code state:

> When only notice pleading is required, reputedly, practicing lawyers often complain that they do not become fully aware of the issue in many cases until after prolonged discovery. This results in increased costs to the litigants and untoward delay in cases reaching the trial stage. Under code pleading, if the pleadings are properly prepared, the issues are apparent immediately upon the filing of a petition

[complaint] and the filing of an answer. If either a petition or an answer does not clearly set forth a litigant's issues, sustaining a motion to make more definite and certain will expeditiously clarify the issues, save the litigants unwarranted expense, promote judicial economy, and avoid unnecessary delay in a case reaching the trial stage.

Christianson v. Educational Service Unit No. 16, 501 N.W.2d 281, 287-88 (Neb. 1993).

iii. The Common Counts

Historically, courts have allowed plaintiffs to state certain claims in a shorthand form called "common counts." Common counts were permitted under the writ system of the common law and basically allow a one-sentence allegation for money had and received, quantum meruit (value of labor done), quantum valebant (value of goods delivered), and for indebitatus assumpsit (for money owed). The common counts for such claims clearly violate the code requirement for a statement of the facts underlying a cause of action. Nonetheless, code states permit them, as do the Federal Rules. Although the Federal Rules do not mention the term, Forms 3, 5, 6, and 8 are essentially common counts.

e. Heightened Specificity Requirements in Certain Cases

Read Rule 9, concentrating on subsections (a), (b), (c), and (g). These provisions are express exceptions to the liberal pleading requirements of Rule 8(a)(2). As courts have become more crowded, and litigation has become more expensive, some courts have required detailed pleadings even in cases not listed in Rule 9. As Professor Marcus demonstrated, several courts developed categories of cases for which they routinely required heightened specificity in pleading. These included claims involving conspiracy, see, e.g., Fullman v. Graddick, 739 F.2d 553, 557 (11th Cir. 1984), and civil rights claims filed under 42 U.S.C. § 1983, which prohibits deprivation of civil rights "under color of state law." See, e.g., Palmer v. San Antonio, 810 F.2d 514 (5th Cir. 1987)(suit against municipality); Elliott v. Perez, 751 F.2d 1472 (5th Cir. 1985)(suit against officer). Richard Marcus, *The Revival of Fact Pleading Under the Federal Rules of Civil Procedure*, 86 COLUM. L. REV. 433 (1986). See also Douglas Blaze, *Presumed Frivolous: Application of Stringent Pleading Requirements in Civil Rights Litigation*, 31 WM. & MARY L. REV. 936 (1990).

Is there a basis in the language of the Federal Rules for imposing a heightened requirement in these cases? Aside from the Rules, are there policy reasons for doing so?

C. The Complaint

Leatherman v. Tarrant County
___ U.S. ___, 113 S. Ct. 1160, 122 L.Ed.2d 517 (1993)

CHIEF JUSTICE REHNQUIST delivered the opinion of the Court.

We granted certiorari to decide whether a federal court may apply a "heightened pleading standard" — more stringent than the usual pleading requirements of Rule 8(a) of the Federal Rules of Civil Procedure — in civil rights cases alleging municipal liability under 42 U.S.C. § 1983. We hold it may not.

We review here a decision granting a motion to dismiss, and therefore must accept as true all the factual allegations in the complaint. This action arose out of two separate incidents involving the execution of search warrants by local law enforcement officers. Each involved the forcible entry into a home based on the detection of odors associated with the manufacture of narcotics. One homeowner claimed that he was assaulted by the officers after they had entered; another claimed that the police had entered her home in her absence and killed her two dogs. The plaintiffs sued several local officials in their official capacity and the county and two municipal corporations that employed the police officers involved in the incidents, asserting that the police conduct had violated the Fourth Amendment to the United States Constitution. The stated basis for municipal liability under Monell v. New York City Dept. of Social Services, 436 U.S. 658 (1978), was the failure of these bodies adequately to train the police officers involved.

The United States District Court for the Northern District of Texas ordered the complaints dismissed, because they failed to meet the "heightened pleading standard" required by the decisional law of the Court of Appeals for the Fifth Circuit. 755 F.Supp. 726 (1991). The Fifth Circuit, in turn, affirmed the judgment of dismissal, 954 F.2d 1054 (1992), and we granted certiorari to resolve a conflict among the Courts of Appeals concerning the applicability of a heightened pleading standard to § 1983 actions alleging municipal liability. Compare, e.g., Karim-Panahi v. Los Angeles Police Dept., 839 F.2d 621, 624 (CA9 1988) ("a claim of municipal liability under section 1983 is sufficient to withstand a motion to dismiss even if the claim is based on nothing more than a bare allegation that the individual officers' conduct conformed to official policy, custom, or practice") (internal quotation marks omitted). We now reverse.

Respondents seek to defend the Fifth Circuit's application of a more rigorous pleading standard on two grounds. First, respondents claim that municipalities' freedom from respondeat superior liability necessarily includes immunity from suit. In this sense, respondents assert, municipalities are not different from state or local officials sued in their individual capacity. Respondents reason that a more relaxed pleading requirement would subject municipalities to expensive and time consuming discovery in every § 1983 case, eviscerating their immunity from suit and disrupting municipal functions.

This argument wrongly equates freedom from liability with immunity from suit. To be sure, we reaffirmed in Monell that "a municipality cannot be held liable under § 1983 on a respondeat superior theory." But, contrary to respondents' assertions, this protection against liability does not encompass immunity from suit. Indeed, this argument is flatly contradicted by Monell and our later decisions involving municipal liability under § 1983. In Monell, we overruled Monroe v. Pape, 365 U.S. 167 (1961), insofar as it held that local governments were wholly immune from suit under § 1983, though we did reserve decision on whether municipalities are entitled to some form of limited immunity. Yet, when we took that issue up again in Owen v. City of Independence, 445 U.S. 622, 650 (1980), we rejected a claim that municipalities should be afforded qualified immunity, much like that afforded individual officials, based on the good faith of their agents. These decisions make it quite clear that, unlike various government officials, municipalities do not enjoy immunity from suit—either absolute or qualified—under § 1983. In short, a municipality can be sued under § 1983, but it cannot be held liable unless a municipal policy or custom caused the constitutional injury. We thus have no occasion to consider whether our qualified immunity jurisprudence would require a heightened pleading in cases involving individual government officials.

Second, respondents contend that the Fifth Circuit's heightened pleading standard is not really that at all. See Brief for Respondents Tarrant County Narcotics Intelligence and Coordination Unit et al. 9-10 ("[T]he Fifth Circuit's so-called 'heightened' pleading requirement is a misnomer"). According to respondents, the degree of factual specificity required of a complaint by the Federal Rules of Civil Procedure varies according to the complexity of the underlying substantive law. To establish municipal liability under § 1983, respondents argue, a plaintiff must do more than plead a single instance of misconduct. This requirement, respondents insist, is consistent with a plaintiff's Rule 11 obligation to make a reasonable pre-filing inquiry into the facts.

But examination of the Fifth Circuit's decision in this case makes it quite evident that the "heightened pleading standard" is just what it purports to be: a more demanding rule for pleading a complaint under § 1983 than for pleading other kinds of claims for relief. See 954 F.2d, at 1057-1058. This rule was adopted by the Fifth Circuit in Elliott v. Perez, 751 F.2d 1472 (1985), and described in this language:

> "In cases against government officials involving the likely defense of immunity we require of trial judges that they demand that the plaintiff's complaints state with factual detail and particularity the basis for the claim which necessarily includes why the defendant-official cannot successfully maintain the defense of immunity." Id. at 1473.

In later cases, the Fifth Circuit extended this rule to complaints against municipal corporations asserting liability under § 1983.

We think that it is impossible to square the "heightened pleading standard" applied by the Fifth Circuit in this case with the liberal system of "notice pleading" set up by the Federal Rules. Rule 8(a)(2) requires that a complaint include only "a short and plain statement of theclaim showing that the pleader is entitled to relief." In Conley v. Gibson, 355 U.S. 41 (1957), we said in effect that the Rule meant what it said:

> "[T]he Federal Rules of Civil Procedure do not require a claimant to set out in detail the facts upon which he bases his claim. To the contrary, all the Rules require is 'a short and plain statement of the claim' that will give the defendant fair notice of what the plaintiff's claim is and the grounds upon which it rests."

Id. at 47 (footnote omitted).

Rule 9(b) does impose a particularity requirement in two specific instances. It provides that "[i]n all averments of fraud or mistake, the circumstances constituting fraud or mistake shall be stated with particularity." Thus, the Federal Rules do address in Rule 9(b) the question of the need for greater particularity in pleading certain actions, but do not include among the enumerated actions any reference to complaints alleging municipal liability under § 1983. *Expressio unius est exclusio alterius.*

The phenomenon of litigation against municipal corporations based on claimed constitutional violations by their employees dates from our decision in *Monell*, where we for the first time construed § 1983 to allow such municipal liability. Perhaps if Rules 8 and 9 were rewritten today, claims against municipalities under § 1983 might be subjected to the added specificity requirement of Rule 9(b). But that is a result which must be obtained by the process of amending the Federal Rules, and not by judicial interpretation. In the absence of such an amendment, federal courts and litigants must rely on summary judgment and control of discovery to weed out unmeritorious claims sooner rather than later.

The judgment of the Court of Appeals is reversed, and the case remanded for further proceedings consistent with this opinion.

It is so ordered.

NOTES AND QUESTIONS

1. In the wake of *Leatherman*, lower courts have rejected a heightened pleading standard for cases involving false arrest, see Mendocino Environmental Ctr. v. Mendocino County, 14 F.3d 457 (9th Cir. 1994); copyright infringement, see Mid-American Title Co. v. Kirk, 991 F.2d 417 (7th Cir. 1993); antitrust, see Storer Cable Communications, Inc. v. City of Montgomery, 826 F.Supp. 1338 (N.D. Ala. 1993); and environmental cleanup, see Warwich Admin. Group. v. Avon Prods., Inc., 820 F. Supp. 116 (S.D. N.Y. 1993).

Nonetheless, some courts continue to impose a heightened pleading requirement in cases involving claims against individual government officials entitled to qualified immunity. These courts have stressed that *Leatherman* specifically left this question open. One example is Kimberlin v. Quinlin, 6 F.3d 789 (D.C. Cir. 1993). There, the plaintiff sued the former Director of Federal Prisons and a Justice Department official, alleging that they incarcerated him before the 1988 elections to stop him from announcing publicly that he had sold marijuana to Dan Quayle years earlier. (Quayle has denied the assertion.) After the defendants claimed qualified immunity, the court required the plaintiff to allege his claims with greater specificity. When he did not, the case was dismissed. See also Branch v. Tunnell, 14 F.3d 449 (9th Cir. 1994). The Supreme Court vacated the judgment in *Kimberlin* and directed the court of appeals to reconsider the case. 115 S.Ct. 2151, 132 L. Ed. 2d 252 (1995).

2. Why should there ever be a heightened specificity requirement? Why should there be such a requirement in the situations listed in Rule 9(b) and 9(g)? Is it to help the plaintiff by making her think more carefully about bringing claims that may be more difficult

to prove? Or is it to help the defendant, by providing some protection from glib assertions of claims, such as fraud, that may be especially damaging to her reputation?

In Romani v. Shearson Lehman Hutton, 929 F.2d 875 (1st Cir. 1991), the court affirmed the dismissal of a securities fraud case, holding that the plaintiff had failed to allege with specificity that the defendants fraudulently induced the plaintiff to invest. After noting that there was no "shred of factual support for the plaintiff's hypothetical tale of deception," the court felt itself "faced with precisely the sort of fishing expedition for fraud that Rule 9(b) is designed to prevent." Id. at 880. Why should the court be looking for "factual support" for the claim? Does the court's reading of Rule 9(b) discount the importance of discovery to the development of the plaintiff's case?

In Semegen v. Weidner, 780 F.2d 727, 731 (9th Cir. 1986), the court concluded that Rule 9(b) was designed to protect "especially professionals whose reputations in their fields of expertise are most sensitive to slander—from the harm that comes from being charged with the commission of fraudulent acts." Does this reading find any support in Rule 9(b)? In Lewis v. Berry, 101 F.R.D. 706 (W.D. Wash. 1984), the court expressly rejected the notion that Rule 9(b) gives professionals a right to more particularized allegations of fraud than other defendants. If slanderous accusations are the real concern, should Rule 9(b) include defamation among the claims that must be pleaded with particularity? Does *Semegen* survive *Leatherman*?

3. What does it mean to plead "with particularity?" Rule 9(b) requires particularity only with regard to "circumstances constituting fraud or mistake." It thus does not require detailed allegations of every element, for example, of a fraud claim. Obviously, the plaintiff must do more than make the blanket statement "the defendant defrauded me." The courts have not been wholly uniform in assessing "particularity." See 2A MOORE'S FEDERAL PRACTICE ¶ 9.03[1]. One court held that the plaintiff "must adequately specify the statements [she] claims were false or misleading, give particulars as to the respect in which the plaintiff contends the statements were fraudulent, state when and where the statements were made, and identify those responsible for the statements." Cosmas v. Hassett, 886 F.2d 8, 11 (2d Cir. 1992).

Review Form 13, paragraph 4. Do the allegations there meet the *Cosmas* prescription? Do they meet Rule 9(b)? (At one level, the answer to the latter question is very easy: they satisfy the Rule because Rule 84 says so.)

4. What policy supports the rule that state of mind, including malice, may be "averred generally" under Rule 9(b)? After all, an allegation that the defendant acted with malice may hold the defendant up to ridicule and defamation. The theory seems to be that conditions of the defendant's mind are within the defendant's knowledge, and thus impossible for the plaintiff to state with particularity. Caliber Partners, Ltd. v. Affeld, 583 F. Supp. 1308, 1311 (N.D. Ill. 1984). Does this reasoning apply, however, when the issue is malice?

5. Note also that satisfaction of conditions precedent may be pleaded generally, although a *denial* of performance "shall be made specifically and with particularity." Rule 9(c). Can you articulate a reason for this different treatment?

6. Special damages are "those which, although resulting from the commission of the wrong, are neither such a necessary result that they will be implied by law nor be deemed within the contemplation of the parties." Cotton Bros. Baking Co. v. Industrial Risk Insurers, 102 F.R.D. 964, 966 (W.D. La. 1983). They are to be contrasted with "general damages," which are said to "flow naturally" from the commission of the wrong. Based upon your studies in other law school courses, can you think of any claims that would constitute special damages?

Consider Rule 9(g) in light of this statement from a medical malpractice case, in which health care providers allegedly failed to diagnose a cancerous tumor, leading to a claim for general damages (including medical expenses already incurred) and to a special damages claim for future medical treatment:

> Decisions on what needs to be pleaded by way of special damages are sparse. The tendency is liberalization. We believe the purpose is to give notice. We are satisfied with 'Karen will incur * * * extensive major medical costs and expenses and will require costly health care services until her death.' The subject had been opened; defendants could seek details by inquiry.

Matos v. Ashford Presbyterian Community Hospital, Inc., 4 F.3d 47, 51-52 (1st Cir. 1993). Does the court in *Matos* equate Rule 9(g) with Rule 8(a)(2)? The court's statement that "defendants could seek details by inquiry" presumably refers to discovery devices. Because these are available in all civil cases, why should we ever require more specificity than is provided by notice pleading?

7. Note how the choice of pleading rules affects the entire system of procedure. After effectively recognizing that Rule 8(a)(2) imposes a very low pleading requirement, Chief Justice Rehnquist said in *Leatherman* that the "courts and litigants must rely on summary judgment and control of discovery to weed out unmeritorious claims sooner rather than later."

8. Recall that under *Hanna v. Plumer*, Chapter 7, a federal court must apply a Federal Rule that is in direct conflict with state law, so long as that rule was properly within the ambit of the Rules Enabling Act, 28 U.S.C. § 2072, and the Constitution. Thus, in a defamation case in which the plaintiff sought special damages, state law, which did not require pleading of special damages, did not control. Brown & Williamson Tobacco Corp. v. Jacobson, 713 F.2d 262 (7th Cir. 1983). See also Whittenburg v. L.J. Holding Co., 830 F. Supp. 557 (D. Kan. 1993).

9. If the defendant feels that allegations in the plaintiff's complaint do not satisfy Rule 9(b) or 9(g), what motion(s) should she make? When may she make such motions? See Rules 12(g) and 12(h).

10. We will address the notion of capacity to sue, mentioned in Rule 9(a), when we discuss joinder of parties in Chapter 12.

f. Pleading Inconsistent Facts and Alternative Theories

McCormick v. Kopmann
161 N.E.2d 720 (Ill. Ct. App. 1959)

REYNOLDS, PRESIDING JUSTICE.

[The plaintiff, Mrs. McCormick, sued to recover damages for the wrongful death of her husband. Mr. McCormick was killed when the car he drove was hit by a truck being operated by defendant Kopmann. In Count I of her complaint, the plaintiff alleged that Kopmann negligently drove his truck across the center line of the street, striking decedent's car and killing him. She also alleged that her husband had acted in a non-negligent manner (apparently to rebut the possibility of contributory negligence).

In Count IV of the same complaint, the plaintiff sued "in the alternative to Count I," and named as defendants three members of the Huls family. The Hulses operated taverns in the area. In Count IV, the plaintiff alleged that the Hulses sold alcoholic beverages to decedent shortly before his death. She asserted that decedent became intoxicated and that "as a result of such intoxication" McCormick drove his automobile "in such a manner as to cause a collision with a truck" being driven by Kopmann. Thus, she alleged, the Hulses were liable under the Illinois Dram Shop Act.—EDS.]

* * *

Kopmann, defendant under Count I, moved to dismiss the complaint on the theory that the allegations of that Count I and Count IV were fatally repugnant and could not stand together, because McCormick could not be free from contributory negligence as alleged in Count I, if his intoxication caused the accident as alleged in Count IV. Kopmann also urged that the allegation in Count IV that McCormick's intoxication was the proximate cause of his death, is a binding judicial admission which precludes an action under the Wrongful Death Act. Kopmann's motion was denied. He raised the same defenses in his answer.

The Huls, defendants under Count IV, answered. They did not file a motion directed against Count IV.

C. The Complaint

* * *

[At trial, the plaintiff] introduced proof that at the time of the collision, McCormick was proceeding North in the northbound traffic lane, and that Kopmann's truck, traveling South, crossed the center line and struck McCormick's car. The plaintiff also introduced testimony that prior to the accident McCormick drank a bottle of beer in Anna Huls' tavern in Penfield and one or two bottles of beer in John and Mary Huls' tavern in Gifford. The plaintiff's witness Roy Lowe, who was with McCormick during the afternoon and evening of November 21, and who was seated in the front seat of McCormick's car when the collision occurred, testified on cross examination that in his opinion McCormick was sober at the time of the accident. * * *

Kopmann, the defendant under the Wrongful Death count, introduced testimony that at the time of the collision, his truck was in the proper lane; that McCormick's automobile was backed across the center line of Main Street, thus encroaching on the southbound lane, and blocking it; that the parking lights on McCormick's automobile were turned on, but not the headlights; that Kopmann tried to swerve to avoid hitting McCormick's car; and that there was an odor of alcohol on McCormick's breath immediately after the accident. Over plaintiff's objection, the trial court permitted Kopmann's counsel to read to the jury the allegations of Count IV relating to McCormick's intoxication, as an admission.

The Huls, defendants under the Dram Shop count, introduced opinion testimony of a number of witnesses that McCormick was not intoxicated at the time of the accident. Anna Huls testified that McCormick drank one bottle of beer in her tavern. Several witnesses testified that McCormick had no alcoholic beverages in John and Mary Huls' tavern.

* * * The jury was instructed that Count IV was an alternative to Count I; that Illinois law permits a party who is uncertain as to which state of facts is true to plead in the alternative, and that it is for the jury to determine the facts. At Kopmann's request, the court instructed the jury on the law of contributory negligence. * * *

The jury returned a verdict against Kopmann for $15,500 under Count I. The jury found the Huls not guilty under Count IV. * * *

Kopmann has appealed. His first contention is that the trial court erred in denying his pre-trial motion to dismiss the complaint. Kopmann is correct in asserting that the complaint contains inconsistent allegations. The allegation of Count I that McCormick was free from contributory negligence, cannot be reconciled with the allegation of Count IV that McCormick's intoxication was the proximate cause of his death. Freedom from contributory negligence is a prerequisite to recovery under the Wrongful Death Act. If the jury had found that McCormick was intoxicated and that his intoxication caused the accident, it could not at the same time have found that McCormick was not contributorily negligent. The Illinois Supreme Court has held that "voluntary intoxication will not excuse a person from exercising such care as may reasonable be expected from who is sober."

* * *

Counts I and IV, therefore, are mutually exclusive; the plaintiff may not recover upon both counts. It does not follow, however, that these counts may not be pleaded together. Section 24(1) of the Illinois Civil Practice Act authorizes joinder of defendants against whom a liability is asserted in the alternative arising out of the same transaction. * * *

CHAPTER 8 PLEADINGS AND JUDGMENTS BASED ON PLEADINGS

Section 34 of the Act states in part that "Relief, whether based on one or more counts, may be asked in the alternative."

Section 43(2) of the Act provides:

"When a party is in doubt as to which of two or more statements of fact is true, he may, regardless of consistency, state them in the alternative or hypothetically in the same or different counts or defenses, whether legal or equitable. A bad alternative does not affect a good one."

Thus, the Civil Practice Act expressly permits a plaintiff to plead inconsistent counts in the alternative, where he is genuinely in doubt as to what the facts are and what the evidence will show. The legal sufficiency of each count presents a separate question. It is not ground for dismissal that allegations in one count contradict those in an alternative count. These principles have been applied recently in cases similar to that at bar. * * *

* * *

The * * * revision of Section 43(2) of the Civil Practice Act was designed to make it clear that inconsistent facts or theories could be pleaded alternatively, whether in the same or different counts. * * * This provision was modeled after Rule 8(e)(2) of the Federal Rules of Civil Procedure. * * *

There is nothing in the record before us to indicate that the plaintiff knew in advance of the trial, that the averments of Count I, and not Count IV, were true. In fact, at the trial, Kopmann attempted to establish the truth of the allegations of Count IV that McCormick was intoxicated at the time of the collision and that his intoxication caused his death. He can hardly be heard now to say that before the trial, the plaintiff should have known that these were not the facts. Where * * * the injured party is still living and able to recollect the events surrounding the accident, pleading in the alternative may not be justified, but where, as in the case at bar, the key witness is deceased, pleading alternative sets of facts is often the only feasible way to proceed. * * *

* * *

We know of no case which supports the position Kopmann takes in this court, viz., that the admission [regarding McCormick's intoxication] is conclusively binding and is a ground for judgment notwithstanding the verdict. If this were the law, the provisions of the Civil Practice Act sanctioning pleading in the alternative, "regardless of consistency," would be a legal snare.

* * *

* * * Plaintiff pleaded alternative counts because she was uncertain as to what the true facts were. Even assuming she introduced proof to support all essential allegations of both Count I and Count IV, she was entitled to have all the evidence submitted to the trier of fact, and to have the jury decide where the truth lay. She was not foreclosed ipso facto from going to the jury under Count

I, merely because she submitted proof, under Count IV, tending to prove that McCormick's intoxication proximately caused his death. If this were the rule, one who in good faith tried his case on alternative theories, pursuant to the authorization, if not the encouragement of Section 43, would run the risk of having his entire case dismissed. The provisions of the Civil Practice Act authorizing alternative pleading, necessarily contemplate that the pleader adduce proof in support of both sets of allegations or legal theories, leaving to the jury the determination of the facts.

* * *

What we have said is not to say that a plaintiff assumes no risks in adducing proof to support inconsistent counts. The proof in support of one inconsistent count necessarily tends to negate the proof under the other count and to have its effect upon the jury. While the fact alone of inconsistent evidence will not bar submission of the case to the jury, it may very well affect the matter of the weight of the evidence and warrant the granting of a new trial, even though, as we held, it does not warrant ipso facto a directed verdict or judgment notwithstanding the verdict.

* * *

Kopmann contends he was prejudiced because Counts I and IV were submitted together to the jury, in that the jury was confused by the plaintiff's inconsistent positions as to liability. We believe this argument is no longer open to Kopmann, since he failed to seek a separate trial pursuant to Section 51 of the Illinois Civil Practice Act. * * *

* * *

We conclude that the verdict and judgment below are correct and the judgment is affirmed.

NOTES AND QUESTIONS

1. *McCormick* is based upon Illinois rules. Read Federal Rules 8(a) and 8(e). How would the case have been decided in federal court?

2. Does *McCormick* stand for the proposition that inconsistent pleading is always acceptable? According to the court, when would it not be? On this point, is the court's view consistent with the provisions of Federal Rules 8(a) and 8(e)?

3. *McCormick* makes clear that a plaintiff need not guess at which of two or more alternative theories might prevail at trial. She can pursue both, and her pleading as to one is not to be treated as a judicial admission on the other point. Thus, Mrs. McCormick's assertion that her husband was drunk at the Hulses' tavern could not be used by Kopmann to rebut her argument that Mr. McCormick was free from negligence when he drove his car.

But what if Mrs. McCormick had sued the two defendants in separate actions? Under federal rules of evidence, the pleadings in one case could be used as an "admission against interest" against the plaintiff in the other case. Dugan v. EMS Helicopters, Inc., 915 F.2d 1428 (10th Cir. 1990)(Federal Rule of Evidence 801(d)(2)). Beside this consideration, can you think of other reasons for Mrs. McCormick to want to sue both the Hulses and Kopmann in a single proceeding?

    4. Is there anything ethically improper about pleading two theories when only one ultimately can be true? Suppose the plaintiff uncovers evidence during discovery which leads her to believe that one of her alternative theories is more likely based upon fact than the other. Should she still be able to pursue the alternative theories?

    5. Rule 8(e) applies to defendants as well as to plaintiffs. Suppose the defendant in a breach of contract case asserts as a defense that there was no contract and also asserts a counterclaim suing the plaintiff for breach of that same contract! Is this be permissible? In Olympia Hotels Corp. v. Johnson Wax Dev. Corp., 908 F.2d 1363 (7th Cir. 1990), the court held that it was.

2. Voluntary Dismissal

A plaintiff institutes suit by filing her complaint. Does she have the power to withdraw that complaint? Why would she want to? Read Rule 41(a). A dismissal "without prejudice" means that the plaintiff can reinstitute the case. A dismissal "with prejudice" or "on the merits" bars the plaintiff from bringing the claim again. Note that Rule 41 permits the plaintiff to act unilaterally in some situations but requires a court order in others.

Are there limits on a court's power to order dismissal without prejudice under Rule 41(a)(2)? Consider Grover v. Eli Lilly Co., 33 F.3d 716 (6th Cir. 1994), which is one of hundreds of cases concerning birth defects allegedly caused by diethylstilbestrol (DES), a female hormone manufactured by Eli Lilly and other pharmaceutical companies, and prescribed to countless pregnant women from the 1940s through the 1960s. It was used to prevent miscarriages, but injured female children in utero. The injuries to the female offspring did not become discernible, however, until those children were of childbearing age. In *Grover*, the alleged injury was a generation further removed. The plaintiff was a boy who had suffered serious birth defects. Those suing on his behalf claimed that the boy was injured because his maternal grandmother had taken DES when she was pregnant with the boy's mother. They claimed that the drug affected the boy's mother in such a way as to cause his birth defects.

C. The Complaint

The plaintiffs sued in state court in 1983 and the defendant removed the case to federal court under diversity of citizenship jurisdiction. Defendant asserted that Ohio law (which governed the dispute) did not recognize a claim in such circumstances. In 1988, the plaintiffs sought certification of the legal question to the Ohio Supreme Court. Over the defendant's objection, the district judge certified the question, noting that the answer would be dispositive of the suit. After the Ohio court held, in a four-to-three decision, that the boy could not sue because he had not ingested the drug directly or in utero, the district judge granted the plaintiffs' motion to dismiss *without prejudice*. He did so because he felt that the Ohio court might change its mind or the legislature might provide a remedy for persons such as the boy involved in *Grover*.

The Sixth Circuit reversed and remanded with instructions to dismiss the case with prejudice. According to the court, "[t]he primary purpose of the rule [41(a)(2)] in interposing the requirement of court approval is to protect the nonmovant from unfair treatment." Id. at 718. Such unfair treatment consisted not of the possibility of being sued a second time, but of "plain legal prejudice," which was shown by the delay and expense of certification and the court's order of dismissal without prejudice in the face of the Ohio court's rejection of the claim. The court concluded: "At the point when the law clearly dictates a result for the defendant, it is unfair to subject him to continued exposure to potential liability by dismissing the case without prejudice." Id. at 719.

Why should the plaintiff in *Grover* be denied the opportunity to take advantage of any subsequent change in Ohio substantive law?

NOTES AND QUESTIONS

1. Under what circumstances may a plaintiff dismiss unilaterally without prejudice?

2. Under what circumstances may a plaintiff dismiss only with the agreement of the other parties who have appeared? Under what circumstances may she do so without prejudice?

3. Under what circumstances may a plaintiff dismiss only with the permission of the court? Under what circumstances may she do so without prejudice?

4. Why should procedural rules limit the number of times a plaintiff can unilaterally dismiss without prejudice? Why should this right be available only relatively early in the case? See generally 5 MOORE'S FEDERAL PRACTICE ¶ 41.02.

5. The plaintiff files and serves her complaint in federal court. Before defendant takes any action, the plaintiff files a notice of dismissal. Now the plaintiff brings the case in federal court a second time, but voluntarily dismisses by stipulation of all parties who have

appeared. Why is this dismissal *not* with prejudice? See Sutton Place Dev. Co. v. Abacus Mortgage Inv. Co., 826 F.2d 637 (7th Cir. 1987)(reaching that conclusion based upon language of Rule 41(a)).

6. Same facts as in Question 5, except the second dismissal is by notice of dismissal. Why is this dismissal with prejudice?

7. Assume that the plaintiff's second case is in federal court and that she dismisses it through notice of dismissal. Assume also that she had dismissed her first case voluntarily. In determining whether the second dismissal is with prejudice, does it matter whether the first case was filed in federal or state court? Should it matter that the state court system does not have a similar rule?

8. If the second action to be dismissed voluntarily was brought in state court, Rule 41 would not apply. Why?

3. Involuntary Dismissal

Any litigant can find herself in trouble for failing to play by the rules. In addition to sanctions under Rule 11 or other provisions, or the court's inherent powers, see infra at 369-85, the court may dismiss the plaintiff's case. Read Rule 41(b).

The rule appears to preclude the court from ordering involuntary dismissal on its own motion, since it provides that "a defendant may move for dismissal" for any of the reasons listed. Despite this language, the Supreme Court has held that the district court may order involuntary dismissal sua sponte. Link v. Wabash R. Co., 370 U.S. 626 (1962). *Link* is the leading case on involuntary dismissal. There, the plaintiff filed his personal injury suit in August 1954; the case lingered on the district court docket until dismissed in October 1960. The plaintiff had consistently sought extensions (including extensions of two trial dates) to perform various tasks, such as respond to discovery requests. The straw that broke the camel's back was the plaintiff's counsel's failure to attend the pretrial conference in October 1960. Counsel called the judge's chambers the day of the conference and left a message for His Honor that counsel was busy working on papers in a state court case and could not make it to the conference. He would be available the two following days, however. The district court dismissed "for failure of the plaintiff's counsel to appear at the pretrial, for failure to prosecute this action." Id. at 629 (quoting opinion of trial court).

The Supreme Court affirmed, with Justice Harlan writing for the majority of four (two justices did not participate in the decision, so only seven took part). Although the delay was not attributable entirely to the plaintiff (indeed, sixteen months were lost while the plaintiff secured a reversal of the district judge's earlier wrongful dismissal of the case), the majority concluded that the district judge had not abused his discretion in ordering the dismissal. Id. at 633.

C. The Complaint

Justice Black wrote a vigorous dissent, arguing, inter alia, that "it seems * * * contrary to the most fundamental ideas of fairness and justice to impose the punishment for the lawyer's failure to prosecute upon the plaintiff who, as far as this record shows, was simply trusting his lawyer to take care of his case as clients generally do." Id. at 643 (Black, J., dissenting). The majority said that "[p]laintiff voluntarily chose this attorney * * * and he cannot now avoid the consequences of the acts or omissions of this freely selected agent." Id. at 633-34.

Aren't there problems with both approaches? Does Justice Black's view lead to the possibility that no dismissal could be entered, no matter how dilatory the lawyer? Would a reasonable client begin to think that something was amiss when, six years after filing, the case had not gone to trial? On the other hand, isn't the majority shortsighted in saying that the involuntary dismissal will clear the district court's docket? After all, won't Mr. Link now be able to file a second suit against his erstwhile lawyer?

The district court in *Link* did not specifically warn the plaintiff's counsel that the case might be dismissed if he failed to attend the pretrial conference. Neither did it set up a proceeding to elicit explanations from the plaintiff's counsel. On the record, however, the majority of the Supreme Court felt that Mr. Link's lawyer understood the gravity of the situation. Still, providing warning and an opportunity to be heard is the preferred course. See generally 5 MOORE'S FEDERAL PRACTICE ¶ 41.11[2]. Indeed, as we will see below, Rule 11 now requires notice and an opportunity to be heard before sanctions can be imposed.

NOTES AND QUESTIONS

1. For what reasons may the court dismiss under Rule 41(b)? Must the court do so? May it dismiss less than the entire case?

2. Rule 83 allows district courts to adopt local rules providing for involuntary dismissal if no action is shown of record within a stated time. Such local rules are quite common. If the plaintiff has taken no action within the given period—say, for example, one year—the court issues an Order to Show Cause (universally referred to as an OSC) to the plaintiff. The OSC requires the plaintiff to show the court why it should not dismiss for lack of prosecution. Many states have similar provisions, granting the trial judge discretion to determine whether the plaintiff has been so dilatory as to justify an order of involuntary dismissal.

California has such a provision for cases that have not gone to trial within two years of filing. CAL. CODE CIV. PROC. § 593(a). Another statute goes further, depriving the trial court of jurisdiction over any case in which trial has not commenced within five years of filing. CAL. CODE CIV. PROC. § 583(b). At some points in the 1970s and 1980s, however, the backlog in Los Angeles Superior Court was so overwhelming that it was impossible even for a diligent plaintiff to get to trial in less than five years! To escape the operation of this provision, the Superior Court would call the case for trial before the five years ran, and "recess" until the case could be heard. This charade is a telling comment on the desirability of provisions depriving the trial judge of discretion in this area.

3. Notice how Rule 60(b) makes involuntary dismissal less harsh.

4. Note Rule 41(b)'s statement of the types of dismissals that operate as an adjudication on the merits. How can it be said that dismissal for failure to prosecute is in any way related to the merits? We will see why this provision is important in Chapter 11, where we will see that only judgments on the merits are entitled to preclusive (claim or issue preclusion) effect.

D. Defendant's Options in Response

The defendant has two basic choices in responding to a complaint: she can bring a motion or file an answer. A motion, as we have seen elsewhere, is a request that the court order something, such as dismissal of the case; it is not a "pleading." The answer, on the other hand, is a pleading which responds to allegations of the complaint and may add new matter as well. In a given case, the defendant might use one or the other. For example, she may eschew bringing a motion and simply file an answer. Or she might bring a motion to dismiss, which, if granted, obviates the need for an answer. In some cases, the defendant may use both, as when her motion to dismiss is denied, and she must thereafter file an answer. In addition, as we will see, she may assert an affirmative claim for relief against the plaintiff.

1. Motions

Read Rule 12(b). In Chapter 6, we discussed the timing of a defendant's motion to dismiss under Rule 12(b), paying special attention to motions to dismiss for lack of personal jurisdiction, subject matter jurisdiction, and venue. Here, our focus is the Rule 12(b)(6) motion to dismiss for failure to state a claim on which relief can be granted. As noted in Section C(1) of this chapter, that motion serves two functions. First, it tests the legal sufficiency of the plaintiff's claim, questioning whether the law accords a remedy on the facts alleged. (This is done by the general demurrer in code states.) Second, it tests the

350

D. Defendant's Options in Response

factual, or formal, sufficiency of the complaint, questioning whether the plaintiff has set forth her claim in appropriate detail. (This is done by the special demurrer in code states.)

Defendant may also seek dismissal on a variety of other grounds. If the facts are undisputed, and the defendant is entitled to judgment as a matter of law, she may bring a motion for summary judgment under Rule 56. Thus, for example, if the statute of limitations has run, or if the claim is barred by claim or issue preclusion (res judicata or collateral estoppel), summary judgment may be a vehicle for early dismissal of a case.

In addition, the defendant may bring motions for relief other than dismissal. Specifically, she may seek a more definite statement under Rule 12(e) or move to strike under Rule 12(f). Read those two subparts. The 1938 version of Rule 12(e) permitted a motion for more definite statement or for a bill of particulars to allow a party to prepare a responsive pleading "or to prepare for trial." The rule was amended in 1946 to strike the reference to trial preparation, in express recognition that the discovery rules were the appropriate avenue for fleshing out details in trial preparation. Neither is the Rule 12(e) motion aimed at pleadings that fail to state a claim. Instead, it "is plainly designed to strike at unintelligibility rather than want of detail." 2A MOORE'S FEDERAL PRACTICE ¶ 12.18, at 12-161.

Despite the provision that the defendant should make a motion to strike before responding to a pleading, courts have inherent power to entertain such motion (or to strike sua sponte) at any time. Hoppe v. G.D. Searle & Co., 779 F. Supp. 1413, 1421 (S.D. N.Y. 1991). Note the categories of allegations that may be stricken. A scandalous allegation has been defined as one that "reflect[s] cruelly" on the defendant's moral character, which uses "repulsive language," or which detracts from the "dignity of the court." Khalid Bin Talal v. E.F. Hutton & Co., 720 F. Supp. 671, 686 (N.D. Ill. 1989).

The motion to strike can serve a similar substantive function to the Rule 12(b)(6) motion. For example, a claim for relief not available as a matter of law can be stricken under Rule 12(f). Brokke v. Stauffer Chem. Co., 703 F. Supp. 215 (D. Conn. 1988)(striking claim for punitive damages).

QUESTIONS

1. Defendant files and serves an answer which the plaintiff finds unintelligible. Why can the plaintiff not file a motion for more definite statement?

2. Why is the plaintiff not able to file a 12(b)(6) motion regarding an answer that is insufficient as a matter of law? What is the appropriate motion?

CHAPTER 8 PLEADINGS AND JUDGMENTS BASED ON PLEADINGS

2. The Answer

Read Rule 8(b), 8(c), and 8(d). These provisions set forth the modern philosophy of defensive pleading. The defendant can do two things in her answer: respond to the allegations of the complaint and raise new matter through an affirmative defense. In all cases, she will do the former; in most cases, she will probably do the latter as well.

a. Responses to the Plaintiff's Allegations

Under Rule 8(b), there are three possible responses to the various allegations of the plaintiff's complaint. The defendant can admit, deny, or claim that she lacks sufficient information to admit or deny. These choices must be read against the backdrop of Rule 8(d), which provides simply that allegations not denied are deemed admitted. Those allegations that are properly denied are said to be "joined," which means that they are in dispute and ripe for adjudication.

i. Admissions

It may seem contrary to the adversary system, but there are many allegations of a complaint which the defendant will admit. For example, allegations of citizenship of the parties for diversity of citizenship purposes, allegations that the parties entered into a contract, and many others, may not be in dispute. It is incumbent on the defendant to admit such allegations. As we will see below, Rule 11 requires the parties to act in good faith and allege matters only if they are supported by evidence. Rule 11 similarly applies to answers. Thus, the pleadings serve to establish undisputed facts on which there need be no trial.

ii. Denials

The *general denial* is a very short pleading, the operative language of which can be as simple as "Defendant denies each and every allegation of the complaint." See Stringfellow v. Perry, 869 F.2d 1140 (8th Cir. 1989). It is acceptable under the Federal Rules and in code pleading, but only if the defendant can in good faith deny all allegations of the complaint. Because there will almost always be at least one material allegation the defendant cannot contest, general denials should be used with great caution.

Almost always, the defendant will use *specific denials* in combination with admissions in responding to the allegations of the complaint. The Rules do not prescribe a particular form for denials, although the fourth and fifth sentences of Rule 8(b) provide some good practical advice. Responding to each paragraph of the complaint individually is a common practice. For example, an answer could say: "Defendant admits the allegations of Para-

D. Defendant's Options in Response

graph One of the Complaint. Defendant denies the allegations of Paragraph Two of the Complaint," and so forth.

But the defendant need not match the complaint paragraph for paragraph, so long as she denies those allegations she needs to deny. For instance, if appropriate on the facts, the answer could provide: "Defendant admits the allegations of Paragraph Five of the Complaint, and denies each and every other allegation of the Complaint." This form is often called a *qualified general denial*. See Form 20, Third Defense, and Form 21.

What if a single paragraph of the complaint contains both material the defendant wishes to admit and material she wishes to deny? Here, the defendant needs to be careful to separate the former from the latter. Suppose, for example, that you represent a corporate defendant in a diversity of citizenship case. Your client is incorporated in Nebraska with its principal place of business in Iowa. Paragraph Four of the complaint alleges that "defendant is an Nebraska corporation with its principal place of business in Nebraska." Your associate suggests that you file an answer responding to that paragraph by saying: "In response to Paragraph Four of the Complaint, Defendant admits that it is a Nebraska corporation and denies the remainder of the Paragraph."

What do you think of the associate's suggestion? Shouldn't the plaintiff's counsel, reading this response, be tipped off to the possibility that the principal place of business is not in Nebraska? Or do you have an ethical obligation to tell the plaintiff that your client's principal place of business is in Iowa?

Some defendants cannot resist the temptation to make their lives more difficult than the rules require. A defendant who wants to deny allegations should simply do so without getting fancy or demanding. For example, an answer that neither admits nor denies allegations but demands proof of the plaintiff's claims at trial is worthless. Because such an answer does not deny anything, all allegations of the complaint are deemed admitted. Unless the court allows amendment, the defendant's lawyer may need to check on the malpractice coverage.

Rule 8(b) requires that "denials shall fairly meet the substance of the averments denied." Thus, counsel should resist the temptation to plead contrary facts. For example, suppose the complaint alleged that on a certain date, "the defendant negligently drove her car on Main Street in Apalachicola, Florida, and ran over the plaintiff." Instead of simply denying the allegations, defendant alleges that on the date mentioned, "defendant was on vacation in Brazil." This is an "argumentative denial," and runs the risk, at least in code states, of being deemed an admission of the facts alleged by the plaintiff. In federal court, it will likely be effective as a denial, but may create problems if it is not clear what allegations are being put in issue. 2A MOORE'S FEDERAL PRACTICE ¶ 8.25.

Another problem is the "negative pregnant," which can result from a denial that is too literal. Suppose again that the plaintiff alleges in Paragraph Four that on a certain date, "the defendant negligently drove her car on Main Street in Apalachicola, Florida, and ran over the plaintiff." The most direct approach would be "Defendant denies the allegations of Paragraph Four." Instead, suppose she says: "Defendant denies that she negligently drove her car on Main Street in Apalachicola, Florida, and ran over the plaintiff." Such a literal denial is "pregnant" with the admission that the defendant negligently drove her car at some other time or in some other place and ran over the plaintiff.

Thus, in Freedom National Bank v. Northern Illinois Corp., 202 F.2d 601 (7th Cir. 1953), the plaintiff alleged that the value of a trailer exceeded $4,718.25. Defendant denied that the value exceeded $4,718.25. The court treated this as an admission that the trailer was worth exactly $4,718.25 or any lesser amount. How should defendant have phrased the denial to avoid the negative pregnant?

Suppose the plaintiff alleges that defendant "made, executed, and delivered" a contract. Defendant's response is: "Defendant denies that he made, executed, and delivered" the contract. Is this response an admission that defendant made and executed the contract? Or that she executed and delivered the contract? Or that she made and delivered the contract? Why? How should she have responded to avoid this problem?

Problems with literal denials and negative pregnants are hypertechnical, and most federal courts today will construe such allegations as denials. Some state courts, however, may be less forgiving.

iii. Denials for Lack of Knowledge or Information

Rule 8(b) allows a party to state that she is "without knowledge or information sufficient to form a belief as to the truth of an averment" and that such an allegation "has the effect of a denial." Because of the requirements of good faith and veracity under Rule 11, however, this defense cannot be used if the defendant has reasonable access to the information or if it is a matter of public record or general knowledge. See 2A MOORE'S FEDERAL PRACTICE ¶ 8.22.

b. Affirmative Defenses

Rule 8(c) requires the defendant to raise affirmative defenses. The rule's list of nineteen such defenses is not exhaustive, as it then requires the assertion of "any other matter constituting an avoidance or affirmative defense." Use of the term "avoidance" is a vestige of common law pleading. At common law, a defendant could use a plea in confession and avoidance, which would admit the plaintiff's allegations but raise new matter that would "avoid" liability for those allegations. For example, a defendant might admit that she had breached a contract, but assert that the contract was unenforceable because it violated the rule that it must be in writing under the statute of frauds.

Affirmative defenses differ from denials by injecting new matter into the dispute. Suppose, for example, that the plaintiff sues for battery, alleging that the defendant struck her. If the defendant did not strike the plaintiff, she will simply deny the plaintiff's allegation. On the other hand, if the defendant struck the plaintiff, but did so in self defense, she will admit the plaintiff's allegation and raise the affirmative defense of self defense. In the first case, the defendant is merely denying the plaintiff's version of the story. In the second, she is injecting a new set of facts upon which her defense is premised. In light of *McCormick*, could the defendant deny the allegation that she struck the plaintiff and raise the affirmative defense of self defense?

Why is self defense an affirmative defense to be pleaded by the defendant, rather than as a part of the plaintiff's claim? In other words, why didn't the plaintiff have to allege that the defendant did not act in self defense? In an influential article, Professor Cleary shed light on this subject in his discussion of the elements of a claim and affirmative defenses as "conditional imperatives." Edward Cleary, *Presuming and Pleading: An Essay on Juristic Immaturity*, 12 STAN. L. REV. 5 (1959).

Under this analysis, for example, a contract claimant might prevail *if* she showed offer, acceptance, consideration, and breach *unless* the contract should have been in writing under the statute of frauds, or the contract was illegal, or a party lacked capacity to contract, etc. Roughly stated, the "ifs" in this equation are elements of the plaintiff's claim, and the "unlesses" are affirmative defenses. The substantive law of each jurisdiction allocates each of the items to the "if" or "unless" category. Thus, in the battery hypothetical above, the substantive law requires the defendant to allege self-defense.

As Professor Cleary discussed, however, the fact that precedent clearly establishes the burden of pleading "does nothing for the inquiring mind." How does each jurisdiction determine the matter of allocation? The answer is largely one of policy, influenced by the fact that a litigant usually has the burden of producing evidence at trial on the elements she must plead. For instance, it would be an intolerable burden if the contract the plaintiff had to plead not only offer, acceptance, consideration, and breach, but also that there had been no accord and satisfaction, that there was no capacity problem, that the statute of limitations had not run, etc. The better approach has the plaintiff assert the prima facie case and allows the defendant to inject whichever of the potential "unlesses" might negate recovery.

While this explanation counsels toward limiting the number of things the plaintiff has to plead and prove, it does not tell us *why* the line is drawn at a particular point. In part, as Cleary examined, the line is drawn because of an assessment of the fairness of requiring

CHAPTER 8 PLEADINGS AND JUDGMENTS BASED ON PLEADINGS

one party or the other to bear the burden of proof at trial. Suppose the plaintiff sues to recover on a note. Defendant claims that she repaid the note. Who should have the burden of pleading and proving the issue of whether payment was made? Think about the case from the plaintiff's viewpoint. How can you prove that the defendant failed to pay? How can one ever prove a negative? *

On the other hand, can't the defendant more readily prove that she made payment (as, for example, by producing a canceled check)? In such a case, doesn't it make sense to prescribe, as Rule 8(c) does, that the issue of payment be raised as an affirmative defense? Such cases represent one of the exceptions to the rule that the burden of proving an issue at trial follows the burden of pleading the issue. In many jurisdictions, both the plaintiff and defendant are required to plead regarding the issue of repayment (plaintiff that it has not been made, defendant that it has). Only the defendant, however, bears the burden of proof at trial. See, e.g., West Coast Credit Corp. v. Pederson, 390 P.2d 551 (Wash. 1964).

NOTES AND QUESTIONS

1. In her answer in a contract case in federal court, defendant asserts that the contract is not enforceable because it was not in writing, as required by the Statute of Frauds.

   (a) Why is this an affirmative defense?
   (b) If the plaintiff thinks that the Statute of Frauds does not apply to this contract, what response does she make? Why?

2. In addition to averring it in her answer, the defendant may be able to raise her affirmative defense in a motion for summary judgment. As we will see in Chapter 10, courts can grant summary judgment if there is no dispute as to a material issue of fact and the moving party is entitled to judgment as a matter of law. So if the facts were clear, and the statute of limitations barred the claim, the defendant could win on summary judgment.

3. Rule 8(c) provides that the defendant "shall" plead her affirmative defenses. A defendant who fails to do so thus waives the defense omitted. As we will see in Section E of this chapter, however, the defendant might be able to amend her answer to assert the affirmative defense.

   Suppose the defendant failed to raise an affirmative defense in her answer, but used it as a basis for a summary judgment motion. Should the court conclude that she waived the affirmative defense? Although courts have reached different conclusions, the

---

* The same problem arises in cases involving defamation, which is the publication of a false statement about the plaintiff, tending to hold her up to ridicule. Suppose defendant publicly called plaintiff a prostitute, or a murderer, or a traitor. How can plaintiff prove that she is none of these?

D. Defendant's Options in Response

trend is to allow the motion. See, e.g., Grant v. Preferred Research, Inc., 885 F.2d 795, 797 (11th Cir. 1989)(no waiver); Funding Systems Leasing Corp. v. Pugh, 530 F.2d 91, 96 (5th Cir. 1976)(waiver). The trend is consistent with the liberal policy of amendment embodied in the Federal Rules.

4. Can you think of a case in which an affirmative defense could be raised by a Rule 12(b)(6) motion?

5. Under the practice in some states, the plaintiff must file a pleading responding to the affirmative defenses. This pleading is usually called a reply. Under Federal Rule 7(a), the reply is not required but may be ordered. Under that Rule, "reply" also refers to a pleading by the plaintiff in response to a counterclaim by the defendant. It is required.

3. Claims by the Defendant

Thus far, we have considered how a defending party may avoid the imposition of liability on herself. A defending party can also assert claims against other parties and, in some circumstances, force the joinder of additional parties. The principal claims by a defending party are the counterclaim (against an opposing party) and the cross-claim (against a co-party). As noted above, the plaintiff must file a reply to a "counterclaim denominated as such." We will discuss counterclaims, cross-claims, and other possible assertions of liability by the defendant in Chapter 12.

4. Failure to Respond: Default and Default Judgment

If a defending party fails to respond in an appropriate and timely way, she may find herself in default. Default must be distinguished from default judgment. The former is simply a ministerial notation on the court's docket sheet that the defendant has failed to plead or otherwise respond in time. The plaintiff cannot obtain money or other relief on the basis of a default. Instead, she must get a default judgment, which is enforced like any other judgment. Entry of default judgment presents a clash of important policies: while we do not want to subject a worthy the plaintiff to untoward delay, also we prefer to decide cases on the merits rather than on technicalities.

Read Rules 6(b), 54(c), and 55 before addressing the following.

NOTES AND QUESTIONS

1. You are Plaintiff's counsel. You file suit on behalf of Plaintiff seeking $95,000 in damages, plus costs and whatever other relief the court may find appropriate. You have

CHAPTER 8 PLEADINGS AND JUDGMENTS BASED ON PLEADINGS

process served upon Defendant properly. Defendant fails to respond in any way within the appropriate period.

    (a) What documents do you prepare, and to whom do you give them, to get the entry of default?

    (b) Assuming you prepare and file the proper documents, *must* the person to whom you go enter the default, or does she have discretion to refuse?

    (c) To whom do you go for entry of the default judgment? What document(s) do you prepare for that step?

    (d) Can the default judgment be for $100,000? Can it be for $20,000?

  2. Same facts, except that the claim is for unspecified damages.

    (a) Is there any difference in acquiring the default from the fact pattern in Question 1?

    (b) To whom do you go for entry of the default judgment? What document(s) do you prepare for this step?

    (c) What proceedings follow? Why does the defendant *not* get notice of these proceedings on these facts? Under what facts would she get notice?

    (d) Can the default judgment be for $100,000? Can it be for $20,000?

  3. Note that the hearing addressed in Rule 55(b) does not necessarily result in default judgment.

> The disposition of a motion for entry of a default judgment by the court lies within the court's sound discretion. In the exercise of its discretion the court may consider a wide variety of factors. Where defendant's failure to plead or otherwise defend is merely technical, or where the default is de minimis, the court should generally refuse to enter a default judgment. On the other hand, where there is reason to believe that defendant's default resulted from bad faith in the party's dealings with the court or opposing party, the district court may properly enter * * * judgment against defendant as a sanction. Other factors which may influence the * * * court's discretion are as follows: the possibility of prejudice to the plaintiff; the merit of the plaintiff's substantive claim; the sufficiency of the complaint; the sum of money at stake in the action; the possibility of a dispute concerning material facts; whether the default was due to excusable neglect; and the strong policy underlying the Federal Rule * * * favoring decisions on the merits.

6 MOORE'S FEDERAL PRACTICE ¶ 55.05[2], pp. 55-28 to 55-31.

  4. It may seem perplexing that a party can be in default even though she has "appeared in the action." There are several ways, however, in which this might happen. For example, the defendant may make a timely motion to dismiss under Rule 12(b). After it is denied, the defendant fails to file an answer. She is in default even though she appeared.

D. Defendant's Options in Response

Or the defendant might mail a document to the court that does not constitute a defensive response but which might be deemed an appearance for these purposes. Indeed, some courts have found an "appearance" even when the defendant addressed its communication to the plaintiff and not to the court. See, e.g., Muniz v. Vidal, 739 F.2d 699, 701 (1st Cir. 1984)(defendant's counsel discussed case with the plaintiff's counsel); H. F. Livermore Corp. v. Aktiengesellschaft Gebruder Loepfe, 432 F.2d 689, 692 (D.C. Cir. 1970)(involvement in settlement negotiations with the plaintiff). Such opinions note the policy favoring resolution of disputes on the merits rather than on technicalities. Other courts have been less liberal, purporting to require a presentation to the court itself. See, e.g., North Central Illinois Laborers' Dist. Council v. S.J. Groves & Sons Co., 842 F.2d 164, 169 (7th Cir. 1988). See 6 MOORE'S FEDERAL PRACTICE ¶ 55.05[3].

Even though such appearances do not save a defendant from being found in default, what consequences flow from the finding that defendant did appear in the action?

5. Defendant fails to respond to the complaint within twenty days. On the twenty-first day, you, as Plaintiff's lawyer, go to the courthouse to ask the clerk to enter default. In front of you in line at the clerk's window is counsel for Defendant, who wants to file an answer on behalf of Defendant. Can she do so? What argument would you make that she was acting improperly in attempting to file an answer? Would you prevail? Probably not. Although a motion for enlargement of time under Rule 6(b) would be the proper course for Defendant to take, in fact few courts pay attention to this requirement. The result is that defendant has a "right" to answer late, so long as no default is on the docket. The bottom line: you should be first in line at the clerk's window. See, e.g., DeTore v. Local No. 245, 511 F. Supp. 171 (D. N.J. 1981).

6. A plaintiff whose claim proceeds to trial may recover whatever relief the evidence supports, even if it is more than she asked for or of a different kind than demanded. See Rule 54(c). As you have seen, that is not true in default judgment cases. Can you articulate a reason for this different rule in default judgment cases? Does this counsel the plaintiffs to "aim high" when filing their complaints?

7. Client comes to your office and tells you that she was sued and has defaulted, although no default judgment has yet been entered. She wants to avoid liability. What should you do on her behalf? How do you do so? Where do you do so? What do you have to show? When do you have to do so?

If the judgment has already been entered, what do you do? How, where, and when do you do it? See Rule 60(b).

E. Amended Pleadings

1. Basic Principles Under Rule 15(a)

Read Rule 15(a) before addressing the following.

NOTES AND QUESTIONS

1. Plaintiff files her complaint. Before Defendant answers, Plaintiff files an amended complaint adding new claims and seeking an additional $6 million in damages. Why did Plaintiff have a right to do this? (Be sure that the phrase "twenty days" is not part of your answer. The provision in Rule 15(a) regarding twenty days is irrelevant here.)

2. Plaintiff files her complaint. Defendant files a motion to dismiss under Rule 12(b)(6). Reading Defendant's motion, Plaintiff realizes that Defendant is correct, since Plaintiff left out material allegations of her claim. Before the hearing on Defendant's motion, Plaintiff files an amended complaint fixing the problem raised by Defendant's motion (and thereby mooting the motion). Plaintiff had an absolute right to do this. Why? Why is Rule 7(a) relevant to your answer? See Alexander v. Fujitsu Bus. Commun. Sys., 818 F. Supp. 462 (D. N.H. 1993). When must Defendant respond to an amended complaint?

3. Plaintiff files and serves her complaint on May 15. Defendant files her answer on June 1 and serves it on Plaintiff on June 3. On June 22, Defendant files an amended answer, correcting some errors in the original answer. Why does Defendant have a right to do this?

4. If Plaintiff in Question 1 and Defendant in Question 3 had waited too long to take advantage of amendment of right, what showing would they have to make to be allowed to amend? Notice that Rule 15(a) instructs the court that "leave shall be freely given when justice so requires."

As we have seen, the Federal Rules embody a preference for deciding controversies on their merits rather than on technicalities. In keeping with this goal, the courts have allowed amendment liberally. For instance, amendment generally will not be denied solely because it will substantially change the character of the action. The court has to find a weightier reason *not* to allow amendment. In the words of the Supreme Court:

> If the underlying facts or circumstances relied upon by a plaintiff may be a proper subject of relief, he ought to be afforded an opportunity to test his claim on the merits. In the absence of any apparent or declared reason—such as undue delay, bad faith or dilatory motive on the part of the movant, repeated failure to cure deficiencies by amendments previously allowed, undue prejudice to the opposing party by virtue of allowance of the amendment, futility of amendment,

E. Amended Pleadings

etc.—the leave sought should, as the rules require, be "freely given." Of course, the grant or denial of an opportunity to amend is within the discretion of the District Court.

Foman v. Davis, 371 U.S. 178, 182 (1962).

Review the list of examples in detail. The moving party may jeopardize her privilege of amendment by undue delay, bad faith, dilatory motive, or failure to cure problems with previous amendments. The court may also refuse amendment if it would result in undue prejudice to the opposing party or if the amendment would be futile. Can you give specific examples of the latter two? When would prejudice become "undue?" Couldn't prejudice always be abated by allowing the party opposing amendment more time to prepare for trial?

5. Although many cases involve amendment by the plaintiff, the rule obviously applies equally to defendants. Suppose Plaintiff sued Manufacturer for injuries sustained while using a water slide. The complaint was filed October 15, 1973. Manufacturer's answer, filed within 20 days of service, admitted that it had manufactured the slide on which Plaintiff was injured, but denied liability. In early 1975, Manufacturer's president inspected the slide and determined that Manufacturer had not built it. Manufacturer sought leave to amend its answer to deny manufacture of the slide. What result? What other factors would you determine relevant? See Beeck v. Aquaslide 'N' Dive Corp., 562 F.2d 537 (8th Cir. 1977)(affirming district court's grant of leave to amend).

6. Rule 15(a) does not limit the time in which one can seek leave to amend. As a practical matter, however, the longer one waits to ask for leave to amend, the more likely it is that the other side can claim prejudice. See Nilsen v. City of Moss Point, 621 F.2d 117 (5th Cir. 1980). Most observers consider the Federal Rules on amendment liberal, and many states have adopted those rules. At least one state has taken amendment of right about as far as it can go. In Georgia, every party has an unfettered right to amend her pleadings anytime before the court enters a pretrial order. CODE GA. ANNOT. § 9-11-15(a). As we will see in Chapter 9, the pretrial order is entered after motions and discovery, usually just a few weeks before trial is scheduled. If no pretrial order is entered, Georgia permits amendment of right until the trial starts! Little wonder the Georgia courts say "[t]he right to amend is as broad as the Atlantic Ocean and as saving as the power of salvation." MCG Devel. Corp. v. Bick Realty Co., 230 S.E.2d 261 (Ga. Ct. App. 1976).

7. Note how the policy of liberal amendment under the Federal Rules is facilitated by Rule 42(b).

2. The Problem of Variance Under Rule 15(b)

Suppose plaintiff's complaint alleges breach of contract, and at trial she introduces evidence that defendant breached a different contract, or committed a tort. The presentation of evidence on a point not covered in pleading is called *variance*. Some older opinions decided under code pleading rules were extremely harsh, holding that a plaintiff's failure to prove exactly what she pleaded was fatal, at least if the defendant raised the objection of variance.

For example, in Wabash Western Rw. v. Friedman, 30 N.E.2d 353 (Ill. 1892), the plaintiff was injured when a train derailed. The wreck occurred between Kirksville and Glenwood Junction, Missouri, which was one leg of a longer trip that the plaintiff was taking from Moberly to Ottumwa. The plaintiff boarded the train at Moberly, bound for Ottumwa, but alleged in his complaint that he became a passenger at Kirksville, bound for Glenwood Junction. The Illinois Supreme Court reversed a $30,000 judgment in the plaintiff's favor, holding that the variance between what was pleaded and what was proved was fatal. See generally Morgan, *The Variance Problem*, 32 NEB. L. REV. 357 (1952).

Wabash Western is an example of elevating form over substance. On the other hand, it is not ridiculous to require plaintiffs to be accurate in what they allege, at least as to things about which they have knowledge. Most likely, all code states today would be more forgiving on this point. The federal provision regarding variance is Rule 15(b). It allows amendment to conform to the evidence presented at trial. Read it before addressing the following.[1]

NOTES AND QUESTIONS

1. Plaintiff sues for breach of Contract 1, and introduces evidence regarding Defendant's breach of Contract 1 and breach of Contract 2. Defendant does not object to introduction of the evidence regarding Contract 2. Does this constitute "implied consent" to trial regarding breach of Contract 2? Some courts say yes, at least if the evidence on Contract 2 did not also relate to Contract 1. If it did, then it seems unfair to conclude that the defendant knowingly consented to trial of Contract 2. See, e.g., Corsica Livestock Sales, Inc. v. Sumitomo Bank of Cal., 726 F.2d 374 (8th Cir. 1983)(finding consent); Southwestern Stationery & Bank Supply, Inc. v. Harris Corp., 624 F.2d 168 (10th Cir. 1980)(no consent where evidence was also relevant to pleaded issues).

The evidence beyond the scope of the pleadings need not relate to a different claim. It might, for example, simply support a different theoretical basis for the same claim already asserted. Thus, in D. Federico Co. v. New Bedford Redev. Auth., 723 F.2d 122

E. Amended Pleadings

(1st Cir. 1983), the court upheld amendment by implied consent to introduce an unpleaded equitable theory of recovery in a contract case.

Amendment to conform to the evidence can benefit defendants as well as the plaintiffs. For example, in Prinz v. Greate Bay Casino Corp., 705 F.2d 692 (3d Cir. 1983), the appellate court reversed the trial court's refusal to allow the jury to consider a defense of claim preclusion (res judicata) which, while not pleaded, was tried by implied consent. Rule 15(b) permits a defendant to overcome the general rule that defenses not pleaded are waived. Fejta v. GAF Co., 800 F.2d 1395 (5th Cir. 1986). See generally 3 MOORE'S FEDERAL PRACTICE ¶ 15.13[2]. Of course, express consent, either by the plaintiff or defendant, will be more obvious, usually being embodied in a stipulation or pretrial conference order.

2. Again, assume Plaintiff sues for breach of Contract 1 and also introduces evidence of breach of Contract 2. Assuming the court finds implied consent to try the second contract claim, *must* it grant plaintiff leave to amend to conform to the evidence? Why? What effect would there be on the proceedings if Plaintiff did not seek leave to amend?

3. Plaintiff sues for patent infringement and then introduces evidence of a claim for unfair competition. Defendant objects to introduction of evidence on the latter claim.

    (a) The court will sustain the objection and bar admission of the evidence. Why?

    (b) After the court sustains the objection, what motion might Plaintiff want to make? What is the standard for granting that motion? How does this standard differ from the standard applied when seeking leave to amend under Rule 15(a)?

4. In Brandon v. Holt, 469 U.S. 464 (1985), the plaintiffs brought a civil rights action against a police officer and a city's director of police. At the time the plaintiffs sued, cities could not be held liable for such violations, but that rule was changed shortly thereafter. The district court held for the plaintiffs, but the court of appeals reversed, holding that the director was immune from suit under relevant law. Id. at 471-72. The Supreme Court reinstated the judgment for the plaintiffs. It treated the complaint as amended to conform to the evidence and as stating a claim against the city itself, under the recent change in the law. The claim against the director was essentially a claim for damages against the city. *Brandon* is unusual in permitting amendment even on appeal. Almost all motions for amendment to conform to the evidence will be made in the trial court.

3. Amendment and the Statute of Limitations Under Rule 15(c)

a. Amendment to Claims or Defenses

The liberal policy of the Federal Rules' amendment provisions may clash with policies underlying other rules. Statutes of limitations, for example, impose temporal limits on the bringing of a claim. Thus, a state may require that the plaintiffs sue for personal injuries within two years of the accrual of the claim. You will recall from Chapter 7 that statutes of limitations and the rules for stopping ("tolling") their running are substantive for *Erie* purposes. Thus, in diversity of citizenship cases, federal courts apply state statutes of limitations. Of course, for federal claims, Congress can provide the limitations period.

Such statutes are said to embody a policy of "repose" — meaning that after passage of a certain period, a defendant should be assured that she will not be sued for an act or omission. In addition, limitations rules may ensure that cases proceed while events are relatively fresh in the minds of witnesses. Imagine that a case is filed before the statute of limitations runs. Then, after the statute would have run, one of the parties to the case seeks leave to amend to state a new claim or defense. Which policy—that supporting liberal amendment or that underlying the limitation of actions—should prevail? Read Rule 15(c).

Marsh v. Coleman Company
774 F. Supp. 608 (D. Kan. 1991)

CROW, DISTRICT JUDGE.

[Marsh started working for Coleman Company in 1960 as an industrial engineer in the Outing Products Group, which manufactured outdoor equipment and various thermal and marine products. After three years, he moved from the manufacturing side of the Outing Products Group to the design side of the same group. He worked in other capacities, as detailed in the opinion below. Coleman terminated Marsh's employment on January 20, 1988. Marsh filed suit on January 19, 1990, alleging that the termination was in breach of contract and violated the federal Age Discrimination in Employment Act, 29 U.S.C. § 621, et seq. On November 5, 1990, Marsh sought leave to amend his complaint to add a claim for fraud, based on alleged representations made by his superiors in 1985. Coleman opposed the motion for leave to amend, and claimed that the fraud claim was barred by the applicable two-year Kansas statute of limitations. Marsh argued that the fraud claim could take advantage of relation back under Rule 15(c).—EDS.]

* * *

E. Amended Pleadings

During his years at the Coleman Company the plaintiff enjoyed several promotions and advancements. One of his highest achievements occurred in 1969, when the plaintiff was made Director of Design Engineering for the Outing Products Group. He held that position until 1985 when he became Director of Manufacturing for the Manufactured Housing (Mobile Home) Division of the Heating and Air Conditioning Group.

The plaintiff's move in 1985 was due to several events. In 1984, Sheldon C. Coleman ("Sheldon Junior") became the General Manager for the Outing Products Group. Around the same time, the Outing Products Group was broken down into several divisions causing the question whether the employees of the Design Department would still have jobs. After the divisionalization occurred, discussions between Sheldon Junior and the plaintiff concluded that no positions remained for the plaintiff in the new organization of the group. Sheldon Junior told the plaintiff that a divisionalization was also occurring in the Heating and Air Conditioning Group and that he should contact Bob Hoffman, Manager of the Manufactured Housing Division of the Heating and Air Conditioning Group, about a position as Director of Manufacturing in the Mobile Home Division. Around this same time, the plaintiff met with Sheldon Senior about the concerns of employees in the Design Department over the reorganization. Sheldon Senior told the plaintiff to assure his employees that there would be jobs for everyone in his department after the divisionalization.

The plaintiff was interviewed and hired by Bob Hoffman for the position of Director of Manufacturing for the Mobile Home Division, effective January, 1985. Hoffman was Marsh's immediate supervisor. Don Berchtold headed up the entire Heating and Air Conditioning Group. In 1985, this group was divided into three divisions: Manufactured Housing (Mobile Homes), Residential, and Recreational Vehicles.

In February of 1985, the Outing Products Group held a party to honor the plaintiff. Sheldon Junior spoke to the Group praising Marsh's accomplishments in design. Marsh recalls that Sheldon Junior said, among other things, that "there will always be a place for Bill Marsh at the Coleman Company."

In May of 1987, Hoffman and Marsh transferred from the Manufactured Housing Division to the Residential Division of the Group. On January 2, 1988, Marsh received a memorandum sent to all weekly and monthly salaried employees from Berchtold dated December 31, 1987, stating that the Manufactured Housing Division and the ResidentialDivision would be merged, explaining the business reasons for that decision, and naming the heads for the various combined departments. Joe Nold was designated to head up the manufacturing operation.

After January 2, 1988, the plaintiff recalled having several conversations with Joe Nold. Nold told Marsh: "Don't worry, you're working for the world's nicest guy now; everything's going to be all right. And what I want you to do is just continue what you're doing and just sit back, relax, don't worry." Marsh also remembered Nold calling on another occasion and saying everything was fine and not to worry.

Nold's responsibility was to decide who was to remain in the combined division and to select a staff who would report directly to him. Nold decided to streamline the manufacturing operation and reduce the number of employees by twenty-nine. Nold and his staff considered each of existing manufacturing employees in both divisions for the remaining positions. The plaintiff was not selected by Nold for any of the positions. Nold's reason was that other employees had skills and abilities better suited for the particular positions required in the streamlined operation. * * *

CHAPTER 8 PLEADINGS AND JUDGMENTS BASED ON PLEADINGS

On January 20, 1988, Nold met with Marsh and told him that he was one of thirty people being let go as a result of the divisions combining. At that time, Nold also went over Marsh's separation package which included regular pay through January 31, 1988, unused vacation pay, and then ten months severance pay at his current base salary. * * * Following the ten months of severance pay, Marsh took early retirement with Coleman Company.

* * *

[In his motion for leave to amend, Marsh] alleges he was defrauded in one or more of the following particulars:

(1) by falsely representing through its agent, Sheldon C. Coleman (Sheldon Junior):

(a) there would be jobs available for everyone in the Design Group, including the plaintiff;

(b) that employees in the Design Group need not be concerned about their jobs;

(c) that the plaintiff would have permanent employment with defendant as long as there was a Coleman Company.

(2) by enticing the plaintiff not to look for other employment as a result of the representations of Sheldon C. Coleman, which representations were relied upon by the plaintiff and which representations caused the plaintiff to forego seeking other job opportunities during the period 1984 until the date of his termination.

(3) by falsely representing through its agent Sheldon Coleman (Sheldon Senior), that there would be jobs for everyone in the plaintiff's group.

(4) by expressly or impliedly approving the false statements of Sheldon C. Coleman, through its then president Sheldon Coleman (Senior).

(5) by falsely representing to the plaintiff through its agent, Joe Nold, on numerous occasions, not to worry about his position in the company and that everything would be fine.

(6) by enticing the plaintiff over a period of years to believe that his position was permanently secure when, in fact, defendant had no intention of providing the plaintiff job security.

The plaintiff did not allege a fraud claim in his original complaint filed January 19, 1990. On November 5, 1990, the plaintiff moved for leave to amend his complaint to include [the claim for fraud.] * * *

Defendant contends the fraud claim is barred by the statute of limitations and does not relate back to the filing of the original complaint. In the alternative, defendant argues the the plaintiff is unable to prove the elements to his claims of fraudulent promises. The plaintiff responds that the fraud claims come within the terms of Fed.R.Civ.P. 15(c) [now 15(c)(2)–EDS.] and properly relate back to the original complaint * * *.

* * * Rule 15(c) is built upon the premise that once notified of pending litigation over particular conduct or a certain transaction or occurrence, the defendant has been given all the notice required for purposes of the statute of limitations. Baldwin County Welcome Center v. Brown, 466 U.S. 147, 149 n.3 (1984). The linchpin to Rule 15(c) is notice before the limitations period expires. Relation back does not offend the notice policies underlying a statute of limitations if the original complaint fairly discloses the general fact situation out of which the new claims arise. 3 JAMES W. MOORE & RICHARD D. FREER, MOORE'S FEDERAL PRACTICE ¶ 15.15[2] at 15-144, 145 (1985). Amendments will relate back if they only flesh out the factual details, change the legal theory, or add another claim arising out of the same transaction, occurrence or conduct. Relation back is denied those

E. Amended Pleadings

amendments which are based on entirely different facts, transactions, and occurrences. Holmes v. Greyhound Lines, Inc., 757 F.2d 1563, 1566 (5th Cir. 1985).

Looking back at the the plaintiff's original complaint, he limited his factual allegations to his termination on January 20, 1988, to the reasons given for his termination, to his replacement being younger, and to the defendant's actions being in breach of his employment contract. All alleged events occurred on January 29, 1988, or after. The complaint made no reference to any transactions or event occurring in 1984 or 1985. None of the claims were based on promises by defendant that the plaintiff would always have employment with it. Not until his amended complaint did the plaintiff ever allege that defendant's agents made fraudulent statements to him prior to his discharge. For that matter, the plaintiff never sought damages for lost employment opportunities until he added his new claim for fraud. The only factual overlap between the plaintiff's fraud claim and his original claims is that his employment with defendant ended on January 20, 1988. Other than this, the claims are based on events and transactions that are distinct in time and not closely related. A reasonably prudent person would not have expected from reading the plaintiff's original complaint that promises made to the plaintiff before termination, in particular those made more than three years earlier, might be called into question through subsequent pleadings. * * *

The plaintiff's promissory fraud claims are based on conduct substantially different in kind and time from that alleged in the plaintiff's original complaint. The crux of a promissory fraud claim is not that the promisor breached his promise to perform, rather it is that the promisor fraudulently represented his present intent to perform. Defendant had no reason to anticipate from reading the plaintiff's original complaint that it should prepare to defend a case based on acts more than three years earlier. For these reasons, the court finds the plaintiff's fraud claim does not relate back to the filing of the original complaint and, therefore, is barred by the two-year statute of limitations.

* * *

NOTES AND QUESTIONS

1. Explain how relation back, if applicable in *Marsh*, would have saved the plaintiff's fraud claim. Explain the justification for allowing relation back.

2. Can you make an argument that the events underlying the fraud claim were part of the same "conduct, transaction, or occurrence" as the termination of Mr. Marsh's employment in 1988?

3. Suppose Mr. Marsh had not sought leave to amend and that his case proceeded to trial. Suppose he then proffered evidence on the fraud claim. If the defendant objected to that evidence on the basis of variance, how would the court rule? If the defendant failed to object to that evidence, would the court amend to conform to the evidence after trial? Would such amendment relate back?

4. Should relation back be permitted if the new claim would add considerably more exposure for the defendant? For example, suppose the amended claim, although meeting the "conduct, transaction or occurrence" standard, allowed the plaintiff to seek

punitive and other damages far exceeding the original claim. Does Rule 15 speak to this possibility?

5. Should Rule 15(c) govern in a diversity of citizenship case if state rules do not allow for relation back of amendments? Why should relation back be treated differently from statute of limitations and tolling, which, as we saw in Chapter 7, are governed by state law in diversity of citizenship cases?

b. Amendment Changing a Party

Marsh involved amendment to add a claim after the statute of limitations had run. A more difficult (but less common) problem deals with relation back when an amendment adds a new party after the statute of limitations has run. The issue is addressed in Rule 15(c)(3), which was clarified by amendment in 1991. Rule 15(c)(3) contemplates a very narrow class of cases, in which the "wrong" party is joined before the statute of limitations runs, but in which the "right" party somehow knows about the case and that it should have been involved.

For example, suppose the plaintiff attempted to sue Fortune magazine for defamation. In her complaint, the plaintiff names "Fortune" as defendant and described it as a New York corporation with its principal place of business in the Time and Life Building in New York. In fact, however, there is no such entity. "Fortune" is a trademark and division of Time, Incorporated, which should have been named as the defendant. The plaintiff filed her complaint before the statute of limitations ran, and had process served on Time's registered agent.

Because of service on Time's registered agent, two requirements of the rule were met: (1) Time, Incorporated, was charged with notice of the suit, and (2) it was obvious to Time that "but for a mistake concerning the identity of the proper party, the action would have been brought against [it]." Rule 15(c)(3)(A) and (B). Relation back would depend upon whether these requirements were met within the time prescribed by the Rule, or "within the period provided by Rule 4(m) for service of the summons and complaint." Thus, if the service on Time, Incorporated were effected within that period — even though that may be after the statute of limitations would have run — the court will allow relation back. (These facts are adapted from Schiavone v. Fortune, 477 U.S. 21 (1986), which led to revision of Rule 15(c) to its current form.)

F. Supplemental Pleadings

Read Rule 15(d).

A supplemental pleading sets forth events occurring after a pleading is filed. This does not include facts that occurred before the original filing but which were discovered after filing. As to such facts, amendment is the proper course. Supplemental pleadings update the dispute by bringing such new facts to the attention of the court, even if they change the relief sought or add additional parties.

A supplemental pleading is allowed only with court permission; there is no such thing as supplementation of right. Nonetheless, the same policies we saw with amendment counsel the liberal reading of Rule 15(d). Thus, courts freely grant leave to supplement, unless there is undue delay, prejudice, or bad faith. For example, in Twin Disc, Inc. v. Big Bud Tractor, Inc., 772 F.2d 1329 (7th Cir. 1985), the plaintiff sought leave to supplement one week before trial to add additional alleged failures to pay for goods delivered to the defendant. The defendant lacked notice of the additional amounts claimed and would require discovery to prepare adequately to meet the allegations. The court denied the plaintiff's motion to file the supplemental pleading, concluding that the trial should not be delayed. The Seventh Circuit affirmed, holding that the district judge had not abused his discretion in so ruling.

G. Veracity in Pleading: Rule 11 and Other Devices

1. Rule 11.

Professor Judith Resnik has written that the "history of procedure is a series of attempts to solve the problems created by the preceding generation's procedural reforms." Judith Resnik, *Tiers*, 57 S. Cal. L. Rev. 837, 1030 (1984). This may be an accurate description of the history of Rule 11. The original version, included in the 1938 Rules, required that attorneys have "good grounds to support" their pleading. The Rule permitted, but did not require, the imposition of sanctions for violations. Courts found violations only if the attorney was guilty of subjective bad faith. In the first forty years of its existence, Rule 11 was invoked in fewer than a dozen reported cases.

This all changed in 1983. The 1970s and 1980s were marked by increasing concern about frivolous litigation and the supposed "litigation explosion". Some have also suggested that there was a growing dislike of the "notice pleading/open discovery revolution embodies in the 1938 Rules." Jeffrey Stempel, *Sanction, Symmetry, and Safe Harbors:*

Limiting Misapplications of Rule 11 By Harmonizing it with Pre-Verdict Dismissal Devices, 60 FORDHAM L. REV. 257, 265 (1991). As a result, the Court in 1983 substantially revised Rule 11.

The 1983 amendments to Rule 11 required that all pleadings and other papers be signed and that the signature of the attorney or party constituted

> a certification by the signer that the signer has read the pleading, motion or other paper, that to the best of the signer's knowledge, information, and belief formed after reasonable inquiry it is well grounded in fact and warranted by existing law or a good faith argument for the extension, modification, or reversal of existing law, and that it is not interposed for any improper purpose, such as to harass or to cause unnecessary delay or needlessly increase in the cost of litigation.

The Rule *required* courts to impose sanctions for violations.[*]

The revised Rule 11 unleashed a torrent of litigation. Over the next decade, there were over 3000 reported Rule 11 decisions. The Court itself decided four cases involving Rule 11. Two of the cases are of particular note. In Cooter & Gell v. Hartmax Corp., 496 U.S. 384 (1990), the Court held that a district court can impose Rule 11 sanctions on the plaintiff and its attorney for inadequate pre-filing inquiry, even after the plaintiff had voluntarily dismissed the suit. According to the Court the voluntary dismissal neither cured the defect nor deprived the court of jurisdiction to impose sanctions.

In Willy v. Coastal Corp., 503 U.S. 131 (1992), the Court held that a district court may impose Rule 11 sanctions in a case in which the court is later determined to be without subject matter jurisdiction. The case was originally filed in state court and the defendant removed it to federal court. The plaintiff objected to the removal on the grounds of lack of subject matter jurisdiction, but the district court rejected this argument. Then the plaintiff moved for partial summary judgment and the defendant moved to dismiss for failure to state a claim. While these motions were pending, the plaintiff twice more moved unsuccessfully for remand. The district court granted the defendant's motion and imposed Rule 11 sanctions on the plaintiff for bringing a baseless motion for summary judgment which confused the proceedings. The court of appeals held that the district court lacked subject matter jurisdiction, but nonetheless affirmed the imposition of sanctions. The Court unanimously affirmed. Plaintiff's lawyer was sanctioned nearly $23,000 because the district court found that the summary judgment motion "create[d] a blur of absolute confusion." Although it

---

[*] Recall the prevailing party in any case will recover "costs" from the losing party under Federal Rule 54(d). "Costs" are limited, however, to various litigation expenses such as filing fees and other charges by the clerk of the court, witness and discovery fees. They do not include attorney's fees, which will always be the most significant amount of expense. One of the reasons Rule 11 has generated such intense debate is that it permits the recovery of attorney's fees.

G. Veracity in Pleading: Rule 11 and Other Devices

ultimately lacked subject matter jurisdiction, the district court had power to impose sanctions.

There has been an enormous amount of writing about Rule 11, including at least two books and innumerable law review articles. See, e.g., GREGORY JOSEPH, SANCTIONS: THE FEDERAL LAW OF LITIGATION ABUSE (1989); GEORGENE VAIRO, RULE 11 SANCTIONS: CASE LAW PERSPECTIVES AND PREVENTATIVE MEASURES (1991); Stephen Burbank, *The Transformation of American Civil Procedure: The Example of Rule 11*, 137 U. PA. L. REV. 1925 (1989); William Schwarzer, *Rule 11 Revisited*, 101 HARV. L. REV. 1013 (1988); Carl Tobias, *Certification and Civil Rights*, 136 F.R.D. 223 (1991).

By the early 1990s, Rule 11 had come under increasing criticism. Critics argued that the Rule chilled appropriate but zealous advocacy, see Melissa Nelken, *Sanction Under Amended Federal Rule 11--Some "Chilling" Problems in the Struggle Between Compensation and Punishment*, 74 GEO. L.J. 1313 (1986), and produced wasteful satellite litigation, see Lawrence Marshall, Herbert Kritzer & Frances Zemans, *The Use and Impact of Rule 11*, 86 Nw. U. L. REV. 943 (1992). In addition, some critics charged that Rule 11 was partially responsible for a deterioration in lawyer professionalism and civility in litigation. One report cites the following comments by lawyers concerning Rule 11:

> In recent years the great problem is Rule 11. It has lead to personal recriminations between lawyers and threats of financial and personal reputation consequences to counsel. These threats lead to defensive incivility and mistrust.
>
> Rule 11 has negatively affected civility by initiating a punitive system.
>
> Certain large law firms have adopted a policy of seeking Rule 11 sanctions as a routine strategy.

Interim Report of the Committee on Civility of the Seventh Circuit, 143 F.R.D. 371, 389 (1991).

In the face of growing criticism, a new version of Rule 11 went in to effect December 1, 1993. The revised version has its critics as well, including Justices Scalia and Thomas, who opposed promulgation of the new Rule, arguing that it "gutted" Rule 11. 113 S.Ct. at 583-84. Professor Jeffrey Stempel has offered the insightful explanation for the divergent views of the Rule:

> [T]he sanctions debate is a distributional political battle that has some unavoidable aspects of a zero-sum game. If Rule 11 is written or interpreted stringently, some claims are sacrificed in the name of efficiency, deterring the unfounded or abusive, and thinning court dockets. If Rule 11's test to application is made more forgiving, some of these values are sacrificed in favor of zealous advocacy, innovative lawyering and claimants' right. Because some lawyers tend to favor the access/advocacy/ innovation goals while others prefer the efficiency/

CHAPTER 8 PLEADINGS AND JUDGMENTS BASED ON PLEADINGS

expense/deterrence goals, no theory of Rule 11 can hope to satisfy all sides of the sanctions debate completely.

Stempel, supra, at 261.

Rule 11 is not the only source of standards for proper conduct in litigation. The Rules of Professional Responsibility also address this issue. Although each state bar has its own rules governing professional responsibility, and there are some important variations among these, we have reproduced below some of the relevant rules from the American Bar Association's Model Code of Professional Responsibility. Read these rules, then read Rule 11 and the 1993 Advisory Committee Notes to Rule 11.

MODEL RULES OF PROFESSIONAL RESPONSIBILITY

Rule 3.1: A lawyer shall not bring or defend a proceeding, or assert or controvert an issue therein, unless there is a basis for doing so that is not frivolous, which includes a good faith argument for an extension, modification or reversal of existing law. A lawyer for the defendant in a criminal proceeding, or the respondent in a proceeding that could result in incarceration, may nonetheless so defend the proceeding as to require that every element of the case be established.

Rule 3.2: A lawyer shall make reasonable efforts to expedite litigation consistent with the interests of the client.

Rule 3.3: (a) A lawyer shall not knowingly:

(1) Make a false statement of material fact or law to a tribunal;

(2) Fail to disclose a material fact to a tribunal when disclosure is necessary to avoid assisting a criminal or fraudulent act by the client;

(3) Fail to disclose to the tribunal legal authority in the controlling jurisdiction known to the lawyer to be directly adverse to the position of the client and not disclosed by opposing counsel; or

(4) Offer evidence that the lawyer knows to be false. If a lawyer has offered material evidence and comes to know of its falsity, the lawyer shall take reasonable remedial measures.

(b) The duties stated in paragraph (a) continue to the conclusion of the proceeding, and apply even if compliance requires disclosure of information otherwise protected by [attorney-client privilege].

(c) A lawyer may refuse to offer evidence that the lawyer reasonably believes is false.

(d) In an ex parte proceeding, a lawyer shall inform the tribunal of all material facts known to the lawyer which will enable the tribunal to make and informed decision, whether or not the facts are adverse.

Rule 3.4: A lawyer shall not:

(a) Unlawfully obstruct another party's access to evidence or unlawfully alter, destroy or conceal a document or other material having

potential evidentiary value. A lawyer shall not counsel or assist another person to do any such act;
   (b) Falsify evidence, counsel or assist a witness to testify falsely, or offer an inducement to a witness that is prohibited by law;
   (c) Knowingly disobey an obligation under the rules of a tribunal except for an open refusal based on an assertion that no valid obligation exists;
   (d) In pretrial procedure, make a frivolous discovery request or fail to comply with a legally proper discovery request by an opposing party;
   (e) In trial, allude to any matter that the lawyer does not reasonably believe is relevant or that will not be supported by admissible evidence, assert personal knowledge of facts in issue except when testifying as a witness, or state a personal opinion as to the justness of a cause, the credibility of a witness, the culpability of a civil litigant or the guilt or innocence of an accused; or
   (f) Request a person other than a client to refrain from voluntarily giving relevant information to another party unless:
   (1) The person is a relative or an employee or other agent of a client; and
   (2) The lawyer reasonably believes that the person's interest will not be adversely affected by refraining from giving such information.

NOTES AND QUESTIONS

1. Who makes the Rule 11 certification? How does she do so? When does she do so? Under the 1983 version, as noted, certification was effective only initially. Now, certification attaches to every "presenting" of any "pleading, written motion, or other paper." When does such presenting occur? Explain how this puts counsel under an ongoing duty to assess whether a position continues to be tenable under Rule 11.

2. What is the certification made under Rule 11? Consider the following:
   (a) What is "an inquiry reasonable under the circumstances?" Suppose Client comes to your office at 5:50 p.m. on the day before the statute of limitations would run. If her complaint is not filed by 5:00 p.m. the following day, her claim will be barred forever. Her story, if true, would entitle her to recovery. What inquiry must you under take before drafting and filing the complaint? How would your answer differ if she came to your office ten days earlier?
   (b) What is a "nonfrivolous" argument for change in the law? If the law was established by a Supreme Court opinion last year, in which one justice dissented, would your advocating the dissent's position be "nonfrivolous?" What if the case were decided ten years ago? What if four justices dissented?

CHAPTER 8 PLEADINGS AND JUDGMENTS BASED ON PLEADINGS

(c) When may a plaintiff allege that she is likely to find evidentiary support later? When may a defendant deny allegations based solely upon her information and belief?

3. Rule 11 no longer *requires* imposition of sanctions for violation. What language of the rule makes this clear? What purpose is served by this change?

(a) On whom can sanctions be imposed? Under what circumstance can a monetary sanction be imposed only on counsel, and not on the party? Why does this limitation make sense? When can a law firm be sanctioned for the errors of its employee?

(b) What is the goal of sanctions? What are appropriate sanctions? What nonmonetary sanctions are possible? (Don't forget to read the 1993 Advisory Committee Note.)

(c) Note that no sanctions of any kind can be imposed without notice and an opportunity to be heard.

(d) When can a party recover attorney's fees under Rule 11?

4. Rule 11 violations may be raised by the court sua sponte. What is the procedure for this?

5. Would the plaintiff's lawyer in *McCormick*, supra, have violated Rule 11 in pleading alternative theories?

6. The most controversial provision in the 1993 amendment to Rule 11 provides a 21 day "safe harbor" for those purportedly violating the rule. The following case addresses this and other aspects of the amended rule, including the requirement of reasonable inquiry.

Hadges v. Yonkers Racing Corp.
48 F. 3d 1320 (2d Cir. 1995)

Feinberg, Circuit Judge.

Plaintiff George Hadges appeals from three rulings of the United States District Court for the Southern District of New York, Gerard L. Goettel, J. The first ruling * * * denied relief to Hadges in his action brought under Fed.R.Civ.P. 60(b) (the Rule 60(b) action) to set aside the judgment of the court in an earlier case, Hadges v. Yonkers Raceway Corp.(*Hadges I*). In *Hadges I*, Judge Goettel had denied Hadges's application for a preliminary injunction and had granted defendant Yonkers Racing Corp. (YRC) summary judgment in Hadges's action against it. We affirmed that judgment. The basis of the present Rule 60(b) action is that YRC had committed a fraud on the court in *Hadges I*. [Rule 60(b) permits a litigant to file an action to set aside the judgment in a prior case. One specific ground for seeking such relief is fraud, misrepresentation or other misconduct of an adverse party. Rule 60(b)(3). -- EDS.]

In the second ruling on appeal, * * * Judge Goettel imposed Rule 11 sanctions on Hadges and his attorney, William M. Kunstler, for misleading the court in the course of the Rule 60(b) action. The judge fined Hadges and censured Kunstler. In the third ruling, two weeks later, the judge denied Hadges and Kunstler permission to reargue the sanctions issues. This appeal followed. For the reasons stated below, we affirm the denial of Rule 60(b) relief, but we reverse the sanction on Hadges and the censure of Kunstler.

I. Background

This appeal concerns the most recent dispute arising out of the efforts of the plaintiff-appellant Hadges to compel various racetracks and state agencies to permit him to pursue his career as a harness racehorse driver, trainer and owner. * * *

A. Facts underlying Rule 60(b) action

Hadges was first licensed by the New York State Racing and Wagering Board (Racing Board) in 1972. His license was suspended and revoked in 1974 because he failed to disclose the full extent of his criminal arrest record in his initial license application. Hadges was relicensed in 1976.

In early 1989, the Racing Board again suspended Hadges's license for six months after determining that Hadges had illegally passed wagering information to a member of the betting public at Roosevelt Raceway in 1986. According to the Racing Board, as Hadges approached the starting gate, he trailed behind the other horses and shouted, "Get the '7'," to someone in the stands. The number seven horse did in fact win, and Hadges's horse, number two, drove erratically and interfered with the other horses.

In September 1989, although the Racing Board had reissued Hadges's license, YRC denied Hadges the right to work at its racetrack, Yonkers Raceway. In response, Hadges filed an action against YRC in the district court under 42 U.S.C. § 1983, which resulted in the decision in *Hadges I*. [§ 1983 provides a cause of action for deprivation of constitutional rights "under color of state law." Thus, it does not apply to deprivations by private (non-state) actors. -- EDS.] Hadges alleged that YRC had violated his Fourteenth Amendment right to due process in banning him. In the course of the *Hadges I* litigation, YRC submitted an affidavit of its General Manager, Robert Galterio, who stated that the YRC ban did not prevent Hadges from pursuing his profession because he could still work at other regional tracks, including the Meadowlands in New Jersey.

In March 1990, the district court granted YRC's motion for summary judgment, finding that YRC's practices were not state action and thus could not give rise to liability under § 1983. In two footnotes, the district court indicated its apparent understanding that Hadges was not barred from racing at other facilities but "that proof that other tracks in the state followed YRC's decision could establish state action."

In 1992, Hadges commenced another suit against YRC, this time in New York state court. He alleged several causes of action including that all the harness tracks in New York State were engaged in a civil conspiracy and that the racetracks had blackballed him in violation of the Donnelly Act, New York's anti-trust law. The state court ruled against Hadges on all of his claims.

In 1993, Hadges brought another § 1983 action, this time against the Meadowlands Raceway, in federal district court in New Jersey (the Meadowlands suit). He alleged that in 1992 Meadow-

CHAPTER 8 PLEADINGS AND JUDGMENTS BASED ON PLEADINGS

lands had improperly banned him from racing without a hearing. Because Meadowlands is run by a state agency, the New Jersey Sports & Exposition Authority (Sports Authority), there was no dispute as to whether the banning constituted state action. The parties settled that litigation.

In the course of that action, Meadowlands General Manager Bruce Garland submitted an affidavit stating that Meadowlands had banned Hadges based on the YRC ban. In particular, Garland said that Meadowlands had acted pursuant to a Sports Authority resolution adopted in 1992, which provided that Meadowlands would exclude those who had been "ruled off from . . . another racetrack." Thus, he stated, "the fact that plaintiff has been barred at Yonkers Raceway would operate as a basis for . . . rejecting plaintiff's application for participation in [a] 1993 . . . meet at the Meadowlands, had such an application been properly filed."

After successfully settling the Meadowlands suit, and with the appeal from dismissal of the New York state court action pending, Hadges brought the instant Rule 60(b) action in the Southern District of New York. He sought to vacate the court's decision in *Hadges I* on the ground that YRC had perpetrated a fraud on the court in that action by submitting the Galterio affidavit stating that Hadges could continue to work at other tracks despite the YRC ban. Hadges did not inform the district court of the then-pending state court appeal. As noted above, the district court ruled against Hadges and granted YRC's motion for summary judgment. In response to a request by YRC, the court also imposed sanctions under Fed.R.Civ.P. 11 on both Hadges and Kunstler.

B. Facts underlying Rule 11 sanctions

In support of his claim for relief in the Rule 60(b) action, Hadges submitted a sworn statement that 1993 was his "fifth year . . . out of work, with the boycott by Yonkers still in effect." In addition, he stated that "there was a secret agreement among all of the racetracks, that barring a licensee from one, will result in his being barred from all." The plaintiff's memorandum of law, signed by Kunstler, also asserted that Hadges "has not worked for more than four years." Hadges claimed that he had applied to race at other tracks in New York State, but that these tracks refused to act upon the applications, thereby barring him from racing. He also asserted that upon the advice of a former attorney, Joseph A. Faraldo, he had written to the general managers of these tracks to apply for driving privileges in mid-1990 but received no reply. Hadges presented the court with an affidavit of Faraldo stating that Faraldo had so advised Hadges.

In response, YRC produced documents revealing that Hadges had in fact raced at Monticello Raceway five times in 1991 and seven times in 1993. The most recent race took place less than one month before Hadges submitted his affidavit stating that he had been banned from racing by all tracks in New York State for more than four years. YRC also submitted letters of current and former Racing Secretaries from race tracks in Saratoga, Batavia Downs, Fairmount Park, Vernon Downs and Buffalo who asserted that Hadges had not applied (or they had no recollection of his having applied) for racing privileges at their respective tracks in the relevant time period.

In a memorandum of law and notice of motion to dismiss the Rule 60(b) action, YRC requested that the court impose sanctions on Hadges and, if warranted, on his counsel for this misrepresentation and for failing to disclose the state court action to the district court. This method of requesting Rule 11 sanctions was, as set forth below, contrary to the procedural requirements of Rule 11 that took effect on December 1, 1993, five days before Hadges filed his complaint in the Rule 60(b) action and 15 days before YRC requested sanctions.

G. Veracity in Pleading: Rule 11 and Other Devices

After YRC requested sanctions, Hadges submitted an affidavit dated December 28, 1993, admitting that he had raced in Monticello in 1991 and 1993, but explaining that he considered the races insignificant because he had earned less than $100 in the two years combined. That affidavit also described a so-called "scratching incident" that Hadges claimed had taken place at Yonkers Raceway on October 31, 1989. He stated that although his state racing license had been restored in 1989, New York State Racing Board judges "scratched" him from that race, in which he was to have ridden the horse "Me Gotta Bret." After this scratching incident, YRC informed him of its independent ban. Hadges argued to the district court that this sequence of events supported his theory that YRC was acting as a state agent in banning him and thus could be held liable in a § 1983 action. Hadges submitted to the court a "scratch sheet," purporting to document his version of the event.

YRC then submitted what the district court later described as "overwhelming proof" that the scratch sheet did not refer to an October 1989 race, but rather to a November 1987 race.

In its decision on the merits of the Rule 60(b) action, the district court found that Hadges had raced at Monticello in 1991 and 1993 but that he had made only a "minimal" amount of money. It also found that the legal basis for Hadges's Rule 60(b) action was not "so frivolous as to warrant Rule 11 sanctions." However, the court was "quite concerned" that Hadges and Kunstler had attempted "to indicate that [Hadges] had not raced in four years when, in fact, he had privileges at Monticello in both 1991 and 1993." The court stated that Hadges had "made matters worse by attempting to strengthen his claim of state involvement alleging that he was scratched from driving Me Gotta Bret on October 31, 1989 by the judges of the racing board." The court further found that submission of the undated scratch sheet was a "flagrant misrepresentation . . . suggesting the need for sanctions, certainly against the plaintiff and possibly against his counsel." The judge invited Hadges and Kunstler to submit papers opposing the imposition of sanctions. The court did not refer to the nondisclosure of the state court action as a possible basis for sanctions.[1]

Thereafter, Hadges submitted an affidavit admitting that he had made a misstatement about the scratching incident but expressing his objection to sanctions. He stated that this error was the result of a simple memory loss, and that the scratch sheet involved was bona fide proof of his having been scratched in 1987 rather than in 1989. He went on to describe yet another 1989 incident in which he had been scratched from racing the horse "Dazzling GT" at YRC. Hadges also submitted an affidavit of his then-assistant Erik Schulman, which also described the 1989 Dazzling GT scratching incident. Further, Hadges repeated that he had written to the General Managers (not the Racing Secretaries relied upon by YRC) of the various tracks to request driving privileges but had received no reply. He attached copies of the letters along with copies of postal receipts.

Kunstler also submitted a sworn response, which stated that he "had no idea" that the scratch sheet was from 1987 rather than 1989, and set forth the facts of the Dazzling GT incident.

---

[1] In fairness, we note that YRC has also hardly been a model of candor in this litigation. YRC submitted documents to the district court making it appear that Hadges has earned nearly $2,000 at Monticello in 1991 and 1993, when in fact, the record is uncontroverted that as the driver earned less than $100.

[2] Kunstler's affidavit also sought to disqualify Judge Goettel, claiming that the judge had gained knowledge of facts in this case through his involvement in a different litigation. In that prior litigation, according to an affidavit of Hadges's then-attorney, Robert A. Schutzman, Judge Goettel had ordered the Racing Board to reissue Hadges's license after his suspension was over. On this basis, Hadges sought to have the judge (1) withdraw his decision in the Rule 60(b) action in its entirety, (2) disqualify himself pursuant to 28 U.S.C. §445 "for personal knowledge of material facts in this case, learned in the course of different litigation," and (3) hold a hearing on above issues. The court denied all of these requests, and Hadges has not appealed from the judge's decision not to recuse himself on this basis.

Kunstler maintained that the error regarding the date of the scratch sheet was unintentional but would not have affected the outcome of the case in any event. Regardless of its date, he argued, the scratch sheet was evidence that YRC was acting as an agent of the state Racing Board and could therefore be held liable in a § 1983 action. Thus, he maintained that submission of the document was not sanctionable. Kunstler's affidavit did not describe the efforts he had undertaken to verify his client's factual claims.[2] YRC then submitted further affidavits stating that it had no records concerning the alleged Dazzling GT incident.

Thereafter, in the second ruling on appeal to us, the judge imposed a Rule 11 sanction of $2,000 on Hadges as an appropriate sanction for his misrepresentations. The judge also censured Kunstler under Rule 11 for failing to make adequate inquiry as to the truth of Hadges's affidavits and for failing to inform the court of the pending state court litigation. In the course of his opinion, the judge stated:

> Mr. Kunstler is apparently one of those attorneys who believes that his sole obligation is to his client and that he has no obligations to the court or to the processes of justice. Unfortunately, he is not alone in this approach to the practice of law, which may be one reason why the legal profession is held in such low esteem by the public at this time.

Kunstler responded in a letter to the court, in which he argued that the court erred in sanctioning his client $2,000 and in censuring him. In particular, he objected to the court's characterization of him as an attorney "who believes that his sole obligation is to his client," and he objected to the court's charge that his approach to law practice was in part responsible for the low public esteem for the legal profession. Kunstler went on to state his opinion that the court's comment was "generated by an animus toward activist practitioners who, like myself, have, over the years, vigorously represented clients wholly disfavored by the establishment."

The court treated the letter as an application to reargue the sanction issues. Its order denying the application is the third ruling on appeal to us. In that order, the court quoted at length from a recent New York state court opinion criticizing Kunstler's law partner, Ronald L. Kuby in an entirely unrelated case. The judge's order further reprimanded Kunstler stating:

> Finally, Mr. Kunstler claims that he is entitled to "consideration" because of his representation of unpopular clients. Undoubtedly an attorney who assumes or is assigned the defense of an unpopular case or client and does so at risk to his practice or standing in the community (such as the fictional attorney Atticus Finch in Harper Lee's "To Kill a Mockingbird") is entitled to some consideration. However, an attorney who aggressively and repeatedly seeks to represent unpopular causes or questionable clients for personal reasons of his own is not deserving of any particular consideration. And an attorney who places himself and his causes above the interests of justice is entitled to none.

This appeal from the judgment for YRC in the Rule 60(b) action and from the two April 1994 rulings on sanctions followed.

II. Discussion

A. The Rule 60(b) action

G. Veracity in Pleading: Rule 11 and Other Devices

* * *

Since we believe that the district court was correct in concluding that there was no fraud on the court, its denial of Rule 60(b) relief must be upheld.

B. Rule 11 sanctions

As we have already noted, not only did the district court rule against Hadges regarding his claims of fraud on the court in *Hadges I*, but it went on to impose Rule 11 sanctions on both Hadges and Kunstler for their own misrepresentations and omissions. This determination was based on two principal grounds: (1) misstatement of the date of the alleged "scratching" incident and (2) misstatement regarding Hadges's lack of work in the years since the YRC ban. In addition, the court based Kunstler's censure on his failure to inform the court of the state court action. The court also found that Hadges's sanction was justified in part by the disqualification motion, referred to in note 2 above, which the court characterized as "bizarre." Hadges and Kunstler argue that the district court abused its discretion in imposing the Rule 11 sanctions.

* * *

The 1993 amendment to Rule 11 is "intended to remedy problems that had arisen" under the 1983 version of the Rule and is expected to "reduce the number of motions for sanctions presented to the court." Advisory committee note on 1993 amendment. The new Rule liberalizes the standard for compliance and provides procedural safeguards to enable parties to avoid sanctions. Of particular relevance here, the 1993 amendment establishes a "safe harbor" of 21 days during which factual or legal contentions may be withdrawn or appropriately corrected in order to avoid sanction. Fed.R.Civ.P. 11(c)(1)(A). In addition, litigants must move for sanctions "separately from other motions or requests." Id. The Rule also provides that "monetary sanctions may not be awarded against a represented party" for frivolous legal arguments advanced by the party's attorney. Fed.R.Civ.P. 11(c)(2)(A). The standard for sanctioning factual contentions is also revised. Under the former Rule, a signature on a document certified that the contentions therein were "well grounded in fact." Under the current Rule, the "certification is that there is (or likely will be) 'evidentiary support' for the allegation." Advisory committee note on 1993 amendment.

1. Hadges's sanction

* * *

In imposing sanctions, the district court apparently did not take into account YRC's failure to comply with the revised procedural requirements of Rule 11. In this case, YRC did not submit the sanction request separately from all other requests, and there is no evidence in the record indicating that YRC served Hadges with the request for sanctions 21 days before presenting it to the court.

Thus, YRC denied Hadges the "safe-harbor" period that the current version of the Rule specifically mandates.

If Hadges had received the benefit of the safe-harbor period, the record indicates that he would have "withdrawn or appropriately corrected" his misstatements, thus avoiding sanctions altogether. Hadges did in fact correct one of his misstatements by admitting in an affidavit, sworn to on December 28, 1993, just 12 days after YRC asked for sanctions, that he had raced at Monticello in 1991 and 1993. Thus, this misstatement is not sanctionable.

Hadges also explained and corrected his misstatement about the 1989 date of the first scratching incident and described another scratching incident in 1989 involving another horse (Dazzling GT). This correction was supported by his own affidavit sworn to on March 17, 1994, and the affidavit of Erik Schulman, sworn to on March 16, 1994. Both were filed with the district court on March 21, 1994, just one week after the court issued its order stating that it was considering imposition of sanctions. * * *

In addition to sanctioning Hadges for his factual misrepresentations, the district court ruled that sanctions were justified in part by the disqualification motion filed on Hadges's behalf. See note 2 above. In relying on the latter ground, the court imposed monetary sanctions on a represented party for making a legal contention that the court believed was not warranted by existing law or by a nonfrivolous argument for a change in existing law. Revised Rule 11 specifically prohibits imposition of monetary sanctions on the party on this basis. Fed.R.Civ.P. 11(b)(2) & 11(c)(2)(A).

Rule 11 also provides that a court may impose sanctions on its own initiative. Fed.R.Civ.P. 11(c)(1)(B). If a court wishes to exercise its discretion to impose sanctions sua sponte, it must "enter an order describing the specific conduct that appears to violate subdivision (b) and directing an attorney, law firm, or party to show cause why it has not violated subdivision (b) with respect thereto." Id. In this case, the court indicated that it was imposing sanctions in response to YRC's request and did not state that it was imposing sanctions on Hadges sua sponte. We doubt that sua sponte sanctions would have been justified here. The advisory committee note on the 1993 amendment specifically states that such sanctions "will ordinarily be [imposed] only in situations that are akin to a contempt of court." Hadges's conduct did not rise to that level.

Thus, under all the circumstances, particularly the failure to afford Hadges the 21-day safe-harbor period provided by revised Rule 11, we believe that the sanction of Hadges should be reversed.

2. Kunstler's censure

Like Hadges, Kunstler did not receive the benefit of the safe-harbor period. The district court imposed sanctions on Kunstler for failing to adequately investigate the truth of Hadges's representations prior to submitting them to the court and for failing to disclose that Hadges had brought an action against YRC in New York state court. Kunstler argues that the court's censure of him was an abuse of discretion because the court was motivated by a personal or political animus against him and because his conduct was not sufficiently egregious to justify imposition of sanctions.

In our decisions concerning the former version of Rule 11 we have had occasion to address the reasonableness of an attorney's reliance on information provided by a client. In Kamen v. American Tel. & Tel. Co., 791 F.2d 1006 (2d Cir. 1986), the plaintiff brought suit against her employer and supervisors under the Rehabilitation Act of 1973 and state law. Employers are not liable under the Rehabilitation Act unless they receive "federal financial assistance." 29 U.S.C. § 794. The

G. Veracity in Pleading: Rule 11 and Other Devices

employer sent letters to the plaintiff's attorney asserting that it did not receive federal financial assistance, but her attorney persisted in prosecuting the Rehabilitation Act suit. The district court agreed with the employer and dismissed the claims. Although the plaintiff's attorney had submitted an affirmation stating that his client had advised him that the employer received federal grants, the district court imposed sanctions. We found that the district court abused its discretion because the attorney's reliance on his client's statements was reasonable.

* * *

The new version of Rule 11 makes it even clearer that an attorney is entitled to rely on the objectively reasonable representations of the client. No longer are attorneys required to certify that their representations are "well grounded in fact." The current version of the Rule requires only that an attorney conduct "an inquiry reasonable under the circumstances" into whether "factual contentions have evidentiary support." Fed.R.Civ.P. 11(b) & (b)(3). * * *

In its first sanction decision in April 1994, the district court here stated:

> With respect to the plaintiff's counsel, William M. Kunstler, the situation is not quite as clear. There is nothing to indicate that, on the serious factual misrepresentations made in the plaintiff's papers, Mr. Kunstler had independent knowledge of their falsity. However, it is equally clear that he made no attempt to verify the truth of the plaintiff's representations prior to submitting them to the court.

Apparently, the district court did not focus, as Rule 11 now requires, on whether the pretrial proceedings provided "evidentiary support" for the factual misrepresentations with which the court was concerned.

It is clear that the record before the district court contained evidentiary support for Kunstler's incorrect statements. As to the scratching incident, the record included a sworn statement by Hadges describing an October 1989 incident in which he claimed to have been scratched from driving the horse "Me Gotta Bret." A scratch sheet, which did not reveal the year in which it was made out, was also part of the record. Kunstler later submitted an affidavit admitting the error and stating that he had no idea that the 1989 date was wrong. He further maintained that regardless of its date, the scratch sheet was relevant to show collaboration between the Racing Board and YRC in 1987, which would subject the latter to § 1983 liability. Moreover, it appears to be undisputed that most of the evidence YRC produced to persuade the court that the event had taken place in 1987 was within its possession, not Hadges's. See *Kamen*, 791 F.2d at 1012 (noting reasonableness of relying on client representations where "the relevant information [is] largely in the control of the defendants").

We also believe that the record contained evidentiary support for the claim that Hadges had not worked for four years. At the time the district court granted YRC summary judgment in Hadges's 60(b) action, it had before it Hadges's affidavit asserting that he had written to racetrack General Managers asking for driving privileges and had not received any replies. The record also contained attorney Faraldo's affidavit asserting that Hadges had followed his advice in writing these letters. Moreover, Kunstler represented Hadges in the Meadowlands suit in which Meadowlands admitted banning Hadges based upon the YRC ban. We believe that in light of his familiarity with the Meadowlands litigation and the sworn statements of his client and another attorney, Kunstler had sufficient evidence to support a belief that Hadges had not participated in harness horse racing in New York since the YRC ban.

The district court also believed that censure of Kunstler was justified because "he had to be aware of the recent state court litigation, still on appeal, but made no mention of it in his initial papers." Kunstler concedes that he was aware of this litigation but maintains that he did not believe that it was necessary to bring the proceedings to the court's attention because the New York Supreme Court had not ruled on the merits of the state law blackballing claim. As noted above, we agree with the view that the state court opinion was not a decision on the merits of that issue. Even if it were, there would be no tactical advantage in not mentioning the state court ruling to the district court since YRC was a party to both actions (indeed, it was represented by the same law firm and the same attorney in both actions) and could be expected to inform the district court of the state court action if it were helpful.

Moreover, the portion of the court's opinion in the Rule 60(b) action that listed the possible bases for imposition of sanctions omitted any reference to Kunstler's nondisclosure of the state court action. Rule 11 specifically requires that those facing sanctions receive adequate notice and the opportunity to respond. See Fed.R.Civ.P. 11(c)(1)(A) & (B). Although YRC had requested sanctions on this ground, as discussed above, that request was procedurally improper. Thus, although Kunstler would have been wiser to alert the court to the state court proceedings, the nondisclosure was not a proper ground for sanctioning him.

YRC maintains that sanctions were justified because the motions to reargue and to disqualify the district court judge were frivolous. As noted above, the court referred to the disqualification motion as a reason for sanctioning Hadges. However, the court did not rely upon it as a ground for the censure of Kunstler, and we decline to do so here.

Finally, the remarks of the district court, which we have quoted in substantial part above, contribute to our conclusion that the sanction of Kunstler was unjustified. These remarks have the appearance of a personal attack against Kunstler, and perhaps more broadly, against activist attorneys who represent unpopular clients or causes. We find the court's criticism of Kunstler's law partner, Ronald L. Kuby, for his activities in another case, especially unwarranted. For all these reasons, we reverse the imposition of the sanction of censure on Kunstler.

III. Conclusion

We have considered all of the parties' remaining arguments and find that they are without merit.

We affirm the ruling of the district court denying Rule 60(b) relief. We reverse the Rule 11 sanction of Hadges and the censure of Kunstler.

NOTES AND QUESTIONS

1. It appears from the court of appeals' description that Kunstler's primary argument to the district court in opposition to sanctions was that he represents unpopular clients. Is this a basis to avoid sanctions under Rule 11? There is no indication that he even pointed

G. Veracity in Pleading: Rule 11 and Other Devices

out the relevant language or provisions of the current Rule 11. Should he have been sanctioned for a frivolous defense to a Rule 11 motion? Are Rule 11 sanctions proper when a lawyer has a non-frivolous argument but only presents the frivolous one?

2. The court of appeals stressed the language of amended Rule 11 requiring only that factual contentions have evidentiary support. In light of this language, must a lawyer ever go beyond what her client tells her? Consider the following:

    (a) Client tells Lawyer about auto accident. Client says that she was hit by another car and that the other car ran a red light. Must lawyer review the police accident report or any other evidence before filing suit to determine if Client's story is consistent with this other evidence? *Probably yes.*

    (b) Lawyer does do some additional investigating and discovers that the police report and all witnesses to the accident (other than Client) state that it was Client who ran the red light and hit the other car. Is it a Rule 11 violation for the lawyer to file suit based on Client's story?

3. The district court sanctioned Kunstler for failing to mention that the state litigation was still on appeal. The court of appeals found that this was not a Rule 11 violation because "there would be no tactical advantage in not mentioning the state court ruling," since YRC's lawyers would be sure to inform the court of the appeal if they thought it was helpful. Couldn't a lawyer who fails to mention contrary authority always say that she assumed the other side would bring it up if it were important? Is this what Rule 11 contemplates?

4. Does the "safe harbor" provision provide too much protection for lawyers who fail to cite contrary authority? Suppose Defendant's lawyer knows there is a case that is largely contrary to her asserted position. Could the lawyer omit reference to the case and wait to see if Plaintiff's lawyer finds it? If Plaintiff's lawyer does find the case and serves a motion for sanctions, Defendant's lawyer can then amend her papers to explain why that case is distinguishable or should be overruled. If Plaintiff's lawyer never finds the case, Defendant does not have to address it.

5. It was clear that YRC did not comply with the safe harbor provisions of Rule 11. Upon receipt of the motion for sanctions should Kunstler have served (but not filed) a motion for sanctions for a frivolous Rule 11 motion? If YRC failed to withdraw its Rule 11 motion, Kunstler could then file his. Under the prior Rule 11, courts occasionally awarded Rule 11 sanctions for frivolous Rule 11 motions.

6. Rule 11 no longer applies to various discovery documents. For these, the discovery rules themselves provide for certification and sanctions, as we will see in Chapter 9.

7. The 1993 amendments to Rule 11 did not change everything about the rule. There is no question, for example, that the rule requires an objective assessment of the signer's inquiry, rather than an assessment of the signer's state of mind. See Business Guides, Inc. v. Chromatic Communications Ent., Inc., 498 U.S. 533 (1991). See 2A MOORE'S FEDERAL PRACTICE ¶ 11.02[3] (2d ed. 1994). Further, district court decisions under Rule 11 are reviewed on appeal by the "abuse of discretion" standard, which we will see in Chapter 14. Cooter & Gell v. Hartmarx Corp., 496 U.S. 384 (1990)(cited with approval in 1993 Note of Advisory Committee).

8. "Verified pleadings" are signed under oath (and, therefore, under penalty of perjury) and once were quite common. Indeed, the Field Code originally required verification of many pleadings, later changing to give the plaintiff an option to file a verified complaint, to which the defendant was required to respond with a verified answer.

Today, the federal courts and many states have abolished verified pleadings except in limited circumstances. Read Rules 23.1, 27(a), and 65(b). What purpose is served by requiring verification in such situations? Verified pleadings are still used widely in a few states. For discussion and review, see FRIEDENTHAL, KANE & MILLER, CIVIL PROCEDURE 264-66.

Verified pleadings may be of especial importance with summary judgment, a procedure which, as we will see in Chapter 10, usually involves the consideration of evidence that would be admissible at trial. Because verified pleadings are executed under penalty of perjury, they can constitute such evidence. Unverified pleadings cannot.

2. Other Sanctions

In addition to Rule 11, 28 U.S.C. § 1927 provides that any lawyer in federal court who "multiplies the proceeding in any case unreasonably and vexatiously may be required by the court to satisfy personally the excess costs, expenses and attorneys' fees reasonably incurred because of such conduct." Although the statute has been in existence since 1813, it, like the original Rule 11, was almost never invoked. However, after the 1983 amendment to Rule 11, courts and lawyers seemed to rediscover § 1927.

Section 1927 applies to all proceedings in any federal court. It can be applied to misconduct that is entirely oral. It also applies only to attorneys, not to parties or pro se litigants. There is a split among the circuits as to whether a showing of bad faith must be made in addition to a showing of objective unreasonableness. Compare Oliveri v. Thompson, 803 F.2d 1265 (2d Cir. 1986), *cert. denied*, 480 U.S. 918 (1987); Ford v. Temple Hospital, 790 F.2d 342 (3d Cir. 1986) (bad faith required), with Coleman v. Commissioner, 791 F.2d 68 (7th Cir. 1986) (objective unreasonableness sufficient).

G. Veracity in Pleading: Rule 11 and Other Devices

Section 1927 can be used to sanction frivolous appeals, but there are two other provisions addressed specifically to appeals — Rule 38 of the Federal Rules of Appellate Procedure and 28 U.S.C. § 1912. Although the language of the statute is not identical to the Rule, courts generally treat the two provisions as if they were redundant and rely primarily on the Rule. Rule 38 provides: "If a court of appeals shall determine that an appeal is frivolous, it may award just damages and single and double costs to the appellee." The damages awarded may include attorney's fees.

In the absence of a statute or rule, courts have the "inherent power" to sanction bad faith conduct by litigants or counsel. This fact was reasserted forcefully in Chambers v. NASCO, 501 U.S. 32 (1991). In that case, the Court affirmed a district court's order that the losing party in a breach of contract case pay nearly $1,000,000 in attorney's fees to the prevailing party. Even though some of the conduct sanctioned was not covered by either Rule 11 or § 1927, the Court upheld the full award, explaining that courts have "inherent power" to police and punish those before it. Notwithstanding *Chambers*, courts are unlikely to rely on inherent power if a rule or statute applies to the conduct in question. In addition, a court must provide procedural safeguards (such as notice and an opportunity to be heard) to the sanctioned party or lawyer.

Rules 11 and 38, sections 1927 and 1912, and "inherent power" are all bases on which a court can impose sanctions intended to punish improper conduct. Other Rules permit the prevailing party to recover "costs" from the losing side. See Rule 54(d); F.R.App.P. 39. These are not intended as punishment but simply as reimbursement for the winning party. As noted before, "costs" include various litigation expenses, but do not include attorney's fees. The "American Rule" is that each side bears its own attorney's fees, though there are some important statutory exceptions to this rule. See, e.g., 15 U.S.C. § 26 (antitrust); 42 U.S.C. § 2000e-5(k)(civil rights). For a helpful discussion, see Thomas Rowe, *The Legal Theory of Attorney Fee Shifting: A Critical Overview*, 1982 DUKE L.J. 651.

CHAPTER 9

DISCOVERY

A. Introduction and Integration

In Chapter 8 we saw that the Federal Rules of Civil Procedure do not require the inclusion of much factual detail in pleadings. Rather, modern procedure leaves the detailed disclosure of facts for the discovery phase of litigation. This chapter focuses on the discovery* provisions of the Federal Rules. Although those provisions apply only in federal court, most states have adopted discovery rules that largely mirror the Federal Rules.

The discovery rules were one of the most significant innovations introduced by the Federal Rules. The Rules vastly expand the availability of discovery over earlier provisions and make the process litigant driven. The quantity and timing of the information sought is left almost entirely to the parties with judicial intervention only when there is a problem.

The discovery rules serve three basic purposes. They permit the preservation of evidence that might otherwise be lost before trial, provide mechanisms for narrowing the issues in dispute between the parties, and permit the parties to acquire greater information about their own and the other side's case. The first two of these purposes are largely uncontroversial and if they were the only goals they probably could be accomplished through far less extensive discovery than is permitted by the rules. It is the last purpose which is both the most unique to the American system and the source of the most debate.

There are two types of information to which the discovery rules permit access. First, the discovery rules allow parties to learn, well in advance of trial, what evidence the other side has in support of its claims or defenses. This is beneficial for several reasons. By eliminating the element of surprise, the trial may be less of a sporting event that rewards quick wits and be more likely to produce a just result. After all, "the purpose of litigation is not to conduct a contest or to oversee a game of skill, but to do justice as between the

---

* There is an enormous range of informal, non-compulsory mechanisms by which lawyers acquire information about a case. Lawyers interview their clients, talk to witnesses, inspect the scene, and hire private detectives. In addition to these mechanisms, the rules of procedure give lawyers tools by which they can *compel* others to disclose, in advance of trial, information relevant to a case. Thus, although there are many ways by which lawyers can discover information, the word "discovery" usually refers to those compulsory processes permitted by the rules of procedure.

CHAPTER 9 DISCOVERY

parties and to decide controversies on their merits." Alexander Holtzoff, *The Elimination of Surprise in Federal Practice*, 7 VAND. L. REV. 576, 577 (1954). The discovery rules were intended to "make a trial less a game of blind man's bluff and more a fair contest with the basic issues and facts disclosed to the fullest practicable extent." United States v. Procter & Gamble Co., 356 U.S. 677, 683 (1958).

Better knowledge of the other side's evidence may also lead to quicker and fairer settlements of disputes. In theory, each party should be willing to settle for the expected value of a claim. The expected value of a claim equals the possible value, discounted by the probability of receiving that judgment, minus the costs. Thus, a plaintiff who believes that she has a 50% likelihood of receiving a $1 million verdict should be willing to settle for $500,000, minus the costs necessary to achieve that verdict. If the defendant agrees that the plaintiff has a 50% likelihood of $1 million verdict, the defendant should be willing to offer $500,000, minus expected costs. By exchanging information, the parties are more likely to reach agreement on both the size of the possible verdict and its likelihood, and, thus, they are more likely to settle without incurring the expense of trial.* See Steven Shavell, *Suit, Settlement, and Trial: A Theoretical Analysis Under Alternative Methods for the Allocation of Legal Costs*, 11 J. LEG. STUD. 55, 57–58 (1982).

The elimination of surprise is not without costs. The possibility of surprise may have the salutary effect of discouraging perjury or other manipulation of evidence. As one judge has written:

> A certain amount of surprise is often the catalyst which precipitates the truth. Alternatively it may serve as a medium by which the court or jury may gauge the accuracy of the account.
>
> If every witness consistently told the truth, and none cut his cloth to the wind, little possible harm and much good might come from maximum pretrial disclosure. Experience indicates, however, that there are facile witnesses whose interest in "knowing the truth before trial" is prompted primarily by a desire to find the most plausible way to defeat the truth.

Margeson v. Boston & M. R.R., 16 F.R.D. 200, 201 (D. Mass. 1954). In criminal cases, discovery is far more limited than in civil cases and a primary justification for this is the fear of witness intimidation and perjury.

The discovery rules also permit parties to acquire information for the purpose of strengthening their own cases. In many types of cases, the strongest evidence of wrongdoing will be in the possession of the alleged wrongdoer. Without access to this information,

---

* Of course, even where parties know a great deal about the other side's proof, cases don't always settle. One side may persist in an unrealistic assessment, or parties may be motivated by a non-economic desire for justice, revenge or to establish a principle.

some wrongful conduct would go uncompensated because the plaintiff would not have the necessary proof.

Some people object to the use of discovery for this purpose. They view it as wrong and unfair to require a party to produce evidence that may ultimately be used against that party. The Fifth Amendment, which protects criminal defendants from self incrimination, reflects this concern. Concern about fairness also partially explains the limited discovery permitted in civil law countries. The German Supreme Court, in describing its discovery rules, has explained:

> A request for evidence is designed to enable the requesting party to prove contested facts that it already knows, not to find out facts that it does not know. For it is fundamental that no party is obligated to help its adversary to victory by furnishing him with information that he does not already have.*

Decision of Supreme Court (Bundesgerichtshof) of May 4, 1964, 17 Neue Juristische Wochenschrift 1414 (1964).

Today, the greatest concerns about our discovery system focus less on the underlying theory of the system and more on how discovery is practiced in modern litigation. Discovery can be expensive and time consuming. Moreover, many lawyers and judges believe that discovery is increasingly used "as a weapon rather than an information gathering mechanism." Interim Report of the Committee on Civility of the Seventh Federal Judicial Circuit, 143 F.R.D. 371, 387 (1991). One report concluded that "[d]iscovery has become a battlefield on which verbal hostility, overly aggressive tactics and often automatic and unreasoned denials of cooperation are the principal weapons." Id. at 383. In response to these concerns, several significant and controversial changes to the discovery rules were promulgated in 1993. We will highlight these changes at appropriate places throughout the Chapter.

Despite criticism and some changes, discovery remains integral to the procedures set forth in the Federal Rules. It is through discovery that the parties identify and refine the issues that are actually disputed. As a result, trials may be shorter and less confusing for the factfinder. Moreover, the honing of issues may permit the court to dispose of issues (or of the entire case) through the device of summary judgment, which we will study in Chapter 10. Thus, modern practice allocates to discovery the important tasks of defining and narrowing the disputed issues for trial, a task earlier systems relegated to the pleading phase.

---

* A number of countries have laws, including criminal sanctions, "designed to thwart efforts by United States courts to secure production of documents situated abroad." Russell Weintraub, *International Litigation and Forum Non Conveniens*, 29 TEX. INT'L. L. J. 321, 337 (1994).

CHAPTER 9 DISCOVERY

B. Overview of the Discovery Devices

The discovery rules offer five basic devices for acquiring information. As you read about each device, you should read the corresponding rules.

1. Depositions (Rules 30, 31)

In a deposition, a witness is placed under oath and responds to questions, in much the same way that a witness testifies at trial. Unlike a trial, at a deposition there is no judge present — only the witness, the lawyers, and a court officer designated to administer oaths. See Rule 28. Anyone with discoverable information can be deposed. When a party seeks information from a corporation or other organization, but does not know who within the organization would be the most knowledgeable, the party can name the organization as the deponent and describe the matters on which information is sought. The organization must then identify the appropriate person to be deposed. See Rule 30(b)(6).

Traditionally, depositions have been stenographically recorded by a court reporter and transcribed. The 1993 amendments to the Rules permit depositions to be recorded electronically, see Rule 30(b)(2), with a transcript required only if the deposition is later offered into evidence. See Rule 32(c).

Depositions can be a very effective way to learn what an individual knows about a particular matter. They can also be quite expensive. Depositions lasting six hours or longer are not uncommon. The cost of a court reporter to record and transcribe a day long deposition can be close to $1000. In addition, each party must bear the expense of the time her attorney spends preparing for and attending the deposition.

As a result of concern that lawyers were over-using depositions, the 1993 revisions impose a presumptive limit of ten depositions per side. See Rule 30(a)(2)(A). This limit may be altered by stipulation of the parties or by court order. In addition, the revisions attempt to expedite depositions by limiting the type and form of objections that can be raised at depositions. See Rule 30(d)(1).

Rule 31 permits a variation of the traditional oral deposition. Under this rule, a party may serve on the other parties a set of questions that will be asked a witness. The court officer then swears in the witness and asks the questions to the witness. The advantage is that the lawyer need not attend the deposition. The disadvantages are that the witness is likely to know in advance exactly the questions that will be asked and there is no opportunity for follow up questions based on the responses received.

QUESTIONS

1. (a) Who can be deposed?
   (b) If you want to take someone's deposition, what do you have to do? 30(b)2
   (c) Where can the deposition of a party be taken? 30(b)4
   (d) Suppose you send a notice of deposition to the other party and she doesn't show up, what sanctions are available? See Rule 37(d). Suppose she shows up but refuses to answer some of your questions. What can you do? What sanctions are available? See Rule 37(a) & (b).
   (e) Where can the deposition of a non-party witness be taken? See Rule 45.
   (f) Suppose you send a notice of deposition to a non-party witness who doesn't show up. What sanctions are available against *you*? See Rule 30(g)(2). What can you do to avoid being subject to sanctions for a no-show witness? See Rule 45. Why do you think party and non-party witnesses are treated differently?

2. Interrogatories (Rule 33)

Under Rule 33, any party may send any other party written questions that require a written response under oath. These can be a far less expensive and more effective device than depositions for acquiring detailed, objective information. In a deposition, a witness is required to answer based on the knowledge and information she has at the time of the deposition. In contrast, in responding to interrogatories, parties are required to provide facts that are reasonably available to them, even if this requires reviewing files of documents, though parties are not required to supply information that they do not already have. Thus, a party would not be required to conduct new tests to answer interrogatories.

Interrogatories also have limitations. Because answers to interrogatories are typically drafted by the party's lawyer, interrogatories are not an effective device for ascertaining the testimony or credibility of particular witnesses. They are, however, a useful way to get objective information including names, dates and lists of documents. They can also pave the way for other discovery by, for example, identifying people with information whom it may be appropriate to depose. Interrogatories can also be used to clarify the allegations set forth in the pleadings. For example, in a tort case in which the plaintiff generally alleged negligence, the defendant could include an interrogatory asking in what respect defendant's conduct was negligent. See Rule 33(c).

The 1993 amendments impose a presumptive limit of 25 interrogatories (including subparts) per party. See Rule 33(a). As with the limit on the number of depositions, this presumptive limit can be modified by stipulation or court order.

CHAPTER 9 DISCOVERY

QUESTIONS

2. (a) To whom may interrogatories be directed?
   (b) How long does the recipient of the interrogatories have to respond?
   (c) Suppose the recipient of interrogatories considers some of the questions burdensome or irrelevant. What can she do?
   (d) Suppose the recipient of the interrogatories does not respond or responds incompletely. What can the sender do? What sanctions are available? See Rule 37(a), (b) & (d).

3. Production of Documents and Things (Rule 34)

There are many situations in which documentary or physical evidence may be critical to proving what happened and why. Rule 34 permits a party to require another party to produce for inspection, copying, or testing all relevant documents or other tangible things. In most cases, Rule 34 is used to compel the production of relevant documents. Note, however, how much more information is available through this device. For example, in a patent infringement case, a party can use Rule 34 to gain access to the allegedly offending widget. In a property dispute, a party can gain access to land to run geologic tests or surveys.

QUESTIONS

3. (a) To whom may requests for production be directed?
   (b) How does a party secure documents or tangible things from a non-party? See Rules 34(c), 45. A subpoena commanding production of items is generally referred to as a "subpoena duces tecum."
   (c) What sanctions are available if a party fails to respond or responds incompletely to the request for production? See Rule 37(a), (b) & (d).

4. Medical Examination (Rule 35)

When the health, physical, or mental condition of a party is in controversy, the court may order the party to submit to a physical or mental examination by a "suitably licensed or certified examiner." Unlike the other discovery devices, for which the intervention of the court is not ordinarily required, Rule 35 requires a court order. The order is appropriate only where the movant shows "good cause" and the mental or physical condition is "in controversy." The Supreme Court has said of these requirements:

> They are not met by mere conclusory allegations of the pleadings — nor by mere relevance to the case — but require an affirmative showing by the movant that each condition as to which the examination is sought is really and genuinely in controversy and that good cause exists for ordering each particular examination. Obviously, what may be good cause for one type of examination may not be so for another. The ability of the movant to obtain the deserved information by other means is also relevant.

Schlagenhauf v. Holder, 379 U.S. 104, 118 (1964).

QUESTIONS

4. (a) If a party refuses to submit to an ordered physical exam, what sanctions are available? See Rule 37(b)(2)(E).
   (b) Under Rule 35(b)(1), the person being examined is entitled to request a copy of the examiner's report. Are there reasons why the person being examined might not request the report? See Rule 35(b)(2).
   (c) Under Rule 35, could the court order a party to submit to an examination by a physical therapist (who is not a physician)? A chiropractor?
   (d) Suppose one party believes that a non-party eyewitness has very poor eye sight. Upon motion, can the court order the witness to submit to an eye exam under Rule 35?
   (e) Following a bus accident, injured passengers sue the bus company (but not the driver). For good cause shown, can the court order a physical exam of the driver?

5. Requests for Admission (Rule 36)

Requests for admission are used to determine what issues are and are not in dispute. By identifying contested issues early, both side can conserve resources. Rule 36 is valuable for its limited purpose of narrowing the issues, but is not an effective device for acquiring detailed knowledge of the evidence.

CHAPTER 9 DISCOVERY

QUESTIONS

5. (a) To whom may requests for admission be directed? *[handwritten: not on non-party]*
   (b) What happens if the recipient simply ignores the requests for admission and does not respond? See Rule 36(a). *[handwritten: it is admitted]*
   (c) Suppose the recipient of a request for admission denies a fact that is later established at trial, what sanctions are available? See Rule 37(c).

6. Practice Problem

Kay Robinson and two of her children were badly burned when the Audi in which they were driving was hit by another car and the Robinsons' car exploded in flames. The Robinsons have filed suit against Audi in federal court alleging defective design and manufacture of the car. The plaintiffs believe that the location of the gas tank made it more susceptible to puncture in a rear end collision and that there was insufficient fire protection between the gas tank and the passenger compartment. They have the name and address of one eye witness to the crash. Prepare a discovery plan for the Robinsons. What types of information would you like to acquire? Which discovery devices should you use for which kinds of information? Which discovery requests would you serve first?*

C. Scope of Discovery

1. General Scope

Rule 26(b)(1) addresses the scope of discovery but does not delineate what evidence will be *admissible* at trial. In federal court, admissibility of evidence is governed by the Federal Rules of Evidence, a set of rules that you will study in detail in an Evidence course. Rule 26(b)(1) specifically provides that "[t]he information sought need not be admissible at the trial if the information sought appears reasonably calculated to lead to the discovery of admissible evidence."

The following questions are based on the Robinsons' suit against Audi. Can you articulate a reason for allowing discovery of the evidence described below even though it would be admissible at trial?

---

* Discovery of information in foreign countries presents some complications. See generally Darrell Prescott & Edwin Alley, *Effective Evidence-Taking Under the Hague Convention*, 22 INT'L LAW 939 (1988). For purposes of this question, you may ignore all of the international issues.

C. Scope of Discovery

(a) "Hearsay" is evidence that comes not from the knowledge of the witness but from mere repetition of what the witness has heard others say. Hearsay is generally inadmissible, although there are a number of exceptions. See Fed. R. Evid. 801-805. Under the hearsay rules, Mrs. Jones, a witness to the Robinsons' accident, would be permitted to testify that she heard brakes screech. She would not be permitted to testify that her husband told her that he heard brakes screech. At a deposition of Mrs. Jones is it permissible to ask here what her husband told her about what he heard?

(b) Evidence of other similar accidents may be inadmissible. Although there is not specific rule addressing this issue, courts will frequently exclude such evidence on the grounds that its prejudicial effect outweighs its probative value. Courts are concerned that a jury may decide that whether or not the defendant is responsible for the injuries in the case at hand, it was responsible for other previous yet unrelated injuries and therefore it is fair to hold the defendant liable in this case. Should the Robinsons be permitted to discover from Audi any evidence Audi has about other similar incidents?

Roesberg v. Johns-Manville Corp.
85 F.R.D. 292 (E.D. Pa. 1980)

TROUTMAN, DISTRICT JUDGE.

Laborers working with, handling and using asbestos, material containing asbestos, and asbestos products and compounds have instituted litigation with increasing frequency to recover compensatory damages for asbestos-related respiratory and cardiovascular diseases such as asbestosis, mesothelioma, scarred lungs, lung cancer and other tissue and bone disorders. Plaintiff, an insulator associated with Local 14 of the Asbestos Workers' Union from 1942 to 1977 and employed by various companies during this time period, continually worked and allegedly came in constant contact with asbestos products mined, manufactured, produced, processed, compounded, converted, sold, merchandised and distributed by defendants, whom plaintiff alleges knew, could or should have known were inherently defective, ultrahazardous, dangerous, deleterious, poisonous and "otherwise highly harmful" to plaintiff and other employees. More specifically, plaintiff charges defendants with failing to take reasonable precautions or to exercise reasonable care in warning plaintiff adequately; to provide plaintiff with knowledge of reasonable safeguards such as wearing apparel and safety equipment and appliances for protection from asbestos dust and fibers; to place on containers of asbestos products warnings emphasizing potential risks, dangers and harm resulting from use and handling thereof; to package asbestos products in a manner designed to avoid contact with, exposure to and inhalation of asbestos dust and fibers from these products; to make efforts reasonably calculated to inform plaintiff of the inherently dangerous and harmful effects thereof; to take any reasonable precaution or to exercise care to protect plaintiff from the harms and dangers thereof; to adopt and enforce safety regulations, plans or methods for plaintiff while working therewith; to test adequately asbestos products before offering them for sale and use by plaintiff; to render asbestos products safe or to provide proper and sufficient safeguards for the use and handling thereof; to remove and recall asbestos products from the stream of commerce upon learning that they could cause injuries similar to those of which plaintiff complains; to comply with the Federal Hazardous Substance Act, 15 U.S.C. § 1261 et seq.; and to advise plaintiff, whom defendants knew, could or should have known had been exposed to long-term contact therewith and to terminate this exposure, to have plaintiff examined by a lung specialist or to receive treatment for any diseases caused by contact, exposure or inhalation thereof.

Continuing, plaintiff alleges breach of an implied warranty that the asbestos products were reasonably fit for use and safe for their intended purposes. Plaintiff complains that the products were defective in that they were incapable of being made safe for their ordinary and intended use and purpose because of their intrinsically dangerous and ultrahazardous nature. Plaintiff also accuses defendants, individually and in conspiracy with one another, of manufacturing, selling and distributing these products despite knowledge on their part of the products' unreasonably dangerous, ultrahazardous and potentially carcinogenic and lethal effects, of concealing this knowledge from plaintiff willfully and fraudulently, and of keeping plaintiff ignorant of his rights not only by concealing the nature and extent of harm suffered by using asbestos products and the causal relationship between them but also by inducing plaintiff to rely in good faith on these fraudulent representations.

Finally, plaintiff claims that defendants intentionally and fraudulently withheld or misrepresented medical conditions *of* and altered other material and significant medical information *about* other asbestos workers and employees, including plaintiff, by reviewing and altering medical records and test results to prevent discovery of plaintiff's actual medical condition, to deter or sacrifice plaintiff's ability to file workmen's compensation or other disability claims, to obtain proper medical care, to increase the risk of harm and further complications arising from asbestos-related diseases, to prevent plaintiff and others from exercising the option of terminating their employment because of unsafe health conditions or taking precautionary safety measures on their own behalf, and to prevent, limit or otherwise bar plaintiff's right to seek compensatory and/or punitive damages. The last portion of the alleged conspiracy involves defendants' efforts to "camouflage and make indistinguishable" these products so that injured plaintiffs would not know the true identity thereof. In furtherance of the alleged conspiracy, defendants supposedly entered into "occult relabelling and distribution agreements" and intentionally and fraudulently manufactured products without labels or salient characteristics and with identical colors, textures and appearances in order to deceive users, including plaintiff, and to limit and exclude liability from claims brought by injured users.

In September 1979 plaintiffs filed fifty-seven separate interrogatories with all defendants, of which one, GAF Corporation (GAF), answered six but objected to the others as "overly broad," "burdensome," "oppressive," "not reasonably calculated to lead to discoverable evidence" and "privileged." [The interrogatories are reproduced in the Appendix at the end of the opinion.] Plaintiffs then moved to compel answers thereto, and the magistrate so ordered. GAF now appeals from that order.

C. Scope of Discovery

Recently describing the scope of discovery under Federal Rule of Civil Procedure 26(b)(1), this court ruled that

> "[r]elevancy, and to a lesser extent burdensomeness, constitute the principal inquiry in ruling upon objections to interrogatories. In the interests of fair trial, eliminating surprise and achieving justice, relevancy, construed liberally, creates a broad vista for discovery, ... and makes trial 'less a game of blind man's bluff and more a fair contest with the basic issues and facts disclosed to the fullest practicable extent.' United States v. Proctor & Gamble Co., 356 U.S. 677, 682 (1958)."

Additionally, the facts and circumstances of each case determine and limit relevance of interrogatories.

In Interrogatory Number Three plaintiff seeks to discover asbestos products which GAF manufactured, processed, compounded, converted, sold, supplied or distributed since 1925. GAF's primary objection to this interrogatory is the broad time frame included by plaintiff, whose employment spanned the years 1942 to 1977. However, plaintiff alleges conspiracies antedating plaintiff's employment history and intended to disguise and distort information which would have suggested to plaintiff the unreasonably dangerous and ultrahazardous nature of working with asbestos. Accordingly, plaintiff's selected time frame is not wholly unreasonable or irrelevant. Such a request for discovery should be considered relevant

> "if there is any possibility that the information sought may be relevant to the subject matter of the action ... Discovery should ordinarily be allowed under the concept of relevancy unless it is clear that the information sought can have no possible bearing upon the subject matter of the action ... The scope of examination by interrogatories should not be curtailed unless the information sought is clearly irrelevant."

Plaintiff's request falls squarely within the limits of the subject matter of this action.

GAF also complains that the word "associated" in subsection (b) is vague and ambiguous. The meaning of this verb is clear in the context of the principal part of the interrogatory, in which plaintiff asks GAF to itemize all asbestos products which GAF manufactured, processed, compounded, converted, sold, supplied and distributed.

Finally, GAF objects generally to this interrogatory as "overly broad, burdensome, oppressive and irrelevant," a complaint which GAF echoes with virtually every other interrogatory. To voice a successful objection to an interrogatory, GAF cannot simply intone this familiar litany. Rather, GAF must show specifically how, despite the broad and liberal construction afforded the federal discovery rules, each interrogatory is not relevant or how each question is overly broad, burdensome or oppressive, by submitting affidavits or offering evidence revealing the nature of the burden. The court is not required to "sift each interrogatory to determine the usefulness of the answer sought." The detail in the complaint specifies the necessary relevance of the interrogatories. The burden now falls upon GAF, the party resisting discovery, to clarify and explain its objections and to provide support therefor. The number and detailed character of interrogatories is not alone sufficient reason for disallowing them unless the questions are "egregiously burdensome or oppressive." Nor is the fact that answering the interrogatories will require the objecting party to expend considerable time, effort and expense, or may interfere with defendant's business operations. General objections without specific support may result in waiver of the objections. In most instances GAF has failed to so elaborate, and the objection to Interrogatory Three is typical.

In Interrogatory Number Four plaintiff seeks to determine the nature and extent of GAF's advertising, if any, in which GAF claimed safety and efficacy of products. Plaintiff has alleged that GAF made false claims about the safety of a product which plaintiff avers in unreasonably dangerous and ultrahazardous. The relevance of this interrogatory to plaintiff's claim is obvious.

In Interrogatory Number Five plaintiff seeks to determine whether defendant ever advised ultimate product purchasers or users of potential cancers or other diseases possibly contractible by use of or exposure to GAF products. GAF specifically claims that the portion of the interrogatory "that your products could cause cancer, asbestosis and other serious diseases" is argumentative, presumptive and conclusory. However, the first part of plaintiff's question simply requires an affirmative or negative response. Did GAF specifically inform purchasers or users of its products that the product could cause cancer? If the products carried no such warning, the appropriate response would be "no," and no conclusion or assumption could be drawn from that answer alone that the products caused cancer. If the products did carry such a warning, plaintiffs are entitled to know exactly what warning appeared on the products. That an interrogatory may contain an element of conclusion is not objectionable on this ground alone, for allegations of negligence in a tort complaint typically teem with legal conclusions which are not ipso facto objectionable or excludable.

In Interrogatory Number Six plaintiff seeks identification of all labeling and/or relabeling agreements between GAF and third parties as defined by the instructions to the interrogatories. In view of plaintiff's allegations of a conspiracy among GAF and other defendants to produce products without labels or with deceptive ones, the relevancy of this information seems clear. That answering the interrogatory requires investigation will not support denying plaintiff's access thereto when GAF has not shown how or why the investigation will be unreasonable.

In Interrogatories Number Seven through Nine plaintiff seeks to discover the chain of distribution in which GAF engaged and/or its suppliers of asbestos products. Alternatively, if GAF does not manufacture or produce asbestos, plaintiff desires information concerning its duties within the commercial chain of distribution. GAF objects to the vagueness and ambiguity of plaintiff's terms "chain of distribution" and "with which you had business contact." Since plaintiffs have not assigned a particular meaning to these phrases, the ordinary, everyday usage and meaning must have been intended. Specifically, in Interrogatory Number Eight, asking GAF to identify its distributors and/or suppliers of raw asbestos, asbestos cement and other asbestos products "with which you had business contact," plaintiff essentially seeks information about any asbestos-type products which GAF has dealt with commercially. In Interrogatory Seven, requesting identification of the "distribution chain" plaintiff simply asks GAF to identify the original source of asbestos and to trace its commercial progress therefrom to GAF and to state to whom GAF sends products once it has completed its process. The requirement that interrogatories be definite is satisfied so long as it is clear what the interrogatory asks. Both phrases which plaintiff used are sufficiently comprehensible in order to allow GAF to respond meaningfully.

* * *

In Interrogatories Number Fourteen through Sixteen plaintiff seeks to elicit whether GAF educated anyone as to the reported dangers resulting from working with and exposure to asbestos and certain enumerated diseases. More specifically, the interrogatories seek to determine when and

C. Scope of Discovery

if GAF has ever been aware that insulators and contractors working inside and outside of confined areas might be subjecting themselves to diseases and other health hazards by using or exposing themselves to asbestos or asbestos products. GAF objects to Interrogatory Fourteen as presumptive and conclusory. However, in light of plaintiff's allegations, defendant cannot avoid answering this interrogatory because the question presumes hazardous conditions or the necessity of safety precautions. If GAF did not inform insulators and customers of any hazards, GAF should so state. At this point in time, before plaintiff has proven any causal connection between his alleged condition and working with asbestos, no adverse inference can be drawn. If GAF did provide such a warning, plaintiff is entitled to know exactly what the warning said.

* * *

In Interrogatories Number Seventeen through Twenty-two plaintiff seeks to elicit GAF's knowledge of findings of governmental agencies relating to potential health hazards associated with asbestos and asbestos products and what procedures (such as medical examination programs, financing of laboratory results) GAF followed. Since GAF did not employ plaintiff, GAF argues, he is not entitled to information concerning GAF's plant. However, in view of plaintiff's allegations that plaintiff handled products which flowed through GAF in a chain of distribution or manufacture, this information may be relevant or *may lead to* relevant information. This "may lead to" requirement means only that the request have a reasonable possibility of leading to admissible evidence. To deny an interrogatory of this type would thwart the purposes of the Federal Rules of Civil Procedure and would "enthrone theoretical considerations of logical symmetry above the practical requirements of everyday litigation." In the case at bar to conclude now that the requested information is clearly irrelevant or has no possible bearing on the subject matter defeats the "no surprise" animating spirit of federal discovery rules. GAF also submits that requiring GAF to answer that part of the interrogatory exploring the programs sponsored by GAF's insurance carrier requires GAF to provide information "which is not and cannot be in the knowledge or control of this Defendant." If, indeed, this statement accurately describes the situation, then GAF should simply state that it has no such knowledge. The expedition which accompanies cooperation of this kind is demonstrated readily by GAF's answer to Interrogatory Eighteen, which inquired of any tests performed by GAF and examining the relationship between asbestos exposure and asbestos-related diseases. GAF answered this interrogatory "GAF did not cause any tests or studies to be done or receive any results there from." A negative response by GAF to this part of the interrogatory will end the inquiry as far as its insurance carrier is concerned.

In Interrogatories Number Twenty-three through Twenty-six plaintiff seeks to determine the extent and nature of GAF's knowledge and relationship with one Dr. Irvin J. Selikoff and the Mount Sinai School of Medicine and whether GAF ever made its employees and others aware of the information and studies conducted by Dr. Selikoff since 1963. "Familiar with," a term used by plaintiff in Interrogatory Twenty-three, is impermissibly vague, argues GAF. However, the term as used certainly seems to ask GAF whether it *knew of* Dr. Selikoff and his work. If GAF did, it should so state.

CHAPTER 9 DISCOVERY

* * *

In Interrogatories Fifty-four and Fifty-five plaintiff seeks to ascertain the identity of present or former GAF employees who testified against GAF in litigation or administrative hearings about diseases and health hazards associated with the use of and exposure to asbestos and asbestos products. Additionally, plaintiff requests GAF to identify any transcripts or notes of testimony engendered thereby. GAF's objections include only the routine ones. Testimony from other lawsuits instigated against GAF by former or present employees to recover for injuries resulting from use of asbestos and asbestos products could hardly be more relevant to plaintiff's claims, and plaintiff tailored this request as narrowly as possible. In Renshaw v. Ravert, 82 F.R.D. 361 (E.D. Pa. 1979), the plaintiff brought a civil rights action against the city and police officers. The court required answers to plaintiff's interrogatories relating to prior suits or disciplinary proceedings against these officers concerning abuse of lawful authority and the eventual disposition of these matters. In Dollar v. Long Manufacturing, N.C., Inc., 561 F.2d 613 (5th Cir. 1971), the Court of Appeals held that the trial court committed reversible error by refusing to compel answers to interrogatories seeking information about the existence and details of other injuries and deaths resulting from the use of a backhoe which caused the death of plaintiff's decedent, even though some of the other injuries occurred after the decedent's death. These later accidents, the court stated, could not be relevant to defendant's prior knowledge or notice of a defective product, but the information would be relevant to the issue of causation. *A fortiori*, in the case at bar information from other actions instituted against GAF will bear directly on both the issues of prior notice and causation.

* * *

In light of plaintiff's panoply of allegations his interrogatories have been tailored carefully to establish both the nature and extent of GAF's knowledge of the interrelationship between handling asbestos products and asbestos-related diseases and what GAF did in connection therewith. Clearly this information relates to any duty GAF may have had to refrain from manufacturing or distributing unreasonably dangerous or ultrahazardous goods and whether GAF breached that duty. In a nutshell these interrogatories aim at establishing notice and causation. The exactitude of discovery, the lawyer's tool for factfinding, properly lies somewhere between the acuity of the surgeon's scalpel and the carpenter's hammer. Ideally, the lawyer probes for facts with the precision and delicacy of a cardiologist incising the aorta to receive a by-pass vehicle. Realistically, the lawyer's factfinding search shares a closer propinquity with the carpenter's trade and pounds much more bluntly. Balancing the one party's need for discovery against the other party's burden in producing it requires honing the need as narrowly as possible to prevent unreasonable burden. In the case at bar plaintiff has attained this desideratum artfully. The magistrate granted plaintiff's motion to compel, and his order is not contrary to law or an abuse of discretion. Accordingly, the order of the magistrate will be affirmed and plaintiff's motion to compel will be granted.

Appendix

1. Identify the registered name of answering defendant, as well as all prior names or predecessor entities by which defendant has existed.

C. Scope of Discovery

2. Identify all divisions, subsidiaries or affiliated companies to answering defendant, having any function which now or in the past engaged in any phase of mining, manufacturing, sale supply or distribution of asbestos or asbestos products. With respect to each of such divisions, subsidiaries or companies, identify the nature and extent of such functions during the relevant periods of time in which such activities have or had occurred.

3. Identify each and every asbestos product, from 1925 to the present, which answering defendant manufactured, processed, compounded, converted, sold, supplied or distributed. With each such product:
   (a) State in which phase of commerce defendant engaged;
   (b) State during what period of time such product has been associated with defendant;
   (c) Identify all sales literature, including brochures, advertisements, pamphlets or other material describing such product, its uses and methods of application or installation;
   (d) State how such product was packaged, transported, stored or supplied;
   (e) Identify any warning labels, inserts or other writings provided with such product and with every such printed warning, state what period of time it has or had accompanied the product, the exact wording of the warning, any amendments made to the wording, where the warning was located on each product or packaging, and on what asbestos products the warnings appear(ed);
   (f) Identify any special instructions provided with such product regarding the use, protection or safety procedures to be employed by Persons handling such product.

4. With respect to your Answer to Interrogatory #3, did you claim your product(s) to be either safe, effective and/or easy to handle? If so, identify all such Documents, including but not limited to brochures or advertisements (radio, television or printed), and revisions thereof by publication(s) and date.

5. With respect to your Answer to Interrogatory #3, did you specifically inform the purchaser or user of your products during the same time period that your products could cause cancer, asbestosis, and other serious diseases? If so, identify the Document containing such information by date and location.

6. Identify any and all labeling or relabeling agreements in existence since 1925 between answering defendant and other Persons, including other defendants.

7. Identify the distribution chain of defendant's asbestos products since 1925 along with any Documents evidencing or confirming such chain, including but not limited to distribution from and to other defendants.

8. Identify your distributors and/or suppliers of raw asbestos, asbestos cement and other asbestos products with which you had business contact.

9. As to any answering defendant *not* engaged in some phase of production, state:
   (a) Whether defendant is or was a supplier, distributor or contractor of asbestos products;
   (b) For which of the other defendants answering defendant engaged in such activities;
   (c) Over what period of time and in what geographical area such activities were conducted;
   (d) With which asbestos products were answering defendants involved in such activities;
   (e) What warnings, safety procedures or methods were employed by answering defendants to protect persons against hazards from exposure to said asbestos or asbestos products.

10. As to any answering defendant engaged, inter alia, in production, state:
    (a) Whether defendant is or was a supplier, distributor or contractor of such products;
    (b) For which of the other defendants answering defendant engaged in such activities;
    (c) Over what period of time and in what geographical area such activities were conducted;
    (d) With which asbestos products were answering defendants involved in such activities;
    (e) What warnings, safety procedures or methods were employed by answering defendant to protect persons against hazards from exposure to said asbestos or asbestos products.

11. Is answering defendant aware or possessed of knowledge concerning the reported causal connection between exposure to asbestos or asbestos products and:
    (a) asbestosis?
    (b) lung cancer?
    (c) mesothelioma?
    (d) other cancers?

12. If your answer to Interrogatory #11, as to any or all of its subparts, is the affirmative, Identify:
    (a) When and how defendant *first* learned of such connection;
    (b) If knowledge was obtained by attendance at any conference, lecture, convention, symposium or meeting, Identify such meeting and provide identity of Persons attending or Documents obtained;
    (c) If knowledge was obtained from medical or scientific studies, or any other published work, Identify same;
    (d) If otherwise obtained, identify manner of receipt of Document or communication.

13. With regard to any knowledge obtained *subsequent* to that identified in your answer to Interrogatory #12(a) above, *identify*:
    (a) All Documents or other communications, oral or written, concerning the causal connection between exposure to asbestos or asbestos products and disease, and identity of Persons so communicating;
    (b) Did answering defendant obtain from or transmit any such information to other defendants in this case? If so, *identify*:
        (1) manner of receipt or communication for each contact;
        (2) all Documents and persons involved.

14. As to any knowledge possessed by answering defendant at any time referred to in your answers to Interrogatories #11, #12 and #13, did you educate your employees, distributors or purchasers of the hazards known to you and the safety precautions necessary to guard against cancer and other diseases arising from the use and handling of your products? If so, *identify*:
    (a) When and in what manner customers, insulators, factory workers and the general public were so informed;
    (b) Documents communicating or otherwise disseminating such information;
    (c) Programs initiated or sponsored to establish or promote safety procedures, methods or usage of equipment;
    (d) Published articles or reports by employees (present or prior), including those of medical directors, scientists, engineers or other professionals;

C. Scope of Discovery

(e) Symposia or lectures sponsored for the benefit of asbestos workers and/or the general public.

15. When and by what manner were you first aware of the hazards relating to exposure to asbestos or asbestos products:
   (a) For inside insulators and contractors;
   (b) For outside insulators and contractors.

16. If you have knowledge or information concerning the following, answer in the affirmative or negative, whether:
   (a) Early detection of mesothelioma results in any appreciable rate of cure or arrest;
   (b) A single exposure to asbestos may cause mesothelioma, other cancers, or asbestosis;
   (c) Cumulative or multiple exposures to asbestos result in a greater risk of harm to the exposed person;
   (d) An outside insulator has a risk of harm from exposure to asbestos or asbestos products;
   (e) Stripping or removing old asbestos creates a greater risk of harm than installation of asbestos or asbestos products;
   (f) Cancer resulting from exposure to asbestos develops generally after:
      (1) 1-5 years
      (2) 6-10 years
      (3) 11-20 years
      (4) more than 20 years
   (g) There is any known relationship between smoking and mesothelioma;
   (h) There is any reported cause of mesothelioma other than exposure to asbestos.

17. As to each answer to Interrogatory #16, identify at least *one* Person or Document upon which answering defendant relies.

18. Did you perform, direct to be performed, finance, sponsor or receive the results of any studies or tests concerning the relationship between asbestos exposure and asbestosis and/or cancer? If so, *identify*:
   (a) When, where, and at what intervals such studies were performed;
   (b) Were such studies in writing or reported at a later date in writing;
   (c) Were the results of such studies published or otherwise disseminated? If so, state to whom and when;
   (d) Who performed such studies;
   (e) Will you produce the results of such studies at this time, or state where the results are maintained.

19. Have any findings been made by any governmental agency, body, commission or health organization, including but not limited to the U.S. Public Health Service, OSHA or NIOSH, concerning specific hazards associated with the use and handling of asbestos and asbestos products in plants or on job sites owned or controlled by you, any restrictions in use of same, requirements for medical surveillance and examinations for your workers, dust monitoring, or availability of safety equipment, all of which were aimed at determination of the degree of exposure to asbestos or asbestos products which would not cause disease among employees, and at the prevention or limitation of inhalation or consumption of asbestos fibers or dust in connection with the insulation process? If such findings were made, *identify*:

(a) The date or dates of such findings and by which organization or entity such findings were made;
(b) The form in which such findings were made and, if written, the exact wording of same or location in regulation, order, bulletin, report or other writing;
(c) What steps were taken to comply with such findings and the dates when such acts of compliance occurred;
(d) How insulators or installers were informed of such findings and if such information was written identify same.

20. Did you perform, direct to be performed, finance, sponsor or receive the results of any dust monitoring tests at job sites where asbestos or asbestos products were being applied and/or removed by insulators? If so, *state*:
(a) The date and location of the *first* such test;
(b) When, where and at what intervals subsequent tests were performed;
(c) Who performed such tests;
(d) Where the results of such tests are maintained;
(e) What steps were taken by you to improve results of such tests, and dates when such improvements were made.

21. If your answer to the above Interrogatory is in the negative, state your reasons for not performing dust monitoring tests.

22. Identify any medical examination programs offered or sponsored by answering defendant or its insurance carrier(s) for employees handling or otherwise exposed to asbestos and asbestos products. With respect to each such program, state:
(a) Manner of communicating with employees about such program;
(b) Whether examination was mandatory or optional;
(c) What percentage of workers permitted to undergo such examination participated;
(d) What percentage of workers were found to have asbestosis or mesothelioma;
(e) With respect to (d), what percentage of such workers were paid disability or workmen's compensation benefits or for whose benefit medical expenses were paid to undergo treatment for such conditions.

23. Is answering defendant familiar with Dr. Irving J. Selikoff and/or The Mt. Sinai School of Medicine? If so, state:
(a) Approximate date and manner of obtaining such familiarity;
(b) Whether any employee or representative of defendant attended a lecture or oral presentation at which Dr. Selikoff spoke on the relationship between asbestos and cancer or asbestosis.

24. Did answering defendant (or its insurance carrier) ever send its employees handling or otherwise exposed to asbestos and asbestos products to be examined by Dr. Selikoff or Mt. Sinai personnel? If so, state:
(a) Dates of such examinations;
(b) Whether answering defendant received the results of such examinations;
(c) Whether answering defendant's insurance carriers received the results of such examinations;
(d) *Identify* all Documents authored or summarizing Dr. Selikoff's reports or findings which you have in your possession or control.

C. Scope of Discovery

25. If your answer to Interrogatory #23 is in the affirmative, *identify*:
    (a) All communications, either written or oral, received by you from or transmitted by you to Dr. Selikoff and/or Mt. Sinai prior to the publication of Dr. Selikoff's article, "Asbestosis Exposure and Neoplasia," JAMA 188 :142 (1963), regarding the relationship between asbestos exposure and disease;
    (b) All communications, either written or oral, received by you from or transmitted by you to Dr. Selikoff after 1963, regarding the relationship between asbestos exposure and disease;
    (c) All Documents, including but not limited to preliminary and/or executed agreements, between you, Dr. Selikoff, Mt. Sinai, any of the defendants in this matter and/or any trade associations, corporations or other business entities, relating to, inter alia, scientific research or studies to be performed, equipment and/or funding to be supplied, publication or non-publication of data, results, findings and/or opinions.

26. With respect to those medical programs identified in defendant's answers to Interrogatories #22 and #24, state:
    (a) Whether defendant had a written or unwritten policy that the results of such medical examinations should not be revealed to defendant's employees;
    (b) If your answer to subpart (a) above is in the affirmative, did such policy extend to those employees whose medical examinations revealed evidence of asbestos-related diseases, including but not limited to asbestosis and mesothelioma;
    (c) If such policy was or is written, identify all doctors, clinics, associations and personnel associated with defendant who were instructed as to defendant's policy;
    (d) Whether there is a central repository where the results of such medical examinations or studies are located;
    (e) Whether defendant's policy included instructions to disclose results of medical examinations to the personal physicians of employees, or others;
    (f) Whether defendant performed, financed or assisted in performing medical examinations on employees of other defendants named in this lawsuit. If the answer is in the affirmative, list the name(s) of such defendant(s);
    (g) Whether defendant performed, financed or assisted in performing medical examinations on employees of other corporations or business entities not named as defendants in this lawsuit. If the answer is in the affirmative, list the name(s) of such corporation(s) or business entities;
    (h) *Identify* all Documents or agreements setting forth conditions under which such programs were to be performed and instructing the examiner(s) as to (non-) disclosure of results;
    (i) Whether answering defendant admits or denies any policy of nondisclosure, have any medical or other corporate personnel employed by defendant now or in the past ever testified as to the existence of such policy of nondisclosure. If so, identify the witness, the date, the proceeding, and the existence of any transcripts, notes of testimony or sworn statements of such witnesses;

CHAPTER 9 DISCOVERY

* * *

48. Identify all Documents which exist, either in the files of answering defendant or which have been produced in other proceedings or "asbestos litigation," that represent communications between any of the defendants to this suit, other manufacturers, suppliers or distributors of asbestos products, the United States government, trade organizations, including but not limited to A.T.I., I.H.F., N.I.M.A., A.I.A., N.I.C.A., T.I.M.A., Q.A.M.A., Q.A.P.A. or P.I.C.A., or scientific or medical foundations, such as Saranac Lake Laboratory or Mt. Sinai School of Medicine:
   (a) Discussing the possible relationship between asbestos exposure and asbestosis, lung cancer, mesothelioma and/or other diseases;
   (b) Medical or scientific studies concerning the relationship between asbestos exposure and asbestosis, lung cancer, mesothelioma and/or other diseases;
   (c) Discussing the publication or non-publication of any medical or scientific findings concerning such relationship.

49. Identify all Persons who have testified and all Documents presented or utilized for the purpose of proving or defending against claims concerning the adverse effects upon human life through exposure to asbestos or asbestos products:
   (a) In any litigation, pending or otherwise, involving answering defendant;
   (b) Before Congressional or OSHA hearings or investigative proceedings of any other governmental agency or unit;
   (c) At any symposium, course, lecture or other meeting;
   (d) With respect to (a)-(c) above, identify the name of the case, court term and number, or other description of proceedings and/or meeting.

50. With respect to your answer to Interrogatory #49, *identify*:
   (a) Any affidavit or transcript of a deposition, trial or hearing at which answering defendant participated;
   (b) Any verdict or settlement resulting in the finding of liability and/or payment of money to claimants alleging personal injury from the exposure to asbestos or asbestos products.

51. Identify all Persons who have testified on your behalf and all Documents presented at or utilized for preparation of testimony at OSHA, NIOSH, Congressional and/or other governmental hearings or investigative proceedings on the subjects of the biological effects on human life of exposure to asbestos and the setting, modification, feasibility and acceptance of allegedly safe or proper levels of such exposure to asbestos and asbestos products. For all such testimony *identify*:
   (a) Dates and descriptions of proceedings;
   (b) Relationship between Persons testifying and answering defendant, i.e., employee or consultant;
   (c) All studies, test results, or other scientific or medical Documents relied upon by said Persons as a basis for any recommendations made or testimony given;
   (d) Whether, at any time prior to or following such testimony, you were possessed or knowledge of Documents suggesting that existing or proposed threshold limit values *were not* safe or proper, or that lower threshold limit values were necessary in order to prevent disease. If your answer is in the affirmative, *identify* origin of knowledge and all Documents relating thereto;

C. Scope of Discovery

(e) Whether, at any time prior to or following such testimony, you were aware that the proper method for determination of safe levels of asbestos was to test concentrations of *fibers* in the air, rather than the total number of *particles*. If your answer is in the affirmative, *identify* origin and said knowledge and all Documents relating thereto;

52. Do you send or have you at any time sent counsel or other representatives to courses aimed at defending asbestos cases? If so, *identify.*

53. Identify all expert witnesses who have testified in other cases, pending or otherwise, *on behalf of* answering defendant.

54. Identify all present or former employees of answering defendant, other than *plaintiffs*, who have testified *against* answering defendant in a litigation matter or before a governmental agency or unit.

55. With respect to your answers to Interrogatories #53 and #54, identify all Documents, including but not limited to transcripts or notes of testimony employed by or resulting from the testimony of such expert witnesses or employees.

56. Identify:
(a) Any expert whom you intend to call as a witness or otherwise utilize in connection with this litigation.
(b) Any co-worker of plaintiff whom you have interviewed or intend to call as a witness in this litigation.

57. If plaintiff was ever employed by answering defendant or worked on a job contracted by answering defendant:
(a) *Identify* any work records, employment records or job records with respect thereto;
(b) *Identify* any invoices, purchase orders or other Documents evidencing the use of a product manufactured by defendant on said job(s);
(c) If answering defendant cannot identify Documents as to (a) and (b) above, confirm or deny the existence and use of defendant's products during the relevant time period;
(d) *Identify* any products not manufactured by, but relabelled or otherwise altered by defendant and used on said job(s).

NOTES AND QUESTIONS

1. As noted earlier, although interrogatories are directed to a party, the answers are usually drafted by the lawyer. If you represented Johns-Manville in *Roesberg*, how would you go about acquiring the information necessary to answer these interrogatories?

2. Responding to all of the interrogatories in *Roesberg* could be extremely time consuming. Instead of writing answers to all the questions, the defendant may produce the business records from which the answers can be derived. See Rule 33(d). Notice, however, that this option is available only where "the burden of deriving or ascertaining the answer is substantially the same for the party serving the interrogatory as for the party

CHAPTER 9 DISCOVERY

served." When a responding party relies on this provision, how can the requesting party challenge the other side's assertion that the burden would be the same for both?

3. If the defendant thoroughly answers all of these interrogatories, won't the defendant have done much of the plaintiffs' work in preparing this suit for trial? Is that fair?

4. One reason that the court permitted such broad discovery, dating back so far, was that the plaintiff had alleged a conspiracy antedating plaintiff's employment. If the court had imposed a heightened pleading requirement on the conspiracy allegation, it is possible that the conspiracy allegation would have been struck, and without that allegation discovery would have been more limited. Thus, the generous pleading rules have implications for the amount and scope of discovery. Is Rule 11 at odds with liberal discovery? Under Rule 11, how much proof of a conspiracy must you have to have in order to allege it? How could you acquire that proof without discovery?

5. *Roesberg* may be an example of a case in which a defendant's "stonewalling" tactic backfired. Because the defendant objected to answering virtually everything, the court may have taken less seriously some legitimate objections.

6. You should note that under Rule 26(e)(2) a party must supplement all discovery responses if a party learns a prior response "is in some material respect incomplete or incorrect."

2. Privileged Material

Rule 26(b)(1) permits discovery only of material that is "not privileged." "Privileged," as it is used in Rule 26, refers to a relatively narrow category of material, delineated under the rules of evidence. The fact that certain information is personal, confidential, or intended to be secret does not necessarily make it privileged for purposes of discovery.

There are several well-established categories of privileged information. The confidential communications between lawyer and client, doctor and patient, priest and parishioner, and husband and wife are all considered privileged. In all of these cases it is only the *communication* itself that is protected and not the underlying facts. Thus, in the Robinsons' case against Audi, it would be improper for Audi to ask Mrs. Robinson the following question either in discovery or at trial: "What did you tell your lawyer about how much gas was in the tank at the time of the accident?" On the other hand, it would be completely permissible to ask: "How much gas was in the tank at the time of the accident?"

The protective veil of privilege conceals information that may be important to fact finding and truth seeking. The recognition of some information as privileged reflects a policy judgment that certain interests are more important than fact finding and truth seeking. For example, the attorney client privilege encourages complete and honest disclosure between client and lawyer, and this, in turn, facilitates better representation. As one treatise explains: "The consequent loss to justice of the power to bring all pertinent facts before the court is, according to the theory, outweighed by the benefit to justice (not to the individual client) of a franker disclosure in the lawyer's office." MCCORMICK ON EVIDENCE 121 (4th ed. 1992). Because recognition of a privilege does conceal information, the privileges are narrowly construed and can be waived by disclosure to third parties.

One issue with which the Supreme Court has struggled is the scope of the attorney-client privilege when the client is a corporation. Should the privilege protect all communications between all employees of the corporation and the corporation's lawyer or only between managers and the lawyer? In Upjohn Co. v. United States, 449 U.S. 383 (1981), the Supreme Court rejected as too narrow the position that the privilege extends only to communications with the "control group," i.e., top managers, of the corporation. The Court declined to articulate a specific alternative test, though it suggested that the privilege would apply only where the communication was needed to supply a basis for legal advice, concerned matters within the scope of the employees duties, and was treated as confidential within the corporation. See id. at 394-95.

All privileged information is protected from disclosure. However, the party from whom the information is sought cannot simply quietly withhold the allegedly privileged information. Rule 26(b)(5) requires a party to claim the privilege "expressly" and to describe in sufficient detail the documents, communications or things not produced so as to enable "other parties to assess the applicability of the privilege or protection." In elaborating on this requirement, one court has held that the party claiming the privilege or protection must set forth the following:

(1) a brief description or summary of the contents of the document,
(2) the date the document was prepared,
(3) the person or persons who prepared the document,
(4) to whom the document was directed, or for whom the document was prepared,
(5) the purpose in preparing the document,
(6) the privilege or privileges asserted as to that document,
(7) how each element of the privilege or privileges is/are met as to that document.

Bennett v. Fieser, 1994 U.S.Dist. LEXIS 4050 (D. Kan. 1994).

What happens if the claimant does not properly claim the privilege or protection? The Advisory Committee comment to Rule 26(b)(5) states that failure properly to claim the privilege "may be viewed as a waiver" and at least one court has so held. See Zapata v. IBP, Inc., 1994 U.S. Dist. LEXIS 16285 (D. Kan. 1994). However, other courts have refused to invoke "the harsh remedy of waiver" without a showing of prejudice. See B. Braun Medical Inc. v. Abbott Laboratories., 1994 U.S.Dist. LEXIS 9445 (E.D. Pa. 1994). Which approach do you think is the correct interpretation of the rules?

As noted above, there is much information that parties consider private and confidential, but which is not "privileged." Any relevant, nonprivileged information is subject to discovery, regardless of how private and embarrassing the information might be. Some courts have held, however, that where confidential information is sought, the burden is on the party seeking discovery to establish that the information sought is relevant and necessary to the case. See Hartley Pen Co. v. United States District Court, 287 F.2d 324, 331 (9th Cir. 1961). A court has authority under Rule 26(c) to issue a protective order placing conditions on the disclosure or protecting against disclosure altogether. If the information is relevant, it ordinarily must be disclosed subject to appropriate protective conditions.

The potential reach of discovery is illustrated by litigation between the Coca-Cola Company and several of its bottlers. The secret formula for Coca-Cola has been described as "one of the best-kept trade secrets in the world." It is known by only two people and the only written record of the formula is kept in a bank vault that can be opened only upon resolution of the company's Board of Directors. The formula was never patented because patents are of finite duration, and Coke wanted to maintain the secret indefinitely. Despite the extraordinarily secret nature of the formula, a court ordered it disclosed in connection with discovery in a civil suit. The circumstances were this. In 1921, Coca-Cola had entered into a consent decree settling a suit by several of its bottlers. The consent decree set the price the bottlers would pay for syrup from Coca-Cola. When Coca-Cola introduced Diet Coke, the company took the position that this was a new product that was not covered by the consent decree. Several bottlers disagreed and filed suit against Coca-Cola alleging that Diet Coke was "simply a version of a product which has undergone evolutionary change but which retains its identity as Coke." Because the major issue in the case was whether Diet Coke and Coke were the same product, the plaintiff sought discovery of the secret formula for Diet Coke and Coca-Cola. The court agreed with the plaintiffs and ordered production of the formula though it granted a protective order that limited disclosure to plaintiff's trial counsel and independent experts.

Not surprisingly, Coca-Cola refused to comply with the order to produce. Although the court did not enter a default judgment, as the plaintiffs had requested, it did enter an order that the bottlers were entitled to a non-rebuttable factual finding that the two formulae were within the range of formulae for syrups that had previously been sold as Coca-Cola syrup. Coca-Cola Bottling Co. v Coca-Cola Co., 110 F.R.D. 363, 371-72 (D. Del. 1986). Notwithstanding this order, Coca-Cola ultimately prevailed, although the litigation lasted 10 years and generated at least eight published opinions. See Coca-Cola Bottling Co. v. Coca-Cola Co. (*Coke VIII*), 988 F.2d 386 (3d Cir.), *cert. denied*, 114 S. Ct. 289 (1993). Do you think the plaintiffs in the Coke case really needed the formula for their suit, or were they trying to use the threat of discovery to pressure Coke into settlement?

C. Scope of Discovery

The potential invasiveness of discovery is not limited to commercial cases. Consider the following description of the A. H. Robins Company's litigation strategy in Dalkon Shield litigation:

> Robins took the position that multiple sex partners, with the accompanying increased risk of contracting sexually transmitted diseases, were a more likely cause of uterine infections than was the Dalkon Shield. Attorneys for the company would ask the plaintiff to identify her sex partners so that these men could be subpoenaed and asked about their medical histories. Women were also asked to describe their sexual practices and the details of their personal hygiene, on the theory that these might relate to the risk of pelvic infection. The courts divided on whether to require answers to these questions, but the mere fact that questions suggesting uncleanliness, promiscuity, or sexual aberration were asked dissuaded many women from pressing forward with their claims (or from making claims at all) and induced others to accept cheap settlements offered by Robbins.

RICHARD SOBOL, BENDING THE LAW 13 (1991).

As the these cases illustrate, discovery can be a potent weapon. One of the potential costs of liberal discovery rules is that litigants with meritorious claims or defenses may be discouraged from pursuing their rights out of fear that private or confidential information will have to be disclosed. The benefits of liberal discovery may be worth this cost, but its cost should be taken into account.

3. Work Product

Hickman v. Taylor
329 U.S. 495, 67 S. Ct. 385, 91 L. Ed. 451 (1947)

JUSTICE MURPHY delivered the opinion of the Court.

This case presents an important problem under the Federal Rules of Civil Procedure as to the extent to which a party may inquire into oral and written statements of witnesses, or other information, secured by an adverse party's counsel in the course of preparation for possible litigation after a claim has arisen. Examination into a person's files and records, including those resulting from the professional activities of an attorney, must be judged with care. It is not without reason that various safeguards have been established to preclude unwarranted excursions into the privacy of a man's work. At the same time, public policy supports reasonable and necessary inquiries. Properly to balance these competing interests is a delicate and difficult task.

On February 7, 1943, the tug "J. M. Taylor" sank while engaged in helping to tow a car float of the Baltimore & Ohio Railroad across the Delaware River at Philadelphia. The accident was apparently unusual in nature, the cause of it still being unknown. Five of the nine crew members were drowned. Three days later the tug owners and the underwriters employed a law firm, of which

CHAPTER 9 DISCOVERY

respondent Fortenbaugh is a member, to defend them against potential suits by representatives of the deceased crew members and to sue the railroad for damages to the tug.

A public hearing was held on March 4, 1943, before the United States Steamboat Inspectors, at which the four survivors were examined. This testimony was recorded and made available to all interested parties. Shortly thereafter, Fortenbaugh privately interviewed the survivors and took statements from them with an eye toward the anticipated litigation; the survivors signed these statements on March 29. Fortenbaugh also interviewed other persons believed to have some information relating to the accident and in some cases he made memoranda of what they told him. At the time when Fortenbaugh secured the statements of the survivors, representatives of two of the deceased crew members had been in communication with him. Ultimately claims were presented by representatives of all five of the deceased; four of the claims, however, were settled without litigation. The fifth claimant, petitioner herein, brought suit in a federal court under the Jones Act on November 26, 1943, naming as defendants the two tug owners, individually and as partners, and the railroad.

One year later, petitioner filed 39 interrogatories directed to the tug owners. The 38th interrogatory read: "State whether any statements of the members of the crews of the Tugs 'J. M. Taylor' and 'Philadelphia' or of any other vessel were taken in connection with the towing of the car float and the sinking of the Tug 'John M. Taylor.' Attach hereto exact copies of all such statements if in writing, and if oral, set forth in detail the exact provisions of any such oral statements or reports."

Supplemental interrogatories asked whether any oral or written statements, records, reports or other memoranda had been made concerning any matter relative to the towing operation, the sinking of the tug, the salvaging and repair of the tug, and the death of the deceased. If the answer was in the affirmative, the tug owners were then requested to set forth the nature of all such records, reports, statements or other memoranda.

The tug owners, through Fortenbaugh, answered all of the interrogatories except No. 38 and the supplemental ones just described. While admitting that statements of the survivors had been taken, they declined to summarize or set forth the contents. They did so on the ground that such requests called "for privileged matter obtained in preparation for litigation" and constituted "an attempt to obtain indirectly counsel's private files." It was claimed that answering these requests "would involve practically turning over not only the complete files, but also the telephone records and, almost, the thoughts of counsel."

In connection with the hearing on these objections, Fortenbaugh made a written statement and gave an informal oral deposition explaining the circumstances under which he had taken the statements. But he was not expressly asked in the deposition to produce the statements. The District Court for the Eastern District of Pennsylvania, sitting en banc, held that the requested matters were not privileged. The court then decreed that the tug owners and Fortenbaugh, as counsel and agent for the tug owners, forthwith "answer Plaintiff's 38th interrogatory and supplementary interrogatories; produce all written statements of witnesses obtained by Mr. Fortenbaugh, as counsel and agent for Defendants; state in substance any fact concerning this case which Defendants learned through oral statements made by witnesses to Mr. Fortenbaugh whether or not included in his private memoranda and produce Mr. Fortenbaugh's memoranda containing statements of fact by witnesses or to submit these memoranda to the Court for determination of those portions which should be revealed to Plaintiff." Upon their refusal, the court adjudged them in contempt and ordered them imprisoned until they complied.

The Third Circuit Court of Appeals, also sitting en banc, reversed the judgment of the District Court. It held that the information here sought was part of the "work product of the lawyer" and hence privileged from discovery under the Federal Rules of Civil Procedure. The importance of the problem, which has engendered a great divergence of views among district courts, led us to grant certiorari.

The pre-trial deposition-discovery mechanism established by Rules 26 to 37 is one of the most significant innovations of the Federal Rules of Civil Procedure. Under the prior federal practice, the pre-trial functions of notice-giving, issue-formulation and fact-revelation were performed primarily and inadequately by the pleadings. Inquiry into the issues and the facts before trial was narrowly confined and was often cumbersome in method. The new rules, however, restrict the pleadings to the task of general notice-giving and invest the deposition-discovery process with a vital role in the preparation for trial. The various instruments of discovery now serve (1) as a device, along with the pre-trial hearing under Rule 16, to narrow and clarify the basic issues between the parties, and (2) as a device for ascertaining the facts, or information as to the existence or whereabouts of facts, relative to those issues. Thus civil trials in the federal courts no longer need be carried on in the dark. The way is now clear, consistent with recognized privileges, for the parties to obtain the fullest possible knowledge of the issues and facts before trial.

There is an initial question as to which of the deposition-discovery rules is involved in this case. Petitioner, in filing his interrogatories, thought he was proceeding under Rule 33. That rule provides that a party may serve upon any adverse party written interrogatories to be answered by the party served. The District Court proceeded on the same assumption in its opinion, although its order to produce and its contempt order stated that both Rules 33 and 34 were involved. * * *

* * *

The matter is not without difficulty in light of the events that transpired below. We believe, however, that petitioner was proceeding primarily under Rule 33. He addressed simple interrogatories solely to the individual tug owners, the adverse parties, as contemplated by that rule. He did not, and could not under Rule 33, address such interrogatories to their counsel, Fortenbaugh. Nor did he direct these interrogatories either to the tug owners or to Fortenbaugh by way of deposition; Rule 26 thus could not come into operation. And it does not appear from the record that petitioner filed a motion under Rule 34 for a court order directing the production of the documents in question. Indeed, such an order could not have been entered as to Fortenbaugh since Rule 34, like Rule 33, is limited to parties to the proceeding, thereby excluding their counsel or agents.

Thus to the extent that petitioner was seeking the production of the memoranda and statements gathered by Fortenbaugh in the course of his activities as counsel, petitioner misconceived his remedy. Rule 33 did not permit him to obtain such memoranda and statements as adjuncts to the interrogatories addressed to the individual tug owners. A party clearly cannot refuse to answer interrogatories on the ground that the information sought is solely within the knowledge of his attorney. But that is not this case. Here production was sought of documents prepared by a party's attorney after the claim has arisen. Rule 33 does not make provision for such production, even when sought in connection with permissible interrogatories. Moreover, since petitioner was also foreclosed from securing them through an order under Rule 34, his only recourse was to take Fortenbaugh's deposition under Rule 26 and to attempt to force Fortenbaugh to produce the materials by use of a subpoena duces tecum in accordance with Rule 45. But despite petitioner's faulty choice of action, the District Court entered an order, apparently under Rule 34, commanding the tug owners and Fortenbaugh, as their agent and counsel, to produce the materials in question. Their refusal led to the anomalous result of holding the tug owners in contempt for failure to produce that which was in the possession of their counsel and of holding Fortenbaugh in contempt for failure to produce that which he could not be compelled to produce under either Rule 33 or Rule 34.

But, under the circumstances, we deem it unnecessary and unwise to rest our decision upon this procedural irregularity, an irregularity which is not strongly urged upon us and which was disregarded in the two courts below. It matters little at this late stage whether Fortenbaugh fails to answer interrogatories filed under Rule 26 or under Rule 33 or whether he refuses to produce the memoranda and statements pursuant to a subpoena under Rule 45 or a court order under Rule 34. The deposition-discovery rules create integrated procedural devices. And the basic question at stake is whether any of those devices may be used to inquire into materials collected by an adverse party's counsel in the course of preparation for possible litigation. The fact that the petitioner may have used the wrong method does not destroy the main thrust of his attempt. Nor does it relieve us of the responsibility of dealing with the problem raised by that attempt. It would be inconsistent with the liberal atmosphere surrounding these rules to insist that petitioner now go through the empty formality of pursuing the right procedural device only to reestablish precisely the same basic problem now confronting us. We do not mean to say, however, that there may not be situations in which the failure to proceed in accordance with a specific rule would be important or decisive. But in the present circumstances, for the purposes of this decision, the procedural irregularity is not material. Having noted the proper procedure, we may accordingly turn our attention to the substance of the underlying problem.

In urging that he has a right to inquire into the materials secured and prepared by Fortenbaugh, petitioner emphasizes that the deposition-discovery portions of the Federal Rules of Civil Procedure are designed to enable the parties to discover the true facts and to compel their disclosure wherever they may be found. It is said that inquiry may be made under these rules, epitomized by Rule 26, as to any relevant matter which is not privileged; and since the discovery provisions are to be applied as broadly and liberally as possible, the privilege limitation must be restricted to its narrowest bounds. On the premise that the attorney-client privilege is the one involved in this case, petitioner argues that it must be strictly confined to confidential communications made by a client to his attorney. And since the materials here in issue were secured by Fortenbaugh from third persons rather than from his clients, the tug owners, the conclusion is reached that these materials are proper subjects for discovery under Rule 26.

As additional support for this result, petitioner claims that to prohibit discovery under these circumstances would give a corporate defendant a tremendous advantage in a suit by an individual plaintiff. Thus in a suit by an injured employee against a railroad or in a suit by an insured person against an insurance company the corporate defendant could pull a dark veil of secrecy over all the pertinent facts it can collect after the claim arises merely on the assertion that such facts were gathered by its large staff of attorneys and claim agents. At the same time, the individual plaintiff, who often has direct knowledge of the matter in issue and has no counsel until some time after his claim arises could be compelled to disclose all the intimate details of his case. By endowing with immunity from disclosure all that a lawyer discovers in the course of his duties, it is said, the rights of individual litigants in such cases are drained of vitality and the lawsuit becomes more of a battle of deception than a search for truth.

But framing the problem in terms of assisting individual plaintiffs in their suits against corporate defendants is unsatisfactory. Discovery concededly may work to the disadvantage as well as to the advantage of individual plaintiffs. Discovery, in other words, is not a one-way proposition. It is available in all types of cases at the behest of any party, individual or corporate, plaintiff or defendant. The problem thus far transcends the situation confronting this petitioner. And we must view that problem in light of the limitless situations where the particular kind of discovery sought by petitioner might be used.

We agree, of course, that the deposition-discovery rules are to be accorded a broad and liberal treatment. No longer can the time-honored cry of "fishing expedition" serve to preclude a party from inquiring into the facts underlying his opponent's case. Mutual knowledge of all the relevant facts gathered by both parties is essential to proper litigation. To that end, either party may compel the other to disgorge whatever facts he has in his possession. The deposition-discovery procedure simply advances the stage at which the disclosure can be compelled from the time of trial to the period preceding it, thus reducing the possibility of surprise. But discovery, like all matters of procedure, has ultimate and necessary boundaries. As indicated by Rules 30(b) and (d) and 31(d), limitations inevitably arise when it can be shown that the examination is being conducted in bad faith or in such a manner as to annoy, embarrass or oppress the person subject to the inquiry. And as Rule 26(b) provides, further limitations come into existence when the inquiry touches upon the irrelevant or encroaches upon the recognized domains of privilege.

We also agree that the memoranda, statements and mental impressions in issue in this case fall outside the scope of the attorney-client privilege and hence are not protected from discovery on that basis. It is unnecessary here to delineate the content and scope of that privilege as recognized in the federal courts. For present purposes, it suffices to note that the protective cloak of this privilege does not extend to information which an attorney secures from a witness while acting for his client in anticipation of litigation. Nor does this privilege concern the memoranda, briefs, communications and other writings prepared by counsel for his own use in prosecuting his client's case; and it is equally unrelated to writings which reflect an attorney's mental impressions, conclusions, opinions or legal theories.

But the impropriety of invoking that privilege does not provide an answer to the problem before us. Petitioner has made more than an ordinary request for relevant, nonprivileged facts in the possession of his adversaries or their counsel. He has sought discovery as of right of oral and written statements of witnesses whose identity is well known and whose availability to petitioner appears unimpaired. He has sought production of these matters after making the most searching inquiries of his opponents as to the circumstances surrounding the fatal accident, which inquiries were sworn to have been answered to the best of their information and belief. Interrogatories were directed toward all the events prior to, during and subsequent to the sinking of the tug. Full and honest answers to such broad inquiries would necessarily have included all pertinent information gleaned by Fortenbaugh through his interviews with the witnesses. Petitioner makes no suggestion, and we cannot assume, that the tug owners or Fortenbaugh were incomplete or dishonest in the framing of their answers. In addition, petitioner was free to examine the public testimony of the witnesses taken before the United States Steamboat Inspectors. We are thus dealing with an attempt to secure the production of written statements and mental impressions contained in the files and the mind of the attorney Fortenbaugh without any showing of necessity or any indication or claim that denial of such production would unduly prejudice the preparation of petitioner's case or cause him any hardship or injustice. For aught that appears, the essence of what petitioner seeks either has been revealed to him already through the interrogatories or is readily available to him direct from the witnesses for the asking.

The District Court, after hearing objections to petitioner's request, commanded Fortenbaugh to produce all written statements of witnesses and to state in substance any facts learned through oral statements of witnesses to him. Fortenbaugh was to submit any memoranda he had made of the oral statements so that the court might determine what portions should be revealed to petitioner. All of this was ordered without any showing by petitioner, or any requirement that he make a proper showing, of the necessity for the production of any of this material or any demonstration that denial of production would cause hardship or injustice. The court simply ordered production on the theory that the facts sought were material and were not privileged as constituting attorney-client communications.

In our opinion, neither Rule 26 nor any other rule dealing with discovery contemplates production under such circumstances. That is not because the subject matter is privileged or irrelevant, as those concepts are used in these rules. Here is simply an attempt, without purported necessity or justification, to secure written statements, private memoranda and personal recollections prepared or formed by an adverse party's counsel in the course of his legal duties. As such, it falls outside the arena of discovery and contravenes the public policy underlying the orderly prosecution and defense of legal claims. Not even the most liberal of discovery theories can justify unwarranted inquiries into the files and the mental impressions of an attorney.

Historically, a lawyer is an officer of the court and is bound to work for the advancement of justice while faithfully protecting the rightful interests of his clients. In performing his various duties, however, it is essential that a lawyer work with a certain degree of privacy, free from unnecessary intrusion by opposing parties and their counsel. Proper preparation of a client's case demands that he assemble information, sift what he considers to be the relevant from the irrelevant facts, prepare his legal theories and plan his strategy without undue and needless interference. That is the historical and the necessary way in which lawyers act within the framework of our system of jurisprudence to promote justice and to protect their clients' interests. This work is reflected, of course, in interviews, statements, memoranda, correspondence, briefs, mental impressions, personal beliefs, and countless other tangible and intangible ways — aptly though roughly termed by the Circuit Court of Appeals in this case as the "work product of the lawyer." Were such materials open to opposing counsel on mere demand, much of what is now put down in writing would remain unwritten. An attorney's thoughts, heretofore inviolate, would not be his own. Inefficiency, unfairness and sharp practices would inevitably develop in the giving of legal advice and in the preparation of cases for trial. The effect on the legal profession would be demoralizing. And the interests of the clients and the cause of justice would be poorly served.

We do not mean to say that all written materials obtained or prepared by an adversary's counsel with an eye toward litigation are necessarily free from discovery in all cases. Where relevant and non-privileged facts remain hidden in an attorney's file and where production of those facts is essential to the preparation of one's case, discovery may properly be had. Such written statements and documents might, under certain circumstances, be admissible in evidence or give clues as to the existence or location of relevant facts. Or they might be useful for purposes of impeachment or corroboration. And production might be justified where the witnesses are no longer available or can be reached only with difficulty. Were production of written statements and documents to be precluded under such circumstances, the liberal ideals of the deposition-discovery portions of the Federal Rules of Civil Procedure would be stripped of much of their meaning. But the general policy

C. Scope of Discovery

against invading the privacy of an attorney's course of preparation is so well recognized and so essential to an orderly working of our system of legal procedure that a burden rests on the one who would invade that privacy to establish adequate reasons to justify production through a subpoena or court order. That burden, we believe, is necessarily implicit in the rules as now constituted.

Rule 30(b), as presently written, gives the trial judge the requisite discretion to make a judgment as to whether discovery should be allowed as to written statements secured from witnesses. But in the instant case there was no room for that discretion to operate in favor of the petitioner. No attempt was made to establish any reason why Fortenbaugh should be forced to produce the written statements. There was only a naked, general demand for these materials as of right and a finding by the District Court that no recognizable privilege was involved. That was insufficient to justify discovery under these circumstances and the court should have sustained the refusal of the tug owners and Fortenbaugh to produce.

But as to oral statements made by witnesses to Fortenbaugh, whether presently in the form of his mental impressions or memoranda, we do not believe that any showing of necessity can be made under the circumstances of this case so as to justify production. Under ordinary conditions, forcing an attorney to repeat or write out all that witnesses have told him and to deliver the account to his adversary gives rise to grave dangers of inaccuracy and untrustworthiness. No legitimate purpose is served by such production. The practice forces the attorney to testify as to what he remembers or what he saw fit to write down regarding witnesses' remarks. Such testimony could not qualify as evidence; and to use it for impeachment or corroborative purposes would make the attorney much less an officer of the court and much more an ordinary witness. The standards of the profession would thereby suffer.

Denial of production of this nature does not mean that any material, non-privileged facts can be hidden from the petitioner in this case. He need not be unduly hindered in the preparation of his case, in the discovery of facts or in his anticipation of his opponents' position. Searching interrogatories directed to Fortenbaugh and the tug owners, production of written documents and statements upon a proper showing and direct interviews with the witnesses themselves all serve to reveal the facts in Fortenbaugh's possession to the fullest possible extent consistent with public policy. Petitioner's counsel frankly admits that he wants the oral statements only to help prepare himself to examine witnesses and to make sure that he has overlooked nothing. That is insufficient under the circumstances to permit him an exception to the policy underlying the privacy of Fortenbaugh's professional activities. If there should be a rare situation justifying production of these matters, petitioner's case is not of that type.

We fully appreciate the wide-spread controversy among the members of the legal profession over the problem raised by this case. It is a problem that rests on what has been one of the most hazy frontiers of the discovery process. But until some rule or statute definitely prescribes otherwise, we are not justified in permitting discovery in a situation of this nature as a matter of unqualified right. When Rule 26 and the other discovery rules were adopted, this Court and the members of the bar in general certainly did not believe or contemplate that all the files and mental processes of lawyers were thereby opened to the free scrutiny of their adversaries. And we refuse to interpret the rules at this time so as to reach so harsh and unwarranted a result.

We therefore affirm the judgment of the Circuit Court of Appeals.

Affirmed.

JUSTICE JACKSON, concurring.

CHAPTER 9 DISCOVERY

* * *

The primary effect of the practice advocated here would be on the legal profession itself. But it too often is overlooked that the lawyer and the law office are indispensable parts of our administration of justice. Law-abiding people can go nowhere else to learn the ever changing and constantly multiplying rules by which they must behave and to obtain redress for their wrongs. The welfare and tone of the legal profession is therefore of prime consequence to society, which would feel the consequences of such a practice as petitioner urges secondarily but certainly.

"Discovery" is one of the working tools of the legal profession. It traces back to the equity bill of discovery in English Chancery practice and seems to have had a forerunner in Continental practice. Since 1848 when the draftsmen of New York's Code of Procedure recognized the importance of a better system of discovery, the impetus to extend and expand discovery, as well as the opposition to it, has come from within the Bar itself. It happens in this case that it is the plaintiff's attorney who demands such unprecedented latitude of discovery and, strangely enough, *amicus* briefs in his support have been filed by several labor unions representing plaintiffs as a class. It is the history of the movement for broader discovery, however, that in actual experience the chief opposition to its extension has come from lawyers who specialize in representing plaintiffs, because defendants have made liberal use of it to force plaintiffs to disclose their cases in advance. Discovery is a two-edged sword and we cannot decide this problem on any doctrine of extending help to one class of litigants.

* * *

Counsel for the petitioner candidly said on argument that he wanted this information to help prepare himself to examine witnesses, to make sure he overlooked nothing. He bases his claim to it in his brief on the view that the Rules were to do away with the old situation where a law suit developed into "a battle of wits between counsel." But a common law trial is and always should be an adversary proceeding. Discovery was hardly intended to enable a learned profession to perform its functions either without wits or on wits borrowed from the adversary.

The real purpose and the probable effect of the practice ordered by the district court would be to put trials on a level even lower than a "battle of wits." I can conceive of no practice more demoralizing to the Bar than to require a lawyer to write out and deliver to his adversary an account of what witnesses have told him. Even if his recollection were perfect, the statement would be his language, permeated with his inferences. Every one who has tried it knows that it is almost impossible so fairly to record the expressions and emphasis of a witness that when he testifies in the environment of the court and under the influence of the leading question there will not be departures in some respects. Whenever the testimony of the witness would differ from the "exact" statement the lawyer had delivered, the lawyer's statement would be whipped out to impeach the witness. Counsel producing his adversary's "inexact" statement could lose nothing by saying, "Here is a contradiction, gentlemen of the jury. I do not know whether it is my adversary or his witness who is not telling the truth, but one is not." Of course, if this practice were adopted, that scene would be repeated over and over again. The lawyer who delivers such statements often would find himself branded a deceiver afraid to take the stand to support his own version of the witness's conversation with him, or else he will have to go on the stand to defend his own credibility — perhaps against that of his chief witness, or possibly even his client.

C. Scope of Discovery

Every lawyer dislikes to take the witness stand and will do so only for grave reasons. This is partly because it is not his role; he is almost invariably a poor witness. But he steps out of professional character to do it. He regrets it; the profession discourages it. But the practice advocated here is one which would force him to be a witness, not as to what he has seen or done but as to other witnesses' stories, and not because he wants to do so but in self-defense.

And what is the lawyer to do who has interviewed one whom he believes to be a biased, lying or hostile witness to get his unfavorable statements and know what to meet? He must record and deliver such statements even though he would not vouch for the credibility of the witness by calling him. Perhaps the other side would not want to call him either, but the attorney is open to the charge of suppressing evidence at the trial if he fails to call such a hostile witness even though he never regarded him as reliable or truthful.

Having been supplied the names of the witnesses, petitioner's lawyer gives no reason why he cannot interview them himself. If an employee-witness refuses to tell his story, he, too, may be examined under the Rules. He may be compelled on discovery, as fully as on the trial, to disclose his version of the facts. But that is his own disclosure — it can be used to impeach him if he contradicts it and such a deposition is not useful to promote an unseemly disagreement between the witness and the counsel in the case.

* * *

I agree to the affirmance of the judgment of the Circuit Court of Appeals which reversed the district court.

NOTES AND QUESTIONS

1. Why were the witness statements not protected by the attorney-client privilege?

2. Why did the plaintiff's attorney want the witness statements? The Court suggests that the plaintiff can learn all the facts contained in these statements through other means. Is that true? Suppose a witness has told the defense lawyer one story and then, at deposition, tells a somewhat different story. How can the plaintiff's lawyer learn of the inconsistency without getting the witness' prior statement?

3. Consider the justifications the Court offers for protecting work product:

(a) "Sharp practices." What "sharp practices" might develop without work product protection? Is the risk of sharp practices any greater with respect to work product than with respect to any other type of discoverable information?

(b) "[M]uch of what is now put down in writing would remain unwritten." Do you agree that the elimination of work product would cause lawyers to stop writing things down? Couldn't a similar argument be made with respect to other types of discovery? For example, if manufacturers know that written reports of safety tests can be discovered, they might stop recording such tests. As a result, information that might improve the safety of a product could be lost. If this argument is not sufficiently compelling to limit discovery from parties, why is it so compelling with respect to discovery from lawyers?

(c) Relying on "wits borrowed from the adversary." Without work product protection, would lawyers stop preparing cases and instead gain a free ride on the work of their opponents?

(d) Lawyers would become witnesses at trial. Doesn't this argument confuse the question of discoverability with the question of admissibility? Couldn't work product be discoverable without its being admissible at trial?

(e) What "demoralizing" effect would the elimination of work product have on the profession?

4. Even if work product protection does encourage greater investigation and preparation, is this greater preparation something we *should* encourage? Judge Frank Easterbrook has asserted that most litigation simply concerns how to divide up the stakes among the parties and that the resources "spent bickering over the distribution of a pile of money" are largely a waste to society. He argues that the attorney-client privilege and work product protection should be restricted because these protections encourage overinvestment in information creation that is useful principally to divide the stakes. "To say, as the Court did, that a restriction of the scope of the attorney-client and work product privileges would reduce the investment in information in litigation may be to praise that result, not to condemn it." Frank Easterbrook, *Insider Trading, Secret Agents, Evidentiary Privileges, and the Production of Information*, 1981 SUP. CT. REV. 309, 361.

5. Regardless of whether greater trial preparation is socially useful, work product protection, like the evidentiary privileges, has the potential cost of concealing relevant information. Professor Elizabeth Thornburg has argued that this cost is not worth the benefits. Do you agree? See Elizabeth Thornburg, *Rethinking Work Product*, 77 VA. L. REV. 1515 (1991).

6. In 1970, Rule 26(b)(3) dealing with work product material was added to the Federal Rules. Read Rule 26(b)(3) carefully. Is the Rule coextensive with *Hickman*? Is there material protected by *Hickman* that is not covered by the Rule or vice versa?

7. Rule 26(b)(3) only applies to "documents and tangible things." In *Hickman* the Supreme Court held that lawyer Fortenbaugh did not have to answer an interrogatory asking for a complete description of what the interviewed witness said. Under the Rule, would Fortenbaugh be required to answer the interrogatory? In Peterson v. United States, 52 F.R.D. 317, 320 (S.D. Ill. 1971), the court stated: "It is clear to this court that discovery of a detailed description of the contents of documents through interrogatories is equivalent to discovery of the documents themselves. The discovery sought by plaintiff through the

C. Scope of Discovery

interrogatories is therefore covered by rule 26(b)(3)." Do you agree with this interpretation?

On the other hand, as *Hickman* also makes clear, work product does not protect the underlying facts. Thus, in the Robinsons' suit against Audi, if Audi sent an interrogatory to the Robinsons asking whether there were skid marks at the scene of the accident, the Robinsons could not decline to answer on the grounds that their lawyer learned the answer to that question while preparing for litigation. What about photographs of the skid marks taken by an investigator hired by the Robinsons' lawyer. Would these be covered by Rule 26(b)(3)?

8. Rule 26(b)(3) protects only material prepared "in anticipation of litigation." Courts generally agree that this language does not require that litigation actually have commenced — it is sufficient that it is anticipated. Professors Wright and Miller have explained the test as follows:

> Prudent parties anticipate litigation, and begin preparation prior to the time suit is formally commenced. Thus the test should be whether, in light of the nature of the document and the factual situation in the particular case, the document can fairly be said to have been prepared or obtained because of the prospect of litigation.

8 WRIGHT & MILLER, FEDERAL PRACTICE & PROCEDURE § 2024 at 343. Some courts have suggested that because of the word "litigation," the protection extends only where adversarial proceedings are contemplated. In one case, a commercial customer had complained to a product manufacturer that a product was defective. In response to the complaint, employees of the manufacturer prepared several internal memoranda discussing the defect in the product and possible solutions. Ultimately, the customer sued the manufacturer and in the course of that litigation, the manufacturer refused to produce the memoranda on grounds of work product. The court held that the documents were not protected because when the documents were prepared, the manufacturer was primarily concerned about maintaining good relations with its customer and with finding a commercial settlement that *avoided* litigation, the documents were not protected. Scott Paper Co. v. Ceilcote Co., 103 F.R.D. 591 (D. Me. 1984). See Binks Manufacturing Co. v. National Presto Indus., Inc., 709 F.2d 1109 (7th Cir. 1983). Doesn't this create disincentives for parties to seek non-adversarial solutions to disputes?

9. Material protected by Rule 26(b)(3) is frequently called "attorney work product." Notice, however, that material does not have to be produced by a lawyer to be protected by the rule. Indeed, the Rule does not use the phrase "work product."

10. The Advisory Committee Notes state that "materials assembled in the ordinary course of business, or pursuant to public requirements unrelated to litigation, or for other nonlitigation purposes are not under the qualified immunity provided by this subdivision."

Relying on this language, some courts have held that where a defendant routinely produces a report about any accident involving its products, those reports are not protected by Rule 26(b)(3). See, e.g., Soeder v. General Dynamics Corp., 90 F.R.D. 253, 255 (D. Nev. 1980); Rakus v. Erie-Lackawanna R.R., 76 F.R.D. 145, 146 (W.D. N.Y. 1977). Along these lines, one court has said,

> a document or thing produced or used by an insurer to evaluate an insured's claim in order to arrive at a claim decision in the ordinary and regular course of business is not work product regardless of the fact it was produced after litigation was reasonably anticipated. It is presumed that a document or thing prepared before a final decision was reached on an insured's claim, and which constitutes part of the factual inquiry into or evaluation of that claim, was prepared in the ordinary and routine course of the insurer's business of claim determination and is not work product.

Harper v. Auto-Owner's Ins. Co., 138 F.R.D. 655, 663 (S.D. Ind. 1991). Are these cases consistent with Rule 26(b)(3)? For an analysis and critique of what is sometimes called the "ordinary course of business exception" to work product, see *Special Project: The Work Product Doctrine*, 68 CORNELL L. REV. 760, 848-855 (1983).

11. Why should the signed, written statement of a witness be protected under work product? Some have argued that witness statements should not be protected. See Kathleen Waits, *Work Product Protection for Witness Statements: Time for Abolition*, 1985 WIS. L. REV. 305. Witness statements are not fully protected in the criminal arena. Under the Jencks Act, 18 U.S.C. § 3500, after a witness has testified on direct examination in federal criminal prosecution, the government is required to disclose any statement previously made by the witness. Should a similar disclosure obligation be imposed in civil cases? Why or why not?

12. Suppose one side, through great expense and ingenuity, locates a previously unknown witness to an accident. Is the name of that witness protected under Rule 26?

13. Review Interrogatory 56(b) in *Roesberg*, supra at 407. Does that question ask for work product protected material?

14. Is material that was produced in anticipation of litigation in one suit, protected from discovery in future litigation? In FTC v. Grolier Inc., 462 U.S. 19, 25 (1983), the Court observed in dicta, "the literal language of [Rule 26(b)(3)] protects materials prepared for *any* litigation or trial as long as they were prepared by or for a party to the subsequent litigation." Some courts have held that the protection continues only if the subsequent litigation is related to the case for which the material was originally prepared. See, e.g., Leonen v. Johns-Manville, 135 F.R.D. 94, 97 (D. N.J. 1990). Moreover, where the entity for which the material was prepared is not a party to the subsequent litigation, courts have held that the material is not protected. See, e.g., Hawkins v. South Plain Int'l Trucks, Inc.,

139 F.R.D. 682 (D. Colo. 1991). See Note, *The Work Product Doctrine in Subsequent Litigation*, 83 COLUM. L. REV. 412 (1983).

15. What must a party show to overcome the work product protection? Suppose one side cannot *now* obtain the substantial equivalent, but should could have obtained it if she had acted earlier? One court allowed discovery of the work product material under these circumstances explaining, "Our role in administering the discovery rules * * * is not to reward diligence or to penalize laziness." Southern R.R. v. Lanham, 403 F.2d 119, 130 (5th Cir. 1968). Other courts have denied discovery where the other party could through diligence have obtained the equivalent. See, e.g., Hoffman v. Owens-Illinois Glass Co., 107 F.R.D. 793 (D. Mass. 1985).

16. Rule 26(b)(3) provides that the court "shall protect against disclosure of the mental impressions, conclusions, opinions, or legal theories of an attorney." Is this provision inconsistent with Rule 33(c) which permits interrogatories that call for "an opinion or contention that relates to fact or the application of law to fact?" The Advisory Committee Notes to Rule 26(b)(3) state:

> Under those rules [33 and 36], a party and his attorney or other representative may be required to disclose, to some extent, mental impressions, opinions, or conclusions. But documents or parts of documents containing these matters are protected against discovery by this subdivision. Even though a party may ultimately have to disclose in response to interrogatories or requests to admit, he is entitled to keep confidential documents containing such matters prepared for internal use.

One commentator has explained this comment as follows:

> The distinction between discoverable and nondiscoverable creative trial preparation material more logically can be expressed if it is described as not merely a distinction between the oral and the written but as primarily one between the general and specific. The general shape of a party's assertions must be known in order to determine what is and what is not in issue. It is not, however, necessary in order to determine the genuine issues in the cases to have detailed knowledge of the other side's contentions. Obtaining detailed knowledge could improperly serve as a substitute for the discovering party's own trial preparation work. This detailed creative trial preparation is more likely to be put in writing in the form of documents prepared for internal office use. Seen in this light the distinction is less one between the oral and written creative trial preparation material than it is a distinction between general assertions, which must be revealed in order to prepare intelligently for trial, and detailed development of contentions, a process that is less essential in the early stages of a case. The detailed assertion, however, are most commonly embodied in written form.

JAMES UNDERWOOD, A GUIDE TO FEDERAL DISCOVERY RULES 40 (2d ed. 1985).

17. Aside from contention interrogatories, are legal opinions absolutely protected? Consider the following case:

Holmgren v. State Farm Mutual Insurance Co.
976 F. 2d 573 (9th Cir. 1992)

FARRIS, CIRCUIT JUDGE.

In these consolidated appeals, State Farm Mutual Automobile Insurance Company appeals the district court's judgment entered on a jury verdict for Julie Holmgren in her action for unfair claim settlement practices under Mont. Code Ann. § 33-18-201. State Farm also appeals the district court's award of attorney expenses under the Federal Rules of Civil Procedure 37(c). We affirm in all respects except the size of the Rule 37(c) award.

I

Julie Holmgren was injured on July 16, 1986, in Helena, Montana, when State Farm's insured, Sharon Cannon, ran a stop sign and collided with the car in which Holmgren was riding. Cannon was intoxicated at the time. She left the scene of the Holmgren accident and collided with three other cars in the vicinity. Cannon pled guilty to several charges, including driving while under the influence of alcohol.

Immediately after the accident, Holmgren was treated at a local emergency room for headache and neck and back pain. She thereafter saw Dr. Bishop, who prescribed physical therapy and recommended that she cease working until January 1987. Holmgren followed his recommendation. Her employer discharged her from her part-time job some time before October 22, 1986. Holmgren received further treatment through 1988.

Within a week of the accident, Holmgren hired an attorney, who promptly contacted State Farm. A State Farm representative, Ron Ashbraner, conducted an initial investigation and concluded that Cannon's liability was clear. At his direction, State Farm reimbursed the Holmgren family for the damage to their automobile, for car rental expenses, and made advance payments for Holmgren's medical expenses and lost wages totaling just over $5,000.

Holmgren's husband had been disabled in 1984 and was unemployed. The Holmgrens lost their home through foreclosure in December 1987. The family's fiscal pressures were regularly communicated to State Farm by Holmgren's counsel.

In December 1987, State Farm's offer to settle for $12,500 was rejected. Unsuccessful settlement attempts led to the July 1988 filing of suit in state court. Cannon's attorney, who had been retained by State Farm, filed an answer admitting injury but denying liability. The suit was settled for $40,000 in October 1989, on the second day of trial. The settlement expressly reserved Holmgren's rights against State Farm for bad faith in the process of adjusting and settling the claim.

Holmgren filed this suit in state court, under Mont. Code Ann. §§ 33-18-201(2), (4), (6) and (13), on November 9, 1989. Invoking diversity jurisdiction, State Farm removed the suit to federal district court. The district court entered judgment of $149,115.40 on a jury verdict for Holmgren, after crediting State Farm for advance payments and the amount paid to settle the Cannon suit. * * *

Holmgren's motion for attorneys' fees under the Federal Rules of Civil Procedure 37(c) for State Farm's denial during discovery of certain requests for admission was granted. Following

C. Scope of Discovery

supplemental briefing, the district court awarded attorneys' fees of $11,639.35. State Farm timely appealed.

II

(1) *Opinion Work Product* — State Farm contends that the district court erred in compelling it to produce and admitting as evidence plaintiff's exhibits 92 and 93. These items are handwritten memoranda drafted during the litigation of the Cannon suit by a State Farm adjuster. They contain a range of values for Holmgren's claims, including aggravation, medical expenses, lost earnings, pain and suffering, loss of course of life and loss of home, fixing the range of potential liability as from $78,000 to $145,000. State Farm argues that these items are opinion work product and protected under the Federal Rules of Civil Procedure 26(b)(3).

Holmgren contends that State Farm failed to object to the admission of the exhibits. We reject the argument. Counsel objected by affidavit to the production of both items as "opinion work product."

* * * The primary purpose of the work product rule is to "prevent exploitation of a party's efforts in preparing for litigation." Admiral Ins. Co. v. United States District Court, 881 F.2d 1486, 1494 (9th Cir. 1989). Like the discovery process that it limits, the work product doctrine encourages efficient development of facts and issues.

Exhibits 92 and 93 meet the threshold requirements for qualification as work product: both are (a) documents sought by Holmgren that were (b) prepared for trial (c) by a representative of State Farm. They reflect the opinion of a State Farm adjuster on the range of potential liability.

We need not decide whether Rule 26(b)(3) provides any protection for material prepared for litigation that has terminated. For even if it does, the rule permits discovery when mental impressions are the pivotal issue in the current litigation and the need for the material is compelling.

A party seeking opinion work product must make a showing beyond the substantial need/ undue hardship test required under Rule 26(b)(3) for non-opinion work product. Upjohn Co. v. United States, 449 U.S. 383, 401-02 (1981). The Supreme Court, however, has so far declined to decide whether opinion work product is absolutely protected from discovery.

The leading case to deny all discovery of opinion work product is Duplan Corp. v. Moulinage et Retorderie de Chavanoz, 509 F.2d 730, 734 (4th Cir. 1974)(*Duplan II*). The *Duplan II* court reasoned, "in our view, no showing of relevance, substantial need or undue hardship should justify compelled disclosure of an attorney's mental impressions, conclusions, opinions or legal theories. This is made clear by the Rule's use of the term 'shall' as opposed to 'may.'" This argument ignores the Advisory Committee notes to the 1970 amendment to Rule 26(b)(3) which state that the Rule "conforms to the holdings of the cases, when viewed in light of their facts." In *Hickman*, the Court stated that "if there should be a rare situation justifying production of [work product], petitioner's case is not of that type."

The Supreme Court, in 1946, rejected a proposed amendment to Rule 30(b) that would have given opinion work product absolute protection. That rejection, followed closely by the *Hickman* decision, which ordained a case-by-case approach to work product questions, suggests that the Court did not view the mandatory language of Rule 26(b)(3) as demanding absolute protection of opinion work product.

We agree with the several courts and commentators that have concluded that opinion work product may be discovered and admitted when mental impressions are *at issue* in a case and the need for the material is compelling.

Both elements are met here. In a bad faith insurance claim settlement case, the "strategy, mental impressions and opinion of [the insurer's] agents concerning the handling of the claim are directly at issue." Further, Holmgren's need for the exhibits was compelling. Montana permits insureds and third party claimants to proceed under § 33-18-201 against an insurer for bad faith in the settlement process. Unless the information is available elsewhere, a plaintiff may be able to establish a compelling need for evidence in the insurer's claim file regarding the insurer's opinion of the viability and value of the claim. We review the question on a case-by-case basis.

If a party has demonstrated the requisite level of need and hardship, the other party must produce the material.

In *Handgards*, "the lawyers who managed and supervised the former litigation for the defendants [were] being called as witnesses to express their opinions as to the merits of the prior suits." This comment, and others like it in "at issue" cases, is a practical acknowledgment of the fact that, in bad faith settlement cases, insurers may call their adjusters to testify to their opinions as to the lack of viability of the underlying claim. When an insurer chooses to remain mute on the subject, the plaintiff is not foreclosed from developing the same evidence.

The district court did not err in ordering discovery of and admitting Exhibits 92 and 93.

* * *

NOTES AND QUESTIONS

1. Insurance companies owe fiduciary duties to their insureds. Among other things, this includes the duty to represent and provide a defense, and to act in good faith in settling claims. If they breach any of these, they can be sued for tort.

2. Given the court's ruling in *Holmgren*, would it also have been permissible for Holmgren to depose the attorney who represented State Farm in the original suit and ask that lawyer about his settlement and litigation strategy?

3. If the memo in question in *Holmgren* had been sent from the claims adjuster to State Farm's attorney, would it have been protected by attorney-client privilege?

4. Attorney-client privilege is waived when the client puts the communication itself at issue. Thus, where the client asserts advice of counsel as a defense or claims that the lawyer gave improper or inadequate advice, the communications between lawyer and client that would otherwise be protected become discoverable. Notice, however, that in these situations it is the client who puts the communication at issue. In *Holmgren*, by contrast, it was the opposing party that raised an issue concerning the contents of the memo.

C. Scope of Discovery

4. Experts

Experts can be extremely valuable, both as consultants who assist in preparation, but do not testify, and as expert witnesses at trial. They are widely used in civil litigation. A survey of California state civil jury cases showed that expert witnesses testified in 86% of these cases with an average of 3.3 experts per trial. Samuel Gross, *Expert Evidence*, 1991 WIS. L. REV. 1113, 1119. Although ordinary witnesses are not permitted to testify as to their opinions, see Fed. R. Evid. 701, qualified experts may offer opinions where "scientific, technical, or other specialized knowledge will assist the trier of fact to understand the evidence or to determine a fact in issue." Fed. R. Evid. 702.

Rule 26 deals specifically with discovery from experts. The 1993 amendments to Rule 26 made some significant changes to the Rule. The rule requires that at least 90 days before trial, each party must identify all experts who may testify at trial. Rule 26(a)(2). This disclosure must be accompanied by a written report prepared and signed by the expert. Rule 26(a)(2)(B). Once the report has been turned over, the expert can be deposed. Rule 26(b)(4)(A). Failure to produce the required expert report can result in the court prohibiting the expert from testifying. See China Resource Prod. v. FAYDA Int'l, 856 F. Supp. 856, 866-67 (D. Del. 1994).

What information must be included in the report? Rule 26(a)(2)(B) provides in particular that the report must include "the data or other information considered by the witness in forming the opinions." How broadly should this phrase be construed? Suppose an attorney gives a testifying expert material that would otherwise be protected by work-product. Does Rule 26(a)(2)(B) mean that the expert must disclose this material? Prior to the adoption of the 1993 amendments, most, though not all, courts that had considered this question had held that giving material to an expert did not remove work-product protection. Compare Bogosian v. Gulf Oil Corp., 738 F.2d 587, 593-95 (3d Cir. 1984) (material protected), with Boring v. Keller, 97 F.R.D. 404, 407 (D. Colo. 1983) (material not protected). The Advisory Committee Notes to the 1993 amendments state that under Rule 26(a)(2)(B), "litigants should no longer be able to argue that materials furnished to their experts to be used in forming their opinions — whether or not ultimately relied upon by the expert — are privileged or otherwise protected from disclosure when such persons are testifying or being deposed." Does this mean that a work-product protected report given to a testifying expert must be disclosed? One district court has held that the 1993 rule does not mean this:

> This court interprets the revised rule and comment to mean only that the *data or information, i.e.,* the facts, considered by the expert must be disclosed notwithstanding the assertion of work product protection or privilege. It does not compel the production of the *documents* that transmitted the data or information to the expert, which may well, as here, contain protected work product other than data or information.

CHAPTER 9 DISCOVERY

All West Pet Supply v. Hill's Pet Products, 152 F.R.D. 634, 639 n.9 (D. Kan. 1993).

Rule 26(b)(4)(B) addresses discovery from non-testifying experts. Study this rule, then consider the following case:

Ager v. Jane C. Stormont Hospital & Training School for Nurses
622 F. 2d 496 (10th Cir. 1980)

BARRETT, CIRCUIT JUDGE.

Lynn R. Johnson, counsel for plaintiff Emily Ager, appeals from an order of the District Court adjudging him guilty of civil contempt. Jurisdiction vests by reason of 28 U.S.C. § 1826(b).

Emily was born April 4, 1955, at Stormont-Vail Hospital in Topeka, Kansas. During the second stage of labor, Emily's mother suffered a massive rupture of the uterine wall. The ensuing loss of blood led to Mrs. Ager's death. Premature separation of the placenta from the uterine wall also occurred, resulting in fetal asphyxia. Following Emily's delivery, it was discovered that she evidenced signs of severe neurological dysfunction. Today, she is mentally impaired and a permanently disabled quadriplegic with essentially no control over her body functions.

In March, 1977, Emily's father filed, on her behalf, a complaint for the damages sustained at her birth. The complaint alleges, in essence, that "the hemorrhaging and resultant death of her mother and the brain damage and other injuries which she sustained...while still in her mother's womb and/or during her delivery, were directly and proximately caused by the negligence and carelessness of the defendants (Stormont-Vail Hospital and Dr. Dan L. Tappen, the attending physician) which joined and concurred in causing plaintiff's mother's death and plaintiff's bodily injuries and damages and resultant disability." After joining the issues, Dr. Tappen propounded a series of interrogatories to the plaintiff. The specific interrogatories at issue here are:

> 1. Have you contacted any person or persons, whether they are going to testify or not, in regard to the care and treatment rendered by Dr. Dan Tappen involved herein?

> 2. If the answer to the question immediately above is in the affirmative, please set forth the name of said person or persons and their present residential and/or business address.

> 3. If the answer to question # 1 is in the affirmative, do you have any statements or written reports from said person or persons?

In response, plaintiff filed written objections, accompanied by a lengthy brief. Dr. Tappen answered the plaintiff's objections. The answer brief was treated by the United States Magistrate as a motion for an order compelling discovery pursuant to the Federal Rules of Civil Procedure, Rule 37(a). Following his review, the Magistrate ordered the plaintiff to answer the interrogatories:

C. Scope of Discovery

Interrogatories No. 1, 2 and 3 should be answered with the single exception, if the plaintiff has contacted an expert who was informally consulted in preparation for trial, but who was never retained or specifically employed and will not be called as a witness, it will not be necessary for the plaintiff to supply the name and address of such person or persons or to set forth any statement or report which such person or persons may have made.

Plaintiff's counsel answered the interrogatories in part, but failed to provide any information concerning consultative experts not expected to testify at trial. Plaintiff apparently based the refusal to answer on her contention that an expert who advises a party that his opinion will not aid the party in the trial of the case falls within the definition of experts informally consulted but not retained or specially employed. At defendant's suggestion, the Magistrate ordered plaintiff to provide further answers to the interrogatories, specifically defining the terms retained or specially employed:

> In the generally accepted meaning of the term in everyday usage, "retained" or "specially employed" ordinarily implies some consideration, a payment or reward of some kind, as consideration for being "retained" or "specially employed." It follows, therefore, that if a medical expert is consulted for the purpose of rendering advice or opinion on a hospital chart, or a physician's medical records pertaining to a case, and is paid or makes a charge for such service, he has been "retained" or "specially employed" within the meaning of the Rule. If [such an] expert is not to be called as a witness, he would be subject to the provisions of Rule 26(b)(4)(B) and, * * * there would be routine access to the names and addresses of such experts; but if they are not to be called as witnesses, facts known or opinions held by such experts would be subject to the requirements of Rule 26(b)(4)(B). However, if the consultation with the medical expert was strictly on an informal basis and such expert was not "retained" or "specially employed," the identity of such expert need not be disclosed.

Rather than complying with the Magistrate's order, Ager sought review by the District Court pursuant to 28 U.S.C. § 636(b)(1)(A). The District Court denied plaintiff's motion for review as untimely. On reconsideration, the Court affirmed the Magistrate's order:

> In the context of this malpractice case the question is whether plaintiff must identify each and every doctor, physician or medical expert plaintiff's counsel retained or specially employed during pretrial investigation and preparation. The courts have been divided on the issue. The Magistrate * * * held the identities of persons retained or specially employed for an opinion (i.e. to whom some consideration had been paid) to be discoverable. We have again read the Magistrate's Order and the suggestions of counsel. We find plaintiff's argument based upon the Advisory Committee Notes to be unpersuasive. After reviewing the cases and the suggestions of counsel we cannot find the Magistrate's Order to be "contrary to law."

Plaintiff's counsel filed a formal response to the Court's order and refused to comply. The Court thereafter entered a civil contempt order against Johnson. Johnson was committed to the custody of the United States Marshal until his compliance with the Court's order. Execution of the custody order was stayed pending appeal, after Johnson posted a recognizance bond. The Court specifically found that the appeal was not frivolous or taken for purposes of delay.

The issues on appeal are whether: (1) the District Court erred in adjudging Johnson guilty of civil contempt; and (2) a party may routinely discover the names of retained or specially employed consultative non-witness experts, pursuant to the Federal Rules of Civil Procedure, rule 26(b)(4)(B), absent a showing of exceptional circumstances justifying disclosure.

The Contempt Power

When a recalcitrant witness fails to obey the duly issued orders of a court, he may be cited for contempt, either criminal, civil, or both. Whether the adjudication of contempt "survives the avoidance of [the] underlying order depends on the nature of the contempt decree. If the contempt is criminal it stands; if it is civil it fails."

The primary purpose of a criminal contempt is to punish defiance of a court's judicial authority. Accordingly, the normal beneficiaries of such an order are the courts and the public interest. On the other hand, civil contempt is characterized by the court's desire "to *compel* obedience of the court order or to compensate the litigant for injuries stained from the disobedience." The remedial aspects outweigh the punitive considerations. Thus, the primary beneficiaries of such an order are the individual litigants. The judicial system benefits to a lesser extent.

Our review of the order, and the proceedings held in connection therewith, convinces us that the citation was framed in the nature of a coercive civil contempt. * * *

Validity of the Underlying Order

Having held that the viability of the contempt citation depends upon the validity of the underlying order, we now turn to the issue of whether a party may routinely discover the identities of non-witness expert consultants absent a showing of exceptional circumstances justifying disclosure.

[Rule 26 of the] Federal Rules of Civil Procedure governs the scope of discovery concerning experts or consultants. Subdivision (b)(4) separates these experts into four categories, applying different discovery limitations to each:

(1) Experts a party expects to use at trial. The opponent may learn by interrogatories the names of these trial witnesses and the substance of their testimony but further discovery concerning them can be had only on motion and court order.

(2) Experts retained or specially employed in anticipation of litigation or preparation for trial but not expected to be used at trial. Except as provided in rule 35 for an examining physician, the facts and opinions of experts in this category can be discovered only on a showing of exceptional circumstances.

(3) Experts informally consulted in preparation for trial but not retained. No discovery may be had of the names or views of experts in this category.

(4) Experts whose information was not acquired in preparation for trial. This class, which includes both regular employees of a party not specially employed on

the case and also experts who were actors or viewers of the occurrences that gave rise to suit, is not included within Rule 26(b)(4) at all and facts and opinions they have are freely discoverable as with any ordinary witness.

WRIGHT & MILLER, FEDERAL PRACTICE AND PROCEDURE : CIVIL § 2029. We are here concerned *only* with the second and third category of experts.

A. Discovery of Experts Informally Consulted, But Not Retained or Specially Employed

No provision in the Federal Rules of Civil Procedure, rule 26(b)(4) expressly deals with non-witness experts who are informally consulted by a party in preparation for trial, but not retained or specially employed in anticipation of litigation. The advisory committee notes to the rule indicated, however, that subdivision (b)(4)(B) "precludes discovery against experts who [are] informally consulted in preparation for trial, but not retained or specially employed." We agree with the District Court that this preclusion not only encompasses information and opinions developed in anticipation of litigation, but also insulates discovery of the identity and other collateral information concerning experts consulted informally. Graham, *Discovery of Experts Under Rule 26(b)(4) of the Federal Rules of Civil Procedure: Part One, an Analytical Study*, 1976 U. ILL. L.F. 895, 938-939.

Relying on Professor Graham's article, Ager urges that "an expert 'would be considered informally consulted if, for any reason, the consulting party did not consider the expert of any assistance,' and that '[a] consulting party may consider the expert of no assistance because of his insufficient credentials, his unattractive demeanor, or his excessive fees.'" This view is, of course, at odds with the Trial Court's ruling that:

> The commonly accepted meaning of the term "informally consulted" necessarily implies a consultation without formality. If one makes an appointment with a medical expert to discuss a case or examine records and give advice or opinion for which a charge is made and the charge is paid or promised what is informal about such consultation? On the other hand, an attorney meets a doctor friend at a social occasion or on the golf course and a discussion occurs concerning the case no charge is made or contemplated no written report rendered such could clearly be an "informal consultation."

We decline to embrace either approach in its entirety. In our view, the status of each expert must be determined on an ad hoc basis. Several factors should be considered: (1) the manner in which the consultation was initiated; (2) the nature, type and extent of information or material provided to, or determined by, the expert in connection with his review; (3) the duration and intensity of the consultative relationship; and, (4) the terms of the consultation, if any (e.g. payment, confidentiality of test data or opinions, etc.). Of course, additional factors bearing on this determination may be examined if relevant.

Thus, while we recognize that an expert witness' lack of qualifications, unattractive demeanor, excessive fees, or adverse opinions may result in a party's decision not to use the expert at trial, nonetheless, there are situations where a witness is retained or specifically employed in anticipation of litigation prior to the discovery of such undesirable information or characteristics. On the other hand, a telephonic inquiry to an expert's office in which only general information is provided may result in informal consultation, even if a fee is charged, provided there is no follow-up consultation.

The determination of the status of the expert rests, in the first instance, with the party resisting discovery. Should the expert be considered informally consulted, that categorization should be provided in response. The propounding party should then be provided the opportunity of requesting a determination of the expert's status based on an in camera review by the court. Inasmuch as the District Court failed to express its views on this question, we deem it appropriate to remand rather than attempt to deal with the merits of this issue on appeal. If the expert is considered to have been only informally consulted in anticipation of litigation, discovery is barred.

B. Discovery of the Identities of Experts Retained or Specially Employed

Subdivision (b)(4)(B) of rule 26 specifically deals with non-witness experts who have been retained or specially employed by a party in anticipation of litigation. The text of that subdivision provides that "facts or opinions" of non-witness experts retained or specially employed may only be discovered upon a showing of "exceptional circumstances under which it is impracticable for the party seeking discovery to obtain facts or opinions on the same subject by other means." Inasmuch as discovery of the identities of these experts, absent a showing of exceptional circumstances, was not expressly precluded by the text of subdivision (b)(4)(B), the District Court found the general provisions of rule 26(b)(1) controlling. * * *

The District Court's ruling on this issue follows [several cases]. Several [other] decisions, however, have held that rule 26(b)(4)(B) requires a showing of exceptional circumstances before names of retained or specially employed consultants may be discovered.

The advisory committee notes indicate that the structure of rule 26 was largely developed around the doctrine of unfairness designed to prevent a party from building his own case by means of his opponent's financial resources, superior diligence and more aggressive preparation. Dr. Tappen contends that "[d]iscoverability of the identity of an expert retained or specially employed by the other party but who is not to be called to testify hardly gives the discovering party a material advantage or benefit at the expense of the opposing party's preparation. Once those identities are disclosed, the discovering party is left to his own diligence and resourcefulness in contacting such experts and seeking to enlist whatever assistance they may be both able and willing to offer." The drafters of rule 26 did not contemplate such a result:

> Subdivision (b)(4)(B) is concerned only with experts retained or specially consulted in relation to trial preparation. Thus the subdivision precludes discovery against experts who were informally consulted in preparation for trial, but not retained or specially employed. As an ancillary procedure, a party may *on a proper showing* require the other party to *name* experts retained or specially employed, but not those informally consulted. (Emphasis supplied).

We hold that the "proper showing" required to compel discovery of a non-witness expert retained or specially employed in anticipation of litigation[5] corresponds to a showing of "exceptional

C. Scope of Discovery

circumstances under which it is impracticable for the party seeking discovery to obtain facts or opinions on the same subject by other means." Federal Rules of Civil Procedure, rule 26(b)(4)(B).

There are several policy considerations supporting our view. Contrary to Dr. Tappen's view, once the identities of retained or specially employed experts are disclosed, the protective provisions of the rule concerning facts known or opinions held by such experts are subverted. The expert may be contacted or his records obtained and information normally non-discoverable, under rule 26(b)(4)(B), revealed. Similarly, although perhaps rarer, the opponent may attempt to compel an expert retained or specially employed by an adverse party in anticipation of trial, but whom the adverse party does not intend to call, to testify at trial.[6] The possibility also exists, although we do not suggest it would occur in this case, or that it would be proper, that a party may call his opponent to the stand and ask if certain experts were retained in anticipation of trial, but not called as a witness, thereby leaving with the jury an inference that the retaining party is attempting to suppress adverse facts or opinions. Finally, we agree with Ager's view that "[d]isclosure of the identities of [medical] consultative experts would inevitably lessen the number of candid opinions available as well as the number of consultants willing to even discuss a potential medical malpractice claim with counsel .... [I]n medical malpractice actions [perhaps] more than any other type of litigation, the limited availability of consultative experts and the widespread aversion of many health care providers to assist plaintiff's counsel require that, absent special circumstances, discovery of the identity of evaluative consultants be denied. If one assumes that access to informed opinions is desirable in both prosecuting valid claims and eliminating groundless ones, a discovery practice that would do harm to these objectives should not be condoned."

In sum, we hold that the identity, and other collateral information concerning an expert who is retained or specially employed in anticipation of litigation, but not expected to be called as a witness at trial, is not discoverable except as "provided in Rule 35(b) or upon a showing of exceptional circumstances under which it is impracticable for the party seeking discovery to obtain facts or opinions on the same subject by other means."[8] Fed. Rules Civ. Proc., rule 26(b)(4)(B). The party "seeking disclosure under Rule 26(b)(4)(B) carries a heavy burden" in demonstrating the existence of exceptional circumstances.

---

[5] The distinction between experts who are retained or specially employed in anticipation of litigation is somewhat unclear.

[6] We do not here decide the propriety of this action.

[8] Professor Albert Sacks, reporter to the advisory committee, listed two examples of exceptional circumstances:

> (a) Circumstances in which an expert employed by the party seeking discovery could not conduct important experiments and test[s] because an item of equipment, etc., needed for the test[s] has been destroyed or is otherwise no longer available. If the party from whom discovery is sought had been able to have its experts test the item before its destruction or nonavailability, then information obtained from those tests might be discoverable.
>
> (b) Circumstances in which it might be impossible for a party to obtain its own expert. Such circumstances would occur when the number of experts in a field is small and their time is already fully retained by others.

See: ALI-ABA, CIVIL TRIAL MANUAL p.189

Disposition

The order of the District Court adjudging Lynn R. Johnson guilty of civil contempt is vacated. The cause is remanded. On remand, the status of the non-witness experts against whom discovery is sought should be undertaken as a two-step process. First, was the expert informally consulted in anticipation of litigation but not retained or specially employed? If so, no discovery may be had as to the identity or opinions of the expert. Second, if the expert was *not* informally consulted, but rather retained or specially employed in anticipation of litigation, but not expected to testify at trial, do exceptional circumstances exist justifying disclosure of the expert's identity, opinions or other collateral information?

Vacated and remanded.

NOTES AND QUESTIONS

1. If you represented the plaintiff in *Ager*, why would you want the names of defendant's *non*-testifying experts?

2. In *Ager* suppose that the court refuses to permit plaintiff to discover the identity of the defendant's non-testifying experts. Nonetheless, in preparing for trial, plaintiff contacts an expert who happens to be one defendant had consulted. Would Rule 26(b)(4) prohibit the plaintiff from consulting that expert or calling her to testify? The cases are in conflict on this issue. See Note, *Must the Show Go On? Defining When One Party May Call or Compel an Opposing Party's Consultative Expert to Testify*, 78 MINN. L. REV. 1191 (1994).

3. Prior to the 1993 amendments, discovery of even testifying experts was more limited. These past limitations were justified by the Advisory Committee of the prior rule because they "reflect[ed] the fear that one side will benefit unduly from the other's better preparation." The 1993 amendments, which allow relatively unfettered discovery from testifying experts, apparently reject this fairness argument, at least as it is applied to testifying experts. Should the argument also be rejected with respect to non-testifying experts? Are there other reasons to protect non-testifying experts from discovery?

4. Why should information from informally consulted experts be absolutely protected?

5. As *Ager* suggests, there is a split of authority on the question whether the names of non-testifying experts are protected under Rule 26(b)(4)(B). In *Roesberg*, the court required defendant to answer Interrogatory 56(a), including identifying non-testifying experts who were "retained or specially employed." The court held that these names were available without a showing of exceptional circumstance. What are the arguments for and

against routine disclosure of such experts' identities? Which argument do you think is stronger? See Note, *Discovery of Retained Nontestifying Experts' Identities Under the Federal Rules of Civil Procedure*, 80 Mich. L. Rev. 513 (1982).

6. Consider the following case: Goldman Paper Company hires a consultant to test land owned by the corporation for contamination. Later the corporation is sold to another entity. When the buyer learns that the land is contaminated, it sues to rescind the purchase and seeks to depose the consultant. Goldman objects to the deposition on the grounds that the consultant is an non-testifying expert whom Goldman has retained to assist in the preparation of litigation. Should the buyer be permitted to depose the consultant? See Bunzl Pulp & Paper Sales, Inc. v. Golder, 1990 U.S. Dist. LEXIS 16355 (E.D. Pa. 1990).

7. In the past, lawyers sometimes used their testifying expert as a colleague and sounding board for possible theories. In light of the uncertainty about the scope of work product protection for information given to testifying experts, see discussion supra at 427, some practitioners now advise using non-testifying experts to assist in the development of theories and factual research, thereby screening the testifying expert from this phase. See 1 Fed. Disc. News 8 (Issue 1, Dec. 1994).

8. Can independent experts, such as research scientists, who have not been hired by any party, be forced to testify? In general, such experts can be forced to testify, but Rule 45 (c)(3)(B) gives the court authority to order appropriate compensation. As the Advisory Committee Notes explain: "Experts are not exempt from the duty to give evidence, * * * but compulsion to give evidence may threaten the intellectual property of experts denied the opportunity to bargain for the value of their services."

9. In both *Ager* and *Hickman*, counsel for one of the parties disobeyed a discovery order, was held in contempt of court, and sent to jail. You may wonder why a lawyer would behave so defiantly. The reason is that the contempt citation is necessary to ensure immediate appellate review of the discovery ruling. As we will see in Chapter 14, in federal court, litigants ordinarily cannot appeal until there is a final judgment which ends the whole case. Because discovery rulings come long before the end of the case, those rulings are not immediately appealable. However, a contempt citation is immediately appealable because it is considered separate proceeding.

10. The discovery dispute in *Ager* was decided in the first instance by a magistrate judge. Magistrate judges are not appointed pursuant to Art. III of the Constitution. They are not appointed by the President and do not enjoy life tenure. Instead they are appointed to eight year terms by the district judges of each district court. 28 U.S.C. § 631. On referral from a district judge, magistrate judges are authorized to decide matters that are not dispositive of a claim or defense. See 28 U.S.C. § 636(b)(1); Rule 72. Most discovery falls into this category and magistrate judges are widely used in scheduling and planning

CHAPTER 9 DISCOVERY

conference under Rule 16 and in resolving discovery disputes. Decisions of a magistrate judge are reviewable by the district court and only a district court can enter a contempt citation. With consent of the parties, magistrate judges can also adjudicate cases. See 28 U.S.C. § 636(c); Rule 73.

5. Review Problem

A tanker owned by Gasson Oil Co. runs aground causing a massive oil spill off the coast of Alaska. Immediately following the spill, Gasson sends a team of investigators to learn all they can about the incident. The investigative team is lead by Gasson's General Counsel and includes lawyers, engineers, environmental specialists, as well as other experts. The team is instructed to inspect the site, interview people and write a report for the Gasson Board of Directors on the causes and effects of the spill.

1. A group of fisherman sue Gasson to recover damages caused to their business by the oil spill. In the course of discovery, plaintiffs make a request for production of documents seeking:

(a) a copy of the report to the Board;
(b) all photos or videos of the accident site taken by the investigative team;
(c) all photos or videos of the accident site taken by witnesses or other non-parties and given or sold to Gasson;
(d) all signed statements given by witnesses;
(e) all audio or video tapes of interviews with witnesses;
(f) all notes and memos concerning the investigation;
(g) the results of all tests conducted by the Gasson investigative team.

The plaintiffs also serve interrogatories which ask for:

(h) names of everyone interviewed as part of the investigation;
(i) a summary of what was said by each person who was interviewed.

Which, if any, of these items are discoverable?

2. Would any of the items listed in Question 1 have to be disclosed if Gasson decided to call as an expert witness at trial one of the experts who participated in the investigation?

3. Plaintiffs' interrogatories also request detailed information concerning how the accident occurred. Can Gasson refuse to answer on the grounds that the information was acquired as part of a work product protected investigation? Can it refuse to answer on the grounds that its attorney has that information?

4. Suppose that in the course of the investigation, the captain of the ship admitted to one of the lawyers that the evening before the ship sailed, he spent time in a bar and had

8 to 10 drinks. In addition, he gave the lawyer the names of the crew who were with him at the bar. In discovery the plaintiffs' interrogatories ask:
- (a) For the 24 hour period immediately prior to the departure of the tanker, state whether the captain consumed any alcohol.
- (b) If the captain did consume any alcohol during the 24 hours prior to the departure of the tanker, state when and where the alcohol was consumed and the quantity consumed. Also state the names and addresses of any people who were present with the captain when he consumed the alcohol.

Does Gasson have to answer these interrogatories?

5. Suppose during the course of the investigation, a witness who was with the captain shortly before the ship ran aground noted that the captain was not wearing his eyeglasses. In his deposition, the captain say he does not remember whether he was wearing his glasses at the time of the accident, but asserted "I don't need them anyway — my vision is fine without glasses." Can plaintiff's counsel have the captain subjected to ophthalmological testing? How?

D. Timing, Scheduling and Mandatory Disclosure

1. Timing

Rule 26(f) requires that all parties or their counsel meet "as soon as practicable and in any event at least 14 days before a scheduling conference is held or a scheduling order is due under Rule 16(b)." The purpose of the conference is to discuss "the nature and basis of their claims and defenses and the possibilities for a prompt settlement or resolution of the case, to make or arrange for the disclosures required by subdivision (a)(1), and to develop a proposed discovery plan." Absent court order or agreement of the parties, no formal discovery can commence until after this meeting has occurred.

Under Rule 16(b), the scheduling order can be issued at any time, but must be issued no later than 90 days after the appearance of the defendant and 120 days after service of the complaint. Thus, where the court complies with the outer limits of Rule 16(b), the Rule 26(f) conference between the parties could be as late as 106 days after service, with no formal discovery permitted during that period.

Within 10 days after the Rule 26(f) conference, the parties must submit a written report of this conference. See Form 35.

2. Mandatory Initial Disclosures

The 1993 amendments to Rule 26 require automatic disclosure of certain information, without the need for a discovery request. The goal of this change is "to accelerate the exchange of basic information about the case and eliminate the paperwork involved in requesting such information." Advisory Committee Notes. These disclosures occur at three different points. First are the "initial disclosures" of basic information relevant to the case. See Rule 26(a)(1). Initial disclosures must be made within 10 days after the Rule 26(f) conference unless the parties agree on or the court orders a different disclosure schedule. Second are the disclosures of expert witnesses which must be made no later than 90 days before trial, unless otherwise ordered or agreed. See Rule 26(a)(2). Third, are pretrial disclosures of expected trial witnesses and evidence. See Rule 26(a)(3). These disclosure must be made at least 30 days before trial, unless otherwise ordered or agreed. Pretrial disclosures are considered in greater detail at the end of this chapter.

In this section we focus on the initial disclosures required under Rule 26(a)(1) — the most controversial of the 1993 changes.

In re Lotus Development Securities Litigation
874 F. Supp. 48 (D. Mass.1995)

SARIS, DISTRICT JUDGE.

Introduction

This is a consolidated class action alleging that defendants Lotus Development Corporation ("Lotus"), James P. Manzi (the Lotus Chief Executive Officer and Chairman) and Edwin J. Gillis (the Chief Financial Officer) knowingly made certain false and misleading public statements in violation of §§ 10(b) and 20(a) of the Securities Exchange Act of 1934, 15 U.S.C. §§ 78j(b) and 78t(a) and Rule 10(b)-5, 17 CFR § 240.10b-5. The purported class purchased shares of common stock between April 20, 1994 and June 20, 1994.

At the scheduling conference held on November 28, 1994, pursuant to Fed. R. Civ. P. 16(b) and Local Rule 16.1, defendants requested a stay of the automatic disclosure required by Fed. R. Civ. P. 26(a)(1) and Local Rule 26.2 (which was amended effective January 2, 1995). Defendants argued that the complaint should be dismissed pursuant to Fed. R. Civ. P. 9(b), and that proceeding with automatic disclosure, as well as discovery, before resolution of their motion to dismiss, would impose on them unnecessary expense.

The Court stayed automatic disclosure subject to an expedited briefing schedule in order to enable defendants to file a motion to stay discovery pending decision on a motion to dismiss, to be supported by a five page memorandum. Such a motion was filed on December 13, 1994, and an opposition of the same length was filed on December 23, 1994. Although defendants seek to stay "discovery," the court assumes, based on the discussions at the scheduling conference, that the term was intended to encompass the concept of "automatic disclosure" as well.

Defendants' motion identifies the tension between the heightened pleading standard of Fed. R. Civ. P. 9(b) and the new automatic disclosure requirement of Fed. R. Civ. P. 26(a)(1), as amended in 1993 and incorporated in Local Rule 26.2. After weighing the policies underlying the two rules, and studying the papers filed, the Court DENIES defendants' motion.

A. Rule 26(a)(1)

Generally, the new Rule 26(a)(1) requires the automatic disclosure of certain materials. * * *

A party may not seek discovery from any source before the parties have met and conferred as required by subdivision (f). Local Rule 26.2(A) further provides that unless otherwise ordered by the Court, a party must provide the information subject to automatic disclosure before the meeting required by Fed. R. Civ. P. 26(f) and before it may initiate discovery.

The advisory committee has made clear that a "court may eliminate or modify the disclosure requirements in a particular case." The notes also offer some guidance on the particularity provisos:

> Broad, vague, and conclusory allegations sometimes tolerated in notice pleading — for example, the assertion that a product with many component parts is defective in some unspecified manner — should not impose upon responding parties the obligation at that point to search for and identify all persons possibly involved in, or all documents affecting the design, manufacture, and assembly of the product. The greater the specificity and clarity of the allegations in the pleadings, the more complete should be the listing of potential witnesses and types of documentary evidence.
>
> . . . The rule contemplates that [the factual disputes defined in the pleadings] would be informally refined and clarified during the meeting of the parties under subdivision (f). . . . The disclosure requirements should, in short, be applied with common sense in light of the principles of Rule 1, keeping in mind the salutary purposes that the rule is intended to accomplish. The litigants should not indulge in gamesmanship. . . .

The salutary purpose identified by the advisory committee is "to accelerate the exchange of basic information about the case and to eliminate the paper work involved in requesting such information." More colorfully put, the committee set out to slay the twin dragons of cost and delay. See William W. Schwarzer, *Slaying the Monsters of Cost and Delay*, 74 JUDICATURE 178, (1991). The reform is expected to "reduce the cost and delay of obtaining plainly relevant core information, while limiting the opportunities to obstruct and delay the disclosure of such information." Schwarzer, *In Defense of "Automatic Disclosure in Discovery,"* 27 GA. L. REV. 655, 660 (1993). "If in the process it also helps raise the level of professionalism and restore a measure of civility, so much the better." Id.

B. Rule 9(b)

The rigors of Rule 9(b) have been recited with frequency in this circuit. In brief, the rule requires a specification of the time, place, and content of each alleged false representation, any where any allegation of fraud is based only on information and belief, the complaint must set forth the source of the information and the reasons for the belief. The objects of the rule are three: to place the defendants on notice; to safeguard defendants from unwarranted damage to their reputations; and to safeguard defendants from the danger of strike suits. "The danger of strike suits" is short-hand for "the possibility that 'a plaintiff with a largely groundless claim [will be able] to simply take up the time of a number of other people [by extensive discovery], with the right to do so representing an in terrorem increment of settlement value, rather than a reasonably founded hope that the process will reveal relevant evidence....'" Ross v. A. H. Robins Co., 607 F.2d 545, 557 (2d Cir. 1979) (quoting Blue Chip Stamps v. Manor Drug Stores, 421 U.S. 723, 741 (1975)). Many have observed that the danger of strike suits is near its apogee in securities law because of the big money at stake.

C. Reconciling the Rules

There are several possible ways of reconciling the policies underpinning Rule 26(a)(1) with Rule 9(b). The first option would be to give primacy to Rule 26(a)(1) and require disclosure to proceed apace without any evaluation of the merits of defendants' claims. This option, however, both disserves the goals of Rule 9(b) and ignores a key stricture of Rule 26(a)(1), avoidance of unnecessary expense. The second solution — that urged by defendants — is to give primacy to Rule 9(b) and stay automatic disclosure until the motion to dismiss is fully briefed and decided, often a lengthy process. The problem with this approach is that it carves out a wholesale exception to automatic disclosure that is not specifically contemplated by the text or committee notes.

Having rejected the extremes, the court explores the middle. The language of Rule 26(a)(1) virtually invites disputes as to which allegations are alleged specifically enough to warrant disclosure of related materials. The advisory committee states that, under the new Rule 26, such disputes "would be informally refined and clarified during the meeting of the parties under subdivision (f)." This hope is echoed by Judge Schwarzer: "The pre-disclosure, pre-discovery conference mandated by amended Rule 26(f), followed by the Rule 16 conference with a judge, leading to an order that would govern disclosure and future discovery ... will help identify and clarify issues, thus cutting through ... amorphous and uninformative allegations...." In the ideal case, parties would immediately disclose all core information, manifestly pertinent to well-pled allegations; wrangle over the rest; and then — if necessary — file a motion for an order compelling disclosure or discovery pursuant to Fed. R. Civ. P. 37. But this offers little guidance where the defendants immediately press the claim that the complaint as a whole is ill-pled and should be dismissed pursuant to established circuit law.

The procedure followed here is meant to be summary. The burden of proof imposed on the party seeking a stay is a stiff one. To create a full-blown procedure, or to make a stay more readily obtainable simply because there is a colorable motion to dismiss, would undermine the spirit of the new rule, and vindicate the critics who cried that the reform was bound to balloon motion practice by introducing new ambiguities that would be seized upon by lawyers trained to operate in an adversarial system. See, e.g., Griffin B. Bell, et al., *Automatic Disclosure in Discovery — The Rush to Reform*, 27 GA. L. REV. 1, 41-42, 46-47 (1992); Virginia E. Hench, *Mandatory Disclosure and Equal Access to*

Justice, 67 TEMP. L. REV. 179, 204-07 (1994). The function of the judiciary is to apply the amendment adopted on a case-by-case basis while attempting to harmonize the subsidiary goals of the various federal rules with each other and with the over arching goal of Rule 1: promoting the "just, speedy, and inexpensive" disposition of each case.

D. The Merits of the Motion to Dismiss

Although they did an admirable job in presenting their case in five pages (with some creative margin and font maneuvering), defendants have not persuaded this court that their motion to dismiss is a likely winner.

Defendants' primary contention is that the complaint fails to plead specific facts, as opposed to hindsight inferences, tending to show that defendants knew that Lotus' financial forecasts were false when made. Overpromising does not in itself imply fraud. As defendants point out, "courts in this district have repeatedly dismissed complaints that merely quote company statements or predictions as supporting facts for fraud." * * *

What were missing in all of the * * * cases [upon which defendant relied] was specific factual support that — at the time the rosy forecasts were made — defendants knew, or recklessly disregarded the likelihood, that those forecasts were false. In this case, plaintiffs point to some specifics.

It is alleged, based on press reports, that, by September and October, 1994, defendant Lotus, Inc., had accumulated 20-30 weeks worth of inventory backlog in its European trade channels, rather than the usual 5-6 weeks worth — an excess valued in the vicinity of $ 100 million. Plaintiffs allege that this backlog did not appear overnight, that Lotus and its officers were aware of the problem as it was developing during the second quarter of 1994, and that they were deceiving the public when they denied rumors of backlog. Unusual backlogs may reasonably be expected to lead to decreased sales. Plaintiffs further allege that there was no realistic basis for believing that such lost sales would be fully offset by other company developments.

To establish defendants' awareness of the developing backlog problem, plaintiffs point to two admissions. First, defendant Gillis, chief financial officer, made a public statement, on June 21, that sales were "below expectations throughout the [second] quarter." Second, in the course of denying rumors that there was excessive inventory backlog in the company's European trade channels, a spokesperson assured the public: "We maintain communication with the [trade] channels." In addition, the complaint alleges that defendant Gillis received weekly sales reports during the class period.

Plaintiffs make well-pled allegations of motive. They allege that all of the defendants gained heavily from an artificially inflated stock price during the class period: the insiders through sizable sales of their personal stock holdings; and the company through an important stock-financed acquisition. The timing of these transactions reinforces the claim that defendants manipulated a market overvaluation during the second quarter, by pushing excessive product on independent Lotus resellers prior to the second quarter.

These are sufficient factual contentions, in combination, to support an inference that the defendants were misrepresenting Lotus' financial status to the public when they made optimistic earnings projections as late as May 25.

This court concludes that the complaint is not so clearly deficient as to justify a stay of automatic disclosure, and, in due course, discovery. After all, automatic disclosure relating to whether or not there was excessive inventory during the class period, and the speed of the build up may well promote settlement and expedited resolution of this litigation. This memorandum and order should not be construed to preclude defendants from pressing their motion to dismiss and for a stay of discovery in fuller form.

Order

Defendants' Motion in Support of Discovery Stay Pending Decision on Motion to Dismiss is DENIED.

NOTES AND QUESTION

1. The mandatory disclosure requirements apply only to disputed facts "alleged with particularity." If one party believes that a fact is not alleged with sufficient particularity to trigger mandatory disclosure, does that party need to "stay" disclosure? Can't the party await a motion to compel under Rule 37(a)(2)(A)? Why then did the defendant in *Lotus* seek a stay? Do you think the defendant could have properly taken the position that there was no disputed fact alleged with sufficient particularity to trigger any mandatory disclosure?

2. Does "alleged with particularity" in Rule 26(a)(1) mean the same as "stated with particularity" in Rule 9(b)? If a fraud complaint is not dismissed under 9(b), does it follow that all allegations in the complaint are sufficiently particular to trigger mandatory disclosure? Lawyers have speculated that whether facts have been pleaded "with particularity" "will likely be a frequent battleground." Robert Pass, *Big Changes in the Federal Rules*, 20 LITIG. 10, 12 (1994).

3. The Advisory Committee Notes quoted in *Lotus* refer to "[b]road, vague, and conclusory allegations sometimes *tolerated* in notice pleading." (Emphasis added.) Is Rule 26(a)(1) a first step toward requiring more detailed pleadings?

4. One commentator has speculated that the disclosure requirements will encourage plaintiffs "to think before filing a complaint. Now, more than ever, an unprepared plaintiff is asking for trouble. If, within a few weeks of filing suit, plaintiff's counsel must make such disclosures, she must take the time to investigate and prepare *before* filing suit." Pass, supra, 20 LITIG. at 12. Do you agree?

5. One commentator has argued that many of the efforts at discovery reform are doomed because they mistakenly assume that "discovery requests may be interpreted fairly and easily if only lawyers chose to do so." Jeffrey Mayer, *Prescribing Cooperation: The Mandatory Pretrial Disclosure Requirement of Proposed Rules 26 and 37 of the Federal Rules of Civil Procedure*, 12 REV. OF LITIG. 77, 95 (1992). Noting the unavoidable

D. Timing, Scheduling and Mandatory Disclosure

indeterminacy of language, he argues that in the context of discovery "unlike the traditional model of written communication, where both parties are committed to understanding, the reader is not committed to understanding the writer's intent. To the contrary, the attorney is committed to serving his client's interest and not in reaching mutual understanding with opposing counsel." Id. at 98. The author concludes that the mandatory disclosure rules

> replicate the very communication problems found in the exchange of initial discovery requests. A lawyer asked to draw a link between disputed facts alleged with particularity and documents and information in his possession is carrying out the same analytical function he would were he to respond to an interrogatory referring to the same fact.

Id. at 113-14. Do you agree?

6. Are there any circumstances under which mandatory disclosure is automatically stayed? Should a district court stay mandatory disclosure pending resolution of any of the Rule 12(b) motions?

7. Suppose one side ignores its obligations under Rule 26(a)(1). Does this relieve the other side of its obligations to disclose?

8. Must one party automatically disclose information which it reasonably believes the other side already knows? In Scheetz v. Bridgestone/Firestone, Inc., 152 F.R.D. 628 (D. Mont. 1993), the court, applying a local rule similar to Rule 26(a)(1), held that disclosure was required in these circumstances. Is this consistent with the Rule's goal of reducing unnecessary cost and delay?

9. Look back at *Roesberg*. Would the disputes at issue there have been avoided if the 1993 amendments had been in effect? Of the information requested in the interrogatories, what of it would have been disclosed automatically through mandatory disclosure?

10. Examine the sanctions provision of Rule 37(c)(1). Will this provision effectively deter violations of the mandatory disclosure requirement? It has been argued that "[i]t would be a poor lawyer indeed who could not provide a good faith reason for under disclosure or explain why a subsequently corrected under disclosure was harmless." Mayer, supra, 12 REV. OF LITIG. at 117. Do you agree?

11. The 1993 amendments reflect a growing perception that discovery has gotten "out of control." JUSTICE FOR ALL — REDUCING COSTS AND DELAY IN CIVIL LITIGATION 19-20 (Brookings Inst. 1989). The amendments included a number of changes — mandatory disclosure requirements, presumptive limits on the number of depositions and interrogatories, a requirement that lawyers meet and confer to establish a discovery schedule, a requirement that the court enter a scheduling discovery scheduling order. The hope was that this set of changes, taken together, would speed up discovery and curb abuse. Notice that most of the changes entail greater judicial, and reduced litigant, control of discovery.

Do you think the drafters of the 1993 amendments trust litigants (and their lawyers) less than the drafters of the original rules?

12. One study of civil cases in state courts, conducted in the early 1990's found that no discovery is taken in over 40% of the cases. Even where parties undertake discovery, the amount of discovery is quite modest in the vast majority of cases. In 86% of such cases, there were 10 or fewer discovery requests in the entire case. See Susan Keilitz, Roger Hanson & Henry Daley, *Is Civil Discovery in State Trial Courts Out of Control?*, 17 ST. CT. J. 8, 11 (1993). These conclusions are consistent with an earlier study of federal courts which likewise suggests that discovery is used extensively in only a small fraction of civil lawsuits. See DAVID TRUBEK, JOEL GROSSMAN, WILLIAM FELSTINER, HERBERT KRITZER & AUSTIN SARAT, CIVIL LITIGATION RESEARCH PROJECT: FINAL REPORT (1983). See generally Linda Mullenix, *Discovery in Disarray: The Pervasive Myth of Pervasive Discovery Abuse and the Consequences for Unfounded Rulemaking*, 46 STAN. L. REV. 1393 (1994). If these studies are accurate, will mandatory disclosure increase or decrease the amount of discovery?

13. The Federal Rules of Civil Procedure are promulgated by the Supreme Court, but do not become effective for seven months after transmittal from the Supreme Court to Congress. See 28 U.S.C. § 2074. This gives Congress an opportunity to review the proposed changes and, if it wishes, to pass legislation blocking the rules from becoming effective. The mandatory disclosure provision of the 1993 amendments was very controversial and opponents mounted a substantial effort in Congress to block this rule. The House of Representatives passed a bill that would have blocked the rule, see H.R. 2814, 103rd Cong., 1st Sess. (1993), and many observers expected that the Senate would do the same. However, the bill did not get to the Senate until shortly before the session ended and came at a time when the Senate was preoccupied with a gun control measure. In addition there was disagreement between key Senators over aspects of the amendments. As a result, the Senate adjourned without passing the bill and all of the proposed 1993 amendments went into effect on Dec. 1, 1993.

14. Justice Scalia, joined by Justices Souter and Thomas, dissented form the adoption of Rule 26(a)(1) by the Supreme Court:

> This proposal is promoted as a means of reducing the unnecessary expense and delay that occur in the present discovery regime. But the duty-to-disclose regime does not replace the current, much-criticized discovery process; rather, it *adds a further layer of discovery*. It will likely *increase* the discovery burdens on district judges, as parties litigate what is "relevant" to "disputed facts," whether those facts have been alleged with particularity, whether the opposing side has adequately disclosed the required information, and whether it has fulfilled its continuing obligation to supplement the initial disclosure. * * *

D. Timing, Scheduling and Mandatory Disclosure

The proposed new regime does not fit comfortably within the American judicial system, which relies on adversarial litigation to develop the facts before a neutral decision maker. By placing upon lawyers the obligation to disclose information damaging to their clients — on their own initiative, and in a context where the lines between what must be disclosed and what need not be disclosed are not clear but require the exercise of considerable judgment — the new Rule would place intolerable strain upon lawyers' ethical duty to represent their clients and not to assist the opposing side. Requiring a lawyer to make a judgment as to what information if "relevant to disputed facts" plainly requires him to use his professional skills in the service of the adversary.

146 F.R.D. 510-11 (1993) (emphasis in original). How persuasive do you find these arguments?

15. In criminal cases, the prosecution has an obligation to disclose exculpatory material to the defense, regardless of whether the material is specifically requested by the defense. See Kyles v. Whitley, 115 S. Ct. 1555 (1995); United States v. Bagley, 473 U.S. 667 (1985); Brady v. Maryland, 373 U.S. 83 (1963). Should a similar obligation be imposed on both sides in civil litigation?

16. Consider what automatic disclosures would be required in the suit between the Robinsons and Audi, described at the beginning of the chapter. Assume that the Robinsons' complaint alleges in pertinent part:

(1) The Robinsons' automobile was hit in the rear by another vehicle.
(2) After their automobile was hit, the Robinsons' car exploded into flames.
(3) The flames spread quickly into the passenger compartment.
(4) Kay Robinson, and her children Eva and Sam were severely burned, hospitalized and suffered great pain.
(5) The Robinsons' automobile was designed and manufactured by Audi.
(6) Audi was negligent in the design and manufacture of the Robinsons' automobile. The automobile was unreasonably dangerous for use by the Robinsons.
(7) The Robinsons seek $4 million in damages.

Audi's answer admits that the accident occurred and that it designed and manufactured the Robinsons' car. It denies paragraph 6. It also denies that the car "exploded into flames" or that the "flames spread quickly into the passenger compartment," though it admits there was a fire in the car. What types of information will the Robinsons and Audi to have to disclose under Rule 26(a)(1)? As a lawyer representing the Robinsons or Audi, how would you go about identifying the necessary information? What would you tell your client they must do to comply with this rule? Consider in particular:

(a) The Robinsons' rear bumper was replaced shortly before the accident. The Robinsons have a service receipt showing that this work was done. Must they

CHAPTER 9 DISCOVERY

disclose the existence of this receipt? Must they disclose the name of the mechanic who performed this work? *Yup — or maybe no (no specifics)*

(b) The Robinsons' medical bills were paid by Blue Cross/Blue Shield. Would they have to produce that insurance policy? *NO, maybe the medical bills*

(c) Would Audi have to automatically disclose witnesses or documents relating to any of the following:
- front impact crash tests; *no — we're dealing w/ rear impact*
- rear impact crash tests done only on the structure of the car and without the gas tank in place; *close call, one can go either way • NO specifically so*
- structural reinforcement around the gas tank; *NO, not in pleadings*
- tests and data concerning fire insulation in the car; *yes*
- tests and data concerning how quickly passengers can exit the car in an emergency; *NO — no facts alleged*
- names of people who have sued Audi about alleged defects in car. *N, unless these people are going to be called witness*

26(a)(3) — pretrial disclosures

3. **Local Rules**

Rule 83 authorizes district courts to issue local rules. Local rules cover a range of matters including admission of attorneys to practice, jury selection methods, procedures for presenting and hearing motions, establishment of a calendar for pretrial conferences, criteria and procedures for seeking continuances, and discovery. There are wide variations among local rules and commentators have criticized both the process by which local rules have been promulgated and the lack of uniformity among districts. See David Roberts, *The Myth of Uniformity in Federal Civil Procedure: Federal Civil Rule 83 and District Court Local Rulemaking Powers*, 8 U. PUGET S. L. REV. 537 (1985).

In 1990, with the passage of the Civil Justice Reform Act (CJRA), Congress encouraged even greater variations among local rules. The CJRA requires each federal district court to appoint an advisory group to analyze the causes of expense and delay in litigation in the district and make recommendations to the court for solutions to the district's problems. See 28 U.S.C. §§ 471-482. As a result many districts have promulgated CJRA plans which specify procedures for pretrial conferences, discovery and alternative dispute resolution. See, e.g., Linda Mullenix, *Civil Justice Reform Comes to the Southern District of Texas: Creating and Implementing a Cost Reduction Plan Under the Civil Justice Reform Act of 1990*, 11 REV. OF LITIG. 165 (192). Rule 26(a)(1) dealing with initial mandatory disclosure explicitly permits districts to opt out and a number of districts have done so. You should note, however, that not all the rules are subject to local variations. For example, with respect to mandatory expert witness and pretrial disclosures, local courts can change the time of these disclosures, but a complete opt-out is not permitted. See Rules 26(a)(2) & (3).

The opt-outs that are permitted have produced significant variations among district courts. Professor Wright describes the current situation as "anarchy." WRIGHT, FEDERAL COURTS iv. For example, in the District of Columbia, parties must meet and confer pursuant to Rule 26(f) within 15 days after the filing of the answer. However, in the neighboring District of Maryland, the meet and confer requirement applies only to certain designated complex cases. In the Eastern District of Virginia (also adjacent to D.C.) all cases are exempted from the meet and confer requirement. This book does not attempt to detail the local rules of the 94 district courts. However, you should be aware of the existence of local rules and should always consult the rules of any district in which you are litigating.

Local rules and districts opting out of Rule 26(a)(1) may create some unforeseen complications. Consider the following: Prior to the 1993 amendments, 26(b)(2) explicitly authorized discovery of the existence and contents of insurance agreements. The theory was that although amount of available insurance is not relevant to the merits, it is essential to informed settlement discussion. The new Rule 26(a)(1)(D) includes insurance as a matter for mandatory disclosure. Will insurance be discoverable in an opt-out district?

E. Sanctions

We have already seen that some actions permit a party to seek an order compelling discovery while others justify the imposition of sanctions. We turn now to a detailed consideration of this latter issue.

Washington State Physicians Ins. Exchange & Ass'n v. Fisons Corp.
858 P. 2d. 1054 (Wash. 1993)

ANDERSEN, CHIEF JUSTICE.

Facts of Case

We are asked in this case to decide whether a physician has a cause of action against a drug company for personal and professional injuries which he suffered when his patient had an adverse reaction to a drug he had prescribed. The physician claimed the drug company failed to warn him of the risks associated with the drug. If such action is legally cognizable, we are then asked to determine whether damages awarded by the jury were excessive and whether attorneys' fees were properly awarded by the trial court. We are also asked to rule that the trial court erred in denying sanctions against the drug company for certain abuses in the discovery process.

CHAPTER 9 DISCOVERY

The physician's action began as part of a malpractice and product liability suit brought on behalf of a child who was the physician's patient. On January 18, 1986, 2-year-old Jennifer Pollock suffered seizures which resulted in severe and permanent brain damage. It was determined that the seizures were caused by an excessive amount of theophylline in her system. The Pollocks sued Dr. James Klicpera (Jennifer's pediatrician), who had prescribed the drug, as well as Fisons Corporation (the drug manufacturer and hereafter drug company) which produced Somophyllin Oral Liquid, the theophylline-based medication prescribed for Jennifer.

Dr. Klicpera cross-claimed against the drug company both for contribution and for damages and attorneys' fees under the Consumer Protection Act as well as for damages for emotional distress.

In January 1989, after nearly 3 years of discovery, Dr. Klicpera, his partner and the Everett Clinic settled with the Pollocks. The settlement agreement essentially provided that the doctors' insurer, Washington State Physicians Insurance Exchange & Association (WSPIE), would loan $500,000 to the Pollocks which would be contributed in the event of a settlement between the Pollocks and the drug company. The Pollocks were guaranteed a minimum total recovery of $1 million, and in the event of trial Dr. Klicpera agreed to remain as a party and to pay a maximum of $1 million. The settlement between the Pollocks and Dr. Klicpera was determined by the trial court to be reasonable pursuant to RCW 4.22.060.

More than 1 year after this settlement, an attorney for the Pollocks provided Dr. Klicpera's attorney a copy of a letter received from an anonymous source. The letter, dated June 30, 1981, indicated that the drug company was aware in 1981 of "life-threatening theophylline toxicity" in children who received the drug while suffering from viral infections. The letter was sent from the drug company to only a small number of what the company considered influential physicians. The letter stated that physicians needed to understand that theophylline can be a "capricious drug."

The Pollocks and Dr. Klicpera contended that their discovery requests should have produced the June 1981 letter and they moved for sanctions against the drug company. The request for sanctions was initially heard by a special discovery master, who denied sanctions, but who required the drug company to deliver all documents requested which related to theophylline. Documents that the drug company and its counsel had immediately available were to be produced by the day following the hearing before the special master. The remainder of the documents were to be produced within 2 weeks. The trial court subsequently denied Dr. Klicpera's request to reverse the discovery master's denial of sanctions and at the close of trial denied a renewed motion for sanctions.

The day after the hearing on sanctions, the drug company delivered approximately 10,000 documents to Dr. Klicpera's and Pollocks' attorneys. Among the documents provided was a July 10, 1985 memorandum from Cedric Grigg, director of medical communications for the drug company, to Bruce Simpson, vice president of sales and marketing for the company.

This 1985 memorandum referred to a dramatic increase in reports of serious toxicity to theophylline in early 1985 and also referred to the current recommended dosage as a significant "mistake" or "poor clinical judgment." The memo alluded to the "sinister aspect" that the physician who was the "pope" of theophylline dosage recommendation was a consultant to the pharmaceutical company that was the leading manufacturer of the drug and that this consultant was "heavily into [that company's] stocks." The memo also noted that the toxicity reports were not reported in the journal read by those who most often prescribed the drug and concluded that those physicians may

E. Sanctions

not be aware of the "alarming increase in adverse reactions such as seizures, permanent brain damage and death." The memo concluded that the "epidemic of theophylline toxicity provides strong justification for our corporate decision to cease promotional activities with our theophylline line of products." The record at trial showed that the drug company continued to promote and sell theophylline after the date of this memo.

On April 27, 1990, shortly after the 1985 memo was revealed, the drug company settled with the Pollocks for $6.9 million. The trial court determined that settlement to be reasonable, dismissed the Pollocks' claims, extinguished Dr. Klicpera's contribution/indemnity claims against Fisons pursuant to RCW 4.22.060 and reserved determination of what claims remained for trial. The trial court then ordered the lawsuit recaptioned, essentially as Dr. James Klicpera, plaintiff v. Fisons Corporation, defendant.

* * *

On a special verdict form, the jury concluded that Dr. Klicpera was entitled to recover against the drug company under his Consumer Protection Act claim and under his product liability claim, but not under the fraud claim. The jury awarded Dr. Klicpera $150,000 for loss of professional consultations, $1,085,000 for injury to professional reputation, and $2,137,500 for physical and mental pain and suffering. The jury further found Dr. Klicpera to be 3.3 percent contributorily negligent. The jury found that WSPIE was not entitled to recover under its fraud claim against the drug company the $500,000 settlement paid to the Pollocks.

The trial court denied the drug company's motion for judgment n.o.v. and for a new trial. On a motion for reduction of the jury award, the trial court reduced the amount awarded for loss of professional consultations from $150,000 to $2,250 but refused to reduce the awards for loss of reputation and for pain and suffering. The trial court also denied WSPIE's motion for judgment n.o.v. or a new trial based on the dismissal of WSPIE's Consumer Protection Act claim.

* * *

ISSUE NINE

Conclusion

The trial court applied an erroneous legal standard when ruling on the motion for sanctions for discovery abuse and erred when it refused to sanction the drug company and/or its attorneys for violation of CR 26(g).

The doctor and his insurer, Washington State Physicians Insurance & Exchange Association (hereinafter referred to collectively as "the doctor"), asked the trial court to sanction the drug company and its lawyers for discovery abuse. This request was based on the fact that at least two documents crucial to the doctor's defense as well as to the injured child's case were not discovered until March of 1990 — more than 1 year after the doctor had settled with the child, nearly 4 years after the complaint was filed and approximately 1 month before the scheduled trial date. The two documents, dubbed the "smoking guns" by the doctor, show that the drug company knew about, and in fact had warned selected physicians about, the dangers of theophylline toxicity in children with viral infections at least as early as June 1981, 4 years before Jennifer Pollock was injured.

Although interrogatories and requests for production should have led to the discovery of the "smoking gun" documents, their existence was not revealed to the doctor until one of them was anonymously delivered to his attorneys.

A motion for sanctions based on discovery abuse was heard first by a special discovery master on March 28, 1990, before the child's case was settled. The special master ruled that he could not find "on the basis of this record that there was an *intentional* withholding of this document." The special master then turned to what he determined was the more relevant issue, additional and full discovery of other theophylline-related documents in the drug company's possession. The special master ordered the drug company's attorneys to turn over any immediately available documents concerning theophylline to attorneys for the child and the doctor by noon the next day and to review the remainder of the drug company's files and produce other relevant documents at the end of 2 weeks. The next day, the second "smoking gun," a 1985 internal memorandum describing theophylline toxicity in children, was delivered along with about 10,000 other documents.

Although other documents were relevant to the case, the two smoking gun documents were the most important. The first, a letter, dated June 30, 1981, discussed an article that contained a study confirming reports "of life threatening theophylline toxicity when pediatric asthmatics ... contract viral infections." The second, an interoffice memorandum, dated July 10, 1985, talks of an "epidemic" of theophylline toxicity and of "a dramatic increase in reports of serious toxicity to theophylline."

Both documents contradicted the position taken by the drug company in the litigation, namely, that it did not know that theophylline-based medications were potentially dangerous when given to children with viral infections.

After the 1985 memorandum was discovered and still prior to trial, the special master's denial of the sanctions motion was appealed and affirmed, without specific findings, by a judge of the Superior Court (Judge Knight), who essentially deferred to the special master.

The motion for sanctions was renewed and heard by another judge of the Superior Court, the trial judge (Judge French), at the close of trial. The trial court declined to impose sanctions, deferring to the earlier decisions of the special master and Judge Knight. The doctor then appealed the denial of his sanctions motion directly to this court.

The standard of review to be applied to sanctions decisions under CR 11 and CR 26(g) has not yet been specifically articulated by this court.

The doctor urges us to review the sanctions decision *de novo*. However, decisions either denying or granting sanctions, under CR 11 or for discovery abuse, are generally reviewed for abuse of discretion. We hold that the proper standard to apply in reviewing sanctions decisions is the abuse of discretion standard.

The abuse of discretion standard again recognizes that deference is owed to the judicial actor who is "better positioned than another to decide the issue in question.'" Cooter & Gell v. Hartmarx Corp., 496 U.S. 384 (1990) (quoting Miller v. Fenton, 474 U.S. 104 (1985)). Further, the sanction rules are "designed to confer wide latitude and discretion upon the trial judge to determine what sanctions are proper in a given case and to 'reduce the reluctance of courts to impose sanctions'.... If a review de novo was the proper standard of review, it could thwart these purposes; it could also have a chilling effect on the trial court's willingness to impose ... sanctions." Cooper v.

Viking Ventures, 53 Wash. App. 739, 742-43, 770 P. 2d 659 (1989) (quoting Fed. R. Civ. P. 11 advisory committee note).

A trial court abuses its discretion when its order is manifestly unreasonable or based on untenable grounds. A trial court would necessarily abuse its discretion if it based its ruling on an erroneous view of the law.

The doctor asked that sanctions be awarded pursuant to CR 11, CR 26(g), CR 37(d), or the inherent power of the court. CR 11 sanctions are not appropriate where, as here, other court rules more properly apply. Similarly, the sanctions provisions of CR 37 do not apply where, as here, the more specific sanction rule better fits the situation. Furthermore, the inherent power of the court should not be resorted to where rules adequately address the problem. Because CR 26(g), the discovery sanctions rule, was adopted to specifically address the type of conduct involved here, it, rather than CR 11, CR 37 or the inherent power of the court, is applicable in the present case.

* * *

CR 26(g) has not yet been interpreted by this court. The rule parallels Federal Rule of Civil Procedure 26(g) (Rule 26(g)) and, like its federal counterpart and like CR 11, CR 26(g) is aimed at reducing delaying tactics, procedural harassment and mounting legal costs. Such practices "tend to impose unjustified burdens on other parties, frustrate those who seek to vindicate their rights in the courts, obstruct the judicial process, and bring the civil justice system into disrepute." Schwarzer, *Sanctions Under the New Federal Rule 11 — A Closer Look*, 104 F.R.D. 181, 182 (1985).

Because it is essentially identical to Rule 26(g), this court may look to federal court decisions interpreting that rule for guidance in construing CR 26(g). In turn, federal courts analyzing the Rule 26 sanctions provision look to interpretations of [Rule] 11. The federal advisory committee notes describe the discovery process and problems that led to the enactment of Rule 26(g) as follows:

> Excessive discovery and evasion or resistance to reasonable discovery requests pose significant problems....

> The purpose of discovery is to provide a mechanism for making relevant information available to the litigants. "Mutual knowledge of all the relevant facts gathered by both parties is essential to proper litigation." Hickman v. Taylor, 329 U.S. 495 (1947). Thus the spirit of the rules is violated when advocates attempt to use discovery tools as tactical weapons rather than to expose the facts and illuminate the issues by overuse of discovery or unnecessary use of defensive weapons or evasive responses. All of this results in excessively costly and time-consuming activities that are disproportionate to the nature of the case, the amount involved, or the issues or values at stake....

> ... Rule 26(g) imposes an affirmative duty to engage in pretrial discovery in a responsible manner that is consistent with the spirit and purposes of Rules 26 through 37. In addition, *Rule 26(g) is designed to curb discovery abuse by explicitly encouraging the imposition of sanctions*.... The term "response" includes answers to interrogatories and to requests to admit as well as responses to production requests....

Concern about discovery abuse has led to widespread recognition that there is a need for more aggressive judicial control and supervision. Sanctions to deter discovery abuse would be more effective if they were diligently applied "not merely to penalize those whose conduct may be deemed to warrant such a sanction, but to deter those who might be tempted to such conduct in the absence of such a deterrent." ... *Thus the premise of Rule 26(g) is that imposing sanctions on attorneys who fail to meet the rule's standards will significantly reduce abuse by imposing disadvantages therefor.*

The concept that a spirit of cooperation and forthrightness during the discovery process is necessary for the proper functioning of modern trials is reflected in decisions of our Court of Appeals. In Gammon v. Clark Equip. Co., 38 Wash. App. 274, 686 P. 2d 1102 (1984), *aff'd*, 104 Wash. 2d 613, 707 P. 2d 685 (1985), the Court of Appeals held that a new trial should have been ordered because of discovery abuse by the defendant. Then Court of Appeals Judge Barbara Durham wrote for the court:

> The Supreme Court has noted that the aim of the liberal federal discovery rules is to "make a trial less a game of blindman's b[l]uff and more a fair contest with the basic issues and facts disclosed to the fullest practicable extent." The availability of liberal discovery means that civil trials
>
>> no longer need be carried on in the dark. The way is now clear ... for the parties to obtain the fullest possible knowledge of the issues and facts before trial.
>
> This system obviously cannot succeed without the full cooperation of the parties. Accordingly, the drafters wisely included a provision authorizing the trial court to impose sanctions for unjustified or unexplained resistance to discovery.

It was after *Gammon* that this court adopted CR 26(g) in order to provide a deterrent to discovery abuses as well as an impetus for candor and reason in the discovery phase of litigation.

It is with these purposes in mind, that we now articulate the standard to be applied by trial courts which are asked to impose sanctions for discovery abuse.

On its face, Rule 26(g) requires an attorney signing a discovery response to certify that the attorney has read the response and that after a reasonable inquiry believes it is (1) consistent with the discovery rules and is warranted by existing law or a good faith argument for the extension, modification or reversal of existing law; (2) not interposed for any improper purpose such as to harass or cause unnecessary delay or needless increase in the cost of litigation; and (3) not unreasonable or unduly burdensome or expensive, given the needs of the case, the discovery already had, the amount in controversy, and the importance of the issues at stake in the litigation.

Whether an attorney has made a reasonable inquiry is to be judged by an objective standard. Subjective belief or good faith alone no longer shields an attorney from sanctions under the rules.

In determining whether an attorney has complied with the rule, the court should consider all of the surrounding circumstances, the importance of the evidence to its proponent, and the ability of the opposing party to formulate a response or to comply with the request.

E. Sanctions

The responses must be consistent with the letter, spirit and purpose of the rules. To be consistent with CR 33, an interrogatory must be "answered separately and fully in writing under oath, unless it is objected to, in which event the reasons for objection shall be stated in lieu of an answer." CR 33(a) (part). A response to a request for production "shall state, with respect to each item or category, that inspection and related activities will be permitted as requested, unless the request is objected to, in which event the reasons for objection shall be stated. If objection is made to part of an item or category, the part shall be specified." CR 34(b) (part).

In applying the rules to the facts of the present case, the trial court should have asked whether the attorneys' certifications to the responses to the interrogatories and requests for production were made after reasonable inquiry *and* (1) were consistent with the rules, (2) were not interposed for any improper purpose and (3) were not unreasonable or unduly burdensome or expensive. The trial court did not have the benefit of our decision to guide it and it did not apply this standard in this case.

Instead, the trial court considered the opinions of attorneys and others as to whether sanctions should be imposed. This was error. Legal opinions on the ultimate *legal* issue before the court are not properly considered under the guise of expert testimony. It is the responsibility of the court deciding a sanction motion to interpret and apply the law.

The trial court then denied sanctions, in part because: (1) The evidence did not support a finding that the drug company *intentionally* misfiled documents to avoid discovery; (2) neither the doctor nor the child had formally moved for a definition of "product" and neither had moved to compel production of documents or answers before requesting sanctions; (3) the conduct of the drug company and its counsel was consistent with the customary and accepted litigation practices of the bar of Snohomish County and of this state; and (4) the doctor failed to meet his burden of proving that the "evidence of discovery abuse is so clear that reasonable minds could not differ on the appropriateness of sanctions."

The trial court erred in concluding as it did. As stated above, intent need not be shown before sanctions are mandated. A motion to compel compliance with the rules is not a prerequisite to a sanctions motion. Conduct is to be measured against the spirit and purpose of the rules, not against the standard of practice of the local bar. Furthermore, the burden placed on the doctor by the trial court in this regard was greater than that mandated under the rule.

Additionally, we agree with the doctor's claim that many of the findings of fact entered by the trial court are, instead, erroneous conclusions of law or are not supported by the evidence. For example, the trial court implicitly found in finding of fact 7, and then again in finding of fact 14b, that the "product scope" had been defined by the plaintiffs early in the litigation. The record does not support this finding. In finding of fact 14c the trial court stated that the doctor had been put on notice by the drug company's discovery responses that production of documents "would be limited to responsive documents from Somophyllin Oral Liquid *files*." (Italics ours.) There is no evidence in the record to support this finding and while findings of fact which are supported by substantial evidence will not be disturbed on appeal, unsupported findings cannot stand.

A remand for a determination as to whether sanctions are warranted would be appropriate but is not necessary. Where, as here, the trial judge has applied the wrong legal standard to evidence consisting entirely of written documents and argument of counsel, an appellate court may independently review the evidence to determine whether a violation of the certification rule occurred. If a violation is found, as it is here, then sanctions are mandated, but in fairness to the attorneys and parties, a remand is required for a hearing on the appropriate sanctions required and against whom they should be imposed.

We now measure the conduct of the drug company and its attorneys against the standard set forth in the rule.

The drug company was persistent in its resistance to discovery requests. Fair and reasoned resistance to discovery is not sanctionable. Rather it is the misleading nature of the drug company's responses that is contrary to the purposes of discovery and which is most damaging to the fairness of the litigation process.

The specific instances alleged to be sanctionable in this case involve misleading or "non" responses to a number of requests which the doctor claims should have produced the smoking gun documents themselves or a way to discover the information they contained. The two smoking gun documents reportedly were contained in files which related to Intal, a cromolyn sodium product, which was manufactured by Fisons and which competed with Somophyllin. The manager of medical communications had a thorough collection of articles, materials and other documents relating to the dangers of theophylline and used the information from those materials to market Intal, as an alternative to Somophyllin Oral Liquid. The drug company avoided production of these theophylline-related materials, and avoided identifying the manager of medical communications as a person with information about the dangers of theophylline, by giving evasive or misleading responses to interrogatories and requests for production.

The following is but a sampling of the discovery between the parties.

The first discovery documents directed to the drug company were prepared by the child's attorney and were dated September 26, 1986. The interrogatories contained a short definition section stating in part:

> The term "the product" as used hereinafter in these interrogatories shall mean the product which is claimed to have caused injury or damage to JENNIFER MARIE POLLOCK as alleged in pleadings filed on her behalf, namely, to wit: "Somophyllin" oral liquid.

These first interrogatories requested information about "the product" which is manufactured by the drug company, Fisons, as well as about theophylline, a drug entity which is the primary ingredient of the drug company's product Somophyllin Oral Liquid. The interrogatory regarding theophylline was answered by the drug company, as were the interrogatories about "the product".

Somophyllin and its primary ingredient, theophylline, were not distinguished in discussions between the attorneys or in drug company literature. The printed package insert for Somophyllin Oral Liquid and marketing brochures refer to the names Somophyllin and theophylline interchangeably. * * *

The drug company's responses to discovery requests contained the following general objection:

> *Requests Regarding Fisons Products Other Than Somophyllin Oral Liquid.*
> Fisons objects to all discovery requests regarding Fisons products other than Somophyllin Oral Liquid as overly broad, unduly burdensome, harassing, and not reasonably calculated to lead to the discovery of admissible evidence.

E. Sanctions

Theophylline is not a Fisons "product". Furthermore, because theophylline is the primary ingredient in Somophyllin Oral Liquid, any document focusing on theophylline would, necessarily, be one *regarding* Somophyllin Oral Liquid.

In November 1986 the doctor served his first requests for production on the drug company. Four requests were made. Three asked for documents concerning Somophyllin. Request 3 stated:

> 3. Produce genuine copies of any letters sent by your company to physicians concerning theophylline toxicity in children.

The drug company's response was:

> Such letters, *if any*, regarding Somophyllin Oral Liquid will be produced at a reasonable time and place convenient to Fisons and its counsel of record.

Had the request, as written, been complied with, the first smoking gun letter (exhibit 3) would have been disclosed early in the litigation. That June 30, 1981 letter concerned theophylline toxicity in children; it was sent by the drug company to physicians.

The child's first requests for production, and the responses thereto, included the following:

> Request for Production No. 12: All documents pertaining to any warning letters including "Dear Doctor letters" or warning correspondence to the medical professions regarding the use of the drug Somophyllin Oral Liquid.
>
> Response: Fisons objects to this request as overbroad in time and scope for the reasons identified in response to request number 2, hereby incorporated by reference. *Without waiver of these objections and subject to these limitations, Fisons will produce documents responsive to this request* at plaintiffs' expense at a mutually agreeable time at Fisons' headquarters.
>
> Request for Production No. 13: All documents of any clinical investigators who at any time stated or recommended to the defendant that the use of the drug Somophyllin Oral Liquid might prove dangerous.
>
> Response: Fisons objects to this request as overbroad in time and scope for the reasons identified in response to request number 2 hereby incorporated by reference. Fisons further objects to this request as calling for materials not within Fisons' possession, custody or control. Fisons further objects to this request to the extent it calls for expert disclosures beyond the scope of CR 26(b)(4) or which may be protected by the work-product and/or attorney-client privilege. *Without waiver of these objections and subject to these limitations, Fisons will produce documents responsive to this interrogatory* at plaintiffs' expense at a mutually agreeable time at Fisons' headquarters.

(Italics ours.)

The doctor further requested:

> Request for Production No. 4: Please produce copies of any and all seminar materials, regardless of their source, in Fisons' possession on or before January

CHAPTER 9 DISCOVERY

> 16, 1986 regarding asthma, bronchopulmonary dysplasia, theophylline and/or allergy.
>
> Response: Fisons objects to this discovery request as overbroad, burdensome, and not reasonably calculated to lead to the discovery of admissible evidence *to the extent it seeks seminar materials regarding subjects other than theophylline.* Without waiving these objections, Fisons answers as follows:
>
> *Fisons has no documents regarding theophylline* and otherwise responsive to this discovery request.

(Some italics ours.)

These requests, and others of a similar tenor, should have led to the production of the smoking gun documents.

When the child or the doctor attempted to see information from the files of other products, the drug company objected. For example:

> Request for Production No. 1: All documents contained in all files from the regulating department, marketing department, drug surveillance department, pharmaceutical development department, product manager department and the medical departments regarding all cromolyn [Intal] products of Fisons Corporation. Regarding this request for production all documents should include from inception of file to the present.
>
> Answer: Defendant Fisons objects to this discovery request as not reasonably calculated to lead to the discovery of admissible evidence, as overbroad in time, and as incredibly burdensome and harassing. This discovery request encompasses approximately *eighty-five* percent of all documents in the subject files and departments — millions of pages of documents. *Neither cromolyn (which should be referred to as cromolyn sodium), nor any cromolyn product, nor the properties or efficacy of cromolyn is at issue in this litigation.* Furthermore, Fisons objects to this discovery request as calling for the production of extremely sensitive trade secret and proprietary material.

(Some italics ours.)

To requests asking for correspondence, memoranda, articles and other documents "concerning," "regarding" or "covering" Somophyllin Oral Liquid, the drug company generally objected to the requests and then stated:

> Without waiver of these objects and subject to these limitations, Fisons will produce documents responsive to this request at plaintiffs' expense at a mutually agreeable time at Fisons' headquarters.

In support of the drug company's motion for a protective order, the drug company's in-house counsel and its Seattle lawyer filed similar affidavits. Seattle counsel's affidavit declares:

> Plaintiffs allege that Fisons failed to provide adequate warnings of possible dangers associated with the use of Somophyllin Oral Liquid, a theophylline-based

E. Sanctions

prescription medication distributed by Fisons ... [Plaintiffs'] discovery requests are extremely broad in scope. Many of these discovery requests are not reasonably related to plaintiffs' failure-to-warn allegations against Fisons.

Following receipt of plaintiffs' First Request for Production, I traveled to Fisons in Bedford, Massachusetts in order to ascertain firsthand the scope and extent of documents responsive to plaintiffs' request for production. At that time I confirmed that to produce all of the documents responsive to plaintiffs' catch-all requests would be extremely burdensome and oppressive to Fisons. Between one and two million pages of documents, most of which have no colorable relevance to the issues in this action, would have to be located, assembled, and made available for review or copying. The time, expense, and intrusion upon the day-to-day business activities of Fisons would be immense.

While at Fisons I identified those documents reasonably related to the claims asserted by plaintiffs in this litigation and arranged to have them copied and forwarded to Seattle for production to plaintiffs.

The affidavit goes on to say that the drug company had "agreed to make available those documents reasonably related to plaintiffs' allegations against Fisons."

In its memorandum to the court in support of the motion for a protective order, the attorney for the drug company outlined the documents contained in the regulatory file on Somophyllin Oral Liquid. That file purportedly contained complete information regarding the drug including: Summaries of adverse reactions associated with the use of the medication that had been reported to Fisons; all promotional or advertising material disseminated by Fisons *with regard to the medication;* the complete product file for Somophyllin Oral Liquid, which contained records of communications with the Food and Drug Administration, internal memoranda, and miscellaneous medical literature regarding theophylline. The memorandum goes on to tell the court

> In short, Fisons' Regulatory File for Somophyllin Oral Liquid contains all or nearly all documents in Fisons' possession that are reasonably related to plaintiffs' failure-to-warn allegations.

A footnote to this comment states "Fisons has also agreed to make available to plaintiffs an index of periodicals maintained in Fisons' internal library as well as certain other documents."

The drug company's responses and answers to discovery requests are misleading. The answers state that all information *regarding* Somophyllin Oral Liquid which had been requested would be provided. They further imply that all documents which are relevant to the plaintiffs' claims were being produced. They do not specifically object to the production of documents that discuss the dangers of theophylline, but which are not within the Somophyllin Oral Liquid files. They state that there is no relevant information within the cromolyn sodium product files.

It appears clear that no conceivable discovery request could have been made by the doctor that would have uncovered the relevant documents, given the above and other responses of the drug company. The objections did not specify that certain documents were not being produced. Instead the general objections were followed by a promise to produce requested documents. These responses did not comply with either the spirit or letter of the discovery rules and thus were signed in violation of the certification requirement.

The drug company does not claim that its inquiry into the records did not uncover the smoking gun documents. Instead, the drug company attempts to justify its responses by arguing as follows: (1) The plaintiffs themselves limited the scope of discovery to documents contained in Somophyllin Oral Liquid *files*. (2) The smoking gun documents were not intended to relate to Somophyllin Oral Liquid, but rather were intended to promote another product of the drug company. (3) The drug company produced all of the documents it agreed to produce or was ordered to produce. (4) The drug company's failure to produce the smoking gun documents resulted from the plaintiffs' failure to specifically ask for those documents or from their failure to move to compel production of those documents. (5) Discovery is an adversarial process and good lawyering required the responses made in this case.

If the discovery rules are to be effective, then the drug company's arguments must be rejected.

First, neither the child nor the doctor limited the scope of discovery in this case. Attorneys for the child, the doctor and the drug company repeatedly referred to both theophylline and Somophyllin Oral Liquid. There was no clear indication from the drug company that it was limiting all discovery *regarding* Somophyllin Oral Liquid to material from that product's file. Nor was there any indication from the drug company that it had information about theophylline, which is not a Fisons "product", or information *regarding* Somophyllin Oral Liquid that it was not producing because the information was in another product's file. The doctor was justified in relying on the statements made by the drug company's attorneys that all relevant documents had been produced and he cannot be determined to have impliedly, albeit unknowingly, acquiesced in limiting the scope of discoverable information.

Second, the drug company argues that the smoking gun documents and other documents relating to theophylline were not documents *regarding* Somophyllin Oral Liquid because they were intended to market another product. No matter what its initial purpose, and regardless of where it had been filed, under the facts of this case, a document that warned of the serious dangers of the primary ingredient of Somophyllin Oral Liquid is a document *regarding* Somophyllin Oral Liquid.

Third, the discovery rules do not require the drug company to produce only what it agreed to produce or what it was ordered to produce. The rules are clear that a party must *fully* answer all interrogatories and all requests for production, unless a specific and clear objection is made. If the drug company did not agree with the scope of production or did not want to respond, then it was required to move for a protective order. In this case, the documents requested were relevant. The drug company did not have the option of determining what it would produce or answer, once discovery requests were made.

Fourth, the drug company further attempts to justify its failure to produce the smoking guns by saying that the request were not specific enough. Having read the record herein, we cannot perceive of *any* request that could have been made to this drug company that would have produced the smoking gun documents. Unless the doctor had been somehow specifically able to request the June 30, 1981, "dear doctor" letter, it is unlikely that the letter would have been discovered. Indeed the drug company claims the letter was not an official "dear doctor" letter and therefore was not required to be produced.

Fifth, the drug company's attorneys claim they were just doing their job, that is, they were vigorously representing their client. The conflict here is between the attorney's duty to represent the client's interest and the attorney's duty as an officer of the court to use, but not abuse the judicial process.

E. Sanctions

> [V]igorous advocacy is not contingent on lawyers being free to pursue litigation tactics that they cannot justify as legitimate. The lawyer's duty to place his client's interests ahead of all others presupposes that the lawyer will live with the rules that govern the system. Unlike the polemicist haranguing the public from his soapbox in the park, the lawyer enjoys the privilege of a professional license that entitles him to entry into the justice system to represent his client, and in doing so, to pursue his profession and earn his living. He is subject to the correlative obligation to comply with the rules and to conduct himself in a manner consistent with the proper functioning of that system.

Schwarzer, *Sanctions Under the New Federal Rule 11 — A Closer Look*, 104 F.R.D. 181, 184 (1985).

Like CR 11, CR 26(g) makes the imposition of sanctions mandatory, if a violation of the rule is found. Sanctions are warranted in this case. What the sanctions should be and against whom they should be imposed is a question that cannot be fairly answered without further factual inquiry, and that is the trial court's function. While we recognize that the issue of imposition of sanctions upon attorneys is a difficult and disagreeable task for a trial judge, it is a necessary one if our system is to remain accessible and responsible.

> Misconduct, once tolerated, will breed more misconduct and those who might seek relief against abuse will instead resort to it in self-defense.

Schwarzer, 104 F.R.D. at 205.

In making its determination, the trial court should use its discretion to fashion "appropriate" sanctions. The rule provides that sanctions may be imposed upon the signing attorney, the party on whose behalf the response is made, or both.

In determining what sanctions are appropriate, the trial court is given wide latitude. However certain principles guide the trial court's consideration of sanctions. First, the least severe sanction that will be adequate to serve the purpose of the particular sanction should be imposed. The sanction must not be so minimal, however, that it undermines the purpose of discovery. The sanction should insure that the wrongdoer does not profit from the wrong. The wrongdoer's lack of intent to violate the rules and the other party's failure to mitigate may be considered by the trial court in fashioning sanctions.

The purposes of sanctions orders are to deter, to punish, to compensate and to educate. Where compensation to litigants is appropriate, then sanctions should include a compensation award. However, we caution that the sanctions rules are not "fee shifting" rules. Furthermore, requests for sanctions should not turn into satellite litigation or become a "cottage industry" for lawyers. To avoid the appeal of sanctions motions as a profession or profitable specialty of law, we encourage trial courts to consider requiring that monetary sanctions awards be paid to a particular court fund or to court-related funds. In the present case, sanctions need to be severe enough to deter these attorneys and others from participating in this kind of conduct in the future.

The trial court's denial of sanctions is reversed and the case is remanded for a determination of appropriate sanctions.

CHAPTER 9 DISCOVERY

* * *

Holmgren v. State Farm Mutual Automobile Insurance Co.
976 F. 2d 573 (9th Cir. 1992)

[The first part of this opinion is reproduced supra at 424.]

(3) *The Rule 37(c) Award* — State Farm argues that the district court erred in awarding expenses to Holmgren under the Federal Rules of Civil Procedure 37(c) for State Farm's failure to qualify its denial of certain requests to admit. But State Farm brought these sanctions upon itself by treating discovery as a game instead of a serious matter. "When good faith requires that a party qualify an answer or deny only a part of the matter of which an admission is requested, the party shall specify so much of it as is true and qualify or deny the remainder." Fed. R. Civ. P. 36(a). State Farm acted as if this rule simply didn't exist.

Request No. 1 asked State Farm to "please admit that the collision [with Holmgren] was caused by Sharon Cannon [the insured] driving through a stop sign." State Farm denied this request without qualification. Its justification: "It was uncertain as to what may have been the proximate cause or causes of the accident. The accident may have been the result of Cannon's having been drinking and driving, or her inattentiveness, or her speed. Neither State Farm nor anyone else really knows what 'caused' the accident ...." State Farm's epistemological doubts speak highly of its philosophical sophistication, but poorly of its respect for Rule 36(a). Even if State Farm's nitpicking of the question could serve as a basis for qualifying its response, it certainly doesn't justify a flat denial.

Request No. 4 asked State Farm to "please admit that after her vehicle collided with three more vehicles, Sharon Cannon attempted to escape the scene of those accidents." State Farm denied this request without qualification, because, it claimed, the word "escape" required knowledge of Cannon's subjective intentions, yet no one could know for sure what Cannon intended at the time. State Farm concedes, however, that Cannon may have tried to leave the accident scene. After-the-fact excuses about the unknowability of intentions don't justify blanket denials. At the very least, the response should have stated the grounds for dispute.

State Farm also denied Request No. 5, which said: "Please admit that at the time of the accident involving Julie Holmgren, Sharon Cannon was operating her vehicle under the influence of alcohol." In its brief before us State Farm freely admits that Cannon had been drinking quite a bit. How, then, does it justify its flat denial? "Being 'under the influence of alcohol' is a physical condition which varies between persons depending upon dozens of physiological and psychological factors, and State Farm was not in a position to admit that Sharon Cannon was 'under the influence of alcohol.'" Even if one were to accept appellant's point, [Rule] 36(a) imposes a duty to "qualify an answer or deny only a part of the matter" by conceding Cannon's drinking, but disputing its significance.

Request No. 6 asked: "Please admit that at the time of the accident involving Julie Holmgren, Sharon Cannon's blood alcohol content was two and one-half times greater than the presumptive level of intoxication under Montana law." State Farm's reply: "No one knows what Cannon's blood alcohol content was at the time of the accident," because "one cannot, with exactness, derive Cannon's blood alcohol content at the time of the accident from" tests taken hours later. This might have been a plausible quibble if it had been given as a qualification to an admission. As a post hoc explanation for a blanket denial, it's totally unacceptable.

Request No. 3 was the simplest of all: "Please admit that immediately after leaving the scene of the accident involving Julie Holmgren, Sharon Cannon's vehicle collided with three more vehicles." State Farm now states that it denied that request because "to the best of counsel's recollection, ... there was some question as to just how many cars the Cannon vehicle collided with." But a denial means "no," not "I'm not sure." If State Farm was genuinely uncertain (after conducting the reasonable inquiry required by [Rule] 36(a)), it should have said so. The lawyer's justification - made only a few months after State Farm responded to Holmgren's requests - provides no factual predicate at all for a flat denial.

The record supports the district court's conclusion that the core of each of the requests for admission had to do with indisputable historical fact. If State Farm had objections to the requests based on issues other than historical fact, good faith required it to qualify its denials to make it clear that it conceded matters of historical fact. State Farm's argument that the requests were indivisible is without merit.

State Farm argues that the district court abused its discretion in fixing the amount of the Rule 37(c) award. It relies upon three items in the affidavit supporting the motion for an award under 37(c) to sustain its contention that the district court awarded expenses incurred prior to denial of the requests. According to the affidavit, all three of those items accrued on or before October 3, 1989. By that date, this litigation had not begun. Those expenses did not flow from State Farm's wrongful failure to qualify its denials during the discovery stage of this suit. The district court therefore abused its discretion in incorporating those sums in its award. We reverse the award to the extent that it incorporates these expenses. We also remand for a determination of whether any of the remaining items included in the award, many of which are not time-specific, were incurred prior to the filing of the denials.

The district court found $200 per hour to be a reasonable rate for calculation of attorney expenses. It considered the expertise of Holmgren's counsel and the contingent nature of the fee arrangement between Holmgren and counsel. It also had before it an affidavit from local counsel indicating that the going non-contingent fee rate in Great Falls was $125. We are unable to find, on this record, that the district court abused its discretion in fixing the hourly rate on which the award is based.

Although the district court has wide discretion to fix the amount of a Rule 37(c) award, the rule provides that such an award must be "reasonable." In fixing the award, we direct the court to consider the strength and clarity of the police and news reports that were admitted as evidence of the denied facts.

III

We exercise our discretion to impose damages on State Farm as a sanction for raising frivolous issues on appeal. See Fed. R. App. P. 38. We could award sanctions based entirely on State Farm's failure to comply with [Rule] 36(a), but we note State Farm also made [other] meritless appellate arguments * * *. We award sanctions in the additional amount of $5,000.

The district court's judgment is AFFIRMED on the merits. The district court's decision to award fees under Rule 37(c) is AFFIRMED. We REMAND for a determination of which expenses were incurred in this litigation as a result of State Farm's denials and what sum is reasonable considering all relevant facts.

AFFIRMED but REMANDED for recalculation of the Rule 37(c) award. The plaintiff shall recover costs.

NOTES AND QUESTIONS

1. The original version of the opinion in *Holmgren* included the following paragraph:

> State Farm's sophistries would be humorous if the implications of such behavior for our legal system weren't so sad. As a large insurer, State Farm is a repeat player in our courts. It has no excuse for flouting our rules, and every incentive to obey them. Tactics like the ones we saw in this case give some parties — even some industries — a bad name. Before displaying such tactics in the future, State Farm's lawyers should think long and hard about their effect on the client's corporate reputation in the minds of the public and the judiciary.

See 1992 U.S. App. LEXIS 29008. The paragraph was deleted from the final published version.

2. On the remand of *Fisons*, Dr. Klicpera's counsel sought a public evidentiary hearing at which Fisons' officials and their lawyers could be cross-examined about their conduct. The hearing never took place. Instead, Fisons and its lawyers settled, agreeing to pay $350,000 for the discovery abuse and to admit publicly that they violated the rules. See Stuart Taylor, Jr., *Sleazy in Seattle*, THE AMERICAN LAWYER, April 1, 1994, at 5.

3. The *Fisons* court states that Rule 11 and 37(d) were not applicable in that case. Why?

4. What sanctions were available against Fisons? Could the court have imposed any of the sanctions enumerated in Rule 37(b)(2)?

5. You will recall that Rule 11 was amended in 1993 to make clear that sanction are for deterrence only and that if monetary sanctions are awarded, the amount should ordinarily be paid to the court, not to the other side. Comparable amendments were not made to Rule 26(g). Should 26(g) be interpreted to include these changes to Rule 11 or does the failure to amend 26(g) suggest that it was meant to function differently from Rule 11?

6. In *Holmgren*, suppose it turned out that the statements State Farm refused to admit were easily provable through public documents such as police reports. Does that makes State Farm's refusal to admit more or less egregious? Does it make the likely sanction bigger or smaller?

E. Sanctions

7. In *Holmgren*, the Rule 37(c) sanctions were awarded against State Farm. Could sanctions have been imposed against the lawyer? At least one court has held not, noting the language in the Rule which states that the court can order "the other party to pay." Apex Oil Co. v. Belcher Co. of New York, Inc., 855 F.2d 1009, 1013-14 (2d Cir. 1988). The *Apex* court went on to hold, however, that the lawyer could be sanctioned under Rule 26(g).

8. Can a defendant be sanctioned under Rule 37(c) for failing to admit an ultimate issue (such as negligence) in response to a Rule 36 request? Consider Marchand v. Mercy Medical Center, 22 F.3d 933 (9th Cir. 1994). In connection with a medical malpractice suit, the plaintiff served on the defendant the following request to admit:

> [a]dmit that the care and treatment provided to [plaintiff by defendant] * * * failed to comply with the applicable standard of care which existed for that person on that date.

The defendant responded, "denied." Following trial, the court imposed Rule 37(c) sanctions of over $205,000 on defendant for failing to admit this statement and the court of appeals upheld the award. The court of appeals explained that although defendant presented an expert witness who testified that the defendant satisfied the standard of care, "[t]he district court had ample evidence to discredit the expert testimony." Id. at 937. The court concluded that the defendant "could not under the circumstances have reasonably denied his negligence." Id.

9. Suppose in *Fisons* that the "smoking gun" documents did not become known until after all the claims had settled or judgments had been entered. Could the court have imposed sanctions after the case was over? In Cooter & Gell v. Hartmarx Corp., 496 U.S. 384 (1990), the Court held that federal courts could impose Rule 11 sanctions after a case had been voluntarily dismissed. "It is well established that a federal court may consider collateral issues after an action is no longer pending." Id. at 395. The Court explained that "whether the attorney has abused the judicial process" is collateral to the merits of the underlying suit and hence "[s]uch a determination may be made after the principal suit has been terminated." Id. at 396. After the 1993 amendments to Rule 11, monetary sanctions can not be awarded unless a show cause order is issued prior to dismissal of the suit, see Rule 11(c)(2)(B), but there is no such limitation in 26(g).

10. Suppose you had been the plaintiff in *Roesberg* and had received the interrogatory answers described in the case. Upon receiving these answers, what would your options have been? What, if any, sanctions were available?

11. The defendant's attorneys in both *Fisons* and *Holmgren* engaged in practices that some lawyers think is appropriate or even required by the zealous advocate. In both cases the lawyers construed each question so as to avoid disclosing or admitting something damaging to their client. Indeed, in *Fisons*, a number of local attorneys submitted affidavits asserting that what the counsel did was consistent with accepted practice of attorneys in the area. Should the court have given greater weight to this argument? Consider how you, as a lawyer, would explain to your client that it must reveal the "smoking gun" document even though there is a way that a request could be construed to not call for the document.

12. One report suggests that the threat of sanctions for improper discovery may have contributed to a deterioration in professionalism rather than improved the situation. See Interim Report of the Committee on Civility of the Seventh Federal Judicial Circuit, 143 F.R.D. 371 (1991). Among the comments from lawyers who were surveyed were the following:

> Rules 11 and 37 have not deterred improper conduct. They have just provided an additional source of argument, some justified, others contrived, as a means of tactical advantage.
>
> Though some may find it ironic, I think Rule 11 and Rule 37 sanctions have actually contributed to the problem. These efforts to legislate professional civility seem to have turned our profession, including both judges and litigators, into a petty society of tattletales, hall monitors and paranoids.

Id. at 390, 406. Consider *Fisons* and *Holmgren*. Do you think sanctions were warranted in those cases? Do you think that the imposition of sanctions in those cases will contribute to an improvement or a deterioration in civility and professionalism? Do you see solutions other than sanctions that might be more effective?

13. The sanctions provisions apply only to conduct that violates the Rules. But given the broad scope of permissible discovery, lots of discovery that one side considers offensive or intrusive is completely permissible. Undoubtedly the plaintiffs in the Dalcon Shield litigation who were asked details of their sexual practices considered this abusive. Nonetheless, many courts permitted the questions on ground that the inquiry was relevant to determining the cause of the plaintiffs' injuries. The distinction between discovery that is "abusive" in some sense and discovery that violates the rules is one that has on occasion caused confusion for courts. Consider the case of McKennon v. Nashville Banner Publishing Co., 115 S. Ct. 879 (1995). There the plaintiff who had been fired from her job sued her employer alleging age discrimination. After the litigation was underway, the defendant learned for the first time that prior to the firing, the plaintiff had copied confidential company documents — conduct that the company alleged would have resulted in her being fired. The Supreme Court held that the "after-acquired" evidence of misconduct does not bar a suit for age discrimination, although it may eliminate the remedies of reinstatement and future pay. That plaintiff had argued that if after-acquired evidence is admissible for any purpose, it will give defendants in discrimination cases an incentive to begin scouring the plaintiff's employment record for previously undiscovered violations of company rules. In response, Justice Kennedy wrote:

> The concern that employers might as a routine matter undertake extensive discovery into employee's background or performance on the job to resist claims under the Act is not an insubstantial one, but we think the authority of the courts to award attorney's fees, mandated under the [Age Discrimination Act], and in appropriate cases to invoke the provisions of Rule 11 of the Federal Rules of Civil Procedure will deter most abuses.

Id. at 887. Given that the Court held that previously undiscovered employee misconduct is relevant, on what bases would a district court impose attorneys fees or other sanctions?

14. Arizona has adopted its own version of automatic disclosure. Ariz. R. Civ. Proc. 26.1. More recently, Arizona has considered a further change, this time to the rules governing lawyer ethics. The proposed change would make it an ethical violation for a lawyer knowingly to fail to disclose a material fact to the other side. Is this going too far or is it a necessary response to lawyer abuse? See Elliot Talenfeld, *Reflections on Professionalism, Quality of Life, and the Disclosure Rule: A Response to Richard Plattner's Petition to Modify Ethical Rules 3.0, 3.3(a)(2), 4.1, and 1.6*, 26 ARIZ. ST. L.J. 797 (1994).

15. Although Rule 37(b)(2)(C) permits a court to dismiss a suit, courts are extremely reluctant to invoke this sanction against *attorney* misconduct. One court has observed that the harsh sanction of dismissal is "usually inappropriate where the neglect is solely the fault of the attorney." Carter v. Memphis, Tennessee, 636 F.2d 159, 161 (6th Cir. 1980). Should dismissal be reserved for cases in which the client was actually involved in the misconduct? Doesn't this remove from the court one of its most powerful sanctions? Clients pay the price for other attorney mistakes such as failing to file within the statute of limitations. If clients paid the price for attorney discovery abuse, would this make overly aggressive or abusive lawyers less attractive in the market place?

16. What is a lawyer's obligation if she discovers that her client has lied at a deposition or presented false evidence? See Model Rules of Professional Conduct, Rule 3.3(a), supra Chapter 8. Several states have held that the obligation to disclose applies even at the pretrial stage. See, e.g., Kath v. Western Media Inc., 684 P. 2d 98 (Wyo. 1984) (attorney had a letter that was inconsistent with deposition testimony; attorney required to disclose letter prior to settlement negotiations). See also Fire Insurance Exchange v. Bell, 643 N.E. 2d 310 (Ind. 1994) (permitting claim of fraudulent misrepresentation against lawyer who misrepresented insurance policy limits in settlement negotiations).

F. Scheduling and Pretrial Conferences and Orders

As we saw earlier, the mandatory disclosure provisions of the Federal Rules include the Rule 26(f) meeting. See supra at 437. This meeting takes place early in the lawsuit and gives the parties an opportunity to discuss settlement and to agree on a discovery plan and schedule. In this Section, we address conferences under Rule 16. A conference differs from a meeting in one very important respect: the judge is a participant. On a practical level, this fact means that the action taken at a conference will be reflected in a court order that "shall control the subsequent course of the action unless modified by a subsequent order." See Rule 16(e).

On a more theoretical level, it reflects the increasing involvement of the federal judge in the management of cases in her court. As we discussed in Chapter 1, the traditional adversary model of litigation envisions a reactive, umpireal judge, largely removed from the day-to-day management of the litigation. Increasingly, modern litigation is marked by more hands-on involvement of the court in keeping the parties' feet to the fire, narrowing the scope of the dispute, and fostering settlement. As Rule 16(a)(2) provides, the court may hold a conference to "establish[] early and continuing control so that the case will not be protracted because of lack of management." With this and similar provisions added to the rule in 1983, "[t]he primary focus of the rule shifted from trial preparation to case management." TEPLY & WHITTEN, CIVIL PROCEDURE 768. The panoply of sanctions available under Rule 16(f) underscores the importance of these conferences.

Rule 16(a) sets out a broad range of proper goals for conferences. Rule 16(c) specifies in great detail the subjects that might be considered in achieving the objectives of Rule 16(a). Since 1983, an express objective has been "facilitating the settlement of the case." Rule 16(a)(5). There had been considerable debate over whether this was an appropriate goal of pretrial conferences under the prior version. Its express recognition reflects concern, voiced in many quarters, that court dockets are too crowded and must be pared through negotiation if possible.

Some commentators feel that the judge's involvement in settlement efforts raises serious problems if the parties do not reach an agreement. Specifically, the judge might be exposed to something in settlement discussions that would not be admissible at trial. Professor Resnik concludes that this responsibility was imposed upon judges without proper consideration of whether it should affect the standards governing when a judge should recuse herself (step aside and let another judge preside over the case). Judith Resnik, *Managerial Judges*, 96 HARV. L. REV. 374 (1982). See generally Carrie Menkel-Meadow, *For and Against Settlement: Uses and Abuses of the Mandatory Settlement Conference*, 33 UCLA L. REV. 485 (1985).

F. Scheduling and Pretrial Conferences and Orders

One way to insulate the judge from compromising her objectivity is to shield her from the settlement process. Federal judges can do this by referring Rule 16 matters to a magistrate judge who may perform a variety of pretrial tasks to facilitate the case and often take part in efforts to settle cases.[*] See Rule 16(b). (We discussed magistrate judges at 435 supra.)

If the case does not settle, Rule 16 arms the court with considerable authority to streamline the trial. To understand Rule 16, it is important to remember that the course of pretrial litigation — from plaintiff's filing the complaint until the start of trial — usually takes months or even years to complete. During that time, the parties are busy with pleadings, motions, discovery and other facets of litigation.

Rule 16(b) requires a *scheduling order* in all cases except those falling into categories exempted by court rule.[**] It permits, but does not require, the court to hold a *scheduling conference* with the parties or their lawyers to assist in her preparation of the scheduling order. The scheduling order is entered early in the lawsuit and *must* establish time limits for joinder of additional claims or parties, amendment of pleadings, motions (including motions challenging jurisdiction or venue or sufficiency of pleadings) and discovery. Rule 16(b)(1)-(3). (The Rule 26(f) plan filed by the parties obviously will assist the judge in determining deadlines for the discovery phase.) The scheduling order is a *blueprint for the pretrial litigation as a whole*, determining when various tasks must be completed and at least suggesting when the case might be ready for trial.

As the case progresses, the court may hold as many *pretrial conferences* as it sees fit. In the federal courts, the same judge presides over a case from inception to completion.[***] This gives the judge an opportunity to learn about the case and the evidence along with the parties. As discovery progresses, for example, parties may stipulate as to certain facts or recognize the need for amended pleadings or perhaps the court will be able to grant summary judgment on some or all issues. Through ongoing monitoring, the court may be able to narrow the number and scope of issues still needing resolution at trial. See Rule 16(c).

Very late in the pretrial stage, "as close to the time of trial as reasonable under the circumstances," the court may hold the *final pretrial conference*. Rule 16(d). At this

---

[*] In discussing settlement, litigants must be aware of the "offer of judgment" provision of Rule 68. Under that rule, the defendant can offer to settle the claim against her on terms she specifies. The plaintiff is not required to accept that offer, of course. If she does not, however, and does not thereafter obtain a judgment more favorable than the offer, she must pay the defendant's costs (not including attorney's fees) incurred after making the offer.

[**] For example, parties can seek federal court review of findings of the Social Security Administration concerning disability benefits. Courts routinely exempt such cases from the requirement of a scheduling order.

[***] This is not true in many state court systems, in which a different judge may preside over issues arising in each phase of the litigation, such as pleadings, motions, discovery, pretrial conferences, and trial.

point, the parties have completed discovery and should be in a position to know what issues remain in contention and their respective evidence and witnesses on those issues. The purpose of the final pretrial conference is to "formulate a plan for trial, including a program for facilitating the admission of evidence." Id. As she does with all pretrial conferences, the court enters an order (the "final pretrial conference order") "reciting the action taken" at the conference. Rule 16(e). Just as the scheduling order was a blueprint for the litigation as a whole, the final pretrial conference order is a blueprint for the trial itself.

Preparing for the pretrial conference is a major task, one that is facilitated by mandatory disclosure under Rule 26(a)(3). Even in those districts opting out of mandatory disclosure, however, local rules invariably require counsel to submit similar information. The order will contain each party's assertion of every factual and legal contention to be raised at trial, every witness she will call and every piece of evidence she will seek to introduce. It is especially important because it governs the conduct of the trial. Thus, stipulations made in the final pretrial conference order are binding.

In addition, the statement of issues to be tried and the witness list embodied in the order will govern at trial. Thus, "[w]hile Rule 16 does not in terms provide that the [final] pretrial order supersedes the pleadings, * * * nevertheless in practice the order sometimes has that effect." 3 MOORE'S FEDERAL PRACTICE 16-96 to 16-97. Issues framed in the pleadings but not included in the final pretrial conference order may not be tried. Conversely, issues not raised in the pleadings but included in the final pretrial conference order may be tried. Moreover, the standard for amending the final pretrial conference order is quite stringent: the order "shall be modified only to prevent manifest injustice." Rule 16(e). This stringent standard emphasizes that "to allow modification of [the] order without restriction would defeat the function of the final pretrial order to structure and control the course of trial." TEPLY & WHITTEN, CIVIL PROCEDURE 773-74. See generally 3 MOORE'S FEDERAL PRACTICE ¶ 16.17.

The strict approach is illustrated by Walker v. Anderson Elec. Connectors, 944 F.2d 841 (11th Cir. 1991), *cert. denied*, 113 S. Ct. 1043 (1993). There, the plaintiff sued her employer, Anderson, and others for sexual harassment. In her complaint, Walker sought damages as well as injunctive and declaratory relief. At the final pretrial conference, however, she abandoned her claims for equitable relief and went to trial seeking damages as her sole remedy. The jury found that Anderson had committed sexual harassment in violation of federal law and invaded plaintiff's privacy. Nonetheless, the jury also found that plaintiff had suffered no monetary damage. Thus, although plaintiff showed a violation, she was entitled to no remedy. The district court entered judgment for the defendant.

Plaintiff then sought to amend the pretrial order to reinstate the claims for injunctive and declaratory relief. She argued that her showing of a violation of federal law not only

F. Scheduling and Pretrial Conferences and Orders

entitled her to this relief, but made her a "prevailing party" entitled to recover attorney's fees under federal employment statutes. The district court refused to amend the final pretrial order and denied her request for attorney's fees. The Eleventh Circuit affirmed.

> The district court's decision to follow the pre-trial order can be reversed on appeal only where the district court has abused its discretion. "[W]e realize that for pretrial procedures to continue as viable mechanisms of court efficiency, appellate courts must exercise minimal interference with trial court discretion in matters such as the modification of its orders." Hodges [v. United States, 597 F.2d 1014, 1018 (5th Cir. 1979).]
>
> While Rule 16(e) requires that the pretrial order be modified to "prevent manifest injustice," in this case the modification requested by Walker would only serve to work an injustice against the defendant [employer]. As the district court pointed out in its Memorandum Opinion of July 9, 1990, "Walker chose her strategy, forcing [defendant] to choose its strategy. It would be disingenuous of any court to find at this late date that this pretrial order can be modified post-trial in order to 'prevent manifest injustice.'"
>
> We agree with this reasoning and find that the district court did not abuse its discretion in following the pre-trial order. Walker pursued a damages trial and got just that. It would be unfair to [defendant] to give Walker relief which she did not request; relief for which [defendant] was never permitted to establish a defense.
>
> Walker's central argument on this matter is that the district court has not complied with Fed. R. Civ. P. 54(c). Rule 54(c) states, in pertinent part, that "every final judgment shall grant the relief to which the party in whose favor it is rendered is entitled, even if the party has not demanded such relief in the party's pleadings." Applying Rule 54(c) to the facts of her case, Walker contends that she is "entitled" to equitable relief based on the jury's finding of sexual harassment even though she abandoned this claim for relief in the pretrial conference and actively pursued a monetary award. Walker further contends that Rule 54(c) and Rule 16(e) conflict under these facts and that Rule 54(c) prevails * * *.
>
> We see no conflict and find that Rule 54(c) does not apply to this case. Rule 54(c) requires that the district court grant Walker only the relief to which she is "entitled," even when that relief is not requested in the pleadings. But Walker *did* request a declaratory judgment and an injunction in her pleadings and then abandoned this form of relief at the pretrial conference in favor of something else, namely a money award. Rule 54(c) simply does not sanction this type of maneuvering. We hold that Walker is not entitled to the relief abandoned in the pretrial order * * *.

944 F.2d at 844.

Should a final pretrial conference order be amended to conform to evidence presented at trial? Recall from Chapter 8 that Rule 15(b) permits the court to amend pleadings to conform to evidence presented at trial by express or implied consent of the parties.

Suppose plaintiff presents evidence at trial of a claim clearly not envisioned in the final pretrial conference order, and that defendant does not object. Should the court permit amendment of the order under Rule 15(b) or must plaintiff satisfy the more stringent standard of Rule 16(e)? Most courts conclude that Rule 15(b) governs. WRIGHT, FEDERAL COURTS 649. Is *Walker* consistent with this conclusion?

At the beginning of Chapter 8, we noted that early procedure systems used pleadings to perform several tasks beyond giving notice to parties and the court. Specifically, they were thought to be a vehicle for narrowing the issues and winnowing out insubstantial claims and defenses. Modern theory asks less of pleadings and provides other mechanisms better suited to these tasks. Broad ranging discovery may put the parties and the court in position to redefine the scope of the dispute, perhaps by permitting summary judgment or by suggesting the need for amended pleadings. Pretrial conferences focus attention on those matters for which resolution is required and the final pretrial conference order further clarifies the issues that need to be tried. Thus, the process begun by pleadings is completed largely by other tools.

CHAPTER 10

ADJUDICATION

WITH AND WITHOUT A TRIAL OR A JURY

A. Introduction and Integration

In prior chapters we saw that courts may dismiss cases early in the litigation for a variety of reasons, including lack of personal or subject matter jurisdiction, failure to state a claim, or default. However, most cases survive such preliminary objections. How are cases that survive adjudicated?

This chapter focuses on two critical aspects of the adjudication process — whether the adjudication process will include an actual trial with witnesses and evidence presented under oath in open court and second, if there is a trial, whether the finder of fact will be a jury or a judge. As you will see, these two questions are interrelated.

B. The Right to a Jury

1. Scope of the Constitutional Right

We begin by considering whether the fact finder will be a jury or a judge. The right to a jury was very important to this country's founders. Breach of the right was one of the British abuses listed in the Declaration of Independence and the failure of the original Constitution to guarantee the right in civil cases was one of the strong arguments of the anti-federalists against the adoption of the Constitution.

The right to a jury appears in three places in the Constitution. Art. III, section 2, and the Sixth Amendment address juries in criminal cases, and the Seventh Amendment address juries in civil cases. Although we will focus on the Seventh Amendment, the Sixth Amendment provides a useful comparison.

Notice that although the Sixth Amendment refers to "all criminal prosecutions," the Seventh Amendment does not provide for juries in all civil cases. Instead, it provides for juries "[i]n suits at common law." As discussed in Chapter 1, Section F, the British had two separate court systems — courts of law and courts of equity. Juries were available in the former, but not the latter. The American Colonies followed this British model and likewise had separate law and equity courts. Thus, the phrase "suits at common law" refers to suits in the courts of law as opposed to the courts of equity. In 1938, federal courts of law and equity were merged into one court system. As you will see, this merger creates some interpretative complications with respect to the Seventh Amendment.

A second important difference in the language of the Sixth and Seventh Amendments is that while the Sixth Amendment explicitly grants a right to a jury, the Seventh Amendment provides that the right shall be "preserved." As we will see, the word "preserved" has been interpreted to impose an historical test, under which the court determines whether there was a right to a jury at the time of the Seventh Amendment's ratification in 1791. In other words, one has a right to a jury trial today if she would have had such a right for her claim in 1791.

One potential difficulty of focusing on whether one would have had a right to a jury in 1791 is that there were some differences among state jury practices at that time. Thus, one might ask, "A right to a jury *where*?" Justice Story answered this question decisively in a case that has never subsequently been questioned:

> Beyond all question, the common law here alluded to is not the common law of any individual state, (for it probably differs in all), but it is the common law of England, the grand reservoir of all our jurisprudence. It cannot be necessary for me to expound the grounds of this opinion, because they must be obvious to every person acquainted with the history of the law.

United States v. Wonson, 28 F. Cas. 745, 750 (No. 16, 750) (C.C.D. Mass. 1812). Of course England, that grand reservoir of our jurisprudence, largely abolished the civil jury in 1920, but that doesn't change the historical practices as of 1791. As we will see, using an historical test to analyze modern claims under modern procedures presents numerous complications.

A final difference between the Sixth and Seventh Amendments is not apparent from the language. At the time of their ratification, the first ten amendments applied only to the federal government and not to the states. After the adoption of the Fourteenth Amendment, the Court began a process of selective incorporation, finding that some of the protections of the first ten amendments were part of the liberty interest protected by the Fourteenth Amendment and thus required of the states. The Court has held that the Sixth Amendment is applicable to the states, see Duncan v. Louisiana, 391 U.S. 145 (1968), but it has never so held with respect to the Seventh Amendment. Thus, in a civil case in state court there is no *federal* constitutional right to a jury, though a state constitutional or statutory provision may ensure the right.

a. "Actions at Common Law" and the Historical Test

Chauffers Local, 391 v. Terry
494 U.S. 558, 110 S. Ct. 1339, 108 L. Ed. 2d 519 (1990)

JUSTICE MARSHALL delivered the opinion of the Court, except as to Part III-A.

This case presents the question whether an employee who seeks relief in the form of backpay for a union's alleged breach of its duty of fair representation has a right to trial by jury. We hold that the Seventh Amendment entitles such a plaintiff to a jury trial.

I

McLean Trucking Company and the Chauffeurs, Teamsters and Helpers Local No. 391 (Union) were parties to a collective-bargaining agreement that governed the terms and conditions of employment at McLean's terminals. The 27 respondents were employed by McLean as truck drivers in bargaining units covered by the agreement, and all were members of the Union. In 1982 McLean implemented a change in operations that resulted in the elimination of some of its terminals and the reorganization of others.

[In connection with reorganization, respondents were laid off and lost seniority rights. Respondents filed two grievances against McLean and were represented by the Union. When respondents filed a third grievance, the union declined to refer the charges to the grievance committee on the grounds that the relevant issue had been determined in prior proceedings.]

In July 1983, respondents filed an action in District Court, alleging that McLean had breached the collective-bargaining agreement in violation of § 301 of the Labor Management Relations Act, 1947, 61 Stat. 156, 29 U.S.C. § 185 (1982 ed.), and that the Union had violated its duty of fair representation. Respondents requested a permanent injunction requiring the defendants to cease their illegal acts and to reinstate them to their proper seniority status; in addition, they sought, inter alia, compensatory damages for lost wages and health benefits. In 1986 McLean filed for bankruptcy; subsequently, the action against it was voluntarily dismissed, along with all claims for injunctive relief.

Respondents had requested a jury trial in their pleadings. The Union moved to strike the jury demand on the ground that no right to a jury trial exists in a duty of fair representation suit. The District Court denied the motion to strike. After an interlocutory appeal, the Fourth Circuit affirmed the trial court, holding that the Seventh Amendment entitled respondents to a jury trial of their claim for monetary relief. 863 F. 2d 334 (1988). We granted the petition for certiorari to resolve a Circuit conflict on this issue, and now affirm the judgment of the Fourth Circuit.

II

The duty of fair representation is inferred from unions' exclusive authority under the National Labor Relations Act to represent all employees in a bargaining unit. The duty requires a union "to serve the interests of all members without hostility or discrimination toward any, to exercise its discretion with complete good faith and honesty, and to avoid arbitrary conduct." A union must discharge its duty both in bargaining with the employer and in its enforcement of the resulting collective-bargaining agreement. Thus, the Union here was required to pursue respondents' grievances in a manner consistent with the principles of fair representation.

Because most collective-bargaining agreements accord finality to grievance or arbitration procedures established by the collective-bargaining agreement, an employee normally cannot bring a § 301 action against an employer unless he can show that the union breached its duty of fair representation in its handling of his grievance. Whether the employee sues both the labor union and the employer or only one of those entities, he must prove the same two facts to recover money damages: that the employer's action violated the terms of the collective-bargaining agreement and that the union breached its duty of fair representation.

III

We turn now to the constitutional issue presented in this case — whether respondents are entitled to a jury trial.[3] The Seventh Amendment provides that "[i]n Suits at common law, where the value in controversy shall exceed twenty dollars, the right of trial by jury shall be preserved." The right to a jury trial includes more than the common-law forms of action recognized in 1791; the phrase "Suits at common law" refers to "suits in which *legal* rights [are] to be ascertained and determined, in contradistinction to those where equitable rights alone [are] recognized, and equitable remedies [are] administered." The right extends to causes of action created by Congress. Tull v. United States, 481 U.S. 412, 417 (1987). Since the merger of the systems of law and equity, see Fed. Rule Civ. Proc. 2, this Court has carefully preserved the right to trial by jury where legal rights are at stake. As the Court noted in Beacon Theatres, Inc. v. Westover, 359 U.S. 500, 501 (1959), "'Maintenance of the jury as a fact-finding body is of such importance and occupies so firm a place in our history and jurisprudence that any seeming curtailment of the right to a jury trial should be scrutinized with the utmost care.'"

To determine whether a particular action will resolve legal rights, we examine both the nature of the issues involved and the remedy sought. "First, we compare the statutory action to 18th-century actions brought in the courts of England prior to the merger of the courts of law and equity. Second, we examine the remedy sought and determine whether it is legal or equitable in nature." *Tull*, supra. The second inquiry is the more important in our analysis. Granfinanciera, S.A. v. Nordberg, 492 U.S. 33, 42 (1989).

A

An action for breach of a union's duty of fair representation was unknown in 18th-century England; in fact, collective bargaining was unlawful. We must therefore look for an analogous cause

---

[3] Because the NLRA, does not expressly create the duty of fair representation, resort to the statute to determine whether Congress provided for a jury trial in an action for breach of that duty is unavailing. Cf. Curtis v. Loether, 415 U.S. 189, 192, n. 6 (1974) (recognizing the "'cardinal principle that this Court will first ascertain whether a construction of the statute is fairly possible by which the [constitutional] question may be avoided'" * * *)

of action that existed in the 18th century to determine whether the nature of this duty of fair representation suit is legal or equitable.

The Union contends that this duty of fair representation action resembles a suit brought to vacate an arbitration award because respondents seek to set aside the result of the grievance process. In the 18th century, an action to set aside an arbitration award was considered equitable. 2 J. STORY, COMMENTARIES ON EQUITY JURISPRUDENCE § 1452, pp. 789-790 (13th ed. 1886) (equity courts had jurisdiction over claims that an award should be set aside on the ground of "mistake of the arbitrators"); see, e.g., Burchell v. Marsh, 17 How. 344 (1855) (reviewing bill in equity to vacate an arbitration award). * * *

The arbitration analogy is inapposite, however, to the Seventh Amendment question posed in this case. No grievance committee has considered respondents' claim that the Union violated its duty of fair representation; the grievance process was concerned only with the employer's alleged breach of the collective-bargaining agreement. Thus, respondents' claim against the Union cannot be characterized as an action to vacate an arbitration award because "'[t]he arbitration proceeding did not, and indeed, could not, resolve the employee's claim against the union.... Because no arbitrator has decided the primary issue presented by this claim, no arbitration award need be undone, even if the employee ultimately prevails.'"

The Union next argues that respondents' duty of fair representation action is comparable to an action by a trust beneficiary against a trustee for breach of fiduciary duty. Such actions were within the exclusive jurisdiction of courts of equity. 2 STORY, supra, § 960, p. 266; RESTATEMENT (SECOND) OF TRUSTS § 199(c) (1959). This analogy is far more persuasive than the arbitration analogy. Just as a trustee must act in the best interests of the beneficiaries, a union, as the exclusive representative of the workers, must exercise its power to act on behalf of the employees in good faith. Moreover, just as a beneficiary does not directly control the actions of a trustee, an individual employee lacks direct control over a union's actions taken on his behalf.

* * *

Respondents contend that their duty of fair representation suit is less like a trust action than an attorney malpractice action, which was historically an action at law, see, e.g., Russell v. Palmer, 2 Wils. K. B. 325, 95 Eng. Rep. 837 (1767). In determining the appropriate statute of limitations for a hybrid § 301/duty of fair representation action, this Court in *DelCostello* [v. Teamsters] noted in dictum that an attorney malpractice action is "the closest state-law analogy for the claim against the union." 462 U.S. 151, 167. The Court in *DelCostello* did not consider the trust analogy, however. Presented with a more complete range of alternatives, we find that, in the context of the Seventh Amendment inquiry, the attorney malpractice analogy does not capture the relationship between the union and the represented employees as fully as the trust analogy does.

The attorney malpractice analogy is inadequate in several respects. Although an attorney malpractice suit is in some ways similar to a suit alleging a union's breach of its fiduciary duty, the two actions are fundamentally different. The nature of an action is in large part controlled by the nature of the underlying relationship between the parties. Unlike employees represented by a union, a client controls the significant decisions concerning his representation. Moreover, a client can fire his attorney if he is dissatisfied with his attorney's performance. This option is not available to an individual employee who is unhappy with a union's representation, unless a majority of the members of the bargaining unit share his dissatisfaction. Thus, we find the malpractice analogy less convincing than the trust analogy.

Nevertheless, the trust analogy does not persuade us to characterize respondents' claim as wholly equitable. The Union's argument mischaracterizes the nature of our comparison of the action before us to 18th-century forms of action. As we observed in Ross v. Bernhard, 396 U.S. 531 (1970), "The Seventh Amendment question depends on the nature of the *issue* to be tried rather than the character of the overall action." Id. at 538 (emphasis added) (finding a right to jury trial in a shareholder's derivative suit, a type of suit traditionally brought in courts of equity, because plaintiffs' case presented legal issues of breach of contract and negligence). As discussed above, to recover from the Union here, respondents must prove both that McLean violated § 301 by breaching the collective-bargaining agreement and that the Union breached its duty of fair representation. When viewed in isolation, the duty of fair representation issue is analogous to a claim against a trustee for breach of fiduciary duty. The § 301 issue, however, is comparable to a breach of contract claim — a legal issue.

Respondents' action against the Union thus encompasses both equitable and legal issues. The first part of our Seventh Amendment inquiry, then, leaves us in equipoise as to whether respondents are entitled to a jury trial.

B

Our determination under the first part of the Seventh Amendment analysis is only preliminary. In this case, the only remedy sought is a request for compensatory damages representing backpay and benefits. Generally, an action for money damages was "the traditional form of relief offered in the courts of law." Curtis v. Loether, 415 U.S. 189, 196 (1974). This Court has not, however, held that "any award of monetary relief must *necessarily* be 'legal' relief." Ibid. (emphasis added). Nonetheless, because we conclude that the remedy respondents seek has none of the attributes that must be present before we will find an exception to the general rule and characterize damages as equitable, we find that the remedy sought by respondents is legal.

First, we have characterized damages as equitable where they are restitutionary, such as in "action[s] for disgorgement of improper profits." The backpay sought by respondents is not money wrongfully held by the Union, but wages and benefits they would have received from McLean had the Union processed the employees' grievances properly. Such relief is not restitutionary.

Second, a monetary award "incidental to or intertwined with injunctive relief" may be equitable. Because respondents seek only money damages, this characteristic is clearly absent from the case.[8]

The Union argues that the backpay relief sought here must nonetheless be considered equitable because this Court has labeled backpay awarded under Title VII of the Civil Rights Act of 1964 as equitable. See Albemarle Paper Co. v. Moody, 422 U.S. 405, 415-418 (1975) (characterizing backpay awarded against employer under Title VII as equitable in context of assessing whether

---

[8] Both the Union and the dissent argue that the backpay award sought here is equitable because it is closely analogous to damages awarded to beneficiaries for a trustee's breach of trust. Such damages were available only in courts of equity because those courts had exclusive jurisdiction over actions involving a trustee's breach of his fiduciary duties.

judge erred in refusing to award such relief). It contends that the Title VII analogy is compelling in the context of the duty of fair representation because the Title VII backpay provision was based on the NLRA provision governing backpay awards for unfair labor practices. We are not convinced.

The Court has never held that a plaintiff seeking backpay under Title VII has a right to a jury trial. Assuming, without deciding, that such a Title VII plaintiff has no right to a jury trial, the Union's argument does not persuade us that respondents are not entitled to a jury trial here. Congress specifically characterized backpay under Title VII as a form of "equitable relief." 42 U.S.C. § 2000e-5(g) (1982 ed.) ("[T]he court may ... order such affirmative action as may be appropriate, which may include, but is not limited to, reinstatement or hiring of employees, with or without back pay ..., or any other equitable relief as the court deems appropriate"). See also Curtis v. Loether, (distinguishing backpay under Title VII from damages under Title VIII, the fair housing provision of the Civil Right Act, which the Court characterized as "legal" for Seventh Amendment purposes). Congress made no similar pronouncement regarding the duty of fair representation. Furthermore, the Court has noted that backpay sought from an employer under Title VII would generally be restitutionary in nature, in contrast to the damages sought here from the Union. Thus, the remedy sought in this duty of fair representation case is clearly different from backpay sought for violations of Title VII.

Moreover, the fact that Title VII's backpay provision may have been modeled on a provision in the NLRA concerning remedies for unfair labor practices does not require that the backpay remedy available here be considered equitable. The Union apparently reasons that if Title VII is comparable to one labor law remedy it is comparable to all remedies available in the NLRA context. Although both the duty of fair representation and the unfair labor practice provisions of the NLRA are components of national labor policy, their purposes are not identical. Unlike the unfair labor practice provisions of the NLRA, which are concerned primarily with the public interest in effecting federal labor policy, the duty of fair representation targets "'the wrong done the individual employee.'" Thus, the remedies appropriate for unfair labor practices may differ from the remedies for a breach of the duty of fair representation, given the need to vindicate different goals. Certainly, the connection between backpay under Title VII and damages under the unfair labor practice provision of the NLRA does not require us to find a parallel connection between Title VII backpay and money damages for breach of the duty of fair representation.

We hold, then, that the remedy of backpay sought in this duty of fair representation action is legal in nature. Considering both parts of the Seventh Amendment inquiry, we find that respondents are entitled to a jury trial on all issues presented in their suit.

The Union's argument, however, conflates the two parts of our Seventh Amendment inquiry. Under the dissent's approach, if the action at issue were analogous to an 18th-century action within the exclusive jurisdiction of the courts of equity, we would necessarily conclude that the remedy sought was also equitable because it would have been unavailable in a court of law. This view would, in effect, make the first part of our inquiry dispositive. We have clearly held, however, that the second part of the inquiry— the nature of the relief— is more important to the Seventh Amendment determination. The second part of the analysis, therefore, should not replicate the "abstruse historical" inquiry of the first part, but requires consideration of the general types of relief provided by courts of law and equity.

IV

On balance, our analysis of the nature of respondents' duty of fair representation action and the remedy they seek convinces us that this action is a legal one. Although the search for an adequate 18th-century analog revealed that the claim includes both legal and equitable issues, the money damages respondents seek are the type of relief traditionally awarded by courts of law. Thus, the Seventh Amendment entitles respondents to a jury trial, and we therefore affirm the judgment of the Court of Appeals.

It is so ordered.

JUSTICE BRENNAN, concurring in part and concurring in the judgment.

I agree with the Court that respondents seek a remedy that is legal in nature and that the Seventh Amendment entitles respondents to a jury trial on their duty of fair representation claims. I therefore join Parts I, II, III-B, and IV of the Court's opinion. I do not join that part of the opinion which reprises the particular historical analysis this Court has employed to determine whether a claim is a "Sui[t] at common law" under the Seventh Amendment, because I believe the historical test can and should be simplified.

The current test, first expounded in *Curtis v. Loether*, requires a court to compare the right at issue to 18th-century English forms of action to determine whether the historically analogous right was vindicated in an action at law or in equity, and to examine whether the remedy sought is legal or equitable in nature. However, this Court, in expounding the test, has repeatedly discounted the significance of the analogous form of action for deciding where the Seventh Amendment applies. I think it is time we dispense with it altogether. I would decide Seventh Amendment questions on the basis of the relief sought. If the relief is legal in nature, i.e., if it is the kind of relief that historically was available from courts of law, I would hold that the parties have a constitutional right to a trial by jury — unless Congress has permissibly delegated the particular dispute to a non-Article III decision maker and jury trials would frustrate Congress' purposes in enacting a particular statutory scheme.

I believe that our insistence that the jury trial right hinges in part on a comparison of the substantive right at issue to forms of action used in English courts 200 years ago needlessly convolutes our Seventh Amendment jurisprudence. For the past decade and a half, this Court has explained that the two parts of the historical test are not equal in weight, that the nature of the remedy is more important than the nature of the right. Since the existence of a right to jury trial therefore turns on the nature of the remedy, absent congressional delegation to a specialized decision maker, there remains little purpose to our rattling through dusty attics of ancient writs. The time has come to borrow William of Occam's razor and sever this portion of our analysis.

We have long acknowledged that, of the factors relevant to the jury trial right, comparison of the claim to ancient forms of action, "requiring extensive and possibly abstruse historical inquiry, is obviously the most difficult to apply." Requiring judges, with neither the training nor time necessary for reputable historical scholarship, to root through the tangle of primary and secondary sources to determine which of a hundred or so writs is analogous to the right at issue has embroiled courts in recondite controversies better left to legal historians. * * *

B. The Right to a Jury

To be sure, it is neither unusual nor embarrassing for members of a court to disagree and disagree vehemently. But it better behooves judges to disagree within the province of judicial expertise. Furthermore, inquiries into the appropriate historical analogs for the rights at issue are not necessarily susceptible of sound resolution under the best of circumstances. As one scholar observes: "[T]he line between law and equity (and therefore between jury and non-jury trial) was not a fixed and static one. There was a continual process of borrowing by one jurisdiction from the other; there were less frequent instances of a sloughing off of older functions....The borrowing by each jurisdiction from the other was not accompanied by an equivalent sloughing off of functions. This led to a very large overlap between law and equity." James, *Right to a Jury Trial in Civil Actions*, 72 YALE L. J. 655, 658-659 (1963).

In addition, modern statutory rights did not exist in the 18th century, and even the most exacting historical research may not elicit a clear historical analog. The right at issue here, for example, is a creature of modern labor law quite foreign to Georgian England. Justice Stewart recognized the perplexities involved in this task in his dissent in *Ross v. Bernhard*, albeit drawing a different conclusion. "The fact is," he said, "that there are, for the most part, no such things as inherently 'legal issues' or inherently 'equitable issues.' There are only factual issues, and, 'like chameleons [they] take their color from surrounding circumstances.' Thus, the Court's 'nature of the issue' approach is hardly meaningful." I have grappled with this kind of inquiry for three decades on this Court and have come to the realization that engaging in such inquiries is impracticable and unilluminating.

To rest the historical test required by the Seventh Amendment solely on the nature of the relief sought would not, of course, offer the federal courts a rule that is in all cases self-executing. Courts will still be required to ask which remedies were traditionally available at law and which only in equity. But this inquiry involves fewer variables and simpler choices, on the whole, and is far more manageable than the scholastic debates in which we have been engaged. Moreover, the rule I propose would remain true to the Seventh Amendment, as it is undisputed that, historically, "[j]urisdictional lines [between law and equity] were primarily a matter of remedy." McCoid, *Procedural Reform and the Right to Jury Trial: A Study of Beacon Theatres, Inc. v. Westover*, 116 U. PA. L. REV. 1 (1967). See also Redish, *Seventh Amendment Right to Jury Trial: A Study in the Irrationality of Rational Decision Making*, 70 NW. U. L. REV. 486, 490 (1975) ("In the majority of cases at common law, the equitable or legal nature of a suit was determined not by the substantive nature of the cause of action but by the remedy sought").[7]

This is not to say that the resulting division between claims entitled to jury trials and claims not so entitled would exactly mirror the division between law and equity in England in 1791. But it is too late in the day for this Court to profess that the Seventh Amendment preserves the right to jury trial only in cases that would have been heard in the British law courts of the 18th century. See, e.g., Curtis v. Loether, 415 U.S., at 193 ("Although the thrust of the Amendment was to preserve the right

---

[7] There are, to be sure, some who advocate abolishing the historical test altogether. See, e.g., Wolfram, *The Constitutional History of the Seventh Amendment*, 57 MINN. L.REV. 639, 742-747 (1973). Contrary to the intimations in Justice Kennedy's dissent, I am not among them. I believe that it is imperative to retain a historical test for determining when parties have a right to jury trial for precisely the same reasons Justice Kennedy does. It is mandated by the language of the Seventh Amendment and it is a bulwark against those who would restrict a right our forefathers held indispensable. Like Justice Kennedy, I have no doubt that courts can and do look to legal history for the answers to constitutional questions, and therefore the Seventh Amendment test I propose today obliges courts to do exactly that.

to jury trial as it existed in 1791, it has long been settled that the right extends beyond the common-law forms of action recognized at that time"); Beacon Theatres, Inc. v. Westover, 359 U.S. 500 (1959) (rejecting the relevance of the chancellor's historic ability to decide legal claims incidental to a case brought in equity and holding that, in mixed cases, the parties are not only entitled to a jury trial on the legal claims but that this jury trial must precede a decision on the equitable claims — with the attendant collateral-estoppel effects); Ross v. Bernhard, 396 U.S. 531 (1970) (requiring a jury trial on the legal issues in a shareholders' derivative suit even though the procedurally equivalent suit in the 18th century would have been heard only in equity).

Indeed, given this Court's repeated insistence that the nature of the remedy is always to be given more weight than the nature of the historically analogous right, it is unlikely that the simplified Seventh Amendment analysis I propose will result in different decisions than the analysis in current use. In the unusual circumstance that the nature of the remedy could be characterized equally as legal or equitable, I submit that the comparison of a contemporary statutory action unheard of in the 18th century to some ill-fitting ancient writ is too shaky a basis for the resolution of an issue as significant as the availability of a trial by jury. If, in the rare case, a tie breaker is needed, let us break the tie in favor of jury trial.

* * *

We can guard this right and save our courts from needless and intractable excursions into increasingly unfamiliar territory simply by retiring that prong of our Seventh Amendment test which we have already cast into a certain doubt. If we are not prepared to accord the nature of the historical analog sufficient weight for this factor to affect the outcome of our inquiry, except in the rarest of hypothetical cases, what reason do we have for insisting that federal judges proceed with this arduous inquiry? It is time we read the writing on the wall, especially as we ourselves put it there.

JUSTICE STEVENS, concurring in part and concurring in the judgment.

Because I believe the Court has made this case unnecessarily difficult by exaggerating the importance of finding a precise common-law analogue to the duty of fair representation, I do not join Part III-A of its opinion. Ironically, by stressing the importance of identifying an exact analogue, the Court has diminished the utility of looking for any analogue.

Where Justice Kennedy and I differ is in our evaluations of which historical test provides the more reliable results. That three learned Justices of the Supreme Court cannot arrive at the same conclusion in this very case, on what is essentially a question of fact, does not speak well for the judicial solvency of the current test. My concern is not merely the competence of courts to delve into this peculiarly recalcitrant aspect of legal history and certainly not, as Justice Kennedy summarizes it, the "competence of the Court to understand legal history" in general. My concern is that all too often the first prong of the current test requires courts to measure modern statutory actions against 18th-century English actions so remote in form and concept that there is no firm basis for comparison. In such cases, the result is less the discovery of a historical analog than the manufacture of a historical fiction. By contrast, the nature of relief available today corresponds more directly to the nature of relief available in Georgian England. Thus the historical test I propose, focusing on the nature of the relief sought, is not only more manageable than the current test, it is more reliably grounded in history.

As I have suggested in the past, I believe the duty of fair representation action resembles a common-law action against an attorney for malpractice more closely than it does any other form of action. * * *

* * *

* * * Duty of fair representation suits are for the most part ordinary civil actions involving the stuff of contract and malpractice disputes. There is accordingly no ground for excluding these actions from the jury right.

* * *

JUSTICE KENNEDY, with whom JUSTICE O'CONNOR and JUSTICE SCALIA join, dissenting.

This case asks whether the Seventh Amendment guarantees the respondent union members a jury trial in a duty of fair representation action against their labor union. The Court is quite correct, in my view, in its formulation of the initial premises that must govern the case. Under *Curtis v. Loether*, the right to a jury trial in a statutory action depends on the presence of "legal rights and remedies." To determine whether rights and remedies in a duty of fair representation action are legal in character, we must compare the action to the 18th-century cases permitted in the law courts of England, and we must examine the nature of the relief sought. I agree also with those Members of the Court who find that the duty of fair representation action resembles an equitable trust action more than a suit for malpractice.

I disagree with the analytic innovation of the Court that identification of the trust action as a model for modern duty of fair representation actions is insufficient to decide the case. The Seventh Amendment requires us to determine whether the duty of fair representation action "is more similar to cases that were tried in courts of law than to suits tried in courts of equity." Tull v. United States, 481 U.S. 412, 417 (1987). Having made this decision in favor of an equitable action, our inquiry should end. Because the Court disagrees with this proposition, I dissent.

* * *

III

The Court must adhere to the historical test in determining the right to a jury because the language of the Constitution requires it. The Seventh Amendment "preserves" the right to jury trial in civil cases. We cannot preserve a right existing in 1791 unless we look to history to identify it. Our precedents are in full agreement with this reasoning and insist on adherence to the historical test. No alternatives short of rewriting the Constitution exist. If we abandon the plain language of the Constitution to expand the jury right, we may expect Courts with opposing views to curtail it in the future.

It is true that a historical inquiry into the distinction between law and equity may require us to enter into a domain becoming less familiar with time. Two centuries have passed since the

Seventh Amendment's ratification, and the incompleteness of our historical records makes it difficult to know the nature of certain actions in 1791. The historical test, nonetheless, has received more criticism than it deserves. Although our application of the analysis in some cases may seem biased in favor of jury trials, the test has not become a nullity. We do not require juries in all statutory actions. The historical test, in fact, resolves most cases without difficulty.

I would hesitate to abandon or curtail the historical test out of concern for the competence of the Court to understand legal history. We do look to history for the answers to constitutional questions. Although opinions will differ on what this history shows, the approach has no less validity in the Seventh Amendment context than elsewhere.

If Congress has not provided for a jury trial, we are confined to the Seventh Amendment to determine whether one is required. Our own views respecting the wisdom of using a jury should be put aside. Like Justice Brennan, I admire the jury process. Other judges have taken the opposite view. See, e.g., J. FRANK, LAW AND THE MODERN MIND 170-185 (1931). But the judgment of our own times is not always preferable to the lessons of history. Our whole constitutional experience teaches that history must inform the judicial inquiry. Our obligation to the Constitution and its Bill of Rights, no less than the compact we have with the generation that wrote them for us, do not permit us to disregard provisions that some may think to be mere matters of historical form.

* * *

NOTES AND QUESTIONS

1. In which, if any, of the following situations is there a Seventh Amendment right to a jury:
   (a) Patty and David sign a contract. A dispute arises and Patty files suit for breach of contract seeking money damages.
   (b) Same as (a), except Patty seeks only specific performance.
   (c) Patty contends that the agreed contract price was $200,000, but because of a typing error the contract reads "$100,000," Patty seeks to have the contract reformed.
   (d) Patty alleges that David fraudulently talked her into signing the contract. She seeks to have the purported agreement rescinded.

2. Under Rule 38, a party must demand a jury "not later than 10 days after the service of the last pleading directed to such issue." Rule 38(b). Failure to request a jury constitutes a waiver, see Rule 38(d), and the case is then tried to a judge. See Rule 39(b). Although the Rule allows the jury demand to be included in a separate document, most parties include the demand in their pleadings. The federal requirement of a demand is in contrast to the practice in some states. In Georgia, for example, a jury is presumed unless explicitly waived by all parties. See GA. CODE ANN. § 9-11-39; Whitaker & Rambo Interior Designs, Inc. v. Prudential Property Cas. Ins. Co., 510 F. Supp. 97 (N.D. Ga. 1981) (under

Rule 81(c) no demand required if case is removed from a state court in which right to a jury is presumed).

3. In Question 1(a) above, suppose the plaintiff requested a judge and the defendant a jury, whose request prevails? 38(b)

4. All of the hypotheticals in Question 1 involve common law claims that existed in 1791. In contrast, *Terry* involved a claim which did not exist in 1791. Notwithstanding that the claim didn't exist in 1791, the Court uses what it calls an historical test. Thus, as noted above, to determine whether a party has a constitutional right to a jury in America today, one asks: "in 1791, in England, to what court would this claim (which didn't exist then) have been assigned?" Isn't this a little like asking in what room of Monticello Thomas Jefferson would have put his television set?

5. Do you agree with Justice Kennedy that an historical test is mandated by the plain language of the Seventh Amendment? Are there any other plausible ways to interpret that Amendment? See Charles Wofran, *The Constitutional History of the Seventh Amendment*, 57 MINN. L. REV. 639, 745 (1973) (arguing that the founders intended a "dynamic" interpretation of the Seventh Amendment, not a fixed historical meaning).

6. What do you think of Justice Brennan's suggestion that the Court should abandon its search for historical analogies and instead confine its inquiry to the historical character of the *remedy* sought?

7. As Justice Brennan notes in his footnote 7, some commentators have urged abandoning an historical approach in favor of a "functional approach" focusing "on whether the judge is in a better position than the jury to decide a particular case in a fashion comporting with notions of fair and efficient justice." Mary Kay Kane, *Civil Jury Trial: The Case for Reasoned Iconoclasm*, 28 HAST. L.J. 1, 2 (1976). Advocates of this approach have drawn some support from a footnote in Ross v. Bernhard, 396 U.S. 531, 538 n.10 (1970), in which the Court observed:

> As our cases indicate, the "legal" nature of an issue is determined by considering, first, the pre-merger custom with reference to such questions. Second, the remedy sought; and third, the practical abilities and limitations of juries. Of the factors, the first, requiring extensive and possible abstruse historical inquiry, is obviously the most difficult to apply.

You will notice that in *Terry*, there is no mention of the third factor listed above. Should the Court consider "the practical abilities and limitations of juries" in deciding whether there is a right to a jury? If so, what are the abilities and limitations of juries? Suppose, for example, the case will be extremely long or complex, is a jury appropriate? See, e.g. In re Japanese Electronic Prods. Antitrust Litigation, 631 F. 2d 1069 (3d Cir. 1980).

The longest jury trial in American history lasted over three and a half years with the jury deliberating for another eights weeks. The case arose out of a train derailment resulting in the spill of crude oil containing small amounts of dioxin. Residents near the spill site brought suit against several defendants, including the railroad and Monsanto, the chemical company whose product spilled. Only the claims against the Monsanto went to trial. The jury found actual damages of $14,500 as to one landowner. For all other plaintiffs the jury awarded $1 in compensatory damages and $16 million in punitive damages. The court of appeals reversed, finding the compensatory damages to be one property owner was unsupported by the evidence, and holding that punitive damages are not permissible when there are only nominal compensatory damages. See Kemner v. Monsanto Co., 576 N.E.2d 1146 (Ill. App. 1991). For a profile of the jury, see Michelle Green, *Never to be Accused of Rushing to Judgment, A Jury Goes Home After a Trying 44 Months*, PEOPLE, Nov. 9, 1987, at 48.

8. In Part III A, of his opinion, Justice Marshall concluded that the "duty of fair representation issue" is equitable while "§ 301 issue" is legal. Isn't this an ahistorical way of analyzing the case? In 1791, courts would not have focused on whether an issue in a claim were legal or equitable. Instead, the entire claim would have gone to one court or the other.

In explaining his analysis, Justice Marshall relied on Ross v. Bernhard, 396 U.S. 531 (1970). *Ross* was a shareholder's derivative suit in which plaintiffs alleged that the defendant breached its contract with the corporation. Although historically shareholder derivative suits could only be brought in courts of equity, the Court held there was nonetheless a right to a jury. The Court explained that a derivative suit "has dual aspects: first, the stockholder's right to sue on behalf of the corporation, historically an equitable matter; second, the claim of the corporation against directors or third parties on which, if the corporation had sued and the claim presented legal issues, the company could demand a jury trial." Id. at 538. The Court concluded:

> The historical rule preventing a court of law from entertaining a shareholder's suit on behalf of the corporation is obsolete; it is no longer tenable for a district court, administering both law and equity in the same action, to deny legal remedies to a corporation, merely because the corporation's spokesmen are its shareholders rather than its directors. Under the rules, law and equity are procedurally combined; nothing turns now upon the form of the action or the procedural devices by which the parties happen to come before the court.

Id. at 540.

Justice Kennedy responded to Justice Marshall's analysis in *Terry* by quoting from Justice Stewart's dissent in *Ross* that "there are, for the most part, no such things as inherently 'legal issues' or inherently 'equitable issues'. There are only factual issues, and 'like chameleons [they] take their color from surrounding circumstances.'" Do you agree? How far can a court go in splitting a claim into its equitable and legal components? Consider, for example, a breach of contract claim seeking specific performance. Could it be said that such a claim has two components, the remedy, which is equitable, and the question of whether the contract was breached, which is legal?

9. In *Terry*, the Court focuses on whether the remedy sought is legal or equitable. This is not always a simple historical inquiry. First, as the Court's discussion of back pay suggests, equitable remedies sometimes closely resemble legal ones. Second, traditionally a precondition for equity was that legal remedies were inadequate. Because the scope of equitable remedies is tied to the scope of legal remedies, the Court has held that "procedural changes which remove the inadequacy of a remedy at law may sharply diminish the scope of traditional equitable remedies by making them unnecessary in many cases." Dairy Queen v. Wood, 369 U.S. 469, 478 n.19 (1962). This principle is well illustrated by *Dairy Queen*. There, the plaintiff sought an "accounting," an historically equitable remedy. Nonetheless, the Court held that there was a right to a jury, explaining:

> The respondents' contention that this money claim is "purely equitable" is based primarily upon the fact that their complaint is cast in terms of an "accounting," rather than in terms of an action for "debt" or "damages." But the constitutional right to trial by jury cannot be made to depend upon the choice of words used in the pleadings. The necessary prerequisite to the right to maintain a suit for an equitable accounting, like all other equitable remedies, is, as we pointed out in *Beacon Theatres*, the absence of an adequate remedy at law. Consequently, in order to maintain such a suit on a cause of action cognizable at law, as this one is, the plaintiff must be able to show that the "accounts between the parties" are of such a "complicated nature" that only a court of equity can satisfactorily unravel them. In view of the powers given to District Courts by Federal Rule of Civil Procedure 53(b) to appoint masters to assist the jury in those exceptional cases where the legal issues are too complicated for the jury adequately to handle alone, the burden of such a showing is considerably increased and it will indeed be a rare case in which it can be met. But be that as it may, this is certainly not such a case. A jury under proper instructions from the court, could readily determine the recovery, if any, to be had here, where the theory finally settled upon is that of breach of contract, that of trademark infringement, or any combination of the two. The legal remedy cannot be characterized as inadequate merely because the measure of damages may necessitate a look into petitioner's business records.

Id. at 477-79.

How far can this analysis be pushed? Consider: a trust beneficiary files suit against a trustee, alleging that the trustee embezzled money. The plaintiff seeks "restitution." Could the defendant argue that it is entitled to a jury since although the plaintiff sought restitution, a legal action for damages would be adequate? If this line of argument works, will back pay ever be equitable?

10. In *Terry*, the Court indicates that when backpay is "restitutionary," it is equitable. Suppose that the plaintiffs in *Terry* had pursued their claim against their employer alleging wrongful firing and seeking back pay. Would this claim be restitutionary? Would there be a right to a jury?

11. In Tull v. United States, 481 U.S. 412 (1987), the Court held that there is a right to a jury in cases seeking civil penalties under the Clean Water Act. The government contended that the defendant had dumped fill material on wetlands in violation of the Act. The Act authorized civil penalties of up to $10,000 per day during the period of the violation and the government sought the maximum penalty of over $22 million. The defendant argued that the suit was analogous to an action in debt, which was a legal claim. The government responded that the suit was more analogous to an action to abate a public nuisance which was equitable. The Court declined to rest its holding on an "'abstruse historical' search for the nearest 18th-century analog." Id. at 421. Instead the Court focused on the remedy. The Court observed that the penalties were not intended simply to restore the status quo — a traditional equitable function, but were designed to deter and punish. It concluded that "the nature of the relief authorized by [the Act] was traditionally available only in a court of law" and therefore the defendant was entitled to jury on the question of liability under the Act. Id. at 423.

Although the Court found a right to a jury on the question of liability, it also held that there was no right to have a jury determine the amount of the civil penalty. According to the Court, "[t]he assessment of a civil penalty is not one of the 'most fundamental elements' [of the system of trial by jury]." Id. at 426. Thus, although the reason the defendant got a jury on liability was because of the remedy, he wasn't allowed a jury on the question of the remedy. Does this make any sense?

In probing whether the assessment of civil penalties is an essential function of the jury trial, *Tull* leaves unanswered whether the Seventh Amendment requires that the jury determine other types of remedies, such as compensatory or punitive damages. Professor Murphy concludes that the Seventh Amendment does not compel a jury assessment of punitive damages. She argues that the assessment of punitive damages, like that of civil penalties, is unconstrained by meaningful standards and that this sort of discretionary decision making is better performed by judges, who have legal training and experience in the civil justice system. Colleen Murphy, *Integrating the Constitutional Authority of Civil and Criminal Juries*, 61 GEO. WASH. L. REV. 723, 739-82 (1993). In contrast, Professor Murphy concludes that the Seventh Amendment does require that juries determine compensatory damages because that assessment is rooted in factfinding and subjective evaluation of the facts are at the heart of the jury's constitutional province. Colleen Murphy,

Determining Compensation: The Tension Between Legislative Power and Jury Authority, 74 TEX. L. REV. __ (1995).

12. Following *Terry*, some unions urged Congress to rewrite § 301 to eliminate a right to a jury in such cases. Assume that you are on the staff of a congressional committee that has been asked to consider ways to amend the statute to achieve this result. Which, if any, of the following devices would be effective:

(a) Add a provision stating that "there shall be no right to a jury in any case brought against a union under § 301."

(b) Add a provision stating that "a plaintiff who proves a violation of § 301 is entitled to back pay and other equitable relief."

(c) Amend the statute to provide that: "Unions have an obligation as trustees to act in the best interest of their members. If a union fails properly to represent its members in a dispute with a member's employer, a union member may bring an equitable claim against the union for breach of fiduciary duty."

(d) Amend § 301 to provide that suits for violation of the act can be brought in any District Court of the United States, but "such court shall sit as a court of equity."

b. The Complications of Merger and the Federal Rules

The Federal Rules not only merge the courts of law and equity, they permit parties to join legal and equitable claims in a single suit. Thus, today in federal and most state courts, parties can raise legal and equitable claims in one suit. Suppose, for example, the plaintiff files suit seeking injunctive relief and the defendant counterclaims with a legal claim. Is there a right to jury?

In Beacon Theatres v. Westover, 359 U.S. 500 (1958), the Supreme Court held that there is a right to a jury on the legal claim and that, therefore, the legal claim should ordinarily be tried first. The reason for trying the legal claim first is tied to the concept of preclusion, which we will study in Chapter 11. Under preclusion doctrine, once a claim or issue has been determined, that decision will generally be binding on future adjudications involving that claim or issue. Therefore, if the equitable claim were decided first, the facts decided in connection with that claim would then be treated as having been established for purposes of the legal claim. This would mean that the only issues left for the jury would be any that were not addressed in connection with the equitable claim. Thus, the Court in *Beacon Theatres* concluded:

> If there should be cases [joining equitable and legal claims] * * * the trial court will necessarily have to use its discretion in deciding whether the legal or equitable cause should be tried first. Since the right to jury trial is a constitutional one,

however, while no similar requirement protects trials by the court, that discretion is very narrowly limited and must, wherever possible, be exercised to preserve jury trial. As this Court said in Scott v. Neely, 140 U.S. 106, 109-110: "In the Federal courts this [jury] right cannot be dispensed with, except by the assent of the parties entitled to it, nor can it be impaired by any blending with a claim, properly cognizable at law, of a demand for equitable relief in aid of the legal action or during its pendency." This long-standing principle of equity dictates that only under the most imperative circumstances, circumstances which in view of the flexible procedures of the Federal Rules we cannot now anticipate, can the right to a jury trial of legal issues be lost through prior determination of equitable claims.

Id. at 510-11.

The Court reaffirmed this holding of *Beacon Theatres* in Dairy Queen v. Wood, 369 U.S. 469 (1962). In *Dairy Queen* the Court stressed that there is a right to a jury on legal issues even if the equitable claims predominate or the legal issues are "incidental" to the equitable ones. Id. at 473.

Another modern innovation is the declaratory judgment, a remedy unknown in 1791, and which we encountered supra at 198. Is there a right to a jury in a declaratory judgment action? In answering this, courts determine in what kind of an action the suit would have been brought absent the availability of the declaratory judgment. See, e.g., Johnson v. Fidelity & Cas. Co. of N.Y., 258 F. 2d 322 (8th Cir. 1956); 9 WRIGHT & MILLER, FEDERAL PRACTICE & PROCEDURE § 2313. For example, if a party to a contract is unable to perform because of some unforeseen circumstance, that party might seek a declaratory judgment that the failure to perform is not a breach of contract. Since the other way the issue of the breach could have arisen would have been in a suit for damages with a jury right, there is a jury right in the declaratory judgment action. Given that many issues could be litigated in either an equitable or legal action, this test can be difficult. Suppose a plaintiff brings a school desegregation claim seeking an injunction. Can the school board get a jury if it counterclaims for a declaratory judgment that it is not liable for damages? See Robinson v. Brown, 320 F. 2d 503 (6th Cir.), *cert. denied*, 376 U.S. 908 (1964).

One modern innovation that has been permitted to diminish in some respects the right to a jury is non-mutual issue preclusion, which we will examine in detail in Chapter 11. In that chaper, we will read Parklane Hosiery Co. v. Shore, 439 U.S. 322 (1979). There, the Securities and Exchange Commission sought a declaratory judgment against a corporation and some of its directors and officers that they had issued false proxy statements in violation of federal laws. After the SEC won that case, private litigants, suing the same defendants for the same proxy statements, asserted that the defendants were estopped to deny that the proxy statements were false. The Court agreed, even though the SEC proceeding had not involved a jury and the assertion of preclusion meant that defendants would never be able to litigate the question before a jury.

B. The Right to a Jury

c. Juries in non-Article III Courts

Article III of the Constitution describes the judicial power of the United States and provides, among other things, for judges with life tenure. However, not all adjudication of federal claims occurs in courts with Art. III judges. First, and most obviously, state courts are not covered by Art. III. Because of concurrent jurisdiction, many federal claims are adjudicated in state court. Indeed prior to the establishment of general federal question jurisdiction in 1875, most federal claims were litigated in state court. In addition, Congress has established numerous federal agencies which, among other powers, have adjudicative authority. These administrative courts are staffed with administrative law judges who are appointed for fixed terms and are not covered by Art. III. In addition to administrative agencies, Congress, pursuant to its powers in Art. I, has created other so called "Art.I courts," including the local courts of the District of Columbia and the Bankruptcy Courts. Is there a Seventh Amendment right to a jury in litigation outside of Article III courts? Consider the following case:

Atlas Roofing Co. v. OSHRC
430 U.S. 442, 97 S. Ct. 1261, 51 L. Ed. 2d 464 (1977)

JUSTICE WHITE delivered the opinion of the Court.

The issue in these cases is whether, consistent with the Seventh Amendment, Congress may create a new cause of action in the Government for civil penalties enforceable in an administrative agency where there is no jury trial.

I

After extensive investigation, Congress concluded, in 1970, that work-related deaths and injuries had become a "drastic" national problem. Finding the existing state statutory remedies as well as state common-law actions for negligence and wrongful death to be inadequate to protect the employee population from death and injury due to unsafe working conditions, Congress enacted the Occupational Safety and Health Act of 1970 (OSHA or Act), 84 Stat. 1590, 29 U.S.C. § 651 et seq. The Act created a new statutory duty to avoid maintaining unsafe or unhealthy working conditions, and empowers the Secretary of Labor to promulgate health and safety standards. Two new remedies were provided — permitting the Federal Government, proceeding before an administrative agency, (1) to obtain abatement orders requiring employers to correct unsafe working conditions and (2) to impose civil penalties on any employer maintaining any unsafe working condition. Each remedy exists whether or not an employee is actually injured or killed as a result of the condition, and existing state statutory and common-law remedies for actual injury and death remain unaffected.

* * *

II

Petitioners were separately cited by the Secretary and ordered immediately to abate pertinent hazards after inspections of their respective work sites conducted in 1972 revealed conditions that assertedly violated a mandatory occupational safety standard. * * *

Petitioners timely contested these citations and were afforded hearings before Administrative Law Judges of the Commission. The judges, and later the Commission, affirmed the findings of violations and accompanying abatement requirements and assessed petitioner Irey a reduced civil penalty of $5,000 and petitioner Atlas the civil penalty of $600 which the Secretary had proposed. Petitioners respectively thereupon sought judicial review in the Courts of Appeals for the Third and Fifth Circuits, challenging both the Commission's factual findings that violations had occurred and the constitutionality of the Act's enforcement procedures.

* * *

III

The Seventh Amendment provides that "[i]n Suits at common law, where the value in controversy shall exceed twenty dollars, the right of trial by jury shall be preserved...." The phrase "Suits at common law" has been construed to refer to cases tried prior to the adoption of the Seventh Amendment in courts of law in which jury trial was customary as distinguished from courts of equity or admiralty in which jury trial was not. Petitioners claim that a suit in a federal court by the Government for civil penalties for violation of a statute is a suit for a money judgment which is classically a suit at common law; and that the defendant therefore has a Seventh Amendment right to a jury determination of all issues of fact in such a case. Petitioners then claim that to permit Congress to assign the function of adjudicating the Government's rights to civil penalties for violation of the statute to a different forum — an administrative agency in which no jury is available — would be to permit Congress to deprive a defendant of his Seventh Amendment jury right. We disagree. At least in cases in which "public rights" are being litigated — e.g., cases in which the Government sues in its sovereign capacity to enforce public rights created by statutes within the power of Congress to enact — the Seventh Amendment does not prohibit Congress from assigning the factfinding function and initial adjudication to an administrative forum with which the jury would be incompatible.[7]

Congress has often created new statutory obligations, provided for civil penalties for their violation, and committed exclusively to an administrative agency the function of deciding whether a violation has in fact occurred. These statutory schemes have been sustained by this Court, albeit

---

[7] These cases do not involve purely "private rights." In cases which do involve only "private rights," this Court has accepted factfinding by an administrative agency, without intervention by a jury, only as an adjunct to an Art. III court, analogizing the agency to a jury or a special master and permitting it in admiralty cases to perform the function of the special master. Crowell v. Benson, 285 U.S. 22, 51-65 (1932). The Court there said: "On the common law side of the federal courts, the aid of juries is not only deemed appropriate but is required by the Constitution itself." Id. at 51.

often without express reference to the Seventh Amendment. Thus taxes may constitutionally be assessed and collected together with penalties, with the relevant facts in some instances being adjudicated only by an administrative agency. * * * Similarly, Congress has entrusted to an administrative agency the task of adjudicating violations of the customs and immigration laws and assessing penalties based thereon.

In Block v. Hirsh, 256 U.S. 135 (1921), the Court sustained Congress' power to pass a statute, applicable to the District of Columbia, temporarily suspending landlords' legal remedy of ejectment and relegating them to an administrative factfinding forum charged with determining fair rents at which tenants could hold over despite the expiration of their leases. In that case the Court squarely rejected a challenge to the statute based on the Seventh Amendment. * * *

In Crowell v. Benson, 285 U.S. 22 (1932), apparently referring to the above-cited line of authority, the Court stated:

> "[T]he distinction is at once apparent between cases of private right and those which arise *between the Government and persons subject to its authority in connection with the performance of the constitutional functions of the executive or legislative departments*.... [T]he Congress, in exercising the powers confided to it may establish 'legislative' courts ... to serve as special tribunals 'to examine and determine various matters, arising between the government and others, which from their nature do not require judicial determination and yet are susceptible of it.' But '*the mode of determining matters of this class is completely within congressional control.* Congress may reserve to itself the power to decide, *may delegate that power to executive officers*, or may commit it to judicial tribunals.' ... Familiar illustrations of *administrative agencies created for the determination of such matters are found in connection with the exercise of the congressional power as to interstate* and foreign *commerce*, taxation, immigration, the public lands, public health, the facilities of the post office, pensions and payments to veterans." Id. at 50-51. (Emphasis added.)

In NLRB v. Jones & Laughlin Steel Corp., 301 U.S. 1 (1937), the Court squarely addressed the Seventh Amendment issue involved when Congress commits the factfinding function under a new statute to an administrative tribunal. Under the National Labor Relations Act, Congress had committed to the National Labor Relations Board, in a proceeding brought by its litigating arm, the task of deciding whether an unfair labor practice had been committed and of ordering backpay where appropriate. The Court stated:

> "The instant case is not a suit at common law or in the nature of such a suit. The proceeding is one unknown to the common law. *It is a statutory proceeding. Reinstatement of the employee and payment for time lost are requirements [administratively] imposed for violation of the statute and are remedies appropriate to its enforcement.* The contention under the Seventh Amendment is without merit." Id. at 48-49.(Emphasis added.)

This passage from *Jones & Laughlin* has recently been explained in Curtis v. Loether, 415 U.S. 189 (1974), in which the Court held the Seventh Amendment applicable to private damages suits in federal courts brought under the housing discrimination provisions of the Civil Rights Act of 1968. The Court rejected the argument that *Jones & Laughlin* held the Seventh Amendment inapplicable to any action based on a statutorily created right even if the action was brought before a tribunal which customarily utilizes a jury as its factfinding arm. Instead, we concluded that *Jones & Laughlin* upheld

> "congressional power to entrust enforcement of statutory rights to *an administrative process or specialized court of equity* free from the strictures of the Seventh Amendment." 415 U.S. at 194-195. (Emphasis added.)

Finally, in Pernell v. Southall Realty, 416 U.S. 363 (1974), in discussing Block v. Hirsh, 256 U.S. 135 (1921), and *Jones & Laughlin*, we stated:

> "*Block v. Hirsh* merely stands for the principle that *the Seventh Amendment is generally inapplicable in administrative proceedings, where jury trials would be incompatible with the whole concept of administrative adjudication....* We may assume that the Seventh Amendment would not be a bar to a congressional effort to entrust landlord-tenant disputes, including those over the right to possession, to an administrative agency. Congress has not seen fit to do so, however, but rather has provided that actions under § 16-1501 be brought as ordinary civil actions in the District of Columbia's court of general jurisdiction. Where it has done so, and where the action involves rights and remedies recognized at common law, it must preserve to parties their right to a jury trial." 416 U.S. at 383. (Emphasis added.)

In sum, the cases discussed above stand clearly for the proposition that when Congress creates new statutory "public rights," it may assign their adjudication to an administrative agency with which a jury trial would be incompatible, without violating the Seventh Amendment's injunction that jury trial is to be "preserved" in "suits at common law." Congress is not required by the Seventh Amendment to choke the already crowded federal courts with new types of litigation or prevented from committing some new types of litigation to administrative agencies with special competence in the relevant field. This is the case even if the Seventh Amendment would have required a jury where the adjudication of those rights is assigned to a federal court of law instead of an administrative agency. * * *

* * *

[The court was unconvinced by] the assertion that the right to jury trial was never intended to depend on the identity of the forum to which Congress has chosen to submit a dispute; otherwise, it is said, Congress could utterly destroy the right to a jury trial by always providing for administrative rather than judicial resolution of the vast range of cases that now arise in the courts. The argument is well put, but it overstates the holdings of our prior cases and is in any event unpersuasive. Our prior cases support administrative factfinding in only those situations involving "public rights," e.g., where the Government is involved in its sovereign capacity under an otherwise valid statute creating enforceable public rights. Wholly private tort, contract, and property cases, as well as a vast range of other cases, are not at all implicated.

* * *

Thus, history and our cases support the proposition that the right to a jury trial turns not solely on the nature of the issue to be resolved but also on the forum in which it is to be resolved. Congress found the common-law and other existing remedies for work injuries resulting from unsafe working conditions to be inadequate to protect the Nation's working men and women. It created a new cause of action, and remedies therefor, unknown to the common law, and placed their enforcement in a tribunal supplying speedy and expert resolutions of the issues involved. The Seventh Amendment is no bar to the creation of new rights or to their enforcement outside the regular courts of law.

The judgments below are affirmed.

It is so ordered.

NOTES AND QUESTIONS

1. In Note 12 following *Terry*, we considered techniques Congress might use if it wanted claims against unions adjudicated without juries. Could Congress achieve this result by assigning such suits to an administrative agency for adjudication? In *Tull*, could suits for civil penalties under the Clean Water Act be adjudicated by an administrative agency without juries?

2. If Congress can eliminate the right to a jury when it assigns claims such as those in *Terry* and *Tull* to administrative courts, why can't it also eliminate juries when it assigns these claims to Art. III courts? The answer might depend on what we understand to be the purpose of the Seventh Amendment. Dean Carrington has argued that "the most elementary aim of the Seventh Amendment [was] to prevent the vesting of factfinding power in elitist life-tenure judges." Paul Carrington, *The Seventh Amendment: Some Bicentennial Reflections*, 1990 U. CHI. LEG. FORUM 33, 77. Under this view, it may be acceptable to dispense with juries where the agency responsible for adjudicating is politically accountable.

3. In response to concern about allowing Congress to "eviscerate the Seventh Amendment," Dean Carrington has argued:

> Two hundred years of experience confirm that a Congress standing every biennium for re-election by voters who are also sometimes jurors is structurally incapable of taking a step to "eviscerate the Seventh Amendment's guarantee by assigning" all cases to courts of equity. We can stop worrying about that. And if Congress were imaginably willing so to affront citizen-jurors, we can be sure that the trial bar is sufficiently organized to meet any political challenge that would "eviscerate" its collective livelihood.

Id. at 76. Do you agree?

4. In Granfinanciera, S.A. v. Norberg, 492 U.S. 33, 51-54 (1989), the Court elaborated on the difference between "public" and "private" rights. The Court explained:

> Congress may devise novel causes of action involving public rights free from the strictures of the Seventh Amendment if it assigns their adjudication to tribunals without statutory authority to employ juries as factfinders. But it lacks the power to strip parties contesting matters of private right of their constitutional right to a trial by jury. As we recognized in *Atlas Roofing*, to hold otherwise would be to permit Congress to eviscerate the Seventh Amendment's guarantee by assigning to administrative agencies or courts of equity all causes of action not grounded in state law, whether they originate in a newly fashioned regulatory scheme or possess a long line of common-law forebears. The Constitution nowhere grants Congress such puissant authority. "[L]egal claims are not magically converted into equitable issues by their presentation to a court of equity," Ross v. Bernhard, 396 U.S. 531, 538 (1970), nor can Congress conjure away the Seventh Amendment by mandating that traditional legal claims be brought there or taken to an administrative tribunal.
>
> In certain situations, of course, Congress may fashion causes of action that are closely *analogous* to common-law claims and place them beyond the ambit of the Seventh Amendment by assigning their resolution to a forum in which jury trials are unavailable. * * * Unless a legal cause of action involves "public rights," Congress may not deprive parties litigating over such a right of the Seventh Amendment's guarantee to a jury trial.
>
> * * *
>
> In our most recent discussion of the "public rights" doctrine as it bears on Congress' power to commit adjudication of a statutory cause of action to a non-Article III tribunal, we rejected the view that "a matter of public rights must at a minimum arise 'between the government and others.'" We held, instead, that the Federal Government need not be a party for a case to revolve around "public rights." The crucial question, in cases not involving the Federal Government, is whether "Congress, acting for a valid legislative purpose pursuant to its constitutional powers under Article I, [has] create[d] a seemingly 'private' right that is so closely integrated into a public regulatory scheme as to be a matter appropriate for agency resolution with limited involvement by the Article III judiciary." If a statutory right is not closely intertwined with a federal regulatory program Congress has power to enact, and if that right neither belongs to nor exists against the Federal Government, then it must be adjudicated by an Article III court. If the right is legal in nature, then it carries with it the Seventh Amendment's guarantee of a jury trial.

5. Suppose Congress decided that all tort cases arising out of airplane crashes should be adjudicated before the Federal Aviation Administration without juries. Would this violate the Seventh Amendment? Does the answer depend on whether airline safety is regulated by a public regulatory scheme?

6. Dean Carrington suggests that rather than focusing on public v. private rights, it would be more appropriate to focus on the difference between state created and federally created rights. He observes that the heart of the concern of the anti-federalists who succeeded in adding the Seventh Amendment to the original Constitution was that "state-created rights might be entrusted for enforcement to aristocratic federal judges unconstrained by juries." Carrington, supra, 1990 U. CHI. LEG. FORUM at 43; see id. at 77-86.

d. Juries in State Courts

As noted earlier, the Seventh Amendment does not apply to litigation in state court. Nonetheless, most state constitutions provide a right to a jury in civil cases comparable to the Seventh Amendment. A few, such as Georgia, North Carolina, Tennessee and Texas grant a right to jury in equity cases. However, among states that limit juries to actions at law, there are significant variations in interpretation. Some, for example, do not follow *Beacon Theatres*, and instead hold that there is no right to a jury on a legal counterclaim filed in response to an equitable claim. See, e.g., Vanier v. Ponsoldt, 251 Kan. 88, 833 P.2d 949 (1992). Similarly, you will recall in Byrd v. Blue Ridge Rural Electric Cooperative, Inc., 356 U.S. 525 (1958), in Chapter 7, South Carolina did not grant a jury on an issue as to which the federal courts did.

Although the Seventh Amendment does not require juries in state court, some federal statutes explicitly provide for a right to a jury trial, see, e.g., The Jones Act, 46 U.S.C. § 688(a), and others, though not explicit, have been interpreted to require a jury. Where the right to a jury is "part and parcel of the remedy afforded" by the federal statute, the Court has held that state courts must provide a jury when claims under that federal statute are litigated in state court. See Dice v. Akron, Canton & Youngstown R.R., 342 U.S. 359 (1952).

2. Selection and Size of the Jury

a. The Venire and Voir Dire

Jurors are summoned from a master roll of prospective jurors. For much of our history, these master lists systematically excluded certain groups such as minorities, and women. Beginning in the 1940s, the Supreme Court began to strike down this exclusion of groups from jury rolls and in 1975 it held that the lists from which juries are summoned must reflect a reasonable cross-section of the population. Taylor v. Louisiana, 419 U.S. 522 (1975). Today, courts rely on a variety of sources for the names on their jury rolls. Voter

CHAPTER 10 ADJUDICATION WITH AND WITHOUT A TRIAL OR A JURY

registration lists are a common source, but increasingly courts rely in addition on lists of licensed drivers, taxpayers or welfare recipients.

The jurors summoned for duty are called the venire. The jury is selected from the venire through the process of voir dire.* The purpose of voir dire is to gather information about prospective jurors' knowledge, bias or opinions about the case. Based on the information gleaned during voir dire, the judge may strike a juror for cause or a lawyer may exercise one of her peremptory challenges. Jurors can be struck for cause when they have a close connection with any of the parties or witnesses or "when they have such fixed opinions that they could not judge impartially the guilt of the defendant." Patton v. Yount, 467 U.S. 1025, 1035 (1984). Peremptory challenges, which are discussed in greater detail below, allow lawyers to strike potential jurors, historically without a need to state a reason.

Different courts conduct voir dire in a variety of ways. Prospective jurors may be questioned in groups or individually and the questioning may be done entirely by the lawyers, entirely by the judge or by both the lawyers and the judge. See Rule 47(a). The judge has wide discretion both as to the conduct of voir dire and the scope of the questions. Sometimes, particularly in cases involving substantial pre-trial publicity, the court may give prospective jurors a written questionnaire in order to expedite voir dire and more easily screen out those with obvious biases.

b. Peremptory Challenges

In England, peremptory challenges, at least in criminal cases, date back to the 13th century. Originally, the crown had unlimited peremptory strikes. To correct what was perceived as an unfairness, however Parliament in 1305 eliminated the prosecution's (but not the defendant's) right to exercise peremptories. Despite this change, the crown retained the power to ask jurors to "stand aside." Under this procedure, no reason for the request was required unless there was an insufficient number of jurors remaining to compose a jury. Peremptories remained entrenched in the British system until Parliament abolished them in 1988.

In the United States, the practice of allowing defendants peremptory challenges dates back to colonial times. After independence, Congress codified the practice, granting defendants twenty peremptories in felonies punishable by death and thirty-five peremptories in trials for treason. In contrast, it was not until the early twentieth century that the prosecutor's right to exercise peremptories was fully established. For a history of peremptory challenges, see Richard Friedman, *An Asymmetrical Approach to the Problem of Peremptories*, 28 CRIM. L. BULL. 507 (Nov.-Dec. 1992); Deborah Zalesne & Kinney Zalesne, *Saving the*

---

* "Voir dire" is traditionally translated either "to speak the truth" or "to see what is said."

Peremptory Challenge: The Case for a Narrow Interpretation of McCollum, 70 Denv. U. L. Rev. 313, 315-19 (1993).

Proponents of peremptory challenges offer several justifications for them. First, particularly in earlier times, the government was perceived as having an inherent advantage in controlling the selection of the venire. Thus, the defendant's peremptories helped equalize the defendant's position. Second, by giving participants some power in the selection of the jury, peremptories helped legitimize verdicts. As Blackstone explained, "a prisoner (when put to defend his life) should have a good opinion of his jury, the want of which might totally disconcert him, the law wills not that he should be tried by any one man against whom he has conceived a prejudice, even without being able to assign a reason for such his dislike." 4 William Blackstone, Commentaries, * 353 (1859). Finally, peremptory challenges supplement the challenges for cause, allowing lawyers to strike jurors whom they believe to be biased, without having to ask the potentially time-consuming and intrusive voir dire questions that would be necessary to establish a challenge for cause.

Today, the number of peremptories is usually fixed by statute. In federal civil cases, each side is entitled to three peremptories. 28 U.S.C. § 1870. In non-capital federal felony prosecutions, the defendant is entitled to ten peremptories, the prosecution six. Fed. R. Crim. P. 24(b). In capital cases, each side is entitled to twenty peremptory strikes. Id.

Traditionally, lawyers could exercise peremptory challenges for any reason or no reason without explanation. As the following case highlights, that tradition is now subject to some important qualifications.

J. E. B. v. Alabama
__ U.S. __, 114 S. Ct. 1419, 128 L. Ed. 2d 89 (1994)

Justice Blackmun delivered the opinion of the Court.

In Batson v. Kentucky, 476 U.S. 79 (1986), this Court held that the Equal Protection Clause of the Fourteenth Amendment governs the exercise of peremptory challenges by a prosecutor in a criminal trial. The Court explained that although a defendant has "no right to a 'petit jury composed in whole or in part of persons of his own race,'" id. at 85, quoting Strauder v. West Virginia, 100 U.S. 303, 305 (1880), the "defendant does have the right to be tried by a jury whose members are selected pursuant to nondiscriminatory criteria." Since *Batson*, we have reaffirmed repeatedly our commitment to jury selection procedures that are fair and nondiscriminatory. We have recognized that whether the trial is criminal or civil, potential jurors, as well as litigants, have an equal protection right to jury selection procedures that are free from state-sponsored group stereotypes rooted in, and reflective of, historical prejudice. See Powers v. Ohio, 499 U.S. 400 (1991); Edmonson v. Leesville Concrete Co., 500 U.S. 614 (1991); Georgia v. McCollum, 505 U.S. 42 (1992).

Although premised on equal protection principles that apply equally to gender discrimination, all our recent cases defining the scope of Batson involved alleged racial discrimination in the exercise of peremptory challenges. Today we are faced with the question whether the Equal Protection Clause forbids intentional discrimination on the basis of gender, just as it prohibits discrimination on the basis of race. We hold that gender, like race, is an unconstitutional proxy for juror competence and impartiality.

I

On behalf of relator T.B., the mother of a minor child, respondent State of Alabama filed a complaint for paternity and child support against petitioner J.E.B. in the District Court of Jackson County, Alabama. On October 21, 1991, the matter was called for trial and jury selection began. The trial court assembled a panel of 36 potential jurors, 12 males and 24 females. After the court excused three jurors for cause, only 10 of the remaining 33 jurors were male. The State then used 9 of its 10 peremptory strikes to remove male jurors; petitioner used all but one of his strikes to remove female jurors. As a result, all the selected jurors were female.

Before the jury was empaneled, petitioner objected to the State's peremptory challenges on the ground that they were exercised against male jurors solely on the basis of gender, in violation of the Equal Protection Clause of the Fourteenth Amendment. Petitioner argued that the logic and reasoning of *Batson v. Kentucky*, which prohibits peremptory strikes solely on the basis of race, similarly forbids intentional discrimination on the basis of gender. The court rejected petitioner's claim and empaneled the all-female jury. The jury found petitioner to be the father of the child and the court entered an order directing him to pay child support. On post-judgment motion, the court reaffirmed its ruling that *Batson* does not extend to gender-based peremptory challenges. The Alabama Court of Civil Appeals affirmed, relying on Alabama precedent. The Supreme Court of Alabama denied certiorari.

We granted certiorari to resolve a question that has created a conflict of authority — whether the Equal Protection Clause forbids peremptory challenges on the basis of gender as well as on the basis of race. Today we reaffirm what, by now, should be axiomatic: Intentional discrimination on the basis of gender by state actors violates the Equal Protection Clause, particularly where, as here, the discrimination serves to ratify and perpetuate invidious, archaic, and overbroad stereotypes about the relative abilities of men and women.

II

Discrimination on the basis of gender in the exercise of peremptory challenges is a relatively recent phenomenon. Gender-based peremptory strikes were hardly practicable for most of our country's existence, since, until the 19th century, women were completely excluded from jury service.[2] So well-entrenched was this exclusion of women that in 1880 this Court, while finding that the

---

[2] There was one brief exception. Between 1870 and 1871, women were permitted to serve on juries in Wyoming Territory. They were no longer allowed on juries after a new chief justice who disfavored the practice was appointed in 1871.

exclusion of African-American men from juries violated the Fourteenth Amendment, expressed no doubt that a State "may confine the selection [of jurors] to males." Strauder v. West Virginia, 100 U.S. 303, 310.

Many States continued to exclude women from jury service well into the present century, despite the fact that women attained suffrage upon ratification of the Nineteenth Amendment in 1920.[3] States that did permit women to serve on juries often erected other barriers, such as registration requirements and automatic exemptions, designed to deter women from exercising their right to jury service.

The prohibition of women on juries was derived from the English common law which, according to Blackstone, rightfully excluded women from juries under "the doctrine of *propter defectum sexus*, literally, the 'defect of sex.'" United States v. DeGross, 960 F. 2d 1433, 1438 (9th Cir. 1992) (*en banc*), quoting 2 W. BLACKSTONE, COMMENTARIES * 362.[4] In this country, supporters of the exclusion of women from juries tended to couch their objections in terms of the ostensible need to protect women from the ugliness and depravity of trials. Women were thought to be too fragile and virginal to withstand the polluted courtroom atmosphere. See Bailey v. State, 215 Ark. 53, 61, 219 S.W. 2d 424, 428 (1949) ("Criminal court trials often involve testimony of the foulest kind, and they sometimes require consideration of indecent conduct, the use of filthy and loathsome words, references to intimate sex relationships, and other elements that would prove humiliating, embarrassing and degrading to a lady"); In re Goodell, 39 Wis. 232, 245-246 (1875) (endorsing statutory ineligibility of women for admission to the bar because "[r]everence for all womanhood would suffer in the public spectacle of women ... so engaged"). Bradwell v. State, 16 Wall. 130, 141 (1872) (concurring opinion) ("[T]he civil law, as well as nature herself, has always recognized a wide difference in the respective spheres and destinies of man and woman. Man is, or should be, woman's protector and defender. The natural and proper timidity and delicacy which belongs to the female sex evidently unfits it for many of the occupations of civil life.... The paramount destiny and mission of woman are to fulfil the noble and benign offices of wife and mother. This is the law of the Creator"). Cf. Frontiero v. Richardson, 411 U.S. 677, 684 (1973) (plurality opinion) (This "attitude of 'romantic paternalism' ... put women, not on a pedestal, but in a cage").

This Court in Ballard v. United States, 329 U.S. 187 (1946), first questioned the fundamental fairness of denying women the right to serve on juries. Relying on its supervisory powers over the federal courts, it held that women may not be excluded from the venire in federal trials in States where women were eligible for jury service under local law. In response to the argument that women have

---

[3] In 1947, women still had not been granted the right to serve on juries in 16 States. As late as 1961, three States, Alabama, Mississippi, and South Carolina, continued to exclude women from jury service. Indeed, Alabama did not recognize women as a "cognizable group" for jury-service purposes until after the 1966 decision in White v. Crook, 251 F. Supp. 401 (M.D. Ala.) (three-judge court).

[4] In England there was at least one deviation from the general rule that only males could serve as jurors. If a woman was subject to capital punishment, or if a widow sought postponement of the disposition of her husband's estate until birth of a child, a writ *de ventre inspiciendo* permitted the use of a jury of matrons to examine the woman to determine whether she was pregnant. But even when a jury of matrons was used, the examination took place in the presence of 12 men, who also composed part of the jury in such cases. The jury of matrons was used in the United States during the Colonial period, but apparently fell into disuse when the medical profession began to perform that function.

no superior or unique perspective, such that defendants are denied a fair trial by virtue of their exclusion from jury panels, the Court explained:

> "It is said ... that an all male panel drawn from the various groups within a community will be as truly representative as if women were included. The thought is that the factors which tend to influence the action of women are the same as those which influence the action of men — personality, background, economic status — and not sex. Yet it is not enough to say that women when sitting as jurors neither act nor tend to act as a class. Men likewise do not act like a class.... The truth is that the two sexes are not fungible; a community made up exclusively of one is different from a community composed of both; the subtle interplay of influence one on the other is among the imponderables. To insulate the courtroom from either may not in a given case make an iota of difference. Yet a flavor, a distinct quality is lost if either sex is excluded."

Fifteen years later, however, the Court still was unwilling to translate its appreciation for the value of women's contribution to civic life into an enforceable right to equal treatment under state laws governing jury service. In Hoyt v. Florida, 368 U.S. at 61, the Court found it reasonable, "despite the enlightened emancipation of women," to exempt women from mandatory jury service by statute, allowing women to serve on juries only if they volunteered to serve. The Court justified the differential exemption policy on the ground that women, unlike men, occupied a unique position "as the center of home and family life."

In 1975, the Court finally repudiated the reasoning of *Hoyt* and struck down, under the Sixth Amendment, an affirmative registration statute nearly identical to the one at issue in *Hoyt*. See Taylor v. Louisiana, 419 U.S. 522 (1975). We explained: "Restricting jury service to only special groups or excluding identifiable segments playing major roles in the community cannot be squared with the constitutional concept of jury trial." The diverse and representative character of the jury must be maintained "partly as assurance of a diffused impartiality and partly because sharing in the administration of justice is a phase of civic responsibility.'"

III

Taylor relied on Sixth Amendment principles, but the opinion's approach is consistent with the heightened equal protection scrutiny afforded gender-based classifications. Since Reed v. Reed, 404 U.S. 71 (1971), this Court consistently has subjected gender-based classifications to heightened scrutiny in recognition of the real danger that government policies that professedly are based on reasonable considerations in fact may be reflective of "archaic and overbroad" generalizations about gender, or based on "outdated misconceptions concerning the role of females in the home rather than in the 'marketplace and world of ideas.'" Craig v. Boren, 429 U.S. 190, 198-199 (1976).

Despite the heightened scrutiny afforded distinctions based on gender, respondent argues that gender discrimination in the selection of the petit jury should be permitted, though discrimination on the basis of race is not. Respondent suggests that "gender discrimination in this country ... has never reached the level of discrimination" against African-Americans, and therefore gender discrimination, unlike racial discrimination, is tolerable in the courtroom.

While the prejudicial attitudes toward women in this country have not been identical to those held toward racial minorities, the similarities between the experiences of racial minorities and women, in some contexts, "overpower those differences." As a plurality of this Court observed in Frontiero v. Richardson, 411 U.S. 677, 685 (1973):

> "[T]hroughout much of the 19th century the position of women in our society was, in many respects, comparable to that of blacks under the pre-Civil War slave codes. Neither slaves nor women could hold office, serve on juries, or bring suit in their own names, and married women traditionally were denied the legal capacity to hold or convey property or to serve as legal guardians of their own children.... And although blacks were guaranteed the right to vote in 1870, women were denied even that right — which is itself 'preservative of other basic civil and political rights' — until adoption of the Nineteenth Amendment half a century later." (Footnotes omitted.)

Certainly, with respect to jury service, African-Americans and women share a history of total exclusion, a history which came to an end for women many years after the embarrassing chapter in our history came to an end for African-Americans.

We need not determine, however, whether women or racial minorities have suffered more at the hands of discriminatory state actors during the decades of our Nation's history. It is necessary only to acknowledge that "our Nation has had a long and unfortunate history of sex discrimination," a history which warrants the heightened scrutiny we afford all gender-based classifications today. Under our equal protection jurisprudence, gender-based classifications require "an exceedingly persuasive justification" in order to survive constitutional scrutiny. Thus, the only question is whether discrimination on the basis of gender in jury selection substantially furthers the State's legitimate interest in achieving a fair and impartial trial.[6] In making this assessment, we do not weigh the value of peremptory challenges as an institution against our asserted commitment to eradicate invidious discrimination from the courtroom.[7] Instead, we consider whether peremptory challenges based on gender stereotypes provide substantial aid to a litigant's effort to secure a fair and impartial jury.[8]

---

[6] Because we conclude that gender-based peremptory challenges are not substantially related to an important government objective, we once again need not decide whether classifications based on gender are inherently suspect.

[7] Although peremptory challenges are valuable tools in jury trials, they "are not constitutionally protected fundamental rights; rather they are but one state-created means to the constitutional end of an impartial jury and a fair trial." Georgia v. McCollum, 505 U.S. 42, 57 (1992).

[8] Respondent argues that we should recognize a special state interest in this case: the State's interest in establishing the paternity of a child born out of wedlock. Respondent contends that this interest justifies the use of gender-based peremptory challenges, since illegitimate children are themselves victims of historical discrimination and entitled to heightened scrutiny under the Equal Protection Clause.

What respondent fails to recognize is that the only legitimate interest it could possibly have in the exercise of its peremptory challenges is securing a fair and impartial jury. See Edmonson v. Leesville Concrete Co., 500 U.S. 614, 620 (1991) ("[T]he sole purpose [of the peremptory challenge] is to permit litigants to assist the government in the selection of an impartial trier of fact"). This interest does not change with the parties or the causes. The State's interest in *every* trial is to see that the proceedings are carried out in a fair, impartial, and nondiscriminatory manner.

Far from proffering an exceptionally persuasive justification for its gender-based peremptory challenges, respondent maintains that its decision to strike virtually all the males from the jury in this case "may reasonably have been based upon the perception, supported by history, that men otherwise totally qualified to serve upon a jury might be more sympathetic and receptive to the arguments of a man alleged in a paternity action to be the father of an out-of-wedlock child, while women equally qualified to serve upon a jury might be more sympathetic and receptive to the arguments of the complaining witness who bore the child." [9]

We shall not accept as a defense to gender-based peremptory challenges "the very stereotype the law condemns." Respondent's rationale, not unlike those regularly expressed for gender-based strikes, is reminiscent of the arguments advanced to justify the total exclusion of women from juries.[10] Respondent offers virtually no support for the conclusion that gender alone is an accurate predictor of juror's attitudes; yet it urges this Court to condone the same stereotypes that justified the wholesale exclusion of women from juries and the ballot box.[11] Respondent seems to assume that gross generalizations that would be deemed impermissible if made on the basis of race are somehow permissible when made on the basis of gender.

---

[9] Respondent cites one study in support of its quasi-empirical claim that women and men may have different attitudes about certain issues justifying the use of gender as a proxy for bias. See R. HASTIE, S. PENROD & N. PENNINGTON, INSIDE THE JURY 140 (1983). The authors conclude: "Neither student nor citizen judgments for typical criminal case material have revealed differences between male and female verdict preferences. * * * The picture differs [only] for rape cases, where female jurors appear to be somewhat more conviction-prone than male jurors." The majority of studies suggest that gender plays no identifiable role in jurors' attitudes. See, e.g., V. HANS & N. VIDMAR, JUDGING THE JURY 76 (1986) ("[I]n the majority of studies there are no significant differences in the way men and women perceive and react to trials; yet a few studies find women more defense-oriented, while still others show women more favorable to the prosecutor"). Even in 1956, before women had a constitutional right to serve on juries, some commentators warned against using gender as a proxy for bias. See 1 F. BUSCH, LAW AND TACTICS IN JURY TRIALS § 143, p. 207 (1949) ("In this age of general and specialized education, availed of generally by both men and women, it would appear unsound to base a peremptory challenge in any case upon the sole ground of sex ....").

[10] A manual formerly used to instruct prosecutors in Dallas, Texas, provided the following advice: "I don't like women jurors because I can't trust them. They do, however, make the best jurors in cases involving crimes against children. It is possible that their 'women's intuition' can help you if you can't win your case with the facts." Another widely circulated trial manual speculated:

> "If counsel is depending upon a clearly applicable rule of law and if he wants to avoid a verdict of 'intuition' or 'sympathy,' if his verdict in amount is to be proved by clearly demonstrated blackboard figures for example, generally he would want a male juror....
>
> "[But women] are desired jurors when the plaintiff is a man. A woman juror may see a man impeached from the beginning of the case to the end, but there is at least the chance with the woman juror (particularly if the man happens to be handsome or appealing) [that] the plaintiff's derelictions in and out of court will be overlooked. A woman is inclined to forgive sin in the opposite sex; but definitely not her own. ..." 3 M. BELLI, MODERN TRIALS §§ 51.67 and 51.68, pp. 446-447 (2d ed. 1982).

[11] Even if a measure of truth can be found in some of the gender stereotypes used to justify gender-based peremptory challenges, that fact alone cannot support discrimination on the basis of gender in jury selection. We have made abundantly clear in past cases that gender classifications that rest on impermissible stereotypes violate the Equal Protection Clause, even when some statistical support can be conjured up for the generalization. The generalization advanced by Alabama in support of its asserted right to discriminate on the basis of gender is, at the

Discrimination in jury selection, whether based on race or on gender, causes harm to the litigants, the community, and the individual jurors who are wrongfully excluded from participation in the judicial process. The litigants are harmed by the risk that the prejudice which motivated the discriminatory selection of the jury will infect the entire proceedings. See *Edmonson*, (discrimination in the courtroom "raises serious questions as to the fairness of the proceedings conducted there"). The community is harmed by the State's participation in the perpetuation of invidious group stereotypes and the inevitable loss of confidence in our judicial system that state-sanctioned discrimination in the courtroom engenders.

When state actors exercise peremptory challenges in reliance on gender stereotypes, they ratify and reinforce prejudicial views of the relative abilities of men and women. Because these stereotypes have wreaked injustice in so many other spheres of our country's public life, active discrimination by litigants on the basis of gender during jury selection "invites cynicism respecting the jury's neutrality and its obligation to adhere to the law." Powers v. Ohio, 499 U.S. at 412. The potential for cynicism is particularly acute in cases where gender-related issues are prominent, such as cases involving rape, sexual harassment, or paternity. Discriminatory use of peremptory challenges may create the impression that the judicial system has acquiesced in suppressing full participation by one gender or that the "deck has been stacked" in favor of one side. See id. at 413 ("The verdict will not be accepted or understood [as fair] if the jury is chosen by unlawful means at the outset").

In recent cases we have emphasized that individual jurors themselves have a right to nondiscriminatory jury selection procedures. Contrary to respondent's suggestion, this right extends to both men and women. See Mississippi University for Women v. Hogan, 458 U.S. at 723 (that a state practice "discriminates against males rather than against females does not exempt it from scrutiny or reduce the standard of review"). All persons, when granted the opportunity to serve on a jury, have the right not to be excluded summarily because of discriminatory and stereotypical presumptions that reflect and reinforce patterns of historical discrimination.[13] Striking individual jurors on the assumption that they hold particular views simply because of their gender is "practically a brand upon them, affixed by law, an assertion of their inferiority." Strauder v. West Virginia, 100 U.S. 303, 308 (1880). It denigrates the dignity of the excluded juror, and, for a woman, reinvokes a history of exclusion from political participation.[14] The message it sends to all those in the court-

---

least, overbroad, and serves only to perpetuate the same "outmoded notions of the relative capabilities of men and women," that we have invalidated in other contexts. The Equal Protection Clause, as interpreted by decisions of this Court, acknowledges that a shred of truth may be contained in some stereotypes, but requires that state actors look beyond the surface before making judgments about people that are likely to stigmatize as well as to perpetuate historical patterns of discrimination.

[13] It is irrelevant that women, unlike African-Americans, are not a numerical minority and therefore are likely to remain on the jury if each side uses its peremptory challenges in an equally discriminatory fashion. Because the right to nondiscriminatory jury selection procedures belongs to the potential jurors, as well as to the litigants, the possibility that members of both genders will get on the jury despite the intentional discrimination is beside the point. The exclusion of even one juror for impermissible reasons harms that juror and undermines public confidence in the fairness of the system.

[14] The popular refrain is that all peremptory challenges are based on stereotypes of some kind, expressing various intuitive and frequently erroneous biases. But where peremptory challenges are made on the basis of group characteristics other than race or gender (like occupation, for example), they do not reinforce the same stereotypes about the group's competence or predispositions that have been used to prevent them from voting, participating on juries, pursuing their chosen professions, or otherwise contributing to civic life. See B. Babcock, *A Place in the Palladium, Women's Rights and Jury Service*, 61 U. CINN. L. REV. 1139, 1173 (1993).

room, and all those who may later learn of the discriminatory act, is that certain individuals, for no reason other than gender, are presumed unqualified by state actors to decide important questions upon which reasonable persons could disagree.[15]

IV

Our conclusion that litigants may not strike potential jurors solely on the basis of gender does not imply the elimination of all peremptory challenges. Neither does it conflict with a State's legitimate interest in using such challenges in its effort to secure a fair and impartial jury. Parties still may remove jurors whom they feel might be less acceptable than others on the panel; gender simply may not serve as a proxy for bias. Parties may also exercise their peremptory challenges to remove from the venire any group or class of individuals normally subject to "rational basis" review. Even strikes based on characteristics that are disproportionately associated with one gender could be appropriate, absent a showing of pretext.[16]

If conducted properly, voir dire can inform litigants about potential jurors, making reliance upon stereotypical and pejorative notions about a particular gender or race both unnecessary and unwise. Voir dire provides a means of discovering actual or implied bias and a firmer basis upon which the parties may exercise their peremptory challenges intelligently. See, e.g., Nebraska Press Ass'n v. Stuart, 427 U.S. 539, 602 (1976) (Brennan, J., concurring in the judgment) (voir dire "facilitate[s] intelligent exercise of peremptory challenges and [helps] uncover factors that would dictate disqualification for cause"); United States v. Whitt, 718 F. 2d 1494, 1497 (10th Cir. 1983) ("Without an adequate foundation [laid by voir dire], counsel cannot exercise sensitive and intelligent peremptory challenges").

The experience in the many jurisdictions that have barred gender-based challenges belies the claim that litigants and trial courts are incapable of complying with a rule barring strikes based on gender.[17] As with race-based *Batson* claims, a party alleging gender discrimination must make a prima

---

[15] Justice Scalia argues that there is no "discrimination and dishonor" in being subject to a race- or gender-based peremptory strike. Justice Scalia's argument has been rejected many times, and we reject it once again. The only support Justice Scalia offers for his conclusion is the fact that race- and gender-based peremptory challenges have a long history in this country. We do not dispute that this Court long has tolerated the discriminatory use of peremptory challenges, but this is not a reason to continue to do so. Many of "our people's traditions," such as de jure segregation and the total exclusion of women from juries, are now unconstitutional even though they once co-existed with the Equal Protection Clause.

[16] For example, challenging all persons who have had military experience would disproportionately affect men at this time, while challenging all persons employed as nurses would disproportionately affect women. Without a showing of pretext, however, these challenges may well not be unconstitutional, since they are not gender- or race-based.

[17] Respondent argues that Alabama's method of jury selection would make the extension of *Batson* to gender particularly burdensome. In Alabama, the "struck-jury" system is employed, a system which requires litigants to strike alternately until 12 persons remain, who then constitute the jury. Respondent suggests that, in some cases at least, it is necessary under this system to continue striking persons from the venire after the litigants no longer have an articulable reason for doing so. As a result, respondent contends, some litigants may be unable to come up with gender-neutral explanations for their strikes.

We find it worthy of note that Alabama has managed to maintain its struck-jury system even after the ruling in *Batson*, despite the fact that there are counties in Alabama that are predominately African-American. In

facie showing of intentional discrimination before the party exercising the challenge is required to explain the basis for the strike. *Batson*. When an explanation is required, it need not rise to the level of a "for cause" challenge; rather, it merely must be based on a juror characteristic other than gender, and the proffered explanation may not be pretextual.

Failing to provide jurors the same protection against gender discrimination as race discrimination could frustrate the purpose of *Batson* itself. Because gender and race are overlapping categories, gender can be used as a pretext for racial discrimination.[18] Allowing parties to remove racial minorities from the jury not because of their race, but because of their gender, contravenes well-established equal protection principles and could insulate effectively racial discrimination from judicial scrutiny.

V

Equal opportunity to participate in the fair administration of justice is fundamental to our democratic system.[19] It not only furthers the goals of the jury system. It reaffirms the promise of equality under the law — that all citizens, regardless of race, ethnicity, or gender, have the chance to take part directly in our democracy. Powers v. Ohio, 499 U.S., at 407 ("Indeed, with the exception of voting, for most citizens the honor and privilege of jury duty is their most significant opportunity to participate in the democratic process"). When persons are excluded from participation in our democratic processes solely because of race or gender, this promise of equality dims, and the integrity of our judicial system is jeopardized.

---

those counties, it presumably would be as difficult to come up with race-neutral explanations for peremptory strikes as it would be to advance gender-neutral explanations. No doubt the voir dire process aids litigants in their ability to articulate race-neutral explanations for their peremptory challenges. The same should be true for gender. Regardless, a State's choice of jury-selection methods cannot insulate it from the strictures of the Equal Protection Clause. Alabama is free to adopt whatever jury-selection procedures it chooses so long as they do not violate the Constitution.

[18] The temptation to use gender as a pretext for racial discrimination may explain why the majority of the lower court decisions extending *Batson* to gender involve the use of peremptory challenges to remove minority women. All four of the gender-based peremptory cases to reach the federal courts of appeals * * * involved the striking of minority women.

[19] This Court almost a half century ago stated:

> "The American tradition of trial by jury, considered in connection with either criminal or civil proceedings, necessarily contemplates an impartial jury drawn from a cross-section of the community.... This does not mean, of course, that every jury must contain representatives of all the economic, social, religious, racial, political and geographical groups of the community; frequently such complete representation would be impossible. But it does mean that prospective jurors shall be selected by court officials without systematic and intentional exclusion of any of these groups. Recognition must be given to the fact that those eligible for jury service are to be found in every stratum of society. Jury competence is an individual rather than a group or class matter. That fact lies at the very heart of the jury system. To disregard it is to open the door to class distinctions and discriminations which are abhorrent to the democratic ideals of trial by jury."

Thiel v. Southern Pacific Co., 328 U.S. 217, 220 (1946).

In view of these concerns, the Equal Protection Clause prohibits discrimination in jury selection on the basis of gender, or on the assumption that an individual will be biased in a particular case for no reason other than the fact that the person happens to be a woman or happens to be a man. As with race, the "core guarantee of equal protection, ensuring citizens that their State will not discriminate ..., would be meaningless were we to approve the exclusion of jurors on the basis of such assumptions, which arise solely from the jurors' [gender]." *Batson*.

The judgment of the Court of Civil Appeals of Alabama is reversed and the case is remanded to that court for further proceedings not inconsistent with this opinion.

It is so ordered.

JUSTICE O'CONNOR, concurring.

I agree with the Court that the Equal Protection Clause prohibits the government from excluding a person from jury service on account of that person's gender. The State's proffered justifications for its gender-based peremptory challenges are far from the "'exceedingly persuasive'" showing required to sustain a gender-based classification. I therefore join the Court's opinion in this case. But today's important blow against gender discrimination is not costless. I write separately to discuss some of these costs, and to express my belief that today's holding should be limited to the government's use of gender-based peremptory strikes.

Batson v. Kentucky, itself was a significant intrusion into the jury selection process. *Batson* mini-hearings are now routine in state and federal trial courts, and Batson appeals have proliferated as well. Demographics indicate that today's holding may have an even greater impact than did *Batson* itself. In further constitutionalizing jury selection procedures, the Court increases the number of cases in which jury selection — once a sideshow — will become part of the main event.

For this same reason, today's decision further erodes the role of the peremptory challenge. The peremptory challenge is "a practice of ancient origin" and is "part of our common law heritage." The principal value of the peremptory is that it helps produce fair and impartial juries. "Peremptory challenges, by enabling each side to exclude those jurors it believes will be most partial toward the other side, are a means of eliminat[ing] extremes of partiality on both sides, thereby assuring the selection of a qualified and unbiased jury." The peremptory's importance is confirmed by its persistence: it was well established at the time of Blackstone and continues to endure in all the States.

Moreover, "[t]he essential nature of the peremptory challenge is that it is one exercised without a reason stated, without inquiry and without being subject to the court's control." Indeed, often a reason for it cannot be stated, for a trial lawyer's judgments about a juror's sympathies are sometimes based on experienced hunches and educated guesses, derived from a juror's responses at voir dire or a juror's "'bare looks and gestures.'" That a trial lawyer's instinctive assessment of a juror's predisposition cannot meet the high standards of a challenge for cause does not mean that the lawyer's instinct is erroneous. Cf. V. STARR & M. MCCORMICK, JURY SELECTION 522 (1993) (nonverbal cues can be better than verbal responses at revealing a juror's disposition). Our belief that experienced lawyers will often correctly intuit which jurors are likely to be the least sympathetic, and our understanding that the lawyer will often be unable to explain the intuition, are the very reason we cherish the peremptory challenge. But, as we add, layer by layer, additional constitutional restraints on the use of the peremptory, we force lawyers to articulate what we know is often inarticulable.

In so doing we make the peremptory challenge less discretionary and more like a challenge for cause. We also increase the possibility that biased jurors will be allowed onto the jury, because sometimes a lawyer will be unable to provide an acceptable gender-neutral explanation even though the lawyer is in fact correct that the juror is unsympathetic. Similarly, in jurisdictions where lawyers exercise their strikes in open court, lawyers may be deterred from using their peremptories, out of the fear that if they are unable to justify the strike the court will seat a juror who knows that the striking party thought him unfit. Because I believe the peremptory remains an important litigator's tool and a fundamental part of the process of selecting impartial juries, our increasing limitation of it gives me pause.

Nor is the value of the peremptory challenge to the litigant diminished when the peremptory is exercised in a gender-based manner. We know that like race, gender matters. A plethora of studies make clear that in rape cases, for example, female jurors are somewhat more likely to vote to convict than male jurors. See R. HASTIE, S. PENROD, & N. PENNINGTON, INSIDE THE JURY 140-141 (1983) (collecting and summarizing empirical studies). Moreover, though there have been no similarly definitive studies regarding, for example, sexual harassment, child custody, or spousal or child abuse, one need not be a sexist to share the intuition that in certain cases a person's gender and resulting life experience will be relevant to his or her view of the case. "'Jurors are not expected to come into the jury box and leave behind all that their human experience has taught them.'" Individuals are not expected to ignore as jurors what they know as men — or women.

Today's decision severely limits a litigant's ability to act on this intuition, for the import of our holding is that any correlation between a juror's gender and attitudes is irrelevant as a matter of constitutional law. But to say that gender makes no difference as a matter of law is not to say that gender makes no difference as a matter of fact. I previously have said with regard to *Batson:* "That the Court will not tolerate prosecutors' racially discriminatory use of the peremptory challenge, in effect, is a special rule of relevance, a statement about what this Nation stands for, rather than a statement of fact." Today's decision is a statement that, in an effort to eliminate the potential discriminatory use of the peremptory, gender is now governed by the special rule of relevance formerly reserved for race. Though we gain much from this statement, we cannot ignore what we lose. In extending *Batson* to gender we have added an additional burden to the state and federal trial process, taken a step closer to eliminating the peremptory challenge, and diminished the ability of litigants to act on sometimes accurate gender-based assumptions about juror attitudes.

These concerns reinforce my conviction that today's decision should be limited to a prohibition on the government's use of gender-based peremptory challenges. The Equal Protection Clause prohibits only discrimination by state actors. In *Edmonson*, we made the mistake of concluding that private civil litigants were state actors when they exercised peremptory challenges; in *Georgia v. McCollum*, we compounded the mistake by holding that criminal defendants were also state actors. Our commitment to eliminating discrimination from the legal process should not allow us to forget that not all that occurs in the courtroom is state action. Private civil litigants are just that — private litigants. "The government erects the platform; it does not thereby become responsible for all that occurs upon it." *Edmonson*, (O'Connor, J., dissenting).

Clearly, criminal defendants are not state actors. "From arrest, to trial, to possible sentencing and punishment, the antagonistic relationship between government and the accused is clear for all to see.... [T]he unique relationship between criminal defendants and the State precludes attributing defendants' actions to the State...." *McCollum*, (O'Connor, J., dissenting). The peremptory challenge is "'one of the most important of the rights secured to the *accused*.' Limiting the accused's use of the peremptory is "a serious misordering of our priorities," for it means "we have exalted the right of citizens to sit on juries over the rights of the criminal defendant, even though it is the defendant, not the jurors, who faces imprisonment or even death." *McCollum*, (Thomas, J., concurring in judgment).

Accordingly, I adhere to my position that the Equal Protection Clause does not limit the exercise of peremptory challenges by private civil litigants and criminal defendants. This case itself presents no state action dilemma, for here the State of Alabama itself filed the paternity suit on behalf of petitioner. But what of the next case? Will we, in the name of fighting gender discrimination, hold that the battered wife — on trial for wounding her abusive husband — is a state actor? Will we preclude her from using her peremptory challenges to ensure that the jury of her peers contains as many women members as possible? I assume we will, but I hope we will not.

JUSTICE KENNEDY, concurring in the judgment.

I am in full agreement with the Court that the Equal Protection Clause prohibits gender discrimination in the exercise of peremptory challenges. * * *

* * *

The importance of individual rights to our analysis prompts a further observation concerning what I conceive to be the intended effect of today's decision. We do not prohibit racial and gender bias in jury selection only to encourage it in jury deliberations. Once seated, a juror should not give free rein to some racial or gender bias of his or her own. The jury system is a kind of compact by which power is transferred from the judge to jury, the jury in turn deciding the case in accord with the instructions defining the relevant issues for consideration. The wise limitation on the authority of courts to inquire into the reasons underlying a jury's verdict does not mean that a jury ought to disregard the court's instructions. A juror who allows racial or gender bias to influence assessment of the case breaches the compact and renounces his or her oath.

In this regard, it is important to recognize that a juror sits not as a representative of a racial or sexual group but as an individual citizen. Nothing would be more pernicious to the jury system than for society to presume that persons of different backgrounds go to the jury room to voice prejudice. The jury pool must be representative of the community, but that is a structural mechanism for preventing bias, not enfranchising it. "Jury competence is an individual rather than a group or class matter. That fact lies at the very heart of the jury system." Thus, the Constitution guarantees a right only to an impartial jury, not to a jury composed of members of a particular race or gender.

* * *

CHIEF JUSTICE REHNQUIST, dissenting.

I agree with the dissent of Justice Scalia, which I have joined. I add these words in support of its conclusion. Accepting Batson v. Kentucky, 476 U.S. 79 (1986) as correctly decided, there are

B. The Right to a Jury

sufficient differences between race and gender discrimination such that the principle of *Batson* should not be extended to peremptory challenges to potential jurors based on sex.

That race and sex discrimination are different is acknowledged by our equal protection jurisprudence, which accords different levels of protection to the two groups. Classifications based on race are inherently suspect, triggering "strict scrutiny," while gender-based classifications are judged under a heightened, but less searching standard of review. Racial groups comprise numerical minorities in our society, warranting in some situations a greater need for protection, whereas the population is divided almost equally between men and women. Furthermore, while substantial discrimination against both groups still lingers in our society, racial equality has proved a more challenging goal to achieve on many fronts than gender equality. See, e.g., D. KIRP, M. YUDOF, M. FRANKS, GENDER JUSTICE 137 (1986).

* * *

Under the Equal Protection Clause, these differences mean that the balance should tilt in favor of peremptory challenges when sex, not race, is the issue. Unlike the Court, I think the State has shown that jury strikes on the basis of gender "substantially further" the State's legitimate interest in achieving a fair and impartial trial through the venerable practice of peremptory challenges. The two sexes differ, both biologically and, to a diminishing extent, in experience. It is not merely "stereotyping" to say that these differences may produce a difference in outlook which is brought to the jury room. Accordingly, use of peremptory challenges on the basis of sex is generally not the sort of derogatory and invidious act which peremptory challenges directed at black jurors may be.

* * *

JUSTICE SCALIA, with whom THE CHIEF JUSTICE and JUSTICE THOMAS join, dissenting.

Today's opinion is an inspiring demonstration of how thoroughly up-to-date and right-thinking we Justices are in matters pertaining to the sexes (or as the Court would have it, the genders), and how sternly we disapprove the male chauvinist attitudes of our predecessors. The price to be paid for this display — a modest price, surely — is that most of the opinion is quite irrelevant to the case at hand. The hasty reader will be surprised to learn, for example, that this lawsuit involves a complaint about the use of peremptory challenges to exclude *men* from a petit jury. To be sure, petitioner, a man, used all but one of *his* peremptory strikes to remove *women* from the jury (he used his last challenge to strike the sole remaining male from the pool), but the validity of *his* strikes is not before us. Nonetheless, the Court treats itself to an extended discussion of the historic exclusion of women not only from jury service, but also from service at the bar (which is rather like jury service, in that it involves going to the courthouse a lot). All this, as I say, is irrelevant, since the case involves state action that allegedly discriminates against men. The parties do not contest that

CHAPTER 10 ADJUDICATION WITH AND WITHOUT A TRIAL OR A JURY

discrimination on the basis of sex[1] is subject to what our cases call "heightened scrutiny," and the citation of one of those cases (preferably one involving men rather than women) is all that was needed.

The Court also spends time establishing that the use of sex as a proxy for particular views or sympathies is unwise and perhaps irrational. The opinion stresses the lack of statistical evidence to support the widely held belief that, at least in certain types of cases, a juror's sex has some statistically significant predictive value as to how the juror will behave. This assertion seems to place the Court in opposition to its earlier Sixth Amendment "fair cross-section" cases. See, e.g., Taylor v. Louisiana, 419 U.S. 522, 532, n.12 (1975) ("Controlled studies ... have concluded that women bring to juries their own perspectives and values that influence both jury deliberation and result"). But times and trends do change, and unisex is unquestionably in fashion. Personally, I am less inclined to demand statistics, and more inclined to credit the perceptions of experienced litigators who have had money on the line. But it does not matter. The Court's fervent defense of the proposition *il n'y a pas de différence entre les hommes et les femmes* (it stereotypes the opposite view as hateful "stereotyping") turns out to be, like its recounting of the history of sex discrimination against women, utterly irrelevant. Even if sex was a remarkably good predictor in certain cases, the Court would find its use in peremptories unconstitutional.

Of course the relationship of sex to partiality *would have been* relevant if the Court had demanded in this case what it ordinarily demands: that the complaining party have suffered some injury. Leaving aside for the moment the reality that the defendant himself had the opportunity to strike women from the jury, the defendant would have some cause to complain about the prosecutor's striking male jurors if male jurors tend to be more favorable towards defendants in paternity suits. But if men and women jurors are (as the Court thinks) fungible, then the only arguable injury from the prosecutor's "impermissible" use of male sex as the basis for his peremptories is injury to the stricken juror, not to the defendant. Indeed, far from having suffered harm, petitioner, a state actor under our precedents, has himself actually *inflicted* harm on female jurors. The Court today presumably supplies petitioner with a cause of action by applying the uniquely expansive third-party standing analysis of Powers v. Ohio, 499 U.S. 400, 415 (1991), according petitioner a remedy because of the wrong done to male jurors. This case illustrates why making restitution to Paul when it is Peter who has been robbed is such a bad idea. Not only has petitioner, by implication of the Court's own reasoning, suffered no harm, but the scientific evidence presented at trial established petitioner's paternity with 99.92% accuracy. Insofar as petitioner is concerned, this is a case of harmless error if there ever was one; a retrial will do nothing but divert the State's judicial and prosecutorial resources, allowing either petitioner or some other malefactor to go free.

The core of the Court's reasoning is that peremptory challenges on the basis of any group characteristic subject to heightened scrutiny are inconsistent with the guarantee of the Equal Protection Clause. That conclusion can be reached only by focusing unrealistically upon individual exercises of the peremptory challenge, and ignoring the totality of the practice. Since all groups are

---

[1] Throughout this opinion, I shall refer to the issue as sex discrimination rather than (as the Court does) gender discrimination. The word "gender" has acquired the new and useful connotation of cultural or attitudinal characteristics (as opposed to physical characteristics) distinctive to the sexes. That is to say, gender is to sex as feminine is to female and masculine to male. The present case does not involve peremptory strikes exercised on the basis of feminity or masculinity (as far as it appears, effeminate men did not survive the prosecution's peremptories). The case involves, therefore, sex discrimination plain and simple.

subject to the peremptory challenge (and will be made the object of it, depending upon the nature of the particular case) it is hard to see how any group is denied equal protection. That explains why peremptory challenges coexisted with the Equal Protection Clause for 120 years. This case is a perfect example of how the system as a whole is even-handed. While the only claim before the Court is petitioner's complaint that the prosecutor struck male jurors, for every man struck by the government petitioner's own lawyer struck a woman. To say that men were singled out for discriminatory treatment in this process is preposterous. The situation would be different if both sides systematically struck individuals of one group, so that the strikes evinced group-based animus and served as a proxy for segregated venire lists. See Swain v. Alabama, 380 U.S. 202, 223-224 (1965). The pattern here, however, displays not a systemic sex-based animus but each side's desire to get a jury favorably disposed to its case. That is why the Court's characterization of respondent's argument as "reminiscent of the arguments advanced to justify the total exclusion of women from juries," is patently false. Women were categorically excluded from juries because of doubt that they were competent; women are stricken from juries by peremptory challenge because of doubt that they are well disposed to the striking party's case. There is discrimination and dishonor in the former, and not in the latter — which explains the 106-year interlude between our holding that exclusion from juries on the basis of race was unconstitutional, and our holding that peremptory challenges on the basis of race were unconstitutional, *Batson v. Kentucky*, supra.

Although the Court's legal reasoning in this case is largely obscured by anti-male-chauvinist oratory, to the extent such reasoning is discernible it invalidates much more than sex-based strikes. After identifying unequal treatment (by separating individual exercises of peremptory challenge from the process as a whole), the Court applies the "heightened scrutiny" mode of equal-protection analysis used for sex-based discrimination, and concludes that the strikes fail heightened scrutiny because they do not substantially further an important government interest. The Court says that the only important government interest that could be served by peremptory strikes is "securing a fair and impartial jury."[3] It refuses to accept respondent's argument that these strikes further that interest by eliminating a group (men) which may be partial to male defendants, because it will not accept any argument based on "'the very stereotype the law condemns.'" This analysis, entirely eliminating the only allowable argument, implies that sex-based strikes do not even rationally further a legitimate government interest, let alone pass heightened scrutiny. That places *all* peremptory strikes based on *any* group characteristic at risk, since they can all be denominated "stereotypes." Perhaps, however (though I do not see why it should be so), only the stereotyping of groups entitled to heightened or strict scrutiny constitutes "the very stereotype the law condemns" — so that other stereotyping (e.g., wide-eyed blondes and football players are dumb) remains OK. Or perhaps when the Court refers to "impermissible stereotypes," it means the adjective to be limiting rather than descriptive — so that we can expect to learn from the Court's peremptory/stereotyping jurisprudence in the future which stereotypes the Constitution frowns upon and which it does not.

Even if the line of our later cases guaranteed by today's decision limits the theoretically boundless *Batson* principle to race, sex, and perhaps other classifications subject to heightened scrutiny

---

[3] It does not seem to me that even this premise is correct. Wise observers have long understood that the appearance of justice is as important as its reality. If the system of peremptory strikes affects the actual impartiality of the jury not a bit, but gives litigants a greater belief in that impartiality, it serves a most important function. See, e.g., 4 W. BLACKSTONE, COMMENTARIES * 353. In point of fact, that may well be its greater value.

(which presumably would include religious belief), much damage has been done. It has been done, first and foremost, to the peremptory challenge system, which loses its whole character when (in order to defend against "impermissible stereotyping" claims) "reasons" for strikes must be given. The right of peremptory challenge "'is, as Blackstone says, an arbitrary and capricious right; and it must be exercised with full freedom, or it fails of its full purpose.'" The loss of the real peremptory will be felt most keenly by the criminal defendant, whom we have until recently thought "should not be held to accept a juror, apparently indifferent, whom he distrusted for any reason or for no reason." And make no mistake about it: there really is no substitute for the peremptory. Voir dire (though it can be expected to expand as a consequence of today's decision) cannot fill the gap. The biases that go along with group characteristics tend to be biases that the juror himself does not perceive, so that it is no use asking about them. It is fruitless to inquire of a male juror whether he harbors any subliminal prejudice in favor of unwed fathers.

And damage has been done, secondarily, to the entire justice system, which will bear the burden of the expanded quest for "reasoned peremptories" that the Court demands. The extension of *Batson* to sex, and almost certainly beyond, will provide the basis for extensive collateral litigation, which especially the criminal defendant (who litigates full-time and cost-free) can be expected to pursue. While demographic reality places some limit on the number of cases in which race-based challenges will be an issue, every case contains a potential sex-based claim. Another consequence, as I have mentioned, is a lengthening of the voir dire process that already burdens trial courts.

The irrationality of today's strike-by-strike approach to equal protection is evident from the consequences of extending it to its logical conclusion. If a fair and impartial trial is a prosecutor's only legitimate goal; if adversarial trial stratagems must be tested against that goal in abstraction from their role within the system as a whole; and if, so tested, sex-based stratagems do not survive heightened scrutiny — then the prosecutor presumably violates the Constitution when he selects a male or female police officer to testify because he believes one or the other sex might be more convincing in the context of the particular case, or because he believes one or the other might be more appealing to a predominantly male or female jury. A decision to stress one line of argument or present certain witnesses before a mostly female jury — for example, to stress that the defendant victimized women — becomes, under the Court's reasoning, intentional discrimination by a state actor on the basis of gender.

* * *

In order, it seems to me, not to eliminate any real denial of equal protection, but simply to pay conspicuous obeisance to the equality of the sexes, the Court imperils a practice that has been considered an essential part of fair jury trial since the dawn of the common law. The Constitution of the United States neither requires nor permits this vandalizing of our people's traditions.

For these reasons, I dissent.

NOTES AND QUESTIONS

1. Does the Court's holding in *Batson* and its progeny elevate concerns for the dignity of excluded jurors over concerns for the fairness of trials? If litigants and the public believe that jurors' attitudes are affected by race and gender, does it increase or decrease the perception of fairness to allow parties to strike those whom they believe (rightly or wrongly) are likely to be more inclined to find for the other side?

2. Jurors are expected to rely on their life experience in deciding cases. Is the experience of being black or female in America different from the experience of being white or male? Would people with different life experiences tend to evaluate certain evidence differently, not because they are biased or prejudiced, but because they view the evidence from a different perspective? Is the possibility of different perspectives an argument for or against constraining the use of peremptory strikes?

3. In Georgia v. McCollum, 505 U.S. 42 (1992), the Court held that a white defendant's use of peremptories to strike black jurors on the basis of race violates the Equal Protection Clause of the Fourteenth Amendment. Justice Thomas, writing separately, agreed that the holding was consistent with the Court's precedents, but he questioned the wisdom of those precedents. He explained:

> The public, in general, continues to believe that the makeup of juries can matter in certain instances. Consider, for example, how the press reports criminal trials. Major newspapers regularly note the number of whites and blacks that sit on juries in important cases. Their editors and readers apparently recognize that conscious and unconscious prejudice persists in our society and that it may influence some juries. Common experience and common sense confirm this understanding.

Id. at 61. He concluded, "I am certain that black criminal defendants will rue the day that this court ventured down this road that inexorably will lead to the elimination of peremptory strikes." Id. at 60. Justice O'Connor suggests a similar concern with respect to women litigants in sexual harassment, child custody or abuse cases. Do you think *Batson* and *McCollum* will harm the interests of women and minority litigants?

4. Challenges to jury selection must ordinarily be raised prior to trial or such arguments will be waived. See United States v. Romero-Reyna, 867 F. 2d 834 (5th Cir. 1989). In *J.E.B*, the defendant's lawyer, did make a timely objection to the governments use of its peremptories. Counsel later explained that he

> raised the *Batson* challenge in this context "not because of some in-depth legal research I had done," but because of a conversation over coffee with some lawyers that morning in which they told him about a 9th U.S. Circuit Court of Appeals case seeking to extend *Batson* to gender-based juror strikes.

"I didn't even know the name of the case," he admits, adding, "We in Alabama quite frankly don't pay much attention to what the courts in California say." Local judges, he explains, often take a dim view of that state's jurisprudence.

Marcia Coyle, *High Court May Strike Sex-Based Challenges*, NAT'L L.J., Nov. 8, 1993, at 27.

5. Are there other cognizable groups to which *Batson* applies? Groups that have been held to be covered by *Batson* are: American Indians, United States v. Chalan, 812 F. 2d 1302 (10th Cir. 1987); Italian-Americans, United States v. Biaggi, 673 F.Supp. 96 (E.D.N.Y. 1987), *aff'd* 853 F. 2d 89 (2d Cir. 1988), but see United States v. Angiulo, 847 F. 2d 956 (1st Cir.), *cert. denied*, 488 U.S. 928 (1988); and Hispanics, United States v. Ruiz, 894 F. 2d 501 (2d Cir. 1990). On the other hand, courts have refused to extend *Batson* to cover these groups: young persons, United States v. Cresta, 825 F. 2d 538 (1st Cir. 1987), *cert. denied*, 486 U.S. 1042 (1988); Irish-Americans, Murchu v. United States 926 F. 2d 50 (1st Cir.), *cert. denied*, 502 U.S. 828 (1991); and homosexuals, State v. Spitter, 75 Ohio App. 3d 341, 599 N.E. 2d 408 (1991).

6. The side challenging the other side's use of peremptories must make a prima facie showing that the removed juror was a member of cognizable group and that the juror was removed "on account of" membership in that group. What is required to make out a prima facie case? Suppose the venire includes four blacks. The government uses two of its six peremptories to strike two of the blacks and one to strike a white. Is there a prima facie case? See United States v. Dennis, 804 F. 2d 1208 (11th Cir. 1986), *cert. denied*, 481 U.S. 1037 (1987) (holding no prima facie case shown). On the other hand, courts have said that striking a single black juror where this is motivated by race violates *Batson* even if other black jurors are seated. United States v. David, 803 F. 2d 1567 (11th Cir. 1986); Fleming v. Kemp, 794 F. 2d 1478 (11th Cir. 1986).

7. What constitutes an adequate non-discriminatory justification? In his concurrence to *Batson*, Justice Marshall argued for the complete elimination of peremptories on the grounds that requiring lawyers to explain their peremptories would not stop them from striking for improper reasons. He explained:

> Any prosecutor can easily assert facially neutral reasons for striking a juror, and trial courts are ill-equipped to second-guess those reasons. How is the court to treat a prosecutor's statement that he struck a juror because the juror had a son about the same age as the defendant, or seemed "uncommunicative," or "never cracked a smile" and, therefore "did not possess the sensitivities necessary to realistically look at the issues and decide the facts in this case?" If such easily generated explanations are sufficient to discharge the prosecutor's obligation to justify his strikes on nonracial grounds, then the protection erected by the Court today may be illusory.

476 U.S. at 106. Which of the following explanations should be acceptable?

(a) The juror's posture and demeanor suggested hostility. See United States v. Forbes, 816 F. 2d 1006 (5th Cir. 1987).
(b) One juror was too grandmotherly, another had a beard, a third was too close in age to the parents of the deceased. See Wallace v. State, 507 So. 2d 466 (Ala. 1987).
(c) In a case in which some testimony would be in Spanish, the struck jurors were fluent in Spanish. See Hernandez v. New York, 500 U.S. 352 (1991); Pemberthy v. Beyer, 19 F. 2d 857 (3rd Cir. 1994).
(d) "I just got a feeling about him." See United States v. Horsley, 864 F. 2d 1543, 1545 (11th Cir. 1989).

8. Suppose that race or gender is part of the motivation for striking a juror, but not the sole reason. Would that violate the Constitution? In Howard v. Senkowski, 986 F. 2d 24 (2d Cir. 1993), the Second Circuit held that *"Batson* challenges may be brought by defendants who can show that racial discrimination was a substantial part of the motivation for a prosecutor's peremptory challenges, leaving to the prosecutor the affirmative defense of showing that the same challenges would have been exercised for race-neutral reasons in the absence of such partially improper motivation." Id. at 30. In that case the prosecutor admitted to the judge that race had been a factor, but asserted that it was not the sole factor. He offered the following "race-neutral" explanations for striking African-American jurors. One juror could not correctly pronounce the word "prejudice" when she read it, indicating to the prosecutor that the lacked the necessary educational level. The other African-American juror was struck because she "had limited work experience; had five children and therefore might be sympathetic to the defendant; had expressed no opinion about mental illness, which might be relevant to one of the trial witnesses; and had no connection with law enforcement, either as a juror in prior cases, as a crime victim, or as a friend of those in law enforcement." Id. at 25. How should the trial court rule on remand?

9. Suppose one side objects to the other side's use of a peremptory challenge and the trial court agrees that there has been a *Baston* violation. Should the trial court dismiss the entire venire and select a new jury, or should it seat the improperly dismissed juror? In *Baston*, the Supreme Court explicitly declined to answer this question, 476 U.S. at 99 n. 24, and the lower courts are split. See Jones v. Maryland, 659 A.2d 361 (Md. Ct. Spec. App. 1995), and cases collected therein.

10. You are on the staff of the House Judiciary Committee. The Committee has asked you to consider whether it should revise 28 U.S.C. § 1870 or Crim. R. 24, dealing with peremptory challenges in civil and criminal cases. Some changes that have been suggested are:
(a) expand the number of peremptories;
(b) eliminate peremptories;

(c) in criminal cases, allow only defendants to exercise peremptories;
(d) prohibit the use of peremptories to strike jurors based on:
- ethnic origin
- religion
- age
- wealth

Would you favor these or any other changes? Should the rules concerning peremptory challenges be different in civil and criminal cases?

11. *J.E.B.* was reversed and remanded for a new trial. In June 1995, on the day before the new trial was to begin, the case settled.

c. Two Views of Voir Dire and Peremptory Strikes

The first of these two excerpts was written by an experienced trial lawyer, the second by a trial judge. They obviously have quite different views about the purposes and value of voir dire.

The Mapplethorpe Obscenity Trial
by Marc Mezibov and H. Louis Sirkin
18 LITIGATION 112 (Summer 1992)

Only the most prescient of lawyers (or perhaps the most cynical) could have anticipated that legal history would be made on a Saturday morning at an art museum. At approximately 10:30 a.m. on Saturday, April 7, 1990, grand jurors were summoned to the Hamilton County Courthouse in Cincinnati, Ohio, and from there marched approximately six blocks south to join several hundred people already waiting in line at the Contemporary Art Center (CAC), one of Cincinnati's premier museums. On public display for the first time that day was *The Perfect Moment*, a retrospective of the works of the late photographer Robert Mapplethorpe, who died of AIDS in 1989.

The Perfect Moment comprised approximately 175 of Mapplethorpe's photographs and surveyed the photographer's view of, among other things, flora, portraiture, and homoerotic, all of which were presented in the "formalist" or "classical" mode of visual art. Not surprisingly, only the homoerotic category engaged the attention of the grand jurors. They were sufficiently offended by several of the images — form, lighting, and composition notwithstanding — that shortly after noon that same day they returned a two-count indictment against the CAC and its director, Dennis Barrie. Barrie and the CAC were each charged by the grand jurors with pandering obscenity and displaying photographs of minors in a state of nudity. The former charge, a misdemeanor carrying a maximum jail term of six months and a fine of $1,000, related specifically to five images contained in Mapplethorpe's *X* portfolio, which has as its thematic core sexual acts and practices prevalent in the homosexual subculture of Greenwich Village during the 1970s. The other charge, also a misdemeanor, involved two pictures of children: "Jessie," a boy approximately five years old, and "Rosie," a three-year-old girl. Both photographs are similar to those in most family albums.

B. The Right to a Jury

* * *

In this new frontier of obscenity prosecution, the challenge to the defense was twofold: first, to pick a jury from an array of potential jurors whose lives revealed an amazing dearth of experience with museums, to say nothing of art museums, much less contemporary art museums displaying photographs of sado-masochistic acts; and second, to creatively adapt a body of case law developed over several decades that dealt primarily with the sort of sexually explicit forms of expression typically available in adult bookstores and cinema.

* * *

Our emphasis in voir dire, * * * was primarily on * * * the artistic value of *The Perfect Moment* exhibition and the individual images in it. Rather than attempt to sell the jurors on the beauty of the photographs, we offered them the notion that to be valued, art need not — indeed sometimes should not — please the eye. Early in the jury selection process, to underscore our argument that art need not be beautiful and to desensitize the jurors to what they would be shown once the trial began, we described in graphic detail the photographs listed in the indictment. * * *

Jury selection took four complete days and involved not only desensitization but a penetrating inquiry into the potential jurors' attitudes toward a variety of topics not necessarily associated with artistic themes. For example, we were especially interested in the jurors' views on choice and privacy issues, clearly subthemes in our defense. To elicit what we hoped would be meaningful responses, we asked open-ended questions about such subjects as abortion rights and legal rights for homosexuals. We also asked each juror's opinion about whether adults should be restricted in what they may see, read, or hear. Most interesting was the uniformity of the jurors' liberalism, or seeming libertarianism, in their response to such general questions as, Do you think adults should be prevented or restricted from seeing movies of their choice? Curiously, the very jurors who answered no invariably responded yes to the more pointed question of whether adults should be restricted from viewing films involving acts of oral sex or group sex. Our exchanges with jurors on those points demonstrated the wisdom of an in-depth inquiry, especially when a case involves the fundamental values to which most Americans give all-too-easy lip service.

* * *

Our Model Juror

Although expert witnesses played a central role in our defense strategy, we did not use jury selection experts, despite the many who offered assistance. Our decision did not result entirely from a professional bias against expert-assisted jury selection. In part, we were skeptical about whether we could take advantage of expert assistance. Because we would not receive the panel lists until immediately before the trial, we would not be able to analyze and factor into our selection process the sparse background information about the jurors. And the trial judge refused to use questionnaires prepared by counsel. Moreover, in the weeks before trial, while the propriety of the Mapplethorpe exhibition was a topic of unprecedented public debate in Cincinnati, the CAC commissioned a survey to assess community attitudes on this issue. Going into trial, we felt that that survey would give us a useful frame of reference in choosing a jury. As it turned out, the results of the survey were more interesting than practical. On the basis of the survey, our model juror was a single black male living within the boundaries of the city of Cincinnati. Out of a jury array of approximately 60 persons, only one fit the model profile. In the end we were forced to rely on our experience, our instincts, an the considerable knowledge we acquired through intensive questioning of prospective jurors.

In voir dire another major theme that we emphasized was the "human factor." We frequently referred to the men and women who, either as paid staff or as volunteers, operate the CAC along with Barrie. We sought not only to humanize our corporate client but to divert the jurors' attention from the controversial photographs toward the people who, as we viewed it, were being held accountable for their principled fidelity to the CAC's cultural and educational mission. To accomplish these twin goals, we asked many of the potential jurors about their familiarity with the CAC's cultural and educational mission. To accomplish these twin goals, we asked many of the potential jurors about their familiarity with the CAC, its purpose, and the various community-based programs for implementing that purpose. We wanted to disabuse the jurors of any notion planted by the prosecution that our clients were "panderers" in the worst sense of the word. During the defense's case in chief, we presented, in addition to Barrie, both the CAC's assistant director and member of its governing board who also serves as the museum's legal counsel. Through the attorney we explained to the jury the nature, purpose, and significance of the CAC's not-for-profit status. That was simply another way of establishing that when it came to the Mapplethorpe exhibition, the case was motivated not by money but by "art for art's sake."

The manner in which prospective jurors are selected in Hamilton County gave us considerable cause for concern. The names of prospective jurors are taken from the lists of registered voters on file with the county elections board. Historically, Hamilton County, which is in the southwest corner of Ohio, is a bastion of conservatism. Traditional values for the most part go unquestioned. Free speech battles are rare. In the last 20 years a community-wide understanding has developed of acceptable forms and means of expression, largely the result of rigorous law enforcement. X-rated movies are not acceptable, nor are adult bookstores. Neither type of establishment exists any longer in Hamilton County.

In Search of Diversity

The Hamilton county voters retain in office political leaders who perpetuate a climate hostile to a diversity of opinion and alternative lifestyles. We were concerned about selecting a jury from among those voters. In Ohio, as in many other states, the law authorizes driver's license registration lists as a source for jury enpanelment. Therefore, we moved that the court strike the entire array of jurors in favor of a panel chosen from driver's license registration lists. We believed that jurors selected from that pool would be more urban and diverse, reflecting a wider spectrum of opinion on social issues in general and on free speech and choice issues in particular. To our disappointment, but not our surprise, the court overruled our motion on the ground that there was no evidence of irregularity in the way this particular group of prospective jurors had been assembled.

In a case as emotionally and politically charged as ours, it was not surprising to find individuals with their own agendas in this politically conservative community. They gave our

B. The Right to a Jury

painstakingly planned and exhaustive jury selection process some peak moments. Perhaps the most memorable occurred during the questioning of a Mrs. Murphy. Her jury questionnaire said she was employed as an administrative secretary to a well-known local clergyman who also happened to be a leader not only locally but nationally in a crusade against pornography. We were confident that because of her professional and personal affiliations, Mrs. Murphy would be excused for cause. That would obviate the need for additional questions of this woman, who we feared would want to educate the jurors about her cause in much the same way we were seeking to educate them about ours. The judge disagreed. Further questioning revealed that Mrs. Murphy's personal involvement and interest in the antiporn movement was such that when *The Perfect Moment* was first announced in the press, she had gone out of her way to be shown photocopies of the two images of the children listed in the indictment. She also acknowledged that she had already formed an opinion about those photographs. In Mrs. Murphy's view, the photographs of the two children were "not morally decent" and should not have been shown in a museum. The following exchange between Mrs. Murphy and defense counsel ensued:

Q: Is it your opinion that the pictures should not be shown for any purpose?
A: Yes.
Q: Anywhere?
A: Yes.
Q: Anytime?
A: Yes.
Q: To anyone?
A: Yes.

We asked again that Mrs. Murphy be excused for cause. Rather than rule immediately on our request, the judge proceeded to serve up a softball, underhanded. He asked Mrs. Murphy whether she could set aside her convictions and be fair to both sides. In dutiful response to whatever cause greater than the truth that Mrs. Murphy served, she hit the judge's pitch a mile. Mrs. Murphy's impartially having been assured to his satisfaction, the judge ruled that although she might be opinionated, she had given him the impression she could follow the law. When the groans of disbelief from the gallery subsided, we exercised our final peremptory challenge to keep Mrs. Murphy off the jury.

Our jury consisted of eight persons, four men and four women, all from rather conventional Cincinnati backgrounds. All were employed. Two had some college education, and one had a college degree. Not one of the jurors had attended the Mapplethorpe exhibition; nor, for that matter, had any ever visited the CAC.

Because the long, involved jury selection process addressed virtually all the legal issues and themes in the case, the evidentiary portion of the trial provided little that was new to the jurors. By design, the testimony of our witnesses dovetailed in all important respects with the voir dire. And imagine our professional satisfaction when we learned that in explaining the verdict to the media after the trial, more than one of the jurors hearkened back to our presentation during voir dire. Biases notwithstanding, it became clear by the case's end that those jurors finally selected were willing to hold themselves open to a broad range of human experiences, as well as the appropriateness of those experiences, as subjects for artistic inquiry. Despite the graphic nature of the photographs, which some jurors described as gross and disgusting, the jury concluded that the prosecution had not made its case because, like a poorly baked apple pie, "it was missing an ingredient. [The exhibition] had artistic value, and that's what kept it from being obscene."

* * *

A Critical Role

The jury's verdict did show how critical the lawyer's role is in jury selection. In many jurisdictions, especially in federal courts, lawyers are losing the opportunity to participate meaningfully in jury selection. We have little doubt that if our role in voir dire had been less than it was, we would now be before an appellate court.

10 Trial Mistakes
by Morris Hoffman
19 THE DOCKET 17 (Spring 1994)

Most prospective jurors report for jury duty angry and skeptical. The first thing most lawyers do is to make them more angry and more skeptical by engaging in a process whose fundamental assumption that there are prospective jurors who must be hunted down like dogs and removed for their "biases." These "biases" are discovered by a series of tricky Rorschach questions designed to open hidden psychiatric vistas in mere minutes.

My trial observations have confirmed my instincts that this entire approach to voir dire is baloney. All any of us can realistically hope for in voir dire is to find out if any jurors have a direct financial interest in the litigation, are related to any of the parties or the lawyers, or for any other gross reason cannot be fair or impartial. In my opinion, all the other energy lawyers waste on pop psychology in voir dire is not just a waste, it is waste which insults the jurors, and does irreparable damage to the legendary "rapport" which is supposed be created at this state of the trial.

The most effective voir dire I've ever seen was by a well-known Denver trial lawyer who stood up, asked about five minutes' worth of questions aimed simply at whether the prospective jurors thought they could be fair, and sat down. That exchange did more to build rapport than a hundred questions about the jurors' children, reading habits and toilet training.

d. Jury Size

At common law both criminal and civil juries were composed of twelve people. In Williams v. Florida, 399 U.S. 78 (1970), the Supreme Court held that the use in criminal cases of juries of fewer than twelve did not violate the Sixth Amendment right to a jury. Similarly, in Colgrove v. Battin, 413 U.S. 149 (1973), the Court upheld the use of six person juries in civil cases. The Court explained that "by referring to the 'common law,' the

Framers of the Seventh Amendment were concerned with preserving the *right* of trial by jury in civil cases where it existed at common law, rather than the various incidents of trial by jury." Id. at 155-56. The size of the jury was an incident of trial by jury, not part of the right.

Rule 48 allows federal courts in civil cases to empanel juries of "not fewer than six and not more than twelve members." Driven by economics, the result is that federal juries are usually six persons. The 1991 amendments to Rule 47 abolished alternative jurors. Now all jurors must participate in the verdict unless excused for good cause. The comment to Rule 48 advises empaneling seven or more jurors so that the jury will still include at least six people in the event a juror is dismissed. Regardless of the size of the jury, Rule 48 requires a unanimous verdict unless the parties otherwise stipulate.

Some commentators have expressed concern about the use of small juries, noting that smaller panels are more likely to reach a verdict than larger panels but show greater variations in the verdicts reached. Moreover, smaller juries are less likely to be representative of the community. See Peter Sperlich, . . . *And Then There Were Six: The Decline of the American Jury*, 63 JUDICATURE 262 (1980); Hans Zeisel & Shari Diamond, *"Convincing Empirical Evidence" on the Six Member Jury*, 41 U. CHI. L. REV. 281 (1974).

3. Jury Nullification and Its Limits

In the criminal arena, the defendant's right to a jury is absolute. Even when the evidence of guilt is overwhelming and the defendant has no defense, the defendant can still demand that the case be sent to a jury. Moreover, if in such a case, the jury returns a verdict of not guilty, that verdict will be allowed to stand even though it is contrary to all the evidence.[*] The criminal jury's absolute authority to acquit reflects, in large part the long accepted principle of jury nullification. Jury nullification occurs "when a jury — based on its own sense of justice or fairness — refuses to follow this law and convict in a particular case even though the facts seem to allow no other conclusion but guilt." Jack Weinstein, *Considering Jury "Nullification" : When May and Should a Jury Reject the Law to Do Justice*, 30 AM. CR. L. REV. 239 (1993). Judge Weinstein has explained the role of jury nullification as follows:

> When jurors return with a "nullification" verdict, then, they have not in reality "nullified" anything: they have done their job. "[N]ullification is inherent in the

---

[*] The jury's discretion in criminal cases is one-sided. The jury may acquit in the face of overwhelming evidence and the judge cannot disturb the verdict. However, where the judge finds there is too little evidence of guilt, the judge may refuse to send the case to the jury and can enter judgment of acquittal herself or enter judgment of acquittal despite a contrary jury verdict. See F.R. Crim. P. 29.

> jury's role as the conscience of the democratic community and a cushion between the citizens and overly harsh or arbitrary government criminal prosecution." Juries are charged not with the task of blindly and mechanically applying the law, but of doing justice in light of the law, the evidence presented at trial, and their own knowledge of society and the world. To decide that some outcomes are just and some are not is not possible without drawing upon personal views.

Id. at 244-45.

We could extend the concept of jury nullification to civil cases and give the parties to a civil suit an absolute right to have their case decided by a jury. A justice system, for example, could allow plaintiffs to argue in essence, "I have no proof to support my claim, but I should win anyway." Do you think this would be a good idea? Are there differences between civil and criminal adjudication that make jury nullification appropriate for one, but not the other? See Murphy, supra, 61 GEO. WASH. L. REV. at 736-54, 762-70.

While one could imagine a system in which the right to a jury is absolute in civil cases, that is not our system. Indeed, in some circumstances, the Court has held that the failure to provide judicial review of jury verdicts violates the due process clause. See Honda Motor Co., Ltd. v. Oberg, 114 S. Ct. 2331 (1994) (state must provide judicial review of jury award of punitive damages). As we will see in the following sections, in cases in which the judge concludes that there is insufficient evidence, several procedural devices permit her to decide the case without a jury or to enter judgment contrary to a jury's verdict.

C. Summary Judgment — Adjudication Without Trial or Jury

Rule 56 authorizes the court to enter judgment whenever it appears that "there is no genuine issue as to any material fact and that the moving party is entitled to a judgment as a matter of law." Rule 56(c). Motions for summary judgment are filed before trial and if the motion is granted, judgment is entered without benefit of a trial (or a jury). The court may hold a hearing on the motion, but such a hearing is not a trial - there is no presentation of evidence. The hearing is simply an opportunity for the lawyers to amplify their motion papers and for the court to ask questions.

There are two basic situations in which summary judgment is appropriate. First, the parties may agree on all the facts and their dispute may be entirely a dispute about the law — whether liability attaches under the particular circumstances. Indeed, sometimes the parties will stipulate to the facts and then file motions for summary judgment, with each side arguing that under these undisputed facts, it is entitled to a judgment. When, as here, the parties agree on the facts and the dispute is entirely one of law, there is no need for a trial or a jury. Matters of law are for the judge to decide. The judge may hold oral argument

C. Summary Judgment — Adjudication Without Trial or Jury

to assist her in understanding the law, but there is no need to have a trial with witnesses testifying about the facts.

Summary judgment also is used when the parties disagree about the facts, but there is no "genuine" dispute, that is, one side has so little evidence that no reasonable jury could find for that side. For example, in Dyer v. MacDougall, 201 F. 2d 265 (2d Cir. 1952), the plaintiff alleged that the defendant slandered him in the presence of two other people. The defendant filed a motion for summary judgment attaching his own affidavit plus the affidavits of the two supposed witnesses and all three affidavits denied that the statements attributed to the defendant were uttered. The plaintiff offered no admissible evidence that the statement was made and the court granted summary judgment.

Summary judgment should be distinguished from a motion to dismiss under 12(b)(6) or a motion for judgment on the pleadings under 12(c). In ruling on the Rule 12 motions, the court relies solely on the pleadings to determine the facts. All undenied facts are treated as true and all denied facts are assumed to be in dispute. In contrast, in ruling on summary judgment, the court looks beyond the pleadings and considers evidence such as affidavits or other sworn statements such as depositions or interrogatories. All the evidence considered is in written form. The court does not take evidence from witnesses in open court as it would at a trial. In addition, in ruling on a motion for summary judgment the court does not assess credibility. Instead, the court views the evidence in the light most favorable to the non-moving party. This is true even if the court believes the defendant's witness is more credible than the plaintiffs witness. The question of which witness is more credible is left to the trier of fact and if the resolution of the case turns on which witness is believed, the court will deny summary judgment.

As we will see, summary judgment is not the only procedure whereby the court enters judgment without a jury verdict. In the next section we will study directed verdicts (now called judgments as a matter of law). Under this procedure, if the court, having heard the evidence at trial, concludes that no reasonable jury could find for one side, the court may enter judgment without submitting the case to the jury. The directed verdict is a close cousin of summary judgment. The standard for granting the two motions is essentially the same. The difference is that in summary judgment, the court makes its ruling on the basis of affidavits, while a direct verdict is granted on the basis of the evidence presented at trial.

Knapp v. Holiday Inns, Inc.
682 S.W.2d 936 (Tenn. Ct. App. 1984)

Koch, Judge.

This is a wrongful death action predicated upon a common law dram shop cause of action * * *. It was concluded prior to trial when the trial court granted a summary judgment for the defendant owner of the cocktail lounge where the person causing the fatal accident had been served alcoholic beverages immediately prior to the accident.

This case presents a unique situation in which the party seeking a summary judgment contends that it is entitled to a judgment as a matter of law because all available witnesses having direct and personal knowledge of the material facts have made statements favorable to the movant thereby precluding any possibility of a genuine dispute of material fact. In response, the opponent to the motion for summary judgment concedes that the statements of all available witnesses with direct knowledge of the facts are in the movant's favor. However, the opponent to the motion contends that a genuine and material factual dispute exists because the credibility of the defendant's witnesses and the weight to be given their testimony should not be decided at the summary judgment stage but should be resolved by the trier of fact at a trial on the merits.

For the reasons stated in this opinion, we find that granting a summary judgment was not appropriate in this case.

On December 3, 1982, Mr. Dennis L. Knapp, acting as the administrator of his son's estate, brought this action * * * against Holiday Inns, Inc., the owner of a cocktail lounge named "Chuggers" located in the Holiday Inn Hotel in Nashville adjacent to I-65. In substance, the complaint alleged that employees of Chuggers lounge had illegally and negligently served alcoholic beverages to Mr. Norman D. Lane, a regular and frequent Chuggers patron, after he had reached an intoxicated condition. The complaint further alleged that immediately after leaving Chuggers, Mr. Lane caused an automobile accident on I-65 which resulted in David L. Knapp's death. The complaint concludes that Holiday Inn, Inc.'s negligence was the proximate cause of David L. Knapp's death.

Holiday Inns, Inc. moved for a summary judgment on October 25, 1983, contending (1) that the complaint failed to state a claim upon which relief can be granted, (2) that it had committed no negligent act that was the proximate cause of the accident in which David L. Knapp was killed, and (3) that David L. Knapp's death resulted from independent and superceding [sic] causes over which Holiday Inns, Inc. had no control. In support of its contentions that there were no genuine factual issues and that it was entitled to a judgment as a matter of law, Holiday Inns, Inc. filed the deposition of Norman D. Lane, an affidavit of one of Mr. Lane's employees, an affidavit of one of Mr. Lane's former clients who was a cocktail waitress at Chuggers on the night David L. Knapp was killed, and affidavits from another waitress and the Food and Beverage Director of the hotel concerning Chuggers' general policy concerning serving alcoholic beverages.

In response to the motion for summary judgment, Mr. Knapp filed the affidavit of a Professor of Toxicology from the Indiana University School of Medicine and the affidavit of the Director of the Crime Laboratory of the Tennessee Bureau of Investigation together with attached exhibits relating to the level of Mr. Lane's intoxication at the time the fatal accident occurred.

C. Summary Judgment — Adjudication Without Trial or Jury

The trial court conducted a hearing on the motion for summary judgment on January 6, 1984. During this hearing both in briefs filed and during argument, Mr. Knapp challenged Holiday Inn, Inc.'s affidavits in support of the motion for summary judgment on the basis of bias and interest of the persons upon whose affidavits the motion for summary judgment was predicated. Likewise, Holiday Inns, Inc. challenged the competency of the affidavits submitted by Mr. Knapp. On January 9, 1984, an order was entered granting Holiday Inns, Inc. a summary judgment.

The dispositive issue both in the trial court and in this appeal is whether there exists a genuine factual dispute concerning whether the employees of Chuggers served alcoholic beverages to Norman Lane when he was visibly intoxicated. This is a material issue because the owner or operator of an establishment selling alcoholic beverages by the drink to the public may only be held liable for injuries proximately caused by serving alcoholic beverages to a person who is visibly intoxicated at the time the alcoholic beverages are served.

Holiday Inns, Inc. sought to show definitively that Mr. Lane was not visibly intoxicated by relying on the deposition of Mr. Lane himself, the affidavits of one of Mr. Lane's former clients who was one of the cocktail waitresses at Chuggers who served Mr. Lane prior to the accident, and Mr. Lane's law clerk who talked with him by telephone while Mr. Lane was at Chuggers.[2]

This proof shows that Mr. Lane began drinking at his law office during the afternoon of the day David Knapp was killed and that he drank more at his law office than he did while he was at Chuggers. He had nothing to eat that day because he was on a diet. While he could not remember when he left his law office, Mr. Lane remembered that he drove directly to Chuggers and that he arrived there some time prior to 6:30 p.m. He planned to stay there until the traffic congestion eased before continuing home. He did not remember how many drinks he was served while he was at Chuggers.

A waitress employed at Chuggers who was a former client and friend of Mr. Lane stated in an affidavit that she served him two drinks during happy hour before she left work at 7:00 p.m. and that Mr. Lane did not appear to be intoxicated when she saw him. Mr. Lane's law clerk stated in an affidavit that he called Mr. Lane at Chuggers at approximately 6:30 p.m. shortly after Mr. Lane arrived and that Mr. Lane did not sound intoxicated during that telephone conversation.

Mr. Lane recalled ordering another drink from another waitress before he left Chuggers, but by affidavit, this waitress had no independent recollection of Mr. Lane or that she ever served him as a customer at Chuggers.

When Mr. Lane left Chuggers at 8:00 p.m. he drove onto I-65. He remembers being concerned about being arrested for driving while intoxicated immediately prior to the accident. Approximately ten minutes after leaving Chuggers, he mistook the gas pedal for the brake pedal and accelerated into the rear of the automobile ahead of him, drove across the highway's medial strip, and struck the automobile being driven by David Knapp head on.

Mr. Knapp was killed, and Mr. Lane was rendered unconscious and remained so for some time after the accident. A sample of Mr. Lame's blood was taken within an hour after the accident. It

---

[2] Holiday Inns, Inc. submitted two other affidavits in support of its motion for summary judgment. They have no bearing on Mr. Lane's demeanor while at Chuggers but rather relate to Chuggers' general policy concerning serving alcoholic beverages to persons who appear intoxicated.

was subsequently analyzed by the Tennessee Bureau of Investigation's crime laboratory and was found to have a blood alcohol concentration of .23%.[3]

Mr. Lane admitted in his pleadings that it was his negligence that caused David Knapp's death and that he was driving while intoxicated when the accident occurred.

The benefits of granting summary judgment in prior cases have been recognized repeatedly. However, our courts have also been quick to point out that summary judgments should not be used as substitutes for trials on the merits when the material facts are in dispute, or when there is uncertainty about whether the material facts are in dispute, or even when the parties disagree about the inferences to be drawn from the facts.

The procedural requirements contained in Tenn.R.Civ.P. 56 used to consider a motion for summary judgment have also been reviewed on prior occasions and need no great elaboration here. Suffice it to say that the party moving for a summary judgment must first carry the burden of demonstrating that no genuine dispute involving material facts exists and that he is entitled to a judgment as a matter of law. Once confronted with a motion for summary judgment, the opponent to the motion cannot take it lightly and is required to demonstrate why granting a motion for summary judgment would be inappropriate. In most instances, the opponent to a motion for summary judgment defeats the motion by demonstrating that genuine disputes concerning material fact exist.

The decisions of our state courts construing Tenn.R.Civ.P. 56 have repeatedly held that when a court is determining whether all the requirements of Tenn.R.Civ.P. 56 have been met in a particular case, the pleadings and other competent factual proof should be viewed in a light most favorable to the opponent of the motion and likewise, that all legitimate conclusions should be drawn in the opponent's favor. The Federal courts construing Fed.R.Civ.P. 56 which is substantially similar to Tenn.R.Civ.P. 56 have stated the same principle another way. * * *

While summary judgments can be granted in negligence cases when the requirements of Tenn.R.Civ.P. 56 have been satisfied, the Tennessee Supreme Court has cautioned that as a general matter, summary judgments should be granted only hesitantly in negligence cases because the ultimate determinative issues in these cases should be decided by the trier of fact after an opportunity to view witnesses' demeanor and to evaluate their credibility. Bowman v. Henard, 547 S.W.2d 527, 530 (Tenn. 1977). * * *

In the *Bowman v. Henard* opinion, the Tennessee Supreme Court, like other courts, has recognized that there are cases in which it is not proper to force a party to try his case on affidavits because to do so would prevent the trier of fact from having the opportunity to view the witnesses as they testify and thus to decide upon their credibility and the weight to be given to their testimony.

This conclusion is in full harmony with the decisions of Federal courts construing Fed.R.Civ.P. 56. These decisions conclude that evidence in the form of affidavits is, on the whole, the least satisfactory form of evidentiary material to use in support of a motion for summary judgment because the use of affidavits deprives the opposing party of an opportunity to cross examine the witness thereby depriving the fact finder of any real opportunity to judge the witness' credibility and to determine the wright to be given to the testimony. Judge Friendly has expressed this proposition as follows:

> "But even if the trial should turn out to be nothing more than a swearing contest, with the parties saying the same thing in the witness chair they have said in

---

[3] TENN. CODE ANN. §§ 55-10-408(b) provides for a presumption that a person is under the influence of alcohol if there is .10% or more by weight of alcohol in his blood.

C. Summary Judgment — Adjudication Without Trial or Jury

affidavits, the court would have the benefit of observing their demeanor, particularly under cross-examination, and the case would come to us [the appellate court] with factual findings on the disputed matters which are lacking in the opinion before us . . ."

Painton & Co. v. Bourns, Inc., 442 F. 2d 216, 233 (2d Cir. 1971).

Courts construing the federal counterpart to Tenn.R.Civ.P. 56 consistently hold that summary judgments should not be granted in cases where the outcome hinges squarely upon the state of mind, intent or credibility of the witnesses. Stated another way, doubt as to the credibility of material witnesses will create a genuine issue of material fact sufficient to render granting a summary judgment improper. This is especially the case when the basic facts are under the control of one of the parties.

A party seeking to defeat a motion for summary judgment by questioning the credibility of witnesses must fairly raise this issue in the trial court at the time the motion for summary judgment is being considered. However, if the opponent to a motion for summary judgment succeeds in raising a genuine doubt concerning a witness' credibility by a sufficient showing of the witness' bias, prejudice or interest, the summary judgment should be denied, and the case should be decided by the trier of fact. Thus, in a wrongful death action, Judge Wisdom cautioned:

> "The court should be cautious in granting a motion for summary judgment when resolution of the dispositive issue requires a determination of state of mind. Much depends upon the credibility of the witnesses testifying as to their own states of mind. In these circumstances the jury should be given an opportunity to observe the demeanor, during direct and cross-examination, of the witnesses whose states of mind are at issue."

Croley v. Matson Navigation Co., 434 F. 2d 73, 77 (5th Cir. 1970).

After analogizing a motion for summary judgment with a motion for a directed verdict, the United States Supreme Court held that the credibility of witnesses and the weight to be given their testimony should be left to the jury and that a summary judgment supported by affidavits of interested witnesses was not proper because ". . . a summary disposition . . . should be on evidence which a jury would not be at liberty to disbelieve and which would require a directed verdict for the moving party." Sartor v. Arkansas Natural Gas Corp., 321 U.S. 620, 624, (1944).

* * *

This case presents a clear situation where a summary judgment is not proper because the outcome of this case rests solely upon the credibility of the witnesses who can be considered competent to testify from personal knowledge about Norman Lane's demeanor and conduct while he was at Chuggers prior to the fatal accident. Mr. Knapp squarely challenged the credibility of these witnesses in the trial court and has sufficiently called the credibility of these witnesses into question to create a genuine issue of material fact.

In fact, this record reveals that there is only one witness other than Mr. Lane himself who has any direct, personal knowledge concerning Mr. Lane's conduct at Chuggers.[12] This witness is the waitress who served Mr. Lane during the first half hour he was at Chuggers. In addition to being an employee of the defendant, this witness admitted that she was a personal friend and former client of Mr. Lane. These relationships are sufficient to raise a question of this witness' credibility which should be resolved at a full hearing on the merits. In other dram shop cases, an employee of the defendant tavern owner has been found to be sufficiently interested in the proceeding to be impeached.

In addition to the question about the weight to be given to this waitress' testimony, it is evident that Holiday Inns, Inc.'s affidavits do not exclude the existence of a dispute with regard to the material facts. None of the proof submitted by Holiday Inns, Inc. provides any evidence concerning Mr. Lane's demeanor at Chuggers for an hour immediately before he left. Mr. Lane was served by two waitresses that night. The first waitress who served him until approximately 7:00 p.m. left the establishment and had no chance to observe Mr. Lane further. The second waitress who would have served Mr. Lane from 7:00 p.m. until the time he left had no independent recollection of Mr. Lane nor any of the events at Chuggers that evening. This absence of proof is not sufficient for Holiday Inns, Inc. to carry its burden required by Tenn.R.Civ.P. 56.03 of demonstrating that there are no genuine disputes of material fact.

While we have determined that the questioned credibility of Holiday Inns, Inc.'s witnesses, by itself, is sufficient to render a summary judgment inappropriate in this case, we also find that a portion of the evidence Mr. Knapp presented in opposition to the summary judgment may also be competent to create a material factual dispute.

In response to Holiday Inns. Inc.'s motion for summary judgment, Mr. Knapp filed an affidavit of the director of the crime laboratory of the Tennessee Bureau of Investigation attaching certified copies of the records relating to the blood alcohol concentration tests conducted upon a sample of Mr. Lane's blood which was taken within an hour after the fatal accident. While proper foundation would be required in order to admit these documents into evidence at trial, TENN. CODE ANN. § 55-10-410(d) provides that this evidence is admissible in any court as evidence of the facts stated therein and of the results of the blood alcohol test itself.

Any material fact can be proved by circumstantial evidence. In certain cases, this Court has recognized that a well connected train of circumstances may be more convincing than direct evidence on the same matters.

Well reasoned authority from other jurisdictions holds that the level of a person's intoxication as well as his demeanor may be proved by circumstantial evidence. While not conclusive, the results of properly conducted blood alcohol concentration tests can assist the trier of fact in determining the state of a person's intoxication.

This authority leads us to conclude that evidence concerning Mr. Lane's blood alcohol concentration and properly admitted expert testimony concerning the conclusions that can be drawn from the results of the blood alcohol concentration test are relevant to the question of whether Mr. Lane was visibly intoxicated while at Chuggers. Using the tolerant standard required when considering the evidence used to oppose a motion for summary judgment, we find that the proof relating to Mr. Lane's blood alcohol concentration, when viewed together with the other proof, creates a material factual dispute thereby rendering a summary judgment inappropriate.

---

[12] Mr. Lane's testimony in his deposition reveals that his memory about his conduct is less than reliable. Mr. Lane's law clerk admits in his affidavit that he never saw Mr. Lane on the day of the accident. Testimony regarding a telephone conversation is barely relevant to the issue of whether Mr. Lane was visibly intoxicated during the ninety minutes Mr. Lane remained at Chuggers after the telephone call.

C. Summary Judgment — Adjudication Without Trial or Jury

The trial court's decision to grant Holiday Inns, Inc. a summary judgment is, therefore, reversed and the case is remanded for further proceedings.

The costs of this appeal will be taxed to Holiday Inns, Inc. and its surety for which execution, if necessary, may issue.

NOTES AND QUESTIONS

1. In *Knapp*, in response to defendant's motion, plaintiff submitted the affidavit of the director of the crime laboratory attaching certified copies of the blood alcohol tests done on Lane. The court is careful to point out that this evidence would be admissible at trial. What difference does it make whether it is admissible?

2. Suppose the defendant produced a videotape of Lane at Chuggers and moved for summary judgment on the grounds that the tape showed that he was not visibly intoxicated. Should the court grant summary judgment? Would your answer be the same if the plaintiff moved for summary judgment on the basis of a videotape showing Lane stumbling and recording his slurred speech?

3. Suppose the issue in the case had been whether Lane had in fact been at Chuggers on the evening in question. Defendant submits the affidavits of several Chuggers waitresses, all of whom deny that Lane was there. Lane himself denies remembering where he was. Plaintiff responds to the motion by pointing out that as employees of the defendant, the waitresses have an incentive to lie. Is this case distinguishable from *Knapp*? Should summary judgment be granted?

4. In Colosi v. Electri-Flex Co., 965 F. 2d 500, 503 (7th Cir. 1992), Judge Posner offered the following analysis:

> If a party presents multiple affidavits on summary judgment, covering the same ground, and some are shown to be unworthy of belief but others are not, do those others entitle the party to summary judgment or can the falsity of some support a negative inference about the others? We should think the latter, at least in extreme cases. If (to choose a number at random) a party presents nine affidavits each saying the same thing, and eight are shown to be perjurious, we would doubt that the party was entitled to summary judgment merely because the last stood uncontradicted.

Do you agree that a summary judgment would not be proper in that situation?

5. Rule 56(d) permits a court to enter partial summary judgment disposing of some, but not all, issues in the case. For example, a court could grant summary judgment on the issue of liability, but not on the issue of damages, or as to one claim, but not another.

6. Summary judgment is not appropriate when there is a "genuine issue as to any material fact." What is a fact? Suppose the parties agree on what the defendant did and the dispute concerns whether that conduct was negligent. Is summary judgment proper? The Supreme Court has written that in such a situation

> it is a matter of judgment and discretion, of sound inference, what is the deduction to be drawn from the undisputed facts. Certain facts we may suppose to be clearly established from which one sensible, impartial man would infer that proper care had not been used, and that negligence existed; another man equally sensible and equally impartial would infer that proper care had been used, and that there was no negligence. It is this class of cases and those akin to it that the law commits to the decision of a jury. * * * It is assumed that twelve men know more of the common affairs of life than does one man, that they can draw wiser and safer conclusions from admitted facts thus occurring than can a single judge.

Railroad Co. v. Stout, 84 U.S. 657, 663-64 (1873). In other contexts, the courts have held that the inferences to be drawn from undisputed historical facts are a matter of law for the court. See e.g., Wolston v. Readers Digest Assoc. Inc., 578 F. 2d 427, 429 (D.C.Cir. 1978) (whether plaintiff is a "public figure" for purposes of libel law); Fox v. Johnson & Wimsatt, Inc., 127 F. 2d 729, 736-37 (D.C.Cir. 1942) (interpretation of a corporate resolution).

Judge Schwarzer has argued that in determining whether an issue is one of fact for purposes of summary judgment, the court should focus on whether "as a matter of precedent or policy, [the issue] should be decided by the jury or by the court." William Schwarzer, *Summary Judgment Under the Federal Rules: Defining Genuine Issues of Material Fact*, 99 F.R.D. 465, 471 (1984). What issues should not be decided by juries?

7. Charles E. Clark, the senior reporter for the committee that drafted the Federal Rules, along with other legal realists, disliked juries. "Jurists of experience find little to say in support of the delays, the expense, and the aleatory results of trial by jury," said Clark. LAURA KALMAN, LEGAL REALISM AT YALE 21 (1986). Indeed, it has been argued that one of the attractions of summary judgment to the drafters of the Rules was that it was a device for taking cases away from juries. See id.

Anderson v. Liberty Lobby, Inc.
477 U.S. 242; 106 S. Ct. 2505; 91 L. Ed. 2d 202 (1986)

JUSTICE WHITE delivered the opinion of the Court.

In New York Times Co. v. Sullivan, 376 U.S. 254, 279-280 (1964), we held that, in a libel suit brought by a public official, the First Amendment requires the plaintiff to show that in publishing the defamatory statement the defendant acted with actual malice — "with knowledge that it was false or with reckless disregard of whether it was false or not." We held further that such actual malice must be shown with "convincing clarity." * * *

This case presents the question whether the clear-and-convincing-evidence requirement must be considered by a court ruling on a motion for summary judgment under Rule 56 of the Federal Rules of Civil Procedure in a case to which *New York Times* applies. The United States Court of Appeals for the District of Columbia Circuit held that that requirement need not be considered at the summary judgment stage. * * * We now reverse.

I

Respondent Liberty Lobby, Inc., is a not-for-profit corporation and self-described "citizens' lobby." Respondent Willis Carto is its founder and treasurer. In October 1981, The Investigator magazine published two articles: "The Private World of Willis Carto" and "Yockey: Profile of an American Hitler." These articles were introduced by a third, shorter article entitled "America's Neo-Nazi Underground: Did *Mein Kampf* Spawn Yockey's *Imperium*, a Book Revived by Carto's Liberty Lobby?" These articles portrayed respondents as neo-Nazi, anti-Semitic, racist, and Fascist.

Respondents filed this diversity libel action in the United States District Court for the District of Columbia, alleging that some 28 statements and 2 illustrations in the 3 articles were false and derogatory. * * *

Following discovery, petitioners moved for summary judgment pursuant to Rule 56. In their motion, petitioners asserted that because respondents are public figures they were required to prove their case under the standards set forth in *New York Times*. Petitioners also asserted that summary judgment was proper because actual malice was absent as a matter of law. In support of this latter assertion, petitioners submitted the affidavit of Charles Bermant, an employee of petitioners and the author of the two longer articles. In this affidavit, Bermant stated that he had spent a substantial amount of time researching and writing the articles and that his facts were obtained from a wide variety of sources. He also stated that he had at all times believed and still believed that the facts contained in the articles were truthful and accurate. Attached to this affidavit was an appendix in which Bermant detailed the sources for each of the statements alleged by respondents to be libelous.

Respondents opposed the motion for summary judgment, asserting that there were numerous inaccuracies in the articles and claiming that an issue of actual malice was presented by virtue of the fact that in preparing the articles Bermant had relied on several sources that respondents asserted were patently unreliable. Generally, respondents charged that petitioners had failed adequately to verify their information before publishing. Respondents also presented evidence that William McGaw, an editor of The Investigator, had told petitioner Adkins before publication that the articles were "terrible" and "ridiculous."

[The district court granted summary judgment and entered judgment in favor of the petitioners. The court of appeals affirmed summary judgment as to some of the allegedly defamatory statements, but reversed as to others.]

II

A

Our inquiry is whether the Court of Appeals erred in holding that the heightened evidentiary requirements that apply to proof of actual malice in this *New York Times* case need not be considered for the purposes of a motion for summary judgment. Rule 56(c) of the Federal Rules of Civil Procedure provides that summary judgment "shall be rendered forthwith if the pleadings, depositions, answers to interrogatories, and admissions on file, together with the affidavits, if any, show that there is no genuine issue as to any material fact and that the moving party is entitled to a judgment as a matter of law." By its very terms, this standard provides that the mere existence of *some* alleged factual dispute between the parties will not defeat an otherwise properly supported motion for summary judgment; the requirement is that there be no *genuine* issue of *material* fact.

As to materiality, the substantive law will identify which facts are material. Only disputes over facts that might affect the outcome of the suit under the governing law will properly preclude the entry of summary judgment. Factual disputes that are irrelevant or unnecessary will not be counted. This materiality inquiry is independent of and separate from the question of the incorporation of the evidentiary standard into the summary judgment determination. That is, while the materiality determination rests on the substantive law, it is the substantive law's identification of which facts are critical and which facts are irrelevant that governs. Any proof or evidentiary requirements imposed by the substantive law are not germane to this inquiry, since materiality is only a criterion for categorizing factual disputes in their relation to the legal elements of the claim and not a criterion for evaluating the evidentiary underpinnings of those disputes.

More important for present purposes, summary judgment will not lie if the dispute about a material fact is "genuine," that is, if the evidence is such that a reasonable jury could return a verdict for the nonmoving party. * * *

* * *

Our prior decisions may not have uniformly recited the same language in describing genuine factual issues under Rule 56, but it is clear enough from our recent cases that at the summary judgment stage the judge's function is not himself to weigh the evidence and determine the truth of the matter but to determine whether there is a genuine issue for trial. * * * [T]here is no issue for trial unless there is sufficient evidence favoring the nonmoving party for a jury to return a verdict for that party. If the evidence is merely colorable, or is not significantly probative, summary judgment may be granted.

That this is the proper focus of the inquiry is strongly suggested by the Rule itself. Rule 56(e) provides that, when a properly supported motion for summary judgment is made, the adverse

C. Summary Judgment — Adjudication Without Trial or Jury

party "must set forth specific facts showing that there is a genuine issue for trial."[5] And, as we noted above, Rule 56(c) provides that the trial judge shall then grant summary judgment if there is no genuine issue as to any material fact and if the moving party is entitled to judgment as a matter of law. There is no requirement that the trial judge make findings of fact. The inquiry performed is the threshold inquiry of determining whether there is the need for a trial — whether, in other words, there are any genuine factual issues that properly can be resolved only by a finder of fact because they may reasonably be resolved in favor of either party.

Petitioners suggest, and we agree, that this standard mirrors the standard for a directed verdict [now called a "motion for judgment as a mater of law" — EDS.] under Federal Rule of Civil Procedure 50(a), which is that the trial judge must direct a verdict if, under the governing law, there can be but one reasonable conclusion as to the verdict. If reasonable minds could differ as to the import of the evidence, however, a verdict should not be directed. As the Court long ago said, and has several times repeated:

> "Nor are judges any longer required to submit a question to a jury merely because some evidence has been introduced by the party having the burden of proof, unless the evidence be of such a character that it would warrant the jury in finding a verdict in favor of that party. Formerly it was held that if there was what is called a *scintilla* of evidence in support of a case the judge was bound to leave it to the jury, but recent decisions of high authority have established a more reasonable rule, that in every case, before the evidence is left to the jury, there is a preliminary question for the judge, not whether there is literally no evidence, but whether there is any upon which a jury could properly proceed to find a verdict for the party producing it, upon whom the *onus* of proof is imposed."

The Court has said that summary judgment should be granted where the evidence is such that it "would require a directed verdict for the moving party." And we have noted that the "genuine issue" summary judgment standard is "very close" to the "reasonable jury" directed verdict standard: "The primary difference between the two motions is procedural; summary judgment motions are usually made before trial and decided on documentary evidence, while directed verdict motions are made at trial and decided on the evidence that has been admitted." In essence, though, the inquiry under each is the same: whether the evidence presents a sufficient disagreement to require submission to a jury or whether it is so one-sided that one party must prevail as a matter of law.

B

Progressing to the specific issue in this case, we are convinced that the inquiry involved in a ruling on a motion for summary judgment or for a directed verdict necessarily implicates the substantive evidentiary standard of proof that would apply at the trial on the merits. If the defendant in a run-of-the-mill civil case moves for summary judgment or for a directed verdict based on the lack of proof of a material fact, the judge must ask himself not whether he thinks the evidence unmistak-

---

[5] This requirement in turn is qualified by Rule 56(f)'s provision that summary judgment be refused where the nonmoving party has not had the opportunity to discover information that is essential to his opposition. In our analysis here, we assume that both parties have had ample opportunity for discovery.

ably favors one side or the other but whether a fair-minded jury could return a verdict for the plaintiff on the evidence presented. The mere existence of a scintilla of evidence in support of the plaintiff's position will be insufficient; there must be evidence on which the jury could reasonably find for the plaintiff. The judge's inquiry, therefore, unavoidably asks whether reasonable jurors could find by a preponderance of the evidence that the plaintiff is entitled to a verdict — "whether there is [evidence] upon which a jury can properly proceed to find a verdict for the party producing it, upon whom the *onus* of proof is imposed."

* * *

Thus, in ruling on a motion for summary judgment, the judge must view the evidence presented through the prism of the substantive evidentiary burden. This conclusion is mandated by the nature of this determination. The question here is whether a jury could reasonably find *either* that the plaintiff proved his case by the quality and quantity of evidence required by the governing law *or* that he did not. Whether a jury could reasonably find for either party, however, cannot be defined except by the criteria governing what evidence would enable the jury to find for either the plaintiff or the defendant: It makes no sense to say that a jury could reasonably find for either party without some benchmark as to what standards govern its deliberations and within what boundaries its ultimate decision must fall, and these standards and boundaries are in fact provided by the applicable evidentiary standards.

Our holding that the clear-and-convincing standard of proof should be taken into account in ruling on summary judgment motions does not denigrate the role of the jury. It by no means authorizes trial on affidavits. Credibility determinations, the weighing of the evidence, and the drawing of legitimate inferences from the facts are jury functions, not those of a judge, whether he is ruling on a motion for summary judgment or for a directed verdict. The evidence of the nonmovant is to be believed, and all justifiable inferences are to be drawn in his favor. Neither do we suggest that the trial courts should act other than with caution in granting summary judgment or that the trial court may not deny summary judgment in a case where there is reason to believe that the better course would be to proceed to a full trial.

In sum, we conclude that the determination of whether a given factual dispute requires submission to a jury must be guided by the substantive evidentiary standards that apply to the case. This is true at both the directed verdict and summary judgment stages. Consequently, where the *New York Times* "clear and convincing" evidence requirement applies, the trial judge's summary judgment inquiry as to whether a genuine issue exists will be whether the evidence presented is such that a jury applying that evidentiary standard could reasonably find for either the plaintiff or the defendant. Thus, where the factual dispute concerns actual malice, clearly a material issue in a *New York Times* case, the appropriate summary judgment question will be whether the evidence in the record could support a reasonable jury finding either that the plaintiff has shown actual malice by clear and convincing evidence or that the plaintiff has not.

III

Respondents argue, however, that whatever may be true of the applicability of the "clear and convincing" standard at the summary judgment or directed verdict stage, the defendant should seldom if ever be granted summary judgment where his state of mind is at issue and the jury might disbelieve him or his witnesses as to this issue. They rely on Poller v. Columbia Broadcasting Co., 368 U.S. 464 (1962), for this proposition. We do not understand *Poller*, however, to hold that a plaintiff may defeat a defendant's properly supported motion for summary judgment in a conspiracy or libel case, for example, without offering any concrete evidence from which a reasonable juror could return a verdict in his favor and by merely asserting that the jury might, and legally could, disbelieve the defendant's denial of a conspiracy or of legal malice. The movant has the burden of showing that there is no genuine issue of fact, but the plaintiff is not thereby relieved of his own burden of producing in turn evidence that would support a jury verdict. Rule 56(e) itself provides that a party opposing a properly supported motion for summary judgment may not rest upon mere allegation or denials of his pleading, but must set forth specific facts showing that there is a genuine issue for trial. * * * As we have recently said, "discredited testimony is not [normally] considered a sufficient basis for drawing a contrary conclusion." Instead, the plaintiff must present affirmative evidence in order to defeat a properly supported motion for summary judgment. This is true even where the evidence is likely to be within the possession of the defendant, as long as the plaintiff has had a full opportunity to conduct discovery. We repeat, however, that the plaintiff, to survive the defendant's motion, need only present evidence from which a jury might return a verdict in his favor. If he does so, there is a genuine issue of fact that requires a trial.

IV

In sum, a court ruling on a motion for summary judgment must be guided by the *New York Times* "clear and convincing" evidentiary standard in determining whether a genuine issue of actual malice exists — that is, whether the evidence presented is such that a reasonable jury might find that actual malice had been shown with convincing clarity. Because the Court of Appeals did not apply the correct standard in reviewing the District Court's grant of summary judgment, we vacate its decision and remand the case for further proceedings consistent with this opinion.

It is so ordered.

JUSTICE BRENNAN, dissenting.

The Court today holds that "whether a given factual dispute requires submission to a jury must be guided by the substantive evidentiary standards that apply to the case." In my view, the Court's analysis is deeply flawed, and rests on a shaky foundation of unconnected and unsupported observations, assertions, and conclusions. Moreover, I am unable to divine from the Court's opinion *how* these evidentiary standards are to be considered, or what a trial judge is actually supposed to do in ruling on a motion for summary judgment. Accordingly, I respectfully dissent.

* * *

But my concern is not only that the Court's decision is unsupported; after all, unsupported views may nonetheless be supportable. I am more troubled by the fact that the Court's opinion sends conflicting signals to trial courts and reviewing courts which must deal with summary judgment motions on a day-to-day basis. This case is about a trial court's responsibility when considering a motion for summary judgment, but in my view, the Court, while instructing the trial judge to "consider" heightened evidentiary standards, fails to explain what that means. In other words, how does a judge assess how one-sided evidence is, or what a "fair-minded" jury could "reasonably" decide? The Court provides conflicting clues to these mysteries, which I fear can lead only to increased confusion in the district and appellate courts.

The Court's opinion is replete with boiler plate language to the effect that trial courts are not to weigh evidence when deciding summary judgment motions:

> "[I]t is clear enough from our recent cases that at the summary judgment stage the judge's function is not himself to weigh the evidence and determine the truth of the matter ...."

> "Our holding ... does not denigrate the role of the jury.... Credibility determinations, the weighing of the evidence, and the drawing of legitimate inferences from the facts are jury functions, not those of a judge, whether he is ruling on a motion for summary judgment or for a directed verdict. The evidence of the nonmovant is to be believed, and all justifiable inferences are to be drawn in his favor."

But the Court's opinion is also full of language which could surely be understood as an invitation — if not an instruction — to trial courts to assess and weigh evidence much as a juror would:

> "When determining if a genuine factual issue ... exists ... , a trial judge must *bear in mind the actual quantum and quality* of proof necessary to support liability .... For example, *there is no genuine issue if the evidence presented in the opposing affidavits is of insufficient caliber or quantity* to allow a rational finder of fact to find actual malice by clear and convincing evidence."

> "[T]he inquiry ... [is] whether the evidence presents a *sufficient* disagreement to require submission to a jury or whether *it is so one-sided* that one party must prevail as a matter of law."

> "[T]he judge must ask himself ... whether a fair-minded jury could return a verdict for the plaintiff on the evidence presented. The mere existence of a scintilla of evidence in support of the plaintiff's position will be insufficient; there must be evidence on which the jury could reasonably find for the plaintiff."

I simply cannot square the direction that the judge "is not himself to weigh the evidence" with the direction that the judge also bear in mind the "quantum" of proof required and consider whether the evidence is of sufficient "caliber or quantity" to meet that "quantum." I would have thought that a determination of the "caliber and quantity," i.e., the importance and value, of the evidence in light of the "quantum," i.e., amount "required," could *only* be performed by weighing the evidence.

If in fact, this is what the Court would, under today's decision, require of district courts, then I am fearful that this new rule — for this surely would be a brand new procedure — will transform what is meant to provide an expedited "summary" procedure into a full-blown paper trial on the merits. It is hard for me to imagine that a responsible counsel, aware that the judge will be assessing the "quantum" of the evidence he is presenting, will risk either moving for or responding to a summary judgment motion without coming forth with *all* of the evidence he can muster in support of his client's case. Moreover, if the judge on motion for summary judgment really is to weigh the evidence, then in my view grave concerns are raised concerning the constitutional right of civil litigants to a jury trial.

It may well be, as Justice Rehnquist suggests, that the Court's decision today will be of little practical effect. I, for one, cannot imagine a case in which a judge might plausibly hold that the evidence on motion for summary judgment was sufficient to enable a plaintiff bearing a mere preponderance burden to get to the jury — i.e., that a prima facie case had been made out — but insufficient for a plaintiff bearing a clear-and-convincing burden to withstand a defendant's summary judgment motion. Imagine a suit for breach of contract. If, for example, the defendant moves for summary judgment and produces one purported eyewitness who states that he was present at the time the parties discussed the possibility of an agreement, and unequivocally denies that the parties ever agreed to enter into a contract, while the plaintiff produces one purported eyewitness who asserts that the parties did in fact come to terms, presumably that case would go to the jury. But if the defendant produced not one, but 100 eyewitnesses, while the plaintiff stuck with his single witness, would that case, under the Court's holding, still go to the jury? After all, although the plaintiff's burden in this hypothetical contract action is to prove his case by a mere preponderance of the evidence, the judge, so the Court tells us, is to "ask himself ... whether a fair-minded jury could return a verdict for the plaintiff on the evidence presented." Is there, in this hypothetical example, "a sufficient disagreement to require submission to a jury," or is the evidence "so one-sided that one party must prevail as a matter of law?" Would the result change if the plaintiff's one witness were now shown to be a convicted perjurer? Would the result change if, instead of a garden-variety contract claim, the plaintiff sued on a fraud theory, thus requiring him to prove his case by clear and convincing evidence?

It seems to me that the Court's decision today unpersuasively answers the question presented, and in doing so raises a host of difficult and troubling questions for which there may well be no adequate solutions. What is particularly unfair is that the mess we make is not, at least in the first instance, our own to deal with; it is the district courts and courts of appeals that must struggle to clean up after us.

In my view, if a plaintiff presents evidence which either directly or by permissible inference (and these inferences are a product of the substantive law of the underlying claim) supports all of the elements he needs to prove in order to prevail on his legal claim, the plaintiff has made out a prima facie case and a defendant's motion for summary judgment must fail regardless of the burden of proof that the plaintiff must meet. In other words, whether evidence is "clear and convincing," or proves a point by a mere preponderance, is for the factfinder to determine. As I read the case law, this is how it has been, and because of my concern that today's decision may erode the constitutionally enshrined role of the jury, and also undermine the usefulness of summary judgment procedure, this is how I believe it should remain.

JUSTICE REHNQUIST, with whom THE CHIEF JUSTICE joins, dissenting.

CHAPTER 10 ADJUDICATION WITH AND WITHOUT A TRIAL OR A JURY

* * *

There is a large class of cases in which the higher standard imposed by the Court today would seem to have no effect at all. Suppose, for example, on motion for summary judgment in a hypothetical libel case, the plaintiff concedes that his only proof of malice is the testimony of witness A. Witness A testifies at his deposition that the reporter who wrote the story in question told him that she, the reporter, had done absolutely no checking on the story and had real doubts about whether or not it was correct as to the plaintiff. The defendant's examination of witness A brings out that he has a prior conviction for perjury.

May the Court grant the defendant's motion for summary judgment on the ground that the plaintiff has failed to produce sufficient proof of malice? Surely not, if the Court means what it says, when it states: "Credibility determinations ... are jury functions, not those of a judge, whether he is ruling on a motion for summary judgment or for a directed verdict. The evidence of the nonmovant is to be believed, and all justifiable inferences are to be drawn in his favor."

The case proceeds to trial, and at the close of the plaintiff's evidence the defendant moves for a directed verdict on the ground that the plaintiff has failed to produce sufficient evidence of malice. The only evidence of malice produced by the plaintiff is the same testimony of witness A, who is duly impeached by the defendant for the prior perjury conviction. In addition, the trial judge has now had an opportunity to observe the demeanor of witness A, and has noticed that he fidgets when answering critical questions, his eyes shift from the floor to the ceiling, and he manifests all other indicia traditionally attributed to perjurers.

May the trial court at this stage grant a directed verdict? Again, surely not; we are still dealing with "credibility determinations."

The defendant now puts on its testimony, and produces three witnesses who were present at the time when witness A alleges that the reporter said she had not checked the story and had grave doubts about its accuracy as to plaintiff. Witness A concedes that these three people were present at the meeting, and that the statement of the reporter took place in the presence of all these witnesses. Each witness categorically denies that the reporter made the claimed statement to witness A.

May the trial court now grant a directed verdict at the close of all the evidence? Certainly the plaintiff's case is appreciably weakened by the testimony of three disinterested witnesses, and one would hope that a properly charged jury would quickly return a verdict for the defendant. But as long as credibility is exclusively for the jury, it seems the Court's analysis would still require this case to be decided by that body.

Thus, in the case that I have posed, it would seem to make no difference whether the standard of proof which the plaintiff had to meet in order to prevail was the preponderance of the evidence, clear and convincing evidence, or proof beyond a reasonable doubt. But if the application of the standards makes no difference in the case that I hypothesize, one may fairly ask in what sort of case *does* the difference in standards make a difference in outcome? Cases may be posed dealing with evidence that is essentially documentary, rather than testimonial; but the Court has held in a related context involving Federal Rule of Civil Procedure 52(a) that inferences from documentary evidence are as much the prerogative of the finder of fact as inferences as to the credibility of witnesses. The Court affords the lower courts no guidance whatsoever as to what, if any, difference the abstract standards that it propounds would make in a particular case.

C. Summary Judgment — Adjudication Without Trial or Jury

* * *

The three differentiated burdens of proof in civil and criminal cases, vague and impressionistic though they necessarily are, probably do make some difference when considered by the finder of fact, whether it be a jury or a judge in a bench trial. Yet it is not a logical or analytical message that the terms convey, but instead almost a state of mind; we have previously said:

> "Candor suggests that, to a degree, efforts to analyze what lay jurors understand concerning the differences among these three tests ... may well be largely an academic exercise.... Indeed, the ultimate truth as to how the standards of proof affect decision making may well be *unknowable*, given that factfinding is a process shared by countless thousands of individuals throughout the country. We probably can assume no more than that the difference between a preponderance of the evidence and proof beyond a reasonable doubt probably is better understood than either of them in relation to the intermediate standard of clear and convincing evidence."

The Court's decision to engraft the standard of proof applicable to a factfinder onto the law governing the procedural motion for a summary judgment (a motion that has always been regarded as raising a question of law rather than a question of fact), will do great mischief with little corresponding benefit. The primary effect of the Court's opinion today will likely be to cause the decisions of trial judges on summary judgment motions in libel cases to be more erratic and inconsistent than before. This is largely because the Court has created a standard that is different from the standard traditionally applied in summary judgment motions without even hinting as to how its new standard will be applied to particular cases.

NOTES AND QUESTIONS

1. In analyzing summary judgment, you should distinguish between burden of production and burden of persuasion (sometimes called burden of proof). Burden of production refers to the obligation of one side to come forward with evidence to support its claim. Burden of persuasion refers to the degree of certainty the fact finder must have before it can find for one side. There are different standards for the degree of certainty the fact finder must have in order to find for the party with the burden of persuasion. In most civil cases the standard is "preponderance of the evidence." The standard means that the fact finder must believe that the claimant's version of events is more probable than not. As a result, if the factfinder concludes that the evidence is evenly balanced, the party with the burden of persuasion must lose. In criminal cases, the government has the burden of proof and must meet a much higher standard of "beyond a reasonable doubts." In a few civil cases the standard is "clear and convincing evidence" which is generally understood to be somewhere between the preponderance and beyond a reasonable doubt standards.

The burdens of production and persuasion usually follow the burden of pleading. Thus, as to elements of a claim, the plaintiff shoulders these burdens, but as to affirmative defense such as those listed in Rule 8(c), the defendant must produce evidence and prove the defense. For example, if contributory negligence is a defense and no evidence is introduced on the question of plaintiff's negligence, the defense fails — plaintiff does not have to produce evidence of her freedom from negligence.

These concepts can be illustrated as follows:

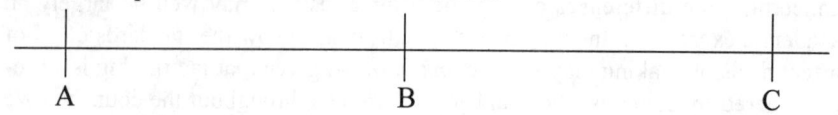

```
|───────────────|───────────────────────────|
A               B                           C
```

The line at A marks the burden of production. The plaintiff must introduce enough evidence to get past line A or the court will grant summary judgment for the defendant. If the evidence is to the right of line C, then the court will enter summary judgment for the plaintiff. If the evidence falls between A and C, then the issue is one for the jury. Line B marks the burden of persuasion. It is up to the factfinder to determine whether the evidence falls to the right or left of that line. In addition, if the factfinder concludes that the evidence falls *on* the line, the burden acts as the tiebreaker the person with the burden on that issue loses. For example, in a slander case, suppose the jury concludes that it is just as likely as it is not that the injurious statement was true. If the plaintiff had the burden of showing falsity, she loses. If, on the other hand, defendant had the burden of showing truth, then she loses.

The majority opinion in *Anderson* suggests that where the burden of persuasion line (B) moves to a higher standard, the burden of production line should also move. Thus if B moves to B', then A should move to A'.

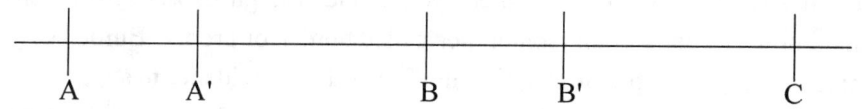

```
|──────|────────|──────|──────────|
A      A'       B      B'         C
```

2. Justice Brennan argues that a court cannot determine whether the evidence is to the right of line A', without weighing the evidence. Do you agree? If you do not think it is appropriate for courts (as opposed to juries) to weigh the evidence, when should summary judgment be granted? Does Justice Brennan appear to believe that a court can determine that the evidence is to the right of line A without weighing the evidence?

3. Dean Friedenthal has argued that summary judgment "rests on the often unarticulated determination that decisions concerning the sufficiency of evidence to get to a trier of fact, even when based on human judgment, are of a different quality than decisions

C. Summary Judgment — Adjudication Without Trial or Jury

by the trier of fact on evidence that it receives, and that the former falls outside the scope of the right to trial by jury." Jack Friedenthal, *Cases on Summary Judgment: Has There Been a Material Change in Standards?* 63 NOTRE DAME L. REV. 770, 783 (1988). Do you agree? Do you think there is a fundamental difference between the two types of determinations he describes?

4. Suppose there is an auto accident at an intersection. The plaintiff's theory is that the defendant ran the red light. Would summary judgment be appropriate in the following cases? Would your answer change depending on whether the burden of persuasion is "preponderance of the evidence" or "clear and convincing?"

(a) Defendant moves for summary judgment and submits the affidavit of a witness who says the light was green. Plaintiff responds by pointing to her complaint which alleges the light was red.

(b) Defendant moves for summary judgment and submits the affidavit of a witness who says the light was green. Plaintiff responds with an affidavit of a witness who says the light was red.

(c) Same as (b), but defendant submits affidavits of 15 witnesses who say the light was green.

(d) Defendant moves for summary judgment and submits the affidavit of one witness who said the light was green. Plaintiff responds with the affidavit of a witness who says she did not see the light, but she saw that cars in the other line of traffic that were going in the same direction as defendant's car (and were controlled by the same traffic light) had stopped.

(e) Defendant moves for summary judgment and submits a videotape taken by a bystander which shows that the light was green. Plaintiff responds with the affidavit of a witness who says the light was red.

(f) Plaintiff moves for summary judgment and submits the affidavit of a witness who says the light was red. Defendant offers no evidence in response.

5. In *Anderson*, the Court did not decide whether summary judgment was appropriate. It held only that the court of appeals applied the wrong standard and therefore reversed and remanded. What should happen on remand? With respect to one of the allegedly defamatory statements, the plaintiff offered evidence that the defendants were aware of a previously published Washington Post article which contradicted the defendants' statement. Is this sufficient to create a jury question on malice? On remand, the district court held that this was not sufficient, reasoning that "defendants' knowledge of the existence of a contradictory source, without more, does not constitute clear and convincing evidence of actual malice." Liberty Lobby, Inc. v. Anderson, 1990 U.S. Dist. LEXIS 19587 (D. D.C. 1990). Do you agree? Could a reasonable jury find that this was constituted clear

CHAPTER 10 ADJUDICATION WITH AND WITHOUT A TRIAL OR A JURY

and convincing evidence? Could a reasonable jury find that this evidence proved malice under a preponderance of the evidence test?

6. In Matsushita Elec. Indus. Co. v. Zenith Radio, 475 U.S. 574 (1986), the Court upheld a grant of summary judgment in an antitrust case. American television manufacturers alleged that Japanese manufacturers conspired to maintain low prices for Japanese televisions sold in the United States. The Court concluded that the scheme alleged by plaintiffs would have been economically irrational. It then observed, "if the factual context renders respondents' claim implausible — if the claim is one that simply makes no economic sense — respondents must come forward with more persuasive evidence to support their claim than would otherwise be necessary." Id. at 587. Should the same be true when a plaintiff alleges other types of "irrational" behavior? Should the court leave it to a jury to determine whether the alleged conduct is irrational or otherwise implausible?

7. In *J.E.B.*, supra at 495, the plaintiff had scientific evidence establishing with 99.92% certainty that the defendant was the father. The defendant contended that he was not with the child's mother at the time of conception and, in addition, was impotent. If the plaintiff had moved for summary judgment, should it have been granted?

Suppose the facts were reversed: the scientific evidence established with 99.92% certainty that the defendant was *not* the father. The mother's affidavit stated that she had sexual relations with the defendant at the time of conception. Should summary judgment be granted for the defendant? Does your answer depend on whether the mother states that the defendant was the only man with whom she had relations? In Simblest v. Maynard, 427 F. 2d 1, 6 (2d Cir. 1970), the court held that "[p]laintiff's testimony * * * in the teeth of the proven physical facts * * * is tantamount to no proof at all on that issue." Could the same be said of the *J.E.B.* hypothetical?

8. Consider the following case. Plaintiff is 64 1/2 years old and is fired two months before her pension would have vested. Under the Age Discrimination in Employment act, it is impermissible to fire someone because of her age or to deprive her of her pension. The defendant moves for summary judgment and submits an affidavit of the plaintiff's boss. In her affidavit the boss denies that the firing was motivated by age or the pension. The boss describes her own conduct as sometimes random and capricious and asserts that the firing of the plaintiff was for no reason. Is evidence that the plaintiff was two months away from receiving her pension sufficient to defeat the motion for summary judgment? If you represented the plaintiff what other evidence might you submit? See Visser v. Packer Engineering Assoc., 924 F. 2d 655 (7th Cir. 1991) (en banc).

9. Although unusual, it is possible for a court to enter summary just for the party with the burden of proof. (Do you see why it is unusual?) In American Airlines v. Ulen, 186 F. 2d 529 (D.C. Cir. 1949), the plaintiff sued for injuries sustained when the airplane in

which he was a passenger crashed into a mountain. Federal Aviation Administration regulations require air carriers to fly at 1000 feet above "the highest obstacle located with a horizontal distance of 5 miles from the center of the course." The filed flight plan called for the plane to fly at 4,000 feet on a course that took it within 1.5 miles of a mountain 4,080 feet high. The court granted the plaintiff's motion for judgment on the question of defendant's negligence.

10. In *Anderson*, the Court says that the test for summary judgment is whether a reasonable jury could find for the non-moving party. However, at the summary judgment stage, the court does not have before it all the evidence that would be used at trial. Instead it has only a few selected pieces offered by counsel. Does it make sense to frame a test for summary judgment in terms of what a reasonable jury would do where the court does not yet have before it all the evidence a jury would have?

11. Suppose in *Anderson* that the district court had denied summary judgment and that the plaintiff had won at trial. Could the defendant appeal the trial verdict on the ground that the court erred in denying summary judgment? Most courts have held that the denial of summary judgment cannot be appealed in these circumstances. See, e.g., Black v. J. I. Case Co., 22 F. 3d 568 (5th Cir.), *cert. denied*, 115 S. Ct. 579 (1994).

12. Most discussions of summary judgment assume that the finder of fact would be a jury (if the case were to go to trial). However, Rule 56 does not differentiate between cases that would go to trial before a jury and those that would be tried before a judge. Judge Schwarzer has suggested that the test for determining whether summary judgment is proper should be somewhat different when the court would be the trier of fact. He argues that in this context the proper question is "What does a trial add to the judge's ability to decide the issue submitted on motion?" Schwarzer, supra, 99 F.R.D. at 476. He explains:

> The point here is not that the provisions of Rule 56 should be ignored in nonjury cases. Rather it is that in the absence of a genuine need to assess testimonial credibility or demeanor, the decision of issues which would otherwise go to the jury may be made on motion for summary judgment when trial is to the court. In such cases it is not enough to classify an issue as one of "law" or "fact" or "ultimate fact" as those terms are conventionally understood; the court must determine whether a trial of the issue would serve any purpose, if it would not, then the issue is one of law *for purposes of Rule 56*, even if it is a fact issue for other purposes, including Rule 56 purposes in *jury* cases.

Id. at 479-80 (emphasis in original). Does it make sense to apply a different test for summary judgment depending on whether the trier of fact is a judge or a jury?

13. In *Anderson*, as in *Dyer*, the moving party came forward with affirmative evidence that contradicted the plaintiff's allegation. Suppose, however, that instead of offering affirmative evidence, the defendant simply asserts that the plaintiff lacks sufficient evidence to prove her claim. In essence, the defendant simply challenges the plaintiff to "put up or shut up." Under these circumstances, must the plaintiff produce some evidence to avoid summary judgment?

Celotex Corp. v. Catrett
477 U.S. 317, 106 S. Ct. 2548, 91 L. Ed. 2d 265 (1986)

JUSTICE REHNQUIST delivered the opinion of the Court.

* * *

Respondent commenced this lawsuit in September 1980, alleging that the death in 1979 of her husband, Louis H. Catrett, resulted from his exposure to products containing asbestos manufactured or distributed by 15 named corporations. Respondent's complaint sounded in negligence, breach of warranty, and strict liability. Two of the defendants filed motions challenging the District Court's in personam jurisdiction, and the remaining 13, including petitioner, filed motions for summary judgment. Petitioner's motion, which was first filed in September 1981, argued that summary judgment was proper because respondent had "failed to produce evidence that any[Celotex] product ... was the proximate cause of the injuries alleged within the jurisdictional limits of [the District] Court." In particular, petitioner noted that respondent had failed to identify, in answering interrogatories specifically requesting such information, any witnesses who could testify about the decedent's exposure to petitioner's asbestos products. In response to petitioner's summary judgment motion, respondent then produced three documents which she claimed "demonstrate that there is a genuine material factual dispute" as to whether the decedent had ever been exposed to petitioner's asbestos products. The three documents included a transcript of a deposition of the decedent, a letter from an official of one of the decedent's former employers whom petitioner planned to call as a trial witness, and a letter from an insurance company to respondent's attorney, all tending to establish that the decedent had been exposed to petitioner's asbestos products in Chicago during 1970-1971. Petitioner, in turn, argued that the three documents were inadmissible hearsay and thus could not be considered in opposition to the summary judgment motion.

In July 1982, almost two years after the commencement of the lawsuit, the District Court granted all of the motions filed by the various defendants. The court explained that it was granting petitioner's summary judgment motion because "there [was] no showing that the plaintiff was exposed to the defendant Celotex's product in the District of Columbia or elsewhere within the statutory period."[2] Respondent appealed only the grant of summary judgment in favor of petitioner, and

---

[2] Justice Stevens, in dissent, argues that the District Court granted summary judgment only because respondent presented no evidence that the decedent was exposed to Celotex asbestos products *in the District of Columbia*. According to Justice Stevens, we should affirm the decision of the Court of Appeals, reversing the District Court, on the "narrower ground" that respondent "made an adequate showing" that the decedent was exposed to Celotex asbestos products in Chicago during 1970-1971.

C. Summary Judgment — Adjudication Without Trial or Jury

a divided panel of the District of Columbia Circuit reversed. The majority of the Court of Appeals held that petitioner's summary judgment motion was rendered "fatally defective" by the fact that petitioner "made no effort to adduce *any* evidence, in the form of affidavits or otherwise, to support its motion." According to the majority, Rule 56(e) of the Federal Rules of Civil Procedure, and this Court's decision in Adickes v. S.H. Kress & Co., 398 U.S. 144, 159 (1970), establish that "the party opposing the motion for summary judgment bears the burden of responding *only after* the moving party has met its burden of coming forward with proof of the absence of any genuine issues of material fact." The majority therefore declined to consider petitioner's argument that none of the evidence produced by respondent in opposition to the motion for summary judgment would have been admissible at trial. * * *

We think that the position taken by the majority of the Court of Appeals is inconsistent with the standard for summary judgment set forth in Rule 56(c) of the Federal Rules of Civil Procedure. Under Rule 56(c), summary judgment is proper "if the pleadings, depositions, answers to interrogatories, and admissions on file, together with the affidavits, if any, show that there is no genuine issue as to any material fact and that the moving party is entitled to a judgment as a matter of law." In our view, the plain language of Rule 56(c) mandates the entry of summary judgment, after adequate time for discovery and upon motion, against a party who fails to make a showing sufficient to establish the existence of an element essential to that party's case, and on which that party will bear the burden of proof at trial. * * *

Of course, a party seeking summary judgment always bears the initial responsibility of informing the district court of the basis for its motion, and identifying those portions of "the pleadings, depositions, answers to interrogatories, and admissions on file, together with the affidavits, if any," which it believes demonstrate the absence of a genuine issue of material fact. But unlike the Court of Appeals, we find no express or implied requirement in Rule 56 that the moving party support its motion with affidavits or other similar materials *negating* the opponent's claim. On the contrary, Rule 56(c), which refers to "the affidavits, *if any*" (emphasis added), suggests the absence of such a requirement. And if there were any doubt about the meaning of Rule 56(c) in this regard, such doubt is clearly removed by Rules 56(a) and (b), which provide that claimants and defendants, respectively, may move for summary judgment "*with or without supporting affidavits*" (emphasis added). The import of these subsections is that, regardless of whether the moving party accompanies its summary judgment motion with affidavits, the motion may, and should, be granted so long as whatever is before the district court demonstrates that the standard for the entry of summary judgment, as set forth in Rule 56(c), is satisfied. One of the principal purposes of the summary judgment rule is to isolate and dispose of factually unsupported claims or defenses, and we think it should be interpreted in a way that allows it to accomplish this purpose.

Respondent argues, however, that Rule 56(e), by its terms, places on the nonmoving party the burden of coming forward with rebuttal affidavits, or other specified kinds of materials, only in response to a motion for summary judgment "made and supported as provided in this rule." According to respondent's argument, since petitioner did not "support" its motion with affidavits, summary judgment was improper in this case. But as we have already explained, a motion for summary judgment may be made pursuant to Rule 56 "with or without supporting affidavits." In cases like the

---

Justice Stevens' position is factually incorrect. The District Court expressly stated that respondent had made no showing of exposure to Celotex asbestos products "in the District of Columbia or *elsewhere*." Unlike Justice Stevens, we assume that the District Court meant what it said. * * *

instant one, where the nonmoving party will bear the burden of proof at trial on a dispositive issue, a summary judgment motion may properly be made in reliance solely on the "pleadings, depositions, answers to interrogatories, and admissions on file." Such a motion, whether or not accompanied by affidavits, will be "made and supported as provided in this rule," and Rule 56(e) therefore requires the nonmoving party to go beyond the pleadings and by her own affidavits, or by the "depositions, answers to interrogatories, and admissions on file," designate "specific facts showing that there is a genuine issue for trial."

We do not mean that the nonmoving party must produce evidence in a form that would be admissible at trial in order to avoid summary judgment. Obviously, Rule 56 does not require the nonmoving party to depose her own witnesses. Rule 56(e) permits a proper summary judgment motion to be opposed by any of the kinds of evidentiary materials listed in Rule 56(c), except the mere pleadings themselves, and it is from this list that one would normally expect the nonmoving party to make the showing to which we have referred.

The Court of Appeals in this case felt itself constrained, however, by language in our decision in Adickes v. S.H. Kress & Co., 398 U.S. 144 (1970). There we held that summary judgment had been improperly entered in favor of the defendant restaurant in an action brought under 42 U.S.C. § 1983. In the course of its opinion, the *Adickes* Court said that "both the commentary on and the background of the 1963 amendment conclusively show that it was not intended to modify the burden of the moving party ... to show initially the absence of a genuine issue concerning any material fact." We think that this statement is accurate in a literal sense, since we fully agree with the *Adickes* Court that the 1963 amendment to Rule 56(e) was not designed to modify the burden of making the showing generally required by Rule 56(c). It also appears to us that, on the basis of the showing before the Court in *Adickes*, the motion for summary judgment in that case should have been denied. But we do not think the *Adickes* language quoted above should be construed to mean that the burden is on the party moving for summary judgment to produce evidence showing the absence of a genuine issue of material fact, even with respect to an issue on which the nonmoving party bears the burden of proof. Instead, as we have explained, the burden on the moving party may be discharged by "showing" — that is, pointing out to the district court — that there is an absence of evidence to support the nonmoving party's case.

The last two sentences of Rule 56(e) were added, as this Court indicated in *Adickes*, to disapprove a line of cases allowing a party opposing summary judgment to resist a properly made motion by reference only to its pleadings. While the *Adickes* Court was undoubtedly correct in concluding that these two sentences were not intended to *reduce* the burden of the moving party, it is also obvious that they were not adopted to *add to* that burden. Yet that is exactly the result which the reasoning of the Court of Appeals would produce; in effect, an amendment to Rule 56(e) designed to *facilitate* the granting of motions for summary judgment would be interpreted to make it *more difficult* to grant such motions. Nothing in the two sentences themselves requires this result, for the reasons we have previously indicated, and we now put to rest any inference that they do so.

Our conclusion is bolstered by the fact that district courts are widely acknowledged to possess the power to enter summary judgments sua sponte, so long as the losing party was on notice that she had to come forward with all of her evidence. It would surely defy common sense to hold that the District Court could have entered summary judgment sua sponte in favor of petitioner in the instant case, but that petitioner's filing of a motion requesting such a disposition precluded the District Court from ordering it.

C. Summary Judgment — Adjudication Without Trial or Jury

Respondent commenced this action in September 1980, and petitioner's motion was filed in September 1981. The parties had conducted discovery, and no serious claim can be made that respondent was in any sense "railroaded" by a premature motion for summary judgment. Any potential problem with such premature motions can be adequately dealt with under Rule 56(f), which allows a summary judgment motion to be denied, or the hearing on the motion to be continued, if the nonmoving party has not had an opportunity to make full discovery.

In this Court, respondent's brief and oral argument have been devoted as much to the proposition that an adequate showing of exposure to petitioner's asbestos products was made as to the proposition that no such showing should have been required. But the Court of Appeals declined to address either the adequacy of the showing made by respondent in opposition to petitioner's motion for summary judgment, or the question whether such a showing, if reduced to admissible evidence, would be sufficient to carry respondent's burden of proof at trial. We think the Court of Appeals with its superior knowledge of local law is better suited than we are to make these determinations in the first instance.

The Federal Rules of Civil Procedure have for almost 50 years authorized motions for summary judgment upon proper showings of the lack of a genuine, triable issue of material fact. Summary judgment procedure is properly regarded not as a disfavored procedural shortcut, but rather as an integral part of the Federal Rules as a whole, which are designed "to secure the just, speedy and inexpensive determination of every action." Fed. Rule Civ. Proc. 1. Before the shift to "notice pleading" accomplished by the Federal Rules, motions to dismiss a complaint or to strike a defense were the principal tools by which factually insufficient claims or defenses could be isolated and prevented from going to trial with the attendant unwarranted consumption of public and private resources. But with the advent of "notice pleading," the motion to dismiss seldom fulfills this function any more, and its place has been taken by the motion for summary judgment. Rule 56 must be construed with due regard not only for the rights of persons asserting claims and defenses that are adequately based in fact to have those claims and defenses tried to a jury, but also for the rights of persons opposing such claims and defenses to demonstrate in the manner provided by the Rule, prior to trial, that the claims and defenses have no factual basis.

The judgment of the Court of Appeals is accordingly reversed, and the case is remanded for further proceedings consistent with this opinion.

It is so ordered.

JUSTICE WHITE, concurring.

I agree that the Court of Appeals was wrong in holding that the moving defendant must always support his motion with evidence or affidavits showing the absence of a genuine dispute about a material fact. I also agree that the movant may rely on depositions, answers to interrogatories, and the like, to demonstrate that the plaintiff has no evidence to prove his case and hence that there can be no factual dispute. But the movant must discharge the burden the Rules place upon him: It is not enough to move for summary judgment without supporting the motion in any way or with a conclusory assertion that the plaintiff has no evidence to prove his case.

A plaintiff need not initiate any discovery or reveal his witnesses or evidence unless required to do so under the discovery Rules or by court order. Of course, he must respond if required to do so; but he need not also depose his witnesses or obtain their affidavits to defeat a summary judgment motion asserting only that he has failed to produce any support for his case. It is the defendant's task to negate, if he can, the claimed basis for the suit.

Petitioner Celotex does not dispute that if respondent has named a witness to support her claim, summary judgment should not be granted without Celotex somehow showing that the named witness' possible testimony raises no genuine issue of material fact. It asserts, however, that respondent has failed on request to produce any basis for her case. Respondent, on the other hand, does not contend that she was not obligated to reveal her witnesses and evidence but insists that she has revealed enough to defeat the motion for summary judgment. Because the Court of Appeals found it unnecessary to address this aspect of the case, I agree that the case should be remanded for further proceedings.

JUSTICE BRENNAN, with whom THE CHIEF JUSTICE and JUSTICE BLACKMUN join, dissenting.

This case requires the Court to determine whether Celotex satisfied its initial burden of production in moving for summary judgment on the ground that the plaintiff lacked evidence to establish an essential element of her case at trial. I do not disagree with the Court's legal analysis. The Court clearly rejects the ruling of the Court of Appeals that the defendant must provide affirmative evidence disproving the plaintiff's case. Beyond this, however, the Court has not clearly explained what is required of a moving party seeking summary judgment on the ground that the nonmoving party cannot prove its case.[1] This lack of clarity is unfortunate: district courts must routinely decide summary judgment motions, and the Court's opinion will very likely create confusion. For this reason, even if I agreed with the Court's result, I would have written separately to explain more clearly the law in this area. However, because I believe that Celotex did not meet its burden of production under Federal Rule of Civil Procedure 56, I respectfully dissent from the Court's judgment.

* * * The burden of establishing the nonexistence of a "genuine issue" is on the party moving for summary judgment. This burden has two distinct components: an initial burden of production, which shifts to the nonmoving party if satisfied by the moving party; and an ultimate burden of persuasion, which always remains on the moving party. The court need not decide whether the moving party has satisfied its ultimate burden of persuasion unless and until the court finds that the moving party has discharged its initial burden of production.

The burden of production imposed by Rule 56 requires the moving party to make a prima facie showing that it is entitled to summary judgment. The manner in which this showing can be made depends upon which party will bear the burden of persuasion on the challenged claim at trial. If the *moving* party will bear the burden of persuasion at trial, that party must support its motion with credible evidence — using any of the materials specified in Rule 56(c) — that would entitle it to a

---

[1] It is also unclear what the Court of Appeals is supposed to do in this case on remand. Justice White— who has provided the Court's fifth vote — plainly believes that the Court of Appeals should reevaluate whether the defendant met its initial burden of production. However, the decision to reverse rather than to vacate the judgment below implies that the Court of Appeals should assume that Celotex has met its initial burden of production and ask only whether the plaintiff responded adequately, and, if so, whether the defendant has met its ultimate burden of persuasion that no genuine issue exists for trial. Absent some clearer expression from the Court to the contrary, Justice White's understanding would seem to be controlling. Cf. Marks v. United States, 430 U.S. 188, 193 (1977).

C. Summary Judgment — Adjudication Without Trial or Jury

directed verdict if not controverted at trial. Such an affirmative showing shifts the burden of production to the party opposing the motion and requires that party either to produce evidentiary materials that demonstrate the existence of a "genuine issue" for trial or to submit an affidavit requesting additional time for discovery.

If the burden of persuasion at trial would be on the *nonmoving* party, the party moving for summary judgment may satisfy Rule 56's burden of production in either of two ways. First, the moving party may submit affirmative evidence that negates an essential element of the nonmoving party's claim. Second, the moving party may demonstrate to the court that the nonmoving party's evidence is insufficient to establish an essential element of the nonmoving party's claim. If the nonmoving party cannot muster sufficient evidence to make out its claim, a trial would be useless and the moving party is entitled to summary judgment as a matter of law. *Anderson v. Liberty Lobby, Inc.*

Where the moving party adopts this second option and seeks summary judgment on the ground that the nonmoving party — who will bear the burden of persuasion at trial — has no evidence, the mechanics of discharging Rule 56's burden of production are somewhat trickier. Plainly, a conclusory assertion that the nonmoving party has no evidence is insufficient. See ante, (White, J., concurring). Such a "burden" of production is no burden at all and would simply permit summary judgment procedure to be converted into a tool for harassment. Rather, as the Court confirms, a party who moves for summary judgment on the ground that the nonmoving party has no evidence must affirmatively show the absence of evidence in the record. This may require the moving party to depose the nonmoving party's witnesses or to establish the inadequacy of documentary evidence. If there is literally no evidence in the record, the moving party may demonstrate this by reviewing for the court the admissions, interrogatories, and other exchanges between the parties that are in the record. Either way, however, the moving party must affirmatively demonstrate that there is no evidence in the record to support a judgment for the nonmoving party.

If the moving party has not fully discharged this initial burden of production, its motion for summary judgment must be denied, and the court need not consider whether the moving party has met its ultimate burden of persuasion. Accordingly, the nonmoving party may defeat a motion for summary judgment that asserts that the nonmoving party has no evidence by calling the court's attention to supporting evidence already in the record that was overlooked or ignored by the moving party. In that event, the moving party must respond by making an attempt to demonstrate the inadequacy of this evidence, for it is only by attacking all the record evidence allegedly supporting the nonmoving party that a party seeking summary judgment satisfies Rule 56's burden of production. Thus, if the record disclosed that the moving party had overlooked a witness who would provide relevant testimony for the nonmoving party at trial, the court could not find that the moving party had discharged its initial burden of production unless the moving party sought to demonstrate the inadequacy of this witness' testimony. Absent such a demonstration, summary judgment would have to be denied on the ground that the moving party had failed to meet its burden of production under Rule 56.

* * *

II

I do not read the Court's opinion to say anything inconsistent with or different than the preceding discussion. My disagreement with the Court concerns the application of these principles to the facts of this case.

* * *

On these facts, there is simply no question that Celotex failed to discharge its initial burden of production. Having chosen to base its motion on the argument that there was no evidence in the record to support plaintiff's claim, Celotex was not free to ignore supporting evidence that the record clearly contained. Rather, Celotex was required, as an initial matter, to attack the adequacy of this evidence. Celotex' failure to fulfill this simple requirement constituted a failure to discharge its initial burden of production under Rule 56, and thereby rendered summary judgment improper.

* * *

JUSTICE STEVENS, dissenting.

As the Court points out, petitioner's motion for summary judgment was based on the proposition that respondent could not prevail unless she proved that her deceased husband had been exposed to petitioner's products "within the jurisdictional limits" of the District of Columbia. Respondent made an adequate showing — albeit possibly not in admissible form — that her husband had been exposed to petitioner's product in Illinois. Although the basis of the motion and the argument had been the lack of exposure *in the District of Columbia*, the District Court stated at the end of the argument: "The Court will grant the defendant Celotex's motion for summary judgment there being no showing that the plaintiff was exposed to the defendant Celotex's product in the District of Columbia or elsewhere within the statutory period." The District Court offered no additional explanation and no written opinion. The Court of Appeals reversed on the basis that Celotex had not met its burden; the court noted the incongruity of the District Court's opinion in the context of the motion and argument, but did not rest on that basis because of the "or elsewhere" language.

Taken in the context of the motion for summary judgment on the basis of no exposure in the District of Columbia, the District Court's decision to grant summary judgment was palpably erroneous. The court's bench reference to "or elsewhere" neither validated that decision nor raised the complex question addressed by this Court today. In light of the District Court's plain error, therefore, it is perfectly clear that, even after this Court's abstract exercise in Rule construction, we should nonetheless affirm the reversal of summary judgment on that narrow ground.

I respectfully dissent.

C. Summary Judgment — Adjudication Without Trial or Jury

NOTES AND QUESTIONS

1. After *Celotex*, suppose the defendant were to file a motion for summary judgment which simply said, "I don't believe the plaintiff can prove her case." If the plaintiff fails to respond and present evidence in support of her claim, should the court enter judgement for the defendant?

2. Rather than awaiting a motion, why shouldn't courts routinely demand that plaintiffs demonstrate that they have sufficient evidence to warrant proceeding to trial? See Friedenthal, supra, 63 NOTRE DAME L. REV. at 779-80.

3. On remand after the Supreme Court decision in *Celotex*, the court of appeals held that summary judgment was not proper. Catrett v. Johns-Manville Sales Corp., 826 F. 2d 33 (D.C.Cir. 1987), *cert. denied*, 484 U.S. 1066 (1988). That court concluded that the letter from the decedent's former employer, Mr. Hoff, established a genuine issue as to whether the decedent had been exposed to defendant's products. Celotex argued that the letter should be disregarded in ruling on the motion because it would be inadmissible at trial. See Rule 56(c). The court rejected this argument on the grounds that Celotex had failed to object to the district court concerning the admissibility of the letter and hence and waived this argument. Judge Bork dissented and argued that defendant had properly objected. He cited the following exchange between counsel for the defendant and the trial court:

> Counsel said: *"Your Honor, there is only a letter from the assistant secretary and that is not"* — at this point the judge interrupted with several questions, but then counsel finished — "We also have, and they rely on this, the deposition of the decedent that was taken of him prior to his death for the compensation claim, *which would not be admissible in this case either.*"

826 F. 2d at 42 n.1 (Bork, J. dissenting) (emphasis in original). Do you think the defendant objected?

One possible explanation for the majority's decision to reverse the summary judgment is found in one of its footnotes:

> In our previous opinion in this case, we observed that during the hearing the District Court focused, almost exclusively, on the notion that the only alleged exposure occurred outside the District of Columbia and on the issue of venue. We repeat that observation here. We nonetheless gave dispositive weight to the District Court's inclusion of the two words, "or elsewhere," because, as we noted, it was only inclusion of that phrase that made the District Court's ruling "even conceivable proper." Justice Stevens discussed this point in his dissent, arguing that the District Court was clearly granting summary judgment "on the basis of no exposure in the District of Columbia," a ruling Justice Stevens described as "palpably erroneous." Although we could agree with Justice Stevens' observations, if that were indeed the trial court's ruling, we are nonetheless constrained not to

pierce the veil, as it were, of the District Judge's actual words; we thus once again treat the District Court's ruling as a bona fide grant of summary judgment on the basis of no evidence of exposure in the District of Columbia *or elsewhere.*

Id. at 36-37 n.9 (emphasis in original). Is this a case where the court of appeals believes that the district court applied an incorrect view of the law, but can't prove it and therefore stretches to find that the Hoff letter was admissible?

4. Suppose that in *Catrett* the plaintiff had responded to the motion for summary judgment by submitting the *affidavit* of Mr. Hoff (not just the letter) and that affidavit stated that Hoff had personal knowledge that Catrett as part of his duties handled asbestos products manufactured by Celotex. Wouldn't this have eliminated objections about the inadmissibility of the Hoff letter and saved years of litigation about the appropriateness of summary judgment?

Why didn't Catrett's lawyer get Hoff's affidavit? In a phone conversation, Catrett's lawyer offered two different explanations. First, he indicated that because the defendant's motion included no affidavits they did not believe they were required to submit one. Second, he suggested that although he didn't really remember for sure, he may have tried to get the affidavit but the witness was uncooperative. Catrett's appellate counsel suggested a third reason — that trial counsel was rushed and just didn't get a chance.

5. It took five and a half years of appellate litigation for the courts finally to determine that summary judgment should not have been granted. Wouldn't it have been quicker just to have tried the case rather than to litigate about summary judgment?

6. *Anderson, Matsushita,* and *Celotex* were all decided the same term. Some commentators have suggested that the significance of these cases is not that they announced a substantive change in the standards for summary judgment, but that they signaled a new receptiveness to such motions. As one observer noted, "Since summary decisions turn less on precise phrasings of legal standards than on attitudes toward the motion, the [Court's] celebration of summary judgment may be more important than any reformulation of standards." Stephen Calkins, *Summary Judgment, Motions to Dismiss, and Other Examples of Equilibrating Tendencies in the Antitrust System,* 74 GEO. L.J. 1065, 1114-15 (1986).

7. You will recall from Chapter 8 that prior to the Supreme Court's decision in *Leatherman,* some lower courts required more detailed pleading in certain categories of cases. Professor Marcus has suggested that the more difficult it is for courts to grant summary judgment, the more likely they are to rely on other devises, such as heightened pleading requirements, to screen non-meritorious cases. Richard Marcus, *The Revival of Fact Pleading Under the Federal Rules of Civil Procedure,* 86 COLUM. L. REV. 433, 484-85 (1986). He argued that summary judgment is a more appropriate device for identifying "suspicious" cases than heightened pleading. Id. at 493. Do you agree?

D. Controlling and Second-Guessing Juries

8. Will the 1993 amendments to Rule 11 make it easier for a defendant to identify the weaknesses in a plaintiff's case? See Rule 11(b)(3).

D. Controlling and Second - Guessing Juries

1. Judgment as a Matter of Law (Directed Verdict and JNOV)

When a case goes to trial before a jury, the court continues to have authority to determine whether there is sufficient evidence to support a jury verdict. If the court determines that there is insufficient evidence, it may decline to submit the case to the jury and instead enter judgment (historically called a directed verdict). In the alternative, the court can submit the case to the jury and if the jury returns a verdict for which there is insufficient evidentiary support, the court may enter judgment notwithstanding the verdict (historically referred to as a JNOV*). The standard for directed verdict and JNOV is the same as the standard for summary judgment — "whether a fair-minded jury could return a verdict for the plaintiff on the evidence presented." *Anderson v. Liberty Lobby.*

Rule 50 was amended in 1991 and changed the terminology. Directed verdict is now a "motion for judgment as a matter of law" (JMOL) and the JNOV is now a renewed motion for judgment as a matter of law. Despite the name change in the Rule, "directed verdict" and "JNOV" are still used routinely in federal practice. No state has adopted the 1991 terminology.

The name change was only that, and did not alter the timing for making these motions or the standards for granting them. Read Rule 50 with care. The timing requirements of this rule present a potential trap for the unwary and must be strictly observed. The sequence at trial is as follows. The plaintiff presents her case first — calling witnesses (whom the defendant can cross-examine) and introducing evidence. When the plaintiff rests, the defendant can move for a JMOL. If it is denied, the defendant then can call her witnesses and put in her evidence. There may be another round for rebuttal evidence, but then all evidence is closed. At that point, both plaintiff and defendant can move for a JMOL. If these motions are denied, the case is submitted to the jury. Following the verdict and entry of judgment, the losing party may "renew" her motion for JMOL. Notice, however, that the renewed motion can be made *only* if that party previously moved for a JMOL at the close of all the evidence. See Rule 50(b).

We turn now to the standard for granting a JMOL.

---

* The letters JNOV stand for "judgment non obstante veredicto."

Lavender v. Kurn
327 U.S. 645, 66 S. Ct., 90 L. Ed. 916 (1946)

JUSTICE MURPHY delivered the opinion of the Court.

The Federal Employers' Liability Act permits recovery for personal injuries to an employee of a railroad engaged in interstate commerce if such injuries result "in whole or in part from the negligence of any of the officers, agents, or employees of such carrier, or by reason of any defect or insufficiency, due to its negligence, in its cars, engines, appliances, machinery, track, roadbed, works, boats, wharves, or other equipment."

Petitioner, the administrator of the estate of L. E. Haney, brought this suit under the Act against the respondent trustees of the St. Louis-San Francisco Railway Company (Frisco) and the respondent Illinois Central Railroad Company. It was charged that Haney, while employed as a switch-tender by the respondents in the switch yard of the Grand Central Station in Memphis, Tennessee, was killed as a result of respondents' negligence. Following a trial in the Circuit Court of the City of St. Louis, Missouri, the jury returned a verdict in favor of petitioner and awarded damages in the amount of $30,000. Judgment was entered accordingly. On appeal, however, the Supreme Court of Missouri reversed the judgment, holding that there was no substantial evidence of negligence to support the submission of the case to the jury. We granted certiorari to review the propriety of the Supreme Court's action under the circumstances of this case.

It was admitted that Haney was employed by the Illinois Central, or a subsidiary corporation thereof, as a switch-tender in the railroad yards near the Grand Central Station, which was owned by the Illinois Central. His duties included the throwing of switches for the Illinois Central as well as for the Frisco and other railroads using that station. For these services, the trustees of Frisco paid the Illinois Central two-twelfths of Haney's wages; they also paid two-twelfths of the wages of two other switch-tenders who worked at the same switches. In addition, the trustees paid Illinois Central $1.87 1/2 for each passenger car switched into Grand Central Station, which included all the cars in the Frisco train being switched into the station at the time Haney was killed.

The Illinois Central tracks run north and south directly past and into the Grand Central Station. About 2,700 feet south of the station the Frisco tracks cross at right angles to the Illinois Central tracks. A west-bound Frisco train wishing to use the station must stop some 250 feet or more west of this crossing and back into the station over a switch line curving east and north. The events in issue center about the switch several feet north of the main Frisco tracks at the point where the switch line branches off. This switch controls the tracks at this point.

It was very dark on the evening of December 21, 1939. At about 7:30 p.m. a west-bound interstate Frisco passenger train stopped on the Frisco main line, its rear some 20 or 30 feet west of the switch. Haney, in the performance of his duties, threw or opened the switch to permit the train to back into the station. The respondents claimed that Haney was then required to cross to the south side of the track before the train passed the switch; and the conductor of the train testified that he saw Haney so cross. But there was also evidence that Haney's duties required him to wait at the switch north of the track until the train had cleared, close the switch, return to his shanty near the crossing and change the signals from red to green to permit trains on the Illinois Central tracks to use the crossing. The Frisco train cleared the switch, backing at the rate of 8 or 10 miles per hour. But the switch remained open and the signals still were red. Upon investigation Haney was found north of the track near the switch lying face down on the ground, unconscious. An ambulance was called, but he was dead upon arrival at the hospital.

Haney had been struck in the back of the head, causing a fractured skull from which he died. There were no known eyewitnesses to the fatal blow. Although it is not clear, there is evidence that his body was extended north and south, the head to the south. Apparently he had fallen forward to the south; his face was bruised on the left side from hitting the ground and there were marks indicating that his toes had dragged a few inches southward as he fell. His head was about 5 1/2 feet north of the Frisco tracks. Estimates ranged from 2 feet to 14 feet as to how far west of the switch he lay.

The injury to Haney's head was evidenced by a gash about two inches long from which blood flowed. The back of Haney's white cap had a corresponding black mark about an inch and a half long and an inch wide, running at an angle downward to the right of the center of the back of the head. A spot of blood was later found at a point 3 or 4 feet north of the tracks. The conclusion following an autopsy was that Haney's skull was fractured by "some fast moving small round object." One of the examining doctors testified that such an object might have been attached to a train backing at the rate of 8 or 10 miles per hour. But he also admitted that the fracture might have resulted from a blow from a pipe or club or some similar round object in the hands of an individual.

Petitioner's theory is that Haney was struck by the curled end or tip of a mail hook hanging down loosely on the outside of the mail car of the backing train. This curled end was 73 inches above the top of the rail, which was 7 inches high. The overhang of the mail car in relation to the rails was about 2 to 2 1/2 feet. The evidence indicated that when the mail car swayed or moved around a curve the mail hook might pivot, its curled end swinging out as much as 12 to 14 inches. The curled end could thus be swung out to a point 3 to 3 1/2 feet from the rail and about 73 inches above the top of the rail. Both east and west of the switch, however, was an uneven mound of cinders and dirt rising at its highest points 18 to 24 inches above the top of the rails. Witnesses differed as to how close the mound approached the rails, the estimates varying from 3 to 15 feet. But taking the figures most favorable to the petitioner, the mound extended to a point 6 to 12 inches north of the overhanging side of the mail car. If the mail hook end swung out 12 to 14 inches it would be 49 to 55 inches above the highest parts of the mound. Haney was 67 1/2 inches tall. If he had been standing on the mound about a foot from the side of the mail car he could have been hit by the end of the mail hook, the exact point of contact depending upon the height of the mound at the particular point. His wound was about 4 inches below the top of his head, or 63 1/2 inches above the point where he stood on the mound — well within the possible range of the mail hook end.

Respondents' theory is that Haney was murdered. They point to the estimates that the mound was 10 to 15 feet north of the rail, making it impossible for the mail hook end to reach a point of contact with Haney's head. Photographs were placed in the record to support the claim that the ground was level north of the rail for at least 10 feet. Moreover, it appears that the area immediately surrounding the switch was quite dark. Witnesses stated that it was so dark that it was impossible to see a 3-inch pipe 25 feet away. It also appears that many hoboes and tramps frequented the area at night in order to get rides on freight trains. Haney carried a pistol to protect himself. This pistol was found loose under his body by those who came to his rescue. It was testified, however, that the pistol had apparently slipped out of his pocket or scabbard as he fell. Haney's clothes were not disarranged and there was no evidence of a struggle or fight. No rods, pipes or weapons of any kind, except Haney's own pistol, were found near the scene. Moreover, his gold watch and diamond ring were still on him after he was struck. Six days later his unsoiled billfold was found on a high board

CHAPTER 10 ADJUDICATION WITH AND WITHOUT A TRIAL OR A JURY

fence about a block from the place where Haney was struck and near the point where he had been placed in an ambulance. It contained his social security card and other effects, but no money. His wife testified that he "never carried very much money, not very much more than $10." Such were the facts in relation to respondents' theory of murder.

Finally, one of the Frisco foremen testified that he arrived at the scene shortly after Haney was found injured. He later examined the fireman's side of the train very carefully and found nothing sticking out or in disorder. In explaining why he examined this side of the train so carefully he stated that while he was at the scene of the accident "someone said they thought that train No. 106 backing into Grand Central Station is what struck this man" and that Haney "was supposed to have been struck by something protruding on the side of this train." The foreman testified that these statements were made by an unknown Illinois Central switchman standing near the fallen body of Haney. The foreman admitted that the switchman "didn't see the accident ..." This testimony was admitted by the trial court over the strenuous objections of respondents' counsel that it was mere hearsay falling outside the *res gestae* rule.

The jury was instructed that Frisco's trustees were liable if it was found that they negligently permitted a rod or other object to extend out from the side of the train as it backed past Haney and that Haney was killed as the direct result of such negligence, if any. The jury was further told that Illinois Central was liable if it was found that the company negligently maintained an unsafe and dangerous place for Haney to work, in that the ground was high and uneven and the light insufficient and inadequate, and that Haney was injured and killed as a direct result of the said place being unsafe and dangerous. This latter instruction as to Illinois Central did not require the jury to find that Haney was killed by something protruding from the train.

The Supreme Court, in upsetting the jury's verdict against both the Frisco trustees and the Illinois Central, admitted that "It could be inferred from the facts that Haney could have been struck by the mail hook knob if he were standing on the south side of the mound and the mail hook extended out as far as 12 or 14 inches." But it held that "all reasonable minds would agree that it would be mere speculation and conjecture to say that Haney was struck by the mail hook" and that "plaintiff failed to make a submissible case on that question." It also ruled that there "was no substantial evidence that the uneven ground and insufficient light were causes or contributing causes of the death of Haney." Finally, the Supreme Court held that the testimony of the foreman as to the statement made to him by the unknown switchman was inadmissible under the *res gestae* rule since the switchman spoke from what he had heard rather than from his own knowledge.

We hold, however, that there was sufficient evidence of negligence on the part of both the Frisco trustees and the Illinois Central to justify the submission of the case to the jury and to require appellate courts to abide by the verdict rendered by the jury.

The evidence we have already detailed demonstrates that there was evidence from which it might be inferred that the end of the mail hook struck Haney in the back of the head, an inference that the Supreme Court admitted could be drawn. That inference is not rendered unreasonable by the fact that Haney apparently fell forward toward the main Frisco track so that his head was 5 1/2 feet north of the rail. He may well have been struck and then wandered in a daze to the point where he fell forward. The testimony as to blood marks some distance away from his head lends credence to that possibility, indicating that he did not fall immediately upon being hit. When that is added to the evidence most favorable to the petitioner as to the height and swing-out of the hook, the height and location of the mound and the nature of Haney's duties, the inference that Haney was killed by the

556

hook cannot be said to be unsupported by probative facts or to be so unreasonable as to warrant taking the case from the jury.

It is true that there is evidence tending to show that it was physically and mathematically impossible for the hook to strike Haney. And there are facts from which it might reasonably be inferred that Haney was murdered. But such evidence has become irrelevant upon appeal, there being a reasonable basis in the record for inferring that the hook struck Haney. The jury having made that inference, the respondents were not free to relitigate the factual dispute in a reviewing court. Under these circumstances it would be an undue invasion of the jury's historic function for an appellate court to weigh the conflicting evidence, judge the credibility of witnesses and arrive at a conclusion opposite from the one reached by the jury.

It is no answer to say that the jury's verdict involved speculation and conjecture. Whenever facts are in dispute or the evidence is such that fair-minded men may draw different inferences, a measure of speculation and conjecture is required on the part of those whose duty it is to settle the dispute by choosing what seems to them to be the most reasonable inference. Only when there is a complete absence of probative facts to support the conclusion reached does a reversible error appear. But where, as here, there is an evidentiary basis for the jury's verdict, the jury is free to discard or disbelieve whatever facts are inconsistent with its conclusion. And the appellate court's function is exhausted when that evidentiary basis becomes apparent, it being immaterial that the court might draw a contrary inference or feel that another conclusion is more reasonable.

We are unable, therefore, to sanction a reversal of the jury's verdict against Frisco's trustees. Nor can we approve any disturbance in the verdict as to Illinois Central. The evidence was uncontradicted that it was very dark at the place where Haney was working and the surrounding ground was high and uneven. The evidence also showed that this area was entirely within the domination and control of Illinois Central despite the fact that the area was technically located in a public street of the City of Memphis. It was not unreasonable to conclude that these conditions constituted an unsafe and dangerous working place and that such conditions contributed in part to Haney's death, assuming that it resulted primarily from the mail hook striking his head.

In view of the foregoing disposition of the case, it is unnecessary to decide whether the allegedly hearsay testimony was admissible under the *res gestae* rule. Rulings on the admissibility of evidence must normally be left to the sound discretion of the trial judge in actions under the Federal Employers' Liability Act. But inasmuch as there is adequate support in the record for the jury's verdict apart from the hearsay testimony, we need not determine whether that discretion was abused in this instance.

The judgment of the Supreme Court of Missouri is reversed and the case is remanded for whatever further proceedings may be necessary not inconsistent with this opinion.

Reversed.

NOTES AND QUESTIONS

1. In *Lavender,* what reasonable rationale could the jury have used to find Illinois Central liable?

2. What reasonable rationale could the jury have used to find Frisco liable?

3. If you had been on the *Lavender* jury, how would you have voted in the case? Why? Would it have been proper for the jury to decide for the plaintiff on the theory that of the two theories (the mail hook vs. the hobo), the mail hook theory was the more likely?

4. Compare *Lavender* with Reid v. San Pedro, Los Angeles & Salt Lake Railroad, 39 Utah 617, 118 P. 1009 (1911). In *Reid* a cow got onto a railroad right-of-way and was killed by a train. The right-of-way was protected by a fence for which the railroad was responsible. If the cow got onto the right-of-way through an open gate, the railroad was not liable but if the cow came through a break in the fence, it was liable. The jury rendered judgment for the cow's owner. In holding that the judge should have entered a JNOV, the Utah Supreme Court explained:

> There is no direct evidence as to where the cow got on to the right of way. It is conceded, however, that she was killed in the immediate vicinity of the gate mentioned, and, as shown by the evidence, about one mile from the point where the fence in closing the right of way was down and out of repair. The inference, therefore, is just a strong, if not stronger, that she entered upon the right of way through the open gate as it is that she entered through the fence at the point where it was out of repair. The plaintiff held the affirmative and the burden was on her to establish the liability of the defendant by a preponderance of the evidence. It is a familiar rule that where the undisputed evidence of the plaintiff, from which the existence of an essential fact is sought to be inferred, points with equal force to two things, one of which renders the defendant liable and the other not, the plaintiff must fail. So in this case, in order to entitle respondent to recover it was essential for her to show by a preponderance of the evidence that the cow entered upon the right of way through the broken down fence. This the respondent failed to do.

Id. at 621. In *Lavender*, as in *Reid*, did the evidence point with equal force to the two possible theories?

5. Consider the facts of Wratchford v. S. J. Groves & Sons Co., 405 F. 2d 1061 (4th Cir. 1969). Late at night, plaintiff parked his car on the eastbound shoulder of a country road. He apparently intended to walk across the east and westbound lanes of the road to a market, where he could purchase groceries on his way home from work. The next morning, plaintiff was found at the bottom of an open highway drainage hole which was in the median of the road, between the east and westbound lanes. The fall into the hole fractured plaintiff's skull and left him totally incapacitated. It also caused retrograde amnesia, meaning that he could recall nothing about the event.

D. Controlling and Second-Guessing Juries

His representative sued the construction company doing work on the median, alleging that it had negligently failed to put a grate over the hole and to erect a barricade or warning light around the hole. The defendant contended that plaintiff had slipped on ice several feet from the open hole, and sustained his head injuries in that slip, after which he slid or crawled into the hole. In defendant's view, then, the fall into the hole was not the proximate cause of plaintiff's injuries. Defendant pointed out that blood stains were found on the ice and snow around the hole.

On these facts, the district judge concluded that the evidence showed that the injury could have been caused with equal probability in either way and he entered judgment as a matter of law for the defendant. The Fourth Circuit reversed and remanded the case, holding that it should have been submitted to a jury "instructed that * * * plaintiffs must persuade them by the preponderance of the evidence that the injury was sustained as a result of a step into the hole rather than in an earlier fall on the ice." 405 F. 2d at 1066.

How could the plaintiff discharge that burden on this evidence without encouraging the jury to engage in speculation? If he could not, then wouldn't entry of judgment as a matter of law for the defendant be proper?

6. In ruling on a motion for JMOL, what evidence should the court consider? Suppose, for example, the defendant had produced a witness who testified that she saw a "hobo" attack Haney, or suppose that it had produced a video tape showing a "hobo" attacking Haney. Should this additional evidence affect the court's ruling on the JMOL? Some courts have held that in ruling on a JMOL, the court should consider only the evidence produced by the non-moving party. However, today in federal court, the generally accepted test is that the court

> may consider all of the evidence favorable to the position of the party opposing the motion as well as any unfavorable evidence that the jury is required to believe. Thus it may take into account evidence supporting the moving party that is uncontradicted and unimpeached, at least to the extent that evidence comes from disinterested witnesses.

9A Wright & Miller, Federal Practice & Procedure § 2529 at 299-300.

7. *Lavender* is an FELA case. Some read the case as adopting a scintilla of evidence test — that is, holding that all the plaintiff need have is some scintilla of evidence to support his theory. You will recall that in *Anderson* the Court rejected the scintilla test for summary judgment and, as we have noted, said that the test for summary judgment is the same as the test for directed verdict and JNOV. Thus, if *Lavender* does adopt a scintilla test, its application may be confined to FELA and other related statutory negligence cases. See Boeing Co. v. Shipman, 411 F. 2d 365, 370-73 (5th Cir. 1969); Edward Cooper, *Directions for Directed Verdicts: A Compass for Federal Court*, 55 Minn. L. Rev. 903, 926-27 (1971).

8. As discussed earlier, a party moving for judgment as a matter of law must so move before submission of the case to the jury. If the judge grants the motion, the jury is dismissed and judgment entered. If the judge denies the motion, and there is an adverse judgment, that party may renew her motion (provided she moved for a JMOL at the close of all the evidence). Given that the test for JMOL before submission to a jury and after a verdict is the same, why would a judge ever deny the motion before submission, but then grant the motion after the verdict? One court of appeals has explained:

> We have in the past cautioned trial judges that it is preferable, "in the best interests of efficient judicial administration," to refrain from granting a motion for a directed verdict and instead to allow the case to be decided — at least in the first instance — by the jury. Pursuant to the recommended practice, if the jury reaches what the judge considers to be an irrational verdict, the judge may grant a motion for judgment notwithstanding the verdict. If this ruling is reversed on appeal, the jury's verdict may simply be reinstated. If, however, a verdict has been directed and that ruling is reversed on appeal, an entire new trial must be held.

Konik v. Champlain Valley Physicians Hosp., 733 F. 2d 1007, 1013 n.4 (1984).

9. Summary judgment and a direct verdict (a JMOL prior to submission to the jury) have the effect of taking some cases away from juries. Why don't these procedures violate the Seventh Amendment? In Galloway v. United States, 319 U.S. 372 (1943), the Court upheld the constitutionality of these procedures explaining that at common law there were equivalent (though not identical) mechanisms for withdrawing cases from juries. A JNOV (a JMOL granted after a jury verdict) presents a somewhat trickier problem. The Seventh Amendment provides "no fact tried by a jury, shall be otherwise re-examined in any Court of the United States, than according to the rules of the common law." At common law there was no procedure equivalent to a JNOV. After first holding that a JNOV was unconstitutional, see Slocum v. New York Life Insurance Co., 228 U.S. 364 (1913), the Court found a way to uphold the procedure. In Baltimore & Carolina Line, Inc. v. Redman, 295 U.S. 654 (1935), the Court upheld a JNOV where the defendant had moved for a directed verdict and the trial court submitted the case to the jury, but expressly reserved its ruling on the motion. The theory was that a JNOV was simply a delayed ruling on a directed verdict. Notice how this principle is now incorporated into Rule 50(b).

10. Is a JMOL proper in any of the following situations?
(a) Plaintiff presents overwhelming evidence in her favor. At the close of the presentation of her evidence, Plaintiff moves for a JMOL.
(b) Plaintiff and Defendant both present their evidence. Neither side moves for a JMOL. After the case has been submitted to the jury, but before a verdict has been returned, Defendant moves for a JMOL.

(c) At the close of Plaintiff's evidence, Defendant moves for a JMOL. The motion is denied. Defendant then presents his evidence and the case is submitted to the jury. Following verdict and judgment for Plaintiff, Defendant immediately renews her motion for JMOL. *NO - ∆ had to do it at the close of all evid.*

(d) At the close of all the evidence, Defendant moves for a JMOL, stating, "Your Honor, plaintiff just hasn't proved her case." The motion is denied. Following a verdict and judgment for Plaintiff, Defendant again moves for a JNOV. *NO*

(e) Defendant moves for a JMOL at the close of all the evidence. After verdict for Plaintiff, the court enters judgment and Defendant immediately makes an oral motion for a JMOL. The Defendant doesn't get around to filing ~~and serving~~ a written motion for JMOL until eleven days after entry of judgment. *NO*

(f) Defendant moves for a JMOL at the close of all the evidence. The court denies the motion. After the jury returns a verdict for Plaintiff, the court, without motion from Defendant, grants a JMOL. *N*

(g) Both sides present their evidence and neither moves for JMOL. Following a verdict for Plaintiff, the judge on her own concludes that there was insufficient evidence. Can the judge enter a JMOL?

2. New Trials

Judgment as a matter of law gives the court one tool to control juries. But JMOL is available only where the evidence is so weak for one side that no reasonable jury could find for that side. It thus permits court intervention only in limited and extreme circumstances. Suppose, however, that there is sufficient evidence that a JMOL is inappropriate. Nonetheless, the court strongly disagrees with the jury's verdict and thinks it was against the heavy weight of the evidence. Under these circumstances, should we give the court any power to override the jury's verdict? If we had complete confidence in juries, the answer to this question would likely be no. Nonetheless, Rule 59 provides a mechanism for some court intervention under these circumstances by allowing the court to order a new trial. Notice that in ordering a new trial, the judge is not directly substituting her view of the evidence. The determination of who wins and loses will be left to a jury — but, to a new jury.

Rule 59 gives courts authority to grant new trials "for any of the reasons for which new trials have heretofore been granted in actions at law in courts of the United States." We consider now the circumstances under which courts may order new trials.

Dadurian v. Underwriters at Lloyd's of London
787 F. 2d 756 (1st Cir. 1986)

CAMPBELL, CHIEF JUDGE.

This diversity case arose out of the refusal of defendant- appellant Lloyd's, London ("Lloyd's") to indemnify plaintiff- appellee Paul Dadurian after he claimed the loss of certain jewelry that he allegedly owned and that had been insured under a Lloyd's insurance policy. As affirmative defenses to the suit for nonpayment, Lloyd's asserted that Dadurian's claim was fraudulent and that Dadurian had knowingly made false statements about facts material to his claim. The jury entered special verdicts favorable to Dadurian, resulting in his recovering $267,000 plus interest. Lloyd's moved for judgment notwithstanding the verdict, or alternatively, for a new trial. The United States District Court for the District of Rhode Island denied the motion, and Lloyd's now appeals. As we find the jury's verdict was against the great weight of the evidence, we vacate and remand for a new trial.

I

Dadurian claimed that he purchased 12 pieces of "specialty" jewelry for investment purposes over a period of 30 months, from August 1977 to January 1980. The pieces allegedly ranged in price from $12,000 to $35,000, costing him $233,000 in total. Dadurian testified that he purchased all the jewelry from James Howe, a jeweler in Providence, Rhode Island, and paid for each item in cash. Dadurian did not present any sales slips, receipts or other documents of transfer reflecting any of his alleged purchases; and Howe not only presented no records of his sale of the jewelry to Dadurian, but he could not remember from whom he had originally obtained the jewelry and had no records showing that the jewelry had ever actually been in his possession.

On or about March 2, 1980, Dadurian purchased a "Jewelry Floater" policy from Lloyd's, which insured him against loss of the 12 items of jewelry. The jewelry pieces were described on an attached schedule, which also set forth the maximum amount recoverable for each piece. The maximum recoverable under the policy was $267,000. Dadurian obtained the insurance coverage on the strength of eight appraisal certificates for the jewelry, which were prepared by Howe at Dadurian's request. Some certificates were dated on the same day as certain of the alleged purchases, while the others were dated months later.

Dadurian claimed that on or about April 12, 1980, armed robbers entered his home and forced him to open his safe, where the jewelry was kept. He was shot in the right shoulder, allegedly by one of the robbers, and was taken to the hospital. It is Dadurian's contention that the insured pieces of jewelry were stolen during the robbery. After preliminary investigation by an adjuster representing Lloyd's, Dadurian was asked to appear for a formal examination under oath by counsel for Lloyd's. The examination took place on September 10, 1980, and again on May 28, 1981. Because of alleged false and fraudulent statements made under oath by Dadurian at this examination, Lloyd's refused to indemnify Dadurian for the claimed losses.

On March 31, 1982, Dadurian brought this action in the district court seeking compensation for his losses under the jewelry insurance policy issued by Lloyd's. The action was tried before a jury from October 29 through November 5, 1984. The jury rendered four special verdicts, all favorable to Dadurian: that Dadurian had been robbed on April 12, 1980; that he had not given false answers or information on any material subject when he was examined under oath before the commencement of this suit; that he had not made any false statement or fraudulent claims as to any of the 12 jewelry items for which he claimed a loss; and that the total fair market value of all the jewelry on April 12, 1980, was $267,000. Judgment was entered for plaintiff in the amount of $267,000 with interest.

Pursuant to Fed.R.Civ.P. 50, Lloyd's moved for judgment n.o.v. or, in the alternative, for a new trial. The district court denied defendant's motion, and this appeal followed.

II

Lloyd's argues on appeal that Dadurian swore falsely, and necessarily knowingly, with respect to at least two key issues, and that either instance of false swearing was sufficient to void the insurance policy. First, Dadurian is said to have clearly lied in asserting that he purchased and owned the 12 pieces of jewelry for which he later obtained the insurance; and second, he is said to have knowingly lied in telling Lloyd's, at the formal examination under oath conducted before this action was begun, that the cash he used to purchase the jewelry came from certain bank loans. Lloyd's contends that evidence presented at trial was so overwhelmingly against Dadurian on both these issues that no reasonable jury could have rendered a verdict in his favor.

A. The Purchase of the Jewelry

Pointing to the suspicious absence of documentation for any of the jewelry purchases, Lloyd's asserts that the record shows that Dadurian had sworn falsely when he testified to having purchased the jewelry at all. Dadurian procured the Lloyd's insurance on the basis of written appraisals executed by Howe, the man from whom he allegedly purchased all 12 pieces. But he obtained no receipts nor did Howe have any records of the alleged sales to Dadurian. Moreover, although Dadurian testified to specific dates and prices paid for each of his jewelry purchases, in support of his story of ownership, his testimony that he had obtained that information from Howe's records was contradicted by testimony that Howe kept no such records.

But whatever may be thought of Dadurian's story, we cannot say, as a matter of law, that no jury could have properly found that Dadurian had purchased the jewelry as he claimed. Nor can we say the verdict on this issue was so far contrary to the clear weight of the evidence as, by itself, to provide grounds for our ordering the district court to grant a new trial. Not only did Howe testify at trial that he sold each one of the jewelry pieces to Dadurian at the prices Dadurian claimed, but Howe's employees, Cheryl Cousineau and Edward Proulx, gave testimony which, in material respects, tended to support the story that Dadurian purchased at least some jewelry items from Howe with cash. And Howe and Cousineau testified that they did not usually give receipts for cash purchases of "investment jewelry" or of jewelry sold "on consignment," thus tending to explain why Dadurian had no receipts. Despite extensive cross-examination by counsel for Lloyd's, the jury apparently chose to credit the testimony of Dadurian and his witnesses, and the jury was entitled to overlook the lack of any documentation for the purchases.

B. The Source of the Funds

Lloyd's also argues that Dadurian knowingly lied under oath at the formal examination when he swore that certain specific bank loans were the source of the cash he used to buy the jewelry. If Dadurian swore falsely and knowingly on this issue, he is not entitled to recover under the insurance contract. This is so because under the Lloyd's policy Dadurian was required to give "such information and evidence as to the property lost and the circumstances of the Loss as the Underwriters may reasonably require and as may be in the Assured's power" — and it is undisputed that under the policy, as well as under established case law, knowingly false testimony by Dadurian as to any fact considered "material" to his claim voids the policy.

The district court instructed the jury, and Dadurian does not dispute, that the issue of where he obtained the cash used for his jewelry purchases was "material" to his claim. To be considered material, a statement need not "relate[] to a matter or subject which ultimately proves to be decisive or significant in the ultimate disposition of the claim"; rather, it is sufficient if the statement was reasonably relevant to the insurance company's investigation of a claim. We agree that where Dadurian got the cash was material to his insurance claim, since Dadurian insisted that he paid Howe a total of $223,000 in cash over a 30-month period for the jewelry, and the credibility of this story, and hence of Dadurian's ownership of the insured items, turned in part on his ability to explain plausibly where he obtained such large sums of cash.[5]

The details of Dadurian's testimony about the bank loans are as follows: Soon after the alleged robbery of the jewelry items in April 1980, Dadurian was interviewed by an adjuster for Lloyd's. At this initial interview Dadurian, to explain the sources of his cash, stated that he "may have borrowed from the bank for the purchase of certain of the personal items of jewelry and [would] check [his] records in this regard." He later submitted to Lloyd's certain promissory notes which he contended represented the bank loans used to finance many of his purchases. Apparently still dissatisfied with the information provided by Dadurian, Lloyd's notified Dadurian in a letter dated August 18, 1980, that he would be required to appear at a formal examination under oath for further questioning at which time he "should be prepared to produce all documents in any way relating to the occurrence of the loss...."

At the first examination session on September 10, 1980, and again at the second session on May 28, 1981, when he was examined under oath by counsel for Lloyd's, Dadurian testified to the effect that most of his cash had come from loans from the Rhode Island Hospital Trust National Bank ("Hospital Trust").[7] During the two sessions, Dadurian was specifically questioned in turn about

---

[5] Lloyd's was understandably interested in hearing Dadurian's explanation of the source of his cash, particularly when it discovered that in 1978, the year Dadurian allegedly bought four of the twelve jewelry items for a total of $90,000 in cash, his income as reported in his federal tax return was only about $3,000.

[7] Dadurian testified during his September 1980 examination as follows:

> If you want to know how I wound up with the cash, how all this jewelry was paid up in cash, how I got all the cash for the jewelry, the insurance company has copies of these. (indicating) These are all bank notes. When a good piece of jewelry came along for the right price, which I had to pay for in cash, I went to the bank. I borrowed from the bank, borrowed the money on notes, and the [insurance] company has these copies which you may take them if you like, and you may make copies of them. That's how I purchased the jewelry.
>
> ...
>
> I have a quarter of a million dollars loss, and the money came from here from bank notes. I still owe this bank. I borrowed this money, and it's as simple as that.

the sources of the cash used to purchase each one of the jewelry pieces. For 11 of the 12 items, Dadurian identified the individual promissory notes of his — by date and by loan amount — that purportedly represented the bank loans he said was used to finance his purchases. In total, he identified 13 specific bank loans as the source of $166,000 of the $233,000 which he claimed to have paid to Howe.

At trial, however, Richard Niedzwiadek, an employee of the bank, testified that the loans associated with four of the jewelry pieces, totaling $49,500, were simply renewals of earlier loans which could not have generated any cash for Dadurian. He also produced bank statements for Dadurian's accounts at Hospital Trust showing that the proceeds from several other loans which Dadurian had identified as having financed a number of the jewelry pieces had been deposited in those accounts and then withdrawn in too small amounts over a period of time to have been used for purchasing the jewelry as Dadurian claimed. Niedzwiadek further testified that the proceeds of yet another loan supposedly associated with a jewelry item had been deposited in the corporate account of a company named U.S. Enterprises, Inc., and that Dadurian had stated the purpose of the loan as "real estate investment."[9] Confronted with this cumulative evidence, Dadurian essentially conceded that some, if not most, of the promissory notes he had selected had been the wrong ones, and that his testimony as to the sources of the funds was therefore in part false. He insisted, however, that he had selected the notes "to the best of [his] recollection" and that he had been honestly mistaken.

Since it is thus uncontroverted that a substantial number of Dadurian's representations under oath about the sources of his cash were untrue, the only remaining question is whether Dadurian made these false statements *knowingly* or whether he was simply mistaken in good faith as he claims. False swearing is "swearing knowingly and intentionally false and not through mere mistake." Black's Law Dictionary 725 (rev. 5th ed. 1979). Lloyd's forcefully contends that where Dadurian testified with such certainty, yet incorrectly, about so many of his own promissory notes and bank loans, the inference of intentional falsehood is so compelling as to render the jury's finding contrary, at very least, to the great weight of the evidence.

After carefully considering the entire record, we find that the great weight of the evidence indicates overwhelmingly that Dadurian knew he was giving false testimony. At the formal examination under oath Dadurian specifically identified 13 promissory notes, apparently from those he had given Lloyd's sometime before the examination, and explicitly linked each note to a particular jewelry purchase. He did not qualify his identifications, but rather couched his testimony in terms of misleading certainty. Only when confronted at trial with the patent falsity of his earlier testimony did Dadurian testify, by way of explanation, that he had made his selections only to the "best of his recollection" in order to satisfy the insurance company's inquiries. It was only then that he explained that because he had "files and files" of such notes in his possession,[10] he must have simply selected the wrong ones under pressure of time and circumstances.

This explanation strains credulity. This was not a case where Dadurian was confronted for the first time at the examination with "files and files" of his promissory notes and asked to come up

---

[9] According to the bank records presented at trial, Dadurian did not state the purchase of jewelry as the purpose for obtaining any of the bank loans; and for four of the nine non-renewal loans, Dadurian specifically stated that he would use the loans for real estate investment, working capital, or his used car business.

[10] At one point in his testimony at trial, Dadurian stated that he had "maybe ... 50, 60, 70 notes" in his possession.

with correct ones "on the spot." Rather it was Dadurian himself who originated and put forward the story that most of his cash had come from bank loans, and it was Dadurian who apparently first tendered the supposedly relevant promissory notes to Lloyd's at some time before the formal examination. Dadurian admitted at trial that he had known before the first examination session that he would be questioned further about the bank loans. He apparently marked each of the notes before the examination sessions with the number of the jewelry piece with which it was supposedly associated. By the first session in September 1980, and certainly by the May 1981 session, Dadurian had had ample notice as well as opportunity to discover the correct promissory notes or, if he found he was wrong or in doubt, to say so. The uncontested facts simply belie Dadurian's excuse that he was pressured into making identifications prematurely.

Dadurian had much to gain by providing a plausible explanation for the sources of his cash. By piecing together notes executed on dates close to the times of the alleged purchases, he could hope to create an impression of credibility. That he linked the notes to the jewelry purchases so positively — without bothering to ascertain readily available information showing that they were not so related — indicates, at the least, a wilful misrepresentation as to the state of his own knowledge concerning the matters to which he was testifying. We think the only fair inference from this kind of total indifference to the truth or falsity of his assertions was that Dadurian knew that he was not telling the truth.

It follows, we believe, that the jury's verdict was against the clear weight of the evidence insofar as it found that Dadurian did not knowingly give false answers or information on any material subject when he was examined under oath before commencement of this suit.[11] We emphasize that Dadurian himself conceded that some of his answers were incorrect, and it is clear the district court properly found them "material." This leaves open only the question of their possible innocence, which, to be sure, Dadurian attested to — but with implausible explanations as to why he put forward these patently unfounded and incorrect assertions. We conclude that the jury's finding that Dadurian did not give knowingly false answers was contrary to the great weight of the evidence. For that aspect of the verdict to stand would, in our view, amount to a manifest miscarriage of justice. We hold, therefore, that the district court abused its discretion in denying defendant's motion for a new trial, and remand the case for retrial by a new jury.

We are mindful of the alternative plea by Lloyd's that we should reverse the court's refusal to grant a judgment n.o.v. and, in effect, direct a finding for Lloyd's rather than order a new trial. Whether to do so is a very close question. A factor weighing against this alternative is that Lloyd's had the burden of proving that Dadurian was lying, and this circuit, like most courts, is reluctant to direct a verdict for the party having the burden of proof. The issue, moreover, involves a determination of credibility. Hence, even though we find it hard to see how a reasonable jury could reach any

---

[11] It strikes us that the jury may not have paid sufficient attention to determining whether Dadurian had knowingly lied as to the sources of his cash. There were many issues raised at trial. Once the jury concluded that Dadurian had indeed purchased the jewelry as he alleged, it could have thought that the issue of Dadurian's false swearing as to the bank loans was a mere technicality. But, as we discussed, a finding that Dadurian had knowingly given false testimony as to any material fact voids the policy just as a finding that Dadurian had not owned the jewelry would have voided it. It is possible that the jury, despite instructions in the jury charge to the contrary, decided on its own that since Lloyd's had insured the jewelry it should pay for its loss, regardless of whether Dadurian lied as to the source of his funds.

result other than that Dadurian was knowingly lying, we believe that the more appropriate relief is a new trial.

A remaining question is whether the new trial should encompass both the issue of Dadurian's ownership of the jewelry and the issue of his knowingly false testimony as to the sources of his funds. We hold that it should, even though it was on the latter issue that the district court erred. Dadurian's credibility is cast into serious doubt by our finding that the clear weight of the evidence shows that he must have knowingly lied about a material issue. It follows that this loss of credibility necessarily affects the jury finding in Dadurian's favor on the issue of his jewelry purchases, since Dadurian was his own main witness for all aspects of his story. A new trial as to both issues also makes sense since the issue of where Dadurian obtained the cash to make his purchases is so interrelated with the question of whether Dadurian bought the jewelry he claimed as to make it difficult to hold a meaningful trial on the first without the second.

Vacated and remanded for a new trial.

NOTES AND QUESTIONS

1. *Dadurian* raises two issues. First, what is the standard by which a district court decides whether to grant a new trial? Second, what is the standard of review by which an appellate court reviews the decision of the district court? These two issues are discussed separately below.

2. A district court may order a new trial on grounds that the verdict is against the weight of the evidence. In ruling on a motion for new trial, a judge is permitted to weigh the evidence herself. There are a variety of verbal formulations, but as Professors Wright and Miller explain, none is particularly helpful:

> Necessarily all such formulations are couched in broad and general terms that furnish no unerring litmus test for a particular case. On the one hand, the trial judge does not sit to approve miscarriages of justice. His power to set aside the verdict is supported by clear precedent at common law, far from being a denigration or a usurpation of jury trial, has long been regarded as an integral part of trial by jury as we know it. On the other hand, a decent respect for the collective wisdom of the jury, and for the function entrusted to it on our system, certainly suggests that in most cases the judge should accept the findings of the jury, regardless of his own doubts in the matter. Probably all that the judge can do is to balance these conflicting principle in the light of the facts of the particular case. If, having given full respect to the jury's findings, the judge on the entire evidence is left with the definite and firm conviction that a mistake has been committed, it is to be expected that he will grant a new trial.

11 WRIGHT & MILLER, FEDERAL PRACTICE & PROCEDURE § 2806 at 49.

CHAPTER 10 ADJUDICATION WITH AND WITHOUT A TRIAL OR A JURY

3. In *Dadurian*, the court of appeals reversed the trial court's denial of a new trial. This is extremely rare, and up until the 1950s, courts routinely announced that the denial of a motion for new trial on grounds of sufficiency of the evidence was not reviewable. See, e.g., Portman v. American Home Products Corp., 201 F. 2d 847, 848 (2d Cir. 1953). Today, courts more commonly assert, as does the court in *Dadurian*, that such denials are reviewable under an abuse of discretion standard. However, some have questioned the constitutionality of this practice, arguing that at common law, only the judge who presided at the trial and heard the witnesses was permitted to determine whether the verdict was contrary to the weight of the evidence. See 11 WRIGHT & MILLER, FEDERAL PRACTICE & PROCEDURE § 2819 at 125. Of course, where the trial court grants a new trial and the court of appeals reverses that grant there is no Seventh Amendment problem. Do you see why?

4. Suppose that following a second trial in *Dadurian*, the jury finds for the plaintiff. Should the trial court grant another new trial?

5. Suppose that the trial in *Lavender* had occurred in federal court:
   (a) Upon a proper motion, would it have been reversible error for the trial court to grant a new trial? *no*
   (b) Upon a proper motion, would it have been reversible error for the trial court *not* to grant a new trial? *no*
   (c) Could the trial court have granted a new trial on its own, without a motion by a party? *yes*
   (d) Suppose that the defendants had never moved for a JMOL. Could they properly move for a new trial? *yes*

6. The judge may grant a new trial on grounds of misconduct by counsel or other unfairness at trial or because of newly discovered evidence. As with all motions for a new trial, even a motion on grounds of new evidence must be made within ten days of the judgment. However, if a party discovers new evidence more than ten days after the judgment, she may move for relief under Rule 60(b)(2), provided the motion is filed no later than one year after entry of the judgment.

7. The court may grant a new trial on grounds that the size of the verdict is contrary to the weight of the evidence. In the alternative, the court may use "remittitur," in which the court offers the plaintiff a verdict of a specified lower amount. The plaintiff is not required to accept the lower amount. If she rejects it, however, the court will order a new trial. The converse of remittitur is "additur," in which the court finds that the verdict is unreasonably low and gives the defendant the choice of a specified higher verdict or a new trial. The Supreme Court has held that remittitur is permitted under the Seventh Amendment but additur is not. See Dimick v. Schredt, 293 U.S. 474 (1935). Additur is permitted, however, in some state courts.

8. A party disappointed with a jury verdict may renew her motion for judgment as a matter of law (assuming she preserved the right to do so) and, in the alternative, request a new trial. If the court grants the JMOL, its ruling on the new trial motion would seem to be unnecessary. However, the moving party can request that the court "conditionally" rule on the new trial motion, that is, that the court state what its ruling on the new trial request would be in the event the JMOL is reversed.

A party wanting to protect the option of a new trial should be sure to press the trial court to rule on the conditional new trial motion. Consider Arenson v. Southern University Law Center, 43 F. 3d 194 (5th Cir. 1995). After a jury returned a verdict in the plaintiff's favor, the defendant renewed his motion for judgment as a matter of law and, moved in the alternative, for a new trial. The district court granted the JMOL and did not rule on the new trial. After the renewed motion was reversed on appeal, the defendant sought a ruling from the district court on the new trial. The district court granted the new trial and the defendant won at the second trial. The plaintiff appealed and won on the ground that the grant of the new trial was improper.

Acknowledging that "no matter how it comes out, our decision will not be entirely just," the court of appeals reversed, explaining that Rule 50(c) is a "use-it-or-lose-it" provision. Id. at 196. Defendant failed to "use" its right to seek a new trial by failing to obtain a ruling after the grant of the JMOL and by failing to note on appeal its new trial motion. Thus, defendant lost the right to seek a new trial after the JMOL was reversed and the district court erred in granting a new trial on remand. Consequently, the defendant's victory in the second trial was reversed. Is this pushing "use-it-or-lose-it" too far?

3. Other Techniques for Controlling Juries

a. Jury Instructions

Earlier we saw that a court may grant summary judgment where there is no genuine issue of material fact. That standard distinguishes between disputes of fact and of law, and is premised on the understanding that matters of law are properly decided by the court, not the jury. This division of responsibility is also reflected in jury instructions. The judge determines what the law is and then instructs the jury about it. The jury's job is to resolve disputes of fact and then apply the law to the facts.

Jury instructions provide another mechanism for controlling juries. They identify and define the elements of each claim or defense, explain which party has the burden of proof and what the burden of persuasion is. Although there is no guaranty that juries will in fact follow instructions, the instructions can focus the juries attention on particular matters and provide a structure for the deliberations.

It is the judge's job to instruct the jury orally on the relevant law. Even in simple cases, the judge's oral instructions can last 30 minutes to an hour. Traditionally, juries were not permitted to take notes on the instructions, nor were they given a written copy. This rule stemmed from a concern that jurors would improperly focus on a single phrase in the instructions rather than taking them as a whole. Faced with increasingly complex law and instructions, resourceful juries have found ways around this. In one libel case, for example, the jury asked that a copy of the instructions be sent into the jury room. The judge refused but told the jurors he would read the instructions again. The jury foreman later explained what the jury did:

> [W]e agreed before we went back in to have the judge read the instructions again that since the judge said we could not take notes, that we would divide up what was being said, and we would all come back and remember the part we were each assigned, and we would write it down when we got back into the jury room.

David Branson & Andrea Johnson, *Aids Needed for Jury to Understand Instructions*, LEGAL TIMES OF WASHINGTON, March 5, 1984 at A9. Increasingly today, judges give jurors written copies of the instructions or a tape recording of the oral instructions.

Errors in jury instructions are a common basis for appeal and reversal. As a result, courts tend to rely on jury instructions that have been previously challenged and upheld. Unfortunately, such instruction while legally accurate are not always easy for lay juries to understand.

Consider this standard jury instruction on proximate cause:

> The proximate cause is that which, in the natural and continuous sequence, unbroken by other causes, produces an event, and without which the event would not have occurred. Proximate cause is that which is nearest in the order of responsible causes, as distinguished from remote, that which stands last in causation, not necessarily in time or place, but in causal relation. It is sometimes called the dominant cause.

1 SUGGESTED PATTERN JURY INSTRUCTIONS 231 (3d ed. 1991) (for Georgia). How helpful do you find this instruction?

b. Form of the Verdict

In most civil cases, the jury renders a general verdict, that is, it announces who wins and how much, but does not indicate its rationale or how it resolved particular issues. Rule 49 offers alternatives to the general verdict.

Rule 49(a) authorizes use of the special verdict by which the court asks the jury to decide one or more specific factual questions but is not asked to decide the bottom-line issue of who wins or loses. Proponents of the special verdict claim because the questions focus the jury's attention on the critical disputed facts, and the jury never actually decide who wins and who loses, its decision will be more scientific and less subject to prejudices. This argument assumes that juries will be unable to determine, or at least guess, which side benefits from a particular factual conclusion. Moreover, some question the desirability of making jury verdicts more scientific. Dissenting from the adoption of the 1963 amendments to the Federal Rules of Civil Procedure, Justices Black and Douglas wrote of Rule 49:

> Such devices are used to impair or wholly take away the power of a jury to render a general verdict. One of the ancient, fundamental reasons for having general jury verdicts was to preserve the right of trial by jury as an indispensable part of a free government. Many of the most famous constitutional controversies in England revolved around litigants' insistence, particularly in seditious libel cases, that a jury had the right to render a general verdict without being compelled to return a number of subsidiary findings to support its general verdict. Some English jurors had to go to jail because they insisted upon their right to render general verdicts over the repeated commands of tyrannical judges not to do so. Rule 49 is but another means utilized by courts to weaken the constitutional power of juries and to vest judges with more power to decide cases according to their own judgments. A scrutiny of the special verdict and written interrogatory cases in appellate courts will show the confusion that necessarily results from the employment of these devices and the ease with which judges can use them to take away the right to trial by jury. We believe that Rule 49 should be repealed, not amplified.

374 U.S. 861, 867-68 (1963).

At a practical level, it is not always easy to write a set of unambiguous questions. Courts that use special verdicts must often deal with apparently inconsistent answers. See, e.g., Gallick v. Baltimore & Ohio R.R., 372 U.S. 108 (1963) (no fatal inconsistency where jury answered foreseeability interrogatories in negative, but still found negligence).

Rule 49(b) allows the use of a general verdict supplemented with one or more specific questions. As with the special verdict, this can be used to focus the jury's attention on particular issues, although, here too, ambiguity and inconsistent answers sometimes result.

c. Judicial Comment

In federal court, the judge is not limited merely to instructing the jury on the law. The judge is also permitted to comment on the evidence and express her opinion on factual issues. As the Supreme Court has explained:

> In a trial by jury in a federal court, the judge is not a mere moderator, but is the governor of the trial for the purpose of assuring its proper conduct and of deter-

mining questions of law. In charging the jury, the trial judge is not limited to instructions of an abstract sort. It is within his province, whenever he thinks it necessary, to assist the jury in arriving at a just conclusion by explaining and commenting upon the evidence, by drawing their attention to the parts of it which he thinks important; and he may express his opinion upon the facts, provided he makes it clear to the jury that all matters of fact are submitted to their determination.

Quercia v. United States, 289 U.S. 466, 469 (1933). Despite this apparently broad range for judicial comment, the Court held that the following comment by the trial judge went too far in invading the province of the jury:

And now I am going to tell you what I think of the defendant's testimony. You may have noticed, Mr. Foreman and gentlemen, that he wiped his hands during his testimony. It is rather a serious thing, but that is almost always an indication of lying. Why it should be so we don't know, but that is the fact. I think that every single word that man said, except when he agreed with the government's testimony, was a lie.

Id. at 468.

d. Juror Misconduct

Suppose that following a jury verdict, interviews with jurors reveal that they misunderstood the instructions, flipped a coin to decide the case, were intoxicated during deliberations or were bribed. Would this information be a basis to overturn the verdict?

The common law rule was that the affidavits of jurors could not be used to impeach their verdict. Although this rule was framed as a rule of evidence, which made jurors' testimony inadmissible, its effect was to insulate from review most types of juror misconduct, because frequently the jurors themselves will be the only source of evidence.

What are the costs and benefits of insulating jury conduct from scrutiny? The justifications for the traditional rule are:

(1) the need for stability of verdicts; (2) the need to protect jurors from fraud and harassment by disappointed litigants; (3) the desire to prevent prolonged litigation; (4) the need to prevent verdicts from being set aside because of subsequent doubts or change of attitude by a juror; (5) the concept of the sanctity of the jury room.

Sopp v. Smith, 377 P.2d 649, 653 (Cal. 1963) (Peters, J. dissenting). To what extent does the traditional rule meet these goals? Are these goals of sufficient importance to justify the rule? Are there some kinds of jury conduct (or misconduct) that should be subject to scrutiny?

D. Controlling and Second-Guessing Juries

Some jurisdictions have modified the traditional approach and adopted instead what has come to be called "the Iowa rule." This approach is based upon the distinction between extrinsic and intrinsic influences. Extrinsic influences involve overt acts which may be objectively corroborated or disproved. Extrinsic influences include a juror conducting an independent investigation of the facts outside the courtroom, or the jury using an illegal method of reaching a verdict (such as flipping a coin). Evidence concerning extrinsic influences is admissible. Intrinsic influences are matters known only to the individual juror, such as a juror's thought processes, motives, misunderstandings or prejudices. Intrinsic influences are not readily capable of being either corroborated or disproved and are, therefore, excluded. Intrinsic influences are sometimes said to "inhere in the verdict".

Rule 606(b) of the Federal Rules of Evidence provides:

> Upon an inquiry into the validity of a verdict or indictment, a juror may not testify as to any matter or statement occurring during the course of the jury's deliberations or to the effect of anything upon his or any other juror's mind or emotions as influencing him to assent to or dissent from the verdict or indictment or concerning his mental processes in connection therewith, except that a juror may testify on the question whether extraneous prejudicial information was improperly brought to the jury's attention or whether any outside influence was improperly brought to bear upon any juror. Nor may his affidavit or evidence of any statement by him concerning a matter about which he would be precluded from testifying be received for these purposes.

Under this rule, could a juror testify that members of the jury were under the influence of drugs or alcohol during the trial or deliberations? Would this constitute an "outside influence" that was improperly brought to bear? In Tanner v. United States, 483 U.S. 107 (1987), the Supreme Court held that such evidence was *not* admissible to impeach a verdict. According to the juror whose testimony was not admissible, several of the jurors regularly had several alcoholic drinks during lunch and regularly smoked marijuana during the trial. Two other jurors ingested cocaine on multiple occasions. Justice O'Connor explained that "[h]owever severe their effect and improper their use, drugs or alcohol voluntarily ingested by a juror seems no more an 'outside influence' than a virus, poorly prepared food, or a lack of sleep." Id. at 122. Is taking cocaine really equivalent to having indigestion? Mr. Tanner's felony conviction was upheld despite the alleged outrageous conduct of the jury. Was this just?

Suppose some jurors made racially derogatory remarks to other jurors concerning one of the parties. Would this be a basis to grant a new trial? The Florida Supreme Court, applying Florida law, held that a new trial was proper under these circumstances. Powell v. Allstate Ins. Co., 652 So.2d 354 (1995). The court concluded that because the racially biased remarks were spoken, not merely thought privately, they constituted "sufficient 'overt acts' to permit trial court inquiry." The court further reasoned that "the conduct alleged herein, established, [would] be violative of the guarantees of both the federal and state constitutions which ensures all litigants a fair and impartial jury and equal protection of the law." Would the verdict in *Powell* be subject to impeachment under Federal Rule 606? See Carson v. Polley, 689 F. 2d 562, 581 (5th Cir. 1982) (racially biased remark by juror not admissible to impeach verdict). Does it make sense for the federal courts to prohibit race-based used of peremptory challenges, but allow blatant racism within the jury once it is selected?

Suppose that after the verdict, you learn that one of the jurors gave an incorrect answer during voir dire. Is that a basis for a new trial? In McDonough Power Equipment, Inc. v. Greenwood, 464 U.S. 548, 555-56 (1984), the Supreme Court held that incorrect voir dire answers provide a basis for a new trial in only limited circumstances:

> To invalidate the result of a 3-week trial because of a juror's mistaken, though honest, response to a question, is to insist on something closer to perfection than our judicial system can be expected to give. A trial represents an important investment of private and social resources, and it ill serves the important end of finality to wipe the slate clean simply to recreate the peremptory challenge process because counsel lacked an item of information which objectively he should have obtained from a juror on voir dire examination. * * * We hold that to obtain a new trial in such a situation, a party must first demonstrate that a juror failed to answer honestly a material question on voir dire, and then further show that a correct response would have provided a valid basis for a challenge for cause. The motives for concealing information may vary, but only those reasons that affect a juror's impartiality can truly be said to affect the fairness of a trial.

4. Motions to Set Aside the Judgment

We have already encountered one other post-trial motion by which a trial court can correct errors — the motion to set aside the judgment under rule 60(b). We discussed this motion in the materials on default judgments in Section D(4) of Chapter 8 and considered the Second Circuit's treatment of such a motion in *DeWeerth v. Baldinger,* in Chapter 7, and *Hadges v. Yonkers Racing Corporation*, in Chapter 8. Note the broad range of grounds on which a party may move to set aside and the rule's limitation on time in which the motion may be brought. In many cases, these bases will not be available to support a motion for JMOL or new trial. Sometimes, however, a party failing to make a timely motion for JMOL, or new trial will attempt to gain relief under Rule 60(b). It is important to note that the motion to set aside is not an appeal; it is made to the trial court that entered the judgment.

Of course, being able to make the motion is no guaranty that it will be granted; the issue is left to the discretion of the trial judge. As you would predict, granting a motion to set aside a judgment is an extraordinary occurrence.

Rule 60(a) is more easily invoked, but addresses only the correction of clerical errors.

CHAPTER 11

THE PRECLUSION DOCTRINES

Judgment Precludes Subsequent Litigation

A. Introduction and Integration

In this Chapter, we study the circumstances under which a judgment precludes subsequent litigation. Obviously, the assessment of such a preclusive effect requires consideration of at least two suits, one of which has gone to judgment. The question then becomes whether the judgment in the first case precludes the parties from litigating anything in the second case. By "first case," we refer to the first case in which a court enters judgment; the order in which they are filed is irrelevant.

A judgment can preclude subsequent litigation in two basic ways, traditionally referred to as *res judicata* ("the thing is adjudicated") and *collateral estoppel*. In recent years, influenced by the Restatement (Second) of Judgments, courts have begun to use the more descriptive terms *claim preclusion* and *issue preclusion*. The confusion over labels is compounded by the fact that some courts refer to the generic effect of preclusion as res judicata and to collateral estoppel as a sub-species of res judicata. For our purposes, what we refer to generically as preclusion is divided into two doctrines, claim preclusion (which many courts still call res judicata or the rule against splitting a cause of action) and issue preclusion (which many courts still call collateral estoppel or, less frequently, estoppel by judgment).

Claim preclusion stands for the proposition that a claimant may only sue on a single claim or "cause of action" once. Obviously, then, a claimant must appreciate the scope of her claim before filing suit. As we will see, one claim can encompass more than one right to relief. For instance, a single act by the defendant may cause personal injuries as well as property damage. If the claim is defined to include all harms caused by the defendant's act, it will encompass both personal injuries and property damage. In such a situation, a claimant who sues only for property damage in the first case will be precluded from bringing a second suit for personal injuries. She has one chance to vindicate *all rights to relief encompassed in a single claim*; failure to do so means that she has lost the right to pursue other aspects of relief encompassed in that claim.

CHAPTER 11   THE PRECLUSION DOCTRINES

Issue preclusion is narrower, and prevents relitigation of particular issues that were actually litigated and determined in the first case. For example, assume that in the first case the claimant litigated and established issues A, B, C and D; assume further that in her second case, to recover on a different claim, the claimant must establish issues A, X, Y and Z. Issue preclusion, if applicable, would operate to deem issue A established in the second case. The defendant could not relitigate that issue, and the plaintiff would establish her right to relief by proving issues X, Y and Z. Of course, issue preclusion will apply only if the second case is permitted to proceed. If claim preclusion bars the second suit, there is no occasion to consider issue preclusion.

One obvious policy justification for preclusion is efficiency. Claim preclusion counsels claimants to seek all rights to relief from a single cause of action in one case. Issue preclusion teaches that one may not relitigate an issue on which she has litigated and lost. There are other policy justifications, as we will see. On the other hand, overzealous application of preclusion might jeopardize a party's opportunity to litigate, and thus might undermine important due process protection. Accordingly, throughout the chapter, consider the relative costs that would be imposed on the parties and the judicial system if the courts did not follow the preclusion doctrines, on the one hand, and the litigant's right to present evidence, on the other.

At the outset, it is useful to contrast claim and issue preclusion with several similar concepts. *Double jeopardy* is the criminal law analog to claim preclusion. While the requirements of the two are not the same, each ensures that no one is made to answer twice for the same wrong. Once a criminal defendant has been tried and acquitted or otherwise put in "jeopardy" of conviction (a point for which there is no particularly easy definition), the prosecution cannot bring the same charge against that defendant in a subsequent proceeding.

Stare decisis, or the doctrine of precedent, requires that courts of a particular jurisdiction follow the legal pronouncements of appellate courts in that jurisdiction. For example, if a state supreme court determines that comparative negligence should supplant the common law rule of contributory negligence, all courts of that state are required to apply comparative negligence. Stare decisis differs from issue preclusion in two important ways. First, it is concerned with appellate pronouncements on questions of law, while preclusion addresses trial court determinations of issues of law or fact.* Second, an opinion's stare decisis effect binds all litigants in all cases in the jurisdiction, while issue preclusion binds only litigants to the particular case (and persons in "privity" with them). Third, the court that

---

* Although issue preclusion can apply both to matters of fact and law, it is most commonly used regarding questions of fact. Issue preclusion on matters of law can raise special problems, as we will see infra at 598.

issued the precedent has the discretion to reverse or alter it whereas there is less discretion with the preclusion rules.

Finally, the doctrine of *law of the case* provides that issues decided in a suit will not be relitigated later in that same suit. For example, if a court decides an issue during pre-trial motions, that determination will bind the parties whenever that issue reappears in the course of the litigation. It differs from issue preclusion in two ways. First, law of the case concerns the same issue being raised multiple times in the same action, while issue preclusion is concerned with raising the same issue in different actions. Second, law of the case is less formal than issue preclusion; a judge is free to depart from an earlier ruling on an issue when appropriate. See generally Allan Vestal, *Law of the Case: Single Suit Preclusion*, 1967 UTAH L. REV. 1.

B. Claim Preclusion

Although the language employed by various courts differs, the standard statement of claim preclusion contains three requirements: (1) the two cases must involve the same claim (or, as some jurisdictions refer to it, cause of action); (2) the parties to the two suits must be identical or in "privity"; and (3) the first case must have ended in a valid final judgment "on the merits." See, e.g., Kale v. Combined Ins. Co., 924 F. 2d 1161 (1st Cir. 1991).

1. Scope of a Claim

a. In General

Courts and commentators agree that defining the scope of a claim (which we use interchangeably with "cause of action") is difficult. For example, the Pennsylvania Supreme Court admits that it "has never adopted a comprehensive definition of what constitutes a cause of action, for the excellent reason that no such definition exists." Kuisis v. Baldwin-Lima-Hamilton Corp., 319 A. 2d 914, 918 n. 7 (Pa. 1974). Because of different contending definitions, one commentator over four decades ago said "on a given set of facts there seems to be at least one rule to buttress any result, and the same tests often can sustain opposite positions." *Developments in the Law—Res Judicata*, 65 HARV. L. REV. 818, 825 (1952). One can say much the same thing today. The continuing uncertainty reflects important policy choices on which jurisdictions may disagree.

Carter v. Hinkle
52 S.E.2d 135 (Va. 1949)

GREGORY, J., delivered the opinion of the Court.

A taxicab owned and driven by Hinkle was involved in a head-on collision with an automobile owned by the defendant, Smith, and operated by his agent, the defendant, Carter. The collision occurred in Alleghany county, on U.S. Route 60, near the town of Covington, on December 20, 1946, and it is conceded that it was the proximate result of the negligence of the defendant, Carter. The taxi was damaged and an action was instituted by the plaintiff, Hinkle, against the defendant, Smith, for $1,000, $750 of which represented damage to the taxi and $250 damages for the loss of the use of it. Judgment was recovered, the full amount paid thereon and it was marked satisfied.

Later, Hinkle instituted another action against the two named defendants seeking to recover for personal injuries received by him by reason of the collision. The defendants pleaded that the judgment and its satisfaction in the first action was a bar to Hinkle's right to bring the second action for the personal injuries. The court overruled that contention and permitted the case to go to the jury. A verdict was returned in favor of the plaintiff for the sum of $1,000, and judgment was entered, from which this writ of error was obtained.

The question involved is one of law: May one who has suffered both damage to his property and injury to his person as the result of a single wrongful act maintain two separate actions therefor, or is a judgment obtained in the first action a bar to the second? We have no Virginia decision upon the point.

The question has been presented to the courts many times and there is a direct conflict of American authority on the subject. The majority of the American courts of last resort are of the view that but one single cause of action exists and that but one action may be brought therefor.

On the other hand a respectable * * * minority of the courts are of the view that a single tort, resulting in damage to both person and property, gives rise to two distinct causes of action, and that, therefore, recovery in one is no bar to an action subsequently commenced for the other. The minority view is based upon the English case of Brunsden v. Humphrey (1884), L.R. 14 Q.B.D. 141.

* * *

Typical of the minority rule are the cases of Vasu v. Kohlers, Inc. (1945), 145 Ohio St. 321, and Reilly v. Sicilian Asphalt Paving Co. (1902), 170 N.Y. 40. In the latter case, which is a leading one, the court had this to say: "The question now before us has been the subject of conflicting decisions in different jurisdictions. In England it has been held by the court of appeals (Lord Coleridge, C.J., dissenting) that damages to the person and to property, though occasioned by the same wrongful act, give rise to different causes of action (*Brunsden v. Humphrey*), while in Massachusetts, Minnesota, and Missouri the contrary doctrine has been declared. The argument of those courts which maintain that an injury to person and property creates but a single cause of action is that, as the defendant's wrongful act was single, the cause of action must be single, and that the different injuries occasioned by it are merely items of damage proceeding from the same wrong, while that of the English court is that the negligent act of the defendant in itself constitutes no cause of action, and becomes an actionable wrong only out of the damage which it causes. 'One wrong was done as soon as the plaintiff's enjoyment of his property was substantially interfered with. A further wrong arose as soon as the driving also caused injury to the plaintiff's person.' *Brunsden v. Humphrey.*"

The court, in that case (*Reilly v. Sicilian Asphalt Paving Co.*), concluded that injury to person and injury to property were essentially different and gave rise to two causes of action; that to hold that only one cause of action exists would be impractical or at least very inconvenient in the administration of justice, and that they should not be blended. The court noted that different periods of limitation applied; that the plaintiff cannot assign his right of action for the injury to his person, while he could assign that for injury to his property; that action for injury to his person would abate or be lost by his death before a recovery; and that injury to property would be an action that would survive and might be seized by creditors or pass to an assignee in bankruptcy. * * *

In *Vasu v. Kohlers, Inc.*, the Ohio court * * * adopted the minority view, * * * and distinguished between torts to the person and torts to property. The court expressed the thought in this language: "A critical and analytical study of the two-causes-of-action rule will demonstrate that it is in harmony and keeping with the historical and logical development of the common law on that subject * * * . The distinctions involved are most important because they involve not only the determination of what constitutes causes of action but the necessary relation of such causes of action to the doctrine of res judicata."

The right of personal security and the right of property which are invaded by a single wrong give rise to two remedial rights, said the court, and further, in giving the reason for the rule, it said that consideration must be given to the fact that where a property right is invaded the title to the property must be shown to be in the plaintiff, whereas there is no such requirement as to personal injuries. * * *

The court further called attention to the fact that nearly all of the cases which support the single-cause-of action rule involve situations where the plaintiff brought the action in his own right to recover both his property and personal injury damages, and that the rule against splitting demands which would limit the plaintiff to a single action is based on the idea of unreasonable vexation of the defendant rather than upon a discriminating conception of a cause of action. However, when a tort-feasor has committed a tort resulting in damage to both person and property there is nothing vexatious or unreasonable in prosecuting separate actions against him. * * *

It will be observed that an argument to support the majority view is that the single-cause-of-action rule will prevent the crowding of courts with unnecessary litigation, prevent vexatious litigation, eliminate added court costs and delay, and expeditiously end litigation.

That argument is answered in *Vasu v. Kohlers, Inc.*, where the court said: "* * * Short cuts and improvisations may be appealing, but if certainty and predictability, qualities so necessary in the law, are to be maintained, the logical and symmetrical distinctions of the substantive common law, carefully developed through the necessities of experience, should be preserved and not destroyed. In the complexity of life the combinations of fact which give rise to legal liability are infinite, and as a consequence a heavy burden is necessarily imposed upon procedural processes. Nevertheless, rights are too important and liability is too oppressive to be determined and administered in wholesale fashion. * * *"

The minority view follows a less practical but a more logical path. Each jurisdiction concerned has chosen a measuring stick regarded by it as the most important. When it is remembered that the plaintiff usually institutes an action in order to obtain compensation for damages done to his rights rather than to punish the defendant for the wrong, it would seem that the question of the number of rights invaded would be the more important one. * * *

In the English case of *Brunsden v. Humphrey*, the plaintiff brought an action to recover for damages done to his cab in a collision caused by the negligence of the defendant's servant, and after having recovered the amount claimed he brought another action against the defendant claiming damages for personal injury sustained through the same negligent act. After he obtained a verdict the court ruled in favor of the defendant on the ground that the action was not for a new wrong but for a consequence of the same wrongful act which was the subject of the former suit. On appeal the judgment was reversed and the judgment on the verdict for the plaintiff was restored. The Master of the Rolls said that the causes of action were distinct and therefore the court was not called upon to apply the doctrine of res judicata. It was suggested that different evidence would be required to support the respective claims for injury to property and to the person of the plaintiff, and on this point Lord Justice Bowen said, "In the one case the identity of the man injured and the character of his injuries would be in issue, and justifications might conceivably be pleaded as to the assault, which would have nothing to do with the damage done to the goods and chattels."

In speaking of the gist of the action, Lord Justice Bowen said, "[I]t is sufficient to say that the gist of an action for negligence seems to me to be the harm to person or property negligently perpetrated. * * * Both causes of action, in one sense, may be said to be founded upon one act of the defendant's servant, but they are not on that account identical causes of action. The wrong consists in the damage done without lawful excuse, not the act of driving, which (if no damage had ensued) would have been legally unimportant."

Lord Chief Justice Coleridge dissented, taking the other view. He said: "It appears to me that whether the negligence of the servant or the impact of the vehicle which the servant drove, be the technical cause of action, equally the cause of action is one and the same; that the injury done to the plaintiff is injury done to him at one and the same moment by one and the same act in respect to different rights, i.e., his person and his goods, I do not in the least deny; but it seems to me a subtlety not warranted by law to hold that a man cannot bring two actions, if he is injured in his arm and in his leg, but can bring two, if besides his arm and leg being injured, his trousers which contain his leg, and his coat sleeve which contains his arm, have been torn."

This case does not hold that it would have been improper to join the two causes of action in one, subject to certain exceptions not important here. The English rule permits a plaintiff to unite in the same action several causes of action, but he is not compelled to do so.

The weight of American authority, as we have previously stated, disagrees with the decision in *Brunsden v. Humphrey*, but we believe that the principles announced in that case, upon which the minority rule is founded, are more logical and better suited to our practice in Virginia.

NOTES AND QUESTIONS

1. Do you agree that the "primary rights" test, adopted in *Carter*, is "less practical but* * * more logical" than the "single wrongful act" test? How is it less practical? How is it more logical? Between these two—pragmatism and logic—which should prevail? Can you articulate how the single wrongful act definition of claim is broader than the primary rights definition?

2. The court supported its conclusion in *Carter* by noting several differences between claims for property damages and for personal injuries. The former is assignable and does not abate at plaintiff's death. The latter is not assignable and does abate. The two have different statutes of limitations. Should these factors be relevant in defining a claim for preclusion purposes? What role should pleading rules have? Suppose, for example, that Virginia's pleading rules restricted a plaintiff's ability to seek recovery for property and personal damage in a single case. Would that rule affect the definition of claim? If so, why shouldn't these other rules?

3. In *Carter*, the plaintiff sued in the first case both for damage to the taxi and loss of its use. Suppose instead he had sought only recovery for damage to the car. Would the Virginia court permit a second case for loss of use?

4. The tests discussed in *Carter* are not the only formulations for determining the scope of a claim. Some courts define claim by a third formula, the "sameness of the evidence" test (which the court mentioned in *Carter*). Under this test, courts assess whether the same evidentiary showing would justify recovery for the claimant in both suits. If so, the cases involve the same claim. It is not always clear, however, how much evidentiary overlap is required for the assertions to be considered a single claim.

For example, consider the facts of *Carter*. If the plaintiff sued only for property damage in the first case, would the sameness of the evidence test lead to dismissal of a second suit for personal injuries? To be sure, the evidence in the two cases will not be exactly the same, since the damages are different in the two cases. Indeed, recall the discussion of this point by Lord Justice Bowen in *Brunsden*, quoted in *Carter*. On the other hand, the evidence showing the defendant's liability will be identical. Is that enough to justify the conclusion that both cases involve the same cause of action? Most courts seem to think so. See, e.g., Sure-Snap Corp. v. State Street Bank & Trust Co., 948 F. 2d 869 (2d Cir. 1991); Buck Creek Indus. v. Alcon Constr., Inc., 631 F. 2d 75 (5th Cir. 1980); Kent County Bd. of Educ. v. Billbrough, 525 A.2d 232 (Md. 1987); Morris v. Union Oil Co., 421 N.E. 2d 278 (Ill. App. 1981).

If that is true, does the sameness of the evidence notion differ from the transactional test in any meaningful way? On the other hand, what was Lord Justice Bowen's conclusion regarding sameness of the evidence in *Brunsden*, as discussed in *Carter*?

5. The clear modern trend is to force claimants to package cases more inclusively, along transactional lines. This trend is typified by § 24(1) of the Restatement (Second) of Judgments, which may be considered a fourth test for claim. The Restatement (Second) considers a claim to encompass all rights to relief "with respect to all or any part of the transaction, or series of connected transactions, out of which the action arose." The drafters of this definition state that a transaction is "a natural grouping or common nucleus of operative facts." RESTATEMENT (SECOND) OF JUDGMENTS § 24 cmt. b (1982). They stress a pragmatic approach, focusing on factors such as whether the facts are closely connected in "time, space, origin, or motivation, * * * whether, taken together, they form a convenient unit for trial purposes," and whether treating them as a single transaction comports with the expectations of the parties and of business practice. Id.

The Restatement (Second) view comports with modern joinder rules and the rules for supplemental jurisdiction, all of which emphasize the transactional test as the appropriate definition of the litigative unit. See Allan Vestal, *Res Judicata/Preclusion: Expansion*, 47 S. CAL. L. REV. 357 (1974) (discussing efficiency fostered by broader definition of cause of action). Consistent with this modern trend, the Ohio Supreme Court overruled *Vasu v. Kohlers, Inc.* (discussed in *Carter*) and adopted a transactional test for claim in Rush v. City of Maple Heights, 147 N.E. 2d 599 (Ohio 1958).

6. How many claims would arise from the following fact patterns under (a) the primary rights definition, (b) the single wrongful act definition, (c) the sameness of the evidence definition, and (d) the Restatement (Second) definition?

(a) D places foreign substances in P's rum jug, thereby ruining the rum and damaging the jug. A week later, P drinks from the jug and becomes ill because of the adulteration. See Boerum v. Taylor, 19 Conn. 122 (1848).

(b) P owns two pieces of rural land, Fields A and C. They are separated by Field B, which is owned by someone else. On Field A, P has his house, a barn with stored crops for sale, a chicken house where he raises eggs for sale and for personal use, and a field of alfalfa almost ready for harvest. On Field C, he has a field of oats, partially harvested. Some of the oats already harvested are stored onsite on Field C and some in the barn on Field A. D negligently starts a fire which spreads from his land across Field A, Field B, and Field C, destroying everything mentioned.

(c) P and D, each driving her own car, collide. P suffers personal injuries and her car is damaged. In addition, two items of personal property in P's car are ruined by the collision—a video camera with which P pursues her livelihood of recording weddings and other special events, and an heirloom hand beveled mirror, which her grandmother had just given to her.

(d) Same facts as in C, but assume that immediately after the collision, D jumps from her car and screams obscenities at P, causing P emotional distress, and defames P by shouting libelous falsehoods about P to the crowd of onlookers.

(e) P enters an oral contract to buy land from D. After P pays, D refuses to convey the land. P sues for specific performance of the contract. D wins, however, because oral contracts for the conveyance of land are violate the statute of frauds and are therefore unenforceable. P then sues D under a theory of restitution, seeking not the conveyance of land, but return of the money she paid to D. Will the second action be dismissed under claim preclusion? See TEPLY & WHITTEN, CIVIL PROCEDURE 878.

In some older cases, courts would permit P to bring the second case, based upon what may be yet another approach to the scope of claim. These courts concluded that the second case involved a different "legal theory" from the first, and thus constituted a separate claim. This view was the product of common law pleading, which, as we saw in Chapter 8, narrowly circumscribed the plaintiff's ability to join claims against the defendant. Under the writ system, the plaintiff could pursue only a single legal theory in one case. Thus, the claim preclusion effect of a judgment in that case was correspondingly narrow.

7. Although most courts today employ relatively broad, transactional definitions of claim, not all jurisdictions have abandoned the primary rights approach. Similarly, do not assume that jurisdictions choose one test for all types of cases. For instance, the Virginia Supreme Court has never overruled *Carter*, although other decisions of that court support other definitions of cause of action. See, e.g., Flora, Flora & Montague, Inc. v. Saunders, 367 S.E. 2d 493 (Va. 1988) (sameness of evidence); Brown v. Haley, 355 S.E. 2d 563 (Va. 1987) (transactional test). Similarly, the New York Court of Appeals has never overruled *Reilly v. Sicilian Asphalt Paving Co.*, upon which the court relied in *Carter*. California and Illinois also have authority supporting application of the primary rights test. See Holmes v. Bricker, 452 P. 2d 647 (Cal. 1969); Stephan v. Yellow Cab Co., 333 N.E. 2d 223 (Ill. App. 1975).

In addition, some states have codified the primary rights approach. For example, a Georgia statute provides that motor vehicle crash cases create two causes of action — one for property damage and one for personal injury. GA. CODE ANN. § 51-1-32. See also OR. REV. STAT. §16.220.

The primary rights approach seems to promote duplicative litigation. In *Carter*, for example, the court's definition of claim permits the claimant to bring separate suits for property damage and for personal injuries. The taxpayers of Virginia therefore may be required to provide judicial machinery — judges, jurors, clerks, etc.—twice for adjudications concerning one set of underlying facts. Indeed, the court in *Carter* admitted that the single wrongful act definition would "expeditiously end litigation." What policy can justify the seeming inefficiency of adopting the primary rights definition? Are certain types of disputes better suited to the primary rights test?

Proponents of the primary rights theory argue that the rule avoids hardship in cases involving insurance coverage. Suppose Insured is injured and suffers property damage in an automobile crash with Bad Driver. Pursuant to Insured's policy, Insco, her insurer, pays her for the property damage. Upon doing so, the insurer is "subrogated" to Insured's right to sue for that property damage; that is, it "stands in the shoes" of the insured for that claim. Before Insurer sues, however, Insured recovers a judgment against Bad Driver for personal injuries. A strict reading of the transaction test could preclude Insurer from suing. The primary rights rule avoids this result by holding that there are two claims. Thus, several jurisdictions adopting a transaction test definition for claim simply make an exception for this subrogation situation. See, e.g. Smith v. Hutchins, 566 P. 2d 1136 (Nev. 1977); *Rush v. City of Maple Heights*, supra (noting that jurisdictions adopting transaction test "almost universally recognize[]" an exception to protect insurers).

There is also an argument that the primary rights definition may not be as inefficient as one might surmise. Consider the facts of *Carter* again. After prevailing in her first case, for property damage, the plaintiff brings a second action to recover for personal injuries. Under the primary rights approach, although the second case is not precluded by claim preclusion, the defendant may be barred *by issue preclusion* from relitigating the question of her negligence. Remember that issue preclusion bars the relitigation of particular issues that were litigated and determined in a prior case between the same parties. Thus, the plaintiff in the second case will not be required to prove the defendant's negligence. In *Andrews v. Christenson*, supra, 692 P. 2d at 690 n. 1, the court noted:

> The total judicial time consumed, even if both parts are actually tried, may not be significantly greater than trying them together. In fact, it is likely that both will not be tried. If the decision in the property damage case is against the plaintiff, there can be no second trial. If it is in favor of the plaintiff, the parties may well settle the damages claim.

8. Whatever definition is used for determining the scope of claim, that claim is personal to each individual harmed. Suppose Pam and Pat are passengers in a car and each is injured. However we define their claims—by primary rights or by transaction, etc.—Pam's is separate from Pat's. The fact that they were hurt in a single transaction may affect the scope of their individual claims, but it does not merge their separate claims into one.

b. Contract Cases

Do the various tests we have seen help us define the scope of a claim in contract and similar suits? Suppose P and D enter an installment sales contract, under which D is to pay P $5000 per month for twelve months. D makes the first two payments, but misses the third; then D makes the fourth and fifth payments, but fails to make the sixth. Can P bring separate suits against D for the two missed payments, or do they constitute a single claim?

Generally, courts conclude that the claim constitutes all amounts owed at the time the claimant files suit. Thus, in this hypothetical, P's claim would include both the breach in the third month and the breach in the sixth month. If P sued for only one of these, claim preclusion would prohibit her seeking damages for the other. If P had sued in the fourth month, however, at which time D had failed to pay only one installment, her claim would have consisted of only that single breach. She could then maintain a separate action for the breach in the sixth month (or could add the later claim in the pending case through a supplemental pleading under Rule 15(d)). The same rule applies to cases involving interest payments on a bond or other security.

This discussion assumes that the payments were due under a single instrument. Generally, each contract or bond gives rise to a separate claim or series of claims. Assume that both Contract-1 and Contract-2 require D to make periodic payments to P. One month, D fails to make the required payments under both contracts. P may maintain separate actions for the breach of Contract-1 and for the breach of Contract-2.

2. Parties or Persons in Privity

a. Who Can Be Bound?

Even if a second case involves the same claim as one that has gone to judgment, claim preclusion requires that the parties to the two suits be the same or in "privity" with a litigant in the prior case. This requirement reflects an abiding theme in our civil justice system: the commonly stated notion that everyone is entitled to her "day in court." Put more accurately, the due process clause generally requires that one cannot be bound by a judgment unless she has had an opportunity to appear and litigate. Martin v. Wilks, 490 U.S. 755 (1989). (We discussed the importance of adequate notice in ensuring this opportunity in Chapter 3.)

This constitutional precept is not absolute, however. Courts have long held that nonparties may be bound by a judgment, as noted above, if they are in "privity" with a party to the litigation. Because binding a nonparty precludes her from her "day in court," it can be done only in carefully circumscribed situations. The word "privity" is a catchall for those situations. Unfortunately, the word is not self-defining. Professor Moore long advocated a pragmatic approach to the concept, emphasizing not the language used but the relationship between the party to the first case and the nonparty to be bound by the judgment. 1B MOORE'S FEDERAL PRACTICE ¶ 0.411[1] at III-215. Thus, the modern approach, as exemplified by the Restatement (Second) of Judgments, is to eschew the term "privity" altogether, focusing generally upon two sorts of relationships between the litigant and the nonparty to be bound. Many courts still use the term, however, and throughout these materials, we will use "privity" as a shorthand for those relationships that justify binding a nonparty.

These relationships fall into two broad categories. First, a nonparty is bound by a judgment if she was "represented" by a party to another case. For example, a trustee litigating on behalf of an estate represents a beneficiary of the estate. As we will see in Chapter 13, the class action device allows a representative to sue or be sued on behalf of a group of similarly situated persons. Assuming the representative is adequate and the class is properly certified, all class members will be bound by the judgment entered. See Hansberry v. Lee, 311 U.S. 32 (1940).

Similarly, a guardian, executor or other fiduciary represents her beneficiaries in litigation, as long as she brings the litigation in that representative capacity. For example, in Virginia v. Johnson, 376 S.E. 2d 787 (Va. Ct. App. 1989), a woman filed a paternity suit against the alleged father of her son, seeking damages. After the court ruled for the man, the child sued him, also asserting paternity. The court refused to apply claim preclusion, because the first case had been brought by the mother in her own stead, and not as representative of the child. Had she sued as the child's guardian, representing his interests in the first suit, the judgment would have precluded the boy from bringing a second action.

Second, substantive legal relationships between a litigant and a nonparty will justify binding the nonparty. For example, successive owners of property are bound by a judgment affecting the property. Similarly, an action by a party to a contract regarding contract rights may bind a person to whom that party assigns the contract rights. An indemnitor (such as an insurance company) may be bound by a judgment against an indemnitee (such as the insured). A decedent's estate may be bound by a judgment against the decedent. For example, assume P is injured in an auto wreck, and sues to recover for personal injuries. After losing, P dies from the injuries. An unfavorable judgment against him in the personal injuries case may preclude his family for suing for wrongful death. See Brown v. Rahman, 282 Cal. Rptr. 815 (Cal. App. 1991). See generally JAMES, HAZARD & LEUBSDORF, CIVIL PROCEDURE 625-37.

NOTES AND QUESTIONS

1. If the opportunity to appear and litigate is a requirement of due process, how can nonparties ever be bound by a judgment? What policy supports binding nonparties in the circumstances discussed above? Consider such policies in light of the following.

(a) P-1, the owner of Greenacre, sues D, the adjoining landowner, to establish that she has a right of way to travel across D's property. After trial, the court enters judgment for D. P-1 sells Greenacre to P-2, who then sues, asserting the same right of way rejected in the prior suit. Should the fact that P-2 was not a party to the first case permit her to maintain this new action? What are the costs to D and to the community if we permit the second action to proceed? What are the costs to P-2 if we do not permit the second action to proceed?

(b) Same facts as in (a) above, but assume that the judgment in the first case was erroneous as a matter of law. To correct that, P-1 could have appealed the judgment. Assume, however, that she did not. Is P-2 bound by the judgment? If not, can you articulate the circumstances under which P-2 should be allowed to proceed? What if it was "possible" that the judgment in the first case was wrong?

2. Can a nonparty be bound by a judgment simply because she is represented by a litigant, or does she have to be notified of the proceedings? Section 41(2) of the Restatement (Second) of Judgments expressly provides that a nonparty represented by a litigant "is bound by the judgment even though [she] does not have notice of the action, is not served with process, or is not subject to service of process." How can this statement be justified, however, in light of other materials we have studied? For most of this course, we have considered the due process ideal to be that no one is bound by a judgment unless she is joined as a party and given notice and an opportunity to participate. Thus, due process restrictions on personal jurisdiction sought to ensure that the defendant not litigate in an unduly burdensome forum. Similarly, the notice we discussed in Chapter 3 was intended to make meaningful a *party's* opportunity to appear and litigate. But if the person to be bound is not going to be joined as a party, why should personal jurisdiction and notice be required?

This notion of binding nonparties because of their relationship to a litigant is controversial, but well accepted under certain circumstances. In addition to those discussed above, we will consider other situations in which a nonparty may be bound in Section C(3) below. The best example of representative litigation is the class action, which we will address in detail in Chapter 13.

b. Configuration of the Parties

Even assuming that the parties to the first and second actions are the same (or closely related enough to justify preclusion), claim preclusion generally requires that they have the same litigation posture in both cases. Claim preclusion basically bars repeat assertions of a claim by the same person. Therefore, it is not enough simply to say that both cases involve the same parties. Instead, in most jurisdictions, both the first and second cases must be brought by the same claimant against the same defendant. Put another way, the second suit must involve the same parties *in the same configuration.*

For instance, suppose in the first case Adams sues Baker for injuries sustained in an auto collision between the two. After a final judgment in that case, Baker sues Adams to recover for injuries sustained in the same wreck. Can Adams assert claim preclusion against Baker? The general principles of claim preclusion would suggest not. Even though the two cases involved the same parties, Baker has not asserted a claim before and thus cannot be guilty of trying to get two bites of the same apple. Another way to look at it is that the first case involved a different claim, since it was for the vindication of Adams's rights, while the second case was for vindication of Baker's rights.

This result emphasizes another aspect of the ingrained sense that a claimant has a right to her "day in court." In general, a potential claimant can sue when and where she pleases, subject, of course, to jurisdictional principles and the statute of limitations. In this scenario, the fact that Adams decided to sue Baker may not preclude Baker from deciding to pursue her own claim in a separate proceeding. Obviously, absolute litigant autonomy in this regard is inefficient. Here, it would require the judicial system to process two pieces of litigation over a single factual occurrence. This may create a risk of inconsistent results, which can erode public confidence in the administration of justice.

Because of concerns about efficiency and consistency, most jurisdictions modify the result suggested by the general principles of claim preclusion by adopting a *compulsory counterclaim rule*. See, e.g., Rule 13(a). Such a rule, which we will study in detail in Chapter 12, requires a defendant to assert all transactionally related claims against the plaintiff in the pending case. Thus, when Adams sues Baker, the compulsory counterclaim rule would require Baker to assert her claim arising from the same accident in that case. If she failed to do so, the same rule would require the court in which Baker brings suit against Adams to dismiss.

This explains why we are careful to use the term "claimant" (instead of "plaintiff") in discussing claim preclusion; parties other than the plaintiff can assert claims. For example, suppose again that Adams sues Baker for injuries sustained in an auto collision between them. Here, however, assume that Baker files a compulsory counterclaim against Adams, seeking to recover for her personal injuries from the same collision. After a valid final judgment is entered in that case, suppose Baker sues Adams again regarding the same claim. Here, claim preclusion may bar the second case. Even though Baker was not the plaintiff in the first action, she was a "claimant."

NOTES AND QUESTIONS

1. The compulsory counterclaim rule requires a person already joined as a party to assert transactionally related claims against another party. It overrides only the defendant's

perceived "right" to choose the forum for her claim. The notion of binding a nonparty to the case, obviously, is a far more serious matter, since it precludes the nonparty from pursuing a claim at all.

2. The compulsory counterclaim rule certainly seems to promote efficiency and avoid inconsistent results. But aren't these policies vindicated by issue preclusion as well? Suppose Adams sues Baker for damages arising from their auto collision. The court finds that Baker was negligent, and enters judgment for Adams. Now, because there is no compulsory counterclaim rule, Baker sues Adams for injuries sustained in the same wreck. Won't issue preclusion prevent Baker from relitigating the issue of his negligence? Will this result foster efficiency and consistency to the same degree as the compulsory counterclaim rule?

3. The permissive counterclaim, recognized in most jurisdictions, allows the defendant to assert transactionally *unrelated* claims against the plaintiff. See Rule 13(b). As the name implies, the defendant is not required to assert such a claim. Thus, assume Adams sues Baker for injuries suffered in their auto crash. If Baker has an unrelated contract claim against Adams, she may choose to file it as a permissive counterclaim in the pending case, or she may assert it in a separate action. If she does assert it, however, she is a "claimant" on that contract claim; claim preclusion will prevent her from suing again on the contract claim.

4. Assume the same auto collision between Adams and Baker, and that there is no compulsory counterclaim rule. Adams sues Baker, and Baker asserts the defense of contributory negligence. Obviously, Baker could have raised this as a permissive counterclaim if she had desired. There is some authority for the proposition that Baker has split her claim by raising the *defense*, and that claim preclusion will prevent her from suing for her own damages arising from Adams's negligence. See Mitchell v. Federal Intermediate Credit Bank, 164 S.E. 2d 136 (S.C. 1932).

3. Valid, Final Judgment On the Merits

a. Validity

Courts accord claim or issue preclusion only to valid judgments. Validity as used here refers to the competence of the court, and requires basically that it have had subject matter and personal jurisdiction. A judgment by a court having both forms of jurisdiction is valid, even though it may have been wrong on the merits. If a party feels that the judgment was erroneous, the proper course is to appeal it in the original jurisdiction. As the Supreme Court has explained, "the res judicata consequences of a final, unappealed judgment on the merits [are not] altered by the fact that the judgment may have been wrong or rested on a legal principle subsequently overruled in another case." Federated Dept. Stores, Inc. v. Moitie, 452 U.S. 394, 398 (1981).

b. Finality

Preclusion attaches only to final judgments. Thus individual rulings during the course of a litigation are not entitled to preclusive effect, since they may be revisited by the judge before decision on the case as a final matter. At best, such nonfinal, or interlocutory, orders are entitled to such deference as dictated by the law of the case doctrine, noted in Section A of this Chapter.

Suppose a court enters a valid final judgment on the merits, and the losing party appeals. It will take months, perhaps even years, for the appellate court to decide the case. In the interim, is the trial court's judgment entitled to claim preclusion effect? The federal courts conclude that it is. See, e.g., Wagner v. Taylor, 836 F. 2d 596 (D.C. Cir. 1987). The state courts, on the other hand, disagree on the issue.

What arguments support recognition of a preclusive effect during appeal? What arguments counsel the opposite result? Suppose the court in the second case affords preclusive effect to a judgment that is later reversed. What can the court that decided the second case do to remedy the problem? See Rule 60.

c. On the Merits

Traditionally, courts have accorded preclusive effect only to judgments "on the merits," meaning judgments "based on the validity of the plaintiff's claim rather than on a technical procedural ground." FRIEDENTHAL, KANE & MILLER, CIVIL PROCEDURE 652. Clearly, a judgment entered after plenary trial would be on the merits. But a trial is not required. For example, summary judgments and directed verdicts constitute decisions on the merits. Id. at 653. Indeed, it is virtually impossible for a claimant to win without establishing her right to recover. Thus virtually any judgment *in favor* of the claimant is considered on the merits. Even a judgment by default is on the merits because it establishes the substantive validity of the claim. Morris v. Jones, 329 U.S. 545 (1947).

The more difficult situations arise when the claimant loses. Again, she may lose after trial, or on summary judgment or pursuant to directed verdict, any of which is on the merits. But she may also lose for a variety of other reasons. For example, the court may dismiss for claimant's failure to prosecute, or as a discovery sanction, or for lack of jurisdiction or venue. Judgments on these bases would appear to have nothing to do with the merits of the underlying dispute. On the other hand, given liberal modern provisions for pleading, amendment, joinder, and discovery, is there any reason to permit a claimant to bring the same claim again after such a dismissal?

In view of such modern provisions, and because of historic difficulty defining "on the merits," the current approach avoids the phrase. The Restatement (Second) of Judgments "does not require that a judgment against the plaintiff be on the merits to be preclusive." JAMES, HAZARD & LEUBSDORF, CIVIL PROCEDURE 607. As Professor Wright explains, "[i]t is sufficient that in the first litigation there was an opportunity to get to the merits." WRIGHT, FEDERAL COURTS 723. Section 20(1)(a) of the Restatement (Second) thus provides a blanket rule that any judgment against the claimant, *except* one "for lack of jurisdiction, for improper venue, or for nonjoinder or misjoinder of parties" is accorded claim preclusive effect.

Federal Rule 41(b) adopts this approach, dictating that any judgment against the claimant, with exceptions similar to those in the Restatement (Second), "operates as an adjudication upon the merits." Under both Rule 41(b) and the Restatement (Second) the court in the first case is free to provide that its judgment will not operate on the merits. Usually, courts do this by providing that the dismissal is entered "without prejudice."

Read Rule 41(b).

NOTES AND QUESTIONS

1. Why should dismissals for lack of jurisdiction, improper venue, and failure to join an indispensable party not preclude a second suit?

2. By "lack of jurisdiction," should Rule 41(b) be construed to refer to personal jurisdiction, subject matter jurisdiction, or both? Why?

3. P sues D for personal injuries suffered in an auto crash with D. Before trial, the court enters judgment for plaintiff because defendant committed abuses under the discovery rules. Now P sues D for property damage suffered in the same crash. Assume the jurisdiction adopts a transactional test for claim. Can D successfully assert claim preclusion against P? Note that Rule 41(b) does not apply. Why?

4. Suppose the court dismisses P's case against D under Rule 12(b)(6), because P failed to state a claim under which relief can be granted. (In some state courts, the functional equivalent would be dismissal based upon D's demurrer.) The court's order says nothing about whether the dismissal is with prejudice. Now P brings a separate case, correcting the allegations of the first complaint in a way that states a claim. Can D successfully assert claim preclusion? Most federal courts say yes. See, e.g., Hall v. Tower Land & Investment Co., 512 F. 2d 481 (5th Cir. 1975). State courts adopting the federal rules generally agree. See, e.g., Velasquez v. Franz, 589 A.2d 143 (N.J. Super. 1991).

Note, however, that some state courts following code pleading rules, in which amendment provisions may not be so liberal, do not prevent plaintiff from filing a second case alleging different facts to support the claim. See, e.g., In re Estate of Cochrane, 391 N.E. 2d 35 (Ill. App. 1979).

Consider this statement of the relationship between liberality of other procedure rules and the scope of preclusion:

> Modern pleading rules allow plaintiffs to allege claim formulations in the alternative and afford liberal opportunity to amend any formulation found insufficient on a demurrer or a motion to dismiss a claim. There is no reason not to expect plaintiffs to avail themselves of these opportunities. Similarly, modern procedure, particularly discovery, allows plaintiffs abundant opportunity to develop all available evidence that could be used at trial. These opportunities thus enlarge the scope of what might have been litigated by the plaintiff in the first action and should correspondingly enlarge the scope of claim preclusion.

JAMES, HAZARD & LEUBSDORF, CIVIL PROCEDURE 606.

Most courts avoid a debate over whether dismissals under Rule 12(b)(6) or state equivalents are on the merits by expressly making them with or without prejudice. The latter seems appropriate, at least if the court is convinced that the error can be remedied by improved pleading. Indeed, it is not unusual for a plaintiff to be allowed several chances to state a claim on which relief can be granted. At some point, however, even a patient judge may conclude that a claimant simply has no claim to state, and may grant a motion under Rule 12(b)(6) or sustain a demurrer with prejudice.

5. Suppose P sues D for medical malpractice, but fails, as required by relevant state law, to proffer an "affidavit of good cause," which is a sworn statement supporting her claim. The court dismisses P's case because of this failure, and does not indicate whether the dismissal is with prejudice. P then files a second case against D, this time including the affidavit of good cause. Assuming Rule 41(b) applies, can D successfully assert claim preclusion? On similar facts, the Supreme Court permitted the plaintiff to proceed with the second action, holding that the failure to satisfy the condition precedent of filing the affidavit constituted a lack of jurisdiction under Rule 41(b). Costello v. United States, 365 U.S. 265 (1961).

Could the same argument be used for other dismissals? For example, suppose the court dismisses the first case because it is brought by the wrong person (for example, someone lacking "standing")? What if the case is brought prematurely? For example, suppose P sues D to recover on a contract. At trial, it is established that D was not required to perform under the contract for six more months. Will the dismissal preclude P from filing a second suit? See Watkins v. Resorts International Hotel & Casino, Inc., 591 A.2d 592

(N.J. 1991) (first case dismissed for plaintiffs' lack of standing deemed a dismissal on jurisdictional grounds; second case not precluded).

6. Many cases use the terms "merger" and "bar" in discussing claim preclusion. The difference focuses on whether the claimant won or lost the first case. If the court entered final judgment in favor of the claimant in the first case, claim preclusion is said to operate as "merger." That is, upon entry of such a judgment, the claim is extinguished and merged into the claimant's judgment. Thus, while claim preclusion precludes her from reasserting the *claim*, she can recover by suing on the *judgment*.

On the other hand, courts refer to the claim preclusion effect of a final judgment for the defendant as "bar." Thus, a claimant who lost the first case is barred from reasserting the claim. As our discussion above shows, it is these "bar" situations that raise the most serious problems concerning whether the judgment is "on the merits," or, under modern principles, to be treated as an adjudication supporting preclusion.

4. Exceptions to the Operation of Claim Preclusion

All courts recognize that claim preclusion is inappropriate in certain circumstances. Section 26(1) of the Restatement (Second) of Judgments provides a helpful list of such circumstances, providing that the doctrine will not apply if:

(a) The parties have agreed in terms or in effect that the plaintiff may split his claim, or the defendant has acquiesced therein; or
(b) The court in the first action has expressly reserved the plaintiff's right to maintain the second action; or
(c) The plaintiff was unable to rely on a certain theory of the case or to seek a certain remedy or form of relief in the first action because of the limitations on the subject matter jurisdiction of the courts or restrictions on their authority to entertain multiple theories or demands for multiple remedies or forms of relief in a single action, and the plaintiff desires in the second action to rely on that theory or to seek that remedy or form of relief; or
(d) The judgment in the first action was plainly inconsistent with the fair and equitable implementation of a statutory or constitutional scheme, or it is the sense of the scheme that the plaintiff should be permitted to split his claim; or
(e) For reasons of substantive policy in a case involving a continuing or recurrent wrong, the plaintiff is given an option to sue once for the total harm, both past and prospective, or to sue from time to time for the damages incurred to the date of suit, and chooses the latter course; or
(f) It is clearly and convincingly shown that the policies favoring preclusion of a second action are overcome for an extraordinary reason, such as the apparent invalidity of a continuing restraint or condition having a vital relation to personal liberty or the failure of the prior litigation to yield a coherent disposition of the controversy.

NOTES AND QUESTIONS

1. D's vessel rams P's motorboat. Although the motorboat was damaged, P did not seem to be hurt. P sued D in small claims court to recover the $500 damage to her boat. After winning a judgment in that case, P experienced neck problems, which, her doctor concluded, resulted from the boat collision. Now P sues D to recover $250,000 for personal injuries. Assume that the jurisdiction adopts a transactional test for claim preclusion. Can D successfully assert claim preclusion?

2. P was involved in a motorcycle accident and suffered both personal injuries and property damage. He filed suit for the property damage in the Justice of the Peace Court (which can hear property cases involving no more than $1500 but cannot hear claims for personal injuries), and won a judgment of $103.60. Now he sues for personal injuries in Superior Court. D asserts claim preclusion, because the jurisdiction adopts the Restatement (Second) definition of cause of action. P attempts to invoke exception (c) from § 26(1) of the Restatement (Second) of Judgments. What result? See Mells v. Billops, 482 A.2d 759, 761 (Del. Super. 1984) (plaintiff "voluntarily chose a court of limited jurisdiction when he could have presented all his claims * * * had he brought the original action in this Court."). Accord City of Los Angeles v. Superior Court, 149 Cal. Rptr. 320 (Cal. Ct. App. 1978); McKibben v. Zamora, 358 So. 2d 866 (Fla. App. 1978).

3. D injures P and destroys P's car in a collision. P files two suits against D in the same court, one seeking damages for personal injury and the other seeking damages for loss of the car. D does not object, and does not seek consolidation of the two cases. After one of the cases goes to judgment for P, D moves to dismiss the other case under claim preclusion. Will the motion be successful? In other words, is claim preclusion a waivable defense? Does Federal Rule 8(c) help in your decision? Compare Lake v. Jones, 598 A.2d 858 (Md. 1991) (claim preclusion waived); with Buchanan v. Dain Bosworth, Inc. 469 N.W. 2d 508 (Minn. App. 1991) (only waived if defendant gives affirmative indication of waiver). Should a court raise claim preclusion sua sponte? When would it do so? See generally TEPLY & WHITTEN, CIVIL PROCEDURE 883-84.

4. P sues D for divorce, based upon irreconcilable differences. After the court enters final judgment granting the divorce, P sues D for emotional distress caused by D's alleged physical abuse of P during their marriage. Because physical abuse is also a basis for divorce, D argues that P's tort claim is barred by claim preclusion because it was not included in P's divorce suit. In Henriksen v. Cameron 622 A.2d 1135 (Me. 1993), the court rejected D's argument. Formulate two arguments: (1) that the two suits involved different claims; and (2) even if they involved the same claim, an exception applies.

5. A group of public school students and their parents sue the local school board to enjoin a state "tuition voucher system" that permits students to attend private schools essentially at public expense. They allege that the law is unconstitutional because it promotes religion. The court upholds the law, and enters final judgment for the school board. Thereafter, in a different case, the United States Supreme Court holds a similar voucher system in another state unconstitutional. The same group of students and parents file a second action against the same local school board, reasserting the same claim rejected in the first suit. What argument can they make to avoid the defense of claim preclusion? See TEPLY & WHITTEN, CIVIL PROCEDURE 885.

In connection with this fact pattern, consider Federated Department Stores, Inc. v. Moitie, 452 U.S. 394 (1981), in which retail purchasers brought several cases against owners of department stores, alleging that the defendants had illegally agreed to fix retail prices in violation of federal antitrust law. The district court dismissed all of the cases, holding that retail purchasers could not show the kind of injury required by the antitrust provisions. Some of the plaintiffs ("Set 1") appealed to the Ninth Circuit. Others ("Set 2") did not, and instead filed new suits in state court, which the defendants removed to federal court. The district court dismissed the claims by the Set 2 plaintiffs under claim preclusion. The Set 2 plaintiffs then appealed to the Ninth Circuit.

While the cases of both Set 1 and Set 2 plaintiffs were on appeal, the Supreme Court decided a different case, and held that retail purchasers can show injury as required by the antitrust laws. The Ninth Circuit reversed and remanded the Set 1 cases for reconsideration in light of this new precedent. As to the Set 2 cases, the Ninth Circuit recognized an exception to claim preclusion, to the effect that "non-appealing parties may benefit from a reversal when their position is closely interwoven with that of appealing parties." That court thus held that the Set 2 plaintiffs could take advantage of the new precedent because claim preclusion should give way to "public policy" and "simple justice."

The Supreme Court reversed, holding that claim preclusion barred the Set 2 plaintiffs from proceeding under the new precedent. The Court rejected the Ninth Circuit's exception, saying:

> [W]e do not see the grave injustice which would be done by the application of accepted principles of res judicata. "Simple justice" is achieved when a complex body of law developed over a period of years is evenhandedly applied. The doctrine of res judicata serves vital public interests beyond any individual judge's ad hoc determination of the equities in a particular case. There is simply "no principle of law or equity which sanctions the rejection by a federal court of the salutary principle of res judicata." The Court of Appeals' reliance on "public policy" is similarly misplaced. This Court has long recognized that "[p]ublic policy dictates that there be an end of litigation; that those who have contested an issue shall be bound by the result of the contest, and that matters once tried shall be considered forever settled as between the parties." We have stressed that "[the] doctrine of res judicata is not a mere matter of practice or procedure inherited from

a more technical time than ours. It is a rule of fundamental and substantial justice
* * *."

452 U.S. at 400.

In light of *Moitie*, would the plaintiffs in the hypothetical set forth at the beginning of this note be subject to claim preclusion because they did not appeal the judgment against them? Does *Moitie* counsel unsuccessful litigants to pursue appeals for which they have no precedent, in the hope that the Supreme Court will take their case or decide another in favor of their position? Is taking such an appeal consistent with Rule 11? Is *Moitie* consistent with *Chicot County*, supra at 261?

6. Note that the provision of § 26(1)(e) of the Restatement (Second) of Judgments embodies the principles we discussed at Section B(1) of this chapter regarding breach of contract and similar claims.

C. Issue Preclusion

Application of issue preclusion requires assessment of five questions: (1) was the same issue litigated and determined in the first case? (2) was the issue essential to the judgment in the first case? (3) was the holding on that issue embodied in a valid, final judgment on the merits? (4) *against whom* may preclusion be asserted? and (5) *by whom* may preclusion be asserted? Because we addressed the third requirement in discussing claim preclusion, we proceed now to the other four.

1. Same Issue Litigated and Determined

Whether the same issue was involved in both cases often will be obvious. Occasionally, however, the second court will be required to review the record from the first case in considerable detail to determine whether the same issue was litigated and determined. In O'Connor v. G & R Packing Co., 423 N.E. 2d 397 (N.Y. 1981), a teenager was injured while trespassing in a railroad yard. In the boy's first case, the defendants prevailed when the judge ruled in their favor at the close of plaintiff's evidence. Among other things, the judge noted that the boy "not only disobeyed * * * statutes which were enacted for the benefit of the public but also deliberately and needlessly exposed himself to a known danger * * *." Id. at 398 (quoting oral opinion of trial court).

Plaintiff brought a second case against a different defendant, who sought preclusion on the issue of the plaintiff's contributory negligence. After a thorough review of the transcript of the trial judge's ruling in the first case, the New York Court of Appeals refused preclusion. Although the quoted language seemed to address contributory negligence, it was also consistent with the finding that the defendant breached no duty to the boy (because it owed minimal duty to a trespasser). The court continued, id. at 399:

> The ambivalence of the words used, and of the holding in relation to that issue, arises from a number of factors: the words "contributory negligence" were not used; the Trial Judge could not have had in mind the effect of his holding on the present action, which was not begun until several months after his dismissal of the action against the railroads; none of the cases cited concerned contributory negligence, nor does the language used indicate that consideration had been given to Anthony's age, experience, intelligence, and degree of development * * *. Litigation of the contributory negligence issue is not precluded by such a nonspecific nonfactual determination.

Cromwell v. County of Sac
94 U.S. 351, 24 L. Ed. 195 (1877)

Mr. JUSTICE FIELD delivered the opinion of the Court.

This was an action on four bonds of the county of Sac, in the State of Iowa, each for $1,000, and four coupons for interest, attached to them, each for $100. The bonds were issued in 1860, and were made payable to bearer, in the city of New York, in the years 1868, 1869, 1870, and 1871, respectively, with annual interest at the rate of ten per cent a year.

To defeat this action, the defendant relied upon the estoppel of a judgment rendered in favor of the county in a prior action brought by one Samuel C. Smith upon certain earlier maturing coupons on the same bonds, accompanied with proof that the plaintiff Cromwell was at the time the owner of the coupons in that action, and that the action was prosecuted for his sole use and benefit.

The questions presented for our determination relate to the operation of this judgment as an estoppel against the prosecution of the present action, and the admissibility of the evidence to connect the present plaintiff with the former action as a real party in interest.

In considering the operation of this judgment, it should be borne in mind, as stated by counsel, that there is a difference between the effect of a judgment as a bar or estoppel against the prosecution of a second action upon the same claim or demand, and its effect as an estoppel in another action between the same parties upon a different claim or cause of action. In the former case, the judgment, if rendered upon the merits, constitutes an absolute bar to a subsequent action. It is a finality as to the claim or demand in controversy, concluding parties and those in privity with them, not only as to every matter which was offered and received to sustain or defeat the claim or demand, but as to any other admissible matter which might have been offered for that purpose. Thus, for example, a judgment rendered upon a promissory note is conclusive as to the validity of the instrument and the amount due upon it, although it be subsequently alleged that perfect defences actually existed, of which no proof was offered, such as forgery, want of consideration, or payment. If such defences were not presented in the action, and established by competent evidence, the subsequent allegation of their existence is of no legal consequence. The judgment is as conclusive, so far as future proceedings at law are concerned, as though the defences never existed. The language, therefore, which is so often used, that a judgment estops not only as to every ground of recovery or defence actually presented in the action, but also as to every ground which might have been presented, is strictly accurate, when applied to the demand or claim in controversy. Such demand or claim, having passed into judgment, cannot again be brought into litigation between the parties in proceedings at law upon any ground whatever.

But where the second action between the same parties is upon a different claim or demand, the judgment in the prior action operates as an estoppel only as to those matters in issue or points controverted, upon the determination of which the finding or verdict was rendered. In all cases, therefore, where it is sought to apply the estoppel of a judgment rendered upon one cause of action to matters arising in a suit upon a different cause of action, the inquiry must always be as to the point or question actually litigated and determined in the original action, not what might have been thus litigated and determined. Only upon such matters is the judgment conclusive in another action.

The difference in the operation of a judgment in the two classes of cases mentioned is seen through all the leading adjudications upon the doctrine of estoppel. Thus, in the case of Outram v. Morewood, 3 East, 346, the defendants were held estopped from averring title to a mine, in an action of trespass for digging out coal from it, because, in a previous action for a similar trespass, they had set up the same title, and it had been determined against them. In commenting upon a decision cited in that case, Lord Ellenborough, in his elaborate opinion, said: "It is not the recovery, but the matter alleged by the party, and upon which the recovery proceeds, which creates the estoppel. The recovery of itself in an action of trespass is only a bar to the future recovery of damages for the same injury; but the estoppel precludes parties and privies from contending to the contrary of that point or matter of fact, which, having been once distinctly put in issue by them, or by those to whom they are privy in estate or law, has been, on such issue joined, solemnly found against them." * * *

* * * [Such] cases, usually cited in support of the doctrine that the determination of a question directly involved in one action is conclusive as to that question in a second suit between the same parties upon a different cause of action, negative the proposition that the estoppel can extend beyond the point actually litigated and determined. * * *

* * *

Various considerations, other than the actual merits, may govern a party in bringing forward grounds of recovery or defence in one action, which may not exist in another action upon a different demand, such as the smallness of the amount or the value of the property in controversy, the difficulty of obtaining the necessary evidence, the expense of the litigation, and his own situation at the time. A party acting upon considerations like these ought not to be precluded from contesting in a subsequent action other demands arising out of the same transaction. * * *

If, now, we consider the main question presented for our determination by the light of the views thus expressed and the authorities cited, its solution will not be difficult. It appears from the findings in the original action of Smith, that the county of Sac, by a vote of its people, authorized the issue of bonds to the amount of $10,000, for the erection of a court-house; that bonds to that amount were issued by the county judge, and delivered to one Meserey, with whom he had made a contract for the erection of the court-house; that immediately upon receipt of the bonds the contractor gave one of them as a gratuity to the county judge; and that the court-house was never constructed by the contractor, or by any other person pursuant to the contract. It also appears that the plaintiff had become, before their maturity, the holder of twenty-five coupons, which had been attached to the bonds, but there was no finding that he had ever given any value for them. The court below held, upon these findings, that the bonds were void as against the county, and gave judgment accordingly. The case coming here on writ of error, this court held that the facts disclosed by the findings were sufficient evidence of fraud and illegality in the inception of the bonds to call upon the holder to show that he had given value for the coupons; and, not having done so, the judgment was affirmed. Reading the record of the lower court by the opinion and judgment of this court, it must be considered that the matters adjudged in that case were these: that the bonds were void as against the county in the hands of parties who did not acquire them before maturity and give value for them, and that the plaintiff, not having proved that he gave such value, was not entitled to recover upon the coupons. Whatever illegality or fraud there was in the issue and delivery to the contractor of the bonds affected equally the coupons for interest attached to them. The finding and judgment upon the invalidity of the bonds, as against the county, must be held to estop the plaintiff here from averring to the contrary. But as the bonds were negotiable instruments, and their issue was authorized by a vote of the county, and they recite on their face a compliance with the law providing for their issue, they would be held as valid obligations against the county in the hands of a bona fide holder taking them for value before maturity, according to repeated decisions of this court upon the character of such obligations. If, therefore, the plaintiff received the bond and coupons in suit before maturity for value, as he offered to prove, he should have been permitted to show that fact. There was nothing adjudged in the former action in the finding that the plaintiff had not made such proof in that case which can preclude the present plaintiff from making such proof here. The fact that a party may not have shown that he gave value for one bond or coupon is not even presumptive, much less conclusive, evidence that he may not have given value for another and different bond or coupon. The exclusion of the evidence offered by the plaintiff was erroneous, and for the ruling of the court in that respect the judgment must be reversed and a new trial had.

Upon the second question presented, we think the court below ruled correctly. Evidence showing that the action of Smith was brought for the sole use and benefit of the present plaintiff was, in our judgment, admissible. The finding that Smith was the holder and owner of the coupons in suit went only to this extent, that he held the legal title to them, which was sufficient for the purpose of the action, and was not inconsistent with an equitable and beneficial interest in another.

Judgment reversed, and cause remanded for a new trial.

NOTES AND QUESTIONS

1. The first case was brought by Smith and the second by Cromwell. Nonetheless, why would that fact not negate claim preclusion? Why, then, did claim preclusion not apply in *Cromwell*?

2. Why can there be no issue preclusion as to the question of whether Cromwell held the bonds as a bona fide purchaser? After all, Smith (as Cromwell's agent) could have raised that issue in the first case. Recall that claim preclusion generally stops a claimant from litigating something that she has never presented to a court. The reason is that she had an opportunity to present those issues in the previous case on the same claim. Issue preclusion, on the other hand, stops someone from relitigating issues which she actually litigated before. Why the difference? What policy is served by the requirement of actual litigation and determination of an issue?

A few courts have not required actual litigation of an issue as a prerequisite for issue preclusion. See, e.g., Sutphin v. Speik, 15 Cal. 2d 195 (1940). The clear majority, however, follows the rule in *Cromwell*.

3. In the case brought by Cromwell, could the county have asserted issue preclusion as to whether the bond issuance was fraudulent?

4. Courts may view the scope of "the issue" determined differently depending upon the party who raised it. For example, suppose P sues D for injuries sustained in an auto crash, alleging that D was negligent because she failed to keep a proper lookout. Suppose D wins, with the court finding that D was not negligent. Now D files a separate action against P to recover for her injuries from the same accident. Assuming that there is no compulsory counterclaim rule, the action will proceed. Can P defend this case by asserting that D was negligent because she drove too fast for road conditions? The drafters of the Restatement (Second) of Judgments conclude that P cannot raise the issue, since P reasonably could be expected to have raised the speeding issue in support of her claim in the first action. See RESTATEMENT (SECOND), § 27, cmt c, illus. 4. In other words, they treat "the issue" as the relatively broad question of whether D was negligent.

In contrast, suppose P sues D to recover an installment payment under an oral contract. D raises a single defense: that the contract is unenforceable under statute of frauds because it is not in writing. The court rejects the defense and enters judgment for P. Then P sues to recover a different installment (coming due after the judgment in the first case) under the same contract. Clearly, D cannot raise the statute of frauds defense. But can she raise the defense that the contract is unenforceable because it violates some fundamental public policy? The drafters of the Restatement (Second) of Judgments conclude that she may. Id. at illus 6. Here, they treat "the issue" as the narrower question of statute of frauds, rather than enforceability of the contract. See TEPLY & WHITTEN, CIVIL PROCEDURE 892-93.

What policy justifies this divergent treatment? As a practical matter, what does the Restatement (Second) approach counsel plaintiffs to do?

C. Issue Preclusion

5. As we saw in Section B(3) of this chapter, a default judgment and dismissal for failure to prosecute carry claim preclusion effect. Why do default judgments and dismissals for failure to prosecute *not* carry issue preclusion consequences? See, e.g., United States v. Ringley, 750 F. Supp. 750 (W.D. Va. 1990) (default judgment). Should stipulations among litigants or judgments pursuant to settlement carry issue preclusion consequences? See Rule 36(b).

6. Recall *Baldwin v. Iowa Men's Traveling Association*, Chapter 6. There, the defendant made a direct attack on the personal jurisdiction of the court in which the plaintiff filed the first case. That court held that it had personal jurisdiction. The defendant failed to seek appellate review and refused to litigate further. The court entered default judgment. When the plaintiff sought to enforce the judgment in another state, the defendant made a collateral attack on the personal jurisdiction of the first court. Although the Supreme Court stated that a collateral attack was precluded on grounds of "res judicata," it used that term in a generic sense. In fact, the case was based upon issue preclusion. In *Baldwin*, the issue of jurisdiction was fully litigated in the first proceeding and could not be relitigated in the second.

7. *The Sally and Joe Hypotheticals*. Here we undertake a series of hypotheticals involving a single fact pattern. Assume that two cars collide and that their respective drivers—Sally and Joe—suffer personal injuries and property damage. Assume further that the jurisdiction recognizes contributory negligence, so that a negligent claimant cannot recover, and that the issues of defendant's negligence and plaintiff's contributory negligence are litigated in each case. Also assume that the jurisdiction does not have a compulsory counterclaim rule.

    (a) Sally sues Joe for negligence. Joe raises the defense of contributory negligence. The jury returns a general verdict in favor of Sally, and the court enters judgment for Sally on the basis of that verdict.

        Now Joe sues Sally to recover his damages arising from the same accident. Can Sally assert issue preclusion against Joe as to (1) Joe's negligence or (2) her freedom from negligence? Can we deduce from the general verdict in the first case what issues must have been determined in the first case? If the only issues proffered were the negligence of the two parties, what two findings must have been made for the jury to find in Sally's favor in the first case?

    (b) Sally sues Joe for negligence. Joe raises the defense of contributory negligence. The jury returns a general verdict in favor of Joe, and the court enters judgment for Joe on the basis of that verdict.

        Now Joe sues Sally to recover his damages arising from the same accident. Can Joe assert issue preclusion against Sally as to (1) his own freedom

CHAPTER 11 THE PRECLUSION DOCTRINES

from negligence or (2) Sally's negligence? Can we know what issues were litigated and determined in the first case?

(c) Sally sues Joe for negligence. Joe raises the defense of contributory negligence. The jury returns a special verdict finding that Sally was negligent, and the court enters judgment for Joe on the basis of that verdict.

Now Joe sues Sally to recover his damages arising from the same accident. Can Joe assert issue preclusion against Sally as to (1) his own freedom from negligence or (2) Sally's negligence? Based upon your conclusion, what, if anything, remains to be litigated in Joe v. Sally?

(d) Sally sues Joe for negligence. Joe raises the defense of contributory negligence. The jury returns a special verdict finding that Sally was not negligent, and that Joe was negligent. The court enters judgment for Sally on the basis of that verdict.

Now Joe sues Sally to recover his damages arising from the same accident. Can Sally assert issue preclusion against Joe as to (1) her own freedom from negligence or (2) Joe's negligence? Legally, which of the prior hypotheticals ((a) through (c)) is the same as this one?

2. Issue Determined Was Essential to the Judgment

Issue preclusion is only proper if the issue litigated and decided was essential to the judgment. This requirement is demonstrated by another twist to our Sally and Joe hypotheticals.

(e) Sally sues Joe for negligence. Joe raises the defense of contributory negligence. The jury returns a special verdict finding that both Sally and Joe were negligent, and the court enters judgment for Joe on the basis of that verdict.

Now Joe sues Sally to recover his damages arising from the same accident. Can Sally assert issue preclusion against Joe as to his negligence? Can Joe assert issue preclusion against Sally as to her negligence? Before concluding, consider the following case.

C. Issue Preclusion

Rios v. Davis
373 S.W. 2d 386 (Tex. Ct. Civ. App. 1963)

COLLINGS, J.

Juan C. Rios brought this suit against Jessie Hubert Davis in the District Court to recover damages in the sum of $17,500.00, alleged to have been sustained as a result of personal injuries received on December 24, 1960, in an automobile collision. Plaintiff alleged that his injuries were proximately caused by negligence on the part of the defendant. The defendant answered alleging that Rios was guilty of contributory negligence. Also, among other defenses, the defendant urged a plea of res judicata and collateral estoppel based upon the findings and the judgment entered on December 17, 1962, in a suit between the same parties in the County Court at Law of El Paso County. The plea of res judicata was sustained and judgment was entered in favor of the defendant Jessie Hubert Davis. Juan C. Rios has appealed.

It is shown by the record that on April 11, 1961, Popular Dry Goods Company brought suit against appellee Davis in the El Paso County Court at Law, seeking to recover for damages to its truck in the sum of $443.97, alleged to have been sustained in the same collision here involved. Davis answered alleging contributory negligence on the part of Popular and joined appellant Juan C. Rios as a third party defendant and sought to recover from Rios $248.50, the alleged amount of damages to his automobile. The jury in the County Court at Law found that Popular Dry Goods Company and Rios were guilty of negligence proximately causing the collision. However, the jury also found that Davis was guilty of negligence proximately causing the collision, and judgment was entered in the County Court at Law denying Popular Dry Goods any recovery against Davis and denying Davis any recovery against Rios.

Appellant Rios in his third point contends that the District Court erred in sustaining appellee's plea of res judicata based upon the judgment of the County Court at Law because the findings on the issues regarding appellant's negligence and liability in the County Court at Law case were immaterial because the judgment entered in that case was in favor of appellant. We sustain this point. We are unable to agree with appellee's contention that the findings in the County Court at Law case that Rios was guilty of negligence in failing to keep a proper lookout and in driving on the left side of the roadway, and that such negligent acts were proximate causes of the accident were essential to the judgment entered therein. The sole basis for the judgment in the County Court at Law as between Rios and Davis was the findings concerning the negligence of Davis. The finding that Rios was negligent was not essential or material to the judgment and the judgment was not based thereon. On the contrary, the finding in the County Court at Law case that Rios was negligent proximately causing the accident would, if it had been controlling, led to a different result. Since the judgment was in favor of Rios he had no right or opportunity to complain of or to appeal from the finding that he was guilty of such negligence even if such finding had been without any support whatever in the evidence. The right of appeal is from a judgment and not from a finding. The principles controlling the fact situation here involved are, in our opinion, stated in the following quoted authorities and cases. The annotation in 133 A.L.R. 840, page 850 states:

> "According to the weight of authority, a finding of a particular fact is not res judicata in a subsequent action, where the finding not only was not essential to

support the judgment, but was found in favor of the party against whom the judgment was rendered, and, if allowed to control, would have led to a result different from that actually reached."

In the case of Word v. Colley, Tex.Civ.App., 173 S.W. 629, at page 634 of its opinion (Error Ref.), the court stated as follows:

"It is the judgment, and not the verdict or the conclusions of fact, filed by a trial court which constitutes the estoppel, and a finding of fact by a jury or a court which does not become the basis or one of the grounds of the judgment rendered is not conclusive against either party to the suit."

For the reasons stated the court erred in entering judgment for Jessie Hubert Davis based upon his plea of res judicata and collateral estoppel. The judgment is, therefore, reversed and the cause is remanded.

NOTES AND QUESTIONS

1. In light of *Rios*, how should hypothetical (e), set out before the case, be decided? Why?

2. What policy supports an essentiality requirement? After all, it is clear that the factfinder in the first case determined that Rios was negligent. We can assume that Rios's self-interest motivated him to litigate the issue seriously. He had his "day in court" and lost on the issue. Why should Rios be able to relitigate that issue?

3. Exactly why was the finding of Rios's negligence in the first case not essential to the judgment? Would a finding that Rios was not negligent have changed the judgment in first case? Once the plaintiff was found negligent in the first case, was Rios's negligence relevant? Is that why the finding on Rios was not essential?

4. The court notes that Rios could not have appealed the finding that he was negligent in the first case, since he won the judgment. Is that why the finding on his negligence was not essential? Again, though, even though he could not appeal, Rios had an opportunity and incentive to litigate the question, and lost. Is availability of an appeal part of one's "day in court?" Does the fact that there is no constitutional right to appeal a civil judgment affect your answer? See Mower v. Boyer, 811 S.W. 2d 560 (Tex. 1991) (inability to appeal finding one reason not to accord issue preclusion effect).

5. Are we more confident that the factfinder assessed an issue more carefully if it was essential to the judgment? If so, is that a sign of faith, or lack of faith, in factfinders?

6. Another aspect of essentiality is raised by our final hypothetical involving Sally and Joe.

(f) Sally sues Joe for negligence. Joe raises the defense of contributory negligence. The jury returns a special verdict finding that Sally was negligent and that Joe was not negligent. The court enters judgment for Joe.

Now Joe sues Sally to recover his damages arising from the same accident. Can Joe assert issue preclusion against Sally as to (1) his own freedom from negligence or (2) Sally's negligence? Why?

The two findings in the first case are "alternative determinations." Do you see why? If only one of the two were made in the first case, would the judgment have been the same? The original Restatement of Judgments § 68, cmt. n, accords preclusive effect to both alternative determinations. The Restatement (Second) of Judgments § 27, denies preclusive effect to both determinations, unless one or both are later affirmed on appeal. See cmt. o.

Does the Restatement (Second) punish a litigant for doing too well? After all, if Joe had won on only one of the two questions, issue preclusion would apply in the second action. Why should he be denied issue preclusion when he wins on both questions? The drafters of the Restatement (Second) explain their reasoning as follows:

> * * * First, a determination in the alternative may not have been as carefully or rigorously considered as it would have if it had been necessary to the result, and in that sense it has some of the characteristics of dicta. Second, and of critical importance, the losing party, although entitled to appeal from both determinations, might be dissuaded from doing so because of the likelihood that at least one of them would be upheld and the others not even reached. If he were to appeal solely for the purpose of avoiding the application of the rule of issue preclusion, then the rule might be responsible for increasing the burdens of litigation on the parties and the courts rather than lightening those burdens. * * *

RESTATEMENT (SECOND) OF JUDGMENTS § 27 cmt. i (1982). Are you persuaded?

Not surprisingly, courts disagree on how the question should be resolved. Some courts take a flexible approach in this area, looking at the facts to determine whether it would be proper to permit issue preclusion on alternative findings. For example, in Malloy v. Trombley, 405 N.E. 2d 213 (N.Y. 1980), the judge in the first case found defendant not negligent and further found, "[although] unnecessary to a decision herein," that the plaintiff was barred by contributory negligence. The court of appeals upheld issue preclusion on contributory negligence in a second action. After reviewing the record, the court was impressed that the "thorough and careful deliberation" by the trial judge showed the alternative holding was not a casual finding.

3. Against Whom Can Issue Preclusion be Asserted?

You will recall that claim preclusion could only be asserted against parties to the prior litigation or nonparties so closely related to them as to be considered in "privity" with a litigant. This requirement is rooted in due process, and, as we saw, there is considerable uncertainty concerning the type of relationship that will justify preclusion of a nonparty. Issue preclusion also is available only against "parties or privies," and allows us to address the question of nonparty preclusion in greater detail.

Hardy v. Johns-Manville Sales Corp.
681 F. 2d 334 (5th Cir. 1982)

GEE, CIRCUIT JUDGE.

[Asbestos is a fireproof, incombustible fibrous building material. It was used for decades in countless structures and appliances such as hand-held hair dryers. Breathing asbestos fibers, however, can cause asbestosis, mesothelioma and other potentially deadly lung diseases. This risk became widely apparent in the 1960s and 1970s, and led to thousands of lawsuits for personal injuries and wrongful death. The federal government ordered that asbestos be removed from existing buildings, which resulted in litigation concerning the liability for clean up damages. In addition, there was widespread litigation concerning insurance coverage for the manufacturers of asbestos. Asbestos-related suits constitute the largest series of related litigation in history.

In one personal injuries case, plaintiffs won a judgment against six manufacturers of asbestos. Borel v. Fibreboard Paper Prod. Corp., 493 F. 2d 1076 (5th Cir. 1974). In *Hardy*, different plaintiffs sued six of the same manufacturers and thirteen additional manufacturers who had not been parties to *Borel*. The trial court in *Hardy* held that the judgment in *Borel* was entitled to issue preclusion effect as to various matters concerning liability, including defendants' breach of a duty to warn workers of the dangers of asbestos. The trial court concluded that the plaintiffs could assert such issue preclusion against all defendants before it in *Hardy*. There is no question that issue preclusion can be asserted against the six manufacturers who were defendants in *Borel*. The question addressed by the court in this part of its lengthy opinion is whether issue preclusion (which this court and many others call collateral estoppel) can be used against those manufacturers who were not parties to *Borel*.]

This is the first and, in our view, insurmountable problem with the trial court's application of collateral estoppel in the case sub judice. The omnibus order under review here does not distinguish between defendants who were parties to *Borel* and those who were not; it purports to estop all defendants because all purportedly share an "identity of interests" sufficient to constitute privity. The trial court's action stretches "privity" beyond meaningful limits. While we acknowledge the manipulability of the notion of "privity," this has not prevented courts from establishing guidelines on the permissibility of binding nonparties through res judicata or collateral estoppel. Without such guidelines, the due process guarantee of a full and fair opportunity to litigate disappears. Thus, we noted in Southwest Airlines Co. v. Texas International Airlines, 546 F. 2d 84, 95 (5th Cir. 1977):

Federal courts have deemed several types of relationships "sufficiently close" to justify preclusion. First, a nonparty who has succeeded to a party's interest in property is bound by any prior judgments against that party.... Second, a nonparty who controlled the original suit will be bound by the resulting judgment.... Third, federal courts will bind a nonparty whose interests were represented adequately by a party in the original suit.

The rationale for these exceptions — all derived from RESTATEMENT (SECOND) OF JUDGMENTS §§ 30, 31, 34, 39-41 (1982) — is obviously that in these instances the nonparty has in effect had his day in court. In this case, the exceptions elaborated in *Southwest Airlines* and in the *Restatement* are inapplicable. First, the *Borel* litigation did not involve any property interests. Second, none of the non-*Borel* defendants have succeeded to any property interest held by the *Borel* defendants. Finally, the plaintiffs did not show that any non-*Borel* defendant had any control whatever over the *Borel* litigation. "To have control of litigation requires that a person have effective choice as to the legal theories and proofs to be advanced in behalf of the party to the action. He must also have control over the opportunity to obtain review." RESTATEMENT (SECOND) OF JUDGMENTS § 39, comment c (1982). In, for example, Sea-Land Services v. Gaudet, 414 U.S. 573, the Supreme Court held that a nonparty may be collaterally estopped from relitigating issues necessarily decided in a suit by a party who acted as a fiduciary responsible for the beneficial interests of the nonparties. Even in this context, however, the Court placed the exception within strict confines: "In such cases, 'the beneficiaries are bound by the judgment with respect to the interest which was the subject of the fiduciary relationship....'" Many of our circuit's cases evince a similar concern with keeping the nonparties' exceptions to res judicata and collateral estoppel within strict confines.

The fact that all the non-*Borel* defendants, like the *Borel* defendants, are engaged in the manufacture of asbestos-containing products does not evince privity among the parties. The plaintiffs did not demonstrate that any of the non-*Borel* defendants participated in any capacity in the *Borel* litigation — whether directly or even through a trade representative — or were even part of a trustee-beneficiary relationship with any *Borel* defendant. On the contrary, several of the defendants indicate on appeal that they were not even aware of the *Borel* litigation until those proceedings were over and that they were not even members of industry or trade associations composed of asbestos product manufacturers.[6]

Plaintiffs can draw little support from the doctrine of "virtual representation" of cases such as Aerojet-General Corp. v. Askew, [511 F. 2d 710 (5th Cir.), cert. denied 423 U.S. 908 (1975)] in which we stated that "[u]nder the federal law of res judicata, a person may be bound by a judgment even though not a party if one of the parties to the suit is so closely aligned with his interests as to be his virtual representative" and that "the question whether a party's interests in a case are virtually representative of the interests of a nonparty is one of fact for the trial court." 511 F. 2d at 719. In that case we approved a district court's determination that the interests of two government entities were so closely aligned that a prior judgment against one entity bound the other. The proposition that governments may represent private interests in litigation, thereby precluding relitigation, while uncertain at the margin, appears to be an unexceptional special instance of the examples noted in RESTATEMENT (SECOND) OF JUDGMENTS §41(1) (1982). The facts here permit no inference of virtual representation of interest. As we explained in Pollard v. Cockrell, 578 F. 2d 1002, 1008-9 (5th Cir. 1978):

---

[6] Since *Borel* was neither designated nor approved as a class action, there can be no claim that any non-*Borel* defendant is bound as representative of a class.

> Virtual representation demands the existence of an express or implied legal relationship in which parties to the first suit are accountable to nonparties who file a subsequent suit raising identical issues. . . . In the instant case . . . the [first] plaintiffs were in no sense legally accountable to the [second] plaintiffs; they shared only an abstract interest in enjoining enforcement of the ordinance. The [first] plaintiffs sued in their individual capacities and not as representatives of a judicially certified class. Representation by the same attorneys cannot furnish the requisite alignment of interest. . . .

Thus, in *Pollard* we rejected the contention that one group of massage parlor owners were bound by a judgment in a prior lawsuit brought by another group. Virtual representation was rejected despite nearly identical pleadings filed by the groups and representation by common attorneys. The court's omnibus order here amounts to collateral estoppel based on similar legal positions — a proposition that has been properly rejected by at least one other district court that considered the identical issue. Mooney v. Fibreboard Corp., 485 F. Supp. 242, 249 (E.D. Tex. 1980). We agree with the Texas Supreme Court that "privity is not established by the mere fact that persons may happen to be interested in the same question or in proving the same state of facts," Benson v. Wanda Petroleum Co., 468 S.W. 2d 361, 363 (Tex. 1971), and hold that the trial court's actions here transgress the bounds of due process.

Our conclusion likewise pertains to those defendants who, while originally parties to the *Borel* litigation, settled before trial. The plaintiffs here did not show that any of these defendants settled out of the *Borel* litigation after the entire trial had run its course and only the judicial act of signing a final known adverse judgment remained. Such action would suggest settlement precisely to avoid offensive collateral estoppel and, in an appropriate case, might preclude relitigation. All the indications here are, however, that the defendants in question settled out of the case early because of, for example, lack of product identification. Like the non-*Borel* defendants, these defendants have likewise been deprived of their day in court by the trial court's omnibus order.

* * *

NOTES AND QUESTIONS

1. According to the court, the application of issue preclusion to the non-*Borel* defendants violated their due process rights. Exactly how did it do so? Was it the fact that they weren't joined in *Borel*? Or that their interests weren't adequately represented in *Borel*? Or both?

2. In rejecting a representation theory for binding the non-*Borel* defendants, the court relied upon § 41(1) of the Restatement (Second) of Judgments, which provides:

> A person who is not a party to an action but who is represented by a party is bound by and entitled to the benefits of a judgment as though he were a party. A person is represented by a party who is:

(a) The trustee of an estate or interest of which the person is a beneficiary; or

(b) Invested by the person with authority to represent him in an action; or

(c) The executor, administrator, guardian, conservator, or similar fiduciary manager of an interest of which the person is a beneficiary; or

(d) An official or agency invested by law with authority to represent the person's interests; or

(e) The representative of a class of persons similarly situated, designated as such with the approval of the court, of which the person is a member.

In *Aerojet-General*, discussed in *Hardy*, the Fifth Circuit held that a Florida county, which was plaintiff in the case before it, was estopped by a judgment in a prior case in which two Florida state boards were defendants. It concluded that the boards had been the "virtual representatives" of the county in the first case, even though they failed to raise a defense which the county sought to assert. According to the court, "a person may be bound by a judgment even though not a party if one of the parties to the suit is so closely aligned with his interests as to be his virtual representative." *Aerojet-General*, 511 F. 2d at 719. Although the case seemed revolutionary when the Fifth Circuit decided it, note how that court in *Hardy* now considers it an "unexceptional" example of the application of the Restatement (Second) provision.

In *Pollard*, also discussed in *Hardy*, the Fifth Circuit began to retreat from a broad reading of *Aerojet-General*. *Pollard* introduced the notion of "accountability," requiring (as quoted in *Hardy*) "an express or implied legal relationship in which parties to the first suit are accountable to nonparties who file a subsequent suit raising identical issues." The court did not define accountability and did not indicate why it was required. It did provide examples of what it meant, however, including estate executors, who would bind beneficiaries, trustees, who would also bind executors, and corporations, which would bind their officers and sole stockholders. *Pollard*, 578 F. 2d at 1008-09. So interpreted, the *Pollard* insistence on "accountability" also seems to limit nonparty preclusion to the Restatement (Second) definition of representation.

For detailed discussion of these and other cases, and criticism that "*Aerojet-General*'s promise of broader preclusion has never been realized," see Robert Bone, *Rethinking the "Day in Court" Ideal and Nonparty Preclusion*, 67 N.Y.U. L. REV. 193, 220 (1992).

3. Why should the binding effect on nonparties be so limited? After all, what will be gained by permitting the non-*Borel* defendants to litigate all issues afresh? What costs will be imposed upon the plaintiffs and upon the community by permitting them to litigate?

4. What is wrong with imposing a binding effect on those raising identical issues in subsequent litigation? Would it be less objectionable if it were clear that the defendants in

Borel litigated intensely and competently, raised the relevant issues, and were represented by competent counsel?

5. The answers to the questions in Notes 3 and 4 seem to be summed up in the court's conclusion in *Hardy* and other cases that no one can be bound without her "day in court." We have already seen, however, that the "day in court" can be constructive, since nonparties can be bound if the litigant is a proper "representative" as that term is used in Restatement (Second) § 41(1). The issue becomes where to draw the line—when is a constructive "day in court" acceptable? Consider Professor Bone's assessment of that issue:

> Courts have hesitated to expand nonparty preclusion * * * even though current nonparty preclusion rules are narrow and formalistic, and even though they tolerate extensive relitigation at substantial social cost. The reason for this reluctance, it is said, is the nonparty's constitutionally protected right to her own "day in court."
>
> The day in court ideal pulls so strongly against preclusion that a person who was not a party to the first suit frequently may relitigate legal and factual issues that have already been determined in that suit. It often makes no difference that the nonparty sues about the same set of events, asserts the same legal theories, seeks the same remedies, or shares the same interests in the outcome * * * as the plaintiff to the first suit. * * *
>
> There is something deeply disturbing about this restrictive approach to nonparty preclusion. The trouble lies not only in the particular limitations themselves, but also, and more importantly, in the way courts and commentators use the day in court ideal to justify them. The "day in court" is often invoked in talismanic fashion to oppose nonparty preclusion without any explanation of why the values underlying the ideal support the result. Even those few decisions that come out in favor of nonparty preclusion offer little in the way of normative rationale. The result is a body of law without much apparent conceptual or normative coherence.

Bone, supra, 67 N.Y.U. L. REV. at 196.

To what "substantial social cost" resulting from overly narrow preclusion do you think Professor Bone might be referring? Do you think his discussion of how courts often invoke the phrase "day in court" accurately describes the opinion in *Hardy*?

6. Is the continuing importance of the "day in court" notion related to a broader notion of justice? Does the opportunity to participate in and control litigation personally contribute to a perception that the process is legitimate, and thus that the result should be respected? Or, more than perceived legitimacy, is such control part of a normative assessment that the process is legitimate? Professor Bone concludes that the fetish for litigant participation and control is not supported by history, or by positive or normative consider-

ations. He argues for broader preclusion of nonparties based upon representation. Bone, supra, 67 N.Y.U. L. REV. 234-36, 288.

Similarly, Professor George concludes that the phrase "day in court" is a "shibboleth" that has unduly stunted the expansion of nonparty exclusion. Lawrence George, *Sweet Uses of Adversity: Parklane Hosiery and the Collateral Class Action*, 32 STAN. L. REV. 655, 658 (1980).

7. Why were those defendants in *Borel* who settled before final judgment not bound by issue preclusion?

8. Note that in *Hardy*, the plaintiffs could use issue preclusion as to some defendants but not as to others. If you represented the defendants as to whom issue preclusion was not permitted, what would you be worried about at trial?

9. In *Hardy,* the court noted the possibility of binding a nonparty who "controlled" litigation in the first case. The leading case is Montana v. United States, 440 U.S. 147 (1979). There, a contractor on a federal dam project challenged a state gross receipts tax, arguing that it discriminated unconstitutionally against the United States and companies contracting with it. The United States was not a party to that case but controlled virtually every aspect of the contractor's litigation. Among other things, it required the contractor to bring the suit, reviewed and approved its complaint, paid all attorney's fees and costs, directed an appeal, and submitted an amicus brief on appeal. After the contractor lost in the state supreme court, the United States proceeded in its own suit against the state, raising the same challenge. The Court held that the United States was bound by issue preclusion from the first case, concluding that "although not a party, the United States plainly had a sufficient 'laboring oar' in the conduct of the state-court litigation to actuate principles of estoppel." Id. at 155.

4. By Whom Can Issue Preclusion be Asserted?

a. Mutuality and Exceptions

We have just seen that due process requires that issue preclusion be asserted only *against* one who was a party (or in "privity" with a party) to the first case. Now we address a completely different issue: *by whom* can issue preclusion be asserted? Traditionally, courts answered this question by invoking the principle of *mutuality of estoppel*, which dictates that issue preclusion can be used only by someone who was a party (or in "privity" with a party) to the first case. Mutuality is based upon a basic fairness rationale: that someone who cannot be hurt by a prior judgment should not be entitled to take advantage of it.

Although it implicates notions of fairness, mutuality is not rooted in due process. It is, instead, a product of history that courts are free to reject. Commentators have urged courts to do so for generations. One of the most strident critics, Jeremy Bentham, felt that mutuality brought to legal actions the "aura of the gaming table." 3 JEREMY BENTHAM, RATIONALE OF JUDICIAL EVIDENCE 579 (1827), reprinted in 7 WORKS OF JEREMY BENTHAM 171 (J. Bowring ed. 1843). Slowly, in response to such criticism and to illogical results from the application of mutuality, courts have moved away from the doctrine. Indeed, the most important development in recent decades has been the widespread jettisoning of the traditional rule to permit *nonmutual* issue preclusion—that is, assertion of issue preclusion by someone who was not a party to the first case.

The mutuality doctrine started to erode when courts recognized two "exceptions" to its operation in vicarious liability cases. For example, consider the employer-employee relationship. The employer is vicariously liable for the acts of the employee. Suppose the employee allegedly committed a tort within the scope of her employment (say, spilling hot soup on a restaurant patron whom she was serving). Assume that Patron sues Employee; the court enters judgment for Employee because it found her not negligent. Now Patron sues Employer, seeking to impose vicarious liability on her. (By the way, why can Employer *not* assert claim preclusion? Despite the close relationship, this is not a situation of "privity.")

Under vicarious liability, Employer is liable only if Employee committed a tort. Because the court in the first case found that Employee had not committed a tort, Employer would like to use issue preclusion. All of the requirements for issue preclusion are met except that it is being asserted by one who was not a party to the first case. A strict view of the mutuality rule would prohibit Employer from asserting preclusion.

But let's consider what could happen in this situation. Suppose the second case (Patron v. Employer) goes forward and Patron wins. Employer then must pay the judgment to Patron. Under vicarious liability, however, Employer is entitled to indemnification from Employee. Obviously, then, she will sue Employee to recover for the judgment she has had to pay to Patron. In this suit by Employer against Employee, a judgment for either party will be anomalous. If Employer wins, what good was Employee's original victory? If Employee wins, what good is Employer's "right" to indemnification?

To avoid these anomalies, courts recognized an exception to mutuality and permitted Employer to assert issue preclusion on the finding from the first case that Employee was not negligent. This is known generally as the "narrow exception" to mutuality.

Now suppose the first case was Patron v. *Employer*, and Employer won. When Patron sues Employee in a second case, could Employee use issue preclusion? Again, the mutuality doctrine would say no, because Employee was not a party to the first case. Does the logic of the narrow exception compel an exception here? No. If Employee loses this case, she has no right to indemnification from Employer. Thus, there will be no second suit for indemnity, and no possibility of the anomalous results we saw above. Despite this lack of logical compulsion, some courts permit the employee to assert nonmutual issue preclusion here. This is known generally as the "broad exception" to mutuality.

Not all jurisdictions in the United States have rejected the mutuality doctrine expressly. Among those still adhering to it, however, all recognize at least the narrow exception; many embrace the broad exception.

b. Rejection of Mutuality for Defensive Use

The exceptions just considered apply only in vicarious liability cases. Eventually, some courts took the further step of rejecting mutuality outright, rather than looking for an exception to its operation. The most influential case was Bernhard v. Bank of America, 122 P. 2d 892 (Cal. 1942). In *Bernhard*, an elderly woman in failing health made her home with the Cooks, a married couple, and permitted Mr. Cook to write checks on her behalf against one of her accounts. Mr. Cook withdrew a large sum of money from the account and deposited it in his own. After the woman died, Mr. Cook became executor of her estate. The decedent's relatives sued to challenge Mr. Cook's accounting, arguing that he should return the money to the estate. The court found that the decedent authorized Mr. Cook to withdraw the money as a gift to him and his wife. It entered judgment in his favor.

Mr. Cook then resigned as executor, and one of the decedent's daughters was appointed executrix. She sued the bank that had handled the accounts, arguing that her mother had never authorized the withdrawal. The bank asserted preclusion on the finding in the first case that the decedent had indeed given the money to Mr. Cook. The mutuality doctrine would not permit the assertion of preclusion; neither would the exceptions for vicarious liability cases. Nonetheless, the California Supreme Court permitted the bank to assert nonmutual issue preclusion. Justice Traynor criticized the mutuality rule:

> No satisfactory rationalization has been advanced for the requirement of mutuality. Just why a party who was not bound by a previous action should be precluded from asserting it as res judicata against a party who was bound by it is difficult to comprehend. Many courts have abandoned the requirement of mutuality and confined the requirement of privity to the party against whom the plea of res judicata is asserted. The commentators are almost unanimously in accord. The courts of most jurisdictions have in effect accomplished the same result by recognizing a broad exception to the requirements of mutuality and privity, namely, that they are not necessary where the liability of the defendant asserting the plea of res judicata is dependent upon or derived from the liability of one who was exonerated in an earlier suit brought by the same plaintiff upon the same facts. Typical

examples of such derivative liability are master and servant, principal and agent, and indemnitor and indemnitee.

* * *

In determining the validity of a plea of res judicata three questions are pertinent: Was the issue decided in the prior adjudication identical with the one presented in the action in question? Was there a final judgment on the merits? Was the party against whom the plea is asserted a party or in privity with a party to the prior adjudication?

122 P. 2d at 895.

Again, the revolutionary aspect of *Bernhard* is that it does not struggle to find an exception to mutuality; it simply *rejects* the concept. Thus, it expands the availability of nonmutual issue preclusion beyond the vicarious liability area. Many courts have followed the lead. Indeed, Professor Wright considers *Bernhard* one of those rare situations in which "a major change in established legal doctrine can be identified with a single decision and judge." WRIGHT, FEDERAL COURTS 729. In addition to numerous state courts, the United States Supreme Court has embraced *Bernhard*.

In Blonder-Tongue Laboratories, Inc. v. University of Illinois Foundation, 402 U.S. 313 (1971), a patent holder sued Defendant-1, alleging patent infringement. The court held plaintiff's patent invalid and entered judgment for the defendant. Then plaintiff sued Defendant-2, asserting that it was infringing the same patent. Adhering to the mutuality principle, the lower courts refused to let Defendant-2 use issue preclusion as to the finding that the patent was invalid. The Supreme Court reversed, and discussed policy reasons for rejecting mutuality.

> The cases and authorities discussed above [principally *Bernhard*] connect erosion of the mutuality requirement to the goal of limiting relitigation of issues where that can be achieved without compromising fairness in particular cases. The courts have often discarded the rule while commenting on crowded dockets and long delays preceding trial. Authorities differ on whether the public interest in efficient judicial administration is a sufficient ground in and of itself for abandoning mutuality, but it is clear that more than crowded dockets is involved. The broader question is whether it is any longer tenable to afford a litigant more than one full and fair opportunity for judicial resolution of the same issue. * * * In any lawsuit where a defendant, because of the mutuality principle, is forced to present a complete defense on the merits to a claim which the plaintiff has fully litigated and lost in a prior action, there is an arguable misallocation of resources. To the extent the defendant in the second suit may not win by asserting, without contradiction, that the plaintiff had fully and fairly, but unsuccessfully, litigated the same claim in the prior suit, the defendant's time and money are diverted from alternative uses—productive or otherwise—to relitigation of a decided issue. And, still as-

suming that the issue was resolved correctly in the first suit, there is reason to be concerned about the plaintiff's allocation of resources. Permitting repeated litigation of the same issue as long as the supply of unrelated defendants holds out reflects either the aura of the gaming table or "a lack of discipline and of disinterestedness on the part of the lower courts, hardly a worthy or wise basis for fashioning rules of procedure." Although neither judges, the parties, nor the adversary system performs perfectly in all cases, the requirement of determining whether the party against whom an estoppel is asserted had a full and fair opportunity to litigate is a most significant safeguard.

402 U.S. at 328-29.

NOTES AND QUESTIONS

1. What, if anything, justifies the Supreme Court's concern in *Blonder-Tongue* with "plaintiff's allocation of resources?" If the plaintiff wants to spend money on repeated litigation, what business is that of the judiciary's?

2. In *Blonder-Tongue* the Court abandoned mutuality so long as the party against whom issue preclusion is used had a "full and fair opportunity to litigate" the relevant issue in the first case. Does this add anything to requirements we have already seen for issue preclusion? Can you think of any situations (short of the court's binding and gagging the party's lawyers) in which a party would not have had a "full and fair opportunity to litigate" in the first case?

3. Each jurisdiction is free to determine its own rules concerning preclusion, including mutuality. As noted, *Bernhard* has been influential among the states. *Blonder-Tongue* represents federal law on the subject, to be applied in cases in which state law does not govern. As we will see, state law will govern if the judgment in the first case was decided in a state court and the second action was filed in federal court.

Still, as noted, outright rejection of mutuality is not universal. Some jurisdictions, with the support of some influential commentators, adhere to mutuality as the standard, while recognizing exceptions in vicarious liability situations. See, e.g., Gilmer v. Porterfield, 212 S.E. 2d 842 (Ga. 1975); Kyreacos v. Smith, 572 P. 2d 425 (Wash. 1978). See also J. Wm. Moore & Thomas Currier, *Mutuality and Conclusiveness of Judgments*, 35 TULANE L. REV. 301 (1961). Can you articulate a reason for this position?

4. Note that in *Blonder-Tongue* and *Bernhard*, the person asserting nonmutual issue preclusion was the defendant in the second case. In other words, both cases involved "nonmutual defensive issue preclusion." Yet, neither opinion seems to make much of that fact, leaving open the possibility that nonmutual issue preclusion might be available to *a* *plaintiff* in the second case. Professor Brainerd Currie foresaw the possibility of such "nonmutual *offensive* issue preclusion" even before *Blonder-Tongue*, and was worried by it. In a justly famous article, he argued against expansion of *Bernhard* to the offensive situation. Brainerd Currie, *Mutuality of Estoppel: Limits of the Bernhard Doctrine*, 9 STAN. L. REV. 281 (1957).

Let us consider a variation of a hypothetical posed by Professor Currie. Suppose an airliner crashes, and 100 passengers (P) are injured.

    (a) In the first case, P-1 sues Airline. The court finds that Airline was not negligent and enters judgment for Airline. In the second case, P-2 sues Airline concerning the same crash. It is clear that Airline cannot assert issue preclusion on the finding that it was not negligent. Why?

    (b) Same facts, but P-1 wins the first case, the court finding Airline negligent. Now P-2 sues Airline concerning the same crash. Unless *Bernhard* and *Blonder-Tongue* are limited to their facts, P-2 can assert issue preclusion against Airline on the finding that it was negligent (assuming, of course, that Airline had a "full and fair opportunity to litigate" the issue in the first case). Why? Indeed, wouldn't P-2 through P-100 *all* be able to "ride" the victory of P-1?

Note that Airline would have to win all one hundred cases individually to escape liability. It could never use issue preclusion against a successive plaintiff. The passengers, however, would simply be able to wait until a single passenger won, and then assert nonmutual offensive issue preclusion based upon that case. Professor Ratliff calls this the "option effect," which he criticizes as an unfair one-way street. Jack Ratliff, *Offensive Collateral Estoppel and the Option Effect*, 67 TEX. L. REV. 63 (1988).

Another fact pattern makes the unfairness clearer. Suppose Airline wins each of the first 55 cases brought against it concerning the crash, defeating P-1 through P-55 by proving that it was not negligent. Then P-56 prevails, with a finding that Airline was negligent. Allowing P-57 through P-100 to "ride" this victory seems especially unpalatable because the victory seems clearly to be an aberration. Can the legal system really give such weight to one victory out of 56? This type of scenario especially bothered Professor Currie, who counseled great caution when it came to nonmutual offensive issue preclusion. Currie, supra, 9 STAN. L. REV. at 304-21. Do these concerns militate toward a flat rejection of nonmutual offensive issue preclusion, or toward its use with appropriate limitations? If the latter, what sorts of limitations would be appropriate?

c. Rejection of Mutuality for Offensive Use

Parklane Hosiery v. Shore
439 U.S. 322, 99 S. Ct. 645, 58 L.Ed. 2d 552 (1979)

MR. JUSTICE STEWART delivered the opinion of the Court.

This case presents the question whether a party who has had issues of fact adjudicated adversely to it in an equitable action may be collaterally estopped from relitigating the same issues before a jury in a subsequent legal action brought against it by a new party.

The respondent brought this stockholder's class action against the petitioners in a Federal District Court. The complaint alleged that the petitioners, Parklane Hosiery Co., Inc. (Parklane), and 13 of its officers, directors, and stockholders, had issued a materially false and misleading proxy statement in connection with a merger. The proxy statement, according to the complaint, had violated §§ 14 (a), 10 (b), and 20 (a) of the Securities Exchange Act of 1934, as well as various rules and regulations promulgated by the Securities and Exchange Commission (SEC). The complaint sought damages, rescission of the merger, and recovery of costs.

Before this action came to trial, the SEC filed suit against the same defendants in the Federal District Court, alleging that the proxy statement that had been issued by Parklane was materially false and misleading in essentially the same respects as those that had been alleged in the respondent's complaint. Injunctive relief was requested. After a 4-day trial, the District Court found that the proxy statement was materially false and misleading in the respects alleged, and entered a declaratory judgment to that effect. The Court of Appeals for the Second Circuit affirmed this judgment.

The respondent in the present case then moved for partial summary judgment against the petitioners, asserting that the petitioners were collaterally estopped from relitigating the issues that had been resolved against them in the action brought by the SEC.[2] The District Court denied the motion on the ground that such an application of collateral estoppel would deny the petitioners their Seventh Amendment right to a jury trial. The Court of Appeals for the Second Circuit reversed, holding that a party who has had issues of fact determined against him after a full and fair opportunity to litigate in a nonjury trial is collaterally estopped from obtaining a subsequent jury trial of these same issues of fact. The appellate court concluded that "the Seventh Amendment preserves the right to jury trial only with respect to issues of fact, [and] once those issues have been fully and fairly adjudicated in a prior proceeding, nothing remains for trial, either with or without a jury." Because of an intercircuit conflict, we granted certiorari.

---

[2] A private plaintiff in an action under the proxy rules is not entitled to relief simply by demonstrating that the proxy solicitation was materially false and misleading. The plaintiff must also show that he was injured and prove damages. Since the SEC action was limited to a determination of whether the proxy statement contained materially false and misleading information, the respondent conceded that he would still have to prove these other elements of his prima facie case in the private action. The petitioners' right to a jury trial on those remaining issues is not contested.

CHAPTER 11 THE PRECLUSION DOCTRINES

I

The threshold question to be considered is whether, quite apart from the right to a jury trial under the Seventh Amendment, the petitioners can be precluded from relitigating facts resolved adversely to them in a prior equitable proceeding with another party under the general law of collateral estoppel. Specifically, we must determine whether a litigant who was not a party to a prior judgment may nevertheless use that judgment "offensively" to prevent a defendant from relitigating issues resolved in the earlier proceeding.

A

Collateral estoppel, like the related doctrine of res judicata, has the dual purpose of protecting litigants from the burden of relitigating an identical issue with the same party or his privy and of promoting judicial economy by preventing needless litigation. Until relatively recently, however, the scope of collateral estoppel was limited by the doctrine of mutuality of parties. Under this mutuality doctrine, neither party could use a prior judgment as an estoppel against the other unless both parties were bound by the judgment. Based on the premise that it is somehow unfair to allow a party to use a prior judgment when he himself would not be so bound, the mutuality requirement provided a party who had litigated and lost in a previous action an opportunity to relitigate identical issues with new parties.

By failing to recognize the obvious difference in position between a party who has never litigated an issue and one who has fully litigated and lost, the mutuality requirement was criticized almost from its inception. Recognizing the validity of this criticism, the Court in *Blonder-Tongue Laboratories, Inc. v. University of Illinois Foundation*, abandoned the mutuality requirement, at least in cases where a patentee seeks to relitigate the validity of a patent after a federal court in a previous lawsuit has already declared it invalid. The "broader question" before the Court, however, was "whether it is any longer tenable to afford a litigant more than one full and fair opportunity for judicial resolution of the same issue." 402 U.S., at 328. The Court strongly suggested a negative answer to that question.

B

The *Blonder-Tongue* case involved defensive use of collateral estoppel — a plaintiff was estopped from asserting a claim that the plaintiff had previously litigated and lost against another defendant. The present case, by contrast, involves offensive use of collateral estoppel — a plaintiff is seeking to estop a defendant from relitigating the issues which the defendant previously litigated and lost against another plaintiff. In both the offensive and defensive use situations, the party against whom estoppel is asserted has litigated and lost in an earlier action. Nevertheless, several reasons have been advanced why the two situations should be treated differently.

First, offensive use of collateral estoppel does not promote judicial economy in the same manner as defensive use does. Defensive use of collateral estoppel precludes a plaintiff from relitigating identical issues by merely "switching adversaries." Thus defensive collateral estoppel gives a plaintiff a strong incentive to join all potential defendants in the first action if possible.

Offensive use of collateral estoppel, on the other hand, creates precisely the opposite incentive. Since a plaintiff will be able to rely on a previous judgment against a defendant but will not be bound by that judgment if the defendant wins, the plaintiff has every incentive to adopt a "wait and see" attitude, in the hope that the first action by another plaintiff will result in a favorable judgment. Thus offensive use of collateral estoppel will likely increase rather than decrease the total amount of litigation, since potential plaintiffs will have everything to gain and nothing to lose by not intervening in the first action.

A second argument against offensive use of collateral estoppel is that it may be unfair to a defendant. If a defendant in the first action is sued for small or nominal damages, he may have little incentive to defend vigorously, particularly if future suits are not foreseeable. Allowing offensive collateral estoppel may also be unfair to a defendant if the judgment relied upon as a basis for the estoppel is itself inconsistent with one or more previous judgments in favor of the defendant. Still another situation where it might be unfair to apply offensive estoppel is where the second action affords the defendant procedural opportunities unavailable in the first action that could readily cause a different result.[15]

C

We have concluded that the preferable approach for dealing with these problems in the federal courts is not to preclude the use of offensive collateral estoppel, but to grant trial courts broad discretion to determine when it should be applied. The general rule should be that in cases where a plaintiff could easily have joined in the earlier action or where, either for the reasons discussed above or for other reasons, the application of offensive estoppel would be unfair to a defendant, a trial judge should not allow the use of offensive collateral estoppel.

In the present case, however, none of the circumstances that might justify reluctance to allow the offensive use of collateral estoppel is present. The application of offensive collateral estoppel will not here reward a private plaintiff who could have joined in the previous action, since the respondent probably could not have joined in the injunctive action brought by the SEC even had he so desired. Similarly, there is no unfairness to the petitioners in applying offensive collateral estoppel in this case. First, in light of the serious allegations made in the SEC's complaint against the petitioners, as well as the foreseeability of subsequent private suits that typically follow a successful Government judgment, the petitioners had every incentive to litigate the SEC lawsuit fully and vigorously.

Second, the judgment in the SEC action was not inconsistent with any previous decision. Finally, there will in the respondent's action be no procedural opportunities available to the petitioners that were unavailable in the first action of a kind that might be likely to cause a different result.

We conclude, therefore, that none of the considerations that would justify a refusal to allow the use of offensive collateral estoppel is present in this case. Since the petitioners received a "full

---

[15] If, for example, the defendant in the first action was forced to defend in an inconvenient forum and therefore was unable to engage in full scale discovery or call witnesses, application of offensive collateral estoppel may be unwarranted. Indeed, differences in available procedures may sometimes justify not allowing a prior judgement to have estoppel effect in a subsequent action even between the same parties* * *. The problem of unfairness is particularly acute in cases of offesnive estoppel, however, because the defendant against whom estoppel is asserted typically will not have chosen the forum in the first action.

and fair" opportunity to litigate their claims in the SEC action, the contemporary law of collateral estoppel leads inescapably to the conclusion that the petitioners are collaterally estopped from relitigating the question of whether the proxy statement was materially false and misleading.

II

[The Court then concluded that application of issue preclusion did not violate the Seventh Amendment right to jury trial.]

NOTES AND QUESTIONS

1. In *Parklane*, the Court abandoned mutuality in the offensive context, but only after arming the district courts with discretion to determine whether the use of preclusion would be fair under the circumstances. Consider them individually.

> (a) *Easy joinder in the first case.* Is the Court correct in its opinion that nonmutual defensive issue preclusion promotes efficiency while nonmutual offensive issue preclusion does not? In an interesting article, Professor Hay demonstrates the Court's point through economic analysis, concluding that "by suing separately from the group, the free rider gets two bites at the apple; if the group loses, he is not bound by the adverse judgment." Bruce Hay, *Some Settlement Effects of Preclusion*, 1993 U. ILL. L. REV. 21, 49.

To deal with this concern, the Court will not let someone who "could easily have joined" in the first case use offensive preclusion. Is this a meaningful limitation? After all, the "penalty" for waiting in the wings is simply that the second plaintiff gets to present her entire case. See Ratliff, supra, 67 TEX. L. REV. at 83.

In Chapter 12, we will see that certain nonparties are able to intervene in a pending case. The ability to intervene depends, of course, on knowledge of the pending case. But assuming knowledge and an ability to intervene, what does "easily" mean? If a case is pending in Philadelphia and the would-be intervenor lives across the river in Camden, New Jersey, could she join "easily?" What if the case were in federal court and she wanted to sue in state court?

> (b) *Foreseeability of litigation/incentive to litigate.* How can this be shown? Will it not be obvious in mass tort cases? Won't the defendant's incentive to litigate in the first case be especially high if the jurisdiction adopts nonmutual offensive issue preclusion?
>
> (c) *Inconsistent judgments.* The Court would not permit nonmutual offensive issue preclusion if there were inconsistent judgments in litigation already com-

pleted. Is there any limit to this notion? Suppose 30 successive plaintiffs proved that defendant was negligent and that defendant had only won one case—the first one, at that. In a well-known pre-*Parklane* decision, the Oregon Supreme Court said "[w]e do not mean to say that one favorable determination can never be overcome and estoppel never applied despite the number of subsequent determinations to the contrary." State Farm Fire & Cas. Co. v. Century Home Components, Inc., 550 P. 2d 1185, 1192 n. 5 (Ore. 1976). In Hoppe v. G.D. Searle & Co., 779 F. Supp. 1425 (S.D. N.Y. 1991), the court rejected nonmutual offensive issue preclusion because the defendant had won sixteen of twenty prior jury adjudications.

(d) *Different procedures.* What examples did the Court give for this factor? Can you think of any others?

2. Would you expect plaintiffs to use nonmutual offensive issue preclusion whenever it is available? While there are few data, one federal judge offers his anecdotal observation that many plaintiffs do not try to take advantage of the doctrine. As he concludes, parties eschew preclusion because it may "eliminate [their] opportunity to present the 'horribles' of defendant's conduct to the jury in each subsequent case." Spencer Williams, *Mass Tort Class Actions: Going, Going, Gone?*, 98 F.R.D. 323, 328-29 (1983). Should plaintiffs be allowed to burden courts with such unnecessary presentation of evidence?

3. Predictably, the advent of nonmutual offensive issue preclusion gave rise to "plaintiff shopping." That is, counsel for numerous plaintiffs might agree that the one with the most compelling case—and thus the best chance to show that the defendant was liable—ought to go forward first. When she wins, the others may then use preclusion to ride that victory. A good example of this type of litigation strategy is found in the asbestos cases. Interestingly, for a variety of reasons, the courts have not readily employed nonmutual offensive issue preclusion there. See Michael Green, *The Inability of Offensive Collateral Estoppel to Fulfill Its Promise: An Examination of Estoppel in Asbestos Litigation*, 70 Iowa L. Rev. 141 (1984).

For example, recall *Hardy v. Johns-Manville Sales Corp.* There, plaintiffs succeeded in a prior case (*Borel*). In *Hardy*, different plaintiffs tried to use *Borel* to establish various issues decided in that first case. As we read, preclusion could only be used against defendants who were parties to *Borel*. As to such defendants, however, the court refused to invoke preclusion. Among other things, it cited inconsistent judgments and different litigation incentives coming from vastly varying exposure in the different cases. It also concluded that the *Borel* court had not decided exactly the same issues on which plaintiffs wanted preclusion.

4. Does *Parklane* address sufficiently Professor Currie's concerns (discussed above at 614)? Recall the mass disaster hypothetical, in which 100 passengers are injured in a single crash. Airline wins the first 55 cases, proving that it was not negligent. Then P-56 wins a judgment, based upon a finding that Airline was negligent. Professor Currie was wary of allowing P-57 through P-100 to use preclusion because it seems that P-56's judgment is an aberration.

Suppose instead P-1 wins the first case to go to judgment. Because it is first, there are obviously no inconsistent judgments. Thus, *Parklane* would appear to permit P-2 through P-100 to use issue preclusion (assuming, of course, that no other fairness factor is violated). But how do we know (especially given the possibility of "plaintiff shopping," discussed above) that the judgment for P-1 is not an aberration? That is, if we litigated all 100 cases separately, is it not possible that Airline would win 99? Even if Airline would win just one, why should it be "railroaded" for 99 judgments just because it lost the first one? Currie, supra, 9 STAN. L. REV. at 308-21. Is there an alternative, such as trying ten test cases to see which way the wind is blowing?

Does *Parklane* tell us why we should repose such confidence in the first judgment?

5. Exceptions to the Operation of Issue Preclusion

As with claim preclusion, the courts recognize exceptions to the operation of issue preclusion. These are cataloged in § 28 of the Restatement (Second) of Judgments, which provides that issue preclusion will not apply if:

(1) The party against whom preclusion is sought could not, as a matter of law, have obtained review of the judgment in the initial action; or
(2) The issue is one of law and (a) the two actions involve claims that are substantially unrelated, or (b) a new determination is warranted in order to take account of an intervening change in the applicable legal context or otherwise to avoid inequitable administration of the laws; or
(3) A new determination of the issue is warranted by differences in the quality or extensiveness of the procedures followed in the two courts or by factors relating to the allocation of jurisdiction between them; or
(4) The party against whom preclusion is sought had a significantly heavier burden of persuasion with respect to the issue in the initial action than in the subsequent action; the burden has shifted to his adversary; or the adversary has a significantly heavier burden than he had in the first action; or
(5) There is a clear and convincing need for a new determination of the issue (a) because of the potential adverse impact of the determination on the public interest or the interests of persons not themselves parties in the initial action, (b) because it was not

sufficiently foreseeable at the time of the initial action that the issue would arise in the context of a subsequent action, or (c) because the party sought to be precluded, as a result of the conduct of his adversary or other special circumstances, did not have an adequate opportunity or incentive to obtain a full and fair adjudication in the initial action.

NOTES AND QUESTIONS

1. At least three of the *Parklane* "fairness" factors seem to be addressed by this list. Which ones? Does this suggest that *Parklane* is not particularly revolutionary?

2. While riding her bicycle, P crashes because of faulty paving on a city street. She is injured, and her bike is damaged. First, she sues the city for $80.00 property damage. She proves that the city was negligent and wins. Second, she sues the city for $1,000,000 in personal injuries. Assuming that the jurisdiction adopts the primary rights definition of claim (so the case is not dismissed for claim preclusion), can she use issue preclusion to establish the city's negligence?

3. Criminal defendants must be convicted by evidence that proves guilt beyond a reasonable doubt. In civil cases, the claimant must prevail by a lesser standard—a preponderance of the evidence.

Suppose the state prosecutes D for theft, and gains a conviction. Then, the person from whom D stole institutes a civil action against D to recover damages. Can the plaintiff in the civil case use issue preclusion on the question of whether D stole the item? Why? See Crowall v. Heritage Mutual Ins. Co., 346 N.W. 2d 327 (Wis. 1984) (criminal conviction for driving under influence given issue preclusive effect in later civil case).

Suppose instead that the state prosecutes D for theft, but the jury returns a verdict of not guilty. Now the person from whom D allegedly stole institutes a civil action against D to recover damages. Aside from the fact that the civil plaintiff was not a party to the criminal case, why can D *not* assert issue preclusion to the effect that he did not steal the item?

4. Inventor patented an invention and entered into Contract-1 with Manufacturer. Under the agreement, Manufacturer made and marketed the invention and paid a royalty to Inventor's spouse. The Internal Revenue Service sued, claiming that the income from Contract-1 ought to be taxed to Inventor and not to Spouse. The court disagreed, holding that the income was taxable to Spouse. (Inventor liked this result because Spouse had a lower income tax rate.)

Because the product continued to sell well at the expiration of Contract-1, Inventor entered Contract-2 with Manufacturer; it was identical to Contract-1 in every detail except dates. The IRS sued concerning tax liabilities for a different year, again claiming that the income—this time from Contract-2—should be taxable to Inventor. Should issue preclusion prevent the IRS from arguing that issue? See Commissioner of Internal Revenue v. Sunnen, 333 U.S. 591, 602 (1948) (no issue preclusion; "For income tax purposes, what is decided as to one contract is not conclusive as to any other contract which is not then in issue, however similar or identical it may be."). In *Sunnen*, the Court was influenced by the fact that relevant case law intervened and made it clear that the income should be taxed to the inventor. Where is the holding in *Sunnen* reflected in § 28 of the Restatement (Second) of Judgments?

Sunnen may be a good example of why issue preclusion should be applied with especial care to issues of law. Although it was once widely stated that there could be no issue preclusion on matters of law, the opposite view now prevails. See Colin Buckley, *Issue Preclusion and Issues of Law: A Doctrinal Framework Based on Rules of Recognition, Jurisdiction and Legal History*, 24 HOUS. L. REV. 875 (1987); Geoffrey Hazard, *Preclusion as to Issues of Law: The Legal System's Interest*, 70 IOWA L. REV. 81 (1984). Still, as *Sunnen* shows, issues of law raise special problems, since allowing a party to use issue preclusion on a matter of law might allow her to avoid the consequences of subsequent changes in the law. This could give one person a preferred position vis a vis other citizens.

5. Nonmutual offensive issue preclusion is unavailable in litigation against the United States. United States v. Mendoza, 464 U.S. 154 (1984). This rule is dictated by policy. The government is involved in litigation around the country, and may litigate the same issue in numerous cases. It would be required to appeal every adverse ruling in an effort to avoid preclusion. This result "might disserve the economy interest in whose name estoppel is advanced by requiring the government to abandon virtually any exercise of discretion in seeking to review judgments unfavorable to it." Id. at 163. Does this exception find support in § 28 of the Restatement (Second) of Judgments? See generally Leo Levin & Susan Leeson, *Issue Preclusion Against the United States Government*, 70 IOWA L. REV. 113 (1984).

D. Problems of Federalism

What preclusion rules apply if judgment is entered in one jurisdiction and the second case is filed in another? In answering this, we need to consider separately the four possible fact patterns: (1) "state-to-state," in which the first judgment is rendered in State A and the second case is filed in State B; (2) "state-to-federal," in which the first judgment is rendered in state court and the second case is filed in federal court; (3) "federal-to-state," in which the first judgment is rendered in federal court and the second case is filed in state court; and (4) "federal-to-federal," in which the first judgment is rendered in one federal district court and the second case is filed in another.

The analysis of what rules apply starts with the Full Faith and Credit Clause of the Constitution, Article IV, §1, and the full faith and credit statute, 28 U.S.C. § 1738. Read both provisions carefully. Two things are noteworthy at this point. First, the constitutional provision is narrower; it covers only the fact pattern (1) above, and requires every state court to give full faith and credit to the judicial proceedings of every other state. The statutory provision covers this situation as well as fact pattern (2) above, and requires every state court *and federal court* to give "the same full faith and credit" to a judgment as it would receive in the judgment-rendering state. Second, neither the Constitution nor the statute covers situations (3) or (4), in which the judgment is rendered in a federal court.

1. State-to-State

In Chapter 2 on personal jurisdiction, we saw that the courts of all states must give full faith and credit to a valid judgment of a court of another state. In determining whether a judgment of State A was valid, the court in State B could inquire only as to whether the court in State A had personal jurisdiction. If it did not, the judgment of State A was void and unenforceable. But if the court in State A had jurisdiction, its judgment was entitled to full faith and credit in State B, even if the judgment was wrong on the merits of the dispute. If the losing party felt that the State A judgment was erroneous, she should have appealed it in State A. We also discussed this topic in Chapter 6, where we saw these distinctions between direct and collateral attacks on personal jurisdiction.

2. State-to-Federal

Here, § 1738 requires a federal court in State B to give full faith and credit to a valid judgment of State A. Thus, this situation is functionally equivalent to the "state-to-state" fact pattern. Allen v. McCurry, 449 U.S. 90, 96 (1980) ("Congress has specifically required all federal courts to give preclusive effect to state court judgments whenever the courts of the State from which the judgments emerged would do so."). See generally William Luneberg, *The Opportunity to be Heard and the Doctrines of Preclusion: Federal Limits on State Law* 31 VILL. L. REV. 81 (1986); Gene Shreve, *Preclusion and Federal Choice of Law*, 64 TEX. L. REV. 1209 (1986).

In each of these two situations, however, does the statutory requirement that the second court give the "same full faith and credit" as the judgment-rendering court mean "same" in every detail? The drafters of the Restatement (Second) of Judgments conclude that it does. To them, § 1738 that requires the second court "to give to the state judgment the same effect—*no more and no less*—than the [judgment-rendering] court would give it." Id. § 86 cmt. g (1982). Although this summarizes the majority view, some commentators argue, and a few courts conclude, that the second court is free to diverge somewhat from the preclusion rules of the judgment-rendering state. There are two possibilities.

First, one can argue that full faith and credit encompasses only the "central doctrines of claim and issue preclusion" and not "every minute detail." WRIGHT, FEDERAL COURTS 732. Under this approach, full faith and credit would be "limited to the rules that support the core values of finality, repose, and reliance, as well as some of the rules that facilitate control by the first court over its own procedure." It would not, however, "demand obeisance to other aspects of preclusion doctrine that are incidental to the central role of preclusion and that may intrude on substantial interests of later courts." Id. Can you think of any such "other aspects of preclusion doctrine?" Perhaps reflecting the difficulty in drawing this line, courts have not accepted this argument.

Second, there is some support for the conclusion that § 1738 does not preclude the second court from giving a judgment a *greater* preclusive effect than it would receive in the first court. According to this view, the main purpose of the statute is to ensure respect for the original court's judgment; giving it greater effect than it would receive in that court does not violate that policy. A few opinions have embraced this proposition. See In re Trans Ocean Tender Offer Securities Litigation, 455 F. Supp. 999 (N.D. Ill. 1978); Hart v. American Airlines, Inc., 304 N.Y.S. 2d 810 (Sup. Ct. 1969). For example, suppose the judgment-rendering state does not allow nonmutual assertion of issue preclusion, but the second court would. In *Trans Ocean*, the second court, a federal district court, extended the effect of the first judgment by enforcing it through nonmutual preclusion. Such holdings are rare, and are widely criticized. TEPLY & WHITTEN, CIVIL PROCEDURE 929 ("wisdom * * * is questionable"); WRIGHT, FEDERAL COURTS 733. What policy counsels against providing greater preclusive effect than the original court would give?

Accordingly, when § 1738 instructs the second court to give the "same full faith and credit" as the original court, "same" means "same." This requirement can create odd situations in the second fact pattern, where a federal court must apply the preclusion law of the judgment–rendering state. In Marrese v. American Academy of Orthopaedic Surgeons, 470 U.S. 373 (1985), doctors sued a professional association in state court, asserting that they were denied membership in violation of various state laws. After losing there, the doctors sued in federal court, asserting a violation of federal antitrust laws. Because the federal antitrust claims invoked exclusive federal jurisdiction, the doctors could not have asserted them in the first proceeding. Nonetheless, the lower courts dismissed the second case under claim preclusion, noting that the plaintiffs could have sued on both the federal and state claims in federal court.

The Supreme Court reversed and remanded for consideration of what the law of the judgment-rendering state would provide in this situation. But what sort of assessment will that be? How can a state have rules of preclusion for claims that cannot be asserted in its courts? Recall that one exception to claim preclusion is that the claim could not have been asserted before because of jurisdictional limitations. See supra Section B(4). Does this exception ensure that the state rules cannot prescribe preclusion on these facts? See JAMES, HAZARD & LEUBSDORF, CIVIL PROCEDURE 601. Indeed, on remand in *Marrese*, the district court denied claim preclusion precisely because the federal claim could not have been joined in the state proceeding. Marrese v. American Academy of Orthopaedic Surgeons, 628 F. Supp. 918 (N.D. Ill. 1986) (court's "task is an exercise in extrapolation because, of course, the Illinois courts never address issue pertaining to exclusively federal lawsuits.").

3. Federal-to-State

As noted, neither the Constitution nor the statute addresses this fact pattern. Nonetheless, courts and commentators agree that the state courts must respect federal judgments. Professor Degnan concluded that this result is compelled by the Supremacy Clause of Article VI of the Constitution. Ronan Degnan, *Federalized Res Judicata*, 85 YALE L.J. 741, 742-49, 768-69 (1976). See also Stephen Burbank, *Federal Judgments Law: Sources of Authority and Sources of Rules*, 70 TEX. L. REV. 1551 (1992).

Isn't this the only reasonable result? After all, what good would a federal court judgment be if other courts were free to ignore it? As Professor Wright concludes, "[t]he suggestion that state courts should be free to disregard the judgments of federal courts is so unthinkable that the rule rejecting any such suggestion has been stated in an unbroken line of cases * * * ." WRIGHT, FEDERAL COURTS 736.

4. Federal-to-Federal

It is not surprising that this fact pattern is not mentioned in either the Constitution or § 1738, since here the litigants do not deal with intersystem enforcement of a judgment; all of the litigation is in a single court system. That does not mean there are not problems, however. If the first case was in federal court based upon federal question jurisdiction, the courts assume that federal common law governs the preclusion question. The Supreme

Court did this in *Blonder-Tongue* and *Parklane*. (Is this result consistent with the Rules of Decision Act?)

But what if the federal court's jurisdiction was based upon diversity of citizenship jurisdiction? Clearly, the *Erie* doctrine, discussed in Chapter 7, requires the federal court to apply state substantive law in diversity cases. Does that mean that the federal court in the second action must look to the preclusion law of the state in which the federal court sat in the first case? Suppose, for example, that the first federal judgment is entered in a district court in Iowa in a diversity of citizenship case, and that the second action is filed in federal district court in Hawaii. Should the Hawaii federal judge use Iowa law of preclusion to determine the preclusive effect of the first judgment? Or is she free to apply a federal law of preclusion?

The Restatement (Second) of Judgments § 87 takes the position that federal law should govern. That section bears the influence of Professor Ronan Degnan, who reached the conclusion that federal law should govern in *Federalized Res Judicata*, supra, 85 YALE L.J. 741. Other commentators disagree. See, e.g., Stephen Burbank, *Interjurisdictional Preclusion, Full Faith and Credit and Federal Common Law: A General Approach*, 71 CORNELL L. REV. 733 (1986). Not surprisingly, the courts have disagreed. Compare Adkins v. Allstate Ins. Co., 729 F. 2d 974 (4th Cir. 1984) (federal law applies) with Bates v. Union Oil Co., 944 F. 2d 647 (9th Cir. 1991) (state law applies).

The majority, and growing, view appears to be that federal law should apply, even if the first case were based upon diversity of citizenship, unless to do so would jeopardize some instate substantive policy. WRIGHT, FEDERAL COURTS 737-38; RESTATEMENT (SECOND) OF JUDGMENTS § 87 cmt. b. What kind of preclusion rules might embody such substantive concerns?

CHAPTER 12

SCOPE OF LITIGATION—

JOINDER AND SUPPLEMENTAL JURISDICTION

A. Introduction and Integration

In this chapter we address the scope of litigation. In other words, what parties can be joined and what claims can they assert in a civil action? At common law, joinder rules were restrictive, resulting in multiple suits for what could easily be seen as a single overall dispute. Equity practice relaxed the joinder rules considerably, with the express goal of determining disputes by the whole, rather than piecemeal. Modern joinder practice, as embodied in the Federal Rules, adopts this theme from equity, and permits (indeed, sometimes compels) the joinder of parties and claims along transactional lines. This trend is supported by the evolution of preclusion doctrines that also focus on "transaction or occurrence" in defining a claim.

This inclination toward "packaging" of disputes brings many benefits. Primarily, it avoids duplicative litigation by putting all transactionally related claims and parties into a single case. This not only avoids unnecessary expense for the litigants, but reduces backlog in burdened court systems. Remember, litigation is publicly funded dispute resolution. The public has some right to insist on efficiency in the process. Packaging also may contribute to public confidence in the judicial system by avoiding inconsistent results that may flow from duplicative litigation. For a classic discussion of the benefits of packaging, see John McCoid, *A Single Package for Multiparty Disputes*, 27 STAN. L. REV. 707 (1976).

But packaging is not a panacea. It makes litigation more complex and therefore may not reduce queuing time significantly. Clearly, the court must be equipped with mechanisms to ensure that multiple claims and parties do not confuse the jury at trial. Moreover, mandatory packaging may override the plaintiff's ability to choose her forum and the scope of the litigation she wishes to pursue. Historically, courts have given great deference to plaintiff autonomy. Today, with growing concerns for efficiency, many argue that the plaintiff must share the decisionmaking authority regarding scope of the litigation.* One of the significant debates in procedure concerns the balance between plaintiff autonomy and efficiency. *See* JAMES, HAZARD & LEUBSDORF, CIVIL PROCEDURE 461-64.

The joinder rules are only part of the story, however. The scope of litigation in federal court is also a function of subject matter jurisdiction. The joinder provisions of the Federal Rules provide procedural mechanisms by which to assert a variety of claims. They do not, however, provide subject matter jurisdiction for those claims. See Rule 82. *Every claim joined in federal court must have a basis of subject matter jurisdiction.* Sometimes the basis will be clear because the claim will be supported by federal question, alienage, or diversity of citizenship jurisdiction. Sometimes, however, the claim will not be supported by one of the bases of jurisdiction we studied in Chapter 4.

In such situations, the court may nonetheless permit assertion of a claim under *supplemental jurisdiction.* This doctrine allows a federal court to hear claims that are so closely related to an underlying dispute that properly invoked federal jurisdiction as to be considered part of the same "case or controversy" as that dispute. As we will see, the courts have defined this close relationship along transactional lines. This has created a confluence between the procedural test for joinder and the supplemental jurisdictional test and has greatly facilitated packaging.

In this chapter, we integrate the discussion of supplemental jurisdiction with the discussion of the joinder rules. Thus, throughout this chapter, there are always two questions. First, is there a joinder Rule that permits the assertion of this claim? If so, second, is the claim supported by subject matter jurisdiction? An affirmative answer to the second question can be based upon any of the bases of subject matter jurisdiction discussed in chapter 4 or upon supplemental jurisdiction. Accordingly, as to the joinder devices throughout the chapter, we will have separate subparts on "procedural aspects" and "jurisdictional aspects."

B. Real Party in Interest, Capacity, and Standing

Our system does not allow everyone who is irked about something to bring a suit. The plaintiff, generally speaking, must have been harmed by the defendant and must be the appropriate recipient of any remedy the court may award.

The first sentence of Rule 17(a) requires that "[e]very action shall be prosecuted in the name of the real party in interest." The second sentence makes it clear that the real

---

* We have already discussed how the plaintiff's choice of forum may be overridden by removal and by transfer of venue. See Chapter 4, Section C(6) and Chapter 5, Section E.

party in interest (RPI) will not necessarily be the person who receives the benefit of a favorable judgment. For example, a trustee suing on behalf of beneficiaries to the trust will not be enriched by a judgment. She is acting merely as a representative of the beneficiaries.

Most of the difficult RPI cases involve assignment or subrogation of the plaintiff's claim. Suppose P has a claim against D, but assigns the right to sue to Z. Common law did not recognize the assignment, and required the case to be brought by P, even though she obviously had no interest in the outcome of the case. Equity, on the other hand, recognized the assignment, and allowed Z to bring suit as the RPI. See generally 3A MOORE'S FEDERAL PRACTICE ¶ 17.08. Rule 17(a) follows this historic equity practice.*

Subrogation is basically an assignment by operation of law and arises commonly in insurance cases. For example, suppose Corporation purchases fire insurance from Insurer to cover fire damage to its manufacturing plant. The plant is destroyed by a fire caused by the negligence of D. Obviously, Corporation has a claim against D. Pursuing litigation, however, will take several years; Corporation wants money now so it can rebuild the plant and get back in business. That is why it bought insurance. Under the policy, Insurer will write a check to Corporation immediately *and will, in return, be subrogated to Corporation's right to sue D.* In other words, Insurer pays Corporation for the loss and receives, by operation of law, an assignment of Corporation's right to sue D. In the case against D, Insurer would be the RPI. If Corporation brought the case, D would move to substitute Insurer as RPI.

RPI inquiries are to be contrasted with the notion of *capacity*. Capacity refers to a person's or an entity's ability to sue and be sued. For example, minors and incompetent persons lack the capacity to represent their own interests in litigation; a case by or against them must be brought by or against such a person's representative. Similarly, some entities, such as labor unions and partnerships, may lack capacity to sue in their common name; litigation by or against them will be brought by or against individual members of the group instead.** Rule 17(b) addresses these and other capacity issues.

Both RPI and capacity must be distinguished from *standing*, a doctrine of surpassing difficulty requiring that the plaintiff have suffered some "injury in fact" before she can sue. Standing is often an issue in cases challenging governmental action. For example, can a private group interested in environmental issues sue to enjoin the government's building of a dam that may endanger certain animals? Can persons opposed to capital punishment sue to enjoin the execution of a convicted murderer? The answers to such questions are not easy, and are addressed in detail in courses on constitutional law and federal courts.

---

* We have already discussed problems that can arise under 28 U.S.C. § 1359 when a claim is assigned for the purpose of creating diversity of citizenship jurisdiction. See supra at 186.

** It may be possible to pursue the litigation as a class action, as we will see in Chapter 13.

NOTES AND QUESTIONS

Read Rule 17(a) and (b) and answer the following.

1. If someone other than an RPI sues a defendant, what can the defendant do?

2. Paula, a citizen of North Carolina, sues Dana, a citizen of Washington, in federal court, seeking damages of $150,000. Under relevant substantive law, assume that the RPI is not Paula, but Pamela, who is a citizen of Washington. Notwithstanding the third sentence of Rule 17(a), why must this action be dismissed? What *two* motions should Dana make?

3. Harvey has a homeowner's insurance policy insuring his house from damage. His house is severely damaged when a small airplane crashes into it. Although the damage is $75,000, his insurance company pays him $74,500 under the policy, because the policy has a $500 deductible. In a suit against the pilot of the airplane, why are *both* Harvey and the insurance company RPIs?

4. Same facts as in Note 3. Assume that Harvey is a citizen of Missouri, the pilot is a citizen of Kansas, and the insurance company is a citizen of Connecticut. Clearly, the insurance company could sue the pilot under diversity of citizenship jurisdiction.

   (a) Could Harvey invoke diversity of citizenship jurisdiction against the pilot? Isn't he an RPI only for a claim of $500? See Travelers Ins. Co. v. Riggs, 671 F.2d 810 (4th Cir. 1982)(similar fact pattern; court allows both insured and insurer to proceed as RPIs without discussing this problem).

   (b) Instead of making an outright payment to Harvey, suppose the insurance company "lent" Harvey $74,500, with the stipulation that he would return any judgment recovered to the insurance company. Who is the RPI? Would your answer differ if the agreement stated that Harvey need never return the money if he recovers no judgment against the pilot?

5. The scenario described in Note 4(b) is quite common, since insurance companies prefer to have the litigation filed and prosecuted in the name of the insured individual rather than in their names. They fear that a jury will be less sympathetic to an insurance company than to an aggrieved individual. Why? Probably, it is because many potential jurors see an insurance company as a "deep pocket" for a judgment. In addition, many jurors may have had their own disagreements with insurance companies. Courts have not been consistent in addressing this "loan receipt" situation. Some see the insured as the RPI, some say it is the insurer. See generally Stephen Boynton, *The Myth of the 'Loan Receipt' Revisited Under Rule 17(a)*, 18 S.C. L. REV. 624 (1966); June Entman, *More*

Reasons for Abolishing Federal Rule of Civil Procedure 17(a): The Problem of the Proper Plaintiff and Insurance Subrogation, 68 N.C. L. REV. 893 (1990).

An insurer may try to achieve anonymity through ratification. In Prosperity Realty Co. v. Haco-Canon, 724 F. Supp. 254 (S.D. N.Y. 1989), the insurer paid all but $1000 of plaintiff's damages, thereby seeming to make it an RPI through subrogation. The court refused to join the insurer, however, for two reasons. First, the insurer had ratified the action brought by the insured when it signed an agreement upon payment of the damages. Second, it had waived all rights to subrogation outside the case brought by the insured. In the court's view, the purpose of Rule 17(a) is to protect the defendant from subsequent actions by the party actually entitled to recovery. The ratification agreement provided such protection.

Does the RPI rule serve any purpose other than that suggested by the court in *Prosperity Realty*? If the *Prosperity Realty* explanation is correct, does the RPI rule add any protection not already accorded by the substantive law? That is, if the "wrong" person sues the defendant, won't the substantive law preclude her from recovering? Noting this and other arguments, some critics argue that the RPI rule is more trouble than it is worth, and ought to be jettisoned. See, e.g., Thomas Atkinson, *The Real Party in Interest Rule: A Plea for its Abolition*, 32 N.Y.U. L. REV. 926 (1957); Entman, supra, 68 N.C.L. Rev. 893; John Kennedy, *Federal Rule 17(a): Will the Real Party in Interest Please Stand?*, 51 MINN. L. REV. 675 (1967).

6. Assume that state law precludes a partnership from suing in its own name. If the partnership desired to sue in federal court, why would a federal court allow it to sue by the common name?

C. Claim Joinder by Plaintiffs

1. Procedural Aspects

Assuming that the plaintiff is an RPI, and that she has capacity and standing, what claims can she assert against a defendant? Read Rule 18(a). Note its breadth; it allows a claimant to assert every claim she has against the opposing party. This rule applies even if the claims are not transactionally related, are based upon different theories, and even if the claimant is seeking different remedies. It declares "open season" on the defendant. It says "anything goes." Such open-ended joinder may facilitate settlement by allowing parties to put their entire dispute in one litigation. There are other points to consider.

First, Rule 18(a) is permissive; the plaintiff is not required to assert all claims she has against the defendant. Remember, however, that the joinder rules are not the only things that animate a plaintiff's choices. The plaintiff must also consider the preclusion rules. Thus, although Rule 18(a) is permissive, the preclusion rules may, as a practical matter, force the plaintiff to join several assertions of liability in a single case. Rule 18(a) is the carrot and claim preclusion is the stick. See Richard Freer, *Avoiding Duplicative Litigation: Rethinking Plaintiff Autonomy and the Court's Role in Defining the Litigative Unit*, 50 U. PITT. L. REV. 809, 822 (1989).

Second, if the plaintiff's claims are *not* transactionally related, and claim preclusion does not act as a stick (why not?), why would the plaintiff ever want to "load up" a case by asserting them together? Can you imagine a less than noble motive? Can you imagine a sensible motive? Read Rule 42(b). Does this allow the court to avoid problems created by overzealous claim joinder by the plaintiff?

Third, note that Rule 18(a) does not empower the "plaintiff," but speaks instead of "[a] party asserting a claim to relief." This excellent drafting recognizes that plaintiffs are not the only litigants who can assert claims. It is important to understand, however, that Rule 18(a) does not automatically grant all litigants the right to assert all claims against all other litigants. Rather, it declares "open season" only for those litigants asserting a claim listed in the rule. For example, as we will see, a cross-claim is a transactionally related claim that one has against a co-party. If a defendant asserts a cross-claim against her co-defendant, *then* Rule 18(a) permits her to declare open season on the co-defendant by joining all other claims. If she does not assert the cross-claim, however, she cannot invoke Rule 18(a).

Fourth, joinder rules such as Rule 18(a) are procedural only, and cannot affect subject matter jurisdiction. Thus, once the procedural propriety of a claim is established, we then must assess whether the claim is supported by federal subject matter jurisdiction.

2. Jurisdictional Aspects

In some cases, multiple claims will have independent bases of subject matter jurisdiction. Suppose, for example, that Paul, a citizen of Georgia, sues Don, a citizen of Arizona, asserting a violation of federal antitrust laws and a completely unrelated $60,000 claim for breach of contract. The antitrust claim invokes federal question jurisdiction, and the contract claim invokes diversity of citizenship jurisdiction.

What happens, however, when a party uses Rule 18(a) to join a claim over which there is no federal question or diversity of citizenship jurisdiction?

C. Claim Joinder by Plaintiffs

United Mine Workers v. Gibbs
383 U.S. 715, 86 S. Ct. 1130, 16 L. Ed. 2d. 218 (1966)

MR JUSTICE BRENNAN delivered the opinion of the Court.

Respondent Paul Gibbs was awarded compensatory and punitive damages in this action against petitioner United Mine Workers of America (UMW) for alleged violations of § 303 of the Labor Management Relations Act, 1947, as amended, and of the common law of Tennessee. The case grew out of the rivalry between the United Mine Workers and the Southern Labor Union over representation of workers in the southern Appalachian coal fields. Tennessee Consolidated Coal Company, not a party here, laid off 100 miners of the UMW's Local 5881 when it closed one of its mines in southern Tennessee during the spring of 1960. Late that summer, Grundy Company, a wholly owned subsidiary of Consolidated, hired respondent as mine superintendent to attempt to open a new mine on Consolidated's property at nearby Gray's Creek through use of members of the Southern Labor Union. As part of the arrangement, Grundy also gave respondent a contract to haul the mine's coal to the nearest railroad loading point.

On August 15 and 16, 1960, armed members of Local 5881 forcibly prevented the opening of the mine, threatening respondent and beating an organizer for the rival union. The members of the local believed Consolidated had promised them the jobs at the new mine; they insisted that if anyone would do the work, they would. * * *

Respondent lost his job as superintendent, and never entered into performance of his haulage contract. He testified that he soon began to lose other trucking contracts and mine leases he held in nearby areas. Claiming these effects to be the result of a concerted union plan against him, he sought recovery not against Local 5881 or its members, but only against petitioner, the international union. The suit was brought in the United States District Court for the Eastern District of Tennessee, and jurisdiction was premised on allegations of secondary boycotts under § 303. The state law claim, for which jurisdiction was based upon the doctrine of pendent jurisdiction, asserted "an unlawful conspiracy and an unlawful boycott aimed at him and [Grundy] to maliciously, wantonly and willfully interfere with his contract of employment and with his contract of haulage."

The trial judge refused to submit to the jury the claims of pressure intended to cause mining firms other than Grundy to cease doing business with Gibbs; he found those claims unsupported by the evidence. The jury's verdict was that the UMW had violated both § 303 and state law. Gibbs was awarded $60,000 as damages under the employment contract and $14,500 under the haulage contract; he was also awarded $100,000 punitive damages. On motion, the trial court set aside the award of damages with respect to the haulage contract on the ground that damage was unproved. It also held that union pressure on Grundy to discharge respondent as supervisor would constitute only a primary dispute with Grundy, as respondent's employer, and hence was not cognizable as a claim under § 303. Interference with the employment relationship was cognizable as a state claim, however, and a remitted award was sustained on the state law claim. The Court of Appeals for the Sixth Circuit affirmed. We granted certiorari. We reverse.

CHAPTER 12 SCOPE OF LITIGATION — JOINDER AND SUPPLEMENTAL JURISDICTION

* * *

A threshold question is whether the District Court properly entertained jurisdiction of the claim based on Tennessee law. There was no need to decide a like question in Teamsters Union v. Morton, 377 U.S. 252, since the pertinent state claim there was based on peaceful secondary activities and we held that state law based on such activities had been pre-empted by § 303. But here respondent's claim is based in part on proofs of violence and intimidation. "We have allowed the States to grant compensation for the consequences, as defined by the traditional law of torts, of conduct marked by violence and imminent threats to the public order....State jurisdiction has prevailed in these situations because the compelling state interest, in the scheme of our federalism, in the maintenance of domestic peace is not overridden in the absence of clearly expressed congressional direction." San Diego Building Trades Council v. Garmon, 359 U.S. 236, 247 [1959].

The fact that state remedies were not entirely pre-empted does not, however, answer the question whether the state claim was properly adjudicated in the District Court absent diversity jurisdiction. The Court held in Hurn v. Oursler, 289 U.S. 238, that state law claims are appropriate for federal court determination if they form a separate but parallel ground for relief also sought in a substantial claim based on federal law. The Court distinguished permissible from nonpermissible exercises of federal judicial power over state law claims by contrasting "a case where two distinct grounds in support of a single cause of action are alleged, one only of which presents a federal question, and a case where two separate and distinct causes of action are alleged, one only of which is federal in character. In the former, where the federal question averred is not plainly wanting in substance, the federal court, even though the federal ground be not established, may nevertheless retain and dispose of the case upon the non-federal *ground*; in the latter it may not do so upon the non-federal *cause of action.*" The question is into which category the present action fell.

Hurn was decided in 1933, before the unification of law and equity by the Federal Rules of Civil Procedure. At the time, the meaning of "cause of action" was a subject of serious dispute; the phrase might "mean one thing for one purpose and something different for another." United States v. Memphis Cotton Oil Co., 288 U.S. 62, 67-68 [1933].. The Court in *Hurn* identified what it meant by the term by citation of Baltimore S.S. Co. v. Phillips, 274 U.S. 316 [1927], a case in which "cause of action" had been used to identify the operative scope of the doctrine of res judicata. In that case the Court had noted that "'the whole tendency of our decisions is to require a plaintiff to try his whole cause of action and his whole case at one time.'" It stated its holding in the following language, quoted in part in the *Hurn* opinion:

> "Upon principle, it is perfectly plain that the respondent [a seaman suing for an injury sustained while working aboard ship] suffered but one actionable wrong and was entitled to but one recovery, whether his injury was due to one or the other of several distinct acts of alleged negligence or to a combination of some or all of them. In either view, there would be but a single wrongful invasion of a single primary right of the plaintiff, namely, the right of bodily safety, whether the acts constituting such invasion were one or many, simple or complex.
>
> "A cause of action does not consist of facts, but of the unlawful violation of a right which the facts show. The number and variety of the facts alleged do not establish more than one cause of action so long as their result, whether they be considered severally or in combination, is the violation of but one right by a single

legal wrong. The mere multiplication of grounds of negligence alleged as causing the same injury does not result in multiplying the causes of action. 'The facts are merely the means, and not the end. They do not constitute the cause of action, but they show its existence by making the wrong appear.'"

* * *

With the adoption of the Federal Rules of Civil Procedure and the unified form of action, Fed. Rule Civ. Proc. 2, much of the controversy over "cause of action" abated. The phrase remained as the keystone of the *Hurn* test, however, and, as commentators have noted, has been the source of considerable confusion. Under the Rules, the impulse is toward entertaining the broadest possible scope of action consistent with fairness to the parties; joinder of claims, parties and remedies is strongly encouraged. Yet because the *Hurn* question involves issues of jurisdiction as well as convenience, there has been some tendency to limit its application to cases in which the state and federal claims are, as in *Hurn*, "little more than the equivalent of different epithets to characterize the same group of circumstances."

This limited approach is unnecessarily grudging. Pendent jurisdiction, in the sense of judicial *power*, exists whenever there is a claim "arising under [the] Constitution, the Laws of the United States, and Treaties made, or which shall be made, under their Authority....," U.S. Const., Art. III, § 2, and the relationship between that claim and the state claim permits the conclusion that the entire action before the court comprises but one constitutional "case." The federal claim must have substance sufficient to confer subject matter jurisdiction on the court. The state and federal claims must derive from a common nucleus of operative fact. But if, considered without regard to their federal or state character, a plaintiff's claims are such that he would ordinarily be expected to try them all in one judicial proceeding, then, assuming substantiality of the federal issues, there is *power* in federal courts to hear the whole.[13]

That power need not be exercised in every case in which it is found to exist. It has consistently been recognized that pendent jurisdiction is a doctrine of discretion, not of plaintiff's right. Its justification lies in considerations of judicial economy, convenience and fairness to litigants; if these are not present a federal court should hesitate to exercise jurisdiction over state claims, even though bound to apply state law to them, Erie R. Co. v Tompkins, 304 U.S. 64 [1938]. Needless decisions of state law should be avoided both as a matter of comity and to promote justice between the parties, by procuring for them a surer-footed reading of applicable law.[15] Certainly, if the federal claims are dismissed before trial, even though not insubstantial in a jurisdictional sense, the state claims

---

[13] While it is commonplace that the Federal Rules of Civil Procedure do not expand the jurisdiction of federal courts, they do embody "the whole tendency of our decisions ... to require a plaintiff to try this ... whole case at one time," and to that extent emphasize the basis of pendent jurisdiction.

[15] Some have seen this consideration as the principal argument against exercise of pendent jurisdiction. Thus, before *Erie*, it was remarked that "the limitations [on pendent jurisdiction] are in the wise discretion of the courts to be fixed in individual cases by the exercise of that statesmanship which is required of any arbiter of the relations of states to nation in a federal system." Shulman & Jaegerman, [45 YALE L.J.] at 408. In his oft-cited concurrence in Strachman v. Palmer, 177 F.2d 427, 431 (C. A. 1st Cir. 1949), Judge Magruder counseled that "federal courts should not be overeager to hold on to the determination of issues that might be more appropriately left to settlement in state court litigation," at 433.

should be dismissed as well. Similarly, if it appears that the state issues substantially predominate, whether in terms of proof, of the scope of the issues raised, or of the comprehensiveness of the remedy sought, the state claims may be dismissed without prejudice and left for resolution to state tribunals. There may, on the other hand, be situations in which the state claim is so closely tied to questions of federal policy that the argument for exercise of pendent jurisdiction is particularly strong. In the present case, for example, the allowable scope of the state claim implicates the federal doctrine of pre-emption; while this interrelationship does not create statutory federal question jurisdiction, Louisville & N. R. Co. v. Mottley, 211 U.S. 149 [1908], its existence is relevant to the exercise of discretion. Finally, there may be reasons independent of jurisdictional considerations, such as the likelihood of jury confusion in treating divergent legal theories of relief, that would justify separating state and federal claims for trial, Fed. Rule Civ. Proc. 42 (b). If so, jurisdiction should ordinarily be refused.

The question of power will ordinarily be resolved on the pleadings. But the issue whether pendent jurisdiction has been properly assumed is one which remains open throughout the litigation. Pretrial procedures or even the trial itself may reveal a substantial hegemony of state law claims, or likelihood of jury confusion, which could not have been anticipated at the pleading stage. Although it will of course be appropriate to take account in this circumstance of the already completed course of the litigation, dismissal of the state claim might even then be merited. For example, it may appear that the plaintiff was well aware of the nature of his proofs and the relative importance of his claims; recognition of a federal court's wide latitude to decide ancillary questions of state law does not imply that it must tolerate a litigant's effort to impose upon it what is in effect only a state law case. Once it appears that a state claim constitutes the real body of a case, to which the federal claim is only an appendage, the state claim may fairly be dismissed.

We are not prepared to say that in the present case the District Court exceeded its discretion in proceeding to judgment on the state claim. We may assume for purposes of decision that the District Court was correct in its holding that the claim of pressure on Grundy to terminate the employment contract was outside the purview of § 303. Even so, the § 303 claims based on secondary pressures on Grundy relative to the haulage contract and on other coal operators generally were substantial. Although § 303 limited recovery to compensatory damages based on secondary pressures, and state law allowed both compensatory and punitive damages, and allowed such damages as to both secondary and primary activity, the state and federal claims arose from the same nucleus of operative fact and reflected alternative remedies. Indeed, the verdict sheet sent in to the jury authorized only one award of damages, so that recovery could not be given separately on the federal and state claims.

It is true that the § 303 claims ultimately failed and that the only recovery allowed respondent was on the state claim. We cannot confidently say, however, that the federal issues were so remote or played such a minor role at the trial that in effect the state claim only was tried. Although the District Court dismissed as unproved the § 303 claims that petitioner's secondary activities included attempts to induce coal operators other than Grundy to cease doing business with respondent, the court submitted the § 303 claims relating to Grundy to the jury. The jury returned verdicts against petitioner on these § 303 claims, and it was only on petitioner's motion for a directed verdict and a judgment *n. o. v.* that the verdicts on those claims were set aside. The District Judge considered the claim as to the haulage contract proved as to liability, and held it failed only for lack of proof of damages. Although there was some risk of confusing the jury in joining the state and federal claims — especially since, as will be developed, differing standards of proof of UMW involvement applied — the possibility of confusion could be lessened by employing a special verdict form, as the District Court did. Moreover, the question whether the permissible scope of the state claim was limited by the doctrine of pre-emption afforded a special reason for the exercise of pendent jurisdiction; the federal courts are particularly appropriate bodies for the application of pre-emption principles. We thus conclude that although it may be that the District Court might, in its sound discretion, have dismissed the state claim, the circumstances show no error in refusing to do so.

[The Court then reviewed the trial record and concluded that respondent had failed to prove the necessary elements for a claim.]

NOTES AND QUESTIONS

1. *Gibbs* allows a federal court to entertain a claim over which there is no diversity of citizenship or federal question jurisdiction. It does so through what the Court calls "pendent jurisdiction." The federal courts have used different terminology through the years to refer to their power to decide such nonfederal, nondiversity claims. Traditionally, courts exercised "pendent jurisdiction" over claims asserted by the plaintiff in a federal question case and "ancillary jurisdiction" over those asserted by some party other than the plaintiff. Several commentators, most notably Dean Matasar, argued that there was no functional difference between the two concepts and that a generic rubric, "supplemental jurisdiction," ought to be employed. Richard Matasar, *A Pendent and Ancillary Jurisdiction Primer: The Scope and Limits of Supplemental Jurisdiction*, 17 U.C. DAVIS L. REV. 103, 150-57 (1983).

Congress has followed this suggestion. Its 1990 statute codifying this area uses the term "supplemental jurisdiction." 28 U.S.C. § 1367(a). Throughout this book, we will use this generic terminology. It is important to remember, though, that the terms pendent and ancillary are employed not only in the older cases, but by many judges and practitioners today. The terminology employed is less important than understanding what such jurisdiction does. Whether we call it pendent, ancillary or supplemental, this form of jurisdiction allows a federal court to hear claims which are not supported by any of the bases of subject matter jurisdiction we studied in Chapter 4. For especially helpful background on § 1367, see Karen Moore, *The Supplemental Jurisdiction Statute: An Important but Controversial Supplement to Federal Jurisdiction*, 41 EMORY L.J. 31 (1992); John Oakley, *Recent Statutory Changes in the Law of Federal Jurisdiction and Venue: The Judicial Improvements Acts of 1988 and 1990*, 24 U.C. DAVIS L. REV. 735 (1991); Arthur Wolf, *Codification of Supplemental Jurisdiction: Anatomy of a Legislative Proposal*, 14 W. NEW. ENGL. L. REV. 1 (1992).

2. How can the result in *Gibbs* be constitutional? After all, as we saw in Chapter 4, the federal courts are of limited subject matter jurisdiction. Nothing in Article III speaks of "pendent" or "ancillary" or "supplemental" jurisdiction—at least not expressly. According to the Court in *Gibbs*, what part of Article III permits supplemental jurisdiction?

3. *Gibbs* had important ancestors. In Osborn v. Bank of the United States, 22 U.S. 738, 820 (1824), Chief Justice John Marshall recognized that "[t]here is scarcely any case, every part of which depends on the constitution, laws, or treaties of the United States." But, he continued, because the federal court takes jurisdiction over an entire "case or controversy," it can determine incidental questions over which there would be no independent basis of subject matter jurisdiction. In Hurn v. Oursler, 289 U.S. 238 (1933), the plaintiff asserted a federal copyright claim and a state unfair competition claim against a nondiverse defendant. The Court upheld jurisdiction over both, calling them "different grounds asserted in support of the same cause of action." Id. at 246. Is *Gibbs* broader than *Hurn*?

4. *Gibbs* defines the *constitutional* power of the federal courts to hear claims that have no independent statutory basis of federal jurisdiction. Review carefully the Court's discussion at 639-40.

   (a) The federal and nonfederal claims must share a "common nucleus of operative fact." Why did the claims in *Gibbs* meet this test? Note the similarity between this test and the modern view of the definition of claim for claim preclusion purposes.

   (b) The federal question must be "substantial." Did the dismissal of the federal question on directed verdict in *Gibbs* mean that the federal question failed this test?

   (c) The *Gibbs* requirement that the federal question be substantial is not revolutionary. For any case to invoke federal question jurisdiction, the federal issue must not be "wholly insubstantial or frivolous." Bell v. Hood, 327 U.S. 678, 682 (1946). We discussed this point in considering federal question jurisdiction, supra at 213. The timing of when the federal question is dismissed may affect whether it was substantial. For example, if the federal claim in *Gibbs* were dismissed on a Rule 12(b)(6) motion three weeks after filing, could it be considered substantial? On the facts of *Gibbs*, the federal claim "survived" until after trial. Is that what made it substantial? What if the claim were dismissed on a Rule 12(b)(6) motion six months after filing?

   (d) The Court seems to require that the federal and nonfederal claims be so related that a plaintiff "would ordinarily be expected to try them all in one judicial proceeding." Note, however, that the Court preceded discussion of this factor with "But if" instead of "And if." Some commentators have argued that this language means that this factor is disjunctive, not conjunctive. See, e.g., Joan

Baker, *Toward a Relaxed View of Federal Ancillary and Pendent Jurisdiction,* 33 U. PITT. L. REV. 759, 764-65 (1972). Courts have not agreed, however, and have treated this as a separate requirement. See Ferguson v. Mobil Oil Corp., 443 F. Supp. 1334, 1340 (S.D. N.Y. 1978), *aff'd,* 607 F. 2d 995 (2d Cir. 1979). Realistically, does this factor add anything to the equation?

5. *Gibbs* established that federal courts can exercise supplemental jurisdiction. But why should they? What purposes are served by it? Let us consider these questions in the context of *Gibbs* itself. If the Supreme Court had rejected supplemental jurisdiction, Mr. Gibbs would have had two options. First, he could have filed the LMRA claim in federal court and the state law claim in state court. Obviously, this course would force Mr. Gibbs, the defendant, and the taxpayers to pay for two suits and endure the inconvenience caused by them.

As his second option, Mr. Gibbs could bring both of his claims in state court. Wouldn't this serve any efficiency rationale as readily as supplemental jurisdiction? The *Gibbs* Court quoted Judge Sobeloff's statement, "the efficiency plaintiff seeks so avidly is available without question in the state courts." Kenrose Mfg. Co. v. Fred Whitaker Co., 512 F. 2d 890, 894 (4th Cir. 1972). What, if any, disadvantage is there to having Mr. Gibbs file his federal claim in state court? Would Mr. Gibbs have any opportunity for federal court review of his federal claim? Does this weigh in favor of supplemental jurisdiction in federal question cases and against it in diversity cases?

6. Would the case for supplemental jurisdiction be stronger if the federal question claim were within the exclusive jurisdiction of the federal court? (Keep this in mind when considering the *Finley* case in the next section.)

7. How would *Gibbs* be decided under § 1367? The legislative history states that "subsection (a) codifies the scope of supplemental jurisdiction first articulated by the Supreme Court in United Mine Workers v. Gibbs." H.R. REP. NO. 734, 101st Cong., 2d Sess. (1990), reprinted in 1990 U.S.C.C.A.N. 6873, 6875 n.15. Would it have been preferable to use the term "common nucleus of operative fact" from *Gibbs*?

8. In *Gibbs*, the Court distinguished between a federal court's *power* to exercise supplemental jurisdiction and its *discretion* to refuse to do so. Under what circumstances does the *Gibbs* Court countenance a refusal to exercise supplemental jurisdiction? Is Congress's codification of discretionary factors in § 1367(c) consistent with *Gibbs*? See Executive Software of N. Am. v. United States Dist. Court, 24 F. 3d 1545 (9th Cir. 1994) (statute gives less discretion). Professor Oakley first questioned whether the statute is consistent with *Gibbs* on this point. See Oakley, supra, 24 U.C. DAVIS L. REV. at 766-68 (1991).

9. In *Gibbs* and other cases for more than a century, the Court allowed supplemental jurisdiction even though no statute expressly permitted it. In Chapter 4, we noted that most of the jurisdictional grants of Article III are not self-executing; they can be used only if Congress so provides. Before Congress passed § 1367, was there any statutory authority for supplemental jurisdiction? Sections 1331 and 1332 authorize jurisdiction over "civil action[s]." Some commentators argued that that phrase could be construed as broadly as Article III's "case or controversy." See David Currie, *Pendent Parties*, 45 U. CHI. L. REV. 753 (1978); Richard Freer, *A Principled Statutory Approach to Supplemental Jurisdiction*, 1987 DUKE L.J. 34.

D. Permissive Party Joinder by Plaintiff

1. Procedural Aspects

We have seen that (procedurally, at least), the plaintiff may assert any *claims* she has against a defendant. Now we turn to *party* joinder options for the plaintiff; specifically, how many plaintiffs and defendants may she join? Rule 20 defines "proper" parties. It determines who *may* (as opposed to *must*) be joined in a single case.* Because Rule 20 is permissive, the plaintiff is not required to join all potential parties who satisfy Rule 20. Instead, she can use it to structure the suit as best serves her purposes. Various considerations (e.g., personal and subject matter jurisdiction, litigation tactics) may affect her choices. Later in this chapter, we will address the tools available for overriding the plaintiff's choices for party structure.

Schwartz v. Swan

211 N.E.2D 122 (Ill. App. 1965)

GOLDENHERSH, J.

Plaintiffs, Dorothy Schwartz, Clarence Schwartz and Adelia Schwartz appeal from judgments entered on jury verdicts finding the issues in favor of defendants, on plaintiffs' claims for personal injuries and loss of consortium. Proper presentation of the issues raised by the appeal requires a review of the pleadings, and of certain procedural questions which arose prior to trial.

Plaintiffs, Dorothy Schwartz and Clarence Schwartz, are husband and wife. Plaintiff, Adelia Schwartz, is the widow of the deceased brother of plaintiff, Clarence Schwartz.

On July 2, 1962, plaintiffs, Dorothy and Clarence Schwartz, filed a four count complaint in the Circuit Court of St. Clair County. In Count I, plaintiff, Dorothy Schwartz, alleges that on August

---

* The question of who *must* be joined in a case is addressed by Rule 19, governing necessary and indispensable parties. See infra at Section F(2).

13, 1960, she was a passenger in an automobile operated by plaintiff, Adelia Schwartz, that while the car in which she was riding was stopped at a stop sign, automobiles driven by the defendants, Vada Abernathy, and Lawrence Allen Bray, collided, causing Vada Abernathy's automobile to strike the automobile in which plaintiff was riding. This count contains the usual allegation of plaintiff's freedom from contributory negligence, and charges the defendants with various acts of negligence.

Count II alleges that on August 23, 1960, plaintiff, Dorothy Schwartz was riding in an automobile being driven by plaintiff, Clarence Schwartz; that the automobile was struck by a car driven by defendant, Mary J. Polivick; that plaintiff was free of contributory negligence and defendant, Mary J. Polivick was negligent.

Count I alleges that in the occurrence on August 13, 1960, plaintiff, Dorothy Schwartz, suffered injuries to her head, neck and shoulders, that on August 23, 1960, her head, neck, shoulders, arms and back were injured, and that she is unable to allege to what extent the occurrence of August 13, 1960, caused or contributed to her condition of ill being.

Count II alleges that the occurrence on August 23, 1960, in addition to the injuries caused thereby, aggravated the injuries suffered on August 13, 1960, and that she is unable to allege to what extent the injuries of which she complains resulted from either of the two occurrences.

In Count III, plaintiff, Clarence Schwartz, sues for loss of consortium resulting from the occurrence of August 13, 1960, and in Count IV seeks to recover damages for loss of consortium suffered by reason of the occurrence of August 23, 1960.

On July 3, 1962, plaintiff, Adelia Schwartz, filed suit seeking to recover damages from defendants Abernathy and Bray for injuries allegedly suffered in the occurrence of August 13, 1960.

Defendants, Bray and Polivick, answered the complaints. The three defendants, Bray, Polivick, and Abernathy, filed separate motions for severance of Counts I and II of the complaint in the case of Dorothy Schwartz and Clarence Schwartz. Defendant Bray, in his motion, stated that he had no part in the occurrence of August 23, 1960, cannot be held responsible for any injury caused plaintiffs on that date, and the trial of issues involving two separate accidents would prejudice a substantial right to a fair and just trial, of the defendant, Bray. Defendant, Polivick, represented by the same counsel, in identical language, moved for severance for the same reasons. Defendant, Abernathy, in her motion, states that Counts I and II constitute entirely separate causes of action, involve claims against different defendants, allege different facts, and the evidence and instructions would be so complicated and cause such confusion as to make it impossible for the jury to comprehend the proceedings, making it impossible for defendant to receive a fair trial.

After hearing arguments of counsel, the court ordered a severance of the cases, directing that the counts pertinent to the occurrence of August 13, 1960, be severed from those pertinent to the occurrence of August 23, 1960, and further directing that they be thereafter treated as two separate cases, with different docket numbers.

* * *

[Subsequently], the court, over the objection of plaintiffs, allowed the motion of defendant, Abernathy, to consolidate the case of Adelia Schwartz with the case of Dorothy Schwartz and Clarence Schwartz, each case seeking to recover from defendants, Bray and Abernathy, for injuries suffered on August 13, 1960.

CHAPTER 12 SCOPE OF LITIGATION — JOINDER AND SUPPLEMENTAL JURISDICTION

The consolidated cases involving the collision on August 13, 1960, came on for trial, the jury found for all defendants as to the claims of all three plaintiffs, judgments were entered on the verdicts, and this appeal followed.

Plaintiffs contend that the Circuit Court erred in ordering a severance in the case of plaintiff, Dorothy Schwartz, and a consolidation of the case of Adelia Schwartz, with that of Dorothy Schwartz. Numerous errors are charged during the course of the trial, and to the extent material to this decision will be hereinafter enumerated and discussed. Since the case of Clarence Schwartz is predicated solely on alleged loss of consortium, the disposition thereof is governed by the result reached in the case of Dorothy Schwartz.

We shall first consider plaintiffs' contention that the court erred in ordering the severance. Section 44 of the Civil Practice Act provides:

> "(1) Subject to rules any plaintiff or plaintiffs may join any causes of action, whether legal or equitable or both, against any defendant or defendants; . . . ."

Section 24 of the Civil Practice Act provides:

> Joinder of defendants. (1) Any person may be made a defendant who, either jointly, severally or in the alternative, is alleged to have or claim an interest in the controversy, or in any part thereof, or in the transaction or series of transactions out of which the controversy arose, or whom it is necessary to make a party for the complete determination or settlement of any question involved therein, or against whom a liability is asserted either jointly, severally or in the alternative arising out of the same transaction or series of transactions, regardless of the number of causes of action joined.
>
> (2) It is not necessary that each defendant be interested as to all the relief prayed for, or as to every cause of action included in any proceeding against him; but the court may make any order that may be just to prevent any defendant from being embarrassed or put to expense by being required to attend any proceedings in which he may have no interest.
>
> (3) If the plaintiff is in doubt as to the person from whom he is entitled to redress, he may join two or more defendants, and state his claim against them in the alternative in the same count or plead separate counts in the alternative against different defendants, to the intent that the question which, if any, of the defendants is liable, and to what extent, may be determined as between the parties."

Section 51 of the Civil Practice Act provides:

> "Consolidation and severance of actions. An action may be severed, and actions pending in the same court may be consolidated, as an aid to convenience, whenever it can be done without prejudice to a substantial right."

In Johnson v. Moon, 121 NE2d 774 [1954], the [Illinois] Supreme Court stated that joinder of multiple plaintiffs and defendants depends broadly upon the assertion of a right to relief, or a liability, arising out of the same transaction or series of transactions, and the existence of a common question of law or fact.

D. Permissive Party Joinder by Plaintiffs

* * *

In our opinion the provisions of the Civil Practice Act, as interpreted in *Johnson v. Moon*, authorize the joinder of these defendants, since the complaint clearly asserts a liability arising out of the series of transactions alleged. Unless it can be determined with reasonable certainty to which occurrence plaintiff's alleged injuries are attributable, the nature and severity of plaintiff's injuries, and the extent to which each collision contributed thereto is a common question of fact.

Having determined this issue, we must consider whether the order of severance is an abuse of the discretion vested in the trial court. Our Supreme and Appellate Courts have consistently held that the disposition of many procedural issues rests within the sound discretion of the trial court. The exercise of sound discretion requires the availability of information sufficient to support the conclusion reached. In this case the order of severance was entered on September 28, 1962 without presenting to the court evidence readily available through appropriate discovery procedures. If after deposition and interrogatory, the defendants were to move for severance on the ground that medical testimony could establish to a reasonable degree of medical certainty which injuries, if any, were attributable to a particular occurrence, severance would not be improper. If, on the other hand, it appears that the cumulative effect of the acts of which plaintiff complains is a single indivisible injury, or that it is unlikely that it can be ascertained to a reasonable degree of medical certainty which occurrence caused the injuries, then severance is prejudicial to the plaintiff. The fact that it might be difficult, under these circumstances to establish the exact proportion of injury caused by each occurrence, is not sufficient reason to deprive plaintiff of the substantial right of a proper evaluation of her damages. To hold otherwise would require plaintiff to prosecute her claim in separate trials, in each of which the defense would be the uncertainty of the injuries resulting from each occurrence. In view of plaintiff, Dorothy Schwartz's status as a passenger in a standing automobile, it is difficult to attribute the verdict in this case to any reason except that here suggested.

* * *

We are not impressed with the contention that the trial of the negligence issues in two comparatively simple fact situations would be beyond the comprehension of a jury. Juries try and determine fact issues in extremely complicated cases involving third party complaints, cross claims, counterclaims, multiple plaintiffs and defendants, with a high degree of perception. One of hundreds of examples is the case of Nelson v. Union Wire Rope Corporation, 187 NE2d 425 [1963], in which the jury assessed damages in 18 separate verdicts, some involving injuries and some wrongful deaths, and distinguished between the defendants in a complicated case to the extent that one was exonerated. Properly instructed, there is no reason to anticipate confusion of the jury, or prejudice to the rights of any of the parties.

Appellants suggest to the court that the evidence might warrant separate verdicts, apportioning the damages between the defendants in the first occurrence, and the defendant in the second. Section 50 of the Civil Practice Act provides:

"More than one judgment or decree may be rendered in the same cause."

In the light of the holding in *Johnson v. Moon* that the effect of the Civil Practice Act is to make applicable to actions at law, the practices which theretofore prevailed in equity, we agree. After proper instruction, if the evidence warrants, such apportionment by the jury would not be objectionable.

We have carefully examined the medical testimony and conclude that justice requires that plaintiff, Dorothy Schwartz, be permitted to prosecute her claims against these defendants in a single trial. As to the consolidation of the case of Adelia Schwartz, that is a matter for the discretion of the trial court, to be determined in the light of the views here expressed.

* * *

Judgment reversed and cause remanded.

NOTES AND QUESTIONS

1. You may wonder why the case is *Schwartz v. Swan*, while the name Swan never appears in the opinion. Vada Abernathy got married after the accident and before the case was filed; she was sued in her married name, Vada Abernathy Swan.

2. *Schwartz* was decided under Illinois state procedural rules. Read Federal Rules 20, 21, and 42.

(a) What is the federal counterpart to state § 44? How do they differ? How are they similar?

(b) What is the federal counterpart to state § 24(1) and § 24(2)? How do they differ? How are they similar?

(c) What is the federal counterpart to state § 51? How do they differ? How are they similar?

(d) How would *Schwartz* have been decided under the Federal Rules?

3. Under Federal Rule 20, why would Abernathy and Bray have been proper co-defendants in a suit concerning the August 13 crash? Under the same rule, why would Mr. and Mrs. Schwartz have been proper co-plaintiffs in a suit concerning either the August 13 or August 23 crash?

Note that the requirement that claims by or against the proper parties involve a common question of law or fact is usually not difficult. Instead, the courts wrestle with the more vexing issue of whether the claims by or against the proper parties have the required transactional relatedness. We have addressed this transactional issue before. Recall that the Restatement (Second) of Judgments definition of "cause of action" for claim preclusion purposes is "transaction or occurrence or series of related transactions or occurrences." As we discovered in studying preclusion, and as *Schwartz* and other cases confirm, the definition of a transaction or occurrence, or even a series thereof, is not always easy, and often involves a pragmatic, case-by-case analysis.*

4. The most difficult issue in *Schwartz* is why the defendants from the two separate crashes could be joined. According to the court in *Schwartz,* why were the two accidents sufficiently related to meet the transactional component of the joinder rule? How important was it that Mrs. Schwartz alleged that the second accident aggravated the condition caused in the first?

In Poster v. Central Gulf Steamship Corp., 25 F.R.D. 18 (E.D. Pa. 1960), a seaman contracted amebiasis, a painful gastric illness, while sailing through the Suez Canal for Company 1. Several months later, while working for Company 2, he again sailed through the Suez Canal, and again contracted amebiasis. Plaintiff alleged that the condition was caused by unsanitary practices of local workers employed to help the ships' cooks, and further asserted that the second episode exacerbated the condition caused by the first. The court recognized that the two bouts were separate "occurrences," but upheld joinder because "the second of which might result in concurrent liability of both companies." In other words, the court was influenced by the fact that the alleged negligence of both defendants contributed to the plaintiff's plight.

How does invocation of a tort theory of concurrent liability affect whether injuries arise from the same transaction or occurrence?

Some courts have shown remarkable ability to expand the notion of transactional relatedness under Rule 20 through tort theories. In Hall v. E.I DuPont De Nemours Co., 345 F. Supp. 353 (E.D. N.Y. 1972), thirteen plaintiffs attempted to join together in a suit against six manufacturers of blasting caps and their trade association. The plaintiffs were representatives of children injured while playing with blasting caps. Their basic theory of liability was that the defendants, who together constituted the entire blasting cap industry in the United States, had failed to warn users that blasting caps were not intended for hours of harmless fun.

Although the children were injured in twelve different explosions in ten states over a four year period, and although no child was certain which of the defendants had made the cap that injured him, the court allowed joinder of all plaintiffs and defendants. Among other things, the court relied on the "enterprise liability" theory, noting that the plaintiffs in essence were suing an entire industry, members of which had joint awareness of the risk and joint capacity to reduce the risk. The court noted "[t]he allegations in this case suggest that the

---

* In fact, we will see more of this problem below. The basic test for compulsory counterclaims under Rule 13(a) and for cross-claims under Rule 13(g) is whether the claim arises from the same "transaction or occurrence" as the underlying dispute. At first glance, the Rule 20 seems broader than Rule 13(a) and 13(g) because it allows for a "series" of transactions or occurrences. In practice, however, most courts construe Rules 13(a) and 13(g) broadly, so "it is unlikely that the distinction is significant." 1B MOORE'S FEDERAL PRACTICE at III-194.

entire blasting cap industry and its trade association provide the logical locus at which precautions should be taken and liability imposed." Id. at 378. What does this rationale have to do with whether the plaintiffs' claims arose from the same transaction or occurrence?

What if it turned out at trial that Mr. Poster's two bouts of amebiasis were completely unrelated? Or that the blasting cap manufacturers did not make an industry-wide decision to eschew labels? Or that Mrs. Schwartz's injuries were divisible?

5. Note that under Rule 21 the penalty for misjoinder of parties is that the claims against the separate defendants (or by the separate plaintiffs) will be "severed and proceeded with separately." Severance is a term of art and should not be confused with the court's power to order separate trials under Rule 42(b). Severance results in two (or more) separate suits, each with its own docket number and judgment. See United States v. O'Neil, 709 F.2d 361 (5th Cir. 1983). In *Schwartz*, severance by the trial court resulted in separate cases, one by Mr. and Mrs. Schwartz against Abernathy and Bray, and one by Mr. and Mrs. Schwartz against Polivick.

In contrast, Rule 42(b) allows a court *in the context of a single case* to order separate trials on various issues or claims. It might do so, for instance, to avoid confusing the jury in a case involving numerous claims. Rule 20(b) makes similar provision.

6. Why would a plaintiff not join all possible plaintiffs and defendants whose joinder would satisfy Rule 20? There may be jurisdictional problems; perhaps she cannot get personal jurisdiction over all defendants or perhaps joinder of a particular person would destroy diversity of citizenship jurisdiction. Another reason for underinclusive joinder by the plaintiff may be litigation strategy. Consider this discussion of litigation incentives:

> As a general rule, underinclusive joinder of defendants would seem less likely than underinclusive joinder of plaintiffs. The typical plaintiff wants to sue once; serial litigation against successive defendants is expensive and time-consuming. Moreover, whatever incentive there may be to sue serially is sapped, to a degree at least, by the adoption of nonmutual defensive issue preclusion. * * *
>
> Further, inclusive joinder of defendants robs the individual defendants of the ability to "whipsaw" the plaintiff by convincing the jury that some absentee is really to blame. A whipsawed plaintiff may well convince two juries that he is entitled to recovery, but end up with nothing, since each jury believed that the defendant before it was not the responsible party. Thus plaintiffs often prefer to join all possible defendants, and may gain from the defendants' efforts to lay the blame on each other. * * *
>
> More commonly, the underinclusive joinder will be on the plaintiff's side. * * * [H]ere there are strong strategic reasons for the plaintiff to eschew joining co-plaintiffs. A single plaintiff may try to strike first, recovering against a defendant of limited resources or an insurance fund before others can do so. She may decide that she is the most attractive of the potential plaintiffs, and that she does not want to go before a jury allied with less sympathetic characters. Most likely,

D. Permissive Party Joinder by Plaintiffs

*** she will be influenced by the widely held view that she can recover more if she is the only plaintiff, since the jury will focus solely on her claim.

Freer, supra, 50 U. PITT. L. REV. at 824-25.

(a) Why do you suppose Mr. and Mrs. Schwartz wanted to have both sets of defendants (Abernathy and Bray for the first collision and Polivick for the second) joined in a single case? What litigation advantages might there be to joining all possible defendants under Rule 20? Was Mrs. Schwartz whipsawed at the trial court?

(b) Why do you suppose Mr. and Mrs. Schwartz, on the one hand, and Adelia Schwartz, on the other, did *not* want to litigate as co-plaintiffs? Could the three Schwartzes have joined as co-plaintiffs in a single case under Rule 20?

(c) Given the nature of Mr. Schwartz's claim, why do you suppose the husband and wife decided to sue together?

(d) Why would the emergence of nonmutual defensive collateral estoppel encourage a plaintiff to sue all potential defendants in a single proceeding?

7. Litigation strategy is often driven by what the plaintiff, as initial architect of the suit, thinks will impress the jury at trial. If the appearance at trial is most important, consider the possible utility of Rule 42(a), governing consolidation. That rule addresses the situation where more than one action is pending in a single district,[*] and allows the separate cases to be treated together for any of various purposes.[**] Consolidation—even for "all purposes"—does not result in merging the two cases; they retain their separate docket numbers and will result in separate judgments. Johnson v. Manhattan Ry. Co., 289 U.S. 479 (1933).

What is the standard for consolidation under Rule 42(a)? How does it differ from the standard for joinder under Rule 20 (a)? Because it is "easier" to meet than Rule 20(a), it might be a valuable safety valve for a plaintiff who is denied joinder.

An instructive case is Stanford v. Tennessee Valley Authority, 18 F.R.D. 152 (M.D. Tenn. 1955), in which the plaintiff sued two chemical companies, each of which spewed

---

[*] If two cases which would benefit from consolidated treatment are pending in different districts, what tool might be available to put the cases in a single district, thereby allowing invocation of Rule 42(a)? Remember Chapter 5.

[**] In federal district courts, cases are assigned to judges of the district at random. Cases are assigned docket numbers according to when they are filed. The lower the docket number, the earlier the case was filed. All districts have local rules allowing related cases to be placed before the judge assigned to the original case. For example, if a series of asbestos cases were filed in a district, the first one being assigned to Judge A, the clerk's office would thereafter assign all related asbestos cases to Judge A, rather than assigning them at random to other judges. This practice is usually called "low numbering." Low numbering does not effect consolidation; it simply puts related cases before a single judge, who is then in a good position to determine whether consolidation is appropriate.

pollutants into the air near his home. In a parsimonious reading of Rule 20(a), the court denied joinder, holding that the claims against the two companies did not meet the transactional test of that rule. Thus, the cases against the two companies were severed. Then, in the same opinion, the court ordered consolidation for the purpose of trial. Would you agree that the plaintiff lost the battle and won the war? Why?

8. For an example of a plaintiff with even tougher luck than Mrs. Schwartz, see Watts v. Smith, 134 N.W.2d 194 (Mich. 1965), in which the plaintiff was injured in separate auto collisions *on the same day!* (Yes, he was allowed to join the drivers from both of the collisions.)

2. Jurisdictional Aspects

Rule 20 permits joinder of multiple plaintiffs and defendants. What if a claim by or against one of them is not supported by basis of subject matter jurisdiction? Suppose, for example, that plaintiff has a claim against one defendant which invokes federal question jurisdiction and a claim against a second defendant that does not have an independent basis of jurisdiction. In other words, suppose in *Gibbs* that the federal claim was against D-1 and the state claim was against D-2, as to whom there was no diversity of citizenship.

This raises what traditionally has been called *pendent parties jurisdiction*. It differs from the situation in *Gibbs* in that the nonfederal, nondiversity claim is against a second defendant against whom no claim invoking federal jurisdiction has been asserted. As long as the state claim shares a nucleus of operative fact with the jurisdiction-invoking claim, assertion of supplemental jurisdiction would appear to be constitutional. Recognizing this, the Second Circuit upheld pendent parties jurisdiction. Leather's Best, Inc. v. S.S. Mormaclynx, 451 F.2d 800 (2d Cir. 1971). Other courts, however, rejected it. See, e.g. Moor v. Madigan, 458 F.2d 1217 (9th Cir. 1972).

The Supreme Court resolved the split, at least as to some cases, in Aldinger v. Howard, 427 U.S. 1 (1976). Although admitting that pendent parties jurisdiction would be constitutional, the Court rejected its use in that case on statutory grounds. In *Aldinger*, the plaintiff asserted a federal civil rights claim under 42 U.S.C. § 1983 against a county official who had fired her for living with her boyfriend. She joined a state law claim against the county itself.* Because she was a co-citizen with the county, the plaintiff's claim against

---

* Section 1983 allows suits for violation of federal constitutional rights "under color of state law." At the time, a municipality could not be sued under § 1983. Monroe v. Pape, 365 U.S. 167 (1961). The Supreme Court changed its position on this point after *Aldinger* was decided. Monell v. Department of Social Servs. of New York, 436 U.S. 658 (1978).

D. Permissive Party Joinder by Plaintiffs

that entity was not supported by federal question or diversity jurisdiction. The Court rejected supplemental jurisdiction over the claim against the county, citing what it called "clear congressional intent" that the civil rights statute not allow a case against the county.

Thus, in *Aldinger*, the Court recognized that supplemental jurisdiction must be supported by a statutory grant. It presumed, however, that such a statutory grant existed so long as Congress had not *precluded* supplemental jurisdiction, as it theoretically had in the civil rights statute. In other words, as it had in *Gibbs* and as it did two years later in another case, Owen Equipment & Erection Co. v. Kroger, 437 U.S. 367 (1978), infra, the Court was willing to *presume that supplemental jurisdiction was proper unless the legislature said otherwise*. The default position (in case of congressional silence), then, was that supplemental jurisdiction would be upheld so long as the constitutional requirements of *Gibbs* were met.

In *Aldinger*, the Court expressly left open the possibility of pendent parties jurisdiction if the plaintiff's federal claim invoked the *exclusive* jurisdiction of the federal courts. The case of Finley v. United States, 490 U.S. 545 (1989), presented that situation. There, plaintiff's husband and two children were killed when the airplane in which they were traveling struck electric transmission lines during its approach to a San Diego airfield. Mrs. Finley brought a Federal Tort Claims Act (FTCA) suit in federal court against the Federal Aviation Administration (FAA) for alleged negligence both in maintaining runway lights and in performing air traffic control duties. She later sought to amend her complaint to add state law tort claims against the city and the utility company that maintained the lines. Because Mrs. Finley and the added defendants were co-citizens, there was no independent basis for jurisdiction over these state law claims, and the issue was whether the court could hear them through supplemental jurisdiction.

Finley presented an especially strong case for supplemental jurisdiction. The federal courts have exclusive jurisdiction over FTCA cases. Thus, the only court that could hear the entire case was a federal court. Moreover, allowing supplemental jurisdiction was not inconsistent with any purpose underlying the FTCA. There was no evidence that Congress had "negated" jurisdiction over claims against the added parties.

In an opinion by Justice Scalia, the Supreme Court rejected supplemental jurisdiction. The Court stressed that no matter how sensible or convenient supplemental jurisdiction might be, the FTCA did not explicitly authorize jurisdiction over additional parties. According to the Court, supplemental jurisdiction required such statutory authorization. The Court acknowledged that *Gibbs* allowed jurisdiction over pendent *claims*, but characterized pendent *parties* jurisdiction as a "departure from prior practice." Although the Court explicitly declined to overrule *Gibbs*, it also declined to expand *Gibbs* to apply in situations involving additional parties. Four justices dissented and criticized the majority opinion as inconsistent with the Court's approach in earlier cases.

NOTES AND QUESTIONS

1. Because Mrs. Finley's FTCA claim was within the exclusive jurisdiction of the federal courts, the result of *Finley* was to *require* Mrs. Finley to pursue two separate cases—one against the government in federal court and one against the city and utility company in state court. In addition to the expense imposed on Mrs. Finley by this result, what strategic difficulties does this result impose?

2. Suppose Mrs. Finley did file two separate actions, and that the first one to go to judgment resulted in favorable findings and a substantial recovery for her. Why could she not employ either res judicata or collateral estoppel against the defendant in the remaining case?

3. While the result in *Finley* can be lamented, at least it is clear on the facts: there can be no pendent parties jurisdiction without an express statutory allowance. The real problem with *Finley* was language — broader than necessary to decide the issue before the Court — that seemed to require express statutory provision for *all* forms of supplemental jurisdiction.

Commentators criticized *Finley* and voiced concern that it threatened all of supplemental jurisdiction by requiring congressional action. One urged that supplemental jurisdiction was endangered unless courts could read *Finley* narrowly, which, she felt, would be difficult to do in a principled way. Wendy Collins Perdue, Finley v. United States: *Unstringing Pendent Jurisdiction*, 76 VA. L. REV. 539 (1990). One concluded that *Finley* presaged the end of all supplemental jurisdiction as we knew it. Thomas Mengler, *The Demise of Pendent and Ancillary Jurisdiction*, 1990 B.Y.U. L. REV. 247. And one urged a cautious approach, emphasizing some language of the opinion and suggesting that a 5-to-4 decision might be read narrowly. Richard Freer, *Compounding Confusion and Hampering Diversity: Life After* Finley *and the Supplemental Jurisdiction Statute*, 40 EMORY L.J. 445, 464-69 (1991).

Although nervous about the reach of *Finley*, the lower federal courts (including the only appellate courts to address the question) agreed that *Finley* should be limited to its facts, not upsetting well established supplemental jurisdiction practice in other areas. See Alumax Mill Prods., Inc. v. Congress Fin. Corp., 912 F.2d 996 (8th Cir. 1990); King Fisher Marine Serv. v. 21st Phoenix Corp., 893 F.2d 1155 (10th Cir. 1990); Olan Mills, Inc. v. Hy-Vee Food Stores, Inc., 731 F. Supp. 1416 (N.D. Iowa 1990); Huberman v. Duane Fellows, Inc., 725 F. Supp. 204 (S.D. N.Y. 1989). There was little authority to the contrary. See Aetna Cas. & Sur. Co. v. Spartan Mech. Corp., 738 F. Supp. 664 (E.D. N.Y. 1990). The debate over the reach of *Finley* will never be resolved conclusively because Congress intervened.

D. Permissive Party Joinder by Plaintiffs

4. Clearly, the unfortunate result in *Finley* itself deserved to be avoided legislatively. Congress did this with 28 U.S.C. § 1367. Because of uncertainty over the reach of *Finley*, Congress felt the need to address all of supplemental jurisdiction. Although the legislature purported to codify "pre-*Finley* practice," we will see that it did not do so in some areas.

Note the structure of the statute. Section (a) gives supplemental jurisdiction to the full extent of the Constitution. Section (b) precludes supplemental jurisdiction in several situations thought by the drafters to have been precluded by precedent. Section (c) gives courts discretion to refuse supplemental jurisdiction, ostensibly along the lines established by *Gibbs*. Section (d) tolls the statute of limitations on supplemental claims that are later dismissed.

Exactly how does § 1367(a) overrule the result in *Finley*? Does it overrule *Aldinger* as well?

5. Mrs. Finley's claim against the United States did not fare well on the merits. After a bench trial, District Judge Edward Schwartz entered judgment for the government because he found that pilot error caused the crash. Finley v. United States, No. 86-1151-S(M), 1993 U.S. Dist. LEXIS 18949 (S.D. Cal. 1993). Why do you suppose Mrs. Finley apparently did not sue the estate of the pilot, who was also killed in the crash?

6. Suppose Alice and Betty are injured when the car in which they are riding is hit by Carol. Alice is a citizen of California; Betty and Carol are citizens of Utah. If Alice and Betty join as plaintiffs in a suit against Carol, can the court exercise supplemental jurisdiction over Betty's claim? (Assume that the amount in controversy requirement would be met.)

7. Before § 1367, Congress had addressed supplemental jurisdiction only in very specialized cases. See, e.g., 28 U.S.C. § 1338(b).

E. Claim Joinder by Defendants

In Chapter 8, we addressed options available to the defendant to avoid the imposition of liability. As you will recall, the defendant could make a Rule 12 motion or file an answer denying liability and raising affirmative defenses. Here, we consider a defending party's ability to assert *offensive claims* against others, that is, to impose liability on someone else in the course of the pending litigation.

1. Counterclaims

Read Federal Rules 13(a), 13(b), 13(c), and 13(f). The modern counterclaim, as reflected in these rules (and in similar state provisions), grew out of the more restrictive early devices of recoupment and set-off. At common law, a defendant could use recoupment to file a claim against the plaintiff if it arose from the same transaction as plaintiff's claim. The claim could not exceed plaintiff's claim, however, and thus was available only to diminish or defeat the plaintiff's assertion. Set-off permitted a defendant to assert a very limited set of claims (basically for contract or on a judgment), again to diminish or defeat the plaintiff's claim. Neither permitted the joinder of new parties. JAMES, HAZARD & LEUBSDORF, CIVIL PROCEDURE 483-85.

Modern practice, as reflected in the Federal Rules, is far more liberal. Note the provisions for two types of counterclaims.

a. Compulsory Counterclaims

i. Procedural Aspects

Dindo v. Whitney
451 F.2d 1 (1st Cir. 1971)

ALDRICH, CHIEF JUDGE.

* * *

Briefly, plaintiff Dindo alleges that defendant Whitney was a passenger in a car belonging to Whitney, but driven by Dindo; that the car went off the road, severely injuring Dindo, and that the cause of the accident was Whitney's putting his hand through the steering wheel in reaching for a flashlight on the steering shaft. Suit was brought in the district court of New Hampshire on October 29, 1968, within the New Hampshire period for suit, the accident having occurred on October 30, 1965. Dindo and Whitney had long been friends, Dindo living in Vermont and Whitney in New Hampshire. In June, 1966 Whitney sued Dindo in the district court of Vermont. Dindo gave the papers to his insurance agent, who forwarded them to Whitney's insurer which, by virtue of a clause in the policy, insured Dindo as a driver of Whitney's car with Whitney's permission. The insurer retained counsel, but informed Dindo that he should retain his own counsel as well, as the *ad damnum* [demand for judgment — EDS.] exceeded the coverage. Dindo did not do so. In March, 1967 the insurer paid Whitney a sum within the policy limit in settlement, and an entry was made on the court docket, "Settled and discontinued." The present action is defended by the same insurer, Whitney, as the car's owner, being covered by the policy that had included coverage of Dindo.

It is clear on the record that before insurance company counsel settled the case they conferred with Dindo on a number of occasions, and apparently saw no defense to the suit. * * * Dindo did not request counsel to file a counterclaim against Whitney. * * * [H]e did not realize, until he spoke with new counsel in September 1968, that he had a basis for so doing, namely, Whitney's conduct in reaching for the flashlight. Dindo, assertedly, had thought that because he was driving the car he could have no claim.

* * *

Dindo claims * * * that the compulsory [counterclaim] rule is inapplicable to him since the original case was settled, rather than pursued to final judgment on the merits. Alternatively, he says that it is inequitable to assert the rule against him when he had not realized he had a counterclaim until afterwards.

The bar arising out of Rule 13(a) has been characterized variously. Some courts have said that a judgment is res judicata of whatever could have been pleaded in a compulsory counterclaim. Other courts have viewed the rule not in terms of res judicata, but as creating an estoppel or waiver. The latter approach seems more appropriate, at least when the case is settled rather than tried. The purposes of the rule are "to prevent multiplicity of actions and to achieve resolution in a single lawsuit of all disputes arising out of common matter." Southern Constr. Co. v. Pickard, 1962, 371 U.S. 57, 60. If a case has been tried, protection both of the court and of the parties dictates that there should be no further directly related litigation. But if the case is settled, normally the court has not been greatly burdened, and the parties can protect themselves by demanding cross-releases. In such circumstances, absent a release, better-tailored justice seems obtainable by applying principles of equitable estoppel.

If, in the case at bar, Dindo, clearly having opportunity to assert it, knew of the existence of a right to counterclaim, the fact that there was no final judgment on the merits should be immaterial, and a Rule 13(a) bar would be appropriate. His conscious inaction not only created the very additional litigation the rule was designed to prevent it exposed the insurer to double liability. We are not persuaded that a final judgment is a *sine qua non* to invocation of the bar; there is nothing in the rule limning the term "judgment."

* * * We are not prepared to say at this time what lesser facts would compel a conclusion of estoppel as a matter of law. There should be a hearing on the merits, the facts to be found by the jury. In this connection the court may consider the effect of the cooperation clause in the policy, if there were such, since Dindo, as the insured, would be bound by such a provision. Regardless of whether he thought he had no cross-claim [sic], Dindo's failure, presently asserted by the insurer, to give it a full and true account of the accident, might well be found by the jury to be a breach of a cooperation clause, which, in turn, might form a basis for estoppel. Or, a matter on which we do not presently express views, without such a clause estoppel might be based upon misrepresentation.

The judgment of the district court is vacated and the action remanded for further proceedings consistent herewith.

Carteret Savings & Loan Assn. v. Jackson
812 F.2d 36 (1st Cir. 1987)

ALDRICH, SENIOR CIRCUIT JUDGE.

Defendants-appellants Dr. Jackson and his wife were led into an allegedly painless get-rich enterprise by one Garfinkel, now absent. Simply by signing a few papers they expected to achieve gains in the form of substantial deductions on their income tax returns. However, as a result of our present affirmance of the district court, they will realize some unexpected, and very tangible, losses.

Without ever leaving [Massachusetts], defendants authorized the purchase of a yacht in Florida that was to be taken to the Virgin Islands and chartered, the charter fees, allegedly, to meet all expenses. The purchase was to be financed by defendants' note to plaintiff, Carteret Savings & Loan Association. From defendants' understanding, the only backing for the note—defendants, allegedly, having been told it was without recourse—was the prospective yacht. Nothing on the note, however, indicated it was without recourse. Following suit, and a default judgment on the note in the Florida District Court, the yacht, still in Florida, was sold by the U.S. Marshal in partial satisfaction of the judgment. The present suit on the judgment in the Massachusetts District Court is to recover the balance. * * * Following summary judgment for plaintiff, defendants appeal.

* * * [Defendants challenge the Massachusetts District Court's] holding that defendants' present claims against plaintiff, for negligence, fraud, abuse of process, and unfair and deceptive business practices, should have been asserted as compulsory counterclaims in the Florida action pursuant to Fed. R. Civ. P. 13(a), and hence are barred. * * *

* * *

Defendants' basic position is a legal one: that since they served no pleading [in the first case, in Florida], the rule did not become applicable.

We could agree that if a pleading had never been required, as, for example, if "the time of serving" had never been reached, * * * the rule would not apply. We hold, however, that when a defendant is defaulted for failure to file a pleading, the default applies to whatever the party should have pleaded.

The purpose of Rule 13(a) is "to prevent multiplicity of actions and to achieve resolution in a single lawsuit of all disputes arising out of common matters." Southern Constr. Co. v. Pickard, 371 U.S. 57, 60 (1962). This has a number of beneficial consequences. The most obvious may be to save judicial effort. On this basis one court has found the rule inapposite when the judgment on the initial cause was by consent. Martino v. McDonald's System, Inc., 598 F.2d 1079, 1082 (7th Cir. 1979) * * *. While we agree with defendants that relatively little judicial effort, also, is involved in entering a default judgment on a note, we can see grounds for considering consent judgments differently. More to the point, there is a purpose in the rule quite apart from concern for the courts—the interest of the plaintiff in obtaining a complete and final resolution of the essential matters of the litigation. If we accepted defendants' position, a default judgment would be of uncertain value, and represent simply one step toward resolving the dispute between the parties. Instead of having a truly final judgment, the judgment creditor would remain faced with a prospect of litigating other aspects of the same transaction or occurrence at some later time, and in a forum of the defendant's choosing.

E. Claim Joinder by Defendants

* * *

As against these considerations, defendants offer a mere wooden interpretation of the rule. We are aided in rejecting it by Fed. R. Civ. P. 1's general principle, that the rules are to "be construed to secure the just, speedy, and inexpensive determination of every action." As we have said earlier, "The policy of the federal rules favors resolving all disputes between the parties in a single litigation." Gutor International AG v. Raymond Packer Co., 493 F.2d 938, 946 (1st Cir. 1974). We hold that this policy applies here, and that all of defendants' present claims that would have been compulsory counterclaims are, accordingly, barred. * * *

Affirmed.

NOTES AND QUESTIONS

1. In *Dindo*, the court was willing to forgive a failure to file a compulsory counterclaim, permitting further litigation as to whether Mr. Dindo was guilty of "conscious inaction" in failing to assert the claim. Among other things, the court noted that the first case had ended in settlement, with little expenditure of court or litigant effort. In *Carteret Savings*, however, the court was unwilling to consider whether the Jacksons were guilty of "conscious inaction," despite the fact that the first case ended in default, which obviously required very little expenditure of effort by the court or the bank.

We often see different approaches to issues by different courts. Interestingly, however, not only were *Dindo* and *Carteret Savings* decided by the same court, they were written by the same judge! Can you articulate differences in the facts of the cases that might explain the different approaches?

2. In *Dindo*, Judge Aldrich noted that some courts characterize a dismissal for failure to plead a compulsory counterclaim as "res judicata." Based on our study of preclusion, however, why could an omitted compulsory counterclaim *not* carry claim preclusion effects? Judge Aldrich also noted that some courts consider the compulsory counterclaim rule to operate on the basis of waiver or estoppel. Another approach, typified by *Carteret Savings*, simply holds that the defendant is precluded from asserting the claim by "rule preclusion" — because the rule says so.

Because estoppel and waiver are equitable doctrines, courts may find an exception if operation of the compulsory counterclaim rule would be unfair or unduly harsh. *Dindo* is an example of this flexible approach. Courts that view the rule as mandating preclusion are less likely to find an exception to it. *Carteret Savings* is an example.

3. In the first case in *Carteret Savings*, Carteret sued the Jacksons in federal court in Florida. In the second case, Carteret sued the Jacksons in federal court in Massachusetts. Why was Carteret's second case not subject to dismissal under claim preclusion?

4. As we saw in Chapters 8 and 10, persons in the Jacksons' position could have asked the district court in Florida to set aside the judgment and permit them to file a counterclaim. See Rule 60(b).

5. The compulsory counterclaim rules in some jurisdictions spell out the preclusive effect flowing from a failure to assert the claim. See, e.g., CAL. CODE CIV. PROC. 426.30(a). Rule 13(a), however, does not expressly provide that a defendant will be precluded from asserting the claim elsewhere if she fails to assert a counterclaim that arises from the same transaction or occurrence as the underlying suit. Nonetheless, what one word in Rule 13(a) accounts for making the assertion of the claim compulsory?

6. One court explained that preclusion under a compulsory counterclaim rule is "in the nature of an estoppel arising from the culpable conduct of a litigant in failing to assert a proper claim." House v. Hanson, 72 N.W.2d 874, 877 (Minn. 1955). If this statement accurately reflects the goal of the rule, the defendant should not be precluded if she was unaware of the claim at the time the counterclaim would have been filed. Does Rule 13(a) expressly address this concern? What other part of Rule 13 might provide a safety valve for the defendant who fails to assert a compulsory counterclaim? The Restatement (Second) of Judgments § 22(2)(a), provides that failure to assert a counterclaim does not preclude subsequent litigation, unless "the counterclaim is required to be interposed by a compulsory counterclaim statute or rule of court."

7. What if the defendant failed to file a compulsory counterclaim because counsel did not tell her she could? One fact pattern routinely gives rise to this possibility. Suppose Plaintiff is injured in an accident with Employee. Assume that Employee is also hurt. Plaintiff sues both Employee and Employer, alleging that the act took place in Employee's normal course of employment activities. Employee turns the process over to Employer's attorney, who undertakes to represent both Employer and Employee. Now suppose the case goes to trial and defendants win. Employee then sues Plaintiff in a second suit for injuries sustained in the same accident. In response to the argument that the claim should have been asserted in the first case, Employee argues that counsel never told her she could do so.

   (a) Should the case by Employee be dismissed? Would your answer be different if the first case had not gone to trial, but had been decided on an early Rule 12 motion? (What does *Carteret Savings* say about saving judicial resources?)
   (b) If the case by Employee is not dismissed, how do you respond to the argument that you have created duplicative litigation and burdened Plaintiff unduly?

E. Claim Joinder by Defendants

(c) If the case by Employee is dismissed, is judicial economy really served? Won't a new case appear on a judicial docket anyway (one which will cause the lawyer to check anxiously whether she has paid the premium on her malpractice insurance)?

8. The court notes in *Carteret Savings* that some courts treat judgments by consent (settlement) as exceptions to the compulsory counterclaim rule. Is there any support for such an exception in the text of Rule 13(a)? Would courts use an exception if the first case were settled on the eve of trial, after two years of litigation?

9. In *Carteret Savings*, why was the Jacksons' fraud claim against Carteret a compulsory counterclaim in the first case? Perhaps the best known case discussing the scope of compulsory counterclaims is Moore v. New York Cotton Exchange, 270 U.S. 593 (1926), decided under the old federal Equity Rule 30, a precursor of today's Federal Rule 13(a). (Before the merger of law and equity in federal court in 1938, there were separate Equity Rules.) In *Moore*, the Cotton Exchange entered a contract with Western Union allowing that telegraph company to furnish quotes throughout the country to persons approved by the Exchange. Upon orders from the Cotton Exchange, Western Union refused to furnish the quotes to a different exchange ("Odd-Lot"). Odd-Lot then sued the Cotton Exchange and Western Union under federal antitrust laws. The defendants filed a counterclaim alleging that Odd-Lot had been stealing Cotton Exchange quotations.

The Court held that the counterclaim was compulsory because it arose from the same "transaction" as the plaintiff's claim. It explained:

> "Transaction" is a word of flexible meaning. It may comprehend a series of many occurrences, depending not so much upon the immediateness of their connection as upon their logical relationship. The refusal to furnish the quotations is one of the links in the chain which constitutes the transaction upon which [Odd-Lot] here bases its cause of action. * * * It is the one circumstance without which neither party would have found it necessary to seek relief. Essential facts alleged by [Odd-Lot] enter into and constitute in part the cause of action set forth in the counterclaim. That they are not precisely identical, or that the counterclaim embraces additional allegations, as, for example, that [Odd-Lot] is unlawfully getting the quotations, does not matter. To hold otherwise would be to rob [the compulsory counterclaim rule] of all serviceable meaning, since the facts relied upon by the plaintiff rarely, if ever, are, in all particulars, the same as those constituting the defendant's counterclaim.

270 U.S. at 610.

The rule addressed in *Moore*, as noted, applied to claims arising from the same "transaction" as the underlying dispute. Rule 13(a) uses the term "transaction or occurrence." Does this difference compel a broader reading than that in *Moore*? What is the difference between a transaction and an occurrence? The trend is toward a broad interpretation; using language from *Moore*, many courts hold that the test is met if the counterclaim is "logically related" to the underlying suit. See, e.g., Crouse-Hinds Co. v. Internorth, Inc., 634 F.2d 690 (2d Cir. 1980). See generally 3 MOORE'S FEDERAL PRACTICE ¶ 13.13.

ii. Jurisdictional Aspects

It is axiomatic that neither Rule 13(a) nor any of the Federal Rules affects the subject matter jurisdiction of the federal courts. Many compulsory counterclaims will be supported by an independent basis of subject matter jurisdiction. Some will not. If they do not invoke federal question or diversity of citizenship jurisdiction, can they invoke supplemental jurisdiction?

One older but still instructive case is Great Lakes Rubber Corp. v. Herbert Cooper Co., 286 F.2d 631 (3d Cir. 1961). In that case, Great Lakes filed a state law claim of unfair competition against Cooper, ostensibly invoking diversity of citizenship jurisdiction. Cooper filed a counterclaim arising under federal antitrust law, alleging that Great Lakes violated that law by, among other things, filing a series of baseless suits against it. The district court then determined that the parties were not of diverse citizenship. It dismissed Great Lakes' complaint, but left pending Cooper's counterclaim, since it properly invoked federal question jurisdiction.

Then Great Lakes refiled its state law unfair competition claim, this time as a compulsory counterclaim to Cooper's federal antitrust claim. Although Great Lakes' claim invoked no independent basis of subject matter jurisdiction (indeed, the court had just dismissed the same claim for lack of jurisdiction), the Third Circuit held that the claim was supported by supplemental jurisdiction! In so doing, the court discussed the confluence between the "same transaction or occurrence" test for compulsory counterclaims and the test for supplemental (which it called ancillary) jurisdiction. The court explained:

> A federal court has ancillary jurisdiction of the subject matter of a counterclaim if it arises out of the transaction or occurrence that is the subject matter of an opposing party's claim of which the court has jurisdiction. Moore v. New York Cotton Exchange, 270 U.S. 593 (1926). Similarly, a counterclaim that arises out of the transaction or occurrence that is the subject matter of an opposing party's claim is a "compulsory counterclaim" within the meaning of Rule 13(a) of the Federal Rules of Civil Procedure. Such a statement of the law relating to ancillary jurisdiction of counterclaims is not intended to suggest that Rule 13(a) extends the jurisdiction of the federal courts to entertain counterclaims for the Federal Rules of Civil Procedure cannot expand the jurisdiction of the United States courts. What is meant is that the issue of the existence of ancillary jurisdiction and the issue as to whether a counterclaim is compulsory are to be answered by the same test. It is not a coincidence that the same considerations that determine whether a counter-

claim is compulsory decide also whether the court has ancillary jurisdiction to adjudicate it. The tests are the same because Rule 13(a) and the doctrine of ancillary jurisdiction are designed to abolish the same evil, viz., piecemeal litigation in the federal courts.

* * *

Cooper alleges that the claims originally asserted in Great Lakes' amended complaint, reiterated in substance in its counterclaim, are "unjustified" and were brought in "bad faith and without color of right with the sole object of harassing and preventing defendant [Cooper] from competing in the manufacture and sale of flexible hose." These are the only allegations set out by Cooper's counterclaim which demonstrate a relationship within the purview of Rule 13(a) to Great Lakes' amended complaint or counterclaim. But that they do demonstrate a relationship is unquestionable. It is clear that a determination that Cooper's claims that the claims asserted in Great Lakes' amended complaint and reiterated in substance in its counterclaim are harassing will entail an extensive airing of the facts and the law relating to Great Lakes' counterclaim. It follows that the court below was in error in dismissing Great Lakes' counterclaim on the ground that it was permissive.

286 F.2d at 633-34.

NOTES AND QUESTIONS

1. *Great Lakes* was decided before *Gibbs*. Why, however, would the *Gibbs* Court approve of the holding in *Great Lakes*? Recall from *Gibbs* that the principal requirement for the constitutional application of supplemental jurisdiction is that the nonfederal, nondiverse claim share a common nucleus of operative fact with the jurisdiction-invoking claim. Is the test for a compulsory counterclaim—that it arise from the "same transaction or occurrence" as the underlying dispute—exactly the same? As we will continue to see, "transaction or occurrence" is a familiar phrase in the joinder rules. Dean Goldberg has traced the confluence of the "transaction or occurrence" test from the joinder rules with the constitutional test for supplemental jurisdiction under *Gibbs*. Carole Goldberg, *The Influence of Procedural Rules on Federal Jurisdiction*, 28 STAN. L. REV. 395 (1976). Indeed, as she noted, the opinion in *Gibbs* "acknowledged the extent to which the procedural policies of the [then-] new Federal Rules influenced its decision." Id at 418.

2. *Great Lakes* was decided before the passage of § 1367. Why would *Great Lakes* have come out the same way under the statute?

3. In *Great Lakes*, the jurisdiction-invoking claim was based upon a federal question. What if the case involves diversity of citizenship? Try these hypotheticals. In each, P, a citizen of Louisiana, sues D, a citizen of North Dakota, for $85,000 damages from an auto collision between the two.

    (a) Suppose D's counterclaim arising from the same accident is for $45,000. Why is supplemental jurisdiction required here? Why is it clearly available under § 1367(a)? Why is it not withdrawn by §1367(b)?

    (b) Suppose D wants to assert a counterclaim for her damages arising from the same accident, and that the damages are $100,000. Why is supplemental jurisdiction irrelevant?

4. Now let's try a variation on *Great Lakes*. Suppose P's claim was for $45,000, against D-1 and D-2, and that each of the defendants had a compulsory counterclaim for $100,000. P files her claim in federal court. Before that court can dismiss for lack of subject matter jurisdiction, D-1 and D-2 file their counterclaims for $100,000 each. As in *Great Lakes*, the counterclaim becomes the jurisdiction-invoking claim. Now P's original claim is dismissed, and she reasserts it as a compulsory counterclaim.

    (a) Is there supplemental jurisdiction over P's counterclaim? Clearly, there is no reason not to exercise such jurisdiction. Under Rule 13(a), she seems required to assert her claim in the pending case, since it is against an opposing party and arises from the same transaction or occurrence as the jurisdiction-invoking claim.

    (b) Look carefully, however, at the language of §1367(b). D-1 and D-2 were joined under Rule 20 (why?). Isn't P's claim precluded under the supplemental jurisdiction statute? After all, isn't it a claim by a plaintiff against a party joined under Rule 20? The court in Miyano Machinery USA, Inc. v. Zonar, 1993 U.S. Dist. LEXIS 5844 (N.D. Ill. 1993), thought so, and denied supplemental jurisdiction. How could §1367(b) have been drafted to avoid this problem?

b. Permissive Counterclaims

i. Procedural Aspects

Rule 13(b) permits a defending party to assert any claim she has against an opposing party. This provision is as broad as the "open season" or "anything goes" rule we saw for plaintiffs under Rule 18(a). If there is some question as to whether a counterclaim arises from the same transaction or occurrence as the underlying dispute, the existence of Rule 13(b) allows the defendant to err on the side of asserting any claim against the plaintiff in the pending case.

E. Claim Joinder by Defendants

NOTES AND QUESTIONS

1. Suppose Manuel quits his job with Unique Concepts and opens his own design business. Unique claims that Manuel's new business is infringing some of its patents, and sues him for that reason. Unique then sends a letter to Manuel's customers, saying that Manuel's products are unsafe and mentioning its pending patent suit. Manuel wants to sue Unique, alleging that its letter defamed him and violated state consumer protection laws. In Unique Concepts, Inc. v. Manuel, 930 F.2d 573 (7th Cir. 1991), the court concluded that Manuel's claims were *not* compulsory counterclaims. Can you fashion an argument that the court was correct? Can you fashion an argument that the court was incorrect?

Assume that Manuel asserts the claims in the pending action under Rule 13(b). What can the judge do if she is concerned that hearing all of the claims in a single trial will be confusing or that evidence of defamation will prejudice the factfinder?

2. Suppose P and D have entered a business contract that is not faring well. In a completely unrelated event, each is driving her own car, and they collide. P sues D to recover damages for the auto collision. D wants to counterclaim for (1) her injuries from the collision and (2) P's alleged breach of contract in the business deal.

   (a) *May* she assert these two in the pending case? Why? Does Rule 13(b) add anything to Rule 18(a)?

   (b) *Must* she assert either of these two in the pending case or risk losing the claim? Why?

   (c) Assume that D asserts both claims in the pending case, and that P had a claim against D arising from the contract dispute. Why is that claim a compulsory counterclaim?

3. After defendant asserts a counterclaim against the plaintiff, how must the plaintiff respond? See Rule 7(a) and Rule 12(a). Why does Rule 12 eschew the labels "plaintiff" and "defendant?"

ii. Jurisdictional Aspects

Again, a procedural rule cannot affect jurisdiction, so each claim must be assessed separately as to whether it can be asserted in federal court. Permissive counterclaims by definition do not arise from the same transaction or occurrence as the underlying dispute between plaintiff and defendant. Can they ever invoke supplemental jurisdiction? In other words, can there be a claim that does not meet Rule 13(a) but does meet *Gibbs*? If not, what is the only way permissive counterclaims can be brought in federal court? Can you develop a hypothetical in which the permissive counterclaim is supported by an independent basis of jurisdiction?

2. Cross-Claims

a. Procedural Aspects

Rule 13(g) allows a party to assert an offensive claim against a *co-party* (not, as with counterclaims, against an opposing party) if it arises from the same transaction or occurrence as the underlying action. Study the rule carefully and answer the following.

NOTES AND QUESTIONS

1. The operative test for the cross-claim is the same as that for the compulsory counterclaim; both arise from the "same transaction or occurrence" as the underlying dispute. But the cross-claim is not compulsory. A litigant may choose to assert it in the pending case or to sue on it in a separate proceeding. What one word in Rule 13(g) provides that cross-claims are permissive?

The fact that cross-claims are permissive can be wasteful. In Davis & Cox v. Summa Corp., 751 F.2d 1507 (9th Cir. 1985), P could have asserted its claim against D as a cross-claim in a prior case in which both were joined as defendants. It did not do so, opting instead to burden the court system (and the taxpayers) with a separate proceeding. The district court dismissed the second case, but the Ninth Circuit reversed. Because Rule 13(g) did not require P to assert the cross-claim in the prior case, it was free to proceed.

What sense does a permissive cross-claim rule make? After all, the purposes of the cross-claim are the same as those underlying the compulsory counterclaim — "to avoid multiple suits and to encourage resolution of the entire controversy among the parties with a minimum of procedural steps." FRIEDENTHAL, KANE & MILLER, CIVIL PROCEDURE 358. Wouldn't those purposes be served better by making the cross-claim mandatory? By definition, a cross-claim injects a transactionally related claim into the suit, and thus does not bring unrelated matters before the court.

Some state statutes make cross-claims compulsory, at least under certain circumstances. See, e.g., KAN. CIV. PROC. CODE ANN. § 60-213(g)(compulsory if asserting comparative negligence). Although Georgia adopts Federal Rule 13(g)'s permissive language, the existence of a general preclusion statute leads courts in that state to conclude that cross-claims are compulsory! See Citizens Exchange Bank of Pearson v. Kirkland, 344 S.E.2d 409 (1986)(OFF. CODE. GA. ANN. § 9-12-40 provides that a judgment is conclusive as to all matters that could have been raised in the case). Some commentators have suggested that Federal Rule 13(g) should be made compulsory, but there seems to be no move toward making it so.

E. Claim Joinder by Defendants

2. Perry is injured when the car she operates is involved in a collision with a car owned by Olive and driven by Donna. Perry sues both Olive and Donna. (By way of review, why is the joinder of Olive and Donna as co-parties proper?) In addition to filing an appropriate defensive response to the complaint, Olive wants to assert offensive claims (1) to recover for the damage to her car and, (2) if Donna was at fault in the collision, to receive indemnification from Donna for the judgment in Perry's favor. Note that the first of these two claims can be asserted against both Perry and Donna.

(a) What pleading may Olive file against Perry? What, if anything, might happen to her claim if she failed to file it?

(b) What pleading may Olive file against Donna? Must she do so? Note the second sentence of Rule 13(g). It clearly allows the indemnity claim against Donna. What part of the rule allows her to sue Donna for damage to the car?

(c) Suppose Olive asserted a claim against Donna for indemnity but not for damage to the car. The entire case, including this claim against Donna, goes to trial, and the court concludes that Donna was solely responsible for the accident. Now Olive files a separate action against Donna to recover for damages to her car. Why would this case be dismissed in most jurisdictions? (Hint: the answer is not based upon Rule 13(g) or Rule 13(a).)

(d) Suppose Olive asserted against Donna both the claim for indemnification and the claim for property damage to her car in the original proceeding. If Olive had a completely unrelated claim against Donna—say, for trespass on her farm—how could Olive assert that claim in the pending case? Must she do so?

(e) Suppose Olive asserted a cross-claim against Donna seeking both indemnification and damages for wrecking her car. Now assume that Donna wants to assert a claim against Olive, alleging that the car Olive lent her had defective brakes, which caused the collision with Perry. What argument can you fashion for the proposition that Donna *must* assert this claim in the pending case? (Hint: the argument has nothing to do with claim preclusion.) Once Olive asserted the cross-claim against Donna, did they cease to be co-parties (at least for purposes of their relationship with each other) and become something else? See 3 MOORE'S FEDERAL PRACTICE ¶ 13.34[1].

(f) Suppose Olive had a claim against Donna that was not transactionally related to the pending case, for which there would be subject matter jurisdiction. Why can she *not* assert that claim alone in the pending case? If she had a claim against Donna that was transactionally related to the pending case, how would she assert it *and* the unrelated claim in the pending suit?

3. Most cross-claims are asserted by a defendant against a co-defendant. Can a plaintiff assert a cross-claim against a co-plaintiff? Some courts have concluded that a

CHAPTER 12 SCOPE OF LITIGATION — JOINDER AND SUPPLEMENTAL JURISDICTION

plaintiff may do so only if a defendant has asserted a counterclaim against the plaintiffs. See Danner v. Anskis, 256 F.2d 123 (3d Cir. 1958). Does this interpretation find any support in Rule 13(g)? In policy? In a different joinder device, as we will see, the drafters of the rules expressly allow a plaintiff to file only after being sued with a counterclaim. See Rule 14(b).

b. Jurisdictional Aspects

The fact that the cross-claim must arise from the same transaction or occurrence as the underlying dispute is helpful because it opens the door for the use of supplemental jurisdiction. Never jump to supplemental jurisdiction, however, without first assessing whether a claim is supported by some independent basis of subject matter jurisdiction.

NOTES AND QUESTIONS

1. P, a citizen of Vermont, D-1, a citizen of Kentucky, and D-2, also a citizen of Kentucky, all were injured when they collided while skiing. Each will seek damages in excess of $50,000. P sues D-1 and D-2, properly invoking diversity of citizenship jurisdiction.

   (a) Why is D-1's claim against P a compulsory counterclaim? Why does it not need supplemental jurisdiction?

   (b) Why is D-1's claim against D-2 a cross-claim? Why does it need supplemental jurisdiction? Review §1367 (a) and (b), and explain why the cross-claim will be supported by supplemental jurisdiction.

2. P-1 drives a car in which P-2 is a passenger. Each is a citizen of Nevada. They collide with a car driven by D, who is a citizen of Colorado. All three suffer damages in excess of $50,000. P-1 and P-2 join as plaintiffs in a suit against D, properly invoking diversity of citizenship jurisdiction. (What rule allows their joinder?) Suppose D files a compulsory counterclaim against P-1 only, alleging that her negligence caused the collision and seeking recovery of damages for her injuries.

   (a) P-1 now wants to assert a claim against P-2, asserting that P-2 should indemnify her if D's counterclaim is successful and that P-2 may be liable for P-1's injuries. She argues that P-2 is at fault because she distracted P-1 while P-1 was trying to drive. What would she file in the pending case?

   (b) Why would the claim by P-1 need supplemental jurisdiction?

(c) Although historically no one would have objected to having P-1's claim invoke supplemental jurisdiction, why does § 1367(b), on its face, preclude such jurisdiction? How could the statute have been drafted to avoid this problem? See Denis McLaughlin, *The Federal Supplemental Jurisdiction Statute—A Constitutional and Statutory Analysis*, 24 ARIZ. ST. L.J. 849 (1992).

F. Overriding Plaintiff's Party Structure

To this point, we have seen that Rule 20 allows the plaintiff to make the initial choice of who the parties to a lawsuit will be, and we have seen the various claims those original parties can make against each other. Note that the defendant has equal freedom in naming parties to her claims. Rule 13(h) allows the defendant to join additional parties to her cross-claims and counterclaims, so long as the joinder meets Rule 20 or (Rule 13(h), curiously, says "and") Rule 19. Rule 13(h) thus puts the defendant on the same procedural footing as plaintiff in selecting parties to her claims. Here, we turn to the issue of whether the plaintiff's choice of parties can be overridden other than through Rule 13(h).

Remember that the plaintiff need not join all Rule 20 parties. For a variety of tactical or jurisdictional reasons, the plaintiff may have been underinclusive in joining parties. Such underinclusiveness may lead to wasteful duplicative litigation, may subject a defending party to risk of multiple liability, or may render it difficult for a nonparty (or "absentee") to protect her interest from practical impairment. Moreover, duplicative litigation may lead to inconsistent results, which can undermine society's confidence in the judicial process.

The Federal Rules address such problems by allowing others to override plaintiff's party structure with various devices, including impleader, compulsory joinder, and intervention. In each, the most important question will be *why* we would allow someone to override the plaintiff's choices. We will see the same themes played out over and over. In addition, pay attention to *who* may invoke these rules.

1. Impleader (Third-Party Practice)

a. Procedural Aspects

The first tool available to override the plaintiff's party structure of a suit is impleader, or third party practice, under Rule 14. It allows a party in a defensive posture to join an absentee in limited situations. The party invoking impleader is called the "third-party plaintiff," while the absentee brought in becomes the "third-party defendant." Read Rule 14. As you will see, Rule 14(a) covers a good deal of ground.

Under what circumstances can a party implead an absentee? Note how narrowly crafted the rule is in this regard, permitting only joinder of one "who is or may be liable to the third-party plaintiff for all or part of the plaintiff's claim against the third-party plaintiff." This generally permits joinder of one who owes the third-party plaintiff indemnity or contribution. Impleader promotes efficiency by litigating the underlying claim and any "claim over" for indemnity or contribution in a single proceeding. Concomitantly, it avoids the possibility of inconsistent results.

Suppose, for example, that P sues D for damages and that D has a right to indemnity for this claim from T. D can implead T. Then, any judgment for P against D can be deflected to T. If D could not implead T, consider the problems she might face. After losing to P, she would have to sue T in a separate proceeding. Thus, she (and the taxpayers) would pay for two suits, delaying the ultimate resolution of the dispute.

Moreover, in that separate action, D could not use collateral estoppel against T. (By way of review, why not?) She therefore runs the risk of losing that case to T, thereby absorbing the entire loss herself. Allowing her to implead here, then, may be seen as a way of avoiding imposition on her of multiple liability or inconsistent obligations. JAMES, HAZARD & LEUBSDORF, CIVIL PROCEDURE 531.

Markvicka v. Brodhead-Garrett Co.
76 F.R.D. 205 (D. Neb. 1977)

DENNY, DISTRICT JUDGE.

This matter is before the Court upon the motion of third-party defendant, the School District of Ralston, to dismiss the third-party complaint against it filed by defendant and third-party plaintiff, Brodhead-Garrett Company.

This action was brought on behalf of a minor child who suffered severe injuries while using a jointer machine manufactured by the defendant. Plaintiff attributes his injuries to the defective design and condition of the jointer machine.

The defendant's third-party complaint against the School District of Ralston alleges that the accident occurred in the course of a woodworking class held by the third-party defendant and charges that the School District's improper maintenance of the machine and inadequate supervision of the students caused plaintiff's injuries.

The third-party complaint alleges a right to indemnity from the School District. However, the Court finds that the third-party complaint more accurately states a claim for contribution. The distinctions between contribution and indemnity, often difficult to apply, are well stated by D. Busick, *Contribution and Indemnity between Tortfeasors in Nebraska*, 7 CREIGHTON L. REV. 182 (1974) and cases cited therein.

F. Overriding Plaintiff's Party Structure

Contribution and indemnity are two separate remedies which may be available to a tortfeasor who seeks to place all or part of the burden of a judgment upon his fellow tortfeasor. Contribution is based upon the common, though not necessarily identical, liability of two or more actors for the same injury. It equalizes the burden on the wrongdoers by requiring each to pay his own proportionate share of damages. Indemnity, on the other hand, enables one tortfeasor to shift the entire burden of the judgment to another. It tempers the harshness of the doctrines of respondeat superior and vicarious liability since it allows one who has been compelled to pay solely because of a certain legal relationship to shift the ultimate burden of the judgment to the actual culprit.

* * *

In sum, Nebraska law seems to permit indemnity when it has been provided for in a specifically drawn contract or when liability has been imposed upon a party simply because of his legal relationship to the negligent party. It appears, however, that indemnity will not be allowed when both parties have been negligent to a certain degree.

In Royal Indem. Co. v. Aetna Cas. & Sur. Co., 229 N.W.2d 183 (1975), the Nebraska Supreme Court clarified the law of contribution among negligent joint tortfeasors in Nebraska.

We, therefore, hold that in this jurisdiction there is no absolute bar to contribution among negligent joint tort-feasors; and also, as in this case, that a right to equitable contribution exists among judgment debtors jointly liable in tort for damages negligently caused, which right becomes enforceable on behalf of any party when he discharges more than his proportionate share of the judgment. * * *

Thus it is now clear that as between defendants against whom a joint judgment in tort has been rendered, contribution is allowed. The court did not directly rule as to contribution between negligent joint tortfeasors against whom judgments have not yet been rendered. However, the statement that "there is no absolute bar to contribution among negligent joint tortfeasors" would seem to envision contribution not only among those against whom a plaintiff has successfully obtained judgments but also among those whose liability remains to be fixed either in a third-party claim in the original plaintiff's suit or in an independent action for contribution by the original defendant.

The third-party complaint alleges a factual basis for contribution from the School District of Ralston should Brodhead-Garrett be found liable to the plaintiff. If the defendant's allegations are true, the School District's negligence was a concurrent cause of the plaintiff's injury.

Fed.R.Civ.P. 14(a) permits the joinder of a party who "is or may be liable" to the defending party for all or part of the plaintiff's claim. Where state law creates a right to contribution or indemnity among tortfeasors, the wrongdoer who has been sued by an injured party may implead his co-wrongdoers before the plaintiff successfully obtains a judgment. "The fact that contribution may not actually be obtained until the original defendant has been cast in judgment and has paid does not prevent impleader; the impleader judgment may be so fashioned as to protect the rights of the other tortfeasors, so that defendant's judgment over against them may not be enforced until the defendant has paid plaintiff's judgment or more than his proportionate share, whichever the law may require." 3 MOORE'S FED. PRACTICE ¶ 14.11 at 14-322 (1976) et seq.

The defendant has alleged that if it was at fault in the design or construction of the jointer machine, so was the School District in its maintenance of the machine and supervision of the students. Both owed the plaintiff a duty of care.

Therefore, as the School District "may be liable" for contribution, it may be joined as third-party defendant in this action in order to determine its accountability. The fact that the defendant erroneously defined its claim as "indemnity" does not alter this conclusion. A claim should not be dismissed for insufficiency "unless it appears to a certainty that plaintiff is entitled to no relief under any state of facts which could be proved in support of the claim." Morton Bldgs. of Neb., Inc. v. Morton Bldgs., 333 F. Supp. 187, 191 (D.Neb. 1971). At this stage of the proceedings, the Court will grant the defendant leave to amend the third-party complaint to state the correct theory for its cause of action. Accordingly,

It is ordered that the motion of third-party defendant, the School District of Ralston, to dismiss the third-party complaint will be denied if, within ten (10) days hereof, the defendant, Brodhead-Garrett Company, amends its third-party complaint against the School District to allege a claim for contribution.

NOTES AND QUESTIONS

1. In *Markvicka*, state law apparently would not allow the defendant to recover against the third-party defendant until it had paid the entire judgment to the plaintiff. Nonetheless, after *Hanna v. Plumer*, Rule 14(a) clearly governs practice in federal court. If the underlying claim by the plaintiff fails, the claim against the third-party defendant obviously fails as well. If plaintiff wins in the underlying suit, then the court can address the impleader claim. Rule 14, then, merely accelerates assertion of the claim against the third-party defendant. Even if this acceleration is contrary to state law, Rule 14(a) governs, since it does not create liability that would ultimately not exist under state law. See Jeub v. B/G Foods, Inc., 2 F.R.D. 238 (D. Minn. 1942). A different result would be required if state law did not permit a claim for indemnity or contribution at all.

2. Suppose P is injured when struck by a car operated by T, but owned by D. T was using the car with D's permission. D is vicariously liable for T's acts and D has a substantive right of indemnity from T. P sues D for damages.

(a) Obviously, D can implead T, seeking indemnification should P prevail in the underlying suit. When may she do so? Does she need court permission to do so? *Must* she do so? Why should she run no claim preclusion risk if she does not implead T?

(b) If D impleads T, can T raise an affirmative defense (say, statute of limitations) that D forgot to raise in the underlying case?

E. Claim Joinder by Defendants

(c) Will D want to assert more than the indemnity claim against T? If the accident is the fault of T, liability for the judgment against D will be deflected to T. But what about D's property damage claim against T for ruining her car? How can she join that claim in the pending case? Note that D needs to use one joinder rule to assert the indemnity claim against T and a separate rule to join the property damage claim.

On the other hand, if D and T were co-defendants (that is, if P had joined them both originally under Rule 20), D could assert both the indemnity claim and the property damage claim against T through a single device — Rule 13(g). The cross-claim under Rule 13(g) permits assertion of all claims arising from the same transaction or occurrence as the underlying dispute. Impleader is narrower, and allows only the indemnity or contribution claim. Additional claims (even if transactionally related, as here) must be joined through Rule 18(a).

(d) In (c), suppose D impleads T, claiming indemnity, but does *not* join the claim for property damage. If D later tries to sue T for property damage, can T assert claim preclusion?

(e) In addition to impleading T and joining the property damage claim against T, what will D assert against P?

(f) If D impleads T and T has a claim against D for lending her a faulty car, how can she assert it in the pending case? Indeed, *must* she assert it here? (Hint: when D impleaded T, did they become opposing parties?)

(g) Suppose applicable law gave D no right of indemnity or contribution against T, but that she still has her claim against T for damage to the car. Even though it is transactionally related to the underlying dispute, why is there no way for her to assert that claim in the pending case?

3. Rule 14(b) permits a plaintiff to implead an absentee who is or may be liable to her for a counterclaim asserted against her by the defendant. In view of Rule 14(a)'s provision that any "defending party" may implead, Rule 14(b) appears unnecessary.

4. Rule 14(a) permits two other claims, neither of which has a widely adopted name. Under what circumstances can the plaintiff assert a claim against the third-party defendant (TPD)? Under what circumstances can a TPD assert a claim against the plaintiff? Some commentators, diagramming the three claims as follows, refer to these latter two as, respectively, "upsloping 14(a) claims" and "downsloping 14(a) claims." Note that these are *not* impleader claims. That term applies only to the initial joinder of the absentee

CHAPTER 12 SCOPE OF LITIGATION — JOINDER AND SUPPLEMENTAL JURISDICTION

for indemnity or contribution. These are merely additional claims permitted by Rule 14(a) to flesh out the suit.

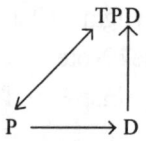

```
         TPD
        ↗ ↑
       ↙  │
      P ——→ D
```

3 MOORE'S FEDERAL PRACTICE ¶ 14.16.

Could both upsloping and downsloping 14(a) claims be asserted in the same case? Once P asserted an upsloping 14(a) claim against TPD, wouldn't any claim by TPD against P be a counterclaim?

b. Jurisdictional Aspects

Obviously, any of the three claims permitted under Rule 14(a)—impleader, upsloping 14(a), and downsloping 14(a)—might be supported by an independent basis of subject matter jurisdiction. It is important to remember that jurisdiction must be assessed for each claim. Thus, suppose P, a citizen of Florida, sues D, a citizen of Wisconsin, invoking diversity of citizenship. D then impleads T, a citizen of Florida, for an indemnity claim exceeding $50,000. The fact that T and P are co-citizens is irrelevant, since there is (as yet) no claim between them. The claim being asserted (the impleader claim) is by a citizen of Wisconsin against a citizen of Florida and exceeds $50,000. Therefore, it has an independent basis of subject matter jurisdiction.

What if one of the three claims does not have an independent basis of subject matter jurisdiction? Can supplemental jurisdiction attach? As always, the first question under § 1367(a) is whether the claim satisfies the *Gibbs* test, sharing a common nucleus of operative fact with the underlying action. The impleader claim seems to, since it requires that the third-party defendant be liable to the defendant for all or part of the plaintiff's claim, that is, the underlying dispute. Similarly, both the upsloping and downsloping 14(a) claims seem to meet the test, since by definition they can be asserted only if they arise from the same transaction or occurrence as the underlying dispute.

For decades, there has been no significant doubt that the impleader claim and the downsloping 14(a) claim invoke supplemental jurisdiction. See, e.g., Agrashell, Inc. v. Bernard Sirotta Co, 344 F.2d 583 (2d Cir. 1965)(impleader); Revere Copper & Brass, Inc. v. Aetna Cas. & Sur. Co., 426 F.2d 709 (5th Cir. 1970)(downsloping 14(a) claim). Upsloping 14(a) claims, however, raise different concerns, as shown in the next case. Note that this case was decided before passage of §1367.

E. Claim Joinder by Defendants

Owen Equipment & Erection Co. v. Kroger
437 U.S. 365, 98 S. Ct. 2396, 57 L. Ed. 2d 274 (1978)

MR JUSTICE STEWART delivered the opinion of the Court.

In an action in which federal jurisdiction is based on diversity of citizenship, may the plaintiff assert a claim against a third-party defendant when there is no independent basis for federal jurisdiction over that claim? The Court of Appeals for the Eighth Circuit held in this case that such a claim is within the ancillary jurisdiction of the federal courts. We granted certiorari, because this decision conflicts with several recent decisions of other Courts of Appeals.

I

On January 18, 1972, James Kroger was electrocuted when the boom of a steel crane next to which he was walking came too close to a high-tension electric power line. The respondent (his widow, who is the administratrix of his estate) filed a wrongful-death action in the United States District Court for the District of Nebraska against the Omaha Public Power District (OPPD). Her complaint alleged that OPPD's negligent construction, maintenance, and operation of the power line had caused Kroger's death. Federal jurisdiction was based on diversity of citizenship, since the respondent was a citizen of Iowa and OPPD was a Nebraska corporation.

OPPD then filed a third-party complaint pursuant to Fed. Rule Civ. Proc. 14(a) against the petitioner, Owen Equipment and Erection Co. (Owen), alleging that the crane was owned and operated by Owen, and that Owen's negligence had been the proximate cause of Kroger's death.[3] OPPD later moved for summary judgment on the respondent's complaint against it. While this motion was pending, the respondent was granted leave to file an amended complaint naming Owen as an additional defendant. Thereafter, the District Court granted OPPD's motion for summary judgment in an unreported opinion. The case thus went to trial between the respondent and the petitioner alone.

The respondent's amended complaint alleged that Owen was "a Nebraska corporation with its principal place of business in Nebraska." Owen's answer admitted that it was "a corporation organized and existing under the laws of the State of Nebraska," and denied every other allegation of the complaint. On the third day of trial, however, it was disclosed that the petitioner's principal place of business was in Iowa, not Nebraska[5] and that the petitioner and the respondent were thus both citizens of Iowa.[6] The petitioner then moved to dismiss the complaint for lack of jurisdiction. The

---

[3] Under Rule 14(a), a third-party defendant may not be impleaded merely because he may be liable to the *plaintiff*. While the third-party complaint in this case alleged merely that Owen's negligence caused Kroger's death, and the basis of Owen's alleged liability *to OPPD* is nowhere spelled out, OPPD evidently relied upon the state common-law right of contribution among joint tortfeasors. The petitioner has never challenged the propriety of the third-party complaint as such.

[5] The problem apparently was one of geography. Although the Missouri River generally marks the boundary between Iowa and Nebraska, Carter Lake, Iowa, where the accident occurred and where Owen had its main office, lies west of the river, adjacent to Omaha, Neb. Apparently the river once avulsed at one of its bends, cutting Carter Lake off from the rest of Iowa.

[6] Title 28 U.S.C. § 1332 (c) provides that "[for] the purposes of [diversity jurisdiction]..., a corporation shall be deemed a citizen of any State by which it has been incorporated and of the State where it has its principal place of business."

District Court reserved decision on the motion, and the jury thereafter returned a verdict in favor of the respondent. In an unreported opinion issued after the trial, the District Court denied the petitioner's motion to dismiss the complaint.

The judgment was affirmed on appeal. The Court of Appeals held that under this Court's decision in *Mine Workers v. Gibbs*, the District Court had jurisdictional power, in its discretion, to adjudicate the respondent's claim against the petitioner because that claim arose from the "core of 'operative facts' giving rise to both [respondent's] claim against OPPD and OPPD's claim against Owen." It further held that the District Court had properly exercised its discretion in proceeding to decide the case even after summary judgment had been granted to OPPD, because the petitioner had concealed its Iowa citizenship from the respondent. Rehearing en banc was denied by an equally divided court.

II

It is undisputed that there was no independent basis of federal jurisdiction over the respondent's state-law tort action against the petitioner, since both are citizens of Iowa. And although Fed. Rule Civ. Proc. 14(a) permits a plaintiff to assert a claim against a third-party defendant, it does not purport to say whether or not such a claim requires an independent basis of federal jurisdiction. Indeed, it could not determine that question, since it is axiomatic that the Federal Rules of Civil Procedure do not create or withdraw federal jurisdiction.

In affirming the District Court's judgment, the Court of Appeals relied upon the doctrine of ancillary jurisdiction, whose contours it believed were defined by this Court's holding in *Mine Workers v. Gibbs* The *Gibbs* case differed from this one in that it involved pendent jurisdiction, which concerns the resolution of a plaintiff's federal- and state-law claims against a single defendant in one action. By contrast, in this case there was no claim based upon substantive federal law, but rather state-law tort claims against two different defendants. Nonetheless, the Court of Appeals was correct in perceiving that *Gibbs* and this case are two species of the same generic problem: Under what circumstances may a federal court hear and decide a state-law claim arising between citizens of the same State?[8] But we believe that the Court of Appeals failed to understand the scope of the doctrine of the *Gibbs* case.

The plaintiff in *Gibbs* alleged that the defendant union had violated the common law of Tennessee as well as the federal prohibition of secondary boycotts. This Court held that, although the parties were not of diverse citizenship, the District Court properly entertained the state-law claim as pendent to the federal claim. The crucial holding was stated as follows:

> "Pendent jurisdiction, in the sense of judicial *power*, exists whenever there is a claim 'arising under [the] Constitution, the Laws of the United States, and Treaties made, or which shall be made, under their Authority . . . ,' U.S. Const., Art. III, § 2, and the relationship between that claim and the state claim permits the conclusion that the entire action before the court comprises but one constitutional 'case.' . . . The state and federal claims must derive from a common nucleus of operative fact. But if, considered without regard to their federal or state character, a plaintiff's

---

[8] No more than in *Aldinger v. Howard* is it necessary to determine here "whether there are any 'principled' differences between pendent and ancillary jurisdiction; or, if there are, what effect *Gibbs* had on such differences."

claims are such that he would ordinarily be expected to try them all in one judicial proceeding, then, assuming substantiality of the federal issues, there is *power* in federal courts to hear the whole.[9]

It is apparent that *Gibbs* delineated the constitutional limits of federal judicial power. But even if it be assumed that the District Court in the present case had constitutional power to decide the respondent's lawsuit against the petitioner, it does not follow that the decision of the Court of Appeals was correct. Constitutional power is merely the first hurdle that must be overcome in determining that a federal court has jurisdiction over a particular controversy. For the jurisdiction of the federal courts is limited not only by the provisions of Art. III of the Constitution, but also by Acts of Congress.

That statutory law as well as the Constitution may limit a federal court's jurisdiction over nonfederal claims[11] is well illustrated by two recent decisions of this Court, Aldinger v. Howard, 427 U.S. 1 [1976], and Zahn v. International Paper Co., 414 U.S. 291 [1974]. In *Aldinger* the Court held that a Federal District Court lacked jurisdiction over a state-law claim against a county, even if that claim was alleged to be pendent to one against county officials under 42 U.S.C. § 1983. In *Zahn* the Court held that in a diversity class action under Fed. Rule Civ. Proc. 23(b)(3), the claim of each member of the plaintiff class must independently satisfy the minimum jurisdictional amount set by 28 U. S. C. § 1332 (a), and rejected the argument that jurisdiction existed over those claims that involved $10,000 or less as ancillary to those that involved more. [At the time, diversity of citizenship cases required an amount in controversy in excess of $10,000-EDS.] In each case, despite the fact that federal and nonfederal claims arose from a "common nucleus of operative fact," the Court held that the statute conferring jurisdiction over the federal claim did not allow the exercise of jurisdiction over the nonfederal claims.

The *Aldinger* and *Zahn* cases thus make clear that a finding that federal and nonfederal claims arise from a "common nucleus of operative fact," the test of *Gibbs*, does not end the inquiry into whether a federal court has power to hear the nonfederal claims along with the federal ones. Beyond this constitutional minimum, there must be an examination of the posture in which the nonfederal claim is asserted and of the specific statute that confers jurisdiction over the federal claim, in order to determine whether "Congress in [that statute] has ... expressly or by implication negated" the exercise of jurisdiction over the particular nonfederal claim.

III

The relevant statute in this case, 28 U. S. C. § 1332 (a)(1), confers upon federal courts jurisdiction over "civil actions where the matter in controversy exceeds the sum or value of $10,000 [now $50,000 — EDS.] ... and is between ... citizens of different States." This statute and its predecessors have consistently been held to require complete diversity of citizenship. That is,

---

[9] The Court further noted that even when such power exists, its exercise remains a matter of discretion based upon "considerations of judicial economy, convenience and fairness to litigants," and held that the District Court had not abused its discretion in retaining jurisdiction of the state-law claim.

[11] As used in this opinion, the term "nonfederal claim" means one as to which there is no independent basis for federal jurisdiction. Conversely, a "federal claim" means one as to which an independent basis for federal jurisdiction exists.

diversity jurisdiction does not exist unless *each* defendant is a citizen of a different State from *each* plaintiff. Over the years Congress has repeatedly re-enacted or amended the statute conferring diversity jurisdiction, leaving intact this rule of complete diversity. Whatever may have been the original purposes of diversity-of-citizenship jurisdiction, this subsequent history clearly demonstrates a congressional mandate that diversity jurisdiction is not to be available when any plaintiff is a citizen of the same State as any defendant.

Thus it is clear that the respondent could not originally have brought suit in federal court naming Owen and OPPD as codefendants, since citizens of Iowa would have been on both sides of the litigation. Yet the identical lawsuit resulted when she amended her complaint. Complete diversity was destroyed just as surely as if she had sued Owen initially. In either situation, in the plain language of the statute, the "matter in controversy" could not be "between . . . citizens of different States."

It is a fundamental precept that federal courts are courts of limited jurisdiction. The limits upon federal jurisdiction, whether imposed by the Constitution or by Congress, must be neither disregarded nor evaded. Yet under the reasoning of the Court of Appeals in this case, a plaintiff could defeat the statutory requirement of complete diversity by the simple expedient of suing only those defendants who were of diverse citizenship and waiting for them to implead nondiverse defendants[17]. If, as the Court of Appeals thought, a "common nucleus of operative fact" were the only requirement for ancillary jurisdiction in a diversity case, there would be no principled reason why the respondent in this case could not have joined her cause of action against Owen in her original complaint as ancillary to her claim against OPPD. Congress' requirement of complete diversity would thus have been evaded completely.

It is true, as the Court of Appeals noted, that the exercise of ancillary jurisdiction over nonfederal claims has often been upheld in situations involving impleader, cross-claims or counterclaims. But in determining whether jurisdiction over a nonfederal claim exists, the context in which the nonfederal claim is asserted is crucial. See Aldinger v. Howard, 427 U.S., at 14. And the claim here arises in a setting quite different from the kinds of nonfederal claims that have been viewed in other cases as falling within the ancillary jurisdiction of the federal courts.

First, the nonfederal claim in this case was simply not ancillary to the federal one in the same sense that, for example, the impleader by a defendant of a third-party defendant always is. A third-party complaint depends at least in part upon the resolution of the primary lawsuit. See n. 3, supra. Its relation to the original complaint is thus not mere factual similarity but logical dependence. Cf. Moore v. New York Cotton Exchange, 270 U.S. 593, 610 [1926]. The respondent's claim against the petitioner, however, was entirely separate from her original claim against OPPD, since the petitioner's liability to her depended not at all upon whether or not OPPD was also liable. Far from being an ancillary and dependent claim, it was a new and independent one.

Second, the nonfederal claim here was asserted by the plaintiff, who voluntarily chose to bring suit upon a state-law claim in a federal court. By contrast, ancillary jurisdiction typically

---

[17] This is not an unlikely hypothesis, since a defendant in a tort suit such as this one would surely try to limit his liability by impleading any joint tortfeasors for indemnity or contribution. Some commentators have suggested that the possible abuse of third-party practice could be dealt with under 28 U.S.C. § 1359, which forbids collusive attempts to create federal jurisdiction. * * * The dissenting opinion today also expresses this view. But there is nothing necessarily collusive about a plaintiff's selectively suing only those tortfeasors of diverse citizenship, or about the named defendants' desire to implead joint tortfeasors. Nonetheless, the requirement of complete diversity would be eviscerated by such a course of events.

involves claims by a defending party haled into court against his will, or by another person whose rights might be irretrievably lost unless he could assert them in an ongoing action in a federal court. A plaintiff cannot complain if ancillary jurisdiction does not encompass all of his possible claims in a case such as this one, since it is he who has chosen the federal rather than the state forum and must thus accept its limitations. "[The] efficiency plaintiff seeks so avidly is available without question in the state courts." Kenrose Mfg. Co. v. Fred Whitaker Co., 512 F.2d 890, 894 (CA4)[1972].[20]

It is not unreasonable to assume that, in generally requiring complete diversity, Congress did not intend to confine the jurisdiction of federal courts so inflexibly that they are unable to protect legal rights or effectively to resolve an entire, logically entwined lawsuit. Those practical needs are the basis of the doctrine of ancillary jurisdiction. But neither the convenience of litigants nor considerations of judicial economy can suffice to justify extension of the doctrine of ancillary jurisdiction to a plaintiff's cause of action against a citizen of the same State in a diversity case. Congress has established the basic rule that diversity jurisdiction exists under 28 U.S.C. § 1332 only when there is complete diversity of citizenship. "The policy of the statute calls for its strict construction." To allow the requirement of complete diversity to be circumvented as it was in this case would simply flout the congressional command.[21]

Accordingly, the judgment of the Court of Appeals is reversed.

It is so ordered.

MR. JUSTICE WHITE, with whom MR. JUSTICE BRENNAN joins, dissenting.

The Court today states that "[it] is not unreasonable to assume that, in generally requiring complete diversity, Congress did not intend to confine the jurisdiction of federal courts so inflexibly that they are unable . . . effectively to resolve an entire, logically entwined lawsuit." In spite of this recognition, the majority goes on to hold that in diversity suits federal courts do not have the jurisdictional power to entertain a claim asserted by a plaintiff against a third-party defendant, no matter how entwined it is with the matter already before the court, unless there is an independent basis for jurisdiction over that claim. Because I find no support for such a requirement in either Art. III of the Constitution or in any statutory law, I dissent from the Court's "unnecessarily grudging" approach. * * *

The majority correctly points out, however, that the analysis cannot stop [with constitutional assessment]. As Aldinger v. Howard, 427 U.S. 1 (1976), teaches, the jurisdictional power of the federal courts may be limited by Congress, as well as by the Constitution. * * *

In the present case, the only indication of congressional intent that the Court can find is that contained in the diversity jurisdictional statute, 28 U.S.C. § 1332(a), which states that "district courts shall have original jurisdiction of all civil actions where the matter in controversy exceeds the sum or value of $10,000 . . . and is between . . . citizens of different States . . . ." Because this statute has been interpreted as requiring complete diversity of citizenship between each plaintiff and each

---

[20] Whether Iowa's statute of limitations would now bar an action by the respondent in an Iowa court is, of course, entirely a matter of state law.

[21] Our holding is that the District Court lacked power to entertain the respondent's lawsuit against the petitioner. Thus, the asserted inequity in the respondent's alleged concealment of its citizenship is irrelevant. Federal judicial power does not depend upon "prior action or consent of the parties."

defendant, Strawbridge v. Curtiss, 3 Cranch 267 (1806), the Court holds that the District Court did not have ancillary jurisdiction over Mrs. Kroger's claim against Owen. In so holding, the Court unnecessarily expands the scope of the complete-diversity requirement while substantially limiting the doctrine of ancillary jurisdiction.

The complete-diversity requirement, of course, could be viewed as meaning that in a diversity case, a federal district court may adjudicate only those claims that are between parties of different States. Thus, in order for a defendant to implead a third-party defendant, there would have to be diversity of citizenship; the same would also be true for cross-claims between defendants and for a third-party defendant's claim against a plaintiff. Even the majority, however, refuses to read the complete-diversity requirement so broadly; it recognizes with seeming approval the exercise of ancillary jurisdiction over nonfederal claims in situations involving impleader, cross-claims, and counterclaims. Given the Court's willingness to recognize ancillary jurisdiction in these contexts, despite the requirements of § 1332(a), I see no justification for the Court's refusal to approve the District Court's exercise of ancillary jurisdiction in the present case.

It is significant that a plaintiff who asserts a claim against a third-party defendant is not seeking to add a new party to the lawsuit. In the present case, for example, Owen had already been brought into the suit by OPPD, and, that having been done, Mrs. Kroger merely sought to assert against Owen a claim arising out of the same transaction that was already before the court. Thus the situation presented here is unlike that in *Aldinger*.

* * *

Because in the instant case Mrs. Kroger merely sought to assert a claim against someone already a party to the suit, considerations of judicial economy, convenience, and fairness to the litigants — the factors relied upon in *Gibbs* — support the recognition of ancillary jurisdiction here. Already before the court was the whole question of the cause of Mr. Kroger's death. Mrs. Kroger initially contended that OPPD was responsible; OPPD in turn contended that Owen's negligence had been the proximate cause of Mr. Kroger's death. In spite of the fact that the question of Owen's negligence was already before the District Court, the majority requires Mrs. Kroger to bring a separate action in state court in order to assert that very claim. Even if the Iowa statute of limitations will still permit such a suit, see ante, n. 20, considerations of judicial economy are certainly not served by requiring such duplicative litigation.

The majority, however, brushes aside such considerations of convenience, judicial economy, and fairness because it concludes that recognizing ancillary jurisdiction over a plaintiff's claim against a third-party defendant would permit the plaintiff to circumvent the complete-diversity requirement and thereby "flout the congressional command." Since the plaintiff in such a case does not bring the third-party defendant into the suit, however, there is no occasion for deliberate circumvention of the diversity requirement, absent collusion with the defendant. In the case of such collusion, of which there is absolutely no indication here, the court can dismiss the action under the authority of 28 U.S.C. § 1359. In the absence of such collusion, there is no reason to adopt an absolute rule prohibiting the plaintiff from asserting those claims that he may properly assert against the third-party defendant pursuant to Fed. Rule Civ. Proc. 14(a). The plaintiff in such a situation brings suit against the defendant only, with absolutely no assurance that the defendant will decide or be able to implead a particular third-party defendant. Since the plaintiff has no control over the

F. Overriding Plaintiff's Party Structure

defendant's decision to implead a third party, the fact that he could not have originally sued that party in federal court should be irrelevant. Moreover, the fact that a plaintiff in some cases may be able to foresee the subsequent chain of events leading to the impleader does not seem to me to be a sufficient reason to declare that a district court does not have the *power* to exercise ancillary jurisdiction over the plaintiff's claims against the third-party defendant.

NOTES AND QUESTIONS

1. Note when *Kroger* was decided—after *Gibbs* and *Aldinger*, but before *Finley*. It seems consistent with *Gibbs* and *Aldinger* in indulging the *presumption* that supplemental jurisdiction applies (if *Gibbs* is met) unless Congress has taken it away. As in *Aldinger*, the Court hunts for legislative action denying supplemental jurisdiction. According to *Kroger*, what statute denies supplemental jurisdiction over upsloping 14(a) claims? How does it do so?

2. Note the Court's statutory analysis in *Kroger*. It seems to stress three factors.
   (a) *Logical dependence.* *Kroger* was the first case to identify "logical dependence" as a factor in supplemental jurisdiction. Of all the claims asserted under the federal rules, only one—the impleader claim—is always logically dependent on the underlying case. If the plaintiff wins, the impleader claim goes to trial; if she loses, it does not. Yet, in *Kroger* the Court recognized that it had long accepted supplemental jurisdiction over other claims not satisfying logical dependence, so long as the *Gibbs* test was met.
   (b) *Defensive initiation.* The Court also said that supplemental jurisdiction is usually employed to support claims by a party in a defensive posture. But what about *Gibbs*? There, it upheld supplemental jurisdiction over a claim by a plaintiff. What is the key distinction between *Gibbs* and *Kroger* on this score? Why do you suppose the Court is more willing to allow supplemental jurisdiction in federal question cases than in diversity cases?
   (c) *The clever plaintiff.* The majority felt that a clever plaintiff could foresee that a defendant would join a third-party defendant and could use an upsloping 14(a) claim as an end-run around the complete diversity rule of *Strawbridge*. Does it strike you as realistic to fear that the plaintiff and defendant will collude in this way? If there were such collusion, wouldn't 28 U.S.C. § 1359 handle the situation?

   At any rate, there was no evidence of such behavior in *Kroger*. Indeed, until the third day of trial, everyone apparently thought that there was diversity between Mrs. Kroger and Owen. Or did everyone? Look very carefully at the allegations of citizenship made by Mrs. Kroger and the response thereto by Owen. Should the response by Owen have caused anyone to look into the issue further?

3. Suppose Mr. Kroger had not been killed, and that he sued OPPD to recover for his personal injuries. Suppose also that after OPPD impleaded Owen, Owen filed a downsloping 14(a) claim against Kroger, alleging that he damaged its equipment. If Kroger then counterclaimed against Owen, would the court have supplemental jurisdiction over the counterclaim? Some courts have upheld supplemental jurisdiction in this context. See, e.g., Finkle v. Gulf & W. Mfg. Co., 744 F.2d 1015 (3d Cir. 1984). How does this situation differ from *Kroger*?

4. Although Mrs. Kroger amended her complaint to include the third-party defendant, the Court chose to treat the assertion as an upsloping 14(a) claim. If treated as an amended complaint, there is no doubt that the case would be dismissed as violating the complete diversity rule. Should the result be different just because of timing—just because she added the claim against Owen later?

5. As a practical matter, what happens to plaintiffs in Mrs. Kroger's situation? The litigation with the defendant and between the defendant and the third-party defendant go forward in federal court, while the transactionally related upsloping 14(a) claim must be asserted in state court. What problems does this scenario raise?

6. What is the effect of the supplemental jurisdiction statute? Consider the following under § 1367.

   (a) Why is there supplemental jurisdiction over an impleader claim filed by a defendant?

   (b) Why is there supplemental jurisdiction over a downsloping 14(a) claim?

   (c) Why is there *not* supplemental jurisdiction over an upsloping 14(a) claim?

   (d) What about an impleader claim filed by the plaintiff? Suppose P, a citizen of New York, sues D, a citizen of Missouri, invoking diversity of citizenship jurisdiction. Now D files a counterclaim against P. P has a claim for indemnity against T, and would like to implead T. T, however, is a citizen of New York, so there is no diversity of citizenship on that claim. Before § 1367, there appears to have been no question that supplemental jurisdiction would attach. By the terms of § 1367(b), however, why is there no supplemental jurisdiction?

Some suggest that courts may avoid finding no jurisdiction in (d) by treating the statutory reference to "plaintiffs" as meaning plaintiffs not filing a claim in a defensive capacity. McLaughlin, supra, 24 Ariz. St. L.J. at 948-49. At least one court has rejected the argument, finding that § 1367(b) changed the prior law in this area. See Guaranteed Systems, Inc. v. American National Can Co., 842 F. Supp. 855, 857 (M.D. N.C. 1994). How could the statute have been drafted to avoid this result?

(e) Suppose the third-party defendant asserts a downsloping 14(a) claim against the nondiverse plaintiff, invoking supplemental jurisdiction. Now plaintiff files a compulsory counterclaim against the third-party defendant. Under pre-*Finley* practice, courts generally invoked supplemental jurisdiction, as discussed in Note 3 above. By the terms of § 1367(b), however, why is there no supplemental jurisdiction?

7. Note the tolling provision of § 1367(d), which is intended to arrest the statute of limitations while claims are pending in federal court. Would the provision have helped Mrs. Kroger? *Kroger* was decided before the statute was passed. Although the Supreme Court expressed uncertainty as to whether the statute of limitations would prevent Mrs. Kroger from refiling, Iowa had a savings statute which gave her 60 days following the dismissal to refile her action. By the time the Supreme Court issued the opinion we just read, Mrs. Kroger had moved and become a Texas citizen. Following the dismissal, Mrs. Kroger filed a new action against Owen. Because she was now of diverse citizenship from Owen, she filed in *federal court* in Iowa! The judgment in the original trial was for $230,000. Iowa law provides for interest to accrue from the time of injury and Mrs. Kroger ultimately settled the second suit for $250,000.

2. Compulsory Joinder (Necessary and Indispensable Parties)

a. Procedural Aspects

Haas v. Jefferson National Bank
442 F.2d 394 (5th Cir. 1971)

ALDISERT, CIRCUIT JUDGE.

* * *

Invoking jurisdiction on the basis of diversity of citizenship, 28 U.S.C. § 1332, Haas, a citizen of Ohio, sought a mandatory injunction from the district court directing the Jefferson National Bank, a citizen of Florida, to issue to him 169 1/2 shares of its common stock. Alternatively, he asked for damages reflecting the stock's value. He alleged a 1963 agreement with Glueck, also an Ohio citizen, under which they were to jointly purchase 250 shares of the bank's stock; the certificates were to issue in the name of Glueck but Haas was to have a one-half ownership of the shares. He also pleaded a similar 1966 agreement with Glueck to purchase 34 additional shares. According to Haas, he paid Glueck amounts representing one-half ownership, the bank had knowledge of his ownership interest, and the certificates and subsequent dividends were issued to Glueck.

CHAPTER 12 SCOPE OF LITIGATION — JOINDER AND SUPPLEMENTAL JURISDICTION

Haas contends, however, that in 1967 he requested Glueck to order the bank to issue certificates in Haas' name, reflecting his ownership of 169 1/2 shares, and that pursuant to this request Glueck presented to the bank properly endorsed certificates for 250 shares with instructions to reissue 170 shares to Haas and the balance to Glueck.

In its answer, the Bank explained that it had refused to make the assignment because at the time of the transfer request Glueck was indebted to it under the terms of a promissory note which required that Glueck pledge, assign, and transfer to the bank property of any kind owned by Glueck and coming into the possession of the Bank. The Bank averred that Glueck withdrew the transfer request and instead pledged the stock certificates with a second bank as collateral for a loan there.

* * *

Following the pre-trial conference * * *, the district court entered an order directing Haas to amend his complaint to join Glueck as a party. The court then denied his motion to dismiss Glueck as a party, and granted the Bank's motion to dismiss the amended complaint on the jurisdictional ground of incomplete diversity.

* * *

* * * [I]f the district court did not err in ordering the joinder of Glueck, it was obviously correct in finding a jurisdictional defect. It is clear beyond any doubt that the diversity statute requires complete diversity of citizenship. "The policy of the statute calls for its strict construction." It is of course immaterial that the nondiverse party has been required to be joined as an indispensable party. It is settled that failure of the district court to acquire jurisdiction over indispensable parties to an action deprives "the court of jurisdiction to proceed in the matter and render a judgment."

In approaching the dispositive question whether Rule 19 required the joinder of Glueck, we begin with the formulation of Shields v. Barrow, 58 U.S. 130, 139 (1854). Indispensable parties were defined as

> persons who not only have an interest in the controversy, but an interest of such a nature that a final decree cannot be made without either affecting that interest, or leaving the controversy in such a condition that its final termination may be wholly inconsistent with equity and good conscience.

As Mr. Justice Harlan declared in Provident Tradesmens Bank & Trust Co. v. Patterson, 390 U.S. 102, 124, [1968] the generalizations of *Shields* "are still valid today, and they are consistent with the requirements of Rule 19. * * * Indeed, the * * * *Shields* definition states, in rather different fashion, the criteria for decision announced in Rule 19(b)." It is essential, however, to bear in mind that the broad statements in *Shields* "are not a substitute for the analysis required by that Rule."

F. Overriding Plaintiff's Party Structure

* * *

The Rule * * * commands that we address ourselves to two broad questions: (1) Was Glueck a party "to be joined if feasible" under section (a)? If so, (2) was the court correct, under section (b), in dismissing the action or should it have proceeded without the additional party?

It is readily apparent that Glueck "falls within the category of persons who, under § (a), should be 'joined if feasible,'" *Provident Tradesmens Bank & Trust Co. v. Patterson*, for his presence is critical to the disposition of the important issues in the litigation. His evidence will either support the complaint or bolster the defense: it will affirm or refute Haas' claim to half ownership of the stock; it will substantiate or undercut Haas' contention that the Bank had knowledge of his alleged ownership interest; it will corroborate or compromise the Bank's contention that Glueck rescinded the transfer order; and it will be crucial to the determination of Glueck's obligation to the Bank under the promissory note. The essence of Haas' action against the Bank is that it "unlawfully and recklessly seized, detained, [and] exercised improper dominion" over his shares in transferring and delivering them to the second bank as collateral for Glueck's loan. Thus, Glueck becomes more than a key witness whose testimony would be of inestimable value. Instead he emerges as an active participant in the alleged conversion of Haas' stock.

Applying the criterion of Rule 19(a)(2)(ii), we believe that Glueck's absence would expose the defendant Bank "to a substantial risk of incurring double, multiple, or otherwise inconsistent obligations by reason of his claimed interest." If Haas prevailed in this litigation in the absence of Glueck and were adjudicated owner of half of the stock, Glueck, not being bound by res adjudicata, could theoretically succeed in later litigation against the Bank in asserting ownership of the whole. In addition, a favorable resolution of Haas' claim against the Bank could, under (a)(2)(i), "as a practical matter impair or impede [the absent party's] ability to protect [his] interest" in all of the shares — an interest that is at least apparent since all of the stock was issued in Glueck's name.

Because Glueck cannot be made a party without destroying diversity, however, it remains to be decided whether, under Rule 19(b), his presence is so vital that "in equity and good conscience the action * * * should be dismissed, the absent person being thus regarded as indispensable." This decision is always a matter of judgment and must be exercised with sufficient knowledge of the facts in order to evaluate the exact role of the absentees. As the Supreme Court has said:

> The decision whether to dismiss (i. e., the decision whether the person missing is "indispensable") must be based on factors varying with the different cases, some such factors being substantive, some procedural, some compelling by themselves, and some subject to balancing against opposing interests. Rule 19 does not prevent the assertion of compelling substantive interests; it merely commands the courts to examine each controversy to make certain that the interests really exist.

The spirit of the Rule is to depart from the tyranny of the old labels of "necessary" and "indispensable," and to solve each problem "in the context of particular litigation."

We turn now to the specific factors enumerated in Rule 19(b), as applied to the facts before us. In our view the first factor tracks the considerations of 19(a)(2)(ii) discussed above: "to what extent a judgment rendered in the person's absence might be prejudicial to him or those already parties." And based on the reasoning previously set forth, we believe this factor supplies weighty reason for a finding of indispensability.[6]

The second factor directs the court to consider the extent to which the shaping of relief might avoid or lessen the prejudice to existing or absent parties.[7] Because the title to the stock certificates, although not the immediate issue in this litigation, assumes such commanding importance, it is difficult to conceptualize a form of relief or protective provisions which would not require as a preliminary matter the determination of the question of title with all the resulting potential for prejudice.

In analyzing the third factor, "whether a judgment rendered in the person's absence will be adequate," Mr. Justice Harlan cautioned:

> [T]here remains the interest of the courts and the public in complete, consistent, and efficient settlement of controversies. We read the Rule's third criterion, whether the judgment issued in the absence of the nonjoined person will be "adequate," to refer to this public stake in settling disputes by wholes, whenever possible, for clearly the plaintiff, who himself chose both the forum and the parties defendant, will not be heard to complain about the sufficiency of the relief obtainable against them. * * *

It seems evident to us that the absence of Glueck in this litigation would, of necessity, result in less than a complete settlement of this controversy. For reasons already discussed, there is no semblance of a guarantee that a judgment on Haas' terms would settle the whole dispute generated by the facts here.

Finally Rule 19(b) requires us to consider whether the plaintiff will have an avenue for relief if the district court's dismissal for nonjoinder is affirmed.[8] Clearly, the state courts of Ohio afford plaintiff Haas an opportunity to adjudicate his rights against Glueck.[9] They provide a ready forum to settle the question of title to the stock. Moreover, assuming the disposition of the preliminary

---

[6] "The defendant may properly wish to avoid multiple litigation, or inconsistent relief, or sole responsibility for a liability he shares with another. * * * There is [also] the interest of the outsider * * *. Of course, since the outsider is not before the court, he cannot be bound by the judgment rendered. This means, however, only that a judgment is not res judicata as to, or legally enforceable against, a nonparty * * *. Instead, as Rule 19(a) expresses it, the court must consider the extent to which the judgment may 'as a practical matter impair or impede his ability to protect' his interest in the subject matter. * * *"

[7] Rule 19(b) also directs a district court to consider the possibility of shaping relief to accommodate these four interests. Commentators had argued that greater attention should be paid to this potential solution to a joinder stymie, and the Rule now makes it explicit that a court should consider modification of a judgment as an alternative to dismissal.

[8] "[T]he plaintiff has an interest in having a forum. Before the trial, the strength of this interest obviously depends upon whether a satisfactory alternative forum exists. * * *" See JAMES, CIVIL PROCEDURE, § 9.20 at 432 (1965):

> [T]he availability of the state court is a factor properly to be considered by the federal court in weighing the relative interests which will be affected by a ruling of indispensability. Even if the plaintiff's preference for the federal forum deserves the court's enthusiastic protection, the disappointment of that choice is not so great a hardship on the plaintiff as the foreclosing of all courts to him.

[9] In response to the court's inquiry at oral argument, Haas' counsel reported that a state action between Haas and Glueck is now pending.

question of title in the Ohio courts, it is not difficult to conceptualize circumstances permitting the possibility of a second action against the Bank in which the problem of nonjoinder will not be so acute.

Accordingly, applying Rule 19(b)'s "equity and good conscience test," we hold that the district court did not abuse its discretion in concluding that Glueck was an indispensable party and in dismissing this action.

Affirmed.

Temple v. Synthes Corp.
498 U.S. 5, 111 S. Ct. 315, 112 L. Ed. 263 (1990)

Per Curiam.

Petitioner Temple, a Mississippi resident [sic], underwent surgery in October 1986 in which a "plate and screw device" was implanted in his lower spine. The device was manufactured by respondent Synthes, Ltd. (U.S.A.) (Synthes), a Pennsylvania corporation. Dr. S. Henry LaRocca performed the surgery at St. Charles General Hospital in New Orleans, Louisiana. Following surgery, the device's screws broke off inside Temple's back.

Temple filed suit against Synthes in the United States District Court for the Eastern District of Louisiana. The suit, which rested on diversity jurisdiction, alleged defective design and manufacture of the device. At the same time, Temple filed a state administrative proceeding against Dr. LaRocca and the hospital for malpractice and negligence. At the conclusion of the administrative proceeding, Temple filed suit against the doctor and the hospital in Louisiana state court.

Synthes did not attempt to bring the doctor and the hospital into the federal action by means of a third-party complaint, as provided in Federal Rule of Civil Procedure 14(a). Instead, Synthes filed a motion to dismiss Temple's federal suit for failure to join necessary parties pursuant to Federal Rule of Civil Procedure 19. Following a hearing, the District Court ordered Temple to join the doctor and the hospital as defendants within 20 days or risk dismissal of the lawsuit. According to the court, the most significant reason for requiring joinder was the interest of judicial economy. The court relied on this Court's decision in Provident Tradesmens Bank & Trust Co. v. Patterson, 390 U.S. 102 (1968), wherein we recognized that one focus of Rule 19 is "the interest of the courts and the public in complete, consistent, and efficient settlement of controversies." When Temple failed to join the doctor and the hospital, the court dismissed the suit with prejudice.

Temple appealed, and the United States Court of Appeals for the Fifth Circuit affirmed. The court deemed it "obviously prejudicial to the defendants to have the separate litigations being carried on," because Synthes' defense might be that the plate was not defective but that the doctor and the hospital were negligent, while the doctor and the hospital, on the other hand, might claim that they were not negligent but that the plate was defective. The Court of Appeals found that the claims overlapped and that the District Court therefore had not abused its discretion in ordering joinder under Rule 19. * * *

In his petition for certiorari to this Court, Temple contends that it was error to label joint tortfeasors as indispensable parties under Rule 19(b) and to dismiss the lawsuit with prejudice for failure to join those parties. We agree. Synthes does not deny that it, the doctor, and the hospital are potential joint tortfeasors. It has long been the rule that it is not necessary for all joint tortfeasors to be named as defendants in a single lawsuit. Nothing in the 1966 revision of Rule 19 changed that principle. The Advisory Committee Notes to Rule 19(a) explicitly state that "a tortfeasor with the usual 'joint-and-several' liability is merely a permissive party to an action against another with like liability." There is nothing in Louisiana tort law to the contrary.

The opinion in *Provident Bank* does speak of the public interest in limiting multiple litigation, but that case is not controlling here. There, the estate of a tort victim brought a declaratory judgment action against an insurance company. We assumed that the policyholder was a person "who, under § (a), should be 'joined if feasible,'" and went on to discuss the appropriate analysis under Rule 19(b), because the policyholder could not be joined without destroying diversity. After examining the factors set forth in Rule 19(b), we determined that the action could proceed without the policyholder; he therefore was not an indispensable party whose absence required dismissal of the suit.

Here, no inquiry under Rule 19(b) is necessary, because the threshold requirements of Rule 19(a) have not been satisfied. As potential joint tortfeasors with Synthes, Dr. LaRocca and the hospital were merely permissive parties. The Court of Appeals erred by failing to hold that the District Court abused its discretion in ordering them joined as defendants and in dismissing the action when Temple failed to comply with the court's order. For these reasons, we grant the petition for certiorari, reverse the judgment of the Court of Appeals for the Fifth Circuit, and remand for further proceedings consistent with this opinion.

It is so ordered.

NOTES AND QUESTIONS

1. Rule 19 analysis proceeds in three steps, "although this fact is obscured by its language." Western Maryland R. Co. v. Harbor Ins. Co., 910 F.2d 960, 968 n. 5 (D.C. Cir. 1990). First, the court must assess whether the absentee is "needed for a just adjudication" under Rule 19(a)(1) or 19(a)(2). Traditionally, such absentees have been called *necessary* parties—persons who should be joined in the pending case. Although Rule 19 does not employ the term "necessary," it is commonly used in practice.

Second, if the absentee is "needed for a just adjudication," the court must assess whether her joinder is "feasible." The factors relevant here are whether service of process is possible, whether venue would be destroyed and, most significantly, whether joinder would destroy subject matter jurisdiction.

Third, if joinder is not feasible, the court must assess whether it should "in equity and good conscience" proceed with the litigation without the absentee or dismiss the pending case. This assessment is guided by the four factors in Rule 19(b). If the court decides that it should dismiss, the absentee is then labeled "indispensable." Thus, an *indispensable* party is one (1) who is "needed for a just adjudication," (2) whose joinder cannot be effectuated (because, for example, it would destroy subject matter jurisdiction) and (3) as to whose absence the court has determined that it should dismiss the pending case rather than run the risk of proceeding without her. See generally Richard Freer, *Rethinking Compulsory Joinder: A Proposal to Restructure Federal Rule 19*, 60 N.Y.U. L. REV. 1061, 1075-80 (1985).

Rule 19 prescribes a pragmatic *process*. The present version of the rule was part of a major amendment of related joinder rules in 1966, spearheaded by trenchant scholarly criticism of the prior practice. Geoffrey Hazard, *Indispensable Party: The Historical Origin of a Procedural Phantom*, 61 COLUM. L. REV. 1254 (1961); John Reed, *Compulsory Joinder of Parties in Civil Actions*, 55 MICH. L.REV. 327 (pt.1) & 483 (pt.2)(1957). In response to criticism, the amendments introduced reasoning for what had become a sometimes mindless exercise of slapping labels on absentees. Professor Wright explained the reasoning behind the current version of the rule aptly:

> Labels are not bad things in the law if they are understood for what they are, a shorthand way of expressing the result of a more complicated reasoning process. Labels become treacherous and misleading if they are applied as a substitute for reasoning. It is perfectly appropriate to say: "this absentee has such a strong interest in this case that it would be unjust to let it go to decision in his absence. Therefore we will refer to him as 'indispensable.'" It is not appropriate to say, as many courts seemed to do, that "this person is 'indispensable.' Therefore we will not let the case go to decision in his absence." The latter reasoning—or nonreasoning—suggests that absent parties wear labels indicating their relation to a controversy and obscures the pragmatic examination of all the circumstances that is required in the light of the very particular facts of a particular case.

WRIGHT, FEDERAL COURTS 496.

2. Let us return to the first step of the Rule 19 analysis. Note that Rule 19(a) gives three alternative reasons for compelling the joinder of an absentee, set out in Rule 19(a)(1), 19(a)(2)(i), and 19(a)(2)(ii). What are the three reasons? What interests are protected by each of the three?

(a) Rule 19(a)(1). In *Haas*, did Glueck satisfy Rule 19(a)(1)? Could the court accord "complete relief * * * among those already parties" if Glueck were not joined? This phrase seems to have two possible readings. First, it might mean that without Glueck, the court could not wrap up things between Haas and the bank. If that is the correct interpretation, will it ever be met? After all, the court is always in a position to determine the respective rights of those before it.

Second, the phrase might mean that without Glueck, the court could not wrap up things in some overall sense between all interested persons. If that is the correct interpretation, won't it always be met? Doesn't such a reading require joinder anytime there is an absentee who threatens multiple litigation? Some courts seem to suggest that the rule means exactly this, although even these courts do not rely exclusively upon Rule 19(a)(1) in ordering joinder. See, e.g., Prestenback v. Employers' Ins. Co., 47 F.R.D. 163 (E.D. La. 1969); Davila Mendez v. Vatican Shrimp Co., 43 F.R.D. 294 (S.D. Tex. 1966).

Because these two possible interpretations seem, respectively, either never or always met, Rule 19(a)(1) has had little, if any, independent impact in compelling joinder of absentees. The more important bases for joinder lie in Rule 19(a)(2). See Freer, supra, 60 N.Y.U. L. REV. at 1080-82.

(b) Rule 19(a)(2)(i). In *Haas*, what was Glueck's interest in the pending case? How would his ability to protect that interest have been impaired or impeded had the case gone to judgment without his joinder? Remember, as a nonparty, Glueck could not have been bound by claim or issue preclusion. Why not? That is why the rule speaks of "practical" (as opposed to "legal") impairment of the absentee's interest. Because Glueck thus would be free to sue the bank in a second proceeding, how can his interest be harmed?

Why would it be easier to conclude that Rule 19(a)(2)(i) was met if Haas had sought to have the Bank cancel Glueck's shares?

The fear of practical harm to the absentee underlies not only this rule, but intervention of right under Rule 24(a)(2) as well. It is also relevant in class actions.

(c) Rule 19(a)(2)(ii). In *Haas*, how did Glueck's absence threaten the bank with "a substantial risk of incurring double, multiple, or otherwise inconsistent obligations?" Remember that the bank could not use the judgment from the case by Haas as a defense to a second case by Glueck. Why not?

The rule defines harm to a party as subjecting her to multiple "obligations," not to multiple "litigation." For instance, suppose Plaintiff sues Airline for injuries sustained in a crash. Fifteen other injured passengers are not joined. Their nonjoinder certainly threatens Airline with multiple suits, some of which the plaintiff might win, others of which the plaintiff might lose. Does this possibility subject Airline to "double, multiple, or otherwise inconsistent obligations?" Apparently not. Most courts seem to feel that the rule does not refer to inconsistent monetary damages awards by successive plaintiffs. How did the potential harm to the bank in *Haas* differ from this?

The fear of subjecting someone to multiple or inconsistent obligations underlies not only this rule, but impleader and interpleader as well. It is also relevant in class actions.

F. Overriding Plaintiff's Party Structure

3. Analyze these cases under Rule 19.
  (a) Black firefighters sue City, alleging racial discrimination in granting promotions in the fire department. Among other things, they seek an order placing them ahead of some white firefighters on the promotion list. The white firefighters who would be displaced by this order are not joined. Are they "needed for a just adjudication?" See Martin v. Wilks, 490 U.S. 755 (1989).
  (b) Why are joint tortfeasors, such as the doctor and hospital in *Synthes*, not necessary parties under Rule 19(a)?
  (c) Plaintiff, representative of persons killed in the crash of a private airplane, sues the manufacturer of the aircraft for wrongful death. The crash may have been caused by the company that owned the plane or by the company that serviced it, but neither of these alleged joint tortfeasors is joined. Are they "needed for a just adjudication?" In Whyham v. Piper Aircraft Corp., 96 F.R.D. 557 (M.D. Pa. 1982), the district court concluded that joinder was required under Rule 19(a)(1), 19(a)(2)(i), *and* 19(a)(2)(ii). Especially after *Temple*, wasn't the court wrong on all three counts?
  (d) Owen contracts to sell his house to Paul. When Nina offers Owen more money, Owen breaches his contract with Paul and contracts with Nina. Paul sues Owen for specific performance. Is Nina a Rule 19(a) party? If so, and she cannot be joined, must the case be dismissed? If Paul sought damages instead of specific performance, could the suit proceed without joinder of Nina?

4. In *Temple*, the Supreme Court took the extraordinary step of reversing the Fifth Circuit's decision solely on the basis of the petition for certiorari. It had no briefing. It heard no oral argument. The justices agreed unanimously and issued a per curiam opinion.

5. The holding in *Temple* that joint tortfeasors are not necessary parties gives the plaintiff significant control over the structuring of such cases. Should the rules require a plaintiff to join all joint tortfeasors? What advantages and disadvantages would such a provision have?

b. Jurisdictional Aspects

Rule 19(a) purports to allow joinder only if, inter alia, "joinder will not deprive the court of jurisdiction over the subject matter of the action." As shown in *Haas*, courts have read this provision to preclude supplemental jurisdiction. If joinder would destroy diversity of citizenship, the court must consider whether to proceed or dismiss under Rule 19(b). Professor Fink long ago objected that the lack of supplemental jurisdiction put the court to this "cruel choice." Howard Fink, *Indispensable Parties and the Proposed Amendment to Federal Rule 19*, 74 YALE L.J. 403, 448 (1965).

One critical factor here is *alignment*. The party proposing to join an absentee under Rule 19 will suggest whether she is to join as a plaintiff or a defendant. This suggestion is not binding, and the court always has the authority to realign the absentee on that side of the dispute with which her interests are most compatible. This realignment may affect subject matter jurisdiction. Suppose the plaintiff is a citizen of New Hampshire and the defendant is a citizen of Vermont, and the absentee to be joined is also a citizen of Vermont. If the absentee is aligned as a defendant, jurisdiction is unaffected. If she is aligned as a plaintiff, however, diversity is destroyed. This power is consistent with the court's power to realign parties at the outset of a diversity of citizenship case.

The absence of supplemental jurisdiction in compulsory joinder seems to be an historical accident. The Supreme Court decided a seminal compulsory joinder case—Shields v. Barrow, 58 U.S. 130 (1855)—just six years before its first major recognition of supplemental jurisdiction—Freeman v. Howe, 65 U.S. 450 (1861). In *Shields*, the Court assumed that a nondiverse absentee could not be joined. The two doctrines simply never intersected as they grew.

Does the supplemental jurisdiction statute change this historic limitation? Remember that § 1367(a) grants supplemental jurisdiction to the full extent of the Constitution and that § 1367(b) cuts it back in certain situations in diversity of citizenship cases. Virtually everyone agrees that claims by or against a party "needed for a just adjudication" would fall within the *Gibbs* test for same case or controversy; thus, the only question is whether § 1367(b) removes that jurisdiction.

NOTES AND QUESTIONS

1. How would § 1367 operate on the facts of *Haas*? Glueck would be joined as a defendant, but has the same citizenship as the plaintiff. Clearly, § 1367(b) denies supplemental jurisdiction over claims asserted by an absentee who is joined as a plaintiff under Rule 19. Because that statute says nothing about claims by a Rule 19 defendant, however, some commentators feel that § 1367 expands the use of supplemental jurisdiction by permitting it in cases such as *Haas*, where the absentee is joined as a defendant. Stephen Burbank, Thomas Rowe & Thomas Mengler, *Compounding or Creating Confusion About Supplemental Jurisdiction? A Reply to Professor Freer*, 40 EMORY L.J. 943, 957 (1991). Thus, they assert, a Rule 19 defendant who is a citizen of the same state as the plaintiff can be joined under § 1367.

Note, however, that § 1367(b) denies supplemental jurisdiction to claims by the original plaintiff against a Rule 19 defendant. So apparently the nondiverse Rule 19 defen-

F. Overriding Plaintiff's Party Structure

dant can be joined, but the plaintiff cannot assert a claim against her. Noting this, some criticize the statute by asking whether it makes sense to join the absentee at all. Thomas Arthur & Richard Freer, *Grasping at Burnt Straws: The Disaster of the Supplemental Jurisdiction Statute*, 40 EMORY L.J. 963, 966-72 (1991).

Can the Rule 19 defendant assert a claim against the nondiverse plaintiff? What would that claim be? We would usually think of it as a counterclaim. But in view of plaintiff's inability to assert a claim against her, how could the defendant's claim be a counterclaim?

2. If the absentee is needed for a just adjudication but her joinder is not feasible, the court decides whether to proceed or dismiss under Rule 19(b). The four factors listed in Rule 19(b) seem redundant of the Rule 19(a)(1) and Rule 19(a)(2) factors, but is there a difference in their thrust?

Note also that the Rule 19(b) factors are neither exclusive nor arranged hierarchically. In practice, however, courts often treat the fourth factor as especially important. It is concerned with whether the plaintiff would have a remedy if the case were dismissed. In other words, is there an alternative forum to which plaintiff can go and effect joinder of all interested parties, including the absentee? Note the discussion of this factor in *Haas*. Because state courts do not need to worry about diversity of citizenship, that alternative forum will almost invariably be a state court. Does dismissal by the federal court in these circumstances constitute an abdication of their responsibility to decide cases properly invoking diversity of citizenship jurisdiction?

3. The availability of other joinder devices may obviate the need to do a full Rule 19 analysis. For example, suppose the defendant complains that nonjoinder of her fellow tortfeasor subjects her to Rule 19(a)(2)(ii) harm because she might be subjected to full liability and later lose a contribution case against the fellow tortfeasor. Rather than address the question under Rule 19, it seems appropriate for the court to point out to the defendant that she can avoid the perceived harm by impleading the fellow tortfeasor under Rule 14(a).

4. The court can raise Rule 19 problems sua sponte. Read Rule 19(c), which is intended to put the court in a position to do so. Unfortunately, it has not worked, because lawyers rarely comply with Rule 19(c). Does counsel's failure to list absentees under Rule 19(c) violate Rule 11?

Thus, the most likely user of Rule 19 will be the defendant. Why is it more likely that she will do so in Rule 19(a)(2)(ii) cases rather than in Rule 19(a)(2)(i) cases? If the potential harm is to the absentee, why (besides altruism) would the defendant raise the issue to the court? She is more likely to do so if joinder of the absentee is not feasible, because then she might possibly get the case dismissed under Rule 19(b). A defendant wanting to join an absentee would make a motion to join her under Rule 19. A defendant wanting to have the case dismissed for nonjoinder of the absentee would move for dismissal under Rule 12(b)(7). See Scott Paper Co. v. National Cas. Co., 151 F.R.D. 577, 579 (E.D. Pa. 1993)(discussing incentives for defendant to raise issue of nonjoinder of absentee).

5. What if the defendant does not raise the nonjoinder issue in a Rule 19(a)(2)(i) case? As we now see, the absentee can protect herself.

6. Do you agree with the court in *Haas* that Glueck should have been aligned as a defendant? Can you articulate an argument for aligning him as a plaintiff? If he had been aligned as a plaintiff, could the court have joined him?

7. Some federal courts recognize an exception to Rule 19(b), refusing to dismiss "public rights" cases for nonjoinder of what would be seen as indispensable parties. Such cases frequently involve citizens' challenge to governmental action. Courts often conclude that such cases ought to proceed even though a judgment might affect absentees. Professor Carl Tobias criticizes this exception in *Rule 19 and the Public Rights Exception to Party Joinder*, 65 N.C. L. REV. 745 (1987).

3. Intervention

a. Procedural Aspects

Read Rule 24. It defines the circumstances in which an absentee can attempt to join a pending case. Thus, it permits an absentee to override the party structure plaintiff chose for the suit.

Note that there are two types of intervention: of right and permissive. As you see from the rule, either type may be granted by statute. The most important of these statutes allow the United States to intervene to protect a government interest. For instance, 28 U.S.C. § 2403 requires notification of the Attorney General and intervention by the United States in any case "wherein the constitutionality of any Act of Congress affecting the public interest is drawn in question."* (Note how Rule 24(c) facilitates the operation of this statute.)

Rule 24 also allows intervention of both types in circumstances not addressed by statute. Note the breadth of the provision for permissive intervention under Rule 24(b)(2). By definition, such intervenors have no "right" to be in the action. Indeed, they could not even be joined as proper parties under Rule 20. (By way of review, why is this so?) How does this test for intervention compare with the test for consolidation of separate actions?

---

* Interestingly, the statute was not followed when the Supreme Court questioned the constitutionality of the Rules of Decision Act in *Erie R.R. v. Tompkins*. Some commentators conclude that this fact should have required the Court to order reargument. 3B MOORE'S FEDERAL PRACTICE at 24-22 n. 1.

Does permissive intervention serve the same purpose as consolidation? Obviously, the court addressing a motion for permissive intervention must weigh the benefits of allowing participation against the disruption and delay caused by the intervention. Such motions are vested in the sound discretion of the district judge, who is guided, at least in theory, by the fact that denial of the motion will not prejudice the absentee. (Why not?)

Intervention of right under Rule 24(a)(2) is more interesting. It has roots in Roman law, which allowed one to enter a case if he "consider[ed] that his interest will be affected [by judgment in that case]." Dalrymple v. Dalrymple, 2 Hagg. Con. Rep. 137 (1811), quoted in 3B MOORE'S FEDERAL PRACTICE ¶ 24.03. Rather than invoking the discretion of the district judge, intervention of right thus serves to avoid harm to the absentee. Note how Rule 24(a)(2) addresses this notion of prejudice to the absentee. It is functionally identical to one of the bases for joining an absentee under Rule 19. (Which one?)

Atlantis Development Corp. v. United States
379 F.2d 818 (5th Cir. 1967)

JOHN R. BROWN, CIRCUIT JUDGE.

This case involves a little bit of nearly everything — a little bit of oceanography, a little bit of marine biology, a little bit of the tidelands oil controversy, a little bit of international law, a little bit of latter day Marco Polo exploration. But these do not command our resolution since the little bits are here controlled by the less exciting bigger, if not big, problem of intervention. The District Court declined to permit mandatory intervention as a matter of right or to allow intervention as permissive. As is so often true, a ruling made to avoid delay, complications, or expense turns out to have generated more of its own. With the main case being stayed by the District Court pending this appeal, it is pretty safe to assume that the case would long have been decided on its merits (or lack of them) had intervention of either kind been allowed. And this seems especially unfortunate since it is difficult to believe that the presence of the attempted intervenor would have added much to the litigation. All of this becomes the more ironic, if not unfortunate, since the intervenor [Atlantis Development Corporation, Ltd., a Bahamian corporation — EDS.] and the Government sparring over why intervention ought or ought not to have been allowed, each try to persuade us the one was bound to win, the other lose on the merits which each proceeds to argue as though the parties were before or in the court. Adding to the problem, or perhaps more accurately, aiding in the solution of it, are the mid-1966 amendments to the Federal Rules of Civil Procedure including specifically those relating to intervention. We reverse.

What the jousting is all about is the ownership in, or right to control the use, development of and building on a number of coral reefs or islands comprising Pacific Reef, Ajax Reef, Long Reef, an unnamed reef and Triumph Reef which the intervenor has called the "Atlantis Group" because of the name given them by Anderson, its predecessor in interest and the supposed discoverer. Discovery in the usual sense of finding a land area, continent or island heretofore unknown could hardly fit this case. For these reefs are, and have been for years, shown on Coast and Geodetic Charts and, more important, they are scarcely 4 1/2 miles off Elliott Key and 10 miles off the Coast of the Florida Mainland. Although the depth of water washing over them at mean low water is likely one of the factual controversies having some possible significance, it seems undisputed that frequently and periodically the bodies of these reefs become very apparent especially in rough seas when the rock or the top surface of the rock becomes plainly visible in the troughs of the seas. Just how or in what manner these reefs were "discovered" is so far unrevealed. Some time in 1962 William T. Anderson discovered the reefs apparently by conceiving the idea of occupying them through the construction of facilities for fishing club, marina, skin diving club, a hotel, and, perhaps as the chief lure, a gambling casino. Anderson made some sort of claim to it and with facilities unavailable to the adventurous explorers of the long past, he gave public notice of this in the United States and in England by newspaper advertisements in late 1962 and early 1963. These "rights" were acquired by Atlantis Development Corporation, Ltd., the proposed intervenor. Reflecting the desire manifested now by the persistent efforts to intervene to have legal rights ascertained in a peaceful fashion through established tribunals and not by self-help or the initiation of physical activities which would precipitate counter moves, physical or legal, or both, Atlantis (and predecessors) patiently sought permission from all governmental agencies, state and federal — just short of the United Nations — but to no avail. The State of Florida through the Trustees of the Internal Improvement Fund responding to a formal request stated that the property is "outside the Constitutional Boundaries of the State of Florida and therefore, not within the jurisdiction of the T.I.I.F." Undaunted, Atlantis turned to the Federal Government. To these entreaties the Department of Interior on September 14, 1962, replied: "The Department of the Interior has no jurisdiction over land that is outside the territorial limits of the United States. Questions concerning such land should be taken up with the Department of State." This was soon echoed by the answer of the Department of State on November 9, 1962, through the Assistant Legal Advisor. "The areas in question are outside of the jurisdiction of the United States and constitute a part of the high seas. The high seas are open to all nations and no state may validly subject any part of them to its sovereignty. * * *" Subsequently, Atlantis spent approximately $50,000 for surveys and the construction of four prefabricated buildings, three of which were destroyed by a hurricane in September 1963. Thereafter upon learning that the United States Corps of Engineers was asserting that permission was needed to erect certain structures on two of the reefs, Triumph and Long Reef, Atlantis commenced its long, but unrewarding, efforts either to convince the Corps of Engineers, the United States Attorney General, or both, that the island reefs were beyond the jurisdiction of United States control or to initiate litigation which would allow a judicial, peaceful resolution. The Engineers ultimately reaffirmed the earlier decision to require permits. In December 1964 on learning that the defendants in the main case had formally sought a permit from the Engineers, Atlantis notified the Government of its claim to ownership of the islands and the threatened unauthorized actions by the defendants. This precipitated further communications with the Department of Justice with Atlantis importuning, apparently successfully, the Government to initiate the present action.

It was against this background that the litigation commenced. The suit is brought by the United States against the main defendants [Acme General Contractors, Inc., and J. H. Coppedge Company, each Florida corporations, and Louis M. Ray, a resident of Dade County, Florida]. The complaint was in two counts seeking injunctive relief. In the first the Government asserted that Triumph and Long Reefs are part of the bed of the Atlantic Ocean included in the Outer Continental Shelf subject to the jurisdiction, control and power of disposition of the United States. The action of the defendants in the erection of caissons on the reefs, the dredging of material from the seabed, and

F. Overriding Plaintiff's Party Structure

the depositing of the dredged material within the caissons without authorization was charged as constituting a trespass on government property. In the second count the Government alleged that the defendants were engaged in the erection of an artificial island or fixed structure on the Outer Continental Shelf in the vicinity of the reefs without a permit from the Secretary of the Army in violation of the Outer Continental Shelf Lands Act, 43 U.S.C.A. § 1333(f) and 33 U.S.C.A. § 403. Denying that the complaint stated a claim, F.R.Civ.P. 12(b), the defendants besides interposing general denial asserted that the Secretary of the Army lacks jurisdiction to require a permit for construction on the Outer Continental Shelf and that the District Court lacks jurisdiction since the reefs and the defendants' actions thereon are outside the territorial limits of the United States. As thus framed, the issues in the main case are whether (1) the District Court has jurisdiction of subject matter, (2) the defendants are engaged in acts which constitute a trespass against government property, and (3) the defendants' construction activities without a permit violate 43 U.S.C.A. § 1333(f) and 33 U.S.C.A. § 403.

Atlantis seeking intervention by proposed answer and cross-claim against the defendants admitted the jurisdiction of the District Court. It asserted that the United States has no territorial jurisdiction, dominion or ownership in or over the reefs and cannot therefore maintain the action for an injunction, and that conversely Atlantis has title to the property by discovery and occupation. In the cross-claim, Atlantis charged the defendants as trespassers against it. Appropriate relief was sought by the prayer.

The District Court without opinion declared in the order that intervenor "does not have such an interest in this cause as will justify its intervention, either as a matter of right or permissively." Leave was granted to appear amicus curiae.

We think without a doubt that under former F.R.Civ.P. 24(a), intervention as a matter of right was not compelled under (a)(2). * * *

This brings us squarely to the effect of the 1966 Amendments and the new F.R.Civ.P. 24(a). * * *

In assaying the new Rule, several things stand out. * * * [T]he revision was a coordinated one to tie more closely together the related situations of joinder, F.R.Civ.P. 19, and class actions, F.R.Civ.P. 23.

As the Advisory Committee's notes reflect, there are competing interests at work in this area. On the one hand, there is the private suitor's interests in having his own lawsuit subject to no one else's direction or meddling. On the other hand, however, is the great public interest, especially in these explosive days of ever-increasing dockets, of having a disposition at a single time of as much of the controversy to as many of the parties as is fairly possible consistent with due process.

In these three Rules the Advisory Committee, unsatisfied with the former Rules which too frequently defined application in terms of rigid legal concepts such as joint, common ownership, res judicata, or the like, as well as court efforts in applying them, deliberately set out on a more pragmatic course. For the purposes of our problem, this course is reflected in the almost, if not quite, uniform language concerning a party who claims an interest relating to the subject of the action and is so situated that the disposition of the action may as a practical matter impair or impede his ability to protect that interest * * *.

Although this is question-begging and is therefore not a real test, this approach shows that the question of whether an intervention as a matter of right exists often turns on the unstated question of whether joinder of the intervenor was called for under new Rule 19. Were this the controlling inquiry, we find ample basis here to answer it in the affirmative. Atlantis — having formally informed the Government in detail of its claim of ownership to the very reefs in suit, that the defendants were trespassing against it, and having successfully urged the Government to institute suit against the defendants — seems clearly to occupy the position of a party who ought to have been joined as a defendant under new Rule 19(a)(2)(i). * * *

* * * [W]e think that both from the terms of new Rule 24(a) and its adoption of 19(a)(2)(i) intervention of right is called for here. Of course F.R.Civ.P. 24(a)(2) requires both the existence of an interest which may be impaired as a practical matter and an absence of adequate representation of the intervenor's interest by existing parties. There can be no difficulty here about the lack of representation. On the basis of the pleadings, Atlantis is without a friend in this litigation. The Government turns on the defendants and takes the same view both administratively and in its brief here toward Atlantis. The defendants, on the other hand, are claiming ownership in and the right to develop the very islands claimed by Atlantis.

Nor can there be any doubt that Atlantis "claims an interest relating to the property or transaction which is the subject of the action." The object of the suit is to assert the sovereign's exclusive dominion and control over two out of a group of islands publicly claimed by Atlantis. This identity with the very property at stake in the main case and with the particular transaction therein involved (the right to build structures with or without permission of the Corps of Engineers) is of exceptional importance. For 24(a)(2) is in the conjunctive requiring both an interest relating to the property or transaction and the practical harm if the party is absent. This sharply reduces the area in which stare decisis may, as we later discuss, supply the element of practical harm.

This brings us then to the question whether these papers reflect that in the absence of Atlantis, a disposition of the main suit may as a practical matter impair or impede its ability to protect that interest — its claim to ownership and the right to control, use and develop without hindrance from the Government, the Department of Defense, or other agencies. Certain things are clear. Foremost, of course, is the plain proposition that the judgment itself as between Government and defendants cannot have any direct, immediate effect upon the rights of Atlantis, not a party to it.

But in a very real and practical sense is not the trial of this lawsuit the trial of Atlantis' suit as well? Quite apart from the contest of Atlantis' claim of sovereignty vis-a-vis the Government resulting from its "discovery" and occupation of the reefs, there are at least two basic substantial legal questions directly at issue, but not yet resolved in any Court at any time between the Government and the defendants which are inescapably present in the claim of Atlantis against the Government. One is whether these coral reefs built up by accretion of marine biology are "submerged lands" under the Outer Continental Shelf Lands Act, 43 U.S.C.A. § 1331 et seq. The second basic question is whether, assuming both from the standpoint of geographical location and their nature they constitute "lands," does the sovereignty of the United States extend to them with respect to any purposes not included in or done for the protection of the "exploring for, developing, removing, and transporting * * *" natural resources therefrom, 43 U.S.C.A. § 1333(a)(1). Another, closely related, is whether the authority of the Secretary of the Army to prevent obstruction of navigation extended by § 1333(f) to "artificial islands and fixed structures," includes structures other than those "erected thereon for the purpose of exploring for, developing, removing, and transporting" mineral resources therefrom. * * *

F. Overriding Plaintiff's Party Structure

* * *

If in its claim against the defendants in the main suit these questions are answered favorably to the Government's position, the claim of Atlantis for all practical purposes is worthless. That statement assumes, of course, that such holding is either approved or made by this Court after an appeal to it and thereafter it is either affirmed, or not taken for review, on certiorari. It also assumes that in the subsequent separate trial of the claim of Atlantis against the Government the prior decision would be followed as a matter of stare decisis. Do these assumptions have a realistic basis? Anyone familiar with the history of the Fifth Circuit could have but a single answer to that query. This Court, unlike some of our sister Circuit Courts who occasionally follow a different course, has long tried earnestly to follow the practice in which a decision announced by one panel of the Court is followed by all others until such time as it is reversed, either outright or by intervening decisions of the Supreme Court, or by the Court itself en banc. That means that if the defendants in the main action do not prevail upon these basic contentions which are part and parcel of the claim of Atlantis, the only way by which Atlantis can win is to secure a rehearing en banc with a successful overruling of the prior decision or, failing in either one or both of those efforts, a reversal of the earlier decision by the Supreme Court on certiorari. With the necessarily limited number of en banc hearings in this Circuit and with the small percentage of cases meriting certiorari, it is an understatement to characterize these prospects as formidable.

That is but a way of saying in a very graphic way that the failure to allow Atlantis an opportunity to advance its own theories both of law and fact in the trial (and appeal) of the pending case will if the disposition is favorable to the Government "as a practical matter impair or impede [its] ability to protect [its] interest." That is, to be sure, a determination by us that in the new language of 24(a)(2) stare decisis may now — unlike the former days under 24 (a)(2) — supply that practical disadvantage which warrants intervention of right. It bears repeating, however, that this holding does not presage one requiring intervention of right in every conceivable circumstance where under the operation of the Circuit's stare decisis practice, the formidable nature of an en banc rehearing or the successful grant of a writ of certiorari, an earlier decision might afford a substantial obstacle. We are dealing here with a conjunction of a claim to and interest in the very property and the very transaction which is the subject of the main action. When those coincide, the Court before whom the potential parties in the second suit must come must itself take the intellectually straight forward, realistic view that the first decision will in all likelihood be the second and the third and the last one. Even the possibility that the decision might be overturned by en banc ruling or reversal on certiorari does not overcome its practical effect, not just as an obstacle, but as the forerunner of the actual outcome. In the face of that, it is "as a practical matter" a certainty that an absent party seeking a right to enter the fray to advance his interest against all or some of the parties as to matters upon which he is for all practical purposes shortly to be foreclosed knows the disposition in his absence will "impair or impede his ability to protect that interest, * * *." F.R.Civ.P. 24(a)(2).

Reversed.

NOTES AND QUESTIONS

1. In *Atlantis*, the court notes the drafters' intent to mesh Rules 19(a)(2)(i) and 24(a)(2). Why should two rules use virtually identical language? Who uses each Rule? See John Kennedy, *Let's All Join In: Intervention Under Federal Rule 24*, 57 KY. L.J. 329 (1969).

2. Would Glueck have had a right to intervene into the pending proceeding in *Haas*, supra at 679? Should the absentee's ability to intervene under Rule 24(a)(2) lead a court to deny Rule 12(b)(7) dismissal? Suppose P sues D and that A, a nonparty, satisfies both Rule 19(a)(2)(i) and 24(a)(2). Suppose further that A cannot be joined because the court lacks personal jurisdiction over her. Should the court deny D's Rule 12(b)(7) motion because A could protect herself by intervening?

3. What three things must be established to grant intervention of right under Rule 24(a)(2)? Of those three, which two are also required for compulsory joinder under Rule 19(a)(2)(i)? How significant is the one difference between Rule 24(a)(2) and Rule 19(a)(2)(i)? Should intervention of right require a greater showing than joinder under Rule 19(a)(2)(i)? Although there was some early confusion, it now seems clear that the intervenor assumes the burden of showing that the extant parties do not adequately represent her interests. According to the Supreme Court, however, this burden is "minimal." Trbovich v. United Mine Workers, 404 U.S. 528, 538 n.10 (1972). It seems to be met simply by showing that the parties have different interests from the intervenor. 3B MOORE'S FEDERAL PRACTICE 24-70. In *Atlantis*, how did the intervenor's interest differ from the plaintiff's? How did it differ from the defendants'?

4. *Atlantis* is one of the very rare cases in which stare decisis constitutes a harm of the type needed to invoke Rule 24 or Rule 19. Note the care with which Judge Brown circumscribes the holding in this regard. Other opinions, even of the same court, have not been as careful. Consider these facts. Insurer insured Development Co. for various casualty and other risks. Development Co.'s airplane crashed, killing several people, whose representatives would eventually sue for wrongful death. Insurer sues Development Co., seeking a declaration that its policy does not cover the plane crash. The representatives of the decedents were not joined. Under the policy, they had the right to sue Insurer directly or to proceed against Development Co.

On these facts, the court in Ranger Ins. Co. v. United Housing of New Mexico, Inc., 488 F.2d 682 (5th Cir. 1974), held that the representatives of decedents satisfied the harm test of Rule 19(a)(2)(i) (and, perforce, Rule 24(a)(2)). Specifically, it felt that stare decisis might apply to determine the representatives' later suits against Insurer if Ranger won its case against Development Co. How is this fact pattern significantly different from that in *Atlantis*? Wouldn't a holding that stare decisis barred a suit by the representatives

F. Overriding Plaintiff's Party Structure

against Insurer violate due process? Most courts have been appropriately parsimonious in finding stare decisis to be a harm under Rule 24 or Rule 19. See, e.g., Ionian Shipping Co. v. British Law Ins. Co., 426 F.2d 186, 191 (2d Cir. 1970).

5. On its face, Rule 24 does not *require* someone who could intervene to do so. Refusal to intervene can create duplicative litigation though. Noting this, Justice Harlan once suggested (as to an absentee who was a witness at trial in a case but who refused to exercise his right to intervene) that the absentee might be estopped from suing separately. Provident Tradesmens Bank & Trust Co. v. Patterson, 390 U.S. 102, 114 (1968). The Supreme Court subsequently rejected this notion in Martin v. Wilks, 490 U.S. 755 (1989).

In *Martin*, black firefighters sued a city, alleging racial discrimination in hiring and promotion. The action resulted in a consent decree ordering promotion of some blacks over some white firefighters. The white firefighters knew of the pendency of the action, but eschewed their clear right to intervene under Rule 24(a)(2). Instead, they sued separately to challenge the consent decree, and the Court held that they could not be bound by the judgment in the prior case. The Court emphasized the interrelation between Rules 19 and 24, noting that the parties to the first case should have joined the white firefighters under Rule 19.

> Joinder as a party, rather than knowledge of a lawsuit and an opportunity to intervene, is the method by which potential parties are subject to the jurisdiction of the court and bound by a judgment. * * * The parties to a lawsuit presumably know better than anyone else the nature and scope of relief sought in the action, and at whose expense such relief might be granted. It makes sense, therefore, to place on them a burden of bringing in additional parties where such a step is indicated, rather than placing on potential additional parties a duty to intervene when they acquire knowledge of the lawsuit.

490 U.S. at 765 (footnote omitted).

6. Obviously, an absentee's ability to intervene is worthless if she does not know of the pendency of the case. In *Atlantis*, as in many cases, the intervenor is fully aware of the litigation. If she is not, however, how can she protect her interest? Read Rule 19(c). The Advisory Committee Report to the 1966 Amendments to that rule suggested that the court contact such absentees identified under Rule 19(c) and notify them of their right to intervene.

Does such notification from the court to a nonparty accord with your view of the court's role? Under what circumstances does Rule 19(c) envision the court's giving notice to a nonparty? Should the parties play a role in notifying the absentee? Should they be prohibited from notifying the absentee?

7. Note that any petition for intervention—of right or permissive—must be "timely." The Rule provides no set time frame for determining timeliness. A representative, albeit nonexclusive, catalogue of relevant factors includes: (1) how long the intervenor knew of her interest before moving to intervene, (2) whether the intervenor's delay will prejudice an extant party, (3) whether denial of intervention will prejudice the absentee, and (4) any unusual circumstances affecting a finding of timeliness. Farmland Dairies v. Commissioner of the New York State Dept. of Agric. & Mkts., 847 F.2d 1038, 1044 (2d Cir. 1988).

Courts generally agree that the timeliness standard should be applied less strictly in intervention of right than in permissive intervention. See, e.g., Fiandaca v. Cunningham, 827 F.2d 825, 832 (1st Cir. 1987). Why should this be so?

8. Not all cases of potential harm to the absentee are as clear as *Atlantis*. Indeed, the difficulty of fathoming the distinction between intervention of right and permissive intervention in some situations, among other things, leads Professor Gene Shreve to question the distinction altogether. Instead, he would favor a rule making all motions for intervention discretionary. Gene Shreve, *Questioning Intervention of Right: Toward a New Methodology of Decisionmaking*, 74 Nw. L. Rev. 894 (1980). Do you agree?

9. Rule 24(c) details the procedure for intervening. The absentee must make a motion — even under Rule 24(a)(2) — and file the appropriate pleading. In *Atlantis*, the absentee sought to join on the defendant's side and proffered an answer in intervention as well as cross-claims against its co-defendants. A plaintiff-intervenor would make the motion, supported by a complaint in intervention. If the court grants intervention, the intervenor becomes a party to the litigation, with all the rights and responsibilities that status entails. In contrast, nonparties sometimes ask for permission to file "amicus curiae" ("friend of the court") briefs setting forth their analysis of an issue before the court. One who files an amicus brief is not a party to the litigation.

10. As we will see in Chapter 14, litigants usually cannot appeal until the trial court has entered a final judgment disposing of the entire case. Nonetheless, federal courts traditionally have allowed immediate appeal of a denial of an absentee's motion to intervene of right. See Wright, Federal Courts 547. As Judge Brown noted in *Atlantis*, such immediate appeal can delay resolution of the underlying case.

b. Jurisdictional Aspects

As always, the court must assess whether a claim joined under the federal rules is supported by subject matter jurisdiction. If a plaintiff-intervenor asserts a federal question claim or a defendant-intervenor defends a federal question claim by the plaintiff, there is, obviously, subject matter jurisdiction. The same is true in a nonfederal claim if the plaintiff-intervenor is of diverse citizenship from all defendants and has a claim in excess of $50,000 or if the defendant-intervenor is of diverse citizenship from all plaintiffs and defends a claim in excess of $50,000.*

But what if there is no such independent basis of subject matter jurisdiction? Traditionally, supplemental jurisdiction supported claims by or against intervenors of right. The reasoning is that if an absentee is so closely related to the fray that her interest may be impeded, her claim (or the claim against her) will share a common nucleus of operative fact with the underlying suit. Thus, under *Gibbs*, the claim by or against the intervenor of right would form part of the same constitutional case or controversy already before the court. See, e.g., Curtis v. Sears, Roebuck & Co., 754 F.2d 781 (8th Cir. 1985).

As to claims by or against permissive intervenors, the tendency has been to reject supplemental jurisdiction. After all, the test of "common question" does not require the same degree of closeness with the underlying case as *Gibbs* required. Some claims involving permissive intervenors, however, would satisfy *Gibbs*. Consider, for example, an intervenor who would satisfy Rule 24(a)(2) except that her interest is adequately represented by existing parties.

The availability of supplemental jurisdiction under Rule 24(a)(2) led to an anomalous situation. Recall that joinder is precluded under Rule 19 if it destroys diversity of citizenship; in such an event the court must proceed or dismiss the entire case under Rule 19(b). Recall also that the operative language of Rule 19(a)(2)(i) and Rule 24(a)(2) is identical. Suppose an absentee will face harm of the type contemplated by these rules, but that her joinder will destroy diversity of citizenship. Rule 19 will not facilitate joinder, because it does not carry supplemental jurisdiction, but Rule 24 will, because it does. Thus, the same absentee in the same situation can be joined under one rule but not the other. Ultimately, joinder depends upon who raises the issue.

Most commentators addressing this issue before Congress passed the supplemental jurisdiction statute, § 1367, recommended that supplemental jurisdiction be expanded to the Rule 19 context. See, e.g., George Fraser, *Ancillary Jurisdiction of Federal Courts of Persons Whose Interest May Be Impaired if Not Joined*, 62 F.R.D. 483, 485-87 (1974); Freer, supra, 60 N.Y.U. L. REV. at 1101-09; Kennedy, supra, 57 KY. L.J. at 362-63. Congress resolved the anomaly the other way, however, when it codified supplemental jurisdiction in 28 U.S.C. § 1367. See also Joan Steinman, *Postremoval Changes in the Party Structure of Diversity Cases: The Old Law, the New Law, and Rule 19*, 38 U. KAN. L. REV. 864, 950 (1990).

---

* As noted above, the intervenor chooses which side of the dispute to enter on. As with Rule 19, the court is free to realign her if it feels that her interests more closely approximate those of the other side.

NOTES AND QUESTIONS

1. Apply § 1367(b) to the following. In each, P, a citizen of California, has sued D, a citizen of Florida, in federal court for $500,000. A is the absentee who seeks to intervene. Let us assume that she, as the absentees in *Atlantis* and *Haas*, would satisfy Rule 24(a)(2).

   (a) Suppose A is a citizen of Florida and would intervene as a plaintiff. What part of §1367(b) precludes supplemental jurisdiction over her claim?

   (b) Suppose A is a citizen of California and would intervene as a defendant. Nothing in §1367(b) seems to prohibit her joinder.

   (i) But can the plaintiff assert a claim against her?

   (ii) After intervening, can A assert a claim against P? What would that claim be called? Can it be a counterclaim if P cannot assert a claim against A? If A can assert a claim against P, can P respond with a compulsory counterclaim? Wouldn't such a claim be prohibited because it is a claim by a plaintiff against one joined under Rule 24?

   (c) Suppose A is a citizen of Florida and would properly be aligned as a plaintiff. Nonetheless, she intervenes as a defendant. May she thus avoid the bar in §1367(b) over claims by absentees who "seek to intervene as plaintiffs?" In Colonial Penn Ins. Co. v. American Centennial Ins. Co., 1992 U.S. Dist. LEXIS 17552 (S.D. N.Y. 1992), the court, sua sponte, realigned the plaintiff-intervenor as a defendant and thus avoided the stricture of the statute. Is this decision sound?

2. After wrestling with questions such as these, several scholars have criticized the supplemental jurisdiction statute's removing of supplemental jurisdiction in intervention of right. See 1 MOORE'S FEDERAL PRACTICE ¶ 0.67 at 700.201; 7C WRIGHT & MILLER, FEDERAL PRACTICE AND PROCEDURE: CIVIL § 1917 (Supp. 1994); Freer, supra, 40 EMORY L.J. at 476-78; McLaughlin, supra, 24 ARIZ. ST. L.J. at 960-61; Oakley, supra, 24 U.C. DAVIS L. REV. at 765-66.

Other commentators disagree. They defend the statute as creating a modest change that brings consistency to the treatment of the area. Rowe, Burbank & Mengler, supra, 40 EMORY L.J. at 956.

CHAPTER 13

SPECIAL MULTIPARTY LITIGATION: INTERPLEADER AND THE CLASS ACTION

A. Introduction and Integration

Starting a new chapter does not mean abandoning a theme. The materials in this chapter build upon the preceding chapter on joinder and supplemental jurisdiction. Here we consider two specialized types of group litigation. Each presents some of the same policy issues underlying those joinder rules that permit parties or the court to override the plaintiff's choice of party joinder. In addition, each presents significant issues relating to litigation management and some interesting jurisdictional problems.

B. Interpleader

1. Background

Interpleader resolves conflicting claims to a tangible res or fund of money. It is instituted by the *stakeholder*, who, as the name implies, is in possession of the res (sometimes called the "stake"). In "true," or "pure" interpleader, the stakeholder is "disinterested," which means she does not claim to own the res. In a proceeding "in the nature of interpleader," however, the stakeholder does claim to own the disputed property. In either event, the stakeholder is aware that others claim ownership of the stake. Rather than engage in successive litigation with each potential claimant, interpleader allows the stakeholder to force all *claimants* into a single proceeding. Thus, interpleader serves the same policies—efficiency and avoidance of inconsistent results—as impleader under Federal Rule 14(a) and joinder of a necessary party under Federal Rule 19(a)(2)(ii).

> The advantages of such a device are both manifest and manifold. A many-sided dispute is settled economically and expeditiously within a single proceed-

ing; the stakeholder is not obliged to determine at his peril which claimant has the rightful claim, and is shielded against the possible multiple liability flowing from inconsistent and adverse determinations of his liability to different claimants in separate suits.

3A MOORE'S FEDERAL PRACTICE ¶ 22.02[1], at 22-4-22-4.

Interpleader litigation proceeds in two stages. First, the stakeholder files the action and joins the claimants. The only issue facing the court at this point is whether interpleader is proper. If so, the stakeholder usually deposits the res with the court and the case then proceeds to the second stage, in which the claimants litigate the ownership of the res. If the case is one of "true" interpleader, the stakeholder does not participate in the second stage. If it is "in the nature of interpleader," the stakeholder does participate as a claimant.

Although most courts regard interpleader as an equitable proceeding, it was first used in the common law courts and "crossed over" into equity centuries ago in England. See generally Geoffrey Hazard & Myron Moskovitz, *An Historical and Critical Analysis of Interpleader*, 52 CALIF. L. REV. 706 (1964). The characterization remains important because it affects the availability of a jury trial. As we saw in Chapter 10, the Seventh Amendment guarantees a jury in actions at law, but not in suits at equity. What do we do in interpleader, which has a history of both? The answer depends upon the stage of the interpleader proceeding. It is clear that there is no right to a jury trial in the first stage. See, e.g., Odum v. Penn Mutual Life Ins. Co., 288 F. 2d 744 (5th Cir. 1961). In the second stage however, most courts recognize a right to jury trial under a typical Seventh Amendment analysis. We will see how one court addressed this issue below.

Because interpleader involves claims to the ownership of a res, courts could have treated it as quasi-in-rem for purposes of personal jurisdiction. Under that view, as we saw in Chapter 2, a court's jurisdiction over the stake would give it authority to determine the relative claimants' interests to the res. In New York Life Ins. Co. v. Dunlevy, 241 U.S. 518 (1916), however, the Supreme Court rejected this contention, and held that an interpleader court must have in personam jurisdiction over the claimants. *Dunlevy* thus imposed a substantial limitation on the usefulness of interpleader.

In *Dunlevy*, New York Life held an insurance policy having a surrender value of approximately $2,500. The insured, Joseph Gould, claimed that it was his. His daughter, Effie Dunlevy, claimed that it was hers because Joseph had assigned the proceeds to her. In addition, a Pittsburgh department store claimed it (or at least a portion thereof) to satisfy a judgment it had recovered against Effie. New York Life instituted interpleader in a state court in Pittsburgh. Although that court lacked in personam jurisdiction over Effie (who had moved to California) it held that the fund belonged to Joseph. Effie then sued New York Life in California, asserting that it had wrongfully paid the proceeds to Joseph and seeking $2,500. The lower courts held in Effie's favor. The Supreme Court affirmed, holding that the Pittsburgh interpleader proceeding did not bind Effie, because that court lacked in personam jurisdiction over her. Thus, the Court required that New York Life pay twice on a single policy. As some observers note:

> This meant that if the claimants of money due under an insurance policy live in different states (as they often do), a state court ordinarily would be impotent to grant effective relief since no state can get service on all claimants. The insurance company, however, is usually answerable to suit in each state where a claimant lives so that it is vulnerable to separate suits, which increases the possibility of double liability.

JAMES, HAZARD & LEUBSDORF, CIVIL PROCEDURE 553.

In reaction to *Dunlevy*, Congress passed the Federal Interpleader Act in 1917. In its present form, the Act is codified at 28 U.S.C. §§ 1335, 1397 and 2361. Of these provisions, § 1335 is an express grant of federal subject matter jurisdiction. A proceeding under the Federal Interpleader Act is usually called *statutory interpleader*.

In addition to (or in lieu of) statutory interpleader, a stakeholder can rely on any of the regular bases of federal subject matter jurisdiction discussed in Chapter 4 and join conflicting claimants under Federal Rule 22. Commonly, the stakeholder using Rule 22 will proceed under diversity of citizenship jurisdiction under 28 U.S.C. § 1332(a)(2), establishing that she is of diverse citizenship from all claimants and that the amount in controversy exceeds $50,000. A proceeding under Rule 22 is usually called *rule interpleader*.

2. The Two Types of Interpleader in Federal Court

Thus, in federal court, there are two mechanisms for invoking interpleader. Review and compare the provisions for statutory interpleader (28 U.S.C. §§ 1335, 1397, and 2361) and rule interpleader (Rule 22) before considering this case.

Pan American Fire & Casualty Co. v. Revere
188 F. Supp. 474 (E.D. La. 1960)

WRIGHT, DISTRICT JUDGE.

On February 3, 1960, a tragic highway accident occurred near Covington, Louisiana. A large tractor and trailer collided head-on with a bus carrying school children. The bus driver and three of the children were killed and 23 others were injured, some very seriously. A few moments later, compounding the disaster, another collision occurred between two cars following the bus. Having stopped in time to avoid ramming the disabled bus obstructing the highway, the first of the following vehicles was struck from the rear by the other, and John Wells, a passenger in the lead car, was injured.

Alleging that three suits against it have already been filed and that numerous other claims have been made, the tractor's liability insurer has instituted this interpleader action, citing all potential claimants. It asks that they be enjoined from initiating legal proceedings elsewhere or further prosecuting the actions already filed and that they be directed to assert their claims in the present suit. Plaintiff has deposited a bond in the full amount of its policy limits, $100,000, and avers that "it has no interest" in these insurance proceeds, being merely "a disinterested stakeholder." On the other hand, the Company denies liability toward any and all claimants. This apparently contradictory position is explained by the statement of its counsel, incorporated in the record as an amendment to the complaint, that plaintiff "has no further claim" on the sum deposited with the court, but cannot technically admit "liability" since that would amount to a concession that its assured was negligent and expose him to a deficiency judgment. [This refers to the possibility that the insured would be personally liable for claims that exceed the amount of his insurance.—EDS.]

The only question presented at this stage of the proceeding is whether, under the circumstances outlined, the remedy of interpleader is available to the insurer. * * *

1. *Jurisdiction.* * * * Plaintiff here invokes both the Interpleader Act and Rule 22 of the Federal Rules of Civil Procedure and alleges diversity of citizenship as a basis for federal jurisdiction.

Considering that four deaths and many serious injuries are involved and that the fund to be distributed is $100,000, the usual jurisdictional amount requirement for diversity suits applicable to an action under the Rule is clearly satisfied. A fortiori, the $500 amount stipulated in the Act is present.

* * * [S]ufficient diversity exists in this instance for an action under either provision. Plaintiff is a citizen of Texas with its principal place of business in that state, while one defendant, Wells, is a citizen of Wisconsin and all the others are Louisiana residents [sic]. Thus, the normal requirement of complete diversity between plaintiff on the one hand and defendants on the other is satisfied. This is viewed as sufficient to support jurisdiction for interpleader under Rule 22. As for the Act, the only requirement, at least for true interpleader, is diversity between some of the defendant claimants, the citizenship of the plaintiff stakeholder being immaterial. The joinder of the Wisconsin resident [sic] together with the Louisiana claimants satisfies this condition. And even if [this] rule * * * does not apply here on the ground that this is not a strict interpleader but rather an action "in the nature of interpleader" in which the plaintiff's citizenship is relevant, sufficient diversity exists since there is both "normal" diversity between the plaintiff and all defendants under § 1332 and "interpleader diversity" between at least two co-claimants.

* * *

4. *Exposure to Multiple Liability.* Though the Interpleader Act makes no such requirement, Rule 22 apparently permits interpleader only if the claims "are such that the plaintiff is or may be exposed to double or multiple liability." In theory at least, this is not necessarily the same thing as exposure to double or multiple vexation on a single obligation. There may be situations in which the debtor, though harassed by many suits on account of one transaction, is never in danger of being compelled to pay the same debt twice. Indeed, here, the argument is advanced that because it has

fixed the limits of its liability in its policy, the insurer is not exposed to multiple liability no matter how many claims are filed, and, therefore, is not entitled to maintain interpleader, at least under the Rule.

* * * The key to the clause requiring exposure to "double or multiple liability" is in the words "may be." The danger need not be immediate; any possibility of having to pay more than is justly due, no matter how improbable or remote, will suffice. At least, it is settled that an insurer with limited contractual liability who faces claims in excess of his policy limits is "exposed" within the intendment of Rule 22, and we need go no further to find the requirement satisfied here.

* * *

7. *Unliquidated Tort Claims as Justifying Interpleader.* Over and above the technical obligations already disposed of, the argument is advanced that interpleader is not an appropriate method of adjudicating unliquidated tort claims. Such a bald proposition might be rejected summarily were it not for the startling fact that there appears to be no precedent in the federal courts for granting interpleader in the present situation. The matter must be examined closely.

At the outset, it seems clear that interpleader will lie when there are several tort claimants who have obtained judgments which aggregate more than the amount of the policy. Indeed, in that case it can make no difference whether the claims originated in tort or contract. Moreover, it is settled that interpleader is available to an insurer whose policy is insufficient to satisfy contract claims, though they have not been reduced to judgment. Why, then, should the remedy be denied to a blameless insurer faced with excessive tort claims? Three reasons have been suggested: (1) As to quantum, at least, tort claims are more conjectural than contract claims; (2) since it is not directly liable to the claimants, the insurer's exposure as to tort claims is "remote" until they have been reduced to judgment; and (3) tort claims "are peculiarly appropriate for jury trial," which would have to be denied under the equitable practice of interpleader.

The effect of the first objection is only this: that it is more difficult in the case of tort claims to determine whether the aggregate will exceed the policy limits so as to render the claimants "adverse" and expose the insurer to "multiple liability." It may be that there are few cases in which this result can be reasonably anticipated, but, clearly, this is one of them.

The second objection * * * is no better. Indeed, under the "may be exposed" clause of Rule 22 and the "may claim" clause of the Interpleader Act, it would not seem to matter how remote the danger might be. But, in any event, prematurity is no defense under the peculiar Louisiana law which allows a direct action against the automobile liability insurer.

8. *Jury Trial.* On the theory that the resort to equity defeats the right of trial by jury, it has been said that once interpleader is granted all issues in the case must be tried to the judge alone. There is, however, eminent authority to the contrary, including Judge Learned Hand, Professor Chafee, and Professor Moore, who hold that legal issues arising in an interpleader action can be tried before a jury. Whatever may be the right solution in another case, here it seems clear that the questions of liability and damages ought to be put to a jury. * * * Nothing in Rule 22 or the Interpleader Act opposes such a procedure. Indeed, the provision of the Federal Rules which permits separate trial of distinct issues invites this solution. Thus, there can be no objection to granting interpleader here on the ground that Seventh Amendment rights are thereby denied. Each claimant can be given a full opportunity to prove his case before a jury, reserving to the court only

CHAPTER 13   SPECIAL MULTIPARTY LITIGATION: INTERPLEADER AND THE CLASS ACTION

the task of apportioning the fund between those who are successful if the aggregate of the verdicts exceeds the amount of the insurance proceeds.

9. *Enjoining of Other Proceedings.* Usually interpleader will not be really effective unless all claimants are brought before the same court in one proceeding and restricted to that single forum in the assertion of their claims. To accomplish that end, absent voluntary self-restraint on the part of all interested parties, it is of course essential that the interpleader court enjoin the institution or prosecution of other suits on the same subject matter elsewhere. Immediately, the question arises whether Section 2283 of Title 28 of the Code presents an obstacle to enjoining state court proceedings.

* * * [T]hat section prohibits a federal court from interfering with a pending state court action except in three situations: (1) Where such a course is "expressly authorized by Act of Congress"; (2) where the issuance of an injunction by the federal court is "necessary in aid of its jurisdiction"; and (3) where the court's action is required "to protect or effectuate its judgments." Clearly, the first exception is applicable to a suit brought under the Interpleader Act since that statute expressly empowers the court to enjoin the claimants "from instituting or prosecuting any proceeding in any State or United States court affecting the property, instrument or obligation involved in the interpleader action * * *." But the exception does not apply to an action under Rule 22, for the quoted provision authorizing stay orders is restricted to statutory interpleader. If state court proceedings can be enjoined when interpleader is brought under the Rule it must be by virtue of the second exception in Section 2283.

The question whether the court entertaining a non-statutory interpleader suit may enjoin state court proceedings on the same issues on the theory that it is "necessary in aid of its jurisdiction" is not free from doubt. * * * [E]very indication is that, regardless of the Interpleader Act, the power of a federal court to enjoin pending state court proceedings in a case like this one will be sustained. Certainly the result is desirable, if not indispensable. If the court had no power to enjoin concurrent state court proceedings, the grant of interpleader would often create more problems than it solved.

10. *Venue and Service of Process.* It has been demonstrated thus far that, except as to strictly jurisdictional matters, the requirements for interpleader under Rule 22 and under the Interpleader Act are identical, and that the present action could be maintained under either provision. But there are two procedural limitations on actions under the Rule which become important whenever the claimants are not all within the territorial jurisdiction of the district court. The first is that the only proper venue for the suit when the defendants do not all reside in the same state is the residence of the plaintiff [this was true at the time this case was decided; the current version of § 1391 does not permit venue to be laid where the plaintiff resides—EDS.]; the second, that process cannot run beyond the boundaries of the state in which the court sits. These restrictions are of course waivable, but if objection is raised by the affected defendant, they usually form an absolute bar to the action. Thus, here, if Rule 22 alone were applicable, absent a waiver of venue by Wells, the suit would have to be instituted at the plaintiff's domicile in Texas, and none of the defendants could be validly served unless they were found in that state.

But the situation is different when jurisdiction exists under the statute, for the Interpleader Act specially provides that the action may be commenced in any district where one defendant resides and that process will run throughout the United States. Unfortunately, these exceptional rules apply only to statutory interpleader. The present suit, then, is maintainable only under the

Interpleader Act unless the Wisconsin defendant waives venue and voluntarily appears or is found in Louisiana.

11. *Conclusion.* Although, because of the venue and service problems just recited, Rule 22 is not available, the court clearly has jurisdiction of the action under the Interpleader Act. Accordingly, the prayer for interpleader will be granted, without, however, discharging the plaintiff who is contractually bound to resist the demands. Injunctions will issue restraining all parties from further prosecuting any pending suits against plaintiff or its assured on account of the accident described, or from instituting like proceedings before this or any other court. All defendants will be required to enter their claims by way of answer in this action within thirty days from notice of this judgment. Thereafter, upon timely demand by any one of the parties, the court will order a joint jury trial of all the claims upon the issues of liability and damages. In the event the aggregate of the verdicts should exceed the amount of plaintiff's liability, the court reserves unto itself the task of apportioning the insurance proceeds in such manner as it deems just.

The motion to dismiss will be denied.

NOTES AND QUESTIONS

1. Note the two important differences for invoking federal jurisdiction under statutory interpleader and under rule interpleader.

(a) Because rule interpleader generally invokes federal jurisdiction through diversity of citizenship under 28 U.S.C. § 1332(a)(1), it must comport with the complete diversity requirement of *Strawbridge v. Curtiss*. Statutory interpleader, on the other hand, invokes federal jurisdiction under § 1335, which repeals *Strawbridge* in such cases, allowing jurisdiction based upon "minimal" diversity. Exactly what language of § 1335 does so?

(b) In addition, rule and statutory interpleader focus on different litigants for determining whether there is diversity of citizenship. Under Rule 22, who has to be of diverse citizenship from whom? Under the statute, who has to be of diverse citizenship from whom?

2. Is the provision for statutory interpleader jurisdiction based upon "minimal" diversity constitutional? The answer depends upon whether the complete diversity rule of *Strawbridge* was based upon the diversity statute or Article III. Most observers felt that Chief Justice John Marshall engaged only in statutory, not constitutional, interpretation in *Strawbridge*. In 1967, the Supreme Court made this clear, holding that the Constitution permits jurisdiction based upon minimal diversity of citizenship, and therefore statutory interpleader is constitutional. That case, State Farm Fire & Cas. Co. v. Tashire, 386 U.S. 523 (1967), is important for other points as well, as we will see below.

CHAPTER 13 SPECIAL MULTIPARTY LITIGATION: INTERPLEADER AND THE CLASS ACTION

3. Based upon the differences in subject matter jurisdiction, assess which kind of interpleader, if either, could be invoked in the following:
   (a) Stakeholder is an insurance company incorporated in Delaware with its principal place of business in Connecticut. It issued a $100,000 automobile policy insuring Anna, a citizen of New York. After an accident, potential claimants to the policy fund are Anna, Betty (a citizen of Delaware), and Claudia (a citizen of Arizona).
   (b) Would the supplemental jurisdiction statute, 28 U.S.C. § 1367, permit the case in (a) to proceed under rule interpleader?
   (c) Same facts as in (a) except that Anna, Betty and Claudia are all citizens of Nevada.
   (d) Same facts as in (c) except the stake at issue is worth $45,000. Why can neither rule nor statutory interpleader be used here?
   (e) In (d), suppose Stakeholder contended that it was entitled to keep the funds because Anna breached the contract. Can you fashion an argument that statutory interpleader should be available?

4. As *Pan American* also makes clear, service of process rules differ between rule and statutory interpleader. Again, because rule interpleader is simply a diversity of citizenship case, the standard rules we addressed in Chapter 3 apply, including the territorial limitations imposed by Federal Rule 4. Under statutory interpleader, though, a district court may issue process for service in "the respective districts where the claimants reside or may be found." 28 U.S.C. § 2361. Thus, the court can exercise nationwide service of process in statutory interpleader.

Suppose, for example, that Stakeholder institutes a statutory interpleader proceeding in federal district court in Maine. One of the claimants to be joined is a citizen of Hawaii, who has never left that state. Because statutory interpleader allows nationwide service of process, the district court in Maine can exercise personal jurisdiction over the Hawaiian. This is so even though that claimant has no contacts with Maine (let alone minimum contacts under *International Shoe*). How, then, can the provision for nationwide service of process be constitutional? (Remember that *International Shoe* and all the cases in Chapter 2 regarding due process limitations on personal jurisdiction addressed the authority of *state* courts). See supra at 61.

5. Compare the two types of interpleader in these additional ways:
   (a) *Amount in controversy.* Under either the rule or statute, "[t]he total amount to be distributed is the amount in controversy, and supports jurisdiction though individual claims may be for less than this amount." WRIGHT, FEDERAL COURTS 535.

(b) *Venue.* Is the statutory provision in § 1397 additional to the general venue provision of § 1391(a), or in lieu thereof? Will it matter in most cases? Under § 1391(a)(2), note that "[t]here is considerable room for speculation—and no case law—on where the claim arises in an action for interpleader." WRIGHT, FEDERAL COURTS 536 n.36.

(c) *Deposit of the res.* Is it required? If not, does the court have discretion to order it? Why might a stakeholder prefer not to deposit the res?

6. Consider how much less useful interpleader would be if the interpleader court could not enjoin others from litigating their claims in other proceedings. Statutory interpleader, of course, expressly provides for such injunctions against parties to state or federal court proceedings. 28 U.S.C. § 2361. Rule interpleader has no similar provision. Nonetheless, most courts agree with Judge Wright's assessment in *Pan American*, and conclude that an such an injunction is "necessary in aid of [the] jurisdiction" of the interpleader court. Thus, it satisfies an exception to the anti-injunction statute, 28 U.S.C. § 2283. See, e.g., General Railway Signal Co. v. Corcoran, 921 F.2d 700 (7th Cir. 1991). In addition, after conclusion of the federal action, a permanent injunction would be proper "to protect or effectuate [the] judgments" of the interpleader court, thereby satisfying another exception to § 2283.

7. What if Stakeholder does not sue first? For example, assume that Stakeholder is in possession of a diamond watch that she found in her house and claims it under a finder's statute. Claimant-1 is the previous owner of the house, and argues that the watch is hers because she left it there. Claimant-2 is a former houseguest of Stakeholder, who claims that she left the watch in the house. Claimant-3 is an insurance company, which claims that it has reimbursed Claimant-1 for the loss of the watch, and thus that it is entitled to it.

Instead of Stakeholder's acting first, however, suppose Claimant-1 sues Stakeholder, naming no other parties, and seeking return of the watch. Can Stakeholder force the joinder of Claimants 2 and 3 through interpleader *in the pending case*? In other words, can a defendant invoke interpleader?

Rule 22 expressly provides that she can. The statute is silent on the point. Nonetheless, Federal Rule 13(h), which applies in statutory interpleader as well as any other case in federal court, allows the addition of parties to a counterclaim if, inter alia, the persons being joined would satisfy Rule 19. See, e.g., Bauer v. Uniroyal Tire Co., 630 F.2d 1287 (8th Cir. 1980); Dove v. Massachusetts Mut. Life Ins. Co., 509 F. Supp. 248 (N.D. Ga. 1981). Why, by definition, do absentee claimants in the interpleader situation satisfy Rule 19? More specifically, why are they always going to satisfy Rule 19(a)(2)(ii)? See generally 3A MOORE'S FEDERAL PRACTICE ¶ 22.15.

Thus, in either statutory or rule interpleader, the defendant-stakeholder could use Rule 13(h) to join the claimants to an interpleader proceeding. But she may have another option as well. Because the nonjoinder of the claimants threatens her with multiple or inconsistent obligations, she could seek compulsory joinder under Rule 19(a)(2)(ii). This overlap of joinder rules is not surprising; again, Rule 19(a)(2)(ii) and interpleader are different devices for raising the same concerns. That does not mean, of course, that they are always available in all cases. With its provision for jurisdiction based upon minimal diversity among claimants, statutory interpleader may be available in cases in which Rule 19 would not work because joinder would destroy diversity.

Suppose, for example, that Plaintiff is a citizen of New York and Defendant (the Stakeholder) is a citizen of Maryland. Absentee claimants are citizens of New York, Maryland, and California. Defendant could interplead the absentees under statutory interpleader, because at least one claimant is of diverse citizenship from one other. She could not join the absentees under Rule 19, however, because the Maryland claimant's joinder would destroy diversity of citizenship. This possibility raises an interesting litigation tactic for Defendant in these cases. If she likes the forum in which she is sued, she can use interpleader to have all claims resolved in a single proceeding there. If she does not like the forum, however, she might seek dismissal under Rule 12(b)(7) by claiming that the absentee-claimants are indispensable.

8. Would the counterclaim under Rule 13(h) be compulsory? It seems clear that since Claimant-1 sued Stakeholder for the same res that is the subject of the interpleader, it should be. Technically, then, Stakeholder files a Rule 13(a) compulsory counterclaim in interpleader against Claimant-1, to which she joins Claimants 2 and 3 as additional parties under Rule 13(h). Because of this relationship, would the counterclaim in interpleader invoke supplemental jurisdiction? The answer seems to be yes. For an interesting discussion, see 6247 Atlas Corp. v. Marine Ins. Co., 155 F.R.D. 454 (S.D. N.Y. 1994). Indeed, Professor Chafee even discussed this possibility over half a century ago. See Zecchariah Chafee, Jr., *Interpleader in the United States Courts*, 41 YALE L.J. 1134, 1145 et seq. (1931). Does anything in the supplemental jurisdiction statute, 28 U.S.C. § 1367, appear to the contrary?

9. Historically, equity courts imposed four significant limitations on interpleader. First, they required that the claimants vie for the same debt. Second, the claims had to share a common origin. Third, the stakeholder could not be interested, that is, she could not claim ownership of the stake. And fourth, the stakeholder could owe no independent liability to any of the claimants. See 3A MOORE'S FEDERAL PRACTICE ¶ 22.11.

Rule 22 and statutory interpleader expressly abolish the first three of these equitable requirements, albeit with language of varying clarity. For example, regarding the third requirement, Rule 22 clearly provides that there is no problem if the stakeholder avers that she is not liable to any claimant. The statute does the same thing by providing for proceedings "in the nature of interpleader." 28 U.S.C. § 1335(a). On the other hand, neither the rule nor the statute expressly addresses the fourth requirement. Although some earlier opinions disagree, the majority of courts conclude that this equity limitation has been abolished as well. See, e.g., Companion Life Ins. Co. v. Schaffer, 442 F. Supp. 826 (S.D. N.Y. 1977). Thus, interpleader can proceed even if the stakeholder is independently liable to one of the claimants.

Of course, the states are free to determine their own rules for interpleader, or whether to permit the procedure at all. Thus, the traditional equitable limitations on interpleader may still exist in some states. See, e.g., Midland National Life Ins. Co. v. Emerson, 174 S.E. 2d 211 (Ga. App. 1970)(interested stakeholder cannot proceed with equitable interpleader; legislation permits "interpleader at law" rejecting this rule).

10. Judge John Skelly Wright authored the opinion in *Pan American* while serving as a federal district judge in Louisiana. President Kennedy appointed him to the United States Court of Appeals for the District of Columbia Circuit in 1962, where he enjoyed a long and distinguished career as one of the nation's leading appellate judges. Such an appointment is somewhat unusual. The more customary course is for a district judge to be elevated to the court of appeals in which her district is located. For Judge Wright, this would have been the Fifth Circuit. If there is no vacancy on the "local" circuit, however, a president might not be able to elevate a capable judge. Thus, some presidents appoint judges from other parts of the country to the D.C. Circuit. Indeed, by statute, judges of every court of appeals except the District of Columbia Circuit must reside in the circuit for which they are appointed. 28 U.S.C. § 44(b).

3. The Limits of Interpleader to Avoid Duplicative Litigation

State Farm Fire & Casualty Co. v. Tashire
386 U.S. 523, 87 S. Ct. 1199, 18 L. Ed. 2d 270 (1967)

MR. JUSTICE FORTAS delivered the opinion of the Court.

Early one September morning in 1964, a Greyhound bus proceeding northward through Shasta County, California, collided with a southbound pickup truck. Two of the passengers aboard the bus were killed. Thirty-three others were injured, as were the bus driver, the driver of the truck and its lone passenger. One of the dead and 10 of the injured passengers were Canadians; the rest of the individuals involved were citizens of five American States. The ensuing litigation led to the present case, which raises important questions concerning administration of the interpleader remedy in the federal courts.

The litigation began when four of the injured passengers filed suit in California state courts, seeking damages in excess of $1,000,000. Named as defendants were Greyhound Lines, Inc., a California corporation; Theron Nauta, the bus driver; Ellis Clark, who drove the truck; and Kenneth Glasgow, the passenger in the truck who was apparently its owner as well. Each of the individual defendants was a citizen and resident of Oregon. Before these cases could come to trial and before other suits were filed in California or elsewhere, petitioner State Farm Fire & Casualty Company, an Illinois corporation, brought this action in the nature of interpleader in the United States District Court for the District of Oregon.

In its complaint State Farm asserted that at the time of the Shasta County collision it had in force an insurance policy with respect to Ellis Clark, driver of the truck, providing for bodily injury liability up to $10,000 per person and $20,000 per occurrence and for legal representation of Clark in actions covered by the policy. It asserted that actions already filed in California and others which it anticipated would be filed far exceeded in aggregate damages sought the amount of its maximum liability under the policy. Accordingly, it paid into court the sum of $20,000 and asked the court (1) to require all claimants to establish their claims against Clark and his insurer in this single proceeding and in no other, and (2) to discharge State Farm from all further obligations under its policy — including its duty to defend Clark in lawsuits arising from the accident. Alternatively, State Farm expressed its conviction that the policy issued to Clark excluded from coverage accidents resulting from his operation of a truck which belonged to another and was being used in the business of another. The complaint, therefore, requested that the court decree that the insurer owed no duty to Clark and was not liable on the policy, and it asked the court to refund the $20,000 deposit.

Joined as defendants were Clark, Glasgow, Nauta, Greyhound Lines, and each of the prospective claimants. Jurisdiction was predicated upon 28 U.S.C. § 1335, the federal interpleader statute, and upon general diversity of citizenship, there being diversity between two or more of the claimants to the fund and between State Farm and all of the named defendants. [At the time, the diversity of citizenship statute required an amount in controversy in excess of only $10,000, which was met by deposit of the $20,000 fund—EDS.]

An order issued, requiring the defendants to show cause why they should not be restrained from filing or prosecuting "any proceeding in any state or United States Court affecting the property or obligation involved in this interpleader action, and specifically against the plaintiff and the defendant Ellis D. Clark." Personal service was effected on each of the American defendants, and registered mail was employed to reach the 11 Canadian claimants. Defendants Nauta, Greyhound, and several of the injured passengers responded, contending that the policy did cover this accident and advancing various arguments for the position that interpleader was either impermissible or inappropriate in the present circumstances. Greyhound, however, soon switched sides and moved that the court broaden any injunction to include Nauta and Greyhound among those who could not be sued except within the confines of the interpleader proceeding.

When a temporary injunction along the lines sought by State Farm was issued by the United States District Court for the District of Oregon, the present respondents moved to dismiss the action * * *. After a hearing, the court declined to dissolve the temporary injunction * * *. The injunction was later broadened to include the protection sought by Greyhound, but modified to permit the filing — although not the prosecution — of suits. The injunction, therefore, provided that all suits against Clark, State Farm, Greyhound, and Nauta be prosecuted in the interpleader proceeding.

On * * * appeal, the Court of Appeals for the Ninth Circuit reversed. The court found it unnecessary to reach respondents' contentions relating to service of process and the scope of the injunction, for it concluded that interpleader was not available in the circumstances of this case. It held that in States like Oregon, which do not permit "direct action" suits against insurance companies until judgments are obtained against the insured, the insurance companies may not invoke federal interpleader until the claims against the insured, the alleged tortfeasor, have been reduced to judgment. Until that is done, said the court, claimants with unliquidated tort claims are not "claimants" within the meaning of § 1335, nor are they "persons having claims against the plaintiff" within the meaning of Rule 22 of the Federal Rules of Civil Procedure.[3] In accord with that view, it directed dissolution of the temporary injunction and dismissal of the action. Because the Court of Appeals' decision on this point conflicts with those of other federal courts, and concerns a matter of significance to the administration of federal interpleader, we granted certiorari. Although we reverse the decision of the Court of Appeals upon the jurisdictional question, we direct a substantial modification of the District Court's injunction for reasons which will appear.

I

[Here the Court upheld the constitutionality of the provision of § 1335 for jurisdiction based upon minimal diversity among claimants. We discussed this point supra at 171.]

II

We do not agree with the Court of Appeals that, in the absence of a state law or contractual provision for "direct action" suits against the insurance company, the company must wait until persons asserting claims against its insured have reduced those claims to judgment before seeking to invoke the benefits of federal interpleader. That may have been a tenable position under the 1926 and 1936 interpleader statutes. These statutes did not carry forward the language in the 1917 Act authorizing interpleader where adverse claimants "may claim" benefits as well as where they "are claiming" them. In 1948, however, in the revision of the Judicial Code, the "may claim" language was restored. Until the decision below, every court confronted by the question has concluded that the 1948 revision removed whatever requirement there might previously have been that the insurance company wait until at least two claimants reduced their claims to judgments. The commentators are in accord.

Considerations of judicial administration demonstrate the soundness of this view which, in any event, seems compelled by the language of the present statute, which is remedial and to be liberally construed. Were an insurance company required to await reduction of claims to judgment,

---

[3] We need not pass upon the Court of Appeals' conclusions with respect to the interpretation of interpleader under Rule 22, which provides that "(1) Persons having claims against the plaintiff may be joined as defendants and required to interplead when their claims are such that the plaintiff is or may be exposed to double or multiple liability...." First, as we indicate today, this action was properly brought under § 1335. Second, State Farm did not purport to invoke Rule 22. Third, State Farm could not have invoked it in light of venue and service of process limitations.* * *

the first claimant to obtain such a judgment or to negotiate a settlement might appropriate all or a disproportionate slice of the fund before his fellow claimants were able to establish their claims. The difficulties such a race to judgment pose for the insurer, and the unfairness which may result to some claimants, were among the principal evils the interpleader device was intended to remedy.

III

The fact that State Farm had properly invoked the interpleader jurisdiction under § 1335 did not, however, entitle it to an order both enjoining prosecution of suits against it outside the confines of the interpleader proceeding and also extending such protection to its insured, the alleged tortfeasor. Still less was Greyhound Lines entitled to have that order expanded so as to protect itself and its driver, also alleged to be tortfeasors, from suits brought by its passengers in various state or federal courts. Here, the scope of the litigation, in terms of parties and claims, was vastly more extensive than the confines of the "fund," the deposited proceeds of the insurance policy. In these circumstances, the mere existence of such a fund cannot, by use of interpleader, be employed to accomplish purposes that exceed the needs of orderly contest with respect to the fund.

There are situations, of a type not present here, where the effect of interpleader is to confine the total litigation to a single forum and proceeding. One such case is where a stakeholder, faced with rival claims to the fund itself, acknowledges — or denies — his liability to one or the other of the claimants. In this situation, the fund itself is the target of the claimants. It marks the outer limits of the controversy. It is, therefore, reasonable and sensible that interpleader, in discharge of its office to protect the fund, should also protect the stakeholder from vexatious and multiple litigation. In this context, the suits sought to be enjoined are squarely within the language of 28 U.S.C. § 2361 * * *.

But the present case is another matter. Here, an accident has happened. Thirty-five passengers or their representatives have claims which they wish to press against a variety of defendants: the bus company, its driver, the owner of the truck, and the truck driver. The circumstance that one of the prospective defendants happens to have an insurance policy is a fortuitous event which should not of itself shape the nature of the ensuing litigation. For example, a resident of California, injured in California aboard a bus owned by a California corporation should not be forced to sue the corporation anywhere but in California simply because another prospective defendant carried an insurance policy. And an insurance company whose maximum interest in the case cannot exceed $20,000 and who in fact asserts that it has no interest at all, should not be allowed to determine that dozens of tort plaintiffs must be compelled to press their claims — even those claims which are not against the insured and which in no event could be satisfied out of the meager insurance fund — in a single forum of the insurance company's choosing. There is nothing in the statutory scheme, and very little in the judicial and academic commentary upon that scheme, which requires that the tail allowed to wag the dog in this fashion.

State Farm's interest in this case, which is the fulcrum of the interpleader procedure, is confined to its $20,000 fund. That interest receives full vindication when the court restrains claimants from seeking to enforce against the insurance company any judgment obtained against its insured, except in the interpleader proceeding itself. To the extent that the District Court sought to control claimants' lawsuits against the insured and other alleged tortfeasors, it exceeded the powers granted to it by the statutory scheme.

We recognize, of course, that our view of interpleader means that it cannot be used to solve all the vexing problems of multiparty litigation arising out of a mass tort. But interpleader was never intended to perform such a function, to be an all-purpose "bill of peace." Had it been so intended, careful provision would necessarily have been made to insure that a party with little or no interest in the outcome of a complex controversy should not strip truly interested parties of substantial rights — such as the right to choose the forum in which to establish their claims, subject to generally applicable rules of jurisdiction, venue, service of process, removal, and change of venue. None of the legislative and academic sponsors of a modern federal interpleader device viewed their accomplishment as a "bill of peace," capable of sweeping dozens of lawsuits out of the various state and federal courts in which they were brought and into a single interpleader proceeding. And only in two reported instances has a federal interpleader court sought to control the underlying litigation against alleged tortfeasors as opposed to the allocation of a fund among successful tort plaintiffs. See Commercial Union Insurance Co. of New York v. Adams, 231 F. Supp. 860 (S.D. Ind. 1964)(where there was virtually no objection and where all of the basic tort suits would in any event have been prosecuted in the forum state), and Pan American Fire & Casualty Co. v. Revere, 188 F. Supp. 474 (E.D. La. 1960). Another district court, on the other hand, has recently held that it lacked statutory authority to enjoin suits against the alleged tortfeasor as opposed to proceedings against the fund itself. Travelers Indemnity Co. v. Greyhound Lines, Inc., 260 F. Supp. 530 (W.D. La. 1966).

In light of the evidence that federal interpleader was not intended to serve the function of a "bill of peace" in the context of multiparty litigation arising out of a mass tort, of the anomalous power which such a construction of the statute would give the stakeholder, and of the thrust of the statute and the purpose it was intended to serve, we hold that the interpleader statute did not authorize the injunction entered in the present case. Upon remand, the injunction is to be modified consistently with this opinion.

IV

The judgment of the Court of Appeals is reversed, and the case is remanded to the United States District Court for proceedings consistent with this opinion.

It is so ordered.

NOTES AND QUESTIONS

1. In *Pan American*, Judge Wright thought it "startling" that there "appears to be no precedent in the federal courts for granting interpleader" for unliquidated tort claims. In Part III of *Tashire*, Justice Fortas mentions *Pan American* critically. Is there a distinction between the two cases that would support the results in each? Or does *Tashire* mean that *Pan American* was wrongly decided?

2. The Court in *Tashire* certainly would not quarrel with Judge Wright's decision in *Pan American* that claims need not be reduced to judgment before interpleader is appropri-

ate. Indeed, *Tashire* makes this clear, even in the absence of a direct action suit, at least in statutory interpleader. Should the same be true under rule interpleader? Why did Judge Wright think so?

3. Justice Fortas explained that interpleader was not intended to be a "'bill of peace,' capable of sweeping dozens of lawsuits out of the various state and federal courts in which they were brought and into a single interpleader proceeding." If interpleader will not force all related claims into a single litigation, what device(s) will? If none comes to mind, should there be any? What policies would favor such a device? What policies would be harmed by such a device?

As to the latter question, consider Justice Fortas's statement that had interpleader "been so intended, careful provision would necessarily have been made to insure that a party with little or no interest in the outcome of a complex controversy should not strip truly interested parties of substantial rights — such as the right to choose the forum in which to establish their claims, subject to generally applicable rules of jurisdiction, venue, service of process, removal, and change of venue." Why is there a "right" to sue in a particular forum? Is the "right" violated by removal of a case from state to federal court? By transfer under 28 U.S.C. § 1404?

4. Statutory interpleader provides a useful model for federal legislation in any situation in which inclusive joinder might be desirable. The allowance of nationwide service of process avoids limitations on the power of individual states to exercise personal jurisdiction. Basing federal jurisdiction on minimal diversity of citizenship permits joinder that would be precluded under *Strawbridge v. Curtiss*.

Several commentators have advocated the use of a similar statute, perhaps augmented by transfer provisions, to avoid duplicative litigation in "complex" cases involving multiple parties and multiple fora. See, e.g., AMERICAN LAW INSTITUTE STUDY ON COMPLEX LITIGATION; Thomas Rowe & Kenneth Sibley, *Beyond Diversity: Federal Multiparty, Multiforum Jurisdiction*, 135 U. PA. L. REV. 7 (1986). Even assuming agreement on what constitutes "complex" litigation, observers disagree over whether federal courts should be empowered to package cases already filed in a *state* court.

C. The Class Action

1. Background

In class action litigation, one or more class representatives (or "named representatives") are formally joined as parties in the case. The members of the group they represent are not joined, and thus are not parties, but are bound by the outcome of the litigation.

Although most class action litigation involves claims asserted by a plaintiff class, the procedural rules generally permit defendant classes as well.

Like so many other procedural devices, the modern class action finds its roots in English equity practice. The law courts of England permitted multiparty litigation based only upon the legal relationship between the parties, such as joint obligors or obligees. Equity developed a broader practice, based not upon legal relationships, but upon the efficiency of deciding transactionally related issues, even when they involved multiple parties. In *Tashire*, recall that Justice Fortas referred to the bill of peace. This was a device developed at equity to permit resolution of disputes between all interested parties. It was limited, however, by the insistence that all interested persons be joined as parties. Knight v. Knight, 24 Eng. Rep. 1088 (Ch. 1734). See generally Zecchariah Chafee, Jr., *Bills of Peace with Multiple Parties*, 45 HARV. L. REV. 1297 (1932).

But what if some interested person could not be joined? Or what if there were so many interested persons that joinder in any traditional sense would not be workable? In such situations, equity developed the notion that parties to litigation might represent nonparties with whom they had a common interest so that the nonparties would be bound by the final decree. The modern class action developed from this equity practice. For an excellent historical treatment, see STEPHEN YEAZELL, FROM MEDIEVAL GROUP LITIGATION TO THE MODERN CLASS ACTION (1987).

The notion that one can be bound by litigation to which she is not made a party raises significant constitutional concerns, which we will address below. Before we do, it is important to set the stage for detailed consideration of the class action by noting some fundamental policy issues raised by its use.

2. Policy and Ethical Issues

The class action is controversial. The fact that it can bind numerous potential claimants to a single judgment leads some commentators to praise its efficiency. Instead of hundreds of potential cases, the judicial system can handle a large dispute with a single proceeding. Critics note, however, that the single class action is potentially an enormous burden on the court in which it proceeds. Moreover, some note that the class action might actually create litigation that otherwise would not exist.

Consider, for example, a class action on behalf of 1,000,000 consumers allegedly overcharged illegally by a retailer. Assume the illegal act resulted in an average overcharged of $10.00 per consumer. Without the class action, there will likely be no litigation in this scenario. No consumer will file suit to recover $10.00, even in a small claims court. It is simply not worth the effort. Thus, allowing a class action here creates litigation. Is this an appropriate result for an ostensibly procedural rule?

On the other hand, if the consumers cannot aggregate through the class action, the retailer may be able to engage in illegal behavior without civil consequence. Some commentators argue that such illegal behavior ought to be addressed by the criminal law or through administrative mechanisms. A problem here, of course, is that criminal proceedings generally do not result in compensation for those harmed. Does the class action properly fill that void? Some observers answer in the affirmative; one cheers the class action as "one of the most socially useful remedies in history." Abraham Pomerantz, *New Developments in Class Actions—Has Their Death Knell Been Sounded?*, 25 BUS. LAWYER 1259, 1259 (1970). The Supreme Court seems to agree.

> The aggregation of individual claims in the context of a classwide suit is an evolutionary response to the existence of injuries unremedied by the regulatory action of government. Where it is not economically feasible to obtain relief within the traditional framework of a multiplicity of small individual suits for damages, aggrieved persons may be without any effective redress unless they may employ the class-action device.

Deposit Guaranty National Bank v. Roper, 445 U.S. 326, 338-39 (1980).

While the class action, like all civil dispute resolution, fills a socially useful role, it must be used with care. It is subject to abuse, and has been abused both by plaintiffs and defendants. Consider, for example, that the class claim against the retailer is very weak on the merits. If the court permits the class action to proceed, the defendant is facing potential aggregated liability of $10,000,000. No matter how good she considers her chances of winning at trial, the defendant may be reluctant to "roll the dice" and proceed in the face of such a huge potential loss. Thus, the incentive to settle the case may become virtually irresistible.

In one interesting empirical study of securities class action cases, Professor Alexander found that the strength of the class's claim on the merits was largely irrelevant to its settlement value. Even weak substantive claims resulted in handsome settlements. See Janet Cooper Alexander, *Do the Merits Matter? A Study of Settlements in Securities Class Actions*, 43 STAN. L. REV. 497 (1991). See also John Coffee, Jr., *The Regulation of Entrepreneurial Litigation: Balancing Fairness and Efficiency in the Large Class Action*, 54 U. CHI. L. REV. 877 (1987). Focusing on this potential to coerce a settlement on claims that otherwise might be defended vigorously, Professor Handler damns the class action as "legalized blackmail." Milton Handler, *The Shift from Substantive to Procedural Innovations in Antitrust Suits*, 71 COLUM. L. REV. 1, 9 (1971).

Now consider the interest of the class member willing to serve as class representative. As we will see, the rules impose various responsibilities on the named representative. Generally, there is no financial reward for undertaking these responsibilities. If the class action is successful, then, the named representative will recover her costs and her individual damages, or about $10.00 in our hypothetical case. Although courts occasionally reward the named representative with a bonus payment, such action is rare. It seems, then, that the named representative is often motivated by principle, not economics.

The class lawyer, on the other hand, may be motivated by economics, not principle. If the defendant settles the case for several millions of dollars, the lawyer may be in a position to recover a substantial fee award without having to go to trial. Thus, class action litigation can create serious ethical tension. The lawyer must be careful that her own self-interest does not conflict with the interests of her clients, the named representative, and the class itself.

The potential abuse of the class action device is not limited to plaintiffs and their lawyers. In some situations, defendants have actually preferred to litigate against a plaintiff class because they may be able to structure a "sweetheart" settlement that binds all class members and thus prevents them from suing separately. In several noteworthy instances, critics charge, defense and plaintiff counsel have struck settlements that are fairly painless to the defendant, which include a significant payment of fees to the class lawyer, and which, by the binding nature of class actions, insulate the defendant from further suit by class members. See, e.g., Pamela Coyle, *When Bigger Isn't Better*, 81 A.B.A. J. 66 (1994).

Because of these potential abuses, and the seemingly inherent potential conflicts between counsel and the group, class action litigation rules place increased burdens on the court. They force the court to assume administrative tasks to ensure that the class is being adequately represented by counsel and to approve settlements. Courts generally do not have this policing job in other types of litigation. Thus, class litigation has contributed to a metamorphosis of the judge from umpire to case manager.

3. Constitutional Considerations

The utility of the class action comes from its binding effect on class members, even though those members are not joined as parties. The leading case on the constitutional problems with binding nonparties in this way, and probably the most famous class action case in American history, is the 1940 Supreme Court decision in *Hansberry v. Lee*. Before reading that case, however, we note two important predecessors.

Smith v. Swormstead, 57 U.S. 288 (1853), involved the split of the Methodist Episcopal Church into southern and northern branches over the issue of slavery. Before the split, the denomination had created the "Book Fund," which totaled about $200,000. After the split, preachers in the northern branch held the property. Six representatives of the preachers in the southern branch sued three representatives of the ministers in the north, seeking their share of the property. Although over 5000 preachers were not joined as parties, the Supreme Court held that they were bound by the outcome. It emphasized that such representation was proper "where the parties interested are numerous, and the suit is for an object common to them all." Id. at 302.

Supreme Tribe of Ben-Hur v. Cauble, 255 U.S. 356 (1921), also involved class members with interests identical to those of their representatives. The class challenged a decision by a fraternal benefits organization to reorganize and reduce benefits for its 70,000 members. Such organizations can provide insurance, pension and other benefits to members, and were especially important before government programs such as social security. In *Ben-Hur*, non-Indiana members sued the organization, purporting to represent all members; the court entered judgment for the defendant. Thereafter, Indiana members sued, arguing that they were not bound by the judgment in the first case, since they could not have invoked diversity of citizenship against the Indiana organization. The Supreme Court held that all members—including the Hoosiers—were bound by the judgment in the first case.

Thus, in *Smith* and *Ben-Hur*, the representatives and the nonparty class members had identical, nonseparable, interests. *Hansberry* involved land allegedly subject to a restrictive covenant. You may study such covenants in your course on property. When effective, they bind landowners in the affected area (usually a subdivision). The covenants are of public record and "run with the land," meaning that they bind all persons who acquire land from the original owner. Such covenants are common today to ensure architectural uniformity in neighborhoods, and work as an adjunct to public zoning rules. Before the Supreme Court declared racially restrictive covenants unconstitutional in Shelley v. Kraemer, 334 U.S. 1 (1948), they were also used to exclude members of particular races from buying or renting in an area.

The litigation in *Hansberry* concerned a racially restrictive covenant in a Chicago neighborhood before *Shelley v. Kraemer*. By its terms, this particular covenant was not to take effect until signed by the owners of 95 percent of the frontage in the neighborhood. The Hansberrys, who were black, bought a home in the neighborhood. Other owners then sued in Illinois state court to rescind the sale to the Hansberrys because it violated the restrictive covenant. At trial, the Hansberrys proved that only 54 percent of the owners had actually signed, and argued, therefore, that the covenant never took effect and could not be enforced.

The trial court agreed that only 54 percent of the owners had ever signed the covenant. Nonetheless, it rescinded the sale and ordered the Hansberrys to move out of the neighborhood. According to that court, the Hansberrys were bound by the judgment of an earlier class action case, Burke v. Kleiman, 277 Ill. App. 519 (1934). In that case, some homeowners sued a white owner (Kleiman) who had rented to a black tenant (Hall) in violation of the covenant. Plaintiffs in *Burke* alleged that 95 percent of the owners had signed the covenant. The defendants in that case stipulated to that as a fact. In *Burke*, the court enforced the covenant and voided the lease to Hall. The Illinois Supreme Court affirmed the trial court's conclusion that the judgment in *Burke* bound the persons who sought to sell to the Hansberrys. The United States Supreme Court then reviewed the case.

Hansberry v. Lee
311 U.S. 32, 61 S. Ct. 115, 85 L. Ed. 22 (1940)

MR. JUSTICE STONE delivered the opinion of the Court.

The question is whether the Supreme Court of Illinois, by its adjudication that petitioners in this case are bound by a judgment rendered in an earlier litigation to which they were not parties, has deprived them of the due process of law guaranteed by the Fourteenth Amendment.

* * *

* * * [T]he Supreme Court of Illinois concluded in the present case that *Burke v. Kleiman* was a "class" or "representative" suit, and that in such a suit, "where the remedy is pursued by a plaintiff who has the right to represent the class to which he belongs, other members of the class are bound by the results in the case unless it is reversed or set aside on direct proceedings"; that petitioners in the present suit were members of the class represented by the plaintiffs in the earlier suit and consequently were bound by its decree, which had rendered the issue of performance of the condition precedent to the restrictive agreement res judicata, so far as petitioners are concerned. The court thought that the circumstance that the stipulation in the earlier suit that owners of 95 per cent of the frontage had signed the agreement was contrary to the fact, as found in the present suit, did not militate against this conclusion, since the court in the earlier suit had jurisdiction to determine the fact as between the parties before it, and that its determination, because of the representative character of the suit, even though erroneous, was binding on petitioners until set aside by a direct attack on the first judgment.

State courts are free to attach such descriptive labels to litigations before them as they may choose and to attribute to them such consequences as they think appropriate under state constitutions and laws, subject only to the requirements of the Constitution of the United States. But when the judgment of a state court, ascribing to the judgment of another court the binding force and effect of res judicata, is challenged for want of due process it becomes the duty of this Court to examine the course of procedure in both litigations to ascertain whether the litigant whose rights have thus been adjudicated has been afforded such notice and opportunity to be heard as are requisite to the due process which the Constitution prescribes.

It is a principle of general application in Anglo-American jurisprudence that one is not bound by a judgment in personam in a litigation in which he is not designated as a party or to which he has not been made a party by service of process. Pennoyer v. Neff, 95 U.S. 714 [1878]. A judgment rendered in such circumstances is not entitled to the full faith and credit which the Constitution and statute of the United States prescribe; and judicial action enforcing it against the person or property of the absent party is not that due process which the Fifth and Fourteenth Amendments require.

To these general rules there is a recognized exception that, to an extent not precisely defined by judicial opinion, the judgment in a "class" or "representative" suit, to which some members of the class were parties, may bind members of the class or those represented who are not made parties to it. *Smith v. Swormstead; Supreme Tribe of Ben-Hur v. Cauble.*

The class suit was an invention of equity to enable it to proceed to a decree in suits where the number of those interested in the subject of the litigation is so great that their joinder as parties in conformity to the usual rules of procedure is impracticable. Courts are not infrequently called upon to proceed with causes in which the number of those interested in the litigation is so great as to make difficult or impossible the joinder of all because some are not within the jurisdiction or because their whereabouts is unknown * * *. In such cases where the interests of those not joined are of the same class as the interests of those who are, and where it is considered that the latter fairly represent the former in the prosecution of the litigation of the issues in which all have a common interest, the court will proceed to a decree.

It is evident that the considerations which may induce a court thus to proceed, despite a technical defect of parties, may differ from those which must be taken into account in determining whether the absent parties are bound by the decree or, if it is adjudged that they are, in ascertaining whether such an adjudication satisfies the requirements of due process and of full faith and credit. Nevertheless, there is scope within the framework of the Constitution for holding in appropriate cases that a judgment rendered in a class suit is res judicata as to members of the class who are not formal parties to the suit. Here, as elsewhere, the Fourteenth Amendment does not compel state courts or legislatures to adopt any particular rule for establishing the conclusiveness of judgments in class suits * * *. With a proper regard for divergent local institutions and interests, this Court is justified in saying that there has been a failure of due process only in those cases where it cannot be said that the procedure adopted, fairly insures the protection of the interests of absent parties who are to be bound by it.

It is familiar doctrine of the federal courts that members of a class not present as parties to the litigation may be bound by the judgment where they are in fact adequately represented by parties who are present, or where they actually participate in the conduct of the litigation in which members of the class are present as parties, or where the interest of the members of the class, some of whom are present as parties, is joint, or where for any other reason the relationship between the parties present and those who are absent is such as legally to entitle the former to stand in judgment for the latter.

In all such cases, so far as it can be said that the members of the class who are present are, by generally recognized rules of law, entitled to stand in judgment for those who are not, we may assume for present purposes that such procedure affords a protection to the parties who are represented, though absent, which would satisfy the requirements of due process and full faith and credit. Nor do we find it necessary for the decision of this case to say that, when the only circumstance defining the class is that the determination of the rights of its members turns upon a single issue of fact or law, a state could not constitutionally adopt a procedure whereby some of the members of the class could stand in judgment for all, provided that the procedure were so devised and applied as to insure that those present are of the same class as those absent and that the litigation is so conducted as to insure the full and fair consideration of the common issue. We decide only that the procedure and the course of litigation sustained here by the plea of res judicata do not satisfy these requirements.

The restrictive agreement did not purport to create a joint obligation or liability. If valid and effective its promises were the several obligations of the signers and those claiming under them. The promises ran severally to every other signer. It is plain that in such circumstances all those alleged to be bound by the agreement would not constitute a single class in any litigation brought to enforce it. Those who sought to secure its benefits by enforcing it could not be said to be in the same class with or represent those whose interest was in resisting performance, for the agreement by its terms imposes obligations and confers rights on the owner of each plot of land who signs it. If those who thus seek to secure the benefits of the agreement were rightly regarded by the state Supreme Court as constituting a class, it is evident that those signers or their successors who are interested in challenging the validity of the agreement and resisting its performance are not of the same class in the sense that their interests are identical so that any group who had elected to enforce rights conferred by the agreement could be said to be acting in the interest of any others who were free to deny its obligation.

* * *

It is one thing to say that some members of a class may represent other members in a litigation where the sole and common interest of the class in the litigation, is either to assert a common right or to challenge an asserted obligation. It is quite another to hold that all those who are free alternatively either to assert rights or to challenge them are of a single class, so that any group, merely because it is of the class so constituted, may be deemed adequately to represent any others of the class in litigating their interests in either alternative. Such a selection of representatives for purposes of litigation, whose substantial interests are not necessarily or even probably the same as those whom they are deemed to represent, does not afford that protection to absent parties which due process requires. The doctrine of representation of absent parties in a class suit has not hitherto been thought to go so far. Apart from the opportunities it would afford for the fraudulent and collusive sacrifice of the rights of absent parties, we think that the representation in this case no more satisfies the requirements of due process than a trial by a judicial officer who is in such situation that he may have an interest in the outcome of the litigation in conflict with that of the litigants.

The plaintiffs in the *Burke* case sought to compel performance of the agreement in behalf of themselves and all others similarly situated. They did not designate the defendants in the suit as a class or seek any injunction or other relief against others than the named defendants, and the decree which was entered did not purport to bind others. In seeking to enforce the agreement the plaintiffs in that suit were not representing the petitioners here whose substantial interest is in resisting performance. The defendants in the first suit were not treated by the pleadings or decree as representing others or as foreclosing by their defense the rights of others; and, even though nominal defendants, it does not appear that their interest in defeating the contract outweighed their interest in establishing its validity. For a court in this situation to ascribe to either the plaintiffs or defendants the performance of such functions on behalf of petitioners here, is to attribute to them a power that it cannot be said that they had assumed to exercise, and a responsibility which, in view of their dual interests it does not appear that they could rightly discharge.

Reversed.

NOTES AND QUESTIONS

1. Exactly why did the judgment in *Burke v. Kleiman* not bind the Hansberrys or the person from whom they bought?

2. For most of this course, we have considered the due process ideal to be one in which no one is bound unless joined as a party to litigation and given notice and an opportunity to participate. For example, due process limitations on a state's power to exercise personal jurisdiction require not only that the defendant have minimum contacts with the forum, but that the court not be so grossly inconvenient as to jeopardize her ability to participate in the litigation. As the Court said in *Burger King*: "jurisdictional rules may not be employed in such a way as to make litigation 'so gravely difficult and inconvenient' that a party unfairly is at a 'severe disadvantage' to his opponent." As another example, provisions for notice must be aimed at actually informing the defendant so that her opportunity to be heard is meaningful.

In materials on the preclusion doctrines, however, we discovered that a judgment can bind nonparties if the relationship between them and a litigant is sufficiently close. As we explored in Chapter 11, such a binding effect is an exception to the general rule that due process precludes binding someone who was not joined as a party. In those materials, we noted that courts consistently consider class action cases as coming within this exception and warranting binding the nonparty class members. *Smith* and *Ben-Hur* are examples of class actions in which the Supreme Court held the nonparties bound. *Hansberry* endorses that general notion, but holds that due process precludes its application as to some members of the "class" in the first action.

Hansberry is not the only case we have read in which the Supreme Court refused on constitutional grounds to bind nonparty absentees. In *Mullane v. Central Hanover Bank*, in Chapter 3, (which was decided after *Hansberry*) the Court held that beneficiaries of a pooled trust fund were entitled to notice before a court could terminate their right to sue the trustee for misfeasance. By notice, the Court envisioned not formal service of process and joinder, but simply notification by first class mail of the filing of the case. Remember, too, that the Court required this notice only as to those persons whose names and addresses were readily available. As to others, the Court held, notice by publication was acceptable.

While *Mullane* did not involve a class action, the beneficiaries of the pooled fund held similar, relatively small, interests. Moreover, the Court clearly did not foresee the participation of all interested persons, explaining that "notice reasonably certain to reach most of those interested in objecting is likely to safeguard the interest of all, since any objection sustained would inure to the benefit of all." 339 U.S. at 319.

Does *Hansberry* countenance bind members of a class even if they receive no notice of the proceedings? Does *Mullane*?

3. In cases involving numerous persons with similar interests, whose interests can be adequately represented, is representative litigation acceptable simply because nothing else will work? Is this sort of litigation a form of "jurisdiction by necessity?" TEPLY & WHITTEN, CIVIL PROCEDURE 331 (saying of *Mullane*: "strong practical considerations point to a particular state as the only realistic forum in which to settle a dispute").

4. Does *Hansberry* mean that a representative is inadequate anytime a class member disagrees with her? Suppose the representative and the class member agree on the goals of the case, but disagree on litigation strategy. Can the representative be adequate under *Hansberry*? What if they disagree over the remedy to be sought? The court in which to file? At what point does disagreement mean that giving the judgment binding effect would violate due process?

5. Reconsider this language from *Hansberry*:

> It is one thing to say that some members of a class may represent other members in a litigation where the sole and common interest of the class in the litigation, is either to assert a common right or to challenge an asserted obligation. It is quite another to hold that all those who are free alternatively either to assert rights or to challenge them are of a single class, so that any group, merely because it is of the class so constituted, may be deemed adequately to represent any other of the class in litigating their interests in either alternative.

(a) Professor Yeazell has asked whether the Court meant what it said to be taken literally. "If, as the Court suggested, the validity of a class depends on the subjective desire of the individuals constituting it to assert their rights, classes could consist only of individuals who had, individually, indicated that they wished to assert the rights in question. Because all persons are always free either to assert their claims or not, classes could consist only of volunteers." STEPHEN YEAZELL, FROM MEDIEVAL GROUP LITIGATION TO THE MODERN CLASS ACTION 234 (1987). If a class action can consist only of volunteers, how useful is it?

(b) Professor Kamp, referring to the same passage from *Hansberry*, says "the language is so sweeping it could apply to and invalidate every class action."

Allen Kamp, *The History Behind Hansberry v. Lee*, 20 U.C. DAVIS L. REV. 481, 497 (1987). How does the language do so?

(c) Read in the context of *Hansberry*, can the second sentence of the passage above be considered as referring to a case in which class members are in conflict? Such a situation is quite different from a case in which class members share an identical interest but are indifferent as to its vindication.

6. Under standard doctrine, why would the judgment in *Burke v. Kleiman* not have been entitled to issue preclusion on the question of whether the covenant was signed by 95 percent of the homeowners?

7. In the article cited in Note 5, Professor Kamp details the rich factual background and human story underlying *Hansberry*. We note just three interesting facts. First, one of the Hansberry's children, Lorraine Hansberry, is the noted playwright who wrote "A Raisin in the Sun," which was both a successful play and motion picture. Events and people in that play are taken from her family's experiences. Second, the litigation was a part of the overall effort to desegregate Chicago's residential neighborhoods. Because of changing demographics and economics the Hansberrys were the only people willing to buy the property; there were no white buyers. Third, and most fascinating, the "Burke" of *Burke v. Kleiman* was the wife of the man who sold to the Hansberrys! Thus, "the husband of the class representative in the first action had become a defendant and sought to subvert the goals of the plaintiff class." Id. at 497.

4. Practice Under Federal Rule 23

a. Background

Hansberry clarified (at least to a degree) the constitutionality of binding nonparties in a class action. Fortunately, few cases involve attempts to bind such disparate groups as those involved in the "class" in *Burke v. Kleiman*. Today, most judicial opinions focus on statutes or rules of procedure prescribing standards for the maintenance of class actions. Federal Rule 23 defines class actions in federal courts. It has also influenced rules and statute drafters in many states; indeed, a majority of states has embraced the federal class action provision. In whatever form, though, such rules serve the salutary function of shifting to the outset of litigation the inquiry into whether the conditions for binding class members—including adequacy of representation—are satisfied. This is a far more efficient way to proceed than what we saw in *Hansberry*, where adequacy of representation could not be challenged until after judgment, in a collateral case.

The present version of Rule 23 differs markedly from the rule originally promulgated in 1938. The older rule liberalized prior practice, but suffered from reliance upon the legal relationships among class members that did not promote liberal use. It permitted three types of class actions: (1) "true" class actions, in which the class right was variously described as "joint" or "common"; (2) "hybrid" class actions, in which class rights were "several" and related to specific property; and (3) "spurious" class actions, in which class rights were "several" and involved a common question and in which the class sought common relief. In the words of the Advisory Committee that amended the rule in 1966, these terms were "obscure and uncertain."

The present version of the rule traces to 1966, and was part of the substantial overhaul of Rules 19, 23, and 24. You will recall from our discussion of Rules 19 and 24 that the 1966 amendments emphasized practicality and pragmatism, and focused on fact patterns rather than legal relationships. Not surprisingly, we will see substantial kinship between parts of Rule 23 andCed Rules 19 and 24.

b. Filing and "Certification" of a Class Action

In a plaintiff class action, the representative(s) institute suit in the usual way: they file a complaint and arrange for service of process. The complaint, however, notes that the representatives sue on behalf of a class of persons similarly situated. At some point after filing, the representatives make what is usually called a motion for class certification. Rule 23 does not set an exact time frame for this; indeed, it does not even refer to "certification." Rule 23(c)(1) provides, however, that "As soon as practicable after the commencement of an action brought as a class action the court shall determine by order whether it is to be so maintained." The court will usually entertain written briefs and oral argument on the issue. The admonition that the decision be made "as soon as practicable" does not mean immediately. It is not unusual for the court to address certification several months after the case is filed. In the interim, the parties might be permitted to pursue discovery on issues relevant to whether the case should proceed as a class action. At the hearing, the class representatives have the burden of establishing that the action satisfies requirements for class treatment.

A court order certifying a class is not cast in stone. As Rule 23(c)(1) also provides, "An order under this subdivision may be conditional, and may be altered or amended before the decision on the merits." The conditional nature of these orders emphasizes the court's continuing duty to monitor the class action. If changes during the course of the litigation make class treatment undesirable or inappropriate, the court can modify the definition or "decertify" the class.

If the court denies certification, the representative's individual suit stays before the court; although litigation may proceed in that suit, the lawyer's incentive may be sapped if the case involves a monetarily insignificant claim. Thus, denial of class certification is often the "death knell" of plaintiff's case. On the other hand, if the court certifies a class action, the defendant's incentive to settle the case increases dramatically because she faces the potential imposition of devastating liability. In many instances, then, the court's decision on certification effectively seals the outcome of the case.

c. Requirements for "Certification" Under Rule 23

Rule 23 provides a two-step process for determining whether a case should proceed as a class action. First, the class must satisfy the prerequisites in Rule 23(a). Second, after doing so, the representatives must demonstrate that their class falls within one of the three types of class actions recognized by Rule 23(b). Although it is tempting to approach such a detailed rule in a mechanical, checklist fashion, keep the bigger picture in mind, always asking why the drafters included each requirement, especially in Rule 23(a). Specifically, assess whether each requirement is dictated by *Hansberry*, or at least contributes to addressing the due process concern addressed in that case.

i. Prerequisites of Rule 23(a)

Rule 23(a) lists four factors as prerequisites to maintenance of a class action. Before addressing them, however, note that the first sentence of the rule presupposes the existence of "a class." It is difficult to state with great precision what factors are relevant to defining a class. Although the representatives generally need not name every member of the class, they must convince the judge at a very practical level that the court will be able to manage the action. For example, a class definition such as "poor people within the state" is simply too vague for a court to consider manageable. See, e.g., Lopez Tijerina v. Henry, 48 F.R.D. 274 (D. N.M. 1969).

Counsel should draft the class definition with great care, considering such things as geographic and temporal limitations. The court must be convinced that it can ultimately determine who is in the class. The relief sought may affect a court's insistence on specificity. Generally, if the class seeks monetary relief, the court may require greater specificity, since it ultimately will need to distribute money to individuals.

Rule 23(a)(1) embodies what some torturers of the English language call *numerosity*. Note two things about the rule. First, it prescribes no "magic number" which automatically satisfies the requirement. Second, it focuses on more than numbers—the class must be "so numerous that joinder of all members is impractical." The court thus must consider other factors beside mere numbers. For example, geographic dispersion and whether joinder of individual members would destroy diversity of citizenship might affect the court's conclusion on whether the class satisfies 23(a)(1). Some courts may deny certification of what would appear to be a large class when all of the members are citizens and residents of a single state, since the parties could join with relative ease. See, e.g., State of Utah v. American Pipe & Construction Co., 49 F.R.D. 17 (C.D. Cal. 1969). On the other hand, one court permitted a discrimination class action to proceed with only 19 members, in part because of the individuals' fear of bringing individual claims. Arkansas Education Assn. v. Board of Education, 446 F.2d 763 (8th Cir. 1971).

Rule 23(a)(2) imposes a *commonality* requirement in very broad and practical terms. It focuses on the facts of the case, and not on legal relationships, and that it refers to questions of fact or law. The nature of class actions would seem to assume this requirement. Not surprisingly, then, courts rarely have trouble finding that this is met. The difficult issue of commonality comes up in class actions under Rule 23(b)(3), in which common questions must "predominate."

Rule 23(a)(3) gives a *typicality* requirement, focusing on whether the representative's claim or defense is typical of that of the rest of the class. This factor is not met, for instance, if the representative suffered a unique harm from the rest of the class members, or if her claim is subject to a defense not available against the rest of the class. Thus, in a class action seeking redress for several harms—e.g., property damage and personal injuries caused by the defendant's acts—there should be a representative who has suffered each of the harms. Or the class might have two representatives, one having suffered personal injuries and the other property damage.

Finally, Rule 23(a)(4) requires that the representatives "fairly and adequately protect the interest of the class." In practice, this factor requires assessment not only of the representatives, but of their lawyers. The court must be satisfied that the case is driven by the class's claims, and not by the lawyer's desire. It must also be satisfied that counsel is competent to handle the burdens of class litigation. In making this assessment, courts often look to the lawyer's experience in class actions, leading some to complain that it is very difficult for young, relatively inexperienced, lawyers to undertake class action litigation.

NOTES AND QUESTIONS

1. The Rule 23(a) factors are not hermetically sealed from one another. Indeed, as the Supreme Court has noted, the latter three factors "tend to merge." General Tel. Co. of the Southwest v. Falcon, 457 U.S. 147, 157 n.13 (1982). Some observers see the requirements of commonality and typicality as ways to ensure that the representative is adequate. Thus, the four prerequisites seem aimed at two major factors: impracticability of joining all interested members and adequacy of representation. See WRIGHT, FEDERAL COURTS 509-10.

2. If *Burke v. Kleiman* had been brought for certification under Rule 23, which requirements would not have been met?

3. During the Vietnam War, it was not uncommon for groups to gather in public protest. Sometimes, police agencies photographed the participants and engaged in other surveillance. In one case, representatives of a class sought to enjoin the police force from engaging in these activities. They defined their class as people "who wish to * * * engage, in the City of Fall River, in peaceful political discussion * * * without surveillance." Yaffe v. Powers, 454 F.2d 1362 (1st Cir. 1972). Who would not be in that class? Doesn't that definition include war protesters, Young Republicans, socialists, and the garden club? How would you redraft the class definition to make it reflect the intended class more accurately?

4. Juana works for Big Co. She claims that Big Co. violated federal employment discrimination law when it refused to promote her because of her national origin. Can she represent a class of persons of the same national origin who allege that Big Co. refused to hire them on that basis? See General Tel. Co. of the Southwest v. Falcon, 457 U.S. 147 (1982). Is the problem with typicality or with commonality or with adequacy of representation?

5. A group of workers claims that the state has not afforded them benefits to which they are entitled under state law. Representative sues on behalf of the group of 750 workers, properly alleging the claim. Representative is subject to deportation from the United States, however, because of a prior criminal conviction. What argument should the state make to defeat his motion for class certification?

6. Suppose a class sues two defendants who allegedly agreed to charge the same price for their products and thus violated antitrust laws by overcharging for products sold to class members. Can a representative who dealt only with one of the two defendants represent the class?

7. Freezer Co. sells freezers door-to-door. It uses a sales force of 100 persons who go to various neighborhoods and engage in face-to-face conversations with potential customers, telling them about their freezers and offering a discount if the person agrees to purchase a freezer on the spot. Freezer Co. collects money from 500 people but never delivers the freezers. Can the 500 proceed in a class action for fraud? Remember that two elements of a fraud claim would be knowing misrepresentation by the seller and reliance by the buyer. How can these be shown en masse? Suppose Freezer Co. gave each salesperson a standard "pitch" which she memorized and stated to each prospective buyer? How would this affect your answer? See Vasquez v. Superior Court, 484 P.2d 964 (Cal. 1971).

8. A statute permits persons of a particular income level to receive public assistance in paying their home heating bills. The agency administering the program treats some applicants with disrespect, causing some eligible persons to eschew participation. Representative sues on behalf of a class of persons eligible for assistance under the program, but

who were dissuaded from applying because of the agency's treatment of others. Can a court define a class based upon subjective intent of its members? How could the court ever determine who was in this class? See Simer v. Rios, 661 F.2d 655 (7th Cir. 1981).

ii. Types of class actions under Rule 23(b).

Once the prerequisites of Rule 23(a) are met, the representative must demonstrate that the class fits a recognized category in Rule 23(b). Although the rule requires only that the class fit one of the types, it is possible to seek certification of a single class under more than one. Throughout these materials, consider why Rule 23(b) imposes additional requirements for maintenance of a class action. What is the function of Rule 23(b)? What does it add to Rule 23(a)? Does it address the concerns expressed in *Hansberry*?

Rule 23(b)(1) mirrors the language of Rule 19. This is not surprising, since, as noted above, the Rules Advisory Committee redrafted the rules together in 1966 to emphasize a pragmatic approach to joinder problems. When the number of persons affected does not preclude it, Rule 19 applies to force joinder of the nonparties. When joinder is impracticable, Rule 23(b)(1) permits a class action to proceed and binds the nonparties through representation.

Rule 23(b)(1) permits class actions in two situations. First, Rule 23(b)(1)(A), like Rule 19(a)(2)(ii), is concerned with the practical effect of a judgment on a party (usually the defendant). Specifically, it permits class litigation where separate actions would create a risk of "establish[ing] incompatible standards of conduct for the party opposing the class." Such cases almost always involve the assertion of common rights in which individual litigation could come to mutually exclusive results. For example, suppose the reorganization of the fraternal benefits organization in *Ben-Hur* had been challenged in individual litigation. One court might have concluded that the organization could go through with its plan and change member benefits, while another might conclude exactly the opposite. Faced with these judgments, the organization would be able to obey one judgment only be disobeying the other. Similarly, suppose shareholders sue a corporation to force the declaration of a dividend. Individual litigation might result in contradictory orders—one commanding the corporation to declare the dividend and one decreeing that it shall not.

As two scholars note, a "unitary decision is essential" in such cases. Arthur Miller & David Crump, *Jurisdiction and Choice of Law in Multistate Class Actions After Phillips Petroleum Co. v. Shutts*, 96 YALE L.J. 1, 46 (1986). They explain, "it is impossible to reorganize a single fraternal benefits organization in inconsistent ways, or to keep two basketball leagues merged and separate, or to distribute and withhold a dividend." Id. Another example involves numerous claims to a specific res or fund. If the number of claimants is manageable, the stakeholder might use interpleader. If joinder through interpleader is impracticable, the case might proceed as a Rule 23(b)(1)(A) class action. Note that it might be the defendant in this situation who wants the plaintiffs to proceed as a class. Does anything in Rule 23 prohibit a defendant from seeking certification of a plaintiff class?

Note that Rule 23(b)(1)(A) usually involves claims for equitable relief such as an injunction or declaratory judgment. The "incompatible standards of conduct" test generally is not met in a case seeking damages. Assume a bus crash injures 80 people, who then sue the busline separately. While these individual actions may reach inconsistent results — Plaintiff-1 may lose and Plaintiff-2 may win — the courts do not consider separate actions for damages as subjecting the airline to the "incompatible standards of conduct." McDonnell Douglas Corp. v. United States District Court, 523 F.2d 1083 (9th Cir. 1975). One reason is that such tort damages are individual, and thus are not the identical, shared sort of interest that class members had in *Smith* and *Ben-Hur* and that the investors had in *Mullane*.

Rule 23(b)(1)(B), like Rule 19(a)(2)(i) and Rule 24(a)(2), is concerned that individual actions will, as a practical matter, impair or impede the ability of nonparties to protect their interests. Such cases often involve claims to a limited fund, and are sometimes called "limited fund class actions." Without unitary adjudication, some claimants will recover, while others, winning their judgments later, may have no fund against which to recover. To avoid this wasteful race to the courthouse, Rule 23(b)(1)(B) allows unitary adjudication.

Rule 23(b)(2) prescribes a remedy as well as a test. It is aimed at equitable relief when the nonclass party "has acted or refused to act on grounds generally applicable to the class." For example, a case seeking an order desegregating schools or ending employment discrimination against a particular group could proceed under Rule 23(b)(2). Although the rule speaks only of equitable relief, there is some authority for recovery of damages but only in that narrow category of cases in which damages flow naturally from the act giving rise to the equitable relief. Thus, class members may win equitable relief ordering their promotion, and recover damages for lost wages for the time they were not promoted. See, e.g., Moody v. Albemarle Paper Co., 474 F.2d 134 (4th Cir. 1973). In light of such authority, would claim preclusion bar class members from suing for damages if their class sought only equitable relief?

The Rule 23(b)(3) class action is sometimes called the "damages" class because that tends to be the type of relief sought in such cases. Note the two requirements: common questions must predominate and the class action must be superior to other methods of adjudication. Obviously, it is not enough that there are common questions; those questions must predominate. That does not mean that every issue in dispute must be common. For example, class members may assert the same bases of defendant liability, but have suffered different damages. The court can certify a class action as to liability only. Once that is determined, it may accommodate individual evidence on damages from each class member.

Along these lines, read Rule 23(c) and (d), and note the breadth of the court's discretion in administering a class action.

In determining whether the class action is the superior method of resolving the dispute, the obvious question is "superior to what?" Rule 23(b)(3) lists four nonexclusive factors for assessment of this issue. Clearly, though, the rule presupposes a detailed knowledge of the joinder rules and other multiparty litigation.

The Rule 23(b)(3) class action poses the greatest tension between the desire for efficiency and the need for due process. Unlike class members under Rule 23(b)(1) and (b)(2), members of a 23(b)(3) class are held together solely by common facts. Their claims are individual and independent. Thus, the fact that some claimants might win and some might lose creates none of the problems we saw under Rule 23(b)(1) and 23(b)(2). In keeping with the joinder rules, which emphasize packaging along transactional lines, however, the 23(b)(3) class action seeks to maximize efficiency in determining factually related claims en masse.

Because class members are more tangentially related here than in other classes, courts will be especially concerned about adequacy of representation. This concern is manifested in two provisions. First, Rule 23(c)(2) requires notice to individual class members under certain circumstances. Second, it also allows members of the Rule 23(b)(3) class to opt out of the proceeding. Class members who do opt out are not bound by the class judgment. See Rule 23(c)(3). Note that Rule 23 does not require such notice or the opportunity to opt out if a class is maintained under Rule (b)(1) or (b)(2). The opt out provision means, as a practical matter, that the class action will rarely work for mass torts in which class members suffer significant damages. In such a case, it is unlikely that a potential plaintiff will forego the right to sue individually.

NOTES AND QUESTIONS

1. What type of class action would have been involved in *Hansberry* and *Smith*? We noted above why *Ben-Hur* might have been maintained under Rule 23(b)(1)(A). Can you make an argument that it could have satisfied Rule 23(b)(1)(B), 23(b)(2) and 23(b)(3) as well? See 3B MOORE'S FEDERAL PRACTICE 23-249 et seq.; 1966 Rules Advisory Committee Notes, Rule 23.

2. Suppose an airplane operated by Airline crashes, killing 80 passengers. The individual wrongful death and punitive damages claims on behalf of the 80 passengers will seek a total of $40,000,000. Airline's net worth and applicable insurance pool totals $8,000,000. If a representative seeks to bring a Rule 23(b)(3) class action, the executors of the other

passengers killed will probably opt out and sue individually, trying to strike first and recover their damages before the available fund is depleted. Can you articulate an argument for certifying a class under Rule 23(b)(1)(B)?

Some lawyers have argued that cases such as this — in which the aggregate claims vastly exceed the resources available to pay them — satisfy Rule 23(b)(1)(B). In their view, the facts present the "constructive bankruptcy" of the defendant. Absent a class, the race to the courthouse will deprive some claimants of a meaningful opportunity to recover anything. This theory has met with mixed success. In one portion of the massive Dalkon Shield litigation, which involved a defective intrauterine device, a district court certified a nationwide Rule 23(b)(1)(B) class of women seeking punitive damages against the manufacturer. (Indeed, the manufacturer, as defendant, moved for the certification of the plaintiff class.) The district judge noted that the punitive damages claims exceeded $2.3 billion, while the net worth of the defendant was slightly more than $280 million. In his view, these numbers "raise[d] the unconscionable possibility that large numbers of plaintiffs who are not first in line at the courthouse door will be deprived of a practical means of redress." In re Northern District of California Dalkon Shield IUD Prods. Liability Litigation, 526 F. Supp. 887, 893 (N.D. Cal. 1981).

The Ninth Circuit reversed the class certification. It criticized the district court for not engaging in sufficient factfinding to determine the defendant's actual assets, whether cases had been settled, and the amount of any insurance coverage for the claims. The Ninth Circuit concluded that on the record, "the detrimental effect of separate punitive damages awards is not clearly inescapable." In re Northern District of California Dalkon Shield IUD Prods. Liability Litigation, 693 F.2d 847, 851 (9th Cir.), *cert. denied* 459 U.S. 1171 (1982). Does anything in Rule 23(b)(1) require a showing that the detriment to absentees from individual litigation be "clearly inescapable?"

Not all courts have been as demanding regarding the showing required to certify a Rule 23(b)(1)(B) class on the constructive bankruptcy theory. In Coburn v. 4-R Corp., 77 F.R.D. 43 (E.D. Ky. 1977), the court estimated that the wrongful death claims emanating from a fire at a supper club, while not precisely calculable, "might reasonably exceed" $16 million. In addition, the court noted that defense counsel estimated the defendants' assets at about $3 million. The court certified a class under Rule 23(b)(1)(B), concluding "[t]here is good reason to believe from the foregoing that total judgments might substantially exceed the ability of defendants to respond." Id. at 45.

d. Notice to class members

Read Rule 23(c)(2) and Rule 23(d)(2). As we have seen, Rule 23(c)(2) requires individual notice to some members of a Rule 23(b)(3) class. In Eisen v. Carlisle & Jacquelin,

417 U.S. 156 (1974), the Supreme Court held that the cost of such notice must be borne initially by the class representatives. Although that expense would ultimately be a taxable "cost" of litigation which the losing party would have to pay, the Court precluded imposing the cost on the nonclass party at the outset of litigation.

Without doubt, the holding in *Eisen* has killed many potential class actions. The facts of *Eisen* demonstrate why. The representative was part of a class of over two million investors alleging violations of federal antitrust and securities laws. Mr. Eisen's personal claim under these federal laws was about $70. To maintain the class action, however, he would have had to pay for individual notice to hundreds of thousands of identifiable class members. Even at the low postal rates of the time, sending this notice would have cost $225,000. Not surprisingly, no potential representative will be willing to put up $225,000 to engage in complex litigation that will, at best, return that cost plus $70 and which, at worst, will return nothing.

It is worth considering whether notice is worth the effort as a practical matter. Although the notice comes from the court, counsel for both sides in the litigation have a hand in drafting it. Plaintiff's counsel usually will want the allegations set out as fact, while the defense will insist that the notice declare that there has been no finding of liability. Often, the result is a notice filled with legalese, unintelligible to the lay person. Professor Miller demonstrated the point by publishing actual responses from persons who had received notice that they were members of a class suing antibiotics manufacturers for alleged violation of antitrust laws. The responses received by the clerk of the court included these:

> Dear Mr. Clerk: I have your notice that I owe you $300 for selling drugs. I have never sold any drugs, especially those you have listed; but I have sold a little whiskey once in a while.

> Dear Sir: I received this paper from you. I guess I really don't understand it, but if I have been given one of those drugs, nobody told me why. If it means what I think it does, I have not been with a man in nine years.

> Dear Sir: I received your pamphlet on drugs, which I think will be of great value to me in the future. I am unable to attend your class, however.

Arthur Miller, *Problems of Giving Notice in Class Actions*, 58 F.R.D. 313, 322 (1972).

NOTES AND QUESTIONS

1. We discussed above why notice is required in the Rule 23(b)(3) class action. But why is it not required in the others? Courts are not required to give notice to members of a Rule 23(b)(1) or (b)(2) class, and nothing in Rule 23 requires that such members be permitted to opt out of the case. Yet they will be bound by the result of the case under Rule 23(c)(3). Is this consistent with *Mullane* and *Hansberry*?

2. What would be the consequence of permitting opt outs in class actions under Rule 23(b)(1) and 23(b)(2)?

3. Is the requirement in Rule 23(c)(2) that the court give the best notice practicable, "including individual notice to all members who can be identified through reasonable effort," more stringent than *Mullane* would require? Did *Mullane* require individual notice to such a broad group? Why do you think Rule 23(c)(2) specifies individual notice?

4. Under what circumstances would a court be likely to give notice to class members under Rule 23(d)(2)? What would be the purpose of such notice? Rule 23 is silent as to whether members of a Rule 23(b)(1) or 23(b)(2) class can opt out. Does any provision of Rule 23(c) or 23(d) give the court sufficient discretion to allow a member of such a class to opt out? If not, why would the court give notice to members in those classes? Recall that in *Mullane*, the Court required notice even without a right to opt out.

5. In *Eisen*, the representative might have lessened the cost of notice by trimming the class definition substantially. For example, he might have pursued a class action on behalf of the investors in a particular city. But what would such a narrow class definition do to the attorney's willingness to pursue the case? Moreover, at some point, she risks failing to satisfy numerosity.

6. Should the representative's lawyer be permitted to advance the cost of notice to her client? In *Eisen*, wasn't the attorney the de facto real party in interest in the case? If so, why shouldn't the lawyer be able to come up with the money? Traditional rules governing professional responsibility of lawyers permit the lawyer to advance certain litigation costs, so long as the client ultimately remain responsible for them. See, e.g., MODEL CODE OF PROFESSIONAL RESPONSIBILITY DR 5-103(B).

In In re Mid-Atlantic Toyota Antitrust Litigation, 93 F.R.D. 485 (D. Md. 1982), the court denied class certification because counsel for the class maintained that it "will not, as a matter of policy, seek reimbursement from the class representatives for the costs and expenses incurred." Id. The court explained that ethical rules such as DR 5-103(B) are intended "to prevent the attorney from acquiring a financial interest in the litigation which might interfere with his/her exercise of independent professional judgment, especially when it comes to deciding whether to settle the case." Id. at 490. Is it realistic to expect that lawyers will not have such a financial interest?

e. Court's Role in Dismissal and Settlement

Read Rule 23(e). In cases other than class actions, the court generally does not need to approve a settlement or voluntary dismissal. The class action is different because the court's role is different. As we have seen, Rules 23(c) and 23(d) envision a very active role for the judge. She is not simply a neutral umpire reacting to parties' actions. Instead, she plays a vital role in assuring and constantly reassessing whether the class members' interests are being represented adequately. Because of the possible conflict of interest between a class and its counsel, the judge is required to assess the fairness of any settlement independently. Note that Rule 23(e) requires the court to give notice to class members. This is done in an effort to solicit members' feedback as to the fairness of a proposed compromise. The assessment of fairness, however, is not a democratic exercise. Some courts have upheld settlements as fair even though they were opposed by a majority of the class. See, e.g., TBK Partners, Ltd. v. Western Union Corp., 675 F.2d 456 (2d Cir. 1982).

Must the court approve a settlement entered after the case was filed but before any class was certified? In other words, is an uncertified class action a "class action" under Rule 23(e)? It seems the answer should depend on what is being compromised. If it is simply the claims of the representatives, perhaps court approval and notice to class members is not necessary. If the settlement purports to compromise the interests of class members, however, the court should (or perhaps must?) proceed under Rule 23(e). Indeed, it is not uncommon to send out notice of certification under Rule 23(c)(2) or 23(d)(2) and notice of proposed settlement under Rule 23(e) simultaneously.

5. Subject Matter Jurisdiction

Many class actions brought in federal court invoke federal question jurisdiction. In these, as you will recall from Chapter 4, the citizenship of the parties and the amount in controversy are irrelevant. But what if a plaintiff class seeks to invoke diversity of citizenship jurisdiction? Must all members of the class be of diverse citizenship from the defendant? Must all members of the class claim an amount exceeding $50,000?

In *Ben-Hur*, the Supreme Court held that only the named representative's citizenship is relevant in determining whether there is complete diversity under *Strawbridge v. Curtiss*. This holding is consistent with the notion that the named representative is a formal party, while the class members are not. It is also consistent with the principle of supplemental jurisdiction. Once the representative properly invokes federal court jurisdiction, *Ben-Hur* permitted binding those whose claims were so closely related to the representative as to constitute part of the same case or controversy.

What about amount in controversy? Remember from our discussion of diversity of citizenship jurisdiction that multiple plaintiffs may not aggregate their claims to satisfy the amount in controversy requirement, unless they assert a joint, common, or undivided right. Recall also that such rights are rare outside the property context. This rule would counsel that every member of a plaintiff class should have to satisfy the amount in controversy requirement. On the other hand, however, the doctrine of supplemental jurisdiction would seem to support class actions so long as the named representative's claim satisfied the amount in controversy requirement. The Supreme Court rejected this argument (actually, the majority opinion ignored it) in Zahn v. International Paper Co., 414 U.S. 291 (1967). *Zahn* made it clear that every member of the class must satisfy the amount in controversy requirement independently.

Obviously, *Ben-Hur* and *Zahn* are completely inconsistent. For determining citizenship, the court looks only to the named representative. But in determining amount in controversy, the court looks to every member of the class. Of the two, commentators have criticized *Zahn* as the aberration. Indeed, as one treatise says: "Put bluntly, *Zahn* is an unprincipled opinion aimed at removing diversity of citizenship cases from the federal courts." 1 MOORE'S FEDERAL PRACTICE 927.

It is possible, however, that the supplemental jurisdiction statute, 28 U.S.C. § 1367, has overruled the result in *Zahn*. Read § 1367(a) and (b). Commentators agree that the literal terms of § 1367 do overrule *Zahn*. Do you see why?

But it seems that Congress did not intend the result dictated by its statute. In a paragraph of the legislative history to the statute, a congressional committee stated that the legislature did not intend to overrule *Zahn*. Three professors involved in the drafting of the statute explain that the statement in the legislative history "was an attempt to correct the oversight" about the effect of the statutory language. Thomas Rowe, Stephen Burbank & Thomas Mengler, *Compounding or Creating Confusion About Supplemental Jurisdiction? A Reply to Professor Freer*, 40 EMORY L.J. 943, 960 n.60 (1991). Professor Wright concludes bluntly that *Zahn* is overruled "[u]nless the legislative history is to prevail over the plain language of the statute." WRIGHT, FEDERAL COURTS 39.

Free v. Abbott Laboratories
51 F. 3d 524 (5th Cir. 1995)

This class action brought under the antitrust laws of the State of Louisiana requires that we decide whether the Judicial Improvements Act of 1990 overrules Zahn v. International Paper Co., 414 U.S. 291 (1973). We hold today that it does. * * *

* * *

III. DIVERSITY AND SUPPLEMENTAL JURISDICTION

A. Diversity Jurisdiction: The Named Plaintiff's Claims

C. The Class Action

* * *

[The complaint alleged that defendants violated state antitrust law by fixing prices on infant formula. Each class member's claim was limited by law to $20,000. Under state law, however, the representative was allowed to seek recovery of attorney's fees. This addition swelled the representative's claim to over $50,000. Thus, the representative's claim satisfied the amount in controversy requirement, while the other class members' claims did not.]

B. Supplemental Jurisdiction: The Unnamed Plaintiff's Claims

Supplemental jurisdiction over the unnamed plaintiffs' claims has been an open question since Congress passed the Judicial Improvements Act of 1990.

* * *

Defendants argue that Congress changed the jurisdictional landscape in 1990 by enacting § 1367. Section 1367(a) grants district courts supplemental jurisdiction over related claims generally, and § 1367(b) carves exceptions. Significantly, class actions are not among the exceptions.

Some commentators have interpreted this silence to mean that Congress overruled *Zahn* and granted supplemental jurisdiction over the claims of class members who individually do not demand the necessary amount in controversy.[5] Some of § 1367's drafters disagree.[6] No appellate court has ruled on the question yet. The district courts are split even within this circuit, although the majority appear to hold that *Zahn* survives the enactment of §1367.

Perhaps, by some measure transcending its language, Congress did not intend the Judicial Improvements Act to overrule *Zahn*. The House Committee on the Judiciary considered the bill that became § 1367 to be a "noncontroversial" collection of "relatively modest proposals," not the sort of legislative action that would upset any long-established precedent like *Zahn*. Plaintiffs argue that the Act was prompted not by a congressional desire for wholesale revisions of the jurisdictional rules, but by the more limited desire to restore traditional understandings of federal jurisdiction, which were upset by Finley v. United States, 490 U.S. 545 (1989). In *Finley*, the Supreme Court held that federal courts could not exercise pendent-party jurisdiction without an express legislative grant, a grant never thought necessary before. In short, Congress intended the Act to "essentially restore the pre-*Finley* understandings of the authorization for and limits on other forms of supplemental

---

[5] See e.g., 1 JAMES W. MOORE ET AL, MOORE'S FEDERAL PRACTICE, ¶ 0.97[5], at 928 (2d ed. 1994); 2 HERBERT B. NEWBERG & ALBA CONTE, NEWBERG ON CLASS ACTIONS. § 6.11, at 6-48 (3d ed. 1992); Joan Steinman, *Section 1367 — Another Party Heard From*, 41 EMORY L. J. 85, 103 (1992); Thomas C. Arthur & Richard D. Freer, *Grasping at Burnt Straws: The Disaster of the Supplemental Jurisdiction Statute*, 40 EMORY L. J. 963, 981 (1991).

[6] See Thomas D. Rowe, Jr., Stephen B. Burbank, & Thomas M. Mengler, *Compounding or Creating Confusion About Supplemental Jurisdiction? A Reply to Professor Freer*, 40 EMORY L.J. 943, 960 n. 90 (1991). Professors Rowe, Burbank, and Mengler all had a hand in crafting the supplemental jurisdiction statute. See Rowe, et al. supra 40 EMORY L.J. at 949 n.27; H.R. REP. No. 734, 101st Cong., 2d Sess. 27, reprinted in 1990 U.S.C.C.A.N. 6860, 6873 n. 13.

jurisdiction," not, arguably, to alter *Zahn.* 1990 U.S.C.C.A.N. at 6874. A disclaimer in the legislative history strives to make this point clear by stating: "The section is not intended to affect the jurisdictional requirements of 28 U.S.C. § 1332 in diversity-only class actions, as those requirements were interpreted prior to *Finley.*" 1990 U.S.C.C.A.N. at 6875. The passage cites *Zahn* as a pre-*Finley* case untouched by the Act. 1990 U.S.C.C.A.N. at 6875 n.17; see also Rowe et al., supra, 40 EMORY L.J. at 960 n.90 (stating that this passage was intended to demonstrate that *Zahn* was to survive the enactment of § 1367).

We cannot search legislative history for congressional intent unless we find the statute unclear or ambiguous. Here, it is neither. The statute's first section vests federal courts with the power to hear supplemental claims generally, subject to limited exceptions set forth in the statute's second section. Class actions are not among the enumerated exceptions.

Omitting the class action from the exception may have been a clerical error. But the statute is the sole repository of congressional intent where the statute is clear and does not demand an absurd result. See West Virginia Univ. Hosps., Inc. v. Casey, 111 S. Ct. 1138, 1147 (1991) (refusing to permit the Court's perception of the 'policy' of the statute to overcome its 'plain language'"); United States v. X-Citement Video, Inc., 115 S. Ct. 464, 467-68 (1994) (rejecting the lower court's "plain language reading" of a statute where that reading would create a "positively absurd" result). Abolishing the strictures of *Zahn* is not an absurd result. Justice Brennan's dissent joined by Justices Douglas and Marshall states the counter position. Some respected commentators would welcome *Zahn*'s demise. See, e.g., 1 MOORE ET AL., supra, § 0.97[5], at 928; Arthur & Freer, supra, 40 EMORY L.J. at 1008 n.6 ("Abrogating *Zahn* would hardly be absurd" since doing so would harmonize case law and "enable federal courts to resolve complex interstate disputes in mass tort situations."). But the wisdom of the statute is not our affair beyond determining that overturning *Zahn* is not absurd. We are persuaded that under § 1367 a district court can exercise supplemental jurisdiction over members of a class, although they did not meet the amount-in-controversy requirement, as did the class representatives.

* * *

* * * We *vacate* the district court's remand order, and *remand* to the district court for further proceedings. The petition for mandamus is *denied.*

NOTES AND QUESTIONS

1. As the court in *Abbott Laboratories* noted, district courts have reached different conclusions on this issue, although most appear to hold that the statute has not overruled *Zahn.* Compare Lindsay v. Kvortek, 865 F. Supp. 264 (W.D. Pa. 1994) (*Zahn* overruled) and Garza v. National American Ins. Co., 807 F. Supp. 1256 (M.D. La. 1992)(same) with Mayo v. Key Fin. Servs., Inc., 812 F. Supp. 277 (D. Mass. 1993)(*Zahn* survives) and Averdick v. Republic Fin. Servs., Inc., 803 F. Supp. 37 (E.D. Ky. 1992)(same).

Before passage of § 1367, filing a diversity of citizenship class action in which only the class representative's claim met the jurisdictional requirement would have violated Rule 11. Now there is appellate authority that the practice is proper. The change was wrought by a statute which, according to Congress, was not intended to change anything on this issue. In view of the state of the case law, should Congress amend § 1367 or await further judicial development? If Congress should act, what should it do?

2. Unless a plaintiff class can invoke federal question jurisdiction, *Zahn* makes it very difficult to bring a class action in federal court. The class action with thousands of people suffering relatively small damages cannot meet the amount in controversy requirement. And if every class member does have a claim exceeding $50,000 and these class actions are brought under Rule 23(b)(3), the odds are high that class members will opt out and pursue claims individually. Thus, some criticized *Zahn* as effectively closing the federal courthouse door to state law consumer class actions, funneling them to state courts. Is there anything wrong with doing that?

3. Recall from our discussion of diversity of citizenship jurisdiction that an unincorporated association takes on the citizenship of all its members. Suppose a partnership of 150 people, who are citizens of Arizona, Nevada, and New Mexico, wants to sue a citizen of New Mexico. If it sued as a partnership, the case would be dismissed for failure to satisfy the complete diversity rule. Assuming the amount in controversy could be met, could the partnership sue as a class? Whom would you, as counsel, select as named representative(s)? See Kerney v. Fort Griffin Fandangel Assn., 624 F.2d 717 (5th Cir. 1980).

6. Personal Jurisdiction

Must the court in which a class action is pending have in personam jurisdiction over all class members? *Mullane*, which we read in Chapter 3, involved a New York statute that established a time limit during which members of a pooled trust fund could sue the trustee for misfeasance. The Supreme Court held, among other things, that the scheme violated due process insofar as it did not provide for individual notice to members whose names and addresses were readily available. Although *Mullane* was not technically a class action, does it help us address the question here?

The Supreme Court addressed the question more directly in Phillips Petroleum Co. v. Shutts, 472 U.S. 797 (1985). In that case, three named representatives brought a Rule 23(b)(3) class action in Kansas state court (Kansas's class action rule was modeled on Federal Rule 23). They purported to represent over 33,000 other owners of royalty interests in gas wells, and sued Phillips Petroleum to recover interest on royalty payments that the company had delayed. The average interest claim of each member of the class was

CHAPTER 13 SPECIAL MULTIPARTY LITIGATION: INTERPLEADER AND THE CLASS ACTION

$100. (Remember, *Zahn* is not a problem here. Why?) Each class member was given the notice required by Rule 23(c)(1). About 3,400 opted out, leaving a class of about 28,000. Of those, about 1,000 were Kansas citizens. Defendant argued that the Kansas court could not enter a binding judgment against the other 27,000, since they did not have minimum contacts with Kansas which would satisfy *International Shoe*.

The Supreme Court rejected the argument, and drew a distinction between members of a plaintiff class and defendants in a nonclass suit:

> The purpose of [the "minimum contacts"] test, of course, is to protect a defendant from the travail of defending in a distant forum, unless the defendant's contacts with the forum make it just to force him to defend there. * * *
>
> * * * An adverse judgment by Kansas courts in this case may extinguish the chose in action forever through res judicata. Such an adverse judgment, petitioner claims, would be every bit as onerous to an absent plaintiff as an adverse judgment on the merits would be to a defendant. Thus, the same due process protections should apply to absent plaintiffs: Kansas should not be able to exert jurisdiction over the plaintiffs' claims unless the plaintiffs have sufficient minimum contacts with Kansas.
>
> We think petitioner's premise is in error. The burdens placed by a State upon an absent class-action plaintiff are not of the same order or magnitude as those it places upon an absent defendant. An out-of-state defendant summoned by a plaintiff is faced with the full powers of the forum State to render judgment *against* it. The defendant must generally hire counsel and travel to the forum to defend itself from the plaintiff's claim, or suffer a default judgment. The defendant may be forced to participate in extended and often costly discovery, and will be forced to respond in damages or to comply with some other form of remedy imposed by the court should it lose the suit. The defendant may also face liability for court costs and attorney's fees. These burdens are substantial, and the minimum contacts requirement of the Due Process Clause prevents the forum State from unfairly imposing them upon the defendant.
>
> A class-action plaintiff, however, is in quite a different posture. * * * In sharp contrast to the predicament of a defendant haled into an out-of-state forum, the plaintiffs in this suit were not haled anywhere to defend themselves upon pain of a default judgment. As commentators have noted, from the plaintiffs' point of view a class action resembles a "quasi-administrative proceeding, conducted by the judge." 3B J. MOORE & J. KENNEDY, MOORE'S FEDERAL PRACTICE ¶ 23.45[4.-5] (1984).
>
> * * *
>
> Unlike a defendant in a normal civil suit, an absent class-action plaintiff is not required to do anything. He may sit back and allow the litigation to runs its course, content in knowing that there are safeguards provided for his protection. In most

class actions an absent plaintiff is provided at least with an opportunity to "opt out" of the class, and if he takes advantage of that opportunity he is removed from the litigation entirely.

* * *

We reject petitioner's contention that the Due Process Clause of the Fourteenth Amendment requires that absent plaintiffs affirmatively "opt in" to the class, rather than be deemed members of the class if they do not "opt out." We think that such a contention is supported by little, if any precedent, and that it ignores the differences between class-action plaintiffs, on the one hand, and defendants in nonclass civil suits on the other. Any plaintiff may consent to jurisdiction. The essential question, then, is how stringent the requirement for a showing of consent will be.

We think that the procedure followed by Kansas, where a fully descriptive notice is sent by first-class mail to each class member, with an explanation of the right to "opt out," satisfies due process.

472 U.S. at 807-12.

NOTES AND QUESTIONS

1. How can a state lacking in personam jurisdiction over a class member force her to take an affirmative act (opt out) to avoid being bound by its judgment?

2. Would *Shutts* permit a binding final judgment against plaintiff class members in actions brought under Rule 23(b)(1) or (b)(2)?

3. In a footnote, the Court limited its holding to plaintiff class actions "concerning claims wholly or predominately for money judgments." The Court would "intimate no view concerning other types of class actions, such as those seeking equitable relief." 472 U.S. at 811-12 n.3. Can you articulate a reason for different treatment when a plaintiff class action seeks equitable relief?

4. In the same footnote, the Court indicated that its discussion did not address defendant classes. Indeed, it seems clear that the Court would not permit defendant class actions to bind members of the defendant class over whom the court lacked in personam jurisdiction. Interestingly, in decisions before *Shutts*, several courts permitted actions against defendant classes even though they only had in personam jurisdiction only the named representative. See, e.g., Dale Electronics, Inc. v. R.C.L. Electronics, Inc., 53 F.R.D. 531 (D. N.H. 1971); Canuel v. Oskoian, 23 F.R.D. 307 (D. R.I. 1959).

5. Remember that the prevailing party in litigation recovers her costs and, in exceptional circumstances, attorney's fees, from the losing party. Suppose a plaintiff class action resulted in judgment for the defendant. From whom can the defendant recover costs and, if appropriate, attorney's fees? Is the representative of the plaintiff class solely responsible for these amounts, or may she seek contribution from the class? If the latter, shouldn't the court be required to have in personam jurisdiction over the class members? The Court in *Shutts* dodged the issue, noting that the petitioner had cited no cases involving such a scenario, and saying "the disposition of these issues is best left to a case which presents them in a more concrete way." 472 U.S. at 810 n.2. Because such issues would only arise when the court entered judgment, how should a court address them at the point of class certification?

6. In a part of the *Shutts* opinion not reproduced above, the Court held that a Kansas court could not apply Kansas substantive law to the claims of class members who had no connection with Kansas. This choice of law issue will be especially important in an upper division course on Conflict of Laws. For our purposes, note that *Shutts* presented the possible use of subclasses. After remand, the trial court could certify subclasses of members to whom the law of a particular state applied. Thus, all claims governed by Kansas, or Missouri, or Oklahoma law could be resolved, respectively, en masse.

7. For extensive and often entertaining commentary on *Shutts*, see John Kennedy, *The Supreme Court Meets the Bride of Frankenstein: Phillips Petroleum Co. v. Shutts and the State Multistate Class Action*, 34 U. KAN. L. REV. 255 (1985); Miller & Crump, supra, 96 YALE L.J. 1.

CHAPTER 14

APPEALS

A. Introduction and Integration

Earlier we examined two mechanisms by which judgments can be re-examined. In one, the rendering court reopens and reconsiders the judgment. In federal court, this approach is controlled by Rule 60. In the second, the dissatisfied litigant attacks the judgment collaterally by challenging its validity or enforceability in a second law suit. This approach is constrained by the rules of preclusion and the full faith and credit provisions. This chapter focuses on a third mechanism for re-examining judgments — appellate review.

In an appeal, a litigant seeks review by a different level of the judiciary. An appeal does not include a new trial — it is a review of what happened in the trial court.[*] Thus, there are no juries and the appellate court does not take evidence. Instead, the appellate court relies on the transcript and other records of the proceedings below. Appellate courts typically sit in multi-judge panels of three or more.

There is no constitutional right to appeal in either civil or criminal cases. See Dohany v. Rogers, 281 U.S. 362, 369 (1930); Reetz v. Michigan, 188 U.S. 505, 508 (1903). See John Leubsdorf, *Constitutional Civil Procedure*, 64 TEX. L. REV. 579, 628-31 (1984). Today the federal system and all state courts have some mechanisms for appeal, although not all states permit appeals "of right." In Virginia and West Virginia, for example, appellate review is entirely discretionary, that is, before addressing the merits of the appeal, the appellate court decides whether to hear the appeal at all. See Thomas Marvell, *Appellate Capacity and Caseload Growth*, 16 AKRON L. REV. 43, 72-74 (1982).

---

[*] Some states permit litigants to "appeal" by seeking a trial *de novo* before a different court. Under this system, which is often used for minor criminal offenses, the defendant is tried first before a court of limited jurisdiction, such as a police traffic court, without a jury. If convicted, the defendant may request a trial de novo before a court of general criminal jurisdiction and a jury. In the trial de novo, the prior trial is ignored — there is no review by the second court of the findings or errors of the first court — and the case is treated as an entirely new proceeding. See generally Ludwig v. Massachusetts, 427 U.S. 618 (1976) (upholding the Massachusetts system of trials de novo). This chapter does not address trials de novo.

Why are appeals allowed at all? One book on appellate courts offers the following justifications:

>*First.* Appellate courts provide a means of ensuring that the law is interpreted and applied correctly and uniformly. ***
>
>*Second.* Appellate courts provide a means for the ongoing development and evolution of the law in the common law tradition. ***
>
>*Third.* Appellate courts heighten the legitimacy and acceptability of judicial decisions. ***
>
>*Fourth.* Appellate courts provide a means for the institutional sharing of judicial responsibility for decisions. ***

DANIEL JOHN MEADOR & JORDANA SIMONE BERNSTEIN, APPELLATE COURTS IN THE UNITED STATES 3-5 (1994). A report by the American Bar Association described appeals as "a fundamental element of procedural fairness as generally understood in this country." ABA COMM. ON STANDARDS OF JUDICIAL ADMINISTRATION: STANDARDS RELATING TO APPELLATE COURTS § 3.10 commentary at 12 (1977). Do you agree? Do the justifications for appeals listed above assume that courts of appeals are more likely to be "correct" than trial courts? Is this assumption warranted? Cf. Brown v. Allen, 344 U.S. 443, 540 (1953) (Jackson, J., concurring)("We are not final because we are infallible, but we are infallible because we are final").

See generally Harlon Dalton, *Taking the Right to Appeal (More or Less) Seriously*, 95 YALE L. J. 62 (1985); Paul Carrington, *The Function of the Civil Appeal: A Late-Century View*, 38 S.C. L. REV. 411 (1987).

B. Appellate Jurisdiction in the Federal Courts

1. Section 1291

The federal appellate courts consist of the United States Courts of Appeals, sometimes called circuit courts, and the United States Supreme Court. (The Supreme Court has trial court jurisdiction over cases involving Ambassadors and cases involving disputes between states.) The courts of appeals primarily review district court decisions, although they also have appellate authority over certain decisions of federal regulatory agencies. The United States Supreme Court primarily reviews decisions of the courts of appeal and of the highest state courts. Congress regulates the jurisdiction of both the courts of appeals and the Supreme Court by statute.

B. Appellate Jurisdiction in the Federal Courts

The primary statute conferring jurisdiction on the courts of appeals is 28 U.S.C. §1291, which provides in relevant part:

> The courts of appeals * * * shall have jurisdiction of appeals from all final decisions of the district courts of the United States, * * * except where a direct review may be had in the Supreme Court. * * *

Notice that §1291 grants an appeal of right in all cases decided by a federal district court. Litigants do not need to persuade the court of appeals that their case warrants review.

The statute nonetheless contains an important qualification — §1291 only grants appellate jurisdiction over "final decisions." The Supreme Court has explained that "[a] 'final decision' generally * * * ends the litigation on the merits and leaves nothing for the court to do but execute the judgment." Catlin v. United States, 324 U.S. 229, 233 (1945). In other words, "final decision" as used in the statute ordinarily means "final judgment" or "final decree."

Would the following rulings be appealable under §1291?
(a) The defendant moves to dismiss the complaint for failure to state a claim. (i) The court grants the motion. (ii) The court denies the motion.
(b) Following a jury verdict, the plaintiff moves for a new trial. (i) The court denies the motion and enters judgment for the defendant. (ii) The court grants the motion for a new trial.

Many decisions made in the course of litigation are "interlocutory," that is, they come before the end of the case and, thus, are not immediately appealable under § 1291. For example, rulings on motions to transfer, discovery, and the admissibility of evidence are all interlocutory. Does it make sense to require litigants to wait until the case is over before appealing? Isn't there a risk of a waste of resources? Suppose, for example, the district court refuses to dismiss a case for lack of jurisdiction and a full trial ensues. On appeal, the court of appeals rules the case should have been dismissed. Wouldn't an early appeal have prevented unnecessary trial expenses? Are there some rights that might be irreparably lost if litigants must await a final judgment before appealing?

What costs might be saved by requiring parties to await a final decision? Does allowing early appeals have any positive or negative effects on the administration of justice? Should decisions about the timing of appeals depend, at least in part, on how likely we think it is that the lower court will be reversed?

In 1991–92, of all civil cases in the district courts that were terminated by some court action, approximately 20% were appealed to the courts of appeal. Of all cases decided by the courts of appeal, approximately 11.7% resulted in a reversal.

2. Collateral Order Doctrine

Suppose a plaintiff who is too poor to pay a filing fee requests that the court waive the fee, and the court denies the motion. At least from the plaintiff's point of view, the ruling is a final decision, because unless the fee is waived, she will never be able to file, let alone proceed to the merits. Should the ruling on the fee waiver be immediately appealable?

The Supreme Court has recognized that in at least some circumstances, a ruling may be immediately appealable even though there is no final ruling on the merits of the case. The leading case is Cohen v. Beneficial Industrial Loan Corp., 337 U.S. 541 (1949), which we first encountered in the chapter on *Erie*, supra at 281. The *Erie* issue in that case was whether the federal court was required to apply a state law that obligated plaintiffs in shareholder derivative actions to post a substantial bond. The district court refused to apply state law, and the defendant immediately appealed. Ultimately, the Supreme Court held that state law should be applied in federal court, but before reaching this issue, the Court had to determine whether the appeal was premature. The Court allowed the interlocutory appeal, explaining:

> The effect of the statute [§1291] is to disallow appeal from any decision which is tentative, informal or incomplete. Appeal gives the upper court a power of review, not one of intervention. So long as the matter remains open, unfinished or inconclusive, there may be no intrusion by appeal. But the District Court's action upon this application was concluded and closed and its decision final in that sense before the appeal was taken.

> Nor does the statute permit appeals, even from fully consummated decisions, where they are but steps towards final judgment in which they will merge. The purpose is to combine in one review all stages of the proceeding that effectively may be reviewed and corrected if and when final judgment results. But this order of the District Court did not make any step toward final disposition of the merits of the case and will not be merged in final judgment. When that time comes, it will be too late effectively to review the present order, and the rights conferred by the statute, if it is applicable, will have been lost, probably irreparably. * * *

> This decision appears to fall in that small class which finally determine claims of right separable from, and collateral to, rights asserted in the action, too important to be denied review and too independent of the cause itself to require that appellate consideration be deferred until the whole case is adjudicated. The Court has long given this provision of the statute this practical rather than a technical construction.

Id. at 546.

Cohen has sometimes been described as an "exception" to the final decision rule, but the Court has explained that "[t]he collateral order doctrine is best understood not as an exception to the 'final decision' rule laid down by Congress in §1291, but as a 'practical construction' of it." Digital Equipment Corp. v. Desktop Direct, Inc., 114 S.Ct. 1992, 1995 (1994). The following case considers how far this "practical construction" extends.

Coopers & Lybrand v. Livesay
437 U.S. 463, 98 S.Ct. 2454, 57 L. Ed. 2d 351 (1978)

JUSTICE STEVENS delivered the opinion of the Court.

The question in this case is whether a district court's determination that an action may not be maintained as a class action pursuant to Fed. Rule Civ. Proc. 23 is a "final decision" within the meaning of 28 U.S.C. § 1291 and therefore appealable as a matter of right. Because there is a conflict in the Circuits over this issue, we granted certiorari and now hold that such an order is not appealable under §1291.

[Plaintiffs brought a class action against an accounting firm, alleging violations of federal securities laws. The district judge certified the class, but then changed his mind. Plaintiff appealed the decertification of the class action under §1291.]

* * *

* * * The Court of Appeals regarded its appellate jurisdiction as depending on whether the decertification order had sounded the "death knell" of the action. After examining the amount of respondents' claims in relation to their financial resources and the probable cost of the litigation, the court concluded that they would not pursue their claims individually. The Court of Appeals therefore held that it had jurisdiction to hear the appeal and, on the merits, reversed the order decertifying the class.

Federal appellate jurisdiction generally depends on the existence of a decision by the District Court that "ends the litigation on the merits and leaves nothing for the court to do but execute the judgment." Catlin v. United States, 324 U.S. 229, 233 (1945).[8] An order refusing to certify, or decertifying, a class does not of its own force terminate the entire litigation because the plaintiff is free to proceed on his individual claim. Such an order is appealable, therefore, only if it comes within an appropriate exception to the final-judgment rule. In this case respondents rely on the "collateral order" exception articulated by this Court in Cohen v. Beneficial Industrial Loan Corp., 337

---

[8] For a unanimous Court in Cobbledick v. United States, 309 U.S. 323, 325 (1940), Justice Frankfurter wrote"

"Since the right to a judgment from more than one court is a matter of grace and not a necessary ingredient of justice, Congress from the very beginning has, by forbidding piecemeal disposition on appeal of what for practical purposes is a single controversy, set itself against enfeebling judicial administration. Thereby is avoided the obstruction to just claims that would come from permitting the harassment and cost of a succession of separate appeals from the various rulings to which a litigation may give rise, from its initiation to entry of judgment. To be effective, judicial administration must not be leaden–footed. Its momentum would be arrested by permitting separate reviews of the component elements in a unified cause."

U.S. 541 [1949], and on the "death knell" doctrine adopted by several Circuits to determine the appealability of orders denying class certification.

I

* * *

To come within the "small class""of decisions excepted from the final-judgment rule by *Cohen*, the order must conclusively determine the disputed question, resolve an important issue completely separate from the merits of the action, and be effectively unreviewable on appeal from a final judgment. An order passing on a request for class certification does not fall in that category. First, such an order is subject to revision in the District Court. Fed. Rule Civ. Proc. 23 (c)(1). Second, the class determination generally involves considerations that are "enmeshed in the factual and legal issues comprising the plaintiff's cause of action."[12] Finally, an order denying class certification is subject to effective review after final judgment at the behest of the named plaintiff or intervening class members. For these reasons, as the Courts of Appeals have consistently recognized, the collateral-order doctrine is not applicable to the kind of order involved in this case.

II

Several Circuits, including the Court of Appeals in this case, have held that an order denying class certification is appealable if it is likely to sound the "death knell" of the litigation. The "death knell" doctrine assumes that without the incentive of a possible group recovery the individual plaintiff may find it economically imprudent to pursue his lawsuit to a final judgment and then seek appellate review of an adverse class determination. Without questioning this assumption, we hold that orders relating to class certification are not independently appealable under §1291 prior to judgment.

* * *

* * * The appealability of any order entered in a class action is determined by the same standards that govern appealability in other types of litigation. Thus, if the "death knell""doctrine has merit, it would apply equally to the many interlocutory orders in ordinary litigation — rulings on discovery, on venue, on summary judgment — that may have such tacticaleconomic significance that a defeat is tantamount to a "death knell" for the entire case.

Though a refusal to certify a class is inherently interlocutory, it may induce a plaintiff to abandon his individual claim. On the other hand, the litigation will often survive an adverse class

---

[12] "Evaluation of many of the questions entering into determination of class action questions is intimately involved with the merits of the claims. The typicality of the representative's claims or defenses, the adequacy of the representative, and the presence of common questions of law or fact are obvious examples. The more complex determinations required in Rule 23 (b)(3) class actions entail even greated entanglement with the merits ...." 15 C. WRIGHT, A. MILLER, & E. COOPER, FEDERAL PRACTICE AND PROCEDURE § 3911, p. 485 n. 45 (1976)

determination. What effect the economic disincentives created by an interlocutory order may have on the fate of any litigation will depend on a variety of factors.[15] Under the "death knell" doctrine, appealability turns on the court's perception of that impact in the individual case. Thus, if the court believes that the plaintiff has adequate incentive to continue, the order is considered interlocutory; but if the court concludes that the ruling, as a practical matter, makes further litigation improbable, it is considered an appealable final decision.

The finality requirement in §1291 evinces a legislative judgment that "[r]estricting appellate review to 'final decisions' prevents the debilitating effect on judicial administration caused by piecemeal appeal disposition of what is, in practical consequence, but a single controversy." Eisen v. Carlisle & Jacquelin, 417 U.S. 156, 170 [1974]. Although a rigid insistence on technical finality would sometimes conflict with the purposes of the statute, even adherents of the "death knell" doctrine acknowledge that a refusal to certify a class does not fall in that limited category of orders which, though nonfinal, may be appealed without undermining the policies served by the general rule. It is undisputed that allowing an appeal from such an order in the ordinary case would run "directly contrary to the policy of the final judgment rule embodied in 28 U.S.C. § 1291 and the sound reasons for it ...." Yet several Courts of Appeals have sought to identify on a case-by-case basis those few interlocutory orders which, when viewed from the standpoint of economic prudence, may induce a plaintiff to abandon the litigation. These orders, then, become appealable as a matter of right.

In administering the "death knell" rule, the courts have used two quite different methods of identifying an appealable class ruling. Some courts have determined their jurisdiction by simply comparing the claims of the named plaintiffs with an arbitrarily selected jurisdictional amount; others have undertaken a thorough study of the possible impact of the class order on the fate of the litigation before determining their jurisdiction. Especially when consideration is given to the consequences of applying these tests to pretrial orders entered in non-class-action litigation, it becomes apparent that neither provides an acceptable basis for the exercise of appellate jurisdiction.

The formulation of an appealability rule that turns on the amount of the plaintiff's claim is plainly a legislative, not a judicial, function. While Congress could grant an appeal of right to those whose claims fall below aspecific amount in controversy, it has not done so. Rather, it has made "finality" the test of appealability. Without a legislative prescription, an amount-in-controversy rule is necessarily an arbitrary measure of finality because it ignores the variables that inform a litigant's decision to proceed, or not to proceed, in the face of an adverse class ruling. Moreover, if the jurisdictional amount is to be measured by the aggregated claims of the named plaintiffs, appellate jurisdiction may turn on the joinder decisions of counsel rather than the finality of the order.

While slightly less arbitrary, the alternative approach to the "death knell" rule would have a serious debilitating effect on the administration of justice. It requires class-action plaintiffs to build a record in the trial court that contains evidence of those factors deemed relevant to the "death knell" issue and district judges to make appropriate findings. And one Court of Appeals has even required that the factual inquiry be extended to all members of the class because the policy against interlocutory appeals can be easily circumvented by joining "only those whose individual claims would not

---

[15] E.g., the plaintiff's resources; the size of his claim and his subjective willingness to finance prosecution of the claim; the probable cost of the litigation and the possibility of joining others who will share that cost; and the prospect of prevailing on the merits and reversing an order denying class certification.

warrant the cost of separate litigation"; to avoid this possibility, the named plaintiff is required to prove that no member of the purported class has a claim that warrants individual litigation.

A threshold inquiry of this kind may, it is true, identify some orders that would truly end the litigation prior to final judgment; allowing an immediate appeal from those orders may enhance the quality of justice afforded a few litigants. But this incremental benefit is outweighed by the impact of such an individualized jurisdictional inquiry on the judicial system's overall capacity to administer justice.

The potential waste of judicial resources is plain. The district court must take evidence, entertain argument, and make findings; and the court of appeals must review that record and those findings simply to determine whether a discretionary class determination is subject to appellate review. And if the record provides an inadequate basis for this determination, a remand for further factual development may be required. Moreover, even if the court makes a "death knell" finding and reviews the class-designation order on the merits, there is no assurance that the trial process will not again be disrupted by interlocutory review. For even if a ruling that the plaintiff does not adequately represent the class is reversed on appeal, the district court may still refuse to certify the class on the ground that, for example, common questions of law or fact do not predominate. Under the "death knell" theory, plaintiff would again be entitled to an appeal as a matter of right pursuant to § 1291. And since other kinds of interlocutory orders may also create the risk of a premature demise, the potential for multiple appeals in every complex case is apparent and serious.

Perhaps the principal vice of the "death knell" doctrine is that it authorizes indiscriminate interlocutory review of decisions made by the trial judge. The Interlocutory Appeals Act of 1958, 28 U.S.C. §1292 (b), was enacted to meet the recognized need for prompt review of certain non final orders. However, Congress carefully confined the availability of such review. Nonfinal orders could never be appealed as a matter of right. Moreover, the discretionary power to permit an interlocutory appeal is not, in the first instance, vested in the courts of appeals. A party seeking review of a nonfinal order must first obtain the consent of the trial judge. This screening procedure serves the dual purpose of ensuring that such review will be confined to appropriate cases and avoiding time-consuming jurisdictional determinations in the court of appeals. Finally, even if the district judge certifies the order under §1292 (b), the appellant still "has the burden of persuading the court of appeals that exceptional circumstances justify a departure from the basic policy of postponing appellate review until after the entry of a final judgment." The appellate court may deny the appeal for any reason, including docket congestion. By permitting appeals of right from class-designation orders after jurisdictional determinations that turn on questions of fact, the "death knell" doctrine circumvents these restrictions.

Additional considerations reinforce our conclusion that the "death knell" doctrine does not support appellate jurisdiction of prejudgment orders denying class certification. First, the doctrine operates only in favor of plaintiffs even though the class issue — whether to certify, and if so, how large the class should be — will often be of critical importance to defendants as well. Certification of a large class may so increase the defendant's potential damages liability and litigation costs that he may find it economically prudent to settle and to abandon a meritorious defense. Yet the Courts of Appeals have correctly concluded that orders granting class certification are interlocutory. Whatever similarities or differences there are between plaintiffs and defendants in this context involve questions of policy for Congress. Moreover, allowing appeals of right from nonfinal orders that turn on the facts of a particular case thrusts appellate courts indiscriminately into the trial process and thus defeats one vital purpose of the final-judgment rule — "that of maintaining the appropriate relationship between the respective courts.... This goal, in the absence of most compelling reasons to the contrary, is very much worth preserving."

Accordingly, we hold that the fact that an interlocutory order may induce a party to abandon his claim before final judgment is not a sufficient reason for considering it a "final decision" within the meaning of §1291. The judgment of the Court of Appeals is reversed with directions to dismiss the appeal.

It is so ordered.

NOTES AND QUESTIONS

1. The Court has wrestled with whether various orders constitute final decisions under § 1291. Do you agree with its resolution of the following?

(a) In a series of cases, the Court held that orders granting or denying motions to disqualify counsel are not immediately appealable. See Richardson-Merrell, Inc. v. Koller, 472 U.S. 424 (1985); Flanagan v. United States, 465 U.S. 259 (1984); Firestone Tire & Rubber Co. v Risjord, 449 U.S. 368 (1981). The Court stressed that these orders can be reviewed effectively on appeal from the final judgment. But consider the situation of a litigant whose lawyer is disqualified. On appeal from the final judgment, would the litigant have to show only that the disqualification was erroneous, or would she also have to show prejudice? As one leading treatise has observed, "Reversal of an otherwise proper judgment without requiring a showing of prejudice would be costly in the extreme, and would be a high price to pay for the abstract desire to protect freedom of choice in representation." 15B WRIGHT & MILLER, FEDERAL PRACTICE & PROCEDURE § 3914.21, at 99. On the other hand, if the litigant must show prejudice, then she would presumably have to show that the representation by substitute counsel was not as good as she would have received from original counsel and that this qualitative difference altered the outcome. How likely is it that any litigant could ever make this showing?

(b) In Moses H. Cone Memorial Hospital v. Mercury Construction Corp., 460 U.S. 1 (1983), the Supreme Court held that an order staying a federal court action pending resolution of a parallel state case was immediately appealable. The Court reasoned that because the state judgment would be binding on the federal court, the plaintiff was "effectively out of court." The Court further explained that the case fell within the "*Cohen* exception." The defendant argued that the ruling on the stay could be reconsidered by the district court because it did not "conclusively determine the disputed question." The Court rejected this argument, explaining: "this is true only in the technical sense that every order short of a final decree is subject to reopening at the discretion of the district judge. * * * He surely would not have made that decision in the first instance unless he had expected the state court to resolve all relevant issues adequately." Id. at 12-13. Was the district court's ruling in this case any more "conclusive" than the ruling in *Coopers & Lybrand*?

(c) In Puerto Rico Aqueduct & Sewer Authority v. Metcalf & Eddy, Inc., 113 S.Ct. 684 (1993), the defendant, an arm of the Puerto Rico government, argued that it sought to dismiss a suit on grounds that it was immune from suit under the Eleventh Amendment. That Amendment prohibits states from being sued in federal court. The Supreme Court held that the denial of this motion was immediately appealable because a central purpose of Eleventh Amendment immunity is to protect the state from the costs and burdens of trial. This benefit would be effectively lost if a case were erroneously permitted to go to trial. See Mitchell v. Forsyth, 472 U.S. 511, 524-30 (1985) (allowing immediate appeal of order denying an official's claim of absolute or qualified immunity).

(d) In Digital Equipment Corp. v. Desktop Direct, Inc., 114 S.Ct. 1992 (1994), the parties had settled a pending lawsuit and pursuant to the settlement, the plaintiff filed a notice of dismissal. Several months later, the district court granted the plaintiff's motion to vacate the dismissal and rescind the settlement on grounds that the defendant had misrepresented certain facts during the settlement negotiations. The Court held that the defendant could not immediately appeal the district court's grant of the motion to vacate. In reaching this conclusion, the Court focused on whether the decision involved an "important" question that was "effectively unreviewable" upon final judgment. Id. at 1996. The Court explained that "the third *Cohen* question, whether a right is 'adequately vindicable' or 'effectively reviewable,' simply cannot be answered without a judgment about the value of the interests that would be lost through rigorous application of a final judgment requirement." Id. at 2001. "Where statutory and constitutional rights are concerned, 'irretrievabl[e] los[s]' can hardly be trivial * * *. But it is one thing to say that the policy of §1291 to avoid piecemeal litigation should be reconciled with policies embodied in other statutes or the Constitution, and quite another to suggest that this public policy may be trumped routinely by the expectations or clever drafting of private parties." Id. as 2002. "[A]n agreement's provision for immunity from trial * * * simply does not rise to the level of importance needed for recognition under §1291." Id. at 2001.

2. Should the denial of a motion to dismiss for lack of personal jurisdiction or for forum non conveniens be appealable immediately? In Van Cauwenberghe v. Biard, 486 U.S. 517 (1988), a criminal defendant was extradited to the United States and upon arrival here was served with civil process. The defendant moved to dismiss, arguing first that under the extradition treaty he was immune from civil process and, second, on grounds of forum non conveniens. The district court refused to dismiss on either ground, and the defendant sought an immediate appeal. The Supreme Court held that the appeal was not proper. Concerning the ruling on immunity from civil process, the Court concluded that this was simply an argument that the district court lacked personal jurisdiction. The Court then explained:

> In the context of due process restrictions on the exercise of personal jurisdiction, this Court has recognized that the individual interest protected is in "not being subject to the binding judgments of a forum with which [the defendant] has established no meaningful 'contacts, ties, or relations.'" *Burger King Corp.*, quoting *International Shoe Co.* Similarly, we believe petitioner's challenge to the District Court's exercise of personal jurisdiction because he is immune from civil process should be characterized as the right not to be subject to a binding judgment of the court. Because the right not to be subject to a binding judgment may be effectively vindicated following final judgment, we have held that the denial of a claim of lack of jurisdiction is not an immediately appealable collateral order.

Id. at 526-27. Isn't one of the purposes of personal jurisdiction "to protect a defendant from the travail of defending in a distant forum?" Phillips Petroleum Co. v. Shutts, 472 U.S. 797, 807 (1985). Can this purpose be vindicated on appeal following a full trial on the merits?

The Court also rejected an immediate appeal of the forum non conveniens ruling, holding that it is not "completely separate from the merits of the action," but requires an evaluation of the "locus of the alleged culpable conduct, often a disputed issue, and the connection of that conduct to the plaintiff's chosen forum." 486 U.S. at 528.

3. Under California law, a litigant who asserts a claim to real property may record a "lis pedens" — a notice of the pendency of the action. CAL. CODE CIV. PRO. § 405.20. Following the recording of the lis pendens, the property can still be transferred, but any subsequent purchaser's rights will be subject to the outcome of the litigation. Without the lis pendens, a subsequent purchaser's rights to the property would be limited only if the purchaser had actual knowledge of the litigation. A lis pendens can be expunged upon motion if the court finds that the "claimant has not established by a preponderance of the evidence the probable validity of the real property's claims." Id. at § 405.32. Assume that Jane sues Fred seeking title to Blackacre. Jane records a lis depends and Fred moves to have that expunged. Would either the grant or the denial of the expungement be immediately appeal-

CHAPTER 14 APPEALS

able under collateral order doctrine? See Orange County Calif. Airport Hotel Assoc. v. The Hongkong & Shanghai Banking Corp., 52 F. 3d. 821 (9th Cir. 1995).

3. Section 1292

The collateral order doctrine provides a means by which some interlocutory orders can be appealed. In addition to this court-made doctrine, Congress has explicitly authorized immediate appeals of certain interlocutory orders. Section 1292(a)(1) permits the immediate appeal of the grant or denial of an injunction. The statute reflects the reality that the erroneous grant or denial of even a preliminary injunction may result in irreparable harm.

In 1958, Congress established a certification procedure to allow immediate appeal of certain other interlocutory orders. Under §1292(b) the district court may certify an order for immediate appeal. The criteria for certification are that (1) there is "an order," (2) involving "a controlling question," (3) "of law," (4) "as to which there is substantial ground for difference of opinion," and (5) "that an immediate appeal from the order may materially advance the ultimate termination of the litigation." Once an order has been certified, an appeal must be taken to the court of appeals within 10 days. That court may, in its discretion, hear the appeal.

NOTES AND QUESTIONS

1. Review §1292(b), and consider whether the following cases would be proper for certification.
    (a) Plaintiff files suit under the Americans with Disabilities Act, 42 U.S.C. §12101 et seq. Plaintiff's right to recover depends on a difficult and unsettled question of statutory interpretation. Can the district court certify this interpretive question?
    (b) The court orders the plaintiff to provide English translations of certain documents produced pursuant to Rule 34. The translations will be quite expensive to procure.
    (c) The defendant moves to dismiss a case for lack of personal jurisdiction. The court expresses uncertainty as to whether the defendant really has sufficient contacts, but the court decides not to dismiss.
    (d) The district court concludes it would be more convenient for the litigation to proceed in a different district and orders the case transferred under § 1404(a).
    (e) Would the judge's decision in *Coopers & Lybrand* not to certify the class action have been appealable under § 1292(b)?

2. In 1990, Congress authorized the Supreme Court to draft rules that "define when a ruling of a district court is final for the purposes of appeal under Section 1291." 28 U.S.C. § 2072(c). In 1992, Congress amended § 1292 to authorize the Supreme Court to prescribe rules providing for appeals of interlocutory decisions not otherwise covered by § 1292. See 28 U.S.C. § 1292(e). This combination of authority to define final decisions and to allow interlocutory appeals gives the Supreme Court great power to amend the rules governing appealability. If the Court were to take up this invitation, what principles should guide it? Should the Court promulgate a general standard, or should it promulgate rules that deal specifically with different types of orders? See generally *Federal Civil Appellate Jurisdiction: An Interlocutory Restatement*, 47 LAW & CONTEMP. PROBS., No. 2, at 13 (1984).

3. Suppose that one ruling in a case is immediately appealable, but other rulings are not. In an appeal of the first ruling, can the court of appeals exercise "pendent appellate jurisdiction" over the other rulings and review them at the same time? In Swint v. Chambers County Commission, 115 S. Ct. 1203 (1995), the Supreme Court has held that at least under the facts of that case pendent appellate jurisdiction was not proper. There, the rulings concerned different parties and were not "inextricably intertwined." Id. at 1212.. The Court specifically declined to "definitively or preemptively settle * * * whether or when it may be proper for a court of appeals with jurisdiction over one ruling to review, conjunctively, related rulings that are not themselves independently reviewable." Id. The Court suggested that the proper way to resolve the scope of pendent appellate jurisdiction was through the rule making authority under §§ 2072(c) and 1292(e).

4. Rule 54(b)

As a result of the liberal joinder rules of the Federal Rules of Civil Procedure, a single case may include multiple parties or claims. It is possible for the court to grant partial summary judgment and dispose of claims involving one party long before the rest of the case is decided. Forcing that party to await the outcome of the entire cases may impose a significant hardship. As the Supreme Court has explained:

> With the Federal Rules of Civil Procedure, there came an increased opportunity for the liberal joinder of claims in multiple claims actions. This, in turn, demonstrated a need for relaxing the restrictions upon what should be treated as a judicial unit for purposes of appellate jurisdiction. Sound judicial administration did not require relaxation of the standard of finality in the disposition of the individual adjudicated claims for the purpose of their appealability. It did, however, demonstrate that, at least in multiple claims actions, some final decisions, on less than all of the claims, should be appealable without waiting for a final decision on *all* of the claims.

Sears, Roebuck & Co. v Mackey, 351 U.S. 427, 432 (1956)(emphasis in original).

NOTES AND QUESTIONS

1. Read Rule 54(b). Would it permit an immediate appeal in these cases?
    (a) The plaintiff brings suit for breach of contract and seeks damages. The court grants plaintiff's motion for partial summary judgment and holds that the defendant did breach the contract, but the court has not yet determined the amount of damages. Is the ruling on partial summary judgment immediately appealable?
    (b) In response to the plaintiff's breach of contract complaint, the defendant files a compulsory counterclaim alleging the contract in question violates the antitrust laws. The court grants plaintiff's motion for summary judgment on the antitrust counterclaim. Is this grant immediately appealable? If the court had denied the plaintiff's motion, would that be immediately appealable?
    (c) Two plaintiffs file suit against one defendant. The court dismisses the claim of one of the plaintiffs, but not the other. Is that dismissal immediately appealable?
    (d) One plaintiff sues a defendant. Later, the plaintiff seeks to amend her complaint to add a second plaintiff. The court refuses to allow joinder of the second plaintiff. Is this ruling immediately appealable?

2. Rule 54(b) requires "more than one claim." What is a claim? One treatise explains: "A single claimant presents multiple claims for relief * * * when his possible recoveries are more than one in number and not mutually exclusive or, stated another way, when the facts give rise to more than one legal right or cause of action." 10 WRIGHT & MILLER, FEDERAL PRACTICE & PROCEDURE § 2657 at 67. How would this apply in the following cases?
    (a) A customer is bitten by a poisonous snake in a pet store. She brings a claim for damages against the store alleging negligence, strict liability, and violation of state or federal licensing provisions. The court dismisses the statutory claims.
    (b) A prison inmate who is injured by a guard brings suit for damages against the government alleging respondeat superior and negligence in the supervision and training of the guard. The court dismisses the claim based on respondeat superior.

3. Why does Rule 54(b) require that the district court make an express finding "that there is no just reason for delay?" Should the district court's refusal to make such a finding be reviewable?

5. Mandamus

The All Writs Act, 28 U.S.C. §1651(a), authorizes federal courts to "issue all writs necessary or appropriate in aid of their respective jurisdictions and agreeable to the usages and principles of law." Pursuant to this provision, courts of appeals can issue writs of mandamus, ordering a district court to take certain actions. Such writs are deemed "extraordinary remedies." In Will v. United States, 389 U.S. 90, 95-96 (1967), the Court explained:

> The peremptory writ of mandamus has traditionally been used in the federal courts only "to confine an inferior court to a lawful exercise of its prescribed jurisdiction or to compel it to exercise its authority when it is its duty to do so." While the courts have never confined themselves to an arbitrary and technical definition of "jurisdiction," it is clear that only exceptional circumstances amounting to a judicial "usurpation of power" will justify the invocation of this extraordinary remedy. Thus the writ has been invoked where unwarranted judicial action threatened "to embarrass the executive arm of the Government in conducting foreign relations," where it was the only means of forestalling intrusion by the federal judiciary on a delicate area of federal-state relations, where it was necessary to confine a lower court to the terms of an appellate tribunal's mandate, and where a district judge displayed a persistent disregard of the Rules of Civil Procedure promulgated by this Court. And the party seeking mandamus has "the burden of showing that its right to issuance of the writ is 'clear and indisputable.'"

In a similar vein, the Court in Allied Chemical Corp. v. Daiflon, Inc., 449 U.S. 33, 36 (1980) (per curiam), explained: "[O]ur cases have answered the question as to the availability of mandamus * * * with the refrain: 'What never? Well, *hardly* ever!'" In *Allied Chemical*, the district court declined to enter judgment on the basis of the jury's verdict and ordered a new trial. The court of appeals issued a writ ordering the lower court to reinstate the jury verdict. The Supreme Court reversed, stating:

> A trial court's ordering of a new trial rarely, if ever, will justify the issuance of a writ of mandamus. On the contrary, such an order is not an uncommon feature of any trial which goes to verdict. A litigant is free to seek review of the propriety of such an order on direct appeal after a final judgment has been entered. Consequently, it cannot be said that the litigant "has no other adequate means to seek the relief he desires." The authority to grant a new trial, moreover, is confided almost entirely to the exercise of discretion on the part of the trial court. Where a matter is committed to discretion, it cannot be said that a litigant's right to a particular result is "clear and indisputable."

Id.

In *Coopers & Lybrand*, the Court held that the denial of class action certification was not immediately appealable under § 1291. Would the grant or denial of class certification be immediately reviewable by writ of mandamus? Compare In re Rhone-Poulenc Rorer Inc., 51 F.3d 1293 (7th Cir.) *pet. for cert. filed*, 64 U.S.L.W.____(1995) (mandamus granted ordering decertification of a class), with Green v. Occidental Petroleum Corp., 541 F.2d 1335 (9th Cir. 1976) (denying mandamus that would have ordered the judge to certify a class). See 7B WRIGHT & MILLER, FEDERAL PRACTICE AND PROCEDURE § 1802 at 481-83.

Courts frequently use mandamus when the right to a jury trial is improperly denied. See *Dairy Queen*, supra at 485; *Beacon Theatres*, supra at 487. Judge Easterbrook has criticized this use:

> Neither *Beacon Theatres* nor *Dairy Queen* answers the question: Why mandamus? * * * Surely the answer is not * * * that there is a constitutional right at stake. Much federal litigation involves constitutional rights, but the nature of the right does not dictate whether review comes in mid-course or at the end of the district court's proceedings. Jury trial is not the most essential of rights, either.

First National Bank of Waukesha v. Warren, 796 F.2d 999, 1002 (7th Cir. 1986). Do you agree?

6. Appealability of Discovery Orders

Discovery orders ordinarily are not "final decisions" for purposes of § 1291. Occasionally, such orders are reviewed as interlocutory appeals under § 1292(b), but usually it will be difficult to show that a discovery order involves a controlling question of law or that an immediate appeal will materially advance the termination of the litigation. Discovery orders are also occasionally reviewed by means of a writ of mandamus. See Schlagenhauf v. Holder, 379 U.S. 104 (1964).

The most effective way to appeal a discovery order is to defy the order and to be held in contempt of court. Because the courts treat the contempt judgment as a separate proceeding, that judgment is then immediately appealable. You will recall that this is the route used in *Hickman v. Taylor*, and *Ager*, Chapter 9. There, the lawyers and clients refused to turn over material that they believed was protected from discovery. They were convicted of contempt and sent to jail by the trial judge. Although they were allowed to appeal immediately, this is obviously a risky mechanism for securing an appeal.

In extraordinary cases, the Court has allowed immediate appeals of discovery rulings. In the Watergate Tapes Case, United States v. Nixon, 418 U.S. 683 (1974), the special prosecutor subpoenaed tapes, and the district court ordered President Nixon to produce the material. The President appealed to the court of appeals and then sought review in the Supreme Court. Before the Court could reach the merits, it had to decide whether the immediate appeal of this interlocutory order was proper. The Court allowed the appeal, without requiring that the President first be held in contempt. The Court explained: "To require a President of the United States to place himself in the posture of disobeying an order of the court merely to trigger the procedural mechanism for review of the ruling would be unseemly, and would present an unnecessary occasion for constitutional confrontation between two branches of the Government." Id. at 691-92. Would the same rationale apply to a subpoena directed at a former, rather than a sitting, President?

Any alleged discovery errors can, of course, be included as a basis for appeal from the final judgment. However, it is frequently difficult to get a judgment reversed on grounds of a discovery error because of the harmless error doctrine, discussed below.

7. Mechanics of Filing an Appeal

The Federal Rules of Appellate Procedure require that a notice of appeal be filed with the district court within 30 days after the entry of the judgment or order from which the appeal is taken. The time limit is 60 days when the United States is a party. Fed R. App. P. 4(a). The time limit runs from the date the district court enters judgment. The fact that the district court must still determine and assess costs does not extend the time for appeal. Budinich v. Becton Dickinson & Co., 486 U.S. 196 (1988). This timeliness requirement is jurisdictional and cannot be waived or extended except as provided by the Rules. See Fed. R. App. P. 4(a)(5).

The notice of appeal must specify the party or parties appealing and the judgment or order from which the appeal is taken. Fed. R. App. P. 3(c). The Supreme Court has strictly construed this rule and held that where there were 16 plaintiffs and one of the plaintiff's names was inadvertently omitted from the notice of appeal, that party waived his right to appeal. Torres v. Oakland Scavenger Co., 487 U.S. 312 (1988). The Court rejected the argument that the exclusion of a name from the list of parties was a permissible "informality of form or title" under Fed. R. App. Proc. 3(c). The Court held further that "et al." was not an acceptable alternative to the separate listing of each name.

The filing of a notice of appeal does not suspend the effect of a judgment. In order to order to prevent the enforceability of a judgment pending the appeal, the appellant may be required to post a "supersedeas bond" guaranteeing that the judgment will be paid if she loses on appeal. See Fed. R. App. Pro. 8(b). Frequently, the bond must be at least as large as the amount of the judgment plus costs. In one famous case, Penzoil sued Texaco for breach of contract and won a $10.5 billion jury verdict. In order to appeal the judgment, Texaco was required to post a bond in excess of $11 billion. Texaco sought unsuccessfully to enjoin the requirement of so large a bond. See Penzoil Co. v. Texaco, Inc., 481 U.S. 1 (1987). Texaco ultimately filed for bankruptcy and Penzoil settled for $3 billion. See Douglas Laycock, *The Remedies Issues: Compensatory Damages, Specific Performance, Punitive Damages, Supersedeas Bonds and Abstention*, 9 LITIG. REV. 473 (1990).

8. Appellate Jurisdiction of the United States Supreme Court

The appellate jurisdiction of the Supreme Court, like that of the courts of appeals, is defined by statute. See 28 U.S.C. §1254. Traditionally, there have been two mechanisms available for Supreme Court review — appeal and certiorari. In theory, the difference between these two mechanisms is that appellate jurisdiction, where applicable, is available as a matter of right, whereas certiorari review is entirely discretionary. In practice, however, the Court treats appellate jurisdiction as if it were discretionary. In 1988, Congress abolished virtually all of the appellate jurisdiction of the Court.

Parties seek Supreme Court review in over 5000 cases each year. The Supreme Court declines to review most of these and reaches the merits in fewer than 200 cases a year. In deciding which cases to accept for review, the Court relies on the unwritten "Rule of Four," under which certiorari is granted upon the vote of four justices. In deciding whether to grant certiorari, error below is one factor, but not the only or even the most important factor. The Court also considers the importance of the issue presented, whether there is a split among the circuits on the issue, and whether the issue of interest to the Court is squarely presented by the case or is entangled in factual or state law disputes. See Rules of the Supreme Court of the United States, Rule 10.1. What does this list tell you about the Court's perception of its role? A decision by the Court not to grant certiorari has no precedential effect, and contrary to the impression sometimes created in the popular press, such a decision indicates nothing about whether the Court agrees with the lower court opinion.

C. Appeals in State Courts

Each state has its own appellate system. All states have a supreme court and most have intermediate courts of appeals, though these courts have different names in different states. All states except Virginia and West Virginia permit at least one appeal of right. See Marvell, supra, 16 AKRON L. REV. at 72-74, for a discussion of the Virginia and West Virginia appellate systems.

The timing of appeals in state courts is governed by state law (not by federal statutes such as § 1291). Some states allow appeals under circumstances that the federal courts would not. For example, New York allows an immediate appeal of any order that "grants or refuses a new trial," "involves some part of the merits," or "affects a substantial right." N.Y. CIV. PRAC. L. & R. 5701(a)(2)(iii-v). What are the advantages and disadvantages of this approach?

In addition, some states permit mandamus or a similar writ called a writ of prohibition under circumstances that the federal courts would not allow. For example, in *World-Wide Volkswagen*, Chapter 2, the trial court denied the motion to dismiss for lack of jurisdiction and the defendants immediately sought a writ of prohibition. Similarly, in *Kulko*, *Burnham*, and *Asahi*, also in Chapter 2, the defendants sought immediate appellate review of the denial of their motions to dismiss by seeking writs of mandate.

D. Scope of Review

Appellate review involves a reexamination of the judge's rulings in the court below. For that reason, appellate courts will only review issues or objections that were raised at trial and appear on the record — in the pleadings, briefs, or transcripts from the proceeding below. In addition, appellate courts will ordinarily consider only those issues that are raised and argued on appeal — they will not search the record on their own looking for errors. Finally, appellate review is limited by the concept of "harmless error." See Federal Rule 61. Under this doctrine, even where there is error the appellate court will not reverse the judgment unless the error materially affected the outcome. The Supreme Court has described the harmless error test as follows:

> If, when all is said and done, the conviction is sure that the error did not influence the jury, or had but very slight effect, the verdict and the judgment should stand, except perhaps where the departure is from a constitutional norm or a specific command of Congress. But if one cannot say, with fair assurance, after pondering all that happened without stripping the erroneous action from the whole, that the judgment was not substantially swayed by the error, it is impossible to conclude that substantial rights were not affected. The inquiry cannot be merely whether there was enough to support the result, apart from the phase affected by the error. It is rather, even so, whether the error itself had substantial influence.

Kotteakos v. United States, 328 U.S. 750, 764-65 (1946).

Before reviewing an issue properly before it, an appellate court must determine by what standard to review the decision. Issues of law are reviewed de novo, meaning there is no presumption in favor of the lower court's determination and the appellate court can substitute its view of the law for that of the lower court. In reaching its determination, the appellate court can consider legal precedents that the lower court did not consider or was unaware of. See Elder v. Holloway, 114 S.Ct. 1019 (1994).

CHAPTER 14 APPEALS

In contrast to legal determinations, factual determinations are reversible only if "clearly erroneous."[*] See Rule 52(a). The Supreme Court has explained that "a finding is 'clearly erroneous' when although there is evidence to support it, the reviewing court on the entire evidence is left with the definite and firm conviction that a mistake has been committed." Anderson v. Bessemer City, 470 U.S. 564, 573 (1985). However,

> [i]f the district court's account of the evidence is plausible in light of the record viewed in its entirety, the court of appeals may not reverse it even though convinced that had it been sitting as the trier of fact, it would have weighed the evidence differently. Where there are two permissible views of the evidence, the factfinder's choice between them cannot be clearly erroneous.

Id. at 513-514.

What about determinations involving the application of law to fact, are these legal or factual? The Supreme Court has acknowledged that there is no easy rule for distinguishing between legal and factual issues. See Pullman-Standard v. Swint, 456 U.S. 273, 288 (1982). Several cases illustrate the problem:

In Bose Corp. v. Consumers Union of United States, Inc., 466 U.S. 485 (1984), Bose sued Consumers Union, claiming that an article published by the defendant constituted trade libel. Under the applicable First Amendment doctrine, the defendant was liable only if it acted with "actual malice," that is, with knowledge of the falsity or with reckless disregard for the truth. The district court found actual malice. In upholding the court of appeals' reversal, the Supreme Court engaged in a de novo review of the record. The Court explained:

> Rule 52(a) applies to findings of fact, including those described as "ultimate facts" because they may determine the outcome of litigation. But Rule 52(a) does not inhibit an appellate court's power to correct errors of law, including those that may infect a so-called mixed finding of law and fact, or a finding of fact that is predicated on a misunderstanding of the governing rule of law.* * *
>
> A finding of fact in some cases is inseparable from the principles through which it was deduced. At some point, the reasoning by which a fact is "found" crosses the line between application of those ordinary principles of logic and common experience which are ordinarily entrusted to the finder of fact into the realm of a legal rule upon which the reviewing court must exercise its own independent judgment. Where the line is drawn varies according to the nature of the substantive law at issue. Regarding certain largely factual questions in some

---

[*] Rulings on some motions such an forum non conveniens, see Piper Aircraft C. v. Reyno, 454 U.S. 235, 257 (1981), certification of class actions, see Gulf Oil Co. v. Bernard, 452 U.S. 89, 103 (1981), and discovery sanctions, see National Hockey League v. Metropolitan Hockey Club, Inc., 427 U.S. 639, 642 (1976), are reviewable for "abuse of discretion." The Court has suggested that review for abuse of discretion is comparable to review under the clearly erroneous standard. See Cooter & Gell v. Hartmarx Corp., 496 U.S. 384, 405 (1990).

areas of the law, the stakes — in terms of impact on future cases and future conduct — are too great to entrust them finally to the judgment of the trier of fact.

Id. at 501 & n.17. The Court then went on to apply these principles to the case at hand:

In a consideration of the possible application of the distinction to the issue of "actual malice," at least three characteristics of the rule enunciated in the *New York Times* case are relevant. First, the common law heritage of the rule itself assigns an especially broad role to the judge in applying it to specific factual situations. Second, the content of the rule is not revealed simply by its literal text, but rather is given meaning through the evolutionary process of common-law adjudication; though the source of the rule is found in the Constitution, it is nevertheless largely a judge-made rule of law. Finally, the constitutional values protected by the rule make it imperative that judges — and in some cases judges of this Court — make sure that it is correctly applied.

Id. at 501-02.

The Court does not always review de novo mixed questions of law and fact. In Pierce v. Underwood, 487 U.S. 552 (1988), the district court held that a legal position taken by the government was not "substantially justified" and therefore the other party was entitled to attorneys fees under the Equal Access to Justice Act. The Supreme Court held that this ruling should not be reviewed de novo even though it was obviously bound up with an assessment of the strength of the government's legal arguments. Similarly, in Cooter & Gell v. Hartmarx Corp., 496 U.S. 384 (1990), the Court held that a district court's finding that a lawyer had violated Rule 11 was subject to the clearly erroneous standard, even where the district court's ruling is based on a determination of whether the lawyer's legal arguments were well grounded.

NOTES AND QUESTIONS

1. Professor Sward has described the role of standards of review as follows:

Standards of review serve to allocate decision-making responsibility among the various levels of courts in a hierarchial judicial system. A standard of review that calls for considerable deference to trial level decision-makers places primary responsibility for resolving disputes in the trial courts. By contrast, a standard of review that allows non-deferential review by appellate courts places primary decision-making authority in appellate courts.

Ellen Sward, *Appellate Review of Judicial Fact-Finding*, 40 KAN. L. REV. 1, 4 (1990). Why do you think the Court chooses to make trial courts the primary decision makers with

CHAPTER 14 APPEALS

respect to attorney's fees and Rule 11 enforcement, but not with respect to findings of malice in libel cases?

2. Lower courts have held that the determination of citizenship for purposes of diversity jurisdiction is a mixed question of law and fact for which "clearly erroneous" is the proper standard of review. See, e.g., Rogers v. Bates, 431 F.2d 16 (8th Cir. 1970); Julien v. Sarkes Tarzian, Inc., 352 F. 2d 845 (7th Cir. 1965). Under what standard should a court of appeals review a district court finding that a defendant had sufficient contacts for personal jurisdiction?

3. Why should appellate courts ordinarily exercise such limited review of factual determinations? Is it that trial courts, having seen the actual presentation of the evidence and witnesses, are more likely to be correct in their determination? Lawyers frequently observe that reading a "cold record" or transcript of a trial can leave a very different impression than seeing the trial live. Is this a reason for deferring to trial courts or for not deferring? Maybe it would be useful to have the court of appeals review the cold record, uninfluenced by the emotion of the live event. What about determinations based entirely on documentary proof in which the evidence is equally available to a court of appeals? See Federal Rule 52(a). Are trial courts any more likely to be correct in their assessment of this evidence? Are "mere facts" simply not important enough for appellate courts to waste their time on? See Mucha v. King, 792 F.2d 602, 605-06 (7th Cir. 1986).

4. Are there some issues *of law* as to which trial judges are more likely to be correct? Courts of appeals had long held that when federal courts apply state law, district court determinations of the content of that law are entitled to great deference. The justification relied on the fact that district judges who sit in that state and who are usually drawn from the bar of that state are more likely to be correct about the content of state law than are appellate judges. As Justice Rehnquist explained: "A judge attempting to predict how a state court would rule must use not only his legal reasoning skills, but also his experience and perceptions of judicial behavior in that State. It therefore makes perfect sense for an appellate court judge with no local experience to accord special weight to a local judge's assessment of state court trends." Salve Regina College v. Russell, 499 U.S. 225, 241 (1991)(Rehnquist, J. dissenting). In *Salve Regina College*, the majority of the Court rejected this argument and held that determinations of state law are subject to de novo review by the court of appeals. The Court explained:

> Independent appellate review of legal issues best serves the dual goals of doctrinal coherence and economy of judicial administration. District judges preside alone over fast-paced trials: Of necessity they devote much of their energy and resources to hearing witnesses and reviewing evidence. Similarly, the logisti-

cal burdens of trial advocacy limit the extent to which trial counsel is able to supplement the district judge's legal research with memoranda and briefs. Thus, trial judges often must resolve complicated legal questions without benefit of "extended reflection [or] extensive information."

* * * Perhaps most important, courts of appeals employ multijudge panels, see 28 U.S.C. §§ 46(b) and (c), that permit reflective dialogue and collective judgment. Over 30 years ago, Justice Frankfurter accurately observed: "Without adequate study there cannot be adequate reflection; without adequate reflection there cannot be adequate discussions; without adequate discussion there cannot be that fruitful interchange of minds which is indispensable to thoughtful, unhurried decision and its formulation in learned and impressive opinions."

Id. at 231-232. See Dan Coenen, *To Defer or Not to Defer: A Study of Federal Circuit Court Deference to District Court Rulings on State Law*, 73 MINN. L. REV. 899 (1989). Wouldn't it be valuable to use the collaborative and reflective process of appellate review which the Court praises to review factual determinations?

5. Federal appellate courts do not always review questions of law de novo. In reviewing the actions of administrative agencies, the courts frequently defer to the agency's interpretation of the law. "[I]f the statute is silent or ambiguous with respect to the specific issue, the question for the court is whether the agency's answer is based on a permissible construction of the statute." Chevron, U.S.A. Inc. v. National Resources Defense Council, Inc., 467 U.S. 837, 843 (1984). It is not necessary "that the agency construction was the only one it permissibly could have adopted, or even the reading the court would have reached if the question had arisen in a judicial proceeding." Id. at 843 n.11.

CHAPTER 15
ALTERNATIVE MODELS
OF DISPUTE RESOLUTION

A. Introduction and Integration

This book has focused on one system of dispute resolution — the American litigation system. In recent years, this system has come under increasing criticism. Many observers complain that litigation takes too long and is too expensive. In addition, some argue that litigation as practiced in this country does not always produce the best outcomes. The partisan nature of the adversary system may obscure the truth. Moreover, adjudicated outcomes are largely "winner-take-all." In at least some situations a compromise in which each side "wins" something may be a more socially desirable outcome.

In this chapter we explore some alternative models of dispute resolution. Some of these are drawn from other cultures, others are available within our system.

B. Models of Greater Judicial Control

The German Advantage in Civil Procedure

John H. Langbein
52 U. Chi. L. Rev. 823 (1985)

Our lawyer-dominated system of civil procedure has often been criticized both for its incentives to distort evidence and for the expense and complexity of its modes of discovery and trial. The shortcomings inhere in a system that leaves to partisans the work of gathering and producing the factual material upon which adjudication depends.

We have comforted ourselves with the thought that a lawyerless system would be worse. The excesses of American adversary justice would seem to pale by comparison with a literally nonadversarial system — one in which litigants would be remitted to faceless bureaucratic adjudicators and denied the safeguards that flow from lawyerly intermediation.

The German advantage. The main theme of this article is drawn from Continental civil procedure, exemplified for me by the system that I know reasonably well, the West German. My theme is that, by assigning judges rather than lawyers to investigate the facts, the Germans avoid the most troublesome aspects of our practice. But I shall emphasize that the familiar contrast between our adversarial procedure and the supposedly nonadversarial procedure of the Continental tradition has been grossly overdrawn.

* * *

I. Overview of German Civil Procedure

There are two fundamental differences between German and Anglo-American civil procedure, and these differences lead in turn to many others. First, the court rather than the parties' lawyers takes the main responsibility for gathering and sifting evidence, although the lawyers exercise a watchful eye over the court's work. Second, there is no distinction between pretrial and trial, between discovering evidence and presenting it. Trial is not a single continuous event. Rather, the court gathers and evaluates evidence over a series of hearings, as many as the circumstances require.

Initiation. The plaintiff's lawyer commences a lawsuit in Germany with a complaint. Like its American counterpart, the German complaint narrates the key facts, sets forth a legal theory, and asks for a remedy in damages or specific relief. Unlike an American complaint, however, the German document proposes means of proof for its main factual contentions. The major documents in the plaintiff's possession that support his claim are scheduled and often appended; other documents (for example, hospital files or government records such as police accident reports or agency files) are indicated; witnesses who are thought to know something helpful to the plaintiff's position are identified. The defendant's answer follows the same pattern. It should be emphasized, however, that neither plaintiff's nor defendant's lawyer will have conducted any significant search for witnesses or for other evidence unknown to his client. Digging for facts is primarily the work of the judge.

Judicial preparation. The judge to whom the case is entrusted examines these pleadings and appended documents. He routinely sends for relevant public records. These materials form the beginnings of the official dossier, the court file. All subsequent submissions of counsel, and all subsequent evidence-gathering, will be entered in the dossier, which is open to counsel's inspection continuously.

When the judge develops a first sense of the dispute from these materials, he will schedule a hearing and notify the lawyers. He will often invite and sometimes summon the parties as well as their lawyers to this or subsequent hearings. If the pleadings have identified witnesses whose testimony seems central, the judge may summon them to the initial hearing as well.

Hearing. The circumstances of the case dictate the course of the hearing. Sometimes the court will be able to resolve the case by discussing it with the lawyers and parties and suggesting avenues of compromise. If the case remains contentious and witness testimony needs to be taken, the court will have learned enough about the case to determine a sequence for examining witnesses.

Examining and recording. The judge serves as the examiner-in-chief. At the conclusion of his interrogation of each witness, counsel for either party may pose additional questions, but counsel are not prominent as examiners. Witness testimony is seldom recorded verbatim; rather, the judge pauses from time to time to dictate a summary of the testimony into the dossier. The lawyers sometimes suggest improvements in the wording of these summaries, in order to preserve or to emphasize nuances important to one side or the other.

Since the proceedings in a difficult case may require several hearings extending across many months, these summaries of concluded testimony — by encapsulating succinctly the results of previous hearings — allow the court to refresh itself rapidly for subsequent hearings. The summaries also serve as building blocks from which the court will ultimately fashion the findings of fact for its written judgment. If the case is appealed, these concise summaries constitute the record for the reviewing court. * * *

Anyone who has had to wade through the long-winded narrative of American pretrial depositions and trial transcripts (which preserve every inconsequential utterance, every false start, every stammer) will see at once the economy of the German approach to taking and preserving evidence. Our incentives run the other way; we pay court reporters by the page and lawyers mostly by the hour.

A related source of dispatch in German procedure is the virtual absence of any counterpart to the Anglo-American law of evidence. German law exhibits expansive notions of testimonial privilege, especially for potential witnesses drawn from the family. But German procedure functions without the main chapters of our law of evidence, those rules (such as hearsay) that exclude probative evidence for fear of the inability of the trier of fact to evaluate the evidence purposively. In civil litigation German judges sit without juries * * *; evidentiary shortcomings that would affect admissibility in our law affect weight or credit in German law.

Expertise. If an issue of technical difficulty arises on which the court or counsel wishes to obtain the views of an expert, the court — in consultation with counsel — will select the expert and define his role. * * *

Further contributions of counsel. After the court takes witness testimony or receives some other infusion of evidence, counsel have the opportunity to comment orally or in writing. Counsel use these submissions in order to suggest further proofs or to advance legal theories. Thus, nonadversarial proof-taking alternates with adversarial dialogue across as many hearings as are necessary. The process merges the investigatory function of our pretrial discovery and the evidence-presenting function of our trial. Another manifestation of the comparative efficiency of German procedure is that a witness is ordinarily examined only once. Contrast the American practice of partisan interview and preparation, pretrial deposition, preparation for trial, and examination and cross-examination at trial. These many steps take their toll in expense and irritation.

Judgment. After developing the facts and hearing the adversaries' views, the court decides the case in a written judgment that must contain full findings of fact and make reasoned application of the law.

II. Judicial Control of Sequence

From the standpoint of comparative civil procedure, the most important consequence of having judges direct fact-gathering in this episodic fashion is that German procedure functions without the sequence rules to which we are accustomed in the Anglo-American procedural world. The implications for procedural economy are large. The very concepts of "plaintiff's case" and "defendant's case" are unknown. In our system those concepts function as traffic rules for the partisan presentation of evidence to a passive and ignorant trier. By contrast, in German procedure the court ranges over the entire case, constantly looking for the jugular — for the issue of law or fact that might dispose of the case. Free of constraints that arise from party presentation of evidence, the court investigates the dispute in the fashion most likely to narrow the inquiry. A major job of counsel is to guide the search by directing the court's attention to particularly cogent lines of inquiry.

Suppose that the court has before it a contract case that involves complicated factual or legal issues about whether the contract was formed, and if so, what its precise terms were. But suppose further that the court quickly recognizes (or is led by submission of counsel to recognize) that some factual investigation might establish an affirmative defense — illegality, let us say — that would vitiate the contract. Because the court functions without sequence rules, it can postpone any consideration of issues that we would think of as the plaintiff's case — here the questions concerning the formation and the terms of the contract. Instead, the court can concentrate the entire initial inquiry on what we would regard as a defense. If, in my example, the court were to unearth enough evidence to allow it to conclude that the contract was illegal, no investigation would ever be done on the issues of formation and terms. A defensive issue that could only surface in Anglo–American procedure following full pretrial and trial ventilation of the whole of the plaintiff's case can be brought to the fore in German procedure.

Part of what makes our discovery system so complex is that, on account of our division into pretrial and trial, we have to discover for the entire case. We investigate everything that could possibly come up at trial, because once we enter the trial phase we can seldom go back and search for further evidence. By contrast, the episodic character of German fact-gathering largely eliminates the danger of surprise; if the case takes an unexpected turn, the disadvantaged litigant can count on developing his response in another hearing at a later time. Because there is no pretrial discovery phase, fact-gathering occurs only once; and because the court establishes the sequence of fact-gathering according to criteria of relevance, unnecessary investigation is minimized. In the Anglo–American procedural world we value the early–disposition mechanism, especially summary judgment, for issues of law. But for fact-laden issues, our fixed-sequence rule (plaintiff's case before defendant's case) and our single-continuous–trial rule largely foreclose it.

The episodic character of German civil procedure * * * has other virtues: It lessens tension and theatrics, and it encourages settlement. Countless novels, movies, plays, and broadcast serials attest to the dramatic potential of the Anglo-American trial. The contest between opposing counsel; the potential for surprise witnesses who cannot be rebutted in time; the tricks of adversary examination and cross-examination; the concentration of proof-taking and verdict into a single, continuous proceeding; the unpredictability of juries and the mysterious opacity of their conclusory verdicts — these attributes of the Anglo–American trial make for good theatre. German civil proceedings have the tone not of the theatre, but of a routine business meeting — serious rather than tense. When the court inquires and directs, it sets no stage for advocates to perform. The forensic skills of counsel can wrest no material advantage, and the appearance of a surprise witness would simply lead to the scheduling of a further hearing. In a system that cannot distinguish between dress rehearsal and opening night, there is scant occasion for stage fright.

In this business-like system of civil procedure the tradition is strong that the court promotes compromise. The judge who gathers the facts soon knows the case as well as the litigants do, and he concentrates each subsequent increment of fact-gathering on the most important issues still unresolved. As the case progresses the judge discusses it with the litigants, sometimes indicating provisional views of the likely outcome. He is therefore, strongly positioned to encourage a litigant to abandon a case that is turning out to be weak or hopeless, or to recommend settlement. The loser-pays system of allocating the costs of litigation gives the parties further incentive to settle short of judgment.

III. Witnesses

* * *

If we had deliberately set out to find a means of impairing the reliability of witness testimony, we could not have done much better than the existing system of having partisans prepare witnesses in advance of trial and examine and cross-examine them at trial. Jerome Frank described the problem a generation ago:

> [The witness] often detects what the lawyer hopes to prove at the trial. If the witness desires to have the lawyer's client win the case, he will often, unconsciously, mold his story accordingly. Telling and re-telling it to the lawyer, he will honestly believe that his story, as he narrates it in court, is true, although it importantly deviates from what he originally believed.[29]

Thus, said Frank, "the partisan nature of trials tends to make partisans of the witnesses."

Cross-examination at trial — our only substantial safeguard against this systematic bias in the testimony that reaches our courts — is a frail and fitful palliative. Cross-examination is too often ineffective to undo the consequences of skillful coaching. Further, because cross-examination allows so much latitude for bullying and other truth-defeating stratagems, it is frequently the source of fresh distortion when brought to bear against truthful testimony. * * *

When we cross the border into German civil procedure, we leave behind all traces of this system of partisan preparation, examination, and cross-examination of witnesses. German law distinguishes parties from witnesses. A German lawyer must necessarily discuss the facts with his client, and based on what his client tells him and on what the documentary record discloses, the lawyer will nominate witnesses whose testimony might turn out to be helpful to his client. As the proofs come in, they may reveal to the lawyer the need to nominate further witnesses for the court to examine. But the lawyer stops at nominating; virtually never will he have occasion for out-of-court contact with a witness. Not only would such contact be a serious ethical breach, it would be self-defeating. * * *

No less a critic than Jerome Frank was prepared to concede that in American procedure the adversaries "sometimes do bring into court evidence which, in a dispassionate inquiry, might be overlooked." That is a telling argument for including adversaries in the fact-gathering process, but not for letting them run it. German civil procedure preserves party interests in fact-gathering. The lawyers nominate witnesses, attend and supplement court questioning, and develop adversary

---

[29] JEROME FRANK, [COURTS ON TRIAL: MYTH AND REALITY IN AMERICAN JUSTICE (1949)].

positions on the significance of the evidence. Yet German procedure totally avoids the distortions incident to our partisan witness practice.

IV. Experts

The European jurist who visits the United States and becomes acquainted with our civil procedure typically expresses amazement at our witness practice. His amazement turns to something bordering on disbelief when he discovers that we extend the sphere of partisan control to the selection and preparation of experts. In the Continental tradition experts are selected and commissioned by the court, although with great attention to safeguarding party interests. In the German system, experts are not even called witnesses. They are thought of as "judges' aides."

Perverse incentives. At the American trial bar, those of us who serve as expert witnesses are known as "saxophones." This is a revealing term, as slang often is. The idea is that the lawyer plays the tune, manipulating the expert as though the expert were a musical instrument on which the lawyer sounds the desired notes. I sometimes serve as an expert in trust and pension cases, and I have experienced the subtle pressures to join the team — to shade one's views, to conceal doubt, to overstate nuance, to downplay weak aspects of the case that one has been hired to bolster. Nobody likes to disappoint a patron; and beyond this psychological pressure is the financial inducement. Money changes hands upon the rendering of expertise, but the expert can run his meter only so long as his patron litigator likes the tune. Opposing counsel undertakes a similar exercise, hiring and schooling another expert to parrot the contrary position. The result is our familiar battle of opposing experts. The more measured and impartial an expert is, the less likely he is to be used by either side.

At trial, the battle of experts tends to baffle the trier, especially in jury courts. If the experts do not cancel each other out, the advantage is likely to be with the expert whose forensic skills are the more enticing. The system invites abusive cross-examination. * * *

Thus, the systematic incentive in our procedure to distort expertise leads to a systematic distrust and devaluation of expertise. Short of forbidding the use of experts altogether, we probably could not have designed a procedure better suited to minimize the influence of expertise.

The Continental tradition. European legal systems are, by contrast, expert-prone. Expertise is frequently sought. The literature emphasizes the value attached to having expert assistance available to the courts in an age in which litigation involves facts of ever-greater technical difficulty. The essential insight of Continental civil procedure is that credible expertise must be neutral expertise. Thus, the responsibility for selecting and informing experts is placed upon the courts, although with important protections for party interests.

Selecting the expert. German courts obtain expert help in lawsuits the way Americans obtain expert help in business or personal affairs. If you need an architect, a dermatologist, or a plumber, you do not commission a pair of them to take preordained and opposing positions on your problem, although you do sometimes take a second opinion. Rather, you take care to find an expert who is qualified to advise you in an objective manner; you probe his advice as best you can; and if you find his advice persuasive, you follow it.

When in the course of winnowing the issues in a lawsuit a German court determines that expertise might help resolve the case, the court selects and instructs the expert. The court may decide to seek expertise on its own motion, or at the request of one of the parties. The code of civil procedure allows the court to request nominations from the parties — indeed, the code requires the court to use any expert upon whom the parties agree — but neither practice is typical. In general, the court takes the initiative in nominating and selecting the expert.

* * *

Preparing the expert. The court that selects the expert instructs him, in the sense of propounding the facts that he is to assume or to investigate, and in framing the questions that the court wishes the expert to address. In formulating the expert's task, as in other important steps in the conduct of the case, the court welcomes adversary suggestions. If the expert should take a view of premises (for example, in an accident case or a building- construction dispute), counsel for both sides will accompany him.

Safeguards. The expert is ordinarily instructed to prepare a written opinion. When the court receives that report, it is circulated to the litigants. The litigants commonly file written comments, to which the expert is asked to reply. The court on its own motion may also request the expert to amplify his views. If the expert's report remains in contention, the court will schedule a hearing at which counsel for a dissatisfied litigant can confront and interrogate the expert.

The code of civil procedure reserves to the court the power to order a further report by another expert if the court should deem the first report unsatisfactory. A litigant dissatisfied with the expert may encourage the court to invoke its power to name a second expert. * * * When * * * a litigant can persuade the court that an expert's report has been sloppy or partial, that it rests upon a view of the field that is not generally shared, or that the question referred to the expert is exceptionally difficult, the court will commission further expertise.

A litigant may also engage his own expert, much as is done in the Anglo-American procedural world, in order to rebut the court-appointed expert. The court will discount the views of a party-selected expert on account of his want of neutrality, but cases occur in which he nevertheless proves to be effective. Ordinarily, I am told, the court will not in such circumstances base its judgment directly upon the views of the party-selected expert; rather, the court will treat the rebuttal as ground for engaging a further court-appointed expert * * * whose opinion will take account of the rebuttal.

To conclude: In the use of expertise German civil procedure strikes an adroit balance between nonadversarial and adversarial values. Expertise is kept impartial, but litigants are protected against error or caprice through a variety of opportunities for consultation, confrontation, and rebuttal.

The American counterpart. It may seem curious that we make so little use of court-appointed experts in our civil practice, since "[t]he inherent power of a trial judge to appoint an expert of his own choosing is virtually unquestioned" and has been extended and codified in the Federal Rules of Evidence and the Uniform Rules of Evidence (Model Expert Testimony Act). The literature displays both widespread agreement that our courts virtually never exercise this authority, and a certain bafflement about why.

* * * The difficulty originates with the locktight segmentation of our procedure into pretrial and trial compartments, and with the tradition of partisan domination of the pretrial. Until lately, it was exceptional for the judge to have detailed acquaintance with the facts of the case until the parties presented their evidence at trial. By then the adversaries would have engaged their own experts, and time would no longer allow a court-appointed expert to be located and prepared. * * *

V. Shortcommings of Adversary Theory

The case against adversary domination of fact-gathering is so compelling that we have cause to wonder why our system tolerates it. Because there is nothing to be said in support of coached witnesses, and very little to be said in favor of litigation-biased experts, defenders of the American status quo are left to argue that the advantages of our adversary procedure counterbalance these grievous, truth-defeating distortions. "You have to take the bad with the good; if you want adversary safeguards, you are stuck with adversary excesses."

The false conflict. This all-or-nothing argument overlooks the fundamental distinction between fact-gathering and the rest of civil litigation. Outside the realm of fact-gathering, German civil procedure is about as adversarial as our own. Both systems welcome the lawyerly contribution to identifying legal issues and sharpening legal analysis. German civil procedure is materially less adversarial than our own only in the fact-gathering function, where partisanship has such potential to pollute the sources of truth.

Accordingly, the proper question is not whether to have lawyers, but how to use them; not whether to have an adversarial component to civil procedure, but how to prevent adversarial excesses. If we were to incorporate the essential lesson of the German system in our own procedure, we would still have a strongly adversarial civil procedure. We would not, however, have coached witnesses and litigation-biased experts.

* * *

Equality of representation. The German system gives us a good perspective on another great defect of adversary theory, the problem that the Germans call "Waffenungleichheit" — literally, inequality of weapons, or in this instance, inequality of counsel. In a fair fight the pugilists must be well matched. You cannot send me into a ring with Muhammed Ali if you expect a fair fight. The simple truth is that very little in our adversary system is designed to match combatants of comparable prowess, even though adversarial prowess is a main factor affecting the outcome of litigation. Adversary theory thus presupposes a condition that adversary practice achieves only indifferently.
* * *

Prejudgment. Perhaps the most influential justification for adversary domination of fact-gathering has been an argument put forward by Lon Fuller: Nonadversarial procedure risks prejudgment — that is, prematurity in judgment. * * *

* * *

In German procedure counsel oversees and has means to prompt a flagging judicial inquiry; but quite apart from that protection, is it really true that a "familiar pattern" would otherwise beguile the judge into investigating sparingly? If so, it seems odd that this asserted "natural human tendency" toward premature judgment does not show up in ordinary business and personal decision-making, whose patterns of inquiry resemble the fact-gathering process in German civil procedure. Since the decision-maker does his own investigating in most of life's decisions, it seems odd to despair of prematurity only when that normal mode of decision-making is found to operate in a courtroom.* * *

Depth. Fuller's concern about prematurity shades into a different issue: how to achieve appropriate levels of depth in fact-gathering. Extra investment in search can almost always turn up further proofs that would be at least tenuously related to the case. Adversary domination of fact-gathering privatizes the decision about what level of resources to invest in the case. The litigants who are directly interested in the outcome decide how much to spend on search. In German procedure, by contrast, these partisan calculations of self-interest are subordinated, for a variety of reasons. The initiative in fact-gathering is shared with the judge; and the German system of reckoning and allocating the costs of litigation is less sensitive to the cost of incremental investigative steps than in our system where each side pays for the proofs that it orders. On the other hand, the German judge cannot refuse to investigate party-nominated proofs without reason, and this measure of party control greatly narrows the difference between the two systems.

* * *

VI. Judicial Incentives

Viewed comparatively from the Anglo–American perspective, the greater authority of the German judge over fact–gathering comes at the expense of the lawyers for the parties. Adversary influence on fact-gathering is deliberately restrained. Furthermore, in routine civil procedure, German judges do not share power with jurors. There is no civil jury.

Because German procedure places upon the judge the responsibility for fact-gathering, the danger arises that the job will not be done well. The American system of partisan fact-gathering has the virtue of its vices: It aligns responsibility with incentive. Each side gathers and presents proofs according to its own calculation of self-interest. This privatization is an undoubted safeguard against official sloth. After all, who among us has not been treated shabbily by some lazy bureaucrat in a government department? And who would want to have that ugly character in charge of one's lawsuit?

The answer to that concern in the German tradition is straightforward: The judicial career must be designed in a fashion that creates incentives for diligence and excellence. The idea is to attract very able people to the bench, and to make their path of career advancement congruent with the legitimate interests of the litigants.

The career judiciary. The distinguishing attribute of the bench in Germany (and virtually everywhere else in Europe) is that the profession of judging is separate from the profession of lawyering. Save in exceptional circumstances, the judge is not an ex-lawyer like his Anglo–American counterpart. Rather, he begins his professional career as a judge.

In Germany judges and lawyers undergo a common preparatory schooling. After completing a prescribed course of university legal education that lasts several years, the young jurist sits a first state examination. After passing this examination satisfactorily, he enters upon an apprenticeship that now lasts two and one-half years. He clerks for judges in the civil and criminal courts, assists in the prosecutor's office, and works in a lawyer's office. At the conclusion of this tour of duty, the young jurist sits a second state examination, remotely akin to our bar examination, which concludes the certification process. Thereafter, the career lines of judge and lawyer diverge.

Recruitment. Although West Germany is a federal state, the state and federal courts comprise an integrated system. The courts of first instance and the first layer of appellate courts are state courts, while the second (and final) layer of appellate jurisdiction operates at the federal level. Thus, even though the basic codes of civil and criminal law and procedure are federal codes, the state courts have exclusive jurisdiction until the final appellate instance. It follows that most judges are state judges; and since appointment to the federal bench is by way of promotion from the state courts, all entry-level recruitment to the bench occurs at the state level.

In each of the eleven federal states, the ministry of justice is responsible for staffing the courts. Entry-level vacancies are advertised and applications entertained from young jurists. The judiciary is a prized career: influential, interesting, secure, and (by comparison with practice of the bar) prestigious and not badly compensated. "[O]nly the graduates with the best examination results have any chance of entering the judicial corps."

Advancement. A candidate who is accepted begins serving as a judge without any prior legal-professional experience, typically in his late twenties. At the outset his position is probationary, although he must be promoted to tenure or dismissed within five years. His first assignment may be to a court of petty jurisdiction * * *, or else he will become the junior member of a collegial chamber of the main court of general jurisdiction * * *, where he can receive guidance from experienced judges.

The work of a German judge is overseen and evaluated by his peers throughout his career, initially in connection with his tenure review, and thereafter for promotion through the several levels of judicial office and salary grades. A judge knows that his every step will be grist for the regular periodic reviews that will fill his lifelong personnel file. His "efficiency rating" is based in part upon objective factors, such as caseload discharge rates and reversal rates, and in part on subjective peer evaluation. The presiding judge of a chamber has special responsibility for evaluating the work of the younger judges who serve with him, but the young judges are rotated through various chambers in the course of their careers, and this reduces the influence of an aberrant rating from any one presiding judge. These evaluations by senior judges pay particular regard to (1) a judge's effectiveness in conducting legal proceedings, including fact-gathering, and his treatment of witnesses and litigants; and (2) the quality of his opinions — his success in mastering and applying the law to his cases.

* * *

American contrasts. If I were put to the choice of civil litigation under the German procedure that I have been praising in this article or under the American procedure that I have been criticizing, I might have qualms about choosing the German. The likely venue of a lawsuit of mine would be the state court in Cook County, Illinois, and I must admit that I distrust the bench of that court. The judges are selected by a process in which the criterion of professional competence is at best an incidental value. Further, while decent people do reach the Cook County bench in surprising numbers, events have shown that some of their colleagues are crooks. If my lawsuit may fall into the hands of a dullard or a thug, I become queasy about increasing his authority over the proceedings.

German-style judicial responsibility for fact-gathering cannot be lodged with the Greylord judiciary. Remodeling of civil procedure is intimately connected to improvement in the selection of judges. I do not believe that we would have to institute a German style career judiciary in order to reform American civil procedure along German lines * * *. The difference in quality between the stat and federal trail benches in places like Cook County is sufficient to remind us that measures far short of adopting the Continental career judiciary can bring about material improvement.

B. Models of Greater Judicial Control

* * *

Cultural differences surely do explain something of why institutional and procedural differences arise in different legal systems. The important question for present purposes is what weight to attach to this factor, and my answer is, "Not much." It is all too easy to allow the cry of "cultural differences" to become the universal apologetic that permanently sheathes the status quo against criticism based upon comparative example. Cultural differences that help explain the origins of superior procedures need not restrict their spread. If Americans were to resolve to officialize the fact-gathering process while preserving the political prominence of the higher bench, we would probably turn initially to some combination of judges, magistrates, and masters for getting the job done. Over time, we would strike a new balance between bench and bar, and between higher and lower judicial office.

* * *

NOTES AND QUESTIONS

1. Are there aspects of the German approach you find particularly appealing? Particularly unappealing? Do you think it would be possible to borrow pieces of the German system without taking the whole system?

2. Professor Reitz has argued that the differences between the United States and German is less a result of positive law, and more a function of "legal culture." John Reitz, *Why We Probably Cannot Adopt the German Advantage in Civil Procedure*, 75 IOWA L. REV. 987 (1990). He notes that "on paper" American judges have broader powers then German judges to call expert witnesses, but that power goes largely unused. Id. at 992. Likewise, although the German system permits lawyers to cross-examine witnesses, vigorous cross-examination is relatively rare. Id. at 993. Reitz concludes, "The primacy of cultural definitions over positive law does not mean that change is impossible, but it suggests that the mechanism of change is an important problem." Id. at 994. How much are our models for dispute resolution shaped by our culture and how much can we reshape our culture by reshaping our methods of dispute resolution?

3. Professor Gross has argued that although the German system may be more efficient, "efficiency is a questionable standard for evaluating a system of adjudication." Samuel Gross, *The American Advantage: The Value of Inefficient Litigation*, 85 MICH. L. REV. 734, 756 (1987). First, he notes that defenders of the adversary system argue that it produces greater accuracy than other adjudicative models and in addition "is uniquely respectful of the autonomy of the individual." Id. at 745. Second, he suggests that the inefficiency of our system can be viewed as a strength rather than a weakness: the inefficiency of our adjudicative system reduces incentives to litigate. Id. at 752. How important is efficiency dispute resolution in a dispute resolution system? Is efficiency a strength or a weakness? What other values are important?

Sempier v. Johnson & Higgins
45 F. 3d 724 (3rd Cir. 1995)

GARTH, CIRCUIT JUDGE.

On March 9, 1994, the district court granted summary judgment in favor of Johnson & Higgins ("J & H"), the employer of appellant Burt Sempier. Sempier now appeals the district court's grant of summary judgment on his Age Discrimination in Employment Act ("ADEA") claim, 29 U.S.C. § 623 (1988), and the discretionary dismissal of his pendent state law claims. He also raises as error the district court's substitution of a "Bill of Particulars" in place of his interrogatories.

We have jurisdiction pursuant to 28 U.S.C. § 1291 to review the March 9, 1994 final order of the district court. Because the record reflects a genuine issue of material fact regarding whether J & H's asserted nondiscriminatory reasons for discharging Sempier are pretextual, we will reverse the summary judgment entered in favor of J & H. We also conclude that the district court abused its discretion in substituting its own "Bill of Particulars" for Sempier's interrogatories.

[The court describes the circumstances surrounding Sempier's hiring and later firing by the defendant.]

At the outset of the litigation, Sempier served two sets of interrogatories and a series of document requests on J & H. When J & H refused to respond to a substantial portion of the discovery requested, Sempier sought an order from the magistrate judge which would have compelled J & H to respond. The magistrate judge denied Sempier's motion. On appeal, the district court judge vacated the order of denial but remanded the dispute to the magistrate judge without entering an order compelling discovery. On remand, the magistrate judge relieved J & H from answering the original two sets of interrogatories and required that Sempier draft a third set of interrogatories. After J & H refused to answer almost all of these interrogatories, Sempier again sought a second order compelling discovery. The magistrate judge denied Sempier's motion to compel answers and ordered J & H to provide information responding to a "Bill of Particulars" drafted by the court. On appeal, the district court affirmed the magistrate judge's order and added one question of its own to the "Bill of Particulars."

Between November and December 1993, the parties disputed whether J & H had complied with the court's orders to answer the court's questions and to provide documents. In December, Sempier filed additional motions for an order to compel discovery and for partial summary judgment. J & H replied with its motion for summary judgment.

The district court granted J & H's summary judgment motion on the ADEA claim and dismissed the remaining pendent claims without prejudice. * * *

Sempier filed a timely appeal.

[The court concludes that there was conflicting evidence as to whether Sempier was fired because of poor performance or age discrimination. The court reverses the grant of summary judgment.]

VI

In addition to challenging the district court's order which granted summary judgment to J & H, an order which we now hold must be reversed, Sempier also complains that the district court abused its discretion in ruling on his discovery efforts. In so doing, Sempier contends that he was prevented from marshaling additional evidence establishing that J & H's proffered reason for his discharge was pretextual.

We normally do not become involved with "nitty gritty" rulings on discovery matters. Nor do we generally engage in exercises to determine whether a party's interrogatories are relevant or are unduly burdensome. This appeal, however, requires that we review the actions taken by the magistrate judge and the district court judge with respect to discovery sought and answered by the parties. While we will not examine each jot and tittle of the discovery process, it is important to our analysis that some background be furnished.

Sempier's complaint was filed in April 1992. In June 1992, Sempier served his first set of interrogatories and a request for production of documents. In July 1992, Sempier served a second set of interrogatories with a second request for production of documents. Unfortunately, not all of the interrogatories that were served have found their way into the record, and thus, into the appendix. We have examined those that have been reproduced in the appendix, and we find it difficult to understand how the magistrate judge could have condoned the answers given by J & H. Moreover, we are perplexed by the failure of the magistrate judge or the district court judge to compel responsive answers to the interrogatories — almost all of which appear to us to be relevant and directed to the issues of Sempier's employment, performance and relationship with J & H.

For example, Interrogatory No. 36 sought the name of each and every person who had supervision and/or control over Sempier from January 1, 1986 through the termination of Sempier's employment. It also sought, with respect to each such supervisor identified, the job title, the department supervised, the duties and responsibilities of the job, the date on which he or she assumed the supervisory position, and, if the individual was not still employed, the date and reason of termination and the last known address. True, that interrogatory sought as well the date of hire, date of birth and educational background, but those three inquiries, if not deemed relevant in the district court's judgment, could have been excised and the remainder of the interrogatory answered. Yet J & H objected to the interrogatory on the grounds that it was "overbroad, unduly burdensome, and exceeding the scope of permissible discovery." J & H then referred Sempier to a J & H Position Statement which does not even appear to be part of the record.

Again, Interrogatory No. 44 asked J & H if it voluntarily terminated the employment and/or relationship of Sempier with J & H. J & H's response reads: "Defendant refers plaintiff to pages 3 through 17 of the J & H Position Statement." The following interrogatory, Interrogatory No. 45, sought the dates on which the decision to terminate Sempier was made, and J & H's response was "See Interrogatory No. 44." Interrogatory No. 46 sought the factual basis for J & H's decision to terminate Sempier and/or the relationship of Sempier with J & H. The answer given by J & H: "Defendant refers plaintiff to the J & H Position Statement." The other interrogatories which we have reviewed — all seemingly relevant — have been answered in much the same manner. All of J & H's answers disregard the requirements of the Federal Rules of Civil Procedure. See Fed. R. Civ. P.

33(a) (requiring separate and complete answers unless specific objections are provided); 26(b) (defining the scope of discovery) (1993 version).[9]

Without dwelling further on this subject, we observe that the magistrate judge did not compel the answers which Sempier sought. Rather, he relieved J & H from answering the various discovery requests and instructed Sempier to issue a third set of interrogatories and a third document request. The latter two discovery requests were no more answered than the earlier ones. In lieu of compelling answers to the third set of interrogatories served by Sempier, the district court instructed J & H to answer a four question "Bill of Particulars."

Against this background, we consider Sempier's arguments. Under the Federal Rules of Civil Procedure and our jurisprudence, district courts have broad discretion to manage discovery. Nonetheless, the district court's discretion has boundaries, and in particular, we frown upon unnecessary discovery limitations in Title VII, and hence ADEA, cases. In such cases, other courts have refused, and now we refuse, "to allow procedural technicalities to impede the full vindication of guaranteed rights." A plaintiff in an ADEA case, as Sempier is here, should not be hamstrung by the district court in limiting his discovery. In substituting a "Bill of Particulars" for those means of discovery authorized by the Federal Rules of Civil Procedure, the district court here far exceeded the outermost limits on its discretion.

Since 1938, civil discovery has been an attorney-initiated, attorney-focused procedure. The vast majority of federal discovery tools operate, when used properly, almost entirely without the court's involvement. See Fed. R. Civ. P. 26(f) (requiring the parties to devise and submit a discovery plan); Fed. R. Civ. P. 30 ("[A] party may take the testimony of any person, including a party, by deposition upon oral examination without leave of court."); Fed. R. Civ. P. 34(b) (production of documents); cf. Fed. R. Civ. P. 35 (providing for physical examinations only by leave of the court); see also William Schwarzer, *The Federal Rules, The Adversary Process, and Discovery Reform*, 50 U. PITT. L. REV. 703, 714-16 (1989).

Indeed under the recent amendments to Federal Rule of Civil Procedure 26(a), which became effective December 1, 1993 in the District of New Jersey, a party must provide discovery "without waiting [for] a discovery request." Under this scheme, when civil litigation proceeds smoothly, the parties conduct discovery with minimal interference from and minimal appeal to the court. Through the discovery process, even before the amendments became effective, the attorneys obtain answers to questions that they feel are relevant to the issues if not determinative of the issues. Nowhere in the process is the district court authorized to initiate its own questioning or to seek documents for itself. See John H. Langbein, *The German Advantage in Civil Procedure*, 52 U. CHI. L. REV. 823, 827-30 (1985) (noting the difference between civil law procedure in which judges initiate the investigation and common law procedure in which the parties conduct the investigation).

When the parties stray from this course, Rule 37 provides the court with tools to give the litigants new and proper bearings. A court may compel answers to interrogatories or deposition questions, compel the production of documents, or conversely, grant protective orders. Fed. R. Civ. P. 37; Fed. R. Civ. P. 26(b)(5)(c). If these measures fail, a court may order facts established, forbid the

---

[9] Lead counsel for J & H is apparently the New York law firm of Sullivan & Cromwell. Perhaps this accounts for the lack of familiarity with New Jersey Federal Court practice. We note, however, that J & H has local counsel. It is a matter of concern to us that the discovery practice in this case was so badly abused when at the least, local counsel had to have recognized the need to conform to the standards of discovery practice which have long been established in the District of New Jersey.

introduction of evidence, strike the pleadings, file a default judgment, dismiss the action, or hold a party in contempt of court. However, none of the weapons in this formidable arsenal include the wholesale substitution of court-engineered discovery.

The district court was evidently not content with the contents of its discovery arsenal. Rather, it abandoned the structure and command of the Rules to revive a procedural device abandoned in civil practice forty-five years ago. Although still used in criminal matters, a "Bill of Particulars" has not graced the shores of federal civil discovery since the 1950s. Even in criminal matters, a "Bill of Particulars" is not generally considered a discovery device. In this case, it was not only an unwelcome and inappropriate incursion by the district court into the parties' dispute, but it severely trenched upon the Rules of Civil Procedure which have been crafted to provide information as to matters relevant to the issues disputed. Fed. R. Civ. P. 26(b)(1).

Sempier had served his interrogatories in compliance with Federal Rule of Civil Procedure 33. The Rule provides, "[e]ach interrogatory shall be answered separately and fully in writing under oath, unless it is objected to, in which event the objecting party shall state the reasons for objection and shall answer to the extent the interrogatory is not objectionable." J & H believed the interrogatories were objectionable and stated its objections. Sempier sought to compel answers.

The court could have denied the discovery on the ground that it was privileged, burdensome, duplicative, or otherwise outside of the scope of discovery. Fed. R. Civ. P. 26(b). It could have compelled answers and awarded attorney's fees and/or sanctions. Fed. R. Civ. P. 37(b). It did none of these things nor did it comply with its obligation to consider and rule upon each interrogatory to which J & H objected. Rather than rule upon the objections, the district court decided that "[the] Magistrate Judge ... provided a mechanism (Bill of Particulars) for further discovery regarding the precise issue outlined in this Court's September 7, 1993 Order."

The district court may have disliked its obligation to examine each interrogatory and review the magistrate judge's ruling. Regardless of its feelings, the district court, guided only by its own discretion and determination of what is important or relevant, could not rewrite a party's questions and in effect serve its own set of interrogatories. When the court took upon itself to author the questions being asked, it virtually became a participant in the parties' controversy in a manner inconsistent with fundamental conceptions of the role of a judge in our common law system.

In this case, the district court reformulated Sempier's interrogatories into four broad questions about Sempier's performance. The magistrate judge reframed specific requests pertaining to the reasons considered by J & H, and the reasons upon which J & H actually relied to terminate Sempier, into a vague question, "[w]hy were Plaintiff's job responsibilities reassigned?" Pertinent and direct interrogatories, that were propounded by Sempier, sought the dates of conversations regarding Sempier's performance and the names of the participants in those discussions. Those interrogatories were replaced by the district court with a vague and general "Bill of Particulars." Because the district court's questions were, with one exception, general, nonspecific, and broad, the resulting answers, to the extent that they answered the questions at all, were uninformative and of little value. Sempier had good reason to draft specific interrogatories and had a right to expect correspondingly specific answers. The district court's substitution of its own work product denied Sempier this opportunity.

We have examined the Supplemental Bill of Particulars which contains the questions framed by the magistrate judge and the district court judge, and we have examined closely J & H's answers. Those answers can best be described as an attempt, if not to outwit, then to frustrate all legitimate efforts to furnish information to an adversary. Moreover, whereas Federal Rule of Civil Procedure 33 provides that interrogatories must be answered under oath and thus may be evidentiary, there is no such provision in the Federal Rules of Civil Procedure for a "Bill of Particulars." Indeed, there is no provision at all for "Bills of Particulars" — and for good reason. As we have noted, "Bills of Particulars" were replaced by the discovery rules of the Federal Rules of Civil Procedure.

The district court's action was unauthorized by the Federal Rules of Civil Procedure and in violation of the principles of our jurisprudence. The Federal Rules of Civil Procedure, which must obtain Supreme Court and Congressional approval, not only prescribe the procedures to be followed by counsel, but they also prescribe the Rules under which the courts operate. By venturing so far outside the parameters set by the Rules, the court abused its discretion.

Our discussion and holding here does not leave the district court powerless to manage the discovery difficulties presented by this and similar cases. On the contrary, the district court has considerable authority and discretion by which to resolve discovery disputes. Indeed, if discovery has reached an impasse or a nonproductive stage either through counsel's obstinacy, intransigence, or even incompetence, the district court can always, through appropriate intervention, suggest the proper manner in which questions should be asked and the answers furnished. A district court's creativity in this respect is unrestricted, although it cannot, of course, disregard the commands of the Federal Rules of Civil Procedure or, as in this case, substitute a "Bill of Particulars" for a party's relevant discovery. It can, however, always give counsel guidance and direction as to the manner in which discovery should proceed.

If, after an examination of a party's interrogatories, the district court determines that the interrogatories are inappropriate, the court can refuse to compel answers. If a party is unable to draft satisfactory interrogatories after a reasonable time for discovery has concluded, the court can limit further discovery. If the court feels either party was acting in bad faith, it can impose sanctions. Certainly, if a party, without justification, refuses to answer interrogatories in the manner required by Federal Rule of Civil Procedure 33, the court can compel answers under threat of sanctions. Any or all of these options could have been employed in this case. Any and all of these options would have received substantial deference upon review.

VII

We will reverse the summary judgment of the district court dated March 9, 1994 and remand. On remand, the district court is directed to vacate the magistrate judge's order of August 7, 1993 and to vacate its own order of November 3, 1993 which approved and modified a "Bill of Particulars." The district court is also directed to permit and schedule additional appropriate and adequate discovery pursuant to the Federal Rules of Civil Procedure so that further proceedings, including trial, may be conducted consistent with the foregoing opinion.

B. Models of Greater Judicial Control

NOTES AND QUESTIONS

1. In light of the Langbein article, would you recommend amending the Federal Rules of Civil Procedure to permit judges to do what the magistrate judge attempted in *Sempier*?

2. Is what the magistrate judge attempted in *Sempier* a reasonable approximation of the German approach to discovery? Or did the judge maintain the basic model of partisanship but simply substituted himself for one of the parties? In other words, did the judge borrow too little?

3. In Gentile v. Missouri Department of Corrections & Human Resources, 986 F. 2d 214 (8th Cir. 1993), a prisoner filed an Eighth Amendment claim against prison officials alleging deliberate indifference to his serious medical needs. The prisoner represented himself and requested leave to proceed in forma pauperis under 28 U.S.C. § 1915.* The case was assigned to a magistrate judge who, after a hearing, granted leave to proceed in forma pauperis. The magistrate judge then conducted a personal investigation into the merits of the plaintiff's claim, holding a series of informal "hearings" at which the magistrate interviewed that plaintiff and defendant's lawyers. Later, the judge held a telephone conference call with plaintiff's physician. The doctor was not put under oath but the magistrate questioned the doctor extensively about the plaintiff's medical condition and treatment. Ultimately, the magistrate granted summary judgment for the defendant on the basis of the doctor's unsworn statements.

The court of appeals criticized the approach taken by the magistrate judge. It explained that the §1915 in forma pauperis procedure "does not mean that the participants at trial are to perform different duties from those they would perform if the plaintiff had been able to pay his filing fee. The goal of § 1915 is to put 'the indigent plaintiff on a similar footing with paying plaintiffs.'" The court then said:

> What happened here seems more akin to a civil-law proceeding, in which the judge takes the initiative to determine the truth. The inquisitional method may have something to commend it, but it is not our system. In common-law countries judicial proceedings are adversarial. The judge (or jury) finds the facts on the basis of evidence properly sworn to and offered by both sides in the customary order.

Id. at 219.

There is a final irony to the case. Although the court of appeals held that it was error for the magistrate judge to rely on the unsworn doctor's statement, it affirmed the

---

* This statute authorizes the court to waive for indigent litigant's fees and costs. It also directs the court to serve process on the indigent's behalf.

grant of summary judgment. The court explained that the defendant's motion for summary judgment had included sworn affidavits and the burden had therefore shifted to the plaintiff "to make a showing of specific factual issues for trial." Id. The court concluded that "[b]ecause the plaintiff did not come forward with enough specific facts to support his deliberate indifference claim, summary judgment was proper." Id. Would unrepresented indigent litigants such as the plaintiff in *Gentile* be better off under a civil-law system?

4. Managerial Judging. Notwithstanding *Sempier*, many have argued that the American system is moving toward a model of "managerial judging." The 1983 amendments to Rules 11, 16, and 26 all encouraged greater judicial involvement and control in pretrial proceedings. A similar approach was reflected two years later in the 1985 edition of the Manual for Complex Litigation, produced by the Federal Judicial Center. It describes in detail techniques for judicial supervision and management of complex cases and explains:

> Lawyers and judges are virtually unanimous both on the critical need for early, active involvement by the judiciary in managing complex litigation and on the characteristics of effective judicial control and supervision. Even those who have criticized some constraint imposed by a judge when exercising these powers have generally acknowledged the propriety, if not the necessity, of judicial control to promote the efficient conduct of the litigation. The accord regarding judicial involvement in complex cases does not evidence any disparagement of the adversarial system or of the competency of the bar. Rather, it stems from an awareness that the tensions between an attorney's responsibilities as an advocate and as an officer of the court frequently are aggravated in complex litigation and that the tactics of counsel may waste time and expense if the judge passively waits until problems have arisen.

MANUAL FOR COMPLEX LITIGATION, SECOND, § 20.1 (1985). Many have praised the trend toward managerial judging. See, e.g., Robert Peckham, *The Federal Judge as a Case Manager: The New Role in Guiding a Case from Filing to Disposition*, 69 CALIF. L. REV. 770 (1981).

Others, however, are not so enthusiastic. As Professor Elliott notes:

> Opponents of managerial judging * * * argue that litigants are being forced, directly or indirectly, to abandon positions on the merits. To make matters worse, they say, judges are making discretionary procedural decisions early on that effectively close off lines of substantive inquiry without benefit of full development and consideration of the merits of the parties' positions. And the "managerial" decisions of these judges are largely immune from appellate review.

Donald Elliott, *Managerial Judging and the Evolution of Procedure*, 53 U. CHI. L. REV. 306, 314 (1986). See Judith Resnik, *Managerial Judges*, 96 HARV. L. REV. 374 (1982), Judith Resnik, *Failing Faith: Adjudicatory Procedure in Decline*, 53 U. CHI. L. REV. 494 (1986).

Professor Elliott offers the following assessment:

> In the long run, * * * the disadvantages that arise from the ad hoc character of managerial judging cannot be eliminated, only reduced. More fundamental reform must proceed by addressing directly the system of incentives that creates the need for managerial judging in the first place. Redesigning incentives with an eye to their effect on the terms of settlements will not only reduce the arbitrariness which is inherent in managerial judging, but will also be more likely than ad hoc intervention by judges to encourage just outcomes. For example, if the existing methods of compensating counsel do in fact create powerful economic incentives for lawyers to act in ways that are not in the best interest of their clients, restructuring the compensation system directly is more likely to be effective than managerial techniques. Similarly, if defendants are encouraged to delay judgment because of rules of law that deny successful litigants the full time-value of money during the pendency of litigation, restructuring the system of incentives is more likely to be successful than is an overlay of counter-incentives imposed on an ad hoc basis by managerial judges.
>
> Reforming procedural incentives to promote just settlements requires a fundamental change in the way that we view civil procedure. Before such changes can be made, we will have to stop thinking of the "pretrial" process as a prelude to trial, and start thinking of it as the "main event" — as the matrix of incentives within which the overwhelming majority of cases are going to be settled by two party-appointed arbitrators (the opposing lawyers).

Elliott, supra, 53 U. CHI. L. REV. at 335. What changes might go along with thinking of pretrial as the main event?

C. Models of Non-Judicial Resolution

Professor Elliott's assessment stresses the need to take into account settlement. Settlement is non-judicial resolution of a dispute. Though settlement may come as a result of the threat of adjudication, the settlement terms are determined by the parties.

There are a variety of social customs as well as other techniques that may facilitate non-judicial settlement of disputes. In an earlier era, dueling was a socially accepted, if not quite legal, mechanism that accomplished this purpose. It had the virtues of relative speed and finality, though also carried some obvious social costs. In this section, we consider some more current models of non-judicial resolution of disputes and their advantages and disadvantages. We summarized these models in Section E of Chapter 1.

CHAPTER 15 ALTERNATIVE MODELS OF DISPUTE RESOLUTION

The Implications of Apology:
Law and Culture in Japan and in the United States

Hiroshi Wagatsuma and Arthur Rosette
20 Law & Soc'y Rev. 461 (1986)

Apology is a social lubricant used every day in on-going human relationships. People constantly utter words of apology in both Japan and the United States, most often to seek indulgence for a minor social breach, to ask for permission to violate conventional rules, or to express sympathetic regret for a mishap. * * *

* * *

I. Apology and Culture

* * *

* * * We believe * * * that there are real differences in the incidence of apologetic behavior by Japanese and Americans faced with a serious claim that they have injured another. We are even more confident, however, that there are differences in the significance that is likely to be attached to apologetic behavior or the failure of a person to apologize. These differences in significance are expressive of important cultural assumptions that influence many forms of social interaction and that form a central part of the foundation supporting the structure of the legal system. Studying them should reveal significant information about the formal and informal operation of both the Japanese and American legal systems and about the connections between culturally influenced behavior and the legal processes used to resolve disputes.

We would agree, for example, with [a] recent suggestion that apology in Japan is one of a number of social behaviors that compensate for the weakness of the formal enforcement sanctions of the law. [This] point also can be turned inside out. The availability of social restorative mechanisms like apology obviates formal legal sanction in many cases. In the United States, the relative absence of recognition of apology may be related to the observed tendency of American society to overwork formal legal processes and to rely too heavily on the adjudication of rights and liabilities by litigation. Alternative means of dispute resolution accordingly receive less attention and social support. The relative absence of apology in American law may also be connected to the legal system's historic preoccupation with reducing all losses to economic terms that can be awarded in a money judgment and its related tendency either not to compensate at all or to award extravagant damages for injuries that are not easily reducible to quantifiable economic losses. Finally, the small role of apology or any other personal contact between criminal and victim also seems related to the disquieting tendency in American law to ignore and even abuse the victim during the formal process of criminal prosecution.

C. Models of Non-Judicial Resolution

* * *

IV. Apology as an Admission of the Wrongfulness of the Act

* * *

Many Japanese seem to think it is better to apologize even when the other party is at fault, while Americans may blame others even when they know they are at least partially at fault. Americans, as a group, seem more ready to deny wrongdoing, to demand proof of their delict, to challenge the officials' right to intervene, and to ask to speak to a lawyer. Japanese criminal offenders are said to be more ready than Americans to admit their guilt and throw themselves of the mercy of an offended authority. Only when an individual "sincerely" acknowledges his transgression against the standards of the community does the community take him back.

An apology in the Japanese cultural context thus is an indication of an individual's wish to maintain or restore a positive relationship with another person who has been harmed by the individual's acts. When compensation or damages are to be paid to the victim, it is extremely important that the person responsible expresses to the victim his feeling of deep regret and apologizes, in addition to paying an appropriate sum. If a person appears too willing to pay the damages, that willingness may be taken as the sign of his lack of regret. He may be regarded as thinking that money can settle anything and as not being sincerely interested in restoring a positive relationship with his victim. In dealing with those who have offended them, the cultural assumption of social harmony would lead the Japanese to accept the external act of apology at face value and not to disturb the superficial concord by challenging the sincerity of the person apologizing. The act of apologizing can be significant for its own sake as an acknowledgment of the authority of the hierarchical structure upon which social harmony is based. * * *

Sincerity of apology thus has different connotations in the two cultures, with the Americans preoccupied with the problematics of wholeheartedness and the Japanese focused on the more attainable externality of submission to order and return to harmonious relationship. Thus it appears that the Japanese view an apology without an acceptance of fault as being insincere, while an American is more likely to treat an exculpatory explanation as the equivalent of an apology at least to the extent that it is accompanied by a declaration of nonhostile intent in the future.

* * *

VI. Legal Aspects of Apology

* * *

C. Apology as an Admission

A crucial inhibition to a person making an apology in an American legal proceeding is the possibility that a sincere apology will be taken as an admission: evidence of the occurrence of the event and of the defendant's liability for it. * * * [W]e have been told that Japanese corporations preparing to send their executives to work in the United States have prepared a training program and materials designed to introduce the Japanese to social situations they are likely to find difficult in America. One topic that is discussed in detail for those coming to California is the operation of an automobile, including the appropriate behavior if one is involved in an accident. Along with advice on the handling of insurance, the police, and injuries, the instructions urgently warn the Japanese, "Do not apologize." This advice is considered necessary because, in a parallel situation in Japan, the cultural assumption would be that both sides would immediately apologize to each other, without regard to where fault for the accident might lie. The Japanese advice might be something of an overreaction, for it is not certain that serious adverse consequences will follow in the United States from the tendering of an apology in these circumstances, but many cautious American lawyers and insurance agents might well be tempted to offer similar advice.

* * *

D. Apology and Liability: Obligation to Make Compensation and Accept Punishment

In both the Japanese and American cultures, acceptance of responsibility for the hurtful act by making compensatory reparations to the person injured and by accepting punishment for the violation of criminal rules are stronger elements of apology than mere admission of the act itself. An apology without reparation is a hollow form, at least when the injured person has suffered a clear economic loss and when the actor has the capacity to make compensation.

At the same time, punishment and compensation for injury alone probably are an insufficient basis for forgiving the offender. A felon who has served his time or a tort-feasor who has paid the damage judgment is not entitled to be restored to social acceptance without some acknowledgment of guilt and remorse. As we mentioned above, in Japan a person too willing to pay damages may be thought to lack regret. When industrial pollution, dangerous pharmaceutical drugs, or a commercial aircraft crash cause injury to a large number of people, the company president, as the most senior official of the wrongdoers, is expected to make a public apology, bowing deeply and preferably shedding tears. In such a situation it is important that compensation not be mentioned openly, because it is felt that money does not bring back the dead or restore health. It is important that the company official not appear too eager to settle the matter with money. It also is important that victims not appear too interested in receiving cash payment; they should mourn instead of displaying greed. This behavior reflects multiple layers of consciousness, for the individuals behave as the culture suggests they should while, at the same time, they are entertaining concerns that are quite inconsistent with the externality.

The important point here is that while there are some injuries that cannot be repaired just by saying you are sorry, there are others that can only be repaired by an apology. Such injuries are the very ones that most trouble American law. They include defamation, insult, degradation, loss of status, and the emotional distress and dislocation that accompany conflict. To the extent that a place may be found for apology in the resolution of such conflicts, American law would be enriched and better able to deal with the heart of what brought the controversy to public attention. It would also be relieved of some of the pressure to convert all damages into dollars — a pressure that produces absurdly large punitive damage judgments when a trier of fact sympathetically identifies with the claim of degradation and emotional distress but the economic loss is fictive. More to the point, society at large might be better off and better able to advance social peace if the law, instead of discouraging apologies in such situations by treating them as admissions of liability, encouraged people to apologize to those they have wronged and to compensate them for their losses. Lawsuits may never be filed in such situations.

VII. Formal Apology and Shimatsusho

A striking difference in apologetic behavior in the two legal cultures is the frequency with which a formal, ceremonial apology is tendered in Japan, often by an abject public apology by the senior official of an organization responsible for injury or by a written letter of apology (shimatsusho). For example, following the crash of a Japan Air Lines DC-8 caused by a mentally unstable pilot in 1982, the president of the airline personally called on the bereaved families of the crash victims and was pictured in the press on his knees, bowing in remorseful apology. The ceremony was accompanied by a large cash payment, which apparently obviated litigation of the legal claims arising from the accident. By contrast, American executives whose enterprise has been accused of injury or wrongdoing are thought to be more likely to deny or evade charges of any responsibility and remorse, and even less likely to call on the victims personally and apologize tearfully. The behavior of Union Carbide officials after the Bhophal disaster in 1985 combined an attempt to meet promptly the human problems engendered by the corporation's operations with a desire to avoid admissions of unlimited legal liability. The efforts appear to have satisfied no one.

Although its origins are not clear, it has long been the custom in Japan that a person who breaks a rule should express regret by writing a shimatsusho, or "letter of apology," in lieu of facing an official punishment. These letters are a common and significant aspect of Japanese apology. The practice suggests the use of a formal, written apologue as the basis for relieving a wrongdoer from the legal consequences of the misbehavior. A number of examples suggest the range of ways in which a shimatsusho may serve the needs of both the wrongdoer and, equally important, the injured person or the official interested in resolving the hurtful situation without recourse to formal legal sanctions.

* * *

During a field study in Japan by one of us, he encountered the case of a sixteen-year-old high school student who took a motorcycle from a parking lot in front of a railway station. Unfortunately for him, the gasoline tank was empty, and he therefore could not start the engine. Undaunted, he rode the cycle downhill without using the motor and was stopped by a policeman. The student had no driver's license, but, since the engine was not running, his act did not legally constitute the offense of driving a motor vehicle without a license. The officer undoubtedly was suspicious of the student's tale of borrowing the motorcycle from a friend, yet he did not want to blow the incident out of proportion by treating it as a theft. Accordingly, the officer summoned the student's father to the station and told the student to sign the following shimatsusho:

> On December 24, 1977, at 1:30 PM, I was found by a police officer while riding on a motorcycle without a driver's license on P Street of Block D of City Z. I was warned by the officer. I regret deeply what I have done and I pledge myself never again to ride a motorcycle without obtaining a driver's license. Please deal with me leniently this time.

Both the student and his father signed the letter, which the police officer kept himself, although it was addressed to the chief of the patrol division. The officers thought that if the student had stolen the motorcycle his father certainly must have discovered this and could be relied on to deal with the boy. If it was not stolen, the father would admonish his son not to drive without a license "In either case," said the officer, "the matter has been dealt with effectively."

* * *

VIII. Conclusion

* * *

* * * In Japan it is believed that the settlement of any amount of compensation will go smoothly if both parties start out apologizing to each other This insight — that apology is an important ingredient in resolving conflict — is hardly unique to the Japanese. It is something every eight-year-old knows, yet somehow it tends to be swallowed up during adult American discussions of law and business. Hegland makes this point nicely in discussing a classroom experience:

> In my first year Contracts class, I wished to review various doctrines we have recently studied. I put the following:
>
>> In a long term instalment contract, seller promises buyer to deliver widgets at the rate of 1,000 a month. The first two deliveries are perfect. However, in the third month seller delivers only 990 widgets. Buyer becomes so incensed that he rejects deliveries and refuses to pay for the widgets already delivered.
>
> After stating the problem, I asked, "If you were Seller, what would you say?" What I was looking for was a discussion of the various common law theories which would force the buyer to pay for the widgets delivered and those which would throw buyer into breach for canceling the remaining deliveries. In short, I wanted the class to come up with the legal doctrines which would allow Seller to crush Buyer.
>
> After asking the question, I looked around the room for a volunteer. As is so often the case with first year students, I found that they were all either writing in

their notebooks or inspecting their shoes. There was, however, one eager face, that of an eight year old son of one of my students. It seems that he was suffering through Contracts due to his mother's sin of failing to find a sitter. Suddenly he raised his hand. Such behavior, even from an eight year old, must be rewarded.

"OK," I said, "What would you say if you were the seller?"

"I'd say, 'I'm sorry'".

The underdevelopment of American legal doctrine based on apology suggests the degree to which other, individualistic values — most notably compensation, declaration of right, punishment, professional self-interest, and administrative convenience — have been elevated at the expense of the restorative capacity of law and social ceremony. The American lawsuit is designed to deal with claims of economic loss; indeed, its lawyer-dominated, adversarial structure is not suited to resolve other kinds of issues. The legal system tends to reduce disputes to the types it is comfortable handling. Claims for personal injury are treated as if the issues is how to put a dollar price on pain and suffering, while claims essentially bases on insult and psychic hurt are not dealt with well, if they are recognized at all.

* * *

* * * Pragmatic Americans realize that an apology is a potentially useful tool of informal or nonlitigated resolution, even if apology is formal and there is some cause to doubt the wholeheartedness of the person tendering it. A process built around apology and compensation would fit well into a justice system that increasingly seeks to resolve conflicts by settlement, mediation, or alternative methods of dispute resolution, rather than trial.

* * *

NOTES AND QUESTIONS

1. Could a more developed mechanism for formal apology exist within our litigation system, or is never having to say you're sorry a necessary corollary of our system? Are there social prerequisites to an effective system of apology?

2. Following a 1985 airplane crash, Delta Airlines consciously reached out to the victims. It sent employees to be with every family and offered help in arranging funerals, locating personal property that might have survived the crash and just lending a friendly and sympathetic ear. The result was that far fewer lawsuits were filed than in other similar crashes. But Delta's strategy had another side as well. Where suits were filed, Delta used the information its employees had gathered to reduce recoveries. In one case, a bereaved family member confided to a sympathetic Delta employee that the decedent had had an extra-marital affair. When the family filed suit, Delta pointed to the affair as a reason why the family's claim was not worth as much as they had sought. In another suit, Delta threatened to disclose that the decedent was homosexual. See Ed Bean, *After 137 People Died in Its Texas Jet Crash, Delta Helped Families*, WALL ST. J., Nov. 7, 1986, at 1. Compare this with the description in Wagatsuma and Rosett of Japan Air Lines' response following the crash of its DC-8.

3. The Japanese system of apology is intertwined with other mechanisms of non-judicial third party intervention. One commentator has explained:

> The availability of suitable third parties who are willing and able to perform this role [of mediator] reduces the need to invoke formal judicial intervention. At the outset, mediation requires the presence of persons who, because of position or personal relationships, command respect and are able to exercise some measure of authority. In other words, to be effective, the mediator must be someone who can command the parties' trust and their obedience to the settlement.
>
> One would thus anticipate that suitable third parties are more readily available in a stable, closely-integrated and hierarchical society like Japan, than in a more geographically mobile, less cohesive society like the United States in which individual autonomy and social equality are emphasized. Societal expectations and habits are equally relevant. The role of the mediator becomes increasingly legitimate for both the mediator and the parties to disputes where there is repeated reliance on third parties to settle disputes. A contrast in police attitudes in Japan and the United States pointed out by David H. Bayley is especially interesting in this respect. Japanese commonly rely on the police for assistance in settling disputes. But despite similar popular demand in the United States, "what is different," says Bayley, "is that American police organizations have not adapted willingly to perform this function." Another Japanese example is the mediating service some companies provide for employees involved in traffic accidents. In short, the Japanese may be more successful in avoiding litigation because of social organization and values more conducive to informal dispute resolution through mediation.

John Haley, *The Myth of the Reluctant Litigant*, 4 J. JAPANESE STUDIES 359, 378-79 (1980).

4. An important point made by Wagatsuma and Rosett is that the goal of the Japanese system is to reestablish social relationships which may have been broken by the dispute. A similar concern is expressed by advocates of mediation. Mediation may offer a vehicle through which human connections can be re-established. Professor Riskin has argued:

> Mediation offers some clear advantages over adversary processing: it is cheaper, faster, and potentially more hospitable to unique solutions that take more fully into account nonmaterial interests of the disputants. It can educate the parties about each other's needs and those of their community. Thus, it can help them learn to work together and to see that through cooperation both can make positive

gains. One reason for these advantages is that mediation is less hemmed-in by rules of procedure or substantive law and certain assumptions that dominate the adversary process. * * * [I]n mediation * * * the ultimate authority resides with the disputants. The conflict is seen as unique and therefore less subject to solution by application of some general principle. The case is neither to be governed by a precedent nor to set one. Thus, all sorts of facts, needs, and interests that would be excluded from consideration in an adversary, rule-oriented proceeding could become relevant in a mediation. Indeed, whatever a party deems relevant is relevant.

Leonard Riskin, *Mediation and Lawyers*, 43 OHIO ST. L.J. 29, 34 (1982). Are the benefits of mediation such that litigants should be required to mediate disputes? Some states, such as California, now require mediation of child custody and visitation disputes. CAL. CIV. CODE § 4607(a). Are there other categories of disputes for which mandatory mediation would be appropriate? What about for standard commercial disputes? If some categories are subject to mandatory mediation and others not, are there risks that our system will be perceived as a two-track system.

5. Mediation, particularly mandatory mediation, has not been universally acclaimed. Professor Grillo has argued:

> It has been said that "[d]isputes are cultural events, evolving within a framework of rules about what is worth fighting for, what is the normal or moral way to fight, what kinds of wrongs warrant action, and what kinds of remedies are acceptable." The process by which a society resolves conflict is closely related to its social structure. Implicit in this choice is a message about what is respectable to do or want or say, what the obligations are of being a member of the society or of a particular group within it, and what it takes to be thought of as a good person leading a virtuous life. In the adversary system, it is acceptable to want to win. It is not only acceptable, but expected, that one will rely on a lawyer and advocate for oneself without looking out for the adversary. The judge, a third party obligated to be neutral and bound by certain formalities, bears the ultimate responsibility for deciding the outcome. To the extent that women are more likely than men to believe in communication as a mode of conflict resolution and to appreciate the importance of an adversary's interests, this system does not always suit their needs.
>
> On the other hand, under a scheme of mediation, the standards of acceptable behavior and desires change fundamentally. Parties are to meet with each other, generally without their lawyers. They are encouraged to look at each other's needs and to reach a cooperative resolution based on compromise. Although there are few restrictions on her role in the process, the mediator bears no ultimate, formal responsibility for the outcome of the mediation. In sum, when mediation is the prototype for dispute resolution, the societal message is that a good person — a person following the rules — cooperates, communicates, and compromises.

> The glories of cooperation, however, are easily exaggerated. If one party appreciates cooperation more than the other, the parties might compromise unequally. Moreover, the self-disclosure that cooperation requires, when imposed and not sought by the parties, may feel and be invasive. Thus, rather than representing a change in the system to accommodate the "feminine voice," in actuality, mandatory mediation overrides real women's voices saying that cooperation might, at least for the time being, be detrimental to their lives and the lives of their children. Under a system of forced mediation, women are made to feel selfish for wanting to assert their own interests based on their need to survive.

Trina Grillo, *The Mediation Alternative: Process Dangers for Women*, 100 YALE L. J. 1545, 1607-08 (1991).

6. Even if mediation is not perfect, is it better for more people more often than litigation? Can't the litigation system be dehumanizing and disempowering? Professor White describes in detail "Mrs. G.'s" hearing concerning her welfare benefits. Professor White concludes:

> Mrs. G. had a hearing in which all of the rituals of due process were scrupulously observed. Yet she did not find her voice welcomed at that hearing. A complex pattern of social, economic, and cultural forces under-wrote the procedural formalities, repressing and devaluing her voice.

Lucie White, *Subordination, Rhetorical Survival Skills, and Sunday Shoes: Notes on the Hearing of Mrs. G*, 38 BUFF. L. REV. 1, 32 (1990).

7. The type of dispute resolution system one favors may depend, at least in part, on one's view of the goal of such a system. Some view the goal as almost entirely private — the peaceful resolution of individual disputes. The government is involved primarily to prevent parties from choosing to resolve disputes through socially costly techniques such as violence Others take a different view. Professor Owen Fiss has argued:

> Som[e] * * * se[e] adjudication in essentially private terms: The purpose of lawsuits and the civil courts is to resolve disputes, and the amount of litigation we encounter is evidence of the needlessly combative and quarrelsome character of Americans. Or as [Derek] Bok put it, using a more diplomatic idiom: "At bottom, ours is a society built on individualism, competition, and success." I, on the other hand, see adjudication in more public terms: Civil litigation is an institutional arrangement for using state power to bring a recalcitrant reality closer to our chosen ideals. We turn to the courts because we need to, not because of some quirk in our personalities. We train our students in the tougher arts so that they may help secure all that the law promises, not because we want them to become gladiators or because we take a special pleasure in combat.
>
> To conceive of the civil lawsuit in public terms as America does might be unique. I am willing to assume that no other country — including Japan, Bok's new paragon — has a case like *Brown v. Board of Education* in which the judicial

power is used to eradicate the caste structure. I am willing to assume that no other country conceives of law and uses law in quite the way we do. But this should be a source of pride rather than shame. What is unique is not the problem, that we live short of our ideals, but that we alone among the nations of the world seem willing to do something about it. Adjudication American-style is not a reflection of our combativeness but rather a tribute to our inventiveness and perhaps even more to our commitment.

Owen Fiss, *Against Settlement*, 93 YALE L.J. 1073, 1089-90 (1984). How might different views about the goals of adjudication affect ones views about the desirability of techniques such as mediation or settlement?

Index

Adversary system, 8-9
Inquisitorial system, 9, 773-83
Role of judges, 789-91

Alienage jurisdiction–*see* **Subject matter jurisdiction**

Alternative dispute resolution, 11-13, 773-801
Arbitration, 12-13
Mediation, 12, 798-801
Negotiation, 11-12

Ancillary jurisdiction–*see* **Supplemental jurisdiction**

Appeals
Collateral order doctrine, 752-60
Discovery orders, 764-65
Finality requirement, 750-51
Interlocutory orders, 760-61
Jurisdictional matters, 759
Mechanics of appeal, 765-66
Purposes of appeal, 749
Rule 54(b), 761-62
Scope of review, 767-71
State appellate courts, 766-67
United State Supreme Court, 766

Attorney's fees, 10

Choice of law, 64-65, 77-78, 273-74

Chancery–*see* **Equity, development of**

Class actions
Appeal of certification orders, 753-57
Constitutional limits on binding effect, 723-30
History, 720-21
Notice, 738-40
Personal jurisdiction, 745-48
Policy and ethical issues, 721-23
Rule 23 requirements, 730-40
Settlement, 740-41

Collateral estoppel–*see* **Preclusion**

Index

Default, 357-59

Discovery, 387-470
Appeals of discovery orders, 764-65
Depositions, 390-91
Experts, 427-36
Interrogatories, 391-92
Local rules, 446-47
Medical examinations, 392-93
Privileged material, 408-11
Production of documents and things, 392
Requests for admission, 393-94
Required disclosures, 438-46
Sanctions, 447-65
Scheduling conferences, 437, 466-70
Scope of, 394-408
Timing, 437
Work product, 411-26

Dismissal
Involuntary, 348-49
Voluntary, 346-48

Diversity of citizenship–*see* **Subject matter jurisdiction**

Equity, development of, 13-15

Erie **doctrine,** 263-312
Ascertaining state law, 312-17
Constitutional basis, 274-76
Determining which state's law applies, 273-74
Door-closing statutes, 281, 286
Federal common law, 317-18
Federal Rules, validity of, 296-302
Forum selection clauses, 303-04
Rules of Decision Act, 263-65, 271-72
Rules Enabling Act, 296-302
Statutes of limitations, 276-80, 281, 302

Federal question jurisdiction–*see* **Subject matter jurisdiction**

Forum non conveniens, 238-48

Full faith and credit, 24, 626-29

Index

Joinder
Claims, 635-65
Compulsory party joinder, 683-91
Counterclaims, 656-62
Cross-claims, 666-68
Impleader (third-party practice), 669-74
Interpleader, 705-20
Intervention, 694-702
Permissive party joinder, 644-52

Judgment as a matter of law, 553-61

Jury
Constitutional right to, 471-95
Instructions to, 569-70
Misconduct, 572-74
Nullification, 521-22
Peremptory challenges, 496-520
Selection of, 495-520
Size, 520-21
State courts, 495
Verdict, 570-71

Magistrate judges, 435-36

Mandamus, 763-64

New trial, 561-69
Additur, 568
Conditional grant, 569
Remittitur, 568

Notice
Due process requirements, 133-41
Statutory requirements, 141-49

Opportunity to be heard, constitutional right, 149-63

Parties
Capacity to sue, 632-33
Joinder of–*see* **Joinder**
Real party in interest, 632-35
Standing, 632-33

Index

Pendent jurisdiction–*see* **Supplemental jurisdiction**

Personal jurisdiction
Appeal of, 759
Challenges to, 249-59
Class actions, 745-48
Domicile, 36-37
Federal court, 61-62
General jurisdiction, 45, 85-94
In rem, 32-33
Long-arm statutes, 125-32
Presence, 108-21
Purposes of, 122-23
Quasi-in-rem, 32-33, 95-108
Special appearance, 38, 249-51
Transient jurisdiction, 108-21

Pleadings, 319-85
Affirmative defenses, 354-57
Alternative and inconsistent allegations, 342-46
Amendments to, 360-68
Answer, 352-54
Code pleading, 322-23, 329-31
Common law pleading, 320-22
Complaint
    Factual sufficiency, 329-36
    Heightened specificity, 336-42
    Legal sufficiency, 326-29
    Requirements of Rule 8, 323-26
Counterclaims, 357, 655-62
    Reply, 357
    Sanctions for frivolous, etc., 369-85
    Supplemental, 369

Preclusion
Claim preclusion (res judicata), 577-98
    Exceptions, 595-98
    Parties bound, 587-91
    Scope of claim, 577-87
Compulsory counterclaim rule, 587-89, 655-62
Double jeopardy compared, 578
Issue preclusion (collateral estoppel)
    Issue actually litigated, 598-604
    Issue essential to judgment, 604-07
    Mutuality, 613-24
    Parties bound, 608-13

Preclusion–*Continued*
Stare decisis compared, 578
State–federal issues, 626-29

Pretrial conferences, 466-70

Remittitur, 568

Res judicata–*see* **Preclusion**

Scheduling conferences, 437, 466-70

Service of process–*see* **Notice**

Settlement, 388, 792-97, 800-01
Class action, 740-41

Seventh Amendment–*see* **Jury**

Subject matter jurisdiction
Alienage, 169
"Arising under" jurisdiction–*see* Federal question jurisdiction
Burden of proving, 168
Challenges to, 259-62
Constitutional limits, 166-67
Diversity of citizenship jurisdiction
    Amount in controversy, 188-93
    Assignment of claims to create, 186-87
    Citizenship of individuals, 172-78
    Citizenship of corporations, 178-86
    Citizenship of representatives, 186-87
    Citizenship of resident aliens, 177-78
    Citizenship of unincorporated entities, 185-86
    Collusive joinder to create, 186-87
    Complete diversity rule, 170-72
    Domestic relations exception, 187-88
    Purposes of, 169-70
Federal question jurisdiction
    Centrality of federal issue, 200-13
    Declaratory judgment cases, 198-200
    Well-pleaded complaint rule, 193-97

Summary judgment, 522-53
Burden of proof, 530-44

Index

Supplemental jurisdiction
Class actions, 741-45
Compulsory party joinder, 691-94
Constitutional basis, 642
Counterclaims
    Additional parties, 662-64
    Compulsory, 662-64
    Permissive, 665-66
Cross-claims, 668-69
Impleader, 674-83
Intervention, 702-03
Pendent claims, 636-44
Pendent parties, 652-55
Rule 14(a) claims, 674-83

Third-party practice, 669-74

Venue
Change of, 233-37
Federal court, basic rules, 225-33
Local actions, 221-22
Multidistrict litigation, 237
Removal cases, 215
State court, 222-25, 233

Vertical choice of law–*see Erie* **doctrine**